Fundamentals of

ABNORMAL PSYCHOLOGY

Fundamentals of ABNORMAL PSYCHOLOGY

THIRD EDITION

Worth Publishers
New York

Ronald J. Comer

Princeton University

Fundamentals of Abnormal Psychology, Third Edition
© 2002, 1999, 1996 by Worth Publishers and W. H. Freeman and Company
All rights reserved.

Printed in the United States of America

First printing 2001

Publisher: Catherine Woods
Sponsoring Editor: Marjorie Byers
Development Editor: Barbara Conover
Executive Marketing Manager: Renee Altier
Project Editor: Bradley Umbaugh
Art Director and Text/Cover Designer: Barbara Reingold
Layout Design: Paul Lacy
Production Manager: Sarah Segal
New Media and Supplements Editor: Graig Donini
Cover Illustration: Wiktor Sadowski
Photo Editor: Meg Kuhta
Photo Researcher: Deborah Goodsite
Composition: Compset, Inc.
Manufacturing: RR Donnelly & Sons Co.

Library of Congress Cataloging-in-Publication Data
Comer, Ronald J.
 Fundamentals of abnormal psychology / Ronald J. Comer.— 3rd ed.
   p. cm.
Includes bibliographical references and index.
 ISBN 0-7167-5111-9
 1. Psychology, Pathological. I. Title.
 RC454 .C6343 2001
 616.89—dc21

                                                    2001002321

We gratefully acknowledge the following for the use of their photos. *Chapter Openers:* p. 1 Courtesy of the George Adams Gallery, p. 30 Olivia Parker/Image Bank, p. 66 Zigy Kaluzny/Stone, p. 94 Rick Raymond/Stone, p. 126 Shoshannah White/Aurora, p. 156 Martin Meyer/Stone, p. 190 Roxann Arwen Mills/Photonica, p. 216 Eric Vialard/Photonica, p. 244 Deborah Jaffe, p. 272 Francisco Cruz/SuperStock, p. 308 Luc Beziat/Stone, p. 344 Kevin Irby/Stone, p. 378 Josh Pulman/Stone, p. 406 Margo Weinstein/Image Bank, p. 440 SuperStock, p. 474 Ann Cutting/Photonica. *Opening timeline:* (top to bottom) Mark Marten/US National Library of Medicine/Photo Researchers; Sigmund Freud Copyrights/Everett Collection; W. H. Freeman & Company; Joe McNally/Sygma; Julie Newdoll, Computer Graphics Laboratory, UCSF; Leif Skoogstor/Woodfin Camp & Associates; Roger Ressmeyer/Corbis; and AP Photo/News & Observer, Scott Lewis.

Worth Publishers
41 Madison Avenue
New York, NY 10010
www.worthpublishers.com

For Marlene

Ronald Comer has been a professor in Princeton University's Department of Psychology for the past 27 years and has served as Director of Clinical Psychology Studies for most of that time. He is also currently the director of the department's undergraduate program.

Professor Comer has received the President's Award for Distinguished Teaching at the university. His course "Abnormal Psychology" is one of the university's most popular, and he has offered it almost every year since his arrival at Princeton.

He is also a practicing clinical psychologist and serves as a consultant to the Eden Institute for Persons with Autism and to hospitals and family practice residency programs throughout New Jersey. Additionally, he holds an adjunct position as Clinical Associate Professor of Family Medicine at the UMDNJ–Robert Wood Johnson Medical School.

In addition to writing *Fundamentals of Abnormal Psychology*, Professor Comer is the author of the textbook *Abnormal Psychology*, now in its fourth edition, and the co-author of *Case Studies in Abnormal Psychology.* He has also published a number of journal articles in clinical psychology, social psychology, and family medicine.

Professor Comer was an undergraduate at the University of Pennsylvania and a graduate student at Clark University. He currently lives in Lawrenceville, New Jersey, with his wife, Marlene, and their dog, Annie. From there, he can keep an eye on his sons—Greg, a resident of New York, and Jon, currently a Philadelphian—and on the resurgent Philadelphia sports teams with whom he grew up.

Abnormal Psychology in Science and Clinical Practice

Problems of Anxiety and Mood

Problems of the Mind and Body

Problems of Psychosis and Cognitive Function

Life-Span Problems

Conclusion

Contents

Writing a textbook on abnormal psychology and developing a course on the subject present the same challenge — to open the doors of this important field for students in an enlightening, provocative, and, yet, humane way.

There are also parallels between writing a new edition of a textbook and revising a course. In each undertaking, one is trying to update the material thoroughly, retain techniques that have been successful previously, change what has been unsuccessful, and develop new forms of presentation that can better enlighten and excite students. Although I am deeply gratified by the very positive responses of professors and students to the past editions of *Fundamentals of Abnormal Psychology,* I have carefully considered how to keep improving this text for a new generation of students. Similarly, I have listened closely to my colleagues in this enterprise—the professors and students who have used the textbook over the past six years—and I have tried to incorporate their ideas into *Fundamentals of Abnormal Psychology,* Third Edition. The result, I believe, is a book that will greatly please both professors and readers. At the risk of seeming shamelessly immodest, I would like to describe what I believe to be special about this book.

Continuing Strengths

In this edition, I have been careful to retain the goals, themes, material, and techniques that have worked successfully and been embraced enthusiastically by past readers.

MODERATE IN LENGTH, SOLID IN CONTENT Even though *Fundamentals of Abnormal Psychology* is of moderate length, it offers probing coverage of its broad subject. It expands and challenges students' thinking rather than short-changing or underestimating their intellectual capacity.

BREADTH AND BALANCE The field's many theories, studies, disorders, and treatments are presented completely and accurately. All major models—psychological, biological, and sociocultural—receive objective, balanced, up-to-date coverage, without bias toward any single approach.

HUMANITY The subject of abnormal psychology is people—very often people in great pain. I have therefore tried to always write with humanity and to impart this awareness to students. The book also speaks with a single voice, in clear and straightforward language—the main advantage of a single-author book.

INTEGRATED COVERAGE OF TREATMENT Discussions of treatment are presented throughout the book. In addition to a complete overview of treatment in the opening chapters, each of the pathology chapters includes a full discussion of relevant treatment approaches.

RICH CASE MATERIAL I integrate numerous clinical examples, to bring theoretical and clinical issues to life.

CROSS-CULTURAL AND GENDER COVERAGE Issues raised by ethnic and gender differences, as well as related problems of bias, are given constant attention, and, in fact, the sociocultural model is presented on an equal footing with the other models of psychological abnormality. Coverage includes such topics as minority groups and the mental health system, gender and depression, and the historical use of labeling to suppress certain groups of individuals.

CD-ROM A student CD-ROM, shrink-wrapped with each textbook, brings text concepts to life through videotaped case study aids.

TOPICS OF SPECIAL INTEREST I devote full chapters to important subjects that are of special interest to college-age readers, such as eating disorders and suicide, and I also cover controversial issues that are currently being spotlighted by the news media, including violations of subjects' rights in clinical research, the right to commit suicide, and the implications of "mad cow" disease.

FOCUS ON CRITICAL THINKING The book provides tools for thinking critically about abnormal psychology.

ADAPTABILITY Chapters are self-contained, so they can be assigned in whatever order makes sense to the professor.

Changes and Features New to This Edition

The study of abnormal psychology continues to grow steadily. Similarly, the field of undergraduate education is in constant motion, with new pedagogical techniques and insights emerging each day. Such developments have spurred me to include a variety of important changes and new features in the current edition.

A truly unique and accessible new design greatly increases pedagogy and draws students into the book. In the spirit of a captivating lecture, text discussions precisely intersect with provocative side points, memorable quotes, key definitions, critical thinking questions, special photos and illustrations, revealing graphs, informative tables, and compelling boxes.

"Stepping Back" boxes feature historical insights into disorders and treatments. Examples include discussions of Karen Carpenter's losing battle with anorexia nervosa, the beginnings of Alcoholics Anonymous, and society's initial reactions to Viagra versus "the Pill."

DSM-IV Checklists, which state the DSM-IV criteria for each disorder, now appear alongside the text discussion of the disorder. At the same time, questions are raised about the reliability and validity of the DSM. The new edition reflects changes found in the DSM-IV Text Revision (APA, 2000).

A full updating of the text incorporates recent theories, research, and events—including more than 1,500 new references from 1999–2001, close to 200 new photographs, and new tables and figures.

Increased cross-cultural coverage, both in photos and within the text, shows students the impact of psychological disorders and treatments on the entire human community, and the effects of special cultural, gender, and economic pressures on psychological functioning.

A significantly enhanced and updated supplements package includes a new *Scientific American Reader*, a new *Casebook*, an expanded *Student CD-ROM*, and a new set of *Video Segments* for lectures.

I have included many learning aids to help students both absorb and enjoy the material. A number of these are brand new to this new edition; others build on and enhance the aids that appeared in the previous edition.

Innovative Boxes are all either new, enhanced, or updated. New topics include bullying, the Y2K scare, suicide by the woman who stalked David Letterman, and books recommended by today's therapists. In addition to the new "Stepping Back" boxes, I've included once again three other types of boxes:

- A Closer Look, which challenge students to closely examine and think critically about significant (and sometimes controversial) issues in the field.

- The Current Scene, which examine cutting-edge issues from the world around us.

- Abnormality and the Arts, which examine abnormal behavior as reflected in the movies, literature, music, and the visual arts.

"Side Views," fascinating side-points strategically placed in margins, have been updated and expanded. These notes, which engage students and make the material more accessible, include topics such as Freud's fee for therapy, famous movie therapists, and the cost of developing a psychotropic drug.

"Consider This" questions have also been expanded. These critical thinking questions, strategically placed in margins and at the end of boxed material, help readers access and question their current beliefs.

Margin Glossaries include hundreds of key words defined in the margins of the pages on which they appear. In addition, a traditional glossary is available at the back of the book.

Profile tables summarize and compare disorders in each chapter.

"Summing Up" sections provide readers with short periodic reviews at critical points throughout the chapter, helping them to process and retain the text material.

"Crossroads" sections, which conclude each chapter, bring together the principles and findings of the competing models of abnormality, ask whether the models can work together in a more integrated approach, and also summarize where the field now stands and where it may well be going.

"CyberStudy" sections, located at the end of each chapter, guide the integration of chapter material with the student CD-ROM.

Chapter-ending "Key Terms" and "Quick Quiz" sections, keyed to appropriate pages in the chapter for easy reference, allow students to review and test their knowledge of chapter material.

Supplements)

The very enthusiastic response to the supplements accompanying previous editions has been gratifying. This edition is able to retain and enhance those supplements and to also add several important new ones.

ENHANCED! STUDENT CD-ROM This interactive CD-ROM by Elaine Cassel of Marymount University and Lord Fairfax Community College, which accompanies each textbook, offers students more than 25 intriguing videos running three to five minutes each. Videos usually center on a real person with a disorder discussed in the text. The students first view the video and then answer a series of thought-provoking questions about it. Additionally, the CD-ROM contains multiple-choice practice test questions, with built-in instructional feedback. The CyberStudy section at the end of each chapter directly ties chapter material to the CD-ROM. Thirteen new videos have been added to this edition's CD-ROM, along with new questions and practice tests.

NEW! THE SCIENTIFIC AMERICAN READER Drawn from *Scientific American*, this collection of classic and cutting-edge articles enhances coverage of important topics within the textbook. I have keyed the articles to specific chapters and provided a preview and discussion questions for each article. The *Scientific American Reader* is available for shrink-wrapping with each textbook.

NEW! CASE STUDIES IN ABNORMAL PSYCHOLOGY This new casebook written by Ethan E. Gorenstein of the Behavorial Medicine Program, Columbia-Presbyterian Hospital, and me, provides 17 case histories based on our clinical experiences. Each case describes in detail the individual's history and symptoms, the theory behind treatment, the specific treatment plan, and the actual treatment conducted. In a unique feature, each case also includes the perspective of a relative or friend. Also unique are interesting *margin notes* that fill the pages of each case to add background information and insights. In addition, the casebook provides three cases without diagnoses or treatment, so students can themselves identify disorders and suggest appropriate therapies, then compare their ideas to current information and trends in the field. The casebook is available at a significant discount to textbook users.

ENHANCED! THE STUDENT WORKBOOK AND STUDY GUIDE This workbook by Carmen R. Wilson VanVoorhis, University of Wisconsin at La Crosse, and Katherine M. Nicolai, Rockhurst College, actively involves students in the text material, using a variety of engaging exercises. Students who complete the exercises can better organize and apply what they have studied.

ENHANCED! ABNORMAL PSYCHOLOGY WEB COMPANION LOCATED AT WWW.WORTHPUBLISHERS.COM/COMER The Web site offers an ever-expanding set of resources for both students and instructors. Features include annotated Web links, on-line quizzing, interactive flashcards, abnormal psychology research activities, and PowerPoint® slides.

NEW! MAKING SENSE OF PSYCHOLOGY ON THE WEB (WITH CD-ROM) Upon request, this supplement by Connie K. Varnhagen, University of Alberta, can be packaged with the textbook at a significant discount. Useful for the novice researcher as well as the experienced Internet user, *Making Sense of Psychology on the Web* helps students to become discriminating Web users and researchers, capable of clipping and compiling bits and pieces from Web sites, video and audio excerpts, and other electronic resources.

ENHANCED! VIDEO SEGMENTS FOR ABNORMAL PSYCHOLOGY Designed by me to bring an added dimension to lectures, this set of four videotapes contains more than 80 one- to eight-minute clips that depict disorders, show historical footage, and illustrate clinical topics, pathologies, treatments, laboratory experiments, and clinical dilemmas. A new fourth tape adds more than one-and-a-half hours of excerpts taken from three outstanding series: *The Mind, The Brain,* and *The World of Abnormal Psychology.*

NEW! POWERPOINT® SLIDES Customizable PowerPoint® slide sets offer textbook outlines, along with numerous figures and charts from the textbook.

ENHANCED! INSTRUCTOR'S TRANSPARENCY SET This set of transparencies contains 50 full-color images, charts, photos, and graphs from the text for use in lectures. Additionally, there are many transparency masters of DSM-IV criteria and of text tables available in the Instructor's Manual.

ENHANCED! INSTRUCTOR'S TEST BANK (PRINTED AND CD-ROM) This updated and enhanced *Test Bank*, by Debra and John Hull of Wheeling Jesuit University, offers more than 2,000 multiple-choice, fill-in-the-blank, and essay questions. Each question is assessed according to difficulty, identified as factual or applied, and keyed to the page in the text where the source information appears. The electronic version on a dual-platform CD-ROM allows instructors to add, edit, re-format, and re-sequence questions. The test bank CD-ROM is also the access point for secure *on-line testing* of students by professors.

ENHANCED! INSTRUCTOR'S RESOURCE MANUAL This extensive teaching resource by Stephen M. Saunders of Marquette University, with added material and a video guide by me, ties together the supplements package for instructors and teaching assistants. The manual includes detailed chapter outlines, lists of learning objectives, and many new ideas for lectures, for launching class discussions, and for the use of the textbook's various supplements. It also lays out precise DSM-IV criteria for each of the disorders and offers most of this material in transparency masters.

Acknowledgements)

I am enormously grateful to the many people who have contributed to writing and producing this book. I particularly thank Marion Kowalewski and Marlene Comer for their wonderful, never-ending work on every aspect of the manuscript, from making editorial judgments to typing. In addition, I am indebted to Vicky Glosson, Arlene Kerch, Vera Sohl, Bernie VanUiter, and Carole Zaffarese for their valuable help on the manuscript. I sincerely appreciate the outstanding work of the book's research assistants, including Linda Chamberlin, Jon Comer, and Greg Comer. And, in particular, I thank Kenworthey Bilz for her superb work in researching and drafting many of the new boxes in this edition.

Throughout three editions of *Fundamentals of Abnormal Psychology*, I have received valuable feedback from academicians and clinicians who have reviewed portions of the manuscript and commented on its clarity, accuracy, and completeness. Their collective knowledge and their willingness to share it with me have in large part shaped the third edition. I am of course indebted to those whose insights contributed to this new edition: Catherine Campbell, University of Southern Mississippi; David Liebert, St. Petersburg Junior College; Ronald G. Ribble, University of Texas at San Antonio; Mary A. Rogers, Inver Hills Community College; Michael Simon, San Francisco State University; Helen Taylor, Bellevue Community College; and Fred Whitford, Montana State University.

In the same vein, I wish to acknowledge and thank once again the reviewers of the previous editions of *Fundamentals of Abnormal Psychology*. Their contributions remain integral to the accuracy and soundness of this edition. They include: Kerm Almos, Capital University; Otto Berliner, Alfred State College; Dorothy M. Bianco, Rhode Island College; Connie R. Borowicz, Milwaukee School of Engineering; Katharine Cimini, Lycoming College; Steve Collins, Rio Hondo Community College; John Conklin, Camosun

College; Eric J. Cooley, Western Oregon University; Laurie M. Corey, Westchester Community College; Andrew L. Dickson, University of Southern Mississippi; Ellen Domm, Green River Community College; Linda E. Flickinger, St. Clair County Community College; Frank Goodkin, Castleton State College; Marjorie Hatch, Southern Methodist University; Debra B. Hull, Wheeling Jesuit University; Heidi M. Inderbitzen-Nolan, University of Nebraska-Lincoln; Mary Livingston, Louisiana Tech University; Marlene Moretti, Simon Fraser University; Shelly Nygard, Lakeland College; Sonia Jean Powell, Olive-Harvey College; Lynn P. Rehm, University of Houston; Beth M. Rienzi, California State University–Bakersfield; Anita Rosenfield, Chaffey Community College; Katherine Elaine Royal, Middle Tennessee State University; Charles Spirrison, Mississippi State University; Irving F. Tucker, Shepherd College; Michael W. Vasey, Ohio State University; Amy R. Wolfson, College of the Holy Cross.

The authors of the book's supplements package have my sincere thanks for again doing splendid jobs with their respective supplements: Debra B. Hull and John H. Hull, Wheeling Jesuit University (*Test Bank*); Stephen M. Saunders, Marquette University (*Instructor's Manual*), Carmen R. Wilson VanVoorhis, University of Wisconsin at LaCrosse, and Katherine M. Nicolai, Rockhurst College (*Study Guide*), Elaine Cassel, Marymount University and Lord Fairfax Community College (*Student CD-ROM*).

I wish to also extend my deep appreciation to the core team of professionals at Worth Publishers and W. H. Freeman and Company who have worked so closely with me to produce this edition. As I have noted before, although the author gets most of the credit, the production of a textbook represents a collaboration by more people than one can possibly imagine. Ultimately, the book's quality reflects the ability, judgment, and dedication of these people. In my case, I was blessed once again with a core team of extraordinary people—several of whom also guided me through previous editions of my textbooks. Each of these team members is extremely talented, committed to excellence, dedicated to the education of readers, and bound by a remarkable work ethic; and, each is a wonderful person. They were indeed my co-authors and co-teachers in this enterprise, and I am forever in their debt. They are, in alphabetical order: Marge Byers, sponsoring editor; Barbara Conover, development editor; Deborah Goodsite, photo researcher; Tracey Kuehn, associate managing editor; Meg Kuhta, photo editor; Paul Lacy, page layout artist; Barbara Reingold, art director; Sarah Segal, production manager; Bradley Umbaugh, project editor; and Catherine Woods, publisher.

In addition to this core team, there are a number of other people at Worth and at Freeman to whom I am indebted. Elizabeth Widdicombe, president of Worth and Freeman, has continued to lead the companies courageously, to create a very supportive environment for my books, and to be a good friend. I am also indebted to Graig Donini, Worth new media and supplements editor, who has so skillfully developed and guided the production of the extraordinary and innovative supplements package that accompanies the text. Still other professionals from Worth and Freeman to whom I am indebted are: Barbara Salazar, copy editor; Barbara Hults and Karen Osborne, proofreaders; Beverly Wehrli, referencer; Ellen Brennan, indexer; Megan Burns, editorial assistant; Thomas J. FitzGerald, project editorial assistant; Nancy Giraldo Walker, rights and permissions manager; and John Philp, for his work on the CyberStudy images and the new video segments.

Finally, not to be overlooked are the superb marketing and sales professionals at Worth and at Freeman who continuously work with remarkable energy, skill, and judgment to bring my books to the attention of professors across the world: Renee Altier, executive marketing manager; Marie Schappert, vice-president and director of sales;

Todd Elder, director of advertising; and the company's wonderful sales representatives. Thank you.

Like all previous editions, a project of this scope would not be possible without a loving and supportive family, and I am truly grateful to mine — Claire Comer, Herman Kramer, Pam Weinstein, Steve Comer, Dave Slotkin, Hadaso Slotkin, Sharon Hardy, Chuck Hardy, and Alan Hershman. As in the past, I offer special thanks and words of love to my wife, Marlene, and my sons, Greg and Jon, who make my life so rich and complete and joyful.

Finally, whenever I speak at a conference, students or professors who have seen the comical video segment of my dog, Annie, invariably ask me how she is doing. Well, as these things go, Annie has grown a lot older and is now rather impaired. However, as she approaches 14, she is still here by my side supervising all aspects of my work on this book, as she has for four editions of *Abnormal Psychology* and the two previous editions of *Fundamentals of Abnormal Psychology*. Thus, odd as it may sound, I'd like to thank Annie for her contributions to these books — and to my life.

Ronald J. Comer
Princeton University
September 2001

Abnormal Psychology: Past and Present

Alexandra cries herself to sleep every night. She is certain that the future holds nothing but misery. Indeed, this is the only thing she does feel certain about. "I'm going to die and my daughters are going to die. We're doomed. The world is ugly. I detest every moment of this life." She has great trouble sleeping. She is afraid to close her eyes, afraid that she will never wake up, and what will happen to her daughters then? When she does drift off to sleep, her dreams are nightmares filled with blood, dismembered bodies, thunder, decay, death, destruction.

One morning Alexandra has trouble getting out of bed. The thought of facing another day overwhelms her. Again she wishes she were dead, and she wishes her daughters were dead. "We'd all be better off." She feels paralyzed by her depression and anxiety, too tired to move and too afraid to leave her house. She decides once again to stay home and to keep her daughters with her.

During the past year Brad has been hearing mysterious voices that tell him to quit his job, leave his family, and prepare for the coming invasion. These voices have brought tremendous confusion and emotional turmoil to Brad's life. He believes that they come from beings in distant parts of the universe who are somehow wired to him. Although it gives him a sense of purpose and specialness to be the chosen target of their communications, they also make him tense and anxious. He dreads the coming invasion. When he refuses an order, the voices insult and threaten him and turn his days into a waking nightmare.

Brad has put himself on a sparse diet against the possibility that his enemies may be contaminating his food. He has found a quiet apartment far from his old haunts where he has laid in a good stock of arms and ammunition. His family and friends have tried to reach out to Brad, to understand his problems, and to dissuade him from the disturbing course he is taking. Every day, however, he retreats further into his world of mysterious voices and imagined dangers.

Most of us would probably consider Alexandra's and Brad's emotions, thoughts, and behavior psychologically abnormal, the result of a state sometimes called *psychopathology, maladjustment, emotional disturbance,* or *mental illness.* These terms have been applied to the many problems that seem closely tied to the human brain or mind. Psychological abnormality affects the famous and the unknown, the rich and the poor. Politicians, actors, writers, and other public figures of the present and the past have struggled with it. Psychological problems can bring great suffering, but they can also be the source of inspiration and energy.

Because they are so common and so personal, these problems capture the interest of us all. Hundreds of novels, plays, films, and television programs have explored what many people see as the dark side of human nature, and self-help books flood the market. Mental health experts are popular guests on both television and radio, and some even have their own shows.

The field devoted to the scientific study of the problems we find so fascinating is usually called **abnormal psychology.** As in the other sciences, workers in this field, called *clinical scientists,* gather information carefully so that they may describe, predict, and explain the phenomena they study. The knowledge that they acquire is then used by *clinical practitioners* to detect, assess, and treat abnormal patterns of functioning.

What Is Psychological Abnormality?

Although their general goals are similar to those of other scientific professionals, clinical scientists and practitioners face problems that make their work especially difficult. One problem is that psychological abnormality is very hard to define. Consider once again Alexandra and Brad. Why are we so ready to call their responses abnormal?

Although many definitions of abnormality have been used over the years, none has won total acceptance (Mechanic, 1999). Still, most of the definitions do have some common features, often called "the four D's": deviance, distress, dysfunction, and danger. That is, patterns of psychological abnormality are typically *deviant* (different, extreme, unusual, perhaps even bizarre); *distressing* (unpleasant and upsetting to the person); *dysfunctional* (interfering with the person's ability to conduct daily activities in a constructive way); and possibly *dangerous.* This definition offers a useful starting point from which to explore psychological abnormality. As we shall see, however, it has key limitations.

Deviance

Abnormal psychological functioning is *deviant,* but deviant from what? Alexandra's and Brad's behaviors, thoughts, and emotions are different from those that are considered normal in our place and time. We do not expect people to cry themselves to sleep every night, wish themselves dead, or obey voices that no one else hears.

Deviance and abnormality *Along the Niger River, men of the Wodaabe tribe put on elaborate makeup and costumes to attract women. In Western society, the same behavior would break behavioral norms and probably would be judged abnormal.*

ABNORMALITY AND THE ARTS

Books to Grow By: Top 10 List

Books written about psychological problems are sometimes insightful and instructive. Eighty percent of today's therapists recommend self-help books to their clients and a third recommend autobiographies that have been written by people with psychological disorders (Clifford, Norcross, & Sommer, 1999). Here are therapists' most recommended autobiographies, in order of popularity:

An Unquiet Mind by K. R. Jamison (bipolar disorder)

Nobody Nowhere: The Extraordinary Autobiography of an Autistic by D. Williams (autism)

Darkness Visible: A Memoir of Madness by W. Styron (depression)

Out of Depths by A. T. Boisin (schizophrenia)

Girl, Interrupted by S. Kaysen (borderline personality disorder)

Too Much Anger, Too Many Tears: A Personal Triumph over Psychiatry by J. Gotkin and P. Gotkin (schizophrenia)

Undercurrents: A Therapist's Reckoning with Depression by M. Manning (depression)

Getting Better: Inside Alcoholics Anonymous by N. Robertson (alcoholism)

Am I Still Visible? A Woman's Triumph over Anorexia Nervosa by S. Heater (anorexia nervosa)

Welcome, Silence: My Triumph over Schizophrenia by C. S. North (schizophrenia)

A Brilliant Madness: Living with Manic-Depressive Illness by P. Duke (bipolar disorder)

In short, abnormal behavior, thoughts, and emotions are those that differ markedly from a society's ideas about proper functioning. Each society establishes **norms**—stated and unstated rules for proper conduct. Behavior that breaks legal norms is called criminal. Behavior, thoughts, and emotions that break norms of psychological functioning are called abnormal.

Judgments of abnormality vary from society to society. A society's norms grow from its particular **culture**—its history, values, institutions, habits, skills, technology, and arts. Thus, a society that values competition and assertiveness may accept aggressive behavior, whereas one that emphasizes cooperation and gentleness may consider aggressive behavior unacceptable and even abnormal. A society's values may also change over time, causing its views of what is psychologically abnormal to change as well. In Western society, for example, a woman's participation in the business world was considered inappropriate and strange a hundred years ago. Today the same behavior is valued.

Judgments of abnormality depend on *specific circumstances* as well as on psychological norms. What if, for example, we were to learn that the desperately unhappy Alexandra lives in Serbia, an area pulled apart by years of combat, and that the happiness she once knew vanished when her husband and son were killed. As year followed year with only temporary relief, Alexandra stopped expecting anything except more of the same. In this light, Alexandra's reactions do not seem so inappropriate. If anything is abnormal here, it is her situation. Many things in our world produce intense reactions—large-scale catastrophes and disasters, rape, child abuse, war, terminal illness, chronic pain (Resick, 2001; Ursano et al., 1999). Is there an "appropriate" way to react to such things? Should we ever call reactions to them abnormal?

Distress

Even functioning that is considered unusual does not necessarily qualify as abnormal. According to many clinical theorists, behavior, ideas, or emotions usually have to cause *distress* before they can be labeled abnormal. Consider the Ice Breakers, a group of people in Michigan who go swimming in lakes throughout the state every weekend from November through February. The colder the weather, the better they like it. One man, a member of the group for seventeen years, says he loves the challenge. Man against nature. Mind versus body. A 37-year-old lawyer believes that the weekly shock is good for her health. "It cleanses me," she says. "It perks me up and gives me strength." Another Ice Breaker likes the special bond the group members share. "When we get together, we know we've done something special, something no one else understands. I can't even tell most of the people I know that I'm an Ice Breaker."

Certainly these people are different from most of us, but is their behavior abnormal? Far from experiencing distress, they feel energized. Their positive feelings cause us to hesitate before we decide they are functioning abnormally.

Should we conclude, then, that feelings of distress must always be present before a person's functioning can be considered abnormal? Not necessarily. Some people who function abnormally continue to hold a positive frame of mind. Consider once again Brad, who hears mysterious voices. Brad does experience severe distress over the coming invasion and the life changes he feels forced to make. But what if, instead, he enjoyed listening to the voices, felt honored to be chosen, and looked forward to saving the world? Shouldn't we still consider his functioning abnormal?

NORM-BUSTERS

In 1971, women in English mental hospitals outnumbered men by 35 to 1. That ratio was reversed, however, in English prisons (Asimov, 1997). Might gender influence how a society interprets norm-breaking behavior?

Patrick Gardin Stringer/AP Photo

Changing times *Two decades ago, a woman's love for bullfighting would have been considered strange, perhaps even abnormal. Today Cristina Sánchez is one of Spain's finest matadors and is considered a role model.*

ABNORMAL PSYCHOLOGY The scientific study of abnormal behavior in order to describe, predict, explain, and change abnormal patterns of functioning.

NORMS A society's stated and unstated rules for proper conduct.

CULTURE A people's common history, values, institutions, habits, skills, technology, and arts.

Dysfunction

Abnormal behavior tends to be *dysfunctional;* that is, it interferes with daily functioning. It so distracts or confuses people that they cannot care for themselves properly, take part in ordinary social relationships, or work productively. Brad, for example, has quit his job, left his family, and prepared to withdraw from the productive life he once led.

Here again culture plays a role in the definition of abnormality. Our society holds that it is important to carry out daily activities in an effective manner. Thus Brad's behavior is likely to be regarded as abnormal and undesirable, whereas that of the Ice Breakers, who continue to perform well in their jobs and have fulfilling relationships, would probably be considered simply unusual.

Danger

Perhaps the ultimate in psychological dysfunctioning is behavior that becomes *dangerous* to oneself or to others. Individuals whose behavior is consistently careless, hostile, or confused may be placing themselves or those around them at risk. Brad, for example, seems to be endangering himself by his diet and others by his buildup of arms and ammunition.

Although danger is often cited as a feature of abnormal functioning, research suggests that it is actually the exception rather than the rule (Linaker, 2000; Monahan, 1993, 1992). Most people struggling with anxiety, depression, and even bizarre thinking pose no immediate danger to themselves or to anyone else.

A spiritual experience *In the Val d'Isère, France, students bury themselves in snow up to their necks. Far from experiencing distress or displaying abnormality, they are engaging in a Japanese practice designed to open their hearts and enlarge their spirits.*

The Elusive Nature of Abnormality

Efforts to define psychological abnormality typically raise as many questions as they answer. The major difficulty is that the concept depends on the norms and values of the society in question. Ultimately a society selects the general criteria for defining abnormality and then uses those criteria to judge particular cases.

One clinical theorist, Thomas Szasz (1997, 1987, 1961), places such emphasis on society's role that he finds the whole concept of mental illness to be invalid. According to Szasz, the deviations that society calls abnormal are simply "problems in living," not signs of something wrong within the person. Societies, he is convinced, invent the concept of mental illness so that they can better control or change people whose unusual patterns of functioning upset or threaten the social order.

Even if we assume that psychological abnormality is an appropriate concept, we may be unable to apply its definition consistently. If a behavior—excessive use of alcohol among college students, say—is familiar enough, the society may fail to recognize that it is deviant, distressful, dysfunctional, and dangerous. Thousands of college students throughout the United States are so dependent on alcohol that it interferes with their personal and academic lives, causes them great discomfort, jeopardizes their health, and often endangers them and the people around them. Yet their problem often goes unnoticed, certainly undiagnosed, by college administrators, other students, and health professionals. Alcohol is so much a part of the college subculture that it is easy to overlook drinking behavior that has become abnormal.

Conversely, a society may have trouble separating an abnormality that needs treatment from an *eccentricity,* an unusual individual pattern that others have no right to interfere with. From time to time we see or hear about people who behave in ways we consider strange, such as a man who lives alone with a dozen cats and rarely talks to other people. The behavior of such people is deviant, and it may well be distressful and dysfunctional, yet many professionals think of it as eccentric rather than abnormal.

ANIMAL HOARDERS

Who collects large numbers of animals? Studies suggest that 75 percent of animal hoarders are women; 70 percent are single, divorced, or widowed; half are over 60 years old (Patronek, 1999). Most such individuals collect only one or two species, usually cats.

Marching to a Different Drummer: Eccentrics

Gary Holloway, an environmental planner in San Francisco, keeps a veritable stable of hobbyhorses. He is also fascinated by Martin Van Buren. . . . He discovered that Van Buren was the only U.S. president not to have a society dedicated to his memory, so he promptly founded the Van Buren Fan Club. Holloway is a lifelong devotee of St. Francis of Assisi, and frequently dresses in the habit of a Franciscan monk. "It's comfortable, fun to wear, and I like the response I get when I wear it," he explains. "People always offer me a seat on the bus."

(WEEKS & JAMES, 1995, pp. 29, 36–37)

The dictionary defines an *eccentric* as a person who deviates from common behavior patterns or displays odd or whimsical behavior. But how can we separate a psychologically healthy person who has unusual habits from a person whose oddness is a symptom of psychopathology? Until recently, little research had been done on eccentrics, but a lighthearted study may have started the ball rolling (Weeks & James, 1995).

The researcher David Weeks studied 1,000 eccentrics over a ten-year period and was able to pinpoint fifteen characteristics common to them. Altogether, he estimates that as many as 1 in 5,000 persons may be "classic, full-time eccentrics." Men and women seem equally prone to such patterns.

Weeks suggests that eccentrics do not typically suffer from mental disorders. Whereas the unusual behavior of persons with mental disorders is thrust upon them and usually causes them suffering, eccentricity is chosen freely and provides pleasure. In short, "Eccentrics know they're different and glory in it" (Weeks & James, 1995, p. 14). Similarly, the thought processes of eccentrics are not severely disrupted, and they do not leave the person dysfunctional.

In fact, Weeks found that eccentrics actually had fewer emotional problems than the general population. Perhaps being an "original" is good for mental health. The eccentrics in his study also seemed physically healthier than others, visiting a doctor only once every eight years on average. Weeks concludes that most eccentrics, despite their deviant behavior—perhaps even because of it—are happy, well-adjusted, and joyful people.

Are You Eccentric?

According to Weeks, the following fifteen qualities (in descending order of importance) are characteristic of eccentrics. The first five are the most definitive, but possessing any ten may qualify a person as an eccentric.

- Nonconforming
- Creative
- Strongly curious
- Idealistic
- Happily obsessed with a hobby (often more than one)
- Aware from early childhood of being different from others
- Intelligent
- Opinionated and outspoken
- Noncompetitive
- Unusual eating or living habits
- Not interested in the opinions or company of others
- Mischievous sense of humor
- Single
- Eldest or only child
- Bad speller

Famous Eccentrics

- **James Joyce** always carried a tiny pair of lady's bloomers, which he waved in the air to show approval.
- **Emily Dickinson** always wore white, never left her room, and hid her poems in tiny boxes.
- **Benjamin Franklin** took "air baths" for his health, sitting naked in front of an open window.
- **President John Quincy Adams** swam nude in the Potomac River each morning.
- **Alexander Graham Bell** covered the windows of his house to keep out the rays of the full moon. He also tried to teach his dog how to talk.
- The writer **D. H. Lawrence** enjoyed removing his clothes and climbing mulberry trees.

(ASIMOV, 1997; WEEKS & JAMES, 1995)

Gamma Liaison

Eccentricity takes a break *Gene Pool, a 37-year-old carpenter, journeys repeatedly around New York City wearing an outfit made of 500 empty cans. The reason? To make a statement about the need for recycling and to be noticed. Here he rests for a while on a city park bench.*

In short, while we may agree to define psychological abnormalities as patterns that are deviant, distressful, dysfunctional, and sometimes dangerous, we should be clear that these criteria are often vague. When is a pattern of behavior deviant, distressful, dysfunctional, and dangerous enough to be considered abnormal? The question may be impossible to answer. Few of the current categories of abnormality that we will meet in this book are as clear-cut as they may seem, and most continue to be debated by clinicians.

SUMMING UP | What Is Psychological Abnormality?

The field devoted to the scientific study of abnormal behavior is called abnormal psychology. Its goals are to understand and to treat abnormal patterns of functioning. Abnormal functioning is generally considered to be deviant, distressful, dysfunctional, and dangerous. Behavior must also be considered in the context in which it occurs, however; the concept of abnormality depends on the norms and values of the society in question.

What Is Treatment?

Once clinicians decide that a person is suffering from some form of psychological abnormality, they seek to treat it. **Treatment,** or *therapy,* is a procedure to help change abnormal behavior into more normal behavior; it, too, requires careful definition (Brent & Kolko, 1998). For clinical scientists, the task is closely related to defining abnormality. Consider the case of Bill:

> **February:** He cannot leave the house; Bill knows that for a fact. Home is the only place where he feels safe—safe from humiliation, danger, even ruin. If he were to go to work, his co-workers would somehow reveal their contempt for him. A pointed remark, a quizzical look—that's all it would take for him to get the message. If he were to go shopping at the store, before long everyone would be staring at him. Surely others would see his dark mood and thoughts; he wouldn't be able to hide them. He dare not even go for a walk alone in the woods—his heart would probably start racing again, bringing him to his knees and leaving him breathless, incoherent, and unable to get home. No, he's much better off staying in his room, trying to get through another evening of this curse called life.

> **July:** Bill's life revolves around his circle of friends: Bob and Jack, whom he knows from the office, where he was recently promoted to director of customer relations, and Frank and Tim, his weekend tennis partners. The gang meets for dinner every week at someone's house, and they chat about life, politics, and their jobs. Particularly special in Bill's life is Janice. They go to movies, restaurants, and shows together. She thinks Bill's just terrific, and Bill finds himself beaming whenever she's around. Bill looks forward to work each day and his one-on-one dealings with customers. He is enjoying life and basking in the glow of his many activities and relationships.

Bill's thoughts, feelings, and behavior interfered with all aspects of his life in February. Yet most of his symptoms had disappeared by July. All sorts of factors may have helped Bill to improve. Friends and family members may have offered support or advice. A new job or vacation may have lifted his spirits. Perhaps he changed his diet or started to exercise. Any or all of these things may have been useful to Bill, but they could not be considered treatment, or therapy. Those terms are usually reserved for special, systematic procedures for helping people overcome their psychological difficulties. According to the clinical theorist Jerome Frank, all forms of therapy have three essential features:

TREATMENT A procedure designed to help change abnormal behavior into more normal behavior. Also called *therapy.*

1. A *sufferer* who seeks relief from the healer.

2. A trained, socially accepted *healer,* whose expertise is accepted by the sufferer and his or her social group.

3. A *series of contacts* between the healer and the sufferer, through which the healer tries to produce certain changes in the sufferer's emotional state, attitudes, and behavior.

(Frank, 1973, pp. 2-3)

Despite this straightforward definition, clinical treatment is surrounded by conflict and confusion. Carl Rogers, a pioneer in the modern clinical field whom we will meet in Chapter 2, noted that "therapists are not in agreement as to their goals or aims. . . . They are not in agreement as to what constitutes a successful outcome of their work. They cannot agree as to what constitutes a failure. It seems as though the field is completely chaotic and divided."

Some clinicians view abnormality as an illness and so consider therapy a procedure that helps *cure* the illness. Others see abnormality as a problem in living and therapists as *teachers* of more useful behavior and thought. Clinicians even differ on what to call the person who receives therapy: those who see abnormality as an illness speak of the "patient," while those who view it as a problem in living refer to the "client." Because both terms are so common, this book will use them interchangeably.

Despite their differences, most clinicians do agree that large numbers of people need therapy of one kind or another. Later, we shall see evidence that therapy is indeed often helpful (Chambless & Ollendick, 2001).

> "Modern medicine . . . does reasonably well at measuring disease, but not that well at measuring health."
>
> —James Neel, geneticist, 1994

SUMMING UP | **What Is Treatment?**

Therapy is a special, systematic process for helping people overcome their psychological difficulties. It may differ from problem to problem and therapist to therapist, but it typically includes a patient, a therapist, and a series of professional contacts.

How Was Abnormality Viewed and Treated in the Past?

In any given year as many as 30 percent of the adults and 20 percent of the children and adolescents in the United States display serious psychological disturbances and are in need of clinical treatment (Kazdin, 2000, 1993; Kessler & Zhao, 1999). Furthermore, most people have difficulty coping at various times in their lives and go through periods of extreme tension, dejection, or other forms of psychological discomfort.

It is tempting to conclude that something about the modern world is responsible for these many emotional problems—rapid technological change, perhaps, or a decline in religious, family, or other support systems. Although the special pressures of modern life probably do contribute to psychological dysfunctioning, they are hardly its primary cause. Every society, past and present, has witnessed psychological abnormality. Perhaps, then, the proper place to begin our examination of abnormal behavior and treatment is in the past.

As we look back, we can see how each society has struggled to understand and treat psychological problems, and we can observe that many present-day ideas and treatments have roots in the past. A look backward makes it clear that progress in the understanding and treatment of mental disorders has hardly been a steady movement forward. In fact, many of the inadequacies and controversies that mark the clinical field today are similar to those of the past. At the same

FINANCIAL TOLL

The total economic cost of psychological disorders, including substance abuse, in the United States—direct treatment costs, lost wages, and the like—is more than $400 billion each year (NIDA, 1998; Rice & Miller, 1998).

John W. Verano

Expelling evil spirits *The two holes in this skull recovered from ancient times indicate that the person underwent trephination, possibly for the purpose of releasing evil spirits and curing mental dysfunctioning.*

Humors in action *Hippocrates believed that imbalances of the four humors affected personality. In these depictions of two of the humors, yellow bile (left) drives a husband to beat his wife, and black bile (right) leaves a man melancholic and sends him to bed.*

Zentralbibliothek, Zurich

Zentralbibliothek, Zurich

time, looking back can help us to appreciate the importance of recent breakthroughs and the importance of the journey that lies ahead.

Ancient Views and Treatments

Historians who have scrutinized the unearthed bones, artwork, and other remnants of ancient societies have concluded that these societies probably regarded abnormal behavior as the work of evil spirits. People in prehistoric societies apparently believed that all events around and within them resulted from the actions of magical beings who controlled the world. In particular, they viewed the human body and mind as battle sites for struggles between external forces of good and evil. Abnormal behavior was typically interpreted as a victory by evil spirits, and the cure for such behavior was to force the demons from a victim's body.

This view of abnormality may have begun as far back as the Stone Age, a half-million years ago. Skulls from that period recovered in Europe and South America show evidence of an operation called **trephination,** in which a stone instrument, or *trephine,* was used to cut away a circular section of the skull. Some historians have concluded that this operation was performed as a treatment for severe abnormal behavior—either hallucinations, in which people saw or heard things not actually present, or melancholia, characterized by extreme sadness and immobility. The purpose of opening the skull was to let out the evil spirits that were supposedly causing the problem (Selling, 1940).

Later societies also explained abnormal behavior by pointing to possession by demons. Egyptian, Chinese, and Hebrew writings, for example, all account for psychological problems this way. The Bible describes how an evil spirit from the Lord affected King Saul and how David pretended to be mad in order to convince his enemies that he was visited by divine forces.

The treatment for abnormality in these early societies was often **exorcism.** The idea was to coax the evil spirits to leave or to make the person's body an uncomfortable place for them to live in. A *shaman,* or priest, might recite prayers, plead with the evil spirits, insult them, perform magic, make loud noises, or have the person drink bitter liquids. If these techniques failed, the shaman performed a more extreme form of exorcism, such as whipping or starving the person.

Greek and Roman Views and Treatments

In the years from about 500 B.C. to A.D. 500, when the Greek and Roman civilizations thrived, philosophers and physicians often offered different explanations for abnormal behaviors. Hippocrates (460–377 B.C.), called the father of modern medicine, taught that illnesses had *natural* causes. He saw abnormal behavior as a disease caused by internal physical problems. Specifically, he believed that some form of brain disease was to blame, and that it resulted—like all other forms of disease, in his view—from an imbalance of four fluids, or **humors,** that flowed through the body: *yellow bile, black bile, blood,* and *phlegm.* An excess of yellow bile, for example, caused frenzied joy; an excess of black bile was the source of unshakable sadness. Hippocrates' focus on internal causes for abnormal behavior was shared by the great Greek philosophers Plato (427–347 B.C.) and Aristotle (384–322 B.C.) and by influential Greek and Roman physicians.

Correspondingly, Greek and Roman physicians treated mental disorders with a mixture of medical and psychological techniques. Before resorting to such extreme methods as bleeding patients or restraining them, many Greek physicians first prescribed a warm and supportive atmosphere, music, massage, exercise, and baths. Roman physicians were even clearer about the need to soothe and comfort patients who had mental disorders.

Europe in the Middle Ages: Demonology Returns

The enlightened views of Greek and Roman physicians and scholars were not enough to shake ordinary people's belief in demons. And with the decline of Rome, demonological views and practices became popular once again. A growing distrust of science spread throughout Europe.

From A.D. 500 to 1350, the period known as the Middle Ages, the power of the clergy increased greatly throughout Europe. In those days, the church rejected scientific forms of investigation, and it controlled all education. Religious beliefs, which were highly superstitious and demonological, came to dominate all aspects of life. Once again behavior was usually viewed as a conflict between good and evil, God and the devil. Deviant behavior, particularly psychological dysfunctioning, was seen as evidence of Satan's influence. Although some scientists and physicians still insisted on medical explanations and treatments, their views carried little weight in this atmosphere.

The Middle Ages were a time of great stress and anxiety, of war, urban uprisings, and plagues. People blamed the devil for these troubles and feared being possessed by him. Abnormal behavior apparently increased greatly during this period. In addition, there were outbreaks of *mass madness,* in which large numbers of people apparently shared delusions and hallucinations. In one such disorder, *tarantism* (also known as *St. Vitus's dance*) groups of people would suddenly start to jump, dance, and go into convulsions (Sigerist, 1943). All were convinced that they had been bitten and possessed by a wolf spider, or tarantula. In another form of madness, *lycanthropy,* people thought they were possessed by wolves or other animals. They acted wolflike and imagined that fur was growing all over their bodies.

Not surprisingly, some of the earlier demonological treatments for psychological abnormality returned during the Middle Ages. Once again the key to cure was to rid the person's body of the devil that possessed it. Exorcisms were revived, and clergymen, who generally were in charge of treatment during this period, would plead, chant, or pray to the devil or evil spirit. They might also make individuals drink holy water or bitter-tasting liquids. If these techniques did not work, they might try to insult the devil and attack his pride (Satan's great weakness), or, in more extreme cases, starve, whip, scald, or stretch the individual.

It was not until the Middle Ages drew to a close that demonology and its methods began to lose favor (Magherini & Biotti, 1998). Cities throughout Europe grew larger, and government officials gained more power and took over nonreligious activities. Among their other responsibilities, they began to run hospitals and direct the care of people suffering from mental disorders. Medical views of abnormality gained favor, and many people with psychological disturbances received treatment in medical hospitals, such as Trinity Hospital in England.

The Renaissance and the Rise of Asylums

During the early part of the Renaissance, a period of widespread cultural and scientific activity (about 1400–1700), demonological views of abnormality continued to decline. The German doctor Johann Weyer (1515–1588), the first physician to specialize in mental illness, believed that the mind was as susceptible to sickness as the body. He is now considered the founder of the modern study of *psychopathology,* or mental dysfunction.

TREPHINATION An ancient operation in which a stone instrument was used to cut away a circular section of the skull, perhaps to treat abnormal behavior.

EXORCISM The practice in early societies of treating abnormality by coaxing evil spirits to leave the person's body.

HUMORS According to Greek and Roman physicians, bodily chemicals that influence mental and physical functioning.

CLERICAL INFLUENCE
During the Middle Ages, there was, on average, one church for every 200 people (Asimov, 1997).

THE BARD ON BEHAVIOR
Writing during the Renaissance, William Shakespeare (1564–1616) speculated on the nature and causes of abnormal behavior in 20 of his 38 plays and in many of his sonnets (Dalby, 1997).

Ascending to a Higher Kingdom

In 1997 the world was shocked to learn of the bizarre beliefs held by the Heaven's Gate cult when thirty-nine of its members committed suicide at an expensive house outside San Diego. Videotapes and writings left behind and postings on the Internet revealed that the members had believed that their bodies were mere "containers" for higher heavenly spirits and that a UFO was hiding in the slipstream of the comet Hale-Bopp, coming to take them home to "their world." Ultimately, they believed, their deaths would free them to enter a higher kingdom.

The public was particularly alarmed by the key role that the mass media and modern communication systems apparently played in the rise and spread of Heaven's Gate. In 1993, trying to create interest in the group, its leader, Marshall Herff Applewhite (see photo), ran an ad in *USA Today* that described the cult's philosophical bonds with other millennial groups—groups that expected the world to end in the year 2000. Beyond this form of publicity, the cult members became experts on the Internet and used it to learn about UFO sightings and other signs of "higher life." In addition, cult members apparently recruited new members by sending messages out to Internet news groups focused on suicide, depression, and substance abuse.

Gamma Liaison

ConsiderThis

What features do the beliefs, behaviors, and circumstances of the Heaven's Gate cult share with past forms of "mass madness," such as tarantism and lycanthropy? • Does the Internet pose a special danger in the emergence and spread of new forms of mass madness?

The care of people with mental disorders continued to improve in this atmosphere. In England such individuals might be kept at home while their families were helped financially by the local parish. Across Europe religious shrines were devoted to the humane and loving treatment of people with mental disorders. Perhaps the best known of these shrines was at Gheel in Belgium. Beginning in the fifteenth century, people came to it from all over the world for psychic healing. Local residents welcomed these pilgrims into their homes, and many stayed on to form the world's first "colony" of mental patients. Gheel was the forerunner of today's community mental health programs, and it continues to show that people with mental disorders can respond to loving care and respectful treatment (Aring, 1975, 1974). Many patients still live in foster homes there, interacting with other residents, until they recover.

Unfortunately, these improvements in care began to disappear by the mid-sixteenth century. City officials discovered that private homes and community residences could house only a small percentage of those with severe mental disorders and that medical hospitals were too few and too small. More and more, they converted hospitals and monasteries into **asylums,** institutions whose primary purpose was to care for people with mental illness. These institutions began with every intention of providing good care. Once the asylums started to overflow, however, they became prisons where patients were held in filthy conditions and treated with unspeakable cruelty.

In 1547, for example, Bethlehem Hospital was given to the city of London by Henry VIII for the sole purpose of confining the mentally ill. In this asylum patients bound in chains cried out for all to hear. The hospital actually became a popular tourist attraction; people were eager to pay to look at the howling and gibbering inmates. The hospital's name, pronounced "Bedlam" by the local people, has come to mean a chaotic uproar. Similarly, in the Lunatics' Tower in Vienna, patients were kept in narrow hallways by the outer walls, so that tourists outside could look up and see them.

Corbis-Bettmann

Bewitched or bewildered? *A great fear of witchcraft swept Europe even during the "enlightened" Renaissance. Tens of thousands of people, mostly women, were thought to have made a pact with the devil. Some appear to have had mental disorders, which caused them to act strangely (Zilboorg & Henry, 1941). This individual is being "dunked" repeatedly until she confesses to witchery.*

The Nineteenth Century: Reform and Moral Treatment

As 1800 approached, the treatment of people with mental disorders began to improve once again. Historians usually point to La Bicêtre, an asylum in Paris for male patients, as the first site of asylum reform. In 1793, during the French Revolution, Philippe Pinel (1745–1826) was named the chief physician there. He argued that the patients were sick people whose illnesses should be treated with support and kindness rather than chains and beatings. He allowed them to move freely about the hospital grounds, replaced the dark dungeons with sunny, well-ventilated rooms, and offered support and advice. Pinel's approach proved remarkably successful. Patients who had been shut away for decades improved greatly over a short period of time and were released. Pinel later brought similar reforms to a mental hospital in Paris for female patients, La Salpetrière.

The "crib" *Outrageous devices and techniques, such as the "crib," were used in asylums, and some continued to be used even during the reforms of the nineteenth century.*

Meanwhile an English Quaker named William Tuke (1732–1819) was bringing similar reforms to northern England. In 1796 he founded the York Retreat, a rural estate where about thirty mental patients lived as guests in quiet country houses and were treated with a combination of rest, talk, prayer, and manual work.

THE SPREAD OF MORAL TREATMENT The methods of Pinel and Tuke, called **moral treatment** because they emphasized moral guidance and humane and respectful techniques, caught on throughout Europe and the United States. Patients with psychological problems were increasingly perceived as potentially productive human beings whose mental functioning had broken down under stress. They were considered deserving of individual care, including discussions of their problems, useful activities, work, companionship, and quiet.

The person most responsible for the early spread of moral treatment in the United States was Benjamin Rush (1745–1813), an eminent physician at Pennsylvania Hospital. Limiting his practice to mental illness, Rush developed new, humane approaches to treatment. For example, he required that the hospital hire intelligent and sensitive attendants to work closely with patients, reading and talking to them and taking them on regular walks. He also suggested that it would be therapeutic for doctors to give small gifts to their patients now and then.

Dance in a madhouse *A popular feature of moral treatment was the "lunatic ball." Hospital officials would bring patients together to dance and enjoy themselves. One such ball is shown in this painting,* Dance in a Madhouse, *by George Bellows.*

Rush's work was influential, but it was a Boston schoolteacher named Dorothea Dix (1802–1887) who made humane care a public concern in the United States. From 1841 to 1881, Dix went from state legislature to state legislature and to Congress speaking of the horrors she had observed at asylums throughout the country and calling for reform. Dix's campaign led to new laws and greater government funding to improve the treatment of people with mental disorders. Each state was made responsible for developing effective public mental hospitals. Dix personally helped establish thirty-two of these **state hospitals,** all intended to offer moral treatment (Bickman & Dokecki, 1989). Similar hospitals were established throughout Europe.

THE DECLINE OF MORAL TREATMENT By the 1850s, a number of mental hospitals throughout Europe and America reported that many of their patients were recovering and being released after treatment with moral approaches. By the end of that century, however, several factors helped lead to a reversal of the moral treatment movement (Bockoven, 1963). One factor was the speed with which the movement had spread. As mental hospitals multiplied, severe money and staffing shortages developed, and recovery rates declined. Another factor was the assumption behind moral treatment that all patients could be cured if treated

ASYLUM A type of institution that first became popular in the sixteenth century to provide care for persons with mental disorders. Most became virtual prisons.

MORAL TREATMENT A nineteenth-century approach to treating people with mental dysfunction which emphasized moral guidance and humane and respectful treatment.

STATE HOSPITALS State-run public mental institutions in the United States.

SOMATOGENIC PERSPECTIVE The view that abnormal psychological functioning has physical causes.

PSYCHOGENIC PERSPECTIVE The view that the chief causes of abnormal functioning are psychological.

PSYCHOANALYSIS Either the theory or the treatment of abnormal mental functioning that emphasizes unconscious psychological forces as the cause of psychopathology.

with humanity and dignity. For some, this was indeed sufficient. Others, however, needed more effective treatments than any that had yet been developed. An additional factor contributing to the decline of moral treatment was the emergence of a new wave of prejudice against people with mental disorders. As more and more patients disappeared into large, distant mental hospitals, the public came to view them as strange and dangerous. In turn, people were less open-handed when it came to making donations or allocating government funds. Moreover, many of the patients in public mental hospitals in the United States in the late nineteenth century were poor foreign immigrants, whom the public had little interest in helping.

By the early years of the twentieth century, the moral treatment movement had ground to a halt in both the United States and Europe. Public mental hospitals were providing only custodial care and ineffective medical treatments and were becoming more overcrowded every year. Long-term hospitalization became the rule once again.

The Early Twentieth Century: The Somatogenic and Psychogenic Perspectives

As the moral movement was declining in the late 1800s, two opposing perspectives began to compete for the attention of clinicians: the *somatogenic perspective,* the view that abnormal psychological functioning has physical causes, and the *psychogenic perspective,* the view that the chief causes of abnormal functioning are psychological. These perspectives came into full bloom during the 1900s.

THE SOMATOGENIC PERSPECTIVE The **somatogenic perspective** has at least a 2,400-year history—remember Hippocrates' view that abnormal behavior resulted from brain disease and an imbalance of humors? Not until the late nineteenth century, however, did this view make a triumphant return and begin to gain wide acceptance.

Two factors were responsible for this rebirth. One was the work of an eminent German researcher, Emil Kraepelin (1856–1926). In 1883 Kraepelin published a textbook which argued that physical factors, such as fatigue, are responsible for mental dysfunction. In addition, as we shall see in Chapter 3, he developed the first modern system for classifying abnormal behavior (Hoff, 1998).

Biological discoveries also triggered the rise of the somatogenic perspective. One of the most important was that an organic disease, *syphilis,* led to *general paresis,* an irreversible disorder with both physical and mental symptoms, including paralysis and delusions of grandeur. In 1897 Richard von Krafft-Ebing (1840–1902), a German neurologist, injected matter from syphilis sores into patients suffering from general paresis and found that none of the patients developed symptoms of syphilis. Their immunity could have been caused only by an earlier case of syphilis. Since all patients with general paresis were now immune to syphilis, Krafft-Ebing theorized that syphilis had been the cause of their general paresis.

The work of Kraepelin and the new understanding of general paresis led many researchers and practitioners to suspect that physical factors were responsible for many mental disorders, perhaps all of them. These theories and the possibility of quick and effective

Back wards *Overcrowding, limited funding, and ineffective hospital treatments led to the creation of crowded, often appalling back wards in state hospitals across the United States, which continued well into the twentieth century.*

medical solutions for mental disorders were especially welcomed by those who worked in mental hospitals, where patient populations were now growing at an alarming rate.

Despite the general optimism, biological approaches yielded mostly disappointing results throughout the first half of the twentieth century. Although many medical treatments were developed for patients in mental hospitals during that time, most of the techniques did not work. Physicians tried tooth extraction, tonsillectomy, hydrotherapy (alternating hot and cold baths), and lobotomy, a surgical cutting of certain nerve fibers in the brain. Not until the 1950s, when a number of effective medications were finally discovered, did the somatogenic perspective truly begin to pay off for patients.

THE PSYCHOGENIC PERSPECTIVE The late nineteenth century also saw the rise of the **psychogenic perspective,** the view that the chief causes of abnormal functioning are often psychological. This view, too, has a long history, but it did not gain much of a following until studies of hypnotism demonstrated its potential.

Hypnotism is a procedure that places people in a trancelike mental state during which they become extremely suggestible. It was used to help treat psychological disorders as far back as 1778, when an Austrian physician named Friedrich Anton Mesmer (1734–1815) started a clinic in Paris. His patients suffered from *hysterical disorders,* bodily ailments, such as paralysis, that had no apparent physical basis. Mesmer had his patients sit in a darkened room filled with music; then he appeared, dressed in a colorful costume, and touched the troubled area of each patient's body with a special rod. A surprising number of patients seemed to be helped by this treatment, called *mesmerism.* Their pain, numbness, or paralysis disappeared. Several scientists believed that Mesmer was producing a trancelike state in his patients and that this state was causing their symptoms to disappear. The treatment was so controversial, however, that eventually Mesmer was banished from Paris.

It was not until years after Mesmer had died that many researchers had the courage to investigate his procedure, later called hypnotism, and its effects on hysterical disorders. The experiments of two physicians practicing in the city of Nancy in France, Hippolyte-Marie Bernheim (1840–1919) and Ambroise-Auguste Liébault (1823–1904), showed that hysterical disorders could actually be produced in otherwise normal subjects while they were under the influence of hypnosis. That is, the physicians could make normal people experience deafness, paralysis, blindness, or numbness by means of hypnotic suggestion—and they could remove these artificial symptoms by the same means. Thus, they established that a *mental* process—hypnotic suggestion—could both cause and cure even a physical dysfunction. Influential scientists concluded that hysterical disorders were largely psychological in origin, and the psychogenic perspective rose in popularity.

Among those who studied the effects of hypnotism on hysterical disorders was Josef Breuer (1842–1925) of Vienna. This physician discovered that his patients sometimes awoke without their hysterical symptoms after speaking freely under hypnosis about past upsetting events. During the 1890s Breuer was joined in his work by another Viennese physician, Sigmund Freud (1856–1939). As we shall see in Chapter 2, Freud's work eventually led him to develop the theory of **psychoanalysis,** which holds that many forms of abnormal and normal psychological functioning are psychogenic. In particular, he believed that unconscious psychological processes are at the root of such functioning.

Freud also developed the *technique* of psychoanalysis, a form of discussion in which clinicians help troubled people gain insight into their unconscious psychological processes. He believed that such insight, even without hypnotic procedures, would help the patients overcome their psychological problems.

DR. DICKENS, I PRESUME
Although controversial in professional circles, Mesmer's treatment attracted many persons outside the clinical field. Charles Dickens, the nineteenth-century English novelist, so strongly believed in mesmerism that he considered himself to be a doctor in this method of healing the sick (Asimov, 1997).

The roots of psychogenic theory *The nineteenth century's leading neurologist, Jean Charcot, gives a clinical lecture in Paris on hypnotism and hysterical disorders.*

Corbis-Bettmann

TOPS IN HIS FIELD

Sigmund Freud's fee for one session of therapy was $20—$160 in today's dollars. That is comparable to the fees of some higher-priced therapists in New York City and Los Angeles.

Freud and his followers applied the psychoanalytic treatment approach primarily to patients with mental disorders who did not require hospitalization. These patients visited therapists in their offices for sessions of approximately an hour and then went about their daily activities—a format of treatment now known as *outpatient therapy*. By the early twentieth century, psychoanalytic theory and treatment were widely accepted throughout the Western world.

SUMMING UP | **How Was Abnormality Viewed and Treated in the Past?**

The history of psychological disorders, stretching back to ancient times, provides us with many clues about the nature of psychological abnormality.

Prehistoric Societies There is evidence that Stone Age cultures used trephination, a primitive form of brain surgery, to treat abnormal behavior. People of early societies also sought to drive out evil spirits by exorcism.

Greeks and Romans Physicians of the Greek and Roman empires offered more enlightened explanations of mental disorders. Hippocrates believed that abnormal behavior was due to an imbalance of the four humors: black bile, yellow bile, blood, and phlegm.

The Middle Ages and Renaissance In the Middle Ages, Europeans returned to demonological explanations of abnormal behavior. The clergy was very influential and held that mental disorders were the work of the devil.

Demonology declined once again as the Middle Ages drew to a close, and care of people with psychological disorders improved during the early part of the Renaissance. A number of religious shrines offered humane treatment. Unfortunately, this enlightened approach was short-lived, and by the middle of the sixteenth century persons with mental disorders were being locked away in asylums.

Moral Treatment Care for those with mental disorders began to improve again in the nineteenth century. Moral treatment began in Europe and spread to the United States, where Dorothea Dix's national campaign helped lead to the establishment of state hospitals.

Moral treatment proved costly, however, and as hospitals grew, it became very difficult to keep applying moral principles. Besides, some psychological disorders did not improve under moral treatment. The system slowly fell apart, and by the late nineteenth century public mental hospitals again became warehouses where the inmates received minimal care.

The Somatogenic and Psychogenic Views The late nineteenth century saw the return of the somatogenic perspective, the view that abnormal psychological functioning is caused largely by physical factors. The same period saw the rise of the psychogenic perspective, the view that the chief causes of abnormal functioning are often psychological. Sigmund Freud's psychogenic approach, psychoanalysis, eventually gained wide acceptance and influenced future generations of clinicians.

BIAS IN THE ASYLUMS

Most of the patients in asylums, from all classes and circumstances, were women (Gold, 1998; Showalter, 1985).

LINGERING BELIEFS

19 percent of Americans believe that people with psychological disorders have too little willpower or self-discipline to deal with their problems.

24 percent believe that persons will not develop psychological disorders if they keep busy and have good family relationships and close friends.

(NMHA, 1999)

Current Trends

It would hardly be accurate to say that we now live in a period of great enlightenment or dependable treatment of mental disorders. In fact, one survey found that 43 percent of those interviewed currently believe that people bring on such disorders themselves and 35 percent consider the disorders to be caused by sinful behavior (Murray, 1993). Nevertheless, the past 50 years have brought major changes in the ways clinicians understand and treat mental disorders. There are more theories and types of treatment, more research studies, more information, and, perhaps for these reasons, more disagreements about abnormal functioning today than at any time in the past. In some ways the study and treatment of psychological disorders have come a long way, but in other respects clinical scientists and practitioners are still struggling to make a difference.

How Are People with Severe Disturbances Cared For?

In the 1950s researchers discovered a number of new **psychotropic medications**—drugs that primarily affect the brain and reduce many symptoms of mental dysfunctioning. They included the first *antipsychotic drugs,* to correct extremely confused and distorted thinking; *antidepressant drugs,* to lift the mood of depressed people; and *antianxiety drugs,* to reduce tension and worry.

When given these drugs, many patients who had spent years in mental hospitals began to show signs of improvement. Hospital administrators, encouraged by these results and pressured by a growing public outcry over the terrible conditions in public mental hospitals, began to discharge patients almost immediately.

Since the discovery of these medications, mental health professionals in most of the developed nations of the world have followed a policy of **deinstitutionalization,** releasing hundreds of thousands of patients from public mental hospitals. On any given day in 1955, close to 600,000 people lived in public mental institutions across the United States (see Figure 1-1). Today the daily patient population in the same kinds of hospitals is around 70,000 (Lang, 1999; Torrey, 1997).

In short, outpatient care has become the main form of treatment for people with severe psychological disturbances as well as for those with more moderate problems. Today, when very disturbed people do need institutionalization, they are usually given *short-term* hospitalization (NAPHS, 1999). Ideally, they are then given outpatient psychotherapy and medication in community programs and residences.

Chapters 2 and 12 will look more closely at this recent emphasis on community care for people with severe psychological disturbances—a philosophy called the *community mental health approach.* The approach has been helpful for many patients, but too few community programs are available to meet current needs in the United States. As a result, hundreds of thousands of persons with severe disturbances fail to make lasting recoveries, and they shuffle back and forth between the mental hospital and the community. After release from the hospital, they at best receive minimal care and often wind up living in decrepit rooming houses or on the streets. In fact, an estimated 150,000 or more persons with severe psychological disturbances are currently homeless on any given day; even more are inmates of jails and prisons (Lang, 1999; Torrey, 1997). Their abandonment is truly a national disgrace.

How Are People with Less Severe Disturbances Treated?

The treatment picture for people with moderate psychological disturbances has been more positive than that for people with severe disorders. Since the 1950s, outpatient care has continued to be the preferred form of treatment for them, and the number and types of facilities that offer such care have increased to meet the need (NAPHS, 1999).

Before the 1950s, almost all outpatient care took the form of *private psychotherapy,* an arrangement by which an individual directly pays a psychotherapist for counseling services. This tended to be an expensive form of treatment, available only to the wealthy. Since the 1950s, however, most health insurance plans have increased coverage to include private psychotherapy, so that it is now also widely available to people with modest incomes (Levin, 1992). In addition, outpatient therapy is now offered at a number of less expensive settings, such as community mental health centers, crisis intervention centers, family service

PATIENT DUMPING

According to a recent study, at least two-thirds of mental hospitals in the United States currently engage in the practice of "patient dumping" (Grinfield, 1998; Schlesinger et al., 1997). They periodically deny care to patients or transfer them to other facilities, largely because the individuals require costly care or are underinsured.

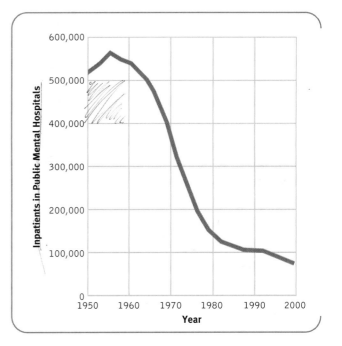

FIGURE 1-1 The impact of deinstitutionalization *The number of patients (70,000) now hospitalized in public mental hospitals in the United States is a small fraction of the number hospitalized in 1955. (Adapted from Lang, 1999; Torrey, 1997, 1988.)*

PSYCHOTROPIC MEDICATIONS Drugs that mainly affect the brain and reduce many symptoms of mental dysfunctioning.

DEINSTITUTIONALIZATION The practice, begun in the 1960s, of releasing hundreds of thousands of patients from public mental hospitals.

Bob Daemmrich/The Image Works

The availability of therapy *Therapy for people with mild to severe psychological disturbances is widely available today in individual, group, and family formats.*

Ron Phillips/The Everett Collection

Therapy in the cinema *The variety and impact of today's mental health professionals are reflected in the work of cinematic therapists such as the late Dr. Malcolm Crowe (*The Sixth Sense*). Other notable film clinicians include Drs. McGuire (*Good Will Hunting*), Berger (*Ordinary People*), Lecter (*The Silence of the Lambs*), Sobel (*Analyze This*), and Petersen and Murchison (*Spellbound*), as well as Nurse Ratchet (*One Flew Over the Cuckoo's Nest*).*

centers, and other social service agencies (Redick et al., 1996; Olfson et al., 1994). The new settings have spurred a dramatic increase in the number of persons seeking outpatient care for psychological problems.

Nationwide surveys suggest that as many as 22 million adults in the United States, one of every eight, receive therapy for psychological problems in the course of a year (Kessler et al., 1994; Narrow et al., 1993). It has also become increasingly common for children to be treated for psychological problems (Kazdin, 1993).

Outpatient treatments are also becoming available for more and more kinds of problems. When Freud and his colleagues first began to practice, most of their patients suffered from anxiety or depression. These problems still dominate therapy today; almost half of all clients suffer from them. However, people with other kinds of disorders are also receiving therapy (Zarin et al., 1998; Narrow et al., 1993). In addition, at least 25 percent of clients enter therapy because of milder problems in living—problems with marital, family, job, social, or school relationships.

In fact, so many persons now seek therapy that private insurance companies have recently changed their plans of coverage for mental health patients. Most companies have developed *managed care programs,* in which the insurance company determines such key issues as which therapists their clients may choose, the cost of sessions, and the number of sessions for which a client may be reimbursed (Manderscheid et al., 1999). As we shall see later in the text, therapists and clients typically dislike these programs. They fear that the programs shorten therapy (often for the worse), unfairly favor treatments whose results are not always lasting (for example, drug therapy), and put control of therapy into the hands of insurance companies rather than of therapists.

Yet another change in outpatient care since the 1950s has been the development of programs that specialize in one kind of psychological problem. We now have, for example, suicide prevention centers, substance abuse programs, eating disorder programs, phobia clinics, and sexual dysfunction programs. Clinicians in these programs offer the kind of expertise that can come only by concentration in a single area.

What Are Today's Leading Theories and Professions?

One of the most important developments in the clinical field has been the growth of numerous theoretical perspectives. Before the 1950s, the *psychoanalytic* perspective, with its emphasis on unconscious psychological problems as the cause of abnormal behavior, was dominant. Then the discovery of effective psychotropic drugs inspired new respect for the somatogenic, or *biological, view.* As we shall see in Chapter 2, other influential perspectives that have come forth since the 1950s are the *behavioral, cognitive, humanistic-existential,* and *sociocultural* schools of thought. At present no single viewpoint commands the clinical field as the psychoanalytic perspective once did. In fact, the perspectives often conflict and compete with one another; yet, as we shall see, in some instances they complement each other and together provide more complete explanations and treatments for psychological disorders (Widiger & Sankis, 2000; Gabbard & Goodwin, 1996).

In addition, a variety of professionals now offer help to people with psychological problems (Peterson et al., 1996). Before the 1950s, psychotherapy was offered only by *psychiatrists,* physicians who complete three to four additional years of training after medical school (a *residency*) in the treatment of abnormal mental functioning. After World War II, however, the need for mental health services increased rapidly, and other professional groups stepped in to fill the need (Humphreys, 1996).

Among those other groups are *clinical psychologists*—professionals who earn a doctorate in clinical psychology by completing four years of graduate training in abnormal functioning and its treatment and also completing a one-year internship at a mental hospital or mental health agency. Psychotherapy and related services are also provided by *counseling psychologists, educational and school psychologists, psychiatric nurses, marriage therapists, family therapists,* and—the largest group—*psychiatric social workers* (see Table 1-1). Each of these specialties has its own graduate training program (Addis, 2000). Theoretically, each does therapy in a different way, but in reality clinicians from the various specialties often use similar techniques. In fact, the individual differences within a professional group are sometimes greater than the general differences between groups.

IT'S THE LAW

Thirty-three states in the United States mandate that every private health insurance policy must include coverage for mental health services.

Table 1-1

Profiles of Mental Health Professionals

	DEGREE	BEGAN TO PRACTICE	CURRENT NUMBER	MEDIAN AGE	PERCENT MALE
Psychiatrists	M.D., D.O.	1840s	33,486	52	75
Psychologists	Ph.D., Psy.D., Ed.D.	Late 1940s	69,817	48	52
Social workers	M.S.W., D.S.W.	Early 1950s	188,792	47	23
Marriage and family therapists	Various	1940s	46,227	52	45

Source: Barber, 1999; Zarin et al., 1998; Peterson et al., 1996; Knowlton, 1995.

One final important development in the study and treatment of mental disorders since World War II has been a growing appreciation of the need for effective research. As theories and forms of treatment have increased, *clinical researchers* have tried to determine which concepts best explain and predict abnormal behavior, which treatments are most effective, and what kinds of changes may be required. Today well-trained clinical researchers carry out studies in universities, laboratories, mental hospitals, mental health centers, and other clinical settings throughout the world. Their work has already produced important discoveries and changed many of our ideas about abnormal psychological functioning.

PROFESSIONAL SHIFT

In 1978, only 28 percent of psychologists were female, compared to 37 percent in 1988 and 48 percent today. The rise in female professionals is likely to continue: women now earn 75 percent of the bachelor degrees in psychology and 66 percent of the advanced degrees (Barber, 1999).

SUMMING UP

Current Trends

In the 1950s, researchers discovered a number of new psychotropic medications, drugs that mainly affect the brain and reduce many symptoms of mental dysfunctioning. Their success led to a policy of deinstitutionalization, under which hundreds of thousands of patients were released from public mental hospitals. In addition, outpatient treatment became the main approach for most persons with mental disorders, both mild and severe.

Today a variety of perspectives and professionals operate in the field of abnormal psychology. Similarly, there are now many well-trained clinical researchers.

"Sure, we need more research in alchemy, necromancy, and sorcery, but where is the money going to come from?"

What Do Clinical Researchers Do?

Research is the key to accuracy in all fields of study, and it is particularly important in abnormal psychology, because wrong beliefs in this field can lead to great suffering. However, clinical researchers face certain challenges that make their work very difficult. They must figure out ways to measure concepts such as unconscious motives, private thoughts, mood change, and human potential, and they must be sure to use ethical guidelines in their work and consider such issues as the rights of subjects. By examining the leading methods used by today's researchers, we can better understand their tasks and challenges and judge their findings.

Clinical researchers, also called clinical scientists, try to discover laws, or principles, of abnormal psychological functioning. They search for **nomothetic,** or general, **understanding** of the nature, causes, and treatments of abnormality. To gather such general insights, they, like scientists in other fields, use the **scientific method**—that is, they collect and evaluate information through careful observations (Beutler et al., 1995). These observations in turn enable them to pinpoint relationships between variables.

Simply stated, a *variable* is any characteristic or event that can vary, whether from time to time, from place to place, or from person to person. Age, sex, and race are human variables. So are eye color, occupation, and social status. Clinical researchers are interested in variables such as childhood upsets, present life experiences, moods, social functioning, and responses to treatments. They try to determine whether two or more such variables change together and whether a change in one variable causes a change in another. Will the death of a parent cause a child to become depressed? If so, will a given therapy reduce that depression?

Such questions cannot be answered by logic alone, because scientists, like all human beings, make frequent errors in thinking (NAMHC, 1996). Thus, clinical researchers rely mainly on three methods of investigation: the case study, which typically observes one individual only; and the *correlational method* and *experimental method,* approaches that usually observe many individuals. Each is best suited to certain circumstances and questions (Beutler et al., 1995). As a group, the methods allow scientists to form and test *hypotheses,* or hunches, that certain variables are related in certain ways—and to draw broad conclusions as to why.

The Case Study

A **case study** is a detailed description of a person's life and psychological problems. It describes the person's background, present circumstances, and symptoms. It may also speculate about how the person's problems developed. It may describe the person's treatment. One of the field's best-known case studies, known as *The Three Faces of Eve,* describes a woman with multiple personality disorder. The case study focuses on the woman's three alternating personalities, each having a distinct set of memories, preferences, and personal habits (Thigpen & Cleckley, 1957).

Most clinicians take notes and keep records in the course of treating their patients, and some further organize their notes into a formal case study to be shared with other professionals. The clues offered by a case study may help a clinician better understand or treat the patient under discussion (Stricker & Trierweiler, 1995). In addition, case studies may play a role that goes far beyond the individual clinical case (Beutler et al., 1995; Smith, 1988).

HOW ARE CASE STUDIES HELPFUL? Case studies often serve as a *source of ideas* about behavior and "open the way for discoveries" (Bolgar, 1965). For example,

A GROWTH PROFESSION
Ninety percent of all scientists who have ever lived are alive today. (Asimov, 1997).

NOMOTHETIC UNDERSTANDING A general understanding of the nature, causes, and treatments of abnormal psychological functioning in the form of laws or principles.

SCIENTIFIC METHOD The process of systematically gathering and evaluating information through careful observations to gain an understanding of a phenomenon.

CASE STUDY A detailed account of a person's life and psychological problems.

STEPPING BACK

Too Obvious to Research?

Each of the following statements was once accepted as gospel. Had their validity not been tested, had they been judged on the basis of conventional wisdom alone, had new ideas not been proposed and investigated, human knowledge and progress would have been severely limited. What enabled thinkers to move beyond such misperceptions? The answer, quite simply, is *research,* the systematic search for facts through the use of careful observations and investigations.

"The brain is an organ of minor importance."

Aristotle, Fourth Century B.C.

"Woman may be said to be an inferior man."

Aristotle

"[Louis Pasteur's] theory of germs is a ridiculous fiction."

Pierre Pochet, Professor of Physiology, 1872

"Everything that can be invented has been invented."

Charles Duell, U.S. Patent Office, 1899

"The theory of relativity [is] worthless and misleading."

T. J. J. See U.S. Government Observatory, 1924

"If excessive smoking actually plays a role in the production of lung cancer, it seems to be a minor one."

W. C. Heuper, National Cancer Institute, 1954

"Space travel is utter bilge."

Richard van der Riet Wooley, British Astronomer Royal, 1956

"There is no reason for any individual to have a computer in their home."

Ken Olson, Digital Equipment Corp., 1977

"The cloning of mammals . . . is biologically impossible."

James McGrath and Davor Solter, Genetic Researchers, 1984

Freud's theory of psychoanalysis was based mainly on the cases he saw in private practice. In addition, a case study may offer *tentative support* for a theory. Freud used case studies in precisely this way, as evidence for the accuracy of his ideas. Conversely, a case study may serve to *challenge a theory's assumptions* (Kratochwill, 1992).

Case studies also may demonstrate the value of *new therapeutic techniques* or unique applications of existing techniques. And, finally, case studies may offer opportunities to study *unusual problems* that do not occur often enough to permit a large number of observations (Lehman, 1991). Investigators of problems such as multiple personality disorder once relied entirely on case studies for information.

WHAT ARE THE LIMITATIONS OF CASE STUDIES? Case studies, although useful in many ways, also have limitations. To begin with, they are reported by *biased observers* (Lehman, 1991). The therapists who write such studies have a personal stake in seeing that their treatments succeed (Stricker & Trierweiler, 1995). They must choose what to include in a case study, and their choices may at times be self-serving. Case studies also rely on *subjective evidence.* Is a client's problem really caused by the events that the therapist or client says are responsible? After all, those are only a fraction of the events that may have contributed to the problem. Finally, case studies provide *little basis for generalization.* Events or treatments that seem important in one case may be of no help at all in efforts to understand or treat others.

The limitations of the case study are largely addressed by two other methods of investigation: the *correlational method* and the *experimental method.* They do not offer the richness of detail that makes case studies so interesting, but they do help investigators draw broad conclusions about abnormality in the population at large. Thus, they are now the preferred methods of clinical investigation (Pincus et al., 1993).

Does mental dysfunctioning run in families?
One of the most celebrated case studies in abnormal psychology is a study of identical quadruplets dubbed the "Genain" sisters by researchers (after the Greek words for "dire birth"). All the sisters developed schizophrenia in their twenties.

Courtesy of Edna Morlok

Case study, Hollywood style *Case studies often find their way into the arts or media and capture the public's attention. Unfortunately, as this movie poster of* The Three Faces of Eve *illustrates, the studies may be trivialized or sensationalized in those venues.*

CAMPUS DEPRESSION

In a survey of 300 college students, 90 percent considered themselves to have been at least mildly depressed since arriving at college. Half of the reported depressions lasted less than one month (Oswalt & Finkelbery, 1995).

Three characteristics of the correlational and experimental methods enable clinical investigators to gain general insights: (1) Researchers typically observe many individuals. That way, they can collect enough information, or *data,* to support a conclusion. (2) Researchers apply procedures uniformly. Therefore, other researchers can repeat, or *replicate,* the study to see whether it consistently gives the same findings. (3) Researchers use *statistical tests* to analyze the results of a study. These tests indicate whether broad conclusions are justified.

The Correlational Method

Correlation is the degree to which events or characteristics vary with each other. The **correlational method** is a research procedure used to determine this "co-relationship" between variables. This method can, for example, answer the question "Is there a correlation between the amount of life stress people confront and the degree of depression they experience?"—that is, as people keep experiencing stressful events, are they more and more likely to become depressed?

To test this question, researchers have collected life stress scores (for example, the number of threatening events experienced during a certain period of time) and depression scores (for example, scores on a depression survey). Typically, they have found that these variables increase or decrease together (Rudolph et al., 2000; Kendler et al., 1999). That is, the greater a particular person's life stress score, the higher his or her score on a depression survey. Correlations of this kind are said to have a positive *direction,* and the correlation is referred to as a *positive correlation.*

Correlations can have a negative rather than a positive direction. In a *negative correlation,* as the value of one variable increases, the value of the other variable decreases. Researchers have found, for example, a negative correlation between depression and activity level. The greater one's depression, the lower the number of one's activities.

There is still a third possible relationship in a correlational study. Two variables may be *unrelated,* meaning that there is no consistent relationship between them. As the measures of one variable increase, those of the other variable sometimes increase and sometimes decrease. Studies have found, for example, that depression and intelligence are unrelated.

In addition to knowing the direction of a correlation, researchers need to know its *magnitude,* or strength. That is, how closely do the two variables correspond? Does one *always* vary along with the other, or is their relationship less exact? When two variables are found to vary together very closely in subject after subject, the correlation is said to be high, or strong.

The direction and magnitude of a correlation are often calculated numerically and expressed by a statistical term called the *correlation coefficient.* The correlation coefficient can vary from +1.00, which indicates a perfect positive correlation between two variables, down to −1.00, which represents a perfect negative correlation. The *sign* of the coefficient (+ or −) signifies the direction of the correlation; the *number* represents its magnitude. The closer the coefficient is to 0, the weaker, or lower in magnitude, it is. Thus, correlations of +.75 and −.75 are of equal magnitude, and a correlation of +.25 is weaker than either.

Everyone's behavior is changeable, and many human responses can be measured only approximately. Most correlations found in psychological research, therefore, fall short of a perfect positive or negative correlation. One study of life stress and depression in sixty-eight adults found a correlation of +.53 between the two variables (Miller et al., 1976). Although hardly perfect, a correlation of this magnitude is considered large in psychological research.

WHEN CAN CORRELATIONS BE TRUSTED? Scientists must decide whether the correlation they find in a given group of subjects accurately reflects a real correlation in the general population. Could the observed correlation have occurred only by chance? They can test their conclusions by a *statistical analysis* of their data, using principles of probability. In essence, they ask how likely it is that the study's particular findings have occurred by chance. If the statistical analysis indicates that chance is unlikely to explain the correlation they found, researchers call the correlation *statistically significant* and conclude that their findings reflect a real correlation in the general population.

WHAT ARE THE MERITS OF THE CORRELATIONAL METHOD? The correlational method has certain advantages over the case study. Because researchers measure their variables, observe numerous subjects, and apply statistical analyses, they are in a better position to generalize their findings to people beyond the ones they have studied. Researchers are also able to repeat correlational studies on new samples of subjects so that they can check the results of such studies.

Although correlational studies allow researchers to describe the relationship between two variables, they do not explain the relationship. When we look at the positive correlation found in many life stress studies, we may be tempted to conclude that increases in recent life stress cause people to feel more depressed. In fact, however, the two variables may be correlated for any one of three reasons: (1) Life stress may cause depression. (2) Depression may cause people to experience more life stress (for example, a depressive approach to life may cause people to mismanage money or may interfere with social relationships). (3) Depression and life stress may each be caused by a third variable such as poverty. Questions about causality call for the use of the experimental method.

SPECIAL FORMS OF CORRELATIONAL RESEARCH Two kinds of correlational research have been widely used by clinical investigators—*epidemiological studies* and *longitudinal studies*. **Epidemiological studies** reveal the incidence and prevalence of a disorder in a given population. **Incidence** is the number of new cases that occur during a given period of time. **Prevalence** is the total number of cases in the population during a given time period; prevalence includes both existing and new cases.

Over the past twenty years, clinical researchers across the United States have worked on the largest epidemiological study ever conducted, called the Epidemiologic Catchment Area Study. They have interviewed more than 20,000 people in five cities to determine the prevalence of many mental disorders and the treatment

CORRELATION The degree to which events or characteristics vary along with each other.

CORRELATIONAL METHOD A research procedure used to determine how much events or characteristics vary along with each other.

EPIDEMIOLOGICAL STUDY A study that measures the incidence and prevalence of a disorder in a given population.

INCIDENCE The number of new cases of a disorder occurring in a population over a specific period of time.

PREVALENCE The total number of cases of a disorder occurring in a population over a specific period of time.

Twins, correlation, and inheritance *Correlational studies of many pairs of twins have suggested a link between genetic factors and certain psychological disorders. Identical twins (who have identical genes) display a higher correlation for some disorders than do fraternal twins (whose genetic makeup is not identical).*

LONGITUDINAL STUDY A study that observes the same subjects on many occasions over a long period of time.

EXPERIMENT A research procedure in which a variable is manipulated and the effect of the manipulation is observed.

INDEPENDENT VARIABLE The variable in an experiment that is manipulated to determine whether it has an effect on another variable.

DEPENDENT VARIABLE The variable in an experiment that is expected to change as the independent variable is manipulated.

CONFOUNDS In an experiment, variables other than the independent variable that may also be affecting the dependent variable.

CONTROL GROUP In an experiment, a group of subjects who are not exposed to the independent variable.

EXPERIMENTAL GROUP In an experiment, the subjects who are exposed to the independent variable under investigation.

RANDOM ASSIGNMENT A selection procedure that ensures that subjects are randomly placed either in the control group or in the experimental group.

programs used for them (Regier et al., 1993). Another large-scale epidemiological study in the United States, the National Comorbidity Survey, has questioned more than 8,000 individuals (Kessler & Zhao, 1999). Both studies have been further compared with epidemiological studies in other countries, to see how rates of mental disorders and treatment programs vary around the world (Alegria et al., 2000).

Such epidemiological studies have helped researchers detect groups at risk for particular disorders. Women, it turns out, have a higher prevalence rate of anxiety disorders and depression than men, while men have a higher rate of alcoholism than women. Elderly people have a higher rate of suicide than younger people. And persons in some non-Western countries (such as Taiwan) have a higher rate of mental dysfunction than people in Western countries. These trends may lead researchers to suspect that something unique about certain groups or settings is helping to cause particular disorders (Rogers & Holloway, 1990). Declining health in elderly people, for example, may make them more likely to commit suicide; cultural pressures or attitudes common in one country may be responsible for a rate of mental dysfunctioning that differs from the rate found in another country.

In **longitudinal studies,** correlational studies of another kind, researchers observe the same subjects on many occasions over a long period of time. In one such study, investigators observed the progress over the years of normally functioning children whose mothers or fathers suffered from schizophrenia (Parnas, 1988; Mednick, 1971). The researchers found, among other things, that the children of the parents with the most severe cases of schizophrenia were more likely to develop a psychological disorder and to commit crimes at later points in their development.

The Experimental Method

An **experiment** is a research procedure in which a variable is manipulated and the manipulation's effect on another variable is observed. The manipulated variable is called the **independent variable,** and the variable being observed is called the **dependent variable.**

One of the questions that clinical scientists most often ask, for example, is "Does a particular therapy reduce the symptoms of a given disorder?" (Kendall, 1998; Lambert & Bergin, 1994). Because this question is about a causal relationship, it can be answered only by an experiment (see Table 1-2). That is, experimenters must give therapy to people who are suffering from a disorder and then observe whether they improve. Here, therapy is the independent variable, while psychological improvement is the dependent variable.

As with correlational studies, investigators must then do a statistical analysis on the data and find out how likely it is that the changes in the dependent variable are due to chance. Again, if this likelihood is very low, the observed differences are called statistically significant, and the experimenter concludes with some confidence that they are due to the independent variable.

If the true cause of changes in the dependent variable cannot be separated from other possible causes, an experiment gives us very little information. Thus, experimenters must try to eliminate all **confounds** from the study—variables other than the independent variable that may also be affecting the dependent variable. When there are confounds in an experiment, they, rather than the independent variable, may be causing the observed changes (Goodwin, 1995).

For example, situational variables such as the location of the particular office (say, a quiet country setting) or a soothing color scheme in the office may have a therapeutic effect on participants

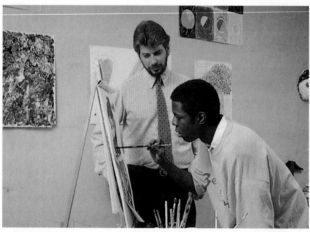

Joel Gordon, New York, NY

What works? *As many as 400 different kinds of therapies are currently used for psychological problems. In one approach,* art therapy, *clients probe, express, and work out their feelings through drawings. An experimental design is needed to determine whether this or any other form of treatment actually causes clients to improve.*

Table 1-2

Strengths and Weaknesses of Research Methods

	PROVIDES INDIVIDUAL INFORMATION	PROVIDES GENERAL INFORMATION	PROVIDES CAUSAL INFORMATION	STATISTICAL ANALYSIS POSSIBLE	REPLICABLE
Case study	Yes	No	No	No	No
Correlational method	No	Yes	No	Yes	Yes
Experimental method	No	Yes	Yes	Yes	Yes

in a therapy study. Or perhaps the participants are unusually motivated or have high expectations that the therapy will work, which thus account for their improvement. To guard against the influence of confounds, researchers include three important features in their experiments—a *control group, random assignment,* and a *blind design* (Goodwin, 1995).

THE CONTROL GROUP A **control group** is a group of subjects who are not exposed to the independent variable under investigation but whose experience is otherwise similar to that of the **experimental group,** the subjects who are exposed to the independent variable. By comparing the two groups, an experimenter can better pinpoint the effect of the independent variable.

To study the effectiveness of therapy, for example, experimenters typically divide subjects into two groups. The experimental group may come into an office and receive the therapy in question for an hour, while the control group may simply come into the office for an hour. If the experimenters find later that the people in the experimental group improve more than the people in the control group, they may conclude that therapy was effective, above and beyond the effects of time, the office setting, and any other confounds. To guard against confounds, experimenters try to provide all participants, both control and experimental, with experiences that are identical in every way—except for the independent variable.

RANDOM ASSIGNMENT Researchers must also watch out for differences that may already exist between participants in the experimental group and those in the control group before a study, since these differences may also confound a study's results. In a therapy study, for example, it may happen that the experimenter has unintentionally put wealthier subjects in the experimental group and poorer subjects in the control group. This difference, rather than therapy, could be the cause of greater improvement later found among the experimental subjects (Persons & Silberschatz, 1998). To reduce the effects of preexisting differences, experimenters typically use **random assignment.** This is the general term for any selection procedure which ensures that every subject in the experiment is as likely to be placed in one group as in the other. We might, for example, try flipping a coin or picking names out of a hat.

STATISTICAL SIGNIFICANCE VS. CLINICAL SIGNIFICANCE

Even if subjects improve because of treatment, we do not know whether the amount of improvement is meaningful in their lives. For example, a subject who is less depressed than previously may still be too unhappy to enjoy life. Thus, although experimenters can determine statistical significance, only individuals and their clinicians can evaluate *clinical* significance.

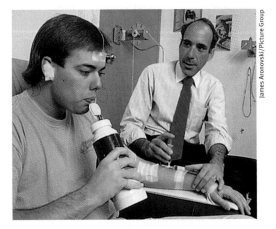

James Aronovski/Picture Group

Overused and overstudied? *The majority of clinical studies have used young white men as subjects, making it difficult to draw clear conclusions about women, members of minority groups, or aged persons. Here one such subject drinks various substances to help determine whether the effects of alcohol are linked to genetic factors.*

Subjects Have Rights

For years researchers have learned about abnormal human behavior from experiments with animals. Animals have sometimes been shocked, prematurely separated from their parents, and starved; they have had their brains surgically changed and even been killed, or "sacrificed," so that researchers could autopsy them. Are such actions always ethically acceptable?

Animal rights activists say no. They have called the undertakings cruel and unnecessary and have fought many forms of animal research with legal protests and demonstrations. Some have even harassed scientists and vandalized their labs. In turn, some researchers accuse the activists of caring more about animals than about human beings. In response to this controversy, a number of state courts have ruled that university researchers must publicly disclose their research proposals to help ensure the well-being of animal subjects. Similarly, government agencies and the American Psychological Association have issued rules and guidelines for animal research. Still the battle goes on.

No less controversial are debates over the rights of human subjects in studies of abnormal behavior. A number of regulations were established in the 1970s to ensure that the rights of all human subjects, particularly those with psychological disorders, were protected in research. In the United States, the Department of Health and Human Services insisted that potential human subjects be clearly informed that they are indeed participating in a study, what procedures will be used, any foreseeable risks, and other such matters. In addition, universities and other research institutions established committees to oversee the well-being of subjects in their facilities.

These efforts have greatly improved the ethics of clinical research, but some problems remain. In fact, the clinical field has been rocked in recent years by a new series of reports that reveal that during the past two decades, many patients with severe mental disorders have been harmed or placed at risk in clinical stud-

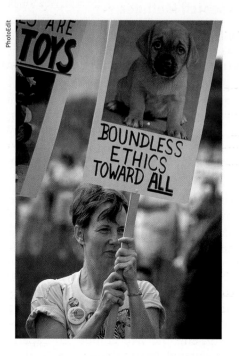

ies (Kong, 1998). The studies in question typically involve antipsychotic drug treatments for patients with psychosis (loss of contact with reality). It appears that many patients in these studies have agreed to receive drug treatments (or not to receive them) without fully understanding the risks involved. In addition, the drugs used in these studies have left some of the subjects with more intense psychotic symptoms. Four types of studies have been cited:

❖ **New Drug Studies** Patients are administered an experimental drug to see whether it reduces their symptoms. The new drug is being tested for effectiveness, safety, undesired effects, and dosage, meaning that the patients may be helped, unaffected, or damaged by the drugs.

❖ **Placebo Studies** When a new drug is being tested on a group of experimental subjects, researchers may administer a *placebo drug* to a group of control subjects (Quitkin, 1999). The improvement of the experimental subjects is then compared with that of the placebo control subjects to determine the new drug's effectiveness. Unfortunately, in such studies, the placebo control subjects—often people with severe

disorders—are receiving no treatment at all.

❖ **Symptom-Exacerbation Studies** Patients are given drugs designed to intensify their symptoms, so that researchers may learn more about the biology of their disorder. For example, people suffering from psychotic disorders have been given apomorphine, amphetamine, ketamine, and other drugs that lead to more delusions, hallucinations, and the like.

❖ **Medication-Withdrawal Studies** Researchers prematurely stop medications for patients who have been symptom-free while taking the medications. The researchers then follow the patients as they relapse, in the hope of learning more about how and when patients can be taken off particular medications.

Each of these kinds of studies seeks to increase understanding of the biology of certain disorders and to improve treatment. Yet at what risk? When does the benefit to many outweigh the suffering of a few? As the clinical community and the public have grown more aware of the risks involved in these studies, they have called for better safeguards to protect research subjects with mental disorders. In 1999 the National Institute of Mental Health suspended some of its symptom-exacerbation studies, and the presidentially appointed National Bioethics Advisory Commission issued a list of recommendations, including the suggestion that a permanent federal panel be created to review high-risk and low-benefit clinical studies. Nevertheless, this important issue is far from being resolved.

Consider This

◉ Do outside restrictions on research interfere with necessary investigations and thus limit potential gains for human beings? • Is there a way to address the concerns and needs of subjects, protesters, *and* researchers?

BLIND DESIGN A final confound problem is *bias.* Participants may bias an experiment's results by trying to please or help the experimenter (Kazdin, 1994). In a therapy experiment, for example, those who receive the treatment, knowing the purpose of the study and knowing which group they are in, might actually work harder to feel better or to fulfill the experimenter's expectations. If so, *subject bias* rather than therapy could be causing their improvement.

To avoid this bias, experimenters can prevent participants from finding out which group they are in. This experimental strategy is called a **blind design** because participants are blind as to their assigned group. In a therapy study, for example, control subjects could receive a **placebo,** something that looks or tastes like real therapy but has none of its key ingredients (Streiner, 1999; Addington, 1995). This "imitation" therapy is called placebo therapy. If the experimental (true therapy) subjects then improve more than the control (placebo therapy) subjects, experimenters have more confidence that the true therapy has caused their improvement.

An experiment may also be confounded by *experimenter bias* (Margraf et al., 1991)—that is, experimenters may have expectations that they unconsciously transmit to their subjects. This bias is referred to as the *Rosenthal effect,* after the psychologist who first identified it (Rosenthal, 1966). Experimenters can eliminate their own bias by arranging to be blind themselves. In a drug therapy study, for example, an aide could make sure that the real medication and the placebo look identical. The experimenter could then give treatment without knowing which participants were receiving true medications and which were receiving false medications.

While either the participants or the experimenter may be kept blind in an experiment, it is best that *both* be blind (a *double-blind design*). In fact, most medication experiments now use double-blind designs to test promising drugs (Morin et al., 1995). Many experimenters also arrange for judges to assess the patients' improvement independently, and the judges, too, are blind to the group each patient is in—*a triple-blind design.*

Alternative Experimental Designs

Clinical experimenters must often settle for experimental designs that are less than ideal. The most common such variations are the quasi-experimental design, the natural experiment, the analogue experiment, and the single-subject experiment.

QUASI-EXPERIMENTAL DESIGN In **quasi-experiments,** or **mixed designs,** investigators do not randomly assign participants to control and experimental groups but instead make use of groups that already exist in the world at large (Kazdin, 1994). For example, because investigators of child abuse cannot actually abuse a randomly chosen group of children, they must instead compare children who already have a history of abuse with children who do not. To make this comparison as valid as possible, they may further use *matched control subjects.* That is, they match the experimental subjects with control subjects who are similar in age, sex, race, number of children in the family, socioeconomic status, or other important characteristics (Kinard, 1982). For every abused child in the experimental group, they choose an unabused child with similar characteristics to be included in the control group.

NATURAL EXPERIMENT In **natural experiments** nature itself manipulates the independent variable, while the experimenter observes the effects. Natural experiments must be used for studying the psychological effects of unusual and unpredictable events, such as floods, earthquakes, plane crashes, and fires. Because the subjects in these studies are

BLIND DESIGN An experiment in which subjects do not know whether they are in the experimental or the control group.

PLACEBO A sham treatment that a subject believes to be genuine.

QUASI-EXPERIMENT An experiment in which investigators make use of control and experimental groups that already exist in the world at large. Also called a *mixed design.*

NATURAL EXPERIMENT An experiment in which nature, rather than an experimenter, manipulates an independent variable.

ConsiderThis

◉ In drug therapy studies, some control subjects who receive placebo pills actually show improvements. Why might sugar pills or other kinds of placebo treatments help people feel better?

Natural experiments *A man surveys the damage wrought by a hurricane upon his home and belongings. Natural experiments conducted in the aftermath of such catastrophes have found that many survivors experience lingering feelings of anxiety and depression.*

Christopher Brown/Stock Boston

Similar enough? *Chimpanzees and human beings share more than 90 percent of their genetic material, but their brains and bodies are very different, as are their perceptions and experiences. Thus, abnormal-like behavior produced in animal analogue experiments may differ from the human abnormality under investigation.*

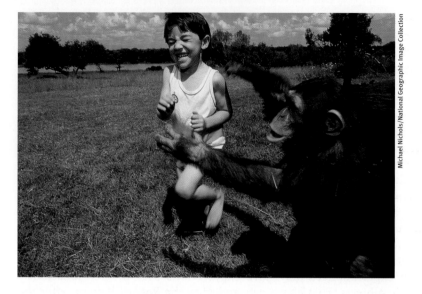

"Ants are so much like human beings as to be an embarrassment. [They] launch armies into wars, use chemical sprays to alarm and confuse enemies, capture slaves, [and] engage in child labor. . . . They exchange information ceaselessly. They do everything but watch television."

—Dr. Lewis Thomas, Memorial Sloan-Kettering Cancer Center

selected by an accident of fate rather than by conscious design, natural experiments are actually a kind of quasi-experiment.

ANALOGUE EXPERIMENT Experimenters often run **analogue experiments** (Plaus, 1996). Here they produce abnormal-like behavior in laboratory subjects—either animals or humans—and then conduct experiments on the subjects in the hope of shedding light on real-life abnormality. For example, the investigator Martin Seligman (1975) has produced depression-like symptoms in laboratory subjects by repeatedly giving them negative reinforcements (shocks, loud noises, task failures) over which they have no control. In these "learned helplessness" studies, the participants seem to give up, lose their initiative, and become sad.

SINGLE-SUBJECT EXPERIMENT Sometimes scientists do not have the luxury of experimenting on many subjects. They may, for example, be investigating a disorder so rare that few subjects are available. Experimentation is still possible, however, with a **single-subject experimental design.** Here a single subject is observed both before and after the manipulation of an independent variable (Goodwin, 1995; Kazdin, 1994).

Single-subject experiments first rely on *baseline data*—information gathered prior to any manipulations. These data set a standard with which later changes may be compared. The experimenter next introduces the independent variable and again observes the subject's behavior. Any changes in behavior are attributed to the effects of the independent variable.

A CLOSER LOOK

Clear as a Bell?

To ensure that subjects know what they are getting into when they sign up for a study, and to guarantee that subjects feel free to leave the study at any time, researchers must inform them about the nature of the study and about their rights. This principle of "informed consent," the foundation of all human research, usually translates into a written form that spells out everything the subjects need to know. But how clear are informed consent forms? Not very, according to some recent studies (Hochhauser, 1999; Uretsky, 1999).

Many such forms are written at an advanced college level, making them incomprehensible to a large percentage of subjects. When investigators used a readability scale to compare various writing samples (higher scores indicated greater reading difficulty), they discovered the following:

An Ann Landers column earned a score of 7.67 (75 percent of the population can understand it).

Reader's Digest magazine earned 9.95 (69 percent can understand it).

New Yorker magazine earned 13.3 (43 percent can understand it).

Typical informed consent forms earned 15.03 (37 percent can understand them).

In an *ABAB*, or *reversal, design,* a common single-subject experimental design, a subject's reactions are measured and compared not only during a baseline period (condition A) and after the introduction of the independent variable (condition B) but also after the independent variable has been removed (condition A) and yet again after it has been reintroduced (condition B). If the subject's responses change back and forth along with changes in the independent variable, the experimenter may conclude that the independent variable is causing the shifting responses (Kratochwill, 1992). Essentially, in an ABAB design a subject is compared with himself or herself under different conditions rather than with control subjects.

One researcher used an ABAB design to determine whether the systematic use of rewards was helping to reduce a teenage boy's habit of disrupting his special education class with loud talk (Deitz, 1977). The treatment program consisted of rewarding the boy, who suffered from mental retardation, with extra teacher time whenever he went 55 minutes without interrupting the class more than three times. When observed during a baseline period, the student was found to disrupt the class frequently with loud talk. Next the boy was given a series of teacher reward sessions (the independent variable); his loud talk decreased dramatically, as expected. Then the rewards from the teacher were stopped, and the student's loud talk increased once again. Apparently the independent variable had indeed been the cause of the improvement. To be still more confident about this conclusion, the researcher had the teacher apply reward sessions yet again. Once again the subject's behavior improved.

What Are the Limits of Clinical Investigations?

We began this discussion by noting that clinical scientists look for general laws that will help them understand, prevent, and treat psychological disorders. As we have seen, however, various circumstances may interfere with their progress.

Each of the methods of investigation addresses some of the problems involved in studying human behavior, but no one approach overcomes them all. Thus it is best to view each research method as part of a team of approaches that together may shed considerable light on abnormal human functioning. When more than one method has been used to investigate a certain disorder, it is important to ask whether all the results seem to point in the same direction. If they do, we are probably that much closer to a clear understanding of the disturbance or an effective treatment for it. Conversely, if the various methods seem to produce conflicting results, we must admit that our knowledge in that particular area is still limited.

ANALOGUE EXPERIMENT A research method in which the experimenter produces abnormal-like behavior in laboratory subjects and then conducts experiments on the subjects.

SINGLE-SUBJECT EXPERIMENT A research method in which a single subject is observed and measured both before and after the manipulation of an independent variable.

"Oh, not bad. The light comes on, I press the bar, they write me a check. How about you?"

SUMMING UP

What Do Clinical Researchers Do?

Clinical researchers use the scientific method to uncover general principles of abnormal psychological functioning. They depend primarily on three methods of investigation: the case study, the correlational method, and the experimental method.

Case Study A case study is a detailed account of a person's life and psychological problems.

Correlational Method Correlational studies systematically observe the degree to which events or characteristics vary together. This method allows researchers to draw broad conclusions about abnormality in the population at large. Two widely used forms of the correlational method are epidemiological studies and longitudinal studies.

Experimental Method In experiments, researchers manipulate suspected causes to see whether expected effects will result. Clinical experimenters must often settle for experimental designs that are less than ideal, including the quasi-experiment, the natural experiment, the analogue experiment, and the single-subject experiment.

IT'S OFFICIAL

The word "scientist" did not exist until it was coined by the nineteenth-century English scholar William Whewell (Asimov, 1997).

*Consider*This

People of the Stone Age did not leave written records, so archaeologists cannot be certain that trephination was in fact an ancient treatment for mental dysfunctioning. How else might we explain the holes found in the skulls recovered from early times?

CROSSROADS:
A Work in Progress

Since ancient times, people have tried to explain, treat, and study abnormal behavior. By examining the responses of past societies to such behaviors, we can better understand the roots of our present views and treatments. In addition, a look backward helps us appreciate just how far we have come—how humane our present views, how impressive our recent discoveries, and how important our current emphasis on research.

At the same time, we must recognize the many problems in abnormal psychology today. The field has yet to agree on one definition of abnormality. It is currently made up of conflicting schools of thought and treatment, whose members are often unimpressed by the claims and accomplishments of the others. Clinical practice is carried out by a variety of professionals trained in different ways. And current research methods each have key flaws that limit our knowledge and use of clinical information.

As we proceed through the topics in this book and look at the nature, treatment, and study of abnormal functioning, we must keep in mind the field's current strengths and weaknesses, the progress that has been made, and the journey that lies ahead. Perhaps the most important lesson to be learned from our look at the history of this field is that our current understanding of abnormal behavior represents a work in progress. The clinical field stands at a *crossroads,* with some of the most important investigations, insights, and changes yet to come.

KEY TERMS

abnormal psychology p. 2

deviance p. 2

norms p. 3

culture p. 3

distress p. 3

dysfunction p. 4

danger p. 4

treatment p. 6

trephination p. 8

exorcism p. 8

humors p. 8

asylum p. 10

moral treatment p. 11

state hospitals p. 11

somatogenic perspective p. 12

general paresis p. 12

psychogenic perspective p. 13

hypnotism p. 13

psychoanalysis p. 13

psychotropic medications p. 15

deinstitutionalization p. 15

private psychotherapy p. 15

nomothetic understanding p. 18

scientific method p. 18

case study p. 18

correlation p. 20

correlational method p. 20

epidemiological study p. 21

incidence p. 21

prevalence p. 21

longitudinal study p. 22

experiment p. 22

independent variable p. 22

dependent variable p. 22

confound p. 22

control group p. 23

experimental group p. 23

random assignment p. 23

blind design p. 25

placebo p. 25

quasi-experiment p. 25

natural experiment p. 25

analogue experiment p. 26

single-subject experimental design p. 26

ABAB design p. 27

QUICK QUIZ

1. What features are common to abnormal psychological functioning? pp. 2–6

2. Name two forms of past treatments that reflect a demonological view of abnormal behavior. pp. 8–10

3. Give examples of the somatogenic view of psychological abnormality from Hippocrates, the Renaissance, the nineteenth century, and the recent past. pp. 8–15

4. Discuss the rise and fall of moral treatment. pp. 11–12

5. Describe the role of hypnotism and hysterical disorders in the development of the psychogenic view. pp. 13–14

6. How did Sigmund Freud come to develop the theory and technique of psychoanalysis? pp. 13–14

7. Describe the major changes in the treatment of people with mental disorders that have occurred since the 1950s. pp. 14–17

8. What are the advantages and disadvantages of the case study, correlational method, and experimental method? What features of each method enable researchers to gain general insights? pp. 18–25

9. What techniques do researchers include in experiments to guard against the influence of confounds? pp. 22–25

10. Describe four alterna[...] experiments that res[...] use. pp. 25–27

CYBER STUDY

▲ *What did past hospital treatments for severe mental disorders look like?* ▲ *How might it have felt to receive or administer these treatments?* ▲ *Are the early treatments behind us?* ▲ *How do researchers measure psychopathology?* ▲ *Observe genetic research in action.*

SEARCH THE *FUNDAMENTALS OF ABNORMAL PSYCHOLOGY* CD-ROM FOR

▲ Chapter 1 video cases and discussions
   Early Procedures in Mental Hospitals
   Mood Disorders: Hereditary Factors

▲ Chapter 1 practice test and feedback

▲ Additional video cases and discussions
   Early Electroconvulsive Therapy
   The Mind of the Psychopath

LOG ON TO THE COMER WEB PAGE FOR

▲ Suggested Web links, research exercises, FAQ page, additional Chapter 1 practice test questions
   <http://www.worthpublishers.com/comer>

Courtesy of the History of Medicine Division, National Library of Medicine

Models of Abnormality

Philip Berman, a 25-year-old single unemployed former copy editor for a large publishing house, . . . had been hospitalized after a suicide attempt in which he deeply gashed his wrist with a razor blade. He described [to the therapist] how he had sat on the bathroom floor and watched the blood drip into the bathtub for some time before he telephoned his father at work for help. He and his father went to the hospital emergency room to have the gash stitched, but he convinced himself and the hospital physician that he did not need hospitalization. The next day when his father suggested he needed help, he knocked his dinner to the floor and angrily stormed to his room. When he was calm again, he allowed his father to take him back to the hospital.

The immediate precipitant for his suicide attempt was that he had run into one of his former girlfriends with her new boyfriend. The patient stated that they had a drink together, but all the while he was with them he could not help thinking that "they were dying to run off and jump in bed." He experienced jealous rage, got up from the table, and walked out of the restaurant. He began to think about how he could "pay her back."

Mr. Berman had felt frequently depressed for brief periods during the previous several years. He was especially critical of himself for his limited social life and his inability to have managed to have sexual intercourse with a woman even once in his life. As he related this to the therapist, he lifted his eyes from the floor and with a sarcastic smirk said, "I'm a 25-year-old virgin. Go ahead, you can laugh now." He has had several girlfriends to date, whom he described as very attractive, but who he said had lost interest in him. On further questioning, however, it became apparent that Mr. Berman soon became very critical of them and demanded that they always meet his every need, often to their own detriment. The women then found the relationship very unrewarding and would soon find someone else.

During the past two years Mr. Berman had seen three psychiatrists briefly, one of whom had given him a drug, the name of which he could not remember, but that had precipitated some sort of unusual reaction for which he had to stay in a hospital overnight. . . . Concerning his hospitalization, the patient said that "It was a dump," that the staff refused to listen to what he had to say or to respond to his needs, and that they, in fact, treated all the patients "sadistically." The referring doctor corroborated that Mr. Berman was a difficult patient who demanded that he be treated as special, and yet was hostile to most staff members throughout his stay. After one angry exchange with an aide, he left the hospital without leave, and subsequently signed out against medical advice.

Mr. Berman is one of two children of a middle-class family. His father is 55 years old and employed in a managerial position for an insurance company. He perceives his father as weak and ineffectual, completely dominated by the patient's overbearing and cruel mother. He states that he hates his mother with "a passion I can barely control." He claims that his mother used to call him names like "pervert" and "sissy" when he was growing up, and that in an argument she once "kicked me in the balls." Together, he sees his parents as rich, powerful, and selfish, and, in turn, thinks that they see him

MODEL A set of assumptions and concepts that help scientists explain and interpret observations. Also called a *paradigm*.

NEURON A nerve cell.

as lazy, irresponsible, and a behavior problem. When his parents called the therapist to discuss their son's treatment, they stated that his problem began with the birth of his younger brother, Arnold, when Philip was 10 years old. After Arnold's birth Philip apparently became an "ornery" child who cursed a lot and was difficult to discipline. Philip recalls this period only vaguely. He reports that his mother once was hospitalized for depression, but that now "she doesn't believe in psychiatry."

Mr. Berman had graduated from college with average grades. Since graduating he had worked at three different publishing houses, but at none of them for more than one year. He always found some justification for quitting. He usually sat around his house doing very little for two or three months after quitting a job, until his parents prodded him into getting a new one. He described innumerable interactions in his life with teachers, friends, and employers in which he felt offended or unfairly treated, . . . and frequent arguments that left him feeling bitter . . . and spent most of his time alone, "bored." He was unable to commit himself to any person, he held no strong convictions, and he felt no allegiance to any group.

The patient appeared as a very thin, bearded, and bespectacled young man with pale skin who maintained little eye contact with the therapist and who had an air of angry bitterness about him. Although he complained of depression, he denied other symptoms of the depressive syndrome. He seemed preoccupied with his rage at his parents, and seemed particularly invested in conveying a despicable image of himself. . . .

(Spitzer et al., 1983, pp. 59–61)

Philip Berman is clearly a troubled person, but how did he come to be that way? How do we explain and correct his many problems? In confronting these questions, we must first look at the wide range of complaints we are trying to understand: Philip's depression and anger, his social failures, his lack of employment, his distrust of those around him, and the problems within his family. Then we must sort through all kinds of potential causes, internal and external, biological and interpersonal, past and present. Which is having the biggest impact on his behavior?

Although we may not realize it, we all use theoretical frameworks as we read about Philip. Over the course of our lives, each of us has developed a perspective that helps us make sense of the things other people say and do. In science, the perspectives used to explain events are known as **models,** or **paradigms.** Each model spells out the scientist's basic assumptions, gives order to the field under study, and sets guidelines for its investigation (Kuhn, 1962). It influences what the investigators observe, as well as the questions they ask, the information they seek, and their interpretation of this information (Plante, 1999; Nietzel et al., 1994). To understand how a clinician explains or treats a specific set of symptoms, such as Philip's, we must know which model shapes his or her view of abnormal functioning.

Until recently, clinical scientists of a given place and time tended to agree on a single model of abnormality—a model greatly influenced by the beliefs of their culture. The demonological model that was used to explain abnormal functioning during the Middle Ages, for example, borrowed heavily from medieval society's concerns with religion, superstition, and warfare. Medieval practitioners would have seen the devil's guiding hand in Philip Berman's efforts to commit suicide and his feelings of depression, rage, jealousy, and hatred. Similarly, their treatments for him—from prayers to whippings—would have sought to drive foreign spirits from his body.

Today several models are used to explain and treat abnormal functioning. This variety has resulted from changes in values and beliefs over the past half-century, as well as improvements in clinical research. At one end of the spectrum is the *biological model,* which sees physical processes as the key to human behavior. At the other end is the *sociocultural model,* which examines the effects of society and

"Men are apt to believe what they least understand."

Michel de Montaigne, 1533–1592

culture on individual behavior. In between are four models that focus on more psychological and personal aspects of human functioning: the *psychodynamic model* looks at people's unconscious internal events and conflicts; the *behavioral model* emphasizes behavior and the ways in which it is learned; the *cognitive model* concentrates on the thinking that underlies behavior; and the *humanistic-existential model* stresses the role of values and choices in human functioning.

Given their different assumptions and concepts, the models are sometimes in conflict. Those who follow one perspective often scoff at the "naive" interpretations, investigations, and treatment efforts of the others. Yet none of the models is complete in itself. Each focuses mainly on one aspect of human functioning, and none can explain all aspects of abnormality.

The Biological Model

Philip Berman is a biological being. His thoughts and feelings are the results of biochemical and bioelectrical processes throughout his brain and body. Proponents of the *biological model* believe that a full understanding of his thoughts, emotions, and behavior must include an understanding of their biological basis. Not surprisingly, they believe that the most effective treatments for Philip's problems will be biological ones.

How Do Biological Theorists Explain Abnormal Behavior?

Adopting a medical perspective, biological theorists view abnormal behavior as an illness brought about by malfunctioning parts of the organism. Typically, they point to a malfunctioning brain as the cause of abnormal behavior (Schwartz, 1999).

BRAIN ANATOMY AND ABNORMAL BEHAVIOR The brain is made up of approximately 100 billion nerve cells, called **neurons,** and thousands of billions of support cells, called *glia* (from the Greek meaning "glue"). Within the brain large groups of neurons form distinct areas, or *brain regions*. To identify the regions of the brain more easily, let us imagine them as continents, countries, and states.

At the bottom of the brain is the "continent" known as the *hindbrain,* which is in turn made up of countrylike regions called the *medulla, pons,* and *cerebellum* (see Figure 2-1). In the middle of the brain is the "continent" called the *midbrain.* And at the top is the "continent" called the *forebrain,* which consists of countrylike regions called the *cerebrum* (the two cerebral hemispheres), the *thalamus,* and the *hypothalamus,* each in turn made up of statelike regions. The cerebrum, for instance, consists of the *cortex, corpus callosum, basal ganglia, hippocampus,* and *amygdala.* The neurons in each of these brain regions control important functions. The hippocampus helps control emotions and memory, for example. Clinical researchers have discovered connections between certain psychological disorders and problems in specific areas of the brain. One such disorder is *Huntington's disease,* a disorder marked by violent emotional outbursts, memory loss, suicidal thinking, involuntary body movements, and absurd beliefs. This disease has been traced to a loss of cells in the basal ganglia.

FIGURE 2-1 **The human brain** *A slice through the center of the brain reveals its major divisions and regions. Each region, composed of numerous neurons, is responsible for certain functions.*

Cerebral hemisphere

Corpus callosum (connects two cerebral hemispheres)

Thalamus

Forebrain (not all subregions visible from this angle)

Hypothalamus (regulates temperature, hunger, thirst, sex)

Midbrain

Cerebellum (regulates smooth coordinated movement)

Pons

Medulla (controls heart rate, breathing, digestion)

Hindbrain

Spinal cord

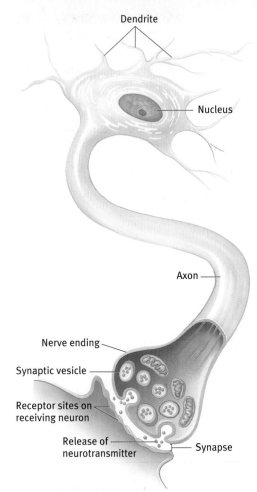

Dendrite

Nucleus

Axon

Nerve ending

Synaptic vesicle

Receptor sites on receiving neuron

Release of neurotransmitter

Synapse

FIGURE 2-2 **A typical neuron** *A message travels down the neuron's axon to the nerve ending, where neurotransmitters carry the message across the synaptic space to a receiving neuron. (Adapted from Bloom et al., 1985, p. 35.)*

More than coincidence? *Studies of twins suggest that some aspects of behavior and personality are influenced by genetic factors. Many identical twins, like these musicians, are found to have similar tastes, behave in similar ways, and make similar life choices. Some even develop similar abnormal behaviors.*

BRAIN CHEMISTRY AND ABNORMAL BEHAVIOR Biological researchers have also learned that psychological disorders can be related to problems in the transmission of messages from neuron to neuron. Information spreads throughout the brain in the form of electrical impulses that travel from one neuron to one or more others. An impulse is first received by a neuron's *dendrites,* antenna-like extensions located at one end of the neuron. From there it travels down the neuron's *axon,* a long fiber extending from the neuron body. Finally, it is transmitted to other neurons through the *nerve endings,* at the far end of the neuron (see Figure 2-2).

But how do messages get from the nerve endings of one neuron to the dendrites of another? After all, the neurons do not actually touch each other. A tiny space, called the **synapse,** separates one neuron from the next, and the message must somehow move across that space. When an electrical impulse reaches a neuron's ending, the nerve ending is stimulated to release a chemical, called a **neurotransmitter,** that travels across the synaptic space to receptors on the dendrites of the adjacent neurons. Upon reception, some neurotransmitters tell the receiving neurons to "fire," that is, to trigger their own electrical impulse. Other neurotransmitters tell receiving neurons to stop all firing. Obviously, neurotransmitters play a key role in moving information through the brain.

Researchers have identified dozens of neurotransmitters in the brain, and they have learned that each neuron uses only certain kinds (Barondes, 1993). Studies indicate that abnormal activity by certain neurotransmitters can lead to specific mental disorders (Robert, Rubin-Brunet, & Darcourt, 1999; Gershon & Rieder, 1992). Certain anxiety disorders, for example, have been linked to low activity of the neurotransmitter *gamma-aminobutyric acid (GABA),* schizophrenia has been linked to excessive activity of the neurotransmitter *dopamine,* and depression has been linked to low activity of the neurotransmitter *serotonin.* Perhaps low serotonin activity is responsible for Philip Berman's pattern of depression and rage.

In addition to focusing on neurons and neurotransmitters, researchers have learned that mental disorders are sometimes related to abnormal chemical activity in the body's *endocrine system.* Endocrine glands, located throughout the body, work along with neurons to control such vital activities as growth, reproduction, sexual activity, heart rate, body temperature, energy, and responses to stress. The glands release chemicals called **hormones** into the bloodstream, and these chemicals then propel body organs into action. During times of stress, for example, the *adrenal glands,* located on top of the kidneys, secrete the hormone *cortisol.* Abnormal secretions of this chemical have been tied to anxiety and mood disorders.

GENETICS AND ABNORMAL BEHAVIOR Abnormalities in brain anatomy or chemistry are sometimes the result of genetic inheritance. Each cell in the human brain and body contains 23 pairs of *chromosomes,* with each chromosome in a pair inherited from one of the person's parents. Every chromosome contains numerous **genes**—segments that control the characteristics and traits a person inherits. Scientists have known for years that genes help determine such physical characteristics as hair color, height, and eyesight. Genes can make people more prone to heart disease, cancer, or diabetes, and perhaps to possessing artistic or musical skill. In recent years, researchers have discovered that genes may also influence behavior, including abnormal behavior.

Studies suggest that inheritance plays a part in mood disorders, schizophrenia, mental retardation, Alzheimer's disease, and other mental disorders (Faraone, Tsuang, & Tsuang, 1999; Hyman, 1999). Yet, with few exceptions, researchers have not been able to identify the specific genes that are the culprits. Nor do they yet know how much genetic factors contribute to various mental disorders. It appears that in most cases no single gene is responsible for a particular behavior or mental disorder. Instead, many genes combine to help bring about our actions and reactions, both functional and dysfunctional.

Biological Treatments

Biological practitioners look for certain kinds of clues when they try to understand abnormal behavior. Does the person's family have a history of that behavior, and hence a possible genetic predisposition to it? (Philip Berman's case history mentions that his mother was once hospitalized for depression.) Does the disorder seem to follow its own course? (Philip's depressed feelings were described as periodic; they seemed to come and go over the course of several years.) Is the behavior increased by events that could have had a physiological effect? (Philip was having a drink when he flew into a jealous rage at the restaurant.)

Once the clinicians have pinpointed physical sources of dysfunctioning, they are in a better position to choose a biological course of treatment. The three

SYNAPSE The tiny space between the nerve ending of one neuron and the dendrite of another.

NEUROTRANSMITTER A chemical that, released by one neuron, crosses the synaptic space to be received at receptors on the dendrites of neighboring neurons.

HORMONES The chemicals released by glands into the bloodstream.

GENES Chromosome segments that control the characteristics and traits we inherit.

THE CURRENT SCENE

Nature's Way

In the United States today, 20 million baby boomers are taking to "herbal" supplements and "natural" hormones to combat ills ranging from arthritis to depression. These supplements are a $6.5 billion industry in the United States, and sales increase by 20 percent each year (Wasik, 1999). This sales explosion can be traced to the 1994 passage of the Dietary Supplement Health and Education Act, which holds that dietary supplements do not need to meet the same legal requirements as medicinal drugs. Whereas drugs must be proved safe and effective by their manufacturers in order to receive approval (through a testing process that costs the manufacturers hundreds of millions of dollars), dietary supplements are assumed to be safe unless proved harmful. In the wake of this law, 4,000 manufacturers have rushed dietary supplements into the marketplace, typically without research and often with extraordinary claims about their healing powers (Musak, 1999).

Melatonin pills are among the most popular supplements in today's marketplace. These pills are modeled after melatonin—a hormone produced in the brains of humans and other animals. Manufacturers of the supplements claim that their product can lift depression, strengthen the immune system, lower cholesterol, extend the life span, increase energy, improve sleep, reduce stress, cure jet lag, and even increase sexual performance, while at the same time preventing cancer, heart disease, cataracts, ulcers, Parkinson's disease, Alzheimer's disease, and pregnancy. But does the reality of this supplement live up to the hype? Not according to a growing body of research.

On the positive side, small doses of melatonin may indeed produce restful sleep in some healthy adults (Wurtman, 1995). Small doses can also help reduce jet lag by resetting the body's internal clock, tricking the body into believing that it is still nighttime (Bonn, 1996). And melatonin can be useful for night-shift workers and the blind, whose circadian rhythms may be out of sync.

On the other hand, melatonin supplements do not seem to improve sexual performance. Nor have studies established any effect of melatonin on heart disease or cholesterol levels. And no reliable evidence exists for melatonin as a fountain of youth (Turek, 1996; Ebihara et al., 1986). Some researchers even worry that melatonin supplements could damage a person's health. Its long-term actions have yet to be investigated, proper dosages are still undetermined, and its effects during pregnancy and puberty and its interactions with other drugs are unknown (Bonn, 1996; Chase, 1996).

In recent years, melatonin supplements have been joined in the marketplace by other mental health remedies such as the depression-fighters *St. John's wort* and *SAMe* and the memory enhancer *ginkgo biloba.* These dietary supplements too are enjoying enormous sales, yet research to determine their proper dosage, effectiveness, and safety—or lack thereof—is really in its infancy.

Before corn flakes *A highly esteemed pioneer in natural treatments, Dr. John Harvey Kellogg was known for using offbeat approaches at his Battle Creek Sanitarium during the late 1800s and early 1900s. Among his cures were high-bran diets and "cleansing enemas" for those who suffered from "ulcers, diabetes, schizophrenia, acne . . . and premature old age."*

Courtesy of the Dr. J. H. Kellogg Discovery Center, Battle Creek, Michigan

Worldwide phenomenon *The psychotropic drug revolution has spread throughout the world. Here a nurse gives medications to patients at Cambodia's largest mental health facility.*

A LONG ROAD

It takes an average of 15 years of testing and $500 million for a pharmaceutical company in the United States to obtain approval for and market a newly discovered drug.

Not that long ago *Before effective psychotropic drugs were developed, clinicians in mental institutions used techniques such as the "wet pack," designed for calming excited patients.*

leading kinds of biological treatments used today are *drug therapy, electroconvulsive therapy,* and *psychosurgery.* Drug therapy is by far the most common of these approaches; psychosurgery is infrequent.

In the 1950s, researchers discovered several effective **psychotropic medications,** drugs that mainly affect emotions and thought processes. These drugs have greatly changed the outlook for a number of mental disorders and today are used widely, either alone or with other forms of therapy. However, the psychotropic drug revolution has also produced some major problems. Many believe, for example, that the drugs are overused. Moreover, while drugs are effective in many cases, they do not help everyone.

Four major psychotropic drug groups are used in therapy: antianxiety, antidepressant, antibipolar, and antipsychotic drugs. **Antianxiety drugs,** also called **minor tranquilizers** or **anxiolytics,** help reduce tension and anxiety. These drugs include *alprazolam* (trade name Xanax) and *diazepam* (Valium). **Antidepressant drugs** help improve the mood of people who are depressed. These drugs, which include *fluoxetine* (Prozac) and *sertraline* (Zoloft), are able to help around 60 percent of those with depression (Parker et al., 2001; Hirschfeld, 1999). **Antibipolar drugs** help steady the moods of those with a bipolar disorder, a condition marked by mood swings from mania to depression. One of the most widely used of these drugs is *lithium,* which, like the antidepressants, is helpful in approximately 60 percent of cases (Maj et al., 1998; Prien, 1992).

Finally, **antipsychotic drugs** help reduce the confusion, hallucinations, and delusions of *psychotic disorders,* disorders marked by a loss of contact with reality. Common antipsychotic drugs are *haloperidol* (Haldol) and *risperidone* (Risperdal). Research has shown that these drugs are more effective than any other single form of treatment for schizophrenia and other psychotic disorders, reducing symptoms in at least 65 percent of patients (Breier, 2001).

The second form of biological treatment, used primarily on depressed patients, is **electroconvulsive therapy (ECT).** Two electrodes are attached to a patient's forehead and an electrical current of 65 to 140 volts is passed briefly through the brain. The current causes a brain seizure that lasts up to a few minutes. After seven to nine ECT sessions, spaced two or three days apart, many patients feel considerably less depressed. The treatment is able to improve the mood of approximately 60 percent of depressed patients (Glass, 2001; Rey & Walter, 1997). It is used on tens of thousands of depressed persons annually, particularly those whose depression fails to respond to other treatments (Cauchon, 1995; Foderaero, 1993).

A third form of biological treatment is **psychosurgery,** brain surgery for mental disorders. It is thought to have roots as far back as trephining, the prehistoric practice of chipping a hole in the skull of a person who behaved strangely. Modern procedures are derived from a technique first developed in the late 1930s by a Portuguese neuropsychiatrist, Antonio de Egas Moniz. In this procedure, known as a *lobotomy,* a surgeon cuts the connections between the brain's frontal lobes and the lower centers of the brain.

Today's brain surgery procedures are much more precise than the lobotomies of the past (Weingarten, 1999). They have fewer unwanted effects and are apparently helpful in some cases of severe depression, anxiety, and obsessive-compulsive disorder. Even so, they are considered experimental and are used only after certain severe disorders have continued for years without responding to any other form of treatment (Goodman et al., 1992).

Assessing the Biological Model

Today the biological model enjoys considerable respect. Biological research constantly produces valuable new information. And biological treatments often bring great relief when other approaches have failed. At the same time, this model has its shortcomings. Some of its followers seem to expect that all human behavior can be explained in biological terms and treated with biological methods. This view can limit rather than enhance our understanding of abnormal functioning (Anderson & Scott, 1999; Miller, 1999). Our mental life is an interplay of biological and nonbiological factors, and it is important to understand that interplay rather than to focus on biological variables alone.

A second shortcoming is that much of the evidence for biological explanations is incomplete or inconclusive. Many brain studies, for example, are conducted on animals in whom symptoms of depression, anxiety, or some other abnormality have been produced by drugs, surgery, or experimental manipulation. Researchers can never be certain that the animals are experiencing the human disorder under investigation.

Finally, several of today's biological treatments are capable of producing significant undesirable effects. Antipsychotic drugs, for example, may produce movement problems such as severe shaking, bizarre-looking contractions of the face and body, and extreme restlessness. Clearly such costs must be weighed against the drug's benefits.

PSYCHOTROPIC MEDICATIONS Drugs that primarily affect the brain and reduce many symptoms of mental dysfunctioning.

ANTIANXIETY DRUGS Psychotropic drugs that help reduce tension and anxiety.

ANTIDEPRESSANT DRUGS Psychotropic drugs that improve the moods of people with depression.

ANTIBIPOLAR DRUGS Psychotropic drugs that help stabilize the moods of people suffering from a bipolar mood disorder.

ANTIPSYCHOTIC DRUGS Psychotropic drugs that help correct the confusion, hallucinations, and delusions found in psychotic disorders.

ELECTROCONVULSIVE THERAPY (ECT) A treatment, used primarily on depressed patients, in which a brain seizure is triggered as an electric current passes through electrodes attached to the patient's forehead.

PSYCHOSURGERY Brain surgery for mental disorders.

SUMMING UP | **The Biological Model**

Biological theorists look inward at the biological processes of human functioning. To explain abnormal behavior, they point to anatomical problems in the brain, abnormalities in the activity of neurotransmitters, or abnormal secretions of certain hormones. Such abnormalities are sometimes the result of genetic inheritance.

Biological therapists use physical and chemical methods to help people overcome their psychological problems. The leading methods are drug therapy, electroconvulsive therapy, and, on rare occasions, psychosurgery.

The Psychodynamic Model

The *psychodynamic model* is the oldest and most famous of the modern psychological models. Psychodynamic theorists believe that a person's behavior, whether normal or abnormal, is determined largely by underlying psychological forces of which he or she is not consciously aware. These internal forces are described as *dynamic*—that is, they interact with one another; and their interaction gives rise to behavior, thoughts, and emotions. Abnormal symptoms are viewed as the result of *conflicts* between these forces.

Psychodynamic theorists would view Philip Berman as a person in conflict. They would want to explore his past experiences because, in their view, psychological conflicts are tied to early relationships and to traumatic experiences that occurred during childhood. Psychodynamic theories rest on the *deterministic* assumption that no symptom or behavior is "accidental": all behavior is determined by past experiences. Thus Philip's hatred for his mother, his memories of her as cruel and overbearing, the weakness and ineffectiveness of his father, and the birth of a younger brother when Philip was 10 may all be important to the understanding of his current problems.

The psychodynamic model was first formulated by the Viennese neurologist Sigmund Freud (1856–1939) at the turn of the twentieth century. After studying hypnosis, Freud developed the theory of *psychoanalysis* to explain both normal and abnormal psychological functioning, and a corresponding method of treat-

Freud and Freud *Anna Freud, the last of Sigmund Freud's six children, studied psychoanalysis with her father and then opened a practice next door to his. (They shared a waiting room.) Her work on defense mechanisms, other ego activities, and child development made her a major figure in her own right.*

ID According to Freud, the psychological force that produces instinctual needs, drives, and impulses.

EGO According to Freud, the psychological force that employs reason and operates in accordance with the reality principle.

EGO DEFENSE MECHANISMS According to psychoanalytic theory, strategies developed by the ego to control unacceptable id impulses and to avoid or reduce the anxiety they arouse.

SUPEREGO According to Freud, the psychological force that represents a person's values and ideals.

FIXATION According to Freud, a condition in which the id, ego, and superego do not mature properly and are frozen at an early stage of development.

Critical training *Freud believed that toilet training is a critical developmental experience. Children whose training is too harsh may become "fixated" at the anal stage and develop an "anal character"—stubborn, contrary, stingy, or controlling.*

Laura Dwight, New York, NY

ment, a conversational approach also called psychoanalysis. During the early 1900s, Freud and several of his colleagues in the Vienna Psychoanalytic Society—including Carl Gustav Jung (1875–1961) and Alfred Adler (1870–1937)—became the most influential clinical theorists in the Western world. Freud's 24 volumes on psychoanalytic theory and treatment are still widely studied today.

How Did Freud Explain Normal and Abnormal Functioning?

Freud believed that three central forces shape the personality—instinctual needs, rational thinking, and moral standards. All these forces, he believed, operate at the *unconscious* level, unavailable to immediate awareness; and he believed them to be dynamic, or interactive. Freud called the forces the *id, ego,* and *superego.*

THE ID Freud used the term **id** to denote instinctual needs, drives, and impulses. The id operates in accordance with the *pleasure principle;* that is, it always seeks gratification. Freud also believed that all id instincts tend to be sexual, noting that from the very earliest stages of life a child's pleasure is obtained from nursing, defecating, masturbating, or engaging in other activities that he considered to have sexual links. He further suggested that a person's *libido,* or sexual energy, fuels the id.

THE EGO During our early years we come to recognize that our environment will not meet every instinctual need. Our mother, for example, is not always available to do our bidding. A part of the id separates off and becomes the **ego.** Like the id, the ego unconsciously seeks gratification, but it does so in accordance with the *reality principle,* the knowledge we acquire through experience that it can be unacceptable to express our id impulses outright. The ego, employing reason, guides us to know when we can and cannot express those impulses.

The ego develops basic strategies, called **ego defense mechanisms,** to control unacceptable id impulses and avoid or reduce the anxiety they arouse. The most basic defense mechanism, *repression,* prevents unacceptable impulses from ever reaching consciousness. There are many other ego defense mechanisms, and each of us tends to favor some over others (see Table 2-1).

THE SUPEREGO The **superego** grows from the ego, just as the ego grows out of the id. As we learn from our parents that many of our id impulses are unacceptable, we unconsciously adopt our parents' values. We identify with our parents and judge ourselves by their standards. When we uphold their values, we feel good; when we go against them, we feel guilty. In short, we develop a *conscience.*

According to Freud, these three parts of the personality—the id, ego, and superego—are often in some degree of conflict. A healthy personality is one in which an effective working relationship, an acceptable compromise, has formed among the three forces. If the id, ego, and superego are in excessive conflict, the person's behavior may show signs of dysfunction.

Freudians would therefore view Philip Berman as someone whose personality forces have a poor working relationship. His ego and superego are unable to control his id impulses, which lead him repeatedly to act in impulsive and often dangerous ways—suicide gestures, jealous rages, job resignations, outbursts of temper, frequent arguments.

DEVELOPMENTAL STAGES Freud proposed that at each stage of development, from infancy to maturity, new events and pressures challenge individuals and require adjustments in their id, ego, and superego. If the adjustments are successful, they lead to personal growth. If not, the person may become **fixated,** or entrapped, at an early stage of development. Then all subsequent development suffers, and the individual may well be headed for abnormal functioning in the future. Because parents

Table 2-1

Defense Mechanisms to the Rescue

DEFENSE	OPERATION	EXAMPLE
Repression	Person avoids anxiety by simply not allowing painful or dangerous thoughts to become conscious.	An executive's desire to run amok and attack his boss and colleagues at a board meeting is denied access to his awareness.
Denial	Person simply refuses to acknowledge the existence of an external source of anxiety.	You are not prepared for tomorrow's final exam, but you tell yourself that it's not actually an important exam and that there's no good reason not to go to a movie tonight.
Projection	Person attributes own unacceptable impulses, motives, or desires to other individuals.	The executive who repressed his destructive desires may project his anger onto his boss and claim that it is actually the boss who is hostile.
Rationalization	Person creates a socially acceptable reason for an action that actually reflects unacceptable motives.	A student explains away poor grades by citing the importance of the "total experience" of going to college and claiming that too much emphasis on grades would actually interfere with a well-rounded education.
Reaction formation	Person adopts behavior that is the exact opposite of impulses he or she is afraid to acknowledge.	A man experiences homosexual feelings and responds by taking a strong antihomosexual stance.
Displacement	Person displaces hostility away from a dangerous object and onto a safer substitute.	After an aggressive driver cuts in front of you and into the last remaining parking spot, you release your pent-up anger by starting a fight with your roommate.
Intellectualization (isolation)	Person represses emotional reactions in favor of overly logical response to a problem.	A woman who has been beaten and raped gives a detached, methodical description of the effects that such attacks may have on victims.
Regression	Person retreats from an upsetting conflict to an early developmental stage at which no one is expected to behave maturely or responsibly.	A boy who cannot cope with the anger he feels toward his rejecting mother regresses to infantile behavior, soiling his clothes and no longer taking care of his basic needs.
Sublimation	Person expresses sexual and aggressive energy in ways that are acceptable to society.	Athletes, artists, surgeons, and other highly dedicated and skilled people may be reaching their high levels of accomplishment by directing otherwise potentially harmful energies into their work.

are the key environmental figures during the early years of life, they are often seen as the cause of improper development.

Freud named each stage of development after the body area that he considered most important to the child at that time. For example, he referred to the first 18 months of life as the *oral stage*. During this stage, children fear that the mother who feeds and comforts them will disappear. Children whose mothers consistently fail to gratify their oral needs may become fixated at the oral stage and display an "oral character" throughout their lives, marked by extreme dependence or extreme mistrust. Such persons are particularly prone to develop depression. As we shall see in later chapters, Freud linked fixations at the other stages of development—*anal* (18 months to 3 years of age), *phallic* (3 to 5 years), *latency* (5 to 12 years), and *genital* (12 years to adulthood)—to yet other kinds of psychological dysfunction.

FREUD'S EARLY YEARS

Freud's parents often favored the precociously intelligent Sigmund over his siblings—for example, by giving him his own room in which to study in peace.

(Gay, 1999)

How Do Other Psychodynamic Explanations Differ from Freud's?

Personal and professional differences between Freud and his colleagues led to a split in the Vienna Psychoanalytic Society early in the twentieth century. Carl Jung, Alfred Adler, and others developed new theories. Although the new theories departed from Freud's ideas in important ways, each held on to Freud's belief that human functioning is shaped by dynamic (interacting) psychological forces. Thus all such theories, including Freud's, are referred to as *psychodynamic*.

Three of today's most influential psychodynamic theories are ego theory, self theory, and object relations theory. **Ego theorists** emphasize the role of the ego and consider it a more independent and powerful force than Freud did. **Self theorists,** in contrast, give greatest attention to the role of the *self*—the unified personality—rather than to any one piece of the personality. They believe that the basic human motive is to save and strengthen the wholeness of the self (Lerner & Ehrlich, 2001; Kohut, 1977). **Object relations theorists** propose that people are motivated mainly by a need to have relationships with others, and that severe problems in the relationships between children and their caregivers may lead to abnormal development and psychological difficulties (Kernberg, 2001, 1997; Fonagy, 1999).

Psychodynamic Therapies

Psychodynamic therapies range from Freudian psychoanalysis to modern therapies based on self theory or object relations theory. All seek to uncover past traumas and the inner conflicts that have resulted from them. All try to help patients resolve, or settle, those conflicts and to resume personal development.

According to most psychodynamic therapists, the search for insight cannot be rushed or imposed. Therapists must subtly guide the discussions so that the patients discover their underlying problems for themselves. To aid in the process, the therapists rely on such techniques as *free association, therapist interpretation, catharsis,* and *working through.*

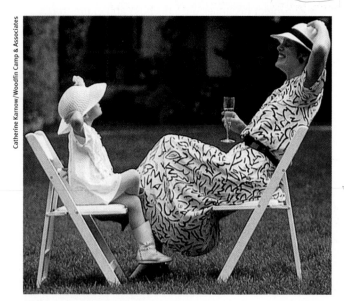

Like mother, like daughter *According to Freud, boys become attracted to their mothers and girls to their fathers during the phallic stage. Children repress these taboo impulses and identify instead with the parent of the same sex, acting like that parent in every way.*

FREE ASSOCIATION In psychodynamic therapies, the patient is responsible for starting and leading each discussion. The therapist tells the patient to describe any thought, feeling, or image that comes to mind, even if it seems unimportant. This practice is known as **free association.** The therapist expects that the person's associations will eventually uncover unconscious events and underlying dynamics. Notice how free association helps this New Yorker to discover threatening impulses and conflicts within herself:

> *Patient:* So I started walking, and walking, and decided to go behind the museum and walk through Central Park. So I walked and went through a back field and felt very excited and wonderful. I saw a park bench next to a clump of bushes and sat down. There was a rustle behind me and I got frightened. I thought of men concealing themselves in the bushes. I thought of the sex perverts I read about in Central Park. I wondered if there was someone behind me exposing himself. The idea is repulsive, but exciting too. I think of father now and feel excited. I think of an erect penis. This is connected with my father. There is something about this pushing in my mind. I don't know what it is, like on the border of my memory. (*Pause*)
>
> *Therapist:* Mm-hmm. (*Pause*) On the border of your memory?
>
> *Patient:* (*The patient breathes rapidly and seems to be under great tension*) As a little girl, I slept with my father. I get a funny feeling. I get a funny feeling over my skin, tingly-like. It's a strange feeling, like a blindness, like not seeing something. My mind blurs and spreads over anything

I look at. I've had this feeling off and on since I walked in the park. My mind seems to blank off like I can't think or absorb anything.

(Wolberg, 1967, p. 662)

THERAPIST INTERPRETATION Psychodynamic therapists listen carefully as patients talk, looking for clues, drawing tentative conclusions, and sharing interpretations when they think the patient is ready to hear them. Interpretations of three phenomena are particularly important—*resistance, transference,* and *dreams.*

Patients are showing **resistance,** an unconscious refusal to participate fully in therapy, when they suddenly cannot free associate or when they change a subject to avoid a painful discussion. They demonstrate **transference** when they act and feel toward the therapist as they did or do toward important persons in their lives, especially their parents, siblings, and spouses. Consider again the woman who walked in Central Park. As she continues talking, the therapist helps her to explore her transference:

Patient: I get so excited by what is happening here. I feel I'm being held back by needing to be nice. I'd like to blast loose sometimes, but I don't dare.
Therapist: Because you fear my reaction?
Patient: The worst thing would be that you wouldn't like me. You wouldn't speak to me friendly; you wouldn't smile; you'd feel you can't treat me and discharge me from treatment. But I know this isn't so, I know it.
Therapist: Where do you think these attitudes come from?
Patient: When I was nine years old, I read a lot about great men in history. I'd quote them and be dramatic. I'd want a sword at my side; I'd dress like an Indian. Mother would scold me. Don't frown, don't talk so much. Sit on your hands, over and over again. I did all kinds of things. I was a naughty child. She told me I'd be hurt. Then at fourteen I fell off a horse and broke my back. I had to be in bed. Mother then told me on the day I went riding not to, that I'd get hurt because the ground was frozen. I was a stubborn, self-willed child. Then I went against her will and suffered an accident that changed my life, a fractured back. Her attitude was, "I told you so." I was put in a cast and kept in bed for months.

(Wolberg, 1967, p. 662)

Finally, many psychodynamic therapists try to help patients interpret their **dreams.** Freud (1924) called dreams the "royal road to the unconscious." He believed that repression and other defense mechanisms operate less completely during sleep and that dreams, correctly interpreted, can reveal unconscious instincts, needs, and wishes. Freud identified two kinds of dream content, manifest and latent. *Manifest content* is the consciously remembered dream, *latent content* its symbolic meaning. To interpret a dream, therapists must translate its manifest content into its latent content.

CATHARSIS Insight must be an emotional as well as intellectual process. Psychodynamic therapists believe that patients must experience **catharsis,** a reliving of past repressed feelings, if they are to settle internal conflicts and overcome their problems.

WORKING THROUGH A single session of interpretation and catharsis will not change a person. The patient and therapist must examine the same issues over and over in the course of many sessions, each time with greater clarity. This process, called **working through,** usually takes a long time, often years.

EGO THEORY The psychodynamic theory that emphasizes the role of the ego and considers it an independent force.

SELF THEORY The psychodynamic theory that emphasizes the role of the self—our unified personality.

OBJECT RELATIONS THEORY The psychodynamic theory that views the desire for relationships as the key motivating force in human behavior.

FREE ASSOCIATION A psychodynamic technique in which the patient describes any thought, feeling, or image that comes to mind, even if it seems unimportant.

RESISTANCE An unconscious refusal to participate fully in therapy.

TRANSFERENCE According to psychodynamic theorists, a process that occurs during psychotherapy, in which patients act toward the therapist as they did or do toward important figures in their lives.

DREAM A series of ideas and images that form during sleep.

CATHARSIS The reliving of past repressed feelings in order to settle internal conflicts and overcome problems.

WORKING THROUGH The psychoanalytic process of facing conflicts, reinterpreting feelings, and overcoming one's problems.

"Don't worry. Fantasies about devouring the doctor are perfectly normal."

The father factor *Because mothers provided almost all infant care in his day, Freud looked largely to maternal influences for explanations of personality development and psychological problems. Today many fathers also actively care for their young children, causing psychodynamic theorists to adapt their explanations accordingly. It turns out that fathers and mothers are more similar than different when it comes to nurturing.*

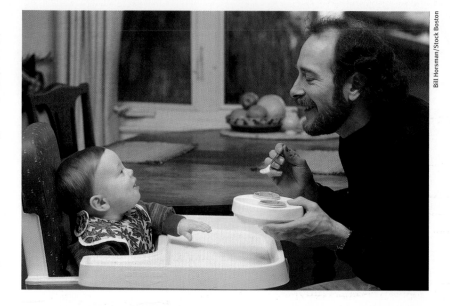

SHORT-TERM PSYCHODYNAMIC THERAPIES In several short versions of psychodynamic therapy, developed over the past few decades, patients choose a single problem—a *dynamic focus*—to work on, such as difficulty getting along with other people (Sifneos, 1992, 1987; Davanloo, 1980). The therapist and patient focus on this problem throughout the treatment and work only on the psychodynamic issues that relate to it (such as unresolved oral needs). Only a limited number of studies have tested the effectiveness of these short-term psychodynamic therapies, but their findings do suggest that the approaches are sometimes quite helpful to patients (Leichsenring, 2001; Messer, 2001).

Assessing the Psychodynamic Model

Freud and his followers have helped change the way abnormal functioning is understood (Nietzel et al., 1994). Largely because of their work, a wide range of theorists today look for answers and explanations outside biological processes. Psychodynamic theorists have also helped us to understand that abnormal functioning may be rooted in the same processes as normal functioning. Psychological conflict is a common experience; it leads to abnormal functioning only if the conflict becomes excessive.

Freud and his many followers have also had a monumental impact on treatment. They were the first to apply theory and techniques systematically to treatment. They were also the first to demonstrate the potential of psychological, as opposed to biological, treatment, and their ideas have served as starting points for many other psychological treatments. At the same time, the psychodynamic model has shortcomings. Its concepts are hard to define and to research (Nietzel et al., 1994; Erdelyi, 1992, 1985). Because processes such as id drives, ego defenses, and fixation are abstract and supposedly operate at an unconscious level, there is no way of knowing for certain if they are occurring. Not surprisingly, then, psychodynamic explanations and treatments have received limited research support, and psychodynamic theorists have been forced to rely largely on evidence provided by individual case studies (Prochaska & Norcross, 1999; Bein, 1998).

Partly in reaction to these problems, other models of abnormality have been developed over the past several decades. Nevertheless, as we can see in Figure 2-3, 19 percent of today's

FIGURE 2-3 Theoretical orientations of today's clinicians *In one survey, almost 27 percent of clinical psychologists labeled themselves as "eclectic," 24 percent considered themselves "cognitive," and 19 percent called their orientation "psychodynamic." (Adapted from Prochaska & Norcross, 1999; Norcross et al., 1997.)*

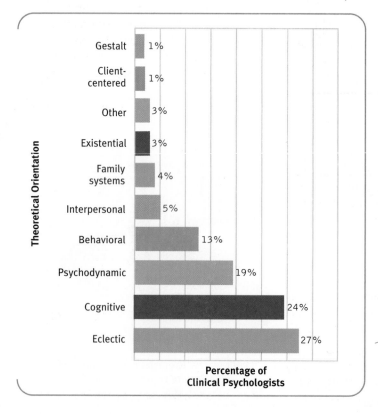

Perchance to Dream

All people dream; so do dogs, and maybe even fish. In fact, although they may not remember them, people average close to 1,500 dreams per year. Some claim that dreams reveal the future; others see them as inner journeys or alternate realities. Sigmund Freud (1900) believed that we express and attempt to fulfill unsatisfied desires with our dreams. His colleague Alfred Adler believed that dreams prepare us for waking life by allowing us to rehearse new behaviors or alerting us to internal problems (Kramer, 1992).

Biological theorists offer a different, though not entirely incompatible, view. Some propose that random signals come from various areas of the brain as we sleep. The brain's *cortex,* the seat of higher cognitive functioning, attempts to make sense of this random bombardment of electrical activity. The result is a dream, often irrational or weird (Reiser, 2001; Flanagan, 2000; Hobson & McCarley, 1977).

According to surveys and studies, two-thirds of people's dreams involve unpleasant material, such as aggression, threats, rejection, confusion, or an inability to communicate (Van de Castle, 1993). Commonly, a dreamer is chased or attacked by a threatening figure, suggesting to some theorists that the dreamer is running from real-life fears, unpleasant issues, or distrusted persons.

Eighty percent of college students report having had dreams of falling. Such dreams are thought to occur when our sense of security is threatened or when we are in fear of losing control. Many people say falling dreams are the first ones they can remember, although people can have them at any stage of life (Van de Castle, 1993; Cartwright & Lamberg, 1992).

Another common theme is public nudity. One study found that 43 percent of American college-age subjects reported

The Nightmare by Johann Heinrich Füssli

Ursula Edelmann, Frankfurt, Germany

having such dreams, compared to 18 percent of Japanese subjects (Vieira, 1993). Freud (1900) viewed dreams of nudity as an unconscious wish to exhibit oneself. Others argue that people who have these dreams may be afraid of being seen for who they really are (Van de Castle, 1993).

Dreams also may differ by gender. In a landmark study in 1951, the researcher Calvin Hall found that men dreamed twice as often about men as they did about women, whereas women dreamed about men and women in equal proportions. In addition, most male dreams took place outdoors, while female dreams were more often set in the home or elsewhere indoors. Men's sexual dreams were more likely to include women they did not know, whereas women dreamed more often about men they cared for. A later study in 1980 found no major changes in these patterns (Van de Castle, 1993). However, studies conducted in the 1980s and 1990s have found that men's and women's dreams are becoming more similar, that women's dreams now take place outdoors more than they did in the past, and that women are now as likely as men to behave aggressively in their dreams.

clinical psychologists, 35 percent of psychiatrists, and 33 percent of social workers identify themselves as psychodynamic therapists (Prochaska & Norcross, 1999). And, interestingly, many practitioners of other models report that when they seek help for their own problems, psychodynamic therapy is their choice (Norcross & Prochaska, 1984).

SUMMING UP

The Psychodynamic Model

Supporters of the psychodynamic model believe that a person's behavior, whether normal or abnormal, results from underlying psychological forces. They consider psychological conflicts to be rooted in early parent-child relationships and traumatic experiences.

Psychodynamic Explanations The psychodynamic model was first developed by Sigmund Freud, who proposed a general theory of psychoanalysis as well as a treatment approach. Freud said that three dynamic forces—the id, ego, and superego—

"We all have much to learn about scientific integrity and commitment from Freud's willingness to study his own dreams, reexamine his theories and persist in a lifelong exploration."

Jerome L. Singer, psychologist, 1989

"I think Freud has been a wholesale disaster for psychology. . . ."

Hans J. Eysenck, psychologist, 1989

CONDITIONING A simple form of learning.

OPERANT CONDITIONING A process of learning in which behavior that leads to satisfying consequences is likely to be repeated.

MODELING A process of learning in which an individual acquires responses by observing and imitating others.

CLASSICAL CONDITIONING A process of learning in which two events that repeatedly occur close together in time become fused in a person's mind and produce the same response.

SYSTEMATIC DESENSITIZATION A behavioral treatment in which clients with phobias learn to react calmly instead of with intense fear to the objects or situations they dread.

interact and produce thought, feeling, and behavior. Other psychodynamic theories are ego theory, self theory, and object relations theory.

Psychodynamic Therapies Psychodynamic therapists help people uncover past traumas and the inner conflicts that have resulted from them. They use a number of techniques such as free association and interpretations of phenomena such as resistance, transference, and dreams.

The Behavioral Model

Like psychodynamic theorists, behavioral theorists believe that our actions are determined largely by our experiences in life. However, the *behavioral model* concentrates on *behaviors,* the responses an organism makes to its environment. Behaviors can be external (going to work, say) or internal (having a feeling or thought). In the behavioral view, people are the sum total of their learned behaviors. Behavioral theorists, therefore, base their explanations and treatments on *principles of learning,* the processes by which these behaviors change in response to the environment.

Many learned behaviors help people to cope with daily challenges and to lead happy, productive lives. However, abnormal behaviors also can be learned. Behaviorists who try to explain Philip Berman's problems might view him as a man who has received improper training: he has learned behaviors that offend others and repeatedly work against him.

Whereas the psychodynamic model had its beginnings in the clinical work of physicians, the behavioral model began in laboratories where psychologists were running experiments on **conditioning,** simple forms of learning. The researchers manipulated *stimuli* and *rewards,* then observed how their manipulations affected their subjects' responses.

During the 1950s, many clinicians became frustrated with what they viewed as the vagueness and slowness of the psychodynamic model. Some of them began to apply the principles of learning to the study and treatment of psychological problems (Wolpe, 1997, 1987). Their efforts gave rise to the behavioral model of abnormality.

How Do Behaviorists Explain Abnormal Functioning?

Learning theorists have identified several different forms of conditioning, and each may produce abnormal behavior as well as normal behavior. In **operant conditioning,** for example, humans and animals learn to behave in certain ways as a result of receiving *rewards*—any satisfying consequences—whenever they do so. In **modeling,** individuals learn responses simply by observing other individuals and repeating their behaviors.

In a third form of conditioning, **classical conditioning,** learning occurs by *temporal association.* When two events repeatedly occur close together in time, they become fused in a person's mind, and before long the person responds in the same way to both events. If one event produces a response of joy, the other brings joy as well; if one event brings feelings of relief, so does the other. A closer look at this form of conditioning illustrates how the behavioral model can account for abnormal functioning.

Ivan Pavlov (1849–1936), a famous Russian physiologist, first demonstrated classical conditioning with animal studies. He placed a bowl of meat powder before a dog, producing the natural response that all dogs have to meat: they start to salivate (see Figure 2-4). Next Pavlov added a step: just before presenting the dog with meat powder, he sounded a metronome. After several such pairings of metronome tone and presentation of meat powder, Pavlov noted

FIGURE 2-4 Working for Pavlov *In Ivan Pavlov's experimental device, the dog's saliva was collected in a tube as it was secreted, and the amount was recorded on a revolving cylinder called a kymograph. The experimenter observed the dog through a one-way glass window.*

that the dog began to salivate as soon as it heard the metronome. The dog had learned to salivate in response to a sound.

In the vocabulary of classical conditioning, the meat in this demonstration is an *unconditioned stimulus (US)*. It produces the *unconditioned response (UR)* of salivation, that is, a natural response with which the dog is born. The sound of the metronome is a *conditioned stimulus (CS)*, a previously neutral stimulus that comes to be linked with meat in the dog's mind. As such, it too produces a salivation response. When the salivation response is produced by the conditioned stimulus rather than by the unconditioned stimulus, it is called a *conditioned response (CR)*.

BEFORE CONDITIONING	AFTER CONDITIONING
CS: Tone → No response	CS: Tone → CR: Salivation
US: Meat → UR: Salivation	US: Meat → UR: Salivation

Classical conditioning explains many familiar behaviors. The romantic feelings a young man experiences when he smells his girlfriend's perfume, say, may represent a conditioned response. Initially this perfume may have had little emotional effect on him, but because the fragrance was present during several romantic encounters, it too came to elicit a romantic response.

Abnormal behaviors, too, can be acquired by classical conditioning. Consider a young boy who is repeatedly frightened by a neighbor's large German shepherd dog. Whenever the child walks past the neighbor's front yard, the dog barks loudly and lunges at him, stopped only by a rope tied to the porch. In this situation, the boy's parents are not surprised to discover that he develops a fear of dogs. They are stumped, however, by another intense fear the child displays, a fear of sand. They cannot understand why he cries whenever they take him to the beach and screams in fear if sand even touches his skin.

Where did this fear of sand come from? Classical conditioning. It turns out that a big sandbox is set up in the neighbor's front yard for the dog to play in. Every time the dog barks and lunges at the boy, the sandbox is there too. After repeated pairings of this kind, the child comes to fear sand as much as he fears the dog.

Behavioral Therapies

Behavioral therapy aims to identify the behaviors that are causing a person's problems and then tries to replace them with more appropriate ones, by applying the principles of classical conditioning, operant conditioning, or modeling (Martin & Pear, 1999). The therapist's attitude toward the client is that of teacher rather than healer. A person's early life matters only for the clues it can provide to current conditioning processes.

Classical conditioning treatments, for example, may be used to change abnormal reactions to particular stimuli. **Systematic desensitization** is one such method, often applied in cases of *phobia*—a specific and unreasonable fear. In this step-by-step procedure, clients learn to react calmly instead of with intense fear to the objects or situations they dread (Wolpe, 1990, 1987, 1958). First, they are taught the skill of relaxation over the course of several sessions. Next, they construct a *fear hierarchy,* a list of feared objects or situations, starting with those that are less feared and ending with the ones that are most dreaded. Here is the hierarchy developed by a man who was afraid of criticism, especially about his mental stability:

1. Friend on the street: "Hi, how are you?"
2. Friend on the street: "How are you feeling these days?"
3. Sister: "You've got to be careful so they don't put you in the hospital."
4. Wife: "You shouldn't drink beer while you are taking medicine."

See and do *Modeling may account for some forms of abnormal behavior. A well-known study by Albert Bandura and his colleagues (1963) demonstrated that children learned to abuse a doll by observing an adult hit it. Children who had not been exposed to the adult model did not mistreat the doll.*

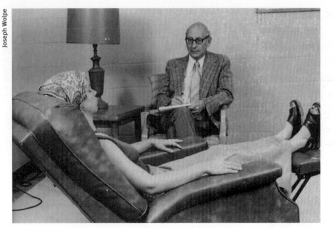

Desensitization *Joseph Wolpe, the psychiatrist who developed the behavioral treatment of systematic desensitization, first teaches a client to relax, then guides her to confront feared objects or situations, real or imagined, while she remains relaxed.*

Conditioning for fun and profit *Pet owners have discovered that they can teach animals a wide assortment of tricks by using the principles of conditioning. Only 3 percent of all dogs have learned to "sing," while 21 percent know how to sit, the most common dog trick (Pet Food Institute).*

5. Mother: "What's the matter, don't you feel good?"

6. Wife: "It's just you yourself, it's all in your head."

7. Service station attendant: "What are you shaking for?"

8. Neighbor borrows rake: "Is there something wrong with your leg? Your knees are shaking."

9. Friend on the job: "Is your blood pressure okay?"

10. Service station attendant: "You are pretty shaky, are you crazy or something?"

(Marquis & Morgan, 1969, p. 28)

Desensitization therapists next have their clients either imagine or actually confront each item on the hierarchy while in a state of relaxation. In step-by-step pairings of feared items and relaxation, clients move up the hierarchy until at last they can face every one of the items without feeling fear. As we shall see in Chapter 4, research has shown systematic desensitization and other classical conditioning techniques to be effective in treating phobias (Wang & Chen, 2000; Ollendick & King, 1998; Wolpe, 1997).

Assessing the Behavioral Model

The number of behavioral clinicians has grown steadily since the 1950s, and the behavioral model has become a powerful force in the clinical field. Various behavioral theories have been proposed over the years, and many treatment techniques have been developed. Approximately 13 percent of today's clinical psychologists report that their approach is mainly behavioral (Prochaska & Norcross, 1999).

Perhaps the greatest appeal of the behavioral model is that it can be tested in the laboratory, whereas psychodynamic theories generally cannot. The behaviorists' basic concepts—stimulus, response, and reward—can be observed and measured. Even more important, the results of research have lent considerable support to the behavioral model (Wolpe, 1997). Experimenters have successfully used the principles of learning to create clinical symptoms in laboratory subjects, suggesting that psychological disorders may indeed develop in the same way. In addition, research has found that behavioral treatments can be helpful to people with specific fears, social deficits, mental retardation, and other problems (DeRubeis & Crits-Christoph, 1998; Emmelkamp, 1994).

At the same time, research has also revealed weaknesses in the model. Certainly behavioral researchers have produced specific symptoms in subjects. But are these symptoms *ordinarily* acquired in this way? There is still no clear evidence that most people with psychological disorders are victims of improper conditioning. Similarly, behavioral therapies have limitations. The improvements noted in the therapist's office do not always carry over to real life. Nor do they necessarily last without continued therapy (Nietzel et al., 1994; Stokes & Osnes, 1989).

Finally, some critics hold that the behavioral view is too simplistic, that its concepts fail to account for the complexity of human behavior. In 1977 Albert Bandura, the behaviorist who earlier had identified modeling as a key conditioning process, argued that in order to feel happy and function effectively people must develop a positive sense of **self-efficacy.** That is, they must know that they can master and perform needed behaviors whenever necessary. Other behaviorists of the 1960s and 1970s similarly recognized that human beings engage in *cognitive behaviors,* such as anticipating or interpreting—ways of thinking that until then had been largely ignored in behavioral theory

THE CURRENT SCENE

Maternal Instincts

On an August day in 1996, a 3-year-old boy climbed over a barrier at the Brookfield Zoo in Illinois and fell 24 feet onto the cement floor of the gorilla compound. An 8-year-old 160-pound gorilla named Binti-Jua picked up

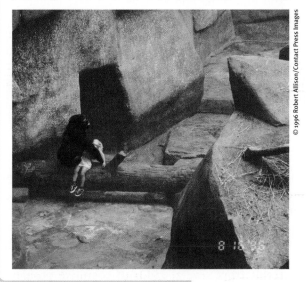

© 1996 Robert Allison/Contact Press Images

the child and cradled his limp body in her arms. The child's mother, fearing the worst, screamed out, "The gorilla's got my baby!" But Binti protected the boy as if he were her own. She held off the other gorillas, rocked him gently, and carried him to the entrance of the gorilla area, where rescue workers were waiting. Within hours, the incident was seen on videotape replays around the world, and Binti was being hailed for her maternal instincts.

When Binti was herself an infant, she had been removed from her mother, Lulu, who did not have enough milk. To make up for this loss, keepers at the zoo worked around the clock to nurture Binti; she was always being held in someone's arms. When Binti be-

came pregnant at age 6, trainers were afraid that the early separation from her mother would leave her ill prepared to raise an infant of her own. So they gave her mothering lessons and taught her to nurse and carry around a stuffed doll.

Consider This

● What was responsible for the gorilla's gentle and nurturing care for the hurt child? • Was it, as object relations theorists might hold, an expression of attachment and bonding, already experienced with her own 17-month-old daughter? • Was it the memory of the nurturing behavior she observed in human models during her own infancy, as behaviorists might claim? • Or might it have been the parenting training she received during her pregnancy?

---

and therapy. These individuals developed *cognitive-behavioral theories* that took unseen cognitive behaviors into greater account (Meichenbaum, 1993; Goldiamond, 1965).

Cognitive-behavioral theorists bridge the behavioral model and the cognitive model, the view we turn to next. On the one hand, their explanations are based squarely on learning principles. These theorists believe, for example, that cognitive processes are learned by classical conditioning, operant conditioning, and modeling. On the other hand, cognitive-behavioral theorists share with other kinds of cognitive theorists a belief that the ability to think is the most important aspect of human functioning (Dougher, 1997; Wilson, Hayes, & Gifford, 1997).

"We are molded and remolded by those who have loved us."

François Mauriac

SUMMING UP
The Behavioral Model

Behaviorists focus on a person's behaviors and propose that they develop in accordance with principles of conditioning.

Behavioral Explanations Behaviorists suggest that three types of conditioning—classical conditioning, operant conditioning, and modeling—account for behavior, whether normal or dysfunctional.

Behavioral Therapies The goal of the behavioral therapies is to identify a person's problematic behaviors and replace them with more appropriate ones. Behavioral therapists use techniques that follow the principles of classical conditioning, operant conditioning, modeling, or a combination of these. The classical conditioning approach of systematic desensitization, for example, has been effective in treating phobias.

SELF-EFFICACY The belief that one can master and perform needed behaviors whenever necessary.

"Stimulus, response! Stimulus, response! Don't you ever think?"

A clinical pioneer *Aaron Beck proposes that many forms of abnormal behavior can be traced to cognitive factors, such as upsetting thoughts and illogical thinking.*

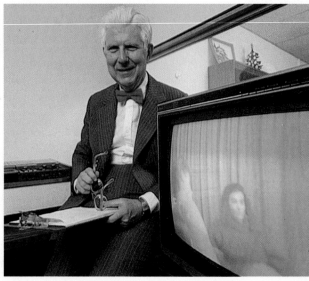

The Cognitive Model

Philip Berman, like the rest of us, has *cognitive* abilities—special intellectual capacities to think, remember, and anticipate. These abilities can help him accomplish a great deal in life. Yet they can also work against him. As he thinks about his experiences, Philip may develop false ideas. He may misinterpret experiences in ways that lead to poor decisions, maladaptive responses, and painful emotions.

In the early 1960s two clinicians, Albert Ellis (1962) and Aaron Beck (1967), proposed that cognitive processes are at the center of behavior, thought, and emotions and that we can best understand abnormal functioning by looking to cognition—a perspective known as the *cognitive model.* Ellis and Beck claimed that clinicians must ask questions about the assumptions and attitudes that color a client's perceptions, the thoughts running through that person's mind, and the conclusions they are leading to. Other theorists and therapists soon embraced and expanded their ideas and techniques.

How Do Cognitive Theorists Explain Abnormal Functioning?

To cognitive theorists, we are all artists. We reproduce and create the world in our minds as we try to understand the events going on around us. If we are effective artists, our cognitions tend to be accurate (they agree with the perceptions of others) and useful. If we are ineffective artists, we may create a cognitive inner world that is painful and harmful to ourselves.

Abnormal functioning can result from several kinds of cognitive problems. Some people may make *assumptions* and adopt *attitudes* that are disturbing and inaccurate (Dryden & Ellis, 2001). Philip Berman, for example, often seems to assume that his past history has locked him in his present situation. He believes that he was victimized by his parents and that he is now forever doomed by his past. He seems to approach all new experiences and relationships with expectations of failure and disaster.

Illogical thinking processes are another source of abnormal functioning, according to cognitive theorists. Beck (1993, 1991, 1967), for example, has found that some people consistently think in illogical ways and keep arriving at self-defeating conclusions. As we shall see in Chapter 6, he has identified a number of illogical thought processes regularly found in depression, such as *overgeneralization,* the drawing of broad negative conclusions on the basis of a single insignificant event. One depressed student couldn't remember the date of Columbus's third voyage to America during a history class. Overgeneralizing, she spent the rest of the day in despair over her general ignorance.

Cognitive Therapies

According to cognitive therapists, people with psychological disorders can overcome their problems by developing new, more functional ways of thinking. Because different forms of abnormality may involve different kinds of cognitive dysfunctioning, cognitive therapists have developed a number of strategies. Beck (1997, 1996, 1967), for example, has developed an approach that is widely used in cases of depression.

In Beck's approach, called simply **cognitive therapy,** therapists help clients recognize the negative thoughts, biased interpretations, and errors in logic that fill their thinking and, according to Beck, cause them to feel depressed. Therapists also guide clients to challenge their dysfunctional thoughts, try out new interpretations, and ultimately apply the new ways of thinking in their daily lives. As we shall see in Chapter 6, people with depression who are treated with Beck's approach improve much more than those who receive no treatment (DeRubeis, Tang, & Beck, 2001).

In the excerpt that follows, a cognitive therapist guides a depressed 26-year-old graduate student to see the tie between the way she interprets her experiences and the way she feels and to begin questioning the accuracy of her interpretations:

> **Therapist:** How do you understand it?
> **Patient:** I get depressed when things go wrong. Like when I fail a test.
> **Therapist:** How can failing a test make you depressed?
> **Patient:** Well, if I fail I'll never get into law school.
> **Therapist:** So failing the test means a lot to you. But if failing a test could drive people into clinical depression, wouldn't you expect everyone who failed the test to have a depression? . . . Did everyone who failed get depressed enough to require treatment?
> **Patient:** No, but it depends on how important the test was to the person.
> **Therapist:** Right, and who decides the importance?
> **Patient:** I do.
> **Therapist:** And so, what we have to examine is your way of viewing the test (or the way that you think about the test) and how it affects your chances of getting into law school. Do you agree?
> **Patient:** Right. . . .
> **Therapist:** Now what did failing mean?
> **Patient:** (*Tearful*) That I couldn't get into law school.
> **Therapist:** And what does that mean to you?
> **Patient:** That I'm just not smart enough.
> **Therapist:** Anything else?
> **Patient:** That I can never be happy.
> **Therapist:** And how do these thoughts make you feel?
> **Patient:** Very unhappy.
> **Therapist:** So it is the meaning of failing a test that makes you very unhappy. In fact, believing that you can never be happy is a powerful factor in producing unhappiness. So, you get yourself into a trap—by definition, failure to get into law school equals "I can never be happy."
>
> *(Beck et al., 1979, pp. 145–146)*

"Life is the art of drawing sufficient conclusions from insufficient premises."

—Samuel Butler (1835–1902)

Assessing the Cognitive Model

The cognitive model has had very broad appeal. In addition to the behaviorists who now include cognitive concepts in their theories about learning, there are a great many clinicians who believe that thinking processes are in fact much more than conditioned reactions. Cognitive theory, research, and treatments have developed in so many interesting ways that the model is now viewed as separate from the behavioral school that gave birth to it.

Approximately 24 percent of today's clinical psychologists identify their approach as cognitive (Prochaska & Norcross, 1999). There are several reasons for the model's popularity. First, it focuses on a process unique to human beings, the process of human thought. Just as our special cognitive abilities are responsible for so many human accomplishments, they may also be responsible for the special problems found in human functioning. Thus many theorists from varied backgrounds find themselves drawn to a model that sees thought as the primary cause of normal or abnormal behavior.

Cognitive theories also lend themselves to research. Investigators have found that many people with psychological disorders do indeed make the kinds of assumptions and errors in thinking that the theorists claim (Clark, Beck, & Alford, 1999; Whisman & McGarvey, 1995). Yet another reason for the popularity of the cognitive model is the impressive performance of cognitive therapies. They

COGNITIVE THERAPY A therapy developed by Aaron Beck that helps people recognize and change their faulty thinking processes.

SELF-ACTUALIZATION The humanistic process by which people fulfill their potential for goodness and growth.

have proved to be very effective for treating depression, panic disorder, and sexual dysfunctions, for example (DeRubeis et al., 2001; DeRubeis & Crits-Christoph, 1998).

Nevertheless, the cognitive model, too, has its drawbacks (Beck, 1997, 1991; Meichenbaum, 1997, 1992). First, although disturbed cognitive processes are found in many forms of abnormality, their precise role has yet to be determined. The cognitions seen in psychologically troubled people could well be a result rather than a cause of their difficulties. Second, although cognitive therapies are clearly of help to many people, they do not help everyone. Research findings have begun to suggest limits to the effectiveness of these approaches. Is it enough to change the cognitive habits of a person with a serious psychological dysfunction? Can such specific changes make a general and lasting difference in the way the person feels and behaves?

Furthermore, like the other models, the cognitive model is narrow in certain ways. Although cognition is a very special human dimension, it is still only one part of human functioning. Aren't human beings more than the sum total of their thoughts, emotions, and behaviors? Shouldn't explanations of human functioning also consider broader issues such as how people approach life, what value they get from it, and how they deal with the question of life's meaning? This is the position of the humanistic-existential perspective.

"It is the mark of an educated mind to be able to entertain a thought without accepting it."

Aristotle

SUMMING UP ⌐ **The Cognitive Model**

The cognitive model claims that we must understand human thought to understand human behavior.

Cognitive Explanations When people display abnormal patterns of functioning, cognitive theorists point to cognitive problems, such as maladaptive assumptions and illogical thinking processes.

Cognitive Therapies Cognitive therapists try to help people recognize and change their faulty ideas and thinking processes. Among the most widely applied cognitive treatments is Beck's cognitive therapy.

The Humanistic-Existential Model

Philip Berman is more than the sum of his psychological conflicts, learned behaviors, or cognitions. Being human, he also has the ability to pursue philosophical goals such as self-awareness, strong values, a sense of meaning in life, and freedom of choice. According to humanistic and existential theorists, Philip's problems can be understood only in the light of such complex goals. Humanistic and existential theorists are usually grouped together—in an approach known as the *humanistic-existential model*—because of their common focus on these broader dimensions of human existence. At the same time, there are important differences between them.

Humanists, the more optimistic of the two groups, believe that human beings are born with a natural tendency to be friendly, cooperative, and constructive. People, these theorists propose, are driven to **self-actualize**—that is, to fulfill this potential for goodness and growth. They can do so, however, only if they honestly recognize and accept their weaknesses as well as their strengths and establish satisfying personal values to live by. Humanists further suggest that self-actualization leads naturally to a concern for the welfare of others and to behavior that is loving, courageous, spontaneous, and independent (Maslow, 1970).

Existentialists agree that human beings must have an accurate awareness of themselves and live meaningful—they say "authentic"—lives in order to be psychologically well adjusted. These theorists do not believe, however, that people

CHARITABLE ACTS

The people of the United States contribute around $150 billion to charity each year (Reese, 1998). Three-fourths of all incoming college freshmen have done volunteer work in the past year—40 percent of them with children and 29 percent for a charity (Kate, 1998).

are naturally inclined to live positively. They believe that from birth we have total freedom, either to face up to our existence and give meaning to our lives or to shrink from that responsibility. Those who choose to "hide" from responsibility and choice will view themselves as helpless and weak and may live empty, inauthentic, and dysfunctional lives as a result.

The humanistic and existential views of abnormality both date back to the 1940s. At that time Carl Rogers (1902–1987), often considered the pioneer of the humanistic perspective, developed *client-centered therapy,* a warm and supportive approach that contrasted sharply with the psychodynamic techniques of the day. He also proposed a theory of personality that paid little attention to irrational instincts and conflicts.

The existential view of personality and abnormality appeared during this same period. Many of its principles came from the ideas of nineteenth-century European existential philosophers who held that human beings are constantly defining and so giving meaning to their existence through their actions. In the late 1950s a book titled *Existence* described a number of major existential ideas and treatment approaches and helped them gain attention (May, Angel, & Ellenberger, 1958).

The humanistic and existential theories, and their uplifting and sometimes spiritual implications, were extremely popular during the 1960s and 1970s, years of considerable soul-searching and social upheaval in Western society. They have since lost some of their popularity, but they continue to influence the ideas and work of many clinicians.

Actualizing the self *Humanists suggest that self-actualized people, such as this hospital volunteer who works with drug-addicted babies, show concern for the welfare of humanity. They are also thought to be highly creative, spontaneous, independent, and humorous.*

Rogers's Humanistic Theory and Therapy

According to Carl Rogers (1987, 1961, 1951), the road to dysfunction begins in infancy. We all have a basic need to receive *positive regard* from the important people in our lives (primarily our parents). Those who receive *unconditional* (nonjudgmental) *positive regard* early in life are likely to develop *unconditional self-regard.* That is, they come to recognize their worth as persons, even while recognizing that they are not perfect. Such people are in a good position to actualize their positive potential.

Unfortunately, some children are repeatedly made to feel that they are not worthy of positive regard. As a result, they acquire *conditions of worth,* standards that tell them they are lovable and acceptable only when they conform to certain guidelines. In order to maintain positive self-regard, these people have to look at themselves very selectively, denying or distorting thoughts and actions that do not measure up to their conditions of worth. They thus acquire a distorted view of themselves and their experiences.

The constant self-deception makes it impossible for these people to self-actualize. They do not know what they are truly feeling, what they genuinely need, or what values and goals would be meaningful for them. Moreover, they spend so much energy trying to protect their self-image that little is left for self-actualizing. Problems in functioning are then inevitable.

Rogers might view Philip Berman as a man who has gone astray. Rather than trying to fulfill his positive human potential, he drifts from job to job, relationship to relationship, and outburst to outburst. In every interaction he is defending himself, trying to interpret events in ways he can live with, usually blaming his problems on other people. Yet his constant efforts at self-defense and self-enhancement are only partly successful. His basic negative self-image keeps breaking through. Rogers would probably link this problem to the critical ways Philip was treated by his mother throughout his childhood.

HUMANISM 101

According to surveys, the attribute admired most by today's college freshmen is *honesty,* cited as number 1 by 28 percent of respondents. This is followed by other humanistic attributes: hard work (cited by 14 percent) and motivation (6 percent) (Kate, 1998).

CLIENT-CENTERED THERAPY The human-istic therapy developed by Carl Rogers in which clinicians try to help clients by con-veying acceptance, accurate empathy, and genuineness.

GESTALT THERAPY The humanistic ther-apy developed by Fritz Perls in which clini-cians actively move clients toward self-recognition and self-acceptance by using techniques such as role-playing and self-discovery exercises.

Clinicians who practice Rogers's **client-centered therapy** try to create a sup-portive climate in which clients feel able to look at themselves honestly and ac-ceptingly (Thorne & Lambers, 1998; Raskin & Rogers, 1995). The therapist must display three important qualities throughout the therapy—unconditional positive regard for the client, accurate empathy, and genuineness.

Therapists show *unconditional positive regard* by offering full and warm accep-tance no matter what clients say, think, or feel. They show *accurate empathy* by accurately hearing what clients are saying and sensitively communicating it back to them. Finally, therapists must convey *genuineness*. Unless therapists' commu-nications are honest and genuine, clients may perceive them as mechanical and false. The following interaction shows the therapist using all these qualities to move the client toward greater self-awareness:

> *Client:* Yes, I know I shouldn't worry about it, but I do. Lots of things— money, people, clothes. In classes I feel that everyone's just waiting for a chance to jump on me. . . . When I meet somebody I wonder what he's actually thinking of me. Then later on I wonder how I match up to what he's come to think of me.
>
> *Therapist:* You feel that you're pretty responsive to the opinions of other people.
>
> *Client:* Yes, but it's things that shouldn't worry me.
>
> *Therapist:* You feel that it's the sort of thing that shouldn't be upsetting, but they do get you pretty much worried anyway.
>
> *Client:* Just some of them. Most of those things do worry me because they're true. The ones I told you, that is. But there are lots of little things that aren't true. . . . Things just seem to be piling up, piling up inside of me. . . . It's a feeling that things were crowding up and they were going to burst.
>
> *Therapist:* You feel that it's a sort of oppression with some frustration and that things are just unmanageable.
>
> *Client:* In a way, but some things just seem illogical. I'm afraid I'm not very clear here but that's the way it comes.
>
> *Therapist:* That's all right. You say just what you think.
>
> *(Snyder, 1947, pp. 2-24)*

In such an atmosphere, persons are expected to feel accepted by their thera-pists. They then may be able to look at themselves with honesty and acceptance— a process called *experiencing*. That is, they begin to value their own emotions, thoughts, and behaviors, and so they are freed from the insecurities and doubts that prevent self-actualization.

Client-centered therapy has not fared very well in research (Patterson, 2000; Greenberg et al., 1998, 1994). Although some studies show that people who re-ceive this therapy improve more than control subjects, many other studies have failed to find any such advantage. All the same, Rogers's therapy has had a posi-tive influence on clinical practice. It was one of the first major alternatives to psychodynamic therapy, and it helped open up the field to new approaches. Rogers also helped pave the way for psychologists to practice psychotherapy; it had previously been considered the territory of psychiatrists. And his commit-ment to clinical research helped promote the systematic study of treatment (Lakin, 1998). Approximately 1 percent of today's clinical psychologists, 2 per-cent of social workers, and 8 percent of counseling psychologists report that they employ the client-centered approach (Prochasca & Norcross, 1999).

Gestalt Theory and Therapy

Gestalt therapy, another humanistic approach, was developed in the 1950s by a charismatic clinician named Frederick (Fritz) Perls (1893–1970). Gestalt thera-pists, like client-centered therapists, guide their clients toward self-recognition

MUSICAL INTERVENTION

Some therapists consider music ther-apy to be a form of humanistic treat-ment because of music's ability to in-spire people, to arouse previously unavailable emotions, insights, and memories, and even to evoke spiritual feelings (Shultis, 1999; Steckler, 1998). The healing power of music has long been recognized; in Greek mythology, Apollo was the god of both music and medicine (Kahn & Fawcett, 1993).

and self-acceptance (Greenberg et al., 1998). But unlike client-centered therapists, they often try to achieve this goal by challenging and even frustrating clients. Gestalt techniques are also meant to shorten the therapy process. Some of Perls's favorite techniques were skillful frustration, role playing, and numerous rules and exercises.

In the technique of *skillful frustration,* gestalt therapists refuse to meet their clients' expectations or demands. This use of frustration is meant to help people see how they often try to manipulate others into meeting their needs. In the technique of *role playing,* the therapists instruct clients to act out various roles. A person may be told to be another person, an object, an alternative self, or even a part of the body (Polster, 1992). Role playing can become intense, as individuals are encouraged to fully express emotions. Many cry out, scream, kick, or pound. Through this experience they may come to "own" (accept) feelings that were previously unknown to them.

Perls also developed a list of *rules* to ensure that clients will look at themselves more closely. In some versions of gestalt therapy, for example, clients may be required to use "I" language rather than "it" language. They must say, "I am frightened" rather than "The situation is frightening." Yet another common rule requires clients to stay in the *here and now.* They have needs now, are hiding their needs now, and must observe them now.

Approximately 1 percent of clinical psychologists and other kinds of clinicians describe themselves as gestalt therapists (Prochaska & Norcross, 1999). Because they believe that personal experiences and self-awareness cannot be measured objectively, controlled research has rarely been done on the gestalt approach (Greenberg et al., 1998, 1994).

Techniques of gestalt therapy *Gestalt therapists may guide their clients to express their needs and feelings in their full intensity through role playing, banging on pillows, and other exercises. In a gestalt therapy group, members may help each other to "get in touch" with their needs and feelings.*

Existential Theories and Therapy

Like humanists, existentialists believe that psychological dysfunctioning is caused by self-deception; but existentialists are talking about a kind of self-deception in which people hide from life's responsibilities and fail to recognize that it is up to them to give meaning to their lives. According to existentialists, many people become overwhelmed by the pressures of present-day society and so look to others for guidance and authority. They overlook their personal freedom of choice and avoid responsibility for their lives and decisions (May & Yalom, 1995, 1989; May, 1987, 1961). Such people are left with empty, inauthentic lives. Their dominant emotions are anxiety, frustration, boredom, alienation, and depression.

Existentialists might view Philip Berman as a man who feels overwhelmed by the forces of society. He sees his parents as "rich, powerful, and selfish," and he views teachers, acquaintances, and employers as abusive and oppressing. He fails

THE TOLL OF BOREDOM

Twenty-one percent of Americans say they are regularly "bored out of their mind." Around 44% of all people eat when they are bored, 27% go for a drive, and 9% have a drink. The most boring time of the week is Sunday for 13% of people, weekday afternoons for 10%, and weeknights for 7% (Kanner, 1999).

EXISTENTIAL THERAPY A therapy that encourages clients to accept responsibility for their lives and to live with greater meaning and values.

to appreciate his choices in life and his capacity for finding meaning and direction. Quitting becomes a habit with him—he leaves job after job, ends every romantic relationship, flees difficult situations, and even tries suicide.

In **existential therapy** people are encouraged to accept responsibility for their lives and for their problems. They are helped to recognize their freedom so that they may choose a different course and live with greater meaning and stronger values (Fischer, McElwain, & DuBoise, 2000). For the most part, existential therapists care more about the *goals* of therapy than the use of specific techniques; methods vary greatly from clinician to clinician (Greenberg et al., 1998; May & Yalom, 1995, 1989). At the same time, most do place great emphasis on the *relationship* between therapist and client and try to create an atmosphere of honesty, hard work, and shared learning and growth (Schneider, 1998; Frankl, 1975, 1963).

> *Patient:* I don't know why I keep coming here. All I do is tell you the same thing over and over. I'm not getting anywhere.
> *Doctor:* I'm getting tired of hearing the same thing over and over, too.
> *Patient:* Maybe I'll stop coming.
> *Doctor:* It's certainly your choice.
> *Patient:* What do you think I should do?
> *Doctor:* What do you want to do?
> *Patient:* I want to get better.
> *Doctor:* I don't blame you.
> *Patient:* If you think I should stay, ok, I will.
> *Doctor:* You want me to tell you to stay?
> *Patient:* You know what's best; you're the doctor.
> *Doctor:* Do I act like a doctor?
>
> *(Keen, 1970, p. 200)*

Existential therapists do not believe that experimental methods can adequately test the effectiveness of their treatments (May & Yalom, 1995, 1989). To them, research dehumanizes individuals by reducing them to test measures or scale scores. Not surprisingly, then, very little controlled research has been devoted to the effectiveness of this approach (Prochaska & Norcross, 1999). Nevertheless, as many as 4 percent of today's therapists use an approach that is primarily existential (Prochaska & Norcross, 1999).

Assessing the Humanistic-Existential Model

The humanistic-existential model appeals to many people in and out of the clinical field. In recognizing the special challenges of human existence, humanistic and existential theorists tap into an aspect of psychological life that is typically missing from the other models (Fuller, 1982). Moreover, the factors that they say are critical to effective functioning—self-acceptance, personal values, personal meaning, and personal choice—are certainly lacking in many people with psychological disturbances.

The optimistic tone of the humanistic-existential model is also an attraction. Theorists who follow these principles offer great hope when they claim that despite the often overwhelming pressures of modern society, we can make our own choices, determine our own destiny, and accomplish much.

Still another attractive feature of the model is its emphasis on health (Cowen, 1991). Unlike clinicians from some of the other models who see individuals as patients with psychological illnesses, humanists and existentialists view them simply as people whose special potential has yet to be fulfilled. Moreover, they believe that a person's behavior can be influenced by his or her own innate good-

ConsiderThis

Many theorists worry about a growing trend toward "victimization" in our society, a tendency to portray undesirable behaviors as inevitable or uncontrollable consequences of early mistreatment or societal stress. What might be some of the dangers of overapplying the "victim" label?

THE**CURRENT SCENE**

Faith Linked to Mental Health

For years, many clinical theorists and practitioners have viewed religion as a negative factor in mental health (Thielman, 1998; Neeleman & Persaud, 1995). They have suspected that people with strong religious beliefs are more superstitious, irrational, guilt-ridden, and unstable than others, and less able to cope with life's difficulties. Recently, however, research has indicated that these views are wrong. Religious faith and mental health can be closely linked (George et al., 2000; Elkins, 1999; Koenig et al., 1998).

A number of studies have examined the mental health of people who view God as warm, caring, helpful, and dependable. Repeatedly, these individuals are found to be less lonely, depressed, or anxious than people who believe that God is cold and unresponsive or those without religious belief of any kind. They also seem to cope better with major life stresses, from illness to war, and they are less likely to abuse drugs (Miller, 1998; Clay, 1996). Accordingly, a growing number of therapists are including a focus on spiritual and religious issues when treating clients with strong religious beliefs (Richards & Bergin, 2000).

ConsiderThis

◉ Why might positive religious beliefs be linked to mental health? • Why have so many clinicians been suspicious of religious beliefs for so long?

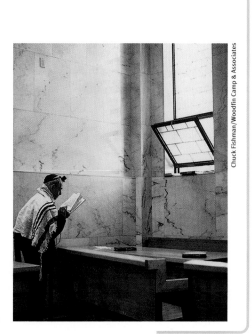

ness and potential, and by a willingness to take responsibility, more than by any factor in the past.

At the same time, the humanistic-existential focus on abstract issues of human fulfillment gives rise to a major problem: these issues are resistant to research. In fact, with the notable exception of Rogers, who spent years investigating his clinical methods, humanists and existentialists tend to reject the research approaches that now dominate the field. They argue the merits of their views using logic, self-observations, and individual case histories.

SUMMING UP | The Humanistic-Existential Model

Followers of the humanistic-existential model focus on the human ability to face challenging philosophical issues such as self-awareness, values, meaning, and choice and to make them part of one's life.

Humanists Humanists believe that people are driven to self-actualize. When this drive is interfered with, abnormal behavior may result. One group of humanistic therapists, client-centered therapists, try to create a very supportive climate in which persons can look at themselves honestly and acceptingly, thus opening the door to self-actualization. Another group, gestalt therapists, try to move persons to recognize and accept their needs through more active techniques.

Existentialists According to existentialists, abnormal behavior is the result of hiding from life's responsibilities. Existential therapists encourage people to accept responsibility for their lives, to recognize their freedom to choose a different course, and to choose to live with greater meaning.

"Creative minds always have been known to survive any kind of bad training."

Anna Freud

FAMILY SYSTEMS THEORY A theory that views the family as a system of interacting parts whose interactions follow consistent patterns and unstated rules.

The Sociocultural Model

Philip Berman is also a social being. He is surrounded by people and by institutions, he is a member of a family and a society, and he is involved in both social and professional relationships. Thus social forces are always operating upon Philip, setting rules and expectations that guide and at times pressure him, helping to shape his behavior, thoughts, and emotions as surely as any internal mechanism.

According to the *sociocultural model,* abnormal behavior is best understood in light of the social and cultural forces that influence an individual (Eaton, 2001; López & Guarnaccia, 2000). What are the norms of the society? What roles does the person play in the social environment? What kind of family structure is the person a part of? And how do other people view and react to him or her? The model borrows concepts and principles from two fields: *sociology,* the study of human relationships and social groups, and *anthropology,* the study of human cultures and institutions.

How Do Sociocultural Theorists Explain Abnormal Functioning?

Because behavior is shaped by social forces, sociocultural theorists hold, we must examine a person's social surroundings if we are to understand abnormal behavior. Sociocultural explanations focus on *family structure and communication, social networks and supports, societal conditions,* and *societal labels and roles.*

FAMILY STRUCTURE AND COMMUNICATION According to **family systems theory,** the family is a system of interacting parts—the family members—who relate to one another in consistent ways and follow the rules unique to each family (McGoldrick, Gerson, & Shellenberger, 1999). Family systems theorists believe that the structure and communication patterns of some families actually force individual members to behave in a way that otherwise seems abnormal. If the members were to behave normally, they would severely strain the family's rules and usual manner of operation, and would actually increase their own and their family's turmoil. The natural responses by other family members would in fact defend against such "normal" behavior.

Family systems theory holds that certain family systems are particularly likely to produce abnormal functioning in individual members (Becvar & Becvar, 1993; Nichols, 1992, 1984). Some families, for example, have an *enmeshed* structure in which the members are grossly overinvolved in each other's activities, thoughts, and feelings. Children from this kind of family may have great difficulty becoming independent in life. Some families display *disengagement,* which is marked by very rigid boundaries between the members. Children from these families may find it hard to function in a group or to give or request support.

In the sociocultural model, Philip Berman's angry and impulsive personal style might be seen as the product of a disturbed family structure. According to family systems theorists, the whole family—mother, father, Philip, and his brother Arnold—relate in such a way as to maintain Philip's behavior. Family theorists might be particularly interested in the conflict between Philip's mother and father and the imbalance between their parental roles. They might see Philip's behavior as both a reaction to and stimulus for his parents' behaviors. With Philip acting out the role of the misbehaving child, or scapegoat, his parents may have little need or time to question their own relationship.

The dysfunctional family *People in dysfunctional families often face special pressures and in addition may be called upon to behave and think in ways that are personally maladaptive. This 8-year-old had to call the police when he saw his father attacking his mother with a knife. The child's rage, frustration, and emotional pain are apparent.*

Family systems theorists would also seek to clarify the precise nature of Philip's relationship with each parent. Is he enmeshed with his mother and/or disengaged from his father? They would look too at the rules governing the sibling relationship in the family, the relationship between the parents and Philip's brother, and the nature of parent-child relationships in previous generations of the family.

SOCIAL NETWORKS AND SUPPORTS Sociocultural theorists are also concerned with the broader social networks in which people operate, including their social and professional relationships. How well do they communicate with others? What kind of signals do they send to or receive from others? Researchers have often found ties between social networks and a person's functioning (Thoits, 1999). They have noted, for example, that people who are isolated and lack social support or intimacy in their lives are more likely to become depressed when under stress and to remain depressed longer than are people with supportive spouses or warm friendships (Husaini, 1997; Paykel & Cooper, 1992).

SOCIETAL CONDITIONS Wide-ranging societal conditions may create special stresses and increase the likelihood of abnormal functioning in some members (Thoits, 1999). Researchers have learned, for example, that psychological abnormality, especially severe psychological abnormality, is more common in the lower socioeconomic classes than in the higher ones (Eaton & Muntaner, 1999). Perhaps the special pressures of lower-class life explain this relationship (Adler et al., 1994). That is, the higher rates of crime, unemployment, overcrowding, and homelessness, the inferior medical care, and the limited educational opportunities of lower-class life may place great stress on members of these groups (Zima et al., 1996). Conversely, it may be that people who suffer from severe mental disturbances are less effective at work and earn less money and, as a result, *drift downward* to a lower socioeconomic class.

Sociocultural researchers have noted that racial and sexual prejudice and discrimination may also contribute to certain forms of abnormal functioning (Clark et al., 1999). Women in Western society receive diagnoses of anxiety and depressive disorders at least twice as often as men (Gold, 1998). Similarly, African Americans experience unusually high rates of anxiety disorders (Blazer et al., 1991). Hispanic persons, particularly young men, have higher rates of alcoholism than members of most other ethnic groups (Helzer, Burnman, & McEvoy, 1991). And Native Americans display exceptionally high alcoholism and suicide rates (Kinzie et al., 1992). Although many factors may combine to produce these differences, racial and sexual prejudice and the problems they pose may contribute to abnormal patterns of tension, unhappiness, low self-esteem, and escape.

SOCIETAL LABELS AND ROLES Sociocultural theorists also believe that abnormal functioning is influenced greatly by the diagnostic labels and roles assigned to troubled people (Szasz, 2000, 1963; Scheff, 1999). When people stray from the norms of their society, the society calls them deviant and, in many cases, "mentally ill." Such labels tend to stick. Moreover, when people are viewed in particular ways, reacted to as "crazy," and perhaps even encouraged to act sick, they gradually learn to accept and play the assigned role. Ultimately the label seems appropriate.

A famous study by the clinical investigator David Rosenhan (1973) supports this position. Eight normal people presented themselves at various mental

The dysfunctional society *The pressures and uncertainty of living in a war-torn environment may contribute to the development of psychological problems. The environment's ongoing violence may leave some individuals feeling numb and confused. This child seems hardly to notice the burning bombed truck behind him as he bicycles through Northern Ireland.*

James Nachtwey/Magnum Photos

PRESSURES OF POVERTY

Each year around 90 of every 1,000 poor persons are victims of violent crime, compared to 50 of every 1,000 middle-income people and 40 of every 1,000 wealthy people (U.S. Bureau of Justice Statistics, 1996).

THE POWER OF DIAGNOSIS
People who are diagnosed with a mental disorder report having twice as much difficulty obtaining and keeping medical insurance as do people with any other condition, including diabetes and hypertension (Druss & Rosenheck, 1998).

hospitals, complaining that they had been hearing voices say the words "empty," "hollow," and "thud." On the basis of this complaint alone, each was diagnosed as having schizophrenia and admitted to the hospital. As the sociocultural model would predict, the "pseudopatients" had a hard time convincing others that they were well once they had been given the diagnostic label. Their hospitalizations ranged from 7 to 52 days, even though they behaved normally as soon as they were admitted. In addition, the label kept influencing the way the staff viewed and dealt with them. For example, one pseudopatient who paced the corridor out of boredom was, in clinical notes, described as "nervous." Finally, the pseudopatients reported that the staff's behavior toward them and other patients was often authoritarian, limited, and counterproductive. Overall, the pseudopatients came to feel powerless, invisible, and bored.

Sociocultural Treatments

Although many clients meet alone with their therapists in *individual therapy,* sociocultural theories have helped spur the growth of other treatment formats and settings. In *group therapy,* therapists meet with a group of clients who all share similar problems. In *family* and *couple therapy,* the therapist and client are joined by other family members. In *community treatment,* the meetings take place in or near the client's everyday environment.

Therapists of any orientation may work with clients in these broad formats, applying the techniques and principles of their preferred models. In such instances the therapy is not purely sociocultural. However, more and more of the clinicians who use these formats believe that psychological problems emerge in a social setting and are best treated in such a setting. In addition, some of these clinicians have developed special sociocultural strategies for use in group, family, couple, and community treatments.

The self-help movement *Thousands of self-help groups around the world help people cope with a variety of problems. Here members of an AIDS support group participate in a group exercise.*

GROUP THERAPY Thousands of therapists specialize in **group therapy,** and countless others run therapy groups as part of their practices. One survey of clinical psychologists, for example, revealed that almost one-third of them devoted some portion of their practice to group therapy (Norcross et al., 1993). Typically, members of a therapy group meet together with a therapist and discuss the problems of one or more of the people in the group. Together they develop important insights, build social skills, strengthen feelings of self-worth, and share useful information or advice (Vinogradov & Yalom, 1994). Many groups are created with particular client populations in mind; for example, there are groups for people with alcoholism, for people who are physically handicapped, and for people who are divorced, abused, or bereaved (Bednar & Kaul, 1994).

Research suggests that group therapy is of help to many clients, often as helpful as individual therapy (McDermut et al., 2001; Bednar & Kaul, 1994). The group format has also been used for purposes that are educational rather than therapeutic, such as "consciousness raising" and spiritual inspiration.

A format similar to group therapy is the **self-help group** (or **mutual help group**). Here people who have similar problems (bereavement, substance abuse, illness, unemployment, divorce) come together to help and support one another without the direct leadership of a professional clinician (Felix et al., 2000; Fehre & White, 1996). These groups have become very popular since the 1970s. Today there are about 500,000 such groups attended by 15 million people in the United States alone. The groups tend to offer more direct advice than do therapy groups and to encourage more exchange of information or "tips" (Silverman, 1992).

Self-help groups are popular for several reasons. Some of the members are looking for inexpensive and interesting alternatives to traditional treatment. Others have simply lost confidence in the ability of clinicians to help with their problems (Silverman, 1992). Still other people find self-help groups less threat-

ConsiderThis
◉ Interest in self-help groups has grown in recent years. What might be the advantages and disadvantages of these groups in comparison with professional treatment?

ening than therapy groups. The rise of these groups may also be tied to the decline of family life and other traditional sources of emotional support in Western society (Bloch, Crouch, & Reibstein, 1982).

FAMILY THERAPY **Family therapy** was first introduced in the 1950s. A therapist meets with all members of a family, points out problem behaviors and interactions, and helps the whole family to change (Minuchin, 1997; Bowen, 1960). Here, the entire family is viewed as the unit under treatment, even if only one of the members receives a clinical diagnosis. The following is a typical interaction between family members and a therapist:

> Tommy sat motionless in a chair gazing out the window. He was fourteen and a bit small for his age. . . . Sissy was eleven. She was sitting on the couch between her Mom and Dad with a smile on her face. Across from them sat Ms. Fargo, the family therapist.
>
> Ms. Fargo spoke. "Could you be a little more specific about the changes you have seen in Tommy and when they came about?"
>
> Mrs. Davis answered first. "Well, I guess it was about two years ago. Tommy started getting in fights at school. When we talked to him at home he said it was none of our business. He became moody and disobedient. He wouldn't do anything that we wanted him to. He began to act mean to his sister and even hit her."
>
> "What about the fights at school?" Ms. Fargo asked.
>
> This time it was Mr. Davis who spoke first. "Ginny was more worried about them than I was. I used to fight a lot when I was in school and I think it is normal. . . . But I was very respectful to my parents, especially my Dad. If I ever got out of line he would smack me one."
>
> "Have you ever had to hit Tommy?" Ms. Fargo inquired softly.
>
> "Sure, a couple of times, but it didn't seem to do any good."
>
> All at once Tommy seemed to be paying attention, his eyes riveted on his father. "Yeah, he hit me a lot, for no reason at all!"
>
> "Now, that's not true, Thomas." Mrs. Davis has a scolding expression on her face. "If you behaved yourself a little better you wouldn't get hit. Ms. Fargo, I can't say that I am in favor of the hitting, but I understand sometimes how frustrating it may be for Bob."
>
> "You don't know how frustrating it is for me, honey." Bob seemed upset. "You don't have to work all day at the office and then come home to contend with all of this. Sometimes I feel like I don't even want to come home."
>
> Ginny gave him a hard stare. "You think things at home are easy all day? I could use some support from you. You think all you have to do is earn the money and I will do everything else. Well, I am not about to do that anymore." . . .
>
> Mrs. Davis began to cry. "I just don't know what to do anymore. Things just seem so hopeless. Why can't people be nice in this family anymore? I don't think I am asking too much, am I?"
>
> Ms. Fargo spoke thoughtfully. "I get the feeling that people in this family would like things to be different. Bob, I can see how frustrating it must be for you to work so hard and not be able to relax when you get home. And, Ginny, your job is not easy either. You have a lot to do at home and Bob can't be there to help because he has to earn a living. And you kids sound like you would like some things to be different too. It must be hard for you, Tommy, to be catching so much flack these days. I think this also makes it hard for you to have fun at home too, Sissy."
>
> She looked at each person briefly and was sure to make eye contact. "There seems to be a lot going on. . . . I think we are going to need to understand a lot of things to see why this is happening. . . ."
>
> *(Sheras & Worchel, 1979, pp. 108–110)*

GROUP THERAPY A therapy format in which a group of people with similar problems meet together with a therapist to work on those problems.

SELF-HELP GROUP A group made up of people with similar problems who help and support one another without the direct leadership of a clinician. Also called a *mutual help group*.

FAMILY THERAPY A therapy format in which the therapist meets with all members of a family and helps them to change in therapeutic ways.

A NEW FAMILY CONSTELLATION

Twenty-six percent of today's families are headed by a single parent, compared to 2 percent 50 years ago (Stacey, 1996; NCHS, 1995).

ConsiderThis

◉ In *Anna Karenina* the writer Leo Tolstoy wrote, "All happy families resemble one another; every unhappy family is unhappy in its own fashion." Would family systems theorists agree with Tolstoy?
• Why are people so affected by their families?

COUPLE THERAPY A therapy format in which the therapist works with two people who share a long-term relationship. Also called *marital therapy*.

COMMUNITY MENTAL HEALTH TREATMENT A treatment approach that emphasizes community care.

Family therapists may follow any of the major theoretical models, but more and more of them are adopting the sociocultural principles of family systems theory. Today 4 percent of all clinical psychologists, 13 percent of social workers, and 1 percent of psychiatrists identify themselves mainly as *family systems therapists* (Prochaska & Norcross, 1999).

As we observed earlier, family systems theory holds that each family has its own rules, structure, and communication patterns that shape the individual members' behavior. In one family systems approach, *structural family therapy,* therapists try to change the family power structure, the roles each person plays, and the alliances between members (Nichols & Minuchin, 1999; Minuchin, 1997, 1974). In another, *conjoint family therapy,* therapists try to help members recognize and change harmful patterns of communication (Satir, 1987, 1967, 1964).

Family therapies of various kinds can be quite helpful for certain persons and problems. Studies have found that the overall improvement rate for families that undergo such treatments is between 50 and 65 percent, compared to 35 percent for families in control groups (Gurman et al., 1986; Todd & Stanton, 1983). The involvement of the father seems greatly to increase the chances of success.

COUPLE THERAPY In **couple therapy,** or **marital therapy,** the therapist works with two individuals who are in a long-term relationship. Often they are husband and wife, but the couple need not be married or even living together. Like family therapy, couple therapy often focuses on the structure and communication patterns in the relationship (Baucom et al., 2000, 1998; Nichols & Minuchin, 1999). A couple approach may also be employed when a child's psychological problems are traced to problems that may exist between the parents (Fauber & Long, 1992).

Shared responsibility *Regardless of the therapist's orientation, individuals in couple therapy are encouraged to recognize and address their own contributions to the relationship.*

Although some degree of conflict exists in any long-term relationship, many adults in our society experience serious marital discord (Bradbury & Karney, 1993). The divorce rate in Canada, the United States, and Europe is now close to 50 percent of the marriage rate (NCHS, 2000, 1999). Many couples who live together without marrying apparently have similar levels of difficulty (Greeley, 1991).

Couple therapy, like family and group therapy, may follow the principles of any of the major therapy orientations. *Behavioral couple therapy,* for example, uses many techniques from the behavioral perspective (Cordova & Jacobson, 1993; Jacobson, 1989). Therapists help spouses recognize and change problem behaviors largely by teaching specific problem-solving and communication skills.

A broader, more sociocultural version, called *integrative couple therapy,* further helps partners accept behaviors that they cannot change and embrace the whole relationship nevertheless (Lawrence et al., 1999; Cordova & Jacobson, 1993). Partners are asked to see such behaviors as an understandable result of basic differences between them.

Couples treated by couple therapy seem to show greater improvement in their relationships than couples with similar problems who fail to receive treatment, but no one form of couple therapy stands out as superior to others (Christensen & Heavey, 1999; Baucom et al., 1998). At the same time, only about half of all treated couples say they are "happily married" at the end of couple therapy. And, according to some studies, as many as 38 percent of successfully treated couples may relapse within two to four years after therapy (Snyder, Wills, & Grady-Fletcher, 1991). Couples who are younger, well adjusted, and less rigid in their gender roles tend to have the best results.

"I've been a cow all my life, honey. Don't ask me to change now."

COMMUNITY TREATMENT Following sociocultural principles, **community mental health treatment** programs allow clients, particularly those with severe psychological difficulties, to receive treatment in familiar surroundings as they try to recover. In 1963 President Kennedy called for such a "bold new approach" to the treatment of mental disorders—a community approach that would enable most people with psychological problems to receive services from nearby agencies rather than distant facilities. Congress passed the Community Mental Health Act soon after, launching the *community mental health movement* across the United States. A number of other countries have launched similar movements.

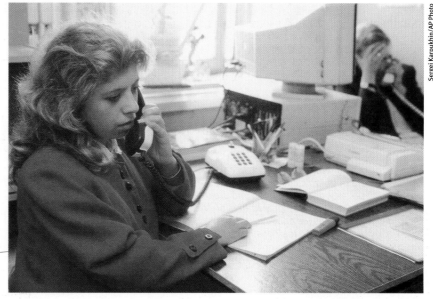

A key principle of community treatment is *prevention* (Pentz, 1999). Here clinicians actively reach out to clients rather than wait for them to seek treatment. Research suggests that prevention efforts are often very successful (Reppucci, Woolard, & Fried, 1999; Heller, 1996). Community workers recognize three types of prevention, which they call *primary, secondary, and tertiary.*

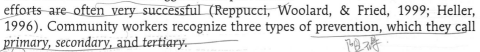

Primary prevention consists of efforts to improve community attitudes and policies. Its goal is to prevent psychological disorders altogether (Burnette, 1996; Martin, 1996). Community workers may lobby for better community recreational programs or child-care facilities, consult with a local school board to help develop a curriculum, or offer health fairs or public workshops on stress reduction.

Secondary prevention consists of identifying and treating psychological disorders in the early stages, before they become serious. Community workers may work with schoolteachers, ministers, or police to help them recognize the early signs of psychological dysfunction and teach them how to help people find treatment (Newman et al., 1996).

The goal of *tertiary prevention* is to provide effective treatment as soon as it is needed so that moderate or severe disorders do not become long-term problems. Today community agencies across the United States do successfully offer tertiary care for millions of people with moderate psychological problems, but, as we observed in Chapter 1, they often fail to provide the services needed by hundreds of thousands with severe disturbances.

Why has the community mental health approach fallen short for so many people with severe disturbances? As we shall see in later chapters, one of the major reasons is lack of funding. In 1981, when only 750 of the planned 2,000 community mental health centers were in place across the United States, almost all federal funding was withdrawn and replaced with smaller financial grants to the states (Humphreys & Rappaport, 1993). Whether or not this trend will continue in the twenty-first century depends on how health care is reformed (Kiesler, 1992) and on how states spend the hundreds of millions of dollars saved by the closing of large state hospitals (Torrey, 1997).

Assessing the Sociocultural Model

The sociocultural model has added greatly to the understanding and treatment of abnormal functioning. Today most clinicians take family, social, and societal issues into account, factors that were overlooked just 30 years ago (Tamplin, Goodyer, & Herbert, 1998). In addition, clinicians have become more aware of the impact of clinical and social labels. Finally, as we have just observed, sociocultural treatment formats sometimes succeed where traditional approaches have failed (Heller, 1996).

Community mental health *Hot-line operators at the Women's Crisis Center in Moscow receive calls from victims of domestic violence and set community programs in motion to help the victims and prevent further abuse.*

ALTERNATIVE "TREATMENT"

It is estimated that jails across the United States admit 700,000 people with severe mental disorders each year. The daily cost of jail is $137 per inmate; the daily cost of community mental health treatment is $60 per patient (Treatment Advocacy Center, 1999; U.S. Public Health Service, 1999).

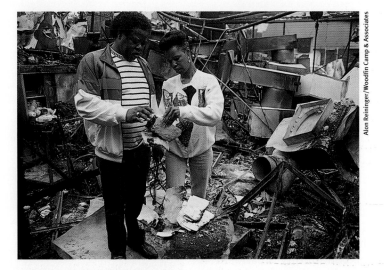

Alon Reininger/Woodfin Camp & Associates

Modern "mass madness"? *Some sociocultural theorists believe that intense social stressors may produce outbreaks of "mass madness" such as the Los Angeles riots of 1992. In a vicious cycle, the riots, which occurred against a backdrop of poverty, unemployment, and prejudice, produced further stress for members of the community, such as Joe and Joyce Wilson, who survey the damage to their business, Pop's Restaurant.*

At the same time, the sociocultural model, like the other models, has certain problems. To begin with, sociocultural research findings are often difficult to interpret. Research may reveal a relationship between certain sociocultural factors and a particular disorder, yet fail to establish that they are its *cause*. Studies show a link between family conflict and schizophrenia, for example, but that finding does not necessarily mean that family dysfunction causes schizophrenia (Miklowitz et al., 1995). It is equally possible that family functioning is disrupted by the tension and conflict created by the schizophrenic behavior of a family member (Eakes, 1995).

Another limitation of the model is its inability to predict abnormality in specific individuals (Reynolds, 1998). For example, if societal conditions such as prejudice and discrimination are key causes of anxiety and depression, why do only some of the people subjected to such forces experience psychological disorders? Are still other factors necessary for the development of the disorders?

Given these limitations, most clinicians view sociocultural explanations as going hand in hand with biological or psychological explanations. They agree that sociocultural factors may create a climate favorable to the development of certain disorders. They believe, however, that biological or psychological conditions or both must also be present in order for the disorders to spring forth.

SUMMING UP | The Sociocultural Model

Followers of the sociocultural model explain and treat abnormality by looking outward at the social forces that affect members of a society.

Sociocultural Explanations Some sociocultural theorists focus on the family system, believing that a family's structure or communication patterns may force members to behave in abnormal ways. Others focus on social networks and support, and still others examine societal conditions to see what special stresses they may pose. Finally, some theorists focus on societal labels and roles; they hold that society calls certain people "mentally ill" and that the label itself may influence how a person behaves and is responded to.

Sociocultural Therapies Sociocultural principles are often on display in such therapy formats as group, family, and couple therapy. Research indicates that these formats are useful for some problems and under some circumstances. In community treatment, therapists try to work with persons in settings close to home, school, and work. Their goal is either primary, secondary, or tertiary prevention.

CROSSROADS:
Integration of the Models

Today's leading models vary widely. They look at behavior differently, begin with different assumptions, arrive at different conclusions, and apply different treatments. Yet none of the models has proved consistently superior. Each helps us appreciate a key aspect of human functioning, and each has important strengths as well as serious limitations (see Table 2-2).

With all their differences, the conclusions and techniques of the different models are often compatible (Friman et al., 1993). Certainly our understanding and treatment of abnormal behavior are more complete if we appreciate the biological, psychological, *and* sociocultural aspects of a person's problem rather than only one of them (Eaton, 2001). Not surprisingly, then, a growing number of clinicians now favor explanations of abnormal behavior that consider more than one kind of cause at a time. These explanations, sometimes called **biopsychosocial theories,** state that abnormality results from the interaction of genetic, biological, developmental, emotional, behavioral, cognitive, social, and societal influences. A case of depression, for example, might best be explained by pointing collectively to an individual's inheritance of unfavorable genes, traumatic losses during childhood, negative ways of thinking, and social isolation.

Some biopsychosocial theorists adopt a **diathesis-stress explanation** of how the various factors work together to cause abnormal functioning ("diathesis" means a predisposed tendency). According to this theory, people must first have a biological, psychological, or sociocultural predisposition to develop a disorder and must then be subjected to episodes of severe stress. In a case of depression, for example, we might find that unfavorable genes and related biochemical

BIOPSYCHOSOCIAL THEORIES Explanations of abnormality as resulting from an interaction of genetic, biological, developmental, emotional, behavioral, cognitive, social, and societal influences.

DIATHESIS-STRESS EXPLANATION The view that a person must first have a predisposition to a disorder and then be subjected to episodes of stress in order to develop the disorder.

Table 2-2

Comparing the Models

	BIOLOGICAL	PSYCHODYNAMIC	BEHAVIORAL	COGNITIVE	HUMANISTIC	EXISTENTIAL	SOCIO-CULTURAL
Cause of dysfunction	Biological malfunction	Underlying conflicts	Maladaptive learning	Maladaptive thinking	Self-deceit	Avoidance of responsibility	Family or social stress
Research support	Strong	Modest	Strong	Strong	Weak	Weak	Moderate
Consumer designation	Patient	Patient	Client	Client	Patient or client	Patient or client	Client
Therapist role	Doctor	Interpreter	Teacher	Persuader	Observer	Collaborator	Social facilitator
Key therapist technique	Biological intervention	Free association and interpretation	Conditioning	Reasoning	Reflection	Varied	Social intervention
Therapy goal	Biological repair	Broad psychological change	Functional behaviors	Adaptive thinking	Self-actualization	Authentic life	Effective family or social system

abnormalities predispose the individual to develop the disorder, while the loss of a loved one actually triggers its onset.

In a similar search for integration, many therapists are now combining treatment techniques from several different models (McDaniel et al., 2001; Norcross et al., 1998). In fact, 27 percent of today's clinical psychologists, 34 percent of social workers, and 53 percent of psychiatrists describe their approach as "eclectic" or "integrative" (Norcross et al., 1997). Studies confirm that clinical problems often respond better to combined approaches than to any one therapy alone (Glass et al., 1998; Beitman, 1996, 1993). For example, as we shall see, drug therapy combined with cognitive therapy is sometimes the most effective treatment for depression (Keller, 1999).

Given the rise in biopsychosocial theories and combination treatments, our look at abnormal behavior throughout this book will take a particular direction. Of course, as different disorders are presented, we will be interested in how today's models explain each disorder and how clinicians who endorse each model treat people with the disorder. Just as important, however, we will also be observing how the explanations and treatments may build upon and strengthen each other, and we will examine current efforts toward integration of the models.

KEY TERMS

model p. 32
neuron p. 33
synapse p. 34
neurotransmitter p. 34
endocrine system p. 34
hormone p. 34
gene p. 34
psychotropic medication p. 36
antianxiety drug p. 36
antidepressant drug p. 36
antibipolar drug p. 36
antipsychotic drug p. 36
electroconvulsive therapy (ECT) p. 36
psychosurgery p. 36
unconscious p. 38
id p. 38

ego p. 38
ego defense mechanisms p. 38
superego p. 38
fixation p. 38
ego theory p. 40
self theory p. 40
object relations theory p. 40
free association p. 40
resistance p. 41
transference p. 41
dream p. 41
catharsis p. 41
working through p. 41
conditioning p. 44
operant conditioning p. 44
modeling p. 44

classical conditioning p. 44
systematic desensitization p. 45
self-efficacy p. 46
cognitive therapy p. 48
self-actualization p. 50
client-centered therapy p. 52
gestalt therapy p. 52
existential therapy p. 54
family systems theory p. 56
group therapy p. 58
self-help group p. 58
family therapy p. 59
couple therapy p. 60
community mental health treatment p. 61
biopsychosocial theories p. 63
diathesis-stress explanation p. 63

QUICK QUIZ

1. What are the key regions of the brain, and how do messages travel throughout the brain? Describe the biological treatments for psychological disorders. pp. 33–36

2. Identify the models associated with learned responses (p. 44), values (p. 50), responsibility (p. 51), underlying conflicts (p. 37), and maladaptive assumptions (p. 48).

3. Identify the treatments that use unconditional positive regard (p. 52), free association (p. 40), classical conditioning (p. 45), skillful frustration (p. 53), and dream interpretation (p. 41).

4. What are the key principles of the psychodynamic (p. 37), behavioral (p. 44), cognitive (p. 48), and humanistic-existential (p. 50) models?

5. According to psychodynamic theorists, what roles do the id, ego, and superego play in the development of both normal and abnormal behavior? What are the key techniques used by psychodynamic therapists? pp. 38–43

6. What forms of conditioning do behaviorists rely on in their explanations and treatments of abnormal behaviors? pp. 44–47

7. What kinds of cognitive dysfunctioning can lead to abnormal behavior? pp. 48–49

8. Compare Rogers's and Perls's humanistic theories and therapies. How do they differ from existential explanations and approaches? pp. 50–55

9. How might family factors, social networks, societal conditions, and societal labels help produce abnormal behavior? pp. 56–58

10. What are the key features of group therapy, family therapy, couple therapy, and community treatment? How effective are these various formats? pp. 58–61

◯ CYBER STUDY

▲ *Observe the biological, psychodynamic, and sociocultural models in action.*
▲ *See how treatments vary.* ▲ *How have biological treatments improved over the years?* ▲ *Are dreams the "royal road to the unconscious"?*

SEARCH THE *FUNDAMENTALS OF ABNORMAL PSYCHOLOGY* CD-ROM FOR

▲ Chapter 2 video cases and discussions
 Early Electroconvulsive Therapies
 "Larry"—Psychoanalytic Therapy Session
 "Jim"—Treating Drug Addiction: A Behavioral Approach

▲ Chapter 2 practice test and feedback

▲ Additional video cases and discussions
 "Meredith"—Mood Disorders: Medication and Talk Therapy
 "Walter"—Alzheimer's Disease

LOG ON TO THE COMER WEB PAGE FOR

▲ Suggested Web links, research exercises, FAQ page, additional Chapter 2 practice test questions
 <http://www.worthpublishers.com/comer>

Source: The Royal Road . . . Psychoanalytic Approaches to the Dream (Producer, Dr. Glenn Gabbard; Menninger Video, 1988)

Clinical Assessment, Diagnosis, and Treatment

Angela Savanti was 22 years old, lived at home with her mother, and was employed as a secretary in a large insurance company. She . . . had had passing periods of "the blues" before, but her present feelings of despondency were of much greater proportion. She was troubled by a severe depression and frequent crying spells, which had not lessened over the past two months. Angela found it hard to concentrate on her job, had great difficulty falling asleep at night, and had a poor appetite. . . . Her depression had begun after she and her boyfriend Jerry broke up two months previously.

(Leon, 1984, p. 109)

Her feelings of despondency led Angela Savanti to make an appointment with a therapist at a local counseling center. The first step the clinician took was to learn as much as possible about Angela and her disturbance. Who is she, what is her life like, and what precisely are her symptoms? The answers might help to reveal the causes and probable course of her present dysfunction and suggest what kinds of strategies would be most likely to help her. Treatment could then be tailored to Angela's needs and particular pattern of abnormal functioning.

In Chapters 1 and 2 we saw how researchers in abnormal psychology build a broad understanding of abnormal functioning. Clinical practitioners apply this general information in their work, but their main focus is to gather **idiographic,** or individual, information about their clients. To help a particular person overcome his or her problems, a practitioner must have the fullest possible understanding of that person and know the circumstances under which the problems arose (Tucker, 1998). Clinicians use the procedures of *assessment* and *diagnosis* to gather individual information about a client. Then they are in a position to apply *treatment*.

Clinical Assessment: How and Why Does the Client Behave Abnormally?

Assessment is simply the collecting of relevant information in an effort to reach a conclusion. It goes on in every realm of life. We make assessments when we decide what cereal to buy or which presidential candidate to vote for. College admissions officers, who have to select the "best" of the students applying to their college, depend on academic records, recommendations, achievement test scores, interviews, and application forms to help them decide. Employers, who have to predict which applicants are most likely to be effective workers, collect information from résumés, interviews, references, and perhaps on-the-job observations.

Clinical assessment is used to determine how and why a person is behaving abnormally and how that person may be helped. It also enables clinicians to evaluate people's progress after they have been in treatment for a while and decide whether the treatment should be changed. The specific tools that are used to do an assessment depend on the clinician's theoretical orientation (Needleman, 1999; Smith, 1998). Psychodynamic clinicians,

IDIOGRAPHIC UNDERSTANDING An understanding of the behavior of a particular individual.

ASSESSMENT The process of collecting and interpreting relevant information about a client or subject.

STANDARDIZATION The process in which a test is administered to a large group of persons whose performance then serves as a common standard or norm against which any individual's score can be measured.

RELIABILITY A measure of the consistency of test or research results.

VALIDITY The accuracy of a test's or study's results; that is, the extent to which the test or study actually measures or shows what it claims.

CLINICAL INTERVIEW A face-to-face encounter in which clinicians ask questions of clients, weigh their responses and reactions, and learn about them and their psychological problems.

for example, use methods that assess a client's personality and probe for any unconscious conflicts he or she may be experiencing. Behavioral and cognitive clinicians are more likely to use assessment methods that reveal specific dysfunctional behaviors and cognitions (Haynes & O'Brien, 2000).

The hundreds of clinical assessment techniques and tools that have been developed fall into three categories: *clinical interviews, tests,* and *observations.* To be useful, these tools must be *standardized* and have clear *reliability* and *validity.*

Characteristics of Assessment Tools

All clinicians must follow the same procedures when they use a particular technique of assessment. To **standardize** a technique is to set up common steps to be followed whenever it is administered. Similarly, clinicians must standardize the way they interpret the results of an assessment tool in order to be able to understand what a particular score means. They may standardize the scores of a test, for example, by first administering it to a group of subjects whose performance will then serve as a common standard, or norm, against which later individual scores can be measured. The group that initially takes the test must be typical of the larger population the test is intended for. If an aggressiveness test meant for the public at large were standardized on a group of marines, for example, the resulting "norm" might turn out to be misleadingly high.

Reliability refers to the *consistency* of assessment measures. A good assessment tool will always yield the same results in the same situation (Wiens, Mueller, & Bryan, 2001; Kline, 1993). An assessment tool has high *test–retest reliability,* one kind of reliability, if it yields the same results every time it is given to the same people. If a woman's responses on a particular test indicate that she is generally a heavy drinker, the test should produce the same result when she takes it again a week later. To measure test–retest reliability, subjects are tested on two occasions and the two scores are correlated. The higher the correlation, the greater the test's reliability (see Chapter 1).

An assessment tool shows high *interrater* (or *interjudge*) *reliability,* another kind of reliability, if different judges independently agree on how to score and interpret it (Moberg et al., 2001). True–false and multiple-choice tests yield consistent scores no matter who evaluates them, but other tests require that the evaluator make a judgment. Consider a test that requires the person to draw a copy of a picture, which a judge then rates for accuracy. Different judges may give different ratings to the same drawing.

Finally, an assessment tool must have **validity:** it must *accurately* measure what it is supposed to be measuring (Haynes, Nelson, & Blaine, 1999). Suppose a weight scale reads 12 pounds every time a 10-pound bag of sugar is placed on it. Although the scale is reliable because its readings are consistent, those readings are not valid, or accurate.

A given assessment tool may appear to be valid simply because it makes sense and seems reasonable. However, this sort of validity, called *face validity,* does not by itself mean that the instrument is trustworthy. A test for depression, for example, might include questions about how often a person cries. Because it makes sense that depressed people would cry, these test questions would have face validity. It turns out, however, that many people cry a great deal for reasons other than depression, and some extremely depressed people fail to cry at all. Thus an assessment tool should not be used unless it has high predictive or concurrent validity.

Predictive validity is a tool's ability to predict future characteristics or behavior. Let us say that a test has been developed to identify elementary school children who are likely to take up cigarette smoking in junior high school. The test gathers information about the children's parents—their personal characteristics, smoking habits, and attitudes toward smoking—and on that basis identifies high-risk

Oops! These judges of a high school diving competition, actually coaches from the opposing teams, arrive at very different assessments of the same diver. The low interrater reliability may reflect evaluator bias or defects in the scoring procedure.

The Palm Beach Post, photo by Mark Mirko

ABNORMALITY AND THE ARTS

Assessing Van Gogh

Vincent van Gogh led a tortured and unhappy life. In a legendary incident the artist cut off one of his ears. Later he was admitted to a mental

Vincent van Gogh, a self-portrait

Courtesy of the Fogg Art Museum, Harvard University Art Museums

institution, and ultimately he committed suicide. Van Gogh wrote a great deal about his pain and anguish, describing mental and physical torment and hallucinations. For years clinicians have speculated that van Gogh suffered from a mood disorder, schizophrenia, or both (Hershman & Lieb, 1998). Recently, however, these assessments have been challenged (Rosenfeld, 1998).

A Harvard neurologist has suggested that van Gogh in fact suffered from *Geschwind's syndrome,* technically known as *interictal personality disorder,* caused by brain seizure disorder, or epilepsy. Van Gogh displayed many of its symptoms, including excessive drawing (hypergraphia), hyperreligiosity, and aggression (Trotter, 1985).

In contrast, medical specialists in Colorado have concluded that van Gogh suffered from an extreme form of *Menière's syndrome,* a disorder marked by an excessive buildup of fluid in the inner ear. The enormous pressure may produce nausea, dizziness, poor balance, pain, deafness, and constant buzzing or ringing sensations. Perhaps van Gogh cut off his ear in an effort to reduce the pain. And perhaps his other problems and pains arose from the severe secondary psychological problems that can accompany Menière's syndrome (Scott, 1990).

ConsiderThis

◉ Would people react to van Gogh's work differently if they thought of him as having had an ear disorder rather than a psychological disorder? • Why do people find it fascinating to assess famous people, particularly those in the arts, long after their death?

---

children. To establish the test's predictive validity, we could administer it to a group of elementary school students, wait until they were in junior high school, and then check to see which children actually did become smokers.

Concurrent validity is the degree to which the measures gathered from one tool agree with measures gathered from other assessment techniques. Subjects' scores on a new test designed to measure anxiety, for example, should correlate highly with their scores on other anxiety tests or with their behavior during clinical interviews.

Clinical Interviews

Most of us feel that the best way to get to know people is to meet with them face to face. Under these circumstances, we can see them react to what we do and say, observe as well as listen as they answer, watch them observing us, and generally get a sense of who they are. A **clinical interview** is just such a face-to-face encounter (Robinson, 2000). If during a clinical interview a man looks as happy as can be while describing his sadness over the recent death of his mother, the clinician may suspect that the man actually has conflicting feelings about this loss. Almost all practitioners use interviews as part of the assessment process.

CONDUCTING THE INTERVIEW The interview is often the first contact between client and clinician. Clinicians use it to collect detailed information about the person's problems and feelings, lifestyle and relationships, and other personal

ConsiderThis

◉ How would you grade the tests you take in school? That is, how reliable and valid are they? • How about the tests you see in magazines?

MENTAL STATUS EXAM A set of interview questions and observations designed to reveal the degree and nature of a client's abnormal functioning.

TEST A device for gathering information about a few aspects of a person's psychological functioning from which broader information about the person can be inferred.

history. They may also ask about the person's expectations of therapy and motives for seeking it. The clinician who worked with Angela Savanti began with a face-to-face interview:

> Angela was dressed neatly when she appeared for her first interview. She answered questions and related information about her life history in a slow, flat tone of voice, which had an impersonal quality to it. She sat stiffly in her chair. . . .
>
> The client stated that the time period just before she and her boyfriend terminated their relationship had been one of extreme emotional turmoil. She was not sure whether she wanted to marry Jerry, and he began to demand that she decide either one way or the other. Mrs. Savanti [Angela's mother] did not seem to like Jerry and was very cold and aloof whenever he came to the house. Angela felt caught in the middle and unable to make a decision about her future. After several confrontations with Jerry over whether she would marry him or not, he told her he felt that she would never decide, so he was not going to see her anymore. . . .
>
> Angela stated that her childhood was a very unhappy period. Her father was seldom home, and when he was present, her parents fought constantly. . . .
>
> Angela recalled feeling very guilty when Mr. Savanti left. . . . She revealed that whenever she thought of her father, she always felt that she had been responsible in some way for his leaving the family. . . .
>
> Angela described her mother as the "long-suffering type" who said that she had sacrificed her life to make her children happy, and the only thing she ever got in return was grief and unhappiness. When Angela and [her sister] began dating, Mrs. Savanti . . . would make disparaging remarks about the boys they had been with and about men in general. . . .
>
> Angela revealed that she had often been troubled with depressed moods. During high school, if she got a lower grade in a subject than she had expected, her initial response was one of anger, followed by depression. Angela also became despondent when she got into an argument with her mother or felt that she was being taken advantage of at work. . . .
>
> The intensity and duration of the [mood change] that she experienced when she broke up with Jerry were much more severe. She was not sure why she was so depressed, but she began to feel it was an effort to walk around and go out to work. Talking with others became difficult. Angela found it hard to concentrate, and she began to forget things she was supposed to do. . . . She preferred to lie in bed rather than be with anyone, and she often cried when alone.
>
> *(Leon, 1984, pp. 110–115)*

Beyond gathering basic information of this kind, clinical interviewers give special attention to whatever topics they consider most important. Psychodynamic interviewers try to learn about the person's needs and memories of past events and relationships (Shea, 1990; Pope, 1983). Behavioral interviewers try to pinpoint the precise nature of the person's abnormal responses, including information about the stimuli that trigger such responses and their consequences (Reyna, 1989). Cognitive interviewers try to discover assumptions and interpretations that influence the person (Kendall, 1990). Humanistic clinicians ask about the person's self-evaluation and self-concept (Aiken, 1985; Brown, 1972). Biological clinicians look for signs of biochemical or brain dysfunction. And sociocultural interviewers ask about the family, social, and cultural environments.

Interviews can be either unstructured or structured (Moberg et al., 2001; Plante, 1999). In an *unstructured interview,* the clinician asks open-ended questions, perhaps as simple as "Would you tell me about yourself?" The lack of structure allows the interviewer to follow interesting leads and explore relevant topics that could not be anticipated before the interview.

FIT TO SERVE

During World War II, recruits were briefly interviewed and tested by clinicians to determine their fitness for military service. When the famous (and witty) pianist Oscar Levant was asked whether he thought he was capable of killing, he is alleged to have pondered the question for a moment and then replied, "I am not sure about strangers, but friends and family, definitely yes" (Bahrick, 1996).

In a *structured interview,* clinicians ask prepared questions. Sometimes they use a published *interview schedule*—a standard set of questions designed for all interviews. Many structured interviews include a **mental status exam,** a set of questions and observations that carefully evaluate the client's awareness, orientation with regard to time and place, attention span, memory, judgment and insight, thought content and processes, mood, and appearance (Robinson, 2000). A structured format ensures that clinicians will cover the same kinds of important issues in all their interviews and enables them to compare the responses of different individuals.

Although most clinical interviews have both unstructured and structured portions, many clinicians favor one kind over the other. Unstructured interviews typically appeal to psychodynamic and humanistic clinicians (Pope, 1983). Structured formats are widely used by behavioral clinicians, who need to do a detailed review of a person's behaviors (Pope, 1983). They are also popular among cognitive interviewers, who need to pinpoint attitudes or thinking processes that may underlie abnormal behavior.

WHAT ARE THE LIMITATIONS OF CLINICAL INTERVIEWS? Although interviews offer valuable information about people (Girón et al., 1998), there are limits to what they can accomplish. One problem is that they sometimes lack validity, or accuracy. Individuals may intentionally mislead in order to present themselves in a positive light or to avoid discussing embarrassing topics (Plante, 1999). Or people may be unable to give an accurate report in an interview. Individuals who suffer from depression, for example, take a pessimistic view of themselves and may describe themselves as poor workers or inadequate parents when that isn't the case at all.

Interviewers too may make mistakes in judgment that slant the information they gather. They usually rely too heavily on first impressions, for example, and give too much weight to unfavorable information about a client (Meehl, 1996, 1960). Interviewer biases, including gender, race, and age biases, may also influence the interviewers' interpretations of what a client says (Plante, 1999).

Interviews, particularly unstructured ones, may also lack reliability (Wiens et al., 2001). People respond differently to different interviewers, providing less information to a cold interviewer than to a warm one (Eisenthal, Koopman, & Lazare, 1983). Similarly, a clinician's race, sex, age, and appearance may influence a client's responses (Paurohit, Dowd, & Cottingham, 1982).

Because different clinicians can obtain different answers and draw different conclusions, even when they ask the same questions of the same person, some researchers believe that interviewing should be discarded as a tool of clinical assessment. This suggestion might be reasonable if there were any problem-free techniques to use instead. As we shall see, however, the two other kinds of clinical assessment methods also have serious limitations.

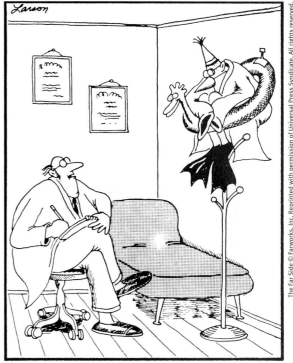

"So, Mr. Fenton, . . . Let's begin with your mother."

The structured interview *In a structured interview, clinicians gather information by asking a set of standard questions regardless of the client's particular symptoms.*

Clinical Tests

Tests are devices for gathering information about a few aspects of a person's psychological functioning, from which broader information about the person can be inferred (Watkins & Campbell, 2000). On the surface, it may look easy to design an effective test. Every month, magazines and newspapers present new tests that supposedly tell us about our personalities, our relationships, our sex lives, our reactions to stress, our ability to succeed. Such tests might sound convincing, but most of them lack reliability, validity, and standardization. That is, they do not yield consistent, accurate information or say anything meaningful about where we stand in comparison with others.

More than 500 different clinical tests are currently in use throughout the United States. The ones that clinicians use most often are of six kinds: *projective*

BELIEVE IT OR NOT

By a strange coincidence, the young schoolmates of Hermann Rorschach, inventor of the widely used inkblot test, gave him the nickname Klex, a variant on the German *Klecks,* which means "inkblot" (Schwartz, 1993).

tests, personality inventories, response inventories, psychophysiological tests, neurological and neuropsychological tests, and *intelligence tests.*

PROJECTIVE TESTS **Projective tests** require that subjects interpret vague stimuli, such as inkblots or ambiguous pictures, or follow open-ended instructions such as "Draw a person." Theoretically, when clues and instructions are so vague, subjects will "project" aspects of their personality into the task. Projective tests are used mainly by psychodynamic clinicians to help assess the unconscious drives and conflicts they believe to be at the root of abnormal functioning (Sugarman & Kanner, 2000). The most widely used projective tests are the *Rorschach test,* the *Thematic Apperception Test, sentence-completion tests,* and *drawings.*

RORSCHACH TEST In 1911 Hermann Rorschach, a Swiss psychiatrist, experimented with the use of inkblots in his clinical work. He made thousands of blots by dropping ink on paper and then folding the paper in half to create a symmetrical but wholly accidental design, such as the one shown in Figure 3-1. Rorschach found that everyone saw images in these blots. In addition, the images a viewer saw seemed to correspond in important ways with his or her psychological condition. People diagnosed with schizophrenia, for example, tended to see images that differed from those described by people with anxiety disorders.

FIGURE 3-1 **An inkblot similar to those used in the Rorschach test**

Rorschach selected ten inkblots and published them in 1921 with instructions for their use in assessment. This set was called the *Rorschach Psychodynamic Inkblot Test.* Rorschach died just eight months later, at the age of 37, but his work was continued by others, and his inkblots took their place among the most widely used projective tests of the twentieth century.

Clinicians administer the "Rorschach," as it is commonly called, by presenting one inkblot card at a time and asking respondents what they see, what the inkblot seems to be, or what it reminds them of. In the early years, Rorschach testers paid special attention to the *themes* and *images* that the inkblots brought to mind (Weiner, 2000). Testers now also pay attention to the *style* of the responses: Do the subjects view the design as a whole or see specific details? Do they focus on the blots or on the white spaces between them? Do they use or do they ignore the shadings and colors in several of the cards?

THEMATIC APPERCEPTION TEST The *Thematic Apperception Test (TAT)* is a pictorial projective test (Conklin & Westen, 2001; Morgan & Murray, 1935). People who take the TAT are commonly shown thirty black-and-white pictures of individuals in vague situations and are asked to make up a dramatic story about each card. They must tell what is happening in the picture, what led up to it, what the characters are feeling and thinking, and what the outcome of the situation will be.

Clinicians who use the TAT believe that people always identify with one of the characters on each card. The stories are thought to reflect the individuals' own circumstances, needs, emotions, and sense of reality and fantasy. For example, a female client seems to be revealing her own feelings in this story about the TAT picture shown in Figure 3-2, one of the few TAT pictures permitted for display in textbooks:

Reprinted by permission of the publishers from Henry A. Murray, *Thematic Apperception Test,* Cambridge, MA: Harvard University Press © 1943 by the President and Fellows of Harvard College, © 1971 by Henry A. Murray

> This is a woman who has been quite troubled by memories of a mother she was resentful toward. She has feelings of sorrow for the way she treated her mother, her memories of her mother plague her. These feelings seem to be increasing as she grows older and sees her children treating her the same way that she treated her mother.

(Aiken, 1985, p. 372)

FIGURE 3-2 **A picture used in the Thematic Apperception Test**

SENTENCE-COMPLETION TEST The *sentence-completion test,* first developed in the 1920s (Payne, 1928), asks people to complete a series of unfinished sentences, such as "I wish _____" or "My father _____." The test is considered a good springboard for discussion and a quick and easy way to pinpoint topics to explore.

DRAWINGS On the assumption that a drawing tells us something about its creator, clinicians often ask clients to draw human figures and talk about them. Evaluations of these drawings are based on the details and shape of the drawing, solidity of the pencil line, location of the drawing on the paper, size of the figures, features of the figures, use of background, and comments made by the respondent during the drawing task. In the *Draw-a-Person (DAP) Test,* the most popular of the drawing tests, subjects are first told to draw "a person," and then are instructed to draw another person of the opposite sex.

Drawing test *Drawing tests are commonly used to assess the functioning of children. Two popular tests are the House-Tree-Person Test, in which subjects draw a house, tree, and person; and the Kinetic Family Drawing test, in which subjects draw their household members performing some activity ("kinetic" means "active").*

WHAT ARE THE MERITS OF PROJECTIVE TESTS? Until the 1950s, projective tests were the most common technique for assessing personality. In recent years, however, clinicians and researchers have used them largely to gain "supplementary" insights (Westen, Feit, & Zittel, 1999). One reason for this shift is that practitioners who follow the newer models have less use for the tests than psychodynamic clinicians do (Kline, 1993). Even more important, the tests have rarely demonstrated much reliability or validity (Halperin & McKay, 1998).

In reliability studies, different clinicians have tended to score the same person's projective test quite differently (Plante, 1999). Similarly, in validity studies, when clinicians try to describe a client's personality and feelings on the basis of responses to projective tests, their conclusions often fail to match those of the client's psychotherapist or those gathered from an extensive case history (Golden, 1964; Sines, 1959).

The art of assessment *Clinicians often view works of art as informal projective tests in which artists reveal their conflicts and mental stability. The sometimes bizarre cat portraits of the early twentieth-century artist Louis Wain, for example, have been interpreted by some as reflections of the psychosis with which he struggled for many years.*

Another validity problem is that projective tests are sometimes biased against minority ethnic groups (Dana, 2000). For example, people are supposed to identify with the characters in the Thematic Apperception Test (TAT) when they make up stories about them, yet no members of minority groups are in the TAT pictures. In response to this problem, some clinicians have developed other TAT-like tests with African American or Hispanic figures (Costantino & Malgady, 2000).

PERSONALITY INVENTORIES An alternative way to collect information about individuals is to ask them to assess themselves. The **personality inventory** asks respondents a wide range of questions about their behavior, beliefs, and feelings. In the typical personality inventory, individuals indicate whether or not each of a long list of statements applies to them. Clinicians then use the responses to draw conclusions about the person's personality and psychological functioning.

PROJECTIVE TEST A test consisting of ambiguous material that people interpret or respond to.

PERSONALITY INVENTORY A test designed to measure broad personality characteristics, consisting of statements about behaviors, beliefs, and feelings that people evaluate as either characteristic or uncharacteristic of them.

NOW TAKING THE LEAD
According to surveys, 80 percent of professionals administering an MMPI in their work use the MMPI-2, 37 percent the MMPI, and 40 percent the MMPI-A (Downey, Sinnett, & Seeberger, 1998). Obviously, many testers use more than one version.

By far the most widely used personality inventory is the *Minnesota Multiphasic Personality Inventory (MMPI)* (Nichols, 2001; Butcher, 1999). Two adult versions are available—the original test, published in 1945, and the *MMPI-2,* a 1989 revision. Currently these two versions are competing for clinicians' favor. A special version of the test for adolescents, the *MMPI-A,* is also used widely.

The traditional MMPI consists of 550 self-statements, to be labeled "true," "false," or "cannot say." The statements describe physical concerns; mood; morale; attitudes toward religion, sex, and social activities; and psychological symptoms, such as fears or hallucinations. The items in the MMPI make up ten clinical scales:

- **Hypochondriasis (HS)** Items showing abnormal concern with bodily functions ("I have chest pains several times a week").
- **Depression (D)** Items showing extreme pessimism and hopelessness ("I often feel hopeless about the future").
- **Conversion hysteria (Hy)** Items suggesting that the person may use physical or mental symptoms as a way of unconsciously avoiding conflicts and responsibilities ("My heart frequently pounds so hard I can feel it").
- **Psychopathic deviate (PD)** Items showing a repeated and gross disregard for social customs and an emotional shallowness ("My activities and interests are often criticized by others").
- **Masculinity-femininity (Mf)** Items that are thought to separate male and female respondents ("I like to arrange flowers").
- **Paranoia (Pa)** Items that show abnormal suspiciousness and delusions of grandeur or persecution ("There are evil people trying to influence my mind").
- **Psychasthenia (Pt)** Items that show obsessions, compulsions, abnormal fears, and guilt and indecisiveness ("I save nearly everything I buy, even after I have no use for it").
- **Schizophrenia (Sc)** Items that show bizarre or unusual thoughts or behavior, including extreme withdrawal, delusions, or hallucinations ("Things around me do not seem real").
- **Hypomania (Ma)** Items that show emotional excitement, overactivity, and flight of ideas ("At times I feel very 'high' or very 'low' for no apparent reason").
- **Social introversion (Si)** Items that show shyness, little interest in people, and insecurity ("I am easily embarrassed").

MODERN CALCULATIONS
Around 68 percent of professionals who administer the MMPI today use computerized scoring, and 44 percent use computerized interpretations of the scores (Downey et al., 1998).

Scores for each scale can range from 0 to 120. When people score above 70, their functioning on that scale is considered deviant. When the scores are connected on a graph, a pattern called the *profile* takes shape, indicating the person's general personality and underlying emotional needs. Figure 3-3 shows the MMPI profile of John, a depressed 27-year-old man. It indicates that he is very depressed, feels anxious and threatened, is socially withdrawn, and is prone to physical complaints.

The MMPI-2, the new version of the MMPI, contains 567 items—many identical to those in the original, some rewritten to reflect current language ("upset stomach," for instance, replaces "acid stomach"), and others that are new. To the original scales the MMPI-2 adds several new scales that cover issues such as eating problems, a tendency to abuse drugs, and poor functioning at work. Before being adopted, the MMPI-2 was tested on a more diverse group of people than was the original test. Thus scores on the new test may be more accurate indicators of personality and abnormal functioning.

Most clinicians have welcomed the MMPI-2 as a needed improvement and update. They have been won over by a growing body of research showing that the MMPI-2 is indeed a useful instrument and that the two versions produce comparable results (Dorfman & Leonard, 2001; Butcher, 1999).

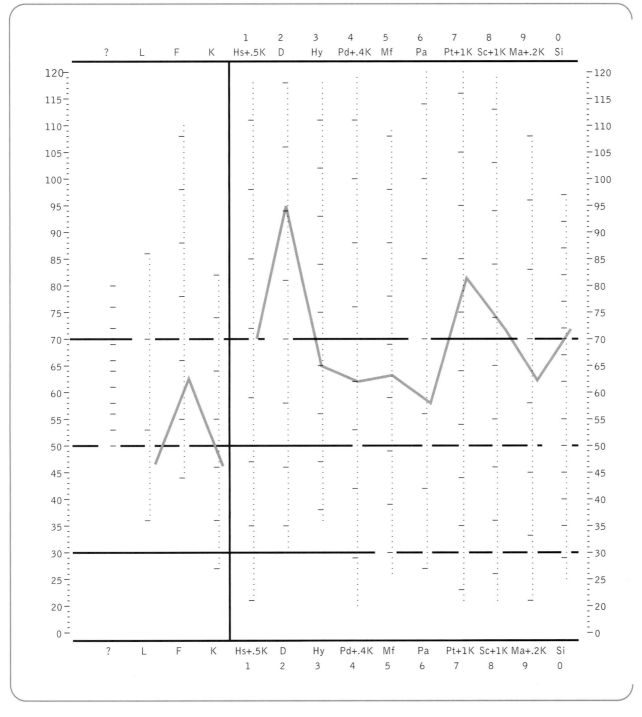

FIGURE 3-3   **An MMPI profile** *The profile of John, a 27-year-old man, suggests that he is depressed. He also appears to be anxious, prone to physical complaints, indecisive, introverted, and insecure. (From Graham, 1977, p. 164.)*

The MMPI and other personality inventories have several advantages over projective tests. Because they are paper-and-pencil tests, they do not take much time to administer, and they are objectively scored. Most of them are standardized, so one person's scores can be compared with those of many others. Moreover, they often display greater test–retest reliability than projective tests. For example, people who take the MMPI a second time after a period of less than two weeks receive approximately the same scores (Graham, 1987, 1977).

Personality inventories also appear to have greater validity, or accuracy, than projective tests (Garb, Florio, & Grove, 1998). However, they can hardly be considered *highly* valid. When clinicians have used these tests alone, they have not typically been able to judge a respondent's personality accurately (Johnson et al., 1996). One problem is that the personality traits that the tests seek to measure cannot be examined directly. How can we fully know a person's character, emotions, and needs from self-reports alone?

ConsiderThis

In 1999, after a number of dog attacks, Spain's Agriculture Ministry proposed a law requiring the owners of potentially dangerous pets to undergo and pass a psychological test. Is this a good idea? • Is the field of clinical assessment equal to such a task?

Despite their limited validity, personality inventories continue to be popular (Archer, 1997). Research indicates that they can help clinicians learn about people's personal styles and disorders as long as they are used in combination with interviews or other assessment tools (Levitt, 1989).

RESPONSE INVENTORIES Like personality inventories, **response inventories** ask people to provide detailed information about themselves, but these tests focus on one specific area of functioning. For example, one such test may measure affect (emotion), another social skills, and still another cognitive processes. Clinicians can use them to determine the role such factors play in a person's disorder.

Affective inventories measure the severity of such emotions as anxiety, depression, and anger (Beidel, Turner, & Morris, 1995). In one of the most widely used affective inventories, the Beck Depression Inventory, shown in Table 3-1, people rate their level of sadness and its effect on their functioning. *Social skill inventories,* used particularly by behavioral and sociocultural clinicians, ask respondents to indicate how they would react in a variety of social situations (Wiggins & Trobst, 1997). *Cognitive inventories* reveal a person's typical thoughts and assumptions, and can uncover counterproductive patterns of thinking that may be at the root of abnormal functioning (Glass & Merluzzi, 2000). They are, not surprisingly, often used by cognitive therapists and researchers.

Because response inventories collect information directly from the clients themselves, they have strong face validity. Thus both the number of these tests and the number of clinicians who use them have increased steadily in the past 25 years. At the same time, however, these inventories have major limitations (Schwarz, 1999; Shedler et al., 1993). Unlike the personality inventories, they rarely include questions to indicate whether people are being careless or inaccurate in their accounts. Moreover, with the notable exceptions of the Beck Depression Inventory and a few others (Canals et al., 2001), only some of them have been subjected to careful standardization, reliability, and validity procedures (Winter et al., 1999). Often they are produced as a need arises, without being tested for accuracy and consistency.

Table 3-1

Sample Items from the Beck Depression Inventory

ITEMS		INVENTORY
Suicidal ideas	0	I don't have any thoughts of killing myself.
	1	I have thoughts of killing myself but I would not carry them out.
	2	I would like to kill myself.
	3	I would kill myself if I had the chance.
Work inhibition	0	I can work about as well as before.
	1	It takes extra effort to get started at doing something.
	2	I have to push myself very hard to do anything.
	3	I can't do any work at all.
Loss of libido	0	I have not noticed any recent change in my interest in sex.
	1	I am less interested in sex than I used to be.
	2	I am much less interested in sex now.
	3	I have lost interest in sex completely.

FEAR WILL OUT

Some persons, so-called *repressive copers,* deny or ignore negative feelings in order to cope with unpleasant circumstances. While watching scary movies in one study, such individuals reported experiencing less fear than did nonrepressors. However, their bodily measures of fear were two to three times higher than those of the nonrepressing moviegoers (Sparks et al., 1999).

PSYCHOPHYSIOLOGICAL TESTS Clinicians may also use **psychophysiological tests,** which measure physiological responses as possible indicators of psychological problems (Cutmore & James, 1999). This practice began three decades ago after several studies suggested that states of anxiety are regularly accompanied by physiological changes, particularly increases in heart rate, body temperature, blood pressure, skin reactions (*galvanic skin response*), and muscle contraction. The measuring of physiological changes has since played a key role in the assessment of certain psychological disorders.

One psychophysiological test is the *polygraph,* popularly known as a *lie detector.* Electrodes attached to various parts of a person's body detect changes in breathing, perspiration, and heart rate while the individual answers questions. The clinician observes these functions while the subject answers yes to *control questions*—questions whose answers are known to be yes, such as "Are your parents both alive?" Then the clinician observes the same physiological functions while the person answers *test questions,* such as "Did you commit this robbery?" If breathing, perspiration, and heart rate suddenly increase, the subject is suspected of lying (Raskin, 1982).

Like other kinds of clinical tests, psychophysiological tests have their drawbacks. Many require expensive equipment that must be carefully tuned and maintained (Cutmore & James, 1999). In addition, psychophysiological measurements can be inaccurate and unreliable. The laboratory equipment itself—impressive, unusual, and sometimes frightening—may arouse a subject's nervous system and thus change his or her physical responses. Physiological responses may also change when they are measured repeatedly in a single session. Galvanic skin responses, for example, often decrease during repeated testing.

RESPONSE INVENTORIES Tests designed to measure a person's responses in one specific area of functioning, such as affect, social skills, or cognitive processes.

PSYCHOPHYSIOLOGICAL TEST A test that measures physical responses (such as heart rate and muscle tension) as possible indicators of psychological problems.

A CLOSER LOOK

Tests, Lies, and Videotapes: The Public Misuse of Assessment

In movies, criminals being grilled by the police reveal their guilt by sweating, shaking, cursing, or twitching. When they are hooked up to a *polygraph* (a lie detector), the needles bounce all over the paper. This image has been with us since World War I, when some clinicians developed the theory that people who are telling lies display certain changes in their breathing, perspiration, and heart rate (Marston, 1917).

The danger of relying on polygraph tests is that there is no clear evidence that they work (Lykken, 1998; Steinbrook, 1992). The public did not pay much attention to this inconvenient fact until the mid-1980s, when the American Psychological Association officially reported that polygraphs were inaccurate and the United States Congress voted to restrict their use in criminal prosecution and employment screening.

With the polygraph's popularity in decline, businesses soon found themselves in need of a test to replace it. They were losing billions of dollars to theft, low productivity, and other dishonest behavior. *Integrity tests* seemed to be the answer. These personality tests seek to measure whether test takers are generally honest or dishonest—and whether it is safe to hire them for a particular job. More than forty of these written tests are now in use, supposedly revealing such characteristics as dependability, deviance, social conformity, wayward impulses, and hostility to rules (Iacono & Patrick, 1997).

Here again, however, research suggests that the tests have little validity, often yielding high rates of false accusations (Camara & Schneider, 1994; Guastello & Reike, 1991).

Other psychological tests too have caused uproars. In Old Town, Maine, a police officer who had been accused of child sexual abuse lost his job after he refused to take a *penile plethysmograph test,* a test meant to evaluate his sexual impulses. To administer this psychophysiological test, a clinician places a rubber tube filled with mercury around a subject's penis and then shows him videotapes or slides of naked adults and children. When the subject becomes sexually aroused, the band stretches and the mercury registers the arousal. Clinicians can chart the results to determine whether a subject is more aroused by adults than by children, by males than by females, or by coerced sex than by consensual sex. Although this test does accurately report sexual arousal, it cannot predict whether a person will act on his feelings (Barker & Howell, 1992). That is, the test cannot determine whether someone has committed a sexual offense or predict whether he is likely to do so.

Although the charges against the police officer in Maine were never confirmed, the police department required him to see a sex-abuse therapist and undergo testing to retain his job. The officer in turn charged the city of Old Town with violation of his civil rights. No government agency, he claimed, had the right to make such an intimate physical test a condition of employment. An arbitrator ordered the police department to reinstate the officer.

Lives can be changed dramatically when people are labeled, whether the label be "dishonest," "criminal," "depressive," or "sexually deviant." Questionable devices such as polygraph, integrity, and plethysmograph tests may violate more than the basic principles of science. They can also violate civil rights and hurt innocent people.

Polygraph, a test that lies?

The EEG *The electroencephalogram, used here to measure the brain waves of a 4-month-old being stimulated with toys, is only a gross indicator of the brain's activity.*

Sadness and the brain *A PET scan of a person thinking sad thoughts shows which areas of brain activity (shown in red, orange, and yellow) are related to such mood changes.*

Crystal clear *This MRI of a person's brain, viewed from the side, is so detailed that it looks more like a photograph than a computer-based image.*

NEUROLOGICAL AND NEUROPSYCHOLOGICAL TESTS Some problems in personality or behavior are caused primarily by damage in the brain or changes in brain activity. Head injury, brain tumors, brain malfunctions, alcoholism, infections, and other disorders can all cause such impairment. If a psychological disorder is to be treated effectively, it is important to know whether its primary cause is a physical abnormality in the brain (Mattis & Wilson, 1997).

A number of techniques may help pinpoint brain abnormalities. Some procedures, such as brain surgery, biopsy, and X ray, have been used for years. More recently, scientists have developed a number of **neurological tests,** designed to measure brain structure and activity directly. One neurological test is the *electroencephalogram (EEG),* which records *brain waves,* the electrical activity taking place within the brain as a result of neurons firing. In this procedure, electrodes placed on the scalp send brain-wave impulses to a machine that records them.

Other neurological tests actually take "pictures" of brain structure or brain activity. These tests, called *neuroimaging techniques,* include *computerized axial tomography (CAT scan or CT scan),* in which X rays of the brain's structure are taken at different angles; *positron emission tomography (PET scan),* a computer-produced motion picture of chemical activity throughout the brain; and *magnetic resonance imaging (MRI),* a procedure that uses the magnetic property of certain atoms in the brain to create a detailed picture of the brain's structure and activity.

Though increasingly used, these various techniques are sometimes unable to detect subtle brain abnormalities. Clinicians have therefore developed less direct but sometimes more revealing **neuropsychological tests** that measure cognitive, perceptual, and motor performances on certain tasks and interpret abnormal performances as an indicator of underlying brain problems (Rao, 2000; Butters et al., 1995). Brain damage is especially likely to affect visual perception, recent memory, and visual-motor coordination, and so neuropsychological tests focus greatly on these areas.

The *Bender Visual-Motor Gestalt Test* (Bender, 1938), one of the most widely used neuropsychological tests, consists of nine cards, each displaying a simple design (see Figure 3-4). Test subjects look at the designs one at a time and copy each one on a piece of paper. Later they try to redraw the designs from memory. By the age of 12, most people can remember and redraw the designs accurately. Notable errors in accuracy are thought to reflect organic brain impairment.

The Bender-Gestalt test can detect *general* organic impairment in approximately 75 percent of cases, suggesting high validity (Heaton, Baade, & Johnson, 1978). However, no single neuropsychological test can consistently distinguish one *specific* kind of brain impairment from another (Lacks, 1999). This is the major limitation of all the neuropsychological tests: at best they are rough and general screening devices for neurological problems. To achieve greater precision and accuracy, clinicians often use a **battery,** or series, of neuropsychological tests, each targeting a specific skill area (Bauer, 2000).

Original　　　　　　　　　　　　　　　Copy

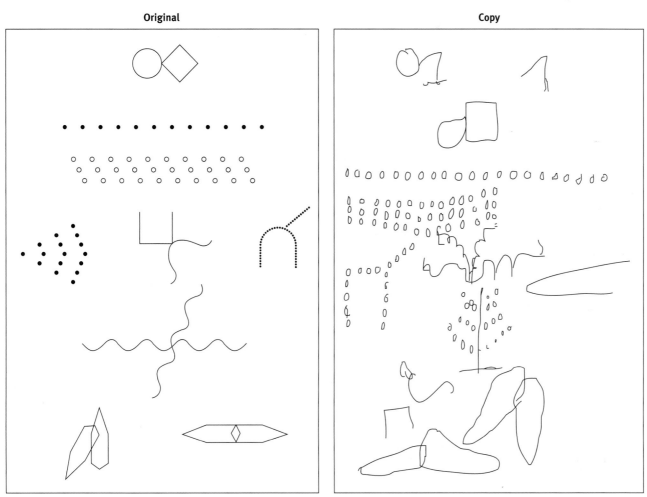

FIGURE 3-4 **The Bender Visual-Motor Gestalt Test** *In this test subjects copy each of nine designs on a piece of paper, then produce them again from memory. Sizable errors in a drawing (as in the one on the right, which was done by a person with brain damage) may reflect organic brain dysfunction of some kind. (Adapted from Lacks, 1984, p. 33.)*

INTELLIGENCE TESTS An early definition of intelligence described it as "the capacity to judge well, to reason well, and to comprehend well" (Binet & Simon, 1916, p. 192). Because intelligence is an *inferred* quality rather than a specific physical process, it can be measured only indirectly. In 1905 the French psychologist Alfred Binet and his associate Theodore Simon produced an **intelligence test** consisting of a series of tasks requiring people to use various verbal and nonverbal skills. The general score derived from this and subsequent intelligence tests is termed an **intelligence quotient,** or **IQ.**

There are now more than 100 intelligence tests available, including the widely used *Wechsler Adult Intelligence Scale, Wechsler Intelligence Scale for Children,* and *Stanford-Binet Intelligence Scale.* As we shall see in Chapter 15, intelligence tests play a key role in the diagnosis of mental retardation, but they can also help clinicians identify other problems (Handler, 1998).

Intelligence tests are among the most carefully produced of all clinical tests. Because they have been standardized on large groups of subjects, clinicians have a good idea how each individual's score compares with the performance of the population at large. These tests have also shown very high reliability: people who repeat the same IQ test years later receive approximately the same score (Kline, 1993). Finally, the major IQ tests appear to have fairly high validity: children's IQ scores often correlate with their performance in school, for example (Sternberg et al., 2001; Ceci & Williams, 1997).

Nevertheless, intelligence tests have some key shortcomings. Factors that have nothing to do with intelligence, such as low motivation and high anxiety, can greatly influence a performance (Van der Molen et al., 1995). In addition, IQ tests may contain cultural biases in their language or tasks that place people of one background at an advantage over those of another (Lee, 1999; Jencks,

NEUROLOGICAL TEST A test that directly measures brain structure or activity.

NEUROPSYCHOLOGICAL TEST A test that detects brain impairment by measuring a person's cognitive, perceptual, and motor performances.

BATTERY A series of tests, each of which produces a different kind of data.

INTELLIGENCE TEST A test designed to measure a person's intellectual ability.

INTELLIGENCE QUOTIENT (IQ) A general score derived from intelligence tests that is considered to represent a person's overall level of intelligence.

The Wechsler Adult Intelligence Scale-III (WAIS-III) *This widely used intelligence test has 11 subtests, which cover such areas as factual information, memory, vocabulary, arithmetic, design, and eye-hand coordination.*

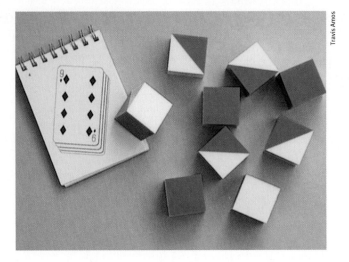

Travis Amos

1998). Similarly, members of some minority groups may have little experience with this kind of test, or they may be uncomfortable with test examiners of a majority ethnic background. Either way, their performances may suffer.

Clinical Observations

In addition to interviewing and testing people, clinicians may systematically observe their behavior. In one technique, called **naturalistic observation,** clinicians observe clients in their everyday environments. In another, **structured observation,** they observe them in an artificial setting, such as a clinical office or laboratory. Finally, in **self-monitoring,** clients are instructed to observe themselves.

NATURALISTIC AND STRUCTURED OBSERVATIONS Naturalistic clinical observations usually take place in homes, schools, institutions such as hospitals and prisons, or community settings. Most of them focus on parent-child, sibling-child, or teacher-child interactions and on fearful, aggressive, or disruptive behavior (Kaplan, 1999). Generally, such observations are made by *participant observers,* key persons in the client's environment, and are then reported to the clinician (Auge & Auge, 1999).

When naturalistic observations are not practical, clinicians may observe people in a structured setting (Haynes, 2001). Observation rooms in offices or laboratories, equipped with videotape or a one-way mirror, have been used to observe children interacting with their parents, married couples trying to settle a disagreement, speech-anxious people giving a speech, and fearful people approaching an object they find frightening.

Although much can be learned from actually witnessing behavior, clinical observations have certain disadvantages. For one thing, they are not always reliable (Banister et al., 1994). It is possible for various clinicians who observe the same person to focus on different aspects of behavior, assess the person differently, and arrive at different conclusions. Careful training of observers and the use of observer checklists can help reduce this problem (Blasko et al., 1998).

Similarly, observers may make errors that affect the validity, or accuracy, of their observations (Banister et al., 1994). The observer may suffer from *overload* and be unable to see or record all the important behaviors and events. Or the observer may experience *observer drift,* a steady decline in accuracy as a result of fatigue or of a gradual unintentional change in the standards used when an observation continues for a long period of time (O'Leary & Kent, 1973). Another possible problem is *observer bias*—the observer's judgments may be influenced by information and expectations he or she already has about the person (Goodwin, 1995).

THE POWER OF OBSERVATION

Everyday observations are more prone to error than clinical observations, and often more damaging. Mistaken eyewitness testimony is the primary cause of the conviction of innocent people (Wells et al., 1998). Confident eyewitnesses are as likely to be wrong as less confident eyewitnesses (Gruneber & Sykes, 1993).

NATURALISTIC OBSERVATION A method for observing behavior in which clinicians or researchers observe people in their everyday environments.

STRUCTURED OBSERVATION A method for observing behavior in which people are observed in artificial settings such as clinicians' offices or laboratories.

SELF-MONITORING A technique for observing behavior in which clients observe themselves.

A client's *reactivity* may also limit the validity of clinical observations; that is, his or her behavior may be affected by the very presence of the observer (Plante, 1999). If schoolchildren are aware that someone special is watching them, for example, they may change their usual classroom behavior, perhaps in the hope of creating a good impression.

Finally, clinical observations may lack *cross-situational validity.* A child who behaves aggressively in school is not necessarily aggressive at home or with friends after school. Because behavior is often specific to particular situations, observations in one setting cannot always be applied to other settings (Haynes, 2001; Simpson & Halpin, 1986).

An ideal observation *Using a one-way mirror, a clinical observer is able to view the classroom behaviors of young children without distracting the children or influencing their behaviors in any way.*

SELF-MONITORING As we saw earlier, personality and response inventories are tests in which persons report their own behaviors, feelings, or cognitions. In a related assessment procedure, *self-monitoring,* people observe themselves and carefully record the frequency of certain behaviors, feelings, or cognitions as they occur over time (Plante, 1999). How frequently, for instance, does a drug user have an urge for drugs or a headache sufferer have a headache? Self-monitoring is especially useful in assessing behavior that occurs so infrequently that it is unlikely to be seen during other kinds of observations. It is also useful for behaviors that occur so frequently that any other method of observing them in detail would be impossible—for example, smoking, drinking, or other drug use. Third, self-monitoring may be the only way to observe and measure private thoughts or perceptions.

Like all other clinical assessment procedures, however, self-monitoring has drawbacks. Here too validity is often a problem (Barker et al., 1994). People do not always receive proper instruction in this form of observation, nor do they always try to record their observations accurately. Furthermore, when people monitor themselves, they may change their behaviors unintentionally (Plante, 1999). Smokers, for example, often smoke fewer cigarettes than usual when they are monitoring themselves, drug users take drugs less frequently, and teachers give more positive and fewer negative comments to their students.

BELIEVING IS SEEING

Persons' beliefs often wrongly influence their observations and recollections. Most moviegoers recall seeing Bambi's mother die in the snow and a knife slash Janet Leigh in the shower in *Psycho,* and hearing Humphrey Bogart say, "Play it again, Sam" in *Casablanca* and Tarzan say, "Me Tarzan, you Jane." Yet none of these events took place in their respective movies.

SUMMING UP | **Clinical Assessment: How and Why Does the Client Behave Abnormally?**

Clinical practitioners are interested primarily in gathering individual information about their clients. They seek a full understanding of the specific nature and origins of a person's problems through assessment.

Most assessment methods fall into three general categories: clinical interviews, tests, and observations. The interview may be either unstructured or structured. Types of tests include projective, personality, response, psychophysiological, neurological, neuropsychological, and intelligence tests. Types of observation include naturalistic observation, structured observation, and self-monitoring.

To be useful, assessment tools must be standardized, reliable, and valid. Each of the methods in current use falls short on at least some of these characteristics. Thus, it is best for clinicians to use a battery of assessment methods.

Diagnosis: Does the Client's Syndrome Match a Known Disorder?

Clinicians use the information from interviews, tests, and observations to construct an integrated picture of the factors that are causing and maintaining a client's disturbance, a construction sometimes known as a *clinical picture* (Stricker & Trierweiler, 1995). The clinical pictures drawn by clinicians are also influenced by their theoretical orientation. The clinician who worked with Angela Savanti held a cognitive-behavioral view of abnormality, and so produced a picture that emphasized modeling and reinforcement principles and Angela's expectations, assumptions, and interpretations:

> Angela was rarely reinforced for any of her accomplishments at school, but she gained her mother's negative attention for what Mrs. Savanti judged to be poor performance at school or at home. Mrs. Savanti repeatedly told her daughter that she was incompetent, and any mishaps that happened to her were her own fault. . . . When Mr. Savanti deserted the family, Angela's first response was that somehow she was responsible. From her mother's past behavior, Angela had learned to expect that in some way she would be blamed. At the time that Angela broke up with her boyfriend, she did not blame Jerry for his behavior, but interpreted this event as a failing solely on her part. As a result, her level of self-esteem was lowered still more.
>
> The type of marital relationship that Angela saw her mother and father model remained her concept of what married life is like. She generalized from her observations of her parents' discordant interactions to an expectation of the type of behavior that she and Jerry would ultimately engage in. . . .
>
> Angela's uncertainties intensified when she was deprived of the major source of gratification she had, her relationship with Jerry. Despite the fact that she was overwhelmed with doubts about whether to marry him or not, she had gained a great deal of pleasure through being with Jerry. Whatever feelings she had been able to express, she had shared with him and no one else. Angela labeled Jerry's termination of their relationship as proof that she was not worthy of another person's interest. She viewed her present unhappiness as likely to continue, and she attributed it to some failing on her part. As a result, she became quite depressed.
>
> *(Leon, 1984, pp. 123-125)*

With the assessment data and clinical picture in hand, clinicians are ready to make a **diagnosis** (from Greek for "discrimination")—that is, a determination that a person's psychological problems constitute a particular disorder (Scotti & Morris, 2001). When clinicians decide, through diagnosis, that a client's pattern of dysfunction reflects a particular disorder, they are saying that the pattern is basically the same as one that has been displayed by many other people, has been investigated in a variety of studies, and perhaps has responded to particular forms of treatment (Bourgeois, 1995). They can then apply what is generally known about the disorder to the particular individual they are trying to help. They can, for example, better predict the future course of the person's problem and the treatments that are likely to be helpful.

Classification Systems

The principle behind diagnosis is straightforward. When certain symptoms regularly occur together—a cluster of symptoms is called a **syndrome**—and follow a particular course, clinicians agree that those symptoms make up a particular mental disorder. When people display this particular pattern of symptoms, diagnosticians assign them to that diagnostic category. A list of such categories, or disorders, with descriptions of the symptoms and guidelines for assigning individuals to the categories, is known as a **classification system.**

SPOTTING DEPRESSION

Family physicians recognize fewer than one-third of all cases of clinical depression that they encounter among their patients. Most undetected cases are mild, however. The physicians tend to identify correctly patients suffering from a major depressive disorder (Coyne, Schwenk, & Fechner-Bates, 1995).

DIAGNOSIS A determination that a person's problems reflect a particular disorder.

SYNDROME A cluster of symptoms that usually occur together.

CLASSIFICATION SYSTEM A list of disorders, along with descriptions of symptoms and guidelines for making appropriate diagnoses.

DSM-IV The fourth, and current, edition of the *Diagnostic and Statistical Manual of Mental Disorders*.

In 1883 Emil Kraepelin developed the first modern classification system for abnormal behavior (see Chapter 1). His categories have formed the foundation for the psychological part of the *International Classification of Diseases (ICD)*, the classification system now used by the World Health Organization (Jablensky, 1995). They have also influenced the *Diagnostic and Statistical Manual of Mental Disorders (DSM)*, a classification system developed by the American Psychiatric Association.

The DSM, like the ICD, has been changed over time. The current edition, **DSM-IV**, published in 1994 and revised slightly in 2000, is by far the most widely used classification system in the United States (APA, 2000, 1994). The descriptions of mental disorders presented throughout this book follow its categories.

STEPPING BACK

Oppression and Mental Health: The Politics of Labeling

Throughout history, governments have applied the label of mental illness as a way of controlling or changing people whose views threaten the social order. This was a common practice in the former Soviet Union. There, political dissent was considered a symptom of abnormal mental functioning, and many dissidents were committed to mental hospitals.

In a more subtle process, a country's cultural values often influence the clinical assessments made by its practitioners. The historians Lynn Gamwell and Nancy Tomes (1995) have noted, for example, the widespread clinical belief in the nineteenth-century United States that freedom would drive such "primitive" people as Native Americans insane. Medical experts of that time went so far as to claim that the forcible movement of tribal groups onto reservations was in their best interest because it would save them from the madness that awaited them in free society. The medical officer who supervised the "removal" of the Cherokees from their homeland to Oklahoma was later pleased to report that during the whole time he oversaw the migration of 20,000 Cherokees (over 4,000 of whom died), he had not observed a single case of insanity.

Slave owners, too, liked to believe that slaves were psychologically comfortable with their situation, and that those who tried to escape either were or would soon become insane. Secretary of State John Calhoun of South Carolina pointed to the 1840 census, conducted by his office, as evidence: it identified almost *no* insanity among slaves in the South, but many cases among former slaves living in the North. Calhoun asserted: "Our nation must conclude that the abolition of slavery would be to the African a curse instead of a blessing."

The work of clinicians at that time lent support to this belief. One specialist claimed that several kinds of mental disorders were unique to African Americans, including *drapetomania* (from the Latin *drapeta,* fugitive)—an obsessive desire for freedom that drove some slaves to try to flee. Any slave who tried to run away more than twice was considered insane.

Drapetomania is long forgotten, but cultural views continue to influence psychological assessments and categories. Indeed, many clinicians have argued that past categories such as "homosexuality," "sexual frigidity," and "masochistic personality"—each of which was a respected clinical category during much of the twentieth century—show all too well the impact of cultural beliefs on clinical assessment and diagnosis.

A ride for liberty *Eastman Johnson's 1862 painting,* A Ride for Liberty—The Fugitive Slaves, *demonstrates the courage and clear-mindedness slaves needed to escape, in stark contrast to the mental instability of which they were accused.*

Francis G. Mayer/Corbis

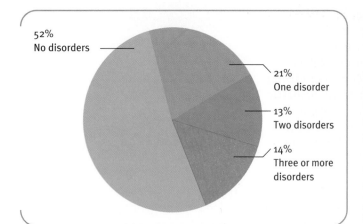

52%
No disorders

21%
One disorder

13%
Two disorders

14%
Three or more disorders

FIGURE 3-5 **How many people in the United States qualify for a DSM diagnosis during their lives?** *Almost half, according to one survey. Some of them even experience two or more different disorders, an occurrence known as comorbidity. (Adapted from Kessler & Zhao, 1999; Kessler et al., 1994.)*

A GROWING LIST

In 1840 the United States census listed only 1 category of psychological dysfunctioning—"idiocy/insanity." The 1880 census cited 7 categories. Today about 400 categories are listed in DSM-IV.

ConsiderThis

⊙ Many people argue for a "people first" approach to clinical labeling, recommending, for example, the phrase "a person with schizophrenia" rather than "a schizophrenic" (Foderaro, 1995). Why might this approach to labeling be preferable?

DSM-IV

DSM-IV lists approximately 400 mental disorders (see Figure 3-5). Each entry describes the criteria for diagnosing the disorder and its key clinical features. The classification system also describes related features, which are often but not always present, and age, culture, or gender trends. Finally, it includes a disorder's prevalence and risk, course, complications, predisposing factors, and family patterns.

DSM-IV requires clinicians to evaluate a client's condition on five separate *axes,* or branches of information, when making a diagnosis. First, they must decide whether the person is displaying one or more of the disorders found on *Axis I,* an extensive list of clinical syndromes that typically cause significant impairment. Some of the most frequently diagnosed disorders listed on this axis are the anxiety disorders and mood disorders—problems we shall discuss in later chapters:

Anxiety disorders People with anxiety disorders may experience general feelings of anxiety and worry (*generalized anxiety disorder*), anxiety centered on a specific situation or object (*phobias*), periods of panic (*panic disorder*), persistent thoughts or repetitive behaviors or both (*obsessive-compulsive disorder*), or lingering anxiety reactions to unusually traumatic events (*acute stress disorder* and *posttraumatic stress disorder*).

Mood disorders People with mood disorders feel extremely sad or elated for long periods of time. These disorders include *major depressive disorder* and *bipolar disorder* (in which episodes of mania alternate with episodes of depression).

Next, diagnosticians must decide whether the person is displaying one of the disorders listed on *Axis II,* which includes long-standing problems that are frequently overlooked in the presence of the disorders on Axis I. There are only two groups of Axis II disorders: mental retardation and personality disorders. We will also examine these patterns in later chapters:

Mental retardation People with this disorder display significantly subaverage intellectual functioning and poor adaptive functioning by 18 years of age.

Personality disorders People with these disorders display a very rigid maladaptive pattern of inner experience and outward behavior that has continued for many years. People with *antisocial personality disorder,* for example, persistently disregard and violate the rights of others. People with *dependent personality disorder* are persistently dependent on others, clinging, obedient, and very afraid of separation.

Although people usually receive a diagnosis from *either* Axis I or Axis II, they may receive diagnoses from both axes. Angela Savanti would first receive a diagnosis of *major depressive disorder* from Axis I (a mood disorder). Let us suppose that the clinician judged that Angela also displayed a life history of dependent behavior. She might then also receive an Axis II diagnosis of *dependent personality disorder.*

The remaining axes of DSM-IV guide diagnosticians in reporting other factors. *Axis III* asks for information concerning relevant general medical conditions from which the person is currently suffering. *Axis IV* asks about special psychosocial or environmental problems the person is facing, such as school or housing problems. And *Axis V* requires the diagnostician to make a *global assessment of functioning (GAF),* that is, to rate the person's psychological, social, and occupational functioning overall.

If Angela Savanti had diabetes, for example, the clinician might include that under Axis III information. Angela's recent breakup with her boyfriend would be noted on Axis IV. And because she seemed fairly dysfunctional at the time of diagnosis, Angela's GAF would probably be around 55 on Axis V, indicating a moderate level of dysfunction. The complete diagnosis for Angela Savanti would then be:

Axis I: Major depressive disorder

Axis II: Dependent personality disorder

Axis III: Diabetes

Axis IV: Problem related to the social environment (termination of engagement)

Axis V: GAF = 55 (current)

Are Classifications Reliable and Valid?

A classification system, like an assessment method, is judged by its reliability and validity. Here *reliability* means that different diagnosticians are likely to agree on the diagnosis when using the system to diagnose the same client. Early versions of the DSM were at best moderately reliable (Nietzel et al., 1994; Kirk & Kutchins, 1992). In the early 1960s, for example, four clinicians, each relying on DSM-I, independently interviewed 153 patients (Beck et al., 1962). Only 54 percent of their diagnoses were in agreement. Because all four clinicians were experienced diagnosticians, their failure to agree suggested deficiencies in the classification system.

DSM-IV appears to have greater reliability than any of its predecessors (Reeb, 2000; Nathan & Lagenbucher, 1999). Its framers conducted extensive reviews of research to pinpoint which categories in past DSMs had been too vague and unreliable (Frances & Egger, 1999). In turn, they developed a number of new diagnostic criteria and categories and then ran *field trials* to make sure that the new criteria and categories were in fact reliable. Still, many clinicians worry that DSM-IV's reliability may not be so strong as its framers claim (Campbell, 1999; Kirk & Kutchins, 1992).

The *validity* of a classification system is the accuracy of the information that its diagnostic categories provide. Categories are of most use to clinicians when they demonstrate *predictive validity*—that is, when they help predict future symptoms or events. A common symptom of major depressive disorder, for example, is either insomnia or excessive sleep. When clinicians give Angela Savanti a diagnosis of major depressive disorder, they expect that she may eventually develop sleep

The power of labeling *When looking at this late nineteenth-century photograph of a baseball team at the State Homeopathic Asylum for the Insane in Middletown, New York, most observers assume that the players are patients. As a result, they tend to "see" depression or confusion in the players' faces and posture. In fact, the players are members of the asylum staff, some of whom even sought their jobs for the express purpose of playing for the hospital team.*

problems even if they are not present now. In addition, they expect her to respond to treatments that are effective for other depressed persons. The more often such predictions are accurate, the greater a category's predictive validity.

DSM-IV's framers tried to ensure the validity of this version of the DSM by again conducting extensive reviews of research and running many field studies. As a result, its criteria and categories appear to have stronger validity than those of earlier versions of the DSM (Reeb, 2000; Nathan & Lagenbucher, 1999). Yet, again, more research is needed to determine the precise strength of DSM-IV's validity (Wakefield, 1999).

Can Diagnosis and Labeling Cause Harm?

Even with trustworthy assessment data and reliable and valid classification categories, clinicians will sometimes arrive at a wrong conclusion (Delahanti et al., 2001; Stricker & Trierweiler, 1995). Like all human beings, they are flawed information processors. Studies show that they may be overly influenced by information gathered early in the assessment process (Meehl, 1996, 1960). They sometimes pay too much attention to certain sources of information, such as a parent's report about a child, and too little to others, such as the child's point of view (McCoy, 1976). Finally, their judgments can be influenced by any number of personal biases—gender, age, race, and socioeconomic status, to name just a few (Delahanti et al., 2001; Baker & Bell, 1999).

Given the limitations of both assessment tools and assessors, it is small wonder that studies sometimes uncover shocking errors in diagnosis, especially in hospitals (Chen, Swann, & Burt, 1996). In one study a clinical team was asked to reevaluate the records of 131 patients at a mental hospital in New York, conduct interviews with many of these persons, and arrive at a diagnosis for each one (Lipton & Simon, 1985). The researchers then compared the team's diagnoses with the original diagnoses for which the patients were hospitalized. Although 89 of the patients had originally received a diagnosis of schizophrenia, only 16 received it upon reevaluation. And whereas 15 patients originally had been given a diagnosis of mood disorder, 50 received it now. It is obviously important for clinicians to be aware that such huge disagreements can occur.

THE CURRENT SCENE

The Battle over Premenstrual Dysphoric Disorder

Some categories of mental dysfunctioning are much more controversial than others, causing clinicians and the public alike to battle over their appropriateness. After long and heated discussions two decades ago, for example, DSM-III dropped homosexuality as a category of mental dysfunctioning, citing a lack of evidence for including it and a concern about the social implications of calling a sexual orientation abnormal.

One of the biggest controversies in the development of DSM-IV centered on the category *premenstrual dysphoric disorder (PMDD)*. A DSM work group recommended in 1993 that PMDD be formally listed as a new kind of depressive disorder. The category was to be applied when a woman was regularly impaired by at least five of eleven symptoms during the week before her menses: sad or hopeless feelings; tense or anxious feelings; marked mood changes; frequent irritability or anger and increased interpersonal conflicts; decreased interest in her usual activities; lack of concentration; lack of energy; changes in appetite; insomnia or sleepiness; a subjective feeling of being overwhelmed or out of control; and physical symptoms such as swollen breasts, headaches, muscle pain, a "bloated" sensation, or weight gain.

This recommendation set off an uproar. Many clinicians (including some dissenting members of the work group), several national organizations, interest groups, and the media warned that this diagnostic category would "pathologize" severe cases of *premenstrual syndrome,* or *PMS,* the premenstrual discomforts that are common and normal, and might cause women's behavior in general to be attributed largely to "raging hormones" (a stereotype that society is finally rejecting). They also argued that few data existed to support the inclusion of the new category (Chase, 1993; DeAngelis, 1993).

The DSM solution? A compromise. PMDD is not currently listed as a formal category in DSM-IV, but the pattern is listed in the DSM appendix, with the suggestion that it be studied more thoroughly in the coming years.

Beyond the potential for misdiagnosis, the very act of classifying people can lead to unintended results. As we observed in Chapter 2, for example, many socioultural theorists believe that diagnostic labels can become self-fulfilling prophecies (Scheff, 1999, 1975; Rosenhan, 1973). When people are diagnosed as mentally disturbed, they may be viewed and reacted to correspondingly. If others see them as deficient and expect them to take on a sick role, they may begin to consider themselves sick as well and act that way. Furthermore, our society attaches a stigma to abnormality (Crisp et al., 2000). People labeled mentally ill may find it difficult to get a job, especially a position of responsibility, or to be welcomed into social relationships. Once a label has been applied, it may stick for a long time.

Because of these problems, some clinicians would like to do away with diagnoses. Others disagree. They believe we must simply work to increase what is known about psychological disorders and improve diagnostic techniques (Cunningham, 2000; Reid, 1997). They hold that classification and diagnosis are critical to understanding and treating people in distress.

> "Newspapers usually take great care not to mention the race of those accused of violent crimes. But how many times have you seen the sentence, 'He had a history of mental illness'?"
>
> Rob Morse, columnist, 1999

SUMMING UP | **Diagnosis: Does the Client's Syndrome Match a Known Disorder?**

After collecting and interpreting the assessment information, clinicians form a clinical picture and reach a diagnosis. The diagnosis is chosen from a classification system. The system used most widely in the United States is the *Diagnostic and Statistical Manual of Mental Disorders* (DSM).

DSM-IV The most recent version of the DSM is known as DSM-IV. Clinicians must evaluate a person's condition on five axes, or categories of information. Because DSM-IV is new, its reliability and validity have yet to receive broad clinical review.

Dangers Even with trustworthy assessment data and reliable and valid classification categories, clinicians will not always arrive at the correct conclusion. Moreover, the prejudices that labels arouse may be damaging to the person being diagnosed.

Treatment: How Might the Client Be Helped?

Over the course of ten months, Angela Savanti was treated for depression and related symptoms. She improved considerably during that time, as the following report describes.

> Angela's depression eased as she began to make progress in therapy. A few months before the termination of treatment, she and Jerry resumed dating. Angela discussed with Jerry her greater comfort in expressing her feelings and her hope that Jerry would also become more expressive with her. They discussed the reasons why Angela was ambivalent about getting married, and they began to talk again about the possibility of marriage. Jerry, however, was not making demands for a decision by a certain date, and Angela felt that she was not as frightened about marriage as she previously had been. . . .
>
> Psychotherapy provided Angela with the opportunity to learn to express her feelings to the persons she was interacting with, and this was quite helpful to her. Most important, she was able to generalize from some of the learning experiences in therapy and modify her behavior in her renewed relationship with Jerry. Angela still had much progress to make in terms of changing the characteristic ways she interacted with others, but she had already made a number of important steps in a potentially happier direction.
>
> *(Leon, 1984, pp. 118, 125)*

HARDENED BELIEFS

One out of five persons surveyed still does not believe that people with psychological disorders can be treated and can improve (National Mental Health Association, 1999).

Clearly, treatment helped Angela, and by its conclusion she was a happier, more functional person than the woman who had first sought help ten months earlier. But how did her therapist decide on the treatment program that proved to be so helpful?

Treatment Decisions

Angela's therapist began, like all therapists, with assessment information and diagnostic decisions. Knowing the specific details and background of Angela's problem (*idiographic knowledge*), and combining this information with established information about the nature and treatment of depression (*nomothetic information*), the clinician could arrive at a treatment plan for her.

Yet therapists may also be influenced by other factors when they make treatment decisions. Their treatment plans typically reflect their theoretical orientations and how they have learned to conduct therapy. As therapists apply a favored model in case after case, they become more and more familiar with its principles and treatment techniques and tend to use them in work with still other clients (Witteman & Koele, 1999).

Current research may also play a role. Most clinicians say that they value research as a guide to practice (Beutler et al., 1995). However, because not all of them actually read research articles, they cannot be directly influenced by them. In fact, according to surveys, today's therapists gather most of their information about the latest developments in the field from colleagues, professional newsletters, workshops, conferences, books, and the like (Goldfried & Wolfe, 1996; Beutler et al., 1995). Unfortunately, the accuracy and usefulness of these sources vary widely.

Finally, clinicians are influenced by the general state of knowledge in the clinical field when they make therapy decisions. What, in fact, does the field currently know about treatment and treatment effectiveness? We turn to this set of questions next.

The Effectiveness of Treatment

Altogether, as many as 400 forms of therapy are currently practiced in the clinical field (Prochaska & Norcross, 1999). Naturally, the most important question to ask about each of them is whether it does what it is supposed to do. Does a particular treatment really help people overcome their psychological problems?

ConsiderThis

How can persons make wise decisions about therapists and treatment approaches when they are seeking treatment? • What kinds of information about their approach and background should clinicians share with clients at the beginning of treatment?

On the surface, the question may seem simple. In fact, it is one of the most difficult questions for clinical researchers to answer (March & Curry, 1998).

The first problem is how to *define* "success" (Strupp, 1996, 1989). If, as Angela's therapist suggests, she still has much progress to make at the conclusion of therapy, should her recovery be considered successful? The second problem is how to *measure* improvement (Luborsky et al., 1999). Should researchers give equal weight to the reports of clients, friends, relatives, therapists, and teachers? Should they use rating scales, inventories, therapy insights, observations, or some other measure?

Perhaps the biggest problem in determining the effectiveness of treatment is the *range* and *complexity* of the treatments currently in use. People differ in their problems, personal styles, and motivations for therapy. Therapists differ in skill, experience, orientation, and personality (Garfield, 1998). And therapies differ in theory, format, and setting. Because an individual's progress is influenced by all these factors and more, the findings of a particular study will not always apply to other clients and therapists.

Proper research procedures address some of these problems. By using control groups, random assignment, matched subjects, and the like, clinicians can draw

A CLOSER LOOK

Minority Groups and the Mental Health System

Researchers and clinicians around the world have become interested in the mental health experiences of members of ethnic and racial minority groups (Flaskerud, 2000; Gray-Little & Kaplan, 2000; Burnett et al., 1999). In country after country, members of minority groups have been found to use mental health services less often than members of majority groups (Flaherty & Adams, 1998; Flaskerud & Hu, 1992). Nowhere is this trend more evident than in the United States.

Several factors may contribute to this underuse of mental health services. In some cases, cultural beliefs, a language barrier, and lack of information about available services prevent minority individuals from seeking help. In other cases, members of minority groups do not trust the establishment, and rely instead on traditional remedies that are available in their immediate social environment (Cunningham, 1999; Lee, 1999). Some Hispanic persons in the United States, for example, continue to practice spiritualism, believing that bad spirits can enter the body and cause mental disorders, and that good spirits can cure those disorders (Rogler, Malgady, & Rodriguez, 1989). These individuals may seek help not from therapists but from folk healers, family members, and friends.

Research also finds that members of minority groups stop therapy sooner than persons from majority groups. In the United States, for example, African Americans, Native Americans, Asian Americans, and Hispanic Americans all have higher therapy dropout rates than white Americans (Flaherty & Adams, 1998; Wierzbicki & Pekarik, 1993). This finding may be a matter of economics. Dropping out of therapy is more common among clients who have less money, and members of minority groups have, on average, lower incomes. In addition, members of such groups may stop treatment because they do not feel they are benefiting from it or because ethnic and racial differences prevent a strong rapport with their therapist (Whaley, 1998).

A number of studies in recent years have attempted to learn more about these patterns of therapy usage (Lee, 1999; Whaley, 1998; Sue, Zane, & Young, 1994). Some preliminary trends have emerged:

❖ In some studies clients from minority groups improve as much as those from the majority group; in others they improve less. In no study, however, do they improve more than majority clients.

❖ Clients from minority groups tend to prefer therapists who are ethnically and racially similar to themselves. Having a similar therapist often improves the outcome of treatment among minority clients.

❖ Features that may increase the effectiveness of treatment are greater therapist sensitivity to cultural issues and inclusion of cultural morals and models in treatment (especially in therapies for children and adolescents).

❖ There is a shortage of therapists from ethnic and racial minority groups.

In light of such findings, clinicians have developed *culture-sensitive therapies,* which are designed to address the unique issues faced by members of minority groups (Tan & Dong, 2000; Trujillo, 2000). These approaches often include features such as (1) raising the consciousness of minority-group clients about the impact of the dominant culture and of their own culture on their self-views and behaviors, (2) helping clients express suppressed anger and pain, and (3) helping clients to make choices that work for them and to achieve a bicultural balance that feels right for them.

certain conclusions about various therapies. Even in studies that are well designed, however, the complexity of treatment limits the conclusions that can be reached (Kazdin, 1994).

Despite these difficulties, the job of evaluating therapies must be done, and clinical researchers have plowed ahead with it. Investigators have, in fact, conducted thousands of *therapy outcome studies,* studies that measure the effects of various treatments, and have tried to draw conclusions about the value of treatment. The studies typically ask one of three questions:

1. Is therapy in *general* effective?
2. Are *particular* therapies generally effective?
3. Are *particular* therapies effective for *particular* problems?

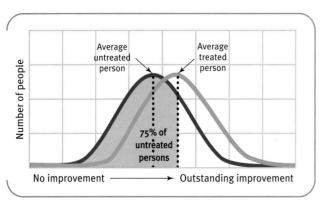

FIGURE 3-6 Does therapy help? *Combining subjects and results from hundreds of studies, investigators have determined that the average person who receives psychotherapy experiences greater improvement than do 75 percent of all untreated people with similar problems. (Adapted from Lambert, Weber, & Sykes, 1993; Smith, Glass, & Miller, 1980; Smith & Glass, 1977.)*

IS THERAPY GENERALLY EFFECTIVE? Studies suggest that therapy is often more helpful than no treatment or than placebos (Cameron et al., 1999). A pioneering review examined 375 controlled studies, covering a total of almost 25,000 people seen in a wide assortment of therapies (Smith, Glass, & Miller, 1980; Smith & Glass, 1977). The reviewers combined the findings of these studies by using a special statistical technique called *meta-analysis.* They rated the level of improvement in each person treated and in each untreated control subject and measured the average difference between the two groups. According to this statistical analysis, the average person who received treatment was better off than were 75 percent of the untreated control subjects (see Figure 3-6). Other meta-analyses have found similar relationships between treatment and improvement (Lambert, Weber, & Sykes, 1993; Crits-Christoph et al., 1991).

The widely read magazine *Consumer Reports* also conducted a survey a few years ago, asking its readers about their experiences and satisfaction in therapy (Seligman, 1995). The 4,000 readers who responded indicated that therapy had often been helpful for them, or at least satisfying. Around 54 percent of the respondents who had felt "very poor" when they first began therapy reported that therapy "made things a lot better."

Some clinicians have concerned themselves with an important related question: Can therapy be harmful? Freud himself believed that therapy had this potential (Kardiner, 1977), and a number of studies agree that more than 5 percent of patients actually seem to get worse because of therapy (Plante, 1999; Lambert & Bergin, 1994). Their symptoms may become more intense, or the individuals may develop new ones, such as a sense of failure, guilt, reduced self-concept, or hopelessness, because of their inability to profit from therapy (Lambert et al., 1986; Hadley & Strupp, 1976).

ARE PARTICULAR THERAPIES GENERALLY EFFECTIVE? The studies we have looked at so far have lumped all therapies together to consider their general effectiveness. Many researchers, however, consider it wrong to treat all therapies alike. One critic suggests that these studies are operating under a *uniformity myth*—a false belief that all therapies are equivalent despite differences in the therapists' training, experience, theoretical orientations, and personalities (Kiesler, 1995, 1966).

Thus, an alternative approach examines the effectiveness of *particular* therapies. Most research of this kind shows each of the major forms of therapy to be superior to no treatment or to placebo treatment (Prochaska & Norcross, 1999, 1994). A number of other studies have compared particular therapies with one another and found that no one form of therapy generally stands out over all others (Luborsky et al., 1999, 1975).

If different kinds of therapy have similar successes, might they have something in common? A **rapprochement movement** has tried to identify a set of common strategies that may run through the work of all effective therapists, regardless of the clinicians' particular orientation (Luborsky et al., 1999; Beutler, Machado, & Neufeldt, 1994). A survey of highly successful therapists suggests, for example, that most give feedback to patients, help patients focus on their own thoughts and behavior, pay attention to the way they and their patients are interacting, and try to promote self-mastery in their patients. In short, effective therapists of any type may practice more similarly than they preach (Korchin & Sands, 1983).

Are Particular Therapies Effective for Particular Problems?

People with different disorders may respond differently to the various forms of therapy. Gordon Paul, an influential clinical theorist, said some years back that the most appropriate question regarding the effectiveness of therapy may be *"What specific treatment, by whom, is most effective for this individual with that specific problem, and under which set of circumstances?"* (Paul, 1967, p. 111). Researchers have investigated how effective particular therapies are at treating particular disorders, and they have often found sizable differences among the various therapies (DeRubeis & Crits-Christoph, 1998). Behavioral therapies, for example, appear to be the most effective of all in treating phobias (McLean & Woody, 2001), whereas drug therapy is the single most effective treatment for schizophrenia (Breier, 2001).

As we observed previously, studies also show that some clinical problems may respond better to *combined* approaches (Kupfer & Frank, 2001). Drug therapy is sometimes combined with certain forms of psychotherapy, for example, to treat depression. In fact, it is now common for clients to be seen by two therapists—one of them a **psychopharmacologist** (or **pharmacotherapist**)—a psychiatrist who primarily prescribes medications—and the other a psychologist, social worker, or other therapist who conducts psychotherapy (Woodward et al., 1993).

Knowledge of how particular therapies fare with particular disorders can help therapists and clients alike make better decisions about treatment (Beutler, 1991, 1979). Thus this is an issue to which we shall keep returning as we examine the disorders the therapies have been devised to combat.

RAPPROCHEMENT MOVEMENT An effort to identify a set of common strategies that run through the work of all effective therapists.

PSYCHOPHARMACOLOGIST A psychiatrist who primarily prescribes medications. Also known as a *pharmacotherapist*.

TREATMENT DELAY

People often wait a long time before seeking treatment for psychological disorders. Most individuals with mood, anxiety, or addictive disorders fail to contact a therapist until at least six years after the initial onset of their symptoms (Kessler, Olfson, & Berglund, 1998).

SUMMING UP | Treatment: How Might the Client Be Helped?

The treatment decisions of therapists may be influenced by assessment information, the diagnosis, the clinician's theoretical orientation and familiarity with research, and the field's state of knowledge.

Determining the effectiveness of treatment is difficult because therapists differ in their ways of defining and measuring success. The range and complexity of today's treatments also present a problem. Therapy outcome studies have led to three general conclusions: (1) People in therapy are usually better off than people with similar problems who receive no treatment. (2) The various therapies do not appear to differ dramatically in their general effectiveness. (3) Certain therapies or combinations of therapies do appear to be more effective than others for certain disorders.

"Fortunately, [psycho]analysis is not the only way to resolve inner conflicts. Life itself still remains a very effective therapist."

Karen Horney,
Our Inner Conflicts, 1945

CROSSROADS:
Renewed Respect for Assessment and Diagnosis

Attitudes toward clinical assessment have changed over the past several decades (Nietzel et al., 1994). For many years, assessment was a highly regarded part of clinical practice. However, as the clinical models grew in number during the 1960s and 1970s, followers of each model favored certain tools over others, and the practice of assessment became fragmented. Meanwhile, research began to reveal that many tools were inaccurate or inconsistent. In this atmosphere, many clinicians lost confidence in systematic assessment and diagnosis, and some came to approach these tasks casually.

Today therapists' respect for the role of assessment and diagnosis is on the rise once again. One reason for the renewed interest is the development of more precise diagnostic criteria, as presented in DSM-IV. Another is the drive by researchers for more rigorous tests to help them select appropriate subjects for clinical studies. Still another factor is the clinical field's growing awareness that certain disorders can be properly identified only after careful assessment procedures.

In Chapter 2 we observed that today's leading models of abnormal behavior often differ widely in their assumptions, conclusions, and treatments. It should not surprise us, then, that clinicians also differ considerably in their approaches to assessment and diagnosis or that those who prefer certain assessment techniques sometimes scoff at those who use other approaches. Yet, when all is said and done, no technique stands out as superior to the rest. Each of the hundreds of available tools has major limitations, and each produces at best an incomplete picture of how a person is functioning and why.

In short, the present state of assessment and diagnosis argues against relying exclusively on any one approach (Bornstein, 1999). As a result, more and more clinicians now use batteries of assessment tools in their work. As we shall see later, such batteries are already providing invaluable guidance in the assessment of Alzheimer's disease and certain other disorders that are particularly difficult to diagnose.

Along with the renewed interest in assessment and diagnosis has come increased research (Chorpita & Lilienfeld, 1999; Exner, 1997). Every major kind of assessment tool—from projective tests to personality inventories—is now undergoing careful scrutiny. This work is helping clinicians perform their work with more accuracy and consistency. Such research, and more generally the newly found respect for systematic clinical assessment, is welcome news for people with psychological problems and for those who wish to help them.

MANAGED TESTS

Most clinicians report that because of managed care directives, they have cut down on assessment testing in recent years and have also used fewer assessment instruments. Particularly affected are the Rorschach, TAT, and Wechsler Intelligence Scale (Piotrowski, Belter, & Keller, 1998).

ConsiderThis

How might IQ scores be misused by school officials, parents, or other individuals? • Why do you think our society is so preoccupied with the concept of intelligence and with IQ scores?

KEY TERMS

idiographic understanding p. 67	*Thematic Apperception Test (TAT)* p. 72	*intelligence test* p. 79
assessment p. 67	*personality inventory* p. 73	*intelligence quotient (IQ)* p. 79
standardization p. 68	*MMPI* p. 74	*naturalistic observation* p. 80
reliability p. 68	*response inventories* p. 76	*structured observation* p. 80
validity p. 68	*psychophysiological test* p. 76	*self-monitoring* p. 80
predictive validity p. 68	*neurological test* p. 78	*diagnosis* p. 82
concurrent validity p. 69	*CAT scan* p. 78	*syndrome* p. 82
clinical interview p. 69	*EEG* p. 78	*classification system* p. 82
mental status exam p. 71	*PET scan* p. 78	*DSM-IV* p. 83
test p. 71	*MRI* p. 78	*therapy outcome study* p. 90
projective test p. 72	*neuropsychological test* p. 78	*rapprochement movement* p. 91
Rorschach test p. 72	*battery* p. 78	*psychopharmacologist* p. 91

QUICK QUIZ

1. What forms of reliability and validity should clinical assessment tools display? pp. 68–69

2. What are the strengths and weaknesses of structured and unstructured interviews? pp. 70–71

3. What are the strengths and weaknesses of projective tests (p. 73), personality inventories (pp. 75–76), and other kinds of clinical tests (pp. 76–80)?

4. List and describe today's leading projective tests. pp. 72–73

5. What are the key features of the MMPI? pp. 74–75

6. How do clinicians determine whether psychological problems are linked to brain damage? p. 78

7. Describe the ways in which clinicians may make observations of clients' behaviors. pp. 80–81

8. What is the purpose of clinical diagnoses? pp. 82–83

9. Describe DSM-IV. What problems may accompany the use of classification systems and the process of clinical diagnosis? pp. 84–87

10. According to therapy outcome studies, how effective is therapy? pp. 88–91

CYBER STUDY

▲ *See neuroimaging in action.* ▲ *How are unstructured and structured interviews conducted?* ▲ *Can violence be predicted?* ▲ *How does an EEG work?*

SEARCH THE *Fundamentals of Abnormal Psychology* CD-ROM FOR

▲ Chapter 3 video cases and discussions
   "Mark"—Aggression, Violence, and the Brain
   The Mind of the Psychopath

▲ Chapter 3 practice test and feedback

▲ Additional video case and discussion
   "Al"—Alcohol Disorders: Hereditary Factors

LOG ON TO THE COMER WEB PAGE FOR

▲ Suggested Web links, research exercises, FAQ page, additional Chapter 3 practice test questions
   <http://www.worthpublishers.com/comer>

Source: *The Brain, Second Edition* (The Annenberg/CPB Collection, 1997)

Generalized Anxiety Disorder and Phobias

Bob Donaldson was a 22-year-old carpenter referred to the psychiatric outpatient department of a community hospital. . . . During the initial interview Bob was visibly distressed. He appeared tense, worried, and frightened. He sat on the edge of his chair, tapping his foot and fidgeting with a pencil on the psychiatrist's desk. He sighed frequently, took deep breaths between sentences, and periodically exhaled audibly and changed his position as he attempted to relate his story:

> *Bob:* It's been an awful month. I can't seem to do anything. I don't know whether I'm coming or going. I'm afraid I'm going crazy or something.
>
> *Doctor:* What makes you think that?
>
> *Bob:* I can't concentrate. My boss tells me to do something and I start to do it, but before I've taken five steps I don't know what I started out to do. I get dizzy and I can feel my heart beating and everything looks like it's shimmering or far away from me or something—it's unbelievable.
>
> *Doctor:* What thoughts come to mind when you're feeling like this?
>
> *Bob:* I just think, "Oh, Christ, my heart is really beating, my head is swimming, my ears are ringing—I'm either going to die or go crazy."
>
> *Doctor:* What happens then?
>
> *Bob:* Well, it doesn't last more than a few seconds, I mean that intense feeling. I come back down to earth, but then I'm worrying what's the matter with me all the time, or checking my pulse to see how fast it's going, or feeling my palms to see if they're sweating.
>
> *Doctor:* Can others see what you're going through?
>
> *Bob:* You know, I doubt it. I hide it. I haven't been seeing my friends. . . . I'm not with them when I'm with them anyway—I'm just sitting there worrying. . . . So, anyway, I just go home and turn on the TV or pick up the sports page, but I can't really get into that either.

Bob went on to say that he had stopped playing softball because of fatigability and trouble concentrating. On several occasions during the past two weeks he was unable to go to work because he was "too nervous."

(Spitzer et al., 1983, pp. 11-12)

One does not need to be as troubled as Bob Donaldson to experience fear and anxiety. Think about a time when your breathing quickened, your muscles tensed, and your heart pounded with a sudden sense of dread. Was it when your car almost skidded off the road in the rain? When your professor announced a pop quiz? What about when the person you were in love with went out with someone else, or your boss suggested that your job performance ought to improve? Any time that you face what seems to be a serious threat to your well-being, you may react with the state of immediate alarm known as **fear.** Sometimes you cannot pinpoint a specific cause for your alarm, but still you feel tense and edgy, as if you expected something unpleasant to happen. The vague sense of being in danger is usually termed **anxiety,** and it has the same features—the same increase in breathing, muscular tension, perspiration, and so forth—as fear.

What the features ∧

FEAR The central nervous system's physiological and emotional response to a serious threat to one's well-being.

ANXIETY The central nervous system's physiological and emotional response to a vague sense of threat or danger.

AUTONOMIC NERVOUS SYSTEM (ANS) The network of nerve fibers that connects the central nervous system to all the other organs of the body.

Although everyday experiences of fear and anxiety are not pleasant, they are often useful: they prepare us for action—for "fight or flight"—when danger threatens. They may lead us to drive more cautiously in a storm, keep up with our reading assignments, treat our dates more sensitively, and work harder at our jobs (Millar & Millar, 1996). Unfortunately, some people suffer such disabling fear and anxiety that they cannot lead normal lives. Their discomfort is too severe or too frequent; it lasts too long; or it is triggered too easily. These people are said to have an *anxiety disorder* or a related kind of disorder.

Anxiety disorders are the most common mental disorders in the United States. In any given year as many as 19 percent of the adult population suffer from one or another of the six anxiety disorders identified by DSM-IV (Kessler & Zhao, 1999). These disorders cost society at least $42 billion each year in health-care expenses, lost wages, and lost productivity (Greenberg et al., 1999; Kessler et al., 1999, 1994).

People with *generalized anxiety disorder* experience general and persistent feelings of anxiety. People with *phobias* experience a persistent and irrational fear of a specific object, activity, or situation. Individuals with *panic disorder* have recurrent attacks of terror. Those with *obsessive-compulsive disorder* feel overrun by re-

A CLOSER LOOK

Adjustment Disorders: A Category of Compromise?

Some people react to a major stressor in their lives with extended and excessive feelings of anxiety, depressed mood, or antisocial behaviors. The symptoms do not quite add up to an anxiety or mood disorder, but they do cause considerable distress or interfere with the person's job, schoolwork, or social life. Should we consider such reactions normal? No, says DSM-IV. Somewhere between effective coping strategies and anxiety disorders lie the *adjustment disorders* (APA, 2000, 1994).

DSM-IV lists several types of adjustment disorders, including *adjustment disorder with anxiety* and *adjustment disorder with depressed mood.* People receive such diagnoses if they develop their symptoms within three months of the onset of a stressor. The symptoms may continue for as long as six months after the stressor subsides. If the stressor is long term, such as a medical condition, the adjustment disorder may last indefinitely. Almost any kind of stressor may trigger an adjustment disorder. Common ones are the breakup of a relationship, marital problems, business difficulties, and living in a crime-ridden neighborhood. The disorder may also be triggered by developmental events such as going away to school, getting married, becoming a parent, or retiring from a job.

Museum of Modern Art Film Stills Archive

Up to 30 percent of all people in outpatient therapy receive this diagnosis—by far the one most frequently submitted to insurance companies for treatment reimbursement (APA, 2000). However, some experts doubt that adjustment disorders are as common as this figure suggests. Rather, the diagnosis seems to be a favorite among clinicians—it can easily be applied to a range of problems, yet is less stigmatizing than many other categories.

ConsiderThis

◉ Have you, a friend, or a relative ever reacted to stress in ways that might suggest this diagnosis? • Is the category "adjustment disorder" too vague or too easily applied?

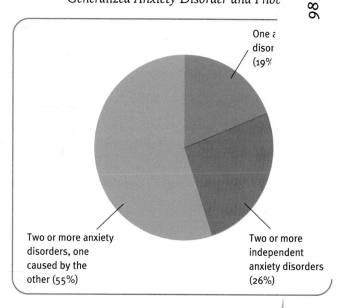

FIGURE 4-1
Does anxiety beget anxiety? *People with one anxiety disorder usually experience another as well, either simultaneously or at another point in their lives. One study of persons with anxiety disorders found that 81 percent actually suffered from multiple disorders. (Adapted from Hunt & Andrews, 1995.)*

One a
disor
(19%

Two or more anxiety
disorders, one
caused by the
other (55%)

Two or more
independent
anxiety disorders
(26%)

peated thoughts that cause anxiety or by the need to perform repetitive actions to reduce anxiety. And those with *acute stress disorder* and *posttraumatic stress disorder* are tormented by fear and related symptoms well after a traumatic event (military combat, rape, torture) has ended. Most individuals with one anxiety disorder suffer from a second one as well (Fong & Silien, 1999) (see Figure 4-1). Bob Donaldson, for example, experiences the excessive worry found in generalized anxiety disorder and the repeated attacks of terror that mark panic disorder.

In this chapter we shall look at generalized anxiety disorder and phobias, the most common anxiety disorders and the ones with the longest history of study. The other anxiety disorders—panic disorder, obsessive-compulsive disorder, and the stress disorders—have come to be understood and successfully treated only in recent years. They are the subject of Chapter 5.

Stress, Coping, and the Anxiety Response

Before we examine the various anxiety disorders, we need to take a closer look at the kinds of situations that normally cause us to feel threatened and the kinds of changes we experience in response to them. Actually, we feel some degree of threat—a state of *stress*—whenever we are faced with demands or opportunities that require us to change in some way. A state of stress has two components: a *stressor,* the event that creates the demands, and a *stress response,* the person's reactions to the demands.

The stressors of life may include annoying everyday hassles, such as rush-hour traffic; turning-point events, such as college graduation or marriage; long-term problems, such as poverty or poor health; or traumatic events, such as major accidents, assaults, or military combat. Our response to such stressors is influenced by the way we judge both the events and our capacity to react to them in an effective way (Pearlin, 1999; Lazarus & Folkman, 1984). People who sense that they have the ability and the resources to cope are more likely to take stressors in stride and to respond effectively (Aldwin et al., 1996).

When we view a stressor as threatening, a natural reaction is fear. Fear is actually a package of responses—physical, emotional, and cognitive. Physically, we perspire, our breathing quickens, our muscles tense, and our hearts beat faster. Turning pale, developing goose bumps, and feeling nauseated are other physical reactions. Emotional responses to extreme threats include horror, dread, and even panic, while in the cognitive realm fear can interfere with our ability to concentrate and change our view of the world. We may exaggerate the harm that actually threatens us or remember things incorrectly after the threat has passed.

These features of the fear and anxiety response are produced by the action of the body's **autonomic nervous system (ANS),** the extensive network of nerve fibers that connects the *central nervous system* (the brain and spinal cord) to all the other organs of the body. The ANS helps control the *involuntary* activities of these organs—breathing, heartbeat, blood pressure, perspiration, and the like (see Figure 4-2 on the next page).

When our brain interprets a situation as dangerous, it excites a special group of ANS fibers that quicken our heartbeat and produce the other changes that we

THE PRESSURES OF EVERYDAY LIFE
Almost one-third of surveyed adults report always feeling rushed, nearly half say they would give up a day's pay for a day off, and more than half say they have felt considerable stress in the past two weeks (American Use of Time Project, 1995).

CORTICOSTEROIDS A group of hormones, including cortisol, released by the adrenal glands at times of stress.

TRAIT ANXIETY The general level of anxiety that a person brings to various events.

SITUATION ANXIETY The various levels of anxiety produced in a person by different situations. Also called *state anxiety*.

GENERALIZED ANXIETY DISORDER A disorder marked by persistent and excessive feelings of anxiety and worry about numerous events and activities.

experience as fear or anxiety. These fibers are referred to collectively as the *sympathetic nervous system* (in a sense, they are "sympathetic" to our emergency needs). When the perceived danger passes, a second group of ANS nerve fibers, the *parasympathetic nervous system,* returns our heartbeat and other body processes to normal. Together, these two parts of the ANS help control our fear and anxiety reactions. They enable our body to operate reliably across all kinds of situations.

The ANS may stimulate organs directly. It may also affect them indirectly by stimulating *endocrine glands,* the structures located throughout the body which release chemicals called *hormones* into the bloodstream. For example, when we are faced with stressors, the ANS triggers the *adrenal glands,* located on top of the kidneys, into action, and these glands release a group of hormones called **corticosteroids.** These corticosteroids, in turn, stimulate various body organs and certain regions of the brain, setting in motion anxiety reactions.

We all have our own ways of experiencing fear and anxiety. Some people are almost always relaxed, while others typically feel some tension, even when no threat is apparent. A person's general level of anxiety is sometimes called **trait anxiety,** because it seems to be a trait or characteristic that each of us brings to the events in our lives (Soric, 1999; Spielberger, 1985, 1972, 1966). Psychologists have found that differences in trait anxiety appear soon after birth (Kagan & Snidman, 1999; Kalin, 1993).

FIGURE 4-2   The autonomic nervous system (ANS) *When the sympathetic division of the ANS is activated, it stimulates some organs and inhibits others. The result is general arousal. In contrast, activation of the parasympathetic division leads to an overall calming effect.*

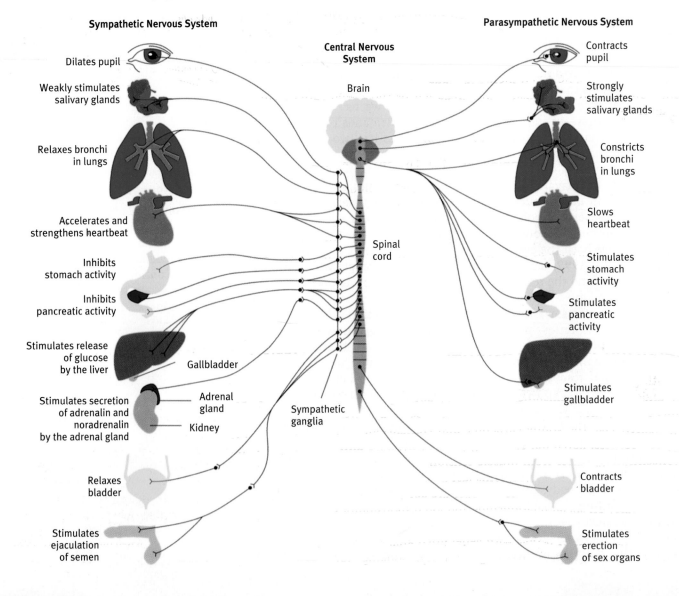

Sympathetic Nervous System

Dilates pupil

Weakly stimulates salivary glands

Relaxes bronchi in lungs

Accelerates and strengthens heartbeat

Inhibits stomach activity

Inhibits pancreatic activity

Stimulates release of glucose by the liver

Gallbladder

Stimulates secretion of adrenalin and noradrenalin by the adrenal gland

Adrenal gland

Kidney

Relaxes bladder

Stimulates ejaculation of semen

Central Nervous System

Brain

Spinal cord

Sympathetic ganglia

Parasympathetic Nervous System

Contracts pupil

Strongly stimulates salivary glands

Constricts bronchi in lungs

Slows heartbeat

Stimulates stomach activity

Stimulates pancreatic activity

Stimulates gallbladder

Contracts bladder

Stimulates erection of sex organs

Computer challenged *The modern world offers all kinds of opportunities for stress, both invited and uninvited. An audience watches as the human chess champion Gary Kasparov struggles against the computer champion Deep Blue.*

Individual experiences of anxiety *Although most people are terrified by the very thought of climbing a mountain, some are stimulated by the experience and others are even calmed by it. Such individual reactions represent differences in situation, or state, anxiety.*

People also differ in their sense of which situations are threatening (Pearlin, 1999; Soric, 1999). Walking through a forest may be fearsome for one person but relaxing for another. Flying in an airplane may arouse terror in some people and boredom in others. Such variations are called differences in **situation,** or **state, anxiety.** In most cases, however, these individual expressions of anxiety are quite different from the waves of tension and dread felt by those who suffer from an anxiety disorder.

SUMMING UP | **Stress, Coping, and the Anxiety Response**

Fear is a state of alarm that occurs in response to a serious threat. Anxiety is the reaction of alarm that occurs when our sense of threat is vague. People with anxiety disorders experience ongoing fear and anxiety that prevent them from leading a normal life. The features of fear and anxiety are produced by the activities of the autonomic nervous system and endocrine glands, including the adrenal glands.

Generalized Anxiety Disorder

People with **generalized anxiety disorder** experience excessive anxiety under most circumstances and worry about practically anything. In fact, their problem is sometimes described as *free-floating anxiety*. Like the young carpenter Bob Donaldson, they typically feel restless, keyed up, or on edge, tire easily, have difficulty concentrating, suffer from muscle tension, and have sleep problems (see Table 4-1). The symptoms last at least six months. Nevertheless, most people with the disorder are able, with some difficulty, to carry on social relationships and job responsibilities (Maier et al., 2000).

Relatives and friends of people with generalized anxiety disorder sometimes accuse them of "wanting" to worry, "looking" for

Table 4-1 **DSM-IV Checklist**

GENERALIZED ANXIETY DISORDER

1. Excessive or ongoing anxiety and worry, for at least six months, about numerous events or activities.
2. Difficulty controlling the worry.
3. At least three of the following symptoms: restlessness • easy fatigue • irritability • muscle tension • sleep disturbance.
4. Significant distress or impairment.

Based on APA, 2000, 1994.

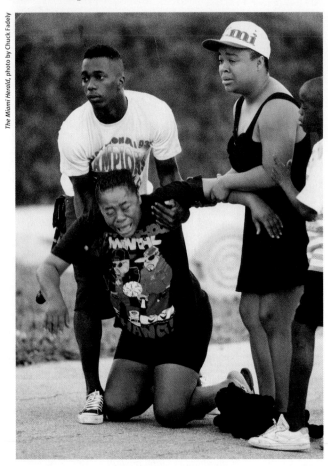

The Miami Herald, photo by Chuck Fadely

The role of society *Upon learning that her son was a victim of a drive-by shooting, a woman collapses in the arms of relatives at the scene. People who live in dangerous environments experience greater anxiety and have a higher rate of generalized anxiety disorder than those residing in other settings.*

ConsiderThis

◉ What kinds of factors might serve to relieve the stresses of modern society, and thus reduce the likelihood of people's developing generalized anxiety disorder?

things to worry about, and being "happy" only when worrying. Most such accusations are unfair: people with the disorder hardly feel happy. They feel that they are in a constant struggle, always threatened and defending themselves, and always trying to escape their pain (Becker et al., 1998).

Generalized anxiety disorder is common in Western society. Surveys suggest that as many as 4 percent of the United States population and 3 percent of Britain's population have the symptoms of this disorder in any given year (Kessler et al., 2001, 1999; Jenkins et al., 1997). It may emerge at any age, but usually it first appears in childhood or adolescence. Women diagnosed with the disorder outnumber men 2 to 1.

A variety of factors have been cited to explain the development of generalized anxiety disorder. Here we shall observe the views and treatments offered by the sociocultural, psychodynamic, humanistic-existential, cognitive, and biological models. The behavioral perspective will be examined when we turn to phobias later in the chapter, because that model's approach to generalized anxiety disorder and phobias is basically the same.

The Sociocultural Perspective

According to sociocultural theorists, generalized anxiety disorder is most likely to develop in people who are faced with societal conditions that are truly dangerous. Studies have found that people in highly threatening environments are indeed more likely to develop the general feelings of tension, anxiety, and fatigue, the exaggerated startle reactions, and the sleep disturbances found in this disorder (Kendler, Karkowski, & Prescott, 1998; Staples, 1996).

Take, for example, the psychological impact of living near the Three Mile Island nuclear power plant after the nuclear reactor accident of March 1979 (Baum, 1990; Bromet et al., 1984, 1982). In the months following the accident, local mothers of preschool children were found to display five times as many anxiety or depression disorders as mothers living elsewhere. Although the number of disorders decreased during the next year, the Three Mile Island mothers still displayed high levels of anxiety or depression a year later.

One of the most powerful forms of societal stress is poverty. People without financial means are likely to live in run-down communities with high crime rates, have fewer educational and job opportunities, and run a greater risk for health problems. As sociocultural theorists would predict, such people also have a higher rate of generalized anxiety disorder. In the United States, the rate is twice as high among people with very low incomes as among those with higher incomes (Blazer et al., 1991). As salaries and wages decrease in this country, the rate of generalized anxiety disorder steadily increases.

Since race is closely tied to income and job opportunity in the United States (Belle, 1990), it is also tied to the prevalence of generalized anxiety disorder. In any given year, approximately 6 percent of all African Americans suffer from this disorder, compared to 3.5 percent of white Americans. African American women, perhaps the country's most socially stressed group (Bennett, 1987), have the highest rate of all—6.6 percent (see Figure 4-3).

Although poverty and other societal pressures may create a climate in which generalized anxiety disorder is more likely to develop, sociocultural variables are not the only factors at work. After all, most people in poor, war-torn, politically oppressed, or dangerous environments do not develop this anxiety disorder. Even if sociocultural factors play a broad role, theorists still must explain why some people develop the disorder and others do not. The psychodynamic, humanistic-existential, cognitive, and biological schools of thought have all tried to explain why and have offered corresponding treatments.

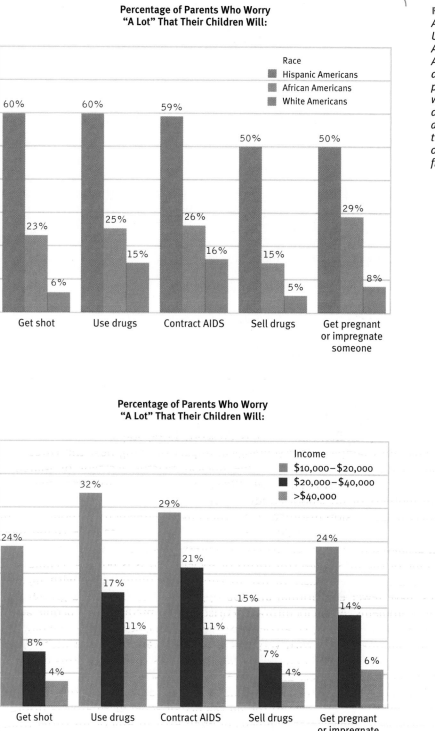

Percentage of Parents Who Worry "A Lot" That Their Children Will:

Race
- Hispanic Americans
- African Americans
- White Americans

Percentage of Parents Who Worry "A Lot" That Their Children Will:

Income
- $10,000–$20,000
- $20,000–$40,000
- >$40,000

FIGURE 4-3 Poverty, race, and anxiety
According to a survey of 1,738 parents in the United States, African Americans and Hispanic Americans are much more likely than white Americans to worry "a lot" about their children's safety, future, and survival. Similarly, poorer parents are much more likely than wealthier parents to worry about their children's welfare, regardless of race. The higher anxiety levels found in racial minority groups, then, may be largely a matter of living in poorer or more dangerous environments. (Adapted from National Commission on Children, 1991.)

CROWDED CONDITIONS

Crowded living conditions are one form of societal stress that may raise anxiety. The most crowded cities in the world are Manila (108,699 people per square mile), Shanghai, Cairo, Paris, and Bombay. The most crowded states in the United States are New Jersey (1,042 people per square mile), Rhode Island, Massachusetts, Connecticut, and Maryland (Cohl, 1997).

The Psychodynamic Perspective

Sigmund Freud (1933, 1917) believed that all children experience some degree of anxiety as part of growing up. They feel *realistic anxiety* when they face actual danger. They experience *neurotic anxiety* when they are repeatedly prevented, by parents or by circumstances, from expressing their id impulses. And they experience *moral anxiety* when they are punished or threatened for expressing their id impulses. According to Freud, we all use ego defense mechanisms to help control these forms of anxiety; in some people, however, the anxiety is so strong and the defense mechanisms are so inadequate that generalized anxiety disorder develops.

PSYCHODYNAMIC EXPLANATIONS: WHEN CHILDHOOD ANXIETY GOES UNRESOLVED

Freud suggested that generalized anxiety disorder arises when a person's defense mechanisms break down under stress and are overrun by neurotic or moral anxiety. It may be that the person's level of anxiety is just too high. Say that a boy is spanked every time he cries for milk as an infant, messes his pants as a 2-year-old, and explores his genitals as a toddler. He may eventually come to believe that his various id impulses are very dangerous, and he may experience overwhelming anxiety whenever he has such impulses. Or perhaps the ego defense mechanisms are too weak to cope with the resulting anxiety. Overprotected children, shielded by their parents from all frustrations and threats, have little opportunity to develop effective defense mechanisms. When they face the pressures of adult life, their defense mechanisms may be too weak to cope with the resulting anxieties. Although today's psychodynamic theorists often disagree with many of Freud's specific notions, they believe, as Freud did, that generalized anxiety disorder can be traced to inadequacies in the early relationships between children and their parents.

Researchers have tested these psychodynamic explanations in various ways. First, they have tried to show that people in general tend to use defense mechanisms in frightening situations. In some studies, experimenters have exposed subjects to threats of various kinds and have then measured how well they remember the fear-arousing events. As psychodynamic theorists would predict, the subjects tend to forget—that is, *repress*—many aspects of the events (Rosenzweig, 1943, 1933).

Second, psychodynamic researchers have tried to show that people with generalized anxiety disorder are particularly likely to use defense mechanisms. In one study, investigators examined the early therapy transcripts of patients with this diagnosis. The transcripts indicated that the patients often reacted defensively. When asked by therapists to discuss upsetting experiences, they would quickly forget (repress) what they had just been talking about, change the direction of the discussion, or deny having negative feelings (Luborsky, 1973).

Third, researchers have studied people who as children suffered extreme punishment for id impulses. As psychodynamic theorists would predict, these people have higher levels of anxiety later in life (Chiu, 1971). In cultures where children are regularly punished and threatened, for example, adults seem to have more fears and anxieties (Whiting et al., 1966). In addition, several studies have supported the psychodynamic position that extreme protectiveness by parents may also lead to high levels of anxiety in their children (Jenkins, 1968; Eisenberg, 1958).

Although these studies are consistent with psychodynamic explanations, some scientists question whether they show what they claim to show. When people have difficulty talking about upsetting events early in therapy, for example, they are not necessarily repressing those events. They may be purposely focusing on the positive aspects of their lives, or they may be too embarrassed to share personal negative events until they develop trust in the therapist.

Another problem is that some research studies and clinical reports have actually contradicted the psychodynamic explanations. In one, 16 people with generalized anxiety disorder were interviewed about their upbringing (Raskin et al., 1982). They reported little of the excessive discipline or disturbed childhood environments that psychodynamic therapists might expect for people with this disorder.

PSYCHODYNAMIC THERAPIES

Psychodynamic therapists use the same general techniques to treat all psychological problems: free association and the therapist's

"Why do you think you cross the road?"

INSECURITY, ADULT STYLE

Children may cling to blankets or cuddly toys to feel more secure. Adults, too, may hug a beloved object in order to relax. One in five adult women and one in twenty men admit to sleeping with a stuffed animal on a regular basis (Kanner, 1995).

Apocalypse Not: The Y2K Scare

As January 1, 2000, approached, more and more people became concerned—even anxious—about what this date would bring. Much of the concern centered on the so-called Y2K problem. Computers around the world, particularly older ones, had not been programmed to recognize the start of the new century, raising questions about their capacity to continue providing governmental, industrial, health, and personal services. As more and more warnings were offered, the public's concern increased.

At first the concerns seemed realistic. There was, after all, a possibility that many services could be interrupted as the year 2000 began. As the countdown to the new millennium continued, however, the anxiety displayed by many people seemed to grow excessive. In one survey, for example, 25 percent of Americans said they were worried because they didn't know what was going to happen in the new century, and 28 percent even agreed with the statement "We're approaching the end of the world" (Roper Starch Worldwide, 1999). Many people talked generally of doom and a number began to hoard food, cash, medicine, and gasoline.

Given such reactions, clinical theorists also suspected psychological reasons for the premillennial anxiety. Some, for example, described the Y2K computer problem as a magnet for the emotions of people who were already highly anxious or experiencing other psychological problems (Strous et al., 2000; Rabasca, 1999). One theorist observed, "People may project some of their anxiety and fears and blame Y2K as a scapegoat" (Goldberg, 1999), and another noted that a person who "fears accidents and disasters is likely to fear the millennial change" (Kupfer, 1999).

Theorists have also pointed out that the anxiety surrounding the Y2K computer problem was similar to that which swept the world in A.D. 999 as people prepared for that millennial change (Landes, 1999; Rhodes, 1999). Doomsaying is as old as humankind. Over the years, numerous religions have taught that the world would end by a particular date, bringing punishment to some people and rewards to others. Nonreligious organizations have also predicted an apocalypse, though for other reasons—a

squandering of natural resources, shortages of food, unchecked population growth, or a natural catastrophe (Moshinsky, 1995). When a new millennium approaches, such beliefs and the people who embrace them increase sharply.

Such theories suggest that the anxiety of the late 1990s was much more than a straightforward reaction to computer dangers, real as some of them were. Like other forms of anxiety, it represented a complex phenomenon in which sociocultural and psychological forces combined in just the right, or wrong, way.

interpretations of transference, resistance, and dreams. *Freudian psychodynamic therapists* use these methods to help clients with generalized anxiety disorder become less afraid of their id impulses and more able to control them successfully. Other psychodynamic therapists, particularly *object relations therapists,* use them to help anxious patients identify and settle the childhood relationship problems that continue to produce anxiety in adulthood (Zerbe, 1990; Diamond, 1987).

Controlled research has not consistently shown psychodynamic approaches to be helpful in cases of generalized anxiety disorder (Goisman et al., 1999; Svartberg & Stiles, 1991). In most studies, such interventions have proved at best modestly helpful. An exception to this overall trend is short-term psychodynamic therapy (see Chapter 2), which has in some cases reduced the levels of anxiety, worry, and social difficulty of patients with this disorder (Crits-Christoph et al., 1996, 1995).

The Humanistic and Existential Perspectives

Humanistic and existential theorists propose that generalized anxiety disorder, like other psychological disorders, arises when people stop looking at themselves honestly and acceptingly. Repeated denials of their true thoughts, emotions, and behavior make these people extremely anxious and unable to fulfill their potential as human beings.

LAY TREATMENT

Besides seeking treatment, people are known to try informal techniques in an effort to feel better. "Worry beads," strings of beads that people rub between their fingers to help relieve anxiety, became very popular in the 1960s and are still used today. The practice began as a custom among peasants in Greece, who fingered sets of beads called *komboloi* in order to keep their hands occupied (Kahn & Fawcett, 1993).

CLIENT-CENTERED THERAPY The humanistic therapy developed by Carl Rogers in which clinicians try to help clients by being accepting, empathizing accurately, and conveying genuineness.

EXISTENTIAL ANXIETY A universal fear of the limits and responsibilities of one's existence.

BASIC IRRATIONAL ASSUMPTIONS The inaccurate and inappropriate beliefs held by people with various psychological problems, according to Albert Ellis.

HUMANISTIC EXPLANATIONS AND TREATMENTS: LACK OF SELF-ACCEPTANCE

The humanistic view of why people develop generalized anxiety disorder is best illustrated by Carl Rogers's explanation. As we saw in Chapter 2, Rogers believed that children who fail to receive *unconditional positive regard* from others may become overly critical of themselves and develop harsh self-standards, what Rogers called *conditions of worth*. They try to meet these standards by repeatedly distorting and denying their true thoughts and experiences. Despite such efforts, however, threatening self-judgments keep breaking through and causing them intense anxiety. This onslaught of anxiety sets the stage for generalized anxiety disorder or some other form of psychological dysfunctioning.

Practitioners of Rogers's treatment approach, **client-centered therapy,** try to show unconditional positive regard for their clients and to empathize with them. The therapists hope that an atmosphere of genuine acceptance and caring will help clients feel secure enough to recognize their true needs, thoughts, and emotions. When clients eventually "experience" themselves—that is, trust their instincts and are honest and comfortable with themselves—their anxiety or other symptoms will subside. In the following excerpt, Rogers describes the progress made by a client with anxiety and related symptoms:

> She was unusually sensitive to the process she was experiencing in herself. To use some of her expressions, she was feeling like pieces of a jigsaw puzzle, she was singing a song without words, she was creating a poem, she was learning a new way of experiencing herself which was like learning to read Braille. Therapy was an experiencing of herself, in all its aspects, in a safe relationship. At first it was her guilt and her concern over being responsible for the maladjustments of others. Then it was her hatred and bitterness toward life for having cheated and frustrated her in so many different areas, particularly the sexual, and then it was the experiencing of her own hurt, of the sorrow she felt for herself for having been so wounded. But along with these went the experiencing of self as having a capacity for wholeness, a self which was not possessively loving toward others but was "without hate," a self that cared about others. This last followed what was, for her, one of the deepest experiences in therapy . . . the realization that the therapist cared, that it really mattered to him how therapy turned out for her, that he really valued her. She experienced the soundness of her basic directions. She gradually became aware of the fact that, though she had searched in every corner of herself, there was nothing fundamentally bad, but rather, at heart she was positive and sound. She realized that the values she deeply held were such as would set her at variance with her culture, but she accepted this calmly. . . .
>
> *(Rogers, 1954, pp. 261–264)*

In spite of such optimistic case reports, controlled studies have only sometimes found client-centered therapy more effective than placebo therapy or no therapy at all (Prochaska & Norcross, 1999; Greenberg et al., 1994). In addition, researchers have found, at best, only limited support for Rogers's explanation of generalized anxiety disorder and other forms of abnormal behavior. Nor have other humanistic theories and treatment received much research support.

EXISTENTIAL EXPLANATIONS AND TREATMENTS: AVOIDING CHOICE AND RESPONSIBILITY
Existentialists believe that generalized anxiety disorder grows out of **existential anxiety,** a universal human fear of the limits and responsibilities of one's existence (May & Yalom, 1995; Tillich, 1952). We all experience existential anxiety, they say, because we know that life is limited and we fear the death that awaits us. We also know that our actions and choices may hurt others. Finally, we suspect that our own personal existence may ultimately lack meaning.

According to existentialists, people can face their existential anxiety by taking responsibility for their actions, making decisions, finding ways to make their lives meaningful, and appreciating their own uniqueness. Or they can shrink from this confrontation and lead "inauthentic lives": deny their fears, overlook

---

PET-CENTERED TREATMENT

To prevent or reduce anxiety in their pets, 33 percent of owners leave a radio or television playing when the pet is to be left alone, 50 percent leave toys out, and 41 percent leave lights on (Klein, 1998). Such efforts may comfort most pets, but for the 5 million dogs with extreme cases of separation anxiety, the Food and Drug Administration has also approved the drug *clomipramine hydrochloride*, brand name Clomicalm.

their freedom of choice, avoid taking responsibility, and conform excessively to society's guidelines (Bugental, 1992, 1965; May, 1967). According to existentialists, such a lifestyle fails to reduce a person's existential anxiety, which continues to erupt in the form of generalized and other anxiety disorders.

Existential therapists use a variety of techniques to help anxious people take more responsibility and live more meaningfully. Sometimes they support their clients; at other times they confront them. Like most humanists, however, existentialists believe that traditional research methods miss subtle human experiences by looking only at what can be observed and defined objectively (Bugental, 1997, 1992). These theorists rely instead on reason, introspection, and case studies as evidence for their views and approaches.

The Cognitive Perspective

Followers of the cognitive model suggest that psychological problems are often caused by dysfunctional ways of thinking. Given that excessive worry—a cognitive symptom—is a key characteristic of generalized anxiety disorder, it is not surprising that cognitive theorists have had much to say about the causes of and treatments for this particular disorder.

Fearful delights *Many people enjoy the feeling of fear as long as it occurs under controlled circumstances, as when they are safely watching the tension grow in the enormously popular The Blair Witch Project.*

COGNITIVE EXPLANATIONS: MALADAPTIVE ASSUMPTIONS Several influential cognitive theories suggest that generalized anxiety disorder is caused by *maladaptive assumptions*. Albert Ellis, for example, believes that many people are guided by irrational beliefs that lead them to act and react in inappropriate ways (Ellis, 1999, 1977, 1962). Ellis calls these **basic irrational assumptions,** and he claims that people with generalized anxiety disorder often hold the following ones:

> "It is a dire necessity for an adult human being to be loved or approved of by virtually every significant other person in his community."
>
> "It is awful and catastrophic when things are not the way one would very much like them to be."
>
> "If something is or may be dangerous or fearsome, one should be terribly concerned about it and should keep dwelling on the possibility of its occurring."
>
> "One should be thoroughly competent, adequate, and achieving in all possible respects if one is to consider oneself worthwhile."
>
> *(Ellis, 1962)*

When people who make these basic assumptions are faced with a stressful event, such as an exam or a blind date, they are likely to interpret it as highly dangerous and threatening, to overreact, and to experience fear. As they apply the assumptions to more and more life events, they may begin to develop a generalized anxiety disorder (Warren, 1997).

Similarly, the cognitive theorist Aaron Beck holds that people with generalized anxiety disorder constantly hold unrealistic silent assumptions that imply they are in imminent danger (Beck, 1997, 1991, 1976; Beck & Emery, 1985):

> "Any strange situation should be regarded as dangerous."
>
> "A situation or a person is unsafe until proven to be safe."
>
> "It is always best to assume the worst."
>
> "My security and safety depend on anticipating and preparing myself at all times for any possible danger."
>
> *(Beck & Emery, 1985, p. 63)*

Researchers have found that people with generalized anxiety disorder do indeed hold maladaptive notions about dangerousness, as Ellis and Beck claim

FACING FEAR

Studies find that subjects with generally high levels of anxiety are more likely than calmer subjects to notice and remember pictures of threatening faces. Attention to happy or neutral faces is about the same in both groups (Bradley et al., 1998).

Fears, Schmears: The Odds Are Usually on Our Side

People with anxiety disorders have many unreasonable fears, but millions of other people, too, worry about disaster every day. Most of the catastrophes they fear are not probable. Perhaps the ability to live by laws of *probability* rather than *possibility* is what separates the fearless from the fearful. What are the odds, then, that commonly feared events will happen? The range of probability is wide, but the odds are usually heavily in our favor.

A city resident will be a victim of a violent crime	1 in 60
A suburbanite will be a victim of a violent crime	1 in 1,000
A small-town resident will be a victim of a violent crime	1 in 2,000
A child will suffer a high-chair injury this year	1 in 6,000
The IRS will audit you this year	1 in 100
You will be bumped off any given airline flight	1 in 4,000
You will be murdered this year	1 in 12,000
You will be killed on your *next* bus ride	1 in 500 million
You will be hit by a baseball at a major-league game	1 in 300,000
You will drown in the tub this year	1 in 685,000
Your house will have a fire this year	1 in 200
You will die in a fire this year	1 in 40,200
Your carton will contain a broken egg	1 in 10
You will develop a tooth cavity	1 in 6

A young child will develop a tooth cavity	1 in 10
You will contract AIDS from a blood transfusion	1 in 100,000
Any given miner will be injured while working this year	1 in 23
Any given factory worker will be injured at work this year	1 in 37
Any given farmer will be injured while working this year	1 in 19
You will die in a fall	1 in 200,000
You will be attacked by a shark	1 in 4 million
You will receive a diagnosis of cancer this year	1 in 8,000
A woman will develop breast cancer during her lifetime	1 in 9

You will develop a brain tumor this year	1 in 25,000
A business owner will become insolvent or declare bankruptcy this year	1 in 55
A piano player will eventually develop lower back pain	1 in 3
You will be killed on your *next* automobile outing	1 in 4 million
You will die in an automobile accident	1 in 5,000
Condom use will eventually fail to prevent pregnancy	1 in 10
An IUD will eventually fail to prevent pregnancy	1 in 10
Coitus interruptus will eventually fail to prevent pregnancy	1 in 5

(Adapted from Krantz, 1992)

Build with care *The chance of a construction worker being injured at work during the year is 1 in 27.*

(Boegels & Zigterman, 2000; Clark, 1999). One study found that 32 participants with this disorder held overblown beliefs that they would come to harm (Beck et al., 1974). Each person reported upsetting assumptions and images regarding such issues as physical injury, illness, or death; psychological dysfunctioning; failure and inability to cope; and rejection. Related studies have also found that people with generalized anxiety symptoms pay unusually close attention to threatening cues (Aikins & Craske, 2001; Mogg & Bradley, 1998).

What kinds of people are likely to have exaggerated expectations of danger? Some cognitive theorists point to those whose lives have been filled with *unpre-*

dictable negative events. These individuals become generally fearful of the unknown and always wait for the boom to drop (Ladouceur et al., 1998; Pekrun, 1992). To avoid being blindsided, they keep trying to predict new and unforeseeable negative events. They look everywhere for signs of danger, and they wind up seeing danger everywhere, thus setting up a life of anxiety. In support of this idea, studies have demonstrated that both animal and human subjects respond more fearfully to unpredictable negative events than to predictable ones (Mineka, 1985) and that people with generalized anxiety disorder worry much more about the future than others do (Dugas et al., 1998). However, researchers have yet to determine whether people with this disorder have, in fact, experienced an unusual number of unpredictable negative events in life.

COGNITIVE THERAPIES Two kinds of cognitive approaches are commonly used in cases of generalized anxiety disorder. In one, based on the theories of Ellis and Beck, therapists help clients change the maladaptive assumptions that are supposedly at the root of their disorders. In the other, therapists teach clients how to cope during stressful situations (see Figure 4-4).

CHANGING MALADAPTIVE ASSUMPTIONS In Ellis's technique of **rational-emotive therapy,** practitioners point out the irrational assumptions held by clients, suggest more appropriate assumptions, and assign homework that gives the individuals practice at challenging old assumptions and applying new ones (Ellis, 1999, 1995, 1962). Research has been limited, but studies do suggest that this approach brings at least modest relief to persons suffering from anxiety (Cowan & Brunero, 1997; Lipsky et al., 1980). The approach is illustrated in the following discussion between Ellis and an anxious client who fears failure and disapproval at work, especially over a testing procedure that she has developed for her company:

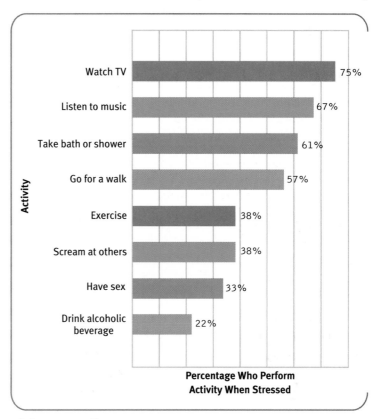

FIGURE 4-4 **What do people do to relieve stress?** *According to one large survey, most of us watch television or listen to music (Kanner, 1995).*

> *Client:* I'm so distraught these days that I can hardly concentrate on anything for more than a minute or two at a time. My mind just keeps wandering to that damn testing procedure I devised, and that they've put so much money into; and whether it's going to work well or be just a waste of all that time and money. . . .
>
> *Ellis:* Point one is that you must admit that you are telling yourself something to start your worrying going, and you must begin to look, and I mean really look, for the specific nonsense with which you keep reindoctrinating yourself. . . . The false statement is: "If, because my testing procedure doesn't work and I am functioning inefficiently on my job, my co-workers do not want me or approve of me, then I shall be a worthless person." . . .
>
> *Client:* But if I want to do what my firm also wants me to do, and I am useless to them, aren't I also useless to me?
>
> *Ellis:* No—not unless you think you are. You are frustrated, of course, if you want to set up a good testing procedure and you can't. But need you be desperately unhappy because you are frustrated? And need you deem yourself completely unworthwhile because you can't do one of the main things you want to do in life?
>
> *(Ellis, 1962, pp. 160-165)*

RATIONAL-EMOTIVE THERAPY A cognitive therapy developed by Albert Ellis which helps clients to identify and change the irrational assumptions and thinking that help cause their psychological disorder.

Beck's similar but more systematic approach, called, simply, *cognitive therapy,* is an adaptation of his influential and very effective treatment for depression

DELICIOUS DANGER

Some individuals overreact to danger, others underreact. In response to a public health warning about contaminated ice cream, 26 percent of the people who heard the warning refused to believe it, and 31 percent ate the ice cream anyway. Many of the latter became sick (Centers for Disease Control and Prevention, 1999).

(which is discussed in Chapter 6). Researchers are already finding that it and similar cognitive approaches often reduce generalized anxiety to more tolerable levels (Overholser & Nasser, 2000; DeRubeis & Crits-Christoph, 1998).

TEACHING CLIENTS TO COPE The clinical innovator Donald Meichenbaum (1997, 1993, 1992, 1977) has developed a cognitive technique for coping with stress called **self-instruction training,** or **stress inoculation training.** It teaches clients to rid themselves of the unpleasant thoughts that keep raising their anxiety during difficult situations (so-called *negative self-statements*) and replace them with *coping self-statements* instead.

In Meichenbaum's approach, people are taught coping self-statements that they can apply during four stages of a stressful situation—say, talking to their boss about a raise. First, they learn to say things to themselves that prepare them for the situation. Second, they learn self-statements that enable them to cope with the stressful situation as it is occurring—for instance, when they are actually in the boss's office. Third, they learn self-statements that will help them through the difficult moments when the situation seems to be going badly, as when the boss glares at them as they ask for more money. Finally, they learn to make self-congratulatory self-statements after they have coped effectively. Here are a few examples of the four kinds of self-statements:

Preparing for a Stressor
What is it you have to do?
You can develop a plan to deal with it.
Just think about what you can do about it. That's better than getting anxious.

Confronting and Handling a Stressor
Just psych yourself up—you can meet this challenge.
This tenseness can be an ally—a cue to cope.
Relax: you're in control. Take a slow, deep breath.

Coping with the Feeling of Being Overwhelmed
When fear comes, just pause.
Keep the focus on the present. What is it you have to do?
You should expect your fear to rise.
Don't try to eliminate fear totally. Just keep it manageable.

Reinforcing Self-Statements
It worked! You did it.
It wasn't as bad as you expected.
You made more out of your fear than it was worth.
Your damn ideas—that's the problem. When you control them, you control your fear.

SPEAKING UP

Apparently most of us talk out loud to ourselves at least occasionally. In one study, researchers bugged the room in which subjects were trying to solve various mental tasks. Fully 132 of the 133 subjects were discovered to be talking to themselves during the tasks! Nevertheless, half of the participants later denied doing so (Duncan et al., 1999).

Self-instruction training has proved to be of modest help in cases of generalized anxiety disorder and moderately helpful to people who suffer from test-taking and performance anxiety, stress associated with life change, and mild forms of anxiety (Rokke & Rehm, 2001; Meichenbaum, 1993, 1992, 1972). It has also been used with some success to help athletes compete better and to encourage people to behave less impulsively, control anger, and control pain (Meichenbaum, 1997, 1993; Novaco, 1977).

In view of the limited effectiveness of self-instruction training in treating generalized and other anxiety disorders, Meichenbaum (1972) himself has suggested that it should be combined with other treatments. In fact, anxious people treated with a combination of self-instruction training and Ellis's rational-emotive therapy improve more than people treated by either approach alone (Glogower, Fremouw, & McCroskey, 1978).

The Biological Perspective

Biological theorists believe that generalized anxiety disorder is caused chiefly by biological factors. For years this claim was supported primarily by **family pedigree studies,** in which researchers determine how many and which relatives of a person with a disorder have the same disorder. If biological tendencies toward generalized anxiety disorder are inherited, people who are biologically related should have similar probabilities of developing this disorder. Studies have in fact found that blood relatives of persons with generalized anxiety disorder are more likely than nonrelatives to have the disorder, too (Kendler et al., 1992; Carey & Gottesman, 1981) (see Table 4-2). Approximately 15 percent of the relatives of people with the disorder display it themselves—much more than the 4 percent found in the general population. And the closer the relative (an identical twin, for example, as opposed to a fraternal twin or other sibling), the greater the likelihood that he or she will also have the disorder (APA, 2000).

Table 4-2

Anxiety Disorders Profile

	ONE-YEAR PREVALENCE (%)	FEMALE:MALE RATIO	TYPICAL AGE AT ONSET	PREVALENCE AMONG CLOSE RELATIVES	PERCENTAGE RECEIVING TREATMENT
Generalized anxiety disorder	4.0%	2:1	0–20 years	Elevated	27%
Specific phobias	9.0	2:1	Variable	Elevated	12%
Social phobias	8.0	3:2	10–20 years	Elevated	21%

Source: Kessler et al., 2001, 1999, 1994; APA, 2000, 1994; Regier et al., 1993; Blazer et al., 1991; Davidson et al., 1991; Eaton et al., 1991.

Of course, investigators cannot have full confidence in biological interpretations of such studies. The findings could also be suggesting that generalized anxiety disorder is caused by environmental experiences. Because relatives are likely to share aspects of the same environment, their shared disorders may reflect similarities in environment and upbringing rather than similarities in biological makeup. The closer the relatives, the more similar their environmental experiences are likely to be (Kendler & Gardner, 1998). Because identical twins are more physically alike than fraternal twins, they may even experience more similarities in their upbringing (Tambs, Harris, & Magnus, 1995).

BIOLOGICAL EXPLANATIONS: GABA INACTIVITY In recent decades important discoveries by brain researchers have offered clearer evidence that generalized anxiety disorder is related to biological factors, in particular to biochemical dysfunction in the brain (Brawman-Mintzer & Lydiard, 1997). One of the first such discoveries occurred in the 1950s, when researchers determined that **benzodiazepines,** the family of drugs that includes *diazepam* (Valium) and *alprazolam* (Xanax), provide relief from anxiety. At first, no one understood why benzodiazepines reduce anxiety. Eventually, however, radioactive techniques were developed which enabled researchers to pinpoint the exact sites in the brain that are affected by benzodiazepines (Mohler & Okada, 1977; Squires & Braestrup, 1977). Apparently certain neurons have receptors that receive the benzodiazepines, just as a lock receives a key.

Investigators soon discovered that these benzodiazepine receptors ordinarily receive **gamma-aminobutyric acid (GABA),** a common and important neurotransmitter in the brain (Leonard, 1999; Costa et al., 1978, 1975). As we observed

SELF-INSTRUCTION TRAINING A cognitive treatment developed by Donald Meichenbaum which teaches clients to use coping self-statements at times of stress. Also known as *stress inoculation training.*

FAMILY PEDIGREE STUDY A research design in which investigators determine how many and which relatives of a person with a disorder have the same disorder.

BENZODIAZEPINES The most common group of antianxiety drugs, which includes Valium and Xanax.

GAMMA-AMINOBUTYRIC ACID (GABA) The neurotransmitter gamma-aminobutyric acid, whose low activity has been linked to generalized anxiety disorder.

in Chapter 2, neurotransmitters are chemicals that carry messages from one neuron to another. GABA carries *inhibitory* messages: when GABA is received at a receptor, it causes the neuron to stop firing.

On the basis of their findings, researchers have pieced together a scenario of how fear reactions occur. In normal fear reactions, key neurons throughout the brain fire more rapidly, triggering the firing of still more neurons and creating a general state of excitability throughout the brain and body. This state is experienced as fear or anxiety. After neuron firing continues for a while, it triggers a feedback system—that is, brain and body activities that reduce the level of excitability. Some neurons throughout the brain release the neurotransmitter GABA, which then binds to GABA receptors on certain neurons and instructs those neurons to stop firing. The state of excitability is thereby reduced, and the experience of fear or anxiety subsides (Sanders & Shekhar, 1995; Costa, 1985, 1983).

Researchers believe that a problem in this feedback system can cause fear or anxiety to go unchecked (Lloyd, Fletcher, & Minchin, 1992). In fact, when some investigators reduced GABA's ability to bind to GABA receptors, they found that animal subjects reacted with a rise in anxiety (Costa, 1985; Mohler, Richards, & Wu, 1981). This finding suggests that people with generalized anxiety disorder may have ongoing problems in their anxiety feedback system. Perhaps their brain supplies of GABA are too low. Perhaps they have too few GABA receptors, or their GABA receptors do not readily capture the neurotransmitter.

Do monkeys experience anxiety? *Clinical researchers must be careful in interpreting the reactions of animal subjects. This infant monkey was considered "fearful" after being separated from its mother. But perhaps it was feeling depression or another emotion, or experiencing a level of arousal that does not correspond to either human emotion.*

This explanation is promising, but it has problems. One is that recent biological discoveries have complicated the picture. It has been found, for example, that GABA is only one of several body chemicals that can bind to the important GABA receptors (Leonard, 1999; Guidotti & Costa, 1998). Could these other chemicals also be critical factors in the brain's control of anxiety? Another problem is that much of the research on the biology of anxiety has been done on laboratory animals. When researchers produce fear responses in animals, they assume that the animals are experiencing something similar to human anxiety, but it is impossible to be certain (Newman & Farley, 1995; Kalin, 1993). The animals may be experiencing a high level of arousal that is quite different from human anxiety.

Finally, biological theorists are faced with the problem of establishing a causal relationship. Although studies do tie physiological functioning to generalized anxiety disorder, they do not establish that the physiological events *cause* the disorder. The biological responses of anxious persons may be the result, rather than the cause, of their anxiety disorders. Perhaps long-term anxiety eventually leads to poorer GABA reception, for example.

BIOLOGICAL TREATMENTS The leading biological approach to treating generalized anxiety disorder is to prescribe *antianxiety drugs.* Indeed, it would be hard to find someone in our society who is not familiar with the words "tranquilizer," or "Valium." Other biological interventions are *relaxation training,* in which people learn to relax the muscles throughout their bodies, and *biofeedback,* in which clients learn to voluntarily control underlying biological processes that may be contributing to their problems.

ANTIANXIETY DRUGS Before the 1950s, a family of drugs labeled *barbiturates* were the major biological treatment for anxiety disorders (Miller, Klamen, & Costa, 1998; Ballenger, 1995). Because these drugs were used in low doses to calm people and in higher doses to help them fall asleep, they were generally known as **sedative-hypnotic drugs.** However, barbiturates created serious problems. They made people very drowsy, too high a dose could lead to death, and those who took them over a long period could become physically dependent on them. In the late 1940s a drug called *meprobamate* was developed and later released as a new

SEDATIVE-HYPNOTIC DRUGS Drugs that calm people at lower doses and help them to fall asleep at higher doses.

RELAXATION TRAINING A treatment procedure that teaches clients to relax at will so they can calm themselves in stressful situations.

kind of sedative-hypnotic medication under the brand name Mil-town (Cole & Yonkers, 1995; Berger, 1970). This drug was less dangerous and less addictive than barbiturates, but it still caused great drowsiness. Finally, in the late 1950s another group of an-tianxiety drugs called *benzodiazepines* was marketed (see Table 4-3). These drugs did not seem to produce as much tiredness as the others and were quickly embraced by both doctors and patients. Initially, the benzodiazepines were considered to be totally safe for use as sedative-hypnotics, and they soon became the most widely prescribed medications in the United States (Strange, 1992).

Only years later did investigators come to understand the rea-sons for the drugs' effectiveness. As we have observed, researchers eventually learned that specific neuron sites in the brain receive benzodiazepines (Mohler & Okada, 1977; Squires & Braestrup, 1977), and that these same receptor sites ordinarily receive the neurotransmitter GABA (Leonard, 1999; Sanders & Shekhar, 1995). Apparently, when benzodiazepines bind to these neuron re-ceptor sites, particularly those receptors known as *GABA-A recep-tors,* they increase the ability of GABA to bind to them as well, and so improve GABA's ability to stop neuron firing, slow bodily arousal, and reduce anxiety.

Benzodiazepines are prescribed for generalized anxiety disorder more than for most other kinds of anxiety disorders (Uhlenhuth et al., 1999, 1995). Controlled studies show that they do sometimes provide temporary and modest relief (Rickels et al., 2000). In recent years, however, clinicians have begun to realize the potential dangers of these drugs. First, when the medications are stopped, many persons' anxieties return as strong as ever. Second, we now know that people who take benzodiazepines in large doses for an extended time can become physically dependent on them. Third, the drugs can produce undesirable effects such as drowsiness, lack of coordination, mem-ory loss, depression, and aggressive behavior. Finally, although benzodiazepines are not directly harmful to the body, clinicians have learned that they do *poten-tiate,* or multiply, the effects of other substances, such as alcohol. Breathing can slow dangerously, sometimes fatally, if people on these antianxiety drugs drink even small amounts of alcohol (Miller, 1999; Elsesser et al., 1996).

Since the 1980s several other kinds of antianxiety drugs have been devel-oped which are now also available for people with generalized anxiety disor-der (Brawman-Mintzer, 2001). One of these drugs, *buspirone,* shows particular promise as a treatment for the disorder. Binding to a different set of receptors in the brain, this drug is often just as effective as benzodiazepines and may be less likely to lead to physical dependence (Schweizer & Rickels, 1997).

RELAXATION TRAINING A nonchemical biological technique commonly used to treat generalized anxiety disorder is **relaxation training.** The notion behind this approach is that physical relaxation will lead to a state of psychological relaxation. In one version, ther-apists teach clients to identify individual muscle groups, tense them, release the tension, and ultimately relax the whole body. With continued practice, they can bring on a state of deep muscle relaxation at will, reducing their anxiety during stress-ful situations.

Research indicates that relaxation training is more effective than no treatment or placebo treatment in cases of generalized anxiety disorder (DeRubeis & Crits-Christoph, 1998). The im-provement it produces, however, tends to be modest (Butler et al., 1991), and other techniques that are known to produce re-laxation, such as *meditation,* often seem to be equally effective (Kabat-Zinn et al., 1992). Relaxation training is of greatest

Table 4-3

Drugs That Reduce Anxiety

CLASS/GENERIC NAME	TRADE NAME
Benzodiazepines	
Alprazolam	Xanax
Chlordiazepoxide	Librium
Clonazepam	Klonopin
Clorazepate dipotassium	Tranxene
Diazepam	Valium
Lorazepam	Ativan
Oxazepam	Serax
Prazepam	Centrax
Azaspirones	
Buspirone	BuSpar
Beta blockers	
Propranolol	Inderal
Atenolol	Tenormin

Modern relaxation *At the Brain Mind Gym, busi-ness executives receive pulsations of light and sound from goggles and headphones, which are meant to lull their brains into deep relaxation.*

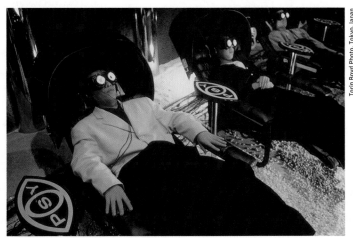

Torin Boyd Photo, Tokyo, Japan

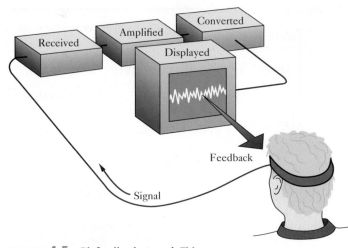

FIGURE 4-5 **Biofeedback at work** *This biofeedback system is recording tension in the forehead muscle of an anxious person. The system receives, amplifies, converts, and displays information about the tension, allowing the client to "observe" it and to try to reduce tension responses.*

Sprinkle lightly *In the early twentieth century, drug companies did not have to prove the safety or value of their products. Brain Salt, a patent medicine for anxiety and related difficulties, promised to cure nervous disability, headaches, indigestion, heart palpitations, and sleep problems.*

help to people with generalized anxiety disorder when it is combined with cognitive therapy or with biofeedback (Overholser & Nasser, 2000; Taylor, 1995).

BIOFEEDBACK In **biofeedback,** therapists use electrical signals from the body to train people to control physiological processes such as heart rate or muscle tension. Clients are connected to a monitor that gives them continuous information about their bodily activities. By attending to the therapist's instructions and the signals from the monitor, they may gradually learn to control even seemingly involuntary physiological processes.

The most widely applied method of biofeedback for the treatment of anxiety uses a device called an **electromyograph (EMG),** which provides feedback about the level of muscular tension in the body. Electrodes are attached to the client's muscles—usually the forehead muscles—where they detect the minute electrical activity that accompanies muscle tension (see Figure 4-5). The device then converts electric potentials coming from the muscles into an image, such as lines on a screen, or into a tone whose pitch changes along with changes in muscle tension. Thus clients "see" or "hear" when their muscles are becoming more or less tense. Through repeated trial and error, the individuals become skilled at voluntarily reducing muscle tension and, theoretically, at reducing tension and anxiety in everyday stressful situations. Research indicates that EMG biofeedback training helps both normal and anxious subjects reduce their anxiety somewhat (Rice, Blanchard, & Purcell, 1993). According to direct comparisons, this approach and relaxation training have similar effects on anxiety levels (Brown, Hertz, & Barlow, 1992).

In the 1960s and 1970s, many hailed biofeedback training as an approach that would change clinical treatment. So far, however, the approach has had its greatest impact when it plays an *adjunct* role in the treatment of certain medical problems, including headaches, back pain, gastrointestinal disorders, seizure disorders, and such neuromuscular disorders as cerebral palsy (Andrasik, 2000; Newton et al., 1995).

SUMMING UP | **Generalized Anxiety Disorder**

People with generalized anxiety disorder experience excessive anxiety and worry about numerous events or activities. Various explanations and treatments for this disorder have received only limited research support, although recent cognitive and biological approaches seem to be promising.

The Sociocultural Perspective According to the sociocultural view, increases in societal dangers and pressures may create a climate in which cases of generalized anxiety disorder are more likely to develop.

The Psychodynamic Perspective Freud said that generalized anxiety disorder may develop when defense mechanisms break down and function poorly. Psychodynamic therapists use free association, interpretation, and related psychodynamic techniques to help people overcome this problem.

The Humanistic and Existential Perspectives Carl Rogers, the leading humanistic theorist, believed that people with generalized anxiety disorder failed to receive unconditional positive regard from key persons during their childhood and so become overly critical of themselves. He applied client-centered therapy to such individuals.

Existentialists believe that generalized anxiety disorder results from the existential anxiety people experience because they know that life is limited and suspect it may have no meaning. Existential therapists help anxious people take more responsibility and live more meaningfully.

The Cognitive Perspective Cognitive theorists believe that generalized anxiety disorder is caused by maladaptive assumptions that lead persons to view most life situations as dangerous. Cognitive therapists help these individuals change such assumptions, and they teach them how to cope during stressful situations.

The Biological Perspective Biological theorists argue that generalized anxiety disorder results from low activity of the neurotransmitter GABA. The most common biological treatment is antianxiety drugs, particularly benzodiazepines. Relaxation training and biofeedback are also applied in many cases.

BIOFEEDBACK A treatment technique in which a client is given information about physiological reactions as they occur and learns to control the reactions voluntarily.

ELECTROMYOGRAPH (EMG) A device that provides feedback about the level of muscular tension in the body.

PHOBIA A persistent and unreasonable fear of a particular object, activity, or situation.

SPECIFIC PHOBIA A severe and persistent fear of a specific object or situation (excluding agoraphobia and social phobia).

SOCIAL PHOBIA A severe and persistent fear of social or performance situations in which embarrassment may occur.

AGORAPHOBIA A severe and persistent fear of venturing into public places, especially when one is alone.

Phobias

A **phobia** (from the Greek for "fear") is a persistent and unreasonable fear of a particular object, activity, or situation. People with a phobia become fearful if they even think about the object or situation they dread, but they usually remain comfortable as long as they avoid the object or thoughts about it. Most are well aware that their fears are excessive and unreasonable. Some have no idea how their fears started.

We all have our areas of special fear, and it is normal for some things to upset us more than other things, perhaps even different things at different stages of our lives. A survey of residents of a community in Burlington, Vermont, found that fears of crowds, death, injury, illness, and separation were more common among people in their 60s than in other age groups (Agras, Sylvester, & Oliveau, 1969). Among 20-year-olds, fears of snakes, heights, storms, enclosures, and social situations were much more common.

How do these common fears differ from phobias? DSM-IV indicates that a phobia is more intense and persistent and the desire to avoid the object or situation is greater (APA, 2000, 1994). People with phobias feel such distress that their fears may interfere dramatically with their personal, social, or occupational lives.

Phobias are common in our society. Surveys suggest that 10 to 11 percent of the adults in the United States suffer from one in any given year, and more than 14 percent develop a phobia at some point in their lives (Magee et al., 1996; Regier et al., 1993). The disorder is more than twice as common in women as in men.

Most phobias technically fall under the category of **specific phobias,** DSM-IV's label for a marked and persistent fear of a specific object or situation. In addition, there are two broader kinds of phobias: **social phobia,** a fear of social or performance situations in which embarrassment may occur; and **agoraphobia,** a fear of venturing into public places, especially when one is alone.

Research indicates that agoraphobia is usually, perhaps always, experienced in conjunction with *panic attacks,* unpredictable attacks of terror that we shall be observing in Chapter 5 (Beck & Weishaar, 1995). People who experience such attacks become fearful of experiencing them again and develop a fear of visiting public places, where the attacks are more likely to occur or where escape from the attacks might be difficult. Because panic is the key feature of agoraphobia, we shall examine this kind of phobia in the next chapter within the discussion of panic disorders, and limit our present discussion to specific phobias and social phobias.

Specific Phobias

As we have observed, a specific phobia is a persistent fear of a specific object or situation (see Table 4-4). When sufferers are exposed to the object or situation, they typically experience

---

Table 4-4 **DSM-IV Checklist**

SPECIFIC PHOBIA

1. Marked and persistent fear of a specific object or situation that is excessive or unreasonable, lasting at least six months.
2. Immediate anxiety usually produced by exposure to the object.
3. Recognition that the fear is excessive or unreasonable.
4. Avoidance of the feared situation.
5. Significant distress or impairment.

Based on APA, 2000, 1994.

immediate fear. Common specific phobias are intense fears of specific animals or insects, heights, enclosed spaces, thunderstorms, and blood. Here are a few first-hand descriptions (all in Melville, 1978):

SPIDERS (ARACHNOPHOBIA)

Seeing a spider makes me rigid with fear, hot, trembling and dizzy. I have occasionally vomited and once fainted in order to escape from the situation. These symptoms last three or four days after seeing a spider. Realistic pictures can cause the same effect, especially if I inadvertently place my hand on one. (p. 44)

THUNDER AND LIGHTNING (BRONTOPHOBIA)

At the end of March each year, I start getting agitated because summer is coming and that means thunderstorms. I have been afraid since my early twenties, but the last three years have been the worst. I have such a heartbeat that for hours after a storm my whole left side is painful. . . . I say I will stay in the room, but when it comes I am a jelly, reduced to nothing. I have a little cupboard and I go there, I press my eyes so hard I can't see for about an hour, and if I sit in the cupboard over an hour my husband has to straighten me up. (p. 104)

FLYING (AEROPHOBIA)

We got on board, and then there was the take-off. There it was again, that horrible feeling as we gathered speed. It was creeping over me again, that old feeling of panic. I kept seeing everyone as puppets, all strapped to their seats with no control over their destinies, me included. Every time the plane did a variation of speed or route, my heart would leap and I would hurriedly ask what was happening. When the plane started to lose height, I was terrified that we were about to crash. (p. 59)

Each year as many as 9 percent of the people in the United States have the symptoms of a specific phobia (APA, 2000; Kessler & Zhao, 1999). Eleven percent develop such phobias at some time during their lives, and many people have more than one at a time. Among people with this disorder, women outnumber men by at least 2 to 1 (Fredrikson et al., 1996).

The impact of a specific phobia on a person's life depends on what arouses the fear. Some things are easier to avoid than others. People whose phobias center on dogs, insects, or water will keep encountering the objects they dread. Their efforts to avoid them must be elaborate and may greatly restrict their activities. People with snake phobias have a much easier time. As we saw in Table 4-2, the vast majority of people with a specific phobia—almost 90 percent of them—do not seek treatment. They try instead to avoid the objects they fear (Bienvenu & Eaton, 1998; Regier et al., 1993).

Specific phobias can develop at any time of life, although some, such as animal phobias, tend to begin during childhood and may disappear on their own before adulthood (APA, 2000). Phobias that last into or begin during adulthood tend to hold on stubbornly and usually lessen only under treatment.

Social Phobias

Many people worry about interacting with others or talking or performing in front of others. The opera singer Maria Callas, for example, would shake with fear before going onstage (Marks, 1987). Such normal social fears are inconvenient, but the people who have them manage to function adequately, some at a very high level.

People with a social phobia, by contrast, have severe, persistent, and unreasonable fears of social or performance situations in which embarrassment may occur (see Table 4-5). A social phobia may be *narrow*, such as a fear of talking or

---

SPIDERS UNDER STRESS

Many people feel threatened by spiders, but what about when the tables are turned? Some species of tarantulas pluck hairs from their stomach and propel them like darts toward any creature that frightens them, causing the creature to itch.

A REALITY CHECK

The odds of being in a plane crash are 1 in 700,000 and of being killed in a plane crash 1 in 25 million.

"Imagine being allergic to people"

Title for a 1999 campaign to heighten awareness of social phobias performing in public, eating in public, using a public bathroom, or writing in front of others, or it may be a *broader* fear of social situations, such as a general fear of functioning inadequately in front of others (Norton et al., 1997). In both forms, people repeatedly judge themselves as performing less adequately than they actually do (Cox et al., 2000).

A social phobia can interfere greatly with one's life (Stein et al., 1999, 1994). A person who is unable to interact with others or speak in public may fail to perform important responsibilities. One who cannot eat in public may reject dinner invitations and other social opportunities. Since most people with this phobia keep their fears secret, their social reluctance is often misinterpreted as snobbery, lack of interest, or hostility.

As many as 8 percent of the population—around three women for every two men—experience a social phobia in any given year (Kessler & Zhao, 1999). The disorder often begins in late childhood or adolescence and may persist for many years, although its intensity may fluctuate (Regier et al., 1998).

Table 4-5 DSM-IV Checklist

SOCIAL PHOBIA

1. Marked and persistent fear of social or performance situations involving exposure to unfamiliar people or possible scrutiny by others, lasting at least six months. Concern about humiliating or embarrassing oneself.
2. Anxiety usually produced by exposure to the social situation.
3. Recognition that the fear is excessive or unreasonable.
4. Avoidance of feared situations.
5. Significant distress or impairment.

Based on APA, 2000, 1994.

What Causes Phobias?

Each of the models offers explanations for phobias. Freud's psychodynamic explanation was once the most influential, but today evidence tends to support the behavioral explanations.

PSYCHODYNAMIC EXPLANATIONS Freud believed that phobias result when people make excessive use of *repression* and *displacement* to control underlying anxiety. The first of these defense mechanisms buries anxiety-producing impulses deep in the unconscious, and the second transfers them to more neutral objects or situations that are easier to cope with and control. Although the new objects of fear may be related to the threatening impulses, the person is not aware of the relationship.

Consider Freud's famous case study of Little Hans, a 4-year-old child who seemed suddenly to develop an extreme fear of horses. Freud (1909) argued that the seeds for this phobia were sown months before its onset. When Hans was 3 years old, he had begun to express sexual feelings toward his mother by handling his penis and asking his mother to place her finger on it. She responded with a threat to cut off his penis and emphasized that his desires were totally improper. According to Freud, this threat so frightened Hans that he became unconsciously afraid that his father, too, would learn of his desires and castrate him. However, Hans did not consciously fear his id impulses, his mother, or his father; rather, he *repressed* the impulses and *displaced* his fears onto a neutral object—horses. Hans unconsciously chose horses, Freud maintained, because he had come to associate them with his father.

Freud's explanation of phobias, like his explanation of generalized anxiety disorder, has received little research support over the years. The same is true of more contemporary psychodynamic theories and of humanistic, cognitive, and biological explanations. In contrast, the explanations developed by *behavioral theorists* have received considerable research support and are today the most influential in the clinical field.

BEHAVIORAL EXPLANATIONS Behaviorists believe that people with phobias first learn to fear certain objects, situations, or events through conditioning (Field & Davey, 2001). Once the fears are acquired, the individuals avoid the dreaded object or situation, permitting the fears to become all the more locked in.

PROPER CREDIT

The oft-cited psychodynamic concept known as the *inferiority complex* was developed by Alfred Adler, not Freud.

WHAT ABOUT MY FEARS?

BEWARE OF DOG

HOW ARE FEARS LEARNED? Behaviorists propose **classical conditioning** as a common way of acquiring fear reactions to objects or situations that are not really dangerous. Here, two events that occur close together in time become closely associated in a person's mind, and, as we saw in Chapter 2, the person then reacts similarly to both of them. If one event triggers a fear response, the other may also.

In the 1920s a clinician described the case of a young woman who apparently acquired a phobia of running water through classical conditioning (Bagby, 1922). As a child of 7 she went on a picnic with her mother and aunt and ran off by herself into the woods after lunch. While she was climbing over some large rocks, her feet were caught between two of them. The harder she tried to free herself, the more trapped she became. No one heard her screams, and she grew more and more terrified. In the language of behaviorists, the entrapment was eliciting a fear response:

A CLOSER LOOK

Phobias, Familiar and Not So Familiar

Air—*aerophobia*
Animals—*zoophobia*
Beards—*pogonophobia*
Being afraid—*phobophobia*
Blood—*hematophobia*
Books—*bibliophobia*
Children—*pediophobia*
Churches—*ecclesiaphobia*
Corpse—*necrophobia*
Crossing a bridge—*gephyrophobia*
Crowds—*ochlophobia*
Darkness—*achluophobia, nyctophobia*
Daylight—*phengophobia*
Demons or devils—*demonophobia*
Dogs—*cynophobia*
Dolls—*pediophobia*
Drugs—*pharmacophobia*
Enclosed space—*claustrophobia*
Eyes—*ommatophobia*
Feces—*coprophobia*
Fire—*pyrophobia*
Flood—*antlophobia*
Flowers—*anthophobia*
Flying—*aerophobia*
Fog—*homichlophobia*
Fur—*doraphobia*
Germs—*spermophobia*
Ghosts—*phasmophobia*
God—*theophobia*
Graves—*taphophobia*
Heat—*thermophobia*
Heights—*acrophobia*

Homosexuality—*homophobia*
Horses—*hippophobia*
Human beings—*anthropophobia*
Ice, frost—*cryophobia*
Insects—*entomophobia*
Machinery—*mechanophobia*
Marriage—*gamophobia*
Meat—*carnophobia*
Mice—*musophobia*
Mirrors—*eisoptrophobia*
Missiles—*ballistophobia*
Money—*chrometrophobia*
Night—*nyctophobia*
Noise or loud talking—*phonophobia*
Odors—*osmophobia*
Odors (body)—*osphresiophobia*

Pleasure—*hedonophobia*
Poison—*toxiphobia*
Poverty—*peniaphobia*
Pregnancy—*maieusiophobia*
Railways—*siderodromophobia*
Rain—*ombrophobia*
Rivers—*potamophobia*
Robbers—*harpaxophobia*
Satan—*Satanophobia*
Sexual intercourse—*coitophobia, cypridophobia*
Shadows—*sciophobia*
Sharp objects—*belonophobia*
Skin—*dermatophobia*
Sleep—*hypnophobia*
Snakes—*ophidiophobia*
Snow—*chionophobia*
Speed—*tachophobia*
Spiders—*arachnophobia*
Stings—*cnidophobia*
Strangers—*xenophobia*
Sun—*heliophobia*
Surgery—*ergasiophobia*
Teeth—*odontophobia*
Travel—*hodophobia*
Trees—*dendrophobia*
Wasps—*spheksophobia*
Water—*hydrophobia*
Wind—*anemophobia*
Worms—*helminthophobia*
Wounds, injury—*traumatophobia*
Writing—*graphophobia*

Michael Melford

Ophidiophobia *A fear of snakes is one of the most common specific phobias.*

(Melville, 1978, pp. 196–202)

Entrapment → Fear response

As she struggled to free her feet, the girl heard a waterfall nearby. The sound of the running water became linked in her mind to her terrifying battle with the rocks, and she developed a fear of running water as well.

Running water → Fear response

Eventually the aunt found the screaming child, freed her from the rocks, and comforted her; but psychological damage had been done. From that day forward, the girl was terrified of running water. For years family members had to hold her down to bathe her. When she traveled on a train, friends had to cover the windows so that she would not have to look at any streams. The young woman had apparently acquired a phobia through classical conditioning.

In conditioning terms, the entrapment was an *unconditioned stimulus (US)* that understandably elicited an *unconditioned response (UR)* of fear. The running water represented a *conditioned stimulus (CS),* a formerly neutral stimulus that became associated with entrapment in the child's mind and came also to elicit a fear reaction. The newly acquired fear was a *conditioned response (CR).*

US: Entrapment → UR: Fear

CS: Running water → CR: Fear

Another way of acquiring a fear reaction is through **modeling;** that is, through observation and imitation (Bandura & Rosenthal, 1966). A person may observe that others are afraid of certain objects or events and develop fears of the same things. Consider a young boy whose mother is afraid of illnesses, doctors, and hospitals. If she frequently states those fears, before long the boy himself may fear illnesses, doctors, and hospitals.

Why should one upsetting experience develop into a long-term phobia? Shouldn't the trapped girl later have seen that running water would bring her no harm? Shouldn't the boy later see that illnesses are temporary and doctors and hospitals helpful? Behaviorists believe that after acquiring a fear response, people try to *avoid* what they fear. Whenever they find themselves near a fearsome object, they quickly move away. They may also plan ahead to ensure that such encounters will not occur. Remember that the girl had friends cover the windows on trains so that she could avoid looking at streams. People with phobias do not get close to the dreaded objects often enough to learn that they are really harmless.

Behaviorists also propose that specific learned fears will blossom into a generalized anxiety disorder when a person acquires a large number of them. This development is presumed to come about through **stimulus generalization:** responses to one stimulus are also produced by similar stimuli. The fear of running water acquired by the girl in the rocks could have generalized to such similar stimuli as milk being poured into a glass or even the sound of bubbly music. Perhaps a person experiences a series of upsetting events, each event produces one or more feared stimuli, and the person's reactions to each of these stimuli generalize to yet other stimuli. That person may then build up a large number of fears and eventually develop generalized anxiety disorder.

HOW HAVE BEHAVIORAL EXPLANATIONS FARED IN RESEARCH? Some laboratory studies have found that animals and humans can indeed be taught to fear objects through classical conditioning (Miller, 1948; Mowrer, 1947, 1939). In one famous

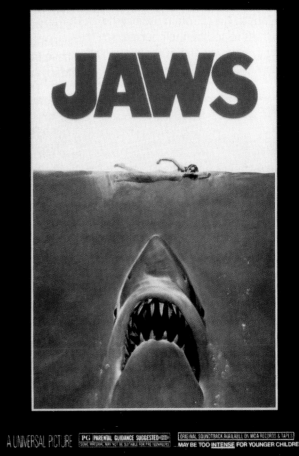

When in Southern California visit **UNIVERSAL STUDIOS TOUR** AN MCA COMPANY

The terrifying motion picture from the terrifying No. 1 best seller.

JAWS

A UNIVERSAL PICTURE | PG PARENTAL GUIDANCE SUGGESTED | ORIGINAL SOUNDTRACK AVAILABLE ON MCA RECORDS & TAPES | ...MAY BE TOO INTENSE FOR YOUNGER CHILDREN

The Everett Collection

Viewer beware *When people observe others (models) cower from or do battle with a threatening object or situation, they themselves may develop a fear of the object. Steven Spielberg's film* Jaws *led to heightened fears of sharks around the world.*

CLASSICAL CONDITIONING A process of learning in which two events that repeatedly occur close together in time become tied together in a person's mind and so produce the same response.

MODELING A process of learning in which a person observes and then imitates others. Also, a therapy approach based on the same principle.

STIMULUS GENERALIZATION A phenomenon in which responses to one stimulus are also produced by similar stimuli.

Sour Notes

Two of every ten orchestra musicians in Great Britain use psychotropic drugs to soothe their nerves, according to a survey of 1,600 professional musicians (Hall, 1997). Overall, 22 percent of the musicians report long stretches of anxiety, and 28 percent experience depression. Around 40 percent have trouble sleeping through the night. Many hyperventilate.

Three-quarters of the surveyed musicians are so anxious about performing that it affects their playing. As a result, one in ten takes *beta blockers,* drugs that are believed to help performance by slowing the heartbeat and stopping shaking. Around 6 percent drink alcohol before a performance.

Paulo Fridman/Gamma Liaison

ConsiderThis

◉ Why do so many professional performers seem particularly prone to social anxiety? • Is it possible that in many cases their fears of performing preceded their choice of profession?

ConsiderThis

◉ Today's human-subject review boards probably would not permit Watson and Rayner to conduct their study on Little Albert. What concerns might they raise about the procedure? • Do these concerns outweigh the insights gained from this study?

FAMOUS MOVIE PHOBIAS

Fear of snakes (*Indiana Jones*), illness (*Hannah and Her Sisters*), the outside world (*Copycat*), social situations (*Annie Hall*), flying (*Rain Man*), heights (*Vertigo*), the color red (*Marnie*), enclosed spaces (*Body Double*).

report, the psychologists John B. Watson and Rosalie Rayner (1920) described how they taught a baby boy called Little Albert to fear white rats. For weeks Albert was allowed to play with a white rat and appeared to enjoy doing so. One time when Albert reached for the rat, however, the experimenter struck a steel bar with a hammer, making a very loud noise that upset and frightened Albert. The next several times that Albert reached for the rat, the experimenter again made the loud noise. Albert acquired a fear and avoidance response to the rat. As Watson (1930) described it, "The instant the rat was shown, the baby began to cry . . . and began to crawl away so rapidly that he was caught with difficulty before he reached the edge of the mattress" (p. 161).

Research has also supported the behavioral position that fears can be acquired through modeling. The psychologists Albert Bandura and Theodore Rosenthal (1966), for example, had human subjects observe a person apparently being shocked by electricity whenever a buzzer sounded. The victim was actually the experimenter's accomplice—in research terminology, a *confederate*—who pretended to be in pain by twitching and yelling whenever the buzzer went on. After the unsuspecting subjects had observed several such episodes, they themselves experienced a fear reaction whenever they heard the buzzer.

Although these studies support behaviorists' explanations of phobias, other research has called those explanations into question (Graham & Gaffan, 1997). Several laboratory studies with children and adults have failed to condition fear reactions (Hallam & Rachman, 1976). In addition, although many case studies trace phobias to possible incidents of classical conditioning or modeling, quite a few fail to do so (King, Eleonora, & Ollendick, 1998). So, although it appears that a phobia *can* be acquired by classical conditioning or modeling, researchers have not established that the disorder is *ordinarily* acquired in this way.

A BEHAVIORAL-BIOLOGICAL EXPLANATION Some phobias are much more common than others (see Figure 4-6). Phobic reactions to animals, heights, and darkness are more common than phobic reactions to meat, grass, and houses. Behaviorists often account for this by proposing that human beings, as a species, have a *predisposition* to develop certain fears (Ohman & Soares, 1993; Seligman, 1971). This idea is referred to as **preparedness,** because human beings, theoretically, are "prepared" to acquire some phobias and not others. The following case description by I. M. Marks (1977) makes the point:

A four-year-old girl was playing in the park. Thinking that she saw a snake, she ran to her parents' car and jumped inside, slamming the door behind her. Unfortunately, the girl's hand was caught by the closing car door, the results of which were severe pain and several visits to the doctor. Before this, she may have been afraid of snakes, but not phobic. After this experience, a phobia developed, not of cars or car doors, but of snakes. The snake phobia persisted into adulthood, at which time she sought treatment from me. (p. 192)

In a series of tests of preparedness, the psychologist Arne Ohman and his colleagues have conditioned different kinds of fears in two groups of human subjects (Ohman & Soares, 1993; Ohman, Erixon, & Lofberg, 1975). In one study they showed all subjects slides of faces, houses, snakes, and spiders. One group received electric shocks whenever they observed the slides of faces and houses, while the other group received shocks when they looked at snakes and spiders. Were subjects more prepared to fear snakes and spiders? Using skin reactions, or *galvanic skin responses (GSRs)*, as a measure of fear, the experimenters found that both groups learned to fear the intended objects after repeated shock pairings. But then they noted an interesting distinction: after a short shock-free period, the persons who had learned to fear faces and houses stopped registering high GSRs in the presence of those objects, but the persons who had learned to fear snakes and spiders continued to show high GSRs in response to them for a long while. One interpretation is that animals and insects are stronger inducers of human phobias than faces or houses.

Researchers do not know whether human predispositions to fear are the result of biological or environmental factors (Poulton et al., 2001). Those who believe in a biological predisposition argue that a tendency to fear has been transmitted genetically through the evolutionary process. Among our ancestors, the ones who more readily acquired a fear of animals, darkness, heights, and the like were more likely to survive long enough to reproduce. Theorists who believe in an environmental predisposition argue instead that experiences teach us early in life that certain objects are legitimate sources of fear, and this training predisposes many people to acquire corresponding phobias.

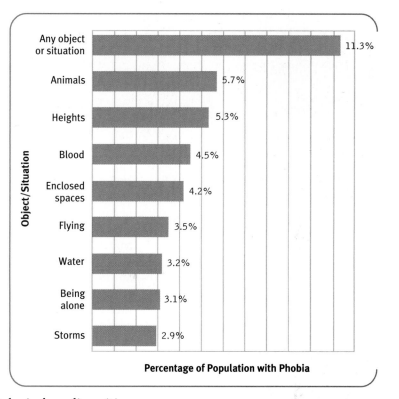

FIGURE 4-6   How common are the specific phobias? *Over the course of their lives, 11.3 percent of people in the United States develop a specific phobia. The most common ones are fears of certain animals and of heights. Most sufferers experience more than one specific phobia. (Adapted from Curtis et al., 1998.)*

How Are Phobias Treated?

Every theoretical model has its own approach to treating phobias, but behavioral techniques are more widely used than the rest, particularly for specific phobias. Research has shown them to be highly effective and to fare better than other approaches in most head-to-head comparisons (Ollendick & King, 1998). Thus we shall focus primarily on the behavioral treatments.

TREATMENTS FOR SPECIFIC PHOBIAS Specific phobias were among the first anxiety disorders to be treated successfully in clinical practice. The major behavioral approaches to treating them are *desensitization, flooding,* and *modeling.* Together, these approaches are called **exposure treatments,** because in all of them individuals are exposed to the objects or situations they dread.

People treated by **systematic desensitization,** a technique developed by Joseph Wolpe (1997, 1987, 1969), learn to relax while gradually facing the objects or situations they fear. Since relaxation and fear are incompatible, the new

PREPAREDNESS A predisposition to develop certain fears.

EXPOSURE TREATMENTS Behavioral treatments in which persons are exposed to the objects or situations they dread.

SYSTEMATIC DESENSITIZATION A behavioral treatment that uses relaxation training and a fear hierarchy to help clients with phobias react calmly to the objects or situations they dread.

Conquering coasterphobia *Missing out on thousands of dollars each year because many persons are afraid of riding on roller coasters, some amusement parks offer behavioral programs to help customers overcome their fears. After "treatment," some clients are able to ride the rails with the best of them. For others, it's back to the relative calm of the Ferris wheel.*

SNAKE DATA

The most dangerous snake in the world is the black mamba, whose bite kills in 95 of 100 cases. The cobra death rate is 18 to 35 percent, depending on the particular type, and the tropical rattlesnake death rate is 18 percent (Ash, 1999).

relaxation response is thought to substitute for the fear response. Desensitization therapists first offer *relaxation training* to clients, teaching them to release all tension from their bodies. With continued practice, the clients are able to bring on a state of deep muscle relaxation at will. In addition, the therapists help clients create a **fear hierarchy,** a list of objects or situations in which the phobia is aroused. The items on the list are ranked from ones that produce only a trace of fear to those that the person finds extremely frightening.

Then clients learn how to pair relaxation with the objects or situations they fear. While the client is in a state of relaxation, the therapist has the client face the event at the bottom of his or her hierarchy. This may be an actual confrontation, a process called *in vivo desensitization.* A person who fears heights, for example, may stand on a chair or climb a stepladder. Or the confrontation may be imagined, a process called *covert desensitization.* In this case, the person imagines the frightening event while the therapist describes it. The client moves through the entire list, pairing his or her relaxation responses with each feared item. Because the first item is only mildly frightening, it is usually only a short while before the person is able to relax totally in its presence. Over the course of several sessions, clients move up the ladder of their fears until they reach and overcome the one that frightens them most of all.

Another behavioral treatment for specific phobias is **flooding.** Flooding therapists believe that people will stop fearing things when they are exposed to them repeatedly and made to see that they are actually harmless. Clients are forced to face their feared objects or situations without relaxation training and without a gradual buildup. The flooding procedure, like desensitization, can be either in vivo or covert.

When flooding therapists guide clients in imagining feared objects or situations, they often exaggerate the description so that the clients experience intense emotional arousal. In the case of a woman with a snake phobia, the therapist had her imagine the following scene, among others:

> Close your eyes again. Picture the snake out in front of you, now make yourself pick it up. Reach down, pick it up, put it in your lap, feel it wiggling around in your lap, leave your hand on it, put your hand out and feel it wiggling around. Kind of explore its body with your fingers and hand. You don't like to do it, make yourself do it. Make yourself do it. Really grab onto the snake. Squeeze it a little bit, feel it. Feel it kind of start to wind around your hand. Let it. Leave your hand there, feel it touching your hand and winding around it, curling around your wrist.
>
> *(Hogan, 1968, pp. 423-431)*

In *modeling,* it is the therapist who confronts the feared object or situation while the fearful person observes (Bandura, 1977, 1971; Bandura, Adams, & Beyer, 1977). The behavioral therapist acts as a model, to demonstrate that the person's fear is groundless. After several sessions many clients are able to approach the objects or situations with composure. In one version of modeling, *participant modeling,* the client is actively encouraged to join in with the therapist.

Clinical researchers have repeatedly found that exposure treatments help with specific phobias (Larkin & Zvolensky, 2001; McGlynn et al., 1999). The key to success in all these therapies appears to be *actual* contact with the feared object or situation (Hellström & Öst, 1996). In vivo desensitization is more effective than covert desensitization, in vivo flooding more effective than covert flooding, and participant modeling more helpful than strictly observational modeling (Menzies & Clarke, 1993). Many behavioral therapists now combine features of each of the exposure approaches.

TREATMENTS FOR SOCIAL PHOBIAS Clinicians have only recently begun to have much success in treating social phobias (Heimberg, 2001; Heimberg et al., 1998). This progress is due in part to the growing recognition that social phobias have two separate features that may feed upon each other: (1) people with the phobias may have overwhelming social fears, and (2) they may lack skill at initiating conversations, communicating their needs, or meeting the needs of others. Armed with this insight, clinicians now treat social phobias by trying to reduce social fears or by providing training in social skills, or both.

HOW CAN SOCIAL FEARS BE REDUCED? Unlike specific phobias, which do not typically respond to psychotropic drugs, social fears are often helped through medication (Schneier, 2001). Somewhat surprisingly, it is antidepressant medications that seem to be most useful for this disorder, often more helpful than benzodiazepines or other kinds of antianxiety drugs (Rivas-Vazquez, 2001). At the same time, several types of psychotherapy have proved at least as effective as medication at reducing social fears. Moreover, people helped by such psychological treatments are apparently less likely to relapse than people treated with drugs alone (Liebowitz et al., 1999, 1997; Davidson, 1998). This finding suggests to some clinicians that the psychological approaches should always be included in the treatment of social fears.

One psychological approach is exposure therapy (DeRubeis & Crits-Christoph, 1998), the behavioral treatment so effective with specific phobias. Exposure therapists guide, encourage, and persuade clients with social fears to expose themselves to the dreaded social situations and to remain until their fears subside. Usually the exposure is gradual, and it is often coupled with homework assignments (Edelman & Chambless, 1995). Group therapy provides an ideal setting for exposure treatments by allowing people to face the social situations they fear in an atmosphere of support and concern (Scholing & Emmelkamp, 1999, 1996). In one group, a man who was afraid that his hands would tremble in the presence of others had to write on a blackboard in front of the group and serve tea to the other members (Emmelkamp, 1982).

Cognitive therapies have also been widely used to treat social fears, often in combination with behavioral techniques (Heimberg, 2001; Turk et al., 1999). In the following discussion, Albert Ellis uses rational-emotive therapy to help a man who fears he will be rejected if he speaks up at gatherings. The discussion took place after the man had done a homework assignment in which he was to observe his self-defeating thoughts and beliefs and force himself to say anything he had on his mind in social situations, no matter how stupid it might seem to him:

> After two weeks of this assignment, the patient came into his next session of therapy and reported: "I did what you told me to do. . . . [Every] time, just as you said, I found myself retreating from people, I said to myself: 'Now, even though you can't see it, there must be some sentences. What are they?' And I finally found them. And there were many of them! And they all seemed to say the same thing."
> "What thing?"
> "That I, uh, was going to be rejected. . . . [If] I related to them I was going to be rejected. And wouldn't that be perfectly awful if I was to be rejected. And there was no reason for me, uh, to take that, uh, sort of thing, and be rejected in that awful manner." . . .
> "And did you do the second part of the homework assignment?"
> "The forcing myself to speak up and express myself?"

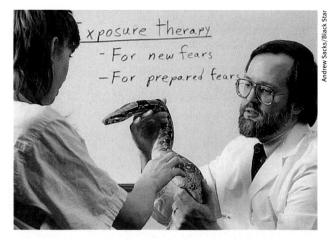

Participant modeling *In the exposure technique of participant modeling, a therapist treats a client with a snake phobia by first handling a snake himself, then encouraging the client to touch and handle it.*

FAMOUS VICTIM OF SOCIAL ANXIETY

Although the poet Emily Dickinson wrote movingly about love, she was not able to interact comfortably with people. She sometimes spoke to her visitors from an adjoining room rather than talking to them face to face (Asimov, 1997).

FEAR HIERARCHY A list of objects or situations that frighten a person, starting with those that are slightly feared and ending with those that are feared greatly.

FLOODING A treatment for phobias in which clients are exposed repeatedly and intensively to a feared object and made to see that it is actually harmless.

SOCIAL SKILLS TRAINING A therapy approach that helps people learn or improve social skills and assertiveness through role playing and rehearsing of desirable behaviors.

"Yes, that part."

"That was worse. That was really hard. Much harder than I thought it would be. But I did it."

"And?"

"Oh, not bad at all. I spoke up several times; more than I've ever done before. Some people were very surprised. Phyllis was very surprised, too. But I spoke up." . . .

"And how did you feel after expressing yourself like that?"

"Remarkable! I don't remember when I last felt this way. I felt, uh, just remarkable—good, that is. It was really something to feel! But it was so hard. I almost didn't make it. And a couple of other times during the week I had to force myself again. But I did. And I was glad!"

(Ellis, 1962, pp. 202–203)

Studies indicate that rational-emotive therapy and similar cognitive approaches help reduce social fears (Heimberg, 2001; Cameron et al., 1999). And these reductions persist for years (Heimberg et al., 1993, 1991). In fact, Ellis's therapy is more effective as a treatment for social anxiety than for most other problems. At the same time, research also suggests that cognitive therapy, like drug therapy and exposure therapy, does not typically overcome social phobias fully (Poulton & Andrews, 1996). It reduces social fear, but it does not consistently help people perform effectively in the social realm (Gardner et al., 1980). This is where social skills training has come to the forefront.

HOW CAN SOCIAL SKILLS BE IMPROVED? In **social skills training,** therapists combine several behavioral techniques to help people improve their social skills. They usually model appropriate social behaviors and encourage the clients to try them out. Clients then role-play with the therapists, rehearsing their new behaviors until they become more effective. Throughout the process, therapists provide frank *feedback* and *reinforcement* (praise) to the clients for effective performances.

Social reinforcement from others with similar social difficulties is often more powerful than reinforcement from a therapist alone. In *social skills training groups* and *assertiveness training groups,* members try out and rehearse new social behavior with or in front of other group members. The group can also offer guidance on what is socially appropriate.

Social skills training helps many people perform better in social situations (Beidel et al., 2000; van Dam Baggen & Kraaimatt, 2000). Some people, however, continue to experience uncomfortable levels of fear despite such treatments (Juster et al., 1996).

No single approach—drug therapy, exposure treatment, cognitive therapy, or social skills training—consistently causes social phobias to disappear, and none is clearly superior to the others (Wlazlo et al., 1990). Yet each is helpful, and when the approaches are combined, the results have been especially encouraging (Spence et al., 2000; Hope & Heimberg, 1993).

GENETICS OR MODELING?

Mothers of very shy preschoolers have a higher rate of anxiety disorders, particularly social phobia, than mothers of children who are not shy. In one study, 78 percent of the mothers of shy young children had a current or past anxiety disorder, a social phobia in half of the cases (Cooper & Eke, 1999).

Contrary to popular belief . . . *The goal of assertiveness training groups is to teach people to express their needs in socially acceptable ways, not to encourage them to lash out at others without restraint.*

SUMMING UP

Phobias

A phobia is a severe, persistent, and unreasonable fear of a particular object, activity, or situation. As many as 11 percent of the adults in the United States suffer from this disorder in any given year. There are three main categories of phobias: agoraphobia, social phobia, and specific phobias.

Explanations for Phobias Behavioral explanations for phobias have been the most influential over the years. Behaviorists believe that phobias are learned from the environment through classical conditioning or modeling and then are maintained because of avoidance behaviors.

Treatments for Phobias Behaviorists have treated specific phobias successfully by using exposure techniques in which people confront the objects they fear. They have also used exposure treatments successfully to treat agoraphobia. Here, people are taught to venture farther and farther from their homes and to enter outside places gradually.

Clinicians typically separate two features of social phobias: social fears and poor social skills. They may try to reduce social fear by using exposure techniques, group therapy, and various cognitive approaches. They may improve social skills with social skills training. And they often use a combination of these approaches.

ConsiderThis

⦿ Ask people what they fear, and you will probably collect a long list of menacing objects and situations. Yet most people get along well every day and never seek treatment. Do these people's fears always differ from phobias? • Or are some people simply better than others at working around their phobias?

CROSSROADS:
Diathesis-Stress in Action

Clinicians and researchers have developed many ideas about generalized anxiety disorder and phobias. At times, however, the sheer number of concepts and findings makes it difficult to grasp what is and what is not really known about the disorders.

Overall, it is fair to say that clinicians do not yet have a clear understanding of generalized anxiety disorder. The explanations offered by each of the models have key limitations. Similarly, most treatments have had only modest success. Partly because progress has been so limited, growing numbers of clinical theorists are coming to believe that they can best understand the disorder by considering the various perspectives together. It may well be that people develop generalized anxiety disorder only when biological, psychological, and sociocultural factors are *all* operating.

Adopting a *diathesis-stress* perspective, for example, some theorists suggest that individuals with this disorder must have a biological predisposition toward experiencing anxiety that is brought to the surface by psychological and sociocultural forces (Kazdin & Weisz, 1998). In fact, genetic investigators have discovered that certain genes may help determine whether a person reacts to life's stressors calmly or in an uptight, anxious way (Plomin et al., 1997; Lesch et al., 1996), and developmental researchers have found that even during the earliest stages of life some infants consistently become very aroused when stimulated while other infants remain quiet (Kalin, 1993; Pekrun, 1992). It may be that the easily aroused infants have inherited defects in GABA functioning or other biological limitations that predispose them to generalized anxiety disorder. If, over the course of their lives, these individuals also face intense societal pressures and learn to interpret the world as a dangerous place, they may be candidates for developing the disorder.

A diathesis-stress perspective may also shed more light on phobias. In one study, almost a third of subjects with a specific phobia had close relatives with a similar phobia (Fyer et al., 1990). And, in a related vein, several studies suggest that certain infants are born with a style of social inhibition or shyness that may

ConsiderThis

⦿ Almost half of all people with a major depressive disorder also experience an anxiety disorder (Regier et al., 1998). In such cases, the anxiety disorder usually begins during adolescence and the depressive disorder during young adulthood. How might problems with anxiety help cause a mood disorder? • How else might the relationship between these disorders be explained?

STRESS MANAGEMENT PROGRAM An approach to treating generalized and other anxiety disorders that teaches clients techniques for reducing and controlling stress.

increase their risk of developing a social phobia (Kagan & Snidman, 1999, 1991). Thus, it could be that people must have both a genetic predisposition and unfortunate conditioning experiences in order to develop particular phobias.

Efforts at integration can also be seen in the treatment of generalized anxiety disorder and phobias. Many clinicians who treat people with these disorders are now combining principles and interventions from various models. As we observed earlier, treatment programs for social phobias may include a combination of medications, exposure therapy, cognitive therapy, and social skills training. Similarly, cognitive techniques such as self-instruction training are now often combined with relaxation training or biofeedback in the treatment of generalized anxiety disorder—a package known as a **stress management program.**

The tendency to combine concepts and techniques from various models has been even more apparent with the remaining anxiety disorders—panic disorder, obsessive-compulsive disorder, and the stress disorders. Over the past 20 years great progress has been made in understanding and treating them. We shall turn to this promising work in Chapter 5.

KEY TERMS

fear p. 95
anxiety p. 95
stressor p. 97
stress response p. 97
autonomic nervous system (ANS) p. 97
sympathetic nervous system p. 98
parasympathetic nervous system p. 98
corticosteroids p. 98
trait anxiety p. 98
situation anxiety p. 99
generalized anxiety disorder p. 99
unconditional positive regard p. 99
conditions of worth p. 99
client-centered therapy p. 104

existential anxiety p. 104
basic irrational assumptions p. 105
rational-emotive therapy p. 107
cognitive therapy p. 107
self-instruction training p. 108
family pedigree study p. 109
benzodiazepines p. 109
gamma-aminobutyric acid (GABA) p. 109
sedative-hypnotic drugs p. 110
relaxation training p. 111
biofeedback p. 112
electromyograph (EMG) p. 112
phobia p. 113
specific phobia p. 113

social phobia p. 113
agoraphobia p. 113
classical conditioning p. 116
modeling p. 117
stimulus generalization p. 117
preparedness p. 118
exposure treatments p. 119
systematic desensitization p. 119
fear hierarchy p. 120
flooding p. 120
participant modeling p. 120
social skills training p. 122
stress management program p. 124

QUICK QUIZ

1. What factors determine how people react to stressors in life? pp. 97–99

2. Describe the relationship between generalized anxiety disorder and sociocultural factors such as societal pressures, including poverty and racial discrimination. pp. 100–101

3. What are the key principles in the psychodynamic and humanistic-existential explanations of generalized anxiety disorder? How have these explanations fared in research? pp. 101–105

4. What are the key principles in the cognitive explanation of generalized anxiety disorder? What research support has this explanation received? pp. 105–108

5. Describe the biological explanations of anxiety and generalized anxiety disorder. pp. 109–110

6. How effective have treatments been for generalized anxiety disorder? pp. 102–112

7. Define and compare the three kinds of phobias. pp. 113–115

8. How do behaviorists explain phobias? What evidence exists for these explanations? pp. 115–119

9. Describe the three behavioral exposure techniques used to treat specific phobias. How effective are they? pp. 119–121

10. What are the two components of a social phobia, and how is each of them addressed in treatment? pp. 121–122

CYBER STUDY

▲ *How might occupational stress affect mental health?* ▲ *How might stress and anxiety affect job performance?* ▲ *Observe the psychoanalytic treatment of an anxious person.* ▲ *See "fight or flight" reactions in action.*

SEARCH THE *FUNDAMENTALS OF ABNORMAL PSYCHOLOGY* CD-ROM FOR

▲ Chapter 4 video case and discussion
  "Claude & Claude"—Emotion, Stress, and Health

▲ Chapter 4 practice test and feedback

▲ Additional video case and discussion
  "Larry"—Psychoanalytic Therapy Session

LOG ON TO THE COMER WEB PAGE FOR

▲ Suggested Web links, research exercises, FAQ page, additional Chapter 4 practice test questions
  <http://www.worthpublishers.com/comer>

Source: *The Brain, Second Edition* (The Annenberg/CPB Collection, 1997)

Panic, Obsessive-Compulsive, and Stress Disorders

I was inside a very busy shopping precinct and all of a sudden it happened: in a matter of seconds I was like a mad woman. It was like a nightmare, only I was awake; everything went black and sweat poured out of me—my body, my hands and even my hair got wet through. All the blood seemed to drain out of me; I went as white as a ghost. I felt as if I were going to collapse; it was as if I had no control over my limbs; my back and legs were very weak and I felt as though it were impossible to move. It was as if I had been taken over by some stronger force. I saw all the people looking at me—just faces, no bodies, all merged into one. My heart started pounding in my head and in my ears; I thought my heart was going to stop. I could see black and yellow lights. I could hear the voices of the people but from a long way off. I could not think of anything except the way I was feeling and that now I had to get out and run quickly or I would die. I must escape and get into the fresh air.

(Hawkrigg, 1975)

Anxiety may take a form that is even more intense than the symptoms discussed in Chapter 4. In the excerpt above, for example, a woman describes a *panic attack,* an outbreak of terror that is the central feature of *panic disorder.* Anxiety may also pose problems that are different from those seen in Chapter 4. People with *obsessive-compulsive disorder* have recurrent unwanted thoughts that cause them anxiety or the need to perform repetitive actions to reduce their anxiety. And people with *acute stress disorder* and *posttraumatic stress disorder* are tormented by fear and related symptoms well after a traumatic event has ended. During most of the twentieth century, clinicians and researchers paid much more attention to generalized anxiety disorder and phobias than to these other anxiety disorders in the belief that panic, obsessive-compulsive, and stress disorders were less common. Certainly they were less understood and treatments for them were less effective.

This situation has changed drastically in the past 20 years. Researchers are discovering that panic, obsessive-compulsive, and stress disorders are more common than anyone had realized. Moreover, they have uncovered very promising clues to the causes of these disorders, and therapists have developed treatments for them that are often quite helpful. In fact, investigators of anxiety disorders are now focusing most of their attention on these particular disorders (Norton et al., 1995).

Panic Disorder

Sometimes an anxiety reaction takes the form of a smothering, nightmarish panic in which people lose control of their behavior and, in fact, are practically unaware of what they are doing. Anyone can react with panic when a real threat suddenly emerges. Some people, however, experience **panic attacks**—periodic, short bouts of panic that occur suddenly, reach a peak within 10 minutes, and gradually pass.

The attacks feature at least four of the following symptoms of panic: palpitations of the heart, tingling in the hands or feet, shortness of breath,

"They just kept pushin' forward and they would just walk right on top of you, just trample over ya like you were a piece of the ground. They wouldn't even help ya; people were just screamin' 'help me' and nobody cared."

Patron at The Who concert, Cincinnati, 1979, where 11 people were trampled to death (Johnson, 1987)

The experience of agoraphobia *George Tooker's painting* Subway *expresses the sense of threat and entrapment that many people with agoraphobia experience when they enter public places.*

sweating, hot and cold flashes, trembling, chest pains, choking sensations, faintness, dizziness, and a feeling of unreality (see Table 5-1). Small wonder that during a panic attack many people fear they will die, go crazy, or lose control.

People with any of the anxiety disorders (or, for that matter, people without an anxiety disorder) may experience a panic attack when they are faced with something they dread. Some people, however, have panic attacks repeatedly and unexpectedly without apparent reason. They may be suffering from **panic disorder.** In addition to the panic attacks, people who are diagnosed with panic disorder also experience dysfunctional changes in their thinking or behavior as a result of attacks that occur over a period of a month or more. For example, they may worry persistently about having another attack, have concerns about what such an attack means ("Am I losing my mind?"), or plan their behavior around the possibility of a future attack.

Panic disorder is often accompanied by **agoraphobia,** one of the three categories of phobia mentioned in Chapter 4. People with agoraphobia (from the Greek for "fear of the marketplace") are afraid to leave the house and travel to public places or other locations where escape might be difficult or help unavailable should panic symptoms develop. The intensity of agoraphobia may fluctuate. In severe cases, people become virtual prisoners in their own homes. Their social life dwindles, and they cannot hold a job.

Until recently, clinicians failed to recognize the close link between agoraphobia and panic

Table 5-1 DSM-IV Checklist

PANIC ATTACK

A discrete period of intense fear in which at least four of the following symptoms develop suddenly and reach a peak within 10 minutes:

- Palpitations, pounding heart, or accelerated heart rate
- Sweating
- Trembling or shaking
- Sensations of shortness of breath or smothering
- A feeling of choking
- Chest pain or discomfort
- Nausea or abdominal distress
- Feeling dizzy, unsteady, lightheaded, or faint
- Derealization or depersonalization
- Fear of losing control or going crazy
- Fear of dying
- Numbness or tingling sensations
- Chills or hot flashes

Based on APA, 2000, 1994.

attacks. They now realize that panic attacks, or at least some paniclike symptoms, typically set the stage for agoraphobia (Langs et al., 2000; Goisman et al., 1995): after experiencing one or more unpredictable attacks, certain individuals become fearful of having new attacks in public places where help or escape might be difficult. Anne Watson's plight illustrates a typical onset of agoraphobia:

Ms. Watson reported that until the onset of her current problems two years ago, she had led a normal and happy life. At that time an uncle to whom she had been extremely close in her childhood died following a sudden unexpected heart attack. . . . Six months after his death she was returning home from work one evening when suddenly she felt that she couldn't catch her breath. Her heart began to pound, and she broke out into a cold sweat. Things began to seem unreal, her legs felt leaden, and she became sure she would die or faint before she reached home. She asked a passerby to help her get a taxi and went to a nearby hospital emergency room. The doctors there found her physical examination, blood count and chemistries, and electrocardiogram all completely normal. . . .

Four weeks later Ms. Watson had a second similar attack while preparing dinner at home. She made an appointment to see her family doctor, but again, all examinations were normal. She decided to put the episodes out of her mind and continue with her normal activities. Within the next several weeks, however, she had four attacks and noticed that she began to worry about when the next one would occur. . . .

She then found herself constantly thinking about her anxieties as attacks continued; she began to dread leaving the house alone for fear she would be stranded, helpless and alone, by an attack. She began to avoid going to movies, parties, and dinners with friends for fear she would have an attack and be embarrassed by her need to leave. When household chores necessitated driving she waited until it was possible to take her children or a friend along for the ride. She also began walking the twenty blocks to her office to avoid the possibility of being trapped in a subway car between stops when an attack occurred.

(Spitzer et al., 1983, pp. 7–8)

Not everyone with panic disorder develops agoraphobia, but many such persons do. Thus DSM-IV distinguishes *panic disorder without agoraphobia* (see Table 5-2) from *panic disorder with agoraphobia*. Around 2.3 percent of all people in the United States suffer from one or the other of these patterns in a given year; 3.5 percent develop one of the patterns at some point in their lives (Kessler & Zhao, 1999; Kessler et al., 1994). Both kinds of panic disorder are likely to develop in late adolescence and early adulthood, and are at least twice as common among women as among men (APA, 2000).

PANIC ATTACK Periodic short bouts of panic that occur suddenly, reach a peak within minutes, and gradually pass.

PANIC DISORDER An anxiety disorder marked by recurrent and unpredictable panic attacks.

AGORAPHOBIA An anxiety disorder in which a person is afraid to be in places or situations from which escape might be difficult (or embarrassing) or help unavailable if paniclike symptoms were to occur.

FEARING FEAR

Researchers had persons with agoraphobia record their thoughts while engaging in fear-arousing situations such as driving alone. The subjects' most common thoughts (29 percent) were about how frightened they were feeling (Williams et al., 1997).

Table 5-2 DSM-IV Checklist

PANIC DISORDER WITHOUT AGORAPHOBIA

1. Recurrent unexpected panic attacks.
2. A month or more of one of the following after at least one of the attacks.
   (a) Persistent concern about having additional attacks.
   (b) Worry about the implications or consequences of the attack.
   (c) Significant change in behavior related to the attacks.

Based on APA, 2000, 1994.

NOCTURNAL PANIC

Around 60 percent of people with panic disorder experience panic attacks at night in addition to their daytime attacks (Sloan et al., 1999; Craske & Rowe, 1997). Usually they are awakened from a deep sleep by their symptoms and fear that they are dying.

DOCTOR VISITS

People with panic disorder report making seven times more visits to physicians than other people do (Carr, 1998).

AGE LIMITS

Typically a person must reach a certain level of physical or cognitive maturity before experiencing a full-blown panic attack (McNally, 2001). One study found that over 5 percent of sixth- and seventh-grade girls had experienced a panic attack (Hayward et al., 1992). In the subgroup of girls rated most physically immature, none reported panic attacks, but 8 percent of those who had completed puberty did report having them.

The Biological Perspective

In the 1960s, clinicians made the surprising discovery that people with panic disorder were helped less by benzodiazepine drugs, the drugs useful in treating generalized anxiety disorder, than by certain *antidepressant drugs,* drugs that are usually used to reduce the symptoms of depression (Klein, 1964; Klein & Fink, 1962). This observation led to the first biological explanations and treatments for panic disorder.

WHAT BIOLOGICAL FACTORS CONTRIBUTE TO PANIC DISORDER? To understand the biology of panic disorder, researchers worked backward from their understanding of the antidepressant drugs that seemed to control it. They knew that many of these antidepressant drugs change the activity of **norepinephrine,** one of the neurotransmitters that carry messages from neuron to neuron in the brain. If the drugs also eliminated panic attacks, researchers wondered, might panic disorder be caused in the first place by abnormal norepinephrine activity?

Several studies have produced evidence that norepinephrine activity is indeed irregular in people who suffer from panic attacks (Gorman et al., 2000, 1995; Levy et al., 1996). For example, the **locus ceruleus** is a brain area rich in neurons that use norepinephrine. When this area is electrically stimulated in monkeys, the monkeys have a paniclike reaction, a finding suggesting that panic reactions are related to changes in norepinephrine activity in the locus ceruleus (Redmond, 1981, 1979, 1977) (see Figure 5-1). In another line of research, scientists have induced panic attacks in human beings by injecting them with chemicals known to affect the activity of norepinephrine (Bourin et al., 1995; Charney et al., 1992, 1983).

These findings strongly tie norepinephrine to panic attacks. Just what goes wrong, however, is still not fully understood. It is not clear, for example, whether the problem is excessive activity, deficient activity, or some other form of dysfunctioning involving norepinephrine. To complicate matters, there is growing evidence that other neurotransmitters also may have roles to play in panic disorder (Gorman et al., 2000, 1995; Emmanuel et al., 1999).

Furthermore, investigators do not know why some people have such biological abnormalities. One possibility is that a predisposition to develop panic disorder is inherited (Stein, Jang, & Livesley, 1999; Kendler et al., 1995; Torgersen, 1990, 1983). If a genetic factor is indeed at work, close relatives should have higher rates of panic disorder than more distant relatives (see Table 5-3). One study did find that among identical twins (twins who share all of their genes), if one twin had panic disorder, the other twin had the same disorder in 24 percent of cases. Among fraternal twins (who share only some of their genes), if one twin had panic disorder, the other twin had the same disorder in only 11 percent of

Table 5-3

Anxiety Disorders Profile

	ONE-YEAR PREVALENCE (%)	FEMALE:MALE RATIO	TYPICAL AGE AT ONSET	PREVALENCE AMONG CLOSE RELATIVES	PERCENTAGE RECEIVING TREATMENT
Panic disorder	2.3%	5:2	15–35 years	Elevated	54.4%
Obsessive-compulsive disorder	2.0	1:1	4–25 years	Elevated	41.3
Acute and posttraumatic stress disorders	3.9	2:1	Variable	Unknown	Unknown

Source: APA, 2000, 1994; Kessler et al., 1994; Regier et al., 1993; Davidson et al., 1991; Eaton et al., 1991; Boyd et al., 1990.

cases (Kendler et al., 1993). Other twin studies, however, have not always provided such clear trends (Stein & Uhde, 1995). Thus the issue of genetic predisposition is still open to debate.

DRUG THERAPIES In 1962 the researchers Donald Klein and Max Fink discovered that certain antidepressant drugs could prevent panic attacks or reduce their frequency. As we have seen, this finding was a surprise at first. Since then, however, studies across the world have repeatedly confirmed this observation (Barlow et al., 2000; Silberman, 1999).

Many of these antidepressant drugs seem to act to restore proper activity of the neurotransmitter norepinephrine, particularly at neurons in the locus ceruleus (Gorman et al., 1995; Redmond, 1985). They bring at least some improvement to 80 percent of patients who have panic disorder (Ballenger, 1998; Hirschfeld, 1992). Approximately 40 to 60 percent recover markedly or fully, and the improvements can last indefinitely, so long as the drugs are not stopped (Tiller et al., 1999; Lecrubier et al., 1997). Otherwise, relapse rates are high. Recently *alprazolam* (Xanax) and a few other powerful benzodiazepine drugs have also proved very effective, yielding similar success rates (Holland, Musch, & Hindmarch, 1999).

Clinicians have also found the antidepressant drugs or powerful benzodiazepines to be helpful in most cases of panic disorder with agoraphobia (Barlow et al., 2000; Uhlenhuth et al., 1995). The drugs apparently help break the cycle of attack, anticipation, and fear. As the drugs eliminate or reduce their panic attacks, people become confident enough to journey out into public places once again. At the same time, such drugs alone are not always enough to overcome panic disorder with agoraphobia. For these people, a combination of medication and behavioral exposure treatment may be more effective than either treatment alone (Antony & Swinson, 2000).

The Cognitive Perspective

Cognitive theorists and practitioners have come to recognize that biological factors are only part of the cause of panic attacks. In their view, full panic reactions are experienced only by people who misinterpret certain physiological events that are occurring within their bodies. Cognitive treatments are aimed at changing such misinterpretations.

THE COGNITIVE EXPLANATION: MISINTERPRETING BODILY SENSATIONS Cognitive theorists believe that panic-prone people may be very sensitive to certain bodily sensations; when such sensations occur unexpectedly, they may misinterpret them as signs of a medical catastrophe (McNally, 2001, 1999). Rather than understanding the probable cause of such sensations as "something I ate" or "a fight with the boss," the panic-prone grow more and more worried about losing control, fear the worst, lose all perspective, and rapidly plunge into panic. They keep expecting that the "dangerous" sensations may return at any time and so set themselves up for future panic attacks.

Why might some people be prone to such misinterpretations? Clinicians have pointed to several possible factors (Stewart et al., 2001; McGlynn & Bates, 1999). Perhaps the individuals have poor coping skills or lack social support. Perhaps their childhoods were filled with unpredictable events, lack of control, chronic illnesses in the family, or parental overreactions to their children's bodily symptoms.

Whatever the precise causes, research suggests that panic-prone persons have a high degree of what cognitive theorists call **anxiety sensitivity:** they focus on their bodily sensations much of the time, are unable to assess them logically, and interpret them as potentially harmful (Muris et al., 2001; Stein & Rapee, 1999).

FIGURE 5-1   The biology of panic *The locus ceruleus sends its major messages to the amygdala, a brain region known to trigger emotional reactions. Many neurons in the locus ceruleus use norepinephrine, a neurotransmitter implicated in panic disorder and in depression.*

NOREPINEPHRINE A neurotransmitter whose abnormal activity is linked to panic disorder and depression.

LOCUS CERULEUS A small area of the brain that seems to be active in the regulation of emotions. Many of its neurons use norepinephrine.

ANXIETY SENSITIVITY A tendency to focus on one's bodily sensations, assess them illogically, and interpret them as harmful.

"I'm sorry, I didn't hear what you said. I was listening to my body."

One study found that people who scored high on an anxiety sensitivity survey were five times more likely than other subjects to develop panic disorder (Maller & Reiss, 1992). Other studies have found that individuals with panic disorder are indeed more aware of and frightened by bodily sensations than other people (McNally, 2001, 1999).

According to cognitive theorists, people with high anxiety sensitivity are likely to experience and misinterpret certain kinds of sensations more than others. Many seem to "overbreathe," or hyperventilate, in stressful situations. Apparently the abnormal breathing makes them think they are in danger or even dying of suffocation, so they panic (Dratcu, 2000). Other physical sensations that can be misinterpreted include excitement, breathing discomfort, fullness in the abdomen, and acute anger (McNally, Hornic, & Donnell, 1995; Verburg et al., 1995). One person, on learning that her artwork had been accepted for exhibit at a gallery, became so excited that she experienced "palpitations of the heart." Misinterpreting them as a sign of a heart attack, she panicked.

In **biological challenge tests,** researchers produce hyperventilation or other biological sensations by administering drugs or by instructing subjects to breathe, exercise, or simply think in certain ways (Stein & Rapee, 1999). As one might expect, people with panic disorder experience greater anxiety during these tests than people without the disorder, particularly when they believe that their bodily sensations are dangerous or out of control.

Although the cognitive explanation of panic disorder is relatively new, researchers have already collected much evidence in its favor. In particular, they have found that people who are prone to panic often interpret bodily sensations in ways that are not at all common. Precisely how different their misinterpretations are and how the misinterpretations interact with biological factors are questions that remain to be answered more fully.

COGNITIVE THERAPY Cognitive therapists try to correct people's misinterpretations of their body sensations (Beck & Weishaar, 1995). The first step is to educate clients about the general nature of panic attacks, the actual causes of bodily sensations, and the tendency of clients to misinterpret their sensations. The next step is to teach clients to apply more accurate interpretations during stressful situations, thus short-circuiting the panic sequence at an early point. Therapists may also teach clients to cope better with anxiety—for example, by applying relaxation and breathing techniques—and to distract themselves from their sensations, perhaps by striking up a conversation with someone.

Cognitive therapists may also use biological challenge procedures to produce panic sensations in therapy, so that clients can apply their new skills under watchful supervision. Individuals whose attacks are typically triggered by a rapid heart rate, for example, may be told to jump up and down for several minutes or to run up a flight of stairs (Clark, 1993; Rapee, 1993). They can then practice interpreting the resulting sensations appropriately and not dwelling on them.

According to research, cognitive treatments often help people with panic disorder (Stuart et al., 2000). In international studies, 85 percent of subjects given these treatments were free of panic for as long as two years or more, compared to only 13 percent of control subjects (Clark & Wells, 1997). As with drug therapy, cognitive treatments are only sometimes sufficient for persons whose panic disorders are accompanied by agoraphobia (Oei, Llamas, & Devilly, 1999). For many such persons, therapists add exposure techniques to the cognitive treatment program.

Cognitive therapy has proved to be at least as helpful as antidepressant drugs or alprazolam in the treatment of panic disorder, sometimes more so (Barlow et al., 2000; Zaubler & Katon, 1998). In view of the effectiveness of both cognitive

BIOLOGICAL CHALLENGE TEST A procedure used to produce panic in subjects or clients by having them exercise vigorously or perform some other potentially panic-inducing task in the presence of a researcher or therapist.

OBSESSION A persistent thought, idea, impulse, or image that is experienced repeatedly, feels intrusive, and causes anxiety.

COMPULSION A repetitive and rigid behavior or mental act that a person feels driven to perform in order to prevent or reduce anxiety.

OBSESSIVE-COMPULSIVE DISORDER A disorder in which a person has recurrent unwanted thoughts, a need to perform repetitive and rigid actions, or both.

and drug treatments, many clinicians have tried combining them. It is not yet clear, however, whether or not this strategy is more effective than cognitive therapy alone (Loerch et al., 1999).

SUMMING UP ⟩ **Panic Disorder**

Panic attacks are periodic limited bouts of panic that occur suddenly. Sufferers of panic disorder experience such attacks repeatedly and unpredictably and without apparent reason.

Biological theorists believe that abnormal norepinephrine activity in the locus ceruleus is the key to panic disorder. Biological therapists use certain antidepressant drugs and benzodiazepine drugs to treat people with this disorder. Patients whose panic disorder is accompanied by agoraphobia may need a combination of drug therapy and behavioral exposure treatment.

Cognitive theorists suggest that panic-prone people are very sensitive to their bodily sensations and often misinterpret them as signs of medical catastrophe. Such persons typically have a high degree of anxiety sensitivity and also experience greater anxiety during biological challenge tests. Cognitive therapists teach patients that their physical sensations are actually harmless.

Obsessive-Compulsive Disorder

Obsessions are persistent thoughts, ideas, impulses, or images that seem to invade a person's consciousness. **Compulsions** are repeated and rigid behaviors or mental acts that people feel they must perform in order to prevent or reduce anxiety. As Figure 5-2 indicates, minor obsessions and compulsions are familiar to almost everyone (Muris, Murckelbach, & Clavan, 1997). We may find ourselves filled with thoughts about an upcoming performance, date, examination, or vacation; worry that we forgot to turn off the stove or lock the door; or be haunted for days by the same song, melody, or poem. We may feel better when we avoid stepping on cracks, turn away from black cats, follow a strict routine every morning, or arrange our closets in a particular way.

Minor obsessions and compulsions can play a helpful role in life. Distracting tunes or little rituals often calm us during times of stress. A person who repeatedly hums a tune or taps his or her fingers during a test may be releasing tension and thus improving performance. Many people find it comforting to repeat religious or cultural rituals, such as touching a mezuzah, sprinkling holy water, or fingering rosary beads.

According to DSM-IV, a diagnosis of **obsessive-compulsive disorder** may be called for when obsessions or compulsions feel excessive or unreasonable, cause great distress, consume considerable time, or interfere with daily functions (see Table 5-4 on the next page). Obsessive-compulsive disorder is classified as an anxiety disorder because the victims' obsessions cause great anxiety, while their compulsions are aimed at preventing or reducing anxiety. In addition, their anxiety rises if they try to resist their obsessions or compulsions. The pattern displayed by Georgia is described by her husband:

FIGURE 5-2 **Normal routines** *Most people find it comforting to follow set routines when they carry out everyday activities, and in fact, 40 percent become irritated if they are forced to depart from their routines. (Adapted from Kanner, 1998, 1995.)*

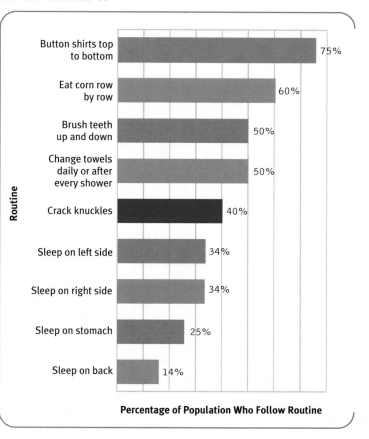

"You remember that old joke about getting up in the middle of the night to go to the john and coming back to the bedroom to find your wife has made the bed? It's no joke. Sometimes I think she never sleeps. I got up one night at 4 A.M. and there she was doing the laundry downstairs. Look at your ash tray! I haven't seen one that dirty in years! I'll tell you what it makes me feel like. If I forget to leave my dirty shoes outside the back door she gives me a look like I had just crapped in the middle of an operating room. I stay out of the house a lot and I'm about half-stoned when I do have to be home. She even made us get rid of the dog because she said he was always filthy. When we used to have people over for supper she would jitterbug around everybody till they couldn't digest their food. I hated to call them up and ask them over because I could always hear them hem and haw and make up excuses not to come over. Even the kids are walking down the street nervous about getting dirt on them. I'm going out of my mind but you can't talk to her. She just blows up and spends twice as much time cleaning things. We have guys in to wash the walls so often I think the house is going to fall down from being scrubbed all the time. About a week ago I had it up to here and told her I couldn't take it any more. I think the only reason she came to see you was because I told her I was going to take off. . . ."

. . . Georgia was aware, in part, of the effect she was having on her family and friends, but she also knew that when she tried to alter her behavior she got so nervous that she felt she was losing her mind. She was frightened by the possibility that "I'm headed for the funny-farm." As she said, "I can't get to sleep unless I am sure everything in the house is in its proper place so that when I get up in the morning, the house is organized. I work like mad to set everything straight before I go to bed, but, when I get up in the morning, I can think of a thousand things that I ought to do. I know some of the things are ridiculous, but I feel better if I get them done, and I can't stand to know something needs doing and I haven't done it."

(McNeil, 1967, pp. 26–28)

As many as 2 percent of the people in the United States and Great Britain suffer from obsessive-compulsive disorder in any given year (APA, 2000; Bebbington, 1998; Regier et al., 1993). It is equally common in men and women and usually begins by young adulthood. As with Georgia, the disorder typically continues for many years, but the symptoms and their severity fluctuate over time. Many sufferers are also depressed, and some have an eating disorder as well (Crino & Andrews, 1996).

What Are the Features of Obsessions and Compulsions?

Obsessions are not the same as excessive worries about real problems, and compulsions are not repeated actions that feel voluntary and seem harmless to the people who perform them (Langlois et al., 2000).

THE FEATURES OF OBSESSIONS Obsessions are thoughts that feel both intrusive and foreign to the people who experience them. Attempts to ignore or resist these thoughts may produce even more anxiety, and before long they come back more strongly than ever. Like Georgia, people with obsessions are usually quite aware that their thoughts are excessive and inappropriate.

Obsessions often take the form of obsessive *wishes* (for example, repeated wishes that one's spouse would die), *impulses* (repeated urges to yell out obscenities at work or in church), *images* (fleeting visions of forbidden sexual scenes), *ideas* (notions that germs are lurking everywhere), or *doubts* (concerns that one has made or will make a wrong

Table 5-4 DSM-IV Checklist

OBSESSIVE-COMPULSIVE DISORDER

1. Recurrent obsessions or compulsions.
2. Past or present recognition that the obsessions or compulsions are excessive or unreasonable.
3. Significant distress or impairment, or disruption by symptoms for more than one hour a day.

Based on APA, 2000, 1994.

decision). In the following excerpt, a clinician describes a 20-year-old college junior who was plagued by obsessive doubts.

> He now spent hours each night "rehashing" the day's events, especially interactions with friends and teachers, endlessly making "right" in his mind any and all regrets. He likened the process to playing a videotape of each event over and over again in his mind, asking himself if he had behaved properly and telling himself that he had done his best, or had said the right thing every step of the way. He would do this while sitting at his desk, supposedly studying; and it was not unusual for him to look at the clock after such a period of rumination and note that, to his surprise, two or three hours had elapsed.
>
> *(Spitzer et al., 1981, pp. 20–21)*

Certain basic themes run through the thoughts of most people troubled by obsessive thinking (APA, 2000, 1994). The most common theme appears to be dirt or contamination. Other common ones are violence and aggression, orderliness, religion, and sexuality.

THE FEATURES OF COMPULSIONS Although compulsive behaviors are technically under voluntary control, the people who feel they must do them have little sense of choice in the matter. Most of these individuals recognize that their behavior is unreasonable, but they believe at the same time something terrible will happen if they don't perform the compulsions (Foa & Kozak, 1995). After performing a compulsive act, they usually feel less anxious for a short while. Some people develop the act into a detailed and often elaborate compulsive *ritual*. They must go through the ritual in exactly the same way every time, according to certain rules.

Like obsessions, compulsions take various forms (Ball, Baer, & Otto, 1996; Tallis, 1996). *Cleaning compulsions* are very common. Like Georgia, people with these compulsions feel they must keep cleaning themselves, their clothing, or their homes. The cleaning may follow ritualistic rules and be repeated dozens or hundreds of times a day. People with *checking compulsions* check the same things over and over—door locks, gas taps, ashtrays, important papers—to make sure that all is as it should be. Another common compulsion is the constant effort to seek *order* or *balance* in one's actions and surroundings. People with this compulsion must place certain items (clothing, books, foods) in perfect order in accordance with strict rules.

> Ted is a 13-year-old referred to a Midwestern inpatient psychiatric research ward because of "senseless rituals and attention to minutiae." He can spend 3 hours centering the toilet paper roll on its holder or rearranging his bed and other objects in his room. When placing objects down, such as books or shoelaces after tying them, he picks them up and replaces them several times until they seem "straight." Although usually placid, he becomes abusive with family members who try to enter his room for fear they will move or break his objects. When he is at school, he worries that people may disturb his room. He sometimes has to be forced to interrupt his routine to attend meals. Last year he hid pieces of his clothing around the house because they wouldn't lie straight in his drawers. Moreover, he often repeats to himself, "This is perfect; you are perfect."
>
> *(Spitzer et al., 1983, p. 15)*

Touching, verbal, and *counting* compulsions are also common. People with touching compulsions repeatedly touch or avoid touching certain items whenever they see them. Individuals with verbal rituals feel compelled to repeat

The great pursuit *Captain Ahab's preoccupation with the great white whale in Herman Melville's* Moby Dick *(1851) is one of literature's most famous presentations of obsessive thinking.*

HARD TO AVOID

People who try to avoid all contamination and rid themselves and their world of all germs are fighting a losing battle. While talking, the average person sprays 300 microscopic saliva droplets per minute, or 2.5 per word.

expressions or chants. And those with counting compulsions constantly count the things they see around them throughout the day.

ARE OBSESSIONS AND COMPULSIONS RELATED? Although some people with obsessive-compulsive disorder experience obsessions only or compulsions only, most of them experience both. In fact, compulsive acts are often a response to obsessive thoughts (Pato & Pato, 1997). One investigation found that in most cases, compulsions seemed to represent a *yielding* to obsessive doubts, ideas, or urges (Akhtar et al., 1975). A woman who keeps doubting that her house is secure may yield to that obsessive doubt by repeatedly checking locks and gas jets. Or a man who obsessively fears contamination may yield to that fear by performing cleaning rituals. The investigation also found that compulsions sometimes serve to help *control* obsessions. Below, a teenager describes how she tried to control her obsessive fears of contamination by performing counting and verbal rituals:

> *Patient:* If I heard the word, like, something that had to do with germs or disease, it would be considered something bad, and so I had things that would go through my mind that were sort of like "cross that out and it'll make it okay" to hear that word.
> *Interviewer:* What sort of things?
> *Patient:* Like numbers or words that seemed to be sort of like a protector.
> *Interviewer:* What numbers and what words were they?
> *Patient:* It started out to be the number 3 and multiples of 3 and then words like "soap and water," something like that; and then the multiples of 3 got really high, and they'd end up to be 124 or something like that. It got real bad then.
>
> *(Spitzer et al., 1981, p. 137)*

Many people with obsessive-compulsive disorder worry that they will act out their obsessions. A man with obsessive images of wounded loved ones may worry that he is but a step away from committing murder; or a woman with obsessive

---

STEPPING BACK

Terror Behind the Smile

*M*any of today's college students grew up watching *Double Dare* and *Family Double Dare,* two of the messiest game shows in television history. Young contestants were regularly splattered with goo and dunked in slime and muck (Summers, 1996). All the while, the host, Marc Summers, seemed to be having a great time, especially when the kids would pick him up and throw him into the mess as well. In 1996, however, Summers revealed that his years on the show had been a personal nightmare. He had an obsessive-compulsive disorder.

Summers says that his disorder dates back to the age of 8. He remembers cleaning his room for hours, removing and dusting every book in his bookcase.

When he got the opportunity to host *Double Dare,* he couldn't turn down the career opportunity. But the price was

Steve Labadessa/Outline

high. After the shows, he would spend hours in the shower. "It was the most uncomfortable feeling in the world—a feeling of physical revulsion." Only in recent years did Summers recognize his disorder. His symptoms decreased as a result of treatment.

ConsiderThis

Might Summers have agreed to host the show to somehow help him face his fears and compulsions? • If it was a form of self-treatment, why did it not help? • What other examples of so-called counterphobic behavior take place in our culture?

urges to yell out in church may worry that she will one day give in to them and embarrass herself. Most such concerns are unfounded. Although many obsessions lead to compulsive acts—particularly to cleaning and checking compulsions—they do not usually lead to violence or immoral conduct.

Obsessive-compulsive disorder, like panic disorder, was once among the least understood of the psychological disorders. In recent years, however, researchers have begun to learn more about it. The most influential explanations and treatments come from the psychodynamic, behavioral, cognitive, and biological models.

The Psychodynamic Perspective

As we have observed, psychodynamic theorists believe that an anxiety disorder develops when children come to fear their own id impulses and use ego defense mechanisms to lessen the resulting anxiety. What distinguishes obsessive-compulsive disorder from other anxiety disorders, in their view, is that here the battle between anxiety-provoking id impulses and anxiety-reducing defense mechanisms is not buried in the unconscious but is played out in explicit and dramatic thoughts and actions. The id impulses usually take the form of obsessive thoughts, and the ego defenses appear as counterthoughts or compulsive actions. A woman who keeps imagining her mother lying broken and bleeding, for example, may counter those thoughts with repeated safety checks throughout the house.

PSYCHODYNAMIC EXPLANATIONS: THE BATTLE BETWEEN THE ID AND THE EGO According to psychodynamic theorists, three ego defense mechanisms are particularly common in obsessive-compulsive disorder: *isolation, undoing,* and *reaction formation* (Hollander et al., 1994). People who resort to **isolation** simply disown their undesirable and unwanted thoughts and experience them as foreign intrusions. People who engage in **undoing** perform acts that are meant to cancel out their undesirable impulses. Those who wash their hands repeatedly, for example, may be symbolically undoing their unacceptable id impulses. People who develop a **reaction formation** take on a lifestyle that directly opposes their unacceptable impulses. A person may live a life of compulsive kindness and devotion to others in order to counter unacceptably aggressive impulses.

Sigmund Freud believed that during the *anal stage* of development (occurring at about 2 years of age) some children experience intense rage and shame that fuel the battle between id and ego. He theorized that children at this stage get pleasure from their bowel movements. When their parents try to toilet train them, the children must learn to delay their anal pleasure. If parents are premature or too harsh in their toilet training, the children may feel such rage that they develop *aggressive id impulses*—antisocial impulses that repeatedly seek expression. They may soil their clothes all the more frequently and become generally destructive, messy, or stubborn.

If parents handle the child's aggressiveness by further pressure and embarrassment, the child may also feel ashamed, guilty, and dirty. The aggressive impulses will now compete with a strong desire to control them; the child who wants to soil will also have a desire to retain. If this intense conflict between the id and the ego continues, it may eventually blossom into obsessive-compulsive disorder.

Not all psychodynamic theorists agree with Freud's explanation. Some believe that the aggressive impulses of people with this disorder are rooted in feelings of insecurity rather than poor toilet-training experiences (Erikson, 1963; Sullivan, 1953; Horney, 1937). Even these theorists,

ISOLATION An ego defense mechanism in which people unconsciously isolate and disown undesirable and unwanted thoughts, experiencing them as foreign intrusions.

UNDOING An ego defense mechanism whereby a person unconsciously cancels out an unacceptable desire or act by performing another act.

REACTION FORMATION An ego defense mechanism whereby a person suppresses an unacceptable desire by taking on a lifestyle that expresses the opposite desire.

At the hospital for mothers whose children stepped on sidewalk cracks

however, agree with Freud that people with the disorder have intense aggressive impulses and a competing need to control them. Overall, research has not clearly supported the various psychodynamic theories (Fitz, 1990).

PSYCHODYNAMIC THERAPIES Psychodynamic therapists try to help people with obsessive-compulsive disorder uncover and overcome their underlying conflicts and defenses, using, once again, the techniques of free association and therapist interpretation. Research has offered little evidence, however, that a traditional psychodynamic approach is of much help (Salzman, 1980).

In fact, there is some suspicion that psychodynamic therapy may actually add to the difficulties of patients with obsessive-compulsive disorder (Salzman, 1980). Free association and interpretation may play into their tendency to "think too much" (Noonan, 1971). Thus some psychodynamic therapists now prefer to treat these patients with *short-term psychodynamic therapies,* which, as we observed in Chapter 2, are more direct and action-oriented than the classical techniques (Salzman, 1985, 1980).

The Behavioral Perspective

Behaviorists have concentrated on explaining and treating compulsions rather than obsessions. Although the behavioral explanation itself has received little support, behavioral treatments for compulsive behaviors have been very successful and have helped change the once gloomy treatment picture for this disorder.

THE BEHAVIORAL EXPLANATION: LEARNING BY CHANCE Behaviorists propose that people happen upon their compulsions randomly. In a fearful situation, they happen just coincidentally to wash their hands, say, or dress a certain way. When the threat lifts, they tie the improvement to that particular action. After repeated accidental associations, they believe that the action is bringing them good luck or actually changing the situation; thus they perform the same actions again and again in similar situations. The act becomes a key method of avoiding or reducing anxiety (Steketee et al., 1996).

The influential clinical investigator Stanley Rachman and his associates have shown that compulsions do appear to be rewarded by a reduction in anxiety. In one of their experiments, for example, 12 people with compulsive hand-washing rituals were placed in contact with objects that they considered contaminated (Hodgson & Rachman, 1972). As behaviorists would predict, the hand-washing rituals of these subjects seemed to lower their anxiety. Of course, although such investigations suggest that compulsions may eventually be rewarded by a reduction in anxiety, they do not show that compulsions are learned in the first place as a result of such reductions.

BEHAVIORAL THERAPY In the mid-1960s, when V. Meyer (1966) was treating two hospitalized patients with chronic obsessive-compulsive disorder, he instructed the staff to keep a watchful eye on them and prevent them from performing their compulsive acts. The patients' compulsive behavior improved significantly and continued to show the same improvement after 14 months. In the 1970s Stanley Rachman dropped the staff supervision: he simply instructed clients to try to stop themselves from performing their compulsive acts.

In Rachman's (1985) procedure, **exposure and response prevention,** people are repeatedly exposed to objects or situations that produce anxiety, obsessive fears, and compulsive behaviors, but they are told to resist performing the behaviors they feel bound to perform. Because people find it very difficult to stop, therapists often set an example. As the clients watch, the therapists put themselves in the upsetting situation without performing any compulsive actions, and then they encourage the clients to do the same.

COMPULSION FOR COMPOSING
Beethoven is said to have habitually dipped his head in cold water before trying to compose music.

Philip Gould/Corbis

Touch for luck *An LSU football player touches a statue of the school mascot, a bulldog, before the homecoming game. Athletes often follow rituals that they believe will help them perform better on the field. Like compulsions, their superstitious behaviors may be reinforced by reductions in anxiety.*

EXPOSURE AND RESPONSE PREVENTION
A behavioral treatment for obsessive-compulsive disorder that exposes clients to anxiety-arousing thoughts or situations and then prevents them from performing their compulsive acts.

Many behavioral therapists now use Rachman's procedure. Some of them have people also carry out *self-help* procedures at home (Emmelkamp, 1994). They assign homework in exposure and response prevention, such as these assignments given to a woman with a cleaning compulsion:

- Do not mop the floor of your bathroom for a week. After this, clean it within three minutes, using an ordinary mop. Use this mop for other chores as well without cleaning it.

- Buy a fluffy mohair sweater and wear it for a week. When taking it off at night do not remove the bits of fluff. Do not clean your house for a week.

- You, your husband, and children all have to keep shoes on. Do not clean the house for a week.

- Drop a cookie on the contaminated floor, pick the cookie up and eat it.

- Leave the sheets and blankets on the floor and then put them on the beds. Do not change these for a week.

(Emmelkamp, 1982, pp. 299–300)

Eventually this woman was able to set up a reasonable routine for cleaning herself and her home.

Exposure and response prevention has been offered in both individual and group therapy. Between 60 and 90 percent of clients with obsessive-compulsive disorder have been found to improve considerably with this approach (Albucher, Abelson, & Nesse, 1998; Riggs & Foa, 1993) (see Figure 5-3). They also show improvements in their family, social, and work lives. These changes continue to be observed for years (Bolton, Luckie, & Steinberg, 1995).

The effectiveness of this approach suggests that people with obsessive-compulsive disorder are like the superstitious man in the old joke who keeps snapping his fingers to keep elephants away. When someone points out, "But there aren't any elephants around here," the man replies, "See? It works!" One review concludes, "With hindsight, it is possible to see that the obsessional individual has been snapping his fingers, and unless he stops (response prevention) and takes a look around at the same time (exposure), he isn't going to learn much of value about elephants" (Berk & Efran, 1983, p. 546).

The same studies and statistics indicate the limitations of exposure and response prevention. Few clients who receive the treatment overcome all their symptoms, and as many as one-quarter fail to improve at all (Marks & Swinson, 1992; Greist, 1990). Also, the approach is of limited help to those who have obsessions but no compulsions (Hohagen et al., 1998; Jenike, 1992). After all, the treatment affects obsessions by blocking closely linked compulsive acts. Finally, the favorable results come mainly from studies of cleaning and checking compulsions. The effectiveness of this approach with other kinds of compulsions is unclear (Ball, Baer, & Otto, 1996).

The Cognitive Perspective

Cognitive theorists have developed a promising explanation and treatment for obsessive-compulsive disorder. Their theory and treatment techniques also include a number of behavioral principles, leading some observers to describe the approach as cognitive-behavioral.

THE COGNITIVE EXPLANATION: OVERINTERPRETING UNWANTED THOUGHTS The cognitive explanation of obsessive-compulsive disorder begins by pointing out that everyone has repetitive, unwanted, and intrusive thoughts. Anyone might

ConsiderThis

⦿ Can you think of instances in your own life when you instinctively tried a simple version of exposure and response prevention in order to stop behaving in certain ways? • Were your efforts successful? • What does this suggest about the need for systematic and perhaps supervised applications of the technique?

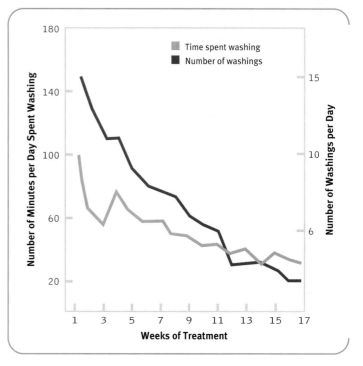

FIGURE 5-3 **Successful treatment for cleaning compulsions** *When a client was treated by exposure and response prevention, he showed a steady decline in the frequency of his daily washings and in the total amount of time he spent at them. (Adapted from Rachman, Hodgson, & Marzillier, 1970, p. 390.)*

Painful thoughts *Like the man in George Cruik-shank's painting* The Blue Devils, *some people may find unwanted thoughts particularly threatening and debilitating. According to cognitive theorists, their reactions to intrusive thoughts may set the stage for obsessive-compulsive disorder.*

NEUTRALIZING An attempt to eliminate unwanted thoughts by thinking or behaving in ways that put matters right internally, that make up for the unacceptable thoughts.

HABITUATION TRAINING A therapeutic technique in which a therapist tries to call forth a client's obsessive thoughts again and again, with the expectation that the thoughts will eventually lose their power to frighten and thus to cause anxiety.

SEROTONIN A neurotransmitter whose abnormal activity is linked to depression, obsessive-compulsive disorder, and eating disorders.

ORBITAL FRONTAL CORTEX A region of the brain in which impulses involving excretion, sexuality, violence, and other primitive activities normally arise.

CAUDATE NUCLEI Structures in the brain, within the region known as the basal ganglia, that help convert sensory information into thoughts and actions.

have thoughts of harming others, engaging in unacceptable sexual acts, or being contaminated by germs, but most people dismiss or ignore them with ease (Baer, 2001). Those who develop obsessive-compulsive disorder, however, typically blame themselves for such thoughts and expect that somehow terrible things will happen (Salkovskis, 1999, 1989, 1985). To avoid such negative outcomes, they try to **neutralize** the thoughts—thinking or behaving in ways meant to put matters right internally or to make up for the thoughts.

Neutralizing acts might include requesting special reassurance from others, deliberately thinking "good" thoughts, washing one's hands, or checking for possible sources of danger (Freeston & Ladouceur, 1997). When a neutralizing effort of some kind brings about a temporary reduction in discomfort, it is reinforced and will likely be repeated. Eventually the neutralizing thought or act is used so often that it becomes, by definition, an obsession or compulsion. At the same time, the individual becomes more and more convinced that his or her unpleasant intrusive thoughts are dangerous. As the person's fear of such thoughts increases, the thoughts begin to occur more frequently and they, too, become obsessions.

Although everyone has undesired thoughts, only some people develop obsessive-compulsive disorder. Why do these people find such normal thoughts so disturbing to begin with? Researchers have found that such individuals tend (1) to be more depressed than other people (Sobin et al., 1999; Clark & Purdon, 1993); (2) to have exceptionally high standards of conduct and morality (Rachman, 1993; Rachman & Hodgson, 1980); (3) to believe that their intrusive negative thoughts are equivalent to actions and capable of causing harm to themselves or others, and to feel responsible for eliminating the imagined danger (Wilson & Chambless, 1999); and (4) generally to believe that they can and should have perfect control over all thoughts and behaviors (Bouchard, Rhéaume, & Ladouceur, 1999).

Other aspects of this cognitive theory have also received support from research. Several investigators have found, for example, that people with obsessive-compulsive disorder have more intrusive thoughts than other people (Clark, 1992). In addition, studies have confirmed that people who develop this disorder resort at least sometimes to more elaborate neutralizing techniques than other people when they try to stop unwanted thoughts (Freeston et al., 1992). The neutralizing techniques do seem to reduce their discomfort temporarily (Roper, Rachman, & Hodgson, 1973).

COGNITIVE THERAPIES Cognitive therapists have developed approaches to obsessive-compulsive disorder that combine cognitive and behavioral techniques (Freeston et al., 1996). Therapists may use **habituation training,** for example, and have clients call forth their obsessive thoughts again and again. The clinicians expect that intense exposure to the thoughts will reduce their power to frighten or threaten, so that the thoughts produce less anxiety and trigger fewer new obsessive thoughts or compulsive acts (Salkovskis & Westbrook, 1989; Rachman & Hodgson, 1980). In one version of habituation training, clients are simply instructed to summon obsessive thoughts or images to mind and hold them for a while. In another version, clients spend up to an hour once or twice a day listening to their own voices on tape stating their obsessive thoughts again and again.

For people who experience obsessions only, habituation training is often the entire plan of treatment (Rachman & Hodgson, 1980). For others, however, therapists may add *covert-response prevention:* they teach clients to prevent or distract themselves from carrying out compulsive actions that may occur during habituation training. So far, support for these approaches has come mostly from case studies (Ladouceur et al., 1995).

The Biological Perspective

Partly because obsessive-compulsive disorder was so difficult to explain in the past, researchers tried repeatedly to identify hidden biological factors that might contribute to it. Their efforts have been rewarded in recent years, and promising biological treatments have been developed as well.

BIOLOGICAL EXPLANATIONS Two lines of research now offer great promise for explaining the biology of obsessive-compulsive disorder. One points to abnormally low activity of the neurotransmitter *serotonin,* the other to abnormal functioning in key areas of the brain.

Serotonin, like GABA and norepinephrine, is a brain chemical that carries messages from neuron to neuron. The first clue to its role in obsessive-compulsive disorder was the surprising finding by clinical researchers that two antidepressant drugs, *clomipramine* and *fluoxetine* (Anafranil and Prozac), reduce obsessive and compulsive symptoms (Klerman et al., 1994; Rapoport, 1991, 1989). Since these particular drugs also increase serotonin activity, some researchers concluded that the disorder is caused by low serotonin activity. In fact, only those antidepressant drugs that increase serotonin activity help in cases of obsessive-compulsive disorder; antidepressants that mainly affect other neurotransmitters have no effect on it (Jenike, 1992).

Another line of research has linked obsessive-compulsive disorder to abnormal brain functioning in specific regions of the brain: the **orbital region of the frontal cortex** (just above each eye) and the **caudate nuclei** (structures located within the brain region known as the *basal ganglia*). Together, these parts set up a brain circuit that converts sensory information into thoughts and actions (see Figure 5-4). The circuit begins in the orbital region, where sexual, violent, and other primitive impulses normally arise. These impulses next move on to the caudate nuclei, which act as filters that send only the most powerful impulses on to the *thalamus,* the next stop on the circuit. If impulses reach the thalamus, the person is driven to think further about them and perhaps to act. Many biological theorists now believe that either the orbital region or the caudate nuclei of some people are too active, leading to a constant breakthrough of troublesome thoughts and actions (Peterson et al., 1998).

In support of this theory, medical scientists have observed for years that obsessive-compulsive symptoms do sometimes arise or subside after the orbital region, caudate nuclei, or related brain areas are damaged by accident or illness (Berthier et al., 2001). Similarly, PET scans, which offer pictures of brain activity, have shown that the caudate nuclei and the orbital region of patients with obsessive-compulsive disorder are more active than those of control subjects (Baxter et al., 2001, 1990).

These biological notions may themselves be linked. It turns out that the neurotransmitter serotonin plays a very active role in the operation of the orbital region and the caudate nuclei; thus low serotonin activity might well interfere with the proper functioning of those brain parts.

BIOLOGICAL THERAPIES As we have seen, researchers have learned that certain antidepressant drugs are very useful in the treatment of obsessive-compulsive disorder (Gorman & Kent, 1999). Not only do they increase brain serotonin activity; they also produce more normal activity in the orbital region and caudate

Basal ganglia

Putamen and globus pallidus

Caudate nucleus

Orbital frontal cortex

Thalamus

FIGURE 5-4 **The biology of obsessive-compulsive disorder** *A three-dimensional view of the brain shows the regions that have been linked to obsessive-compulsive disorder. These areas may be too active in people with the disorder. (Adapted from Rapoport, 1989, p. 85.)*

nuclei, the brain areas that have been implicated in the disorder (Baxter et al., 2001, 1992). Studies have found that clomipramine, fluoxetine, and fluvoxamine (Anafranil, Prozac, and Luvox) bring improvement to between 50 and 80 percent of those with obsessive-compulsive disorder (Black et al., 1997; Taylor, 1995). The obsessions and compulsions do not usually disappear totally, but on average they are cut almost in half within eight weeks of treatment (DeVeaugh-Geiss et al., 1992). People whose improvement is based on the drugs alone, however, tend to relapse if the medication is stopped (Maina, Albert, & Bogetta, 2001).

Thus the treatment of obsessive-compulsive disorder, like that of panic disorder, has improved greatly over the past decade. Once a very stubborn problem, obsessive-compulsive disorder is now helped by several forms of treatment, particularly exposure and response prevention and antidepressant drugs, often used in combination (Foster & Eisler, 2001). In fact, at least two important studies suggest that the behavioral and biological approaches may ultimately have the same effect on the brain. In these investigations, subjects who responded to exposure and response prevention and those who responded to antidepressant drugs all showed marked reductions in activity in the caudate nuclei (Schwartz et al., 1996; Baxter et al., 1992).

A LAST RESORT

Obsessive-compulsive disorder is one of the few psychological problems still treated by psychosurgery, but only as a last resort after all other treatments have failed (Weingarten & Cummings, 2001). The procedure, which involves making narrow surgical lesions in one of the brain areas implicated in obsessive-compulsive disorder, may help as many as 30 percent of patients (Jenike et al., 1991).

SUMMING UP
Obsessive-Compulsive Disorder

People with obsessive-compulsive disorder experience obsessions or perform compulsions or do both. The compulsions are often a response to the obsessive thoughts.

According to the psychodynamic view, obsessive-compulsive disorder arises out of a battle between id impulses, which appear as obsessive thoughts, and ego defense mechanisms, which take the form of counterthoughts or compulsive actions.

Behaviorists believe that compulsive behaviors often develop through chance associations. The leading behavioral treatment combines prolonged exposure with response prevention.

Cognitive theorists believe that obsessive-compulsive disorder grows from a normal human tendency to have unwanted and unpleasant thoughts. The efforts of some people to understand, eliminate, or avoid such thoughts actually lead to obsessions and compulsions. A promising cognitive-behavioral approach is habituation training.

Biological researchers have tied obsessive-compulsive disorder to low serotonin activity and abnormal functioning in the brain's orbital frontal cortex and caudate nuclei. Antidepressant drugs that raise serotonin activity are a useful form of treatment.

Stress Disorders

Mark remembers his first "firefight" and encountering the VC [Viet Cong] for the first time. He lost all bladder and bowel control—in a matter of a few minutes. In his own words, "I was scared and literally shitless; I pissed all over myself, and shit all over myself too. Man, all hell broke loose. I tell you, I was so scared, I thought I would never make it out alive. I was convinced of that. Charlie had us pinned down and [was] hitting the shit out of us for hours. We had to call in the napalm and the bombing." During the first fight, Mark, an infantryman, experienced gruesome sights and strange sounds in battle. He witnessed headless bodies. "One guy said to me, 'Hey, Mark, new greenhorn boy, you saw that head go flying off that gook's shoulder. Isn't that something?'" Within 2 weeks Mark saw the head of a running comrade blown off his shoulders, the headless body

ACUTE STRESS DISORDER An anxiety disorder in which fear and related symptoms are experienced soon after a traumatic event and last less than a month.

POSTTRAUMATIC STRESS DISORDER An anxiety disorder in which fear and related symptoms continue to be experienced long after a traumatic event.

moving for a few feet before falling to the ground. Mark, nauseous and vomiting for a long time, couldn't see himself surviving much longer: "I couldn't get that sight out of my head; it just kept on coming back to me in my dreams, nightmares. Like clockwork, I'd see R's head flying, and his headless body falling to the ground. I knew the guy. He was very good to me when I first got to the unit. Nobody else seemed to give a damn about me; he broke me in. It's like I would see his head and body, you know, man, wow!" Mark often found himself crying during his first weeks of combat. "I wanted to go home. I was so lonely, helpless, and really scared. But I knew I could not go home until my year was up."

(Brende & Parson, 1985, pp. 23–24)

Mark's reaction to combat experience is normal and understandable. During or immediately after a traumatic situation, many people become highly anxious and depressed. For some, however, anxiety and depression persist well after the situation is over. These people may be suffering from **acute stress disorder** or **posttraumatic stress disorder,** patterns that arise in reaction to a psychologically traumatic event. The event usually involves actual or threatened serious injury to the person or to a family member or friend. Unlike other anxiety disorders, which typically are triggered by situations that most people would not find threatening, the situations that cause acute stress disorder or posttraumatic stress disorder—combat, rape, an earthquake, an airplane crash—would be traumatic for anyone.

If the symptoms begin within four weeks of the traumatic event and last for less than a month, DSM-IV assigns a diagnosis of *acute stress disorder* (APA, 2000, 1994). If the symptoms continue longer than a month, a diagnosis of *posttraumatic stress disorder* is appropriate. The symptoms of posttraumatic stress disorder may begin either shortly after the traumatic event or months or years afterward. Many cases of acute stress disorder develop into posttraumatic stress disorder (Brewin et al., 1999). Aside from the differences in onset and how long they last, the symptoms of these two anxiety disorders are almost identical (Taylor et al., 1998):

Reexperiencing the traumatic event People may be battered by recurring memories, dreams, or nightmares connected to the event. A few relive the event so vividly in their minds (flashbacks) that they think it is actually happening again.

Avoidance People will usually avoid activities that remind them of the traumatic event and will try to avoid related thoughts, feelings, or conversations.

Reduced responsiveness People may feel detached from other people or lose interest in activities that once brought enjoyment. They may lose their ability to experience such intimate emotions as tenderness and sexuality. Some even experience symptoms of *dissociation,* or psychological separation: they feel dazed, have trouble remembering things, or have a sense of derealization (feeling that the environment is unreal or strange).

Increased arousal, anxiety, and guilt People with these disorders may feel overly alert, be easily startled, develop sleep problems, and have trouble concentrating. They may feel extreme guilt because they survived the traumatic event while others did not. Some also feel guilty about what they may have had to do to survive.

We can see these symptoms in the recollections of Vietnam combat veterans years after they returned home:

I can't get the memories out of my mind! The images come flooding back in vivid detail, triggered by the most inconsequential things, like a door slamming or the smell of stir-fried pork. Last night I went to bed, was having a good sleep for a change. Then in the early morning a storm-front passed through and there was a

The horror of combat *Soldiers often react to combat with severe anxiety or depression or both. These immediate responses to battle have at various times been called "shell shock," "combat fatigue," or, most recently, "acute stress disorder."*

RETURNING HOME

One-quarter of the 1.5 million combat soldiers who returned from Vietnam were arrested within two years of their return. The divorce rate among the veterans was nearly double that of the general population, and their suicide rate was nearly 25 percent higher (Williams, 1983).

RAPE Forced sexual intercourse or another sexual act upon a nonconsenting person or intercourse with an underage person.

bolt of crackling thunder. I awoke instantly, frozen in fear. I am right back in Vietnam, in the middle of the monsoon season at my guard post. I am sure I'll get hit in the next volley and convinced I will die. My hands are freezing, yet sweat pours from my entire body. I feel each hair on the back of my neck standing on end. I can't catch my breath and my heart is pounding. I smell a damp sulfur smell.

(Davis, 1992)

What Triggers Stress Disorders?

An acute or posttraumatic stress disorder can occur at any age, even in childhood (Yule et al., 2001), and can affect one's personal, family, social, or occupational life (Resick, 2001). People with a stress disorder may also experience depression or substance abuse. Some become suicidal (Kotler et al., 2001; Amir et al., 1999). Around 3.9 percent of people in the United States experience one of the stress disorders in any given year; 7.6 percent suffer from one of them within their lifetimes (Kessler & Zhao, 1999; Kessler et al., 1994). Women are at least twice as likely as men to develop the disorders: around 20 percent of women who are exposed to a severe trauma may develop one, compared to 8 percent of men (Ursano et al., 1999; Kessler et al., 1995). Although any traumatic event can trigger a stress disorder, some are particularly likely to do so. Among the most common are combat, disasters, and abuse and victimization.

COMBAT AND STRESS DISORDERS For years clinicians have recognized that many soldiers develop symptoms of severe anxiety and depression *during* combat (Oei, Lim, & Hennessy, 1990). The pattern of symptoms was called "nostalgia" during the American Civil War because it was considered to be the result of extended absence from home (Bourne, 1970). It was called "shell shock" during World War I because it was thought to result from small brain hemorrhages or concussions caused by constant artillery explosions. During World War II and the Korean War, it was referred to as "combat fatigue" (Figley, 1978). Not until after the Vietnam War, however, did clinicians learn that many soldiers also experience serious psychological symptoms *after* combat (Schlenger et al., 1998).

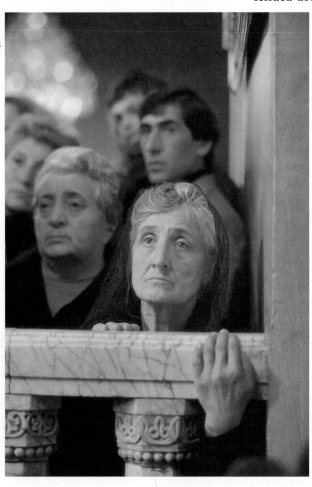

Human aftershocks *These Armenian citizens seek solace in church after a devastating earthquake. Strong institutional and social ties can sometimes, but not always, reduce individual stress reactions after disasters and other traumatic events.*

Peter Turnley/Black Star

In the first years after the Vietnam War, the psychological problems of combat veterans were generally overlooked, perhaps in part because of the nation's desire to leave this unpopular war behind. By the late 1970s, however, it had become apparent that many Vietnam combat veterans were still experiencing war-related psychological problems (Williams, 1983). We now know that as many as 29 percent of all veterans, male and female, who served in Vietnam suffered an acute or posttraumatic stress disorder, while another 22 percent suffered from at least some stress symptoms (Weiss et al., 1992). In fact, 10 percent of the veterans of this war still experience significant posttraumatic stress symptoms, including flashbacks, night terrors, nightmares, and persistent images and thoughts. Similarly, in studies of combat veterans of the Persian Gulf War, over one-third reported six months later that they were experiencing nightmares and were drinking more than before (Erickson et al., 2001; Labbate & Snow, 1992).

DISASTERS AND STRESS DISORDERS Acute and posttraumatic stress disorders may also follow natural and accidental disasters such as earthquakes, floods, tornadoes, fires, airplane crashes, and serious car accidents (see Table 5-5). Studies have found, for example, that around one-third of victims—adult or child—of serious traffic accidents may develop posttraumatic stress disorder within a year of the accident (Lowenstein, 2001; Ursano et al., 1999).

Table 5-5

Worst Natural Disasters of the Twentieth Century

DISASTER	YEAR	LOCATION	NUMBER KILLED
Flood	1931	Huang He River, China	3,700,000
Earthquake	1926	Tangshan, China	242,419
Volcanic eruption	1902	Mont-Pélée, Martinique	40,000
Landslide	1970	Yungay, Peru	17,500
Tidal wave	1960	Agadir, Morocco	12,000
Avalanche	1916	Italian Alps	10,000
Tornado	1989	Shaturia, Bangladesh	1,300

Adapted from Ash, 1999, 1998.

Similarly, several studies found stress reactions among the survivors of Hurricane Andrew, the storm that ravaged Florida and other parts of the southeastern United States in 1992 (Vernberg et al., 1996). By a month after the storm the number of calls received by the domestic violence hot line in Miami and the number of women applying for police protection had doubled (Treaster, 1992). By six months after the storm it was apparent that many elementary-school-age children were also victims of posttraumatic stress disorder; their symptoms ranged from misbehavior in school to failing grades and problems with sleep (Vernberg et al., 1996; Gelman & Katel, 1993).

VICTIMIZATION AND STRESS DISORDERS People who have been abused or victimized often experience lingering stress symptoms. For example, interviews with survivors of Nazi concentration camps years after their liberation found that as many as 46 percent of them eventually qualified for a diagnosis of posttraumatic stress disorder (Kuch & Cox, 1992; Eitinger, 1973, 1969, 1964).

A common form of victimization in our society today is sexual assault. **Rape** is forced sexual intercourse or another sexual act upon a nonconsenting person or intercourse with an underage person. Surveys suggest that in the United States more than 876,000 persons are victims of rape each year (NCVS, 1996). Most rapists are men, and most victims are women. Approximately one in seven women is raped at some time during her life. Surveys also suggest that most rape victims are young: 29 percent are under 11 years old, 32 percent are between the ages of 11 and 17, and 29 percent are between 18 and 29. More than 80 percent of the victims are raped by acquaintances or relatives (NCVS, 1996; Koss, 1992; Youngstrom, 1992).

The psychological impact of rape on a victim is immediate and may last a long time (Koss & Kilpatrick, 2001). Rape victims typically experience enormous distress during the week after the assault. Stress continues to rise for the next three weeks, maintains a peak level for another month or so, and then starts to improve (Koss, 1993). In one study, 94 percent of rape victims fully qualified for a clinical diagnosis of acute stress disorder when they were observed an average of twelve days after the assault (Rothbaum et al., 1992). Although most rape victims improve psychologically within three or four months, the effects may persist for up to eighteen

Victimization and posttraumatic stress disorder *Many survivors of Nazi concentration camps faced a long road back to psychological health. Because knowledge of posttraumatic stress disorder was nonexistent until recent years, most survivors had to find their way back without professional help.*

months or longer. Victims typically continue to have higher than average levels of anxiety, suspiciousness, depression, self-esteem problems, self-blame, flashbacks, sleep problems, and sexual dysfunction (Arata, 1999; Moncrieff et al., 1996). The lingering psychological impact of rape is apparent in the following case description:

> Mary Billings is a 33-year-old divorced nurse, referred to the Victim Clinic at Bedford Psychiatric Hospital for counseling by her supervisory head nurse. Mary had been raped two months ago. The assailant gained entry to her apartment while she was sleeping, and she awoke to find him on top of her. He was armed with a knife and threatened to kill her and her child (who was asleep in the next room) if she did not submit to his demands. He forced her to undress and repeatedly raped her vaginally over a period of 1 hour. He then admonished her that if she told anyone or reported the incident to the police he would return and assault her child.
>
> After he left, she called her boyfriend, who came to her apartment right away. He helped her contact the Sex Crimes Unit of the Police Department, which is currently investigating the case. He then took her to a local hospital for a physical examination and collection of evidence for the police (traces of sperm, pubic hair samples, fingernail scrapings). She was given antibiotics as prophylaxis against venereal disease. Mary then returned home with a girlfriend who spent the remainder of the night with her.
>
> Over the next few weeks Mary continued to be afraid of being alone and had her girlfriend move in with her. She became preoccupied with thoughts of what had happened to her and the possibility that it could happen again. Mary was frightened that the rapist might return to her apartment and therefore had additional locks installed on both the door and the windows. She was so upset and had such difficulty concentrating that she decided she could not yet return to work. When she did return to work several weeks later, she was still clearly upset, and her supervisor suggested that she might be helped by counseling.
>
> During the clinic interview, Mary was coherent and spoke quite rationally in a hushed voice. She reported recurrent and intrusive thoughts about the sexual assault, to the extent that her concentration was impaired and she had difficulty doing chores such as making meals for herself and her daughter. She felt she was not able to be effective at work, still felt afraid to leave her home, to answer her phone, and had little interest in contacting friends or relatives.
>
> . . . [Mary] talked in the same tone of voice whether discussing the assault or less emotionally charged topics, such as her work history. She was easily startled by an unexpected noise. She also was unable to fall asleep because she kept thinking about the assault. She had no desire to eat, and when she did attempt it, she felt nauseated. Mary was repelled by the thought of sex and stated that she did not want to have sex for a long time, although she was willing to be held and comforted by her boyfriend.
>
> *(Spitzer et al., 1983, pp. 20–21)*

Although many rape victims are injured by their attacker or experience other physical problems as a result of their assault, only half receive the kind of formal medical care afforded Mary (Beebe, 1991; Koss, Woodruff, & Koss, 1991). Between 4 and 30 percent of victims develop a sexually transmitted disease (Koss, 1993; Murphy, 1990) and 5 percent become pregnant (Beebe, 1991; Koss et al., 1991), yet a national survey revealed that 60 percent of rape victims received no pregnancy testing or preventive measures and 73 percent received no information or testing for exposure to HIV (National Victims Center, 1992).

Female victims of rape and other crimes are also much more likely than other women to suffer serious long-term health problems (Leserman et al., 1996; Koss & Heslet, 1992). Interviews with 390 women revealed that such victims had

GENDER DIFFERENCES

Rates of reported rape and other sexual assaults against women are 10 times higher than those against men (U.S. Dept. of Justice, 1995). Over 80 percent of male rapes are committed by other men (NCVS, 1998, 1993).

VIOLENCE TIMETABLE

In the United States, a violent crime is committed every 16 seconds, a rape every 5 minutes, a murder every 21 minutes (FBI Uniform Crime Report).

poorer physical well-being for at least five years after the crime and made twice as many visits to physicians. It is not yet clear why rape and other assaults lead to these long-term health problems.

Ongoing victimization and abuse in the family—specifically spouse and child abuse—may also lead to stress disorders (Jones et al., 2001; McLeer et al., 1998). Because these forms of abuse may occur over the long term and violate family roles and trust, many victims develop other symptoms and disorders as well (Kemp et al., 1995).

Finally, living in a violent neighborhood or attending schools plagued by violence can be a source of ongoing trauma (Purnell, 1999; Kliewer et al., 1998). A study of one neighborhood found that fully 14 percent of fifth- and sixth-graders had witnessed a shooting and 43 percent had observed a mugging. These children showed more symptoms of stress than other children (Martinez & Richters, 1993).

Recovery from trauma *Many people eventually overcome the effects of traumatic stress. During a reunion, these concentration camp survivors proudly display their tattooed camp identification numbers as symbols of their triumph over their psychological wounds.*

Why Do People Develop Stress Disorders?

Clearly, extraordinary trauma can cause a stress disorder. The stressful event alone, however, may not be completely to blame. Certainly, anyone who experiences an unusual trauma will be affected by it, but only some people develop a disorder (McNally, 2001). To understand the development of stress disorders more fully, researchers have looked to the survivors' biological processes, personalities, childhood experiences, and social support systems and to the severity of the traumas (Resick, 2001).

BIOLOGICAL AND GENETIC FACTORS Investigators have gathered evidence that traumatic events trigger physical changes in the brain and body that may lead to severe stress reactions and, in some cases, to stress disorders. They have, for example, found abnormal activity of the neurotransmitter *norepinephrine* and the hormone *cortisol* in the urine and blood of combat soldiers, rape victims, concentration camp survivors, and survivors of other severe stresses (Tobin, 2001; Yehuda et al., 1998, 1995, 1994).

Perhaps people whose biochemical reactions to stress are particularly strong are more likely than others to develop acute and posttraumatic stress disorders (Kellner & Yehuda, 1999; Shalev, 1999). But why would certain people be prone to such strong biological reactions? It may be that they inherit a genetic tendency to react in these ways. One study of approximately 4,000 pairs of twins who had served in the Vietnam War found that if one twin developed stress symptoms after combat, an identical twin was more likely than a fraternal twin to develop the same problems (True & Lyons, 1999; True et al., 1993). We must remember, though, that the similarities seen in identical twins do not always reflect genetic influences: childhood experiences, personalities, and support systems may also be more similar in identical twins than in fraternal twins and explain the greater similarity in their reactions to stress.

PERSONALITY Some studies suggest that people with certain personality profiles, attitudes, and coping styles are more likely to develop stress disorders (McFarlane, 1999; Schnurr & Vielhauer, 1999). In the aftermath of Hurricane

ConsiderThis

● What types of events in modern society might be likely to trigger acute and posttraumatic stress disorders? ● Do you think the vivid images seen daily on television, in movies, in rock videos, and the like would make people more vulnerable to developing such disorders or less vulnerable?

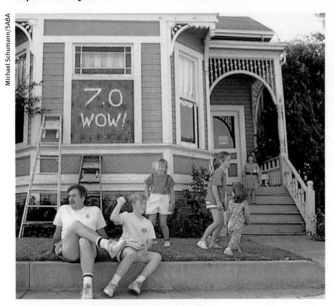

Protection by personality *Millions reacted to the San Francisco earthquake of 1989 with dread and panic, but some laid-back individuals thrived on all the excitement. Their "hardy" personality styles may have helped to protect them from the development of stress disorders.*

Hugo, for example, children who had been highly anxious before the storm were more likely than other children to develop severe stress reactions (Lonigan et al., 1994). Similarly, the victims who are most likely to develop stress disorders after being raped are the ones who had psychological problems before they were raped or who were struggling with stressful life situations (Darvres-Bornoz et al., 1995). The same is true of war veterans who had psychological problems before they went into combat (Orsillo et al., 1996). Finally, people who generally view life's negative events as beyond their control tend to develop more severe stress symptoms after sexual or other kinds of criminal assaults than do people who feel greater control over their lives (Regehr, Cadell, & Jansen, 1999; Kushner et al., 1992).

CHILDHOOD EXPERIENCES A recent wave of studies has found that certain childhood experiences seem to leave some people at risk for later acute and posttraumatic stress disorders. People whose childhoods have been marked by poverty appear more likely to develop these disorders in the face of later trauma. So do people whose family members suffered from psychological disorders; who experienced assault, abuse, or catastrophe at an early age; or who were younger than 10 when their parents separated or divorced (Breslau et al., 1999; Bremner et al., 1993).

SOCIAL SUPPORT It has been found that people whose social support systems are weak are also more likely to develop a stress disorder after a traumatic event (Perry et al., 1992). Rape victims who feel loved, cared for, valued, and accepted by their friends and relatives recover more successfully. So do those treated with dignity and respect by the criminal justice system (Davis, Brickman, & Baker,

THE CURRENT SCENE

Working with Death

One of the least pleasant jobs in our society is to tie up loose ends after a horrifying disaster or murder. Yet the work must be done, regardless of the toll it may take on the workers. It turns out that reactions to such responsibilities vary widely.

In 1993, 83 persons died in the fire at the Branch Davidian compound in Waco, Texas. Thirty-one dentists had to examine the dental remains of the dead. A study later revealed that these dentists had more symptoms of posttraumatic stress disorder than were observed in a control group of other dentists (McCarroll et al., 1996).

Then there are Ray and Louise Barnes (see photo), who run a business called Crime Scene Clean-Up. They and their staffers are hired by police departments, funeral homes, and grieving families to clean up after homicides, suicides, and

accidents. They use latex gloves, mops, respirators, and other tools of the trade

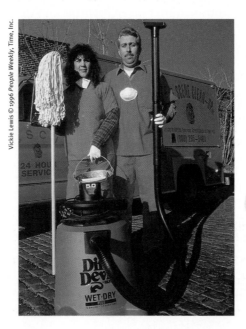

to "scrub away the detritus of human disaster" (Howe & Nugent, 1996). Ray Barnes says that his former jobs with a funeral home and a medical examiner's office helped prepare him for this work. While hardly indifferent to the grisly scenes, he has grown somewhat used to them, and he and his wife now have a thriving business.

ConsiderThis
◉ Why might the dentists and the Barneses react so differently to the situations they have faced? • What other jobs in our society might be traumatizing?

1991; Sales, Baum, & Shore, 1984). In contrast, clinical reports have suggested that poor social support has contributed to the development of posttraumatic stress disorder in some combat veterans (Taft et al., 1999; Figley & Leventman, 1990).

SEVERITY OF TRAUMA As one might expect, the severity and nature of traumatic events help determine whether an individual will develop a stress disorder. Some events can override even a nurturing childhood, positive attitudes, and social support. One study examined 253 Vietnam War prisoners five years after their release. Some 23 percent qualified for a clinical diagnosis, though all had been evaluated as well adjusted before their imprisonment (Ursano, Boydstun, & Wheatley, 1981).

Generally, the more severe the trauma and the more direct one's exposure to it, the greater the likelihood of developing a stress disorder (King et al., 1996; Putnam, 1996). Among the Vietnam prisoners of war, for example, it was the men who had been imprisoned longest and treated most harshly who had the highest percentage of disorders. Mutilation and severe physical injury in particular seem to increase the risk of stress reactions, as does witnessing the injury or death of other people (Putnam, 1996; Kessler et al., 1995). It is, as a survivor of trauma once said, "hard to be a survivor" (Kolff & Doan, 1985, p. 45).

How Do Clinicians Treat Stress Disorders?

Treatment can make a major difference to a person with a stress disorder. One survey found that posttraumatic stress symptoms lasted an average of three years with treatment but five and a half years without (Kessler & Zhao, 1999; Kessler et al., 1995). Today's treatment procedures for troubled survivors typically vary from trauma to trauma. Was it combat, sexual molestation, or a major accident? Yet all the programs share basic goals: they try to help survivors put an end to the lingering stress reactions, gain perspective on their traumatic experiences, and return to constructive living. Programs for combat veterans who suffer from posttraumatic stress disorder illustrate how these issues may be addressed.

TREATMENT FOR COMBAT VETERANS Therapists have used a variety of techniques to reduce veterans' posttraumatic symptoms. Among the most common are *drug therapy, exposure techniques, insight therapy, family therapy,* and *group therapy*. Typically the approaches are combined, as no one of them successfully reduces all the symptoms (Boudewyns, 1996).

Antianxiety drugs help reduce the tension and exaggerated startle responses that many veterans experience. In addition, antidepressant medications may reduce the occurrence of nightmares, panic attacks, flashbacks, unwanted recollections, and feelings of depression (van der Kolk, 2001; Friedman, 1999).

Behavioral exposure techniques, too, have helped reduce specific symptoms, and they have often led to improvements in overall adjustment (DeRubeis & Crits-Christoph, 1998; Woodward et al., 1997). Flooding, along with relaxation training, helped rid a 31-year-old veteran of frightening flashbacks and nightmares (Fairbank & Keane, 1982). The therapist and the veteran first singled out combat scenes that the man had been reexperiencing frequently. The therapist then helped the veteran to imagine one of these scenes in great detail and urged him to hold on to the image until his anxiety stopped. After each of these flooding exercises, the therapist had the veteran switch to a positive image and led him through relaxation exercises.

Although drug therapy and exposure techniques bring some relief, most clinicians believe that veterans with posttraumatic stress disorder cannot fully recover with these approaches alone: they must also come to grips in some way with their combat experiences and the impact those experiences continue to have (Marmar et al., 1993). Thus clinicians often try to help veterans bring out deep-seated feelings, accept what they have done and experienced, become less judgmental of themselves, and learn to trust other people once again (Shay & Munroe, 1999).

ConsiderThis

○ Rape victims need support from the medical and legal systems in order to deal effectively with their trauma and its aftermath. How might physicians, police, the courts, and other agents better meet the needs of these victims?

REBOUND EFFECT

In one study, rape victims suffering from posttraumatic stress disorder were instructed to deliberately suppress all thoughts about their sexual assault. This strategy not only failed to help them but led to a rise in rape-related thoughts (Shipherd & Beck, 1999).

Spouse Abuse: Victimization in the Family

❚ He told me that he was never going to let me go. He said that he married me, and whether he loved me or not, and whether I loved him or not, I was going to stay with him, and if I tried to leave him, he was going to kill me—one day at a time, like dripping water on a rock, until I broke apart. Although I never knew exactly what he would do, I knew that he was capable of torture. He broke my arm once and dangled it in front of me, playing with it, telling me it wasn't broken. ❚

(JONES & SCHECHTER, 1992)

Spouse abuse, the physical mistreatment or misuse of one spouse by the other, takes numerous forms, from shoving to battering. Ninety-three percent of abused spouses are women, married or cohabiting (Walker, 1999). It is estimated that spouse abuse occurs in 2 to 4 million homes in the United States each year and that as many as a third of all U.S. women have been abused at least once by their husbands (Brannen et al., 1999; Dearwater et al., 1998). Spouse abuse is seen in all races, religions, educational levels, and socioeconomic groups. The U.S. surgeon general has ranked it as the leading cause of injuries to women between the ages of 15 and 44.

For years this behavior was viewed as a private matter; until 1874 a husband actually had a legal right to beat his wife in the United States. Even after that time, abusers were rarely punished. Police were reluctant to do anything other than try to calm down an episode of domestic violence, and the courts rarely prosecuted an abuser. Thanks to the civil rights movement in the 1970s and the efforts of women's groups, state legislatures have increasingly passed laws that empower the courts to prosecute abusers and protect victims. As a result, the police are now able to intervene more actively, and nearly half of all U.S. police departments have special units to deal with spouse abuse. In fact, 25 states have laws requiring the police to make an arrest when they are called to a scene. Arrests do not necessarily lead to convictions, however, nor do convictions always produce sentences that prevent future abuse.

Abusers

There is no one personality profile for abusers. Many of them, though, have a need to control their wives, but are emotionally dependent on them at the same time and fear losing them (Murphy et al., 1994). Often these men consider their wives to be their personal property, and they become most assaultive when the wife shows independence. In some cases the abuse increases when the wives seek outside friendships, attempt to work outside the home, or even attend to the children's needs first. These husbands may also belittle and isolate their wives and make them feel inept, worthless, and dependent.

"Honeymoon phases" seem to be common in abusive relationships (Walker, 1984, 1979). Periodically the husband, concerned that the latest violent incident will cause his wife to leave him, performs acts of kindness and sorrow, and promises that the abuse will never happen again (Jones & Schechter, 1992). Unfortunately, in most cases the abuse does happen again, and over time, battering may even increase.

Many persons who abuse their spouses have alcohol-related or other substance-related problems (Mollerstrom et al., 1992), but these problems are not usually the key cause of battering, and treating only an abuser's substance problem seldom stops the violence (ADVTP, 1996; Jones & Schechter, 1992). Many abusers were themselves beaten as children or saw their mothers beaten (Walker, 1999; Saunders, 1992). Often they suffer from low self-esteem and feel generally stressed and frustrated with their lives (Russell & Hulson, 1992).

Victims

As a result of physical abuse, threats, and intimidation, a victim of abuse typically feels very dependent on her husband and unable to function on her own.

People who have a stress disorder are sometimes helped to express their feelings and develop insight in couple or family therapy formats (Glynn et al., 1995; Johnson, Feldman, & Lubin, 1995). The symptoms of posttraumatic stress disorder tend to be particularly apparent to family members, who may be directly affected by the client's anxieties, depressive mood, or angry outbursts (Catherall, 1999). With the help and support of their family members, individuals may come to recognize the feelings they are grappling with, examine their impact on others, learn to communicate better, and improve their problem-solving skills.

Veterans may also benefit from **rap groups,** where they meet with others like themselves to share experiences and feelings, develop insights, and give mutual support. Many veterans find it easier to recall events in a rap group and to face feelings they have been trying to avoid for years (Ford & Stewart, 1999). One of the major issues rap groups deal with is guilt—guilt about things the members may have done to survive or about the very fact that they did survive while close friends died. Once the veterans are finally able to talk openly about their combat experiences and guilt feelings, they may finally start to recover from them and

RAP GROUP A group that meets to talk about and explore members' problems in an atmosphere of mutual support.

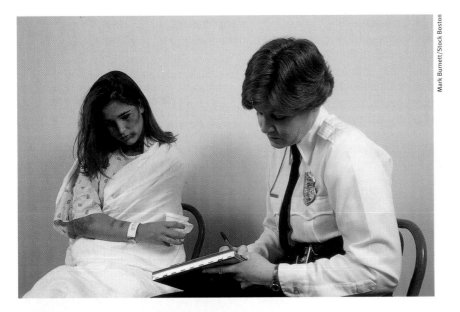

Police intervention *A victim of spouse abuse is interviewed by a police officer after being hospitalized. Many police departments now have special units to ensure that victims receive medical help, counseling, and legal guidance.*

These feelings tend to keep her in the relationship despite the obvious physical dangers. Abused women are not masochistic, as many clinical theorists once believed (Walker, 1984). In fact, 80 percent of them try to defend themselves either physically or verbally. This is the same as the percentage of women in general who defend themselves when assaulted by a stranger (U.S. Dept. of Justice, 1994).

Many victims stay with their husbands out of economic need. Research shows that most women's standard of living falls drastically after a divorce (Glazer, 1993; Heise & Chapman, 1990). Others stay for fear of what their husbands may do if they go. This fear is often justified: violence against the victim increases by as much as 75 percent when she tries to leave the relationship (Hart, 1993; U.S. Dept. of Justice, 1992). In one study of spouse abuse, 70 percent of the reported injuries were inflicted *after* the couple separated (Liss & Stahly, 1993). Another study found that half of all women murdered by their husbands were killed after they had left home (Hart, 1993).

About half of victims of spouse abuse grew up in homes where they or their mothers were abused, and most come from families in which male and female roles follow old stereotypes. Many victims have very low self-esteem, partly as a result of the ongoing abuse (Cornell & Gelles, 1983). They often blame themselves for the abuse and agree when their husbands accuse them of triggering it (Street & Arias, 2001). Usually the pattern of abuse did not begin until after the couple married.

To help victims address their dangerous situation, community programs have been set up which provide such women with a safe place to live, away from their abusive husbands, and which counsel them to help them understand their situation, see their choices, and develop a more positive self-image. The programs often include hot lines; emergency shelters, or "safe houses;" and public organizations and self-help groups to provide education and aid (Monnier et al., 2001; Page, 1996; Sullivan et al., 1992). In some areas, the legal system also plays a role by requiring that arrested abusers attend a batterers' program as an alternative to jail (Walker, 1999).

weigh their responsibility for past actions more accurately (Lifton, 1973). Rap groups may also focus on the rage many combat veterans feel.

Today hundreds of small *Veteran Outreach Centers* across the country, as well as numerous treatment programs in Veterans Administration hospitals and mental health clinics, specialize in rap groups (Ford & Stewart, 1999). These agencies also offer individual therapy, counseling for the spouses and children of troubled veterans, family therapy, and aid in seeking jobs, education, and benefits. Research into the effectiveness of these programs has been limited (Funari, Piekarski, & Sherwood, 1991). However, the clinical reports and empirical studies that have been done suggest that they offer a necessary, sometimes life-saving treatment opportunity.

COMMUNITY THERAPY: THE SOCIOCULTURAL MODEL IN ACTION People who are traumatized by disasters, victimization, or accidents may profit from many of the same treatments that are used to help survivors of combat. In addition, because their traumas occur in their own community, where mental health

WARTIME LEGACY

Vietnam veterans who continue to suffer from posttraumatic stress disorder display a higher than average rate of circulatory, digestive, muscle and skeletal, endocrine, nervous system, respiratory, and infectious diseases (Boscarino, 1997).

Disaster Counseling: The Other Side

Rapid-mobilization mental health programs for disaster victims are growing in number and popularity. Studies of these programs typically yield favorable results, and personal testimonials are supportive as well. At the same time, a number of clinical theorists question the effectiveness of these interventions (Gist & Woodall, 1999).

An investigation conducted several years ago was among the first to raise concerns about the disaster mental health programs (Bisson & Deahl, 1994). Crisis counselors worked with 62 British soldiers whose job during the Gulf War was to handle and identify the bodies of individuals who had been killed. After receiving nine months of crisis counseling, half of the soldiers nevertheless displayed posttraumatic stress symptoms, a finding that led some theorists to conclude that disaster intervention programs do not really make much difference. Still worse, some clinicians now worry that the programs may encourage victims to dwell too long on the traumatic events that they have experienced. Moreover, certain clinicians are concerned that early disaster counseling may actually "suggest" problems to victims, thus helping to produce stress disorders in the first place (McClelland, 1998).

The current clinical climate continues to favor disaster counseling, and such programs may indeed prove to be as helpful as many clinicians believe. However, the concerns that have been raised merit serious consideration. We are reminded here, as elsewhere, of the constant need for careful research in the field of abnormal psychology.

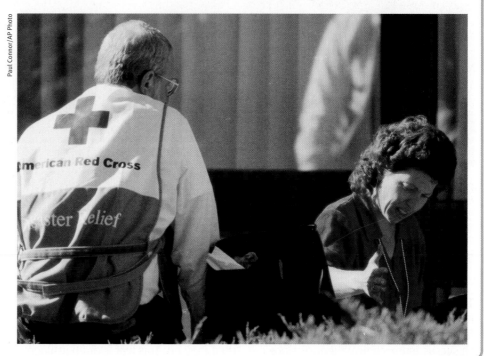

Paul Connor/AP Photo

Essential or excessive? *A relief worker comforts the family member of a victim of Egypt Air Flight 990, the plane that crashed off Nantucket Island in 1999 under mysterious circumstances, killing all 217 aboard.*

resources are close at hand, these individuals may profit from immediate community interventions. A case in point is the rapidly mobilized psychological care now offered at the site of large-scale disasters. These professionals typically receive training in the delivery of emergency mental health services, called **critical incident stress debriefing.**

One of the largest community intervention programs is the *Disaster Response Network (DRN)*, developed in 1991 by the American Psychological Association and the American Red Cross. The network is made up of more than 2,500 volunteer psychologists who offer free emergency mental health services at disaster sites throughout North America (Peterson, 1996). They have been mobilized for such disasters as Hurricane Andrew in 1992, earthquakes in Southern California, the Oklahoma City bombing, the World Trade Center bombing, the explosion of TWA Flight 800, and the 1999 shooting of 23 persons at Columbine High School in Littleton, Colorado.

Traditional long-term mental health services may not always be appropriate, available, or sought after a disaster. In fact, many survivors do not even recognize their own degree of upset in the face of a disaster (Michaelson, 1993). Thus the short-term community intervention provided by the Disaster Response Network and similar programs seems to fill a real need (Joyner & Swenson, 1993). People who live in poverty are in particular need of community-level interventions. These survivors apparently suffer more psychological distress after disasters than survivors with higher incomes (Gibbs, 1989), they cannot afford private counseling, and they are less likely to know where to seek counseling.

CRITICAL INCIDENT STRESS DEBRIEFING
Training in how to help victims talk about their feelings and reactions to traumatic incidents.

The first aim of mental health professionals in disaster settings is to help survivors meet their basic needs as quickly as possible. During the Midwest flood of 1993, for example, professionals worked in shelters and service centers and rode in Red Cross emergency vehicles to deliver food and water along with counseling services. Some counselors joined flood victims in piling sandbags to protect their homes from further damage. The counselors also used these early contacts to determine which victims were most in need of psychological help.

Once mental health volunteers become involved in the community, they may act more directly to help meet the psychological needs of the disaster victims. They often use a four-stage approach (Michaelson, 1993):

1. **Normalize people's responses to the disaster.** The counselors educate survivors about the symptoms they may be experiencing, such as sleep disturbances, difficulty concentrating, or feelings of grief. Essentially, survivors are given permission to have these reactions and told that they are normal responses to a disaster.

2. **Encourage expressions of anxiety, anger, and frustration.** To reduce the anxiety, anger, and frustration that survivors often feel after a disaster, counselors help them talk about their experiences and their feelings.

3. **Teach self-helping skills.** Counselors train survivors to develop stress management and other self-help skills.

4. **Provide referrals.** The workers eventually may refer survivors to other professionals who can provide long-term counseling (Sleek, 1997). It is estimated that between 15 and 25 percent of survivors need this specialized assistance.

Relief workers, too, can become overwhelmed by the traumas they witness (Ursano et al., 1999). During the Los Angeles riots, for example, a key responsibility of many counselors was to help Red Cross workers vent and accept their own feelings as well as teach them about stress disorders and how to identify victims who need further treatment. Many mental health professionals who live in a disaster area need counseling themselves, since they, too, are survivors. The dual role they are thrown into may make it hard for them to deal with their own experiences.

Everyone is affected *A fire captain cradles one-year-old Baylee Almon, a child killed in the bombing of the Oklahoma City federal building. This famous photograph reminds us that rescue workers are themselves subjected to enormous stress and trauma during disasters (Bryant & Harvey, 1995).*

SUMMING UP / Stress Disorders

People with acute stress disorder or posttraumatic stress disorder react with anxiety and related symptoms after a traumatic event. The symptoms of acute stress disorder begin soon after the trauma and last less than a month. Those of posttraumatic stress disorder may begin at any time (even years) after the trauma and may last for months or years.

In attempting to explain why some people develop a stress disorder and others do not, researchers have focused on biological factors, childhood experiences, personal variables, social support, and the severity of the traumatic event.

Techniques used to treat the stress disorders include drug therapy and behavioral exposure techniques. Clinicians may also use insight therapy, family therapy, and group therapy (including rap groups for combat veterans) to help sufferers develop useful insights and perspective. Community therapy, such as that offered by the Disaster Response Network, can also be very helpful after large-scale disasters.

"IT COULD HAVE BEEN SAMMY"
Disaster workers who deal with the remains of deceased victims are more likely to develop a stress disorder if they identify with the victims—"It could have been my family" (Ursano et al., 1999).

CROSSROADS:
Lessons to Be Learned

Panic, obsessive-compulsive, and stress disorders have received intense study over the past decade. Lessons can be learned from the history of these disorders, not just about the disorders themselves, but about the general study and treatment of psychological abnormality.

First, we learn that effort pays off. For many years, the study and treatment of panic disorder and obsessive-compulsive disorder seemed to be going nowhere. Early explanations provided few insights, and clinical treatments brought little change. Recent work in the biological, cognitive, and behavioral spheres has changed all that. Today research into these problems is flourishing, the new explanations are enlightening, and treatment is highly effective.

A second lesson is that insights and techniques from the various models not only *can* be combined but often *should* be combined for greater clarity and effectiveness. Not until clinical theorists took a cross-model look at the disorders discussed in this chapter were they able to develop explanations and treatments that were informative and helpful. The cognitive explanation of panic disorder, for example, builds squarely on the biological idea that the disorder begins with unusual physical sensations. Similarly, therapists have found that treatment is at least sometimes more effective when medications are combined with cognitive techniques to treat panic disorder and with behavioral techniques to treat obsessive-compulsive disorder. For the millions of people who suffer from these anxiety disorders, such integrated insights and treatments are momentous developments.

Finally, we can learn a lesson of caution from the recent work on these disorders. When problems are heavily studied, it is common for researchers and clinicians to make claims and draw conclusions that may be too bold. An example is posttraumatic stress disorder. Because its symptoms are many, because a variety of life events can be considered traumatic, and because the disorder has received so much attention, many people—perhaps too many—are now receiving this diagnosis. We shall see this potential problem again when we look at attention-deficit/hyperactivity disorder, repressed memories of childhood abuse, and multiple personality disorder. The line between enlightenment and overenthusiasm is often thin.

KEY TERMS

QUICK QUIZ

1. What biological factors contribute to panic disorder, and what biological approaches effectively treat this disorder? pp. 130–131

2. How do cognitive theorists explain and treat panic disorder? pp. 131–133

3. What are biological challenge tests, and how are they used by researchers and by therapists? p. 132

4. Describe various types of obsessions and compulsions. pp. 134–137

5. Which defense mechanisms do psychodynamic theorists believe are particularly common in obsessive-compulsive disorder? p. 137

6. How might normal thinking processes and "neutralizing" combine to produce obsessive-compulsive disorder? What kinds of research support has the cognitive explanation received? pp. 139–140

7. What biological factors have been linked to obsessive-compulsive disorder? p. 141

8. Describe and compare the effectiveness of the behavioral treatment (exposure and response prevention) and the biological treatment (antidepressant medications) for obsessive-compulsive disorder. pp. 138–139, 141–142

9. What factors seem to help influence whether a person will develop a stress disorder after experiencing a traumatic event? pp. 144–149

10. What treatment approaches have been used with people suffering from stress disorders? pp. 149–153

CYBER STUDY

▲ *How do persons with obsessive-compulsive disorder explain their behaviors?*
▲ *How disruptive are obsessions and compulsions?* ▲ *How do obsessions and compulsions interrelate?* ▲ *How do persons react to the trauma of losing a loved one to suicide?*

SEARCH THE *FUNDAMENTALS OF ABNORMAL PSYCHOLOGY* CD-ROM FOR

▲ Chapter 5 video cases and discussions
   "Jennifer"—Obsessive-Compulsive Disorder
   "Bill"—Obsessive-Compulsive Disorder

▲ Chapter 5 practice test and feedback

▲ Additional video case and discussion
   "Bonnie"—Suicide

LOG ON TO THE COMER WEB PAGE FOR

▲ Suggested Web links, research exercises, FAQ page, additional Chapter 5 practice test questions
   <http://www.worthpublishers.com/comer>

Source: UCLA Neuropsychiatric Institute & Hospital

CHAPTER

6

Mood Disorders

DEPRESSION A low, sad state marked by significant levels of sadness, lack of energy, low self-worth, guilt, or related symptoms.

MANIA A state of euphoria or frenzied activity in which people may have an exaggerated sense of well-being.

UNIPOLAR DEPRESSION Depression without a history of mania.

BIPOLAR DISORDER A disorder marked by alternating or intermixed periods of mania and depression.

For . . . a six-month period, her irritability bordered on the irrational. She screamed in anger or sobbed in despair at every dirty dish left on the coffee table or on the bedroom floor. Each day the need to plan the dinner menu provoked agonizing indecision. How could all the virtues or, more likely, vices of hamburgers be accurately compared to those of spaghetti? . . . She had her whole family walking on eggs. She thought they would be better off if she were dead.

Beatrice could not cope with her job. As a branch manager of a large chain store, she had many decisions to make. Unable to make them herself, she would ask employees who were much less competent for advice, but then she could not decide whose advice to take. . . .

Beatrice's husband . . . thought that she would improve if he made her life easier by taking over more housework, cooking, and child care. His attempt to help only made Beatrice feel more guilty and worthless. She wanted to make a contribution to her family. She wanted to do the chores "like normal people" did but broke down crying at the smallest impediment to a perfect job. . . . Months passed, and Beatrice's problem became more serious. Some days she was too upset to go to work. She stopped seeing her friends. She spent most of her time at home either yelling or crying.

(Lickey & Gordon, 1991, p. 181)

Most people's moods come and go. Their feelings of joy or sadness are understandable reactions to daily events and do not affect their lives greatly. The moods of people with mood disorders, in contrast, tend to last a long time. As in Beatrice's case, the mood colors all of their interactions with the world and interferes with normal functioning.

Depression and mania are the key emotions in mood disorders. **Depression** is a low, sad state in which life seems dark and its challenges overwhelming. **Mania,** the opposite of depression, is a state of breathless euphoria, or at least frenzied energy, in which people may have an exaggerated belief that the world is theirs for the taking. Most people with a mood disorder suffer only from depression, a pattern called **unipolar depression.** They have no history of mania and return to a normal or nearly normal mood when their depression lifts. Others experience periods of mania that alternate with periods of depression, a pattern called **bipolar disorder.**

Mood disorders have always captured people's interest, in part because so many famous people have suffered from them. The Bible speaks of the severe depressions of Nebuchadnezzar, Saul, and Moses. Queen Victoria of England and Abraham Lincoln seem to have experienced recurring depressions. Mood disorders also have plagued such writers as Ernest Hemingway, Eugene O'Neill, Virginia Woolf, and Sylvia Plath. Their mood problems have been shared by millions, and today the economic costs (work loss, treatment, hospitalization) amount to more than $40 billion each year (Nordenberg, 1998). Of course, the human suffering that the disorders cause is beyond calculation.

Unipolar Depression

Whenever we feel particularly unhappy, we are likely to describe ourselves as "depressed." In all likelihood, we are merely responding to sad events, fatigue, or unhappy thoughts (see Figure 6-1). This loose use of the term confuses a perfectly normal mood swing with a clinical syndrome. All of us experience dejection from time to time, but only some experience unipolar depression. Clinical depression brings severe and long-lasting psychological pain that may intensify as time goes by. Those who suffer from it may lose their will to carry out the simplest of life's activities; some even lose their will to live.

How Common Is Unipolar Depression?

Between 5 and 10 percent of adults in the United States suffer from a pattern of severe unipolar depression in any given year, while another 3 to 5 percent suffer from mild forms (Kessler & Zhao, 1999; Regier et al., 1993). These results are similar in Canada, England, and many other countries (Smith & Weissman, 1992). Around 17 percent of all adults in the world may experience an episode of severe unipolar depression at some point in their lives (Angst, 1999, 1995). A worldwide research project suggests that the risk of experiencing this problem has steadily increased since 1915 (Weissman et al., 1992, 1991).

In almost all countries, women are at least twice as likely as men to experience episodes of severe unipolar depression (Maier et al., 1999; Weissman et al., 1995). As many as 26 percent of women may have an episode at some time in their lives, compared with 12 percent of men (APA, 1993). Among children, the prevalence of unipolar depression is similar for girls and boys (Hankin et al., 1998).

All of these rates hold steady across the various socioeconomic classes. Similarly, few differences in prevalence of unipolar depression have been found among ethnic groups. In the United States, middle-aged white Americans have a somewhat higher rate than middle-aged African Americans, but the rates for younger and older adults are the same in both populations (Weissman et al., 1991). Approximately two-thirds of people with unipolar depression recover within four to six months, some without treatment (APA, 2000, 1994; Keller, 1988). However, most of them have at least one other episode of depression later in their lives (Angst, 1999).

What Are the Symptoms of Depression?

The picture of depression may differ from person to person. Earlier, we saw how Beatrice's indecisiveness, uncontrollable sobbing, and feelings of despair, anger, and worthlessness brought her job and social life to a standstill. Other depressed people have symptoms that are less severe. They manage to function, although their depression typically robs them of much effectiveness or pleasure, as we see in the case of Derek:

> Derek has probably suffered from depression all of his adult life but was unaware of it for many years. Derek called himself a night person, claiming that he could not think clearly until after noon even though he was often awake by 4:00 A.M. He tried to schedule his work as editorial writer for a small-town newspaper so that it was compatible with his depressed mood at the beginning of the day. Therefore, he scheduled meetings for the mornings; talking with people got him moving. He saved writing and decision making for later in the day.
>
> . . . Derek's private thoughts were rarely cheerful and self-confident. He felt that his marriage was a mere business partnership. He provided the money, and she provided a home and children. Derek and his wife rarely expressed affection

FIGURE 6-1 **Where do college students turn when they feel depressed?** *Typically they turn to friends and to themselves. Fewer than one-third go to a counseling center. (Adapted from Oswalt & Finkelberg, 1995.)*

ConsiderThis

◉ Almost every day we experience ups and downs in mood. How can we separate the everyday blues from clinical depression?

DUBIOUS DISTINCTION

The World Health Organization cites depression as the leading cause of disability in the world (Kaufman, 1999).

for each other. Occasionally, he had images of his own violent death in a bicycle crash, in a plane crash, or in a murder by an unidentified assailant.

Derek felt that he was constantly on the edge of job failure. He was disappointed that his editorials had not attracted the attention of larger papers. He was certain that several of the younger people on the paper had better ideas and wrote more skillfully than he did. He scolded himself for a bad editorial that he had written ten years earlier. Although that particular piece had not been up to his usual standards, everyone else on the paper had forgotten it a week after it appeared. But ten years later, Derek was still ruminating over that one editorial. . . .

Derek brushed off his morning confusion as a lack of quick intelligence. He had no way to know that it was a symptom of depression. He never realized that his death images might be suicidal thinking. People do not talk about such things. For all Derek knew, everyone had similar thoughts.

(Lickey & Gordon, 1991, pp. 183–185)

As the cases of Beatrice and Derek indicate, depression has many symptoms other than sadness. The symptoms, which often feed upon one another, span five areas of functioning: emotional, motivational, behavioral, cognitive, and physical.

EMOTIONAL SYMPTOMS Most people who are depressed feel sad and dejected. They describe themselves as feeling "miserable," "empty," and "humiliated." They report getting little pleasure from anything, and they tend to lose their sense of humor. Some also experience anxiety, anger, or agitation (Noyes, 2001). This sea of misery may lead to crying spells.

MOTIVATIONAL SYMPTOMS Depressed people typically lose the desire to participate in their usual activities. Almost all report a lack of drive, initiative, and spontaneity. They may have to force themselves to go to work, talk with friends, eat meals, or have sex (Buchwald & Rudick-Davis, 1993). One individual recalls, "I didn't want to do anything—just wanted to stay put and be let alone" (Kraines & Thetford, 1972, p. 20).

Suicide represents the ultimate escape from life's challenges. As we shall see in Chapter 7, many depressed people become uninterested in life or wish to die; others wish they could kill themselves, and some actually try. It has been estimated that between 6 and 15 percent of people who suffer from severe depression commit suicide (Inskip, Harris, & Barraclough, 1998; Rossow & Amundsen, 1995).

BEHAVIORAL SYMPTOMS Depressed people are usually less active and less productive than others. They spend more time alone and may stay in bed for long periods. One man recalls, "I'd awaken early, but I'd just lie there—what was the use of getting up to a miserable day?" (Kraines & Thetford, 1972, p. 21). Depressed people may also move and even speak more slowly (Sobin & Sackeim, 1997).

COGNITIVE SYMPTOMS Depressed people hold extremely negative views of themselves (Gable & Shean, 2000). They consider themselves inadequate, undesirable, inferior, perhaps evil. They also blame themselves for nearly every unfortunate event, even things that have nothing to do with them, and they rarely credit themselves for positive achievements.

Another cognitive symptom of depression is pessimism. Sufferers are usually convinced that nothing will ever improve, and they feel helpless to change any aspect of their lives (Metalsky et al., 1993).

THE DARKNESS OF DEPRESSION In Western society, black is often the color of choice in describing depression. The British prime minister Winston Churchill called his recurrent episodes a "black dog always waiting to bare its teeth." The American novelist Ernest Hemingway referred to his bouts as "black-assed" days. And the Rolling Stones sing about depressive thinking: "I see a red door and I want to paint it black."

Lincoln's private war *In 1841, Abraham Lincoln wrote to a friend, "I am now the most miserable man living. If what I feel were equally distributed to the whole human family, there would be not one cheerful face on earth."*

George P.A. Healy, 1887, The National Portrait Gallery, Smithsonian Institution

ConsiderThis

⦿ In one study, students who listened to a sad song became more depressed than those who listened to a happy song (Stratton & Zalanowski, 1999, 1994). Yet the sad-song students reported "enjoying" their musical experience more than the happy-song students. What might be going on here?

Because they expect the worst, they are likely to procrastinate. Their sense of hopelessness and helplessness makes them especially prone to suicidal thinking.

People with depression frequently complain that their intellectual ability is poor. They feel confused, unable to remember things, easily distracted, and unable to solve even small problems. In laboratory studies, depressed subjects do perform more poorly than nondepressed subjects on some tasks of memory, attention, and reasoning (Kalska et al., 1999; Hertel, 1998). It may be, however, that these difficulties reflect motivational problems rather than cognitive ones (Lachner & Engel, 1994).

PHYSICAL SYMPTOMS People who are depressed often have such physical ailments as headaches, indigestion, constipation, dizzy spells, and general pain (Fishbain, 2000). In fact, many depressions are misdiagnosed as medical problems at first (Simon & Katzelnick, 1997). Disturbances in appetite and sleep are particularly common. Most depressed people eat less, sleep less, and feel more fatigued than they did prior to the disorder. Some, however, eat and sleep excessively. Even if they get rest and sleep, they feel tired most of the time (Kazes et al., 1994).

Diagnosing Unipolar Depression

According to DSM-IV, a *major depressive episode* is a period marked by at least five symptoms of depression and lasting for two weeks or more (see Table 6-1). In extreme cases, the episode may include psychotic symptoms, ones marked by a loss

---

STEPPING BACK

Depression, Politics, and Public Perceptions

When George McGovern ran for president of the United States in 1972, word leaked out that his running mate, Senator Thomas Eagleton, had once suffered from depression and had received electroconvulsive therapy. The news, as well as the perception that Eagleton may have tried to hide his past problems, led to Eagleton's withdrawal from the race and no doubt contributed to McGovern's overwhelming defeat.

When General Colin Powell was being touted as a possible presidential

candidate in 1996, rumors emerged that his wife, Alma, had suffered from depression. During a news conference announcing his decision not to run, Powell straightforwardly acknowledged his wife's past episode of depression, discussed her successful response to antidepressant drug treatment, and encouraged everyone with this problem to seek treatment. In this instance, the public responded with admiration and respect. Indeed, support for Powell seemed to rise.

Similarly, in 1999 Tipper Gore, wife of then–Vice President Al Gore, disclosed at a White House conference that she had experienced a major depressive episode ten years earlier after her son had been hit by a car. Again the public reacted with empathy and admiration.

ConsiderThis

⦿ Do the different public reactions to Eagleton, Powell, and Gore suggest that the perception of depression is less negative in our society today than it was a generation ago? • If Colin Powell and Al Gore themselves, rather than their wives, had experienced bouts of depression, would the public reaction have been more similar to that accorded Senator Eagleton?

Greg Gibson/AP/Wide World Photos

Triggers of depression *At a 1999 White House conference, Mike Wallace (CBS newsman) and Tipper Gore (wife of then–Vice President Al Gore) discuss their bouts of depression. Wallace's episode was triggered by a lengthy civil trial, Gore's by her son's near-fatal accident.*

> ## Table 6-1 DSM-IV Checklist
>
> ### MAJOR DEPRESSIVE EPISODE
>
> 1. The presence of at least five of the following symptoms during the same two-week period: • depressed mood most of the day, nearly every day • markedly diminished interest or pleasure in almost all activities most of the day, nearly every day • significant weight loss or weight gain, or decrease or increase in appetite nearly every day • insomnia or hypersomnia nearly every day • psychomotor agitation or retardation nearly every day • fatigue or loss of energy nearly every day • feelings of worthlessness or excessive guilt nearly every day • reduced ability to think or concentrate, or indecisiveness, nearly every day • recurrent thoughts of death or suicide, a suicide attempt, or a specific plan for committing suicide.
> 2. Significant distress or impairment.
>
> ### MAJOR DEPRESSIVE DISORDER
>
> 1. The presence of a major depressive episode.
> 2. No history of a manic or hypomanic episode.
>
> Based on APA, 2000, 1994.

MAJOR DEPRESSIVE DISORDER A severe pattern of depression that is disabling and is not caused by such factors as drugs or a general medical condition.

DYSTHYMIC DISORDER A mood disorder that is similar to but longer lasting and less disabling than a major depressive disorder.

of contact with reality, such as *delusions*—bizarre ideas without foundation—or *hallucinations*—perceptions of things that are not actually present (Parker et al., 1997). A depressed man with psychotic symptoms may imagine that he can't eat "because my intestines are deteriorating and will soon stop working," or he may believe that he sees his dead wife.

People who experience a major depressive episode, without having any history of mania, receive a diagnosis of **major depressive disorder.** People who display a longer-lasting but less disabling pattern of unipolar depression may receive a diagnosis of **dysthymic disorder.** When dysthymic disorder leads to major depressive disorder, the sequence is called *double depression* (Miller, Norman, & Keitner, 1999).

GREEK ROOTS

The term "dysthymia" comes from the Greek for "despondent."

Stress and Unipolar Depression

Episodes of unipolar depression often seem to be triggered by stressful events. In fact, researchers have found that depressed people experience a greater number of stressful life events during the month just before the onset of their disorder than do other people during the same period of time (Kohn et al., 2001; Kendler et al., 1999). Stressful life events also precede other psychological disorders, but depressed people report more such events than anybody else.

Some clinicians consider it important to separate a *reactive (exogenous) depression,* which follows clear-cut stressful events, from an *endogenous depression,* which seems to be a response to internal factors (Vetter et al., 2001). But can one ever know for certain whether a depression is reactive or not? Even if stressful events occurred before the onset of depression, that depression may not be reactive. The events could actually be a coincidence (Paykel et al., 1984; Paykel, 1982). Thus, today's clinicians usually concentrate on recognizing both the situational and the internal aspects of any given case of unipolar depression.

EARLY CONTACT

Therapists are not necessarily the first health professionals to be contacted when depression strikes. Initially, 41 percent of depressed persons go to a physician with complaints of feeling generally ill, 37 percent complain of pain, and 12 percent report tiredness and fatigue (Katon & Walker, 1998).

The Biological Model of Unipolar Depression

Medical researchers have been aware for years that certain diseases and drugs produce mood changes. Could unipolar depression itself have biological causes? Evidence from genetic and biochemical studies suggests that often it does (Judd, 1995).

GENETIC EXPLANATIONS Family pedigree studies and twin studies suggest that some people inherit a predisposition to unipolar depression; as we have observed, however, findings from such studies can also be interpreted in other ways. *Family pedigree studies* select people with unipolar depression, examine their relatives, and see whether depression also afflicts other members of the family. If a predisposition to unipolar depression is inherited, relatives should have a higher rate of depression than the population at large. Researchers have in fact found that as many as 20 percent of those relatives are depressed (see Table 6-2), compared with fewer than 10 percent of the general population (Harrington et al., 1993).

If a predisposition to unipolar depression is inherited, we would also expect a particularly large number of cases among the close relatives of depressed persons. *Twin studies* have supported this expectation (Nurnberger & Gershon, 1992, 1984). One study looked at nearly 200 pairs of twins. When an identical twin had unipolar depression, there was a 46 percent chance that the other twin would have the same disorder. In contrast, when a fraternal twin had unipolar depression, the other twin had only a 20 percent chance of developing the disorder (McGuffin et al., 1996).

Table 6-2

Mood Disorders Profile

	ONE-YEAR PREVALENCE (%)	FEMALE: MALE RATIO	TYPICAL AGE AT ONSET (YEARS)	PREVALENCE AMONG FIRST-DEGREE RELATIVES	PERCENTAGE RECEIVING TREATMENT
Major depressive disorder	5–10%	2:1	24–29	Elevated	49%
Dysthymic disorder	2.5–5.4	Between 3:2 and 2:1	10–25	Elevated	37.8
Bipolar I disorder	0.7	1:1	15–44	Elevated	58.9
Bipolar II disorder	0.5	1:1	15–44	Elevated	58.9
Cyclothymic disorder	0.4	1:1	15–25	Elevated	Unknown

Source: APA, 2000, 1994; Kessler et al., 1994; Regier et al., 1993; Weissman et al., 1991.

BIOCHEMICAL EXPLANATIONS As we have seen, neurotransmitters are the brain chemicals that carry messages from one nerve cell, or neuron, to another. Low activity of two such chemicals, **norepinephrine** and **serotonin,** has been strongly linked to unipolar depression (Delgado & Moreno, 2000). In the 1950s, several pieces of evidence began to point to this relationship. First, medical researchers discovered that certain medications for high blood pressure often caused depression (Ayd, 1956). As it turned out, some of these medications lowered norepinephrine activity and others lowered serotonin. A second piece of evidence was the discovery of the first truly effective antidepressant drugs. Although these drugs were discovered by accident, researchers soon learned that they relieve depression by increasing either norepinephrine or serotonin activity.

For years it was thought that low activity of *either* noreprinephine or serotonin was capable of producing depression, but researchers now believe that the relationship of these chemicals to depression is more complicated than that (Delgado & Moreno, 2000). Recent investigations suggest that interactions between serotonin and norepinephrine activity, or between these neurotransmitters and yet other neurotransmitters in the brain, rather than the operation of any one neurotransmitter alone, may account for unipolar depression (Rampello, Nicoletti, & Nicoletti, 2000).

Biological researchers have also learned that the body's *endocrine system* may play a role in unipolar depression. Endocrine glands throughout the body release

THE IMPORTANCE OF SEROTONIN

The researcher Marie Asberg and her colleagues (1976) found that depressed subjects with particularly low serotonin activity were more apathetic and suicidal than other depressed subjects and that suicide attempts made by depressed patients with extremely low serotonin activity were more frequent and more violent than those made by other depressed people.

hormones, chemicals that in turn spur body organs into action (see Chapter 2). People with unipolar depression have been found to have abnormal levels of *cortisol,* a hormone released by the adrenal glands during times of stress (Holsboer, 2001). This relationship is not all that surprising, given that stressful events often seem to trigger depression. Still another hormone that has been tied to depression is *melatonin,* sometimes called the "Dracula hormone" because it is released only in the dark. People who experience a recurrence of unipolar depression each winter (a pattern called *seasonal affective disorder,* or *SAD*) may secrete more melatonin during the winter season's long nights than other individuals do (Goldman, 1999; Rosenthal & Blehar, 1989).

The biological explanations of unipolar depression have produced much enthusiasm, but research in this area has key limitations. Some of it has relied on studies that create depression-like symptoms in laboratory animals. Researchers cannot be certain that these symptoms do in fact reflect the human disorder (Cox et al., 1999). Similarly, until recent years, technology was limited, and biological studies of human depression had to measure brain activity indirectly. As a result, investigators could never be certain of the biological events that were occurring in the brain. Current studies using newer technology, such as PET and MRI scans, are helping to eliminate such inaccuracies and uncertainties regarding brain activity.

WHAT ARE THE BIOLOGICAL TREATMENTS FOR UNIPOLAR DEPRESSION? Usually biological treatment for unipolar depression means antidepressant drugs, but for severely depressed persons who do not respond to other forms of treatment, it sometimes means electroconvulsive therapy. Many people are surprised to learn that electroconvulsive therapy is, in fact, a highly effective approach for unipolar depression.

ELECTROCONVULSIVE THERAPY One of the most controversial forms of treatment for depression is **electroconvulsive therapy, or ECT.** In this procedure, two electrodes are attached to the patient's head, and an electric current of 65 to 140 volts is sent through the brain for half a second or less. The current causes a *brain seizure* that lasts from 25 seconds to a few minutes. After six to twelve such treatments, spaced over two to four weeks, most patients feel less depressed (Fink, 2001, 1992). In *bilateral ECT* one electrode is applied to each side of the forehead and a current passes through both sides of the brain. In *unilateral ECT,* a method used increasingly in recent years, the electrodes are placed so that the current passes through only one side.

The discovery that electric shock can be therapeutic was made by accident. In the 1930s, clinical researchers mistakenly came to believe that brain seizures, or the convulsions (severe body spasms) that accompany them, could cure schizophrenia and other psychotic disorders, and they searched for ways to produce seizures as a treatment for patients with psychosis. One early technique was to give the patients the drug *metrazol.* Another was to give them large doses of insulin (*insulin coma therapy*). These procedures produced brain seizures, but each was dangerous and sometimes even caused death. Finally, the Italian psychiatrist Ugo Cerletti discovered that he could produce seizures more safely by applying electric currents to patients' heads (Cerletti & Bini, 1938). ECT soon became popular and was tried out on a wide range of psychological problems, as new techniques so often are. Its effectiveness with severe depression in particular became apparent.

In the early years of ECT, broken bones and dislocations of the jaw or shoulders sometimes resulted from ECT's severe convulsions. Today's practitioners avoid this problem by giving

The importance of light *These children who live 200 miles north of the Arctic Circle receive a daily dose of ultraviolet light to compensate for the lack of midwinter sun. Similarly, people who suffer from seasonal affective disorder are often treated with light therapy.*

ECT today *During ECT, patients are now given drugs to help them sleep, muscle relaxants to prevent severe jerks of the body and broken bones, and oxygen to guard against brain damage.*

Sadness at the Happiest of Times

Women usually expect the birth of a child to be a happy experience. But for 10 to 30 percent of new mothers, the weeks and months after childbirth bring clinical depression (Nonacs & Cohen, 1998; Terry, Mayocchi, & Hynes, 1996). Postpartum depression typically begins within four weeks after the birth of a child (APA, 2000, 1994), and it is far more severe than simple "baby blues."

The "baby blues" are so common—as many as 80 percent of women experience them—that most researchers consider them normal. As new mothers try to cope with the wakeful nights, rattled emotions, and other stresses that accompany the arrival of a new baby, they may experience crying spells, fatigue, anxiety, insomnia, and sadness. These symptoms usually disappear within days or weeks (Najman et al., 2000; Horowitz et al., 1995).

In postpartum depression, however, depressive symptoms continue, and may last up to a year (Terry et al., 1996). The symptoms include extreme sadness, despair, tearfulness, insomnia, anxiety, intrusive thoughts, compulsions, panic attacks, feelings of inability to cope, and suicidal thoughts. The mother-infant relationship and the health of the child may suffer as a result (Weinberg et al., 2001).

Many clinicians believe that the hormonal changes accompanying childbirth trigger postpartum depression (Parry, 1999). All women experience a kind of hormone "withdrawal" after delivery, as estrogen and progesterone levels, which rise as much as 50 times above normal during pregnancy, now drop sharply to levels far below normal (Horowitz et al., 1995). Perhaps some women are particularly influenced by these dramatic hormone changes (Horowitz et al., 1995). Still other theo-

rists suggest a genetic predisposition to postpartum depression (APA, 2000, 1994; Steiner & Tam, 1999).

At the same time, psychological and sociocultural factors may play important roles in the disorder. The birth of a baby brings enormous psychological and social change (Nicholson, 1999; Hopkins et al., 1984). A woman typically faces changes in her marital relationship, daily routines, and social roles. Sleep and relaxation are likely to decrease and financial pressures may increase. Perhaps she feels the added stress of giving up a career—or of trying to maintain one. This pileup of stress may heighten the risk of depression (Swendsen & Mazure, 2000; Terry et al., 1996).

Fortunately, treatment can make a big difference for most women with postpartum depression. Self-help support groups have proved extremely helpful for many women with the disorder (Honikman, 1999; Taylor, 1999). In addition, many

respond well to the same approaches that are applied to other forms of unipolar depression—antidepressant medications, cognitive therapy, interpersonal psychotherapy, or a combination of these approaches (Stuart, 1999; Stowe et al., 1995).

However, many women who would benefit from treatment do not seek help because they feel ashamed about being sad at a time that is supposed to be joyous or they are concerned about being judged harshly (APA, 1994). For them, and for the spouses and family members close to them, a large dose of education is in order. Even positive events can be stressful and upsetting if they also bring major change to one's life. Recognizing and addressing such upsets are in everyone's best interest.

Behind the smile *Singer Marie Osmond, performing here with her brother Donny, recently revealed that she suffered from postpartum depression after giving birth in 1999.*

Corbis

---

patients strong *muscle relaxants* to minimize convulsions. They also use *anesthetics* (*barbiturates*) to put patients to sleep during the procedure, reducing their terror (Mehta & Bedient, 1999).

Patients who receive ECT typically have difficulty remembering the events before and immediately after their treatments. In most cases, this memory loss clears up within a few months (Calev et al., 1995, 1991). Some patients, however, experience gaps in more distant memory, and this form of amnesia can be permanent (Fink, 2001; Squire, 1977).

MAO INHIBITOR An antidepressant drug that prevents the action of the enzyme monoamine oxidase.

TRICYCLIC An antidepressant drug that has three rings in its molecular structure.

ECT is clearly effective in treating unipolar depression. Studies find that between 60 and 70 percent of ECT patients improve (Fink, 2001; Rey & Walters, 1997). The procedure seems to be particularly effective in severe cases of depression that include delusions. It has been difficult, however, to determine exactly why ECT works so well.

Although ECT is effective and ECT techniques have improved, its use has generally declined since the 1950s. It is estimated that more than 100,000 patients a year underwent ECT during the 1940s and 1950s. Today as few as 50,000 per year are believed to receive it (Cauchon, 1999; Foderaero, 1993). Two of the reasons for this decline are the memory loss caused by ECT and the frightening nature of this procedure. Another is the emergence of effective *antidepressant drugs.*

ANTIDEPRESSANT DRUGS Two kinds of drugs discovered in the 1950s reduce the symptoms of depression: *monoamine oxidase (MAO) inhibitors* and *tricyclics.* These drugs have recently been joined by a third group, the so-called *second-generation antidepressants* (see Table 6-3).

The effectiveness of **MAO inhibitors** as a treatment for unipolar depression was discovered accidentally. Physicians noted that *iproniazid,* a drug being tested on patients with tuberculosis, had an interesting effect: it seemed to make the patients happier (Sandler, 1990). It was found to have the same effect on depressed patients (Kline, 1958; Loomer, Saunders, & Kline, 1957). What this and several related drugs had in common biochemically was that they slowed down the body's production of the enzyme *monoamine oxidase (MAO).* Thus they were called MAO inhibitors.

Normally, brain supplies of the enzyme MAO break down the neurotransmitter norepinephrine. MAO inhibitors block MAO from carrying out this activity and thereby stop the destruction of norepinephrine. The result is a rise in norepinephrine activity and, in turn, a reduction of depressive symptoms. Approximately half of depressed patients who take MAO inhibitors are helped by them (Thase, Trivedi, & Rush, 1995). There is, however, a potential danger to taking MAO inhibitors. People who take the drug will experience a dangerous rise in blood pressure if they eat foods containing the chemical *tyramine*—including such common foods as cheese, bananas, and certain wines. Thus those who take MAO inhibitors must stick to a rigid diet.

The discovery of **tricyclics** in the 1950s was also accidental. Researchers who were looking for a new drug to combat schizophrenia ran tests on a drug called *imipramine* (Kuhn, 1958). They discovered that imipramine was of no help in cases of schizophrenia, but it did relieve unipolar depression in many people. This drug and related ones became known as tricyclic antidepressants because they all share a three-ring molecular structure.

In hundreds of studies, depressed patients taking tricyclics have improved much more than similar patients taking placebos. About 60 to 65 percent of patients who take these drugs are helped by them (Einarson et al., 1999; Hirschfeld, 1999). If depressed people stop taking tricyclics immediately after obtaining relief, they run a high risk of relapsing within a year (Montgomery et al., 1993). If, however, they continue taking the drugs for five months or more after being free of symptoms—a practice called "continuation therapy"—their chances of relapse decrease considerably (Kocsis et al., 1995). As a result, some clinicians keep patients on antidepressant drugs indefinitely (Kupfer, 1995).

Most researchers have concluded that tricyclics reduce depression by acting on neurotransmitter "reuptake" mechanisms (Stahl, 1998). We have seen that messages are carried from one neuron across the synaptic

Table 6-3

Drugs That Reduce Unipolar Depression

CLASS/GENERIC NAME	TRADE NAME
Monoamine Oxidase Inhibitors	
Isocarboxazid	Marplan
Phenelzine	Nardil
Tranylcypromine	Parnate
Tricyclics	
Imipramine	Tofranil
Amitriptyline	Elavil
Doxepin	Adapin; Sinequan
Trimipramine	Surmontil
Desipramine	Norpramin; Pertofrane
Nortriptyline	Aventyl; Pamelor
Protriptyline	Vivactil
Second-Generation Antidepressants	
Maprotiline	Ludiomil
Amoxapine	Asendin
Trazodone	Desyrel
Clomipramine	Anafranil
Fluoxetine	Prozac
Sertraline	Zoloft
Paroxetine	Paxil
Venlafaxine	Effexor
Fluvoxamine	Luvox
Nefazodone	Serzone
Bupropion	Wellbutrin
Mirtazapine	Remeron
Reboxetine	Edronex
Citalopram	Celexa

A biological alternative *Recent research suggests that extracts from the shrub* hypericum perforatum, *popularly known as St. John's wort, may be of help to 60 percent of people with mild to moderate depression (Schrader, 2000).*

Patrick Johns/Corbis

FIGURE 6-2 **Reuptake and anti-depressants** *(Left) When a neuron releases norepinephrine or serotonin from its endings, a pumplike reuptake mechanism immediately starts to recapture the neurotransmitters before they are received by the postsynaptic (receptor) neuron. (Right) Tricyclic and most second-generation antidepressant drugs block this reuptake process, enabling more norepinephrine or serotonin to reach the postsynaptic neuron. (Adapted from Snyder, 1986, p. 106.)*

Presynaptic neuron

Norepinephrine or serotonin release

Norepinephrine or serotonin reuptake

Postsynaptic neuron

Presynaptic neuron

Tricyclic or second-generation antidepressant

Postsynaptic neuron

space to a receiving neuron by a neurotransmitter, a chemical released from the nerve ending of the sending neuron. However, there is a complication in this process. While the nerve ending is releasing the neurotransmitter, a pumplike mechanism in the same ending is trying to recapture it. The purpose of this reuptake mechanism is to prevent the neurotransmitter from remaining in the synapse too long and repeatedly stimulating the receiving neuron. Perhaps this pumplike mechanism is too successful in some people, reducing norepinephrine or serotonin activity too much. The reduced activity of these neurotransmitters may, in turn, result in clinical depression. Apparently tricyclics block this reuptake process, thus increasing neurotransmitter activity (see Figure 6-2).

Today tricyclics are prescribed more often than MAO inhibitors. They do not require restrictions of the person's diet as MAO inhibitors do, and persons taking tricyclics typically show higher rates of improvement than those taking MAO inhibitors. On the other hand, some individuals respond better to MAO inhibitors than to either tricyclics or the new antidepressants described next, and they continue to be given these drugs (Parker et al., 2001; Paykel, 1995).

A third group of antidepressant drugs, structurally different from the MAO inhibitors and tricyclics, has been developed during the past several years. Most of these second-generation antidepressants are labeled **selective serotonin reuptake inhibitors (SSRIs),** because they increase serotonin activity specifically, without affecting norepinephrine or other neurotransmitters. The SSRIs include *fluoxetine* (trade name Prozac) and *sertraline* (Zoloft). Newly developed *selective norepinephrine reuptake inhibitors* (which increase norepinephrine activity only) and *serotonin-norepinephrine reuptake inhibitors* (which increase both serotonin and norepinephrine activity) are also now available (Rivas-Vazquez, 2001; Montgomery, 1999).

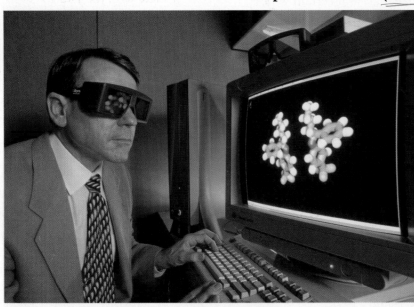

The antidepressant revolution *A clinical scientist studies the molecular structure of Prozac. Sales of antidepressant drugs total $10 billion each year, with Prozac accounting for one-third of this amount.*

In effectiveness the second-generation antidepressant drugs are about on a par with the tricyclics (Hirschfeld, 1999), yet their sales have skyrocketed. Prozac alone produces nearly $3 billion in sales each year. Clinicians often prefer the new antidepressants because it is harder to overdose on them than on the other kinds of antidepressants. In addition, they do not pose the dietary problems of the MAO inhibitors or produce the unpleasant effects of the tricyclics, such

THE CURRENT SCENE

THE CURRENT SCENE

Prozac, Dog's Best Friend?

The popularity of Prozac and related antidepressant drugs skyrocketed in the 1990s. Many clinicians believe that Prozac is being prescribed much too often. They worry in particular about its

Renee Lynn/Photo Researchers

use with children, elderly people, and people whose psychological problems are relatively minor. Now they have been given something else to worry about: Prozac is also being prescribed for dogs with mood or behavioral problems (Millward, 1996).

In a 1996 article for *Dogs Today* magazine, for example, an expert on animal behavior described dogs who were given Prozac. Jannie, a pointer with a shadow-chasing problem, was prescribed the drug for an obsessive-compulsive disorder. George, a

Staffordshire bull terrier, was given it to combat "sustained rage assaults" on other dogs. And Henry, an English bull terrier, kept pinning his owner every time she tried to leave home (Millward, 1996).

ConsiderThis

⊙ Is there something odd or wrong about human beings serving as a testing ground for a medication that is later given to animals? • What other human treatments (psychological or medical) are applied to pets? • Is the prescription of Prozac for troubled pets inappropriate?

as dry mouth and constipation (Leonard, 1997). At the same time, the new anti-depressants can result in undesired effects of their own. Some people, for example, experience a reduction in their sex drive (Segraves, 1998).

However (handwritten annotation)

Psychological Models of Unipolar Depression

The psychological models that have been most widely applied to unipolar depression are the psychodynamic, behavioral, and cognitive models. The psychodynamic perspective has not been strongly supported by research, and the behavioral perspective has received only modest support. In contrast, cognitive explanations and treatments have received considerable research support and have gained a large following.

THE PSYCHODYNAMIC MODEL Sigmund Freud and his student Karl Abraham developed the first psychodynamic explanation and treatment for unipolar depression (Freud, 1917; Abraham, 1916, 1911). Their emphasis on issues such as dependence and loss continues to influence today's psychodynamic clinicians.

PSYCHODYNAMIC EXPLANATIONS Freud and Abraham began by noting the similarity between clinical depression and grief in people who lose loved ones: constant weeping, loss of appetite, difficulty sleeping, loss of pleasure in life, and general withdrawal. According to Freud and Abraham, a series of unconscious processes is set in motion when a loved one dies. Unable to accept the loss, mourners at first regress to the *oral stage* of development, the period of total dependency when infants cannot separate themselves from their parents. By regressing to this stage, the mourners merge their own identity with that of the person they have lost, and so symbolically regain the lost person. They direct all their feelings for the loved one, including sadness and anger, toward themselves.

For most mourners, this process is temporary. For some, however, grief worsens. They feel empty, they continue to avoid social relationships, and their sense of loss increases. They become depressed. Freud and Abraham believed that two kinds of people are particularly likely to become clinically depressed in the face of

NEW KID ON THE BLOCK

In 1999, *s-adenosylmethionine*, or SAMe (pronounced "Sammy"), joined antidepressant drugs and St. John's wort in the United States marketplace as a popular biological treatment for unipolar depression. Sold as an over-the-counter dietary supplement, SAMe is a common molecule produced by all living cells. Although sold in Italy and 13 other countries for more than 20 years, SAMe is just now beginning to receive broad and systematic study.

SELECTIVE SEROTONIN REUPTAKE IN-HIBITORS (SSRIs) A group of second-generation antidepressant drugs that increase serotonin activity specifically, without affecting other neurotransmitters.

Early loss *Research has found that people who lose their parents as children have an increased likelihood of experiencing depression as adults.*

loss: those whose parents failed to meet their needs during the oral stage and those whose parents gratified those needs excessively. People of either kind may devote their lives to others, desperately in search of love and approval (Bemporad, 1992). They are likely to feel a greater sense of loss when a loved one dies.

Of course, many people become depressed without losing a loved one. To explain why, Freud proposed the concept of **symbolic,** or **imagined, loss,** in which other kinds of events are equated with loss of a loved one. A college student may, for example, experience failure in a calculus course as the loss of her parents, believing that they love her only when she excels academically.

Although many psychodynamic theorists have parted company with Freud and Abraham's theory of depression (Bemporad & Vasile, 1999), it continues to influence current psychodynamic thinking. For example, *object relations theorists,* the psychodynamic theorists who emphasize relationships, propose that depression results when people's relationships leave them feeling unsafe and insecure (Kernberg, 1997, 1976). People whose parents pushed them toward either excessive dependence or excessive self-reliance are more likely to become depressed when they later lose important relationships.

The following therapist description of a depressed middle-aged woman illustrates the psychodynamic concepts of dependence, loss of a loved one, and symbolic loss:

> Mrs. Marie Carls . . . had always felt very attached to her mother. As a matter of fact, they used to call her "Stamp" because she stuck to her mother as a stamp to a letter. She always tried to placate her volcanic mother, to please her in every possible way. . . .
>
> After marriage [to Julius], she continued her pattern of submission and compliance. Before her marriage she had difficulty in complying with a volcanic mother, and after her marriage she almost automatically assumed a submissive role. . . .
>
> [W]hen she was thirty years old . . . [she] and her husband invited Ignatius, who was single, to come and live with them. Ignatius and the patient soon discovered that they had an attraction for each other. They both tried to fight that feeling; but when Julius had to go to another city for a few days, the so-called infatuation became much more than that. There were a few physical contacts. . . . There was an intense spiritual affinity. . . . A few months later everybody had to leave the city. . . . Nothing was done to maintain contact. Two years later, approximately a year after the end of the war, Marie heard that Ignatius had married. She felt terribly alone and despondent. . . .
>
> Her suffering had become more acute as she realized that old age was approaching and she had lost all her chances. Ignatius remained as the memory of lost opportunities. . . . Her life of compliance and obedience had not permitted her to reach her goal. . . . When she became aware of these ideas, she felt even more depressed. . . . She felt that everything she had built in her life was false or based on a false premise.
>
> *(Arieti & Bemporad, 1978, pp. 275–284)*

Studies have offered support for the psychodynamic idea that losses suffered early in life may set the stage for later depression (Agid et al., 1999; Lara & Klein, 1999). When, for example, a depression scale was administered to 1,250 medical patients during visits to their family physicians, the patients whose fathers had died during their childhood scored higher on depression (Barnes & Prosen, 1985).

Related research supports the psychodynamic idea that people whose childhood needs were improperly met are particularly likely to become depressed after

VIRTUAL LOSS

Throughout North America, Europe, and Japan, large numbers of people have purchased "virtual pets," electronic interactive toys. Owners must press buttons to stroke, feed, and exercise their pets; if neglected, the pets will die. Clinicians have warned that some owners, especially vulnerable and lonely children, suffer real feelings of loss and bereavement at the death of their virtual dog or cat (O'Neill, 1997).

LOSS OF A FATHER

Before the 1960s, the most common cause of fatherlessness was death. Since then, the leading cause has been separation or divorce (Coney & Mackey, 1998).

experiencing loss (Young et al., 1997; Parker, 1992, 1983). In some studies, depressed subjects have filled out a scale called the Parental Bonding Instrument, which indicates how much care and protection people feel they received as children. Many have identified their parents' child-rearing style as "affectionless control," consisting of a mixture of low care and high protection (Shah & Waller, 2000; Parker et al., 1995).

These studies offer some support for the psychodynamic view of unipolar depression, but this support has key limitations. First, although the findings suggest that early losses and inadequate parenting *sometimes* relate to depression,

SYMBOLIC LOSS According to Freudian theory, the loss of a valued object (for example, a loss of employment) which is unconsciously interpreted as the loss of a loved one. Also called *imagined loss*.

STEPPING BACK

The Grieving Process

Each year tens of millions of people experience the death of a close relative or friend. Reactions to such painful losses can be so similar to clinical depression that Freud and Abraham based the psychoanalytic explanation of depression on them. But mourning is a natural process that allows us eventually to come to grips with our loss and to resume our lives.

Unfortunately, there are many common misconceptions about grieving. The most common is the belief that there is a set timetable for mourning (Doka, 1999). Friends and acquaintances often allow the mourner only a few weeks to return to normal life. In fact, it is sometimes many months before a person is ready to do so (Jacobs, 1999). The amount of time needed depends on such factors as the relationship of the mourner to the deceased, the age of the mourner, and, clearly, the mourner's personality (Stroebe et al., 2000).

The bereavement process is also experienced differently in different cultural groups (Stroebe et al., 1992). Japanese Buddhists believe in maintaining contact with dead ancestors, and almost all homes have an altar dedicated to them. Offering food and speaking to the dead are common practices. The Hopi Indians, though, believe that contact with death brings pollution, so they quickly rid the home of all reminders of their deceased relatives. Muslims in Egypt believe that the bereaved should dwell on their loss and surround themselves with others who share their sorrow, but Muslims in Bali are taught to contain their grief, to laugh and be joyful (Wikan, 1991).

Western society tends to view bereavement as an interference in the daily routine of life, a troublesome, debilitating emotional response that one must overcome as quickly and efficiently as possible. This view was not always the norm in the West. In the mid-nineteenth century, for example, communication with the dead through séances and mediums was popular. The amount of grief one felt after the death of a loved one was held to indicate the relationship's strength and significance, and the bereaved were expected to focus on a reunion with the deceased in heaven.

Whatever a culture's or individual's reaction to grief may be, research suggests that social support plays an important role during the bereavement process (Doka, 1999). Thus it is not surprising that numerous self-help bereavement groups have emerged across the world, giving mourners opportunities to gather with others who have lost loved ones and discuss the emotional and practical problems they all face. These groups, which are apparently helpful for many mourners, allow a necessary process to proceed as it should—without pressure, misinterpretion, or judgment (Allumbaugh & Hoyt, 1999).

Mass grief *The recent deaths of Princess Diana, John Kennedy, Jr., and the Columbine High School students have each triggered mass grief reactions. Tens of thousands of people spontaneously came together to mourn these losses and built extemporaneous memorial sites with endless offerings of flowers, candles, notes, drawings, balloons, and other personal items, as at this site honoring Diana outside Kensington Palace in London.*

David Brauchli/AP/Wide World Photos

Mark Lennihan/AP Wide World Photos

ANIMAL SUPPORT
There are 66 million pet cats and 58 million pet dogs in the United States (Ash, 1998). Studies find that animal companionship often helps prevent or reduce depression, improve cardiovascular functioning, lower stress, and enhance self-esteem (Barker, 1999).

Saying goodbye *As highlights of his glorious career appear on a screen, Wayne Gretzky announces his retirement from ice hockey. According to behaviorists, the reduction in rewards brought about by retirement places sports stars and other high achievers at risk for depression unless they can develop a healthy perspective about the change and add new sources of gratification to their lives.*

they do not establish that such factors are *typically* responsible for the disorder. In fact, it is estimated that less than 10 percent of all people who experience major losses in life actually become depressed (Paykel & Cooper, 1992; Paykel, 1982). Second, many of the findings are inconsistent. Though some studies find evidence of a relationship between childhood loss and later depression, others do not (Parker, 1992; Owen, Lancee, & Freeman, 1986). Finally, certain features of the psychodynamic explanation are nearly impossible to test. Because symbolic loss is said to operate at an unconscious level, for example, it is difficult for researchers to determine if and when it is occurring.

WHAT ARE THE PSYCHODYNAMIC TREATMENTS FOR UNIPOLAR DEPRESSION? Psychodynamic therapists use the same basic procedures with depressed clients as they use with others: they encourage the client to associate freely during therapy; suggest interpretations of the client's associations, dreams, and displays of resistance and transference; and help the person reexperience and review past events and feelings. Free association, for example, helped one man recall the early experiences of loss that, according to his therapist, had set the stage for his depression:

> Among his earliest memories, possibly the earliest of all, was the recollection of being wheeled in his baby cart under the elevated train structure and left there alone. Another memory that recurred vividly during the analysis was of an operation around the age of five. He was anesthetized and his mother left him with the doctor. He recalled how he had kicked and screamed, raging at her for leaving him.
>
> *(Lorand, 1968, pp. 325–326)*

Despite some successful case reports, researchers have found that long-term psychodynamic therapy is only occasionally helpful in cases of unipolar depression (APA, 1993; Prochaska, 1984). Two features of the approach may help limit its effectiveness. First, depressed clients may be too passive and feel too fatigued to join fully in the subtle therapy discussions (Widloecher, 2001). Second, they may become discouraged and end treatment too early when this long-term approach is unable to provide the quick relief that they desperately seek. Generally, psychodynamic therapy seems to be of greatest help in cases of depression that clearly involve a history of childhood loss or trauma, a long-term sense of emptiness, perfectionism, and extreme self-criticism (Blatt, 1999, 1995). Short-term psychodynamic therapies have performed better than the traditional approaches (Leichsenring, 2001; Jefferson & Greist, 1994).

THE BEHAVIORAL MODEL Behaviorists believe that unipolar depression results from changes in the rewards and punishments people receive in their lives, and they treat depressed people by helping them to build more favorable patterns of reinforcement. During the 1970s and 1980s, the clinical researcher Peter Lewinsohn developed one of the leading behavioral explanations and treatments (Lewinsohn et al., 1990, 1984).

THE BEHAVIORAL EXPLANATION Lewinsohn suggested that the positive rewards in life dwindle for some persons, leading them to perform fewer and fewer constructive behaviors. The rewards of campus life, for example, may disappear when a young woman graduates from college and takes a job; or an aging baseball player may lose the rewards of high salary and praise when his skills deteriorate. Although many people manage to fill their lives with other forms of gratification, some become disheartened. The positive features of their lives decrease even more, and the decline in rewards leads them to perform still fewer constructive behaviors. In this manner, a person may spiral toward depression.

Lewinsohn and his colleagues found that the number of rewards people receive in life is indeed related to the presence or absence of depression. Not only did depressed subjects in his studies report fewer positive rewards than nondepressed subjects, but when their rewards began to increase, their mood improved as well (Lewinsohn, Youngren, & Grosscup, 1979). Similarly, recent investigations have found a strong relationship between positive life events and feelings of life satisfaction and happiness (Lu, 1999).

Lewinsohn and other behaviorists further suggested that *social* rewards are particularly important in the downward spiral of depression (Peterson, 1993; Lewinsohn et al., 1984). Their idea is supported by research showing that depressed persons experience fewer social rewards than nondepressed persons, and that as their mood improves, their social rewards increase. Although depressed people are sometimes the victims of social circumstances, it may be that their flat behaviors and dark mood help produce a decline in social rewards (Coyne, 2001).

WHAT ARE THE BEHAVIORAL TREATMENTS FOR UNIPOLAR DEPRESSION? In Lewinsohn's treatment for unipolar depression, therapists use a variety of strategies to help increase the positive behaviors of their clients (Lewinsohn et al., 1990, 1982). First, the therapist selects activities that the client considers pleasurable, such as going shopping or taking photographs, and encourages the person to set up a weekly schedule for engaging in them. Adding positive activities to a person's life is expected to lead to a better mood (Leenstra, Ormel, & Giel, 1995; Teri & Lewinsohn, 1986). Second, while reintroducing pleasurable events into a client's life, the therapist makes sure that the person's various behaviors are rewarded correctly. Behaviorists have argued that when people become depressed, their negative behaviors—crying, complaining, or self-depreciation—keep others at a distance, reducing chances for positive reinforcement. To change this pattern, the therapist may try to ignore a client's depressive behaviors while praising or otherwise rewarding constructive statements and behavior, such as going to work. Finally, behavioral therapists may train clients in effective social skills (Segrin, 2000; Hersen et al., 1984). In group therapy programs, for example, members may work together to improve eye contact, facial expression, posture, and other behaviors that send social messages.

These behavioral techniques seem to be of only limited help when just one of them is applied. A group of depressed people who were instructed to increase their pleasant activities, for example, showed no more improvement than a control group who were told simply to keep track of their activities (Hammen & Glass, 1975). However, when the treatment program combines two or three of these behavioral techniques, much as Lewinsohn had envisioned, it does appear to reduce depressive symptoms, particularly if the depression is mild (Jacobson et al., 1996; Teri & Lewinsohn, 1986).

THE COGNITIVE MODEL Cognitive theorists believe that people with unipolar depression repeatedly view events in negative ways and that such perceptions lead to their disorder. In turn, cognitive therapists focus largely on the thinking processes rather than the mood of these individuals. The two most influential cognitive explanations are the *theory of learned helplessness* and the *theory of negative thinking*.

LEARNED HELPLESSNESS Feelings of helplessness fill this account of a young woman's depression:

> Mary was 25 years old and had just begun her senior year in college. . . . Asked to recount how her life had been going recently, Mary began to weep. Sobbing, she said that for the last year or so she felt she was losing control of her life and that recent stresses (starting school again, friction with her boyfriend) had left her feeling worthless and frightened. Because of a gradual deterioration in her

ConsiderThis

◉ One-third of people who feel unhappy as children continue to feel unhappy as adults. In contrast, fewer than one-tenth of those who are happy as children become unhappy adults (Freeman, Templer, & Hill, 1999). How might different theorists explain this correlation between childhood and adult happiness?

Rick Rickman/Matrix

Preventing depression among the elderly *Behaviorists propose that people need pleasurable events in their lives in order to thrive and to avoid depression. With this in mind, more and more activities, such as the Senior Olympics, are being made available to elderly persons, providing important rewards, stimulation, and satisfaction.*

DECONSTRUCTIVE CRITICISM

College students who seek and receive negative feedback from their roommates feel more depressed than students who do not receive such feedback (Joiner, 1995).

LEARNED HELPLESSNESS The perception, based on past experiences, that one has no control over one's reinforcements.

vision, she was now forced to wear glasses all day. "The glasses make me look terrible," she said, and "I don't look people in the eye much any more." Also, to her dismay, Mary had gained 20 pounds in the past year. She viewed herself as overweight and unattractive. At times she was convinced that with enough money to buy contact lenses and enough time to exercise she could cast off her depression; at other times she believed nothing would help. . . . Mary saw her life deteriorating in other spheres, as well. She felt overwhelmed by schoolwork and, for the first time in her life, was on academic probation. . . . In addition to her dissatisfaction with her appearance and her fears about her academic future, Mary complained of a lack of friends. Her social network consisted solely of her boyfriend, with whom she was living. Although there were times when she experienced this relationship as almost unbearably frustrating, she felt helpless to change it and was pessimistic about its permanence.

(Spitzer et al., 1983, pp. 122–123)

Mary feels that she is "losing control of her life." According to the psychologist Martin Seligman, such feelings of helplessness are at the center of her depression. Since the mid-1960s Seligman has developed the **learned helplessness** theory of depression (Seligman 1992, 1975). It holds that people become depressed when they think (1) that they no longer have control over the reinforcements in their lives and (2) that they themselves are responsible for this helpless state.

A CLOSER LOOK

Depressing News for Women

Women in places as far apart as Paris, Sweden, Beirut, New Zealand, and the United States are at least twice as likely as men to receive a diagnosis of unipolar depression (Schreiber, 2001; Maier et al., 1999). Women also appear to be younger when depression strikes, to have more frequent and longer-lasting bouts, and to respond less successfully to treatment (Pajer, 1995; Weissman & Olfson, 1995). Why the huge difference between the sexes? Several theories have been offered (Blehar & Oren, 1995; Nolen-Hoeksema, 1995, 1990, 1987).

The Artifact Theory

One theory holds that women and men are equally prone to depression, but that clinicians fail to detect depression in men. Perhaps men find it less socially acceptable to admit feeling depressed or to seek treatment. This explanation lacks consistent research support (Fennig, Schwartz, & Bromet, 1994). It turns out that women are actually no more willing or able than men to identify their depressive symptoms and seek treatment (Nolen-Hoeksema, 1990).

The Hormone Theory

Another theory holds that hormone changes trigger depression in many women (Young & Korszun, 1999; Pajer, 1995). A woman's biological life from her early teens to middle age is marked by frequent changes in hormone levels. Gender differences in rates of depression also span these same years. It is unlikely, however, that hormone changes alone are responsible for the high levels of depression in women. Important social and life events that occur at puberty, pregnancy, and menopause could likewise have an effect. Hormone explanations have also been criticized as sexist, since they imply that a woman's normal biology is flawed.

The Quality-of-Life Theory

Perhaps women in our society experience more stress than men (Stoppard, 2000; Gold, 1998). On average they face more poverty, more menial jobs, less adequate housing, and more discrimination than men—all factors that have been linked to depression (Wu & DeMaris, 1996; Brems, 1995). And in many homes, women bear a dispropor-

tionate share of responsibility for child care and housework.

The Societal Pressure Theory

Almost from birth, females in Western society are pressured to seek a low body weight and slender body shape—goals that are unreasonable, unhealthy, and often unattainable. The cultural standard for males is much more lenient. As girls approach adolescence, peer pressure may produce greater and greater dissatisfaction with their weight and body, increasing the likelihood of depression. Consistent with this theory, gender differences in depression do indeed first appear during adolescence (Wichstrom, 1999; Nolen-Hoeksema & Girgus, 1995) and persons with eating disorders often experience high levels of depression. However, it is not clear that eating and weight concerns actually cause depression; they may instead be the result of depression.

The Lack-of-Control Theory

According to this theory, women are more prone to depression because they feel less control over their lives. Studies

Seligman's theory first began to take shape when he was working with laboratory dogs. In one procedure, he strapped dogs into an apparatus called a hammock, in which they received shocks periodically no matter what they would do. The next day each dog was placed in a *shuttle box*, a box divided in half by a barrier over which the animal could jump to reach the other side (see Figure 6-3). Seligman applied shocks to the dogs in the box, expecting that they, like other dogs in this situation, would soon learn to escape by jumping over the barrier. However, most of these dogs failed to learn anything in the shuttle box. After a flurry of activity, they simply "lay down and quietly whined" and accepted the shock.

Seligman decided that while receiving inescapable shocks in the hammock the day before, the dogs had learned that they had no control over unpleasant reinforcements (shocks) in their lives. That is, they had learned that they were helpless to do anything to change negative situations. Thus, when later they were placed in a new situation (the shuttle box) where they could in fact control their fate, they continued to believe that they were generally helpless. Seligman noted that the effects of learned helplessness greatly resemble the symptoms of human depression, and he proposed that people in fact become depressed after developing a general belief that they have no control over reinforcements in their lives.

In numerous human and animal studies, subjects who undergo helplessness training have displayed reactions similar to depressive symptoms. When human subjects are given uncontrollable negative reinforcements, they later score higher

FIGURE 6-3 **Jumping to safety** *Experimental animals learn to escape or avoid shocks that are administered on one side of a shuttle box by jumping to the other (safe) side.*

have, in fact, confirmed that women are more prone to develop learned helplessness in the laboratory than men (Le Unes, Nation, & Turley, 1980). In addition, it has been found that victimization of any kind, from burglary to rape, often produces a general sense of helplessness and increases the symptoms of depres-

sion; and women in our society are more likely than men to be victims, particularly of sexual assault and child abuse (Zuravin & Fontanella, 1999).

The Self-Blame Theory

Research indicates that women are more likely than men to blame their failures

on lack of ability and to attribute their successes to luck—an attribution style that has also been linked to depression (Wolfe & Russianoff, 1997). Perhaps not so coincidentally, these gender differences in attribution begin during adolescence, about the same time that the gender differences in depression first appear (Cyranowski et al., 2000). On the other hand, recent research suggests that today's women and men may not differ as much as they used to in their levels of self-esteem and self-blame (Kling et al., 1999).

Each of these explanations for the gender difference in unipolar depression offers food for thought. Each has gathered just enough supporting evidence to make it interesting and just enough nonsupporting evidence to raise questions about its usefulness. Thus, at present, the gender difference in depression remains one of the most talked-about but least understood phenomena in the clinical field.

Edvard Munch, *Melancholia, Laura, 1899, Oslo kommunes kunstsamlinger Munch-Museet*

Female melancholy *Edvard Munch's painting* Melancholy (Laura) *was inspired by his sister's bouts of severe depression.*

© 1998 Sidney Harris

"I FEEL BETTER TODAY TOO, BUT AROUND HERE I'VE LEARNED NOT TO BE TOO OPTIMISTIC."

REVERSING LEARNED HELPLESSNESS

If attributions are so important, then helplessness may be preventable or reversible by teaching people to attribute losses of control to external causes or to internal causes that are specific or unstable. Helplessness has been prevented in grade school children in just this way: in several studies they have been guided to make alternative attributions for their classroom problems or failures (Gillham et al., 2001, 1995; Dweck, 1976).

"There is nothing either good or bad, but thinking makes it so."

William Shakespeare, *Hamlet*

on a depressive mood survey than other subjects (Miller & Seligman, 1975). Similarly, helplessness-trained animal subjects lose interest in sexual and social activities—a common symptom of human depression (Lindner, 1968). Finally, uncontrollable negative events result in lower norepinephrine and serotonin activity in rats (Wu et al., 1999; Neumaier et al., 1997). This, of course, is similar to the neurotransmitter activity found in the brains of people with unipolar depression.

The learned helplessness explanation of depression has been revised somewhat over the past two decades. According to a new version of the theory, when people view events as beyond their control, they ask themselves why this is so (Abramson et al., 1989, 1978). If they attribute their present lack of control to some *internal* cause that is both *global* and *stable* ("I am inadequate at everything and I always will be"), they may well feel helpless to prevent future negative outcomes and they may experience depression. If they make other kinds of **attributions,** this reaction is unlikely.

Consider a college student whose girlfriend breaks up with him. If he attributes this loss of control to an internal cause that is both global and stable—"It's my fault [internal], I ruin everything I touch [global], and I always will [stable]"—he then has reason to expect similar losses of control in the future and may generally experience a sense of helplessness. According to the learned helplessness view, he is a prime candidate for depression. If the student had instead attributed the breakup to causes that were more *specific* ("The way I've behaved the past couple of weeks blew this relationship"), *unstable* ("I don't usually act like that"), or *external* ("She never did know what she wanted"), he might not expect to lose control again and would probably not experience helplessness and depression.

Hundreds of studies have supported the relationship between styles of attribution, helplessness, and depression (Kinderman & Bentall, 1997). In one study, depressed persons were asked to fill out an Attributional Style Questionnaire both before and after successful therapy. Before therapy, their depression was accompanied by the internal/global/stable pattern of attribution. At the end of therapy and again one year later, their depression was improved and their attribution styles were less likely to be internal, global, and stable (Seligman et al., 1988).

It is worth noting that some theorists have refined the helplessness model yet again in recent years. They suggest that attributions are likely to cause depression only when they further produce a sense of *hopelessness* in an individual (Abramson et al., 1999, 1989; Alloy et al., 1990). By taking this factor into consideration, clinicians are often able to predict depression with still greater precision (Waikar & Craske, 1997).

Although the learned helplessness model of unipolar depression has been widely applied, it too has imperfections. First, much of the learned helplessness research relies on animal subjects. It is impossible to know whether animals' symptoms do in fact reflect the clinical depression found in humans. Second, the attributional feature of the theory raises difficult questions. What about the dogs and rats who learn helplessness? Can animals make attributions, even implicitly?

NEGATIVE THINKING Like Seligman, Aaron Beck believes that negative thinking lies at the heart of depression (Clark, Beck, & Alford, 1999; Beck, 1997, 1991, 1967). According to Beck, however, *maladaptive attitudes, a cognitive triad, errors in thinking,* and *automatic thoughts* combine to produce the clinical syndrome.

Beck believes that some people develop *maladaptive attitudes* as children, such as "My general worth is tied to every task I perform" or "If I fail, others will feel repelled by me." Many failures are inevitable in a full, active life, so such attitudes are self-defeating (Young et al., 1993). Beck suggests that later in these people's lives, upsetting situations can trigger an extended round of negative thinking (see Figure 6-4). The thinking typically takes three forms, which he calls the **cognitive triad:** the individuals repeatedly interpret (1) their *experiences,* (2) *themselves,* and (3) their *futures* in negative ways that lead them to feel depressed. The cognitive triad is at work in the thinking of this depressed person:

> I can't bear it. I can't stand the humiliating fact that I'm the only woman in the world who can't take care of her family, take her place as a real wife and mother, and be respected in her community. When I speak to my young son Billy, I know I can't let him down, but I feel so ill-equipped to take care of him; that's what frightens me. I don't know what to do or where to turn; the whole thing is too overwhelming. . . . I must be a laughingstock. It's more than I can do to go out and meet people and have the fact pointed up to me so clearly.
>
> *(Fieve, 1975)*

According to Beck, depressed people also make *errors in their thinking.* In one common error of logic, they draw *arbitrary inferences*—negative conclusions based on little evidence. A man walking through the park, for example, passes a woman who is looking at nearby flowers, and he concludes, "She's avoiding looking at me." Similarly, depressed people often *minimize* the significance of positive experiences or *magnify* that of negative ones. A college student receives an A on a difficult English exam, for example, but concludes that the grade reflects the professor's generosity rather than her own ability (minimization). Later in the week the same student must miss an English class and is convinced that she will be unable to keep up the rest of the semester (magnification).

Finally, depressed people experience **automatic thoughts,** a steady train of unpleasant thoughts that keep suggesting to them that they are inadequate and that their situation is hopeless. Beck labels these thoughts "automatic" because they seem to just happen, as if by reflex. In the course of only a few hours, depressed people may be visited by hundreds of such thoughts: "I'm worthless. . . . I let everyone down. . . . Everyone hates me. . . . My responsibilities are overwhelming. . . . I've failed as a parent. . . . I'm stupid. . . . Everything is difficult for me. . . . Things will never change."

Numerous studies have produced evidence in support of Beck's explanation. Several, for example, confirm that depressed people hold maladaptive attitudes,

ATTRIBUTION An explanation of events as resulting from particular causes.

COGNITIVE TRIAD The three forms of negative thinking that Aaron Beck theorizes lead people to feel depressed.

AUTOMATIC THOUGHTS Numerous unpleasant thoughts that help to cause or maintain depression, anxiety, or other forms of psychological dysfunction.

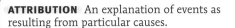

ConsiderThis

● Many comedians report that they have grappled with depression. Is there something about performing that might improve their mood? ● Is there something about being depressed that might make them more skilled at thinking or acting funny?

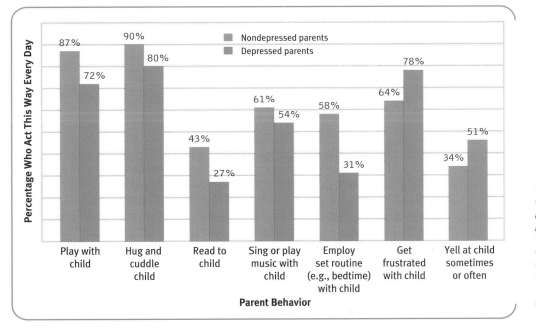

FIGURE 6-4 **How depressed parents and their children interact** *Depressed parents are less likely than nondepressed parents to play with, hug, read to, or sing to their young children each day or to employ the same routine each day. They are also more likely to get frustrated with their children on a daily basis. (Adapted from Princeton Survey Research Associates, 1996.)*

	Monday	Tuesday	Wednesday	Thursday	Fr
9-10		Go to grocery store	Go to museum	Get ready to go out	
10-11		Go to grocery store	Go to museum	Drive to doctor's appointment	
11-12	Doctor's appointment	Call friend	Go to museum	Doctor's appointment	
12-1	Lunch	Lunch	Lunch at museum		
1-2	Drive home	Clean front room	Drive home		
2-3	Read novel	Clean front room	Washing		
3-4	Clean bedroom	Read novel	Washing		
4-5	Watch TV	Watch TV	Watch TV		
5-6	Fix dinner	Fix dinner	Fix dinner		
6-7	Eat with family	Eat with family	Eat with family		
7-8	Clean kitchen	Clean kitchen	Clean kitchen		
8-12	Watch TV, read novel, sleep	Call sister, watch TV, read novel, sleep	Work on rug, read novel, sleep		

FIGURE 6-5 **Increasing activity** *In the early stages of cognitive therapy for depression, the client and therapist prepare an activity schedule such as this. Activities as simple as watching television and calling a friend are specified. (Adapted from Beck et al., 1979, p. 122.)*

"Depression is an insidious vacuum that crawls into your brain and pushes your mind out of the way."

Depressed woman (Karp, 1996)

ConsiderThis

◉ Friends and family members try, with limited success, to convince depressed people that their gloom-and-doom view of things is wrong. How does the successful cognitive approach to unipolar depression differ from such efforts at friendly persuasion?

and the more of these maladaptive attitudes they hold, the more depressed they tend to be (Whisman & McGarvey, 1995; Garber, Weiss, & Shanley, 1993). Still other research has found the cognitive triad at work in depressed people (Cole & Turner, 1993). In various studies, depressed subjects seem to recall unpleasant experiences more readily than positive ones, rate their performances on laboratory tasks lower than nondepressed subjects do, and select pessimistic statements in storytelling tests (for example, "I expect my plans will fail").

Beck's claims about errors in logic have also received research support (Cole & Turner, 1993). In one study, female subjects—some depressed, some not—were asked to read and interpret paragraphs about women in difficult situations. Depressed subjects made more errors in logic (such as arbitrary inference) in their interpretations than nondepressed women did (Hammen & Krantz, 1976).

Finally, research has supported Beck's claim that automatic thoughts are tied to depression. In several studies, nondepressed subjects who are manipulated into reading negative automatic thought–like statements about themselves become more and more depressed (Bates, Thompson, & Flanagan, 1999; Strickland, Hale, & Anderson, 1975).

This body of research shows that negative thinking is indeed linked to depression, but it fails to show that such patterns of thought are the cause and core of unipolar depression. It could be that a central mood problem leads to thinking difficulties that then take a further toll on mood, behavior, and physiology (Scott, Winters, & Beevers, 2000).

WHAT IS BECK'S COGNITIVE TREATMENT FOR UNIPOLAR DEPRESSION? Beck has developed the leading *cognitive therapy* for unipolar depression, designed to help clients recognize and change their maladaptive assumptions and negative thinking and thus to improve both their mood and their behavior (Beck, 1997, 1985, 1967). The approach is similar to Albert Ellis's rational-emotive therapy (discussed in Chapters 2 and 4), but it is tailored to the specific thinking errors found in depression. Beck's approach follows four phases and usually requires fewer than 20 sessions.

Phase 1: Increasing activities and elevating mood Using behavioral techniques to set the stage for cognitive treatment, therapists first encourage individuals to become more active and confident. Clients spend time during each session preparing a detailed schedule of hourly activities for the coming week (see Figure 6-5). As they become more active from week to week, their mood is expected to improve.

Phase 2: Challenging automatic thoughts Once people are more active and feeling some emotional relief, cognitive therapists begin to educate them about their negative automatic thoughts. The individuals are instructed to recognize and record automatic thoughts as they occur and bring their lists to each session. Therapist and client then test the reality behind the thoughts, often concluding that they are groundless.

Phase 3: Identifying negative thinking and biases As people begin to recognize the flaws in their automatic thoughts, cognitive therapists show them how illogical thinking processes are contributing to these thoughts. The therapists also guide clients to see that almost all their interpretations of events have a negative bias and to change that style of interpretation.

Phase 4: Changing primary attitudes Therapists help clients change the maladaptive attitudes that set the stage for their depression in the first place. As part of the process, therapists often encourage clients to test their attitudes, as in the following therapy discussion:

> *Therapist:* On what do you base this belief that you can't be happy without a man?
> *Patient:* I was really depressed for a year and a half when I didn't have a man.
> *Therapist:* Is there another reason why you were depressed?
> *Patient:* As we discussed, I was looking at everything in a distorted way. But I still don't know if I could be happy if no one was interested in me.
> *Therapist:* I don't know either. Is there a way we could find out?
> *Patient:* Well, as an experiment, I could not go out on dates for a while and see how I feel.
> *Therapist:* I think that's a good idea. Although it has its flaws, the experimental method is still the best way currently available to discover the facts. You're fortunate in being able to run this type of experiment. Now, for the first time in your adult life you aren't attached to a man. If you find you can be happy without a man, this will greatly strengthen you and also make your future relationships all the better.
>
> *(Beck et al., 1979, pp. 253–254)*

Over the past three decades, literally hundreds of studies have shown that cognitive therapy helps with unipolar depression (DeRubeis et al., 2000). Depressed people who receive this therapy improve much more than those who receive placebos or no treatment at all (Shaw & Segal, 1999; Hollon & Beck, 1994). Around 50 to 60 percent show a near total elimination of their symptoms. In view of this strong research support, many therapists have adopted the approach.

The Sociocultural Model of Unipolar Depression

Sociocultural theorists propose that unipolar depression is greatly influenced by the social structure in which people live. Their belief is supported by the finding, discussed earlier, that this disorder is often triggered by outside stressors. In addition, researchers have found ties between depression and factors such as culture, gender and race, and social support.

HOW ARE CULTURE AND DEPRESSION RELATED? On the one hand, depression is a worldwide phenomenon: persons in all countries and cultures are at risk for it (Chen, Rubin, & Li, 1995). On the other hand, the precise picture of depression varies from culture to culture. Depressed people in non-Western countries, for example, are more likely to be troubled by physical symptoms such as fatigue, weakness, sleep disturbances, and weight loss (Manson & Good, 1993; Marsella, 1980). Depression in these countries is less often marked by such psychological symptoms as self-blame and guilt. As these countries have become more Westernized, depression there has taken on the more psychological character it has in the West.

HOW DO GENDER AND RACE RELATE TO DEPRESSION? The rates of unipolar depression vary from subgroup to subgroup within a society. As we have already seen, the rate of depression is much higher among women than among men. One sociocultural theory holds that the complexities of women's roles in society leaves them particularly prone to depression.

Similarly, although few differences in the overall rate of unipolar depression have been found among white Americans, African Americans, and Hispanic Americans (Weissman et al., 1991), researchers sometimes find striking differences when they look at specific ethnic populations living under special circumstances. A study of one Native American village in the United States, for example, showed that the lifetime risk of developing depression was 37 percent among women,

Non-Western depression *Depressed people in non-Western countries tend to have fewer cognitive symptoms, such as self-blame, and more physical symptoms, such as fatigue, weakness, and sleep disturbances.*

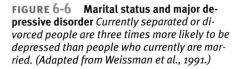

FIGURE 6-6 **Marital status and major depressive disorder** *Currently separated or divorced people are three times more likely to be depressed than people who currently are married. (Adapted from Weissman et al., 1991.)*

19 percent among men, and 28 percent overall, much higher than the risk in the general United States population (Kinzie et al., 1992). Many sociocultural theorists explain high rates of this kind by pointing to the terrible social and economic pressures faced by the people who live on Native American reservations.

HOW DOES SOCIAL SUPPORT RELATE TO DEPRESSION? The availability of social support seems to influence the likelihood of depression (Hammen, 1999; Champion & Power, 1995). As we see in Figure 6-6, across the United States, people who are separated or divorced display three times the depression rate of married or widowed persons and double the rate of people who have never been married. In some cases, the spouse's depression may contribute to a separation or divorce (Spangenberg & Theron, 1999), but often the interpersonal conflicts and low social support found in troubled relationships seem to lead to depression (Whisman, 2001; Bruce & Kim, 1992).

People whose lives are isolated and without intimacy seem particularly likely to become depressed at times of stress (Nezlek et al., 2000; Paykel & Cooper, 1992). Some highly publicized studies conducted in England a few decades ago showed that women who had three or more young children, lacked a close confidante, and had no outside employment were more likely than other women to become depressed after experiencing stressful life events (Brown, 1988; Brown & Harris, 1978). Studies have also found that depressed people who lack social support remain depressed longer than those who have a supportive spouse or warm friendships (Moos & Cronkite, 1999; Goodyer et al., 1997).

WHAT ARE THE SOCIOCULTURAL TREATMENTS FOR UNIPOLAR DEPRESSION? The most effective sociocultural approaches to depression are *interpersonal psychotherapy* and *couple therapy.* The techniques used in these approaches often borrow from the other models, but they are used in this instance to help persons overcome the social difficulties that may underlie their depression.

INTERPERSONAL PSYCHOTHERAPY Developed during the 1980s by the clinical researchers Gerald Klerman and Myrna Weissman, **interpersonal psychotherapy (IPT)** holds that any of four interpersonal problem areas may lead to depression and must be addressed: interpersonal loss, interpersonal role dispute, interpersonal role transition, and interpersonal deficits (Klerman & Weissman, 1992; Klerman et al., 1984). Over the course of around 16 sessions, IPT therapists address these areas.

First, depressed persons may, as psychodynamic theorists suggest, be experiencing a grief reaction over an *interpersonal loss,* the loss of an important loved one. In such cases, IPT therapists encourage clients to explore their relationship with the lost person and express any feelings of anger they may discover. Eventually clients develop new ways of remembering the lost person and also seek new relationships.

Second, depressed people may find themselves in the midst of an *interpersonal role dispute.* Role disputes occur when two people have different expectations of their relationship and of the role each should play. IPT therapists help clients examine whatever role disputes they may be involved in and to develop ways of solving them.

Depressed people may also be experiencing an *interpersonal role transition,* brought about by major life changes such as divorce or the birth of a child. They may feel overwhelmed by the role changes that accompany the life change. In such cases IPT therapists help them develop the social supports and skills the new roles require.

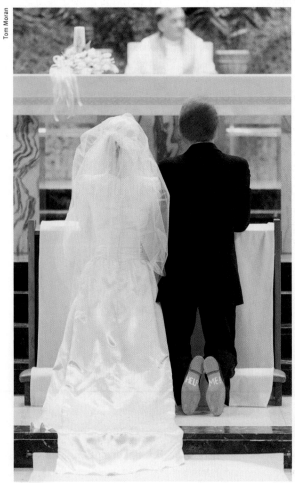

Role transition *A major life change such as marriage, the birth of a child, or divorce can present difficulties in role transition, one of the interpersonal problem areas addressed by IPT therapists in their work with depressed clients.*

THE CURRENT SCENE

Happiness: More Common Than We Think

Judging from the evening news and the spread of self-help books, one would think that happiness was rare. Even psychologists seem far more interested in studying heartache than happiness (Myers, 2000).

But there's good news. A growing body of research indicates that most people's lives are more upbeat than we think. In fact, most people around the world say they're happy—including most of those who are poor, unemployed, elderly, and disabled (Myers & Diener, 1996). Over 90 percent of people with quadriplegia say they're glad to be alive, and overall, people with spinal cord injuries report feeling only slightly less happy than other people (Diener & Diener, 1996). Men and women are equally likely to declare themselves satisfied or very happy. Wealthy people appear only slightly happier than those of modest means (Diener et al., 1993). Overall, only one person in ten reports being "not too happy" (Myers, 2000; Myers & Diener, 1996).

Although people aren't happy every day, most seem able to bounce back well from disappointments. Happy people also seem to remain happy from decade to decade, regardless of job changes, moves, and family changes (Myers & Diener, 1996). Some research indicates that happiness is only briefly affected by events in life (Suh, Diener, & Fujita, 1996). Happy people adjust to negative events and return to their usual cheerful state within a few months (Diener et al., 1992). Conversely, unhappy people are not cheered in the long term even by positive events.

Myrleen Ferguson/Stone

If gender, race, income, and life events have but limited effects on long-term happiness, what makes so many people upbeat? Some studies suggest that happiness is dependent on personality characteristics and interpretive styles (Diener, 2000). Happy people are generally optimistic, outgoing, and tender minded, and they tend to have several close friends (Doyle & Youn, 2000; Francis, 1999; Lu, 1999). Happy people also have high self-esteem and believe that they have control over their lives.

Several theorists further believe that people have a "happiness set point" to which they consistently return, despite life's ups and downs. An investigation of 2,300 twins suggested to the researchers who conducted the study that as much as half of one's sense of happiness is related to genetic factors (Lykken & Tellegen, 1996).

A better understanding of the roots of happiness may come from the present flurry of research, perhaps providing useful solutions to people who are not so happy and even those who are clinically depressed. In the meantime, we have the comfort of knowing that the human condition isn't quite as unhappy as news stories (and textbooks on abnormal psychology) may make it seem.

Finally, some depressed people display *interpersonal deficits*, such as extreme shyness or social awkwardness, which prevent them from having intimate relationships. According to Klerman and Weissman, many depressed people experienced disrupted relationships as children and have failed to establish intimate relationships as adults. IPT therapists may help them recognize their deficits and may teach them social skills and assertiveness in order to improve their social effectiveness. In the following discussion, the therapist encourages a depressed man to recognize the effect his behavior has on others:

> **Client:** *(After a long pause with eyes downcast, a sad facial expression, and slumped posture)* People always make fun of me. I guess I'm just the type of guy who really was meant to be a loner, damn it. *(Deep sigh)*
> **Therapist:** Could you do that again for me?
> **Client:** What?
> **Therapist:** The sigh, only a bit deeper.
> **Client:** Why? *(Pause)* Okay, but I don't see what . . . okay. *(Client sighs again and smiles)*
> **Therapist:** Well, that time you smiled, but mostly when you sigh and look so sad I get the feeling that I better leave you alone in your misery, that I

INTERPERSONAL PSYCHOTHERAPY (IPT) A treatment for unipolar depression that is based on the belief that clarifying and changing one's interpersonal problems will help lead to recovery.

COUPLE THERAPY A therapy format in which the therapist works with two people who share a long-term relationship. Also called *marital therapy*.

should walk on eggshells and not get too chummy or I might hurt you even more.

Client: (*A bit of anger in his voice*) Well, excuse me! I was only trying to tell you how I felt.

Therapist: I know you felt miserable, but I also got the message that you wanted to keep me at a distance, that I have no way to reach you.

Client: (*Slowly*) I feel like a loner, I feel that even you don't care about me—making fun of me.

Therapist: I wonder if other folks need to pass this test too?

(*Young & Blier, 1984, p. 270*)

A number of studies suggests that IPT and related interpersonal treatments for depression have a success rate similar to that of cognitive therapy (Santor & Kusumakar, 2001; Swartz, 1999). That is, symptoms almost totally disappear in 50 to 60 percent of clients who receive treatment. Not surprisingly, IPT is considered especially useful for depressed people who are struggling with social conflicts or undergoing changes in their careers or social roles (APA, 1993).

COUPLE THERAPY As we have seen, depression can result from marital discord, and recovery from depression is often slower for people who do not receive support from their spouse (Bruce & Kim, 1992). In fact, as many as half of all depressed clients may be in a dysfunctional relationship. Thus it is not surprising that many cases of depression have been treated by **couple therapy,** the approach in which a therapist works with two people who share a long-term relationship.

Therapists who offer *behavioral marital therapy* help spouses change harmful marital behavior by teaching them specific communication and problem-solving skills (see Chapter 2). When the depressed person's marriage is filled with conflict, this approach and similar ones may be as effective as individual cognitive therapy, interpersonal psychotherapy, or drug therapy in helping to reduce unipolar depression (Beach, 2001; Baucom et al., 1998).

SPECIAL TRAINING NOT REQUIRED

Any psychotherapist, trained in couple therapy or not, may practice this complex form of treatment. The majority of clinicians now doing couple therapy have had no formal training in it (Doherty, 1999).

ConsiderThis

◉ Some clinicians argue that antidepressant drugs serve to curb useful behaviors, destroy individuality, and blunt people's concerns about societal ills. Are such concerns justified?

SUMMING UP | **Unipolar Depression**

Victims of unipolar depression, the most common pattern of mood disorder, suffer from depression only. The symptoms of depression span five areas of functioning: emotional, motivational, behavioral, cognitive, and physical. Depressed people are also at greater risk for suicidal thinking and behavior. Women are more likely than men to experience unipolar depression.

The Biological Perspective Low activity by two neurotransmitters, norepinephrine and serotonin, appears to play a role in depression. Similarly, abnormal functioning of certain hormones, such as cortisol and melatonin, may contribute. Such biological problems may be linked to genetic factors.

Electroconvulsive therapy (ECT), although controversial, is an effective and fast-acting technique for unipolar depression. Three kinds of antidepressant drugs—MAO inhibitors, tricyclics, and second-generation antidepressants—are also effective treatments, and drug therapy is widely used.

The Psychodynamic Perspective According to the psychodynamic view, certain people who experience real or imagined losses may regress to an earlier stage of development, fuse with the person they have lost, and become depressed. Psychodynamic therapists try to help persons with unipolar depression recognize and work through their losses and excessive dependence on others.

The Behavioral Perspective The behavioral view says that when people experience a large reduction in their positive rewards, they are more likely to become depressed. Behavioral therapists reintroduce clients to events and activities that the clients once found pleasurable, reward nondepressive behaviors, and teach effective interpersonal skills.

The Cognitive Perspective According to the learned helplessness theory, people become depressed when they believe that they have lost control over the reinforcements in their lives and when they attribute this loss to causes that are internal, global, and stable. According to Beck's negative-thinking explanation, maladaptive attitudes, the cognitive triad, errors in thinking, and automatic thoughts help produce unipolar depression.

Cognitive therapy for depression helps persons increase their activities, challenge their automatic thoughts, identify their negative thinking and biases, and change their attitudes.

The Sociocultural Perspective Sociocultural theorists point to broader social factors that help cause depression, including stressors, cultural factors, gender, race, and immediate social environment.

Interpersonal psychotherapy (IPT) addresses the interpersonal problem areas of depression, such as interpersonal loss, interpersonal role dispute, interpersonal role transition, and interpersonal deficits. Couple therapy may also be of help when depression is tied to a troubled long-term relationship.

THE INSURANCE FACTOR

Insurance coverage helps dictate the type of treatment people receive for depression. Privately insured patients are more likely than Medicaid patients to receive psychotherapy. Moreover, among those receiving medications, the privately insured are more likely to receive selective serotonin reuptake inhibitors than the cheaper tricyclics (Melfi, Croghan, & Hanna, 1999).

Bipolar Disorders

People with a *bipolar disorder* experience both the lows of depression and the highs of mania. Many describe their life as an emotional roller coaster. They shift back and forth between extreme moods. This roller-coaster ride and its impact on relatives and friends are seen in the following case study:

In his early school years he had been a remarkable student and had shown a gift for watercolor and oils. Later he had studied art in Paris and married an English girl he had met there. Eventually they had settled in London.

Ten years later, when he was thirty-four years old, he had persuaded his wife and only son to accompany him to Honolulu, where, he assured them, he would be considered famous. He felt he would be able to sell his paintings at many times the prices he could get in London. According to his wife, he had been in an accelerated state, but at that time the family had left, unsuspecting, believing with the patient in their imminent good fortune. When they arrived they found almost no one in the art world that he was supposed to know. There were no connections for sales and deals in Hawaii that he had anticipated. Settling down, the patient began to behave more peculiarly than ever. After enduring several months of the patient's exhilaration, overactivity, weight loss, constant talking, and unbelievably little sleep, the young wife and child began to fear for his sanity. None of his plans materialized. After five months in the Pacific, with finances growing thin, the patient's overactivity subsided and he fell into a depression. During that period he refused to move, paint, or leave the house. He lost twenty pounds, became utterly dependent on his wife, and insisted on seeing none of the friends he had accumulated in his manic state. His despondency became so severe that several doctors came to the house and advised psychiatric hospitalization. He quickly agreed and received twelve electroshock treatments, which relieved his depressed state. Soon afterward he began to paint again and to sell his work modestly. Recognition began to come from galleries and critics in the Far East. Several reviews acclaimed his work as exceptionally brilliant.

"Depression is terrifying, and elation, its nonidentical twin sister, is even more terrifying—attractive as she may be for a moment."

Film director Joshua Logan, describing his bipolar disorder, 1973

> This was the beginning of the lifelong career of his mood swing. In 1952, while still in Honolulu, he once again became severely depressed. . . . Four years later he returned to London in a high. . . . When this manic period subsided and he surveyed the wreckage of his life, an eight-month interval of normal mood followed, after which he again switched into a profound depression.
>
> *(Fieve, 1975, pp. 64–65)*

What Are the Symptoms of Mania?

Unlike people sunk in the gloom of depression, those in a state of mania typically experience dramatic and inappropriate rises in mood. The symptoms of mania span the same areas of functioning—*emotional, motivational, behavioral, cognitive,* and *physical*—as those of depression, but mania affects those areas in an opposite way.

In mania a person has active, powerful emotions in search of an outlet. The mood of euphoric joy and well-being is out of all proportion to the actual happenings in the person's life. One person with mania explained, "I feel no sense of restriction or censorship whatsoever. I am afraid of nothing and no one" (Fieve, 1975, p. 68). Not every person with mania is a picture of happiness, however. Some instead become irritable and angry—especially when others get in the way of their exaggerated ambitions.

In the motivational realm, people with mania seem to want constant excitement, involvement, and companionship. They enthusiastically seek out new friends and old, new interests and old, and have little awareness that their social style is overwhelming, domineering, and excessive.

The behavior of people with mania is usually very active. They move quickly, as though there were not enough time to do everything they want to do. They may talk rapidly and loudly, their conversations filled with jokes and efforts to be clever or, conversely, with complaints and verbal outbursts. Flamboyance is not uncommon: dressing in flashy clothes, giving large sums of money to strangers, or even getting involved in dangerous activities.

In the cognitive realm, people with mania usually show poor judgment and planning, as if they feel too good or move too fast to consider possible pitfalls. Filled with optimism, they rarely listen when others try to slow them down, interrupt their buying sprees, or prevent them from investing money unwisely. They may also hold an inflated opinion of themselves, and sometimes their self-esteem approaches grandiosity (Silverstone & Hunt, 1992). During severe episodes of mania, some have trouble remaining coherent or in touch with reality.

Finally, in the physical realm, people with mania feel remarkably energetic. They typically get little sleep, yet feel and act wide awake (Silverstone & Hunt, 1992). Even if they miss a night or two of sleep, their energy level may remain high.

"Those? Oh, just a few souvenirs from my bipolar-disorder days."

Diagnosing Bipolar Disorders

People are considered to be in a full *manic episode* when for at least one week they display an abnormally high or irritable mood, along with at least three other symptoms of mania (see Table 6-4). The episode may include psychotic features such as delusions or hallucinations. When the symptoms of mania are less severe (causing little impairment), the person is said to be experiencing a *hypomanic episode* (APA, 2000, 1994).

DSM-IV distinguishes two kinds of bipolar disorders—bipolar I and bipolar II. People with **bipolar I disorder** have full manic and major depressive episodes. Most of them experience an *alternation* of the episodes; for example, months of

Table 6-4 DSM-IV Checklist

MANIC EPISODE

1. A period of abnormally and persistently elevated, expansive, or irritable mood, lasting at least one week.
2. Persistence of at least three of the following: • inflated self-esteem or grandiosity • decreased need for sleep • more talkativeness than usual, or pressure to keep talking • flight of ideas or the experience that thoughts are racing • distractibility • increase in activity or psychomotor agitation • excessive involvement in pleasurable activities that have a high potential for painful consequences.
3. Significant distress or impairment.

BIPOLAR I DISORDER

1. The presence of a manic, hypomanic, or major depressive episode.
2. If currently in a hypomanic or major depressive episode, history of a manic episode.
3. Significant distress or impairment.

BIPOLAR II DISORDER

1. The presence of a hypomanic or major depressive episode.
2. If currently in a major depressive episode, history of a hypomanic episode. If currently in a hypomanic episode, history of a major depressive episode. No history of a manic episode.
3. Significant distress or impairment.

Based on APA, 2000, 1994.

FRENZIED MASTERPIECE
George Frideric Handel wrote his *Messiah* in less than a month during a manic episode (Roesch, 1991).

GRADING ONESELF
People do not have to be hypomanic or manic in order to think highly of themselves. According to one survey, large numbers of adults consider themselves kinder (45 percent of the population), funnier (42 percent), more patient (34 percent), and smarter (27 percent) than average (Kanner, 1995).

depression followed by months of mania. Some, however, have *mixed* episodes, in which they swing from manic to depressive symptoms and back again on the same day. In **bipolar II disorder,** hypomanic—that is, mildly manic—episodes alternate with major depressive episodes over the course of time (MacQueen & Young, 2001). Without treatment, the mood episodes tend to recur for people with either type of bipolar disorder.

Surveys from around the world indicate that between 1 and 1.5 percent of all adults suffer from a bipolar disorder at any given time (Bebbington & Ramana, 1995; Kessler et al., 1994). The disorders are equally common in women and men and among all socioeconomic classes and ethnic groups (APA, 2000; Weissman et al., 1991). Onset usually occurs between the ages of 15 and 44 years. In most untreated cases, the manic and depressive episodes eventually subside, only to recur at a later time (APA, 2000, 1994).

When a person experiences numerous periods of hypomanic symptoms and mild depressive symptoms, DSM-IV assigns a diagnosis of **cyclothymic disorder.** The symptoms of this milder form of bipolar disorder continue for two or more years, interrupted occasionally by normal moods that may last for only days or weeks. This disorder, like bipolar I and bipolar II disorders, usually begins in adolescence or early adulthood and is equally common among women and men. At least 0.4 percent of the population develops cyclothymic disorder (APA, 2000). In some cases, the milder symptoms eventually blossom into a bipolar I or II disorder.

What Causes Bipolar Disorders?

Throughout the first half of the twentieth century, the search for the cause of bipolar disorders made little progress. More recently, biological research has

BIPOLAR I DISORDER A type of bipolar disorder marked by full manic and major depressive episodes.

BIPOLAR II DISORDER A type of bipolar disorder marked by mildly manic (hypomanic) episodes and major depressive episodes.

CYCLOTHYMIC DISORDER A disorder marked by numerous periods of hypomanic symptoms and mild depressive symptoms.

Abnormality and Creativity: A Delicate Balance

Up to a point, states of depression, mania, anxiety, and even confusion can actually be useful. This may be particularly true in the arts. The ancient Greeks believed that various forms of "divine madness" inspired creative acts, from poetry to performance (Ludwig, 1995). Even today many people expect "creative geniuses" to be psychologically disturbed. A popular image of the artist includes a glass of liquor, a cigarette, and a tormented expression. Classic examples include the poet Sylvia Plath, who experienced depression most of her life and eventually committed suicide, and the dancer Vaslav Nijinsky, who suffered from schizophrenia and spent many years in institutions. In fact, a number of studies indicate that artists and writers are somewhat more likely than others to suffer from mental disorders, particularly mood disorders (Jamison, 1995; Ludwig, 1995, 1994).

Why might creative people be prone to psychological disorders? Some may be predisposed to such disorders long before they begin their artistic careers; the careers may simply bring attention to their emotional struggles (Ludwig, 1995). Indeed, creative people often have a family history of psychological problems. A number also have experienced intense psychological upsets during childhood. Virginia Woolf, for example, endured sexual abuse as a child.

Another reason for the creativity link may be that creative endeavors create emotional turmoil that is overwhelming. Truman Capote said that writing his famous book *In Cold Blood* "killed" him psychologically. Before writing this account of a brutal murder, he considered himself "a stable person. . . . Afterward something happened to me" (Ludwig, 1995).

Yet a third explanation for the link between creativity and psychological disorders is that the creative professions offer a welcome climate for those with psychological disturbances. In the worlds of poetry, painting, and acting, for example, emotional expression and personal turmoil are valued as sources of inspiration and success (Ludwig, 1995).

Corbis

Much remains to be learned about the relationship between emotional turmoil and creativity, but work in this area has already clarified two important points. First, psychological disturbance is hardly a requirement for creativity. Many "creative geniuses" are, in fact, psychologically stable and happy throughout their entire lives. Second, *mild* psychological disturbances relate to creative achievement much more strongly than severe disturbances do (Jamison, 1995). For example, the nineteenth-century composer Robert Schumann, who suffered from a bipolar disorder, produced twenty-seven works during one mildly manic year but next to nothing during years when he was severely depressed and suicidal (Jamison, 1995).

Some artists worry that if their psychological suffering stops, their creativity will disappear as well. In fact, however, research suggests that successful treatment for severe psychological disorders can actually improve the creative process (Jamison, 1995; Ludwig, 1995). Romantic notions aside, severe mental dysfunctioning has little redeeming value, in the arts or anywhere else.

Famous victim *The English novelist and essayist Virginia Woolf (1882–1941) had an enormous influence on the development of the twentieth-century novel. Yet she suffered from severe mood disturbances, possibly a bipolar disorder, that eventually led her to take her own life by drowning.*

POPULAR SEARCH

Depression is the most common health-care topic searched for on the Internet each year (19 percent of searches), followed by allergies/sinuses (16 percent), bipolar disorder (14 percent), and arthritis/rheumatism (10 percent) (Harris Poll, 1999).

produced some promising clues. New biological insights have come from research into *neurotransmitter activity, ion activity,* and *genetic factors.*

NEUROTRANSMITTERS Could overactivity of norepinephrine be related to mania? This was the expectation of clinicians back in the 1960s after investigators first found a relationship between low norepinephrine activity and unipolar depression (Schildkraut, 1965). One study did indeed find the norepinephrine activity of persons with mania to be higher than that of depressed or control subjects (Post et al., 1980, 1978). In another study patients with a bipolar disorder were given *reserpine,* the blood pressure drug known to reduce norepinephrine activity in the brain, and the manic symptoms of some subsided (Telner et al., 1986).

Because serotonin activity often parallels norepinephrine activity in unipolar depression, theorists at first expected that mania would also be related to high serotonin activity, but no such relationship has been found. Instead, research suggests that mania, like depression, may be linked to *low* serotonin activity (Price,

1990). Perhaps low serotonin activity opens the door to a mood disorder and *permits* the activity of norepinephrine to define the particular form the disorder will take. That is, low serotonin activity accompanied by low norepinephrine activity may lead to depression; low serotonin activity accompanied by high norepinephrine activity may lead to mania.

ION ACTIVITY On both sides of the cell membrane of each neuron sit positively charged *sodium ions.* The ions play a critical role in sending incoming messages down the neuron to the nerve endings. When the neuron is at rest, most of the sodium ions sit on the outer side of the membrane. When the neuron is stimulated by an incoming message at its receptor site, however, the sodium ions from the outer side of the membrane travel across to the inner side. This movement, in turn, starts a wave of electrochemical activity that continues down the length of the neuron and results in its "firing." Afterward, a flow of *potassium ions* from the inside to the outside of the neuron helps it to return to its original resting state (see Figure 6-7).

If brain messages are to be sent and received appropriately, the ions must travel properly back and forth between the outside and the inside of the neural membrane. Some theorists believe that improper transport of these ions may cause neurons to fire too easily (resulting in mania) or to stubbornly resist firing (resulting in depression) (El Mallakh & Huff, 2001). Not surprisingly, researchers have found membrane defects in the neurons of persons with bipolar disorders and have observed abnormal functioning in the proteins that help transport ions across a neuron's membrane (Wang et al., 1999; Meltzer, 1991).

GENETIC FACTORS Many experts believe that people inherit a biological predisposition to develop bipolar disorders. Findings from family pedigree studies support this idea. Identical twins of persons with a bipolar disorder have a 40 percent likelihood of developing the same disorder, and fraternal twins, siblings, and other close relatives of such persons have a 5 to 10 percent likelihood, compared to the 1 percent rate in the general population (Craddock & Jones, 1999; Gershon & Nurnberger, 1995).

Researchers have also conducted *genetic linkage studies* to identify possible patterns in the inheritance of bipolar disorders. They select large families that have had high rates of the disorder over several generations, observe the pattern of distribution of the disorder among family members, and determine whether it closely follows a predictable pattern of inheritance. Still other researchers have used techniques from *molecular biology* to examine possible genetic patterns of the disorder in large families. These various undertakings have linked bipolar disorders to genes on chromosomes 4, 6, 11, 12, 13, 15, 18, 22, and x (Berrettini, 2000). Such wide-ranging findings may mean that the logic behind the various gene studies is flawed (Gershon, 2000). Alternatively, it may be that a variety of gene abnormalities combine to bring about bipolar disorders (Meltzer, 2000).

What Are the Treatments for Bipolar Disorders?

Until the past few decades, people with bipolar disorders were destined to spend their lives on an emotional roller coaster. Psychotherapists reported almost no success (Lickey & Gordon, 1991), and antidepressant drugs were of limited help (Prien et al., 1974). In fact, the drugs sometimes triggered a manic episode (Bowden, 2001). ECT, too, only occasionally relieved either the depressive or the manic episodes of bipolar disorders (Jefferson & Greist, 1994).

LITHIUM THERAPY The use of **lithium** has so dramatically changed this gloomy picture that many people view the silvery-white element—found in various simple mineral salts throughout the natural world—as a true miracle drug. Its effectiveness in the treatment of bipolar disorders was first discovered in 1949 by the Australian psychiatrist John Cade.

FIGURE 6-7 **Ions and the firing of neurons**
Neurons relay messages in the form of electrical impulses that travel down the axon toward the nerve endings. As an impulse travels along the axon, sodium ions (Na+), which had been resting on the outside of the neuron's membrane, flow to the inside, causing the impulse to continue down the axon. Once sodium ions flow in, potassium ions (K+) flow out, thus helping the membrane's electrical balance return to its resting state, ready for the arrival of a new impulse. (Adapted from Snyder, 1986, p. 7.)

LITHIUM A metallic element that occurs in nature as a mineral salt and is an effective treatment for bipolar disorders.

"More lithium."

Determining the correct lithium dosage for a given patient is a delicate process (Schou, 1997). Too low a dose will have little or no effect on the bipolar mood swings, but too high a dose can result in lithium *intoxication* (literally, poisoning), which can cause nausea, vomiting, sluggishness, tremors, dizziness, slurred speech, seizures, kidney dysfunction, and even death (Moncrieff, 1997). With the correct dose, however, lithium often produces a noticeable change in mood within five to fourteen days. Some patients respond better to other drugs, such as the antiseizure drug *carbamazepine (Tegretol)* or *valproate (Depakote)*, or to a combination of such drugs (Lennkh & Simhandl, 2000; Nolen, 1999).

All manner of research has indicated that lithium is effective in treating manic episodes. More than 60 percent of patients with mania improve on this medication. In addition, most of them experience fewer new episodes as long as they continue taking lithium (Viguera et al., 2000). One study found that the risk of relapse is twenty-eight times greater if patients stop taking lithium (Suppes et al., 1991). Thus, today's clinicians usually continue patients on some level of lithium even after their manic episodes subside (Nolen, 1999).

Lithium also helps those with bipolar disorder overcome their depressive episodes, though to a lesser degree than it helps with their manic episodes (Hlastala et al., 1997). In addition, continued doses of lithium apparently reduce the risk of future depressive episodes, just as they seem to prevent the return of manic episodes (Baldessarini, Tondo, & Hennen, 1999).

Researchers do not fully understand how lithium operates. They suspect that it changes synaptic activity in neurons, but in a way different from that of antidepressant drugs (Ghaemi, Boiman, & Goodwin, 1999). The firing of a neuron actually consists of several phases that unfold at lightning speed. When a neurotransmitter binds to a receptor on the receiving neuron, a series of changes occur within the receiving neuron to set the stage for firing. The substances in the neuron that carry out those changes are often called **second messengers** because they relay the original message from the receptor site to the firing mechanism of the neuron. Whereas antidepressant drugs affect a neuron's initial reception of neurotransmitters, lithium appears to affect a neuron's second messengers.

Different second-messenger systems are at work in different neurons. In one of the most important systems, chemicals called *phosphoinositides* are produced once neurotransmitters are received. Lithium apparently affects this particular messenger system (Manji et al., 1999; Belmaker et al., 1995). Lithium may in fact affect the activity of any neuron that uses this second-messenger system, and in so doing may correct the biological abnormalities that lead to bipolar disorders.

ADJUNCTIVE PSYCHOTHERAPY Psychotherapy alone is rarely helpful for persons with bipolar disorders (Klerman et al., 1994). At the same time, clinicians have learned that lithium therapy alone is not always sufficient either. Thirty percent or more of patients with these disorders may not respond to lithium or a related drug, may not receive the proper dose, or may relapse while taking it (Kulhara et al., 1999; Solomon et al., 1995). In addition, a number of patients stop taking lithium on their own (Goodwin & Jamison, 1990).

In view of these problems, many clinicians now use individual, group, or family therapy as an *adjunct* to lithium treatment (George, Friedman, & Miklowitz, 2000; Scott, 1995). Most often, therapists use these formats to stress the need for proper management of medications, to improve social skills and relationships that may be affected by bipolar episodes, to educate patients and families about bipolar disorders, and to help patients solve the special family, school, and occupational problems caused by their disorder.

Few controlled studies have tested the effectiveness of psychotherapy as an adjunct to drug therapy for severe bipolar disorders, but a growing number of clinical reports suggest that it helps reduce hospitalization, improves social

GOING IT ALONE

During the first year after their lithium was stopped, two-thirds of successfully treated bipolar patients in one study developed a new depressive or manic episode. The suicide rate of these individuals also increased twentyfold during this period, although it dropped afterwards (Baldessarini et al., 1999).

SECOND MESSENGERS Chemical changes within a neuron just after the neuron receives a neurotransmitter message and just before it responds.

functioning, and increases clients' ability to obtain and hold a job (Frank, 1999; Scott, 1995; Werder, 1995).

SUMMING UP | **Bipolar Disorders**

In bipolar disorders, episodes of mania alternate or intermix with episodes of depression. These disorders are much less common than unipolar depression. They may take the form of bipolar I disorder, bipolar II disorder, or cyclothymic disorder.

Explanations of Bipolar Disorders Mania has been related to high norepinephrine activity. In addition, bipolar disorders have been linked to improper transportation of ions back and forth between the outside and the inside of the neuron's membrane. Genetic studies suggest that people may inherit a predisposition to these biological abnormalities.

Treatments for Bipolar Disorders Lithium or another mood-stabilizing drug effectively reduces and prevents both the manic and the depressive episodes of bipolar disorders. Some researchers suspect that lithium achieves its effect by acting on second messengers in key neurons throughout the brain. In recent years it has become clear that patients may fare better when lithium is combined with psychotherapy.

ConsiderThis

● What issues of lifestyle, family and social relationships, and other areas of functioning might need to be addressed in adjunctive psychotherapy for persons with a bipolar disorder?

CROSSROADS:
Making Sense of All That Is Known

During the past thirty years, researchers and clinicians have made tremendous gains in the understanding and treatment of mood disorders. Unipolar depression, for example, has also become one of the most treatable of all psychological disorders. Cognitive therapy, interpersonal psychotherapy, and antidepressant drugs are all helpful in cases of any severity; couple therapy is helpful in select cases; behavioral therapy helps in mild to moderate cases; and ECT is useful and effective in severe cases. During the same period of time, several factors have been closely tied to unipolar depression, including biological abnormalities, a reduction in positive reinforcements, a perception of helplessness, negative ways of thinking, and sociocultural influences. Precisely how these various factors relate to unipolar depression remains unclear, however (Flett, Vredenburg, & Krames, 1997). Several relationships are possible:

1. *One* of the factors may be the key cause of unipolar depression. If so, cognitive or biological factors are leading candidates, for these kinds of factors have each been found, at times, to precede and predict depression.

2. *Different* factors may be capable of setting up unipolar depression in different persons. Some people may, for example, begin with low serotonin activity, which predisposes them to react helplessly in stressful situations, interpret events negatively, and enjoy fewer pleasures in life. Others may first suffer a severe loss, which triggers helplessness reactions, low serotonin activity, and reductions in positive rewards.

3. An *interaction* between two or more specific factors may be necessary to produce unipolar depression (Klocek, Oliver, & Ross, 1997). Perhaps people will become depressed only if they have low levels of serotonin activity, feel helpless, *and* repeatedly blame themselves for negative events.

4. The various factors may play *different* roles in unipolar depression. Some may cause the disorder, some may result from it, and some may keep it going.

DRUGS FOR EVERYONE?

Can antidepressants also improve the spirits of nondepressed persons? Yes and no, it appears. When given to volunteers who had no clinical symptoms, antidepressants seemed to help reduce negative emotions such as hostility and fear, but failed to increase positive feelings such as happiness and excitement (Knutson et al., 1998).

EXERCISE REALLY HELPS

Numerous studies clarify that various kinds of regular exercise often alleviate mild to moderate depression and sometimes play a useful role in more severe episodes (Lawlor & Hopker, 2001; Tkachuk & Martin, 1999).

As with unipolar depression, clinicians and researchers have learned much about bipolar disorders during the past 30 years. But, unlike unipolar depression, bipolar disorders appear to be best explained by focusing largely on one kind of variable—biological factors. The evidence suggests that biological abnormalities, perhaps inherited and perhaps triggered by life stress, cause bipolar disorders. In addition, the choice of treatment for these disorders is narrow and simple—lithium (or a related drug), perhaps combined with psychotherapy.

There is no question that an enormous body of information has been gathered about mood disorders and effective interventions have been developed, and that these developments offer great promise for people with such disorders. On the other hand, the sobering fact remains that as many as 40 percent of people with a mood disorder do not improve under treatment and must suffer their mania or depression until it runs its course. Now that clinical researchers have gathered so many important puzzle pieces, they must put the pieces together into a still more meaningful picture that will suggest even better ways to predict, prevent, and treat these disorders.

KEY TERMS

depression p. 157

mania p. 157

unipolar depression p. 157

bipolar disorder p. 157

major depressive disorder p. 161

dysthymic disorder p. 161

reactive depression p. 161

endogenous depression p. 161

norepinephrine p. 162

serotonin p. p. 162

endocrine system p. p. 162

cortisol p. 163

melatonin p. 163

electroconvulsive therapy (ECT) p. 163

MAO inhibitors p. 165

tyramine p. 165

tricyclics p. 165

selective serotonin reuptake inhibitors (SSRIs) p. 166

symbolic loss p. 168

learned helplessness p. 172

attribution p. 174

cognitive triad p. 175

automatic thoughts p. 175

cognitive therapy p. 176

interpersonal psychotherapy (IPT) p. 178

couple therapy p. 180

hypomanic episode p. 182

bipolar I disorder p. 182

bipolar II disorder p. 183

cyclothymic disorder p. 183

sodium ion p. 185

lithium p. 185

carbamazepine (Tegretol) p. 186

valproate (Depakote) p. 186

second messengers p. 186

QUICK QUIZ

1. What are the key symptoms of depression and mania? What is the difference between unipolar depression and bipolar disorder? pp. 157–161, 181–183

2. Describe the differences in prevalence, gender, age, and ethnicity shown by the various mood disorders. pp. 158, 183

3. Describe the role of the neurotransmitters norepinephrine and serotonin in unipolar depression. pp. 162–163

4. Describe Freud and Abraham's psychodynamic theory of depression and the evidence for it. pp. 167–170

5. How do behaviorists describe the role of rewards in depression? pp. 170–171

6. How might laboratory learned helplessness be related to human depression? pp. 171–174

7. What kinds of negative thinking may lead to mood problems? pp. 174–176

8. How do sociocultural theorists account for unipolar depression? pp. 177–178

9. What roles do biological and genetic factors seem to play in bipolar disorders? pp. 183–185

10. Discuss the leading treatments for unipolar depression and bipolar disorders. How effective are these various approaches? pp. 163–167, 170, 171, 176–177, 178–180, 185–187

⊙ CYBER STUDY

Observe the symptoms of depression. ▲ How might stressful events be tied to depression? ▲ Search for genetic causes of mood disorders. ▲ How do medications alleviate mood disorders? ▲ How has ECT changed over the years?

SEARCH THE *FUNDAMENTALS OF ABNORMAL PSYCHOLOGY* CD-ROM FOR

▲ Chapter 6 video cases and discussions
   "Meredith"—Mood Disorders: Medication and Talk Therapy
   Early Electroconvulsive Therapy

▲ Chapter 6 practice test and feedback

▲ Additional video case and discussion
   Mood Disorders: Hereditary Factors

LOG ON TO THE COMER WEB PAGE FOR

▲ Suggested Web links, research exercises, FAQ page, additional Chapter 6 practice test questions
   <www.worthpublishers.com/comer>

The Mind, Second Edition. (WNET/Worth Publishers, 1999)

I had done all I could and I was still sinking. I sat many hours seeking answers, and all there was was a silent wind. The answer was in my head. It was all clear now: Die. . . .

The next day a friend offered to sell me a gun, a .357 magnum pistol. I bought it. My first thought was: What a mess this is going to make. That day I began to say goodbye to people: not actually saying it but expressing it silently.

Friends were around, but I didn't let them see what was wrong with me. I could not let them know lest they prevent it. My mind became locked on my target. My thoughts were: Soon it will all be over. I would obtain the peace I had so long sought. The will to survive and succeed had been crushed and defeated. I was like a general on a battlefield being encroached on by my enemy and its hordes: fear, hate, self-depreciation, desolation. I felt I had to have the upper hand, to control my environment, so I sought to die rather than surrender. . . .

I was only aware of myself and my plight. Death swallowed me long before I pulled the trigger. The world through my eyes seemed to die with me. It was like I was to push the final button to end this world. I committed myself to the arms of death. There comes a time when all things cease to shine, when the rays of hope are lost.

I placed the gun to my head. Then, I remember a tremendous explosion of lights like fireworks. Thus did the pain become glorious, an army rallied to the side of death to help destroy my life, which I could feel leaving my body with each rushing surge of blood. I was engulfed in total darkness.

(Shneidman, 1987, p. 56)

Salmon spawn and then die, after an exhausting upstream swim to their breeding ground. Lemmings rush to the sea and drown. But only humans knowingly take their own lives. The actions of salmon and lemmings are instinctual responses that may even help their species survive in the long run. Only in the human act of suicide do beings act for the specific purpose of putting an end to their lives.

Suicide has been recorded throughout history. The Old Testament described King Saul's suicide: "There Saul took a sword and fell on it." The ancient Chinese, Greeks, and Romans also provided examples. In more recent times, suicides by such famous individuals as the writer Ernest Hemingway, the actress Marilyn Monroe, and the rock star Kurt Cobain have both shocked and fascinated the public. Even more disturbing are mass suicides such as those of the Heaven's Gate cult in 1997.

Before you finish reading this page, someone in the United States will try to kill himself. At least 60 Americans will have taken their own lives by this time tomorrow. . . . Many of those who attempted will try again, a number with lethal success.

(Shneidman & Mandelkorn, 1983)

Suicide in the Family

On July 1, 1996, the model and actress Margaux Hemingway killed herself by taking an overdose of barbiturates. She was the fifth person in four generations of her family to commit suicide. Her death came almost 35 years to the day after the suicide of her famous grandfather, the novelist Ernest Hemingway, by shotgun. Severely depressed about his progressive physical illness, he had failed to respond to two series of electroconvulsive treatments.

Margaux Hemingway had suffered from severe depression, alcoholism, and bulimia nervosa. She had had a successful modeling and acting career in the 1970s, but in later years her work consisted primarily of infomercials and low-budget movies. According to friends, she had tried for years to handle her anguish and setbacks with grace. "I was taught it was Hemingwayesque to take your blows and walk stoically through them."

Marc C. Biggins/Gamma Liaison

Karsh/Woodfin Camp & Associates

ConsiderThis

⬤ Suicide sometimes runs in families. Why might this be the case? • Some family names bring instant recognition, as "Hemingway" does. What special challenges and pressures might such recognition bring to a person's life?

Today suicide ranks among the top ten causes of death in the world. It has been estimated that as many as 700,000 people may die by it each year, 31,000 in the United States alone (Kaplan, 1999; Phillips, Liu, & Zhang, 1999) (see Table 7-1 on page 194). Millions of other people throughout the world—600,000 in the United States—make unsuccessful attempts to kill themselves; such attempts are called **parasuicides** (Welch, 2001). Actually, it is hard to obtain accurate figures on suicide, and many investigators believe that estimates are often low. For one thing, suicide can be difficult to distinguish from unintentional drug overdoses, automobile crashes, drownings, and other accidents (Ohberg, Penttila, & Lonnqvist, 1997). Many apparent "accidents" were probably intentional. For another, suicide is frowned on in our society, causing relatives and friends to refuse to admit that loved ones have taken their own lives.

Suicide is not classified as a mental disorder by DSM-IV, but clinicians are aware of the key role that psychological dysfunctioning—a breakdown of coping skills, emotional turmoil, a distorted view of life—often plays in this act. The majority of cases have in fact been linked to clinical depression, schizophrenia, or other psychological disorders (Murphy, 1998).

What Is Suicide?

Not every self-inflicted death is a suicide. A man who crashes his car into a tree after falling asleep at the steering wheel is not trying to kill himself. Thus Edwin Shneidman (2001, 1993, 1981, 1963), one of the most influential writers on this topic, defines **suicide** as an intentioned death—a self-inflicted death in which one makes an intentional, direct, and conscious effort to end one's life.

Intentioned deaths may take various forms. Consider the following examples. All three of these people intended to die, but their motives, concerns, and actions differed greatly.

WHALE DEATHS

Whales that beach themselves are not committing suicide. The sand disturbs their sonar and throws them off course (Jordan, 1997).

Dave was a successful man. By the age of 50 he had risen to the vice presidency of a small but profitable office machine firm. He had a devoted wife and two teenage sons who respected him. They lived in an upper-middle-class neighborhood, had a spacious house, and enjoyed a life of comfort.

In August of his fiftieth year, everything changed. Dave was fired. Just like that, after many years of loyal and effective service. The firm's profits were down and the president wanted to try new, fresher marketing approaches.

Dave was shocked. The experience of rejection, loss, and emptiness was overwhelming. He looked for another position, but found only low-paying jobs for which he was overqualified. Each day as he looked for work Dave became more depressed, anxious, and desperate. He kept sinking, withdrew from others, and became increasingly hopeless.

Six months after losing his job, Dave began to consider ending his life. The pain was too great, the humiliation unending. He hated the present and dreaded the future. Throughout February he went back and forth. On some days he was sure he wanted to die. On other days, an enjoyable evening or uplifting conversation might change his mind temporarily. On a Monday late in February he heard about a job possibility, and the anticipation of the next day's interview seemed to lift his spirits. But Tuesday's interview did not go well. It was clear to him that he would not be offered the job. He went home, took a recently purchased gun from his locked desk drawer, and shot himself.

Billy never truly recovered from his mother's death. He was only 7 years old and unprepared for such a loss. His father sent him to live with his grandparents for a time, to a new school with new kids and a new way of life. In Billy's mind, all these changes were for the worse. He missed the joy and laughter of the past. He missed his home, his father, and his friends. Most of all he missed his mother.

He did not really understand her death. His father said that she was in heaven now, at peace, happy. Billy's unhappiness and loneliness continued day after day and he began to put things together in his own way. He believed he would be happy again if he could join his mother. He felt she was waiting for him, waiting for him to come to her. These thoughts seemed so right to him; they brought him comfort and hope. One evening, shortly after saying good night to his grandparents, Billy climbed out of bed, went up the stairs to the roof of their apartment house, and jumped to his death. In his mind he was joining his mother in heaven.

Margaret and Bob had been going together for a year. It was Margaret's first serious relationship; it was her whole life. Thus when Bob told her that he no longer loved her and was leaving her for someone else, Margaret was shocked and shaken.

As the weeks went by, Margaret was filled with two competing feelings—depression and anger. Several times she called Bob, begged him to reconsider, and pleaded for a chance to win him back. At the same time, she hated him for putting her through such misery.

Margaret's friends became more and more worried about her. At first they sympathized with her pain, assuming it would soon lift. But as time went on, her depression and anger worsened, and Margaret began to act strangely. She started to drink heavily and to mix her drinks with all kinds of pills. She seemed to be flirting with danger.

One night Margaret went into her bathroom, reached for a bottle of sleeping pills, and swallowed a handful of them. She wanted to make her pain go away, and she wanted Bob to know just how much pain he had caused her. She continued swallowing pill after pill, crying and swearing as she gulped them down. When she began to feel drowsy, she decided to call her close friend Cindy. She was not sure why she was calling, perhaps to say good-bye, to explain her actions, or to make sure that Bob was told; or perhaps to be talked out of it. Cindy pleaded and reasoned with Margaret and tried to motivate her to live. Margaret was trying to listen, but she became less and less clear. Cindy hung up the

PARASUICIDE A suicide attempt that does not result in death.

SUICIDE A self-inflicted death in which the person acts intentionally, directly, and consciously.

Fatal attraction *A tiny male redback spider prepares to be eaten by his large female partner during copulation, and even aids in his own death. While placing his intromittent organ into his partner, he also spins around and dangles his enticing abdomen in front of her mouth. The male may be shortsighted, but he is not intending to die. In fact, by keeping his partner busy eating him, he can deposit a maximum amount of sperm, thus increasing the chances of reproduction and the birth of an offspring with similar tendencies (Andrade, 1996).*

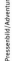

CRITICAL DOCTOR CALLS

Around 83 percent of persons who commit suicide have seen a family doctor in the previous year, 66 percent in the previous month, 40 percent in the previous week, and 20 percent within the past day (Pirkis & Burgess, 1998; Hirschfeld & Russell, 1997).

phone and quickly called Margaret's neighbor and the police. When reached by her neighbor, Margaret was already in a coma. Seven hours later, while her friends and family waited for news in the hospital lounge, Margaret died.

While Margaret seemed to have mixed feelings about her death, Dave was clear in his wish to die. Whereas Billy viewed death as a trip to heaven, Dave saw it as an end to his existence. Such differences can be important in efforts to understand and treat suicidal persons. Accordingly, Shneidman has described four kinds of people who intentionally end their lives: the *death seeker, death initiator, death ignorer,* and *death darer.*

Death seekers clearly intend to end their lives at the time they attempt suicide. This singleness of purpose may last only a short time. It can change to confusion the very next hour or day, and then return again in short order. Dave, the middle-aged executive, was a death seeker. He had many misgivings about suicide and had mixed feelings about it for weeks, but on Tuesday night he was a death seeker—clear in his desire to die and acting in a manner that virtually guaranteed a fatal outcome.

Death initiators also clearly intend to end their lives, but they act out of a belief that the process of death is already under way and that they are simply quickening the process. Some expect that they will die in a matter of days or weeks. Many suicides among the elderly and very sick fall into this category (Clark, 1999). The robust novelist Ernest Hemingway was deeply concerned about his failing body—a concern that some observers believe was at the center of his suicide.

Death ignorers do not believe that their self-inflicted death will mean the end of their existence. They believe they are trading their present lives for a better or happier existence. Many child suicides, like Billy's, fall into this category, as do those of adult believers in a hereafter who commit suicide to reach another form of life. The 39 members of the Heaven's Gate cult acted out of the belief that their deaths would free their spirits and enable them to climb to a "Higher Kingdom."

Death darers experience mixed feelings, or ambivalence, in their intent to die even at the moment of their attempt, and they

Death darers? *A sky surfer tries to ride the perfect cloud over Sweden. Are thrill-seekers daredevils searching for new highs, as many of them claim, or are some actually death darers?*

STATE BY STATE

Suicide rates vary by state in the United States. Western states have the highest rate of suicide (15 per 100,000 persons), followed by the South (13 per 100,000), the Midwest (10 per 100,000), and the Northeast (8 per 100,000). (Klein, 1998).

Table 7-1

Most Common Causes of Death in the United States

RANK	CAUSE	DEATHS PER YEAR	PERCENTAGE OF TOTAL DEATHS
1	Heart disease	733,834	31.6%
2	Cancer	544,278	23.4
3	Stroke	160,431	6.9
4	Lung diseases	106,146	4.6
5	Accidents	93,874	4.0
6	Pneumonia and influenza	82,579	3.6
7	Diabetes	61,559	2.7
8	AIDS	32,655	1.4
9	Suicide	30,862	1.3
10	Liver disease	25,135	1.1

Source: Ash, 1999; U.S. National Center for Health Statistics.

show this ambivalence in the act itself. Although to some degree they wish to die, and they often do die, their risk-taking behavior does not guarantee death. The person who plays Russian roulette—that is, pulls the trigger of a revolver randomly loaded with one bullet—is a death darer. Many death darers are as interested in gaining attention, making someone feel guilty, or expressing anger as in dying per se. Margaret might be considered a death darer. Although her unhappiness and anger were great, she was not sure that she wanted to die. Even while taking pills, she called her friend, reported her actions, and listened to her friend's pleas.

When individuals *play indirect, hidden, partial,* or *unconscious* roles in their own deaths, Shneidman (2001, 1993, 1981) classifies them in a suicidelike category called **subintentional death.** Seriously ill people who consistently mismanage their medicines may belong in this category. Although their deaths may represent a form of suicide, their true intent is unclear.

How Is Suicide Studied?

Suicide researchers face a major problem: their subjects are no longer alive. How can investigators draw accurate conclusions about the intentions, feelings, and circumstances of people who can no longer explain their actions? Two research methods attempt to deal with this problem, each with only partial success.

One strategy is *retrospective analysis,* a kind of psychological autopsy in which clinicians and researchers piece together information from the suicide victim's past (Houston, Hawton, & Sheppard, 2001). Relatives, friends, therapists, or physicians may remember past statements, conversations, and behavior that shed light on a suicide. Retrospective information may also be provided by the suicide notes that some victims leave behind (Leenaars et al., 2001). However, such sources of information are not always available. Less than one-quarter of all suicide victims have been in psychotherapy (Fleer & Pasework, 1982), and less than one-third leave notes (Black, 1993).

Because of these limitations, many researchers also use a second strategy— *studying people who survive their suicide attempts.* Of course, people who survive suicide may differ in important ways from those who do not (Cutler, Glaeser, & Norberg, 2001; Diekstra et al., 1995). Many of them may not really have wanted to die, for example. Nevertheless, suicide researchers have found it useful to study survivors of suicide; and we shall consider those who attempt suicide and those who commit suicide as more or less alike.

Patterns and Statistics

Suicide happens within a larger social setting, and researchers have gathered many statistics regarding the social contexts in which such deaths take place. They have found, for example, that suicide rates vary from country to country (Schmidtke et al., 1999). Russia, Hungary, Germany, Austria, Finland, Denmark, China, and Japan have very high rates, more than 20 suicides annually per 100,000 persons; conversely, Egypt, Mexico, Greece, and Spain have relatively low rates, fewer than 5 per 100,000. The United States and Canada fall in between, each with a suicide rate of around 12 per 100,000 persons, and England has a rate of 9 per 100,000.

Religious affiliation and beliefs may help account for these national differences (Kelleher et al., 1998). For example, countries that are largely Catholic, Jewish, or Muslim tend to have low suicide rates. Perhaps in these countries, strict prohibitions against suicide or a strong religious tradition discourage many people from committing suicide. Yet there are exceptions to this apparent rule. Austria, a largely Roman Catholic country, has one of the highest suicide rates in the world.

Research is beginning to suggest that religious affiliation may not help prevent suicide as much as the degree of an individual's *devoutness.* Regardless of their particular persuasion, very religious people seem less likely to commit suicide (Jahangir, ur-Rehman, & Jan, 1998). Similarly, it seems that people who hold

DEATH SEEKER A person who clearly intends to end his or her life at the time of a suicide attempt.

DEATH INITIATOR A person who attempts suicide believing that the process of death is already under way and that he or she is simply hastening the process.

DEATH IGNORER A person who attempts suicide without recognizing the finality of death.

DEATH DARER A person who is ambivalent about the wish to die even as he or she attempts suicide.

SUBINTENTIONAL DEATH A death in which the victim plays an indirect, hidden, partial, or unconscious role.

Final record *Paul Bern left this suicide note to his wife, the famed actress Jean Harlow, in 1932.*

ConsiderThis
Suicide rates vary widely from country to country. What factors besides religion might help account for the differences?

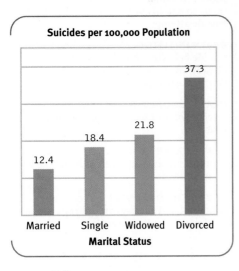

Suicides per 100,000 Population

12.4 — Married
18.4 — Single
21.8 — Widowed
37.3 — Divorced

Marital Status

FIGURE 7-1 **Suicide and marital status**
Approximately 37 of every 100,000 divorced persons commit suicide, more than three times the rate of married persons. (Adapted from McIntosh, 1991, p. 64.)

a greater respect for life are less prone to consider or attempt self-destruction (Lee, 1985).

The suicide rates of men and women also differ. Three times as many women attempt suicide as men, yet men succeed at more than three times the rate of women (Moscicki, 1999). Around the world 19 of every 100,000 men kill themselves each year; the suicide rate for women, which has been increasing in recent years, is 5 per 100,000 (Schmidtke et al., 1999).

One reason for these differing rates appears to be the different methods used by men and women (Ayd & Palma, 1999). Men tend to use more violent methods, such as shooting, stabbing, or hanging themselves, whereas women use less violent methods, such as drug overdose. Guns are used in nearly two-thirds of the male suicides in the United States, compared to 40 percent of the female suicides (Canetto & Lester, 1995).

Suicide is also related to marital status and level of social support (Palmer, 2001) (see Figure 7-1). Married people, especially those with children, have a fairly low suicide rate; single and widowed people have higher rates; and divorced people have the highest rate of all (Weissman et al., 1999; Canetto & Lester, 1995). One study compared 90 persons who committed suicide with 90 psychologically troubled patients who had never attempted suicide (Roy, 1982). Only 16 percent of the suicides were married or living with someone else at the time of the suicide, compared to 30 percent of the control group.

Finally, in the United States at least, suicide rates seem to vary according to race (Wasserman & Stack, 2000) (see Figure 7-2). The suicide rate of white Americans, 12 per 100,000 persons, is almost twice as high as that of African Americans and members of other racial groups (Stillion & McDowell, 1996). A major exception to this pattern is the very high suicide rate of Native Americans, which overall is one and a half times the national average (NCIPC, 1999). Some Native American groups have rates as high as four to ten times the national average (Berlin, 1987; Willard, 1979). Although the extreme poverty of many Native Americans may partly explain such trends, studies show that such factors as alcohol use, modeling, and the availability of guns may also play a role (Berman & Jobes, 1995, 1991; Young, 1991). Studies of Native Americans in Canada yield similar results (Strickland, 1997; Bagley, 1991).

Some of these statistics on suicide have been questioned in recent years. One analysis suggests that the actual rate of suicide may be 15 percent higher for African Americans and 6 percent higher for women than usually reported (Phillips & Ruth, 1993). People in these groups are more likely than others to use methods of suicide that can be mistaken for causes of accidental death, such as poisoning, drug overdose, single car crashes, and pedestrian accidents.

UNACCEPTABLE ACT

According to surveys, African Americans consider suicide "less acceptable" than do white Americans and are more opposed to voluntary euthanasia. These attitudes have been linked to African Americans' higher degrees of orthodox religious belief and personal devotion and to their fear of giving others the power to end one's life (MacDonald, 1998; Neeleman et al., 1998).

SUMMING UP **What Is Suicide?**

Suicide is a self-inflicted death in which one makes an intentional, direct, and conscious effort to end one's life. Edwin Shneidman has described four kinds of people who intentionally end their lives: the death seeker, the death initiator, the death ignorer, and the death darer. He has also identified a suicidelike category called subintentional death, in which people play indirect, hidden, partial, or unconscious roles in their own deaths.

Research Strategies Two major approaches are used in the study of suicide: retrospective analysis (a psychological autopsy) and the study of people who survive suicide attempts, on the assumption that they are similar to those who commit fatal suicides. Each strategy has limitations.

Patterns and Statistics Suicide ranks among the top ten causes of death in Western society. Rates vary from country to country. One reason seems to be cultural differences in religious affiliation, beliefs, or degree of devoutness. Suicide rates also vary according to race, gender, and marital status.

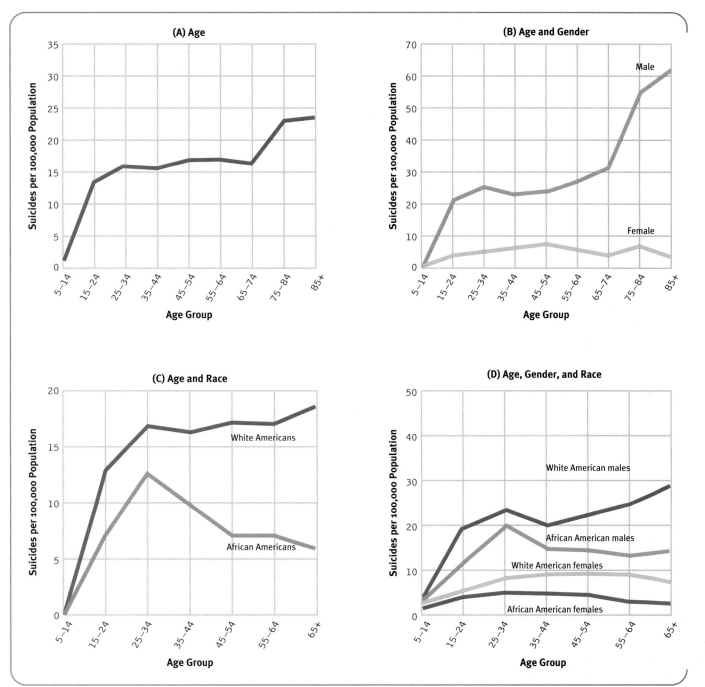

FIGURE 7-2 **Current U.S. suicide rates**
(A) People over the age of 63 are more likely to commit suicide than those in any other age group; (B) males commit suicide at higher rates than females of corresponding ages; (C) white Americans commit suicide at higher rates than African Americans of corresponding ages; (D) elderly white American men have the highest risk of suicide. (Adapted from Stillion & McDowell, 1996; U.S. Bureau of the Census, 1994, 1990; McIntosh, 1991, pp. 62–63.)

What Triggers a Suicide?

Suicidal acts may be connected to recent events or current conditions in a person's life. Although such factors may not be the basic motivation for the suicide, they can trigger it. Common triggering factors include *stressful events, mood and thought changes, alcohol and other drug use, mental disorders,* and *modeling.*

Stressful Events and Situations

Researchers have counted more stressful events in the lives of suicide attempters than in the lives of matched control subjects (Jacobs, Brewer, & Klein-Benheim, 1999). One form of *immediate stress* seen in cases of suicide is the loss of a loved

HOPELESSNESS A pessimistic belief that one's present circumstances, problems, or mood will not change.

DICHOTOMOUS THINKING Viewing problems and solutions in rigid "either/or" terms.

THE IMPACT OF INTERNMENT

The suicide rate among the 110,000 Japanese Americans who were interned in "relocation centers" during World War II rose to double that of the national population (Jensen, 1998).

Multiple risks *People who experience multiple suicide factors are at particular risk for self-destruction. The actor Herve Villechaize (right) killed himself after losing his lucrative role in the television series* Fantasy Island *and also developing a chronic, painful medical condition.*

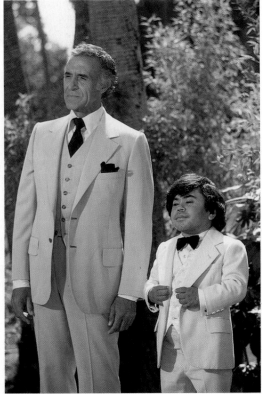

Everett Collection

one through death, divorce, or rejection. Another is the loss of a job (Caces & Harford, 1998). Still another is the stress experienced during hurricanes or other natural disasters, even by very young children (Krug et al., 1998; Cytryn & McKnew, 1996). People may also attempt suicide in response to long-term rather than recent stress. Three *long-term stressors* are particularly common—serious illness, an abusive environment, and occupational stress.

SERIOUS ILLNESS People whose illnesses cause them great pain or severe disability may try to commit suicide, believing that death is unavoidable and imminent (Hendin, 1999). They may also believe that the suffering and problems caused by their illnesses are more than they can endure. One study found that 37 percent of the subjects who died by suicide had been in poor physical health (Conwell, Caine, & Olsen, 1990). Illness-linked suicides have become more common, and controversial, in recent years (Leenaars et al., 2001). Medical progress is partly responsible. Although physicians can now keep seriously ill people alive much longer, they often fail to extend the quality and comfort of the patients' lives (Werth, 1995).

ABUSIVE ENVIRONMENT Victims of an abusive or repressive environment from which they have little hope of escape sometimes commit suicide. For example, prisoners of war, inmates of concentration camps, abused spouses, abused children, and prison inmates have tried to end their lives (Gore, 1999; McKee, 1998). Like those who have serious illnesses, these people may have felt that they could endure no more suffering and believed that there was no hope for improvement in their condition.

OCCUPATIONAL STRESS Some jobs create feelings of tension or dissatisfaction that may trigger suicide attempts. Research has found particularly high suicide rates among psychiatrists and psychologists, physicians, dentists, lawyers, and unskilled laborers (Aasland, Ekeberg, & Schweder, 2001; Holmes & Rich, 1990). Such findings do not necessarily mean that occupational pressures directly cause suicidal actions. Perhaps unskilled workers are responding to financial insecurity rather than job stress when they attempt suicide (Wasserman & Stack, 2000). Similarly, rather than reacting to the emotional strain of their work, suicidal psychiatrists and psychologists may have long-standing emotional problems that stimulated their career interest in the first place.

Clinicians once believed that married women who held jobs outside the home had higher suicide rates than other women, perhaps because of conflicts between the demands of their families and their jobs (Stack, 1987; Stillion, 1985). However, recent studies call these notions into question and some even suggest that work outside the home may be linked to lower suicide rates among women, just as it is among men (Stack, 1998; Yang & Lester, 1995).

Mood and Thought Changes

Many suicide attempts are preceded by a change in mood. The change may not be severe enough to call for a diagnosis of a mental disorder, but it does represent a shift from the person's past mood. The most common change is an increase in sadness (Kienhorst et al., 1995). Also common are rises in feelings of anxiety, tension, frustration, anger, or shame (Fawcett, 1999; Kienhorst et al., 1995). In fact, Shneidman (2001, 1991) suggests that the key to suicide is "psychache," a feeling of psychological pain that seems intolerable to the person.

Suicide attempts may also be preceded by shifts in patterns of thinking. Individuals may become preoccupied with their problems, lose perspective, and see suicide as the only effective solution to their difficulties (Shneidman, 2001, 1999, 1987). They often develop a sense of **hopelessness**—a pessimistic belief that their present circumstances, problems, or mood will not change (Weishaar, 2000). Some clinicians believe that a feeling of hopelessness is the single most likely indicator of suicidal intent, and they take special care to look for signs of hopelessness when they assess the risk of suicide (Hewitt et al., 1997).

Many people who attempt suicide fall victim to **dichotomous thinking,** viewing problems and solutions in rigid either/or terms (Shneidman, 2001, 1993; Weishaar, 2000). In the following statement a woman who survived her leap from a building describes her dichotomous thinking at the time. She saw death as the only alternative to her pain:

> I was so desperate. I felt, my God, I couldn't face this thing. Everything was like a terrible whirlpool of confusion. And I thought to myself: There's only one thing to do. I just have to lose consciousness. That's the only way to get away from it. The only way to lose consciousness, I thought, was to jump off something good and high. . . .
>
> *(Shneidman, 1987, p. 56)*

"To be, or not to be: that is the question . . ."

William Shakespeare, *Hamlet*

Alcohol and Other Drug Use

Studies indicate that as many as 60 percent of the people who attempt suicide drink alcohol just before the act (Suokas & Lonnqvist, 1995; Hirschfeld & Davidson, 1988). Autopsies reveal that about one-fourth of these people are legally intoxicated (Flavin et al., 1990; Abel & Zeidenberg, 1985). Such statistics suggest to many clinical researchers that alcohol often helps trigger suicidal behavior (Lester, 1998). Research shows that the use of other kinds of drugs may have a similar tie to suicide, particularly in teenagers and young adults (Rich et al., 1998). A high level of heroin, for example, was found in the blood of Kurt Cobain at the time of his suicide in 1994 (Colburn, 1996).

MOST COMMON KILLINGS
More suicides (31,000) than homicides (23,000) are committed in the United States each year.

Mental Disorders

Although people who attempt suicide may be troubled or anxious, they do not necessarily have a psychological disorder as defined in DSM-IV. Nevertheless, more than half of all suicide attempters do display such a disorder (Jacobs et al., 1999; Harris & Barraclough, 1997). The ones linked most strongly to suicide are *mood disorders* (unipolar and bipolar depression), *substance-related disorders* (particularly alcoholism), and *schizophrenia* (see Table 7-2). Research suggests that as many as 15 percent of people with each of these disorders try to kill themselves (Kelleher et al., 1998; Meltzer, 1998). People who are both depressed and dependent on alcohol seem particularly prone to suicidal impulses (Weiss & Hufford, 1999; Cornelius et al., 1995).

As we observed in Chapter 6, people with major depressive disorder often experience suicidal thoughts. Those whose disorder includes a particularly strong sense of hopelessness seem most likely to attempt suicide (Fawcett et al., 1987). One program in Sweden was able to reduce the community suicide rate by teaching physicians how to recognize and treat depression at an early stage (Rihmer, Rutz, & Pihlgren, 1995). Even when depressed people are showing improvements in mood, however, they may remain high suicide risks. In fact, among those who are severely depressed, the risk of suicide may actually increase as their mood improves and they have more energy to act on their suicidal wishes.

Table 7-2

Common Predictors of Suicide

1. Depressive disorder and certain other mental disorders
2. Alcoholism and other forms of substance abuse
3. Suicide ideation, talk, preparation; certain religious ideas
4. Prior suicide attempts
5. Lethal methods
6. Isolation, living alone, loss of support
7. Hopelessness, cognitive rigidity
8. Being an older white male
9. Modeling, suicide in the family, genetics
10. Economic or work problems; certain occupations
11. Marital problems, family pathology
12. Stress and stressful events
13. Anger, aggression, irritability
14. Physical illness
15. Repetition and combination of factors 1 to 14

Source: Adapted from Maris, 1992.

Severe depression also may play a key role in suicide attempts by persons with serious physical illnesses (Akechi et al., 2001; Henriksson et al., 1995). A study of 44 patients with terminal illnesses revealed that at most one-quarter of them had thoughts of suicide or wished for an early death, and that those who did were all suffering from major depressive disorder (Brown et al., 1986).

A number of the people who drink alcohol or use drugs just before a suicide attempt actually have a long history of abusing such substances (Rossow & Lauritzen, 2001; Jones, 1997). The basis for the link between substance-related disorders and suicide is not clear (Weiss & Hufford, 1999). Perhaps the tragic lifestyle of many persons with these disorders or their sense of being hopelessly trapped by a substance leads to suicidal thinking. Alternatively, a third factor—psychological pain, for instance, or desperation—may cause both substance abuse and suicidal thinking (Frances & Franklin, 1988). Such people may be caught in a downward spiral: they are driven toward substance use by psychological pain or loss, only to find themselves caught in a pattern of substance abuse that aggravates rather than solves their problems (Downey, 1991).

People with schizophrenia, as we shall see in Chapter 12, may hear voices that are not actually present (hallucinations) or hold beliefs that are clearly false and perhaps bizarre (delusions). There is a popular notion that when such people kill themselves, they must be responding to an imagined voice commanding them to do so or to a delusion that suicide is a grand and noble gesture. Research indicates, however, that suicides by people with schizophrenia more often reflect feelings of *demoralization* (Reid, 1998). For example, many young and unemployed sufferers who have had relapses over several years come to believe that the disorder will forever disrupt their lives. Still others seem to be disheartened by their unfortunate, sometimes dreadful, living conditions. Suicide is the leading cause of premature death in this population (Raymont, 2001; Tsuang et al., 1999).

Modeling: The Contagion of Suicide

It is not unusual for people, particularly teenagers, to try to commit suicide after observing or reading about someone else who has done so (Grossman & Kruesi, 2000; Joiner, 1999). Perhaps these people have been struggling with major problems, and the other person's suicide seems to reveal a possible solution; or they have been thinking about suicide and the other person's suicide seems to give them permission or finally persuades them to act. Either way, one suicidal act apparently serves as a *model* for another. Suicides by celebrities, other highly publicized suicides, and suicides by co-workers are particularly common triggers.

CELEBRITIES When the researcher Steven Stack (1987) analyzed U.S. suicide data spanning 1948 to 1983, he found that suicides by entertainers and political figures are regularly followed by unusual increases in the number of suicides across the United States. During the week after the suicide of Marilyn Monroe in 1963, for example, the national suicide rate rose 12 percent (Phillips, 1974).

OTHER HIGHLY PUBLICIZED CASES Suicides with bizarre or unusual aspects often receive special coverage by the news media. Such highly publicized accounts may lead to similar suicides (Etzersdorfer & Sonneck, 1998). During the year after a widely publicized, politically motivated suicide by self-burning in England, for example, 82 other people set themselves on fire, with equally fatal results (Ashton & Donnan, 1981). Inquest reports revealed that most of those people had histories of emotional problems and that none of the suicides had the political motivation of the publicized suicide. The imitators seemed to be responding to their own problems in a manner triggered by the suicide they had observed or read about.

THE DANGER OF COMORBIDITY
A European study found that people with three or more mental disorders (for example, depression, panic disorder, and a substance-related disorder) are 18 times more likely to attempt suicide than people without a disorder (Wunderlich et al., 1998).

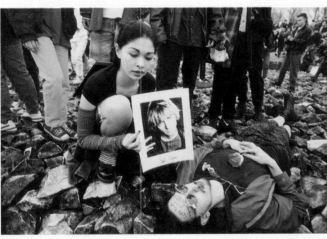

Suicide's broad impact *The suicide of Nirvana's Kurt Cobain in April 1994 shocked young rock fans throughout the world and led to widespread grief and confusion. In Seattle, Cobain's hometown, a candlelight vigil was attended by about 5,000 people, including these two fans.*

Grant Haller, Seattle Post Intelligencer/Corbis-Sygma

THE CURRENT SCENE

"I'm All Traveled Out"

On October 5, 1998, Margaret Mary Ray knelt down in front of an on-coming 105-car coal train in Hotchkiss, Colorado, and brought her life to an immediate end. Ms. Ray, 46, had suffered from schizophrenia for years, holding delusions that she was in intimate relationships with famous people and even stalking them in their residences. Like a number of other people with schizophrenia, she eventually grew weary and hopeless about the chances that her disorder would ever improve. In a suicide note sent to her mother, she said, "I'm all traveled out. . . . I choose a painless and instantaneous way to end my life. . . ."

One difference between Ms. Ray and most other people with schizophrenia is that millions of people knew something about her dysfunction. She gained notoriety during her last decade as the woman who believed that she was

Peter Cosgrove/AP Photo

A weary Margaret Ray faces charges of stalking in 1997.

romantically involved with the television comedian David Letterman, repeatedly breaking into his home, sleeping on his tennis court, and on one occasion stealing his car. Her delusion first came to light in 1988 when she was arrested while driving Letterman's car at the entrance to the Lincoln Tunnel in New York City. When she was unable to pay the toll, she identified herself as Letterman's wife and her son as his son. Over the next decade, she was arrested repeatedly for trespassing and was forced to spend a total of ten months in prison and fourteen months in a state hospital. Newspaper accounts usually described her exploits in a lighthearted way, and readers generally considered her to be a strange and comical character.

Not until Ms. Ray killed herself did most people become aware of just how disturbed she was. In fact, two of her three brothers had also suffered from schizophrenia and killed themselves years earlier. Her adult life consisted of sudden trips across the country, strange ideas, and impulsive and erratic behavior that extended well beyond her focus on Letterman. Her surviving brother remembers times when she spoke in sentences that made no sense and warm days when she wore three layers of clothing (Bruni, 1998). Medications often seemed to help her, but she usually stopped taking them outside of prison or the state hospital.

Letterman himself recognized the seriousness of Ms. Ray's problem and grappled with how best to handle things. He rarely talked about her, never mentioned her name on the air, and often declined

CBS Photo Archive

to press charges against her. Expressing compassion for her, he recalls that she sent him many letters between her uninvited house visits, and it was apparent in each letter whether she was taking her medications (Bruni, 1998). "When she was on them, it was like hearing from your aunt. When she was off them, it was like hearing from your aunt on Neptune." On the day after her death, he observed, "This is a sad end to a confused life."

ConsiderThis

● Why do people tend to overlook or dismiss the psychological pain of people with bizarre ideas or erratic behaviors? • How might such oversights add to the suffering or symptoms of such people?

Some clinicians argue that more responsible reporting could reduce this frightening impact of highly publicized suicides (Etzersdorfer & Sonneck, 1998; Mulder, 1996). One such approach to reporting was seen in the media's coverage of the suicide of Kurt Cobain. MTV's repeated theme on the evening of the suicide was "Don't do it!" In fact, thousands of young people called MTV and other radio and television stations in the hours after Cobain's death, upset, frightened, and in some cases suicidal. Some of the stations responded by posting the phone numbers of suicide prevention centers, presenting interviews with suicide experts, and offering counseling services and advice directly to callers. Perhaps because of such efforts, the usual rate of suicide both in Seattle, Cobain's hometown, and elsewhere held steady during the weeks that followed (Colburn, 1996).

ConsiderThis

● What precautions or actions should the media and the arts take in their presentations of famous cases of suicide?

COPYCAT SUICIDES

In 1999 a character in the popular British medical television show *Casualty* intentionally killed himself by overdosing on a drug. During the two weeks after the episode was aired, the number of attempted suicides in England rose 17 percent, most of them involving the same method (O'Connor et al., 1999).

CO-WORKERS AND COLLEAGUES The word-of-mouth publicity that attends suicides in a school, workplace, or small community may trigger suicide attempts. The suicide of a recruit at a U.S. Navy training school, for example, was followed within two weeks by another and also by an attempted suicide at the school. To head off what threatened to become a suicide epidemic, the school began a program of staff education on suicide and group therapy sessions for recruits who had been close to the suicide victims (Grigg, 1988).

SUMMING UP | **What Triggers a Suicide?**

Many suicidal acts are triggered by current conditions in a person's life. The acts may be triggered by recent stressors such as loss of a loved one and job loss, or long-term stressors such as serious illness, an abusive environment, and job stress. They may also be preceded by changes in mood or thought, particularly increases in one's sense of hopelessness or dichotomous thinking. In addition, the use of alcohol or other kinds of drugs often precedes suicide.

More than half of all people who attempt suicide are experiencing a psychological disorder, particularly a mood disorder, a substance-related disorder, or schizophrenia. Finally, many people who try to kill themselves have recently observed or read about someone else—a celebrity, for example—who has done so.

What Are the Underlying Causes of Suicide?

HOLIDAY EFFECTS

Studies in countries throughout Europe indicate that suicide rates tend to drop before Christmas and Easter, but then increase after those holidays (Jessen et al., 1999). How might we explain these trends?

Most people faced with difficult situations never try to kill themselves. In an effort to understand why some people are more prone to suicide than others, theorists have proposed broad explanations for self-destructive action. The leading theories come from the psychodynamic, sociocultural, and biological perspectives. As a group, however, these explanations have received limited research support and fail to address the full range of suicidal acts. Thus the clinical field currently lacks a clear understanding of suicide.

The Psychodynamic View

Many psychodynamic theorists believe that suicide results from depression and from anger at others that is redirected toward oneself. This theory was first stated by Wilhelm Stekel at a meeting in Vienna in 1910, when he proclaimed that "no one kills himself who has not wanted to kill another or at least wished the death of another" (Shneidman, 1979).

As we saw in Chapter 6, Freud (1917) and Abraham (1916, 1911) proposed that when people experience the real or symbolic loss of a loved one, they unconsciously incorporate the person into their own identity and feel toward themselves as they had felt toward the other. For a short while, negative feelings toward the lost loved one are experienced as self-hatred. Anger toward the loved one may turn into intense anger against oneself and finally into depression. Suicide is thought to be an extreme expression of this self-hatred. The following description of a suicidal patient demonstrates how such forces may operate:

EGOISTIC SUICIDE Suicide committed by people over whom society has little or no control, people who are not inhibited by the norms or rules of society.

ALTRUISTIC SUICIDE Suicide committed by people who intentionally sacrifice their lives for the well-being of society.

ANOMIC SUICIDE Suicide committed by individuals whose social environment fails to provide stability, thus leaving them without a sense of belonging.

> A 27-year-old conscientious and responsible woman took a knife to her wrists to punish herself for being tyrannical, unreliable, self-centered, and abusive. She was perplexed and frightened by this uncharacteristic self-destructive episode and was enormously relieved when her therapist pointed out that her invective described her recently deceased father much better than it did herself.
>
> *(Gill, 1982, p. 15)*

In support of Freud's view, researchers have often found a relationship between childhood losses and later suicidal behaviors (Kaslow et al., 1998; Lester, 1998). One study of 200 family histories found that the loss of a parent at a young age was much more common among suicide attempters (48 percent) than among nonsuicidal control subjects (24 percent) (Adam, Bouckoms, & Streiner, 1982). Common forms of loss were death of the father and divorce or separation of the parents.

Late in his career, Freud proposed that human beings have a basic "death instinct." He called this instinct *Thanatos,* and said that it opposes the "life instinct." According to Freud, while most people learn to redirect their death instinct, by aiming it toward others, suicidal people, caught in a web of self-anger, direct it squarely upon themselves.

Sociological findings are consistent with this explanation of suicide. National suicide rates have been found to drop in times of war, when, one could argue, people are encouraged to direct their self-destructive energy against "the enemy." In addition, societies with high rates of homicide tend to have low rates of suicide, and vice versa (Somasundaram & Rajadurai, 1995). However, research has failed to establish that suicidal people are in fact overwhelmed by intense feelings of anger. Although hostility is an important element in some suicides, several studies find that other emotional states are even more common (Castrogiovanni, Pieraccini, & DiMuro, 1998).

By the end of his career, Freud himself expressed dissatisfaction with his theory of suicide. Other psychodynamic theorists have also challenged his ideas over the years, yet themes of loss and self-directed aggression generally remain at the center of their explanations (Maltsberger, 1999).

The Sociocultural View

Toward the end of the nineteenth century, Emile Durkheim (1897), a sociologist, developed a broad theory of suicidal behavior. Today this theory continues to be influential. According to Durkheim, the probability of suicide is determined by how attached a person is to such social groups as the family, religious institutions, and community. The more thoroughly a person belongs, the lower the risk of suicide. Conversely, people who have poor relationships with their society are at greater risk of killing themselves. He defined several categories of suicide, including *egoistic, altruistic,* and *anomic* suicide.

Egoistic suicides are committed by people over whom society has little or no control. These people are not concerned with the norms or rules of society, nor are they part of the social fabric. According to Durkheim, this kind of suicide is more likely in people who are isolated, alienated, and nonreligious. The larger the number of such people living in a society, the higher that society's suicide rate.

Altruistic suicides, in contrast, are committed by people who are so well integrated into their society that they intentionally sacrifice their lives for its well-being. Soldiers who threw themselves on top of a live grenade to save others, Japanese kamikaze pilots who gave their lives in air attacks, and Buddhist monks and nuns who protested the Vietnam War by setting themselves on fire—all were committing altruistic suicide. According to Durkheim, societies that encourage altruistic deaths and deaths to preserve one's honor (as Far Eastern societies do) are likely to have higher suicide rates.

Anomic suicides, another category proposed by Durkheim, are those committed by people whose social environment fails to provide stable structures, such as family and religion, to support and give meaning to life. Such a societal condition, called *anomie* (literally, "without law"), leaves individuals without a sense of belonging. Unlike egoistic suicide, which is the act of a person who rejects the structures of a society, anomic suicide is the act of a person who has been let down by a disorganized, inadequate, often decaying society.

Durkheim argued that when societies go through periods of anomie, their suicide rates increase. Historical trends support this claim. Periods of economic

POLITICAL INTEGRATION AND DISINTEGRATION

After the reunification of Germany, East Germany's suicide rate dropped by one-third and West Germany's declined by one-quarter (Schmidtke et al., 1999). In contrast, suicide rates increased in the nations formed after the formal breakup of the Soviet Union in 1991 (Lester, 1998).

In the service of others *According to Emile Durkheim, people who intentionally sacrifice their lives for others are committing altruistic suicide. Betsy Smith, a heart transplant recipient who was warned that she would probably die if she did not terminate her pregnancy, elected to have the baby and died giving birth.*

depression may bring about anomie in a country, and national suicide rates tend to rise during such times (Yang et al., 1992; Lester, 1991). Periods of population change and increased immigration, too, tend to bring about a state of anomie, and again suicide rates rise (Burvill, 1998; Ferrada et al., 1995).

A major change in an individual's immediate surroundings, rather than general societal problems, can also lead to anomic suicide. People who suddenly inherit a great deal of money, for example, may go through a period of anomie as their relationships with social, economic, and occupational structures are changed. Thus Durkheim predicted that societies with greater opportunities for change in individual wealth or status would have higher suicide rates, and this prediction, too, is supported by research (Cutright & Fernquist, 2001; Lester, 1985).

Clash of cultures *The sudden introduction of modern technology into a relatively undeveloped society, illustrated by this satellite television disk alongside a nomad's ger in Mongolia, can produce a climate of disorganization and anomie, leaving some members confused and troubled.*

Durkheim's theory of suicide highlights the importance of social and societal factors. Although today's sociocultural theorists do not always embrace Durkheim's particular ideas, most agree that social structure and cultural stress often play major roles in suicide (Hassan, 1998). In fact, the sociocultural view pervades the study of suicide. We saw its impact earlier when we observed the many studies linking suicide to broad factors such as religious affiliation, marital status, gender, race, and societal stress. We will also see it when we consider the ties between suicide and age.

Despite the influence of sociocultural theories, they cannot by themselves explain why some people who experience particular societal pressures commit suicide whereas the majority do not. Durkheim himself concluded that the final explanation probably lies in the interaction between societal and individual factors.

The Biological View

For years biological researchers relied largely on family pedigree studies to support their position that biological factors contribute to suicidal behavior. They have repeatedly found higher rates of suicide among the parents and close relatives of suicidal people than among those of nonsuicidal people (Brent et al., 1998, 1996). Such findings may suggest that genetic, and thus biological, factors are at work.

Studies of twins also have supported this view of suicide. Researchers who studied twins born in Denmark between 1870 and 1920, for example, located 19 identical pairs and 58 fraternal pairs in which at least one twin had committed suicide (Juel-Nielsen & Videbech, 1970). In four of the identical pairs the other twin also committed suicide (21 percent), while none of the other twins among the fraternal pairs had done so.

As with all such family and twin research, there are nonbiological interpretations for these findings as well (Brent et al., 1998). Psychodynamic clinicians might argue that children whose close relatives commit suicide are prone to depression and suicide because they have lost a loved one at a critical stage of development (Stimming & Stimming, 1999). Behavioral theorists might emphasize the modeling role played by parents or close relatives who attempt suicide.

In the past two decades, laboratory research has offered more direct support for a biological view of suicide. The activity level of the neurotransmitter *serotonin* has often been found to be low in people who commit suicide (Mann et al., 2001, 1999). An early hint of this relationship came from a study by the psychiatric researcher Marie Asberg and her colleagues (1976). They studied 68 depressed patients and found that 20 of the patients had particularly low levels of serotonin activity. It turned out that 40 percent of the low-serotonin people attempted suicide, compared with 15 percent of the higher-serotonin subjects. The

ConsiderThis

● Although findings are sometimes mixed, many studies suggest that suicides committed by violent methods are highest during the spring and lowest in late fall (Pretti & Miotto, 2000). How might this trend be explained?

Adrian Arbib/Corbis

STEPPING BACK

Punishment, After the Fact

Today a completed suicide is viewed as a private act—not as a crime against society. We have laws and rules against helping people to commit suicide, but, otherwise, once people actually commit this act, they and their surviving relatives are left alone by legal authorities. This was not always the case.

In times past, the bodies of people who had committed suicide were sometimes treated disrespectfully and their estates fined. Indeed, surviving relatives could be left penniless. In France and England, for example, up through the eighteenth century, the bodies of suicide victims might be dragged through the streets on a frame, head downward, the way criminals were dragged to their executions. Consider the following court ruling in the case of a 55-year-old peasant found hanged in his house in Brittany in 1773:

I [Regarding the case of] the late Christophe Caud, duly charged and proven guilty of having done away with and murdered himself. . . [the court] orders that his memory remain extinguished and suppressed in perpetuity, that his cadaver be attached to a hurdle to be dragged through the streets and common crossings and then . . . hanged by the feet from the gallows set up there, remain there for three hours, and then be thrown into the common refuse heap. . . . [The bench further] declares that his movable goods be acquired and confiscated. . . , and furthermore decrees. . . a fine of 3 *livres*. . . to be taken from his other possessions. . . . I

(BARREAU, 1971)

It is important to note that not everyone who committed suicide was dealt with in this manner. In fact, eighteenth-century law held that coroners had to first rule whether suspicious deaths were suicides or mere accidents. If the ruling was suicide, a coroner's jury then had to determine whether the suicide was a *felo de se* (a "self-murder") or *non compos menti* (due to "mental incompetence"). Only the former kind of suicide was penalized. Families had obvious incentives to disguise suicides, and community members were reluctant to further humiliate or impoverish the innocent survivors of such tragedies, so most suicides were ruled "insane"—that is, due to mental incompetence. Over the course of the eighteenth century, coroners and coroner's juries further came to interpret the act of suicide itself as evidence of insanity. In those rare cases where people who had committed suicide *were* judged guilty and their estates confiscated, the judgment could often be traced to the Crown's need for money.

Religious leaders in Western countries typically followed suit as the eighteenth century unfolded. Although officially they saw the shadow of the devil behind every suicide, their practices were usually generous and humane. If a person had shown any evidence of repentance before committing suicide, he or she was absolved; if even one witness professed to have seen such a sign, the clergyman was instructed to accept it at face value (Minois, 1999). Religious leaders rarely denied a proper sacred burial to persons who had committed suicide.

These judicial and religious trends eventually led to formal changes in the law. By the beginning of the nineteenth century, most legal punishments for suicide had been abolished across Europe and America. England was the last country to give up such punishments. In fact, it was not until 1823 that the Right to Burial Act in that country put a formal end to the practice of highway internment and 1870 that the Abolition of Forfeiture Act stopped the confiscation of suicides' estates. Not until *1961* did England fully remove suicide from its penal code (Hoffman & Webb, 1981).

In contrast to penalties for "successful" suicides, punishments for attempted suicide continued to be imposed well into the twentieth century. In England, as late as the 1950s, people who attempted suicide could be imprisoned for up to two years (Fay, 1995). In the United States, the last prosecution for attempted suicide apparently occurred in 1961, although the prosecution was not successful. Today, people who attempt suicide (or threaten to do so) may still be confined; however, their confinement is in a hospital or mental health facility, not a jail, with goals of prevention and treatment, rather than of punishment.

ConsiderThis

⦿ Why might people in past times have been inclined to punish those who committed suicide and their surviving relatives? • Why do most people take a different view today?

---

researchers interpreted this finding to mean that low serotonin activity may be "a predictor of suicidal acts." Later studies found that suicide attempters with low serotonin activity are 10 times more likely to make a repeat attempt and succeed than are suicide attempters with higher serotonin activity (Roy, 1982; Asberg et al., 1976). Studies that examine the autopsied brains of suicide victims point in the same direction (Mann & Arango, 1999).

At first glance, these studies may appear to tell us only that depressed people often attempt suicide. After all, depression is itself related to low serotonin activity. On the other hand, there is evidence of low serotonin activity even among suicidal subjects who have no history of depression (Van Praag, 1983; Brown et al., 1982). That is, low serotonin activity seems also to have a role in suicide apart from depression.

Murder-suicide *The lives of the comedic actor Phil Hartman and his wife, Brynne, ended in 1998 when she shot him and then herself. Around 1.5 percent of all suicides occur in the context of murder-suicide, usually involving spouses or lovers who have been in conflict (Nock & Marzuk, 1999).*

How, then, might low serotonin activity increase the likelihood of suicidal behavior? One possibility is that it contributes to aggressive behavior. It has been found, for example, that serotonin activity is lower in aggressive men than in nonaggressive men and that serotonin activity is often low in those who commit such aggressive acts as arson and murder (Stanley et al., 2000; Bourgeois, 1991). Such findings suggest that low serotonin activity helps produce aggressive feelings and perhaps impulsive behavior (Mann et al., 2001; Mann & Arango, 1999). In people who are clinically depressed, low serotonin activity may produce aggressive tendencies that cause them to be particularly prone to suicidal thinking and action. Even in the absence of a depressive disorder, however, people with low serotonin activity may develop such aggressive feelings that they too are dangerous to themselves or to others.

SUMMING UP | **What Are the Underlying Causes of Suicide?**

The leading explanations of suicide come from the psychodynamic, sociocultural, and biological models. Each has received only limited research support. Psychodynamic theorists believe that suicide usually results from depression and self-directed anger. Emile Durkheim's sociocultural theory includes three categories of suicide based on the person's relationship with society: egoistic suicides, altruistic suicides, and anomic suicides. And biological theorists suggest that the activity of the neurotransmitter serotonin is particularly low in individuals who commit suicide.

Is Suicide Linked to Age?

The likelihood of committing suicide generally increases with age, although people of all ages may try to kill themselves. Recently clinicians have paid particular attention to self-destructive behavior in three age groups: *children, adolescents,* and the *elderly.* Although the features and theories of suicide discussed throughout this chapter apply to all age groups, each group faces unique problems that may play key roles in the suicidal acts of its members (Richman, 1999).

Children

Although suicide is infrequent among children, it has been increasing over the past several decades (Pfeffer, 2000). Approximately 500 children under 14 years of age in the United States now commit suicide each year—around 0.9 per 100,000 in this age group, a rate nearly 800 percent higher than that in 1950 (Goldman & Beardslee, 1999; Stillion & McDowell, 1996). They use methods ranging from drug overdose to guns. Boys outnumber girls by as much as five to one. In addition, it has been estimated that one of every 100 children tries to harm him- or herself, and many thousands of children are hospitalized each year for deliberately self-destructive acts, such as cutting, burning, or jumping from high places.

Researchers have found that suicide attempts by the very young are commonly preceded by such behavioral patterns as running away from home, accident-proneness, acting out, temper tantrums, social withdrawal and loneliness, extreme sensitivity to criticism, low tolerance of frustration, dark fantasies and daydreams, marked personality change, and overwhelming interest in death and suicide (Cytryn & McKnew, 1996; McGuire, 1982). Studies have further linked child suicides to the recent or upcoming loss of a loved one, family stress and parent unemployment, abuse by parents, and a clinical level of depression (Pfeffer, 2000; Goldman & Beardsley, 1999).

Most people find it hard to believe that children fully understand the meaning of a suicidal act. They argue that because a child's thinking is so limited, children who attempt suicide fall into Shneidman's category of "death ignorers," like Billy, who sought to join his mother in heaven (Fasko & Fasko, 1991). Many child suicides, however, appear to be based on a clear understanding of death and on a clear wish to die (Carlson et al., 1994, 1991; Pfeffer, 1993, 1986). In addition, suicidal thinking among even normal children is apparently more common than most people once believed (Kovacs et al., 1993; Pfeffer et al., 1984). Clinical interviews with schoolchildren have revealed that between 6 and 33 percent have thought about suicide (Culp, Clyman, & Culp, 1995; Jacobsen et al., 1994).

Adolescents

> Dear Mom, Dad, and everyone else,
>
> I'm sorry for what I've done, but I loved you all and I always will, for eternity. Please, please, please don't blame it on yourselves. It was all my fault and not yours or anyone else's. If I didn't do this now, I would have done it later anyway. We all die some day, I just died sooner.
>
> Love,
> John
>
> *(Berman, 1986)*

The suicide of John, age 17, was not an unusual event. Suicidal actions become much more common after the age of 14 than at any earlier age. According to official records, over 2,000 teenagers, or 11 of every 100,000, commit suicide in the United States each year, although some clinicians believe the actual rate to be up to three times higher than this (Madge & Harvey, 1999). In addition, as many as 500,000 teenagers may make attempts (Popenhagen & Qualley, 1998). Because fatal illnesses are uncommon among the young, suicide has become the third leading cause of death in this age group, after accidents and homicides. Furthermore, as many as half of all teenagers have thought about killing themselves (Goldman & Beardsley, 1999).

Although young white Americans are more prone to suicide than young African Americans, the rates of the two groups are becoming closer (Center for Disease Control, 1998). The white American rate was 157 percent greater than the African American rate in 1980; today it is only 42 percent greater. This trend may reflect increasingly similar pressures on young African Americans and young white Americans—competition for grades and college opportunities, for example, is now intense for both groups. The rising suicide rate for young African Americans may also be linked to rising unemployment among them, the many anxieties of inner-city life, and the rage felt by many young African Americans over racial inequities in our society (Burr, Hartman, & Matteson, 1999).

About half of teenage suicides, like those of people in other age groups, have been tied to clinical depression, low self-esteem, and feelings of hopelessness, but many teenagers who try to kill themselves also appear to struggle with anger and impulsiveness

THE HEAVY METAL LINK
Research finds that fans of heavy metal rock consider suicide more acceptable than do people who are not fans (Stack, 1998). But this attitude does not seem to result from the music or the lifestyle it espouses. Rather, heavy metal fans tend to be low in religiosity, and low religiosity relates to greater acceptability of suicide. Fans who are religious rate suicide just as unacceptable as non-fans do.

Difficult years *The angst, confusion, conflict, and impulsivity that typically characterize adolescence provide fertile ground for the growth of suicidal thoughts and attempts.*

Jeff Isaac Greenberg/Photo Researchers

WHERE TO TURN

One survey of 396 high school students indicated that teenagers are unlikely to initiate contact with a counselor during a suicidal crisis, but over half would probably tell a friend (Henning, Crabtree, & Baum, 1998).

TEENAGE ANOMIE

In a study across several midwestern states, half of 300 homeless and runaway teenagers said that they had thoughts of suicide, and over one-quarter had attempted suicide in the previous year (Yoder et al., 1998).

(Sheras, 2001). In addition, some adolescents who consider or attempt suicide may have deficiencies in their ability to sort out and solve problems (Carris, Sheeber, & Howe, 1998). Furthermore, such teenagers are often under great stress. Many of them experience long-term pressures such as poor (or missing) relationships with parents, family conflict, inadequate peer relationships, and social isolation (Houston et al., 2001; Sourander et al., 2001). Their actions also may be triggered by more immediate stress, such as a parent's unemployment or physical illness, financial setbacks for the family, or problems with a boyfriend or girlfriend (Fergusson et al., 2000). Stress at school seems to be a particularly common problem for teenagers who attempt suicide (Ho et al., 1995). Some have trouble keeping up at school, while others may be high achievers who feel pressured to be perfect and to stay at the top of the class (Delisle, 1986; Leroux, 1986).

Some theorists believe that adolescence itself produces a stressful climate in which suicidal actions are more likely (Goldman & Beardsley, 1999). Adolescence is a period of rapid growth, and it is often marked by conflicts, depressed feelings, tensions, and difficulties at home and school. Adolescents tend to react to events more sensitively, angrily, dramatically, and impulsively than people in other age groups; thus the likelihood of suicidal acts during times of stress is increased (Taylor & Stansfeld, 1984). Finally, the suggestibility of adolescents and their eagerness to imitate others, including others who attempt suicide, may set the stage for suicidal action (Hazell & Lewin, 1993). One study found that 93 percent of adolescent suicide attempters had known someone who had attempted suicide (Conrad, 1992).

Far more teenagers attempt suicide than actually kill themselves—the ratio may be as high as 200 to 1. The unusually large number of unsuccessful suicides may mean that teenagers are less certain of their intentions than older persons who make such attempts. While some do indeed wish to die, many may simply want to make others understand how desperate they are, get help, or teach others a lesson (Leenaars et al., 2001; Boergers et al., 1998). Up to half of teenage attempters make new suicide attempts in the future, and as many as 14 percent eventually die by suicide (Diekstra et al., 1995; Diekstra, 1989).

In countries around the world, the suicide rate for adolescents is not only high but increasing (Hawton et al., 2000). Overall, it has more than doubled in recent decades, as has the rate for young adults (Mehlum et al., 1999; McIntosh, 1996) (see Figure 7-3). Several theories, most pointing to societal changes, have been proposed to explain the dramatic rises in these two age groups. First, as the number and proportion of teenagers and young adults in the general population keep rising, the competition for jobs, college positions, and academic and athletic honors intensifies for them, leading increasingly to shattered dreams and ambitions (Holinger & Offer, 1993, 1991, 1982). Other explanations point to weakening ties in the family (which may produce feelings of alienation and rejection in many of today's young people) and to the increased availability of drugs and the pressure to use them among teenagers and young adults (Cutler et al., 2001; Jones, 1997).

The publicity given to suicide attempts by teenagers and young adults may also contribute to the rise in the suicide rate among the young (Grossman & Kruesi, 2000). The detailed descriptions of teenage suicide that the media and the arts have offered in recent years may serve as models for young people who are thinking about suicide. Within days of the highly publicized suicides of four adolescents in one New Jersey town in 1987, dozens of teenagers across the United States took similar actions (at least twelve of them fatal)—two in the same garage just one week later.

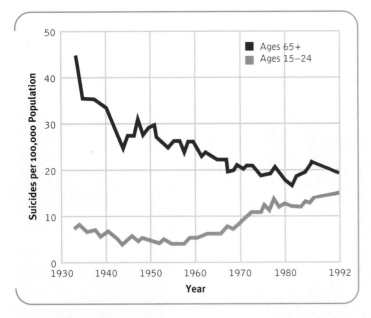

FIGURE 7-3 **Changing suicide rates** *The suicide rate of elderly people has been generally declining for at least a half-century, while that of young adults is increasing. Still, older people continue to be at higher risk for suicide. (Adapted from McIntosh, 1996, 1991, 1987.)*

The Elderly

In Western society the elderly are more likely to commit suicide than people in any other age group. About 19 of every 100,000 persons over the age of 65 in the United States commit suicide (McIntosh, 1995, 1992). Elderly persons committed over 19 percent of all suicides in the United States during the 1980s, yet they accounted for only 12 percent of the total population (McIntosh, 1992).

Many factors contribute to this high suicide rate (Pearson, 2000). As people grow older, all too often they become ill, lose close friends and relatives, lose control over their lives, and lose status in our society. Such experiences may result in feelings of hopelessness, loneliness, or depression among aged persons and so increase the likelihood that they will attempt suicide. In one study, 44 percent of elderly people who committed suicide gave some indication that their act was prompted by the fear of being placed in a nursing home (Loebel et al., 1991). Also, the suicide rate of elderly people who have recently lost a spouse is relatively high (Duberstein, Conwell, & Cox, 1998).

Elderly persons are typically more determined than younger persons in their decision to die, so their success rate is much higher (De Leo et al., 2001; Clark, 1999). Apparently one of every four elderly persons who attempts suicide succeeds. Given the determination of aged persons and their physical decline, some people argue that older persons who want to die are clear in their thinking and should be allowed to carry out their wishes. However, clinical depression appears to play an important role in as many as 60 percent of suicides by the elderly, suggesting that more elderly people who are suicidal should be receiving treatment for their depressive disorders (Harwood et al., 2001).

The suicide rate among the elderly in the United States is lower in some minority groups (Kettl, 1998). Although Native Americans have the highest overall suicide rate, for example, the rate among elderly Native Americans is relatively low (NIH, 1999; McIntosh & Santos, 1982). The aged are held in high esteem by Native Americans and looked to for the wisdom and experience they have acquired over the years—factors that may help account for their low suicide rate. Such high regard is in sharp contrast to the loss of status often experienced by elderly white Americans (Butler, 1975).

Similarly, the suicide rate is only one-third as high among elderly African Americans as among elderly white Americans (McIntosh, 1992). One reason for this low suicide rate may be the pressures faced by African Americans: "only the strongest survive" (Seiden, 1981). Those who reach an advanced age have overcome great adversity and often feel proud of what they have accomplished. Because reaching old age is not in itself a form of success for white Americans, their attitude toward aging is more negative.

ConsiderThis

● Often people view the suicide of an elderly or chronically sick person as less tragic than that of a young or healthy person. Why might they think this way, and is their reasoning valid?

"The man, who in a fit of melancholy, kills himself today, would have wished to live had he waited a week."

Voltaire, "Cato," *Philosophical Dictionary*, 1764

Lawrence Migdale

The power of respect *Elderly persons are held in high esteem in many traditional societies because of the store of knowledge they have accumulated. Perhaps not so coincidentally, suicides among the elderly seem to be less common in these cultures than in those of many modern industrialized nations.*

The Right to Commit Suicide

In the fall of 1989, a Michigan doctor, Jack Kevorkian, built a "suicide device." A person using it could, at the touch of a button, change a saline solution being fed intravenously into the arm to one containing chemicals that would bring unconsciousness and a swift death. The following June, under the doctor's supervision, Mrs. J. Adkins took her life. She left a note explaining: "This is a decision taken in a normal state of mind and is fully considered. I have Alzheimer's disease and I do not want to let it progress any further. I do not want to put my family or myself through the agony of this terrible disease." Mrs. Adkins believed that she had a right to choose death. Michigan authorities promptly prohibited further use of Kevorkian's device, but the physician continued to assist in the suicides of medically ill persons throughout the 1990s until his conviction in 1999 for second-degree murder in one case.

(ADAPTED FROM BELKIN, 1990; MALCOLM, 1990)

*D*o individuals have a right to commit suicide, or does society have the right to stop them? Dr. Kevorkian's series of court battles have made many people ask just that.

The ancient Greeks valued physical and mental well-being in life and dignity in death. Therefore, individuals with a grave illness or mental anguish were permitted to commit suicide. Athenians could obtain official permission from the Senate to take their own lives, and judges were allowed to give them hemlock (Humphry & Wickett, 1986).

American traditions, in contrast, discourage suicide, on the basis of belief in the "sanctity of life" (Eser, 1981). We speak of "committing" suicide, as though it were a criminal act (Barrington, 1980), and we allow the state to use force, including involuntary commitment to a mental hospital, to prevent it. But times and attitudes are changing. Today the ideas of a "right to suicide" and "rational suicide" are receiving more support from the public, psychotherapists, and physicians (Leenaars et al., 2001). In fact, surveys suggest that half of today's physicians believe that suicide can be rational in some circumstances (Ganzini et al., 2000; Duberstein et al., 1995).

Public support for a right to suicide seems strongest in connection with great pain and terminal illness (Werth, 2000, 1999, 1996; Palmore, 1999). Studies show that about half or more of all Americans believe that terminally ill persons should be free to take their lives or to seek a physician's assistance to do so (Drane, 1995; Duberstein et al., 1995). There is also evidence that doctors and patients are acting on these beliefs. One survey of 118 doctors specializing in AIDS in San Francisco found that half of the respondents had helped patients commit suicide by giving them prescriptions for lethal amounts of narcotics (Slome et al., 1997).

Many people consider suicide a "natural right," comparable to the rights to life, ownership of property, and freedom of speech (Battin, 1999, 1982). Most, however, would limit this right to situations in which the act of suicide is indeed "rational," a choice made only when life stops being enriching and fulfilling (Ganzini et al., 2000; Weir, 1992). Most do not believe suicide appropriate in "irrational" cases, those motivated by psychological disorders such as depression (Battin, 1999, 1982; Weir, 1992). In line with such reasoning, the state of Oregon in 1997 passed the "Death with Dignity" Act, allowing a doctor to assist a suicide (by administering a lethal dose of drugs) if two physicians determine that the patient has less than six months to live and is not basing his or her decision to die on depression or another mental disorder.

It turns out, however, that even in cases of severe illness it is difficult to know whether a person's wish to commit suicide is rational (Kelly et al., 1999). Is the hopelessness of an AIDS patient realistic or a symptom of depression? Some research suggests that the suicidal acts of cancer and AIDS patients often spring largely from psychological and social distress (Akechi et al., 2001; Breitbart, Rosenfeld, & Passik, 1996). Half or more

Dr. Jack Kevorkian and his suicide device.

of those patients who are suicidal may be clinically depressed (Chochinov et al., 1995; Brown et al., 1986). Thus, in some cases, it may be more beneficial to help individuals come to terms with a fatal illness than to offer them a license to end their lives (Hendin, 1999).

Some clinicians also worry that the right to suicide could be experienced more as a "duty to die" than as the ultimate freedom (McIntosh, 1999; Seale & Addington-Hall, 1995). Elderly people might feel selfish in expecting relatives to support and care for them when suicide is a socially approved alternative (Sherlock, 1983). Indeed, many already feel that they are "too old" and a burden to their families (Breitbart et al., 1996). Moreover, as care for the terminally ill grows ever more costly, would suicide be subtly encouraged among the poor and disadvantaged? Could assisted suicide become a form of medical cost control (Hendin, 1999; SHHV Task Force, 1995)?

How are these issues to be resolved? Understanding and preventing suicide remain challenges for the future, as do questions about whether and when we should stand back and do nothing. Whatever one's position on this issue, it is a matter of life and death.

Is Suicide Linked to Age?

The likelihood, patterns, and causes of suicide vary with age.

Children Suicide is uncommon among children, although it has been increasing in that group during the past several decades.

Adolescents Suicide by adolescents is increasing. In particular, attempts by this age group are numerous. Adolescent suicide is sometimes linked to clinical depression, anger, impulsiveness, major stress, and adolescent life itself. The rising suicide rate among adolescents and young adults may be related to the growing number and proportion of these young people in the general population, the weakening of family ties, the increased availability and use of drugs among the young, and the broad media coverage of suicide attempts by the young.

Elderly Persons In Western society the elderly are more likely to commit suicide than people in any other age group. The loss of health, friends, control, and status may produce feelings of hopelessness, loneliness, or depression in this age group. The suicide rate among the elderly in the United States is lower in some minority groups, possibly because of differing attitudes toward the elderly in those groups.

LINGERING IMPACT OF CHILD ABUSE
Adults who were sexually or physically abused in childhood harm themselves, think about suicide, and attempt suicide more than do adults without this history (Dinwiddie et al., 2000; Santa Mina & Gallop, 1998).

Treatment and Suicide

Treatment of suicidal people falls into two major categories: *treatment after suicide has been attempted* and *suicide prevention*. While treatment may also be beneficial to relatives and friends, whose feelings of loss, guilt, and anger after a suicide fatality or attempt can be intense, the discussion here is limited to the treatment given to suicidal people themselves (Provini et al., 2000; McIntosh, 1999).

What Treatments Are Used after Suicide Attempts?

After a suicide attempt, most victims need medical care. Some are left with severe injuries, brain damage, or other medical problems. Once the physical damage is treated, psychotherapy or drug therapy may begin, on either an inpatient or an outpatient basis.

Unfortunately, even after trying to kill themselves, many suicidal people fail to continue systematic psychotherapy (Beautrais, Joyce, & Mulder, 2000). In a random survey of several hundred teenagers, 9 percent were found to have made at least one suicide attempt, and of those only half had received later psychological treatment (Harkavy & Asnis, 1985). Similarly, in another study, one-third of adolescent attempters reported that they had not received any help after trying to end their lives (Larsson & Ivarsson, 1998). In some cases, health-care professionals are at fault. In others, the person who has attempted suicide refuses follow-up therapy (Piacentini et al., 1995).

The goals of therapy are to keep people alive, help them achieve a nonsuicidal state of mind, and guide them to develop better ways of handling stress (Shneidman, 2001, 1999, 1993). Various therapies have been employed, including drug, psychodynamic, cognitive, group, and family therapies (Rudd et al., 2001; Salzman, 1999). Treatment appears to help. Studies have found that 30 percent of suicide attempters who do not receive treatment try again, compared with 16 percent of patients in treatment (Nordstrom, Samuelsson, & Asberg, 1995; Allard et al., 1992). It is not clear, however, whether any one approach is more effective than the others (Canetto, 1995).

What Is Suicide Prevention?

During the past 30 years, emphasis around the world has shifted from suicide treatment to suicide prevention (Kosky et al., 1998). In some respects this change

SUICIDE AND HOSPITALIZATION
Suicidal behavior or thinking is the most common precipitant for admission to a mental hospital. Between 60 and 75 percent of patients who are admitted have aroused concern that they will harm themselves (Jacobson, 1999).

FATAL REPETITION
In Finland 19 percent of all males and 39 percent of all females who committed suicide in the late 1980s had made an earlier attempt the previous year (Isometsae & Loennqvist, 1998).

Rob Sollett / Staten Island Advance

Working with suicide *An individual breaks free from police and falls from a bridge in New York City. The scene reminds us that many kinds of professionals face suicidal behavior. Police departments typically provide special crisis intervention training so that officers can develop the skills to address suicidal individuals.*

ConsiderThis

◉ A person's wish to die is often ambivalent. In addition, most people who think about suicide do not act. How, then, should clinicians decide whether to hospitalize a person who is considering suicide or even one who has made an attempt?

is most appropriate: the last opportunity to keep many potential suicide victims alive comes before the first attempt.

The first **suicide prevention program** in the United States was started in Los Angeles in 1955; the first in England, called the *Samaritans,* began in 1953. There are now hundreds of suicide prevention centers in the United States and in England. In addition, many of today's mental health centers, hospital emergency rooms, pastoral counseling centers, and poison control centers include suicide prevention programs among their services (Dorwart & Ostacher, 1999).

There are also hundreds of *suicide hot lines* in the United States, 24-hour-a-day telephone services. Callers reach a counselor, typically a *paraprofessional,* a person trained in counseling but without a formal degree, who provides services under the supervision of a mental health professional (Neimeyer & Bonnelle, 1997).

Suicide prevention programs and hot lines respond to suicidal people as individuals *in crisis—* that is, under great stress, unable to cope, feeling threatened or hurt, and interpreting their situations as unchangeable. Thus the programs offer **crisis intervention:** they try to help suicidal people see their situations more accurately, make better decisions, act more constructively, and overcome their crises (Frankish, 1994). Because crises can occur at any time, the centers advertise their hot lines and also welcome people who walk in without appointments.

Although specific features vary from center to center, the general approach used by the Los Angeles Suicide Prevention Center reflects the goals and techniques of many such organizations (Jacobs, 1999; Litman, 1995). During the first contact, the counselor has several tasks (Shneidman & Farberow, 1968):

Establishing a positive relationship As callers must trust counselors in order to confide in them and follow their suggestions, counselors try to set a positive tone for the discussion. They give the message that they are listening, understanding, interested, nonjudgmental, and available.

Understanding and clarifying the problem Counselors first try to understand the full scope of the caller's crisis and then help the person see the crisis in clear and constructive terms. In particular, they try to help callers see the central issues and the short-term nature of their crises and recognize the alternatives to suicide.

Assessing suicide potential Crisis workers at the Los Angeles Suicide Prevention Center fill out a questionnaire, often called a *lethality scale,* to estimate the caller's potential for suicide. It helps them determine the degree of stress the caller is under, relevant personality characteristics, how detailed the suicide plan is, the severity of symptoms, and the coping resources available to the caller.

Assessing and mobilizing the caller's resources Although they may view themselves as ineffective and helpless, people who are suicidal usually have many strengths and resources, including relatives and friends. It is the counselor's job to recognize, point out, and activate those resources.

Formulating a plan Together the crisis worker and caller develop a plan of action. In essence, they are agreeing on a way out of the crisis, an alternative to suicidal action. Most plans include a series of follow-up counseling sessions over the next few days or weeks, either in person at the center or by phone. Each plan also requires the caller to take certain actions and make certain changes in his or her personal life. Counselors usually negotiate a *no-suicide contract* with the caller—a promise not to attempt suicide, or at least a promise to reestablish contact if the caller again considers suicide. Although popular, the usefulness of such contracts has been called into question in recent years (Miller et al., 1998). In addition, if callers are in the midst of a suicide attempt, counselors will try to find out their whereabouts and get medical help to them immediately.

Although crisis intervention appears to be sufficient treatment for some suicidal people (Hawton, 1986), longer-term therapy is needed for most (Rudd, 2000; Berman & Jobes, 1995). If the crisis intervention center does not offer this kind of therapy, the counselors will refer the clients elsewhere.

As the suicide prevention movement spread during the 1960s, many clinicians came to believe that crisis intervention techniques should also be applied to problems other than suicide. Crisis intervention has emerged during the past three decades as a respected form of treatment for such wide-ranging problems as teenage confusion, drug and alcohol abuse, rape victimization, and spouse abuse.

Do Suicide Prevention Programs Work?

It is difficult for researchers to measure the effectiveness of suicide prevention programs (Reisch, Schlatter, & Tschacher, 1999; Goldney, 1998). There are many kinds of programs, each with its own procedures and serving populations that vary in number, age, and environmental pressures. Communities with high suicide risk factors, such as a high elderly population or economic problems, may continue to have higher suicide rates than other communities regardless of the effectiveness of their local prevention centers.

Do suicide prevention centers reduce the number of suicides in a community? Clinical researchers do not know (Dorwart & Ostacher, 1999; Canetto, 1995). Studies comparing local suicide rates before and after the establishment of community prevention centers have yielded different findings. Some find a decline in a community's suicide rates, others no change, and still others an increase (Lester, 1997; Dew et al., 1987). However, even an increase may represent a positive impact, if it is lower than the larger society's overall increase in suicidal behavior (Lester, 1991, 1974).

Do suicidal people contact prevention centers? Apparently only a small percentage do. Moreover, the typical caller to an urban prevention center appears to be young, African American, and female, whereas the greatest number of suicides are committed by elderly white men (Canetto, 1995; Lester, 1989, 1972).

Prevention programs do seem to reduce the number of suicides among those high-risk people who do call. One study identified 8,000 high-risk individuals who contacted the Los Angeles Suicide Prevention Center (Farberow & Litman, 1970). Approximately 2 percent of these callers later committed suicide, compared to the 6 percent suicide rate usually found in similar high-risk groups. Clearly, centers need to be more visible and available to people who are thinking of suicide. The growing number of advertisements and announcements in newspapers and on television, radio, and billboards indicates a movement in this direction.

Several theorists have called for more effective public education about suicide as the ultimate form of prevention, and at least some *suicide education* programs—most of them concentrating on teachers and students—have begun to emerge (Kalafat & Ryerson, 1999; Mauk & Sharpnack, 1998). The curriculum for such programs has been the subject of much debate (Dorwart & Ostacher, 1999), but clinicians typically agree with the goals behind them and, more generally, with Shneidman when he states:

SUICIDE PREVENTION PROGRAM A program that tries to identify people who are at risk of killing themselves and to offer them crisis intervention.

CRISIS INTERVENTION A treatment approach that tries to help people in a psychological crisis to view their situation more accurately, make better decisions, act more constructively, and overcome the crisis.

Nick Ut/AP/Wide World Photos

Mass suicide *Group suicides are not well understood or effectively prevented by the clinical field. The nation will not soon forget the suicide by 39 members of the Heaven's Gate cult near San Diego, California, or the eerie death scene. Each member lay neatly in new black sneakers, under a diamond-shaped purple shroud. Nearby was an overnight bag, packed with clothes, a notebook, and lip balm.*

ConsiderThis

⦿ Some schools are reluctant to offer suicide education programs, especially if they have never experienced a suicide attempt by one of their students. What might be their concerns? • How valid is their position?

> The primary prevention of suicide lies in education. The route is through teaching one another and . . . the public that suicide can happen to anyone, that there are verbal and behavioral clues that can be looked for . . . , and that help is available. . . .
>
> In the last analysis, the prevention of suicide is everybody's business.
>
> *(Shneidman, 1985, p. 238)*

SUMMING UP

Treatment and Suicide

Treatment may follow a suicide attempt. In such cases, therapists seek to help the person achieve a nonsuicidal state of mind and develop better ways of handling stress and solving problems.

Over the past 30 years, the emphasis of clinicians and educators has shifted to suicide prevention. Suicide prevention programs include 24-hour-a-day hot lines and walk-in centers staffed largely by paraprofessionals who follow a crisis intervention model. Most suicidal people also need longer-term therapy. Suicide education programs for the public are beginning to appear.

CROSSROADS:
Psychological and Biological Insights Lag Behind

PSYCHOLOGICAL DAMAGE CONTROL

The term "postvention" describes services offered after a trauma (for example, after a schoolmate's suicide) to head off psychological aftereffects.

Once a mysterious and hidden problem, hardly acknowledged by the public and barely investigated by professionals, suicide today is the focus of much attention. During the past 25 years in particular, investigators have learned a great deal about this life-or-death problem.

In contrast to most other problems covered in this textbook, suicide has received much more examination from the sociocultural model than from any other (Aldridge, 1998). Sociocultural theorists have, for example, highlighted the importance of societal change and stress, national and religious affiliation, marital status, gender, race, and the mass media. The insights and information gathered by psychological and biological researchers have been more limited.

Although sociocultural factors certainly shed light on the general background and triggers of suicide, they typically leave us unable to predict that a given person will attempt suicide. When all is said and done, clinicians do not yet fully understand why some people kill themselves while others in similar circumstances manage to find better ways of dealing with their problems. Psychological and biological insights must catch up to the sociocultural insights if clinicians are truly to explain and understand suicide.

Treatments for suicide also pose some difficult problems. Clinicians have yet to develop clearly successful therapies for suicidal persons. Although suicide prevention programs certainly show the clinical field's commitment to helping people who are suicidal, it is not yet clear how much such programs actually reduce the overall risk or rate of suicide.

THE CHINA PROFILE

China's 300,000 annual suicides, ten times the United States' toll, represent 40 percent of all suicides in the world. China is the only country in which female suicides are more common than male suicides, accounting for half of suicides by women worldwide (Ji et al., 2001; Kaplan, 1999; Phillips et al., 1999).

At the same time, the growth in the amount of research on suicide offers great promise. And perhaps most promising of all, clinicians are now enlisting the public in the fight against this problem. They are calling for broader public education about suicide—programs aimed at both young and old. It is reasonable to expect that the current climate will lead to a better understanding of suicide and to more successful interventions. Such goals are of importance to everyone. Although suicide itself is typically a lonely and desperate act, the impact of such acts is very broad indeed.

QUICK QUIZ

1. Define suicide and subintentional death. Describe four different kinds of people who attempt suicide. pp. 192–195

2. What techniques do researchers use to study suicide? p. 195

3. How do statistics on suicide vary according to country, religion, gender, marital status, and race? pp. 195–196

4. What kinds of immediate and long-term stresses have been linked to suicide? pp. 197–198

5. What other current events or conditions may help trigger suicidal acts? pp. 198–202

6. How do psychodynamic, sociocultural, and biological theorists explain suicide, and how well supported are their theories? pp. 202–206

7. How do theorists explain the increase in suicide attempts by adolescents and young adults? pp. 207–208

8. Compare the risk, rate, and causes of suicide among children, adolescents, and elderly persons. pp. 206–209

9. Describe the nature and goals of treatment given to people after they have attempted suicide. Do many people receive such treatments? p. 211

10. Describe the principles of suicide prevention programs. What procedures are employed by counselors in these programs? How effective are the programs? pp. 211–214

CYBER STUDY

▲ Observe the behaviors, thought processes, and feelings of suicidal persons. ▲ What role might alcohol or a weapon play in suicide? ▲ Does treatment eliminate (or reduce) suicidal thinking? ▲ What are the reactions of relatives and friends after a suicide?

SEARCH THE *FUNDAMENTALS OF ABNORMAL PSYCHOLOGY* CD-ROM FOR

▲ Chapter 7 video cases and discussions
   "Andy"—Suicide
   "Bonnie"—Suicide
▲ Chapter 7 practice test and feedback
▲ Additional video case and discussion
   "Meredith"—Mood Disorders: Medication and Talk Therapy

LOG ON TO THE COMER WEB PAGE FOR

▲ Suggested Web links, research exercises, FAQ page, additional Chapter 7 practice test questions

   <http://www.worthpublishers.com/comer>

UCLA Neuropsychiatric Institute & Hospital

Psychosocial Factors in Physical Disorders

"Mental disorders arise from physical ones, and likewise physical disorders arise from mental ones."

The Mahabharata, c. A.D. 200

It was Wednesday. The big day. Midterms in History and Physics back to back, beginning at 11:30, and an oral presentation in Psych at 3:30. Jerry had been preparing for, and dreading, this day for weeks, calling it "D-day" to his friends. He had been up until 3:30 A.M. the night before, studying, trying to nail everything down. It seemed as though he had fallen asleep only minutes ago, yet here it was 9:30 A.M. and the killer day was under way.

As soon as he woke, Jerry felt a tight pain grip his stomach. He also noticed buzzing in his ears, a lightheadedness, and even aches throughout his body. He wasn't surprised, given the day he was about to face. One test might bring a few butterflies of anxiety; two and a presentation were probably good for a platoon of dragonflies.

As he tried to get going, however, Jerry began to suspect that this was more than butterflies. His stomach pain soon turned to spasms, and his lightheadedness became outright dizziness. He could barely make it to the bathroom without falling. Thoughts of breakfast made him nauseous. He knew he couldn't keep anything down.

Jerry began to worry, even panic. This was hardly the best way to face what was in store for him today. He tried to shake it off, but the symptoms stayed. Finally, his roommate convinced him that he had better go to a doctor. At 10:30, just an hour before the first exam, he entered the big brick building called "Student Health." He felt embarrassed, like a wimp, but what could he do? Persevering and taking two tests under these conditions wouldn't prove anything—except maybe that he was foolish.

Psychosocial factors—factors that are either psychological or sociocultural—may contribute to somatic, or bodily, illnesses in a variety of ways. The physician who sees Jerry has some possibilities to sort out. Jerry could be *faking* his pain and dizziness to avoid taking a tough test. Alternatively, he might be *imagining* his illness, that is, faking to himself. Or his physical symptoms could be very real, yet triggered by *stress:* whenever he feels extreme pressure, such as a person can feel before an important test, Jerry's gastric juices may become more active and irritate his intestines, and his blood pressure may rise and cause him to become dizzy. Or he may be coming down with the flu. Even this *purely medical problem,* however, could be linked to psychosocial factors. Perhaps weeks of constant worry about the exams and presentation have weakened Jerry's body so that he was not able to fight off the flu virus. Whatever the diagnosis, Jerry's state of mind and his social environment are affecting his body. The physician's view of the role played by these psychosocial factors will in turn affect the treatment Jerry receives.

We have observed that psychological disorders frequently have physical causes. Abnormal neurotransmitter activity, for example, contributes to generalized anxiety disorder, panic disorder, and depression. Is it surprising, then, that bodily illnesses may have psychosocial causes? Today's clinicians recognize the wisdom of Socrates' claim in the fourth century B.C.: "You should not treat body without soul."

STRETCHING THE TRUTH

Almost 60 percent of American adults have called in sick to work when they were perfectly healthy (Kanner, 1995).

The idea that psychological and sociocultural factors may contribute to somatic illnesses has ancient roots, yet it had few supporters before the twentieth century. The seventeenth century French philosopher René Descartes went so far as to claim that the mind, or soul, is separate from the body—a position called **mind-body dualism.**

Not until the twentieth century were medical scientists persuaded that psychosocial factors such as stress, worry, and unconscious needs can contribute in major ways to physical illness. Today, in fact, certain kinds of physical illnesses, known as *factitious disorder* and the *somatoform disorders,* are thought to be caused almost entirely by psychosocial factors. Other kinds, called *psychophysiological disorders,* are believed to result from an interaction of biological, psychological, and sociocultural factors.

Factitious Disorder

Like Jerry, people who become physically sick usually go to a physician. Sometimes, however, the physician cannot find a medical cause for the problem and may suspect that other factors are involved. Perhaps the patient is *malingering*—intentionally faking illness to achieve some external gain, such as financial compensation or deferment from military service (LoPiccolo, Goodkin, & Baldewicz, 1999).

Alternatively, a patient may intentionally produce or fake physical symptoms simply from a wish to be a patient; that is, the motivation for assuming the sick role may be the role itself. Physicians would then decide that the patient is displaying **factitious disorder** (see Table 8-1).

A 29-year-old female laboratory technician was admitted to the medical service via the emergency room because of bloody urine. The patient said that she was being treated for lupus erythematosus by a physician in a different city. She also mentioned that she had had Von Willebrand's disease (a rare hereditary blood disorder) as a child. On the third day of her hospitalization, a medical student mentioned to the resident that she had seen this patient several weeks before at a different hospital in the area, where the patient had been admitted for the same problem. A search of the patient's belongings revealed a cache of anticoagulant medication. When confronted with this information she refused to discuss the matter and hurriedly signed out of the hospital against medical advice.

(Spitzer et al., 1981, p. 33)

People with factitious disorder often go to extremes to create the appearance of illness. Many give themselves medications secretly. Some, like the woman just described, inject drugs to cause bleeding. Still others use laxatives to produce chronic diarrhea. High fevers are especially easy to create. In one study of patients with prolonged mysterious fever, more than 9 percent were eventually diagnosed with factitious disorder (Feldman, Ford, & Reinhold, 1994).

People with factitious disorder often research their supposed ailments and may become very knowledgeable about medicine (Miner & Feldman, 1998). Many eagerly undergo painful testing or treatment, even surgery (Stern & Cremens, 1998). When confronted with evidence that their symptoms are factitious, they typically deny the charges and leave the hospital; they may enter another hospital the same day.

Munchausen syndrome is the extreme and long-term form of factitious disorder. It is named after Baron Munchausen, an eighteenth-century cavalry officer who journeyed from tavern to tavern in Europe telling fantastic tales about his supposed military adventures (Feldman et al., 1994). In a related disorder, **Munchausen syndrome by proxy,** parents make up or produce physical illnesses in their children, leading in some cases to repeated painful diagnostic tests, medication, and surgery

Table 8-1 DSM-IV Checklist

FACTITIOUS DISORDER

1. Intentional production or feigning of physical signs or symptoms.
2. Physical symptoms motivated by a desire to assume the sick role.
3. Absence of economic or other external incentives for the behavior.

Based on APA, 2000, 1994.

A CLOSER LOOK

Munchausen Syndrome by Proxy

| [Jennifer] had been hospitalized 200 times and undergone 40 operations. Physicians removed her gallbladder, her appendix and part of her intestines, and inserted tubes into her chest, stomach and intestines. [The 9-year-old from Florida] was befriended by the Florida Marlins and served as a poster child for health care reform, posing with Hillary Rodham Clinton at a White House rally. Then police notified her mother that she was under investigation for child abuse. Suddenly, Jennifer's condition improved dramatically. In the next nine months, she was hospitalized only once, for a viral infection. . . . Experts said Jennifer's numerous baffling infections were "consistent with someone smearing fecal matter" into her feeding line and urinary catheter. |

(KATEL & BECK, 1996)

Recent cases like Jennifer's have horrified the public and called attention to *Munchausen syndrome by proxy*. This disorder is caused by a caregiver who uses various techniques to induce symptoms in a child—giving the child drugs, tampering with medications, contaminating a feeding tube, or even smothering the child, for example. The illness can take almost any form, but the most common symptoms are bleeding, seizures, comas, diarrhea, vomiting, "accidental" poisonings, infections, fevers, and sudden infant death syndrome (Libow & Schreier, 1998; Boros et al., 1995).

Between 10 and 30 percent of the victims of Munchausen syndrome by proxy die as a result of their symptoms, and 8 percent of those who survive are permanently disfigured or physically impaired (Boros et al., 1995; Von Burg & Hibbard, 1995). Psychological, educational, and physical development are also affected (Libow & Schreier, 1998). Jennifer missed so much school that at age 9 she could barely read or write.

The syndrome is very hard to diagnose (Pankratz, 1999) and may be more common than clinicians once thought. The parent (usually the mother) seems to be so devoted and caring that others sympathize with and admire her. Yet the physical problems disappear when child and parent are separated. In many cases siblings of the sick child have also been victimized (Skau & Mouridsen, 1995; Smith & Killam, 1994).

What kind of parent carefully inflicts pain and illness on her own child? The typical Munchausen mother is emotionally needy: she craves the attention and praise she receives for the devoted care of her sick child. She may have little social support outside the medical system, and her husband tends to be absent, physically or emotionally. Many of these mothers are intelligent; often they have a medical background of some kind—perhaps having worked formerly in a doctor's office. Typically they deny their actions, even in the face of clear evidence, and refuse to undergo therapy. In fact, successful treatment has rarely been documented (Ayoub et al., 2000).

Law enforcement authorities are reluctant to consider Munchausen syndrome by proxy a psychological disorder and instead approach it as a crime—a carefully planned form of child abuse (Libow & Schreier, 1998). They almost always require that the child be separated from the mother (Ayoub et al., 2000; Skau & Mouridsen, 1995). At the same time, a parent who resorts to such actions is obviously experiencing severe psychological disturbance and greatly needs clinical help. Thus clinical researchers and practitioners must now work to develop clearer insights and more effective treatments for such parents and for their small victims.

Convalescent, **1994**, by Frank Holl

Frank Holl, *Convalescent*, Christopher Wood Gallery, London, Bridgeman/Art Resource, NY

(Alexander, 2000). If the children are removed from their parents and placed in the care of others, their symptoms disappear (Ayoub et al., 2000).

Clinical researchers have had a hard time determining the prevalence of factitious disorder, since patients hide the true nature of their problem. Overall, the pattern is more common in women than men (APA, 2000). Severe cases, however, seem to be more frequent among men. The disorder usually begins during early adulthood.

Factitious disorder seems to be most common among people who (1) as children received extensive medical treatment for a true physical disorder, (2) experienced family problems or physical or emotional abuse in childhood, (3) carry a grudge against the medical profession, (4) have worked as a nurse, laboratory

PSEUDOLOGIA FANTASTICA

Some people with factitious disorder are able to provide an elaborate (and false) medical history, a fabrication called *pseudologia fantastica.*

"I hope you're not going to be like the twenty incompetent doctors who couldn't find anything wrong with me."

technician, or medical aide, or (5) have an underlying personality problem such as extreme dependence (APA, 2000; Feldman et al., 1994). They often have poor social support, few long-term social relationships, and little family life.

The precise causes of factitious disorder are not understood, although clinical reports have suggested depression, unsupportive parental relationships during childhood, and an extreme need for social support that is not otherwise forthcoming (Ozden & Canat, 1999; Feldman et al., 1994). Nor have clinicians been able to develop dependably effective treatments for it (Simon, 1998; Feldman & Feldman, 1995). Some cases, however, have responded to joint treatment by psychotherapists and medical practitioners (Parker, 1993; Schwarz et al., 1993).

Psychotherapists and medical practitioners often become annoyed or angry at people with factitious disorder, feeling that these people are, at the very least, wasting their time. Yet people with this disorder, like most people with psychological disorders, feel little control over their problem, and they often experience great distress. They need effective therapy rather than scorn, but such help is often not available to them.

SUMMING UP ⎤ **Factitious Disorder**

Before the twentieth century, medical theory was dominated by mind-body dualism, the belief that the mind and body were totally separate entities. Today's clinicians recognize that bodily illnesses can have psychosocial causes.

Factitious Disorder Patients with a factitious disorder fake or produce physical disorders in order to assume the role of a sick person. Munchausen syndrome is the extreme and long-term form of factitious disorder. In Munchausen syndrome by proxy, a parent fakes or produces a physical illness in his or her child.

Somatoform Disorders

When a physical illness has no apparent medical cause, physicians may also suspect a **somatoform disorder,** another pattern of physical complaints with largely psychosocial causes. In contrast to people with factitious disorder, those with somatoform disorders do not consciously want or purposely produce their symptoms; they almost always believe that their problems are genuinely medical. In some somatoform disorders, known as *hysterical somatoform disorders,* there is an actual change in physical functioning. In others, the *preoccupation somatoform disorders,* people who are healthy become worried mistakenly that there is something physically wrong with them.

What Are Hysterical Somatoform Disorders?

People with **hysterical somatoform disorders** suffer actual changes in their physical functioning. These somatoform disorders are often hard to distinguish from genuine medical problems (Hickie et al., 2000). In fact, it is always possible that a diagnosis of hysterical disorder is a mistake and that the patient's problem actually has an undetected organic cause (Moene et al., 2000). DSM-IV lists three hysterical somatoform disorders: *conversion disorder, somatization disorder,* and *pain disorder associated with psychological factors.*

CONVERSION DISORDER In **conversion disorder,** a psychosocial conflict or need is converted into dramatic physical symptoms that affect voluntary motor

---

GENDER CONFUSION

In some cultures, fathers follow the custom of *couvade:* they feel ill and stay in bed before and during the deliveries of their children. They may even show some symptoms of pregnancy and experience the pangs of childbirth (Kahn & Fawcett, 1993).

Table 8-2 DSM-IV Checklist

CONVERSION DISORDER

1. One or more physical symptoms or deficits affecting voluntary motor or sensory function that suggest a neurological or other general medical condition.
2. Psychological factors judged to be associated with the symptom or deficit.
3. Symptom or deficit not intentionally produced or feigned.
4. Symptom or deficit not fully explained by a general medical condition or a substance.
5. Significant distress or impairment.

SOMATIZATION DISORDER

1. A history of many physical complaints, beginning before the age of 30, that occur over a period of several years and result in treatment being sought or in significant impairment.
2. Physical complaints over the period include all of the following:
   (a) Four different kinds of pain symptoms.
   (b) Two gastrointestinal symptoms.
   (c) One sexual symptom.
   (d) One neurological-type symptom.
3. Physical complaints not fully explained by a known general medical condition or a drug, or extending beyond the usual impact of such a condition.
4. Symptoms not intentionally produced or feigned.

PAIN DISORDER ASSOCIATED WITH PSYCHOLOGICAL FACTORS

1. Significant pain as the primary problem.
2. Psychological factors judged to have the major role in the onset, severity, exacerbation, or maintenance of the pain.
3. Symptom or deficit not intentionally produced or feigned.
4. Significant distress or impairment.

Based on APA, 2000, 1994.

MISTAKEN IDENTITY

Many medical problems with vague and confusing symptoms—hyperparathyroidism, multiple sclerosis, and lupus are examples—are frequently misdiagnosed as hysterical disorders. In the past, whiplash was regularly diagnosed as hysteria (Merskey, 1986).

HARD TO SWALLOW

The sense of having a "lump in the throat" when anxious is known in medical circles as *globus hystericus*.

or sensory functioning (see Table 8-2). The symptoms often seem neurological, such as paralysis, blindness, or loss of feeling (APA, 2000, 1994). One woman developed dizziness in apparent response to her unhappy marriage:

A 46-year-old married housewife . . . described being overcome with feelings of extreme dizziness, accompanied by slight nausea, four or five nights a week. During these attacks, the room around her would take on a "shimmering" appearance, and she would have the feeling that she was "floating" and unable to keep her balance. Inexplicably, the attacks almost always occurred at about 4:00 P.M. She usually had to lie down on the couch and often did not feel better until 7:00 or 8:00 P.M. After recovering, she generally spent the rest of the evening watching TV; and more often than not, she would fall asleep in the living room, not going to bed in the bedroom until 2:00 or 3:00 in the morning.

The patient had been pronounced physically fit by her internist, a neurologist, and an ear, nose, and throat specialist on more than one occasion. Hypoglycemia had been ruled out by glucose tolerance tests.

When asked about her marriage, the patient described her husband as a tyrant, frequently demanding and verbally abusive of her and their four children. She admitted that she dreaded his arrival home from work each day, knowing that he would comment that the house was a mess and the dinner, if prepared,

SOMATOFORM DISORDER A physical illness or ailment that is explained largely by psychosocial causes, in which the patient experiences no sense of wanting or guiding the symptoms.

HYSTERICAL SOMATOFORM DISORDERS Somatoform disorders in which people suffer actual changes in their physical functioning.

CONVERSION DISORDER A somatoform disorder in which a psychosocial need or conflict is converted into dramatic physical symptoms that affect voluntary motor or sensory function.

SOMATIZATION DISORDER A somatoform disorder marked by numerous recurring physical ailments without an organic basis. Also known as *Briquet's syndrome.*

PAIN DISORDER ASSOCIATED WITH PSYCHOLOGICAL FACTORS A somatoform disorder marked by pain, with psychosocial factors playing a central role in the onset, severity, or continuation of the pain.

PREOCCUPATION SOMATOFORM DISORDERS Somatoform disorders in which people misinterpret and overreact to minor, even normal, bodily symptoms or features.

HYPOCHONDRIASIS A somatoform disorder in which people mistakenly fear that minor changes in their physical functioning indicate a serious disease.

not to his liking. Recently, since the onset of her attacks, when she was unable to make dinner he and the four kids would go to McDonald's or the local pizza parlor. After that, he would settle in to watch a ballgame in the bedroom, and their conversation was minimal. In spite of their troubles, the patient claimed that she loved her husband and needed him very much.

(Spitzer et al., 1981, pp. 92–93)

Most conversion disorders begin between late childhood and young adulthood; they are diagnosed at least twice as often in women as in men (APA, 2000; Deaton, 1998). They usually appear suddenly, at times of extreme stress, and last a matter of weeks. Conversion disorders are thought to be rare, occurring in at most 5 of every 1,000 persons.

SOMATIZATION DISORDER Sheila baffled medical specialists with the wide range of her symptoms:

Sheila reported having abdominal pain since age 17, necessitating exploratory surgery that yielded no specific diagnosis. She had several pregnancies, each with severe nausea, vomiting, and abdominal pain; she ultimately had a hysterectomy for a "tipped uterus." Since age 40 she had experienced dizziness and "blackouts," which she eventually was told might be multiple sclerosis or a brain tumor. She continued to be bedridden for extended periods of time, with weakness, blurred vision, and difficulty urinating. At age 43 she was worked up for a hiatal hernia because of complaints of bloating and intolerance of a variety of foods. She also had additional hospitalizations for neurological, hypertensive, and renal workups, all of which failed to reveal a definitive diagnosis.

(Spitzer et al., 1981, pp. 185, 260)

Like Sheila, people with **somatization disorder** have numerous long-lasting physical ailments that have little or no organic basis. This hysterical pattern, first described by Pierre Briquet in 1859, is also known as **Briquet's syndrome.** To receive this diagnosis, a person must have multiple ailments that include several pain symptoms (such as headaches and chest pain), gastrointestinal symptoms (such as nausea and diarrhea), a sexual symptom (such as erectile or menstrual difficulties), and a neurological symptom (such as double vision or paralysis) (APA, 2000, 1994). People with somatization disorder usually go from doctor to doctor in search of relief. They often describe their many symptoms in dramatic and exaggerated terms. Most also feel anxious and depressed (Fink, 1995).

Between 0.2 and 2.0 percent of all women in the United States are believed to experience a somatization disorder in any given year, compared to less than 0.2 percent of men (APA, 2000; Regier et al., 1993). The disorder often runs in families; 10 to 20 percent of the close female relatives of women with the disorder also develop it. It usually begins between adolescence and young adulthood (APA, 2000, 1994; Eisendrath, 1995).

A somatization disorder lasts much longer than a conversion disorder, typically for many years (Simon & Gureje, 1999). The symptoms may fluctuate over time but rarely disappear completely without psychotherapy (Smith, Rost, & Kashner, 1995). Two-thirds of the people with this disorder in the United States receive treatment for their physical ailments from a medical or mental health professional in any given year (Regier et al., 1993).

PAIN DISORDER ASSOCIATED WITH PSYCHOLOGICAL FACTORS When psychosocial factors play a central role in the onset, severity, or continuation of pain, patients may receive a diagnosis of **pain disorder associated with psychological factors.** Patients with a conversion or somatization disorder may also experience pain, but it is the key symptom in this disorder (Mogale, 1999).

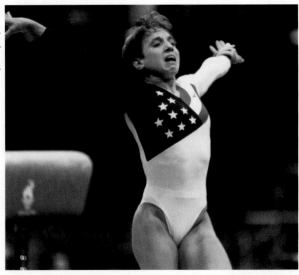

Mind over matter *The opposite of hysterical disorders—though again demonstrating the power of psychological processes—are instances in which people "ignore" pain or other physical symptoms. Despite a badly injured leg, Kerri Strug completes a near-perfect vault routine and landing, leading the United States gymnastics team to an Olympic gold medal in 1996.*

John Gaps III/AP Photo

Although the precise prevalence has not been determined, pain disorder associated with psychological factors appears to be fairly common (McGrady et al., 1999). The disorder may begin at any age, and more women than men seem to experience it (APA, 2000). Often it develops after an accident or during an illness that has caused genuine pain, which then takes on a life of its own. Laura, a 36-year-old woman, reported pains that went far beyond the usual symptoms of her tubercular disease, called sarcoidosis:

> Before the operation I would have little joint pains, nothing that really bothered me that much. After the operation I was having severe pains in my chest and in my ribs, and those were the type of problems I'd been having after the operation, that I didn't have before. . . . I'd go to an emergency room at night, 11:00, 12:00, 1:00 or so. I'd take the medicine, and the next day it stopped hurting, and I'd go back again. In the meantime this is when I went to the other doctors, to complain about the same thing, to find out what was wrong; and they could never find out what was wrong with me either. . . .
> . . . At certain points when I go out or my husband and I go out, we have to leave early because I start hurting. . . . A lot of times I just won't do things because my chest is hurting for one reason or another. . . . Two months ago when the doctor checked me and another doctor looked at the x-rays, he said he didn't see any signs of the sarcoid then and that they were doing a study now, on blood and various things, to see if it was connected to sarcoid. . . .
>
> *(Green, 1985, pp. 60-63)*

HYSTERICAL VERSUS MEDICAL SYMPTOMS Because hysterical somatoform disorders are so similar to "true" medical problems, physicians sometimes rely on oddities in the patient's medical picture to help distinguish the two. The symptoms of a hysterical disorder may, for example, be at odds with the way the nervous system is known to work (APA, 2000, 1994). In a conversion symptom called *glove anesthesia,* numbness begins sharply at the wrist and extends evenly right to the fingertips. As Figure 8-1 shows, real neurological damage is rarely so abrupt or equally distributed.

The physical effects of a hysterical disorder may also differ from those of the corresponding medical problem (Levy, 1985). For example, when paralysis from the waist down, or paraplegia, is caused by damage to the spinal cord, a person's leg muscles may *atrophy,* or waste away, unless physical therapy is applied. People whose paralysis is the result of a conversion disorder, in contrast, do not usually experience atrophy. Perhaps they exercise their muscles without being aware that they are doing so. Similarly, people with conversion blindness have fewer accidents than people who are organically blind, an indication that they have at least some vision even if they are unaware of it.

What Are Preoccupation Somatoform Disorders?

Hypochondriasis and *body dysmorphic disorder* are **preoccupation somatoform disorders.** People with these problems misinterpret and overreact to bodily symptoms or features no matter what friends, relatives, and physicians may say. Although preoccupation disorders also cause great distress, their impact on one's personal, social, and occupational life differs from that of hysterical disorders.

HYPOCHONDRIASIS People who suffer from **hypochondriasis** unrealistically interpret bodily symptoms as signs of a serious illness (see Table 8-3 on the next page). Often their symptoms are merely normal bodily changes, such as occasional coughing, sores, or sweating. Although some patients recognize that their concerns are excessive, many do not.

Although hypochondriasis can begin at any age, it starts most often in early adulthood, among men and women in equal numbers (APA, 2000, 1994). Between 1 and 5 percent of all people experience the disorder. As with pain

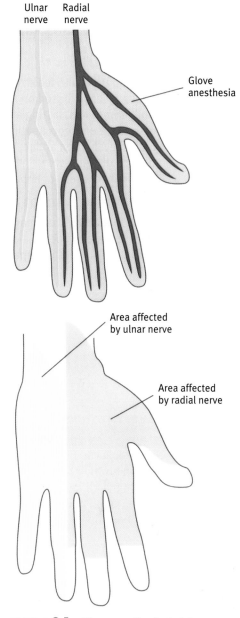

FIGURE 8-1 **Glove anesthesia** *In this conversion symptom the entire hand, extending from the fingertips to the wrist, becomes numb. Actual physical damage to the ulnar nerve, in contrast, causes anesthesia in the ring finger and little finger and beyond the wrist partway up the arm; and damage to the radial nerve causes loss of feeling only in parts of the ring, middle, and index fingers and the thumb and partway up the arm. (Adapted from Gray, 1959.)*

STRICTLY A COINCIDENCE?

On Feb. 17, 1673, the actor-playwright Molière collapsed on stage and died while performing in *Le Malade imaginaire (The Hypochondriac)* (Ash, 1999).

Table 8-3 DSM-IV Checklist

HYPOCHONDRIASIS

1. Preoccupation with fears or beliefs that one has a serious disease, based on misinterpretation of bodily symptoms, lasting at least six months.
2. Persistence of preoccupation despite appropriate medical evaluation and reassurance.
3. Absence of delusions.
4. Significant distress or impairment.

BODY DYSMORPHIC DISORDER

1. Preoccupation with an imagined or exaggerated defect in appearance.
2. Significant distress or impairment.

Based on APA, 2000, 1994.

FOLLICULAR SUBSTITUTIONS

Around 41% of men with significant hair loss wear hats and caps, compared to 23% of men with low hair loss. About 36% of men with high hair loss grow a beard or mustache, compared to 18% of other men (Kanner, 1995).

An extreme case of hypochondriasis? *Not necessarily. After the 1918 flu epidemic killed 20 million people, people in Japan started wearing a masuku to protect them from stray germs. Some, like this commuter, continue the tradition during cold and flu season.*

Torin Boyd Photo, Tokyo, Japan

disorder associated with psychological factors, physicians report seeing many cases (Fink et al., 1999). For most patients, the symptoms rise and fall over the years.

BODY DYSMORPHIC DISORDER People who experience **body dysmorphic disorder,** also known as **dysmorphophobia,** become deeply concerned about some imagined or minor defect in their appearance. Most often, they focus on wrinkles, spots on the skin, excessive facial hair, swelling of the face, or a misshapen nose, mouth, jaw, or eyebrow. Some worry about the appearance of their feet, hands, breasts, penis, or other body parts. Still others are concerned about bad odors coming from sweat, breath, genitals, or the rectum (Neziroglu, 1998; Marks, 1987).

It is common in our society to worry about appearance. Many teenagers and young adults worry about acne, for instance. The concerns of people with body dysmorphic disorder, however, are extreme. Sufferers may be unable to look others in the eye, or they may go to great lengths to conceal their "defects"—say, always wearing sunglasses to hide their supposedly misshapen eyes. Some seek plastic surgery (Hollander & Aronowitz, 1999). One study found that 30 percent of subjects with the disorder were housebound and 17 percent had attempted suicide (Phillips et al., 1993).

Most cases of the disorder begin during adolescence. Often, however, people don't reveal their concerns for many years. Up to 2 percent of people in the United States suffer from body dysmorphic disorder (Hollander & Aronowitz, 1999). Clinical reports suggest that it may be equally common among men and women (APA, 2000).

What Causes Somatoform Disorders?

Theorists typically explain the preoccupation somatoform disorders much as they do anxiety disorders (Noyes, 2001, 1999). Behaviorists, for example, believe that the fears found in hypochondriasis and body dysmorphic disorder have been acquired earlier in life through classical conditioning or modeling (Whitehead et al., 1994) (see Figure 8-2). Cognitive theorists suggest that people with the disorders are so sensitive to and threatened by bodily cues that they come to overinterpret them (Salkovskis & Warwick, 2001; Marcus, 1999).

In contrast, the hysterical somatoform disorders—conversion, somatization, and pain disorders—are widely considered unique and in need of special explanations. The ancient Greeks believed that only women had hysterical disorders. The uterus of a sexually ungratified woman was supposed to wander throughout her body in search of fulfillment, producing a physical symptom wherever it lodged. Thus Hippocrates suggested marriage as the most effective treatment for such disorders. Today's leading explanations for hysterical somatoform disorders come from the psychodynamic, behavioral, and cognitive models. None has received strong research support, however, and the disorders are still poorly understood (Lautenbacher & Rollman, 1999; Kirmayer, Robbins, & Paris, 1994).

THE PSYCHODYNAMIC VIEW As we observed in Chapter 1, Freud's theory of psychoanalysis began with his efforts to explain hysterical symptoms. Indeed, he was one of the few clinicians of his day to treat patients with these symptoms seriously, as people with a genuine problem. After studying hypnosis in Paris, Freud became interested in the work of an older physician, Josef Breuer (1842–1925). Breuer had successfully used hypnosis to treat a woman he called Anna O., who suffered from hysterical deafness, disorganized speech, and paralysis. Critics have since questioned

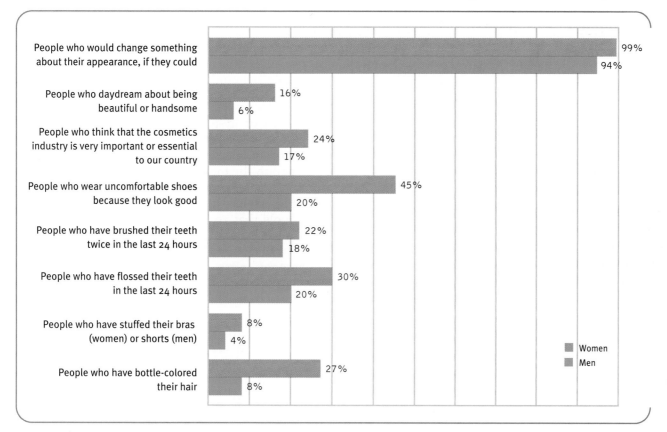

	Women	Men
People who would change something about their appearance, if they could	99%	94%
People who daydream about being beautiful or handsome	16%	6%
People who think that the cosmetics industry is very important or essential to our country	24%	17%
People who wear uncomfortable shoes because they look good	45%	20%
People who have brushed their teeth twice in the last 24 hours	22%	18%
People who have flossed their teeth in the last 24 hours	30%	20%
People who have stuffed their bras (women) or shorts (men)	8%	4%
People who have bottle-colored their hair	27%	8%

whether Anna's ailments were entirely hysterical and whether Breuer's treatment helped her as much as he claimed (Ellenberger, 1972). But on the basis of this and similar cases, Freud (1894) came to believe that hysterical disorders represented a *conversion* of underlying emotional conflicts into physical symptoms.

Observing that most of his patients with hysterical disorders were women, Freud centered his explanation of hysterical disorders on the needs and conflicts experienced by girls during their *phallic stage* (ages 3 through 5). At that time in life, he believed, all girls develop a pattern of desires called the *Electra complex*: each girl experiences sexual feelings for her father and, at the same time, recognizes that she must compete with her mother for his affection. However, aware of her mother's more powerful position and of cultural taboos, the child typically represses her sexual feelings and rejects these early desires for her father.

Freud believed that if a child's parents overreact to her sexual feelings—with strong punishments, for example—the Electra conflict will be unresolved and the child may reexperience sexual anxiety throughout her life. Whenever events trigger sexual feelings, she may experience an unconscious need to hide them from both herself and others. Freud concluded that some women hide their sexual feelings by unconsciously converting them into physical symptoms.

Most of today's psychodynamic theorists take exception to Freud's explanation of hysterical disorders, particularly his notion that the disorders can always be traced to an unresolved Electra conflict. They continue to believe, however, that sufferers of these disorders have unconscious conflicts carried forth from childhood which arouse anxiety and that the individuals convert this anxiety into "more tolerable" physical symptoms (Roth, 2000; Stuart & Noyes, 1999).

Psychodynamic theorists propose that two mechanisms are at work in hysterical somatoform disorders—primary gain and secondary gain. People achieve **primary gain** when their hysterical symptoms keep their internal conflicts out of awareness. During an argument, for example, a man who has underlying fears about expressing anger may develop a conversion paralysis of the arm, thus preventing his feelings of rage from reaching consciousness. People achieve **secondary gain** when their hysterical symptoms further enable them to avoid

FIGURE 8-2 **"Mirror, mirror, on the wall . . ."** *People with body dysmorphic disorder are not the only ones who have concerns about their appearance. Surveys find that in our appearance-conscious society, large percentages of people regularly think about and try to change the way they look (Kimball, 1993; Poretz & Sinrod, 1991; Weiss, 1991; Simmon, 1990).*

BODY DYSMORPHIC DISORDER A somatoform disorder marked by excessive worry that some aspect of one's physical appearance is defective. Also known as *dysmorphophobia*.

PRIMARY GAIN In psychodynamic theory, the gain achieved when hysterical symptoms keep internal conflicts out of awareness.

SECONDARY GAIN In psychodynamic theory, the gain achieved when hysterical symptoms elicit kindness from others or provide an excuse to avoid unpleasant activities.

Young-Wolff/PhotoEdit

Electra complex goes awry *Freud argued that a hysterical disorder may result when parents overreact to their daughter's early displays of affection for her father. The child may go on to exhibit sexual repression in adulthood and convert sexual feelings into physical ailments.*

unpleasant activities or to receive kindness or sympathy from others. When, for example, a conversion paralysis allows a soldier to avoid combat duty or conversion blindness prevents the breakup of a relationship, secondary gain may be operating. Both forms of gain help to lock in the conversion symptoms.

THE BEHAVIORAL VIEW Behavioral theorists propose that the physical symptoms of hysterical disorders bring *rewards* to sufferers (see Table 8-4). Perhaps the symptoms remove the individuals from an unpleasant work situation or relationship or bring attention to the individuals (Whitehead et al., 1994; Ullmann & Krasner, 1975). In response to such rewards, the sufferers learn to display the symptoms more and more. Behaviorists also hold that people who are familiar with an illness will more readily adopt its physical symptoms (Garralda, 1996). In fact, studies find that many sufferers develop their hysterical symptoms after they or their close relatives or friends have had similar medical problems (Stuart & Noyes, 1999).

The behavioral focus on rewards is similar to the psychodynamic idea of secondary gains. The key difference is that psychodynamic theorists view the gains as indeed secondary—that is, as rewards that come only after underlying conflicts produce the disorder. Behaviorists view them as the primary cause of the development of the disorder.

Like the psychodynamic explanation, the behavioral view of hysterical disorders has received little support from empirical research. Even clinical case reports only occasionally support this position. In many cases the pain and upset that surround the disorders seem to outweigh any rewards the symptoms may bring.

THE COGNITIVE VIEW Some cognitive theorists propose that hysterical disorders are forms of *communication,* providing a means for people to express emotions that would otherwise be difficult to state (Sundbom et al., 1999; Lipowski, 1987). Like their psychodynamic colleagues, these theorists hold that the emotions of patients with hysterical disorders are being converted into physical symptoms. They suggest, however, that the purpose of the conversion is not to defend against anxiety but to communicate extreme feelings—anger, fear, depression, guilt, jealousy—in a "physical language" that is familiar to the patient and therefore comfortable (Fry, 1993; Barsky & Klerman, 1983).

Table 8-4

Disorders That Have Physical Symptoms

DISORDER	VOLUNTARY CONTROL OF SYMPTOMS?	SYMPTOMS LINKED TO PSYCHOSOCIAL FACTOR?	AN APPARENT GOAL?
Malingering	Yes	Maybe	Yes
Factitious disorder	Yes	Yes	No*
Somatoform disorder	No	Yes	Maybe
Psychophysiological disorder	No	Yes	Maybe
Physical illness	No	Maybe	No

*Except for medical attention.

Source: Adapted from Hyler & Spitzer, 1978.

Cultural Dysmorphophobia?

People almost everywhere want to be attractive, and they tend to worry about how they appear in the eyes of others. At the same time, these concerns take different forms in different cultures.

Whereas people in Western society worry in particular about their body size and facial features, women of the Padaung tribe in Burma focus on the length of their neck and wear heavy stacks of brass rings to try to extend it. Although many such women are trying to make money as a tourist attraction, others are seeking desperately to achieve what their culture has taught them is the perfect neck size. Said one, "It is most beautiful when the neck is really long. The longer it is, the more beautiful it is. I will never take off my rings . . . I'll be buried in them" (Mydans, 1996).

ConsiderThis

⦿ How might a culture help create individual cases of body dysmorphic disorder (dysmorphophobia)? • Why do some people in a society carry cultural ideals to an extreme, while others stay within normal bounds?

Steve McCurry/Magnum Photo

According to this view, people who find it particularly hard to recognize or express their emotions are candidates for a hysterical disorder, especially when they are in the midst of relationship difficulties. So are those who "know" the language of physical symptoms through firsthand experience with a genuine physical problem either in themselves or in a relative or friend. Because children have less ability to express their emotions verbally, they are particularly likely to develop physical symptoms as a form of communication (Garralda, 1996). Like the other explanations, however, this cognitive view has not been widely tested or supported by research.

How Are Somatoform Disorders Treated?

People with somatoform disorders usually seek psychotherapy only as a last resort (Asaad, 2000). They fully believe that their problems are medical and at first reject all suggestions to the contrary. When a physician tells them that their problems have no physical basis, they simply go to another physician. Eventually, however, many patients with these disorders do turn to psychotherapy.

Individuals with preoccupation somatoform disorders typically receive the kinds of treatment that are applied to anxiety disorders (Warwick & Salkovskis, 2001; Foa & Franklin, 1999). In one study, more than half of patients with body

SOMATIC PREDICTORS

According to a Canadian study, young teenagers with a somatization-like pattern are more likely than their peers to experience major depressive or panic disorder within the next four years. The somatic symptoms are as predictive of these disorders as are emotional symptoms (Zwaigenbaum et al., 1999).

"He didn't really die of anything. He was a hypochondriac."

dysmorphic disorder improved considerably when treated with *selective serotonin reuptake inhibitors,* the antidepressant drugs that are also helpful in cases of obsessive-compulsive disorder (Albertini & Phillips, 1999). In another study, 17 patients with body dysmorphic disorder were treated with *exposure and response prevention*—the behavioral approach that often helps persons with obsessive-compulsive disorder. Over the course of four weeks, the clients were repeatedly reminded of their perceived physical defects and prevented from doing anything (for example, checking their appearance) to help reduce their discomfort (Neziroglu et al., 1996). By the end of treatment, they were less concerned with their "defects" and spent less time checking their body parts, looking in the mirror, and avoiding social interactions. The effectiveness of such approaches, however, has yet to be tested widely (Phillips, 2000).

People with hysterical somatoform disorders are typically treated with approaches that emphasize either insight, suggestion, reinforcement, or confrontation. A commonly applied *insight* approach has been psychodynamic therapy, which helps people become conscious of and overcome their anxiety-arousing conflicts, theoretically eliminating the need to convert anxiety into physical symptoms. Therapists who employ *suggestion* offer emotional support to patients and tell them persuasively that their physical symptoms will soon disappear (Anooshian, Streltzer, & Goebert, 1999), or they suggest the same thing to them under hypnosis (Moene & Hoogduin, 1999). Therapists who take a *reinforcement* approach arrange the removal of rewards for a client's "sick" behavior and an increase of rewards for healthy behaviors (Campo & Negrini, 2000). Finally, therapists who take a *confrontational* approach attempt to force patients out of the sick role by straightforwardly telling them that their symptoms are without medical basis (Brady & Lind, 1961).

Researchers have not fully studied the effects of these various forms of treatment on hysterical disorders (Lock & Giammona, 1999). Case studies suggest, however, that conversion disorder and pain disorder respond better to therapy than does somatization disorder and that approaches using insight, suggestion, and reinforcement bring more lasting improvement than the confrontation strategy. A growing number of today's physicians and psychiatrists have also begun to use antidepressant medications to treat people with hysterical disorders, particularly those with a pain disorder (Fishbain et al., 1998).

ConsiderThis

◉ In the past, physicians failed to recognize that psychosocial factors often contribute to physical illness. Some observers now fear that today there may be too much emphasis on such factors. What problems might result from an overemphasis on the role of psychosocial factors in physical illness?

SUMMING UP | **Somatoform Disorders**

Patients with somatoform disorders have physical complaints whose causes are largely psychosocial. Unlike people with a factitious disorder, these sufferers believe that their illnesses are organic.

Hysterical Somatoform Disorders Hysterical somatoform disorders involve the actual loss or change of physical functioning. They include conversion disorder, somatization disorder (or Briquet's syndrome), and pain disorder associated with psychological factors.

Preoccupation Somatoform Disorders People with preoccupation somatoform disorders are gravely concerned that something is wrong with them physically. In this category are hypochondriasis and body dysmorphic disorder.

Explanations and Treatment Theorists explain preoccupation somatoform disorders much as they do anxiety disorders. Correspondingly, treatments for these disorders include exposure and response prevention and other treatments from the realm of anxiety disorders. In contrast, hysterical somatoform disorders are viewed as unique disorders that are still poorly understood. Treatments for them emphasize either insight, suggestion, reinforcement, or confrontation.

Psychophysiological Disorders

About 75 years ago clinicians identified a group of physical illnesses that seemed to result from an *interaction* of psychosocial and physical factors (Dunbar, 1948; Bott, 1928). These illnesses differed from somatoform disorders in that both psychosocial *and* physical factors helped cause them and the illnesses further brought about actual physical damage. Whereas early versions of the DSM labeled these illnesses **psychophysiological,** or **psychosomatic, disorders,** DSM-IV labels them *psychological factors affecting medical condition* (see Table 8-5). We shall use the more familiar term "psychophysiological" in discussing them.

Traditional Psychophysiological Disorders

Before the 1970s, clinicians believed that only a limited number of illnesses were psychophysiological. The best known and most common of these were ulcers, asthma, insomnia, chronic headaches, high blood pressure, and coronary heart disease. Recent research, however, has shown that many other physical illnesses—including bacterial and viral infections—may be caused by an interaction of psychosocial and physical factors. We will look first at the traditional psychophysiological disorders and then the newer illnesses in this category.

Ulcers are lesions (holes) that form in the wall of the stomach or of the duodenum, resulting in burning sensations or pain in the stomach, occasional vomiting, and stomach bleeding. This disorder is experienced by up to 10 percent of all people in the United States and is responsible for more than 6,000 deaths each year. Ulcers are often caused by an interaction of psychosocial factors, such as environmental stress, intense feelings of anger or anxiety, or a dependent personality style (Overmier & Murison, 2000; Weiner et al., 1957), and physiological factors, such as bacterial infections (Levenstein, 2000).

Asthma causes the body's airways (the trachea and bronchi) to narrow periodically, making it hard for air to pass to and from the lungs (Simeonsson et al., 1995). The resulting symptoms are shortness of breath, wheezing, coughing, and a terrifying choking sensation. Some 15 million people in the United States suffer from asthma, twice as many as 15 years ago (NCHS, 1999). Most victims are children or young teenagers at the time of the first attack (DeAngelis, 1994). Seventy percent of all cases appear to be caused by an interaction of psychosocial factors, such as environmental pressures, troubled family relationships, anxiety, or high dependency needs, and physiological factors, such as allergies to specific substances, a slow-acting sympathetic nervous system, or a weakened respiratory system (Lehrer, 1998; Godding, Kruth, & Jamart, 1997).

PSYCHOPHYSIOLOGICAL DISORDERS Illnesses that result from an interaction of psychosocial and organic factors. Also known as *psychosomatic disorders.*

ULCER A lesion that forms in the wall of the stomach or of the duodenum.

ASTHMA A medical problem marked by narrowing of the trachea and bronchi, which results in shortness of breath, wheezing, coughing, and a choking sensation.

Treating asthma *Children who suffer from asthma may use an aerochamber, or inhaler, to help them inhale helpful medications. The child pumps the medication into the device's plastic tube and then inhales it.*

Lester Sloan/Woodfin Camp & Associates

Table 8-5 DSM-IV Checklist

PSYCHOLOGICAL FACTORS AFFECTING GENERAL MEDICAL CONDITION

1. The presence of a general medical condition.
2. Psychological factors adversely affecting the general medical condition in one of the following ways:
   (a) Influencing the course of the general medical condition.
   (b) Interfering with the treatment of the general medical condition.
   (c) Posing additional health risks.
   (d) Stress-related physiological responses precipitating or exacerbating the general medical condition.

Based on APA, 2000, 1994.

"When the heart is at ease, the body is healthy."

Chinese proverb

INSOMNIA Difficulty falling or staying asleep.

MUSCLE CONTRACTION HEADACHE A headache caused by the narrowing of muscles surrounding the skull. Also known as *tension headache.*

MIGRAINE HEADACHE An extremely severe headache that occurs on one side of the head, often preceded by a warning sensation and sometimes accompanied by dizziness, nausea, or vomiting.

HYPERTENSION Chronic high blood pressure.

CORONARY HEART DISEASE Illness of the heart caused by a blocking of the coronary arteries.

DISREGULATION MODEL A theory that explains psychophysiological disorders as breakdowns in the body's negative feedback loops, which lead to interruption of the body's smooth, self-regulating operation.

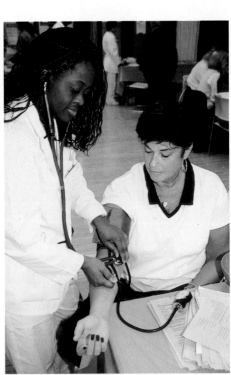

The silent killer *High blood pressure, a psychophysiological disorder with few outward signs, kills tens of thousands of people each year, prompting health-care professionals to regularly provide free blood pressure checks in the workplace or other community settings.*

Insomnia, difficulty falling asleep or maintaining sleep, affects 20 to 45 percent of the population each year (APA, 2000; Mendelson et al., 1999). Although many of us have temporary bouts of insomnia that last a few nights or so, a large number of people experience insomnia that lasts months or years. They feel as though they are almost constantly awake. Chronic insomniacs are often very sleepy during the day and may have difficulty functioning effectively. Their problem may be caused by a combination of psychosocial factors, such as high levels of anxiety or depression, and physiological problems, such as an overactive arousal system or certain medical ailments (Hauri, 2000; Mendelson et al., 1999).

Chronic headaches are frequent intense aches of the head or neck that are not caused by another physical disorder. There are two types. **Muscle contraction,** or **tension, headaches** are identified by pain at the back or front of the head or the back of the neck. These occur when the muscles surrounding the skull tighten, narrowing the blood vessels. Approximately 40 million Americans suffer from such headaches. **Migraine headaches** are extremely severe, often near-paralyzing aches located on one side of the head. They are often preceded by a warning sensation called an *aura* and are sometimes accompanied by dizziness, nausea, or vomiting. Migraine headaches are thought by some medical theorists to develop in two phases: (1) blood vessels in the brain narrow, so that the flow of blood to parts of the brain is reduced; and (2) the same blood vessels later expand, so that blood flows through them rapidly, stimulating many neuron endings and causing pain. Migraines are suffered by about 23 million people in the United States.

Research suggests that chronic headaches are caused by an interaction of psychosocial factors, such as environmental pressures, a passive personality style, or general feelings of helplessness, anger, anxiety, or depression (McGrath & Hillier, 2001), and physiological factors, such as abnormal activity of the neurotransmitter serotonin, vascular problems, or muscle weakness (Hargreaves & Shepheard, 1999; Park, 1996).

Hypertension is a state of chronic high blood pressure. That is, the blood pumped through the body's arteries by the heart produces too much pressure against the artery walls. Hypertension has few outward symptoms (Fahrenberg et al., 1995), but it interferes with the proper functioning of the entire cardiovascular system, greatly increasing the likelihood of stroke, coronary heart disease, and kidney problems. It is estimated that 40 million people in the United States have hypertension, 14,000 die directly from it annually, and millions more perish because of illnesses caused by it (NCHS, 1999; Johnson, Gentry, & Julius, 1992). Fewer than 15 percent of all cases are caused by physiological abnormalities alone; the rest result from a combination of psychosocial and physiological factors and are called *essential hypertension* (McDaniel et al., 1994). Some of the leading psychosocial causes of essential hypertension are constant environmental danger, general feelings of anger or depression, and an unexpressed need for power (Gidron, Davidson, & Bata, 1999; Dubbert, 1995). Physiological causes include faulty *baroreceptors*—sensitive nerves in the blood vessels responsible for signaling the brain that blood pressure is becoming too high (Julius, 1992; Schwartz, 1977).

Coronary heart disease is caused by a blocking of the *coronary arteries*—the blood vessels that surround the heart and are responsible for carrying oxygen to the heart muscle. The term actually refers to several problems, including partial or complete blockage of the coronary arteries and *myocardial infarction* (a "heart attack"). Together such problems are the leading cause of death in men over the age of 35 and of women over 40 in the United States, accounting for over 700,000 deaths each year, almost one-third of all deaths in the nation (Blanchard, 1994). The majority of all cases of coronary heart disease are related to an interaction of psychosocial factors, such as job stress or high levels of anger or depression, and physiological factors, such as a high level of cholesterol, obesity, hypertension, the effects of smoking, or lack of exercise (Sher, 2000; Gallacher et al., 1999).

DISREGULATION AND PSYCHOPHYSIOLOGICAL DISORDERS By definition, psychophysiological disorders are caused by an interaction of psychosocial and physical factors. How do these factors combine to produce a given illness? Gary Schwartz, a leading researcher, has proposed the **disregulation model** to answer this question (see Figure 8-3). Schwartz (1982, 1977) suggests that the brain and body ordinarily set up *negative feedback* loops that guarantee smooth operation of the body. The brain receives information about events from the environment, processes this information, and then stimulates body organs to act. Mechanisms in the organs then provide critical negative feedback, telling the brain that its stimulation has been sufficient and should now stop.

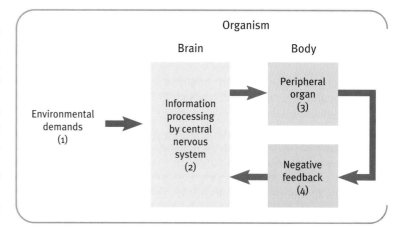

FIGURE 8-3   Negative feedback loop
According to Schwartz's disregulation model, in the normal process of regulation the organism receives environmental pressure (1); the brain processes information about this pressure (2); the brain stimulates body organs into action (3); and the organs provide negative feedback to the brain, sending the message that the stimulation has been sufficient and should stop (4). (Adapted from Schwartz, 1977.)

A typical feedback loop is the one that governs blood pressure (Egan, 1992; Julius, 1992). In one part of the loop the brain receives information that dangers exist in the environment, such as nearby lightning or cars speeding by. In the next part of the loop, the brain processes this information and alerts the nervous system, which causes bodily organs to raise blood pressure. In a subsequent part of the loop, *baroreceptors,* the pressure-sensitive cells in the body's blood vessels, alert the nervous system when the blood pressure rises too high, and the nervous system then lowers the blood pressure. In short, the various parts of the feedback loop work together to help keep blood pressure at a proper level.

According to Schwartz, if one part of a feedback loop fails to operate properly, the body will enter a state of *disregulation,* problems will occur throughout the loop, and a psychophysiological disorder may ultimately develop. Hypertension, for example, may result from a problem in any part of the blood-pressure feedback loop. Should information from the environment be excessive (as when one is faced with continuous job stress or long-term unemployment), should the processing of information be mistaken (as when one keeps misinterpreting everyday events), should an organ malfunction (as when the aorta narrows abnormally), or should a feedback mechanism fail (as when baroreceptors fail to inform the brain that blood pressure is rising too high), inaccurate messages will be fed to the next part of the loop and then relayed to the next, until every part in the loop has been alerted to keep the blood pressure high (Landsbergis et al., 1994).

WHAT FACTORS CONTRIBUTE TO PSYCHOPHYSIOLOGICAL DISORDERS? Over the years, clinicians have identified sociocultural, psychological, and biological variables that may contribute to disregulation and to the development of psychophysiological disorders. Some are particularly common.

SOCIOCULTURAL FACTORS The stressful demands placed on people by their culture or social group may lead to disregulation and set the stage for psychophysiological disorders. The stress may be wide-ranging, such as that produced by wars or natural disasters. After a 1979 nuclear accident at Three Mile Island in Pennsylvania, for example, people who lived near the nuclear plant experienced a high number of psychophysiological disorders, and they continued to do so for years (Schneiderman & Baum, 1992; Baum et al., 1983). Alternatively, local social conditions may produce persistent feelings of tension, such as life in a crime-ridden neighborhood or working in an unsatisfying job (Landsbergis et al., 1994). For example, hypertension is twice as common among African Americans as among white Americans (Johnson et al., 1992). Although physiological factors may largely explain this difference, some theorists believe that it is also linked to the dangerous environments in which so many African Americans live, the unsatisfying jobs at which so many must work, and the racial discrimination most face (Clark et al., 1999; Dorr, 1999).

Risky business *A currency dealer shouts orders during trading at the Paris Stock Exchange. The stresses of working in high-pressure environments apparently increase one's risk of developing a medical illness, including coronary heart disease.*

Lionel Cihes/AP/Wide World Photos

Sleep and Sleep Disorders: Another Mind-Body Connection

Sleep, a physical activity crucial to health and well-being, is affected by both physical and psychosocial factors. Sleep deprivation for 100 hours or more leads to hallucinations, paranoia, and bizarre behavior. When people remain awake for over 200 hours, they frequently experience periods of "microsleep," naps lasting two to three seconds. The body simply refuses to be entirely deprived of sleep for long.

To learn more about sleep, researchers bring people into the laboratory and record their activities as they sleep, using various kinds of recording devices. One important discovery has been that eyes move rapidly about 25 percent of the time a person is asleep (Aserinsky & Kleitman, 1953), a phenomenon known as *rapid eye movement,* or *REM.* REM sleep is often called "paradoxical sleep" because it resembles both deep sleep and wakefulness. Despite small movements and muscle twitches, the body is immobilized—almost paralyzed. At the same time, the eyes are darting back and forth, blood flow to the brain increases, and brain-wave activity is almost identical to that of an awake and alert person. Eighty percent of subjects who are awakened from REM sleep report that they were dreaming.

DSM-IV identifies a number of sleep disorders. Like psychophysiological disorders, most of them result from an interaction of physical and psychosocial causes. The *dyssomnias* are sleep disorders that involve disturbances in the amount, quality, or timing of sleep. The *parasomnias* involve abnormal events that occur during sleep.

Dyssomnias

Insomnia, difficulty falling or staying asleep, is the most common dyssomnia. For a diagnosis of *primary insomnia,* this problem must be the main complaint, last at least one month, and cause significant dysfunctioning (APA, 2000, 1994). Between 1 and 10 percent of all adults qualify for a diagnosis of primary insomnia each year. Contrasting with insomnia, *primary hypersomnia* is a dyssomnia marked by excessive sleepiness that lasts for at least a month. Sufferers may need extra hours of sleep each night and may need to sleep during the daytime as well (APA, 2000, 1994).

Narcolepsy, a disorder marked by more than three months of sudden bouts of REM sleep during waking hours, afflicts more than 135,000 people in the United States. Although narcolepsy is a biological disorder, the bouts of REM sleep are often triggered by strong emotion. Sufferers may fall into REM sleep in the midst of an argument or during an exciting part of a football game.

Breathing-related sleep disorder disrupts sleep by depriving the brain of oxygen. *Sleep apnea,* the most common form of this disorder, is found in up to 10 percent of the adult population (APA, 2000). Its victims, typically overweight men who are heavy snorers, actually

---

TYPE A PERSONALITY STYLE A personality pattern characterized by hostility, cynicism, drivenness, impatience, competitiveness, and ambition.

TYPE B PERSONALITY STYLE A personality pattern characterized by relaxation, less aggressiveness, and less concern about time.

PSYCHOLOGICAL FACTORS According to many theorists, certain needs, attitudes, emotions, or coping styles may cause people to overreact repeatedly to stressors, and so increase their chances of developing psychophysiological disorders (Smith, 2001). Researchers have found, for example, that men with a *repressive coping style* (a reluctance to express discomfort, anger, or hostility) tend to experience a particularly sharp rise in blood pressure and heart rate when they are stressed (Coy, 1998; NAMHC, 1996).

Another personality style that may contribute to psychophysiological disorders is the **Type A personality style,** an idea introduced by two cardiologists, Meyer Friedman and Raymond Rosenman (1959). People with this personality style are said to be consistently angry, cynical, driven, impatient, competitive, and ambitious. They interact with the world in a way that, according to Friedman and Rosenman, produces continual stress and often leads to coronary heart disease. People with a **Type B personality style,** by contrast, are thought to be more relaxed, less aggressive, and less concerned about time. They are less likely to experience cardiovascular deterioration. In reality, of course, most people fall between these two extremes, tending toward one or the other but showing features of both.

The link between the Type A personality style and coronary heart disease has been supported by many studies. In one well-known investigation of more than 3,000 people, Friedman and Rosenman (1974) separated healthy men in their 40s and 50s into Type A and Type B categories and then followed their health over the next eight years. More than twice as many Type A men developed coronary heart disease. Later studies found that Type A functioning relates similarly with heart disease in women (Haynes, Feinleib, & Kannel, 1980).

stop breathing for up to 30 seconds or more as they sleep. Hundreds of episodes may occur nightly without the victim's awareness.

People with *circadian rhythm sleep disorder* experience excessive sleepiness or insomnia as a result of a mismatch between their own sleep-wake pattern and the sleep-wake schedule of most other people in their environment. Often the disorder takes the form of falling asleep late and awakening late. This dyssomnia can result from night-shift work, frequent changes in work shifts, or repeated episodes of jet lag.

Parasomnias

Nightmare disorder is the most common of the parasomnias. Although most of us experience nightmares from time to time, in this disorder nightmares become frequent and cause such great distress that the individual must receive treatment. Such nightmares often increase under stress.

Persons with *sleep terror disorder* awaken suddenly during the first third of their evening sleep, screaming in extreme fear and agitation. They are in a state of panic, are often incoherent, and have a heart rate to match. Sleep terrors most often appear in children and disappear during adolescence.

Sleep, by George Tooker

People with a *sleepwalking disorder*—usually children—repeatedly leave their beds and walk around, without being conscious of the episode or remembering it later. The episodes occur in the first third of the night. People who are awakened while sleepwalking are confused for several moments. If allowed to continue sleepwalking, they eventually return to bed. Sleepwalkers usually manage to avoid obstacles, climb stairs, and perform complex activities, in a seemingly emotionless state. Accidents do happen, however: tripping, bumping into furniture, and even falling out of windows have all been reported. Sleepwalking usually disappears by age 15 (APA, 2000, 1994).

In recent studies the link found between the Type A personality style and heart disease has not been as strong as the earlier studies suggest. They do show, nevertheless, that some of the characteristics that supposedly make up the Type A style, particularly *hostility,* are very likely to be related to heart disease (Siegman et al., 2000; Gallacher et al., 1999).

BIOLOGICAL FACTORS We saw in Chapter 2 that the brain activates body organs through the operation of the *autonomic nervous system (ANS),* the network of nerve fibers that connect the central nervous system to the body's organs. If we see a frightening animal, for example, a group of ANS fibers known as the *sympathetic nervous system* increases its activity. As the danger passes, another group of ANS fibers, the *parasympathetic nervous system,* takes over to counter the activity of the ANS, causing our heartbeat, respiration, and other bodily functions to return to normal. These two parts of the ANS are constantly working in opposition to help our bodies operate in a smooth and stable manner (Selye, 1976; Cannon, 1927). Defects in the ANS are believed to contribute to the development of psychophysiological disorders. If one's ANS is stimulated too easily, for example, it may overreact to situations that most people find only mildly stressful, eventually damaging certain organs and causing a psychophysiological disorder (Boyce et al., 1995; Hugdahl, 1995).

Other more specific biological problems may also contribute to psychophysiological disorders. A person with a weak gastrointestinal system, for example, may be a prime candidate for an ulcer, whereas someone with a weak respiratory system may develop asthma readily. In a related vein, people may display individual biological reactions that heighten their chances of developing psychophysiological disorders (Fahrenberg, Foerster, & Wilmers, 1995). Some infants, for example, produce

WHITE COAT HYPERTENSION

A British study found that one-third of patients who had high blood pressure during a doctor's visit were merely experiencing a temporary rise, caused largely by nervousness about the visit or test (Lahiri et al., 1998). Their blood pressure dropped to near normal levels once they left the doctor's office.

ACID STOMACH

Each day the stomach produces as much as 3.5 pints (2 liters) of hydrochloric acid. Around 500,000 cells are replaced every minute so the acid will not damage the stomach walls (Ash, 1999).

much more gastric acid under stress than other infants (Weiner, 1977; Mirsky, 1958). Perhaps, over the years, this physical reaction wears down the lining of the stomach or duodenum, leaving the individuals more vulnerable to ulcers.

Clearly, sociocultural, psychological, and biological variables combine to produce psychophysiological disorders. The interaction of such variables to produce medical problems was once considered an unusual occurrence. According to the disregulation model, however, the interaction of psychosocial and physical factors is the rule of bodily functioning, not the exception, and as the years have passed, more and more illnesses have been added to the list of traditional psychophysiological disorders. Let us turn next to the "new" psychophysiological disorders.

New Psychophysiological Disorders

Since the 1960s, researchers have found many links between psychosocial stress and a wide range of physical illnesses. Let us look first at how these links were established and then at *psychoneuroimmunology,* the area of study that ties stress and illness to the body's immune system.

MEDICAL EXPENSES

The medical expenses of people who feel under constant stress are 46 percent higher than those of stress-free persons (Goetzel et al., 1998).

ARE PHYSICAL ILLNESSES RELATED TO STRESS? In 1967 two researchers, Thomas Holmes and Richard Rahe, developed the *Social Adjustment Rating Scale,* which assigns numerical values to the stresses that most people experience at some time in their lives (see Table 8-6). Answers given by a large sample of sub-

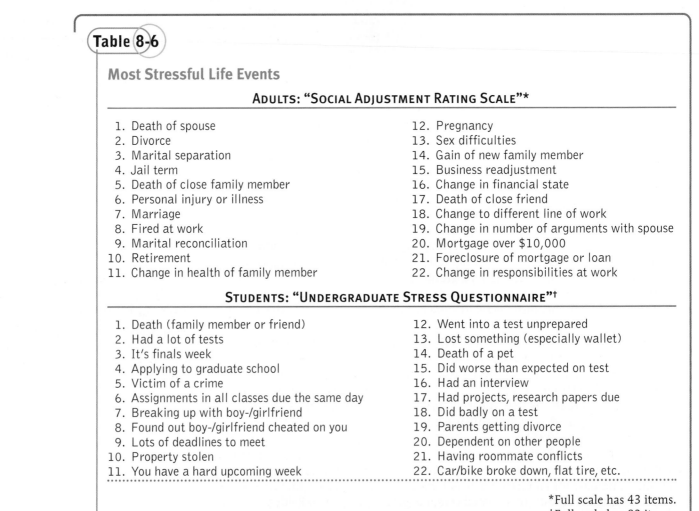

Table 8-6

Most Stressful Life Events

ADULTS: "SOCIAL ADJUSTMENT RATING SCALE"*

1. Death of spouse
2. Divorce
3. Marital separation
4. Jail term
5. Death of close family member
6. Personal injury or illness
7. Marriage
8. Fired at work
9. Marital reconciliation
10. Retirement
11. Change in health of family member
12. Pregnancy
13. Sex difficulties
14. Gain of new family member
15. Business readjustment
16. Change in financial state
17. Death of close friend
18. Change to different line of work
19. Change in number of arguments with spouse
20. Mortgage over $10,000
21. Foreclosure of mortgage or loan
22. Change in responsibilities at work

STUDENTS: "UNDERGRADUATE STRESS QUESTIONNAIRE"†

1. Death (family member or friend)
2. Had a lot of tests
3. It's finals week
4. Applying to graduate school
5. Victim of a crime
6. Assignments in all classes due the same day
7. Breaking up with boy-/girlfriend
8. Found out boy-/girlfriend cheated on you
9. Lots of deadlines to meet
10. Property stolen
11. You have a hard upcoming week
12. Went into a test unprepared
13. Lost something (especially wallet)
14. Death of a pet
15. Did worse than expected on test
16. Had an interview
17. Had projects, research papers due
18. Did badly on a test
19. Parents getting divorce
20. Dependent on other people
21. Having roommate conflicts
22. Car/bike broke down, flat tire, etc.

*Full scale has 43 items.
†Full scale has 83 items.
Source: Holmes & Rahe, 1967; Crandall et al., 1992.

jects indicated that the most stressful event on the scale should be the death of a spouse, which receives a score of 100 *life change units (LCUs)*. Lower on the scale is retirement (45 LCUs), and still lower is a minor violation of the law (11 LCUs). Even positive events, such as an outstanding personal achievement (28 LCUs), are somewhat stressful. This scale gave researchers a yardstick for measuring the total amount of stress a person faces over a period of time. If, for example, in the course of a year a businesswoman started a new business (39 LCUs), sent her son off to college (29 LCUs), moved to a new house (20 LCUs), and witnessed the death of a close friend (37 LCUs), her stress score for the year would be 125 LCUs, a considerable amount of stress for such a period of time.

With the Social Adjustment Rating Scale in hand, the researchers were able to examine the relationship between life stress and the onset of illness. They found that the LCU scores of sick people during the year before they fell ill were much higher than those of healthy people (Holmes & Rahe, 1989, 1967). If a person's life changes totaled more than 300 LCUs over the course of a year, that person was particularly likely to develop a serious health problem.

The Social Adjustment Rating Scale has been updated and revised by various researchers over the years (Hobson et al., 1998; Miller & Rabe, 1997). Using either the original or the revised scales, studies have linked stresses of various kinds to a wide range of physical conditions, from trench mouth and upper respiratory infection to cancer (Cobb & Steptoe, 1998; Kiecolt-Glaser et al., 1991). Overall, the greater the amount of life stress, the greater the likelihood of illness. Researchers even have found a relationship between traumatic stress and death. A particularly striking instance of death after severe psychological stress is seen in the following case:

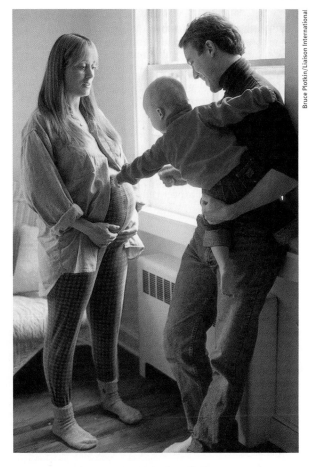

Joyful stress *According to the Social Adjustment Rating Scale, even positive events such as pregnancy are stressful for everyone involved.*

Charlie and Josephine had been inseparable companions for 13 years. In a senseless act of violence Charlie, in full view of Josephine, was shot and killed in a melee with police. Josephine first stood motionless, then slowly approached his prostrate form, sunk to her knees, and silently rested her head on the dead and bloody body. Concerned persons attempted to help her away, but she refused to move. Hoping she would soon surmount her overwhelming grief, they let her be. But she never rose again; in 15 minutes she was dead. Now the remarkable part of the story is that Charlie and Josephine were llamas in the zoo! They had escaped from their pen during a snow storm and Charlie, a mean animal to begin with, was shot when he proved unmanageable. I was able to establish from the zoo keeper that to all intents and purposes Josephine had been normally frisky and healthy right up to the moment of the tragic event.

(Engel, 1968)

One shortcoming of Holmes and Rahe's Social Adjustment Rating Scale is that it does not take into consideration the particular life stress reactions of specific populations. For example, recent studies have shown that women and men differ in their reactions to certain life changes on the scale (Miller & Rahe, 1997). Women, for example, tend to experience more stress than men when faced with the death of a close family member, loss of a job, a major injury or illness, a decrease in income, credit problems, or a change in residence. Similarly, college students may face stressors in their lives that are different from those listed in the scale. Instead of having marital difficulties, being fired, or applying for a job, a college student may have trouble with a roommate, fail a course, or apply to graduate school. When researchers developed special scales to measure life events more accurately in this population (see bottom half of Table 8-6), they found the expected relationships between stressful events and illness (Crandall et al., 1992).

ConsiderThis

⦿ The Social Adjustment Rating Scale has been criticized for assigning a specific number to each major life event. Why might this number fail to be a good indicator of the amount of stress the event actually causes for a particular individual?

PSYCHONEUROIMMUNOLOGY The study of the connections between stress, the body's immune system, and illness.

IMMUNE SYSTEM The body's network of activities and cells that identify and destroy antigens and cancer cells.

ANTIGEN A foreign invader of the body, such as a bacterium or virus.

LYMPHOCYTES White blood cells that circulate through the lymph system and bloodstream, helping the body identify and destroy antigens and cancer cells.

PSYCHONEUROIMMUNOLOGY How do stressful events result in a viral or bacterial infection? Researchers have increasingly looked to the body's immune system as the key to this relationship and have developed an area of study called **psychoneuroimmunology** to examine the links between psychosocial stress, the immune system, and health (Ader, Felton, & Cohen, 2001).

The **immune system** is the body's network of activities and cells that identify and destroy **antigens**—foreign invaders, such as bacteria, viruses, fungi, and parasites—and cancer cells (Cohen & Herbert, 1996). Among the most important cells in this system are billions of **lymphocytes,** white blood cells that circulate through the lymph system and the bloodstream. When stimulated by antigens, lymphocytes spring into action to help the body overcome the invaders.

One group of lymphocytes, called *helper T-cells,* identify antigens and then multiply and trigger the production of other kinds of immune cells. Another group, *natural killer T-cells,* seek out and destroy body cells that have already been infected by viruses, thus helping to stop the spread of a viral infection. A third group of lymphocytes, *B-cells,* produce *antibodies,* protein molecules that recognize and bind to antigens, target them for destruction, and prevent them from causing infection.

Researchers now believe that stress can interfere with the activity of lymphocytes, slowing them down and thus increasing a person's susceptibility to viral and bacterial infections (Ader et al., 2001). In a landmark study, R. W. Bartrop and his colleagues (1977) in New South Wales, Australia, compared the immune systems of 26 people whose spouses had died eight weeks earlier with those of 26 matched control subjects whose spouses had not died. Blood samples revealed that lymphocyte functioning was much lower in the bereaved people than in the controls. Still other studies have shown slow immune functioning in persons who are exposed to long-term stress. For example, researchers have found poorer immune functioning among people who face the challenge of providing ongoing care for a relative with Alzheimer's disease (Kiecolt-Glaser et al., 1996, 1991, 1987).

These studies seem to be telling a remarkable story. During periods when healthy individuals happened to experience unusual levels of stress, they remained healthy on the surface, but their experiences apparently slowed their immune systems so that they became susceptible to illness. If stress affects our capacity to fight off illness, it is no wonder that researchers have repeatedly found a relationship between life stress and illnesses of various kinds. But why and when does stress interfere with the immune system? Several factors influence whether stress will result in a slowdown of the system, including *biochemical activity, behavioral changes, personality style,* and *degree of social support.*

Killer T-cells at work *These killer T-cells surround a larger cancer cell and destroy it, thus helping to prevent the spread of cancer.*

BIOCHEMICAL ACTIVITY As we have seen, stress leads to increased activity by the sympathetic nervous system, including an increase in the release of the neurotransmitter *norepinephrine* throughout the brain and body. It appears that, beyond supporting the activity of the sympathetic nervous system, this chemical eventually helps slow the functioning of the immune system (Ader et al., 2001; McEwen, 2000). During low stress or early stages of stress, norepinephrine travels to certain lymphocyte receptors and gives a message for the lymphocytes to increase their activity. As the stress continues or heightens, however, the neurotransmitter travels to yet other receptors on the lymphocytes and gives them an *inhibitory message* to stop their activity. Thus, while the release of norepinephrine improves immune functioning at low levels of stress, it actually slows down immune functioning at higher levels.

Similarly, the body's endocrine glands reduce immune system functioning during periods of prolonged stress. Remember that under various circumstances, glands throughout the body release *hormones,* chemical messengers that propel

MARITAL STRESS

During and after marital spats, women typically experience a greater release of stress hormones than men, and so a greater decrease in immune functioning (Kiecolt-Glaser et al., 1996).

THE CURRENT SCENE

The Psychological Effects of HIV and AIDS

The *human immunodeficiency virus (HIV)* is a virus that invades certain cells and causes their death. The virus particularly infects *T-4 helper lymphocytes,* the immune cells that normally protect the body from disease by telling the rest of the immune system which invaders to kill (Richardson, 1997; Batchelor, 1988). The infected lymphocytes in turn carry the killer deep into the immune system, where it produces further destruction. In many cases, HIV develops into *acquired immune deficiency syndrome (AIDS),* a full-scale attack on the immune system.

Without treatment, the progression from HIV infection to AIDS may take weeks, months, or years (Barroso, 1999; Travis, 1996). In recent years, scientists have developed powerful combinations of drugs that can suppress the virus and greatly delay the onset of AIDS (Ostrow et al., 1999). Generally, however, much remains to be learned about how and why persons who are infected with HIV develop AIDS, whether slowly or rapidly. Most sufferers do not die of AIDS per se but instead fall victim to infections that would not survive in a healthy immune system. The psychological suffering of both people who are HIV-positive and people with AIDS is increasingly receiving attention from researchers and health-care workers (Roberts et al., 2001; Crystal & Schlosser, 1999).

Psychological disorders associated with HIV may be caused by factors that are primarily organic. The HIV may invade the brain, for example, causing *AIDS dementia complex (ADC),* a disease that can result in lack of energy, manic-depressive symptoms, and psychosis. More commonly, the disease is marked by a general decline in cognitive functioning—it takes longer to think or remember (Clifford, 2000; Brew, 1999). In a vicious cycle, the patient's psychological well-being declines, and this decline causes the immune system to weaken further.

Psychological problems of HIV sufferers may also result from sociocultural factors (Crystal & Schlosser, 1999; Kaplan, Marks, & Mertends, 1997). Society does not provide AIDS sufferers with a supportive environment in which to wage their war. Indeed, it attaches considerable stigma to the disease and to those who contract it. Surveys show that some people view AIDS as a proper punishment for gay men, intravenous drug users, and people who associate with them. Although experts agree that casual contact with AIDS sufferers does not lead to infection, prejudice and misunderstanding continue (Herek & Capitanio, 1999, 1997, 1994, 1993). Patients with HIV may face discrimination and harassment, along with loss of their jobs, health insurance, and police protection. Many victims must also deal with the loss of friends who die of AIDS and with others who reject them, along with the possibility of their own death. The stress can lead to apathy, depression, preoccupation with the illness, anxiety-related disorders, and other problems (Carels et al., 1998; Lyketsos et al., 1996). In a vicious cycle, all of these stressors can themselves affect the ability of the immune system to fight off the disease (Nott & Vedhara, 1999).

Some promising studies find that psychological treatments, particularly cognitive-behavioral stress management techniques, can help prevent or reduce the anxiety and depression in HIV sufferers and may even slow down progression of the disease (Inouye et al., 2001; Schneiderman, 1999; Lutgendorf et al., 1997). More generally, to reduce the psychological problems that accompany HIV and AIDS, society must give victims the support, compassion, and hope that is available to sufferers of other life-threatening illnesses. Only when sufferers are accepted as people deserving of help and understanding will their social environment serve to help their recovery rather than hasten their deaths.

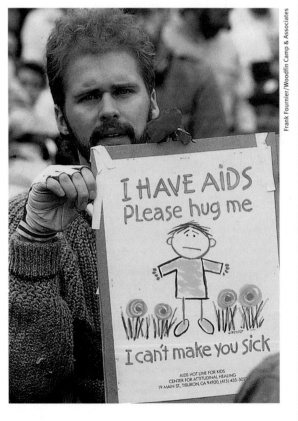

Frank Fournier/Woodfin Camp & Associates

body organs into action. When a person is under stress, the adrenal glands, which are located on top of the kidneys, release *corticosteroids*—cortisone and other so-called stress hormones. At first the body's release of the corticosteroids stimulates body organs to greater activity. After stress continues for 30 minutes or more, however, the stress hormones travel to certain receptor sites in the body and give inhibitory messages, which help calm down the overstressed body (Manuck et al., 1991). One such group of receptor sites is located on the

Laboratory insights *Laboratory animals are widely used in research on the immune system. The destruction of the immune systems of these mice, which has caused their hair to fall out, enables researchers to produce and investigate invasions by various cells and viruses.*

lymphocytes. When the corticosteroids bind to these receptors, their inhibitory messages actually slow down the activity of the lymphocytes (Bellinger et al., 1994). Thus, again, the very chemicals that initially help people to deal with stress eventually act to slow the immune system.

BEHAVIORAL CHANGES Stress may set in motion a series of behavioral changes that indirectly affect the immune system. Some people under intense or long-term stress may, for example, become anxious or depressed, perhaps even develop an anxiety or mood disorder. As a result, they may sleep badly, eat poorly, exercise less, or smoke or drink more—behaviors known to slow down the immune system (Kiecolt-Glaser & Glaser, 1999, 1988; Cohen & Herbert, 1996).

PERSONALITY STYLE An individual's personality style may also play a role in determining how much the immune system is slowed down by stress (Kemeny & Laudenslager, 1999). According to research, people who generally respond to life stress with optimism, constructive coping strategies, and resilience—that is, people who welcome challenge and are willing to take control in their daily encounters—experience better immune system functioning and are better prepared to fight off illness (Taylor et al., 2000; Lee et al., 1998). Some studies find, for example, that people with a so-called hardy personality remain healthy after stressful events, while those whose personalities are less hardy seem more susceptible to illness (Kobasa, 1990, 1987, 1984, 1982). One study even discovered that men with a general sense of hopelessness die at above-average rates from heart disease, cancer, and other causes (Everson et al., 1996) (see Figure 8-4).

FIGURE 8-4 **Warning: psychological disorders may be dangerous to your health** *Psychological disorders are themselves a source of stress that can lead to medical problems. People with such disorders are twice as likely to die of natural causes (medical illnesses) as people in the same age group without psychological difficulties. (Adapted from Harris & Barraclough, 1998.)*

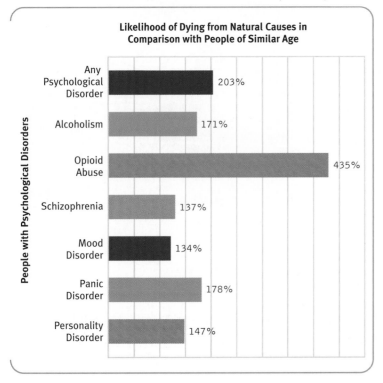

Likelihood of Dying from Natural Causes in Comparison with People of Similar Age

People with Psychological Disorders

- Any Psychological Disorder — 203%
- Alcoholism — 171%
- Opioid Abuse — 435%
- Schizophrenia — 137%
- Mood Disorder — 134%
- Panic Disorder — 178%
- Personality Disorder — 147%

In related work, some studies have noted a relationship between certain personality characteristics and recovery from cancer (Greer, 1999; Garssen & Goodkin, 1999). They have found that patients with certain forms of cancer who display a helpless coping style and who cannot easily express their feelings, particularly anger, tend to have less successful recoveries than patients who do express their emotions. Other studies, however, have found no relationship between personality and cancer outcome (Garssen & Goodkin, 1999; Holland, 1996).

SOCIAL SUPPORT Finally, people who have few social supports and feel lonely seem to display poorer immune functioning in the face of stress than people who do not feel lonely (Cohen & Herbert, 1996; Kiecolt-Glaser et al., 1988, 1987). In one study, medical students were given the *UCLA Loneliness Scale* and then divided into "high" and "low" loneliness groups (Kiecolt-Glaser et al., 1984). The high-loneliness group showed lower lymphocyte responses during a final exam period. Still other studies have found that social support and affiliation may actually help speed up a person's recovery from illness or surgery (Kiecolt-Glaser et al., 1998, 1991). And some studies have suggested that patients with certain forms of cancer

One More for the Road

*P*eople in Toronto are flocking to a new kind of bar, the O₂ Spa Bar. There they pay their hard-earned money for a 20-minute drink of fresh air. Customers hook up to oxygen tanks and inhale nearly pure oxygen. Patrons swear that repeated "drinks" of oxygen help them feel more energetic and less stressed. Many claim to be cured of everything from hangovers to hot flashes. Similar oxygen bars have been around for a while in Asian cities; only recently have they started catching on in North America.

ConsiderThis

⬤ Might a placebo effect be operating for at least some of the people who respond so positively to oxygen bars or other health-enhancement techniques? • Why do people in our society keep searching for new ways to bring about more pleasant physical or psychological states?

Peter Sterling, New York, NY

who receive social support in their personal lives or supportive therapy often have better immune system functioning and, in turn, more successful recoveries than patients without such supports (Spiegel & Classen, 2000; Garssen & Goodkin, 1999).

SUMMING UP Psychophysiological Disorders

Psychophysiological disorders are those in which psychosocial and physiological factors interact to cause a physical problem. These disorders have been explained by the disregulation model, which proposes that the brain and body ordinarily set up negative feedback loops that ensure the smooth operation of the body. When this system fails, psychophysiological problems may result.

Traditional Psychophysiological Disorders For years clinical researchers singled out a limited number of illnesses as psychophysiological. These traditional psychophysiological disorders include ulcers, asthma, chronic headaches, hypertension, and coronary heart disease.

New Psychophysiological Disorders Recently many other psychophysiological disorders have been identified. Scientists have linked many physical illnesses to stress and have developed a new area of study called psychoneuroimmunology.

The body's immune system consists of lymphocytes and other activities and cells that fight off antigens—bacteria, viruses, and other foreign invaders—and cancer cells. Stress can slow lymphocyte activity, thereby interfering with the immune system's ability to protect against illness during times of stress. Factors that seem to affect the immune system's functioning include norepinephrine and hormone activity, behavior changes, personality style, and social support.

SURGICAL RISK

People who experience more fear or stress before surgery tend to experience more pain and more complications after surgery and stay longer in the hospital (Kiecolt-Glaser et al., 1998).

PET PROTECTION

Elderly Americans who own a pet visit a physician an average of 8.42 times each year, compared to 9.49 for people without pets. Elderly dog owners see doctors the least of all: 8.2 visits per year (Spiegel, 1990).

Psychological Treatments for Physical Disorders

As clinicians have discovered that psychosocial factors may contribute to physical disorders, they have applied psychological treatments to more and more medical problems (Compas et al., 1998). The most common of these interventions are relaxation training, biofeedback training, meditation, hypnosis, cognitive interventions, insight therapy, and support groups. The field of treatment that combines psychological and physical interventions to treat or prevent medical problems is known as **behavioral medicine.**

BEHAVIORAL MEDICINE A field of treatment that combines psychological and physical interventions to treat or prevent medical problems.

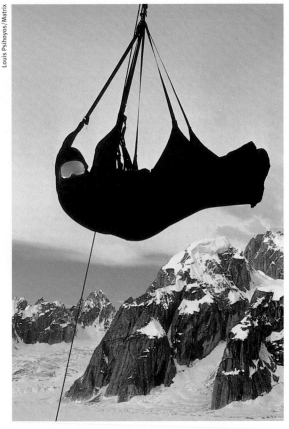

Relaxation, the hard way *Clinicians are always developing techniques to help people relax. A climber dangles from Alaska's Mount Barrile to demonstrate the use of "Tranquilite" sleep goggles, which are supposed to produce relaxation with blue light and a soothing "pink sound."*

Blocking out worldly events *In the past, meditation served as a pathway to enlightenment and spiritual awakening. Though still often used for such ends, today the technique is commonly employed by people who seek a better state of physical or psychological health.*

RELAXATION TRAINING As we saw in Chapter 4, people can be taught to relax their muscles at will, a process that sometimes reduces feelings of anxiety. Given the positive effects of relaxation on anxiety and the nervous system, clinicians believe that **relaxation training** can be of help in preventing or treating medical illnesses that are related to stress.

Relaxation training, often in combination with medication, has been widely used in the treatment of high blood pressure (Dubbert, 1995). It has also been of some help in treating headaches, insomnia, asthma, the undesirable effects of cancer treatments, pain after surgery, and Raynaud's disease, a disorder of the vascular system marked by throbbing, aching, and pain (Powers et al., 2001; Good et al., 1999).

BIOFEEDBACK TRAINING As we also have seen, patients given **biofeedback training** are connected to machinery that gives them continuous readings about their involuntary body activities. This information enables them gradually to gain control over those activities. Somewhat helpful in the treatment of anxiety disorders, the procedure has also been applied to a growing number of physical disorders.

In one study, *electromyograph (EMG)* feedback was used to treat sixteen patients who were experiencing facial pain caused in part by tension in their jaw muscles (Dohrmann & Laskin, 1978). In an EMG procedure, electrodes are attached to a person's muscles so that the muscle contractions are detected and converted into a tone for the individual to hear (see p. 112). Changes in the pitch and volume of the tone indicate changes in muscle tension. After "listening" to EMG feedback repeatedly, the sixteen patients in this study learned how to relax their jaw muscles at will and later reported a reduction in facial pain. In contrast, eight control subjects, who were wired to similar equipment but not given biofeedback training, showed little improvement in muscle tension or pain.

EMG feedback has also been used successfully in the treatment of headaches and muscular disabilities caused by strokes or accidents (Brauer, 1999; Blanchard, 1994). Still other forms of biofeedback training have been of some help in the treatment of heartbeat irregularities, asthma, migraine headaches, high blood pressure, stuttering, pain from burns, and Raynaud's disease (McGrath, 1999; Compas et al., 1998).

MEDITATION Although meditation has been practiced since ancient times, Western health-care professionals have only recently become aware of its effectiveness in relieving physical distress. **Meditation** is a technique of turning one's concentration inward, achieving a slightly changed state of consciousness, and temporarily ignoring all stressors. In the most common approach, meditators go to a quiet place, assume a comfortable posture, utter or think a particular sound (called a *mantra*) to help focus their attention, and allow their minds to turn away from all outside thoughts and concerns.

Many people who meditate regularly report feeling more peaceful, engaged, and creative (Carrington, 1993, 1978). Meditation has been used to help manage pain in cancer patients (Goleman & Gurin, 1993) and to help treat high blood pressure, heart problems, asthma, skin disorders, diabetes, and even viral infections (Andresen, 2000).

HYPNOSIS Individuals who undergo **hypnosis** are guided by a hypnotist into a sleeplike, suggestible state during which they can be directed to act in unusual ways, to experience unusual sensations, to remember seemingly forgotten events, or to forget remembered events. With training some people can even induce their own hypnotic state (*self-hypnosis*). Hypnosis is now used as an aid to psychotherapy and to help treat many physical conditions (Temes, 1999; Barber, 1993, 1984).

Hypnosis seems to be particularly helpful in the control of pain, whether caused by a medical condition or by medical procedures (Kiecolt-

Glaser et al., 1998). One case study describes a patient who underwent dental surgery under hypnotic suggestion: after a hypnotic state was produced, the dentist suggested to the patient that he was in a pleasant and relaxed setting listening to a friend describe his own success at undergoing similar dental surgery under hypnosis. The dentist then proceeded to perform a successful 25-minute operation (Gheorghiu & Orleanu, 1982). Although only some people are able to undergo surgery while anesthetized by hypnosis alone, hypnosis combined with chemical forms of anesthesia is apparently helpful to many patients (Fredericks, 2001). Beyond its use in the control of pain, hypnosis has been used successfully to help treat such problems as skin diseases, asthma, insomnia, high blood pressure, warts, and other forms of infection (Hackman et al., 2000; Hornyak et al., 2000).

Fighting HIV on all fronts *As part of his treatment at the Wellness Center in San Francisco, this man meditates and writes letters to his HIV virus.*

COGNITIVE INTERVENTIONS People with physical ailments have sometimes been taught new attitudes or cognitive responses toward their ailments as part of treatment (Compas et al., 1998; Kiecolt-Glaser et al., 1998). For example, **self-instruction training** has helped patients cope with severe pain, including pain from burns, arthritis, surgical procedures, headaches, back disorders, ulcers, multiple sclerosis, and cancer treatment (Meichenbaum, 1997, 1993, 1977, 1975; Vlaeyen et al., 1995). As we saw in Chapter 4, self-instruction therapists teach people to rid themselves of negative self-statements ("Oh, no, I can't take this pain") and to replace them with coping self-statements ("When pain comes, just pause; keep focusing on what you have to do").

INSIGHT THERAPY AND SUPPORT GROUPS If anxiety, depression, anger, and the like contribute to a person's physical ills, therapy to reduce these negative emotions should help reduce the ills. In such cases, physicians may recommend insight therapy, support groups, or both to help patients overcome their medical difficulties (Dobkin & DaCosta, 2000). Research suggests that the discussion of past and present upsets may indeed improve a person's health (Francis & Pennebaker, 1992). In one study, asthma and arthritis patients who simply wrote down their thoughts and feelings about stressful events for a handful of days showed lasting improvements in their conditions (Smyth et al., 1999). In addition, as we have seen, recovery from cancer and certain other illnesses is sometimes improved by participation in support groups (Spiegel & Diamond, 2001; Garssen & Goodkin, 1999).

VIRTUES OF LAUGHTER

After watching a humorous video, subjects who had laughed at and enjoyed the film showed decreases in stress and improvements in natural killer cell activity (Bennett, 1998).

COMBINATION APPROACHES Studies have found that the various psychological treatments for physical problems tend to be equal in effectiveness (Brauer, 1999; Newton et al., 1995). Relaxation and biofeedback training, for example, are equally helpful (and more helpful than placebos) in the treatment of high blood pressure, headaches, asthma, and Raynaud's disease. Psychological interventions are, in fact, often of greatest help when they are combined with other psychological interventions and with medical treatments (Hermann et al., 1995). In one study, ulcer patients who were given relaxation, self-instruction, and assertiveness training along with medication were found to be less anxious and more comfortable, to have fewer symptoms, and to have a better long-term outcome than patients who received medication only (Brooks & Richardson, 1980). Combination interventions have also been helpful in changing Type A behavior patterns and in reducing the risk of coronary heart disease among Type A people (Sebregts, Falger, & Baer, 2000; Cohen, Ardjoen, & Sewpersad, 1997).

Clearly, the treatment picture for physical illnesses has been changing markedly. While medical treatments continue to dominate, the use of psychological approaches is on the rise. Today's scientists and practitioners are traveling a course far removed from the mind-body dualism of centuries past.

RELAXATION TRAINING A treatment procedure that teaches clients to relax at will.

BIOFEEDBACK TRAINING A treatment technique in which a client receives information about physiological reactions as they occur and learns to control the reactions voluntarily.

MEDITATION A technique of turning one's concentration inward and achieving a slightly changed state of consciousness.

HYPNOSIS A sleeplike suggestible state during which a person can be directed to act in unusual ways, to experience unusual sensations, to remember seemingly forgotten events, or to forget remembered events.

SELF-INSTRUCTION TRAINING A treatment that teaches clients to use coping self-statements at times of stress or discomfort.

SUMMING UP ┐ Psychological Treatments for Physical Disorders

Behavioral medicine combines psychological and physical interventions to treat or prevent medical problems. Psychological approaches such as relaxation training, biofeedback training, meditation, hypnosis, cognitive techniques, insight therapy, and support groups are increasingly being included in the treatment of various medical problems.

CROSSROADS:
Expanding the Boundaries of Abnormal Psychology

Once considered outside the field of abnormal psychology, physical disorders are now seen as problems that fall squarely within its boundaries. Just as physical factors have long been recognized as playing a role in abnormal mental functioning, psychosocial events are now considered important contributors to abnormal physical functioning. In fact, many of today's clinicians believe that psychological and sociocultural factors contribute to the onset and course of virtually all physical ailments.

The number of studies devoted to this relationship has risen steadily during the past 30 years. What researchers once saw as a vague tie between stress and physical illness is now understood as a complex interaction of many variables. Such factors as life stress, individual psychological reactions, neurotransmitter activity, and slowdowns of the immune system are all recognized as contributors to disorders once considered purely physical.

Insights into the treatment of physical illnesses have been growing just as rapidly. Psychological approaches such as relaxation training and cognitive therapy are being applied more and more to physical ills, usually in combination with traditional medical treatments. Although such approaches have yielded only modest results so far, many clinicians are convinced that psychological interventions will become more and more important in the treatment of physical ailments.

"Under our holistic approach, Mr. Wyndot, we not only treat your symptoms, we also treat your dog."

While the increasing focus on psychosocial aspects of physical illness seems promising, perhaps even more exciting is the growing emphasis on the *interrelationship* of the social environment, the brain, and the rest of the body. Researchers have observed repeatedly that mental disorders are often best understood and treated when sociocultural, psychological, and biological factors are all taken into consideration. They now know that this interaction also helps explain medical problems. We are reminded that the brain is part of the body and that both are part of a social context. For better and for worse, the three are closely linked.

KEY TERMS

QUICK QUIZ

1. How does a factitious disorder differ from a somatoform disorder? pp. 218–220

2. What are the symptoms of each of the hysterical somatoform disorders? How do practitioners distinguish hysterical disorders from "true" medical problems? pp. 220–223

3. List the central features of each of the preoccupation somatoform disorders. pp. 223–224

4. What are the leading explanations and treatments for the somatoform disorders? How well does research support them? pp. 224–228

5. What are the key causes of ulcers, asthma, insomnia, headaches, hypertension, and coronary heart disease? pp. 229–230

6. What kinds of sociocultural, psychological, and biological factors appear to contribute to psychophysiological disorders? pp. 231–234

7. What kinds of links have been found between life stress and physical illnesses? What scale has helped researchers investigate this relationship? pp. 234–235

8. Describe the relationship between stress, the immune system, and physical illness. Explain the specific roles played by lymphocytes. pp. 236–238

9. Discuss how immune system functioning at times of stress may be affected by a person's biochemical activity, behavioral changes, personality style, and social support. pp. 236–239

10. What psychological treatments have been used to help treat physical illnesses? To which specific illnesses has each been applied? How effective are such approaches? pp. 239–242

CYBER STUDY

▲ *How do physical, psychological, and sociocultural factors combine to exacerbate pain?* ▲ *Observe pain interventions in action.* ▲ *See the impact of stress on judgment, emotions, job performance, and health.* ▲ *Compare body dysmorphic disorder with a compulsion to check oneself in the mirror and with eating disorders.*

SEARCH THE *FUNDAMENTALS OF ABNORMAL PSYCHOLOGY* CD-ROM FOR

▲ Chapter 8 video case and discussion
   "Fran"—Treating Chronic Pain

▲ Chapter 8 practice test and feedback

▲ Additional video cases and discussions
   "Claude & Claude"—Emotion, Stress, and Health
   "Jennifer"—Obsessive-Compulsive Disorder
   "Liz"—Bulimia Nervosa

LOG ON TO THE COMER WEB PAGE FOR

▲ Suggested Web links, research exercises, FAQ page, additional Chapter 8 practice test questions
   <www.worthpublishers.com/comer>

The Mind, Second Edition (WNET/Worth Publishers, 1999)

Eating Disorders

Janet Caldwell was . . . five feet, two inches tall and weighed 62 pounds. . . . Janet began dieting at the age of 12 when she weighed 115 pounds and was chided by her family and friends for being "pudgy." She continued to restrict her food intake over a two-year period, and as she grew thinner, her parents became increasingly more concerned about her eating behavior. . . .

Janet . . . felt that her weight problem began at the time of puberty. She said that her family and friends had supported her efforts to achieve a ten-pound weight loss when she first began dieting at age 12. Janet did not go on any special kind of diet. Instead, she restricted her food intake at meals, generally cut down on carbohydrates and protein intake, tended to eat a lot of salads, and completely stopped snacking between meals. At first, she was quite pleased with her progressive weight reduction, and she was able to ignore her feelings of hunger by remembering the weight loss goal she had set for herself. However, each time she lost the number of pounds she had set for her goal she decided to lose just a few more pounds. Therefore she continued to set new weight goals for herself. In this manner, her weight dropped from 115 pounds to 88 pounds during the first year of her weight loss regimen.

Janet felt that, in her second year of dieting, her weight loss had continued beyond her control. . . . She became convinced that there was something inside of her that would not let her gain weight. . . . Janet commented that although there had been occasions over the past few years when she had been fairly "down" or unhappy, she still felt driven to keep on dieting. As a result, she frequently went for walks, ran errands for her family, and spent a great deal of time cleaning her room and keeping it in a meticulously neat and unaltered arrangement.

When Janet's weight loss continued beyond the first year, her parents insisted that she see their family physician, and Mrs. Caldwell accompanied Janet to her appointment. Their family practitioner was quite alarmed at Janet's appearance and prescribed a high-calorie diet. Janet said that she often responded to her parents' entreaties that she eat by telling them that she indeed had eaten but they had not seen her do so. She often listed foods that she said she had consumed which in fact she had flushed down the toilet. She estimated that she only was eating about 300 calories a day.

(Leon, 1984, pp. 179-184)

It has not always done so, but Western society today equates thinness with health and beauty. In fact, in the United States, thinness has become a national obsession. Most of us are as preoccupied with how much we eat as with the taste and nutritional value of our food. Thus it is not surprising that during the past three decades we have also witnessed an increase in two eating disorders that have at their core a morbid fear of gaining weight (Gordon, 2000; Russell, 1995). Sufferers of *anorexia nervosa,* like Janet Caldwell, are convinced that they need to be extremely thin, and they lose so much weight that they may starve themselves to death. People with

"All philosophy in two words—sustain and abstain."

Epictetus (A.D. c. 55–c. 135)

bulimia nervosa go on frequent eating binges, during which they uncontrollably consume large quantities of food, then force themselves to vomit or take other extreme steps to keep from gaining weight.

The news media have published many reports about anorexic or bulimic behavior. One reason for the surge in public interest is the frightening medical effects that can result. The death in 1983 of Karen Carpenter, a popular singer and entertainer, from medical problems related to anorexia nervosa serves as a reminder. Another reason for concern is the disproportionate prevalence of these disorders among adolescent girls and young women (Russell, 1995).

Anorexia Nervosa

Janet Caldwell, 14 years old and in the eighth grade, displays many symptoms of **anorexia nervosa:** she refuses to maintain more than 85 percent of her normal body weight, intensely fears becoming overweight, has a distorted view of her weight and shape, and has stopped menstruating (see Table 9-1).

Like Janet, at least half of the people with anorexia nervosa reduce their weight by restricting their intake of food, a pattern called *restricting-type anorexia nervosa.* At first they tend to cut out sweets and fattening snacks and then, increasingly, other foods (APA, 2000, 1994). Eventually people with this kind of anorexia nervosa show almost no variability in diet. Others, however, lose weight by forcing themselves to vomit after meals or by abusing laxatives or diuretics, and they may even engage in eating binges, a pattern called *binge-eating/purging-type anorexia nervosa,* which we shall observe in more detail when we turn to bulimia nervosa (APA, 2000, 1994).

Approximately 90 to 95 percent of all cases of anorexia nervosa occur in females. Although the disorder can appear at any age, the peak age of onset is between 14 and 18 years (APA, 2000). Around 0.5 percent of all females in Western countries develop the disorder in their lifetime, and many more display at least some of its symptoms. It seems to be on the increase in North America, Europe, and Japan (Battle & Brownell, 1996; Szmukler & Patton, 1995).

Typically the disorder begins after a person who is slightly overweight or of normal weight has been on a diet. The escalation toward anorexia nervosa may follow a stressful event such as separation of parents, a move away from home, or an experience of personal failure (Gowers et al., 1996; Horesh et al., 1995). Although most victims recover, between 2 and 6 percent of them become so seriously ill that they die, usually from medical problems brought about by starvation or from suicide (Nielson et al., 1998; Slade, 1995).

Table 9-1 DSM-IV Checklist

ANOREXIA NERVOSA

1. Refusal to maintain body weight above a minimally normal weight for age and height.
2. Intense fear of gaining weight, even though underweight.
3. Disturbed body perception, undue influence of weight or shape on self-evaluation, or denial of the seriousness of the current low weight.
4. In postmenarcheal females, amenorrhea.

Based on APA, 2000, 1994.

The Clinical Picture

Becoming thin is the key goal for people with anorexia nervosa, but fear fuels their motivation (Russell, 1995). People with this disorder are afraid of becoming obese, of giving in to their growing desire to eat, and more generally of losing control over the size and shape of their bodies. In addition, despite their focus on thinness and the severe restrictions they may place on their food intake, people with anorexia are *preoccupied with food.* They may spend considerable time thinking and even reading about food and planning their limited meals (King, Polivy, & Herman, 1991). Many report that their dreams are filled with images of food and eating (Frayn, 1991; Levitan, 1981).

This preoccupation with food may in fact be a result of food deprivation rather than its cause. In a famous "starvation study" conducted in the late 1940s, 36 normal-weight conscientious objectors were put on a semistarvation diet for six months (Keys et al., 1950). Like people with anorexia nervosa, the volunteers became preoccupied with food and eating. They spent hours each day planning their small meals, talked more about food than about any other topic,

CULTURAL DIFFERENCES

In Hong Kong and India, anorexia nervosa is often motivated not by a fear of weight gain but rather by a desire to fast for religious purposes or by eccentric nutritional ideas (Castillo, 1997).

"We've Only Just Begun"

Given the hard-living, substance-abusing, risk-taking image cultivated by many pop music artists, we are hardly shocked anymore to read about the untimely demise of one of them, from Elvis Presley, Jimi Hendrix, or Sid Vicious, to Kurt Cobain, Tupac Shakur, or Notorious B.I.G. The 1983 death of Karen Carpenter, from the effects of anorexia nervosa, in contrast, stunned the country. Karen, the 32-year-old velvet-voiced lead singer of the soft-rock, brother-and-sister duo *The Carpenters,* did not drink, take drugs, drive fast cars, or tear up the roadside in motorcycles. She never appeared in the pages of the tabloids. Until her late 20s—well into her fame—she even continued to live at home with her parents and brother, Richard, in suburban Downey, California. Indeed, she and Richard were icons of unrebellious, quiet, youthful virtue.

The pressure to maintain this wholesome image may have contributed to Karen's destruction. After reading an early concert review describing her as "chubby," Karen began a downward spiral into anorexia nervosa. This disorder has been dubbed the "good girl's disease," because it often afflicts perfectionist, high-achieving young women who try to meet every family, school, and career demand. Always a dutiful family member and content to let Richard make all of the management and artistic decisions for their group, Karen seemed to have little control over her ride to fame. One friend and fellow sufferer later said about Karen's eating disorder, "When you start denying yourself food, and begin feeling you have control over a life that has been pretty much controlled for you, it's exhilarating" (O'Neill, as cited in Levin, 1983).

For nine years, Karen starved herself, abused laxatives and thyroid pills, and purged by repeatedly swallowing ipecac (a drug that induces vomiting). Her weight dropped from a high of 140 pounds at the beginning of her singing career, to a devastating low of 80 pounds. Ironically, in the last year of her life, it looked as though she had gotten a handle on her disorder. She had increased her weight to an almost-normal 108 pounds after a year of therapy in New York City. Yet on a visit home to her parent's house in California, on February 4, 1983, she collapsed. Paramedics could not revive her, and she died an hour later of cardiac arrest. Traces of ipecac were found in her bloodstream.

Until Karen's death, the public knew little about anorexia nervosa, and what it knew did not sound serious—more like the latest celebrity fad diet than a dangerous, potentially fatal condition. But that lighthearted view changed dramatically with her death, as scores of articles in newspapers and magazines detailed not only the tragically short life of Karen, but also the disease that killed her. Anorexia nervosa was no longer something to be taken casually.

Karen Carpenter was not the last celebrity to suffer the ravages of an eating disorder. Many other famous personalities in diverse fields have gone public about their own struggles with eating disorders: actress Jane Fonda, singer Cherry Boone O'Neill (daughter of Pat Boone), tennis star Zina Garrison, diver Megan Neyer, gymnasts Nadia Comaneci and Cathy Rigby, actresses Tracey Gold and Margaux Hemingway, Princess Diana, and more. And sadly,

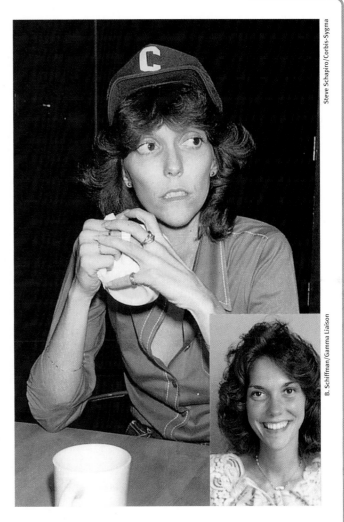

Karen has not been the only celebrity to lose the battle. In 1994, for example, gymnastic star Christy Henrich died from multiple organ failure after a six-year struggle with anorexia nervosa. One-hundred pounds of solid muscle at the height of her athletic career, Christy's weight at one point plummeted to a shocking 42 pounds. Whereas the publicity surrounding Karen Carpenter's death brought anorexia nervosa to the public's attention, the subsequent struggles of Christy Henrich and so many other successful young women remind us of the need for enlightening research on this problem and for the development of still more effective treatments.

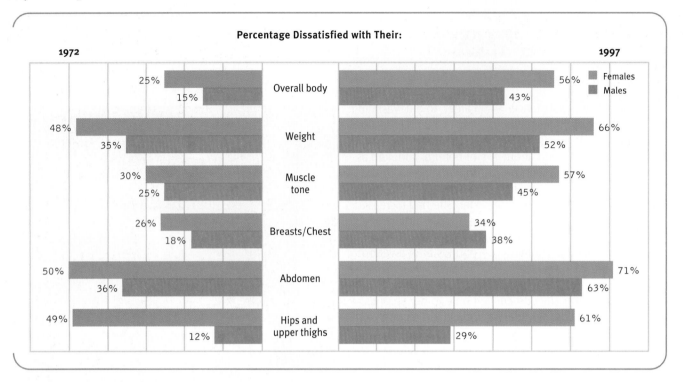

Percentage Dissatisfied with Their:

1972 / 1997, Females / Males

	1972 Females	1972 Males	1997 Females	1997 Males
Overall body	25%	15%	56%	43%
Weight	48%	35%	66%	52%
Muscle tone	30%	25%	57%	45%
Breasts/Chest	26%	18%	34%	38%
Abdomen	50%	36%	71%	63%
Hips and upper thighs	49%	12%	61%	29%

FIGURE 9-1 Body dissatisfaction on the rise
According to surveys on body image, people in our society are much more dissatisfied with their bodies now than they were a generation ago. Women are still more dissatisfied than men, but today's men are more dissatisfied with their bodies than the men of a generation past. (Adapted from Garner, Cooke, & Marano, 1997, p. 42; Rodin, 1992, p. 57.)

studied cookbooks and recipes, mixed food in odd combinations, and dawdled over their meals. Many also had vivid dreams about food.

Persons with anorexia nervosa also *think in distorted ways.* They usually have a low opinion of their body shape, for example, and consider themselves unattractive (Gupta & Johnson, 2000). In addition, they are likely to overestimate their actual proportions. While most women in Western society overestimate their body size (see Figure 9-1), the estimates of those with anorexia nervosa are particularly high. A 23-year-old patient said:

> I look in a full-length mirror at least four or five times daily and I really cannot see myself as too thin. Sometimes after several days of strict dieting, I feel that my shape is tolerable, but most of the time, odd as it may seem, I look in the mirror and believe that I am too fat.
>
> *(Bruch, 1973)*

This tendency to overestimate body size has been tested in the laboratory (Rushford & Ostermeyer, 1997). In a popular assessment technique, subjects look at a photograph of themselves through an adjustable lens. They are asked to adjust the lens until the image that they see matches their actual body size. The

Seeing is deceiving *In one research technique, people look at photographs of themselves through a special lens and adjust the lens until they see what they believe is their actual image. A subject may change her actual image (left) from 20 percent thinner (middle) to 20 percent larger (right).*

image can be made to vary from 20 percent thinner to 20 percent larger than actual appearance. In one study, more than half of the subjects with anorexia nervosa were found to overestimate their body size, stopping the lens when the image was larger than they actually were.

The distorted thinking of anorexia nervosa also takes the form of certain maladaptive attitudes and misperceptions (De Silva, 1995; Garner & Bemis, 1985, 1982). Sufferers tend to hold such beliefs as "I must be perfect in every way"; "I will become a better person if I deprive myself"; and "I can avoid guilt by not eating."

People with anorexia nervosa also display certain *psychological problems,* such as at least mild depression and anxiety and low self-esteem (APA, 2000; Wiederman & Pryor, 2000; Halmi, 1995). Some also experience insomnia or other sleep disturbances. A number grapple with substance abuse. And many display obsessive-compulsive patterns. They may set rigid rules for food preparation or even cut food into specific shapes. Broader obsessive-compulsive patterns are common as well. In one study, people with anorexia nervosa and others with obsessive-compulsive disorder scored equally high for obsessiveness and compulsiveness (Bastiani et al., 1996). Similarly, persons with anorexia nervosa tend to be perfectionists (Bastiani et al., 1995). Again, studies of normal subjects placed on semistarvation diets have reported similar psychological problems, suggesting that some of these features too may be the result of starvation (Fichter & Pirke, 1995; Keys et al., 1950).

Medical Problems

The starvation habits of anorexia nervosa cause medical problems (Mickley, 2001; Casper, 1995). Women develop **amenorrhea,** the absence of menstrual cycles. Other problems include lowered body temperature, low blood pressure, body swelling, reduced bone mineral density, and slow heart rate. Metabolic and electrolyte imbalances also may occur and can lead to heart failure or circulatory collapse (Froelich et al., 2001). The severe nutritional deficiencies of anorexia nervosa may also cause skin to become rough, dry, and cracked; nails to become brittle; and hands and feet to be cold and blue. Some people lose hair from the scalp and some grow *lanugo* (the fine, silky hair that covers some newborns) on their trunk, extremities, and face.

Clearly, people with this disorder are caught in a vicious cycle. Their fear of obesity and distorted body image lead them to starve themselves. Starvation in turn leads to a preoccupation with food, increased anxiety and depression, and medical problems, causing them to feel even more afraid that they will lose control over their weight, their eating, and themselves. They then try still harder to achieve thinness by not eating.

Changing times Seated Bather, *by Pierre-Auguste Renoir (1841–1919), shows that the aesthetically ideal woman of the past was considerably larger than today's ideal.*

Pierre August Renoir, *Seated Bather, 1903–1906, Detroit Institute of the Arts, bequest of Robert H. Tannahill*

SUMMING UP | Anorexia Nervosa

Eating disorders have increased dramatically since thinness has become a national obsession. People with anorexia nervosa pursue extreme thinness and lose dangerous amounts of weight. They may follow a pattern of restricting-type anorexia nervosa or binge-eating/purging-type anorexia nervosa.

The central features of anorexia nervosa are a drive for thinness, fear of weight, preoccupation with food, cognitive disturbances, psychological problems, and medical problems, including amenorrhea. The disorder most often appears between the ages of 14 and 18; over 90 percent of its sufferers are female; and it strikes around 0.5 percent of all females in the Western countries in their lifetime.

Bulimia Nervosa

People with **bulimia nervosa**—a disorder also known as **binge-purge syndrome**—engage in repeated episodes of uncontrollable overeating, or **binges.** A binge occurs over a limited period of time, often an hour, during which the person eats much more food than most people would eat during a similar time span (APA, 2000, 1994). In addition, people with this disorder repeatedly perform inappropriate *compensatory behaviors,* such as forcing themselves to vomit; misusing laxatives, diuretics, or enemas; fasting; or exercising excessively (see Table 9-2 on the next page). A married woman with bulimia nervosa, since recovered, describes a morning during her disorder:

AMENORRHEA Absence of menstrual cycles.

BULIMIA NERVOSA A disorder marked by frequent eating binges that are followed by forced vomiting or other extreme compensatory behaviors to avoid gaining weight. Also known as *binge-purge syndrome.*

BINGE An episode of uncontrollable eating during which a person ingests a very large quantity of food.

BINGE-EATING DISORDER A type of eating disorder in which a person displays a pattern of binge eating without any accompanying compensatory behaviors.

ConsiderThis

● Many, perhaps most, women in Western society feel as if they are dieting, or between diets, their entire adult lives. Is it possible to be a woman in this society and not struggle with at least some issues of eating and appearance?
• Who is responsible for the standards and pressures that affect so many women?

Today I am going to be really good and that means eating certain predetermined portions of food and not taking one more bite than I think I am allowed. I am very careful to see that I don't take more than Doug does. I judge by his body. I can feel the tension building. I wish Doug would hurry up and leave so I can get going!

As soon as he shuts the door, I try to get involved with one of the myriad of responsibilities on the list. I hate them all! I just want to crawl into a hole. I don't want to do anything. I'd rather eat. I am alone, I am nervous, I am no good, I always do everything wrong anyway, I am not in control, I can't make it through the day, I just know it. It has been the same for so long.

I remember the starchy cereal I ate for breakfast. I am into the bathroom and onto the scale. It measures the same, BUT I DON'T WANT TO STAY THE SAME! I want to be thinner! I look in the mirror, I think my thighs are ugly and deformed looking. I see a lumpy, clumsy, pear-shaped wimp. There is always something wrong with what I see. I feel frustrated trapped in this body and I don't know what to do about it.

I float to the refrigerator knowing exactly what is there. I begin with last night's brownies. I always begin with the sweets. At first I try to make it look like nothing is missing, but my appetite is huge and I resolve to make another batch of brownies. I know there is half of a bag of cookies in the bathroom, thrown out the night before, and I polish them off immediately. I take some milk so my vomiting will be smoother. I like the full feeling I get after downing a big glass. I get out six pieces of bread and toast one side in the broiler, turn them over and load them with patties of butter and put them under the broiler again till they are bubbling. I take all six pieces on a plate to the television and go back for a bowl of cereal and a banana to have along with them. Before the last toast is finished, I am already preparing the next batch of six more pieces. Maybe another brownie or five, and a couple of large bowlfuls of ice cream, yogurt or cottage cheese. My stomach is stretched into a huge ball below my ribcage. I know I'll have to go into the bathroom soon, but I want to postpone it. I am in never-never land. I am waiting, feeling the pressure, pacing the floor in and out of the rooms. Time is passing. Time is passing. It is getting to be time.

I wander aimlessly through each of the rooms again tidying, making the whole house neat and put back together. I finally make the turn into the bathroom. I brace my feet, pull my hair back and stick my finger down my throat, stroking twice, and get up a huge pile of food. Three times, four and another pile of food. I can see everything come back. I am glad to see those brownies because they are SO fattening. The rhythm of the emptying is broken and my head is beginning to hurt. I stand up feeling dizzy, empty and weak. The whole episode has taken about an hour.

(Hall, 1980, pp. 5–6)

Table 9-2 DSM-IV Checklist

BULIMIA NERVOSA

1. Recurrent episodes of binge eating.
2. Recurrent inappropriate compensatory behavior in order to prevent weight gain.
3. Symptoms continuing, on average, at least twice a week for three months.
4. Undue influence of weight or shape on self-evaluation.

Based on APA, 2000, 1994.

Like anorexia nervosa, bulimia nervosa usually occurs in females (again in 90 to 95 percent of the cases) and begins in adolescence or young adulthood (most often between 15 and 21 years of age). It often lasts for several years, with periodic letup. The weight of people with bulimia nervosa usually stays within a normal range, although it may fluctuate markedly within that range (APA, 2000, 1994). Some people with this disorder, however, become seriously underweight and may eventually qualify for a diagnosis of anorexia nervosa instead (see Figure 9-2). Clinicians have also observed that certain people, a number of them overweight, display a pattern of binge eating without vomiting or other inappropriate compensatory behaviors. This pattern, often called **binge-eating disorder,** is not yet listed in the DSM (Striegel-Moore et al., 2001). As many as 30 percent of people in weight-control programs may experience this disorder (Ricca et al., 2000; Spitzer et al., 1992).

Many teenagers and young adults go on occasional eating binges or experiment with vomiting or laxatives after they hear

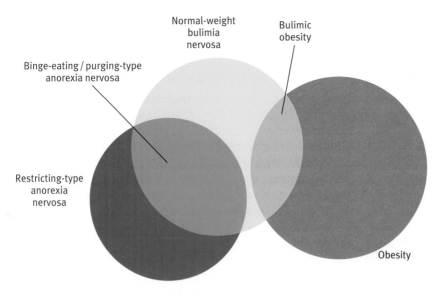

Normal-weight
bulimia
nervosa

Bulimic
obesity

Binge-eating / purging-type
anorexia nervosa

Restricting-type
anorexia
nervosa

Obesity

FIGURE 9-2 **Overlapping patterns of anorexia nervosa, bulimia nervosa, and obesity** *Some people with anorexia nervosa binge and purge their way to weight loss, and some obese persons binge-eat. However, most people with bulimia nervosa are not obese, and most overweight people are not bulimic. (Adapted from APA, 2000, 1994; Garner & Fairburn, 1988; Russell, 1979.)*

about these behaviors from their friends or the media (Pyle, 1999). In one study, 50 percent of the college students surveyed reported periodic binges, 6 percent had tried vomiting, and 8 percent had experimented with laxatives at least once (Mitchell et al., 1982). Only some of these individuals, however, qualify for a diagnosis of bulimia nervosa. Surveys in several countries suggest that as many as 3 percent of women develop the full syndrome (APA, 2000; Foreyt et al., 1996).

Binges

People with bulimia nervosa may have two to forty binge episodes per week, although the number is usually closer to ten (Mizes, 1995, 1993). In most cases, the binges are carried out in secret. The person eats massive amounts of food very rapidly, with minimal chewing—usually sweet, high-calorie foods with a soft texture, such as ice cream, cookies, doughnuts, and sandwiches. As suggested by the Greek term *bous limos,* or "cattle hunger," from which the word "bulimia" is derived, the food is hardly tasted or thought about. Binge-eaters commonly take in more than 1,500 calories (often more than 3,000) during an episode (Agras, 1995).

Binges are usually preceded by feelings of great tension (Crowther et al., 2001; Johnson et al., 1995). The person feels irritable, "unreal," and powerless to control an overwhelming need to eat "forbidden" foods (Levine, 1987). During the binge, the person feels unable to stop eating. Although the binge itself may be experienced as pleasurable in the sense that it relieves the unbearable tension, it is followed by feelings of extreme self-blame, guilt, and depression, as

DIETARY TRIGGERS

Although most dieters do not develop an eating disorder, female teenagers who follow a severely restrictive diet are 18 times more likely than nondieters to develop an eating disorder within one year of the diet (Patton et al., 1999).

Lee Stone/Corbis-Sygma

Calvin Klein Jeans

Harmful advertising *When Calvin Klein posed young teenagers in sexually suggestive clothing ads in 1995, the public protested and the ads were halted. However, what some researchers consider even more damaging—the use of very thin young models who influence the body ideals and dietary habits of millions of teenage girls—has continued uninterrupted.*

Laboratory starvation *Thirty-six conscientious objectors who were put on a semistarvation diet for six months developed many of the symptoms seen in anorexia nervosa and bulimia nervosa (Keys et al., 1950).*

well as fears of gaining weight and being discovered (APA, 2000; Porzelius et al., 1999).

Compensatory Behaviors

After a binge, people with bulimia nervosa try to compensate for and undo its effects. Many resort to vomiting. But vomiting actually fails to prevent the absorption of half of the calories taken in during a binge. Furthermore, repeated vomiting affects one's general ability to feel full; thus it leads to greater hunger and more frequent and intense binges (Wooley & Wooley, 1985). Similarly, the use of laxatives or diuretics fails almost completely to undo the caloric effects of bingeing (Garner et al., 1985).

Vomiting and other compensatory behaviors may temporarily relieve the uncomfortable physical feelings of fullness or lower the feelings of anxiety, self-disgust, and lack of control attached to binge eating (Mizes, 1995). Over time, however, a cycle develops in which purging allows more bingeing and bingeing requires more purging (Porzelius et al., 1999). The cycle eventually causes people with this disorder to feel powerless, useless, and disgusted with themselves (Kanakis & Thelen, 1995). Most recognize fully that they have an eating disorder. The woman we met earlier recalls how the pattern of bingeing, purging, and self-disgust took hold while she was a teenager in boarding school:

> Every bite that went into my mouth was a naughty and selfish indulgence, and I became more and more disgusted with myself. . . .
>
> The first time I stuck my fingers down my throat was during the last week of school. I saw a girl come out of the bathroom with her face all red and her eyes puffy. She had always talked about her weight and how she should be dieting even though her body was really shapely. I knew instantly what she had just done and I had to try it. . . .
>
> I began with breakfasts which were served buffet-style on the main floor of the dorm. I learned which foods I could eat that would come back up easily. When I woke in the morning, I had to make the decision whether to stuff myself for half an hour and throw up before class, or whether to try and make it through the whole day without overeating. . . . I always thought people noticed when I took huge portions at mealtimes, but I figured they assumed that because I was an athlete, I burned it off. . . . Once a binge was under way, I did not stop until my stomach looked pregnant and I felt like I could not swallow one more time.
>
> That year was the first of my nine years of obsessive eating and throwing up. . . . I didn't want to tell anyone what I was doing, and I didn't want to stop. . . . [Though] being in love or other distractions occasionally lessened the cravings, I always returned to the food.
>
> *(Hall, 1980, pp. 9-12)*

WEIGHING IN

Five percent of Americans weigh themselves more than once per day, 8 percent once per day, 10 percent twice per week, and 36 percent twice per month. Women are three times more likely than men to check the scale (Kanner, 1995).

As with anorexia nervosa, a bulimic pattern typically begins during or after a period of intense dieting, often one that has been successful and earned praise from family members and friends (Lowe et al., 1996; Szmukler & Patton, 1995). Research has found that normal subjects placed on very strict diets also develop a tendency to binge. Some of the subjects in the conscientious objector "starvation study," for example, later binged when they were allowed to return to regular eating, and a number of them continued to be hungry even after large meals (Keys et al., 1950). A more recent study examined the binge-eating behavior of subjects at the end of a very low-calorie weight-loss program (Telch & Agras, 1993). Immediately after the program, 62 percent of the subjects, who had not previously been binge eaters, reported binge-eating episodes, although the episodes did decrease during the three months after treatment stopped.

A CLOSER LOOK

Not for Women Only

The number of young men with eating disorders appears to be on the rise, and more men are now seeking treatment for these disorders (Gilbert, 1996). Nevertheless, males account for only 5 to 10 percent of all cases of eating disorders (Frasciello & Willard, 1995). The reasons for this striking gender difference are not entirely clear (Smolak & Murnen, 2001).

One possible explanation is that men and women are subject to different sociocultural pressures. For example, a survey of college men found that the majority selected "muscular, strong and broad shoulders" to describe the ideal male body and "thin, slim, slightly underweight" to describe the ideal female body (Kearney-Cooke & Steichen-Ash, 1990). Although the emphasis on a muscular, strong, and athletic body as the male ideal tends to lower the likelihood of eating disorders in men, it may nevertheless create other problems, such as steroid abuse or excessive weight lifting to increase muscle mass and strength (Mickalide, 1990).

A second reason for the different rates of eating disorders may be the different methods of weight loss favored by men and women. According to some clinical observations, men are more likely to use exercise to lose weight, whereas women more often diet (Braun, 1996; Mickalide, 1990). And dieting often causes the onset of eating disorders.

Perhaps a third reason for the difference in reported cases is that eating disorders in men may be underdiagnosed. Some men do not want to admit that they have what many consider a "female problem."

Many of the men who develop eating disorders struggle with the same issues as women. Some, for example, report that they want a "lean, toned, thin" shape similar to the ideal female body, rather than the muscular, broad-shouldered shape of the typical male ideal (Kearney-Cooke & Steichen-Ash, 1990). In many cases, however, the triggers of male eating disorders are different from those of female eating problems (Joiner et al., 2000; Costanzo et al., 1999). For example, males are more likely than women to develop eating disturbances because of the requirements and pressures of a job or sport (Thompson & Sherman, 1993). According to one study, 37 percent of males with eating disorders had jobs or played sports for which weight control was important, compared to 13 percent of women (Braun, 1996). The highest rates have been found among jockeys, wrestlers, distance runners, bodybuilders, and swimmers. Jockeys commonly spend hours before a race in a sauna, shedding up to seven pounds of weight, and may restrict their food intake, abuse laxatives and diuretics, and force vomiting (King & Mezey, 1987). Similarly, male wrestlers in high school and college commonly restrict their food for up to three days before a match in order to "make weight." Some lose up to five pounds of water weight by practicing or running in several layers of warm or rubber clothing before weighing in for a match (Thompson & Sherman, 1993).

Whereas most women with eating disorders are obsessed with thinness at all times, wrestlers and jockeys are usually concerned with weight reduction only during their active season. After "making weight," many wrestlers go on eating

The weigh-in *Although this jockey does not have an eating disorder, his prerace weigh-in illustrates the weight standards and pressures to which such athletes are subjected.*

and drinking binges in order to gain strength for the upcoming match, only to return to a weight-loss strategy after the match in preparation for the next weigh-in. A cycle of losing and regaining weight each season changes metabolic activity and jeopardizes the person's health and future efforts at weight control (Mickalide, 1990; Steen et al., 1988).

As the number of males with eating disturbances increases, researchers are increasing their efforts to understand both the similarities and the differences between males and females with these disorders (Andersen, 1992). Since eating disturbances cause problems for both men and women, investigators must unravel and deal with the important factors that operate across the gender divide.

Bulimia Nervosa vs. Anorexia Nervosa

Bulimia nervosa is similar to anorexia nervosa in many ways. Both disorders typically begin after a period of dieting by people who are fearful of becoming obese; driven to become thin; preoccupied with food, weight, and appearance; and struggling with feelings of depression, anxiety, and the need to be perfect (Lehoux, Steiger, & Jabalpurlawa, 2000; Joiner et al., 1997, 1995). Substance abuse may accompany either disorder, perhaps beginning with the excessive use

Models and mannequins *Mannequins were once made extra-thin to show the lines of the clothing for sale to best advantage. Today the shape of the ideal woman is indistinguishable from that of a mannequin.*

of diet pills (APA, 2000). People with either disorder believe that they weigh too much and look too heavy regardless of their actual weight or appearance (Mizes, 1995). And both disorders are marked by disturbed attitudes toward eating (Porzelius et al., 1999).

Yet the two disorders also differ in important ways (see Table 9-3). Although people with either disorder worry about the opinions of others, those with bulimia nervosa tend to be more concerned about pleasing others, being attractive to others, and having intimate relationships (Striegel-Moore, Silberstein, & Rodin, 1993; Muuss, 1986). They also tend to be more sexually experienced and active than people with anorexia nervosa. On the positive side, people with bulimia nervosa display fewer of the obsessive qualities that drive people with restricting-type anorexia nervosa to control their caloric intake so rigidly (Halmi, 1995; Andersen, 1985). On the negative side, they are more likely to have long histories of mood swings, become easily frustrated or bored, and have trouble coping effectively or controlling their impulses (Keel et al., 2001; APA, 2000). Individuals with bulimia nervosa also tend to be ruled by strong emotions and may change friends and relationships frequently. And more than one-third of them display the characteristics of a personality disorder, which we shall observe more closely in Chapter 14 (Matsunaga et al., 2000; Braun et al., 1995).

Table 9-3

Anorexia Nervosa vs. Bulimia Nervosa

RESTRICTING-TYPE ANOREXIA NERVOSA	BULIMIA NERVOSA
Refusal to maintain a minimum body weight for healthy functioning	Underweight, normal weight, near-normal weight, or overweight
Hunger and disorder denied; often proud of weight management and more satisfied with body	Intense hunger experienced; binge–purge experienced as abnormal; greater body dissatisfaction
Less antisocial behavior	Greater tendency to antisocial behavior and alcohol abuse
Amenorrhea of at least 3 months' duration common	Irregular menstrual periods common; amenorrhea uncommon unless body weight is low
Mistrust of others, particularly professionals	More trusting of people who wish to help
Tend to be obsessional	Tend to be dramatic
Greater self-control, but emotionally overcontrolled, with problems experiencing and expressing feelings	More impulsivity and emotional instability
More likely to be sexually immature and inexperienced	More sexually experienced and sexually active
Females more likely to reject traditional feminine role	Females more likely to embrace traditional feminine role
Age of onset often around 14–18	Age of onset around 15–21
Greater tendency for maximum pre-disorder weight to be near normal for age	Greater tendency for maximum pre-disorder weight to be slightly greater than normal
Lesser familial predisposition to obesity	Greater familial predisposition to obesity
Greater tendency toward pre-disorder compliance with parents	Greater tendency toward pre-disorder conflict with parents
Tendency to deny family conflict	Tendency to perceive intense family conflict

Source: APA, 2000, 1994; Levine, 1987; Andersen, 1985; Garner et al., 1985; Neuman & Halvorson, 1983.

Another difference is the nature of the medical complications that accompany each disorder (Mickley, 2001). Only half of women with bulimia nervosa are amenorrheic or have very irregular menstrual periods, compared to almost all of those with anorexia nervosa (Treasure & Szmukler, 1995). On the other hand, repeated vomiting bathes teeth and gums in hydrochloric acid, leading some women with bulimia nervosa to experience serious dental problems, such as breakdown of enamel and even loss of teeth (Casper, 1995; Treasure & Szmukler, 1995). Moreover, frequent vomiting or chronic diarrhea (from the use of laxatives) can cause dangerous potassium deficiencies, which may lead to weakness, intestinal disorders, kidney disease, or heart damage (Turner et al., 2000; Halmi et al., 1994).

MULTIDIMENSIONAL RISK PERSPECTIVE
A theory that identifies several kinds of risk factors that are thought to combine to help cause a disorder. The more factors present, the greater the risk of developing the disorder.

SUMMING UP
Bulimia Nervosa

Sufferers of bulimia nervosa go on frequent eating binges and then force themselves to vomit or perform other compensatory behaviors. The binges often occur in response to increasing tension and are followed by feelings of guilt and self-blame.

Compensatory behavior is at first reinforced by the temporary relief from uncomfortable feelings of fullness or the reduction of feelings of anxiety, self-disgust, and loss of control attached to bingeing. Over time, however, people feel generally disgusted with themselves, depressed, and guilty.

Bulimia nervosa usually appears in as many as 3 percent of women. The disorder most often appears between the ages of 15 and 21 and over 90 percent of sufferers are female. And these young women usually maintain their body weight within a normal range.

What Causes Eating Disorders?

Currently, theorists and researchers are using a **multidimensional risk perspective** to explain eating disorders. That is, they cite several key factors that place individuals at risk for these disorders (Lask, 2000). The more of these factors that are present, the greater is the likelihood that a person will develop an eating disorder (Lyon et al., 1997). Among the leading factors identified to date are sociocultural conditions (societal and family pressures), psychological problems (ego, cognitive, and mood disturbances), and biological factors.

Societal Pressures

Many theorists believe that the current Western standards of female attractiveness have contributed to increases in eating disorders (Jambor, 2001; Wertheim et al., 1997). These standards have changed throughout history, with a noticeable shift toward preference for a thin female frame in recent decades. One study that tracked the height, weight, and age of contestants in the Miss America Pageant from 1959 through 1978 found an average decline of 0.28 pound per year among the contestants and 0.37 pound per year among winners (Garner et al., 1980). The researchers also examined data on all *Playboy* magazine centerfold models over the same time period and found that the average weight, bust, and hip measurements of these women had decreased steadily. More recent studies of Miss America contestants and *Playboy* centerfolds indicate that these trends have continued (Rubinstein & Caballero, 2000; Wiseman et al., 1992).

Because thinness is especially valued in the subcultures of fashion models, actors, dancers, and certain athletes, members of these groups are likely to be particularly concerned about their weight (Taylor & Ste-Marie, 2001; Williamson et al., 1995). As sociocultural theorists would predict, studies have found that people in these professions are more prone than others to eating disorders

SAINTLY RESTRAINT

During the Middle Ages, the restrained eating or prolonged fasting of a number of women saints was greatly admired, and was even counted among their miracles. Catherine of Siena sometimes pushed twigs down her throat to bring up food; Mary of Oignes and Beatrice of Nazareth vomited from the mere smell of meat; and Columba of Rieti died of self-starvation (Brumberg, 1988).

ConsiderThis

● The prevalence of eating disorders is particularly low in cultures that restrict female social roles and reduce a woman's freedom to make decisions about her life (Miller & Pumariega, 1999; Bemporad, 1996). How might you explain this relationship?

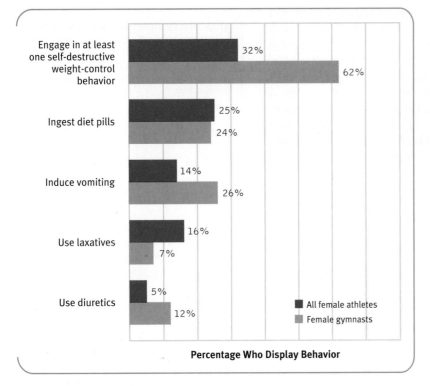

Engage in at least self-destructive weight-control behavior — 32% / 62%

Ingest diet pills — 25% / 24%

Induce vomiting — 14% / 26%

Use laxatives — 16% / 7%

Use diuretics — 5% / 12%

Percentage Who Display Behavior

■ All female athletes
■ Female gymnasts

FIGURE 9-3   Dangerous shortcuts
According to surveys, in sports ranging from field hockey to gymnastics, numerous female athletes engage in one or more self-destructive behaviors to control their weight (Taylor & Ste-Marie, 2001). One study found that close to two-thirds of female college gymnasts engage in at least one such behavior. (Adapted from Rosen & Hough, 1988; Rosen et al., 1986.)

(Thompson & Sherman, 1999; Attie & Brooks-Gunn, 1992), and a number of famous young women in these fields have publicly acknowledged grossly disordered eating patterns in recent years. One survey of 1,443 athletes at ten colleges around the United States revealed that more than 9 percent of female college athletes suffer from an eating disorder and another 50 percent admit to eating behaviors that put them at risk for such disorders (Johnson, 1995). A full 20 percent of the gymnasts surveyed manifested an eating disorder (see Figure 9-3).

Attitudes toward thinness may also help explain economic and racial differences in the rates of eating disorders. In the past, white American women in the upper socioeconomic classes expressed more concern about thinness and dieting than did African American women or white American women of the lower socioeconomic classes (Margo, 1985; Stunkard, 1975). Correspondingly, eating disorders were more common among white American women higher on the socioeconomic scale (Foreyt et al., 1996; Rosen et al., 1991). In more recent years, however, dieting and preoccupation with thinness have increased to some degree in all classes and minority groups, as has the prevalence of eating disorders (Mulholland & Mintz, 2001; Striegel-Moore & Smolak, 2000).

Cultural differences may also help explain the striking gender gap for eating disorders. Our society's emphasis on a thin appearance is aimed at women much more than men (Nichter & Nichter, 1991). Some theorists believe that this double standard has made women much more inclined to diet and prone to eating disorders (Rand & Kuldau, 1991).

Western society not only glorifies thinness but creates a climate of prejudice against overweight people of all ages. Whereas slurs based on ethnicity, race, and gender are considered unacceptable, cruel jokes about obesity are standard fare on television shows and in movies, books, and magazines. Research indicates that the prejudice against obese people is deep-rooted (Tiggeman & Wilson-Barrett, 1998). Prospective parents who were shown pictures of a chubby child and a medium-weight or thin child rated the former as less friendly, energetic, intelligent, and desirable than the latter. In another study, preschool children who were given a choice between a chubby and a thin rag doll chose the thin one, although

Unfair game *In Western society, overweight people are typically treated with insensitivity. They are also the targets of humor in magazines, books, television shows, and movies, such as the highly successful film* The Nutty Professor.

Bruce McBroom/The Everett Collection

THE CURRENT SCENE

Body Image: A Matter of Race?

In the popular movie *Clueless*, Cher and Dionne, wealthy teenage friends of different races, have similar tastes, beliefs, and values about everything from boys to schoolwork. In particular, they have the same kinds of eating habits and beauty ideals, and they are even similar in weight and physical form. But does the story of these young women reflect the realities of white and African American females in our society? The answer, according to some recent investigations, appears to be no (Lovejoy, 2001; Miller et al., 2000; Cash & Henry, 1995).

Although young African American women seem to be more worried about their weight and more prone to diet and to develop eating disorders today than in the past, their values, goals, and behaviors in these areas remain healthier than those of young white women. A widely publicized study done at the University of Arizona explored the body image ideals and dieting behaviors of 296 eighth- and ninth-grade girls over a three-year span (Parker et al., 1995). Its findings: nearly 90 percent of the white teens said they were dissatisfied with their weight and body shape, whereas nearly 70 percent of the African American teens were satisfied with their bodies. The African American teens expressed satisfaction regardless of their actual weight; even those who were overweight described themselves as happy.

Beauty Ideals

The study also suggests that white and African American adolescent girls have very different ideals of beauty. The white teens, asked to define the "perfect girl," described a girl of 5′7″ weighing between 100 and 110 pounds—proportions that mirror those of today's so-called supermodels. Attaining a perfect weight, many said, was the key to being "totally happy," and they indicated that thinness was a requirement for popularity. Several explained that "being skinny makes you fit in more."

In contrast, the African American respondents tended to emphasize personality traits over physical characteristics when they described the ideal girl. They defined the "perfect" African American girl as smart, fun, easy to talk to, not conceited, and funny; she did not necessarily need to be "pretty," as long as she was well groomed. The body dimensions the African American teens described were more attainable for the typical girl; they favored fuller hips, for example. Perhaps the key difference was the African American subjects' greater emphasis on true beauty as an inner quality. Two-thirds of them defined beauty as "the right attitude," and about the same percentage indicated that women become more beautiful as they grow older.

Health and Diet

Given such definitions of beauty, it is not surprising that the African American subjects were far less likely than the white American respondents to diet for extended periods. Although a full 52 percent of the African American teens had dieted at some point in the previous year, they did not tend to stick to a strict diet, explaining that it is better to be a "little" overweight than underweight. Meanwhile, the white teens, 61 percent of whom had dieted in the previous year, stressed dieting as a way both to become thinner and to gain control over other aspects of their lives, such as their social life.

Although the African American teenagers in this study, and in other settings as well, expressed positive feelings about their bodies and about beauty in general, clinical theorists warn that problems may lie ahead for them (Williamson, 1998). The University of Arizona investigators observe, "It remains to be seen whether they will be able to maintain these self-perceptions as they become older and obtain jobs in mainstream American society. . . . [They] may be more likely to deemphasize their black identities in order to get ahead. . . . Will this translate into discipline dieting to obtain a thin body by girls who aspire to make it?" (Parker et al., 1995, p. 111).

Racial differences *Although women within each race differ, evidence is mounting that African American teens are, on average, more satisfied with their weight and body shape than white American teens and less inclined to diet for extended periods.*

Mary Kate Denny/PhotoEdit

ENMESHED FAMILY PATTERN A family system in which members are overinvolved with each other's affairs and overconcerned about each other's welfare.

ConsiderThis

◉ The most successful of today's fashion models, often referred to as supermodels, have a celebrity status that was not conferred upon models in the past. Why do you think the fame and status of models have risen in this way?

they could not say why. It is small wonder that as many as half of elementary school girls have tried to lose weight and 61 percent of middle school girls are currently dieting (Shisslak et al., 1998; Hunnicut & Newman, 1993).

Family Environment

Families may play a critical role in the development of eating disorders. Research suggests that as many as half of the families of people with eating disorders have a long history of emphasizing thinness, physical appearance, and dieting (Haworth-Hoeppner, 2000; Lieberman, 1995). In fact, the mothers in these families are more likely to diet themselves and to be generally perfectionistic than are the mothers in other families (Pike & Rodin, 1991). Abnormal interactions and forms of communication within a family may also set the stage for an eating disorder. Family systems theorists argue that the families of people who develop eating disorders are often dysfunctional to begin with and that the eating disorder of one member is simply a reflection of the larger problem (Rowa, Kerig, & Geller, 2001; Dalzell, 2000). The influential family theorist Salvador Minuchin, for example, believes that what he calls an **enmeshed family pattern** often leads to eating disorders (Minuchin, Rosman, & Baker, 1978).

In an enmeshed system, family members are overinvolved in each other's affairs and overconcerned with the details of each other's lives. On the positive side, enmeshed families can be affectionate and loyal. On the negative side, they can be clinging and foster dependency. Parents are too involved in the lives of their children, allowing little room for individuality and independence. Minuchin argues that adolescence poses a special problem for these families. The teenager's normal push for independence threatens the family's apparent harmony and closeness. In response, the family may subtly force the child to take on a "sick" role—to develop an eating disorder or some other illness. The child's disorder enables the family to maintain its appearance of harmony. A sick child needs her family, and family members can rally to protect her. Some case studies have supported such family systems explanations, but empirical studies fail to show that particular family patterns consistently set the stage for the development of eating disorders (Wilson et al., 1996). In fact, the families of people with either anorexia nervosa or bulimia nervosa vary widely (Eisler, 1995).

Ego Deficiencies and Cognitive Disturbances

Hilde Bruch, a pioneer in the study and treatment of eating disorders, developed a theory built on both psychodynamic and cognitive notions. She argued that disturbed mother–child interactions lead to serious *ego deficiencies* in the child (including a poor sense of independence and control) and to severe *cognitive disturbances* that jointly help produce disordered eating patterns (Bruch, 1991, 1983, 1962).

According to Bruch, parents may respond to their children either effectively or ineffectively. *Effective parents* accurately attend to their children's biological and emotional needs, giving them food when they are crying from hunger and comfort when they are crying out of fear. *Ineffective parents,* by contrast, fail to attend to their children's internal needs, deciding that their children are hungry, cold, or tired without correctly interpreting the children's actual condition. They may feed the children at times of anxiety rather than hunger or comfort them at times of tiredness rather than anxiety. Children who receive such parenting may grow up confused and unaware of their own internal needs, not knowing for themselves when they are hungry or full, and unable to identify their own emotions.

Unable to rely on internal signals, these children turn instead to external guides, such as their parents. They seem to be "model children," but they fail to develop genuine self-reliance and "experience themselves as not being in control of their behavior, needs, and impulses, as not owning their own bodies" (Bruch,

1973, p. 55). Adolescence increases their basic desire to establish independence, yet they feel unable to do so (Strauss & Ryan, 1987). To overcome their sense of helplessness, they seek excessive control over their body size and shape and over their eating habits. Helen, an 18-year-old, describes her experience:

> There is a peculiar contradiction—everybody thinks you're doing so well and everybody thinks you're great, but your real problem is that you think that you are not good enough. You are afraid of not living up to what you think you are expected to do. You have one great fear, namely that of being ordinary, or average, or common—just not good enough. This peculiar dieting begins with such anxiety. You want to prove that you have control, that you can do it. The peculiar part of it is that it makes you feel good about yourself, makes you feel "I can accomplish something." It makes you feel "I can do something nobody else can do."
>
> *(Bruch, 1978, p. 128)*

Clinical reports and research have provided some support for Bruch's theory. Clinicians have observed that the parents of teenagers with eating disorders do tend to define their children's needs rather than allow the children to define their own needs (Hart & Kenny, 1995; Steiner et al., 1991). When Bruch interviewed the mothers of 51 children with anorexia nervosa, many proudly recalled that they had always "anticipated" their young child's needs, never permitting the child to "feel hungry" (Bruch, 1973).

Research has also supported Bruch's belief that people with eating disorders perceive internal cues inaccurately (Fukunishi, 1998; Halmi et al., 1989). When subjects with bulimia nervosa are anxious or upset, for example, many of them mistakenly think they are also hungry, and they respond as they might respond to hunger—by eating (Rebert, Stanton, & Schwarz, 1991) (see Figure 9-4). Finally, studies support Bruch's argument that people with eating disorders rely excessively on the opinions, wishes, and views of others. They are more likely than

UPSETTING ADS

Immediately after looking at ads from fashion magazines and the models in those ads, undergraduate female subjects showed a greater rise in depression and hostility than did women exposed to ads without pictures of people (Pinhas et al., 1999).

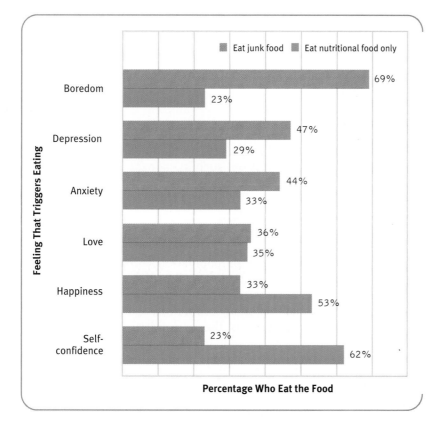

Percentage Who Eat the Food

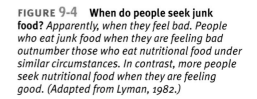

FIGURE 9-4 **When do people seek junk food?** *Apparently, when they feel bad. People who eat junk food when they are feeling bad outnumber those who eat nutritional food under similar circumstances. In contrast, more people seek nutritional food when they are feeling good. (Adapted from Lyman, 1982.)*

A Big McProblem

If the aesthetic ideal is a small frame, if people want to curb their eating, and if rates of eating disorders are increasing, why are fast-food servings getting bigger and more profitable? A Macho Meal sold by the Del Taco Mexican fast-food chain weighs almost four pounds—more than the Manhattan telephone book (Horowitz, 1996). A Double Gulp drink from 7-Eleven is larger than five cans of cola. Four slices of Pizza Hut's Triple Decker pizza contain more than the average allowance of calories, salt, and saturated fat for an entire day.

Meanwhile, McLean Deluxe lower-fat burgers and Taco Bell's Border Lights have struggled in the marketplace. Altogether, customers spend more than $2.5 billion on "big" fast-food products each year.

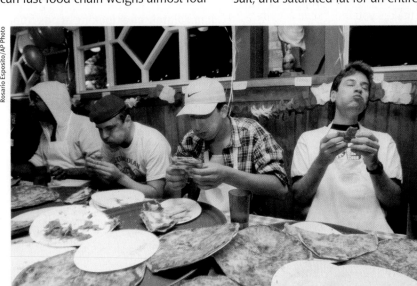

Rosario Esposito/AP Photo

ConsiderThis

⊙ • Does the availability of such generously sized food products create a climate for bingeing and purging? • Or are people actually driven to consume such products by the effects of excessive concern about dieting and eating?

Eating for sport *Few people go to the extremes of these participants at the World Pizza Eating Championships in New York City, but eating outrageous portions at fast-food restaurants and pizzerias is a growing trend around the United States.*

other people to worry about how others view them, to seek approval, to be conforming, and to feel a lack of control over their lives (Button & Warren, 2001; Walters & Kendler, 1995).

Mood Disorders

Many people with eating disorders, particularly those with bulimia nervosa, experience symptoms of depression, such as sadness, low self-esteem, shame, pessimism, and errors in logic (Burney & Irwin, 2000; Lehoux et al., 2000). This finding has led some theorists to suggest that mood disorders set the stage for eating disorders (Hsu et al., 1992).

Their claim is supported by four kinds of evidence. First, many more people with an eating disorder qualify for a clinical diagnosis of major depressive disorder than do people in the general population (Brewerton et al., 1995). Second, the close relatives of people with eating disorders seem to have a higher rate of mood disorders than do close relatives of people without such disorders (APA, 2000). Third, as we shall see, many people with eating disorders, particularly bulimia nervosa, have low activity of the neurotransmitter serotonin, similar to the serotonin abnormalities found in depressed people. And finally, people with eating disorders are often helped by some of the same antidepressant drugs that reduce depression (Advokat & Kutlesic, 1995).

Although such findings suggest that depression may be linked to eating disorders, other explanations are possible (Wade et al., 2000). For example, the pres-

SPECIAL FACTOR?

Although some clinicians claim that eating disorders are frequently the result of experiences of physical or sexual abuse during childhood or adolescence, research indicates that the disorders are only *sometimes* linked to such experiences. Moreover, the elevated rate of past abuse found among people with eating disorders is no higher than that of people with mood, anxiety, and other psychological disorders (Welch & Fairburn, 1996, 1994; Pope & Hudson, 1992).

sure and pain of having an eating disorder may *cause* a mood disorder (Silverstone, 1990). Whatever the correct interpretation, many people struggling with eating disorders also suffer from depression, among other psychological problems.

Biological Factors

Biological theorists suspect that some people inherit a genetic tendency to develop an eating disorder. Consistent with this idea, relatives of people with these disorders are up to six times more likely than other individuals to develop the disorders themselves (Strober et al., 2001, 2000; Gorwood et al., 1998). Moreover, if one identical twin has bulimia nervosa, the other twin also develops the disorder in 23 percent of cases; in contrast, the rate for fraternal twins, who are genetically less similar, is 9 percent (Walters & Kendler, 1995; Kendler et al., 1991). Although such findings do not rule out environmental explanations, they have encouraged biological researchers to look further still for specific biological causes.

One factor that has interested investigators is the possible role of *serotonin*. Several research teams have found a link between eating disorders and the genes responsible for the production of this neurotransmitter (Enoch et al., 1998), while others have measured low serotonin activity in many people with eating disorders (Carrasco et al., 2000). Thus some theorists believe that low serotonin activity causes the body to crave and binge on higher-carbohydrate foods (Kaye et al., 2000; Wurtman, 1987).

Other biological theorists explain eating disorders by pointing to the **hypothalamus**, a part of the brain that controls many bodily functions (Tataranni et al., 1999; Liebowitz & Hoebel, 1998). Researchers have located two separate areas in the hypothalamus that help control eating. One, the **lateral hypothalamus (LH),** produces hunger when it is activated. When the LH of a laboratory animal is stimulated electrically, the animal eats, even if it has been fed recently. In contrast, another area, the **ventromedial hypothalamus (VMH),** reduces hunger when it is activated. When the VMH is electrically stimulated, laboratory animals stop eating.

These different centers of the hypothalamus are apparently activated by chemicals from the brain and body, depending on whether the person is eating or fasting. One such brain chemical is *glucagon-like peptide-1 (GLP-1),* a natural appetite suppressant. When a team of researchers collected and injected GLP-1 into the brains of rats, the chemical traveled to the hypothalamus and caused the rats to reduce their food intake almost entirely even though they had not eaten for 24 hours (Turton et al., 1996). Conversely, when "full" rats were injected with a

HYPOTHALAMUS A part of the brain that helps regulate various bodily functions, including eating and hunger.

LATERAL HYPOTHALAMUS (LH) The region of the hypothalamus that, when activated, produces hunger.

VENTROMEDIAL HYPOTHALAMUS (VMH) The region of the hypothalamus that, when activated, depresses hunger.

FOOD PROCESSING

The adult human stomach can hold up to two liters. Ingested food remains in the stomach for three to five hours, exiting the body completely in fifteen hours or so.

Common goal *As we are reminded by these junior high school students in gym class, children approach puberty with a wide range of body sizes and metabolism rates. Yet, because of societal and psychological influences, the majority of them, particularly girls, aspire to a similar ultra-thin body size that is unattainable for most.*

Obesity: To Lose or Not to Lose

By medical standards, one-third of adults in the United States weigh at least 20 percent more than people of their height typically do (Foreyt et al., 1996). In fact, despite the public's focus on thinness, obesity has become increasingly common in the United States (NCHS, 1999; Kuczmarski et al., 1994). Being overweight is not a mental disorder, nor in most cases is it the result of abnormal psychological processes. Nevertheless, it causes great anguish, and not just because of its physical effects. The media, people on the streets, and even many health professionals treat obesity as shameful. Obese people are often the unrecognized victims of discrimination in efforts to gain admission to college, jobs, and promotions (Rothblum, 1992).

Mounting evidence indicates that overweight persons are not to be sneered at as weak and that obesity results from multiple factors. First, genetic and biological factors seem to play a large role. Researchers have found that children of obese biological parents are more likely to be obese than children whose biological parents are not obese, whether or not the people who raise those children are obese (Stunkard et al., 1986). Other researchers have identified several genes that seem to be linked to obesity (Nagle et al., 1999; Halaas et al., 1995). And still others have identified chemicals in the body, including a hormone called *leptin* and a protein called *glucagon-like peptide-1 (GLP-1)*, that apparently act as natural appetite suppressants (Turton et al., 1996; Tartaglia et al., 1995). Suspicion is growing that the brain receptors for these chemicals may be defective in overweight persons.

Environment also plays a causal role in obesity. Studies have shown that people eat more when they are in the company of others, particularly if the other people are eating (Logue, 1991). In addition, research finds that people from low socioeconomic environments are more likely to be obese than those from high socioeconomic backgrounds (Ernst & Harlan, 1991).

Health Risk?

Do mildly to moderately obese people have a greater risk of coronary disease or cancer or other disease? Investigations have produced conflicting results (Bender et al., 1999; Lean, Han, & Seidell, 1999). One long-term study found that while moderately overweight subjects had a 30 percent higher risk of early death, underweight subjects had a low likelihood of dying at an early age as long as their thinness could not be attributed to smoking or illness (Manson et al., 1995). However, another study found that the mortality rate of underweight subjects was as high as that of overweight subjects regardless of smoking behavior or illness (Troiano et al., 1996). These findings suggest that the jury is still out on this issue.

Does Dieting Work?

There are scores of diets and diet pills. There is almost no evidence, however, that any diet yet devised can ensure long-term weight loss (Wilson, 1994). In

WEIGHT SET POINT The weight level that a person is predisposed to maintain, controlled in part by the hypothalamus.

substance that blocked the reception of GLP-1 in the hypothalamus, they more than doubled their food intake.

Some researchers believe that the LH and VMH and chemicals such as GLP-1, working together, set up a "weight thermostat" of sorts in the body, responsible for keeping an individual at a particular weight level called the **weight set point** (Garner et al., 1985; Keesey & Corbett, 1983). Genetic inheritance and early eating practices seem to determine each person's weight set point. When a person's weight falls below his or her particular set point, the LH is activated and seeks to restore the lost weight by producing hunger and lowering the body's *metabolic* rate, the rate at which the body expends energy. When a person's weight rises above his or her set point, the VMH is activated, and it seeks to remove the excess weight by reducing hunger and increasing the body's metabolic rate.

According to the weight set point theory, when people diet and fall to a weight below their weight set point, their brain begins to try to restore the lost weight. Hypothalamic activity produces a preoccupation with food and a desire to binge. It also triggers bodily changes that make it harder to lose weight and easier to gain weight, however little is eaten (Spalter et al., 1993; Hill & Robinson, 1991). Once the brain and body begin acting to raise weight in this way, dieters actually enter into a battle against themselves. Some people apparently manage to shut down the inner "thermostat" and control their eating almost completely. These people move toward restricting-type anorexia nervosa. For others, the battle spirals toward a binge-purge pattern.

fact, long-term studies reveal a *rebound effect,* an eventual gain in weight in obese people who have lost weight on very low-calorie diets. Research also suggests that the feelings of failure that accompany diet rebounds may lead to dysfunctional eating patterns, including binge eating (Venditti et al., 1996). In cases of extreme obesity, where weight is indeed a clear health hazard and weight loss is advisable, establishing a realistic, attainable goal rather than an unrealistic ideal appears to be the most promising and healthful path to long-term weight loss (Brownell & O'Neil, 1993; Brownell & Wadden, 1992).

Efforts are now under way to develop new kinds of drugs that will operate directly on the genes, hormones, and proteins that have been linked to obesity (Carek & Dickerson, 1999; Greenberg, Chan, & Blackburn, 1999). Theoretically, these treatments will counteract the bodily reactions that undermine efforts at di-

Richard Howard © 1991 Discover

Laboratory obesity *By electrically stimulating parts of a rodent's hypothalamus, researchers can induce overeating and massive weight gain.*

eting. Whether such interventions can provide safe and permanent weight loss remains to be seen.

What Is the Proper Goal?

Some researchers argue that attempts to reduce obesity should focus less on weight loss and more on improving general health and attitudes (Painot et al., 2001; Rosen et al., 1995). If poor eating habits can be corrected, if a poor self-concept and distorted body image can be improved, and if overweight people can be educated about the myths and truths regarding obesity, perhaps everyone will be better off.

Thus a growing number of experts are suggesting that people who are mildly and perhaps even moderately obese should be left alone, at least so far as weight loss is concerned. At the very least, their weight-loss programs should set more modest and realistic goals. In addition, it is critical that the public overcome its prejudice against people who are overweight and come to appreciate that obesity is, at worst, a problem that requires treatment, and perhaps simply another version of the normal human condition.

SUMMING UP | **What Causes Eating Disorders?**

Today's theorists usually apply a multidimensional risk perspective to explain eating disorders, and they identify several key factors that may place a person at risk for such a disorder. The leading factors that have been proposed are society's emphasis on thinness and bias against obesity; family environment, including, perhaps, an enmeshed family pattern; ego and cognitive disturbances, including a poor sense of independence; a mood disorder; and biological factors such as activity of the hypothalamus and of chemicals such as GLP-1 and the weight set point.

How Are Eating Disorders Treated?

Today's treatments for eating disorders have two goals. The first is to correct as quickly as possible the abnormal eating pattern that is endangering the person's health. The second is to address the broader psychological and situational factors that have led to and now maintain the eating problem. Family and friends can also play an important role in helping to overcome the disorder (Sherman & Thompson, 1990).

MISLEADING LABEL

The term "anorexia," which means "lack of appetite," is actually a misnomer. Sufferers usually continue to have strong feelings of hunger.

Treatments for Anorexia Nervosa

The initial aims of treatment for anorexia nervosa are to help individuals regain their lost weight, recover from malnourishment, and eat normally again. Therapists must then help them to make psychological and perhaps family changes to lock in those gains.

HOW ARE PROPER WEIGHT AND NORMAL EATING RESTORED? A variety of treatment methods are used to help patients with anorexia nervosa gain weight quickly and return to health within weeks. In the past, treatment almost always took place in a hospital, but now it is often offered in outpatient settings (Pyle, 1999; Battle & Brownell, 1996).

In life-threatening cases, clinicians may need to use *forced tube and intravenous feedings* on a patient who refuses to eat. Unfortunately, this use of force may breed distrust in the patient and set up a power struggle between patient and therapist (Treasure, Todd, & Szmuckler, 1995; Zerbe, 1993). In contrast, in behavioral weight-restoration approaches clinicians use *rewards* whenever patients eat properly or gain weight and offer no rewards when they eat improperly or fail to gain weight (Tacon & Caldera, 2001; Griffiths et al., 1998).

Perhaps the most popular weight-restoration technique of recent years has been a combination of *supportive nursing care* and a high-calorie diet (Roloff, 2001; Treasure et al., 1995). Here nurses gradually increase a patient's diet over the course of several weeks to more than 2,500 calories a day. The nurses educate patients about the program, track their progress, provide encouragement, and help them recognize that their weight gain is under control and will not be permitted to go overboard into obesity. Studies find that patients in nursing-care programs usually gain the necessary weight over eight to twelve weeks (Treasure et al., 1995).

HOW ARE LASTING CHANGES ACHIEVED? Clinical researchers have found that people with anorexia nervosa must overcome their underlying psychological problems in order to achieve lasting improvement. Therapists typically offer a mixture of therapy and education to achieve this broader goal, using a combination of individual, group, and family approaches (King, 2001; Pyle, 1999).

BUILDING AUTONOMY AND SELF-AWARENESS One focus of treatment is to help patients with anorexia nervosa recognize their need for independence and teach them more appropriate ways to exercise control (Dare & Crowther, 1995; Robin et al., 1995). Therapists may also teach them to recognize and trust their internal sensations and feelings (Kaplan & Garfinkel, 1999). In the following exchange, a therapist tries to help a 15-year-old client recognize and share her feelings:

> *Patient:* I don't talk about my feelings; I never did.
> *Therapist:* Do you think I'll respond like others?
> *Patient:* What do you mean?
> *Therapist:* I think you may be afraid that I won't pay close attention to what you feel inside, or that I'll tell you not to feel the way you do—that it's foolish to feel frightened, to feel fat, to doubt yourself, considering how well you do in school, how you're appreciated by teachers, how pretty you are.
> *Patient:* (*Looking somewhat tense and agitated*) Well, I was always told to be polite and respect other people, just like a stupid, faceless doll.
> *Therapist:* Do I give you the impression that it would be disrespectful for you to share your feelings, whatever they may be?
> *Patient:* Not really; I don't know.
> *Therapist:* I can't, and won't, tell you that this is easy for you to do. . . . But I can promise you that you are free to speak your mind, and that I won't turn away.
>
> (*Strober & Yager, 1985, pp. 368-369*)

IN SEARCH OF A NAME

In the past, names for anorexia nervosa and its victims have included *inedia prodigiosa* ("a great starvation"), *fasting girl, wasting disease, morbid appetite, sitophobia* (fear of grain), and *hysterical anorexia.*

ConsiderThis

Research suggests that young girls who aspire to be superwomen—ideal women who are warm, nurturing, and attractive and at the same time competitive, accomplished, and successful—are more likely to have eating problems than those who reject the model (Gordon, 1990; Steiner-Adair, 1986). How might this relationship be explained?

Daily record *A teenager with anorexia nervosa writes in her journal as part of an inpatient treatment program. The writing helps her identify the fears, emotions, and needs that have contributed to her disorder.*

CORRECTING DISTURBED COGNITIONS Another focus of treatment is to help people with anorexia nervosa change their misconceptions and attitudes about eating and weight (Christie, 2000) (see Table 9-4 on the next page). Using cognitive approaches, therapists may guide clients to focus on, challenge, and change maladaptive assumptions, such as "I must always be perfect" or "My weight and shape determine my value" (Lask & Bryant-Waugh, 2000; Freeman, 1995). Therapists may also educate clients about the body distortions typical of anorexia nervosa and help them see that their own assessments of their size are incorrect (Wegner & Wegner, 2001; Mitchell & Peterson, 1997).

CHANGING FAMILY INTERACTIONS Family therapy is often part of the treatment program for anorexia nervosa (Levitt, 2001; Honig, 2000). As in other family therapy situations, the therapist meets with the family as a whole, points out troublesome family patterns, and helps the members make appropriate changes. In particular, family therapists may try to help the person with anorexia nervosa separate her feelings and needs from those of other family members. Research strongly suggests that family therapy (or at least parent counseling) can be helpful in the treatment of this disorder (Dare & Eisler, 1997, 1995; Russell et al., 1992).

POETIC CONCERNS

The famed poet Lord Byron (1788–1824), author of *Don Juan*, wrote: "A woman should never be seen eating and drinking unless it be lobster salad and champagne." Acquaintances of Byron noted that the poet himself had "a horror of fat." He regularly abstained from eating, believing that he would lose his creativity if he ate normally (Brumberg, 1988).

Mother:	I think I know what [Susan] is going through: all the doubt and insecurity of growing up and establishing her own identity. (*Turning to the patient, with tears*) If you just place trust in yourself, with the support of those around you who care, everything will turn out for the better.
Therapist:	Are you making yourself available to her? Should she turn to you, rely on you for guidance and emotional support?
Mother:	Well, that's what parents are for.
Therapist:	(*Turning to patient*) What do you think?
Susan:	(*To mother*) I can't keep depending on you, Mom, or everyone else. That's what I've been doing, and it gave me anorexia. . . .
Therapist:	Do you think your mom would prefer that there be no secrets between her and the kids—an open door, so to speak?
Older sister:	Sometimes I do.
Therapist:	(*To patient and younger sister*) How about you two?
Susan:	Yeah. Sometimes it's like whatever I feel, she has to feel.
Younger sister:	Yeah.

(Strober & Yager, 1985, pp. 381-382)

Table 9-4

Sample Items from the Eating Disorder Inventory II

For each item, decide if the item is true about you ALWAYS (A), USUALLY (U), OFTEN (O), SOMETIMES (S), RARELY (R), or NEVER (N). Circle the letter that corresponds to your rating.

A	U	O	S	R	N	I think that my stomach is too big.
A	U	O	S	R	N	I eat when I am upset.
A	U	O	S	R	N	I think about dieting.
A	U	O	S	R	N	I think that my thighs are too large.
A	U	O	S	R	N	I feel ineffective as a person.
A	U	O	S	R	N	I feel extremely guilty after overeating.
A	U	O	S	R	N	I am terrified of gaining weight.
A	U	O	S	R	N	I get confused about what emotion I am feeling.
A	U	O	S	R	N	I have gone on eating binges where I felt that I could not stop.
A	U	O	S	R	N	I have trouble expressing my emotions to others.
A	U	O	S	R	N	I get confused as to whether or not I am hungry.
A	U	O	S	R	N	I think my hips are too big.
A	U	O	S	R	N	If I gain a pound, I worry that I will keep gaining.
A	U	O	S	R	N	I think my buttocks are too large.
A	U	O	S	R	N	I eat or drink in secrecy.
A	U	O	S	R	N	I would like to be in total control of my bodily urges.

Source: Garner, Olmsted, & Polivy, 1991, 1984.

> "Girls should be encouraged to take an interest in their appearance when they are very young."
>
> *Ladies' Home Journal,* 1940

WHAT IS THE AFTERMATH OF ANOREXIA NERVOSA? The use of combined treatment approaches has greatly improved the outlook for people with anorexia nervosa, although the road to recovery can be difficult. The course and outcome of this disorder vary from person to person (Miller, 1996), but researchers have noted certain trends.

On the positive side, weight is often quickly restored once treatment begins, and treatment gains may continue for years. In one study, 83 percent of patients continued to show improvement when they were interviewed several years or more after their initial recovery: around 33 percent were fully recovered and 50 percent partially improved (Herzog et al., 1999; Treasure et al., 1995). Other studies have found that most individuals perform effectively at their jobs and express job satisfaction years after their recovery (Fombonne, 1995; Theander, 1970).

Another positive note is that most females with anorexia nervosa menstruate again when they regain their weight (Fombonne, 1995; Crisp, 1981), and other medical improvements follow (Iketani et al., 1995). Also encouraging is that the death rate from anorexia nervosa seems to be declining (Neumarker, 1997; Treasure & Szmukler, 1995). Earlier diagnosis and safer and faster weight-restoration techniques may account for this trend. Deaths that do occur are usually caused by suicide, starvation, infection, gastrointestinal problems, or electrolyte imbalance (Nielson et al., 1998; Treasure & Szmukler, 1995).

On the negative side, close to 20 percent of persons with anorexia nervosa remain seriously troubled for years (APA, 2000; Halmi et al., 1991). Furthermore, recovery, when it does occur, is not always permanent (Herzog et al., 1999). Anorexic behavior recurs in one-third of recovered patients, usually triggered by new stresses, such as marriage, pregnancy, or a major relocation (Strober, Freeman, & Morrell, 1997). Even years later, many recovered individuals continue to express concerns about their weight and appearance. Some continue to restrict their diets to a degree, experience anxiety when they eat with other people, or hold some distorted ideas about food, eating, and weight (Fichter & Pirke, 1995; Pirke et al., 1992).

About half of those who have suffered from anorexia nervosa continue to experience certain emotional problems—particularly depression, social anxiety, and obsessiveness—years after treatment. Such problems are particularly common in those who have not succeeded in reaching a fully normal weight (Halmi, 1995; Hsu et al., 1992).

The more weight persons have lost and the more time that has passed before they entered treatment, the poorer the recovery rate (Pyle, 1999; Steinhausen, 1997). Individuals who had psychological or sexual problems before the onset of the disorder tend to have a poorer recovery rate than those without such a history (Lewis & Chatoor, 1994). Teenagers seem to have a better recovery rate than older patients (APA, 2000; Steinhausen et al., 2000). Females have a better recovery rate than males.

Treatments for Bulimia Nervosa

Treatment programs tailored to bulimia nervosa are relatively new, but they have risen rapidly in popularity. Many of these programs are offered in eating disorder clinics. All share the immediate goal of helping clients to eliminate their binge-purge patterns and establish good eating habits and the more general goal of eliminating the underlying causes of bulimic patterns. The programs emphasize education as much as therapy (Davis et al., 1997; Button, 1993). Like programs for anorexia nervosa, they often combine several treatment strategies, including individual insight therapy, group therapy, behavioral therapy, and antidepressant drug therapy (King, 2001; Tobin, 2000).

INDIVIDUAL INSIGHT THERAPY Psychodynamic therapy has often been applied to cases of bulimia nervosa (Bloom et al., 1994; Fichter, 1990). The therapist uses free association and gentle interpretations to help patients uncover and work through their frustrations, lack of self-trust, need for control, and feelings of powerlessness (Dare & Crowther, 1995; Lerner, 1986). Only a few research studies have tested the effectiveness of psychodynamic therapy in bulimia nervosa, but those studies are generally supportive (Valbak, 2001; Yager, 1985).

The insight approach that is now receiving the most attention in cases of bulimia nervosa is cognitive therapy, which tries to help clients recognize and change their maladaptive attitudes toward food, eating, weight, and shape (Wegner & Wegner, 2001; Porzelius et al., 1999). Cognitive therapists typically teach the individuals to identify and challenge the negative thoughts that regularly precede their urge to binge—"I have no self-control," "I might as well give up," "I look fat" (Mitchell & Peterson, 1997; Fairburn, 1985). They may also guide clients to recognize, question, and eventually change their perfectionistic standards, sense of helplessness, and low self-concept (Freeman, 1995; Mizes, 1995).

Cognitive therapy seems to help as many as 65 percent of patients to stop bingeing and purging (Compas et al., 1998; Walsh et al., 1997). Approaches that mix cognitive and psychodynamic techniques also appear to be helpful (Brisman, 1992; Yager, 1985). Therapists have had considerable success with *interpersonal psychotherapy* as well, a treatment that seeks to improve interpersonal

A new look for Barbie *Partly in response to clinical concerns, the manufacturer of "Barbie" recently changed the proportions of the doll with whom so many women grow up. A 5-foot-2, 125-pound woman who aspires to Barbie's old proportions would have to grow to be 7-foot-2, add 5 inches to her chest and 3.2 inches to her neck length, and lose 6 inches from her waist (Brownell & Napolitano, 1995).*

And She Lived Happily Ever After?

Marcus/Sipa Press

In May 1996 Alicia Machado, a 19-year-old woman from Venezuela, was crowned Miss Universe. Then her problems began. During the first eight months of her reign, her weight rose from 118 to 160 pounds, angering pageant officials and sparking rumors that she was about to be relieved of her crown. The "problem" received broad newspaper and television coverage and much ridicule on talk radio programs around the world.

Ms. Machado explained, "I was a normal girl, but my life has had big changes. I travel to many countries, eat different foods." Nevertheless, in response to all the pressure, she undertook a special diet and an extensive exercise program to lose at least some of the weight she had gained. Her trainer claimed that a weight of 118 pounds was too low for her frame and explained that she had originally attained it by taking diet pills.

Consider This
◉ • Why did so many people hold such strong, often critical opinions about Ms. Machado's weight? • What messages did this controversy and its resolution convey to women around the world?

THE IMPACT OF SATELLITE TV

In 1995 satellite TV began beaming Western shows and fashions to remote parts of the Fiji Islands in the South Pacific. Just a few years later, researchers found that Fijian teenage girls who watched television at least three nights per week were more likely than others to feel "too big or fat." In addition, almost two-thirds of them had dieted in the previous month, and 15 percent had vomited to control weight within the previous year (compared to 3 percent before television) (Becker, 1999).

---

functioning (Wegner & Wegner, 2001; Wilfley & Cohen, 1997), and with *self-care manuals,* which describe education and treatment strategies for sufferers (Garvin et al., 2001; Schmidt et al., 1993).

GROUP THERAPY Most bulimia nervosa programs now include group therapy to give people an opportunity to share their thoughts, concerns, and experiences with one another (Leung et al., 2000; Pyle, 1999). Group members learn that their disorder is not unique or shameful, and they receive support and understanding from one another, along with open feedback and insights (Manley & Needham, 1995). In the group they can also work directly on underlying fears of displeasing others or being criticized. Research suggests that group therapy is at least somewhat helpful in as many as 75 percent of bulimia nervosa cases, particularly when it is combined with individual insight therapy (Valbak, 2001; McKisack & Waller, 1997).

BEHAVIORAL THERAPY Behavioral techniques are often included in treatment programs for bulimia nervosa (Tacon & Caldera, 2001). Clients may, for example, be asked to keep diaries of their eating behavior, changes in sensations of hunger and fullness, and the ebb and flow of other feelings (Mitchell & Peterson, 1997; Goleman, 1995). This approach helps them to observe their eating patterns more objectively and recognize the emotions that trigger their desire to binge.

Some behaviorists use the technique of *exposure and response prevention* to help break the binge-purge cycle. As we saw in Chapter 5, this approach consists of exposing people to situations that would ordinarily raise anxiety and then preventing them from performing their usual compulsive responses until they learn that the situations are actually harmless and their compulsive acts unnecessary. For bulimia nervosa, the therapists require clients to eat particular kinds and amounts of food and then prevent them from vomiting, to show that eating can be a harmless and even constructive activity that needs no undoing (Rosen & Leitenberg, 1985, 1982). Typically the therapist sits with the client during the eating of forbidden foods and stays until the urge to purge has passed (Porzelius et al., 1999). Studies find that this treatment often helps reduce eating-related anxieties, bingeing, and vomiting (Bulik et al., 1998).

ANTIDEPRESSANT MEDICATIONS During the past decade, antidepressant drugs such as fluoxetine, or Prozac, have been used in treatments for bulimia nervosa (Mitchell, 2001; Walsh et al., 1997). According to research, the drugs help 25 to 40 percent of patients, reducing their binges by an average of 67 percent and vomiting by 56 percent. Once again, drug therapy seems to work best in combination with other forms of therapy.

WHAT IS THE AFTERMATH OF BULIMIA NERVOSA? Left untreated, bulimia nervosa can last for years, sometimes improving temporarily but then returning (APA, 2000). Treatment, however, produces immediate, significant improvement in approximately 40 percent of clients: they stop or greatly reduce their bingeing and purging, eat properly, and maintain a normal weight. Another 40 percent show a moderate response—at least some decrease in bingeing and purging. As many as 20 percent show little immediate improvement (Keel & Mitchell, 1997; Button, 1993). Follow-up studies suggest that by 10 years after treatment, 89 percent of persons with bulimia nervosa have recovered either fully (70 percent) or partially (19 percent) (Herzog et al., 1999; Keel et al., 1999). Those with partial recoveries continue to have recurrent binges or purges.

Relapse can be a problem even among people who respond successfully to treatment (Herzog et al., 1999; Keel & Mitchell, 1997). As with anorexia nervosa, relapses are usually triggered by a new life stress, such as an upcoming exam, job change, illness, marriage, or divorce (Abraham & Llewellyn-Jones, 1984). One study found that close to one-third of persons who had recovered from bulimia nervosa relapsed within two years of treatment, usually within six months (Olmsted, Kaplan, & Rockert, 1994). Relapse is more likely among persons who had longer histories of bulimia nervosa before treatment, had vomited more frequently during their disorder, had histories of substance abuse, and continue to distrust others after treatment (Keel et al., 2000, 1999; Olmsted et al., 1994).

Research also indicates that treatment helps many, but not all, people with bulimia nervosa to attain lasting improvements in their overall psychological and social functioning (Keel et al., 2000; Yager et al., 1995). Follow-up studies find former patients to be less depressed than they had been at the time of diagnosis (Halmi, 1995). Approximately one-third of former patients interact in healthier ways at work, at home, and in social settings, while another third interact effectively in two of these areas (Hsu & Holder, 1986).

SOCIETAL DISAPPROVAL

In 1992 Canada canceled national beauty contests, claiming they were too degrading.

SUMMING UP | **How Are Eating Disorders Treated?**

Therapists aim first to help people with eating disorders resume normal eating and regain their health; then they tackle the broader problems that led to the disorder.

Treatments for Anorexia Nervosa The first step in treating anorexia nervosa is to increase calorie intake and restore the person's weight quickly, using a strategy such as supportive nursing care. The second step is to deal with the underlying psychological and perhaps family problems, using a mixture of therapy and education. About 83 percent of people with anorexia nervosa recover markedly. However, some later relapse, and many continue to be concerned about their weight and appearance. Most who do recover are later found to enjoy work and perform effectively at their jobs.

Treatments for Bulimia Nervosa Treatments for bulimia nervosa focus first on stopping the binge-purge pattern and then on the underlying causes of the disorder. Often several treatment strategies, including individual insight therapy, group therapy, behavioral therapy, and antidepressant medications, are combined. Approximately 40 percent of people show an outstanding response to treatment, another 40 percent a moderate response. Relapse can be a problem and may be triggered by a new stress. At the same time, treatment leads to lasting improvements in psychological and social functioning for many individuals.

IS PREVENTION POSSIBLE?

In a psychoeducation program, 11- to 13-year-old girls who were extremely worried about gaining weight were taught that female weight gain after puberty is normal and that excessive restriction of food can actually lead to weight gain. The concerns of the girls lessened markedly, in contrast to those of similar subjects who did not receive the instruction (Killen, 1996; Killen et al., 1994).

CROSSROADS:
A Standard for Integrating Perspectives

We have observed throughout this book that it is often useful to consider socio-cultural, psychological, and biological factors jointly when one tries to explain or treat various forms of abnormal functioning. Nowhere is the argument for combining these perspectives more powerful than in the case of eating disorders. According to the multidimensional risk perspective, embraced by many theorists, varied factors act together to encourage the development of eating disorders (Lyon et al., 1997). One case may be the result of societal pressures, autonomy problems, the changes of adolescence, and hypothalamic overactivity, while another case may result from family pressures, depression, and the effects of dieting. No wonder that the most helpful treatment programs for eating disorders combine sociocultural, psychological, and biological approaches. It makes sense that treatment programs need to be wide-ranging and flexible, tailored to the unique interacting problems of the patient. When the multidimensional risk perspective is applied to eating disorders, it demonstrates that scientists and practitioners who follow very different models can work together effectively in an atmosphere of mutual respect.

Today's many investigations of eating disorders keep revealing new surprises that force clinicians to adjust their theories and treatment programs. For example, in recent years researchers have learned that people with bulimia nervosa sometimes feel strangely positive about their symptoms. A recovered patient said, "I still miss my bulimia as I would an old friend who has died" (Cauwels, 1983, p. 173). Only when feelings like these are understood will treatment become fully effective—another reason why the cooperative efforts of different kinds of theorists, clinicians, and researchers are so important.

While clinicians and researchers seek more answers about eating disorders, clients themselves have begun to take an active role. A number of patient-run organizations now provide information, education, and support through a national telephone hot line, professional referrals, newsletters, workshops, and conferences. The National Anorexic Aid Society, the American Anorexia and Bulimia Association, the National Association of Anorexia Nervosa and Associated Disorders, and Anorexia Nervosa and Related Eating Disorders, Inc., help fight the feelings of isolation and shame experienced by people with eating disorders. The organizations show countless sufferers that they are hardly alone or powerless.

FORBIDDEN FRUIT (AND CRACKERS)

In one study, preschool children showed no special interest in fruit bars and Goldfish crackers until the foods were placed in a "no-no" jar. Once the foods had been given taboo status, the children made more positive comments about them, requested them more often, tried to gain access to them, and grabbed more of them when they were available (Fisher & Birch, 1999).

KEY TERMS

anorexia nervosa p. 246

restricting-type anorexia nervosa p. 246

amenorrhea p. 249

bulimia nervosa p. 249

binge p. 249

compensatory behavior p. 249

binge-eating disorder p. 250

multidimensional risk perspective p. 255

enmeshed family pattern p. 258

effective parents p. 258

hypothalamus p. 261

lateral hypothalamus (LH) p. 261

ventromedial hypothalamus (VMH) p. 261

weight set point p. 262

supportive nursing care p. 264

QUICK QUIZ

1. What are the symptoms and main features of anorexia nervosa? pp. 246–249

2. What are the symptoms and main features of bulimia nervosa? pp. 249–252

3. How are people with anorexia nervosa similar to those with bulimia nervosa? How are they different? pp. 253–255

4. Theorists usually apply a multi-dimensional risk perspective to explain the eating disorders. What does this mean? p. 255

5. What evidence suggests that socio-cultural pressures and factors may set the stage for eating disorders? pp. 255–258

6. According to Hilde Bruch, how might parents' failure to attend appropriately to their baby's internal needs and emotions be contributing to the later development of an eating disorder? pp. 258–260

7. How might a person's hypothalamus and weight set point contribute to the development of an eating disorder? pp. 261–262

8. When clinicians treat people with anorexia nervosa, what are their short-term and long-term goals? What approaches do they use to accomplish them? pp. 264–265

9. How well do people with anorexia nervosa recover from their disorder? What factors affect a person's recovery? What risks and problems linger after recovery? pp. 266–267

10. What are the key goals and approaches used in the treatment of bulimia nervosa? How successful are they? What factors affect a person's recovery? What are the risks of relapse? pp. 267–269

CYBER STUDY

▲ *Witness the feelings behind bingeing and purging.* ▲ *How does bulimia nervosa begin?* ▲ *Why might relapse occur in cases of eating disorders?* ▲ *How do individuals feel toward their eating disorders?* ▲ *Do either obsessive-compulsive disorders or body dysmorphic disorders set the stage for eating disorders?*

SEARCH THE *FUNDAMENTALS OF ABNORMAL PSYCHOLOGY* CD-ROM FOR

▲ Chapter 9 video case and discussion
   "Liz"—Bulimia Nervosa

▲ Chapter 9 practice test and feedback

▲ Additional video case and discussion
   "Jennifer"—Obsessive-Compulsive Disorder

LOG ON TO THE COMER WEB PAGE FOR:

▲ Suggested Web links, research exercises, FAQ page, additional Chapter 9 practice test questions
   <www.worthpublishers.com/comer>

Source: *The Waist Land: Eating Disorders in America* (Coronet/MTI, 1985)

Substance-Related Disorders

"I am Duncan. I am an alcoholic." The audience settled deeper into their chairs at these familiar words. Another chronicle of death and rebirth would shortly begin [at] Alcoholics Anonymous. . . .

. . . "I must have been just past my 15th birthday when I had that first drink that everybody talks about. And like so many of them . . . it was like a miracle. With a little beer in my gut, the world was transformed. I wasn't a weakling anymore, I could lick almost anybody on the block. And girls? Well, you can imagine how a couple of beers made me feel, like I could have any girl I wanted. . . .

"Though it's obvious to me now that my drinking even then, in high school, and after I got to college, was a problem, I didn't think so at the time. After all, everybody was drinking and getting drunk and acting stupid, and I didn't really think I was different. . . . I guess the fact that I hadn't really had any blackouts and that I could go for days without having to drink reassured me that things hadn't gotten out of control. And that's the way it went, until I found myself drinking even more—and more often—and suffering more from my drinking, along about my third year of college.

. . . "My roommate, a friend from high school, started bugging me about my drinking. It wasn't even that I'd have to sleep it off the whole next day and miss class, it was that he had begun to hear other friends talking about me, about the fool I'd made of myself at parties. He saw how shaky I was the morning after, and he saw how different I was when I'd been drinking a lot—almost out of my head was the way he put it. And he could count the bottles that I'd leave around the room, and he knew what the drinking and carousing was doing to my grades. . . . [P]artly because I really cared about my roommate and didn't want to lose him as a friend, I did cut down on my drinking by half or more. I only drank on weekends—and then only at night. . . . And that got me through the rest of college and, actually, through law school as well. . . .

"Shortly after getting my law degree, I married my first wife, and . . . for the first time since I started, my drinking was no problem at all. I would go for weeks at a time without touching a drop. . . .

"My marriage started to go bad after our second son, our third child, was born. I was very much career-and-success oriented, and I had little time to spend at home with my family. . . . My traveling had increased a lot, there were stimulating people on those trips, and, let's face it, there were some pretty exciting women available, too. So home got to be little else but a nagging, boring wife and children I wasn't very interested in. My drinking had gotten bad again, too, with being on the road so much, having to do a lot of entertaining at lunch when I wasn't away, and trying to soften the hassles at home. I guess I was putting down close to a gallon of very good scotch a week, with one thing or another.

"And as that went on, the drinking began to affect both my marriage and my career. With enough booze in me and under the pressures of guilt over my failure to carry out my responsibilities to my wife and children, I sometimes got kind of rough physically with them. I would break furniture, throw things

SUBSTANCE ABUSE A pattern of behavior in which people rely on a drug excessively and regularly, bringing damage to their relationships, functioning poorly at work, or putting themselves or others in danger.

SUBSTANCE DEPENDENCE A pattern of behavior in which people organize their lives around a drug, possibly building a tolerance to it or experiencing withdrawal symptoms when they stop taking it, or both. Also called *addiction*.

TOLERANCE The adjustment that the brain and the body make to the regular use of certain drugs so that ever larger doses are needed to achieve the earlier effects.

WITHDRAWAL Unpleasant, sometimes dangerous reactions that may occur when people who use a drug regularly stop taking or reduce their dosage of the drug.

ALCOHOL Any beverage containing ethyl alcohol, including beer, wine, and liquor.

around, then rush out and drive off in the car. I had a couple of wrecks, lost my license for two years because of one of them. Worst of all was when I tried to stop. By then I was totally hooked, so every time I tried to stop drinking, I'd experience withdrawal in all its horrors . . . with the vomiting and the "shakes" and being unable to sit still or to lie down. And that would go on for days at a time. . . .

"Then, about four years ago, with my life in ruins, my wife given up on me and the kids with her, out of a job, and way down on my luck, [Alcoholics Anonymous] and I found each other. . . . I've been dry now for a little over two years, and with luck and support, I may stay sober. . . ."

(Spitzer et al., 1983, pp. 87–89)

Human beings enjoy a remarkable variety of foods and drinks. Every substance on earth probably has been tried by someone, somewhere, at some time. We also have discovered substances that have interesting effects—both medical and pleasurable—on our brains and the rest of our bodies. We may swallow an aspirin to quiet a headache, an antibiotic to fight an infection, or a tranquilizer to calm us down. We may drink coffee to get going in the morning or wine to relax with friends. We may smoke cigarettes to soothe our nerves. However, many of the substances we consume can harm us or disrupt our behavior or mood. The misuse of such substances has become one of society's biggest problems; it has been estimated that the cost of drug misuse is at least $276 billion each year in the United States alone (Mark et al., 2001; NIDA, 1998).

A *drug* is typically considered to be any substance other than food that affects our bodies or minds. It need not be a medicine or be illegal. The term *substance* is now frequently used in place of "drug," in part because many people fail to see that such substances as alcohol, tobacco, and caffeine are drugs, too. When a person ingests a substance—whether it be alcohol, cocaine, marijuana, or some form of medication—trillions of powerful molecules surge through the bloodstream and into the brain (Nash, 1997). Once there, the molecules set off a series of biochemical events that disturb the normal operation of the brain and body. Not surprisingly, substance misuse may lead to various kinds of abnormal functioning.

Drugs may cause *temporary* changes in behavior, emotion, or thought. As Duncan found out, for example, an excessive amount of alcohol may lead to *intoxication* (literally, "poisoning"), a temporary state of poor judgment, mood changes, irritability, slurred speech, and poor coordination. Drugs such as LSD may produce a particular form of intoxication, sometimes called *hallucinosis,* consisting of perceptual distortions and hallucinations.

Some substances can also lead to *long-term* problems. People who regularly ingest them may develop maladaptive patterns of behavior and changes in their body's physical responses (APA, 2000). In one such pattern, called **substance abuse,** they rely on the drug excessively and repeatedly, and in so doing damage their family and social relationships, perform poorly at work, or put themselves and others in danger. A more advanced pattern, **substance dependence,** is also known as **addiction.** In this pattern, people not only abuse the drug but center their lives on it and perhaps acquire a physical dependence on it, marked by a *tolerance* for it, *withdrawal* symptoms, or both (see Table 10-1). When people develop **tolerance,** they need increasing doses of a drug in order to keep getting the desired effect. **Withdrawal** consists of unpleasant and even dangerous symptoms—cramps, anxiety attacks, sweating, nausea—that occur when individuals suddenly stop taking or cut back on the drug.

Duncan, who described his problems to fellow members at an Alcoholics Anonymous meeting, was caught in a pattern of alcohol dependence. When he was a college student and later a lawyer, alcohol damaged his family, social, aca-

Liam Longman/Miramax/The Kobal Collection

Heroin chic *Over the years, different substances may rise and fall and rise again in popularity. During the 1980s heroin was associated with crime, immorality, and street life, and its use declined. In the 1990s, however, its popularity rose greatly. For a time the drug even defined a new look in the fashion industry—"heroin chic"—and it was prominently featured in movies such as* Trainspotting.

demic, and work life. He also built up a tolerance for the substance over time and experienced withdrawal symptoms such as vomiting and shaking when he tried to stop using it. In any given year, 11.3 percent of all adults in the United States display substance abuse or dependence. Only 20 percent of them receive treatment (Kessler & Zhao, 1999; Regier et al., 1993).

Many drugs are available in our society, and new ones appear almost every day. Some are found in nature, others derived from natural substances, and still others produced in the laboratory. Some, such as antianxiety drugs and barbiturates, require a physician's prescription for legal use. Others, such as alcohol and nicotine, are legally available to adults. Still others, such as heroin, are illegal under all circumstances. In 1962 only 4 million people in the United States had ever used marijuana, cocaine, heroin, or another illegal substance; today the number has climbed to more than 72 million (NHSDA, 1998; Kleber, 1995). In fact, over 23 million people have used illegal substances within the past year, and 14 million are using one of them currently. Ten percent of all teenagers have used an illegal drug within the past month.

The substances people misuse fall into several categories: *depressants,* such as alcohol and opioids, which slow the central nervous system; *stimulants* of the central nervous system, such as cocaine and amphetamines; *hallucinogens,* such as LSD, which cause delusions, hallucinations, and other powerful changes in sensory perception; and *cannabis* substances, such as marijuana, which cause a mixture of hallucinogenic, depressant, and stimulant effects. Many people take more than one of these substances at a time, a practice known as *polydrug use.* In this chapter we shall look at some of the most problematic substances and the abnormal patterns they may produce. After first examining the substances separately, we shall consider the causes and treatments of substance-related disorders as a group.

Table 10-1 DSM-IV Checklist

SUBSTANCE ABUSE

1. A maladaptive pattern of substance use leading to significant impairment or distress
2. At least one of the following features occurring within one year:
   (a) Recurrent substance use, resulting in failure to fulfill major role obligations at work, school, or home
   (b) Recurrent substance use in situations in which it is physically hazardous
   (c) Recurrent substance-related legal problems
   (d) Substance use that continues despite its causing or increasing persistent social or interpersonal problems

SUBSTANCE DEPENDENCE

1. A maladaptive pattern of substance use leading to significant impairment or distress
2. At least three of the following:
   (a) Tolerance
   (b) Withdrawal
   (c) Substance often taken in larger amounts over a longer period than was intended
   (d) Persistent desire for substance or unsuccessful efforts to control substance use
   (e) Considerable time spent trying to obtain, use, or recover from the substance
   (f) Substance use in place of important activities
   (g) Substance use that continues despite its causing or increasing persistent physical or psychological problems

Based on APA, 2000, 1994.

Depressants

Depressants slow the activity of the central nervous system. They reduce tension and inhibitions and may interfere with a person's judgment, motor activity, and concentration. The three most widely used groups of depressants are *alcohol, sedative-hypnotic drugs,* and *opioids.*

Alcohol

Two-thirds of the people in the United States at least from time to time drink beverages that contain **alcohol.** Purchases of beer, wine, and liquor amount to tens of billions of dollars each year in the United States alone. Around 6 percent of all adults are heavy drinkers, having at least five drinks on at least five occasions each month (NHSDA, 1998). Among heavy drinkers, men outnumber women by more than 4 to 1 (Wilsnack et al., 2000).

All alcoholic beverages contain *ethyl alcohol,* a chemical that is quickly absorbed into the blood through the lining of the stomach and the intestine. The ethyl alcohol immediately begins to take effect as it is carried in the bloodstream to the central nervous system (the brain and spinal cord), where it acts to depress, or slow, functioning by binding to various neurons. One important group

BEER SALES

Each year Americans pay $60 billion for 196 million barrels of beer. Light beer accounts for more than one-third of beer sales. The state of Nevada has the highest beer consumption (on average 49 gallons per person) and Utah the lowest (21 gallons) (Weissman, 1999).

of neurons to which ethyl alcohol binds are those that normally receive the neurotransmitter GABA. As we observed in Chapter 4, GABA carries an *inhibitory* message—a message to stop firing—when it is received at certain neurons. When alcohol binds to receptors on those neurons, it apparently helps GABA to shut down the neurons, thus helping to relax the drinker (Heinz et al., 2001; Loh & Ball, 2000).

At first ethyl alcohol depresses the areas of the brain that control judgment and inhibition; people become looser, more talkative, and often more friendly. As their inner control breaks down, they may feel relaxed, confident, and happy. When more alcohol is absorbed, it slows down additional areas in the central nervous system, leaving the drinkers less able to make sound judgments, their speech less careful and less clear, and their memory weaker. Many people become highly emotional and perhaps loud and aggressive.

Motor difficulties increase as drinking continues, and reaction times slow. People may be unsteady when they stand or walk and clumsy in performing even simple activities. Their vision becomes blurred, particularly side vision, and they have trouble hearing. As a result, people who have drunk too much alcohol may have great difficulty driving or solving simple problems.

The extent of the effect of ethyl alcohol is determined by its *concentration,* or proportion, in the blood. Thus a given amount of alcohol will have less effect on a large person than on a small one (see Table 10-2). Gender also affects the concentration of alcohol in the blood. Women have less of the stomach enzyme *alco-*

FIGHTING BLACK DEATH

A popular theory in the mid-1300s was that strong drinks of alcohol offered protection from the Black Death, the bubonic plague, which was sweeping Europe. This mistaken belief led to a plague of drunkenness as widespread as the plague of contagion (Asimov, 1997).

Table 10-2

Relationships between Sex, Weight, Oral Alcohol Consumption, and Blood Alcohol Level

| ABSOLUTE ALCOHOL (OUNCES) | BEVERAGE INTAKE* | BLOOD ALCOHOL LEVEL (PERCENT) | | | | | |
		FEMALE (100 LB.)	MALE (100 LB.)	FEMALE (150 LB.)	MALE (150 LB.)	FEMALE (200 LB.)	MALE (200 LB.)
1/2	1 oz. spirits† 1 glass wine 1 can beer	0.045	0.037	0.03	0.025	0.022	0.019
1	2 oz. spirits 2 glasses wine 2 cans beer	0.090	0.075	0.06	0.050	0.045	0.037
2	4 oz. spirits 4 glasses wine 4 cans beer	0.180	0.150	0.12	0.100	0.090	0.070
3	6 oz. spirits 6 glasses wine 6 cans beer	0.270	0.220	0.18	0.150	0.130	0.110
4	8 oz. spirits 8 glasses wine 8 cans beer	0.360	0.300	0.24	0.200	0.180	0.150
5	10 oz. spirits 10 glasses wine 10 cans beer	0.450	0.370	0.30	0.250	0.220	0.180

*In 1 hour.
†100-proof spirits

Source: Ray & Ksir, 1993, p. 194.

hol dehydrogenase, which breaks down alcohol in the stomach before it enters the blood. So women become more intoxicated than men on equal doses of alcohol.

Levels of impairment are closely tied to the concentration of ethyl alcohol in the blood. When the alcohol concentration reaches 0.06 percent of the blood volume, a person usually feels relaxed and comfortable. By the time it reaches 0.09 percent, however, the drinker crosses the line into intoxication. If the level goes as high as 0.55 percent, death will probably result. Most people, however, lose consciousness before they can drink enough to reach this level.

The effects of alcohol subside only when the alcohol concentration in the blood declines. Most of the alcohol is broken down, or *metabolized,* by the liver into carbon dioxide and water, which can be exhaled and excreted. Because different people's livers work at different speeds, rates of "sobering up" vary. Despite popular belief, only time and metabolism can make a person sober. Drinking black coffee, splashing cold water on one's face, or "pulling oneself together" cannot hurry the process.

ALCOHOL ABUSE AND DEPENDENCE Though legal, alcohol is actually one of the most dangerous of recreational drugs, and its reach extends across the life span (Scheier & Botvin, 1997). In fact, around 10 percent of elementary school students admit to some alcohol use, while 51 percent of high school seniors drink alcohol each month (most to the point of intoxication) and 3.5 percent report drinking every day (Johnston et al., 1999, 1993; NIDA, 1995) (see Figure 10-1). Similarly, alcohol misuse is a major problem on college campuses (Schulenberg et al., 2001).

Surveys indicate that over a one-year period, as many as 10 percent of all adults in the United States fall into a long-term pattern of alcohol abuse or dependence, either of which is known in popular terms as *alcoholism* (Kessler & Zhao, 1999; Regier et al., 1993). Between 13 and 18 percent of the nation's adults display one of the patterns at some time in their lives, with men outnumbering women by as much as 5 to 1. Many teenagers also experience alcohol abuse and dependence (Scheier & Botvin, 1997).

"Wine is the most healthful and most hygienic of beverages."

Louis Pasteur

COLLEGE EXPENSES

Each year college students spend $5.5 billion on alcohol (mostly beer)—more than they spend on books, soda, coffee, juice, and milk combined (Eigan, 1991).

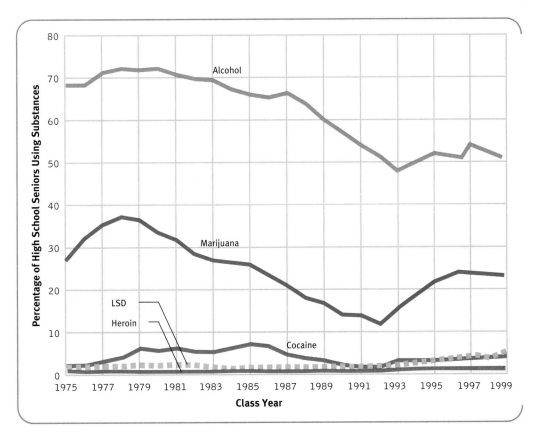

FIGURE 10-1 **Teenagers and substance use** *The overall percentage of high school seniors who admitted to using substances illicitly at least once within 30 days of being surveyed rose in the 1970s, declined in the 1980s, and rose again in the 1990s (Johnston et al., 1999; NIDA, 1996).*

DELIRIUM TREMENS (DTs) A dramatic withdrawal reaction experienced by some people who are alcohol-dependent. It consists of confusion, clouded consciousness, and terrifying visual hallucinations.

The prevalence of alcoholism in a given year is around 7 percent for both whites and African Americans and 9 percent for Hispanic Americans (APA, 2000; Anthony et al., 1995; Helzer et al., 1991). Generally, Asians in the United States and elsewhere have lower rates of alcoholism than do people from other cultures. As many as one-half of these individuals have a deficiency of alcohol dehydrogenase, the chemical responsible for breaking down alcohol, so they react negatively to even a modest intake of alcohol. Such reactions in turn prevent extended use (Wall et al., 2001; APA, 2000).

ALCOHOL ABUSE Generally speaking, people who abuse alcohol drink large amounts regularly and rely on it to help them to do things that would otherwise make them anxious. Eventually the drinking interferes with their social behavior and ability to think and work. They may have frequent arguments with family members or friends, miss work repeatedly, and even lose their jobs (Schmidt et al., 2000).

Individually, however, people vary in their patterns of alcohol abuse. Some drink large amounts of alcohol every day and keep drinking until intoxicated. Others go on periodic binges of heavy drinking that can last weeks or months. They may remain intoxicated for days and later be unable to remember anything about the period. Still others may limit their excessive drinking to weekends or evenings, or both. The actor Dick Van Dyke commented:

> I didn't miss work ever because of drinking. And I never drank at work. Never drank during the day—only at home and only in the evenings. . . . I never craved a drink during the day. I was never a morning drinker—I didn't want one then. The idea made me as sick as it would make anyone else. But evening drinking is a form of alcoholism, just like periodic drinking is a form of alcoholism.
>
> *(HEW, 1976, p. 76)*

AT RISK

Individuals who begin drinking before age 15 are twice as likely to develop alcohol abuse and four times as likely to develop alcohol dependence as those who begin drinking at age 21 (Grant & Dawson, 1997).

ALCOHOL DEPENDENCE For many people, the pattern of alcohol misuse includes dependence. Their bodies build up a tolerance for alcohol and they need to drink ever greater amounts to feel its effects. They also experience withdrawal when they stop drinking. Within hours their hands, tongue, and eyelids begin to shake; they feel weak and nauseated; they sweat and vomit; their heart beats rapidly; and their blood pressure rises. They may also become anxious, depressed, unable to sleep, or irritable (APA, 2000).

A small percentage of people who are dependent on alcohol experience a particularly dramatic withdrawal reaction called **delirium tremens ("the DTs").** It consists of terrifying visual hallucinations that begin within three days after they stop or reduce their drinking. Some people see small, frightening animals chasing or crawling on them, or objects dancing about in front of their eyes. Like most other alcohol withdrawal symptoms, the DTs usually run their course in two to three days. However, people who experience them or a related severe withdrawal reaction may also have seizures, lose consciousness, suffer a stroke, or even die. Today certain medical procedures can help prevent or reduce such extreme reactions (D'Onofrio et al., 1999).

Spreading the word *Educating the public with billboard, television, and radio ads about the dangers of alcohol has helped reduce the number of alcohol-related automobile deaths by over 25 percent in recent years (CDC, 1997).*

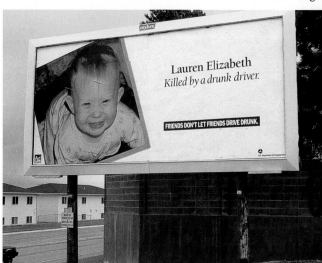

Kevin & Betty Collins/Visuals Unlimited

WHAT ARE THE PERSONAL AND SOCIAL CONSEQUENCES OF ALCOHOLISM? Alcoholism destroys millions of families, social relationships, and careers. Medical treatment, lost productivity, and losses due to deaths from alcoholism cost society as much as $148 billion annually (NIDA, 1998; Cornish et al., 1995). The disorder also plays a role in more than one-third of all suicides, homicides, assaults, rapes, and accidental deaths, including 41 percent of all fatal automobile accidents in the United States (CDC, 1998; Mustaine & Tewksbury, 1998). Altogether, intoxicated drivers are responsible for

THE CURRENT SCENE

College Binge Drinking: An Extracurricular Crisis

Drinking large amounts of alcohol in a short time, or *binge drinking,* is a serious problem on college campuses. Studies show that more than one-third of college students binge-drink at times, around half of them at least six times per month (Wechsler et al., 2000, 1997, 1994; Bennett et al., 1999). These are higher rates than those displayed by people of the same age who are not in college. In fact, college students drink an estimated 430 million gallons of alcohol each year, and spend $5.5 billion to do so (Eigan, 1991).

In many circles, alcohol use is an accepted aspect of college life (Schulenberg et al., 2001). Are we as a society taking the issue too lightly? Consider some of the following statistics:

‡ Alcohol is a factor in nearly 40 percent of academic problems and 28 percent of all college dropouts (Anderson, 1994).

‡ Although 84 percent of incoming freshmen consider heavy alcohol use to be a problem on campus, 68 percent drink during their first semester, at least half of them during their first week on campus (Harvard School of Public Health, 1995).

‡ Binge drinking has been linked to severe health problems and serious injury, auto crashes, unplanned and unprotected sex, aggressive behaviors, and various psychological problems (Wechsler et al., 1995; Wechsler & Isaac, 1992).

These findings have led some educators to describe binge drinking as "the No. 1 public health hazard" for full-time college students, and many researchers and clinicians have turned their attention to it. Henry Wechsler and his colleagues (1995) at the Harvard School of Public Health mailed a questionnaire about

Testing the limits *Binge drinking, similar to this display at a college campus party, has led to a number of deaths in recent years.*

drinking patterns to students at 140 college campuses around the United States and received close to 18,000 replies. According to the responses, people most likely to binge-drink were those who lived in a fraternity or sorority, pursued a party-centered lifestyle, and engaged in high-risk behaviors such as smoking marijuana, having multiple sex partners, and smoking cigarettes. Other variables—including being male, white, involved in athletics, and a business major—also raised the risk of binge drinking. These variables have been cited in other studies as well (Meilman et al., 1999). The studies also found that students who were binge drinkers in high school were more likely to binge-drink in college.

The results of such studies are based on self-administered questionnaires, and subjects' responses may have been biased. Perhaps binge drinkers are more likely than nondrinkers to respond to such questionnaires. Still, the implications are clear: college drinking, certainly binge drinking, may be more common and more harmful than was previously believed. At the very least, it is a problem whose research time has come.

17,000 deaths each year (CDC, 1998). At the same time, intoxicated pedestrians are four times more likely than sober pedestrians to be hit by a car (Painter, 1992).

Alcoholism has serious effects on the 30 million children of persons with this disorder. Home life for these children is likely to include high levels of conflict and perhaps sexual or other forms of abuse (Mathew et al., 1993; Velleman & Orford, 1993). In turn, the children themselves have higher rates of psychological problems such as anxiety, depression, phobias, conduct disorder, attention-deficit disorder, and substance-related disorders during their lifetimes (Kuperman et al., 1999; Hill & Muka, 1996). Many have low self-esteem, poor communication skills, poor sociability, and marital problems (Lewis-Harter, 2000; Kelly & Myers, 1996).

Long-term excessive drinking can also seriously damage physical health. It so overworks the liver that people may develop an irreversible condition called *cirrhosis,* in which the liver becomes scarred and dysfunctional. Cirrhosis is the tenth most frequent cause of death in the United States, accounting for some 25,000 deaths each year (NCHS, 1999). Alcohol abuse and dependence may also damage the heart and lower the immune system's ability to fight off cancer and bacterial infections and to resist the onset of AIDS after infection (NIAAA, 1992).

IMPAIRED DRIVING

Each year over 1.4 million arrests are made in the United States for driving under the influence of alcohol or opioids, involving one of every 123 drivers (Uniform Crime Reports, 1997). In 60 percent of the 500 child passenger deaths linked to alcohol in 1996, it was the driver of the child's own car who was alcohol-impaired (CDC, 1997).

Long-term excessive drinking also causes major nutritional problems. Alcohol makes people feel full and lowers their desire for food, yet it has no nutritional value. As a result, heavy drinkers become malnourished, weak, and prone to disease. Their vitamin and mineral deficiencies may also cause certain mental disorders. An alcohol-related deficiency of vitamin B (thiamine), for example, may lead to **Korsakoff's syndrome,** a disease marked by extreme confusion, memory loss, and other neurological symptoms (Krabbendam et al., 2000). People with Korsakoff's syndrome cannot remember the past or learn new information, and may make up for their memory losses by *confabulating*—reciting made-up events to fill in the gaps.

Finally, women who drink during pregnancy place their fetuses at risk. Excessive alcohol use during pregnancy may cause a baby to be born with **fetal alcohol syndrome,** a pattern of abnormalities that can include mental retardation, hyperactivity, head and face deformities, heart defects, and slow growth (Doweiko, 1999; CDC, 1998). It has been estimated that in the overall population nearly 3 of every 1,000 babies are born with this syndrome. The rate increases to as many as 29 of every 1,000 babies of women who are problem drinkers (Doweiko, 1999; Ray & Ksir, 1993). In addition, heavy drinking early in pregnancy often leads to a miscarriage.

Sedative-Hypnotic Drugs

Sedative-hypnotic drugs produce feelings of relaxation and drowsiness. At low dosages, the drugs have a calming or sedative effect. At higher dosages, they are sleep inducers, or hypnotics. The sedative-hypnotic drugs include *barbiturates* and *benzodiazepines.*

BARBITURATES First discovered in Germany more than 100 years ago, **barbiturates** were widely prescribed in the first half of the twentieth century to fight anxiety and to help people sleep. Despite the recent development of the safer benzodiazepines, some physicians still prescribe barbiturates, especially for sleep problems. The drugs can cause many problems, however, not the least of which are abuse and dependence. Several thousand deaths a year are caused by accidental or suicidal overdoses.

Barbiturates are usually taken in pill or capsule form. In low doses they reduce a person's level of excitement in the same way that alcohol does, by attaching to the neuron receptors that receive the inhibitory neurotransmitter GABA and by helping GABA operate at those receptors (Doweiko, 1999; Frey et al., 1995). People can get intoxicated from large doses of barbiturates, just as they do from alcohol. And, like alcohol, barbiturates are broken down in the liver. At high doses, barbiturates also depress the *reticular formation,* the part of the brain that normally keeps people awake, thus causing the person to get sleepy. At too high a level, the drugs can stop breathing, lower blood pressure, and lead to coma and death.

Repeated use of barbiturates can quickly result in a pattern of abuse. Users may spend much of the day intoxicated, irritable, and unable to do their work. Dependence can also result. The user organizes his or her life around the drug and needs increasing amounts of it to calm down or fall asleep. A great danger of barbiturate dependence is that the lethal dose of the drug remains the same even while the body is building up a tolerance for its sedating effects (Landry, 1994; Gold, 1986). Once the prescribed dose stops reducing anxiety or inducing sleep, the user is all too likely to increase it without medical supervision, and eventually may take a dose that proves fatal. Those caught in a pattern of barbiturate dependence may also experience withdrawal symptoms such as nausea, anxiety, and sleep problems. Barbiturate withdrawal is particularly dangerous, for it can cause convulsions.

BENZODIAZEPINES Chapter 4 described **benzodiazepines,** the antianxiety drugs developed in the 1950s, as the most popular sedative-hypnotic drugs available. Xanax and Valium are just two of the dozens of these compounds in clinical use. Like alcohol and barbiturates, they calm people by binding to neuron recep-

KORSAKOFF'S SYNDROME An alcohol-related disorder marked by extreme confusion, memory impairment, and other neurological symptoms.

FETAL ALCOHOL SYNDROME A cluster of problems in a child, including heart defects, irregularities in the head and face, slow growth, and intellectual deficits, caused by excessive alcohol intake by the mother during pregnancy.

SEDATIVE-HYPNOTIC DRUG A drug used in low doses to reduce anxiety and in higher doses to help people sleep. Also called *anxiolytic drug.*

BARBITURATES Addictive sedative-hypnotic drugs used to reduce anxiety or to help people fall asleep.

BENZODIAZEPINES The most common group of antianxiety drugs, which includes Valium and Xanax.

OPIOID Opium or any of the drugs derived from opium, including morphine, heroin, and codeine.

OPIUM A highly addictive substance made from the sap of the opium poppy.

MORPHINE A highly addictive substance derived from opium that is particularly effective in relieving pain.

HEROIN One of the most addictive substances derived from opium, illegal in the United States under all circumstances.

Table 10-3

Risks and Consequences of Drug Misuse

	INTOXICATION POTENTIAL	DEPENDENCY POTENTIAL	RISK OF ORGAN DAMAGE OR DEATH	RISK OF SEVERE SOCIAL OR ECONOMIC CONSEQUENCES	RISK OF SEVERE OR LONG-LASTING MENTAL AND BEHAVIORAL CHANGE
Opioids	High	High	Low	High	Moderate to high
Sedative-hypnotics Barbiturates	Moderate	Moderate to high	Moderate to high	Moderate to high	Low
Benzodiazepines	Moderate	Low	Low	Low	Low
Stimulants (cocaine, amphetamines)	High	High	Moderate	Moderate to high	Moderate to high
Alcohol	High	Moderate	High	High	High
Cannabis	High	Low to moderate	Low	Low to moderate	Low to moderate
Mixed drug classes	High	High	High	High	High

Source: APA, 2000, 1994; Gold, 1986, p. 28.

tors that receive GABA and by increasing GABA's activity at those receptors. These drugs, however, relieve anxiety without making people as drowsy as other kinds of sedative-hypnotics. Because they are also less likely to slow a person's breathing, they are less likely to cause death in the event of an overdose (Nishino et al., 1995).

When benzodiazepines were first discovered, they seemed so safe and effective that physicians prescribed them generously, and their use spread. Eventually it became clear that in high enough doses the drugs can cause intoxication and lead to abuse or dependence (Ashton, 1995). As many as 1 percent of the adults in the United States abuse or become physically dependent on these antianxiety drugs at some point in their lives (APA, 2000) and thus become subject to some of the same dangers that researchers have identified in barbiturate misuse.

Opioids

Opioids include opium—taken from the sap of the opium poppy—and the drugs derived from it, such as heroin, morphine, and codeine. **Opium** itself has been in use for thousands of years. In the past it was used widely in the treatment of medical disorders because of its ability to reduce both physical and emotional pain. Physicians eventually discovered, however, that the drug was physically addictive.

In 1804 a new substance, **morphine,** was derived from opium. It relieved pain even more effectively than opium and was originally touted as safe. However, wide use of this drug eventually revealed that it too could lead to addiction. So many wounded soldiers in the United States received morphine injections during the Civil War that morphine dependence became known as "soldiers' disease."

In 1898 morphine was converted into yet another new pain reliever, **heroin.** For several years heroin was viewed as a wonder drug and was used as a cough medicine and for other medical purposes. Eventually, however, physicians learned that heroin is even more addictive than the other opioids. By 1917 the U.S. Congress concluded that all drugs produced from opium were addictive (see Table 10-3), and it passed a law making opioids illegal except for medical purposes.

HOW POTENT IS HEROIN?

When heroin is injected intravenously, 68 percent of it is absorbed in the brain, compared to less than 5 percent of injected morphine (Sporer, 1999).

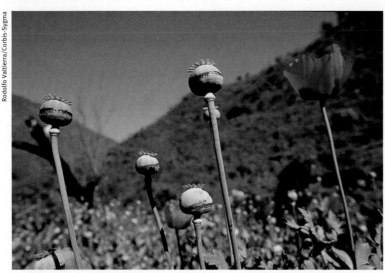

Purer blend *Heroin, derived from poppy fields such as this one in Mexico, was usually injected in the past. Today's heroin, however, is purer than the heroin distributed in the 1980s (65 percent pure vs. 5 percent), so that users can achieve considerable impact by snorting or smoking the drug.*

Still other drugs have been derived from opium, and *synthetic* (laboratory-blended) opioids such as *methadone* have also been developed. All these opioid drugs—natural and synthetic—are known collectively as *narcotics*. Each drug has a different strength, speed of action, and tolerance level. Morphine and *codeine* are medical narcotics usually prescribed to relieve pain. Heroin is illegal in the United States under all circumstances.

Narcotics are smoked, inhaled, snorted, injected by needle just beneath the skin ("skin popped"), or injected directly into the bloodstream ("mainlined"). Injection seems to be the most common method of narcotic use, although the other techniques have been used increasingly in recent years (NHSDA, 1998). An injection quickly brings on a *rush*—a spasm of warmth and ecstasy that is sometimes compared with orgasm. The brief spasm is followed by several hours of a pleasant feeling called a *high* or *nod*. During a high, the drug user feels relaxed, happy, and unconcerned about food, sex, or other bodily needs.

Opioids create these effects by depressing the central nervous system, particularly the centers that help control emotion. The drugs attach to brain receptor sites that ordinarily receive **endorphins**—neurotransmitters that help relieve pain and reduce emotional tension (Doweiko, 1999; Snyder, 1991, 1986). When neurons at these receptor sites receive opioids, they produce pleasurable and calming feelings just as they would do if they were receiving endorphins. In addition to reducing pain and tension, opioids cause nausea, narrowing of the pupils ("pinpoint pupils"), and constipation—bodily reactions that can also be brought about by releases of endorphins in the brain.

HEROIN ABUSE AND DEPENDENCE Heroin use exemplifies the kinds of problems posed by opioids. After taking heroin repeatedly for just a few weeks, users may become caught in a pattern of abuse: the drug interferes significantly with their social and occupational functioning. In most cases, heroin abuse leads to a pattern of dependence as well, and users soon center their lives on the substance, build a tolerance for it, and experience a withdrawal reaction when they stop taking it. At first the withdrawal symptoms are anxiety, restlessness, sweating, and rapid breathing; later they include severe twitching, aches, fever, vomiting, diarrhea, loss of appetite, high blood pressure, and weight loss of up to 15 pounds (due to loss of bodily fluids). These symptoms usually peak by the third day, gradually subside, and disappear by the eighth day. A person in withdrawal can either wait out the symptoms or end withdrawal by taking heroin again.

People who are dependent on heroin soon need the drug just to avoid going into withdrawal, and they must continually increase their doses in order to achieve even that relief. The temporary high becomes less strong and less important. Most such individuals organize their lives around efforts to get their next dose, in many cases turning to criminal activities, such as theft and prostitution, to support the expensive "habit."

Surveys suggest that close to 1 percent of adults in the United States become addicted to heroin or other opioids at some time in their lives (APA, 2000, 1994). The rate of addiction dropped considerably during the 1980s, rose in the early 1990s, and now seems to have fallen once again. The number of persons currently addicted to these drugs is estimated to be less than 150,000 (Morral et al., 2000; NHSDA, 1998). The actual number may be even higher, however, given the reluctance of many people to admit to participation in an illegal activity.

WHAT ARE THE DANGERS OF HEROIN ABUSE? The most immediate danger of heroin use is an overdose, which closes down the respiratory center in the brain, almost paralyzing breathing and in many cases causing death. Death is particularly likely during sleep, when a person is unable to fight this effect by con-

DELICATE BALANCE

The drug *quinine* is often added to heroin to counteract potential infections. Although quinine does have this effect, too much of it can be lethal. Many deaths attributed to heroin may actually have been caused by a quinine-induced flooding of the lungs.

sciously working to breathe. People who resume heroin use after having resisted it for some time often make the fatal mistake of taking the same dose they had built up to before. Because their bodies have been without heroin for some time, however, they can no longer tolerate this high level. Each year approximately 2 percent of persons dependent on heroin and other opioids die under the drug's influence, usually from an overdose (APA, 2000; Sporer, 1999).

Users run other risks as well. Often pushers mix heroin with a cheaper drug, such as a barbiturate or LSD, or even a deadly substance such as cyanide or battery acid. In addition, dirty needles and other unsterile equipment spread infections such as AIDS, hepatitis, and skin abscesses (Ferrando, 2001). In some areas of the United States the HIV infection rate among persons dependent on heroin is reported to be as high as 60 percent (APA, 2000, 1994).

Injecting heroin *Opioids may be taken by mouth, inhaled, snorted, injected just beneath the surface of the skin, or, as here, injected intravenously. Those who share needles to inject themselves risk developing AIDS or hepatitis.*

SUMMING UP / **Depressants**

The misuse of substances (or drugs) may lead to temporary changes in behavior, emotion, or thought, such as intoxication. Regular and excessive use can lead to either substance abuse, a pattern in which people rely heavily on a substance and so damage relationships, work performance, or other areas of functioning; or substance dependence, in which they center their lives on the substance, develop a tolerance for it, and perhaps experience unpleasant withdrawal symptoms when they stop taking it.

Depressants are substances that slow the activity of the central nervous system. Each of the major depressants presents certain problems and dangers. Regular and excessive use of these substances can lead to a pattern of abuse or dependence.

Alcohol Alcoholic beverages contain ethyl alcohol, which is carried by the blood to the central nervous system, depressing its function. Among other actions, alcohol increases the activity of the neurotransmitter GABA at key sites in the brain.

Sedative-Hypnotic Drugs The sedative-hypnotic drugs, which produce feelings of relaxation and drowsiness, include barbiturates and benzodiazepines. Both increase the activity of GABA.

Opioids Opioids include opium and drugs derived from it, such as morphine and heroin, as well as laboratory-made opioids. They all reduce tension and pain and cause other reactions. Opioids operate by binding to neurons that ordinarily receive endorphins.

VIOLATIONS OF THE LAW

The leading reasons for arrests in the United States include drug abuse violations (first place), driving under the influence (third), drunkenness (fifth), and violation of liquor laws (sixth) (Ash, 1998).

Stimulants

Stimulants are substances that increase the activity of the central nervous system, resulting in increased blood pressure and heart rate, greater alertness, and speeded-up behavior and thinking. Among the most troublesome stimulants are *cocaine* and *amphetamines,* which have effects on behavior and emotions that are very similar. When users report different effects, it is often because they have ingested different amounts of the drugs. Two other widely used and legal stimulants are *caffeine* and *nicotine.*

Cocaine

Cocaine—the central active ingredient of the coca plant, found in South America—is the most powerful natural stimulant now known. The drug was first separated from the plant in 1865. Native people of South America, however, have

ENDORPHINS Neurotransmitters that help relieve pain and reduce emotional tension. They are sometimes referred to as the body's own opioids.

COCAINE An addictive stimulant obtained from the coca plant. It is the most powerful natural stimulant known.

Tobacco, Nicotine, and Addiction

Almost 28 percent of all Americans over the age of 12 regularly smoke tobacco (NHSDA, 1998). Surveys also suggest that more than one-third of all high school seniors have smoked within the past month, at least half of them on a regular basis (Johnston et al., 1999). At the same time, 430,000 persons in the United States die each year as a result of smoking (Carpenter, 2001). Smoking is directly tied to high blood pressure, coronary heart disease, lung disease, cancer, strokes, and other deadly medical problems. Nonsmokers who inhale cigarette smoke from their environment have a higher risk of lung cancer and other diseases (Report of the Surgeon General, 1987). And pregnant women who smoke are more likely than nonsmokers to deliver premature and underweight babies (Goldstein, 1994).

Research suggests that smoking may actually increase stress levels (Parrott, 2000, 1999), and most smokers know that smoking is unhealthful, so why do they continue to smoke? Because *nicotine,* the active substance in tobacco and a stimulant of the central nervous system, is as addictive as heroin, perhaps even more so (Report of the Surgeon General, 1988). Regular smokers develop a tolerance for nicotine and must smoke more and more in order to achieve the same results. When they try to stop smoking, they experience withdrawal symptoms—irritability, increased appetite, sleep disturbances, slower metabolism, cognitive difficulties, and a powerful desire to smoke (APA, 2000). Nicotine acts on the same neurotransmitters and reward center in the brain as amphetamines and cocaine (McGehee et al., 1995). Inhaling a puff of cigarette smoke delivers a dose of nicotine to the brain faster than it could be delivered by injection into the bloodstream.

The decline in the acceptability of smoking in our society has created a market for techniques to help people kick the habit. Most of these methods do not work very well. Self-help kits, commercial programs, and support groups are of limited help. Most people who stop smoking after receiving such interventions start smoking again within one year (Hall et al., 1985). Smokers who do quit permanently tend to be successful only after several failed attempts (Spanier et al., 1996).

Several biological treatments have been developed. A common one is the use of *nicotine gum,* which contains a high level of nicotine that is released as the smoker chews. Theoretically, people who obtain nicotine by chewing will no longer feel a need to smoke (Moss, 1999; Fortmann & Killen, 1995). A similar approach is the *nicotine patch,* which is attached to the skin like a Band-Aid. Its nicotine is absorbed through the skin throughout the day, supposedly easing withdrawal and reducing the smoker's need for nicotine. *Nicotine nasal spray,* a relatively new biological approach, delivers nicotine much more rapidly than other methods (Perkins et al., 1996). It can be used several times an hour, whenever the urge to smoke arises. Finally, the antidepressant drug *bupropion* (brand names Zyban and Wellbutrin) has demonstrated some success as a treatment for cigarette smoking. Studies suggest that people who take this drug do better in their efforts to stop smoking than people who take placebos; and some have greater success than people who use a nicotine patch (Jorenby et al., 1999).

The more one smokes, the harder it is to quit. On the positive side, however, former smokers' risk of disease and death decreases steadily the longer they continue to avoid smoking (Goldstein, 1994; Jaffe, 1985). This assurance may be a powerful motivator for many smokers, and, in fact, around 45 percent of regular smokers are eventually able to stop permanently (APA, 2000). In the meantime, more than 1,000 people die of smoking-related diseases each day.

An early start *An Albanian boy in Kosovo is already acquainted with the powers of nicotine.*

chewed the leaves of the plant since prehistoric times for the energy and alertness the drug offers. Processed cocaine is an odorless, white, fluffy powder. For recreational use, it is most often snorted so that it is absorbed through the mucous membrane of the nose. Some users prefer the more powerful effects of injecting cocaine intravenously or smoking it in a pipe or cigarette.

For years people believed that cocaine posed few problems aside from intoxication and, on occasion, temporary psychosis. Only later did researchers come to appreciate its many dangers. Their insights came only after society witnessed a dramatic increase in the drug's popularity and in problems related to its use. In the early 1960s an estimated 10,000 persons in the United States had tried cocaine. Today more than 21 million people have tried it, and 1.8 million—most of them teenagers or young adults—are using it currently (NHSDA, 1998; Kleber, 1995). Altogether, close to 3 percent of the population become dependent on cocaine at some point in their lives (Anthony et al., 1995).

Cocaine brings on a euphoric rush of well-being and confidence. Given a high enough dose, this rush can be almost orgasmic, like the one produced by heroin. At first cocaine stimulates the higher centers of the central nervous system, making users feel excited, energetic, talkative, and even euphoric. As more is taken, it stimulates other centers of the central nervous system, producing a faster pulse, higher blood pressure, faster and deeper breathing, and further arousal and wakefulness.

Cocaine apparently produces these effects largely by increasing supplies of the neurotransmitter *dopamine* at key neurons throughout the brain (see Figure 10-2). Excessive amounts of dopamine travel to receiving neurons throughout the central nervous system and overstimulate them. In addition, cocaine appears to increase the activity of the neurotransmitters *norepinephrine* and *serotonin* in some areas of the brain (Panikkar, 1999; Volkow et al., 1999, 1997).

High doses of the drug produce *cocaine intoxication,* whose symptoms are poor muscle coordination, grandiosity, bad judgment, anger, aggression, compulsive behavior, anxiety, and confusion. Some people experience hallucinations or delusions, or both, a condition known as *cocaine-induced psychotic disorder* (APA, 2000).

Wonder drug *Legal in the United States until 1914, cocaine was an ingredient in over-the-counter medicines, such as Cocaine Toothache Drops. This 1885 ad shows that it was used to treat children as well as adults. Cocaine was also part of Coca-Cola's formula until 1903.*

> A young man described how, after free-basing, he went to his closet to get his clothes, but his suit asked him, "What do you want?" Afraid, he walked toward the door, which told him, "Get back!" Retreating, he then heard the sofa say, "If you sit on me, I'll kick your ass." With a sense of impending doom, intense anxiety, and momentary panic, the young man ran to the hospital where he received help.
>
> *(Allen, 1985, pp. 19-20)*

POPULAR NICKNAMES

Descriptive street terms for cocaine include angel, blow, candy, cane, Dr. White, go powder, happy dust, icicles, joy flakes, lady, nose candy, rails, reindeer dust, rock candy, snort, snow, stardust, toot, uptown, white stuff, and wings (Spignesi, 1994).

As the stimulant effects of cocaine subside, the user experiences a depression-like letdown, popularly called *crashing,* a pattern that may also include headaches, dizziness, and fainting (Cornish et al., 1995). For occasional users, the aftereffects usually disappear within 24 hours, but they may last longer for people

FIGURE 10-2 **Biochemical euphoria** *The subjective experiences of euphoria after a cocaine injection closely parallel cocaine's action at dopamine-using neurons. The peak experience of euphoria seems to occur around the same time as the peak of neuron activity (Fowler, Volkow, & Wolf, 1994, p. 110; Cook, Jeffcoat, & Perez-Reyes, 1985).*

Smoking crack *Crack, a powerful form of free-base cocaine, is produced by boiling cocaine down into crystalline balls and is smoked with a special crack pipe.*

Prenatal concerns *This baby, born prematurely to a woman dependent on cocaine, lived only a few months. The use of cocaine, alcohol, or other drugs during pregnancy greatly increases the risk of miscarriage, premature birth, and child abnormalities.*

FREUD'S FOLLY

Early in his career, Sigmund Freud was a staunch advocate of cocaine use. He proclaimed, "Cocaine brings about an exhilaration and lasting euphoria . . . an increase in self-control and . . . more vitality and capacity for work. . . . In other words, you are simply normal" (Freud, 1885).

who have taken a particularly high dose. These individuals may sink into a stupor, deep sleep, or, in some cases, coma (Coambs & McAndrews, 1994).

COCAINE ABUSE AND DEPENDENCE   Regular use of cocaine may lead to a pattern of abuse in which the person remains under its effects much of each day and functions poorly in social relationships and at work. Regular drug use may also cause problems in short-term memory or attention (Rosselli & Ardila, 1996). Dependence may also develop, so that cocaine dominates the person's life, higher doses are needed to gain the desired effects, and stopping it results in depression, fatigue, sleep problems, irritability, and anxiety (APA, 2000). These withdrawal symptoms may last for weeks or even months after drug use has stopped.

In the past, cocaine's use and impact were limited by the drug's high cost. Moreover, cocaine was usually snorted, a form of ingestion that has less powerful effects than either injection or smoking. Since 1984, however, the availability of newer, more powerful, and sometimes cheaper forms of cocaine has produced an enormous increase in abuse and dependence. Currently, one user in five falls into a pattern of abuse or dependence. Many people now ingest cocaine by **free-basing,** a technique in which the pure cocaine basic alkaloid is chemically separated, or "freed," from processed cocaine, vaporized by heat from a flame, and inhaled through a pipe.

Millions more people use **crack,** a powerful form of free-base cocaine that has been boiled down into crystalline balls. It is smoked with a special pipe and makes a crackling sound as it is inhaled (hence the name). Crack is sold in small quantities at a fairly low cost, a practice that has resulted in crack epidemics among people who previously could not have afforded cocaine, primarily those in poor urban areas. The crack epidemic is particularly disturbing because of the violent crime and risky sex-for-drugs behaviors reported in the crack-using population (Booth et al., 2000). Approximately 3 percent of high school seniors report using crack within the past year, up from 1.5 percent in 1993 (Johnston et al., 1999).

WHAT ARE THE DANGERS OF COCAINE?   Aside from cocaine's harmful effects on behavior, the drug poses serious physical dangers. Its growing use in powerful forms has caused the annual number of cocaine-related emergency room incidents in the United States to multiply 40 times since 1982, from around 4,000 cases to more than 160,000 (DAWN, 1998). In addition, cocaine has been linked

A CLOSER LOOK

"My Life's Great Big Secret"

On one of her shows in January 1995, the popular talk show host Oprah Winfrey revealed, with great emotion, that she had been physically dependent on cocaine in the mid-1970s. "That is my life's great big secret that has been held over my head," she said. "I understand the shame. I understand the guilt." Although surprised by this admission, her television audience responded with compassion and understanding, and thousands sent letters of support and appreciation for her candor.

Steve Sands/Outline

ConsiderThis

⦿ What impact might admissions like Winfrey's have on people's willingness to seek treatment for substance abuse?
• Does drug abuse by a middle-aged, highly regarded person conjure up a different image than drug abuse by a younger, less famous individual?

---

to as many as 20 percent of all suicides by persons under 61 years of age (Marzuk et al., 1992).

The greatest danger of cocaine use is an overdose. Excessive doses have a strong effect on the respiratory center of the brain, at first stimulating it and then depressing it, to the point where breathing may stop. Cocaine can also create major, even fatal, heart problems (Mittleman et al., 1999). The heart beats rapidly and irregularly under the drug's influence and at the same time must work harder to pump blood through the vessels that have narrowed as a result of cocaine's effects (Kaufman et al., 1998). For some people, this strain on the heart causes a brain seizure that brings breathing or heart functioning to a sudden stop. In addition, pregnant women who use cocaine run the risk of having a miscarriage (Ness et al., 1999) and of having children with abnormalities in immune functioning, attention and learning, thyroid size, and dopamine and serotonin activity in the brain (Adler, 1992).

Amphetamines

The **amphetamines** are stimulant drugs that are manufactured in the laboratory. Some common examples are amphetamine (Benzedrine), dextroamphetamine (Dexedrine), and methamphetamine (Methedrine). First produced in the 1930s to help treat asthma, these drugs soon became popular among people trying to lose weight; athletes seeking an extra burst of energy; soldiers, truck drivers, and pilots trying to stay awake; and students studying for exams through the night. Physicians now know the drugs are far too dangerous to be used so casually, and they prescribe them much less freely (Fawcett & Busch, 1995). However, the illicit use of amphetamines seems to be increasing (Baberg, Nelesen, & Dimsdale, 1996).

Amphetamines are most often taken in pill or capsule form, although some people inject the drugs intravenously for a quicker, more powerful effect. Others take the drugs in such forms as "ice" and "crank," counterparts of free-base cocaine and crack, respectively. Like cocaine, amphetamines increase energy and alertness and lower appetite when taken in small doses; produce a rush, intoxication, and psychosis in high doses; and cause an emotional letdown as they leave the body. Also like cocaine, amphetamines stimulate the central nervous system by increasing the release of the neurotransmitters dopamine, norepinephrine, and serotonin throughout the brain, although the actions of amphetamines differ somewhat from those of cocaine (Doweiko, 1999).

CARDIAC RISK
During the first hour after taking cocaine, a user's risk of heart attack increases nearly 24 times (Mittleman et al., 1999).

FREE-BASING A technique for ingesting cocaine in which the pure cocaine basic alkaloid is chemically separated from processed cocaine, vaporized by heat from a flame, and inhaled with a pipe.

CRACK A powerful, ready-to-smoke free-base cocaine.

AMPHETAMINE A stimulant drug that is manufactured in the laboratory.

ANIMAL HIGHS

Animals sometimes use substances to get high or relieve stress. Llamas in Peru get frisky eating coca leaves (which contain cocaine). Grasshoppers that eat wild marijuana leaves jump unusually high. Elephants seek out fermented ripe fruit (Siegel, 1990).

Tolerance to amphetamines builds very quickly, so users are at great risk of becoming dependent. People who start using the drug to reduce their appetite and weight, for example, may soon find they are as hungry as ever, and increase their dose in response. Athletes who use amphetamines to increase their energy may also find before long that larger and larger amounts of the drug are needed. So-called speed freaks, who pop pills all day for days at a time, have built a tolerance so high that they now take as much as 200 times their first amphetamine dose. When people who depend on the drug stop taking it, they plunge into a deep depression and extended sleep identical to the withdrawal from cocaine. Around 1.5 to 2 percent of the population in the United States become dependent on amphetamines at some point in their lives (APA, 2000; Anthony et al., 1995).

SUMMING UP | **Stimulants**

Stimulants are substances that increase the activity of the central nervous system. They may lead to intoxication, abuse, and dependence, including a withdrawal pattern marked by depression, fatigue, and irritability. Cocaine produces a euphoric effect by stimulating the activity of dopamine, norepinephrine, and serotonin in the brain. Amphetamines, stimulant drugs that are manufactured in a laboratory, act in a similar manner.

Hallucinogens, Cannabis, and Combinations of Substances

Other kinds of substances may also cause problems for their users and for society. *Hallucinogens* produce delusions, hallucinations, and other sensory changes. *Cannabis substances* produce sensory changes, but they also have depressant and stimulant effects, and so they are considered apart from hallucinogens in DSM-IV. And many individuals take *combinations of drugs.*

Hallucinogens

Hallucinogens are substances that cause powerful changes in sensory perception, from strengthening a person's normal perceptions to producing illusions and hallucinations. They produce sensations so out of the ordinary that they are sometimes called "trips." The trips may be exciting or frightening, depending on how a person's mind interacts with the drugs. Also called **psychedelic drugs,** the hallucinogens include LSD, mescaline, psilocybin, and MDMA ("Ecstasy"). Many of these substances come from plants or animals; others are laboratory-produced rearrangements of natural psychedelics.

LSD (lysergic acid diethylamide), one of the most famous and most powerful hallucinogens, was derived by the Swiss chemist Albert Hoffman in 1938 from a group of naturally occurring drugs called *ergot alkaloids.* During the 1960s, a decade of social rebellion and experimentation, millions of persons turned to the drug as a way of expanding their experience. Within two hours of being swallowed, LSD brings on a state of *hallucinogen intoxication,* sometimes called *hallucinosis,* marked by a general strengthening of perceptions, particularly visual perceptions, along with psychological changes and physical symptoms. People may focus on small details—the pores of the skin, for example, or individual blades of grass. Colors may seem enhanced or take on a shade of purple. Illusions may be experienced in which objects seem distorted and may appear to move, breathe, or change shape. A person under the influ-

Inspired art *Psychedelic art seemed all-pervasive in the 1960s. Displayed on advertisements, clothing, record albums, and book covers, it was inspired by the kinds of images and sensations produced by psychedelic drugs such as LSD.*

ence of LSD may also hallucinate—seeing people, objects, or forms that are not actually present.

Hallucinosis may also cause one to hear sounds more clearly, feel tingling or numbness in the limbs, or confuse the sensations of hot and cold. Some people have been badly burned after touching flames that felt cool to them under the influence of LSD. The drug may also cause different senses to cross, an effect called *synesthesia.* Colors, for example, may be "heard" or "felt."

LSD can also produce strong emotions, from joy to anxiety or depression. The perception of time may slow dramatically. Long-forgotten thoughts and feelings may return. Physical symptoms can include sweating, palpitations, blurred vision, tremors, and poor coordination. All these effects take place while the user is fully awake and alert, and they wear off in about six hours.

It seems that LSD produces these symptoms primarily by binding to some of the neurons that normally receive the neurotransmitter *serotonin,* changing the neurotransmitter's activity at those sites (Jacobs, 1994, 1984). These neurons ordinarily help the brain send visual information and control emotions (as we observed in Chapter 6); thus LSD's activity there produces various visual and emotional symptoms.

More than 10 percent of all persons in the United States have used LSD or another hallucinogen at some point in their lives (APA, 2000). Around 2 percent use such drugs currently (APA, 2000; NHSDA, 1998). Although people do not usually develop tolerance to LSD or have withdrawal symptoms when they stop taking it, the drug poses dangers for both one-time and long-term users. It is so powerful that any dose, no matter how small, is likely to produce enormous perceptual, emotional, and behavioral reactions. Sometimes the reactions are extremely unpleasant—an experience called a "bad trip." Reports of LSD users who injure themselves or others usually involve a reaction of this kind.

> A 21-year-old woman was admitted to the hospital along with her lover. He had had a number of LSD experiences and had convinced her to take it to make her less constrained sexually. About half an hour after ingestion of approximately 200 microgm., she noticed that the bricks in the wall began to go in and out and that light affected her strangely. She became frightened when she realized that she was unable to distinguish her body from the chair she was sitting on or from her lover's body. Her fear became more marked after she thought that she would not get back into herself. At the time of admission she was hyperactive and laughed inappropriately. Her stream of talk was illogical and affect labile. Two days later, this reaction had ceased.
>
> *(Frosch, Robbins, & Stern, 1965)*

Another danger is the long-term effect that LSD may have. Some users eventually develop psychosis or a mood or anxiety disorder. About one-quarter of users have **flashbacks**—a recurrence of sensory and emotional changes after the LSD has left the body (APA, 2000). Flashbacks may occur days or even months after the last LSD experience. Although they typically become less severe and disappear within several months, some people report flashbacks a year or more after taking the drug.

Cannabis

Cannabis sativa, the hemp plant, grows in warm climates throughout the world. The drugs produced from varieties of hemp are, as a group, called **cannabis.** The most powerful of them is *hashish;* the weaker ones include the best-known form of cannabis, **marijuana,** a mixture of the crushed leaves and flowering tops. Of the several hundred active chemicals in cannabis, **tetrahydrocannabinol (THC)** appears to be the one most responsible for its effects. The greater the THC content, the more powerful the cannabis.

PARTY DRUG DU JOUR

In recent years, *methylenedioxmethamphetamine,* or *MDMA,* known to the public as Ecstasy, has gained enormous popularity among teenagers and young adults as a "club drug," widely available at dance clubs, rock concerts, and raves (all-night social gatherings). Ingested by 4.4 percent of tenth-graders and 5.6 percent of twelfth-graders in 1998, this hallucinogen apparently can significantly impair memory (Reneman et al., 2000; Johnston et al., 1999; Bolla et al., 1998).

HALLUCINOGEN A substance that causes powerful changes primarily in sensory perception, including strengthening perceptions and producing illusions and hallucinations. Also called *psychedelic drug.*

LSD (LYSERGIC ACID DIETHYLAMIDE) A hallucinogenic drug derived from ergot alkaloids.

FLASHBACK LSD-induced sensory and emotional changes that recur long after the drug has left the body.

CANNABIS DRUGS Drugs produced from the different varieties of the hemp plant, *Cannabis sativa.* They cause a mixture of hallucinogenic, depressant, and stimulant effects.

MARIJUANA One of the cannabis drugs, derived from the leaves and flowering tops of the hemp plant, *Cannabis sativa.*

TETRAHYDROCANNABINOL (THC) The main active ingredient of cannabis substances.

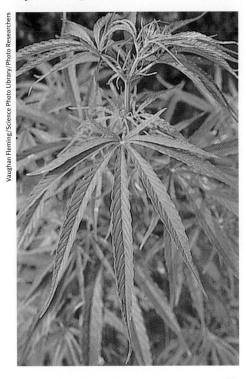

The source of marijuana *Marijuana is made from the leaves of the hemp plant,* Cannabis sativa. *The plant is an annual herb, reaches a height of between 3 and 15 feet, and is grown in a wide range of altitudes, climates, and soils.*

Open for business *The legalization of cannabis use in Holland has given rise to an industry of marijuana shops. This man lights up a marijuana pipe in the Cannabis Castle, where some of the drug's most potent strains are available.*

When smoked, cannabis produces a mixture of hallucinogenic, depressant, and stimulant effects. At low doses, the smoker typically has feelings of joy and relaxation and may become either quiet or talkative. Some smokers, however, become anxious, suspicious, or irritated, especially if they have been in a bad mood or are smoking in an upsetting environment. Many smokers report sharpened perceptions and fascination with the intensified sounds and sights around them. Time seems to slow down, and distances and sizes seem greater than they actually are. This overall "high" is technically called *cannabis intoxication.* Physical changes include reddening of the eyes, fast heartbeat, increases in blood pressure and appetite, dryness in the mouth, and dizziness. Some people become drowsy and may fall asleep.

In high doses, cannabis produces odd visual experiences, changes in body image, and hallucinations (Mathew et al., 1993). Smokers may become confused or impulsive. Some worry that other people are trying to hurt them. Most of the effects of cannabis last three to six hours. The changes in mood, however, may continue longer (Chait, Fishman, & Schuster, 1985).

MARIJUANA ABUSE AND DEPENDENCE Until the early 1970s, the use of marijuana, the weak form of cannabis, rarely led to a pattern of abuse or dependence. Today, however, many people, including large numbers of high school students, are caught in a pattern of marijuana abuse, getting high on marijuana regularly and finding their social and occupational or academic lives greatly affected (see Figure 10-3). Many regular users also become physically dependent on marijuana (Johns, 2001). They develop a tolerance for it and may experience flulike symptoms, restlessness, and irritability when they stop smoking (Kouri & Pope, 2000). Between 4 and 5 percent of all persons in the United States become dependent on marijuana at some point in their lives (APA, 2000; Anthony et al., 1995).

Why have patterns of marijuana abuse and dependence increased in the last three decades? Mainly because the drug has changed. The marijuana widely available in the United States today is two to ten times more powerful than that used in the early 1970s. The THC content of today's marijuana is as high as 10 to 15 percent, compared to 1 to 5 percent in the late 1960s (APA, 2000). Marijuana is now grown in places with a hot, dry climate, which increases the THC content (Weisheit, 1990).

IS MARIJUANA DANGEROUS? As the strength and use of marijuana have increased, researchers have discovered that smoking it may pose certain dangers. It occasionally causes panic reactions similar to the ones caused by hallucinogens, and some smokers may fear they are losing their minds (APA, 2000; Ray & Ksir, 1993). Typically such reactions end in three to six hours, along with marijuana's other effects.

Because marijuana can interfere with the performance of complex sensorimotor tasks (Ashton, 2001; Volkow et al., 1995) and with cognitive functioning (Quiroga, 2001; Hall & Solowij, 1997), it has been implicated in many automobile accidents. Furthermore, people on a marijuana high often fail to remember information, especially anything that has been recently learned, no matter how hard they try to concentrate; thus heavy marijuana smokers are at a serious disadvantage at school or work.

There are indications that regular marijuana smoking may also lead to long-term problems. It may, for example, contribute to lung disease. Studies show that marijuana smoking reduces the ability to expel air from the lungs even more than tobacco smoking does (Nahas et al., 1999). In addition, marijuana smoke contains more tar and

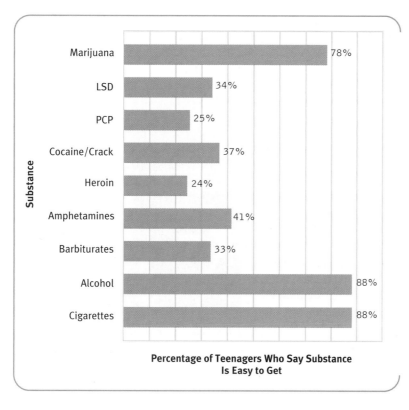

FIGURE 10-3 **How easy is it for teenagers to acquire substances?** *Very easy in the case of cigarettes, alcohol, and marijuana. Fewer than 35 percent of surveyed tenth-graders, however, say it is easy to get LSD, PCP, heroin, or barbiturates (Johnston et al., 1999).*

benzopyrene than tobacco smoke. Both of these substances have been linked to cancer (Ray & Ksir, 1993). Another concern is the effect of regular marijuana smoking on human reproduction. Studies since the late 1970s have discovered lower sperm counts in men who are chronic smokers of marijuana, and abnormal ovulation has been found in female smokers (Nahas et al., 1999).

Efforts to educate the public about the growing dangers of regular marijuana use appeared to have paid off throughout the 1980s. The percentage of high school seniors who smoked the substance on a daily basis decreased from 11 percent in 1978 to 2 percent in 1992 (Johnston et al., 1993). Furthermore, in 1992 about 77 percent of high school seniors believed that regular marijuana smoking poses a serious health risk, a much higher percentage than that in earlier years (Johnston et al., 1993). However, marijuana use among the young jumped up again during the 1990s. Today 6 percent of high school seniors smoke marijuana daily, and fewer than 60 percent believe that regular use can be harmful (Johnston et al., 1999, 1996).

Combinations of Substances

Because people often take more than one drug at a time, a pattern called *polysubstance use,* researchers have studied the ways in which drugs interact with one another. When different drugs are in the body at the same time, they may multiply, or potentiate, each other's effects. The combined impact, called a **synergistic effect,** is often greater than the sum of the effects of each drug taken alone: a small dose of one drug mixed with a small dose of another can produce an enormous change in body chemistry.

One kind of synergistic effect occurs when two or more drugs have *similar actions.* For instance, alcohol, benzodiazepines, barbiturates, and opioids—all depressants—may severely depress the central nervous system when mixed (Miller & Gold, 1990). Combining them, even in small doses, can lead to extreme intoxication, coma, and even death (Nishino et al., 1995). A young man may have just a few alcoholic drinks at a party, for example, and shortly afterward take a moderate dose of barbiturates to help him fall asleep. He believes he has acted with restraint and good judgment—yet he may never wake up.

"Those addicted to marihuana, after an early feeling of exhilaration, soon lose all restraints, all inhibitions. They become bestial demoniacs, filled with the mad lust to kill."

Kenneth Clark,
social psychologist, 1936

SYNERGISTIC EFFECT In pharmacology, an increase of effects that occurs when more than one substance is acting on the body at the same time.

Cannabis and Society: A Rocky Relationship

For centuries cannabis played a respected role in medicine. It was recommended as a surgical anesthetic by Chinese physicians 2,000 years ago and was used in other lands to treat cholera, malaria, coughs, insomnia, and rheumatism. When cannabis entered the United States in the early twentieth century, mainly in the form of marijuana, it was likewise used for various medical purposes. Soon, however, more effective medicines replaced it, and the favorable view of cannabis began to change. Marijuana began to be used as a recreational drug, and its illegal distribution became a law enforcement problem. Authorities assumed it was highly dangerous and outlawed the "killer weed."

But marijuana didn't go away. During the 1960s, a time of disillusionment, protest, and self-exploration, young people discovered the pleasures of getting high from smoking marijuana. By the end of the 1970s, 16 million people reported using it at least once, and 11 percent of the population were recent users.

In the 1980s researchers developed precise techniques for measuring THC, the key ingredient in cannabis, and for extracting pure THC from cannabis; they also developed laboratory forms of THC. These inventions opened the door to new medical applications for cannabis (Ogborne et al., 2000; Watson et al., 2000), such as its use in treating glaucoma, a severe eye disease. Cannabis was also found to help patients with asthma, to reduce the nausea and vomiting of cancer patients in chemotherapy, and to improve the appetites of AIDS patients and so combat weight loss in people with that disorder (Johnson, 1996; Plasse et al., 1991).

In light of these findings, several interest groups campaigned during the late 1980s for the medical legalization of marijuana, which operates on the brain and body more quickly than the THC capsules developed in the laboratory. In 1992, however, the Drug Enforcement Administration opposed this measure, and the Food and Drug Administration stopped reviewing requests for the "compassionate use" of marijuana (Karel, 1992). They held that prescriptions for pure THC served all needed medical functions.

Advocates of the medical use of marijuana challenged this position again during the elections of 1996. Voter referendums, which have the force of law, were passed in California and Arizona, giving physicians the right to prescribe marijuana for "seriously ill" or "terminally ill" patients. Voters in the states of Alaska, Washington, Oregon, Colorado, and Nevada followed suit in 1998. The federal government responded by threatening to revoke the prescription-writing privilege of any physician who prescribed marijuana, and even to prosecute such physicians. Angered by the government's position on this complex issue, many more physicians openly joined the battle, and in 1997 the *New England Journal of Medicine*, one of the world's most prestigious medical publications, published an editorial favoring the medical use of marijuana. This position was countered once again in 2001, however, when the Supreme Court upheld the authority of the federal government to bar doctors and clinics from prescribing marijuana to treat ill patients. Clearly we have not heard the last of this issue.

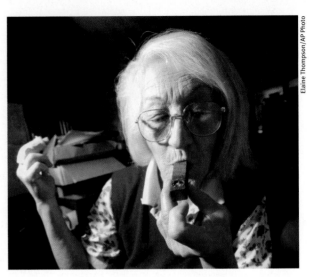

Medicinal use *Suffering from severe arthritis and an eye condition similar to glaucoma, this woman puffs on a pipe filled with marijuana several times a day. It apparently eases her pain and helps clear her vision.*

A different kind of synergistic effect results when drugs have *opposite*, or *antagonistic*, *actions*. Stimulant drugs, for example, interfere with the liver's usual disposal of barbiturates and alcohol. Thus people who combine barbiturates or alcohol with cocaine or amphetamines may build up toxic, even lethal, levels of the depressant drugs in their systems. Students who take amphetamines to help them study late into the night and then take barbiturates to help them fall asleep are unintentionally placing themselves in serious danger.

Each year tens of thousands of people are admitted to hospitals with a multiple drug emergency, and several thousand of them die (DAWN, 1997). Sometimes the cause is carelessness or ignorance. Often, however, people use multiple drugs precisely because they enjoy the synergistic effects. In fact, **polysubstance-related disorders** are becoming as common as individual substance-related disorders in the United States, Canada, and Europe (Schuckit et al., 2001; Galanter

POLYSUBSTANCE-RELATED DISORDER A long-term pattern of maladaptive behavior centered on abuse of or dependence on a combination of drugs.

Déjà vu *Polysubstance use, particularly a mixture of cocaine and opioids, proved fatal for
John Belushi (left) and Chris Farley (right), each
a featured actor on the television show* Saturday Night Live. *Farley had often stated his admiration for Belushi's talent and lifestyle.*

& Castañeda, 1999). As many as 90 percent of persons who use one illegal drug
are also using another to some extent (Cornish et al., 1995).

Fans still mourn the deaths of many celebrities who have been the victims of
polysubstance use. Elvis Presley's delicate balancing act of stimulants and depressants eventually killed him. Janis Joplin's mixtures of wine and heroin were ultimately fatal. And John Belushi's, River Phoenix's, and Chris Farley's liking for the
combined effect of cocaine and opioids ("speedballs") also ended in tragedy.

SUMMING UP | **Hallucinogens, Cannabis, and Combinations
of Substances**

Hallucinogens Hallucinogens, such as LSD, are substances that cause powerful
changes primarily in sensory perception. Perceptions are strengthened and illusions
and hallucinations can occur. LSD apparently causes such effects by disturbing the
release of the neurotransmitter serotonin.

Cannabis The main ingredient of *Cannabis sativa,* the hemp plant, is tetrahydrocannabinol (THC). Marijuana, the most popular form of cannabis, is more powerful
today than it was in years past. It can cause intoxication, and regular use can lead to
abuse and dependence.

Combinations of Substances Many people take more than one drug at a time, and
the drugs interact. The use of two or more drugs at the same time has become increasingly common. Similarly, polysubstance-related disorders have become a
major problem.

What Causes Substance-Related Disorders?

Clinical theorists have developed sociocultural, psychological, and biological explanations for why people abuse or become dependent on various substances. No
single explanation, however, has gained broad support. Like so many other disorders, excessive and regular drug use is increasingly viewed as the result of a combination of these factors.

The Sociocultural View

A number of sociocultural theorists propose that people are most likely to develop patterns of substance abuse or dependence when they live under stressful
socioeconomic conditions. In fact, studies have found that regions with higher
levels of unemployment have higher rates of alcoholism (Linsky, Strauss, &
Colby, 1985). Similarly, lower socioeconomic classes have substance-abuse rates

MISUSE OF INHALANTS

In 1998 more than one-fourth of all
eighth-graders and one-third of all
tenth-graders in the United States tried
to get high by inhaling the fumes of
household products (such as colored
markers, model glue, or spray paint),
despite public warnings about the dangerous—sometimes fatal—effects of
this practice (Johnston et al., 1999).

that are higher than those of other classes (Dohrenwend, 2000; Smith, North, & Spitznagel, 1993).

Other sociocultural theorists propose that substance abuse and dependence are more likely to appear in families and social environments where substance use is valued, or at least accepted (see Table 10-4). Researchers have, in fact, found that problem drinking is more common among teenagers whose parents and peers drink, as well as among teenagers whose family environments are stressful and unsupportive (Shucksmith, Glendinning, & Hendry, 1997; Wills et al., 1996). Moreover, lower rates of alcohol abuse are found among Jews and Protestants, groups in which drinking is typically acceptable only as long as it remains within clear limits, whereas alcoholism rates are higher among the Irish and Eastern Europeans, who do not, on average, draw as clear a line (Kohn & Levav, 1995; Vaillant & Milofsky, 1982).

In sum, the sociocultural explanations of substance abuse and dependence are supported by studies that generally compare drug use among people of different environments or cultures. As with sociocultural explanations of other mental disorders, however, they fail to explain why only some people who live under unfavorable social conditions develop substance-related disorders. Psychological (psychodynamic and behavioral) and biological theorists have provided some insight into this issue.

The Psychodynamic View

Psychodynamic theorists believe that people who abuse substances have powerful *dependency* needs that can be traced to their early years (Shedler & Block, 1990; Abadi, 1984). They claim that when parents fail to satisfy a young child's need for nurturance, the child is likely to grow up depending excessively on others for help and comfort, trying to find the nurturance that was lacking during the early years. If this search for outside support includes experimentation with a drug, the person may well develop a dependent relationship with the substance.

Some psychodynamic theorists also believe that certain people respond to their early deprivations by developing a *substance abuse personality* that leaves them particularly prone to drug abuse. Personality inventories and patient interviews have in fact indicated that people who abuse or depend on drugs tend to be more dependent, antisocial, impulsive, novelty-seeking, and depressive than other people (Finn et al., 2000; Mâsse & Tremblay, 1997). These findings are correlational, however, and do not clarify whether such personality traits lead to drug use or whether drug use causes people to be dependent, impulsive, and the like (Galanter & Castañeda, 1999).

In an effort to establish causation, one study measured the personality traits of a large group of nonalcoholic young men and then kept track of each man's development (Jones, 1971, 1968). Years later, the traits of the men who developed alcohol problems in middle age were compared with the traits of those who did not. The men who developed alcohol problems had been more impulsive as teenagers and continued to be so in middle age, a finding suggesting that impulsive men are indeed more prone to develop alcohol problems. Similarly, in one laboratory investigation, "impulsive" rats—those that generally had trouble delaying their rewards—were found to drink more alcohol when offered it than other rats (Poulos, Le, & Parker, 1995).

A major problem with these studies is the wide range of personality traits that has been tied to sub-

ConsiderThis

● Different ethnic, religious, and national groups have different rates of alcohol abuse. What social factors might help explain this observation? • Can we be certain that biological factors are not involved?

Table 10-4

Annual Alcohol Consumption around the World*

	WINE	BEER	LIQUOR
France	63.5	40.1	2.5
Italy	58.0	25.1	0.9
Switzerland	46.0	65.0	1.7
Australia	15.7	102.1	1.2
Britain	12.2	100.0	1.5
U.S.A.	8.9	87.8	2.0
Russia	2.7	17.1	3.8
Czech Republic	1.7	140.0	1.0
Japan	1.0	55.0	2.1
Mexico	0.2	50.4	0.8

*Consumption in liters per capita.

Source: Shapiro, 1996; World Drink Trends, 1994; World Health Organization; Wine Market Council; Adams/Jobson Publishing Corp.

stance abuse and dependence. In fact, different studies point to different "key" traits. Inasmuch as some people with a drug addiction appear to be dependent, others impulsive, and still others antisocial, researchers cannot conclude that any one personality trait or group of traits stands out in substance-related disorders (Rozin & Stoess, 1993).

The Behavioral View

According to *reinforcement* theorists, the temporary reduction of tension or raising of spirits produced by a drug has a rewarding effect, thus increasing the likelihood that the user will seek this reaction again (Carpenter & Hasin, 1998). The rewarding effects of substances may also lead users eventually to try higher dosages or more powerful methods of ingestion (see Table 10-5). In support of this behavioral theory, studies have found that many subjects do in fact drink more alcohol or seek heroin when they feel tense (Cooney et al., 1997; Cooper, 1994). In one study, as subjects worked on a difficult anagram task, a confederate planted by the researchers unfairly criticized and belittled them (Marlatt, Kosturn, & Lang, 1975). The subjects were then asked to participate in an "alcohol taste task," supposedly to compare and rate alcoholic beverages. The subjects who had been harassed drank more alcohol during the taste task than did control subjects who had not been criticized.

In a manner of speaking, the reinforcement theorists are arguing that many people take drugs to "medicate" themselves when they feel tense (Anthony et al., 1995). If so, one would expect higher rates of drug abuse among people who suffer from anxiety, depression, or intense anger. In fact, substance abuse and dependence do appear to be fairly common among people with mood disorders (Swendsen & Merikangas, 2000). One study of 835 clinically depressed patients found that more than one-fourth abused drugs during episodes of depression (Hasin, Endicott, & Lewis, 1985). Similarly, higher-than-usual rates of drug abuse have been found among people with posttraumatic stress disorder (Najavitis et al., 1998), eating disorders (Higuchi et al., 1993), schizophrenia (Regier et al., 1990), antisocial personality disorder (Brooner et al., 1997), histories of being abused (Yama et al., 1993), and other psychological problems (Kessler et al., 1997).

Other behaviorists have proposed that *classical conditioning* may play a role in drug abuse and dependence (Robbins et al., 2000; Remington et al., 1997).

SONGS OF SUBSTANCE

Substance use—illegal, legal, and medical—is a popular theme in today's music, particularly that favored by teenagers and young adults. Hit groups include Morphine, Xanax 25, and Halcion. Hit songs have ranged from the Velvet Underground's "Heroin" and "Sweet Jane" and Eric Clapton's "Cocaine" to Cyprus Hill's "I Wanna Get High" and "Insane in the Brain," Nirvana's "Lithium," Lil-Kim's "Drugs," and Jimmy Buffet's "Margaritaville."

"When tempted, reach for a Lucky."

Ad for Lucky Strikes cigarettes, 1930, targeting diet-conscious women

Table 10-5

Methods of Taking Substances

METHOD	ROUTE	TIME TO REACH BRAIN
Inhaling	Drug in vapor form is inhaled through mouth and lungs into circulatory system.	7 seconds
Snorting	Drug in powdered form is snorted into the nose. Some of the drug lands on the nasal mucous membranes, is absorbed by blood vessels, and enters the bloodstream.	4 minutes
Injection	Drug in liquid form directly enters the body through a needle. Injection may be intravenous or intramuscular (subcutaneous).	20 seconds (intravenous); 4 minutes (intramuscular)
Oral ingestion	Drug in solid or liquid form passes through esophagus and stomach and finally to the small intestines. It is absorbed by blood vessels in the intestines.	30 minutes
Other routes	Drugs can be absorbed through areas that contain mucous membranes. Drugs can be placed under the tongue, inserted anally and vaginally, and administered as eyedrops.	Variable

Source: Landry, 1994, p. 24.

Objects present at the time drugs are taken may act as classically conditioned stimuli and come to produce some of the same pleasure brought on by the drugs themselves. Just the sight of a hypodermic needle or a regular supplier, for example, has been known to comfort people who abuse heroin or amphetamines and to relieve their withdrawal symptoms (Meyer, 1995).

In a similar manner, objects that are present during withdrawal distress may produce withdrawal-like symptoms (Meyer, 1995; Childress et al., 1993, 1984). One man who had formerly been dependent on heroin experienced nausea and other withdrawal symptoms when he returned to the neighborhood where he had gone through withdrawal in the past—a reaction that led him to start taking heroin again (O'Brien et al., 1975).

The Biological View

In recent years researchers have come to suspect that drug misuse may have biological causes. Studies on genetic predisposition and specific biochemical processes have provided some support for these suspicions.

GENETIC PREDISPOSITION For years breeding experiments have been conducted to see whether certain animals are genetically predisposed to become dependent on drugs (Li, 2000; Kurtz et al., 1996). In several studies, for example, investigators have first identified animals that prefer alcohol to other beverages and then mated them to one another. Generally, the offspring of these animals have been found also to display an unusual preference for alcohol (Melo et al., 1996).

Similarly, research with human twins has suggested that people may inherit a predisposition to abuse substances in response to unfavorable life circumstances (Kendler et al., 1994, 1992). One classic study found an alcohol abuse *concordance* rate of 54 percent in a group of identical twins; that is, if one identical twin abused alcohol, the other twin also abused alcohol in 54 percent of the cases. In contrast, a group of fraternal twins had a concordance rate of only 28 percent (Kaij, 1960). As we have observed, however, such findings do not rule out other interpretations. For one thing, the parenting received by two identical twins may be more similar than that received by two fraternal twins.

ABNORMALITY AND THE ARTS

Chasing Highs Wherever They May Lead

Jonathan Melvoin, a backup keyboard player for the rock group Smashing Pumpkins, died of a heroin overdose in July 1996. Word soon spread that the brand of heroin he had taken was Red Rum, a strain smuggled in from Colombia. Its name—"murder" spelled backward—comes from the Stephen King novel *The Shining*.

Within hours the demand for Red Rum rose dramatically on the streets of Manhattan's Lower East Side. "It's kind of

sick," a narcotics officer told the *New York Times*. "But when people die from something or nearly die, all of a sudden there's this rush to get it."

Smashing aftermath *The Smashing Pumpkins, posing here for a studio photo a year before the keyboardist Melvoin died of an overdose, fired the band's drummer after learning that he had been using drugs with Melvoin.*

ConsiderThis

Why might people actively seek drugs that are known to endanger their lives? • Who has the greater impact on the drug behaviors of teenagers and young adults: rock performers who speak out against drugs or rock performers who praise the virtues of drugs?

A stronger indication that genetics may play a role in substance abuse and dependence comes from studies of alcoholism rates in people adopted shortly after birth (Cadoret et al., 1995; Goldstein, 1994). These studies have compared adoptees whose biological parents are dependent on alcohol with adoptees whose biological parents are not. By adulthood, the individuals whose biological parents are dependent on alcohol typically show higher rates of alcohol abuse than those with nonalcoholic biological parents.

Genetic linkage strategies and *molecular biology* techniques (see p. 185) provide more direct evidence in support of the genetic hypothesis (Crabbe, 2001; Li, 2000). One line of investigation has found an abnormal form of the so-called *dopamine-2 (D2) receptor gene* in a majority of subjects with alcohol dependence and half of subjects with cocaine dependence, but in less than 20 percent of nondependent subjects (Lawford et al., 1997; Blum & Noble, 1993). Other studies have tied still other kinds of dopamine-linked genes to substance-related disorders (Nash, 1997).

BIOCHEMICAL FACTORS Over the past few decades, investigators have pieced together a general biological understanding of drug tolerance and withdrawal symptoms (Wise, 1996). As we have seen, when a particular drug is ingested, it increases the activity of certain neurotransmitters whose normal purpose is to calm, reduce pain, lift mood, or increase alertness. When a person keeps on taking the drug, the brain apparently makes an adjustment and reduces its own production of the neurotransmitters. Because the drug is increasing neurotransmitter activity or efficiency, action by the brain is less necessary. As drug intake increases, the body's production of the neurotransmitters continues to decrease, leaving the person in need of more and more of the drug to achieve its effects. In this way, drug takers build tolerance for a drug, becoming more and more reliant on it rather than on their own biological processes to feel calm, comfortable, happy, or alert. If they suddenly stop taking the drug, their supply of neurotransmitters will be low for a time, producing the symptoms of withdrawal. Withdrawal continues until the brain resumes its normal production of the necessary neurotransmitters.

Which neurotransmitters are affected depends on the drug used. A regular and excessive use of alcohol or benzodiazepines may lower the brain's production of the neurotransmitter GABA; regular use of opioids may reduce the brain's production of endorphins; and regular use of cocaine or amphetamines may lower the brain's production of dopamine (Volkow, Fowler, & Wang, 1999). In addition, researchers have identified neurotransmitters called *anandamides* (from the Sanskrit word for "bliss") that operate much like THC; excessive use of marijuana may reduce the production of these neurotransmitters (Johns, 2001; Biegon & Kerman, 1995).

This model helps explain why people who regularly take substances experience tolerance and withdrawal reactions. But why are drugs so rewarding, and why do certain people turn to them in the first place? A recent flurry of brain-imaging studies suggest that many, perhaps all, drugs eventually activate a single **reward center,** or "pleasure pathway," in the brain (Volkow & Fowler, 2000). A key neurotransmitter in this pleasure pathway appears to be *dopamine.* When dopamine is activated there, a person experiences pleasure. Music may activate dopamine in the reward center. So may a hug or a word of praise. And so may drugs.

Certain drugs apparently stimulate the reward center directly. Remember that cocaine and amphetamines directly increase dopamine activity. Other drugs seem to stimulate the reward center in roundabout ways. The biochemical reactions triggered by alcohol, opioids, and marijuana probably set in motion a series of chemical events that eventually lead to increased dopamine activity in the reward center.

A number of theorists suspect that people who abuse drugs suffer from a **reward-deficiency syndrome;** their reward center is not readily activated by the usual events in their lives (Blum et al., 2000; Nash, 1997), so they turn to drugs to stimulate this pleasure pathway, particularly at times of stress. Abnormal

REWARD CENTER A dopamine-rich pathway in the brain that produces feelings of pleasure when activated.

REWARD-DEFICIENCY SYNDROME A condition, suspected to be present in some individuals, in which the brain's reward center is not readily activated by the usual events in their lives.

"Alcohol is like love. The first kiss is magic, the second is intimate, the third is routine."

Raymond Chandler,
The Long Good-bye

Addicted to chocolate? *Recent studies suggest that the craving for chocolate may be more than just a state of mind. Apparently some chemicals in chocolate may bind to the same neuron receptors that receive cannabis substances (di Tomaso, Beltramo, & Piomelli, 1996). At the same time, however, a person would have to eat 25 pounds of chocolate in one sitting to experience a cannabis-like effect. Then again, for chocolate lovers . . .*

genes, such as the abnormal D2 receptor gene, have been cited as a possible cause of this syndrome (Lawford et al., 1997).

SUMMING UP ❘ **What Causes Substance-Related Disorders?**

Several explanations for substance abuse and dependence have been put forward. None has gained clear research support, but together they are beginning to shed light on the disorders.

According to the sociocultural view, people most likely to abuse drugs are those whose societies create an atmosphere of stress or whose families value or tolerate drug use. In the psychodynamic view, people who turn to substance abuse have excessive dependency needs traceable to the early stages of life. Some theorists from the model also believe that certain people have a substance-abuse personality that makes them prone to drug use. The leading behavioral view proposes that drug use is reinforced at first because it reduces tension and raises spirits.

Biological explanations suggest that people may inherit a predisposition to substance dependence. Researchers have also learned that drug tolerance and withdrawal symptoms may be caused by cutbacks in the brain's production of particular neurotransmitters during excessive and regular drug use. Finally, biological studies suggest that many, perhaps all, drugs eventually lead to increased dopamine activity in the brain's reward center.

How Are Substance-Related Disorders Treated?

Many approaches have been used to treat substance-related disorders, including psychodynamic, behavioral, cognitive-behavioral, biological, and sociocultural therapies. Although these treatments sometimes meet with great success, more often they are only moderately helpful (Miller et al., 2001; Rabasca, 1998). Today the treatments are typically used in combination (Galanter & Brooks, 2001) on both an outpatient and an inpatient basis (Rychtarik et al., 2000).

Psychodynamic Therapies

Psychodynamic therapists try to help people with substance-related disorders become aware of and correct the psychological problems that they believe are at the root of the disorders. They first guide clients to uncover and work through their underlying conflicts, and then they try to help them change their substance-related styles of living (Hopper, 1995; Levinson, 1985). Although this approach has often been applied to substance-related disorders, research has not found it to be highly effective (Cornish et al., 1995; Holder et al., 1991). It may be that drug abuse or dependence, regardless of its causes, eventually becomes a stubborn independent problem that must be the direct target of treatment if people are to become drug-free. Psychodynamic therapy tends to be of greater help when combined with other approaches in a multidimensional treatment program. It has had some success, for example, when combined with behavioral and biological therapies (Galanter & Brook, 2001; Carroll & Rounsaville, 1995).

Behavioral Therapies

AVERSION THERAPY A treatment in which clients are repeatedly presented with unpleasant stimuli while performing undesirable behaviors such as taking a drug.

BEHAVIORAL SELF-CONTROL TRAINING (BSCT) A cognitive-behavioral approach to treating alcohol abuse and dependence in which clients are taught to keep track of their drinking behavior and to apply coping strategies in situations that typically trigger excessive drinking.

A widely used behavioral treatment for substance-related disorders is **aversion therapy,** an approach based on the principles of classical conditioning (Frawley & Smith, 1992). Individuals are repeatedly presented with an unpleasant stimulus (for example, an electric shock) at the very moment that they are taking a drug. After repeated pairings, they are expected to react negatively to the substance itself and to lose their craving for it.

Aversion therapy has been applied to alcohol abuse and dependence more than to other substance-related disorders. In one version of this therapy, drinking behavior is paired with drug-induced nausea and vomiting (Elkins, 1991; Cannon et al., 1986, 1981). Another version, *covert sensitization,* requires people with alcoholism to imagine extremely upsetting, repulsive, or frightening scenes while they are drinking (Kassel, Wagner, & Unrod, 1999). The pairing of the imagined scenes with liquor is expected to produce negative responses to liquor itself. Here is the kind of scene therapists may guide a client to imagine:

> I'd like you to vividly imagine that you are tasting the (beer, whiskey, etc.). See yourself tasting it, capture the exact taste, colour and consistency. Use all of your senses. After you've tasted the drink you notice that there is something small and white floating in the glass—it stands out. You bend closer to examine it more carefully, your nose is right over the glass now and the smell fills your nostrils as you remember exactly what the drink tastes like. Now you can see what's in the glass. There are several maggots floating on the surface. As you watch, revolted, one manages to get a grip on the glass and, undulating, creeps up the glass. There are even more of the repulsive creatures in the glass than you first thought. You realise that you have swallowed some of them and you're very aware of the taste in your mouth. You feel very sick and wish you'd never reached for the glass and had the drink at all.
>
> *(Clarke & Saunders, 1988, pp. 143–144)*

A behavioral approach that has been effective in the short-term treatment of people who abuse cocaine and some other drugs is *contingency management,* which makes incentives (such as program privileges) contingent on the submission of drug-free urine specimens (Katz et al., 2001; Petry, 2000). In one study, 68 percent of cocaine abusers who completed a six-month contingency training program achieved at least eight weeks of continuous abstinence (Higgins et al., 1993).

Behavioral interventions for substance abuse and dependence have usually had only limited success when they are the sole form of treatment (Carroll & Rounsaville, 1995). A major problem is that the approaches can be effective only when individuals are motivated to continue with them despite their unpleasantness or demands. Generally, behavioral treatments work best in combination with either biological or cognitive approaches (Kassel et al., 1999; Whorley, 1996).

Cognitive-Behavioral Therapies

Two popular approaches combine cognitive and behavioral techniques to help people gain *control* over their substance-related behaviors. In one, **behavioral self-control training (BSCT),** applied to alcoholism in particular, therapists first have clients keep track of their own drinking behavior (Miller et al., 1992; Miller, 1983). Writing down the times, locations, emotions, bodily changes, and other circumstances of their drinking, they become more aware of the situations that place them at risk for excessive drinking. They are then taught coping strategies to use when such situations arise. They learn, for example, to set limits on their drinking, to recognize when the limits are being approached, to control their rate of drinking (perhaps by spacing their drinks or by sipping them rather than gulping), and to practice relaxation techniques, assertiveness skills, and other coping behaviors in situations in which they would otherwise be drinking. Approximately 70 percent of the people who complete this training apparently show some improvement, particularly those who are young and not physically dependent on alcohol (Walters, 2000; Hester, 1995).

DRASTIC MEASURE

In one early form of aversion therapy, people with alcoholism were injected with succinylcholine, a drug that actually paralyzed their bodies while they tasted alcoholic beverages (Sanderson, Campbell, & Laverty, 1963). These clients did sometimes develop an aversion to alcohol, but concerns about the safety and ethics of this approach led to its discontinuation.

Jeff Mermelstein, New York, NY

Carrot juice on the rocks *Both public officials and clinical experts welcome the recent growth of juice bars (such as this one in New York City) and similar establishments, where substances other than alcohol are valued by patrons and help to trigger social interactions and activities.*

Controlled Drug Use vs. Abstinence

Is total abstinence the only cure for drug abuse and dependence, or can people with substance-related disorders learn to keep drug use under control? This issue has been debated for years, especially when the drug in question is alcohol (King & Tucker, 2000).

Some cognitive-behavioral theorists believe that people can continue to drink in moderation if they learn to set appropriate drinking limits. They argue that demanding strict abstinence of people may in fact cause people to lose self-control entirely if they have a single drink (Marlatt et al., 2001; Peele, 1989; Heather et al., 1982). In contrast, those who view alcoholism as a disease take the AA position of "Once an alcoholic, always an alcoholic," and argue that people with alcoholism are in fact more

likely to relapse when they believe that they can safely take one drink (Pendery et al., 1982). This misguided belief, they hold, will sooner or later open the door to alcohol once again and lead back to uncontrollable drinking.

Feelings run so strongly that the people on one side have at times challenged the motives and honesty of those on the other (Sobell & Sobell, 1984, 1973; Pendery et al., 1982). Research indicates, however, that both controlled drinking and abstinence may be useful treatment goals, depending on the individual's personality and on the nature of the particular drinking problem. Studies suggest, for example, that abstinence is a more appropriate goal for people who have a long-standing dependence on alcohol, while controlled drinking can be helpful

to younger drinkers whose pattern does not include physical dependence. They may in fact need to be taught a nonabusive form of drinking (Peele, 1992; Marlatt, 1985). Studies also suggest that abstinence is appropriate for people who believe that abstinence is the only answer for them (Rosenberg, 1993). These individuals are indeed more likely to relapse after having just one drink.

Generally speaking, both abstinence and controlled drinking are extremely difficult for persons with alcoholism to achieve. Although treatment may help them to improve for a while, many of them relapse (Allsop et al., 2000). Such statistics serve as a harsh reminder that substance abuse and dependence remain among society's most disabling problems.

In another cognitive-behavioral approach, **relapse-prevention training,** heavy drinkers are assigned many of the same tasks as clients in BSCT (Parks & Marlatt, 2000, 1999). They are also taught to plan ahead of time how many drinks are appropriate, what to drink, and under what circumstances. The approach sometimes lowers the frequency of intoxication (Kassel et al., 1999). Like BSCT, it seems most effective for people who abuse alcohol but are not physically dependent on it (Meyer et al., 1989). The approach has also been used, with some success, in the treatment of marijuana and cocaine abuse (Foxhall, 2001).

Biological Treatments

Biological approaches may be used to help people withdraw from substances, abstain from them, or simply maintain their level of use without further increases (Moss, 1999). As with the other forms of treatment, biological approaches alone rarely bring long-term improvement, but they can be helpful when combined with other approaches (Cornish et al., 1995; Kleber, 1995).

DETOXIFICATION **Detoxification** is systematic and medically supervised withdrawal from a drug. Some detoxification programs are offered on an outpatient basis (Allan, Smith, & Mellin, 2000). Others are located in hospitals and clinics and may also offer individual and group therapy, a "full-service" institutional approach that has become popular. One detoxification approach is to have clients withdraw gradually from the substance, taking smaller and smaller doses until they are off it completely. A second detoxification technique is to give clients other drugs that reduce the symptoms of withdrawal (Schuckit, 1999). Antianxiety drugs, for example, are sometimes used to reduce severe alcohol withdrawal reactions such as delirium tremens and seizures (D'Onofrio et al., 1999). Detoxification programs seem to help motivated people withdraw from drugs (Allan et al., 2000). For people who fail to receive psychotherapy after withdrawal, however, relapse rates tend to be high (Pickens & Fletcher, 1991).

ANTAGONIST DRUGS After successfully stopping a drug, people must avoid falling back into a pattern of abuse or dependence. As an aid to resisting tempta-

RELAPSE-PREVENTION TRAINING An approach to treating alcohol abuse that is similar to BSCT and also has clients plan ahead for risky situations and reactions.

DETOXIFICATION Systematic and medically supervised withdrawal from a drug.

ANTAGONIST DRUGS Drugs that block or change the effects of an addictive drug.

METHADONE MAINTENANCE PROGRAM An approach to treating heroin dependence in which clients are given legally and medically supervised doses of a substitute drug, methadone.

Forced detoxification *Abstinence does not always take place in a planned, medically supervised, or voluntary manner. This sufferer of alcoholism begins to experience symptoms of withdrawal soon after being imprisoned for public intoxication.*

tion, some people with substance-related disorders are given **antagonist drugs,** which block or change the effects of the addictive drug. *Disulfiram (Antabuse),* for example, is often given to people who are trying to stay away from alcohol (Moss, 1999; Landry, 1994). By itself a low dose of this drug seems to have few negative effects, but a person who drinks alcohol while taking disulfiram will experience intense nausea, vomiting, blushing, faster heart rate, dizziness, and perhaps fainting. People taking disulfiram are less likely to drink alcohol because they know the terrible reaction that awaits them should they have even one drink. Disulfiram has proved helpful, but again only with people who are motivated to take it as prescribed (Cornish et al., 1995).

Narcotic antagonists are sometimes used to treat people who are dependent on opioids. These drugs attach to endorphin receptor sites throughout the brain and make it impossible for the opioids to have their usual effect. Without the rush or high, continued drug use becomes pointless. Although narcotic antagonists have been helpful—particularly in emergencies, to rescue people from an overdose of opioids—some clinicians consider them too dangerous for regular treatment of opioid dependence. These antagonists must be given very carefully because of their ability to throw a person with an addiction into severe withdrawal (Rosen et al., 1996; Goldstein, 1994). In recent years, so-called *partial antagonists,* narcotic antagonists that produce less severe withdrawal symptoms, have been developed (Amass et al., 2000).

Recent studies indicate that narcotic antagonists may also be useful in the treatment of alcohol and cocaine dependence (Anton et al., 2001; Schuckit, 1999). In some studies, for example, the narcotic antagonist *naltrexone* has helped reduce cravings for alcohol (O'Malley et al., 2000, 1996, 1992). Why should narcotic antagonists, which operate at the brain's endorphin receptors, help with alcoholism, which has been tied largely to activity at GABA sites? The answer may lie in the reward center of the brain. If various drugs eventually stimulate the same pleasure pathway, it seems reasonable to expect that antagonists for one drug may, in a roundabout way, affect the impact of other drugs as well.

DRUG MAINTENANCE THERAPY A drug-related lifestyle may be a greater problem than the drug's direct effects. Much of the damage caused by heroin addiction, for example, comes from overdoses, unsterile needles, and an accompanying life of crime. Thus clinicians were very enthusiastic when **methadone maintenance programs** were developed in the 1960s to treat heroin addiction (Dole & Nyswander, 1967, 1965). In these programs, people with an addiction are given the laboratory opioid *methadone* as a substitute for heroin. Although they then become dependent on methadone, their new addiction is maintained

"Water is the only drink for a wise man."

Henry David Thoreau, *Walden*

DRUGS AND CRIME
About 57% of state prisoners and 45% of federal prisoners in the United States report using illicit drugs in the month before committing their offense (Bureau of Justice Statistics, 1999).

ConsiderThis

○ Inasmuch as the major dangers of heroin come from overdose, unsterilized needles, and criminal lifestyle, society has periodically tried legal, medically supervised use of heroin (in Great Britain) or of a heroin substitute (in the United States) to combat this drug problem. Generally, such approaches have had limited effectiveness. Why?

under safe medical supervision. Unlike heroin, methadone can be taken by mouth, thus eliminating the dangers of needles, and needs to be taken only once a day.

At first, methadone programs seemed very effective, and many of them were set up throughout the United States, Canada, and England (Payte, 1989). These programs became less popular during the 1980s, however, because of the dangers of methadone itself. Many clinicians came to believe that substituting one addiction for another is not an acceptable "solution" for drug dependence, and many people with an addiction complained that methadone addiction was creating an additional drug problem that simply complicated their original one (Cornish et al., 1995). In fact, methadone is harder to withdraw from than heroin. Moreover, pregnant women maintained on methadone have the added concern of the drug's effect on their fetus (DeCubas & Field, 1993).

Despite such concerns, maintenance treatment with methadone (or with *buprenorphine,* a newly developed substitute drug) has again sparked interest among clinicians in recent years, partly because of new research support (Gossop et al., 2001; Ritter, 2001) and partly because of the rapid spread of the HIV virus among intravenous drug abusers and their sex partners and children (Cornish et al., 1995). More than one-quarter of AIDS cases reported in the early 1990s were directly tied to drug abuse, and intravenous drug abuse is the indirect cause in 60 percent of childhood AIDS cases (Brown, 1993; NIDA, 1991). Not only is methadone treatment safer than street opioid use, but many methadone programs now include AIDS education and other health instructions in their services (Sorensen & Copeland, 2000). Research suggests that methadone maintenance programs are most effective when they are combined with education, regular psychotherapy, family therapy, and employment counseling (Woody et al., 1998). Today more than 900 methadone clinics across the United States dispense the drug to as many as 115,000 patients at an average cost of $13 a day (Marks, 1998).

Sociocultural Therapies

As we have seen, sociocultural theorists believe that psychological problems emerge in a social setting and are best treated in a social context. Three sociocultural approaches have been applied to substance-related disorders: (1) *self-help programs*; (2) *culture- and gender-sensitive programs*; and (3) *community prevention programs.*

SELF-HELP AND RESIDENTIAL TREATMENT PROGRAMS Many people who abuse drugs have organized among themselves to help one another recover without

Changing an image *All kinds of persons in all kinds of places now use the principles of self-help programs to help them overcome and control problems with alcohol or other substances. Here sober bikers get together at The Dry Gulch, a favorite spot in St. Paul, Minnesota.*

STEPPING BACK

In the Beginning

In the summer of 1935, Bill W. sat defeated in a hotel room far from home, longing for a drink.

Six months earlier, this high-risk stock analyst had climbed on the wagon of sobriety and managed to convince his long-suffering employer to give him one more chance. The New York brokerage firm for which he worked reluctantly agreed to let him lead a proxy-fight at an annual stockholders meeting in Akron, Ohio. But Bill failed in this task, and he now felt as if his last hope for restoring his career and his dignity had vanished. In such moments of misery, his usual action would be to reach for a bottle of gin.

This time, however, Bill picked up a phone book and dialed a church at random. He asked the minister who answered if there were any other "hopeless drunks" he could talk to. The minister directed him to Dr. Bob, a local physician who was "drying out" in a hospital in his umpteenth attempt to stop drinking. Bill went to Dr. Bob's bedside and, over the course of several hours, shared his story with the physician. The two men began searching for other "alcoholics" to talk to, and before long they were holding regular meetings in their homes where recovering individuals would join together to tell their stories and exchange thoughts and advice about the road to sobriety.

From such humble beginnings Alcoholics Anonymous (AA) was born, a movement with the singular purpose of helping fellow problem drinkers reclaim their lives. The philosophy of the group is simple: AA members gather to share their experiences with anyone who desires to stop drinking.

For an international organization with more than 2 million members, AA is remarkably decentralized. It works steadfastly to remain "nonprofessional" and strives to create a low-key, humble, and quiet atmosphere. There are no dues for membership, local and national leadership rotates regularly, and organization is kept to a minimum. AA does not actively solicit members, sponsor research or education, or provide any social services, such as medical or financial help, for persons struggling with alcoholism. It does not officially take any position on alcohol-related issues such as "driving under the influence" or minimum-drinking age laws. It makes little effort to publicize its activities, and it even refuses outside donations, funding itself solely by "passing the hat" at meetings and by selling its literature to members.

It wasn't always so. Flush with its early successes, Bill W. envisioned alcoholic hospitals and recovery centers across the country, paid missionaries who would seek out excessive drinkers and urge them to recover, and the publication of books that would generate millions of dollars for the cause. To do all this, however, the organization needed a considerable amount of seed money. Knowing that John D. Rockefeller Jr. was impressed with the fledgling organization, Bill W. convinced the industrialist to sponsor a dinner with 75 of New York's wealthiest and most influential citizens, where he could describe AA and its aspirations. After Bill W. confidently delivered his pitch, Rockefeller's son Nelson lauded AA and announced, "Gentlemen, you can all see that this is a work of good will. Its power lies in the fact that one member carries the good message to the next, without any thought of financial income or reward. Therefore, it is our belief that Alcoholics Anonymous should be self-supporting so far as money is concerned. It needs only our good will." (Bill W., 1957/1975, pp. 184–185)

After several funding disappointments of this kind, AA decided to make its corporate poverty and its narrow goal into a strength. At an international convention in 1950, the membership agreed that "[a]n AA group ought never endorse, finance or lend the AA name to any related facility or outside purpose, lest problems of money, property and prestige divert us from our primary purpose." Since then, the self-supporting, modest, and single-minded nature of AA, has, in the view of many, become central to its mission, its message, and it success. The organization's yearly revenues from member donations and book sales represent but a small fraction of the billions of dollars that America spends more generally on treatment for alcohol abuse and dependence.

professional assistance. The drug self-help movement dates back to 1935, when two Ohio men suffering from alcoholism met to discuss alternative treatment possibilities. The first discussion led to others and to the eventual formation of a self-help group whose members discussed alcohol-related problems, traded ideas, and provided support. The organization became known as **Alcoholics Anonymous (AA).**

Today AA has more than 2 million members in 98,000 groups across the United States and 150 other countries (AA World Services, 2000, 1998). It offers peer support along with moral and spiritual guidelines to help people overcome alcoholism. Different members apparently find different aspects of AA helpful. For some it is the peer support (Galanter et al., 1990); for others it is the spiritual dimension (Swora, 2001). Meetings take place regularly, and members are available to help each other 24 hours a day.

ALCOHOLICS ANONYMOUS (AA) A self-help organization that provides support and guidance for persons with alcohol abuse or dependence.

RESIDENTIAL TREATMENT CENTER A place where people formerly dependent on drugs live, work, and socialize in a drug-free environment. Also called a *therapeutic community*.

By offering guidelines for living, the organization helps members abstain "one day at a time," urging them to accept as "fact" the idea that they are powerless over alcohol and that they must stop drinking entirely and permanently if they are to live normal lives. Related self-help organizations, Al-Anon and Alateen, offer support for people who live with and care about persons with alcoholism. Self-help programs such as Narcotics Anonymous and Cocaine Anonymous have been developed for other substance-related disorders.

Many self-help programs have expanded into **residential treatment centers,** or **therapeutic communities**—such as Daytop Village and Phoenix House—where people formerly dependent on drugs live, work, and socialize in a drug-free environment while undergoing individual, group, and family therapies and making a transition back to community life (Landry, 1994).

The evidence that keeps self-help and residential treatment programs going comes largely in the form of individual testimonials. Many tens of thousands of persons have revealed that they are members of these programs and credit them with turning their lives around (Gleick, 1995). Studies of the programs have also had favorable findings (Tonigan, 2001; Timko et al., 2000), but their numbers have been limited (Watson et al., 1997).

CULTURE- AND GENDER-SENSITIVE PROGRAMS Many persons who abuse substances live in a poor and perhaps violent setting. A growing number of today's treatment programs try to be sensitive to the special sociocultural pressures and problems faced by drug abusers who are poor, homeless, or members of ethnic minority groups (Straussner, 2001). Therapists who are sensitive to their clients' life challenges can do more to address the stresses that often lead to relapse.

Similarly, therapists have become more aware that women often require treatment methods different from those designed for men (Knowlton, 1998; Lisansky-Gomberg, 1993). Women and men have different physical and psychological reactions to drugs, for example (Hamilton, 1991). In addition, treatment of women who abuse substances may be complicated by the impact of sexual abuse, the possibility that they may become pregnant while taking drugs, the stresses of raising children, and the fear of criminal prosecution for abusing drugs during pregnancy (Thompson & Kingree, 1998; Cornish et al., 1995). Thus many women with such disorders feel more comfortable seeking help at gender-sensitive clinics or residential programs; some such programs also allow children to live with their recovering mothers (Clark, 2001).

COMMUNITY PREVENTION PROGRAMS Perhaps the most effective approach to substance-related disorders is to prevent them (Schuckit, 2000). The first drug-prevention efforts took place in schools. Today prevention programs are also offered in workplaces, activity centers, and other community settings, and even through the media (St. Pierre, 2001; Guild & Lowe, 1998). Some prevention programs argue for total abstinence from drugs, while others teach "responsible" use. Some seek to interrupt drug use; others try to delay the age at which people first experiment with drugs. Programs may also differ in whether they offer drug education, teach alternatives to drug use, try to change the psychological state of the potential user, seek to change relationships with peers, or combine these techniques.

Prevention programs may focus on the *individual* (for example, by providing education about unpleasant drug effects), the *family* (by teaching parenting skills), the *peer group* (by teaching resistance to peer pressure), the *school* (by setting up firm enforcement of drug policies), or the *community* at large (by public service announcements such as the "Just say no" campaign several years ago). The most effective prevention efforts focus on several of these areas to

Before it begins *Community prevention programs for substance-related disorders often target very young children. Here children pledge abstinence from drug use by releasing balloons on Red Ribbon Day.*

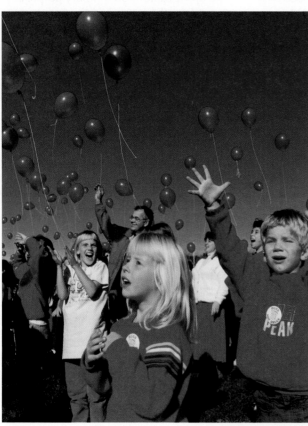

Marc R. Wood, Marinette, Wisconsin

provide a consistent message about drug abuse in all areas of individuals' lives (Smith, 2001; Wagenaar et al., 2000). Some prevention programs have even been developed for preschool children (Hall & Zigler, 1997).

SUMMING UP | How Are Substance-Related Disorders Treated?

Treatments for substance abuse and dependence vary widely. Usually several approaches are combined. Psychodynamic therapies try to help clients become aware of and correct the underlying psychological forces that may have led to their use of drugs. A common behavioral technique is aversion therapy, in which an unpleasant stimulus is paired with the drug that the person is abusing. Cognitive and behavioral techniques have been combined in such forms as behavioral self-control training (BSCT) and relapse-prevention training. Biological treatments include detoxification, antagonist drugs, and drug maintenance therapy. And sociocultural treatments approach substance-related disorders in a social context, using approaches such as self-help groups, like Alcoholics Anonymous; culture- and gender-sensitive treatments; and community prevention programs.

CROSSROADS:
New Wrinkles to a Familiar Story

In some respects the story of the misuse of drugs is the same today as in the past. Substance use is still rampant, often creating damaging psychological disorders. New drugs keep emerging, and the public goes through periods of believing, naively, that they are "safe." Only gradually do people learn that these drugs, too, pose dangers. And treatments for substance-related disorders continue to have only limited effect.

Yet there are important new wrinkles in this familiar story. Researchers have begun to develop a clearer understanding of how drugs act on the brain and body. In treatment, self-help groups and rehabilitation programs are flourishing. And preventive education to make people aware of the dangers of drug misuse is also expanding and seems to be having an effect. One reason for these improvements is that investigators and clinicians have stopped working in isolation and are instead looking for intersections between their own work and that from other models. The same kind of integrated efforts that have helped with other psychological disorders are bringing new promise and hope to the study and treatment of substance-related disorders.

Perhaps the most important insight to be gained from these integrated efforts is that several of the models were already on the right track. Social pressures, personality characteristics, rewards, and genetic predispositions all seem to play a role in substance-related disorders, and in fact to operate together. For example, some people may inherit a malfunction of the biological reward center and so may need special doses of external stimulation—say, intense relationships, an abundance of certain foods, or drugs—to stimulate their reward center. Their pursuit of external rewards may take on the character of an addictive personality. Such individuals may be especially prone to experimenting with drugs, particularly when their social group makes the drugs available or when they are faced with intense social and personal stress.

Just as each model has identified important factors in the development of substance-related disorders, each has made important contributions to treatment. As we have seen, the various forms of treatment seem to work best when they are combined with approaches from the other models, making integrated treatment the most productive approach.

ConsiderThis

◉ Only one-third of the $15 billion the U.S. government spends on drug abuse goes to prevention and treatment. Does the focus on the criminalization of drugs ultimately add to the stigma of drug abuse and, in turn, make effective treatment more difficult (Nash, 1997)?

These recent developments are encouraging. At the same time, however, enormous and increasing levels of drug use continue. New drugs and drug combinations are discovered almost daily, and with them come new problems, new questions, and needs for new research and new treatments. Perhaps the most valuable lesson is an old one. There is no free lunch. The pleasures derived from these substances come with high psychological and biological costs, some not yet even known.

KEY TERMS

intoxication p. 274
hallucinosis p. 274
substance abuse p. 274
substance dependence p. 274
tolerance p. 274
withdrawal p. 274
alcohol p. 275
ethyl alcohol p. 275
alcohol dehydrogenase p. 276
delirium tremens (DTs) p. 278
cirrhosis p. 279
Korsakoff's syndrome p. 280
confabulation p. 280
fetal alcohol syndrome p. 280
sedative-hypnotic drug p. 280
barbiturates p. 280
benzodiazepines p. 280
opioid p. 281
opium p. 281
morphine p. 281

heroin p. 281
methadone p. 282
codeine p. 282
rush p. 282
endorphin p. 282
cocaine p. 283
crashing p. 285
free-basing p. 286
crack p. 286
amphetamine p. 287
hallucinogen p. 288
LSD (lysergic acid diethylamide) p. 288
ergot alkaloids p. 288
flashback p. 289
Cannabis sativa p. 289
cannabis drugs p. 289
hashish p. 289
marijuana p. 289
tetrahydrocannabinol (THC) p. 289
synergistic effect p. 291

polysubstance-related disorder p. 292
substance abuse personality p. 294
dopamine-2 (D2) receptor gene p. 297
reward center p. 297
reward-deficiency syndrome p. 297
aversion therapy p. 298
contingency management p. 299
behavioral self-control training (BSCT) p. 299
relapse-prevention training p. 300
detoxification p. 300
antagonist drugs p. 301
disulfiram (Antabuse) p. 301
narcotic antagonist p. 301
naltrexone p. 301
methadone maintenance program p. 301
self-help program p. 302
culture- and gender-sensitive program p. 302
community prevention program p. 302
Alcoholics Anonymous (AA) p. 303
residential treatment center p. 304

QUICK QUIZ

1. How does alcohol act on the brain and body? What are the problems and dangers of alcohol misuse? pp. 275–280

2. Describe the features and problems of the misuse of barbiturates and benzodiazepines. pp. 280–281

3. Compare the various opioids (opium, heroin, morphine, and codeine). What problems may result from their use, particularly from the use of heroin? pp. 281–283

4. List and compare two kinds of stimulant drugs. Describe their biological actions and the problems caused by each of them. pp. 283–288

5. Why has cocaine use become a major problem in recent years? pp. 286–287

6. What are the effects of hallucinogens, particularly LSD? pp. 288–289

7. What are the effects of marijuana and other cannabis substances?

Why is marijuana a greater danger today than it was 25 years ago? pp. 289–291

8. What special problems does polysubstance use pose? pp. 291–293

9. Describe the leading explanations for substance-related disorders. How well supported are these explanations? pp. 293–298

10. What are the leading treatments for substance-related disorders? How effective are they? pp. 298–305

▲ *Is alcoholism inherited?* ▲ *How does substance abuse affect personal, family, and occupational functioning?* ▲ *Observe behavioral and cognitive treatments for cocaine dependence and other substance-related disorders.* ▲ *What triggers a user's cravings for alcohol, cocaine, or nicotine?* ▲ *How might alcohol use relate to suicide attempts?*

SEARCH THE *FUNDAMENTALS OF ABNORMAL PSYCHOLOGY* CD-ROM FOR

▲ Chapter 10 video cases and discussions
  "Al"—Alcohol Disorders: Hereditary Factors
  "Jim"—Treating Drug Addiction: A Behavioral Approach
  "Greg"—Treating Drug Addiction: A Behavioral Approach

▲ Chapter 10 practice test and feedback

▲ Additional video cases and discussions
  "Claude & Claude"—Emotion, Stress, and Health
  "Andy"—Suicide

LOG ON TO THE COMER WEB PAGE FOR:

▲ Suggested Web links, research exercises, FAQ page, additional Chapter 10 practice test questions
  <www.worthpublishers.com/comer>

Source: *The Mind, Second Edition* (WNET/Worth Publishers, 1999)

Sexual Disorders and Gender Identity Disorder

Robert, a 57-year-old man, came to sex therapy with his wife because of his inability to get erections. He had not had a problem with erections until six months earlier, when they attempted to have sex after an evening out, during which he had had several drinks. They attributed his failure to get an erection to his being "a little drunk," but he found himself worrying over the next few days that he was perhaps becoming impotent. When they next attempted intercourse, he found himself unable to get involved in what they were doing because he was so intent on watching himself to see if he would get an erection. Once again he did not, and they were both very upset. His failure to get an erection continued over the next few months. Robert's wife was very upset and . . . frustrated, accusing him of having an affair, or of no longer finding her attractive. Robert wondered if he was getting too old, or if his medication for high blood pressure, which he had been taking for about a year, might be interfering with erection. . . . When they came for sex therapy, they had not attempted any sexual activity for over two months.

(LoPiccolo, 1992, p. 492)

Sexual behavior is a major focus of both our private thoughts and public discussions. Sexual feelings are a key part of our development and daily functioning, sexual activity is tied to the satisfaction of our basic needs, and sexual performance is linked to our self-esteem. Most people are fascinated by the abnormal sexual behavior of others and worry about the normality of their own sexuality.

Experts recognize two general categories of sexual disorders: sexual dysfunctions and paraphilias. People with *sexual dysfunctions* experience problems with their sexual responses. Robert, for example, had a dysfunction known as erectile disorder, a repeated failure to attain or maintain an erection during sexual activity. People with *paraphilias* have repeated and intense sexual urges or fantasies in response to objects or situations that society deems inappropriate, and they may behave inappropriately as well. They may be aroused by the thought of sexual activity with a child, for example, or of exposing their genitals to strangers, and they may act on those urges. In addition to the sexual disorders, DSM includes a diagnosis called *gender identity disorder,* a sex-related disorder in which people feel that they have been assigned to the wrong sex and in fact identify with the other gender.

Sexual Dysfunctions

Sexual dysfunctions, disorders in which people cannot respond normally in key areas of sexual functioning, make it difficult or impossible to enjoy sexual intercourse. A large study suggests that as many as 31 percent of men and 43 percent of women in the United States suffer from such a dysfunction during their lives (Laumann et al., 1999, 1994). Sexual dysfunctions are typically very distressing, and they often lead to sexual frustration, guilt, loss of self-esteem, and interpersonal problems (Basson et al., 2001). Often these dysfunctions are interrelated, so that many patients

SEXUAL DYSFUNCTION A disorder marked by a persistent inability to function normally in some area of the human sexual response cycle.

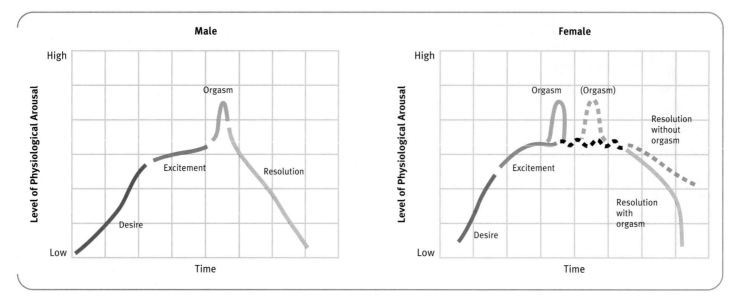

FIGURE 11-1 The normal sexual response cycle *Researchers have found a similar sequence of phases in both males and females. Sometimes, however, women do not experience orgasm; in that case, the resolution phase is less sudden. And sometimes women experience two or more orgasms in succession before the resolution phase. (Adapted from Kaplan, 1974; Masters & Johnson, 1970, 1966.)*

with one experience another as well. Sexual dysfunctioning will be described here for heterosexual couples, the majority of couples seen in therapy. Homosexual couples have the same dysfunctions, however, and therapists use the same basic techniques to treat them (LoPiccolo, 1995).

The human sexual response can be described as a *cycle* with four phases: *desire, excitement, orgasm,* and *resolution* (see Figure 11-1). Sexual dysfunctions affect one or more of the first three phases. Resolution consists simply of the relaxation and reduction in arousal that follow orgasm. Some people struggle with a sexual dysfunction their whole lives; in other cases, normal sexual functioning preceded the dysfunction. In some cases the dysfunction is present during all sexual situations; in others it is tied to particular situations (APA, 1994).

Disorders of Desire

The **desire phase** of the sexual response cycle consists of an urge to have sex, sexual fantasies, and sexual attraction to others (see Figure 11-2). Two dysfunctions—*hypoactive sexual desire* and *sexual aversion*—affect the desire phase. A client named Ms. Bryarton experiences both of these disorders:

FIGURE 11-2 Normal female sexual anatomy *Changes in the female anatomy occur during the different phases of the sexual response cycle. (Adapted from Hyde, 1990, p. 200.)*

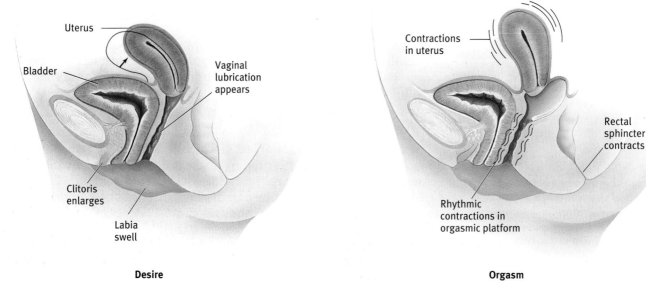

Mr. and Ms. [Bryarton] have been married for 14 years and have three children, ages 8 through 12. They [complain that Ms. Bryarton] has never enjoyed [sex] since they have been married.

Before their marriage, although they had intercourse only twice, Ms. Bryarton had been highly aroused by kissing and petting and felt she used her attractiveness to "seduce" her husband into marriage. She did, however, feel intense guilt about their two episodes of premarital intercourse; during their honeymoon, she began to think of sex as a chore that could not be pleasing. Although she periodically passively complied with intercourse, she had almost no spontaneous desire for sex. She never masturbated, had never reached orgasm, thought of all variations such as oral sex as completely repulsive, and was preoccupied with a fantasy of how disapproving her family would be if she ever engaged in any of these activities.

Ms. Bryarton is almost totally certain that no woman she respects in any older generation has enjoyed sex, and that despite the "new vogue" of sexuality, only sleazy, crude women let themselves act like "animals." These beliefs have led to a pattern of regular, but infrequent, sex that at best is accommodating and gives little or no pleasure to her or her husband. Whenever Ms. Bryarton comes close to having a feeling of sexual arousal, numerous negative thoughts come into her mind, such as "What am I, a tramp?" "If I like this, he'll just want it more often." Or "How could I look myself in the mirror after something like this?" These thoughts almost inevitably are accompanied by a cold feeling and an insensitivity to sensual pleasure. As a result, sex is invariably an unhappy experience. Almost any excuse, such as fatigue or being busy, is sufficient for her to rationalize avoiding intercourse.

Yet, intellectually Ms. Bryarton wonders, "Is something wrong with me?" . . .

(Spitzer et al., 1994, p. 251)

Hypoactive sexual desire is a lack of interest in sex and, in turn, a low level of sexual activity (see Table 11-1). Nevertheless, when people with hypoactive sexual desire do have sex, their physical responses may be normal and they may enjoy the experience. While our culture portrays men as wanting all the sex they can get, hypoactive sexual desire may be found in as many as 15 percent of men (Laumann et al., 1999; Rosen & Leiblum, 1995), and the number seeking therapy has increased during the past decade. It may also be found in 33 percent of women (APA, 2000; Laumann et al., 1999).

DSM-IV defines hypoactive sexual desire as "deficient or absent sexual fantasies and desire for sexual activity," but it does not specify what a "deficient" level is (LoPiccolo, 1995). In fact, this criterion is difficult to define. Age, number of years married, education, social class, race, and other factors may all influence the frequency of sex. In one survey, 93 happily married couples were asked to report how often they desire sexual encounters. Almost all of them said that they desire sex at least once every two weeks, and around 85 percent reported a desire rate of several times a week or more. On the basis of this survey, sexual desire would be considered hypoactive only when a person desires sex less frequently than once every two weeks.

People with **sexual aversion disorder** find sex distinctly unpleasant or repulsive. Sexual advances may sicken, disgust, or frighten them. Some people are repelled by a particular aspect of sex, such as penetration of the vagina; others experience a general aversion to all sexual stimuli, including kissing or touching. Aversion to sex seems to be rare in men and somewhat more common in women.

A person's sex drive is determined by a combination of biological, psychological, and sociocultural factors, and any of them may reduce sexual desire. Most cases of low sexual desire

DESIRE PHASE The phase of the sexual response cycle consisting of an urge to have sex, sexual fantasies, and sexual attraction to others.

HYPOACTIVE SEXUAL DESIRE DISORDER A disorder marked by a lack of interest in sex and hence a low level of sexual activity.

SEXUAL AVERSION DISORDER A disorder characterized by an aversion to and avoidance of genital sexual interplay.

A MATTER OF CHOICE

A number of people experience normal sexual interest and arousal but choose, as a matter of lifestyle, not to engage in sexual relations. These individuals would not be diagnosed as having hypoactive sexual desire.

Table 11-1 DSM-IV Checklist

HYPOACTIVE SEXUAL DESIRE DISORDER

1. Persistent or recurrent deficiency of sexual fantasies and desire for sexual activity.
2. Significant distress or interpersonal difficulty.

SEXUAL AVERSION DISORDER

1. Persistent or recurrent extreme aversion to, and avoidance of, almost all genital contact with a sexual partner.
2. Significant distress or interpersonal difficulty.

Based on APA, 2000, 1994.

Lifetime Patterns of Sexual Behavior

Sexual dysfunctions are, by definition, different from the usual patterns of sexual functioning. But in the sexual realm, what is "the usual"? In the mid-1980s, clinicians found their efforts to prevent the spread of AIDS hindered by a lack of available data on this issue and began to conduct large surveys on sexual behavior. Collectively, recent studies provide a wealth of useful, sometimes eye-opening information about sexual patterns in the "normal" populations of North America (Bortz, Wallace, & Wiley, 1999; Laumann et al., 1999, 1994; Seidman & Rieder, 1995; Janus & Janus, 1993).

Teenagers

More than 90 percent of boys masturbate by the end of adolescence, compared to 50 percent of girls. For the vast majority of them, masturbation began by age 14. Males report masturbating an average of one to two times a week, females once a month.

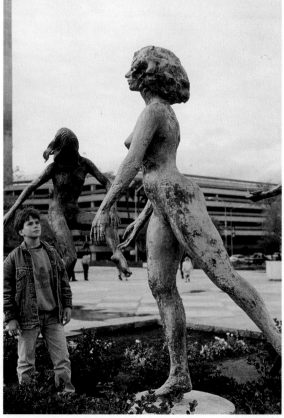

Around 20 percent of teenagers have heterosexual intercourse by the age of 15, and 80 percent by age 19. Today's teenagers are having intercourse younger than those of past generations. Most teens who are sexually experienced engage in only one sexual relationship at a time. Over the course of their teen years, however, most have at least two sex partners.

Extended periods without sex are still common, even for teenagers in a relationship. Half of sexually experienced adolescent girls have intercourse once a month or less. Sexually experienced teenage boys spend an average of six months of the year without intercourse.

Condom use by teenagers has increased somewhat during the past decade, partly because of warnings about AIDS. However, at most half of teenagers report having used a condom the last time they had sex. Less than a third of teenagers use condoms consistently and appropriately.

Early Adulthood (Ages 18–24)

More than 80 percent of unmarried young adults have intercourse in a given year. Of those who are sexually active, around a third have intercourse two or three times a month and another third engage in it two or three times a week. Masturbation remains common in young adulthood: close to 60 percent of men masturbate, a third of them at least once a week, and 36 percent of women masturbate, a tenth of them at least once a week.

Early interest *Sexual curiosity and feelings typically begin well before the teen years. Children may first discover such feelings in unexpected places and may be confused and anxious about them for a while.*

Mid-Adulthood (Ages 25–59)

From the ages of 25 to 59, sexual relationships last longer and are more monogamous. More than 90 percent of people in this age range have sexual intercourse in a given year. Half of the unmarried men have two or more partners in a given year, compared to a quarter of the unmarried women.

Among sexually active adults, close to 60 percent of men have intercourse up to three times a week and around 60 percent of women once or twice a week. Middle-aged adults are still masturbating. Half of all middle-aged men masturbate at least monthly. Half of all women between 25 and 50 masturbate at least monthly, but only a third of those between 51 and 64 do so.

Old Age (Over Age 60)

More and more people stop having intercourse as the years go by—a total of 10 percent in their 40s, 15 percent in their 50s, 30 percent in their 60s, and 45 percent in their 70s. The decline in men's sexual activity usually comes gradually as they advance in age and their health fails. Sexual activity is more likely to drop off sharply for elderly women, commonly because of the death or illness of a partner. Elderly women also seem to lose interest in sex before elderly men do. Half of the women in their 60s report limited sexual interest, compared to fewer than 10 percent of the men.

Among elderly persons who remain sexually active, those in their 60s have intercourse an average of four times a month, those in their 70s two or three times a month. Around 70 percent of elderly men and 50 percent of elderly women continue to have sexual fantasies. Around half of men and a fourth of women continue to masturbate into their 90s.

Clearly sexual interests and behaviors remain an important part of life for large numbers of people, even as they grow older and as their sexual responses change to some degree.

or sexual aversion are caused primarily by sociocultural and psychological factors, but biological conditions can also lower sex drive significantly (Kresin, 1993).

BIOLOGICAL CAUSES A number of hormones interact to produce sexual desire and behavior, and abnormalities in their activity can lower the sex drive (Davis, 2001; Rosen & Leiblum, 1995). In both men and women, a high level of the hormone *prolactin,* a low level of the male sex hormone *testosterone,* and either a high or low level of the female sex hormone *estrogen* can lead to low sex drive. Low sex drive has been linked to the high levels of estrogen contained in some birth control pills, for example. Conversely, it has also been tied to the low level of estrogen found in many postmenopausal women or women who have recently given birth. Long-term physical illness can also lower the sex drive (Kalayjian & Morrell, 2000). The low drive may be a direct result of the illness or an indirect result due to stress, pain, or depression brought on by the illness.

Sex drive can be lowered by some pain medications, certain psychotropic drugs, and a number of illegal drugs such as cocaine, marijuana, amphetamines, and heroin (Stahl, 2001; Rosen, Lane, & Menza, 1999; Segraves, 1995). Low levels of alcohol may increase the sex drive, by lowering a person's inhibitions, yet high levels will reduce it (Roehrich & Kinder, 1991).

PSYCHOLOGICAL CAUSES A general increase in anxiety or anger may reduce sexual desire in both men and women (Beck & Bozman, 1996). Frequently, as cognitive theorists have noted, people with hypoactive sexual desire and sexual aversion have particular attitudes, fears, or memories that contribute to their dysfunction, such as a belief that sex is immoral or dangerous (LoPiccolo, 1995). Other people are so afraid of losing control over their sexual urges that they try to resist them completely. And still others fear pregnancy.

Certain psychological disorders may also lead to hypoactive sexual desire and sexual aversion. Even a mild level of depression can interfere with sexual desire, and some people with obsessive-compulsive symptoms find contact with another person's body fluids and odors to be highly unpleasant (Clayton, 2001; LoPiccolo, 1995).

SOCIOCULTURAL CAUSES The attitudes, fears, and psychological disorders that contribute to hypoactive sexual desire and sexual aversion occur within a social context, and thus certain sociocultural factors have also been linked to these dysfunctions. Many sufferers are feeling situational pressures—divorce, a death in the family, job stress, infertility difficulties, having a baby (Burns, 1995; Letourneau & O'Donohue, 1993). Others may be having problems in their relationships (LoPiccolo, 1997). People who are in an unhappy relationship, have lost affection for their partner, or feel powerless and dominated by their partner can lose interest in sex. Even in basically happy relationships, if one partner is a very unskilled, unenthusiastic lover, the other can begin to lose interest in sex. And sometimes partners differ in their needs for closeness. The one who needs more personal space may develop hypoactive sexual desire as a way of keeping distance (LoPiccolo, 1997, 1995).

Cultural standards can also set the stage for hypoactive sexual desire and sexual aversion. Some men adopt our culture's double standard and thus cannot feel sexual desire for a woman they love and respect. A man may lose sexual interest in his wife when she has their first child, as he cannot think of a mother as a sexually exciting woman. More generally, because our society equates sexual attractiveness with youthfulness, many aging men and women lose interest in sex as their self-image or their attraction to their partner diminishes with age (LoPiccolo, 1995).

The trauma of sexual molestation or assault is especially likely to produce the fears, attitudes, and memories found in these sexual dysfunctions. Sexual aversion is very common in victims of sexual abuse and may persist for years, even decades (Jackson et al., 1990; McCarthy, 1990). In extreme cases, individuals may experience vivid flashbacks of the assault during adult sexual activity.

HARSH JUDGMENT
Two hundred years ago a Boston ship captain who publicly kissed his wife upon returning from a three-year voyage was made to sit two hours in stocks for the crime of "lewd and unseemly behavior" (Asimov, 1997).

ConsiderThis
⦿ Some theorists suggest that recent increases in the number of men receiving treatment for hypoactive sexual desire disorder may be linked to the impact of the women's movement (LoPiccolo, 1995). If this is true, what factors might account for it?

A Kiss Felt 'Round the World

In September 1996, 6-year-old Jonathan Prevette came home from school in Lexington, North Carolina, and admitted to his mother that he was in big trouble. His terrible deed? Not truancy, disrespect for the teacher, or fighting. To his mother's astonishment, the school had charged little Jonathan with sexual harassment for kissing another child on the cheek and suspended him for a day. The school later explained that by his kiss he had broken a rule against unwarranted and unwelcome touching of one student by another.

Within a day, Jonathan's photograph appeared in newspapers throughout the nation. People everywhere wondered how a 6-year-old child could be charged with so serious an offense. For his part, Jonathan seemed understandably confused by his suspension—and more than

Donald C. Roberts/Gamma Liaison

a little saddened that he had missed an ice cream party at school.

Consider This

• Is a 6-year-old capable of understanding the implications of planting an uninvited kiss on another person?
• When school officials react so powerfully to behaviors that would be considered sexual in an adult, might they unintentionally be teaching the child and other young onlookers that sex is dirty, undesirable, and even dangerous?
• Does misapplying this label to the behavior of a young child trivialize the problem and implications of sexual harassment in the teenage and adult worlds?

Disorders of Excitement

The **excitement phase** of the sexual response cycle is marked by changes in the pelvic region, general physical arousal, and increases in heart rate, muscle tension, blood pressure, and rate of breathing. In men, blood pools in the pelvis and leads to erection of the penis; in women, this phase produces swelling of the clitoris and labia, as well as lubrication of the vagina. Dysfunctions affecting the excitement phase are *female sexual arousal disorder* (once referred to as "frigidity") and *male erectile disorder* (once called "impotence").

FEMALE SEXUAL AROUSAL DISORDER Women with a **sexual arousal disorder** are repeatedly unable to attain or maintain proper lubrication or genital swelling during sexual activity (see Table 11-2). Understandably, many of them also experience an orgasmic disorder or other sexual dysfunction. In fact, this disorder is rarely diagnosed alone (Segraves & Segraves, 1991). Studies vary widely in their estimates of its prevalence, but most agree that more than 10 percent of women experience it (Laumann et al., 1999, 1994; Rosen et al., 1993). Because lack of sexual arousal in women is so often tied to an orgasmic disorder, researchers usually study and explain the two problems together. Correspondingly, we shall consider the causes of these problems together when we look at female orgasmic disorder.

MALE ERECTILE DISORDER Men with **erectile disorder** persistently fail to attain or maintain an adequate erection during sexual activity. This problem occurs in about 10 percent of the general male population, including Robert, the man whose difficulties opened this chapter (APA, 2000; Laumann et al., 1999). Carlos Domera also has erectile disorder:

Table 11-2 DSM-IV Checklist

FEMALE SEXUAL AROUSAL DISORDER

1. Persistent or recurrent inability to attain, or to maintain until completion of the sexual activity, adequate lubrication or swelling response of sexual excitement.
2. Significant distress or interpersonal difficulty.

MALE ERECTILE DISORDER

1. Persistent or recurrent inability to attain, or to maintain until completion of the sexual activity, an adequate erection.
2. Significant distress or interpersonal difficulty.

Based on APA, 2000, 1994.

Carlos Domera is a 30-year-old dress manufacturer who came to the United States from Argentina at age 22. He is married to an American woman, Phyllis, also age 30. They have no children. Mr. Domera's problem was that he had been unable to have sexual intercourse for over a year due to his inability to achieve or maintain an erection. He had avoided all sexual contact with his wife for the prior five months, except for two brief attempts at lovemaking which ended when he failed to maintain his erection.

The couple separated a month ago by mutual agreement due to the tension that surrounded their sexual problem and their inability to feel comfortable with each other. Both professed love and concern for the other, but had serious doubts regarding their ability to resolve the sexual problem. . . .

Mr. Domera conformed to the stereotype of the "macho Latin lover," believing that he "should always have erections easily and be able to make love at any time." Since he couldn't "perform" sexually, he felt humiliated and inadequate, and he dealt with this by avoiding not only sex, but any expression of affection for his wife.

Ms. Domera felt "he is not trying; perhaps he doesn't love me, and I can't live with no sex, no affection, and his bad moods." She had requested the separation temporarily, and he readily agreed. However, they had recently been seeing each other twice a week. . . .

During the evaluation he reported that the onset of his erectile difficulties was concurrent with a tense period in his business. After several "failures" to complete intercourse, he concluded he was "useless as a husband" and therefore a "total failure." The anxiety of attempting lovemaking was too much for him to deal with.

He reluctantly admitted that he was occasionally able to masturbate alone to a full, firm erection and reach a satisfying orgasm. However, he felt ashamed and guilty about this, from both childhood masturbatory guilt and a feeling that he was "cheating" his wife. It was also noted that he had occasional firm erections upon awakening in the morning. Other than the antidepressant, the patient was taking no drugs, and he was not using much alcohol. There was no evidence of physical illness.

(Spitzer et al., 1983, pp. 105-106)

EXCITEMENT PHASE The phase of the sexual response cycle marked by changes in the pelvic region, general physical arousal, and increases in heart rate, muscle tension, blood pressure, and rate of breathing.

FEMALE SEXUAL AROUSAL DISORDER A female dysfunction marked by a persistent inability to attain sexual excitement, including adequate lubrication or genital swelling, during sexual activity.

MALE ERECTILE DISORDER A dysfunction in which a man repeatedly fails to attain or maintain an erection during sexual activity.

Unlike Mr. Domera, most men with an erectile disorder are over the age of 50, largely because so many cases are associated with ailments or diseases of older adults (Seidman & Rieder, 1995). The disorder is experienced by 5 to 9 percent of all men who are 40 years old and increases to at least 15 percent at age 60 (Laumann et al., 1999; Feldman et al., 1994). Moreover, according to surveys, half of all adult men experience erectile difficulty during intercourse at least some of the time (Feldman et al., 1994). Erectile dysfunction accounts for more than 400,000 visits to physicians in the United States each year (Ackerman & Carey, 1995).

Most cases of erectile disorder result from an interaction of biological, psychological, and sociocultural processes. One study found that only ten of sixty-three cases of this disorder were caused by purely psychosocial factors, and only five were the result of physical impairment alone (LoPiccolo, 1991).

BIOLOGICAL CAUSES The same hormonal imbalances that can cause hypoactive sexual desire can also produce erectile disorder. More commonly, however, vascular problems—problems with the body's blood vessels—are involved (Althof & Seftel, 1995; Carey et al., 1993). An erection occurs when the chambers in the penis fill with blood, so any condition that reduces blood flow into the penis, such as heart disease or clogging of the arteries, may lead to the disorder (Stahl, 2001; LoPiccolo, 1997). It can also be caused by damage to the nervous system as a result of diabetes, spinal cord injuries, multiple sclerosis, kidney failure, or treatment with an artificial kidney machine (Newton, 1999; Leiblum & Segraves, 1995). In addition, as is the case with hypoactive sexual desire, the use of certain

"Erection is chiefly caused by scuraum, eringoes, cresses, crymon, parsnips, artichokes, turnips, asparagus, candied ginger, acorns bruised to powder and drank in muscadel, scallion, sea shell fish, etc."

Aristotle, *The Masterpiece,*
fourth century B.C.

Joseph Piccolo

Psychological or organic? *The snap-gauge, worn around the penis at night, is a fabric band with three plastic filaments. If the filaments are broken in the morning, the man knows that he has experienced normal erections during REM sleep and that erectile failures during intercourse are probably due to psychological factors.*

NOCTURNAL PENILE TUMESCENCE (NPT) Erection during sleep.

PERFORMANCE ANXIETY The fear of performing inadequately and a related tension experienced during sex.

SPECTATOR ROLE A state of mind that some people experience during sex, focusing on their sexual performance to such an extent that their performance and their enjoyment are reduced.

ORGASM PHASE The phase of the sexual response cycle during which an individual's sexual pleasure peaks and sexual tension is released as muscles in the pelvic region contract rhythmically.

PREMATURE EJACULATION A dysfunction in which a man reaches orgasm and ejaculates before, on, or shortly after penetration and before he wishes to.

medications and various forms of substance abuse, from alcohol abuse to cigarette smoking, may interfere with erections (Keene & Davies, 1999; Segraves, 1998).

Medical procedures, including ultrasound recordings and blood tests, have been developed for diagnosing biological causes of erectile disorder. Measuring **nocturnal penile tumescence (NPT),** or erections during sleep, is particularly useful in assessing whether physical factors are responsible (Althof & Seftel, 1995; Schiavi et al., 1993). Men typically have erections during rapid eye movement (REM) sleep, the phase of sleep in which dreaming takes place. A healthy man is likely to have two to five REM periods each night, and perhaps two to three hours of penile erections. Abnormal or absent nightly erections usually (but not always) indicate some physical basis for erectile failure. As a rough screening device, a patient may be instructed to fasten a simple "snap-gauge" band around his penis before going to sleep and then check it the next morning. A broken band indicates that penile erection has occurred during the night. An unbroken band indicates a lack of nighttime erections and suggests that the person's general erectile problem may have a physical basis (Mohr & Beutler, 1990).

PSYCHOLOGICAL CAUSES Any of the psychological causes of hypoactive sexual desire can also interfere with arousal and lead to erectile disorder. As many as 90 percent of all men with severe depression, for example, experience some degree of erectile dysfunction (Leiblum & Segraves, 1995).

One well-supported psychological explanation for erectile disorder is a cognitive theory developed by William Masters and Virginia Johnson (1970). The explanation emphasizes **performance anxiety** and the **spectator role.** Once a man begins to experience erectile problems, for whatever reason, he becomes fearful about failing to have an erection and worries during each sexual encounter. Instead of relaxing and enjoying the sensations of sexual pleasure, he remains distanced from the activity, watching himself and focusing on the goal of reaching erection. Instead of being an aroused participant, he becomes a judge and spectator. Whatever the initial reason for the erectile dysfunction, the resulting spectator role becomes the reason for the ongoing problem. In this vicious cycle, the original cause of the erectile failure becomes less important than fear of failure.

SOCIOCULTURAL CAUSES Each of the sociocultural factors that contribute to hypoactive sexual desire has also been tied to erectile disorder. Men who have lost their jobs and are under financial stress, for example, are more likely to develop erectile difficulties than other men (Morokoff & Gillilland, 1993). Marital stress, too, has been tied to this dysfunction. Two relationship patterns in particular may contribute to it (LoPiccolo, 1991). In one, the wife provides too little physical stimulation for her aging husband, who, because of normal aging changes, now requires more intense, direct, and lengthy physical stimulation of the penis for erection to occur. In the second relationship pattern, a couple believes that only intercourse can give the wife an orgasm. This idea increases the pressure on the man to have an erection and makes him more prone to erectile dysfunction. If the wife reaches orgasm manually or orally during their sexual encounter, his pressure to perform is reduced.

Disorders of Orgasm

During the **orgasm phase** of the sexual response cycle, an individual's sexual pleasure peaks and sexual tension is released as the muscles in the pelvic region contract, or draw together, rhythmically (see Figure 11-3). The man's semen is ejaculated, and the outer third of the woman's vaginal wall contracts. Dysfunctions of this phase of the sexual response cycle are *premature ejaculation, male orgasmic disorder,* and *female orgasmic disorder.*

Desire

Full erection

Partially stimulated state

Unstimulated state

Partial elevation of testes

Orgasm

Internal sphincter of bladder closes

Penile contractions

Urethral contractions

Contractions force the seminal fluid through the urethra

Seminal vesicles contract

Prostate gland contracts

Rectal sphincter contracts

FIGURE 11-3 **Normal male sexual anatomy** *Changes in the male anatomy occur during the various phases of the sexual response cycle. (Adapted from Hyde, 1990, p. 199.)*

PREMATURE EJACULATION Eddie is typical of many men in his experience of premature ejaculation:

> Eddie, a 20-year-old student, sought treatment after his girlfriend ended their relationship because his premature ejaculation left her sexually frustrated. Eddie had had only one previous sexual relationship, during his senior year in high school. With two friends he would drive to a neighboring town and find a certain prostitute. After picking her up, they would drive to a deserted area and take turns having sex with her, while the others waited outside the car. Both the prostitute and his friends urged him to hurry up because they feared discovery by the police, and besides, in the winter it was cold. When Eddie began his sexual relationship with his girlfriend, his entire sexual history consisted of this rapid intercourse, with virtually no foreplay. He found caressing his girlfriend's breasts and genitals and her touching of his penis to be so arousing that he sometimes ejaculated before complete entry of the penis, or after at most only a minute or so of intercourse.
>
> *(LoPiccolo, 1995, p. 495)*

A man suffering from **premature ejaculation** persistently reaches orgasm and ejaculates with very little sexual stimulation before, on, or shortly after penetration, and before he wishes to (see Table 11-3 on the next page). Around 27 percent of men in the United States experience premature ejaculation at some time (Laumann et al., 1999, 1994; St. Lawrence & Madakasira, 1992). The typical length of intercourse in our society has increased over the past several decades, in turn increasing the distress of men who suffer from premature ejaculation, typically men under the age of 30 (Bancroft, 1989).

Psychological, particularly behavioral, explanations of premature ejaculation have received more research support than other kinds of explanations. The dysfunction seems to be typical of young, sexually inexperienced men such as Eddie, who simply have not learned to slow down, control their arousal, and extend the pleasurable process of making love (Metz & Pryor, 2000). In fact, premature ejaculation is very common when a young man has his first sexual encounter. With continued sexual experience, most men gain greater control over their sexual responses. Men of any age who have sex only occasionally are also prone to ejaculate prematurely (LoPiccolo, 1985).

SEXUAL DURATION

In an extensive survey of people in the United States, respondents estimated that their average sexual experience lasts 39 minutes, including foreplay (Kanner, 1995).

Table 11-3 DSM-IV Checklist

PREMATURE EJACULATION

1. Persistent or recurrent ejaculation with minimal sexual stimulation before, on, or shortly after penetration and before the person wishes it.
2. Significant distress or interpersonal difficulty.

MALE ORGASMIC DISORDER

1. Persistent or recurrent delay in, or absence of, orgasm following a normal sexual excitement phase during sexual activity.
2. Significant distress or interpersonal difficulty.

FEMALE ORGASMIC DISORDER

1. Persistent or recurrent delay in, or absence of, orgasm following a normal sexual excitement phase during sexual activity.
2. Significant distress or interpersonal difficulty.

Based on APA, 2000, 1994.

"When [masturbation] is discovered, it must in young children be put a stop to by such means as tying the hands, strapping the knees together with a pad between them, or some mechanical plan."

From Cradle to School, a Book for Mothers, 1902

Clinicians have also suggested that premature ejaculation may be related to anxiety, hurried masturbation experiences during adolescence (in fear of being "caught" by parents), or poor recognition of one's own sexual arousal. However, these theories have only sometimes received clear research support (Dunn, Croft, & Hackette, 1999).

MALE ORGASMIC DISORDER A man with **male orgasmic disorder** repeatedly cannot reach orgasm or is very delayed in reaching orgasm after normal sexual excitement. The disorder occurs in 10 percent of the male population (APA, 2000; Laumann et al., 1999) and is typically a source of great upset, as in the case of John:

John, a 38-year-old sales representative, had been married for 9 years. At the insistence of his 32-year-old wife, the couple sought counseling for their sexual problem—his inability to ejaculate during intercourse. During the early years of the marriage, his wife had experienced difficulty reaching orgasm until he learned to delay his ejaculation for a long period of time. To do this, he used mental distraction techniques and regularly smoked marijuana before making love. Initially, John felt very satisfied that he could make love for longer and longer periods of time without ejaculation and regarded his ability as a sign of masculinity.

About 3 years prior to seeking counseling, after the birth of their only child, John found that he was losing his erection before he was able to ejaculate. His wife suggested different intercourse positions, but the harder he tried, the more difficulty he had in reaching orgasm. Because of his frustration, the couple began to avoid sex altogether. John experienced increasing performance anxiety with each successive failure, and an increasing sense of helplessness in the face of his problem.

(Rosen & Rosen, 1981, pp. 317–318)

MALE ORGASMIC DISORDER A male dysfunction characterized by a repeated inability to reach orgasm or long delays in reaching orgasm after normal sexual excitement.

FEMALE ORGASMIC DISORDER A dysfunction in which a woman rarely has an orgasm or repeatedly experiences a very delayed one.

A low testosterone level, certain neurological diseases, and some head or spinal cord injuries can interfere with ejaculation (Stahl, 2001; LoPiccolo, 1997, 1995, 1985). Drugs that slow down the sympathetic nervous system (such as alcohol, some medications for high blood pressure, certain antidepressants, and many antianxiety and antipsychotic medications) can also affect ejaculation

(Altman, 2001; Segraves, 1998, 1995, 1993). For example, the antidepressant *fluoxetine,* or Prozac, appears to interfere with ejaculation in 15 to 25 percent of men who take it (Hirschfeld, 1999; Rosen et al., 1999).

A leading psychological cause of male orgasmic disorder appears to be performance anxiety and the spectator role, the cognitive factors also involved in male erectile disorder. Once a man begins to focus on reaching orgasm, he may stop being an aroused participant in his sexual activity and instead become an unaroused, self-critical, and fearful observer (Wiederman, 2001). Finally, male orgasmic disorder may develop out of hypoactive sexual desire (Rosen & Leiblum, 1995). A man who engages in sex primarily because of pressure from his partner, without any real desire for it, simply may not get aroused enough to reach orgasm.

FEMALE ORGASMIC DISORDER Stephanie and Bill, married for three years, came for sex therapy because of her lack of orgasm.

> Stephanie had never had an orgasm in any way, but because of Bill's concern, she had been faking orgasm during intercourse until recently. Finally she told him the truth, and they sought therapy together. Stephanie had been raised by a strictly religious family. She could not recall ever seeing her parents kiss or show physical affection for each other. She was severely punished on one occasion when her mother found her looking at her own genitals, at about age 7. Stephanie received no sex education from her parents, and when she began to menstruate, her mother told her only that this meant that she could become pregnant, so she mustn't ever kiss a boy or let a boy touch her. Her mother restricted her dating severely, with repeated warnings that "boys only want one thing." While her parents were rather critical and demanding of her (asking her why she got one B among otherwise straight A's on her report card, for example), they were loving parents and their approval was very important to her.
>
> *(LoPiccolo, 1995, p. 496)*

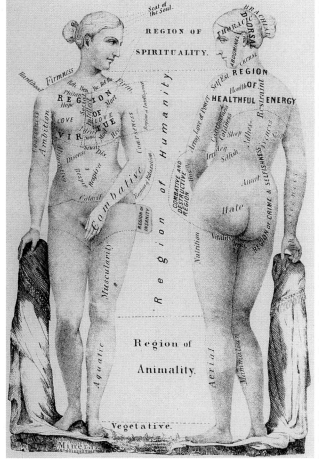

"**The region of insanity**" *Women of the nineteenth century were expected to experience limited sexual arousal. In fact, medical authorities described "excessive passion" in Victorian women as dangerous and as a possible cause of insanity (Gamwell & Tomes, 1995). This illustration from a nineteenth-century medical textbook even labels a woman's reproductive organs as her "region of insanity" (Buchanan, 1854).*

Women with **female orgasmic disorder** rarely reach orgasm or generally experience a very delayed one. Around 25 percent of women apparently have this problem—including more than a third of postmenopausal women (Laumann et al., 1999, 1994; Rosen & Leiblum, 1995). Studies indicate that 10 percent or more of women today have never had an orgasm, either alone or during intercourse, and at least another 10 percent rarely have orgasms (LoPiccolo, 1995). At the same time, half of all women experience orgasm in intercourse at least fairly regularly (LoPiccolo & Stock, 1987). Women who are more sexually assertive (Hurlbert, 1991) and more comfortable with masturbation (Kelly, Stressberg, & Kircher, 1990) tend to have orgasms more regularly. Female orgasmic disorder appears to be more common among single women than among women who are married or cohabiting (Laumann et al., 1999, 1994).

Most clinicians agree that orgasm during intercourse is not mandatory for normal sexual functioning. Many women instead reach orgasm with their partners by direct stimulation of the clitoris (LoPiccolo, 1995). Although early psychoanalytic theory considered a lack of orgasm during intercourse to be pathological, evidence suggests that women who rely on stimulation of the clitoris for orgasm are entirely normal and healthy (Stock, 1993).

As we observed earlier, female orgasmic disorder typically is linked to female sexual arousal disorder, and the two tend to be studied, explained, and treated together (APA, 1995). Once again, biological, psychological, and sociocultural factors may combine to produce these disorders.

Some Sex-Role Myths

Myths of Male Sexuality

❖ *The man must take charge and orchestrate sex.* A man who thinks this way does not let the woman guide him to do what she likes to have done to her, nor is he likely to learn to receive pleasure from what the woman does to him.

❖ *A man always wants and is always ready to have sex.* This myth pressures men to try to have sex in situations or relationships in which they are not emotionally comfortable, with predictably unpleasant results.

❖ *All physical contact must lead to sex.* This mistaken notion prevents men from simply enjoying kissing, hugging, cuddling, and caressing, as they see these activities as only a prelude to "the real thing."

❖ *Good sex is a linear progression of increasing excitement terminated only by orgasm.* Acceptance of this myth eliminates the pleasure of leisurely, playful sex, which may include breaks to talk, rest, and enjoy each other fully as people rather than as just genital organs.

❖ *Sex should be natural and spontaneous.* For today's busy couples, it is often necessary to make very non-spontaneous plans for sex, designating a time when both are likely to be relaxed, not exhausted, and capable of responding sexually.

(ZILBERGELD, 1978)

Myths of Female Sexuality

❖ *Sex is only for women under 30.* Many women don't reach their peak of sexual responsiveness until their mid-30s, and there is no real decline thereafter.

❖ *All women can have multiple orgasms.* There is no relationship between sexual adjustment or satisfaction and the number of orgasms a woman has each time she has sex.

❖ *Pregnancy and delivery reduce women's sexual responsiveness.* While discomfort during the last months of pregnancy and just after delivery can temporarily inhibit sex, the increased blood supply to the pelvis that develops during pregnancy can actually increase sexual responsiveness.

❖ *Nice women aren't aroused by erotic books or films.* Research indicates that women are just as aroused by erotica as men are.

❖ *You are frigid if you don't like the more exotic forms of sex.* Many very sexual women aren't interested in oral or anal sex, sex toys such as vibrators, or group sex.

❖ *If you can't have an orgasm quickly and easily, there's something wrong with you.* The threshold for orgasm varies naturally among women.

(HEIMAN & LOPICCOLO, 1988)

NIGHTLY VISITS

Orgasms can sometimes occur during sleep. Ancient Babylonians said that such nocturnal orgasms were caused by a "maid of the night" who visited men in their sleep and a "little night man" who visited women (Kahn & Fawcett, 1993).

VAGINISMUS A condition marked by involuntary contractions of the muscles around the outer third of the vagina, preventing entry of the penis.

BIOLOGICAL CAUSES A variety of physiological conditions can affect a woman's arousal and orgasm. Diabetes can damage the nervous system in ways that interfere with arousal, lubrication of the vagina, and orgasm. Lack of orgasm has sometimes been linked to multiple sclerosis and other neurological diseases, to the same drugs and medications that may interfere with ejaculation in men, and to postmenopausal changes in skin sensitivity and in the structure of the clitoris and of the vaginal walls (Stahl, 2001; Kalayjian & Morrell, 2000).

PSYCHOLOGICAL CAUSES The psychological causes of hypoactive sexual desire and sexual aversion may also lead to the female arousal and orgasmic disorders (Heiman, 2000). In addition, as psychodynamic theorists might predict, memories of childhood traumas and relationships have sometimes been linked to these disorders. In one large study, memories of an unhappy childhood or loss of a parent during childhood were tied to lack of orgasm in adulthood (Raboch & Raboch, 1992). In another, childhood memories of a positive relationship with one's mother, affection between the parents, the mother's positive personality, and the mother's expression of positive emotions were all predictors of orgasm (Heiman et al., 1986).

SOCIOCULTURAL CAUSES For years many clinicians have believed that female arousal and orgasmic disorders may result from society's repeated message to women that they should hold back and deny their sexuality. And, in fact, many women with these problems report that they had a strict religious upbringing, were punished for childhood masturbation, received no preparation for the onset of menstruation, were restricted in their dating as teenagers, and were told that "nice girls don't" (LoPiccolo, 1997; Masters & Johnson, 1970).

A sexually restrictive history, however, is just as common among women who function well in sexual encounters (LoPiccolo, 1997; LoPiccolo & Stock, 1987).

In addition, cultural messages about female sexuality have been more positive in recent years (see Figure 11-4), while the rate of female arousal and orgasmic disorders remains the same. Why, then, do some women and not others develop sexual arousal and orgasmic dysfunctions? Researchers suggest that unusually stressful events, traumas, or relationships may help produce the fears, memories, and attitudes that often characterize these dysfunctions. For example, more than half of women molested as children or raped as adults have arousal and orgasm dysfunctions (Browne & Finklehor, 1986).

Research has also related orgasmic behavior to certain qualities in a woman's intimate relationships. One study found that the likelihood of reaching orgasm was tied to how much emotional involvement each subject had during her first experience of intercourse and how long that relationship lasted, the pleasure the woman obtained during the experience, her current attraction to her partner's body, and her marital happiness (Heiman et al., 1986). Interestingly, the same study found that erotic fantasies during sex with their current partner were much more common in orgasmic than in nonorgasmic women.

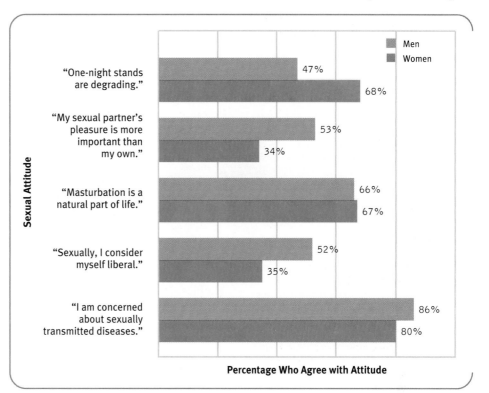

FIGURE 11-4 Sexual attitudes and gender
According to surveys, women are more likely than men to consider "one-night stands" degrading, whereas, contrary to stereotypes, men are more likely than women to say that their sex partner's pleasure is more important than their own. (Adapted from Janus & Janus, 1993.)

Disorders of Sexual Pain

Two sexual dysfunctions do not fit neatly into a specific phase of the sexual response cycle. These are the sexual pain disorders, *vaginismus* and *dyspareunia*, each marked by enormous physical discomfort when sexual activity is attempted.

VAGINISMUS In **vaginismus,** involuntary contractions of the muscles around the outer third of the vagina prevent entry of the penis (see Table 11-4). Severe cases can prevent a couple from ever having intercourse. Perhaps 20 percent of women occasionally experience pain during intercourse, but vaginismus probably occurs in less than 1 percent of all women (Leiblum, 2000; LoPiccolo, 1995).

Most clinicians agree with the cognitive-behavioral position that vaginismus is usually a learned fear response, set off by a woman's expectation that intercourse will be painful and damaging. A variety of factors apparently can set the stage for this fear, including anxiety and ignorance about intercourse, exaggerated stories about how painful and bloody the first occasion of intercourse is for women, trauma caused by an unskilled lover who forces his penis into the vagina before the woman is aroused and lubricated, and, of course, the trauma of childhood sexual abuse or adult rape (Reissing, Binik, & Khalife, 1999; LoPiccolo, 1995).

Some women experience painful intercourse because of an infection of the vagina or urinary tract, a gynecological disease such as herpes simplex, or the physical effects of menopause. It may lead to their developing what is sometimes called "rational" vaginismus, in which the insertion of the penis will indeed cause them problems unless they receive medical treatment for these conditions (LoPiccolo, 1995). Most women who have vaginismus also have other sexual dysfunctions. Some, however, enjoy sex greatly, have a strong sex drive, and reach orgasm with stimulation of the clitoris. They just fear penetration of the vagina.

Table 11-4 DSM-IV Checklist

VAGINISMUS

1. Recurrent or persistent involuntary spasm of the muscles of the outer third of the vagina that interferes with sexual intercourse.
2. Significant distress or interpersonal difficulty.

DYSPAREUNIA

1. Recurrent or persistent genital pain associated with sexual intercourse in either a male or female.
2. Significant distress or interpersonal difficulty.

Based on APA, 2000, 1994.

Rite of passage *A teenage girl in the Samburu highlands of Kenya has her genitals (clitoris and labia) cut so that she may be admitted into the society of mature women. Educated women across Africa are increasingly condemning this tradition, practiced by ethnic groups in 28 countries throughout the continent (Dugger, 1996). They argue that circumcision can lead to various sexual dysfunctions, deprives women of sexual pleasure, and also may create medical problems, both generally and during childbirth.*

RELIABLE SOURCES?

Today almost one-third of teenagers say that they learn about sex primarily from television, compared to 11 percent of teenagers back in 1986. Around 45 percent acquire their sex knowledge from friends and 7 percent from parents, the same percentages as in the past (Time/CNN poll, 1998).

DYSPAREUNIA A disorder in which a person experiences severe pain in the genitals during sexual activity.

DYSPAREUNIA A person with **dyspareunia** (from Latin words meaning "painful mating") experiences severe pain in the genitals during sexual activity. Surveys suggest that 15 percent of women and 3 percent of men suffer from this problem to some degree (APA, 2000; Laumann et al., 1999). Sufferers typically enjoy sex and get aroused but find their sex lives very limited by the pain that accompanies what used to be a positive event.

Dyspareunia in women usually has a physical cause (LoPiccolo, 1995; Steege & Ling, 1993). Among the most common are injury to the vagina, cervix, uterus, or pelvic ligaments during childbirth (Barrett et al., 1999). Similarly, the scar left by an episiotomy (a cut often made to enlarge the vaginal entrance and ease delivery) can cause pain. Dyspareunia has also been tied to collision of the penis with remaining parts of the hymen; infection of the vagina; wiry pubic hair that rubs against the labia during intercourse; pelvic diseases; tumors; cysts; and allergic reactions to the chemicals in vaginal douches and contraceptive creams, the rubber in condoms or diaphragms, or the protein in semen (LoPiccolo & Stock, 1987).

Although relationship problems or the psychological aftereffects of sexual abuse may contribute to this disorder, psychosocial factors alone are rarely responsible for it (Pukall et al., 2000; LoPiccolo, 1995). In cases that are truly psychogenic, the woman is in fact likely to be suffering from hypoactive sexual desire (Steege & Ling, 1993). That is, penetration into an unaroused, unlubricated vagina is painful.

SUMMING UP | **Sexual Dysfunctions**

Sexual dysfunctions make it difficult or impossible for a person to have or enjoy sexual intercourse.

Disorders of Desire Disorders of the desire phase of the sexual response cycle are hypoactive sexual desire disorder, marked by a lack of interest in sex, and sexual aversion disorder, marked by a revulsion to sexual activity. Biological causes for these disorders include abnormal hormone levels, certain drugs, and some medical illnesses. Psychological and sociocultural causes include particular fears, situational pressures, relationship problems, and the trauma of having been sexually molested or assaulted.

Disorders of Excitement Disorders of the excitement phase are female sexual arousal disorder, marked by a repeated inability to attain proper lubrication or genital swelling during sexual activity, and male erectile disorder, a repeated inability to attain or maintain an erection during sexual activity.

Biological causes of male erectile disorder include abnormal hormone levels, vascular problems, other medical conditions, and certain medications. Psychological and sociocultural causes include performance anxiety and the spectator role, situational pressures such as job loss, and relationship problems.

Disorders of Orgasm Premature ejaculation, repeatedly reaching orgasm and ejaculating before or shortly after penetration, has been related to behavioral causes, such as inappropriate early learning and inexperience. Male orgasmic disorder, a repeated absence of or long delay in reaching orgasm, has been linked to biological causes such as low testosterone levels, neurological diseases, and certain drugs and to psychological causes such as performance anxiety and the taking of a spectator role.

Female orgasmic disorder is a repeated absence of or long delay in orgasm in women. Along with female sexual arousal disorder, it has been tied to biological causes such as medical diseases and changes that occur after menopause, psychological causes such as memories of childhood traumas, and sociocultural causes such as relationship problems.

Disorders of Sexual Pain In vaginismus, involuntary contractions of the muscles around the outer third of the vagina prevent entry of the penis. In dyspareunia, the person experiences severe pain in the genitals during sexual activity. Dyspareunia usually occurs in women and typically has a physical cause such as injury resulting from childbirth.

UNEQUAL DISTRIBUTION

Sex is not distributed equally across the population of the United States. Half of all sexual activity is engaged in by 15 percent of adults (General Social Survey, 1998).

Treatments for Sexual Dysfunctions

The last 30 years have brought major changes in the treatment of sexual dysfunctions. For the first half of the twentieth century, the leading approach was long-term psychodynamic therapy. Clinicians assumed that sexual dysfunctioning was caused by failure to move properly through the psychosexual stages of development, and they used techniques of free association and therapist interpretations to help clients gain insight about themselves and their problems. Although it was expected that broad personality changes would lead to improvement in sexual functioning, psychodynamic therapy was typically unsuccessful (Bergler, 1951).

In the 1950s and 1960s, behavioral therapists offered new treatments for sexual dysfunctions. Usually they tried to reduce the fears that they believed were causing the dysfunctions, by applying such procedures as relaxation training and systematic desensitization (Lazarus, 1965; Wolpe, 1958). These approaches had some success, but they failed to work in cases where the key problems were misinformation, negative attitudes, and lack of effective sexual technique (LoPiccolo, 1995).

A revolution in the treatment of sexual dysfunctions occurred with the publication of William Masters and Virginia Johnson's landmark book *Human Sexual Inadequacy* in 1970. The *sex therapy* program they introduced has evolved into a complex approach, which now includes techniques from the various models, particularly cognitive, behavioral, couple, and family systems therapies (Leiblum & Rosen, 2000; LoPiccolo, 1997).

SEXUAL CENSUS

The World Health Organization estimates that around 115 million acts of sexual intercourse occur each day.

What Are the General Features of Sex Therapy?

Modern sex therapy is short-term and instructive, typically lasting 15 to 20 sessions. As the sex therapist and researcher Joseph LoPiccolo (1997, 1995) has explained, it centers on specific sexual problems rather than on broad personality issues. Carlos Domera, the Argentine man with an erectile disorder whom we met earlier, responded successfully to the multiple techniques of modern sex therapy:

> At the end of the evaluation session the psychiatrist reassured the couple that Mr. Domera had a "reversible psychological" sexual problem that was due to several factors, including his depression, but also more currently his anxiety and embarrassment, his high standards, and some cultural and relationship difficulties that made communication awkward and relaxation nearly impossible. The couple was advised that a brief trial of therapy, focused directly on the sexual problem, would very likely produce significant improvement within ten to fourteen sessions. They were assured that the problem was almost certainly not physical in origin, but rather psychogenic, and that therefore the prognosis was excellent.
>
> Mr. Domera was shocked and skeptical, but the couple agreed to commence the therapy on a weekly basis, and they were given a typical first "assignment" to do at home: a caressing massage exercise to try together with specific instructions not to attempt genital stimulation or intercourse at all, even if an erection might occur.

SEEKING TREATMENT

The single largest group of men who enter sex therapy consists of those with erectile difficulties (Spector & Carey, 1990).

Not surprisingly, during the second session Mr. Domera reported with a cautious smile that they had "cheated" and had had intercourse "against the rules." This was their first successful intercourse in more than a year. Their success and happiness were acknowledged by the therapist, but they were cautioned strongly that rapid initial improvement often occurs, only to be followed by increased performance anxiety in subsequent weeks and a return of the initial problem. They were humorously chastised and encouraged to try again to have sexual contact involving caressing and non-demand light genital stimulation, without an expectation of erection or orgasm, and to avoid intercourse.

During the second and fourth weeks Mr. Domera did not achieve erections during the love play, and the therapy sessions dealt with helping him to accept himself with or without erections and to learn to enjoy sensual contact without intercourse. His wife helped him to believe genuinely that he could please her with manual or oral stimulation and that, although she enjoyed intercourse, she enjoyed these other stimulations as much, as long as he was relaxed.

Mr. Domera struggled with his cultural image of what a "man" does, but he had to admit that his wife seemed pleased and that he, too, was enjoying the nonintercourse caressing techniques. He was encouraged to view his new love-making skills as a "success" and to recognize that in many ways he was becoming a better lover than many husbands, because he was listening to his wife and responding to her requests.

By the fifth week the patient was attempting intercourse successfully with relaxed confidence, and by the ninth session he was responding regularly with erections. If they both agreed, they would either have intercourse or choose another sexual technique to achieve orgasm. Treatment was terminated after ten sessions.

(Spitzer et al., 1983, pp. 106–107)

As Mr. Domera's treatment indicates, modern sex therapy includes a variety of principles and techniques. The following ones are applied in almost all cases, regardless of the dysfunction:

1. ***Assessment and conceptualization of the problem.*** Patients are initially given a medical examination and are interviewed concerning their "sex history" (Warren & Sampson, 1995) (see Figure 11-5). The therapist's focus during the interview is on gathering information about past life events and, in particular, current factors that are contributing to the dysfunction. Sometimes, proper assessment requires a team of specialists, perhaps including a psychologist, urologist, and neurologist.

2. ***Mutual responsibility.*** Therapists stress the principle of *mutual responsibility.* Both partners in the relationship share the sexual problem, regardless of who has the actual dysfunction, and treatment will be more successful when both are in therapy (Heiman et al., 1981).

3. ***Education about sexuality.*** Many patients who suffer from sexual dysfunctions know very little about the physiology and techniques of sexual activity. Thus sex therapists may discuss these topics and offer educational materials, including instructional books and videotapes.

4. ***Attitude change.*** Therapists help patients examine and change any beliefs about sexuality that are preventing sexual arousal and pleasure (Rosen, Leiblum, & Spector, 1994). These mistaken beliefs, some of which are widely shared in our society, can result from past traumatic events, family attitudes, or cultural ideas.

5. ***Elimination of performance anxiety and the spectator role.*** Therapists often teach couples *sensate focus,* or *nondemand pleasuring,* a series of sensual tasks, sometimes called "petting" exercises, in which the partners focus on the sexual pleasure that can be achieved by exploring and

caressing each other's bodies at home, without demands to have intercourse or reach orgasm—demands that may be interfering with arousal. Couples are told at first to resist intercourse at home and to restrict their sexual activity to kissing, hugging, and sensual massage of various parts of the body, but not of the breasts or genitals. Over time, they learn how to give and receive greater sexual pleasure and they build back up to the activity of sexual intercourse.

6. ***Increasing sexual communication skills.*** Couples are told to use their sensate-focus sessions at home to try sexual positions in which the person being caressed can guide the other's hands and control the speed, pressure, and location of the caressing. Couples are also taught to give instructions in a nonthreatening, informative manner ("It feels better over here, with a little less pressure"), rather than a threatening uninformative manner ("The way you're touching me doesn't turn me on").

7. ***Changing destructive lifestyles and marital interactions.*** A therapist may encourage a couple to change their lifestyle or take other steps to improve a situation that is having a destructive effect on their relationship—to distance themselves from interfering in-laws, for example, or to change or even quit a job that is too demanding. Similarly, if the couple's general relationship is in conflict, the therapist will try to help them improve it.

8. ***Addressing physical and medical factors.*** When sexual dysfunctions are caused by a medical problem, such as disease, injury, medication, or substance abuse, therapists try to address that problem (Winton, 2000). If antidepressant medications are causing a man's erectile disorder, for example, the clinician may lower the dosage of the medication, change the time of day when the drug is taken, or prescribe a different antidepressant (Segraves, 1998, 1995).

ConsiderThis

● A key technique in sex therapy is to have a couple explore and caress each other's body (sensate focus) while resisting orgasm or intercourse. Why might people become more aroused during sexual caressing if they are prohibited from reaching orgasm or having intercourse?

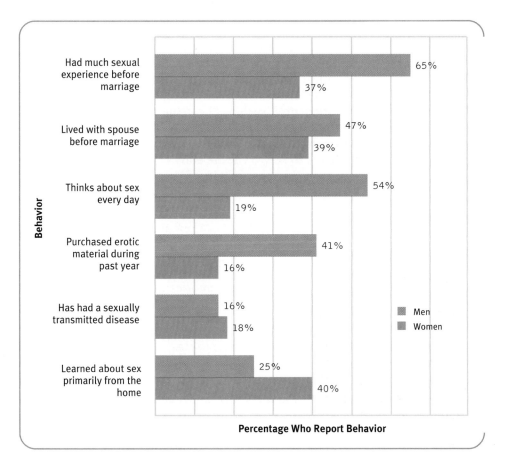

FIGURE 11-5 **Sexual behavior and gender**
According to questionnaires, men are much more likely than women to think about sex on a daily basis and to have purchased sexual material, such as erotic magazines, within the past year. Women are more likely to have learned about sex from the home. (Adapted from Michael et al., 1994; Janus & Janus, 1993.)

Improving a Dog's Life

A company in Buckner, Missouri, has developed a new product: artificial testicles for dogs. Called "neuticles," the testicle substitutes are slipped into a dog's scrotum immediately after neutering to protect the animal from emotional trauma. They are made of polypropylene, a material used to coat some human implants and surgical equipment. Over a thousand pairs were sold in 1996 alone. One dog owner explained, "A dog is like a kid. Same thing. Consideration for his feelings" (Steinberg, 1996). But many veterinarians have questioned "whether the plastic substitutes would improve a dog's esteem" (Uhlig, 1996).

ConsiderThis

🔘 Why might some pet owners believe that this product is necessary or useful? • Are pet owners sometimes too quick to project human discomforts and fears onto animals? • On the other hand, why are other people often critical of the concern, kindness, and affection that many people lavish on their pets?

What Techniques Are Applied to Particular Dysfunctions?

In addition to the universal components of sex therapy, specific techniques can help in each of the sexual dysfunctions.

> "If [a woman] . . . is normally developed mentally and well-bred, her sexual desire is small. If this were not so, the whole world would become a brothel and marriage and a family impossible."
>
> *Health and Longevity,* 1909

HYPOACTIVE SEXUAL DESIRE AND SEXUAL AVERSION Hypoactive sexual desire and sexual aversion are among the most difficult dysfunctions to treat because of the many issues that may feed into them (LoPiccolo, 1997, 1995; Rosen & Leiblum, 1995). Thus therapists typically apply a combination of techniques (LoPiccolo & Friedman, 1988). In a technique called *affectual awareness,* patients visualize sexual scenes in order to discover any feelings of anxiety, vulnerability, and other negative emotions they may have concerning sex. In another technique, patients receive cognitive *self-instruction training* to help them change their negative reactions to sex. That is, they learn to replace negative statements during sex with "coping statements," such as "I can allow myself to enjoy sex; it doesn't mean I'll lose control."

Therapists may also use behavioral approaches to help increase a patient's sex drive. They may instruct clients to keep a "desire diary" in which they record sexual thoughts and feelings, to read books and view films with erotic content, and to fantasize about sex. Pleasurable shared activities such as dancing and walking together are also encouraged (LoPiccolo, 1997, 1995).

For sexual aversion that has resulted from sexual assault or childhood molestation, additional techniques may be needed. A patient may be encouraged to remember, talk, and think about the assault until the memories no longer arouse fear or tension. Or the individual may be instructed to have a mock dialogue with the molester, in order to express lingering feelings of rage and powerlessness (LoPiccolo, 1997, 1995).

These and related approaches apparently help many women and men with hypoactive sexual desire and aversion disorders eventually to have intercourse more than once a week (Hurlbert, 1993; Schover & LoPiccolo, 1982). However, only a few controlled studies have

"You're wasting your time. I'm asexual."

been conducted (Beck, 1995). Finally, biological interventions, such as hormone treatments, have been used, particularly among women whose problems arose after removal of their ovaries or later in life; these interventions have received some research support (Davis, 2000, 1998; Warnock et al., 1999, 1997).

ERECTILE DISORDER Treatments for erectile disorder focus on reducing a man's performance anxiety or increasing his stimulation or both (Rosen, 2000; LoPiccolo, 1995). During sensate focus exercises, the couple may be instructed to try the *tease technique:* the partner keeps caressing the man, but if the man gets an erection, the partner stops caressing him until he loses it. This exercise reduces pressure on the man to perform and at the same time teaches the couple that erections occur naturally in response to stimulation, so long as the partners do not keep focusing on performance. In another technique, the couple may be instructed to use manual or oral sex to try to achieve the woman's orgasm, again reducing pressure on the man to perform (LoPiccolo, 1997, 1995).

Biological approaches, applied particularly when erectile disorder has biological causes, have gained great momentum with the recent development of *sildenafil* (trade name Viagra). This drug increases blood flow to the penis within one hour of ingestion by blocking the activity of certain enzymes; the increased blood flow enables the user to attain an erection during sexual activity. Sildenafil appears to be safe except for men with certain coronary heart diseases and cardiovascular diseases, particularly those who are taking nitroglycerin and other heart medications (Speakman & Kloner, 1999).

Most of the other biological approaches for erectile disorder have been around for years (Morganthaler, 1999). These include gel suppositories, injections of drugs into the penis, and a *vacuum erection device (VED),* a hollow cylinder that is placed over the penis (Braatvedt, 1999). Here a man uses a hand pump to pump air out of the cylinder, drawing blood into his penis and producing an erection. In another biological approach, expensive but widely used, surgeons may implant a *penile prosthesis*—a semirigid rod made of rubber and wire—to produce an artificial erection (Kupeli, Aydos, & Budak, 1999). However, because Viagra is easy to take and helpful to between 40 and 70 percent of patients, drug therapy is the approach now receiving the most attention. In fact, a number of other drugs for erectile disorder are currently in development (Padma, 1999).

MALE ORGASMIC DISORDER Like treatment for male erectile disorder, therapies for male orgasmic disorder include techniques to reduce performance anxiety and increase stimulation (LoPiccolo, 1997; Rosen & Leiblum, 1995). In one technique, a man may be instructed to masturbate to orgasm in the presence of his partner or to masturbate just short of orgasm before inserting his penis for intercourse (Marshall, 1997). This increases the likelihood that he will ejaculate during intercourse. He then is instructed to insert his penis at ever earlier stages of masturbation.

When male orgasmic disorder is caused by physical factors such as neurological damage or injury, treatment may include a drug to increase arousal of the sympathetic nervous system (Murphy & Lipshultz, 1988). However, few studies have systematically tested the effectiveness of such treatments (Rosen & Leiblum, 1995).

PREMATURE EJACULATION Premature ejaculation has been treated successfully for years by behavioral procedures (Polonsky, 2000; Masters & Johnson, 1970). In the *stop-start,* or *pause,* procedure, the penis is manually stimulated until the man is highly aroused. The couple then pause until his arousal subsides, after which the stimulation is resumed. This sequence is repeated several times before stimulation is carried through to ejaculation, so the man ultimately experiences much more total time of stimulation than he has ever experienced before (LoPiccolo, 1995). Eventually the couple progresses to putting the penis in the vagina, making sure to withdraw it and to pause

ConsiderThis

Some theorists cite performance anxiety and the spectator role as contributing factors in certain sexual dysfunctions. Are there other important areas of dysfunction in life that might also be explained by performance anxiety and the spectator role?

"When I touch him he rolls into a ball."

Viagra vs. the Pill: Sexism in Health Care?

Many of us believe that we live in an enlightened world, where sexism is declining and where health care and benefits are available in equal measure to men and women alike. Periodically, however, such illusions are shattered. The responses of government agencies and insurance companies to the discovery and marketing of Viagra in 1998 may be a case in point.

Consider, first, the nation of Japan. In early 1999, just six months after Viagra's sensational introduction in the United States, the drug was approved for use among men in Japan (Martin, 2000). In contrast, low-dose contraceptives—"the pill"—were not approved for use among women in that country until June of 1999—a full 40 years after their invention! Many observers believe that birth control pills would still be unavailable to women in Japan had Viagra not received its quick approval. That is, the country's agency for the approval of medications simply could not withstand the public outrage that was developing over its different responses to the two forms of medical intervention.

Has the United States been able to avoid such an apparent double standard in its health-care system? Not really. Before Viagra was introduced, insurance companies were not required to reimburse women for the cost of prescription contraceptives. As a result, women had to pay 68 percent more out-of-pocket expenses for health care than did men, due largely to uncovered reproductive health–care costs (Hayden, 1998). Some legislators had sought to correct this problem by requiring contraceptive coverage in health insurance plans, but their efforts failed in state after state for more than a decade (Hayden, 1998).

In contrast, when Viagra was introduced in 1998, many insurance companies readily agreed to cover the new drug. In addition, in July of 1998, President Clinton's Health Care Financing Administration mandated that states provide Viagra as part of Medicaid coverage. As the public outcry grew over the contrast between Viagra coverage for men and oral contraceptive coverage for women, laws across the country finally began to change. In fact, by the end of 1998, nine states required prescription contraceptive coverage (Hayden, 1998). Today, 21 states require such coverage by private insurance companies and 35 states require it for state employees (NARAL, 2001). Moreover, if the proposed Prescription and Contraceptive Coverage Act is passed by Congress, all insurers in the nation will be required to reimburse women for the cost of oral contraceptives.

In the meantime, wishful thinkers express hope that generous donors will help defray the cost of oral contraceptives as some donors have done for the cost of Viagra. Immediately after Viagra's approval, for example, one noted philanthropist donated $1 million to provide this drug to the needy. In explaining his action, he said, "I saw an article saying that at $10 apiece, a lot of impotent men wouldn't be able to afford it. So I said [to my wife], . . . 'let's help,' and by Tuesday we had it done" (Carlson, 1998).

Tom Lyle/Medichrome/The Stock Shop

A social phenomenon *Physicians wrote 120,000 prescriptions for Viagra during its first month on the market in 1998, making it the fastest-selling new prescription drug in history (Adler, 1998).*

ConsiderThis

● Although Viagra and "the pill" both relate to sexual behavior, they serve, in fact, different purposes and have different religious implications. Could these differences, rather than sexism, explain the responses of insurance companies and government agencies?

whenever the man becomes too highly aroused. According to clinical reports, after two or three months many couples can enjoy prolonged intercourse without any need for pauses (LoPiccolo, 1997, 1995).

Some clinicians treat premature ejaculation with *fluoxetine* (Prozac) and other serotonin-enhancing antidepressant drugs. Because these drugs often reduce sexual arousal or orgasm, the reasoning goes, they may be helpful to men who experience premature ejaculation. Although some studies have reported positive results (Althof, 1995; Althof et al., 1994), researchers have yet to examine the long-term impact of these drugs on men with premature ejaculation. Nor have they determined whether such drugs may be combined effectively with psychological and interpersonal techniques (Rosen & Leiblum, 1995).

FEMALE AROUSAL AND ORGASMIC DISORDERS Specific treatment techniques for female arousal and orgasmic dysfunctions include self-exploration, enhancement of body awareness, and directed masturbation training (Heiman, 2000; LoPiccolo, 1997). These procedures are especially useful for women who have never had an orgasm under any circumstances. Hormone therapy is also being used increasingly (Davis, 2000, 1998; Warnock et al., 1999).

In **directed masturbation training,** a woman is taught step by step how to masturbate effectively and eventually to reach orgasm during sexual interactions (Hulbert & Apt, 1995; Hulbert et al., 1993). The training includes use of diagrams and reading material, private self-stimulation, erotic material and fantasies, "orgasm triggers" such as holding her breath or thrusting her pelvis, sensate focus with her partner, and sexual positioning that produces stimulation of the clitoris during intercourse. This training program appears to be highly effective: over 90 percent of women learn to have an orgasm during masturbation, about 80 percent during caressing by their partners, and about 30 percent during intercourse (LoPiccolo, 1997; Heiman & LoPiccolo, 1988).

As we observed earlier, a lack of orgasm during intercourse is not necessarily a sexual dysfunction, provided the woman enjoys intercourse and can reach orgasm through caressing, either by her partner or by herself. For this reason some therapists believe that the wisest course is to simply educate women whose only concern is lack of orgasm during intercourse, informing them that they are quite normal.

VAGINISMUS Specific treatment for vaginismus, involuntary contractions of the muscles around the vagina, takes two approaches. First, a woman may practice tightening and relaxing her vaginal muscles until she gains more voluntary control over them (LoPiccolo, 1995; Rosen & Leiblum, 1995). Second, she may receive gradual behavioral exposure treatment to help her overcome her fear of penetration, beginning by inserting increasingly large dilators in her vagina at home and at her own pace and eventually ending with the insertion of her partner's penis. Over 90 percent of the women treated for vaginismus eventually have pain-free intercourse (Beck, 1993; LoPiccolo, 1990). Many women with this problem, however, report that they received ineffective or inaccurate forms of treatment when they first sought help from their physicians (Ogden & Ward, 1995).

DYSPAREUNIA We saw earlier that the most common cause of dyspareunia, genital pain during intercourse, is physical, such as pain-causing scars or tears. When the cause is known, a couple can learn intercourse positions that avoid putting pressure on the injured area. A medical intervention may also be tried, but it must still be combined with other sex therapy techniques to overcome the years of sexual anxiety and lack of arousal (Binik et al., 2000; Leiblum, 1996). Because many cases of dyspareunia are in fact caused by undiagnosed physical problems, it is very important that clients receive expert gynecological exams (Reid & Lininger, 1993).

What Are the Current Trends in Sex Therapy?

Over the past 30 years, sex therapists have moved well beyond the approach first developed by Masters and Johnson (Kring, 2000; Rosen & Leiblum, 1995). For example, today's sex therapists regularly treat partners who are living together but not married. They also treat sexual dysfunctions that arise from psychological disorders such as depression, mania, schizophrenia, and certain personality disorders (Rowlands, 1995). In addition, sex therapists no longer screen out clients with severe marital discord, the elderly, the medically ill, or the physically handicapped (Schover, 2000; Dupont, 1995) or clients with a homosexual orientation or those who have no long-term sex partner (Stravynski et al., 1997). Sex therapists are also paying more attention to excessive sexuality, sometimes called *sexual addiction* (Kafka, 2000).

"[Masturbation] produces seminal weakness, impotence, dysury, tabes dorsalis, pulmonary consumption, dyspepsia, dimness of sight, vertigo, epilepsy, hypochondriasis, loss of memory, manalgia, fatuity, and death."

Benjamin Rush, "the father of American psychiatry," 1812

DIRECTED MASTURBATION TRAINING A sex therapy approach that teaches women with female arousal or orgasmic disorders how to masturbate effectively and eventually to reach orgasm during sexual interactions.

A new message *Over the past several decades, Western society has increasingly viewed female sexual arousal and expression as normal and healthful and has sent this message to women through novels, movies, television shows, and magazines. This Diet Coke ad in which two women openly ogle a sexy construction worker was one of the most discussed television commercials of the 1990s.*

Many sex therapists currently worry about the sharp increase in the use of drugs and other medical interventions for sexual dysfunctions, particularly for hypoactive sexual desire and male erectile disorder (Winton, 2000; Ackerman, 1995). Their concern is that therapists will increasingly choose the biological interventions rather than integrating biological, psychological, and sociocultural interventions (Kring, 2000; Hartmann & Langer, 1993). In fact, narrow approaches of any kind probably cannot fully address the complex factors that cause most sexual problems. It took sex therapists years to recognize the considerable advantages of an integrated approach to sexual dysfunctions. The development of new medical interventions should not lead to its abandonment.

SUMMING UP | **Treatments for Sexual Dysfunctions**

In the 1970s the work of William Masters and Virginia Johnson led to the development of sex therapy. Today sex therapy combines a variety of cognitive, behavioral, couple, and family systems therapies. It includes features such as careful assessment, mutual responsibility, education, attitude changes, sensate-focus exercises to help eliminate performance anxiety and the spectator role, improvements in communication, and couple therapy. In addition, specific techniques have been developed for each of the sexual dysfunctions. Biological treatments for sexual dysfunctions are also increasing.

CYBERSEX

Almost 9 million Americans regularly visit adult Web sites to talk in chat rooms, view erotica, or the like. Almost 8 percent of them spend more than 11 hours a week at such sites (Cooper et al., 1999). Female visitors tend to join chat rooms, while male users are much more prone to visit visual erotica sites.

Paraphilias

Paraphilias are disorders in which individuals repeatedly have intense sexual urges or fantasies or display sexual behaviors that involve nonhuman objects, children, nonconsenting adults, or the experience of suffering or humiliation. Many people with a paraphilia can become aroused only when a paraphilic stimulus is present, fantasized about, or acted out. Others need the stimulus only occasionally, perhaps during times of stress.

According to DSM-IV, a diagnosis of paraphilia should be applied only when the urges, fantasies, or behaviors last at least six months (see Table 11-5). For most paraphilias, the urges, fantasies, or behaviors must also cause great distress or interfere with one's social life or job performance in order for a diagnosis to be applied (APA, 2000). For certain paraphilias, however, performance of the sexual behavior indicates a disorder even if the individual experiences no distress or impairment (APA, 2000). People who initiate sexual contact with children, for example, warrant a diagnosis of pedophilia regardless of how troubled the individuals may or may not be over their behavior.

Some people with one kind of paraphilia display others as well (Abel & Osborn, 1992). Relatively few people receive a formal diagnosis of paraphilia, but the large market in paraphilic pornography leads clinicians to suspect that the patterns may be quite common (APA, 2000). People whose paraphilias involve children or nonconsenting adults often come to the attention of clinicians when they get into legal trouble. Some experts argue that, with the exception of nonconsensual paraphilias, paraphilic activities should be considered a disorder only when they are the exclusive means of achieving sexual excitement and orgasm.

Although theorists have proposed various explanations for paraphilias, there is little formal evidence to support them (Bradford, 1999). Moreover, none of the many treatments applied to paraphilias has proved clearly effective (Bradford, 1999, 1995). Psychological and sociocultural treatments for paraphilias have been available the longest, but today's professionals are also using biological interventions. Some clinicians administer drugs called *antiandrogens* that lower the production of testosterone, the male sex hormone, and reduce sex drive (Roesler & Witztum, 2000; Balon, 1998). Although such drugs do indeed reduce paraphilic behavior patterns, several of them disrupt normal sexual feelings and behavior as well. Thus the drugs tend to be applied primarily when the paraphilias are of danger either to the individuals themselves or to other people (Bender, 1998). Clinicians have also become interested in the possible use of second-generation antidepressant medications to treat persons with paraphilias, hoping that the drugs will reduce these compulsion-like sexual behaviors just as they help reduce other kinds of compulsions (Balon, 1998; Leo & Kim, 1995).

Fetishism

The key features of **fetishism** are recurrent intense sexual urges, sexually arousing fantasies, or behaviors that involve the use of a nonliving object, often to the exclusion of all other stimuli. Usually the disorder begins in adolescence. Almost anything can be a fetish; women's underwear, shoes, and boots are particularly common (APA, 2000, 1994). Some people with fetishism commit thievery in order to collect as many of the desired objects as possible. The objects may be touched, smelled, worn, or used in some other way while the person masturbates, or the individual may ask a partner to wear the object when they have sex. Several of these features are seen in the following case:

> A 32-year-old, single male . . . related that although he was somewhat sexually attracted by women, he was far more attracted by "their panties."
>
> To the best of the patient's memory, sexual excitement began at about age 7, when he came upon a pornographic magazine and felt stimulated by pictures of partially nude women wearing "panties." His first ejaculation occurred at 13 via masturbation to fantasies of women wearing panties. He masturbated into his older sister's panties, which he had stolen without her knowledge. Subsequently he stole panties from her friends and from other women he met socially. He found pretexts to "wander" into the bedrooms of women during social occasions, and would quickly rummage through their possessions until he found a

Table 11-5 DSM-IV Checklist

PARAPHILIA

1. Over a period of at least six months, recurrent, intense sexually arousing fantasies, sexual urges, or behaviors involving certain inappropriate stimuli or situations (nonhuman objects; the suffering or humiliation of oneself or one's partner; or children or other nonconsenting persons).
2. Significant distress or impairment over the fantasies, urges, or behaviors. (In some paraphilias—pedophilia, exhibitionism, voyeurism, frotteurism, and sexual sadism—the performance of paraphilic behaviors indicates a disorder, even in the absence of distress or impairment.)

Based on APA, 2000.

CHEMICAL CASTRATION

In 1996 the California state legislature passed the first law in the United States allowing state judges to order antiandrogen drug treatments, often referred to as "chemical castration," for repeat sex crime offenders, such as men who repeatedly commit pedophiliac acts or rape.

PARAPHILIAS Disorders characterized by recurrent and intense sexual urges, fantasies, or behaviors involving nonhuman objects, children, nonconsenting adults, or experiences of suffering or humiliation.

FETISHISM A paraphilia consisting of recurrent and intense sexual urges, fantasies, or behaviors that involve the use of a nonliving object, often to the exclusion of all other stimuli.

> pair of panties to his satisfaction. He later used these to masturbate into, and then "saved them" in a "private cache." The pattern of masturbating into women's underwear had been his preferred method of achieving sexual excitement and orgasm from adolescence until the present consultation.
>
> *(Spitzer et al., 1994, p. 247)*

Researchers have not been able to pinpoint the causes of fetishism (Wise, 1985). Psychodynamic theorists view fetishes as defense mechanisms that help people avoid the anxiety produced by normal sexual contact. Psychodynamic treatment for this problem, however, has met with little success (LoPiccolo, 1992).

Behaviorists propose that fetishes are learned through classical conditioning. In one behavioral study, male subjects were shown a series of slides of nude women along with slides of boots (Rachman, 1966). After many trials, the subjects became aroused by the boot photos alone. If early sexual experiences similarly occur in the presence of particular objects, perhaps the stage is set for development of fetishes.

Behaviorists have sometimes treated fetishism with *aversion therapy* (Kilmann et al., 1982). In one study, an electric shock was administered to the arms or legs of subjects with fetishes while they imagined their objects of desire (Marks & Gelder, 1967). After two weeks of therapy all subjects in the study showed at least some improvement. In another aversion technique, *covert sensitization,* people with fetishism are guided to imagine the pleasurable object and repeatedly to pair this image with an *imagined* aversive stimulus, until the object of sexual pleasure is no longer desired.

Another behavioral treatment for fetishism is **masturbatory satiation** (Quinsey & Earls, 1990; Marshall & Lippens, 1977). In this method, the client masturbates to orgasm while fantasizing about a sexually appropriate object, then switches to fantasizing in detail about fetishistic objects while masturbating again and continues the fetishistic fantasy for an hour. The procedure is meant to produce a feeling of boredom, which in turn becomes linked to the fetishistic object.

Yet another behavioral approach to fetishism, also used for other paraphilias, is **orgasmic reorientation,** which teaches individuals to respond to more appropriate sources of sexual stimulation. People are shown conventional stimuli while they are responding to unconventional objects. A person with a shoe fetish, for example, may be instructed to obtain an erection from pictures of shoes and then to begin masturbating to a picture of a nude woman. If he starts to lose the erection, he must return to the pictures of shoes until he is masturbating effectively, then change back to the picture of the nude woman. When orgasm approaches, he must direct all attention to the conventional stimulus.

"Man is the only animal that blushes. Or needs to."

Mark Twain

A group approach *"Crossroads" is a self-help group for men with transvestic fetishism, a recurrent need to dress in women's clothing as a means to achieve sexual arousal.*

Transvestic Fetishism

Transvestic fetishism, also known as **transvestism** or **cross-dressing,** is a repeated need or desire to dress in clothes of the opposite sex in order to achieve sexual arousal. In the following passage, a 42-year-old married father describes his pattern:

> I have been told that when I dress in drag, at times I look like Whistler's Mother [laughs], especially when I haven't shaved closely. I usually am good at detail, and I make sure when I dress as a woman that I have my nails done just so, and that my colors match. Honestly, it's hard to pin a date on when I began cross dressing. . . . If pressed, I would have to say it began when I was about 10 years of age, fooling around with and putting on my mom's clothes. . . . I was always careful to put everything back in its exact place, and in 18 years of doing this in her home, my

Peter Yates/Picture Group

mother never, I mean never, suspected, or questioned me about putting on her clothes. I belong to a transvestite support group . . . , a group for men who cross dress. Some of the group are homosexuals, but most are not. A true transvestite—and I am one, so I know—is not homosexual. We don't discriminate against them in the group at all; hey, we have enough trouble getting acceptance as normal people and not just a bunch of weirdos ourselves. They are a bunch of nice guys . . . really. Most of them are like me.

Most of [the men in the group] have told their families about their dressing inclinations, but those that are married are a mixed lot; some wives know and some don't, they just suspect. I believe in honesty, and told my wife about this before we were married. We're separated now, but I don't think it's because of my cross dressing. . . . I have been asked many times why I cross dress, and it's hard to explain, other than it makes me feel good. There is something deep down that it gratifies. Some of my friends, when I was growing up, suggested psychotherapy, but I don't regard this as a problem. . . . I function perfectly well sexually with my wife, though it took her some time to be comfortable with me wearing feminine underwear; yes, sometimes I wear it while making love, it just makes it more exciting.

(Janus & Janus, 1993, p. 121)

MASTURBATORY SATIATION A behavioral treatment in which a client masturbates for a very long period of time while fantasizing in detail about a paraphilic object. The procedure is expected to produce a feeling of boredom that in turn becomes linked to the object.

ORGASMIC REORIENTATION A procedure for treating certain paraphilias by teaching clients to respond to new, more appropriate sources of sexual stimulation.

TRANSVESTIC FETISHISM A paraphilia consisting of repeated and intense sexual urges, fantasies, or behaviors that involve dressing in clothes of the opposite sex. Also known as *transvestism* or *cross-dressing*.

EXHIBITIONISM A paraphilia in which persons have repeated sexually arousing urges or fantasies about exposing their genitals to another person, and may act upon those urges.

Like this man, the typical person with transvestism, almost always a heterosexual male, begins cross-dressing in childhood or adolescence (Docter & Prince, 1997; Bradley, 1995). He is the picture of characteristic masculinity in everyday life and is usually alone when he cross-dresses. A small percentage of such men cross-dress to visit bars or social clubs. Some wear a single item of women's clothing, such as underwear or hosiery, under their masculine clothes. Others wear makeup and dress fully as women. Many married men with transvestism involve their wives in their cross-dressing behavior (Kolodny, Masters, & Johnson, 1979). This pattern is often confused with *gender identity disorder (transsexualism)*, but, as we shall see, they are two separate disorders.

The development of transvestic fetishism sometimes seems to follow the behavioral principles of operant conditioning. In such cases, parents or other adults may openly encourage the individuals to cross-dress as children or even reward them for this behavior. In one case, a woman was delighted to discover that her young nephew enjoyed dressing in girls' clothes. She had always wanted a niece, and she proceeded to buy him dresses and jewelry and sometimes dressed him as a girl and took him out shopping.

Exhibitionism

A person with **exhibitionism** has recurrent urges to expose his genitals to another person, almost always a member of the opposite sex, or has sexually arousing fantasies of doing so. He may also carry out those urges, but rarely attempts to initiate sexual activity with the person to whom he exposes himself (APA, 2000, 1994; Abel, 1989). More often, he wants to provoke shock or surprise. Sometimes a so-called flasher will expose himself in a particular neighborhood at particular hours. The urges typically become stronger when the person has free time or is under significant stress.

Generally the disorder begins before age 18 and is most prevalent in males (APA, 2000, 1994). Persons with exhibitionism are typically immature in their dealings with the opposite sex and have difficulty in interpersonal relationships. Over half of them are married, but their sexual relations with their wives are not usually satisfactory (Blair & Lanyon, 1981; Mohr et al., 1964). Many have doubts or fears about their masculinity, and some apparently have a strong bond to a possessive mother.

As with other paraphilias, treatment generally includes aversion therapy and masturbatory satiation, possibly combined with orgasmic reorientation, social skills training, or psychodynamic therapy (LoPiccolo, 1992; McNally & Lukach,

LEGAL REPERCUSSIONS

The majority of arrests for sexual offenses involve acts of exhibitionism, pedophilia, or voyeurism (APA, 2000).

Playful context *Dressing in clothes of the opposite sex does not necessarily convey a paraphilia. The context of sexual-like behaviors must be weighed. Here members of Harvard University's Hasty Pudding Theatricals Club, known for staging musicals in which male undergraduates dress like women, flank actor Samuel L. Jackson, the 1999 recipient of their Man of the Year award. Jackson's outfit is meant to spoof his famous "hamburger royal with cheese" discussion in the movie Pulp Fiction.*

VOYEURISM A paraphilia in which a person has repeated and intense sexual desires to observe unsuspecting people in secret as they undress or to spy on couples having intercourse, and may act upon those desires.

FROTTEURISM A paraphilia consisting of repeated and intense sexual urges, fantasies, or behaviors that involve touching and rubbing against a nonconsenting person.

PEDOPHILIA A paraphilia in which a person has repeated and intense sexual urges or fantasies about watching, touching, or engaging in sexual acts with prepubescent children, and may carry out those urges or fantasies.

SEXUAL MASOCHISM A paraphilia characterized by repeated and intense sexual urges, fantasies, or behaviors that involve being humiliated, beaten, bound, or otherwise made to suffer.

1991). Clinicians have also reported some success with hypnotherapy (Epstein, 1983; Polk, 1983).

Voyeurism

A person who engages in **voyeurism** has recurrent and intense urges to secretly observe unsuspecting people as they undress or to spy on couples having intercourse. The person may also masturbate during the act of observing or when thinking about it afterward but does not generally seek to have sex with the person being spied on. This disorder usually begins before the age of 15 and tends to persist (APA, 2000, 1994).

The vulnerability of the people being observed and the probability that they would feel humiliated if they knew they were under observation are often part of the individual's enjoyment. In addition, the risk of being discovered often adds to the excitement.

Exhibitionism and voyeurism can play a role in normal sexuality, but in such cases they are done with the consent or understanding of the partner. The clinical disorder of voyeurism is marked by the repeated invasion of other people's privacy. Some people with voyeurism are unable to have normal sexual relations; others, however, have a normal sex life apart from their voyeurism.

Many psychodynamic clinicians propose that people with voyeurism are seeking by their actions to gain power over others, possibly because they feel inadequate or are sexually or socially shy. Others have explained voyeurism as an attempt to reduce fears of castration, originally produced by the sight of an adult's genitals. Theoretically, people with voyeurism are repeating the behavior that produced the original fright, to reassure themselves that there is nothing to fear (Fenichel, 1945). Behaviorists explain the disorder as a learned behavior that can be traced to a chance and secret observation of a sexually arousing scene. If such observations are repeated on several occasions while the onlooker masturbates, a voyeuristic pattern may develop.

Frotteurism

A person who develops **frotteurism** has repeated and intense sexual urges to touch and rub against a nonconsenting person, or has sexually arousing fantasies of doing so. The person may also act on the urges. Frottage (from French *frotter,* "to rub") is usually committed in a crowded place, such as a subway or a busy sidewalk (APA, 2000, 1994; Krueger & Kaplan, 2000). The person, almost always a male, may rub his genitals against the victim's thighs or buttocks or fondle her genital area or breasts with his hands. Typically he fantasizes during the act that he is having a caring relationship with the victim. This paraphilia usually begins in the teenage years or earlier, often after the person observes others committing an act of frottage. After the person reaches the age of about 25, the acts gradually decrease and often disappear (APA, 2000, 1994).

Pedophilia

A person with **pedophilia,** literally "love of children," gains sexual gratification by watching, touching, or engaging in sexual acts with prepubescent children, usually 13 years or younger. Some people with this disorder are satisfied by child pornography (Linz & Imrich, 2001) or seemingly innocent material such as children's underwear ads; others are driven to actually watching, fondling, or engaging in sexual intercourse with children (Howitt, 1995). Some people with pedophilia are attracted only to children; others are attracted to adults as well (APA, 2000, 1994). Both boys and girls can be pedophilia victims, but there is evidence suggesting that three-quarters of them are girls (Koss & Heslet, 1992).

STEPPING BACK

Serving the Public Good

As clinical practitioners and researchers conduct their work, should they consider the potential impact of their decisions on society? Many people, including a large number of clinicians, believe that the answer to this question is a resounding yes. Two clashes between the clinical field and the public interest in the 1990s—each centering on the disorder of *pedophilia*—brought this issue to life.

In 1994, the newly published DSM-IV ruled that people should receive a diagnosis of pedophilia only if their recurrent fantasies, urges, or behaviors involving sexual activity with children cause them significant distress or impairment in social, occupational, or other spheres of functioning. Critics worried that this criterion seemed to suggest that pedophilic behavior is acceptable, even normal, as

long as it causes no distress or impairment. Even the U.S. Congress condemned the DSM-IV definition.

In response to these criticisms, the American Psychiatric Association clarified its position in 1997, stating, "An adult who engages in sexual activity with a child is performing a criminal and immoral act which never can be considered moral or socially acceptable behavior." In 2000 the Association went further still and changed the DSM criteria for pedophilia, so that the disorder is now diagnosed if persons act on their sexual urges, regardless of whether they experience distress or impairment (APA, 2000). Similarly, acting on one's recurrent sexual urges or fantasies warrants a diagnosis in cases of exhibitionism, voyeurism, frotteurism, and sexual sadism.

Another clash between the clinical field and public sensibilities occurred in 1998 when a review article in the prestigious journal *Psychological Bulletin* concluded that the effects of child sexual abuse are not as long-lasting as usually believed. The study set off a firestorm, with critics arguing that the conclusion runs counter to evidence from a number of studies. Furthermore, many people worried that the article's conclusions could be used to legitimize pedophilia. After a groundswell of criticism, the American Psychological Association, publisher of the journal, acknowledged in 1999 that it should have given more thought to how the study would be received, and said that it will more carefully weigh the potential consequences of research publications (Fowler, 1999).

People with pedophilia usually develop their disorder during adolescence. Many were themselves sexually abused as children (Berlin, 2000; Howitt, 1995). It is not unusual for them to be married and to have sexual difficulties or other frustrations in life that lead them to seek an area in which they can be masters. Often these people are immature: their social and sexual skills may be underdeveloped, and thoughts of normal sexual relationships fill them with anxiety. Some people with pedophilia also display faulty thinking, such as "It's all right to have sex with children as long as they agree" (Abel et al., 1984). A recent study of 45 men with this disorder found that 93 percent had at least one additional psychological disorder (Raymond et al., 1999). More than two-thirds of the men had a mood disorder at some time during their lives, 64 percent an anxiety disorder, 60 percent a substance-related disorder, 53 percent another paraphilia, and 24 percent a sexual dysfunction.

Most pedophilic offenders are imprisoned or forced into treatment if they are caught (Stone, Winslade, & Klugman, 2000). After all, they are committing child sexual abuse when they take any steps toward sexual contact with a child. Treatments include those already mentioned for other paraphilias, such as aversion therapy, masturbatory satiation, and orgasmic reorientation (LoPiccolo, 1992; Enright, 1989). There is also a cognitive-behavioral treatment for pedophilia: *relapse-prevention training*, modeled after the relapse-prevention programs used in the treatment of substance dependence (see p. 300). In this approach, clients identify the kinds of situations that typically trigger their pedophilic fantasies and actions (such as depressed mood or distorted thinking). They then learn strategies for avoiding the situations or coping with them more effectively (Fisher, Beech, & Browne, 2000; Pithers, 1990). Relapse-prevention training has sometimes been of help in pedophilia and in certain other paraphilias.

DANGEROUS INTERACTIONS

A study of Internet chat rooms for children and teens estimated that two-thirds of the visitors were actually adults pretending to be children and seeking to engage in sex talk or to acquire or trade pornographic material (Lamb, 1998).

Sexual Masochism

A person with **sexual masochism** is intensely sexually aroused by the act or thought of being humiliated, beaten, bound, or otherwise made to suffer. Many people have fantasies of being forced into sexual acts against their will, but only those who are very upset or impaired by the fantasies receive this diagnosis. Some people with the disorder act on the masochistic urges by themselves, perhaps tying, sticking pins into, or even cutting themselves. Others have their sexual partners restrain, tie up, blindfold, spank, paddle, whip, beat, electrically shock, "pin and pierce," or humiliate them (APA, 2000, 1994).

An industry of products and services has formed to meet the desires of people with sexual masochism. Here a 34-year-old woman describes her work as the operator of a sadomasochism house:

> I get people here who have been all over looking for the right kind of pain they feel they deserve. Don't ask me why they want pain, I'm not a psychologist; but when they have found us, they usually don't go elsewhere. It may take some of the other girls an hour or even two hours to make these guys feel like they've had their treatment—I can achieve that in about 20 minutes. . . . Remember, these are businessmen, and they are not only buying my time, but they have to get back to work, so time is important.
>
> Among the things I do, that work really quickly and well, are: I put clothespins on their nipples, or pins in their [testicles]. Some of them need to see their own blood to be able to get off. . . .
>
> . . . All the time that a torture scene is going on, there is constant dialogue. . . . I scream at the guy, and tell him what a no-good rotten bastard he is, how this is even too good for him, that he knows he deserves worse, and I begin to list his sins. It works every time. Hey, I'm not nuts, I know what I'm doing. I act very tough and hard, but I'm really a very sensitive woman. But you have to watch out for a guy's health . . . you must not kill him, or have him get a heart attack. . . . I know of other places that have had guys die there. I've never lost a customer to death, though they may have wished for it during my "treatment." Remember, these are repeat customers. I have a clientele and a reputation that I value.
>
> (Janus & Janus, 1993, p. 115)

In one form of sexual masochism, *hypoxyphilia,* people strangle or smother themselves (or ask their partner to strangle them) in order to enhance their sexual pleasure. There have, in fact, been a disturbing number of clinical reports of *autoerotic asphyxia,* in which individuals, usually males and as young as 10 years old, accidentally bring about a fatal lack of oxygen by hanging, suffocating, or strangling themselves while masturbating. There is some debate as to whether the practice should be considered sexual masochism, but it is commonly accompanied by other acts of bondage (Blanchard & Hucker, 1991).

Most masochistic sexual fantasies begin in childhood. However, the person does not act out the urges until later, usually by early adulthood. The disorder typically continues for many years. Some people practice more and more dangerous acts over time or during times of particular stress (APA, 2000, 1994).

In many cases sexual masochism seems to have developed through the behavioral process of classical conditioning. One case study tells of a teenage boy with a broken arm who was caressed and held close by an attractive nurse as the physician set his fracture without anesthesia (Gebhard, 1965). The powerful combination of pain and sexual arousal he felt then may have been the cause of his later masochistic urges and acts.

Sexual Sadism

A person with **sexual sadism,** usually male, is intensely sexually aroused by the thought or act of inflicting suffering on others, by dominating, restraining, blindfolding, cutting, strangling, mutilating, or even killing the victim. The label is derived from the name of the famous Marquis de Sade (1740–1814), who tor-

SEXUAL SADISM A paraphilia characterized by repeated and intense sexual urges, fantasies, or behaviors that involve inflicting suffering on others.

tured others in order to satisfy his sexual desires. People who fanta-size about sadism typically imagine that they have total control over a sexual victim who is terrified by the sadistic act. Many carry out sadistic acts with a consenting partner, often a person with sexual masochism. Some, however, act out their urges on nonconsenting victims. A number of rapists, for example, display sexual sadism. In all cases, the real or fantasized victim's suffering is the key to arousal.

Fantasies of sexual sadism, like those of sexual masochism, may first appear in childhood (Johnson & Becker, 1997); the sadistic acts, when they occur, develop by early adulthood (APA, 2000, 1994). The pattern is long-term. Sadistic acts sometimes stay at the same level of cruelty, but more often they become more and more severe over the years. Obviously, people with severe forms of the dis-order may be highly dangerous to others.

Some behaviorists believe that classical conditioning is at work in sexual sadism. While inflicting pain, perhaps unintentionally, on an animal or person, a teenager may feel intense emotions and sexual arousal. The association between inflicting pain and being aroused sexually sets the stage for a pattern of sexual sadism. Behaviorists also propose that the disorder may result from modeling, when ado-lescents observe others achieving sexual satisfaction by inflicting pain. The many sexual magazines, books, and videotapes in our soci-ety make such models readily available (Lebegue, 1991).

Psychodynamic and cognitive theorists view people with sexual sadism as having underlying feelings of sexual inadequacy; they in-flict pain in order to gain a sense of power, which in turn increases their sexual arousal. In contrast, certain biological studies have found signs of possible abnormalities in the endocrine systems of persons with sadism (Langevin et al., 1988). None of these explanations, however, has been fully investigated.

Sexual sadism has been treated by aversion therapy. The public's view of and distaste for this procedure has been influenced by Anthony Burgess's novel (later a movie) *A Clockwork Orange,* which describes simultaneous presenta-tions of sadistic images and drug-induced stomach spasms to a sadistic young man until he is conditioned to feel nausea at the sight of such images. It is not clear that aversion therapy is helpful in cases of sexual sadism. However, relapse-prevention training, used in some criminal cases, seems to be of value (Vaillant & Antonowicz, 1992; Pithers & Cumming, 1989).

S&M *People with sexual sadism and those with sexual masochism often achieve satisfaction with one another. Although many such relation-ships stay within safe bounds and are often por-trayed with humor in photos, novels, and movies, they can cross the line and result in se-vere physical or psychological damage.*

Cinematic introduction *In one of filmdom's most famous scenes, Alex, the sexually sadistic char-acter in* A Clockwork Orange, *is forced to observe violent images while he experiences painful stomach spasms. Public attitudes toward aver-sion therapy were greatly influenced by this 1971 portrayal of the treatment approach.*

SEXUAL RULING

According to a narrow (5 to 4) Supreme Court decision in the 1997 case of *Kansas v. Hendricks,* convicted sex offenders (e.g. rapists) may be removed from prison prior to release and subjected to involuntary civil commitment in a mental hospital if a court judges them likely to engage in further "predatory acts of sexual violence" as the result of a "mental abnormality" or "personality disorder." They must then remain institutionalized until their disorder and sexual dangerousness are rectified.

A Word of Caution

The definitions of the paraphilias, like those of sexual dysfunctions, are strongly influenced by the norms of the particular society in which they occur (Leiblum, 2001; APA, 2000). Some clinicians argue that except when people are hurt by them, many paraphilic behaviors should not be considered disorders at all. We need to be very careful about applying these labels to others or to ourselves. Keep in mind that for years clinical professionals considered homosexuality a paraphilia, and their judgment was used to justify laws and even police actions against homosexual persons (Kirby, 2000). Only when the gay rights movement helped change society's understanding of and attitudes toward homosexuality did clinicians stop considering it a disorder. In the meantime, the clinical field had unintentionally contributed to the persecution, anxiety, and humiliation of millions of people because of personal sexual behavior that differed from the conventional norms.

SUMMING UP ⎮ **Paraphilias**

Paraphilias are disorders marked by repeated and intense sexual urges, fantasies, or behaviors involving either nonhuman objects, children, nonconsenting adults, or experiences of suffering or humiliation. The disorders are found primarily in men. The paraphilias include fetishism, transvestic fetishism (transvestism), exhibitionism, voyeurism, frotteurism, pedophilia, sexual masochism, and sexual sadism.

Although various explanations have been proposed for these disorders, research has revealed little about their causes. A range of treatments has been tried, including aversion therapy, masturbatory satiation, orgasmic reorientation, and relapse-prevention training. However, research into the effectiveness of such treatments has been limited.

Gender Identity Disorder

One of the most fascinating disorders related to sexuality is **gender identity disorder,** or **transsexualism,** a disorder in which people persistently feel that a vast mistake has been made—they have been assigned to the wrong sex (see Table 11-6). Such persons would like to get rid of their primary and secondary sex characteristics—many of them find their own genitals repulsive—and acquire the characteristics of the other sex (APA, 2000, 1994). Men with gender identity disorder outnumber women by around two to one. People with the problem often experience depression and may have thoughts of suicide (Bradley, 1995).

People with gender identity disorder usually feel uncomfortable wearing the clothes of their own sex and dress instead in clothes of the opposite sex. Their condition is not, however, transvestic fetishism (transvestism). People with that paraphilia cross-dress in order to become sexually aroused; persons with gender identity disorder have much deeper reasons for cross-dressing, reasons of gender identity (Bradley, 1995). In addition to engaging in cross-dressing, individuals with gender identity disorder often take up roles and activities that are traditionally associated with the other sex (Brown et al., 1996).

Sometimes gender identity disorder emerges in children (Zucker, 2000). Like adults with this disorder, they feel

Table 11-6 DSM-IV Checklist

GENDER IDENTITY DISORDER

1. Strong and persistent cross-gender identification (for example, a stated desire to be the other sex, frequent passing as the other sex, desire to live or be treated as the other sex, or the conviction that one has the typical feelings and reactions of the other sex).
2. Persistent discomfort with one's sex or a sense of inappropriateness in the gender role of that sex (for example, preoccupation with getting rid of primary and secondary sex characteristics or belief that one was born the wrong sex).
3. Significant distress or impairment.

Based on APA, 2000, 1994.

uncomfortable about their assigned sex and yearn to be members of the opposite sex. This childhood pattern usually disappears by adolescence or adulthood, but in some cases it develops into adult gender identity disorder (Cohen-Kettenis, 2001; Bradley, 1995). Thus adults with this disorder may have had a childhood gender identity disorder, but most children with the disorder do not become transsexual adults. Some adults with gender identity disorder do not develop any symptoms until mid-adulthood.

Various theories have been proposed to explain this disorder (Zucker, 2000; Sugar, 1995), but research to test the ideas has been limited and generally weak. Some clinicians suspect that biological factors play a key role in the disorder (Green, 2000), and one biological study has received considerable attention (Zhou et al., 1995). Dutch investigators autopsied the brains of six people who had changed their sex from male to female. They found that a cluster of cells in the hypothalamus called the *bed nucleus of stria terminalis (BST)* was only half as large in these subjects as it was in a control group of normal men. Normally, a woman's BST is much smaller than a man's, so in effect the subjects with gender identity disorder were found to have a female-sized BST. Scientists do not know for certain what the BST does in humans, but they know that it helps regulate sexual behavior in male rats. Although other interpretations of these findings are possible, it may well be that men who develop gender identity disorder have a key biological difference that leaves them very uncomfortable with their assigned sex characteristics.

Some adults with this disorder change their sexual characteristics by means of *hormone treatments* (Bradley, 1995). Physicians prescribe the female sex hormone *estrogen* for male patients, causing breast development, loss of body and facial hair, and change in body fat distribution. Similar treatments with the male sex hormone *testosterone* are given to women with gender identity disorder.

Hormone therapy and psychotherapy enable many persons with this disorder to lead a satisfactory existence in the gender role that they believe represents their true identity. For others, however, this is not enough, and their dissatisfaction leads them to undergo one of the most controversial practices in medicine: **sex-change surgery** (Liedl, 1999; Bradley, 1995). This surgery is preceded by one to two years of hormone therapy. The operation itself involves, for men, amputation of the penis, creation of an artificial vagina, and face-changing plastic surgery. For women, surgery may include bilateral mastectomy and hysterectomy. The procedure for creating a functioning penis, called *phalloplasty,* is performed

GENDER IDENTITY DISORDER A disorder in which a person persistently feels extremely uncomfortable about his or her assigned sex and strongly wishes to be a member of the opposite sex. Also known as *transsexualism.*

SEX-CHANGE SURGERY A surgical procedure that changes a person's sex organs and features, and, in turn, sexual identity.

James and Jan *Feeling like a woman trapped in a man's body, the British writer James Morris (left) underwent sex-change surgery, described in his 1974 autobiography,* Conundrum. *Today Jan Morris (right) is a successful author and seems comfortable with her change of gender.*

Homosexuality and Society

Homosexuality is not new; it has always existed in all cultures, as has the controversy that surrounds it. While most cultures do not openly advocate homosexuality, over the course of history few have condemned it so fiercely as Western culture does today. Nevertheless, research shows that a society's acceptance or rejection of people who engage in homosexual behavior does not affect the rate of the behavior.

Before 1973, the DSM listed homosexuality as a sexual disorder. Protests by gay activist groups and many psychotherapists eventually led to its elimination from the diagnostic manual as a sexual disorder. Most clinicians in the Western world now view homosexuality as a variant of normal sexual behavior, not a disorder (King & Bartlett, 1999).

Despite the growing acceptance of homosexuality by the clinical field, many people in Western society continue to hold antihomosexual attitudes and to spread myths about the lifestyles of homosexual persons (Kirby, 2000; Parker & Bhugra, 2000). Contrary to these myths, research has shown that homosexual persons do not suffer from gender confusion; they are not more prone to psychopathology than others; and there is not an identifiable "homosexual personality." Homosexual people are found in every socioeconomic group, every race, and every profession.

Today many organizations exist to support and lobby for homosexual people's rights, demanding equal treatment under the law and in society (Freiberg, 1994). One of the key issues affecting support for homosexual rights has been

the debate over whether homosexual people choose their lifestyle or whether it is a natural part of their physiological makeup. This debate has been fueled by findings—pro and con—from the scientific community. Some research suggests that homosexuality is not simply a lifestyle choice but linked to a physiological predisposition (Dawood et al., 2000; Pillard & Bailey, 1995; LeVay & Hamer et al., 1994). Such findings support the claim of the gay community that homosexuality is a naturally occurring phenomenon.

Some studies, for example, have suggested that homosexuality has a genetic component. In the early 1990s, two influential genetic linkage studies concluded that homosexuality may in some instances be passed on by the mother's genes (Hu et al., 1995; Hamer et al., 1993), although recent research has failed to support this particular conclusion (Rice et al., 1999). In addition, two studies found that when one identical twin was homosexual, his twin was also homosexual in more than 50 percent of the cases sampled. The number dropped to less than 20 percent when the siblings

were fraternal twins or nontwins and to under 10 percent when the siblings were adopted and biologically unrelated (Bailey et al., 1997, 1993, 1991). Although environmental factors also have a major impact on homosexuality— otherwise all persons with a homosexual identical twin would be homosexual— genetics may well play a key role in it.

Homosexuality continues to be a lifestyle that many people adopt, whether because of environmental or genetic factors. Now that most clinicians agree that homosexuality is not a disorder, a key issue remains: How will society react to a significant proportion of its population that typically differs from the rest in but one way—their sexual orientation? So far, Western society cannot claim to have dealt very effectively or fairly with this question, but at least a trend toward understanding and equality seems to be emerging. Research suggests that, through education and exposure, people of different sexual orientations can indeed learn to accept and work with one another (Beaty, 1999; Herek & Capitanio, 1993).

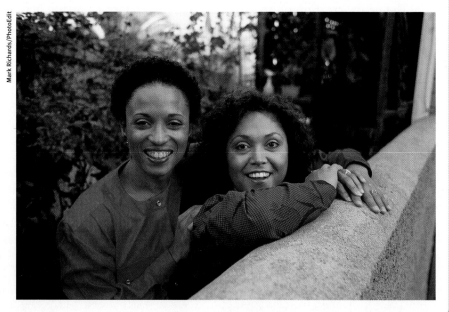

Mark Richards/PhotoEdit

Familiarity fosters acceptance *Although prejudice certainly remains, surveys indicate that the heterosexual public is growing more comfortable with displays of affection by homosexual couples—an important step toward the acceptance of differences in sexual orientation.*

in some cases, but it is not yet perfected. Doctors have, however, developed a silicone prosthesis that gives the patient the appearance of having male genitals (Hage & Bouman, 1992). Studies in Europe suggest that one of every 30,000 men and one of every 100,000 women seek sex-change surgery (APA, 2000).

Clinicians have heatedly debated whether surgery is an appropriate treatment for gender identity disorder. Some consider it a humane solution, perhaps the most satisfying one to people with the disorder (Cohen-Kettenis & Gooren, 1999; Cohen-Kettenis & van Goozen, 1997). Others argue that transsexual surgery is a "drastic nonsolution" for a largely psychological problem. The long-term psychological outcome of surgical sex reassignment is not clear. Some people seem to function well for years after such treatments (Rehman et al., 1999; Bradley, 1995), but others experience psychological difficulties. Without any form of treatment, gender identity disorder among adults is usually long-term, but some cases of recovery without intervention have reportedly occurred (Marks et al., 2000).

Our gender is so basic to our sense of identity that it is hard for most of us to imagine wanting to change it, much less to imagine the feelings of conflict and stress experienced by those who question their assigned gender. Whether the underlying cause is biological, psychological, or sociocultural, gender identity disorder is a dramatic dysfunction that shakes the foundations of the sufferer's existence.

SUMMING UP
Gender Identity Disorder

People with gender identity disorder persistently feel that they have been assigned to the wrong sex and would like to acquire the physical characteristics of the other sex. Men apparently outnumber women with this disorder by around 2 to 1. Its causes are not well understood. Hormone treatments and psychotherapy have been used in many cases of this disorder. Sex-change operations have also been performed, but the appropriateness of surgery as a form of "treatment" has been hotly debated.

CROSSROADS:
A Private Topic Draws Public Attention

For all the public interest in sexual disorders, clinical theorists and practitioners have only recently begun to understand their nature and how to treat them. Although insights about the causes and treatment of paraphilias and gender identity disorder remain limited, 30 years of studying sexual dysfunctions are now paying dividends, and people with such dysfunctions are no longer doomed to a lifetime of sexual frustration.

Studies of sexual dysfunctions have pointed to many psychological, sociocultural, and biological causes. Often, as we have seen with so many disorders, the various causes may *interact* to produce a particular dysfunction, as in erectile disorder and female orgasmic disorder. For some dysfunctions, however, *one cause* alone is dominant, and integrated explanations may be inaccurate and unproductive. Premature ejaculation, for example, appears to have largely psychological causes, while dyspareunia usually has a physical cause.

The past three decades have also witnessed important progress in the treatment of sexual dysfunctions, and people with such problems are now often helped greatly by therapy. Sex therapy today is usually a complex program tailored to the particular problems of an individual or couple. Techniques from the various models may be combined, although in some instances the particular problem calls primarily for one approach.

One of the most important insights to emerge from all this work is that *education* about sexual dysfunctions can be as important as therapy. Sexual myths are still taken so seriously that they often lead to feelings of shame, self-hatred,

ConsiderThis

● The prevalence rates for sexual behavior are typically based on surveys of the general population. However, many people feel that sex is a private matter and refuse to participate in such surveys, and those who do respond tend to be more liberal, sexually experienced, and unconventional than the norm. What problems might this cause for researchers of sexual dysfunctioning?

isolation, and hopelessness—feelings that themselves contribute to sexual difficulty. Even a modest amount of education can help persons who are in treatment.

In fact, most people can benefit from a more accurate understanding of sexual functioning. Public education about sexual functioning—through books, television and radio, school programs, group presentations, and the like—has become a major clinical focus. It is important that these efforts continue and even increase in the coming years.

KEY TERMS

sexual dysfunction p. 309
sexual response cycle p. 310
desire phase p. 310
hypoactive sexual desire p. 311
sexual aversion disorder p. 311
prolactin p. 313
testosterone p. 313
estrogen p. 313
excitement phase p. 314
female sexual arousal disorder p. 314
male erectile disorder p. 314
nocturnal penile tumescence (NPT) p. 316
performance anxiety p. 316
spectator role p. 316

orgasm phase p. 316
premature ejaculation p. 317
male orgasmic disorder p. 318
female orgasmic disorder p. 319
vaginismus p. 321
dyspareunia p. 322
sex therapy p. 323
sensate focus p. 324
affectual awareness p. 326
tease technique p. 327
sildenafil (Viagra) p. 327
directed masturbation training p. 329
paraphilia p. 330
fetishism p. 331

aversion therapy p. 332
masturbatory satiation p. 332
orgasmic reorientation p. 332
transvestic fetishism p. 332
exhibitionism p. 333
voyeurism p. 334
frotteurism p. 334
pedophilia p. 334
relapse-prevention training p. 335
sexual masochism p. 335
sexual sadism p. 336
gender identity disorder p. 338
hormone treatments p. 339
sex-change surgery p. 339

QUICK QUIZ

1. What sexual dysfunctions are associated with the desire phase of the sexual response cycle? How common are they, and what causes them? pp. 310–313

2. What are the symptoms and prevalence of female sexual arousal disorder and male erectile disorder? To which phase of the sexual response cycle are they related? pp. 314–315

3. What are the possible causes of male erectile disorder? pp. 315–316

4. Which sexual dysfunctions seem to involve performance anxiety and the spectator role? pp. 316–319

5. What are the symptoms, rates, and leading causes of premature ejaculation, male orgasmic disorder, and female orgasmic disorder? To which phase of the sexual response cycle are they related? pp. 317–321

6. Identify, describe, and explain the sexual pain disorders. pp. 321–322

7. What are the general features of modern sex therapy? What particular techniques are further used to treat specific sexual dysfunctions? pp. 323–330

8. List, describe, and explain the leading paraphilias. pp. 330–338

9. Describe the treatment techniques of antiandrogens, aversion therapy, masturbatory satiation, orgasmic reorientation, and relapse-prevention training. Which paraphilias have they been used to treat, and how successful are they? pp. 331–337

10. Distinguish transvestism from gender identity disorder (transsexualism). What are the leading treatments for gender identity disorder? pp. 332–333, 338–341

How do people with gender identity disorder feel about themselves and their bodies? ▲ *How does gender identity disorder affect a person's life and functioning?* ▲ *Weigh the pros and cons of sex-change surgery.* ▲ *Observe the results of sex-change surgery.* ▲ *How might sexual feelings be expressed in dreams?*

Search the *Fundamentals of Abnormal Psychology* CD-ROM for

▲ Chapter 11 video case and discussion
   "Brad"—Gender Identity Disorder

▲ Chapter 11 practice test and feedback

▲ Additional video case and discussion
   "Larry"—Psychoanalytic Therapy Session

Log on to the Comer Web Page for

▲ Suggested Web links, research exercises, FAQ page, additional Chapter 11 practice test questions
   <www.worthpublishers.com/comer>

Source: *The World of Abnormal Psychology* (The Annenberg/CPB Collection, 1992)

Schizophrenia

SCHIZOPHRENIA A psychotic disorder in which personal, social, and occupational functioning deteriorate as a result of strange perceptions, disturbed thought processes, unusual emotions, and motor abnormalities.

PSYCHOSIS A state in which a person loses contact with reality in key ways.

What . . . does schizophrenia mean to me? It means fatigue and confusion, it means trying to separate every experience into the real and the unreal and sometimes not being aware of where the edges overlap. It means trying to think straight when there is a maze of experiences getting in the way, and when thoughts are continually being sucked out of your head so that you become embarrassed to speak at meetings. It means feeling sometimes that you are inside your head and visualizing yourself walking over your brain, or watching another girl wearing your clothes and carrying out actions as you think them. It means knowing that you are continually "watched," that you can never succeed in life because the laws are all against you and knowing that your ultimate destruction is never far away.

(Rollin, 1980, p. 162)

Does it surprise you to see such a clear firsthand description of how it feels to suffer from **schizophrenia?** People who have this disorder, though they previously functioned well, or at least acceptably, deteriorate into an isolated world of unusual perceptions, odd thoughts, disturbed emotions, and motor abnormalities. They experience **psychosis,** a loss of contact with reality. Their ability to perceive and respond to the environment becomes so disturbed that they may not be able to function at home, with friends, in school, or at work. They may have hallucinations (false sensory perceptions) or delusions (false beliefs), or they may withdraw into a private world. Taking LSD or abusing amphetamines or cocaine may produce psychosis (see Chapter 10). So may injuries or diseases of the brain. Most commonly, however, psychosis appears in the form of schizophrenia.

Approximately 1 of every 100 people in the world suffers from schizophrenia during his or her lifetime (APA, 2000). An estimated 2.5 million with the disorder are currently living in the United States (McGuire, 2000). Its financial cost is enormous—estimated at more than $100 billion annually, including the costs of hospitalization, lost wages, and disability benefits (Black & Andreasen, 1994). The emotional cost is even greater. In addition, sufferers have an increased risk of suicide and of physical—often fatal—illness (Gilmore et al., 2001; Meltzer, 1998; Brown, 1997). As we discussed in Chapter 7, up to 15 percent of persons with the disorder commit suicide (Andreasen, 1999).

Although schizophrenia appears in all socioeconomic groups, it is found more frequently in the lower levels (see Figure 12-1 on the next page), leading some theorists to believe that the stress of poverty is itself a cause of the disorder. However, it could also be that schizophrenia causes its victims to fall from a higher to a lower socioeconomic level or to remain poor because they are unable to function effectively (Munk & Mortensen, 1992). This is sometimes called the *downward drift* theory.

Equal numbers of men and women receive a diagnosis of schizophrenia. In men, however, the disorder often begins earlier and may be more severe (Moriarty et al., 2001; Gold, 1998). Almost 3 percent of all those who are divorced or separated suffer from schizophrenia sometime during their lives, compared with 1 percent of married people and 2 percent of people

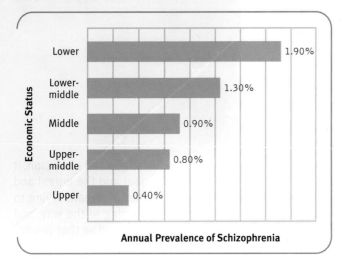

FIGURE 12-1 **Socioeconomic class and schizophrenia** *According to surveys, poor people in the United States are much more likely than wealthy people to experience schizophrenia. (Adapted from Keith et al., 1991.)*

who remain single (Keith et al., 1991). Again, however, it is not clear whether marital problems are a cause or a result.

As many as 2.1 percent of African Americans receive a diagnosis of schizophrenia, compared with 1.4 percent of white Americans (Keith et al., 1991). According to census findings, however, African Americans are also more likely to be poor and to experience marital separation. When these two factors are controlled for, the rates of schizophrenia are equal for both racial groups.

People today, like those of the past, show great interest in schizophrenia, flocking to plays and movies (including the remarkably popular horror movies) whose plots center on the disorder. Yet, as we shall see, all too many people with schizophrenia are neglected in our country, their needs almost entirely ignored. Although effective interventions have been developed, most sufferers live without adequate treatment and without fulfilling their potential as human beings (Torrey, 1997).

The Clinical Picture of Schizophrenia

The symptoms of schizophrenia vary greatly, and so do its triggers, course, and responsiveness to treatment (APA, 2000). In fact, a number of clinicians believe that schizophrenia is actually a group of separate disorders that happen to have some common features. To see the variety of forms schizophrenia may take, consider three people who were diagnosed as suffering from it. The cases are taken from the files of Silvano Arieti (1974), a famous theorist on the disorder.

Inner torment *Like this young woman, people with schizophrenia often appear to be trying to fight off the strange thoughts and perceptions that pervade their minds.*

"I feel cheated by having this illness."

Individual with schizophrenia, 1996

Ann, 26 years old: Ann graduated from high school and from a school for commercial art. . . . At the age of 18 she began going out with Henry. . . . They became engaged shortly thereafter and went out together frequently until their marriage. . . . Married life was considered a boring routine by both Ann and Henry. There was very little conversation between them. . . .

Ann's disappointment in Henry increased. They had nothing in common; she was artistically inclined, whereas he had only an ordinary, conventional outlook toward life. It was at this time that she started to go dancing and then met Charles. Her interest in him increased, but . . . a divorce was not compatible with the precepts of the Catholic church. Her conflict grew and put her in a state of great agitation. . . .

. . . One evening she came home from dancing and told her mother that she was going to give up her husband Henry, marry Charles, go to Brazil with him, and have twenty babies. She was talking very fast and saying many things, several of which were incomprehensible. At the same time she also told her mother that she was seeing the Virgin Mary in visions. She then went to her mother-in-law and told her to take back her son Henry, because he was too immature. The following day Ann went to work and tried to get the entire office down on their knees with her to recite the rosary. A few days later, her mother took her to a priest, whom she "told off" in no uncertain terms. She finally spit at him. A psychiatrist was consulted, and he recommended hospitalization.

(Arieti, 1974, pp. 173–177)

THE WRONG SPLIT
Although people with schizophrenia experience a split from reality, they do not display a "split" or multiple personality. Despite popular misconceptions, that pattern is indicative of a *dissociative disorder*.

Richard, 23 years old: In high school, Richard was an average student. After graduation from high school, he was drafted into the army. . . . Richard remembered [the] period . . . after his discharge from the army . . . as one of the worst in his life. . . . Any, even remote, anticipation of disappointment was able to provoke attacks of anxiety in him. . . .

Approximately two years after his return to civilian life, Richard left his job because he became overwhelmed by these feelings of lack of confidence in himself, and he refused to go look for another one. He stayed home most of the day. His mother would nag him that he was too lazy and unwilling to do anything. He became slower and slower in dressing and undressing and taking care of himself. When he went out of the house, he felt compelled "to give interpretations" to everything he looked at. He did not know what to do outside the house, where to go, where to turn. If he saw a red light at a crossing, he would interpret it as a message that he should not go in that direction. If he saw an arrow, he would follow the arrow interpreting it as a sign sent by God that he should go in that direction. Feeling lost and horrified, he would go home and stay there, afraid to go out because going out meant making decisions or choices that he felt unable to make. He reached the point where he stayed home most of the time. But even at home, he was tortured by his symptoms. He could not act; any motion that he felt like making seemed to him an insurmountable obstacle, because he did not know whether he should make it or not. He was increasingly afraid of doing the wrong thing. Such fears prevented him from dressing, undressing, eating, and so forth. He felt paralyzed and lay motionless in bed. He gradually became worse, was completely motionless, and had to be hospitalized. . . .

Being undecided, he felt blocked, and often would remain mute and motionless, like a statue, even for days.

(Arieti, 1974, pp. 153–155)

"What's so great about reality?"

Individual with schizophrenia, 1988

Laura, 40 years old: Laura's desire was to become independent and leave home [in Austria] as soon as possible. . . . She became a professional dancer at the age of 20 . . . and was booked for vaudeville theaters in many European countries. . . .

It was during one of her tours in Germany that Laura met her husband. . . . They were married and went to live in a small provincial town in France where the husband's business was. . . . She spent a year in that town and was very unhappy. . . . [Finally] Laura and her husband decided to emigrate to the United States. . . .

They had no children, and Laura . . . showed interest in pets. She had a dog to whom she was very devoted. The dog became sick and partially paralyzed, and veterinarians felt that there was no hope of recovery. . . . Finally [her husband] broached the problem to his wife, asking her "Should the dog be destroyed or not?" From that time on Laura became restless, agitated, and depressed. . . .

"I shouldn't precisely have chosen madness if there had been any choice, but once such a thing has taken hold of you, you can't very well get out of it."

Vincent van Gogh, 1889

POSITIVE SYMPTOMS Symptoms of schizophrenia that seem to be excesses of or bizarre additions to normal thoughts, emotions, or behaviors.

DELUSION A strange false belief firmly held despite evidence to the contrary.

FORMAL THOUGHT DISORDER A disturbance in the production and organization of thought.

LOOSE ASSOCIATIONS A common thinking disturbance in schizophrenia, characterized by rapid shifts from one topic of conversation to another. Also known as *derailment*.

HALLUCINATION The experiencing of sights, sounds, or other perceptions in the absence of external stimuli.

> . . . Later Laura started to complain about the neighbors. A woman who lived on the floor beneath them was knocking on the wall to irritate her. According to the husband, this woman had really knocked on the wall a few times; he had heard the noises. However, Laura became more and more concerned about it. She would wake up in the middle of the night under the impression that she was hearing noises from the apartment downstairs. She would become upset and angry at the neighbors. . . . Later she became more disturbed. She started to feel that the neighbors were now recording everything she said; maybe they had hidden wires in the apartment. She started to feel "funny" sensations. There were many strange things happening, which she did not know how to explain; people were looking at her in a funny way in the street; in the butcher shop, the butcher had purposely served her last, although she was in the middle of the line. During the next few days she felt that people were planning to harm either her or her husband. . . . In the evening when she looked at television, it became obvious to her that the programs referred to her life. Often the people on the programs were just repeating what she had thought. They were stealing her ideas. She wanted to go to the police and report them.
>
> *(Arieti, 1974, pp. 165–168)*

What Are the Symptoms of Schizophrenia?

Ann, Richard, and Laura all deteriorated from a normal level of functioning to become ineffective in dealing with the world. Each experienced some of the symptoms found in schizophrenia. The symptoms can be grouped into three categories: *positive symptoms* (excesses of thought, emotion, and behavior), *negative symptoms* (deficits of thought, emotion, and behavior), and *psychomotor symptoms*.

POSITIVE SYMPTOMS **Positive symptoms** are "pathological excesses," or bizarre additions, to a person's behavior. *Delusions, disorganized thinking and speech, heightened perceptions and hallucinations,* and *inappropriate affect* are the ones most often found in schizophrenia.

Delusions of grandeur *In 1892, an artist who was a patient at a mental hospital claimed credit for this painting,* Self-Portrait as Christ. *Although few people with schizophrenia have his artistic skill, a number display similar delusions of grandeur.*

Mutter Museum, College of Physicians of Philadelphia

DELUSIONS Many people with schizophrenia develop **delusions,** ideas that they believe wholeheartedly but that have no basis in fact. Some people hold a single delusion that dominates their lives and behavior, whereas others have many delusions. *Delusions of persecution* are the most common in schizophrenia (APA, 2000). People with such delusions believe that they are being plotted or discriminated against, spied on, slandered, threatened, attacked, or deliberately victimized. Laura believed that her neighbors were trying to irritate her and that other people were trying to harm her and her husband. People with schizophrenia may also experience *delusions of reference,* in which they attach special and personal meaning to the actions of others or to various objects or events. Richard, for example, interpreted arrows on street signs as indicators of the direction he should take. People who experience *delusions of grandeur* believe themselves to be great inventors, religious saviors, or other specially empowered persons. And those with *delusions of control* believe their feelings, thoughts, and actions are being controlled by other people.

DISORGANIZED THINKING AND SPEECH People with schizophrenia may not be able to think logically and may speak in peculiar ways. These **formal thought disorders** can cause the sufferer great confusion and make communication extremely difficult (Docherty, DeRosa, & Andreasen, 1996). Often they take the form of positive symptoms (that is, pathological excesses), as in *loose associations, neologisms, perseveration,* and *clang.*

People who
mon formal thou
lieving that their inc **associations,** or **derailment,** the most com-
ophrenia, asked about . rapidly shift from one topic to another, be-
tements make sense. One man with schiz-
ms, responded:

The problem is insects. My
5 foot 10 inches. You know, 10 ed to collect insects. He's now a man
draw, and watch television. rite number. I also like to dance,

Some people with schizophrenia use
typically have meaning only to the person isms, made-up words that
stated, for example, "I am here from a foreign them. One individual
to have a *plausity* of all acts of amendment to g ersity ... and you have
code ... it is an *amorition* law ... the children h gh for the children's
tive law ..." (Vetter, 1969, p. 189). Others may disp to have this *accentua-*
disorder of *perseveration,* in which they repeat their wo the formal thought
again and again (Capleton, 1996). Finally, some use *cla* and statements
think or express themselves. When asked how she was feeling one person
replied, "Well, hell, it's well to tell." Another described the weather as "So
hot, you know it runs on a cot." Research suggests that some disorganized
speech or thinking may appear long before a full pattern of schizophreni
unfolds (Amminger et al., 1999).

HEIGHTENED PERCEPTIONS AND HALLUCINATIONS The perceptions and atter-
tion of some people with schizophrenia seem to intensify. The persons may
feel that their senses are being flooded by all the sights and sounds that surround
them. This makes it almost impossible for them to attend to anything important:

> Everything seems to grip my attention ... I am speaking to you just now, but I
> can hear noises going on next door and in the corridor. I find it difficult to shut
> these out, and it makes it more difficult for me to concentrate on what I am say-
> ing to you.
>
> *(McGhie and Chapman, 1961)*

Laboratory studies have repeatedly found problems of perception and attention among people with schizophrenia (Kent & Turpin, 2000). Such problems
also contribute to memory impairment, another difficulty experienced by many
individuals with the disorder (APA, 2000; Nieman et al., 2000). The perception
and attention problems may develop years before the onset of the actual disorder
(Sabin et al., 2001; Cornblatt & Keilp, 1994).

Another kind of perceptual problem in schizophrenia consists of **hallucinations,** perceptions that occur in the absence of external stimuli. People who have
auditory hallucinations, by far the most common kind in schizophrenia, hear
sounds and voices that seem to come from outside their heads (APA, 1994;
Mueser, Bellack, & Brady, 1990). The voices may talk directly to the hallucinator,
perhaps giving commands or warning of dangers, or they may be experienced as
overheard:

> The voices ... were mostly heard in my head, though I often heard them in the
> air, or in different parts of the room. Every voice was different, and each beauti-
> ful, and generally, speaking or singing in a different tone and measure, and re-
> sembling those of relations or friends. There appeared to be many in my head, I
> should say upwards of fourteen. I divide them, as they styled themselves, or one
> another, into voices of contrition and voices of joy and honour.
>
> *("Perceval's Narrative" in Bateson, 1974)*

No, it's not "the King" *But surveys
as many as one of every eight Amer
lieves that Elvis Presley is still alive
that has led to numerous Elvis sight
Eleven stores around the country an
aged an army of Elvis impersonators
stop short of calling such beliefs del
however, noting that the Elvis loyali
hold on to their beliefs with a high d
conviction. Most can be persuaded t
has indeed "left the building."*

"Last night I saw upon the stair
A little man who wasn't there.
He wasn't there again today.
Oh, how I wish he'd go away!"

Nurse

D. Silbersweig, M.D., and E. Stern, M.D., Functional Neuroimaging Laboratory,

Relationships of the Mind

While playing in a professional tennis tournament in 1993, Monica Seles (right) was stabbed by a 38-year-old man from Germany. The attacker was obsessed with another tennis star, Steffi Graf, and believed that it was his responsibility to help Graf's career by striking down her rival. Seles did not return to professional tennis for two years.

In 1989 the actress Rebecca Shaeffer of the television show *My Sister Sam* was shot and killed outside her West Hollywood apartment by a fan. He had closely followed Shaeffer's career for months, and eventually he journeyed to her apartment building. When she failed to greet him warmly, he took her rebuff as a sign of arrogance and shot her.

At least 200,000 people are victimized by stalkers in the United States each year (Corwin, 1993). As many as 1 in 12 women and 1 in 50 men are stalked during their lifetimes (Abrams & Robinson, 1998; Klein, 1998). The majority of victims experience substantial stress; indeed, many develop posttraumatic stress

symptoms (Kamphuis & Emmelkamp, 2001) Some stalkers suffer from *erotomanic delusions*, beliefs without any basis watsoever that they are loved by someone who may actually be a casual acquaintance or a complete stranger (Silva et al., 2000; Anderson, 1993). Some pople with such delusions, like Shaeffe's and Graf's pursuers, develop fantasis in which they feel driven to protect, harm, or even kill the object of their desire (Menzies et al., 1995).

Consider This

◉ Some experts believe that erotomanic delusions are more common today than they were in the past. Why might this be? • Do high-profile cases such as Seles's and Shaeffer's heighten or lower the probability that other cases of erotomanic delusions and stalking will emerge?

The human brain during hallucinations *This PET scan, taken at the moment a subject was experiencing auditory and visual hallucinations, shows heightened activity (yellow-orange) in hearing-related tissues at the brain's surface (Silbersweig et al., 1995). Conversely, the front of the brain, which is responsible for determining the source of sounds and other sensations, was quiet. Thus a person who is hallucinating seems to hear sounds produced by his or her own brain, but the brain cannot recognize that the sounds are actually coming from within.*

Research suggests that people with auditory hallucinations actually produce the nerve signals of sounds in their brains, "hear" them, and then believe that external sources are responsible. One study measured blood flow in *Broca's area*, the region of the brain that helps people produce speech (McGuire et al., 1996, 1995, 1993). The researchers found more blood flow in Broca's area while patients were having auditory hallucinations. A related study instructed six men with schizophrenia to press a button whenever they experienced an auditory hallucination (Silbersweig et al., 1995). PET scans revealed increased activity near the brain's surface, in the tissues that are needed for hearing, when they pressed the button.

Hallucinations can also involve any of the other senses. *Tactile* hallucinations may take the form of tingling, burning, or electric-shock sensations. *Somatic* hallucinations feel as if something is happening inside the body, such as a snake crawling inside one's stomach. Visual hallucinations may produce vague perceptions of colors or clouds or distinct visions of people or objects. People with *gustatory* hallucinations regularly find that their food or drink tastes strange, and people with *olfactory* hallucinations smell odors that no one else does, such as the smell of poison or smoke.

Hallucinations and delusions often occur together. A woman who hears voices issuing commands, for example, may have the delusion that the commands are being placed in her head by someone else. Similarly, a man with delusions of persecution may hallucinate the smell of poison in his bedroom or the taste of poison in his coffee. Regardless of which comes first, the hallucination and delusion eventually feed into each other:

> I thought the voices I heard were being transmitted through the walls of my apartment and through the washer and dryer and that these machines were talking and telling me things. I felt that the government agencies had planted transmitters and receivers in my apartment so that I could hear what they were saying and they could hear what I was saying.
>
> *(Anonymous, 1996, p. 183)*

INAPPROPRIATE AFFECT Many people with schizophrenia display **inappropriate affect,** emotions that are unsuited to the situation. They may smile when making a serious statement or on being told terrible news, or they may become upset in situations that should make them happy. They may also undergo inappropriate shifts in mood. During a tender conversation with his wife, for example, a man with schizophrenia suddenly started yelling obscenities at her and complaining about her inadequacies.

In some cases, at least, these emotions may be merely a response to other features of the disorder. Consider a woman with schizophrenia who smiles when told of her husband's serious illness. She may not actually be happy about the news; she may not even be understanding or hearing it. She could, for example, be responding instead to a joke coming from an auditory hallucination.

NEGATIVE SYMPTOMS **Negative symptoms** are those that seem to be "pathological deficits," characteristics that are lacking in an individual (Buchanan & Carpenter, 2001). *Poverty of speech, blunted and flat affect, loss of volition,* and *social withdrawal* are commonly found in schizophrenia. These deficits greatly affect one's life and activities.

POVERTY OF SPEECH People with schizophrenia often display **alogia,** or **poverty of speech,** a reduction in speech or speech content. Some people with this symptom think and say very little. Others say quite a bit but still manage to convey little meaning (Baltaxe & Simmons, 1995).

BLUNTED AND FLAT AFFECT Many people with schizophrenia have a *blunted affect*—they show less anger, sadness, joy, and other feelings than do most people. And some show almost no emotions at all, a condition known as **flat affect.** Their faces are still, their eye contact is poor, and their voices are monotonous. It may be that people with these problems continue to feel emotion but cannot express it as others do. One study had people view very emotional film clips. Those with schizophrenia showed less facial expression than the others; however, they reported feeling just as much positive and negative emotion and in fact displayed greater skin arousal (Kring & Neale, 1996).

LOSS OF VOLITION Many people with schizophrenia experience **avolition,** or apathy, feeling drained of energy and interest in normal goals and unable to start or follow through on a course of action (Lysaker & Bell, 1995). This problem is particularly common in people who have had schizophrenia for many years, as if they have been worn down by it. The avolition and indecisiveness of Richard, the young man whose case was presented earlier, made eating, dressing, and undressing impossible ordeals for him.

SOCIAL WITHDRAWAL People with schizophrenia may withdraw from their social environment and attend only to their own ideas and fantasies. Because their ideas are illogical and confused, the withdrawal helps distance them still further from reality. The social withdrawal seems also to lead to a breakdown of social skills, including the ability to recognize other people's needs and emotions accurately (Trumbetta & Mueser, 2001; Penn et al., 1997).

PSYCHOMOTOR SYMPTOMS People with schizophrenia sometimes experience *psychomotor symptoms,* for example, awkward movements or repeated grimaces

INAPPROPRIATE AFFECT A symptom of schizophrenia in which a person displays emotions that are unsuited to the situation.

NEGATIVE SYMPTOMS Symptoms of schizophrenia that seem to be deficits in normal thought, emotions, or behaviors.

ALOGIA A symptom of schizophrenia in which the person shows a decrease in speech or speech content. Also known as *poverty of speech.*

FLAT AFFECT A symptom of schizophrenia in which the person shows almost no emotions at all.

AVOLITION A symptom of schizophrenia marked by apathy and an inability to start or complete a course of action.

SOCIAL IMPACT
One study indicates that people with schizophrenia who maintain frequent social interactions live 25 percent longer on average than those with few such interactions (Christensen et al., 1999).

The Oskar Diethelm Library, History of Psychiatry Section, Department of Psychiatry, Cornell University Medical College and The New York Hospital, New York.

A catatonic pose *These patients, photographed in the early 1900s, display features of catatonia, including catatonic posturing, in which they assume bizarre positions for long periods of time.*

and odd gestures (Carnahan, Elliott, & Velamoor, 1996). The unusual gestures often seem to have a private purpose—perhaps magical.

The psychomotor symptoms of schizophrenia may take extreme forms, collectively called **catatonia.** People in a *catatonic stupor* stop responding to their environment, remaining motionless and silent for long stretches of time. Recall how Richard would lie motionless and mute in bed for days. Some people show *catatonic rigidity,* maintaining a rigid, upright posture for hours and resisting efforts to be moved. Others exhibit *catatonic posturing,* assuming awkward, bizarre positions for long periods of time. Finally, people who display *catatonic excitement,* a different form of catatonia, move excitedly, sometimes with wild waving of arms and legs.

What Is the Course of Schizophrenia?

Schizophrenia usually first appears between the person's late teens and mid-30s (APA, 2000). Many sufferers seem to go through three phases—prodromal, active, and residual. During the *prodromal phase,* schizophrenic symptoms are not yet obvious, but persons are beginning to deteriorate. They may withdraw socially, speak in vague or odd ways, or express little emotion. During the *active phase,* schizophrenic symptoms become apparent. Sometimes this phase is triggered by stress in the person's life. For Laura, the middle-aged woman described earlier, the immediate trigger was the failing health and eventual death of her cherished dog. Finally, many persons eventually enter a *residual phase,* in which they return to a prodromal-like level of functioning. The striking symptoms of the active phase lessen, but some negative symptoms, such as blunted emotions, may remain. Although as many as one-quarter of patients recover completely from schizophrenia (McGuire, 2000), the majority continue to have at least some residual problems for the rest of their lives (Putnam et al., 1996).

Each of these phases may last for days or for years. A fuller recovery from schizophrenia is more likely in subjects who functioned quite well before the disorder (had good *premorbid functioning*) or whose disorder was first triggered by stress, came on quickly, or developed during middle age (Lindström, 1996; Tolbert, 1996). Relapses are apparently more likely during times of stress (Norman & Malla, 2001, 1995; Hultman et al., 1997).

Diagnosing Schizophrenia

DSM-IV calls for a diagnosis of schizophrenia only after signs of the disorder continue for six months or more (see Table 12-1). In addition, people must show a deterioration in their work, social relations,

Table 12-1 DSM-IV Checklist

SCHIZOPHRENIA

1. At least two of the following symptoms, each present for a significant portion of time during a one-month period:
   a. Delusions.
   b. Hallucinations.
   c. Disorganized speech.
   d. Grossly disorganized or catatonic behavior.
   e. Negative symptoms.
2. Functioning markedly below the level achieved prior to onset.
3. Continuous signs of the disturbance for at least six months, at least one month of which includes symptoms in full and active form (as opposed to attentuated form).

Based on APA, 2000, 1994.

and ability to care for themselves. The DSM distinguishes five patterns of the disorder.

The central symptoms of **disorganized type of schizophrenia** are confusion, incoherence, and flat or inappropriate affect. Attention and perception problems, extreme social withdrawal, and odd mannerisms or grimaces are also common. So is silliness: some patients giggle constantly without apparent reason. This is why the pattern was first called "hebephrenic," after Hebe, the Greek goddess who, according to Greek mythology, often acted like a clown.

The central feature of **catatonic type of schizophrenia** is a psychomotor disturbance of some sort. Some of the people in this category spend their time in a catatonic stupor; others display catatonic excitement. Richard, the unemployed young man who became mute and statuelike, might receive a diagnosis of this type of schizophrenia.

People with **paranoid type of schizophrenia** have an organized system of delusions and auditory hallucinations that may guide their lives. Laura would receive this diagnosis. She believed that people were out to get her (delusions of persecution) and that persons on television were stealing her ideas (delusions of reference). In addition, she heard "noises" from the apartment downstairs and felt "funny sensations" that supported her beliefs.

CATATONIA A pattern of extreme psychomotor symptoms found in some forms of schizophrenia, which may include catatonic stupor, rigidity, or posturing.

DISORGANIZED TYPE OF SCHIZOPHRENIA A type of schizophrenia marked primarily by confusion, incoherence, and flat or inappropriate affect.

CATATONIC TYPE OF SCHIZOPHRENIA A type of schizophrenia dominated by severe psychomotor disturbances.

PARANOID TYPE OF SCHIZOPHRENIA A type of schizophrenia in which the person has an organized system of delusions and hallucinations.

A CLOSER LOOK

Howling for Attention

It's when I was bitten by a rabid dog.... When I'm emotionally upset, I feel as if I am turning into something else: my fingers go numb, as if I had pins and needles right in the middle of my hand; I can no longer control myself.... I get the feeling I'm becoming a wolf. I look at myself in the mirror and I witness my transformation. It's no longer my face; it changes completely. I stare, my pupils dilate, and I feel as if hairs are growing all over my body, as if my teeth are getting longer.... I feel as if my skin is no longer mine.

(BENEZECH, DEWITTE, & BOURGEOIS, 1989)

*L*ycanthropy, the delusion of being an animal, is a rare psychological syndrome. The word "lycanthropy" comes from the Greek *lykos*, wolf, and *anthropos*, man. Accounts have been found all over the world of people who take on the characteristics and behavior of wolves or other animals. Belief in these tales has persisted for centuries. In the Middle Ages, lycanthropy was thought to be the result of demonic possession (Lehmann, 1985). In some societies it occurred after special ointments, probably hallucinogenic drugs, were applied, often for religious purposes (Lévi-Strauss, 1977). In other societies, cases seem to have been closely linked to mental disorders, including schizophrenia, severe mood disorders, and certain forms of brain damage.

Mention of lycanthropy continues to produce an image of a werewolf baring its fangs at a terrified villager on a fog-shrouded moor. The legend was that the former had been bitten by another werewolf in an unbroken chain that passes on the legacy. But there are now more reasonable explanations for this type of behavior. One explanation is that some people afflicted with lycanthropy actually suffer from *congenital generalized hypertrichosis,* an extremely rare disease marked by excessive amounts of hair on the face and upper body (Maugh, 1995). Others may suffer from *porphyria,* an inherited blood disease whose victims sprout extra facial hair and are sensitive to sunlight. Still another current explanation ties lycanthropy to a disturbance in the activity of the temporal lobe of the brain, which is close to areas of the brain that may be responsible for visual hallucinations.

Crying wolf? *In the film* An American Werewolf in London, *a possessed man watches in terror as his hand stretches into the forepaw of a wolf.*

Despite these rational hypotheses, beliefs in werewolves as supernatural beings are likely to continue for the foreseeable future. Tales of demonic possession are more exciting than histories of congenital disease or temporal lobe abnormalities. Nor are publishers or movie producers likely to say good-bye to such good friends. Old explanations of lycanthropy may be flawed scientifically, but the profits they produce are far from a delusion.

The Kobal Collection

UNDIFFERENTIATED TYPE OF SCHIZO-PHRENIA A type of schizophrenia in which no single set of psychotic symptoms dominates.

RESIDUAL TYPE OF SCHIZOPHRENIA A type of schizophrenia in which the acute symptoms of the disorder have lessened in strength and number, yet remain in residual form.

TYPE I SCHIZOPHRENIA A type of schizophrenia characterized mainly by positive symptoms, such as delusions, hallucinations, and certain formal thought disorders.

TYPE II SCHIZOPHRENIA A type of schizophrenia in which the person experiences mostly negative symptoms, such as flat affect, poverty of speech, and loss of volition.

When people with this disorder do not fall neatly into one of the other categories, they are diagnosed with **undifferentiated type of schizophrenia.** Because this category is somewhat vague, it has been assigned to a wide assortment of unusual patterns over the years. Many clinicians believe that the category is in fact overused.

When the symptoms of schizophrenia lessen in strength and number yet remain in a residual form, the patient's diagnosis is usually changed to **residual type of schizophrenia.** As we observed earlier, people with this pattern may continue to display blunted or inappropriate emotions, as well as social withdrawal, eccentric behavior, and some illogical thinking.

Apart from these DSM-IV categories, many researchers believe that a distinction between so-called Type I and Type II schizophrenia helps predict the course of the disorder. **Type I schizophrenia** is dominated by positive symptoms, such as delusions, hallucinations, and certain formal thought disorders (Crow, 1995, 1985, 1982, 1980). **Type II schizophrenia** features negative symptoms, such as flat affect, poverty of speech, and loss of volition. Type I patients generally have a better adjustment before the onset of the disorder, later onset of symptoms, and greater likelihood of improvement. In addition, the positive symptoms of Type I schizophrenia seem to be closely linked to *biochemical* abnormalities in the brain, whereas the negative symptoms of Type II schizophrenia have been tied to *structural* abnormalities in the brain (Crow, 1995).

SUMMING UP
The Clinical Picture of Schizophrenia

Schizophrenia is a disorder in which personal, social, and occupational functioning deteriorate as a result of disturbed thought processes, strange perceptions, unusual emotional states, and motor abnormalities. Approximately 1 percent of the world's population suffers from this disorder.

Symptoms of Schizophrenia The symptoms of schizophrenia fall into three categories: Positive symptoms include delusions, certain formal thought disorders, hallucinations and other disturbances in perception, and inappropriate affect. Negative symptoms include poverty of speech, flat affect, loss of volition, and social withdrawal. The disorder may also be marked by psychomotor symptoms. Schizophrenia usually emerges during late adolescence or early adulthood and progresses through three phases: prodromal, active, and residual.

Diagnosing Schizophrenia DSM-IV identifies five patterns of schizophrenia: disorganized, catatonic, paranoid, undifferentiated, and residual type. In addition, clinicians have distinguished between Type I schizophrenia, characterized primarily by positive symptoms, and Type II schizophrenia, whose symptoms are largely negative.

ConsiderThis

The philosopher F. W. Nietzsche said: "Insanity in individuals is something rare—but in groups, parties, nations, and epochs, it is the rule." What behaviors committed by groups might be considered psychotic if an individual were to perform them?

How Do Theorists Explain Schizophrenia?

As with many other kinds of disorders, biological, psychological, and sociocultural theorists have proposed explanations for schizophrenia. So far, the biological explanations have received by far the most research support. This is not to say that psychological and sociocultural factors play no role in the disorder. Rather, a *diathesis-stress* relationship may be at work: people with a biological predisposition will develop schizophrenia only if certain kinds of events or stressors are also present (Moldin & Gottesman, 1997).

Biological Views

Genetic and biological studies of schizophrenia have dominated clinical research during the past few decades. They have revealed the key roles of inheritance and brain activity in the development of this disorder and have opened the door to important changes in its treatment.

GENETIC FACTORS Following the principles of the diathesis-stress model, genetic researchers believe that some people inherit a biological predisposition to schizophrenia and develop the disorder later when they face extreme stress, usually during late adolescence or early adulthood (Tsuang et al., 2001; Tsuang, 2000). The genetic view has been supported by studies of (1) relatives of people with schizophrenia, (2) twins with this disorder, (3) people with schizophrenia who are adopted, and (4) genetic linkage and molecular biology.

ARE RELATIVES VULNERABLE? Family pedigree studies have found repeatedly that schizophrenia is more common among relatives of people with the disorder (Mortensen et al., 1999; Kendler et al., 1994, 1993). And the more closely related the relatives are to the person with schizophrenia, the greater their likelihood of developing the disorder (see Figure 12-2).

IS AN IDENTICAL TWIN MORE VULNERABLE THAN A FRATERNAL TWIN? Twins, who are among the closest of relatives, have received particular study by schizophrenia researchers. If both members of a pair of twins have a particular trait, they are said to be *concordant* for that trait. If genetic factors are at work in schizophrenia, identical twins (who share all genes) should have a higher concordance rate for this disorder than fraternal twins (who share only some genes). This expectation has been supported repeatedly by research (APA, 2000; Tsuang, 2000; Gottesman, 1991). Studies have found that if one identical twin develops schizophrenia, there is a 48 percent chance that the other twin will do so as well. If the twins are fraternal, on the other hand, the second twin has approximately a 17 percent chance of developing the disorder.

ARE THE BIOLOGICAL RELATIVES OF AN ADOPTEE VULNERABLE? Adoption studies look at adults with schizophrenia who were adopted as infants and compare them with both their biological and their adoptive relatives. Because they were reared apart from their biological relatives, similar symptoms in those relatives would indicate genetic influences. Conversely, similarities to their adoptive relatives would suggest environmental influences. Repeatedly, researchers have found that the biological relatives of adoptees with schizophrenia are more likely to display schizophrenic symptoms than their adoptive relatives (Wahlberg et al., 1997; Gottesman, 1991).

WHAT DO GENETIC LINKAGE AND MOLECULAR BIOLOGY STUDIES SUGGEST? As with bipolar disorders (see Chapter 6), researchers have run studies of *genetic linkage* and *molecular biology* to pinpoint the possible genetic factors in schizophrenia. In one approach, they select large families in which schizophrenia is very common, take blood and DNA samples from all members of the families, and then

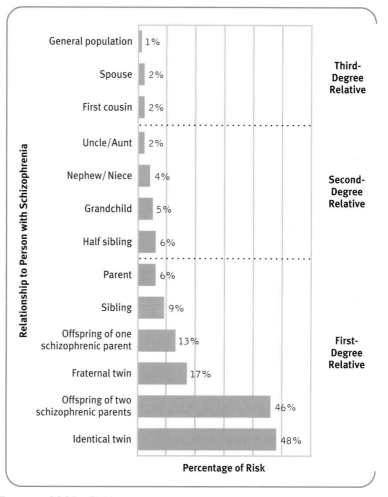

Relationship to Person with Schizophrenia	Percentage of Risk	
General population	1%	Third-Degree Relative
Spouse	2%	
First cousin	2%	
Uncle/Aunt	2%	Second-Degree Relative
Nephew/Niece	4%	
Grandchild	5%	
Half sibling	6%	
Parent	6%	First-Degree Relative
Sibling	9%	
Offspring of one schizophrenic parent	13%	
Fraternal twin	17%	
Offspring of two schizophrenic parents	46%	
Identical twin	48%	

FIGURE 12-2 **Family links** *Biological relatives of people with schizophrenia have a heightened risk of developing the disorder. The closer the biological relationship (that is, the more similar the genetic makeup), the greater the risk of developing the disorder. (Adapted from Gottesman, 1991, p. 96.)*

The brain bank *At St. Elizabeth's Hospital in Washington, D.C., schizophrenia researcher E. Fuller Torrey holds the brain of a person who had schizophrenia. Under Torrey's direction, more than 100 such brains have been gathered at the hospital brain bank, where they sit frozen in bucket-sized plastic tubs, available for study by researchers around the world.*

Chris Usher, Alexandria, Virginia

GENETIC FOUNDATION

More than half of the estimated 100,000 genes in human DNA seem to be dedicated to building and maintaining the nervous system (Cuticchia, 2000; Nash, 1997).

compare the gene fragments taken from members with and without schizophrenia. Applying this procedure to families from around the world, various studies have identified possible gene defects on chromosomes 5, 6, 8, 9, 10, 11, 13, 18, 19, and 22, each of which may predispose individuals to develop schizophrenia (Kendler et al., 2000; Pulver, 2000).

These varied findings may indicate that some of the suspected gene sites are cases of mistaken identity and do not actually contribute to schizophrenia. Alternatively, it may be that different kinds of schizophrenia are linked to different genes. Or perhaps, like a number of other disorders, schizophrenia is caused by a combination of gene defects (Meltzer, Moldin, & Gottesman, 1997).

How might genetic factors lead to the development of schizophrenia? Research has pointed to two kinds of biological abnormalities that could conceivably be inherited—*biochemical abnormalities* and *abnormal brain structure.*

BIOCHEMICAL ABNORMALITIES We have seen that the brain is made up of neurons whose impulses (or "messages") are carried from one neuron to another by neurotransmitters. After an impulse arrives at a receiving neuron, it travels down the body of that neuron until it reaches the nerve ending. The nerve ending then releases neurotransmitters that travel to and attach to receptors on yet another neuron, thus relaying the message by causing that neuron to fire. Over the past two decades, researchers have developed a **dopamine hypothesis** to explain their findings on schizophrenia: neurons that use the neurotransmitter dopamine fire too often and transmit too many messages, thus producing the symptoms of the disorder. This hypothesis has undergone challenges and adjustments in recent years (Schwartz, 1999), but it is still the foundation for present biochemical explanations of schizophrenia. The chain of events leading to this hypothesis began with the accidental discovery of **antipsychotic drugs,** medications that help remove the symptoms of schizophrenia. The first group of antipsychotic medications, the **phenothiazines,** were discovered in the 1950s by researchers who were looking for better *antihistamine* drugs to treat allergies. Although phenothiazines failed as antihistamines, their effectiveness in reducing schizophrenic symptoms became obvious, and clinicians began to prescribe them widely.

Researchers soon learned that these antipsychotic drugs often produce troublesome muscular tremors, symptoms that are identical to the central symptoms of *Parkinson's disease,* a disabling neurological illness. This undesired reaction to antipsychotic drugs gave researchers their first important clue to the biology of schizophrenia. Scientists already knew that people who suffer from Parkinson's disease have abnormally low levels of the neurotransmitter dopamine in some areas of the brain and that lack of dopamine is the reason for their uncontrollable shaking. If antipsychotic drugs produce Parkinsonian symptoms in persons with schizophrenia while removing their psychotic symptoms, perhaps the drugs reduce dopamine activity. And, scientists reasoned further, if lowering dopamine activity helps remove the symptoms of schizophrenia, perhaps schizophrenia is related to excessive dopamine activity in the first place.

Since the 1960s, research has supported and helped clarify the dopamine hypothesis. It has been found, for example, that some people with Parkinson's disease develop schizophrenic symptoms if they take too much *L-dopa,* a medication that raises dopamine levels in patients with that disease (Carey et al., 1995). The L-dopa apparently raises their dopamine activity so much that it produces psychosis. Support has also come from research on *amphetamines,* drugs that, as we saw in Chapter 10, stimulate the central nervous system. Investigators first noticed during the 1970s that people who take high doses of amphetamines may develop *amphetamine psychosis,* a syndrome very similar to schizophrenia. They also found that antipsychotic drugs can reduce the symptoms of ampheta-

"God told me to do it."

Christopher Scarver, inmate who beat fellow prisoner Jeffrey Dahmer to death in 1994

"And only you can hear this whistle?"

mine psychosis, just as they reduce the symptoms of schizophrenia (Janowsky & Davis, 1976; Janowsky et al., 1973). Eventually it was learned that amphetamines increase dopamine activity in the brain, thus producing schizophrenic symptoms (Laruelle & Abi-Dargham, 1999).

Investigators have located areas of the brain that are rich in dopamine receptors and have found that phenothiazines and other antipsychotic drugs bind to many of these receptors (Burt et al., 1977; Creese et al., 1977). Apparently the drugs are *dopamine antagonists*—drugs that bind to dopamine receptors, prevent dopamine from binding there, and so prevent the neurons from firing (Iversen, 1975). Researchers have identified five kinds of dopamine receptors in the brain—called D-1, D-2, D-3, D-4, and D-5 receptors—and have found that phenothiazines bind most strongly to the *D-2 receptors* (Strange, 1992).

These and related findings suggest that in schizophrenia, messages traveling from dopamine-sending neurons to dopamine receptors on other neurons, particularly to the D-2 receptors, may be transmitted too easily or too often. This theory is appealing because certain dopamine neurons are known to play a key role in guiding attention (Cohen et al., 1988). People whose attention is severely disturbed by excessive dopamine activity might well be expected to suffer from the problems of attention, perception, and thought found in schizophrenia.

Why might dopamine be overactive in people with schizophrenia? It may be that people with this disorder have a larger-than-usual number of dopamine receptors, particularly D-2 receptors (Sedvall, 1990; Seidman, 1990). Remember that when dopamine carries a message to a receiving neuron, it must bind to a receptor on the neuron. A greater number of receptors will ensure more dopamine activity and thus more neuron firing.

Though enlightening, the dopamine hypothesis has certain problems. The greatest challenge to it has come with the discovery of a new group of antipsychotic drugs, referred to as **atypical antipsychotics,** which are often more effective than the traditional ones. The new drugs bind not only to D-2 dopamine receptors, like the traditional drugs, but also to many D-1 receptors and to receptors for other neurotransmitters, such as *serotonin* (Kasper et al., 1999). Thus it may be that schizophrenia is related to abnormal activity of both dopamine and serotonin and perhaps other neurotransmitters as well, rather than abnormal dopamine activity alone (Taber, Lewis, & Hurley, 2001).

ABNORMAL BRAIN STRUCTURE During the past decade, researchers have also linked schizophrenia, particularly Type II schizophrenia, to abnormalities in brain structure (Buchanan & Carpenter, 1997). Using scanning techniques, they have found, for example, that many people with schizophrenia have *enlarged ventricles*—the brain cavities that contain cerebrospinal fluid (Lieberman et al., 2001; Wright et al., 2000). Furthermore, patients who have enlarged ventricles tend to display Type II rather than Type I schizophrenia; that is, more negative symptoms of schizophrenia, fewer positive symptoms, a poorer social adjustment before the onset of the disorder, and greater cognitive disturbances (Bornstein et al., 1992; Klausner et al., 1992).

It may be that enlarged ventricles are actually a sign that nearby parts of the brain have not developed properly or have been damaged, and perhaps these problems are the ones that help produce schizophrenia, at least Type II schizophrenia. In fact, some studies suggest that patients with this disorder also have smaller temporal lobes and frontal lobes than other people, smaller amounts of cortical gray matter, and, perhaps most important, abnormal blood flow in certain areas of the brain (Sigmundsson et al., 2001; Kim et al., 2000).

VIRAL PROBLEMS What might cause the biochemical and structural abnormalities found in many cases of schizophrenia? Various studies have pointed to genetic factors, poor nutrition, fetal development, birth complications, immune reactions, and toxins (McNeil & Cantor-Graae, 2001; Susser et al., 1996). In

DOPAMINE HYPOTHESIS The theory that schizophrenia results from excessive activity of the neurotransmitter dopamine.

ANTIPSYCHOTIC DRUGS Drugs that help correct grossly confused or distorted thinking.

PHENOTHIAZINES A group of antihistamine drugs that became the first group of effective antipsychotic medications.

ATYPICAL ANTIPSYCHOTIC DRUGS A new group of antipsychotic drugs whose biological action is different from that of the traditional antipsychotic drugs.

Joe McNally / Matrix

Not-so-identical twins *The man on the left is normal, while his identical twin, on the right, has schizophrenia. Magnetic resonance imaging (MRI), shown in the background, clarifies that the brain of the twin with schizophrenia is smaller overall than his brother's and has larger ventricles, indicated by the dark butterfly-shaped spaces.*

SCHIZOPHRENOGENIC MOTHER A type of mother—supposedly cold, domineering, and uninterested in the needs of others—who was once thought to cause schizophrenia in her child.

addition, a growing number of investigators suggest that the brain abnormalities may result from exposure to *viruses* before birth. Perhaps the viruses enter the fetus's brain and remain quiet until puberty or young adulthood, when, activated by changes in hormones or by another viral infection, they may help to cause schizophrenic symptoms (Torrey et al., 1993; Torrey, 1991).

Circumstantial evidence for the viral theory comes from the unusually large number of people with schizophrenia born during the winter (Battle et al., 1999; Torrey et al., 1997, 1993). This finding could be due to an increase in fetal or infant exposure to viruses at that time of year (Sponheim et al., 1997). More direct evidence comes from studies showing that mothers of persons with schizophrenia were more often exposed to the influenza virus during pregnancy (particularly during the second trimester) than mothers of people without schizophrenia (de Messias et al., 2001; Torrey et al., 1994). And finally, studies have found antibodies to *pestiviruses,* a particular group of viruses usually found in animals, in the blood of 40 percent of subjects with schizophrenia (Torrey et al., 1994; Yolken et al., 2000, 1993). The presence of such antibodies suggests that the subjects were at some time exposed to pestiviruses.

Together, the biochemical, brain structure, and viral findings are beginning to shed much light on the mysteries of schizophrenia. At the same time, it is important to recognize that many people who have these biological problems never develop schizophrenia. Why not? Possibly, as noted earlier, because biological factors merely set the stage for schizophrenia, while key psychological and sociocultural factors must be present for the disorder to appear (Wahlberg et al., 1997).

Psychological Views

When schizophrenia investigators began to identify genetic and biological factors during the 1950s and 1960s, many clinicians abandoned psychological theories of the disorder. During the past decade, however, psychological factors are once again being considered important pieces of the puzzle of schizophrenia. The leading psychological explanations have come from the psychodynamic and cognitive perspectives.

Ballet artist Vaslav Nijinsky *The renowned dancer, performing here in* Schéhérazade, *developed severe schizophrenia and spent the last years of his life in a mental institution.*

THE PSYCHODYNAMIC EXPLANATION Freud (1924, 1915, 1914) believed that schizophrenia develops from two psychological processes: (1) *regression* to a pre-ego stage and (2) efforts to *reestablish* ego control. He proposed that when their world is extremely harsh or withholding—for example, when parents are cold or unnurturing—people who develop schizophrenia regress to the earliest point in their development, to the pre-ego state of *primary narcissism,* in which they recognize and meet only their own needs. Their near-total regression leads to self-centered symptoms such as neologisms, loose associations, and delusions of grandeur. Once people regress to such an infantile state, Freud continued, they try to reestablish ego control and contact with reality. Their efforts give rise to yet other schizophrenic symptoms. Auditory hallucinations, for example, may be an individual's attempt to substitute for a lost sense of reality.

Years later, the noted psychodynamic clinician Frieda Fromm-Reichmann (1948) elaborated on Freud's notion that cold or unnurturing parents may set schizophrenia in motion. She described the mothers of people who develop this disorder as cold, domineering, and uninterested in their children's needs. According to Fromm-Reichmann, these mothers appear to be self-sacrificing but are actually using their children to meet their own needs. At once overprotective and rejecting, they confuse their children and set the stage for schizophrenic functioning. She called them **schizophrenogenic** (schizophrenia-causing) **mothers.**

Fromm-Reichmann's theory, like Freud's, has received little research support (Willick, 2001). The majority of people with schizophrenia do not appear to have mothers who fit the schizophrenogenic description. Most of today's psychodynamic theorists have, in fact, rejected the views of

Freud and Fromm-Reichmann. Although the theorists may retain some of the early notions (Spielrein, 1995), more and more of them believe that biological abnormalities leave certain persons particularly prone to extreme regression and other unconscious acts that may contribute to schizophrenia (Willick et al., 1998).

THE COGNITIVE EXPLANATION A leading cognitive explanation of schizophrenia agrees with the biological view that during hallucinations and other perceptual difficulties, the brains of people with schizophrenia are actually producing strange and unreal sensations—sensations triggered by biological factors. According to the cognitive explanation, however, further features of the disorder develop when the individuals attempt to understand their unusual sensations. When first confronted by voices, visions, or other troubling sensations, these people turn to friends and relatives. Naturally, the friends and relatives deny the reality of the sensations, and eventually the sufferers conclude that the others are trying to hide the truth. They begin to reject all feedback and may develop beliefs (delusions) that they are being persecuted (Garety, 1991; Maher, 1974).

Researchers have established that people with schizophrenia do indeed experience sensory and perceptual problems. As we saw earlier, for example, many of them have hallucinations, and most have trouble keeping their attention focused (APA, 2000; Elkins & Cromwell, 1994). But researchers have yet to provide clear, direct support for the cognitive notion that misinterpretations of such sensory problems actually produce the syndrome of schizophrenia.

Sociocultural Views

Sociocultural theorists, believing that persons with mental disorders are victims of social forces, claim that *social labeling* and *family dysfunctioning* contribute to the development of schizophrenia. Although societal and family forces are considered important in the development of this disorder, research has not yet clarified what the precise causal relationships might be.

SOCIAL LABELING Many sociocultural theorists believe that the features of schizophrenia are influenced by the diagnosis itself (Modrow, 1992). In their opinion, society assigns the label "schizophrenic" to people who fail to follow certain norms of behavior. Once the label is assigned, justified or not, it becomes a self-fulfilling prophecy that leads to the development of many schizophrenic symptoms.

We have already seen the very real dangers of diagnostic labeling. In the famous Rosenhan (1973) study, discussed in Chapter 2, eight normal people presented themselves at various mental hospitals, complaining that they had been hearing voices speak the words "empty," "hollow," and "thud." They were quickly diagnosed as schizophrenic, and all eight were hospitalized. Although the pseudopatients then dropped all symptoms and behaved normally, they had great difficulty getting rid of the label and gaining release from the hospital. They also reported that staff members treated them and other patients as though they were invisible. "A nurse unbuttoned her uniform to adjust her brassiere in the presence of an entire ward of viewing men. One did not have the sense that she was being seductive. Rather, she didn't notice us." In addition, the pseudopatients described feeling powerless, bored, tired, and uninterested. The investigation demonstrates that the label "schizophrenic" can have a negative effect not just on how people are viewed but on how they themselves feel and behave.

FAMILY DYSFUNCTIONING A number of studies suggest that schizophrenia, like certain other mental disorders, is often linked to *family stress* (Miklowitz et al., 1995; Velligan et al., 1995). Parents of people with this disorder often (1) display more conflict, (2) have greater difficulty

ConsiderThis

◉ The psychodynamic explanations of schizophrenia reflect a long-standing tradition in the clinical field and in society of pointing to parents as key causes of mental disorders, even in cases where evidence is lacking. Why are parents and family life so likely to be blamed, and why are these explanations so resistant to change?

"Is there anybody out there?" *Schizophrenia is a popular subject throughout the arts, where it is often depicted in positive terms. Pink Floyd's hugely popular album and movie* The Wall, *for example, follows the lead of certain sociocultural theorists and portrays the disorder as an inward search undertaken by some persons to help cure themselves of confusion and unhappiness caused by their families or by society.*

Courtesy of the artist, Gerald Scharfe, and Tin Blue Ltd.

ConsiderThis

● Rosenhan's pseudopatient study is one of the most controversial in the clinical field. What kinds of ethical, legal, and therapeutic concerns does it raise?

"When you tell people their disease is lifelong, you may be creating self-fulfilling prophesies."

Nancy Andreasen, M.D. (2000), schizophrenia researcher

ConsiderThis

● Was the voice heard by Ray Kinsella ("If you build it, they will come") in the movie *Field of Dreams* a form of spiritual inspiration or an auditory hallucination?

communicating with one another, and (3) are more critical of and overinvolved with their children than other parents.

Negative family climates of this kind may help cause schizophrenia, keep the disorder going, and contribute to relapses among recovering individuals. Family theorists have long recognized that some families are high in **expressed emotion**—that is, members frequently express criticism, disapproval, and hostility toward each other and intrude on one another's privacy. Individuals who are trying to recover from schizophrenia are almost four times more likely to relapse if they live with such a family than if they live with one low in expressed emotion (Linszen et al., 1997; Brown et al., 1962). Do such findings mean that family dysfunctioning helps cause and maintain schizophrenia? Not necessarily. It is also the case that individuals with schizophrenia greatly disrupt family life. In so doing, they themselves may help create the family problems that clinicians and researchers continue to observe (Woo, Goldstein, & Neuchterlein, 1997; Rosenfarb et al., 1995).

Although the sociocultural causes of schizophrenia, like the psychological causes, have yet to be fully understood, many of today's clinicians believe that such factors play an important role in the disorder. As we have noted, most hold a diathesis-stress view of schizophrenia, believing that genetic and biological factors set up a predisposition to develop the disorder but that psychological and sociocultural factors help bring it to life. Perhaps a biological predisposition will lead to schizophrenia only when individuals face personal upsets, inappropriate patterns of reinforcement, or family or social stress. Moreover, once schizophrenia emerges, the forces of social labeling or family dysfunction may help increase or maintain its symptoms.

SUMMING UP ⌐ How Do Theorists Explain Schizophrenia?

A range of biological, psychological, and sociocultural explanations have been offered for schizophrenia.

Biological Explanations The biological explanations point to genetic, biochemical, structural, and viral causes. Researchers have identified a number of gene abnormalities that may predispose persons to develop schizophrenia. According to biochemical research, the brains of people with Type I schizophrenia may contain an unusually large number of dopamine receptors, particularly D-2 receptors, leading to excessive dopamine activity. Other studies have found abnormal brain structures in people with Type II schizophrenia, including enlarged ventricles and reduced blood flow in certain parts of the brain. Finally, some researchers believe that schizophrenia is related to a virus that settles in the fetus and then lies quiet until adolescence or young adulthood.

Psychological Explanations The leading psychological explanations for schizophrenia come from the psychodynamic and cognitive models. Freud believed that schizophrenia involves regression to a state of primary narcissism, and Fromm-Reichmann proposed that schizophrenogenic mothers help produce this disorder. Cognitive theorists hold that when people with schizophrenia try to explain biologically caused strange sensations, they develop delusional thinking. None of these theories has received much research support.

Sociocultural Explanations One sociocultural explanation holds that society expects persons who are labeled as having schizophrenia to behave in certain ways and that these expectations lead to further symptoms. Other sociocultural views point to family stress as a cause of schizophrenia. Research has not yet pinpointed the specific roles of such factors.

Diathesis-Stress Explanation Most clinical theorists now believe that schizophrenia can probably be traced to a combination of biological, psychological, and sociocultural factors, although the biological factors have been identified more precisely.

How Is Schizophrenia Treated?

How can a patient and a therapist communicate when they speak virtually different languages? For years, efforts to treat schizophrenia brought only frustration. Lara Jefferson, a young woman with this disorder, wrote of her treatment experience in the 1940s:

> They call us insane—and in reality they are as inconsistent as we are, as flighty and changeable. This one in particular. One day he derides and ridicules me unmercifully; the next he talks to me sadly and this morning his eyes misted over with tears as he told me of the fate ahead. Damn him and all of his wisdom!
>
> He has dinned into my ears a monotonous dirge—"Too Egotistical—too Egotistical—too Egotistical. Learn to think differently."—And how can I do it? How—how—can I do it? How the hell can I do it? I have tried to follow his suggestions but have not learned to think a bit differently. It was all wasted effort. Where has it got me?
>
> *(Jefferson, 1948)*

For much of human history, patients with schizophrenia, like this woman, were considered beyond help. The disorder is still extremely difficult to treat, but clinicians are more successful today than they were in the past (McGuire, 2000). Much of the credit goes to *antipsychotic drugs,* the medications that help many people with schizophrenia think clearly and profit from therapies that previously would have had little effect on them. A look at how treatment has progressed over the years will help us understand the nature, problems, and promise of today's approaches.

Institutional Care in the Past

For more than half of the twentieth century, most people with schizophrenia were *institutionalized* in a public mental hospital. Because patients with this disorder failed to respond to traditional therapies, the primary goals of these institutions were to restrain them and give them food, shelter, and clothing. Patients rarely saw therapists and were generally neglected. Many were abused. Oddly enough, this state of affairs unfolded in an atmosphere of good intentions.

As we saw in Chapter 1, the move toward institutionalization began in 1793, when the French physician Philippe Pinel "unchained the insane" at La Bicêtre asylum and began the practice of "moral treatment." For the first time in centuries, patients with severe disturbances were viewed as human beings who should be cared for with sympathy and kindness. As Pinel's ideas spread throughout Europe and the United States, they led to the creation of large mental hospitals rather than asylums to care for those with severe mental disorders (Goshen, 1967).

These new mental hospitals were meant to protect patients from the stresses of daily life and offer them a healthful psychological environment in which they could work closely with therapists (Grob, 1966). States throughout the United States were even required by law to establish public mental institutions, **state hospitals,** for patients who could not afford private ones. Eventually, however, the state hospital system developed serious problems. Between 1845 and 1955 nearly 300 opened in the United States, and the number of hospitalized patients on any given day rose from 2,000 in

EXPRESSED EMOTION The general level of criticism, disapproval, and hostility expressed in a family. People recovering from schizophrenia are considered more likely to relapse if their families rate high in expressed emotion.

STATE HOSPITALS Public mental hospitals in the United States, run by each state.

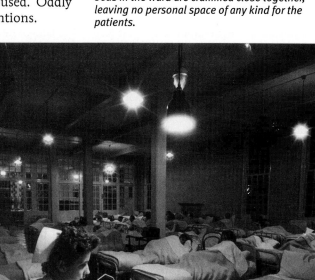

Overcrowded conditions *A night nurse sits in the ward of a public mental hospital in 1956 darning socks while the patients sleep. The beds in the ward are crammed close together, leaving no personal space of any kind for the patients.*

Hulton Getty/Liaison Agency

1845 to nearly 600,000 in 1955. During this expansion, wards became overcrowded, admissions kept rising, and state funding could not keep up with the increasing need for therapists.

The priorities of the public mental hospitals and the quality of care they provided changed during those 110 years. In the face of overcrowding and understaffing, the emphasis shifted from giving humanitarian care to keeping order. In a throwback to the asylum period, difficult patients were restrained and pun-

STEPPING BACK

Lobotomy: How Could It Happen?

In 1949 a *New York Times* article reported on a medical procedure that appeared to offer hope to sufferers of severe mental disorders, people for whom no future had seemed possible outside of overcrowded state mental institutions:

> Hypochondriacs no longer thought they were going to die, would-be suicides found life acceptable, sufferers from persecution complex forgot the machinations of imaginary conspirators. Prefrontal lobotomy, as the operation is called, was made possible by the localization of fears, hates, and instincts [in the prefrontal cortex of the brain]. It is fitting, then, that the Nobel Prize in medicine should be shared by Hess and Moniz. Surgeons now think no more of operations on the brain than they do of removing an appendix.

We now know that the *lobotomy* was hardly a miracle treatment. Far from "curing" people with mental disorders, the procedure left thousands upon thousands extremely withdrawn, subdued, and even stuporous. The first lobotomy was performed by the Portuguese neuropsychiatrist Egas Moniz in 1935 (Tierney, 2000). His particular procedure, called a *prefrontal leukotomy,* consisted of drilling two holes in either side of the skull and inserting an instrument resembling an icepick into the brain tissue to cut or destroy nerve fibers. Moniz believed that severe abnormal thinking could be changed by cutting the nerve pathways that carried such thoughts from one part of the brain to another. In the 1940s Walter Freeman and his surgical partner, James Watts, developed a second kind of psychosurgery called the *transorbital lobotomy,* in which the sur-

geon inserted a needle into the brain through the eye socket and rotated it in order to destroy the brain tissue.

Why was the lobotomy so enthusiastically accepted by the medical community in the 1940s and 1950s? The neuroscientist Elliot Valenstein (1986) points first to the extreme overcrowding in mental hospitals at the time. This crowding was making it difficult to maintain decent standards in the hospitals. Valenstein also points to the personalities of the inventors of the procedure as important factors. Although they were gifted and dedicated physicians, Valenstein also believes that their professional ambitions led them to move too quickly and boldly in applying the procedure. Indeed, in 1949 Moniz was awarded the Nobel Prize for his work.

The prestige and diplomatic skills of Moniz and Freeman were so great and the field of neurology was so small that their procedures drew little criticism. Physicians may also have been misled by the seemingly positive findings of early studies of the lobotomy, which, as it turned out, were not based on sound methodology (Swayze, 1995; Valenstein, 1986).

By the 1950s, better studies revealed that in addition to having a fatality rate of 1.5 to 6 percent, lobotomies could cause serious problems such as brain seizures, huge weight gain, loss of motor coordination, partial paralysis, incontinence, endocrine malfunctions, and very

poor intellectual and emotional responsiveness. When the public became concerned that the procedure might be used to control violent criminals, the lobotomy became a civil rights issue as well. Finally, the discovery of effective antipsychotic drugs put an end to this inhumane treatment for mental disorders (Tierney, 2000).

Today's psychosurgical procedures are greatly refined and hardly resemble the lobotomies of 50 years back. Moreover, such procedures are considered experimental and used only as a last resort in the most severe cases of obsessive-compulsive disorder and depression (Weingarten & Cummings, 2001; Goodman et al., 1992). Even so, many professionals believe that any kind of surgery that destroys brain tissue is inappropriate and perhaps unethical.

Lessons in psychosurgery *The neuropsychiatrist Walter Freeman performs a lobotomy in 1949 before a group of interested onlookers by inserting a needle through a patient's eye socket into the brain.*

ished; individual attention disappeared. Patients were transferred to *back wards,* or chronic wards, if they failed to improve quickly (Bloom, 1984). Most of the patients on these wards suffered from schizophrenia (Hafner & van der Heiden, 1988). The back wards were in fact human warehouses filled with hopelessness. Staff members relied on straitjackets and handcuffs to deal with difficult patients. More "advanced" forms of treatment included medical approaches such as the lobotomy.

Institutional Care Takes a Turn for the Better

In the 1950s, clinicians developed two institutional approaches that finally brought some hope to patients who had lived in institutions for years: *milieu therapy,* based on humanistic principles, and the *token economy program,* based on behavioral principles. These approaches particularly helped improve the personal care and self-image of patients, problem areas that had been worsened by institutionalization. The approaches were soon adopted by many institutions and are now standard features of institutional care.

MILIEU THERAPY The principle behind **milieu therapy** is that institutions can help patients make clinical progress by creating a social climate, or milieu, that builds productive activities, self-respect, and individual responsibility. In such settings, patients are often given the right to run their own lives and make their own decisions. They may take part in institutional government and work with staff members to set up rules and decide penalties. The atmosphere is one of mutual respect, support, and openness. Persons may also take on special projects, jobs, and recreational activities. In short, their daily schedule is designed to resemble life outside the hospital.

Milieu-style programs have been set up in institutions throughout the Western world. The programs vary from setting to setting, but at a minimum staff members try to encourage interactions (especially group interactions) between patients and staff, to keep patients active, and to raise patients' expectations of what they can accomplish.

Research over the years has shown that patients with schizophrenia in milieu hospital programs often improve and that they leave the hospital at higher rates than patients in programs offering primarily custodial care (Paul & Lentz, 1977; Cumming & Cumming, 1962). Many of these persons remain impaired, however, and must live in sheltered settings after their release. Despite such limitations, milieu therapy continues to be practiced in many institutions, often combined with other hospital approaches (Dobson et al., 1995; Ciompi et al., 1992).

THE TOKEN ECONOMY In the 1950s behaviorists discovered that the systematic application of *operant conditioning* techniques on hospital wards could help change the behaviors of patients with schizophrenia (Ayllon, 1963; Ayllon & Michael, 1959). Programs that applied such techniques were named **token economy programs.**

In token economies patients are rewarded whenever they behave acceptably and are not rewarded when they behave unacceptably. The immediate rewards for acceptable behavior are often tokens that can later be exchanged for food, cigarettes, hospital privileges, and other desirable items, thus creating a "token economy." Acceptable behaviors likely to be targeted include caring for oneself (making one's bed, dressing oneself), going to a work program, speaking normally, following ward rules, and showing self-control.

Researchers have found that token economies do help change psychotic and related behaviors (Emmelkamp, 1994; Belcher, 1988). In one very successful program, Gordon Paul and R. L. Lentz (1977) set up such a hospital token economy for 28 patients with long-term schizophrenia, most of whom improved greatly. After four and a half years, 98 percent of the

MILIEU THERAPY A humanistic approach to institutional treatment based on the belief that institutions can help patients recover by creating a climate that promotes self-respect, responsible behavior, and meaningful activity.

TOKEN ECONOMY PROGRAM A behavioral program in which a person's desirable behaviors are reinforced systematically throughout the day by the awarding of tokens that can be exchanged for goods or privileges.

The chain technique *Unimpressed by the success of milieu and token economy programs, some institutions around the world continue to use approaches that seem unenlightened at best. Despite constant criticism by the clinical establishment, the Longfa Tang Temple in southern Taiwan makes use of chains to "treat" the 700 patients who reside there. Often a severely disturbed patient is chained to a more stable patient and is led around to various activities and work assignments throughout the day.*

VOICE IN THE WILDERNESS

Suffering from delusions, a business-man named Clifford Beers spent two years in mental institutions during the early 1900s. His later description of conditions there in an autobiography, *A Mind That Found Itself*, spurred a widespread reform movement in the United States, called the "mental hygiene movement," which led to some key improvements in hospital conditions.

SHORTER STAYS

In 1997 the average length of stay in a mental hospital in the United States was 10.2 days, down 11 percent from the previous year (NAPHS, 1999).

subjects had been released, mostly to sheltered-care facilities, compared to 71 percent of patients treated in a milieu program and 45 percent of patients who received custodial care only.

Despite the effectiveness of token economies, some clinicians have raised ethical and legal concerns about them. If token economy programs are to be effective, administrators need to control the important rewards in a patient's life, perhaps including such basic ones as food and a comfortable bed. But aren't there some things in life to which all human beings are entitled? Court decisions have now ruled that patients do indeed have certain basic rights that clinicians cannot violate, regardless of the positive goals of a treatment program. They have a right to food, storage space, and furniture, as well as freedom of movement (Emmelkamp, 1994).

Still other clinicians have questioned the quality of the improvements made under token economy programs. Are behaviorists changing a patient's psychotic thoughts and perceptions or simply improving the patient's ability to imitate normal behavior? This question is raised by the case of a middle-aged man named John, who had the delusion that he was the U.S. government. Whenever he spoke, he spoke as the government. "We are happy to see you. . . . We need people like you in our service. . . . We are carrying out our activities in John's body." When John's hospital ward was made into a token economy, the staff members targeted his delusional statements and required him to identify himself properly to earn tokens. After a few months on the token economy program, John stopped presenting himself as the government. When asked his name, he would say, "John." Although staff members were understandably pleased by his improvement, John himself had a different view of the situation. In a private discussion, he said:

> We're tired of it. Every damn time we want a cigarette, we have to go through their bullshit. "What's your name? . . . Who wants the cigarette? . . . Where is the government?" Today, we were desperate for a smoke and went to Simpson, the damn nurse, and she made us do her bidding. "Tell me your name if you want a cigarette. What's your name?" Of course, we said, "John." We needed the cigarettes. If we told her the truth, no cigarettes. But we don't have time for this nonsense. We've got business to do, international business, laws to change, people to recruit. And these people keep playing their games.
>
> *(Comer, 1973)*

Critics of the behavioral approach would argue that John was still delusional and therefore as psychotic as before. Behaviorists, however, would argue that at the very least, John's judgment about the results of his behavior had improved.

Token economy programs are no longer as popular as they once were (Glynn, 1990), but they are still used in many mental hospitals, usually along with medication. The approach has also been applied to other clinical problems, including mental retardation, delinquency, and hyperactivity, as well as in other fields, such as education and business.

Antipsychotic Drugs

Milieu therapy and token economy programs helped improve the gloomy outlook for patients with schizophrenia, but it was the discovery of *antipsychotic drugs* in the 1950s that truly revolutionized treatment for this disorder. These drugs eliminate many of its symptoms and today are almost always a part of treatment.

As noted earlier, the discovery of antipsychotic medications actually dates back to the 1940s, when researchers developed the first *antihistamine drugs* to treat allergies. The French surgeon Henri Laborit soon discovered that one group of antihistamines, *phenothiazines*, could also be used to help calm patients about

NEUROLEPTIC DRUGS Conventional antipsychotic drugs, so called because they often produce undesired effects similar to the symptoms of neurological disorders.

The drug revolution *Since the 1950s medications have become the center of treatment for patients hospitalized with schizophrenia and other severe mental disorders. The medications have resulted in shorter hospitalizations that last weeks rather than years.*

to undergo surgery. Laborit suspected that the drugs might also have a calming effect on persons with severe psychological disorders. One of the phenothiazines, *chlorpromazine,* was eventually tested on six patients with psychotic symptoms and found to reduce their symptoms sharply (Delay & Deniker, 1952). In 1954, after a series of laboratory and clinical tests, it went on the market in the United States as an antipsychotic medication under the trade name Thorazine.

Since the discovery of the phenothiazines, other kinds of antipsychotic drugs have also been developed (see Table 12-2). The ones developed throughout the 1960s, 1970s, and 1980s are now referred to as *"conventional" antipsychotic drugs,* to distinguish them from the *"atypical" antipsychotics* that have been developed in recent years. The conventional drugs are also known as **neuroleptic drugs,** because they often produce undesired effects similar to the symptoms of neurological diseases. As we saw earlier, the various antipsychotic drugs reduce the symptoms of schizophrenia at least in part by decreasing excessive activity of the neurotransmitter dopamine, particularly at the brain's D-2 dopamine receptors (Holcomb et al., 1996).

HOW EFFECTIVE ARE ANTIPSYCHOTIC DRUGS? Research has repeatedly shown that antipsychotic drugs reduce schizophrenic symptoms in the majority of patients (Lieberman et al., 1996). Moreover, in direct comparisons the drugs appear to be a more effective treatment for schizophrenia than any of the other approaches used alone, such as psychodynamic therapy, milieu therapy, and electroconvulsive therapy (May, Tuma, & Dixon, 1981; May & Tuma, 1964). At the same time, symptoms may return if patients stop taking the drugs too soon (Davis et al., 1993).

Although antipsychotic drugs are now widely accepted, patients often dislike the powerful effects of the drugs, and some refuse to take them (Olfson et al., 2000). But like Edward Snow, a writer who overcame schizophrenia, many are greatly helped by the medications:

Table 12-2 DSM-IV Checklist

Antipsychotic Drugs

CLASS/GENERIC NAME	TRADE NAME
Chlorpromazine	Thorazine
Risperidone	Risperdal
Triflupromazine	Vesprin
Thioridazine	Mellaril
Mesoridazine besylate	Serentil
Piperacetazine	Quide
Trifluoperazine	Stelazine
Fluphenazine	Prolixin, Permitil
Perphenazine	Trilafon
Acetophenazine maleate	Tindal
Chlorprothixene	Taractan
Thiothixene	Navane
Haloperidol	Haldol
Loxapine	Loxitane
Molindone hydrochloride	Moban, Lidone
Pimozide	Orap
Clozapine	Clozaril
Olanzapine	Zyprexa
Quetiapine	Seroquel

In my case it was necessary to come to terms with a specified drug program. I am a legalized addict. My dose: 100 milligrams of Thorazine and 60 milligrams of Stelazine daily. I don't feel this dope at all, but I have been told it is strong enough to flatten a normal person. It keeps me—as the doctors agree—sane and in good spirits. Without the brain candy, as I call it, I would go—zoom—right back into the bin. I've made the institution scene enough already to be familiar with what it's like and to know I don't want to go back.

(Snow, 1976)

UNWANTED EFFECTS OF CONVENTIONAL ANTIPSYCHOTIC DRUGS In addition to reducing schizophrenic symptoms, the conventional antipsychotic drugs sometimes produce disturbing movement problems. These effects are called **extrapyramidal effects** because they appear to be caused by the drugs' action in the extrapyramidal areas of the brain, areas that help control motor activity.

The most common extrapyramidal effects are *Parkinsonian symptoms,* reactions that closely resemble the features of the neurological disorder Parkinson's disease. Patients may have severe muscle tremors and muscle rigidity; they may shake, move very slowly, shuffle their feet, and show little facial expression. Some also display bizarre movements of the face, neck, tongue, and back, and a number experience great restlessness and discomfort in the limbs. In most cases, these symptoms can be reversed if an anti-Parkinsonian drug is taken along with the antipsychotic drug (Silver et al., 1995).

Whereas most undesired drug effects appear within days or weeks, a reaction called **tardive dyskinesia** (meaning "late-appearing movement disorder") does not usually unfold until after a person has taken conventional antipsychotic drugs for more than a year. The syndrome may include involuntary writhing or ticlike movements of the tongue, mouth, face, or whole body; involuntary chewing, sucking, and lip smacking; and jerky movements of the arms, legs, or entire body.

Most cases of tardive dyskinesia are mild and involve a single symptom such as tongue flicking; however, some are severe and include such features as irregular breathing and grotesque twisting of the face and body. It is believed that over 20 percent of the people who take conventional antipsychotic drugs for an extended time develop tardive dyskinesia to some degree, and the longer the drugs are taken, the greater the risk becomes (APA, 2000; Chakos et al., 1996). Patients over 45 years of age seem to be at greatest risk (Jeste et al., 1996). Tardive dyskinesia can be difficult, sometimes impossible, to eliminate. The longer patients are on the drugs, the less likely it is that their tardive dyskinesia will disappear, even when the drugs are stopped.

Since learning about the unwanted effects of conventional antipsychotic drugs, clinicians have become wiser and more careful in their prescription practices. Previously, when a patient did not improve with such a drug, clinicians would increase the dose (Kane, 1992); today they typically stop the drug (Coryell et al., 1998). Similarly, today's clinicians try to prescribe the lowest effective dose for each patient and to gradually reduce or stop medication weeks or months after the patient begins functioning normally (Gilbert et al., 1995). However, many patients cannot function without these medications (Lerner et al., 1995), and they may be put back on them rather quickly, sometimes at doses that are higher than recommended (Remington et al., 1993).

NEW ANTIPSYCHOTIC DRUGS In recent years, new antipsychotic drugs have been developed (Breier, 2001; Schultz, 2000). The most effective and widely used of these new drugs are *clozapine* (trade name Clozaril), *risperidone* (trade name Risperdal), *olanzapine* (Zyprexa), and *quetiapine* (Seroquel). These drugs are

Unwanted effects *This man has a severe case of Parkinson's disease, a disorder caused by low dopamine activity, and his muscle tremors prevent him from shaving himself. The conventional antipsychotic drugs often produce similar Parkinsonian symptoms.*

IMPROPER DOSAGE

Recent interviews with over 700 people suffering from schizophrenia revealed that 39 percent of them were receiving too low a dosage of antipsychotic medication, 32 percent too high a dosage, and only 29 percent an appropriate dosage (PORT, 1998).

called *atypical* because their biological operation differs from that of conventional antipsychotic medications. In fact, they appear to be more effective than the conventional drugs, helping as many as 85 percent of persons with schizophrenia, compared with the 65 percent helped by most of the conventional drugs (Chakos et al., 2001; Lieberman, 1998). It is particularly promising that the new drugs also help patients who experience primarily negative symptoms (Type II schizophrenia)—people who do not typically respond well to the conventional drugs (Lieberman et al., 1996). Another major benefit of the atypical antipsychotic drugs is that they cause few extrapyramidal symptoms and do not seem to produce tardive dyskinesia (Kane, 2001; APA, 2000).

Yet the new drugs have some serious problems. People who use clozapine, for example, have around a 1 percent risk of developing **agranulocytosis,** a life-threatening drop in white blood cells (Alvir, Lieberman, & Safferman, 1995). Patients who take this drug must therefore have frequent blood tests so that this effect can be spotted early and the drug stopped (Perry, 2000; Honigfeld et al., 1998).

Psychotherapy

Before the discovery of antipsychotic drugs, psychotherapy was not really an option for persons with schizophrenia. Most were simply too far removed from reality to profit from it. Today, however, psychotherapy is successful in many cases of schizophrenia. By helping to relieve thought and perceptual disturbances, antipsychotic drugs allow people with schizophrenia to learn about their disorder, participate actively in therapy, think more clearly about themselves and their relationships, and make changes in their behavior (Svensson et al., 2000; Liberman et al., 1998). The most helpful forms of psychotherapy include *insight therapy* and two broader sociocultural therapies—*family therapy* and *social therapy.* Often these approaches are combined and tailored to the particular needs of patients (Jeffries, 1995; Prendergast, 1995).

INSIGHT THERAPY A variety of insight therapies may be used in cases of schizophrenia (Gould et al., 2001; Scott & Wright, 1997). Studies suggest that the particular orientations of insight therapists are less important than their levels of experience with schizophrenia (Karon & Vanden-Bos, 1996). In addition, the therapists who are most successful tend to be those who take an active role, setting limits, expressing opinions, challenging patients' statements, providing guidance, displaying empathy, and gaining trust (Fox, 2000; Whitehorn & Betz, 1975).

FAMILY THERAPY Between 25 and 40 percent of persons who are recovering from schizophrenia live with their family: parents, siblings, spouses, or children (Torrey, Wolfe, & Flynn, 1988). Such situations create special pressures, so that even if family stress was not a factor in the onset of the disorder, a patient's recovery may be greatly affected by the behavior and reactions of the relatives at home. As we observed earlier, those living with relatives who display high levels of *expressed emotion*—that is, relatives who are very critical, emotionally overinvolved, and hostile—often have a higher relapse rate than those living with more positive and supportive relatives (Penn & Mueser, 1996; Vaughan et al., 1992).

For their part, family members may be greatly affected by the social withdrawal and unusual behaviors of a relative with schizophrenia (Bloch et al., 1995; Creer & Wing, 1974). One individual complained, "In the evening you go into the sitting room and it's in darkness. You turn on the light and there he is just sitting there, staring in front of him."

EXTRAPYRAMIDAL EFFECTS Unwanted movements, such as severe shaking, bizarre-looking grimaces, twisting of the body, and extreme restlessness, sometimes produced by conventional antipsychotic drugs.

TARDIVE DYSKINESIA Extrapyramidal effects that appear in some patients after they have taken conventional antipsychotic drugs for an extended time.

AGRANULOCYTOSIS A life-threatening reduction in white blood cells. This condition is sometimes produced by clozapine, one of the atypical antipsychotic drugs.

© 1998 Sidney Harris

"I'M GLAD YOU CAME TO ME. VISIONS OF GHOSTS OF CHRISTMAS PAST, PRESENT AND FUTURE ARE CLEARLY DELUSIONS BASED ON UNDERLYING PSYCHOLOGICAL CONFLICTS."

"The Monkeys Are Eating My Brain"

For much of the 1990s, Michael Laudor was an inspiration for anyone who had ever suffered from schizophrenia. In 1998 he became a cautionary note about the precarious nature of this disorder—a reminder that excessive stress or premature cessation of medications can lead to relapse and, in some instances, to dire consequences.

A brilliant young man who graduated *summa cum laude* from Yale University, Laudor developed schizophrenia at the age of 24 and was hospitalized for eight months. With antipsychotic medications, psychotherapy, and strong family support, he apparently overcame his many delusions and hallucinations and was accepted at Yale Law School. Still grappling with schizophrenia when he first learned of his acceptance, he screamed, "The monkeys are eating my brain." But he continued to recover during his years at Yale, and he became known for his brilliant mind, charismatic personality, and mastery of the jazz guitar (Morganthau, 1998).

Courageous and concerned about the plight of others with schizophrenia, Laudor openly discussed his disorder in a lengthy interview in the *New York Times* in 1995. "People with schizophrenia are negated constantly," he said then. "But I can . . . say I am a person with schizophrenia who has been a senior editor of *The Yale Law Review,* who is a reasonable candidate to be a law professor. And if I am not doing that, I will be doing something else of value to society."

The interview changed his life. It led to a $600,000 advance for an autobiographical book and $1.5 million for the movie rights to it. He moved to a quiet New York suburb with his fiancée, Caroline Costello, the two of them prepared for the birth of a child, and Michael went to work on his book.

But on a summer day in 1998, Caroline was murdered—stabbed

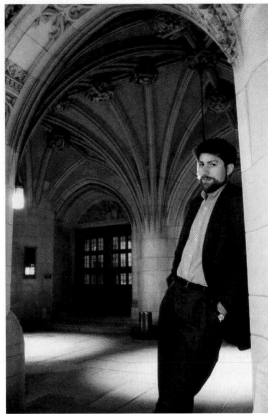

James Estrin/The New York Times

ConsiderThis

◉ In the early years of antipsychotic drug use, patients who failed to respond to these drugs were likely to receive higher and higher dosages until many of them seemed to be walking zombies. Why might clinicians have used this medication strategy, even when the drugs failed to reduce symptoms?

To address such issues, clinicians now commonly include family therapy in their treatment of schizophrenia, providing family members with guidance, training, practical advice, psychoeducation about the disorder, and emotional support and empathy (Pitschel et al., 2001). In family therapy, relatives develop more realistic expectations and become more tolerant, less guilt-ridden, and more willing to try new patterns of communication. Family therapists also try to help the person with schizophrenia cope with the pressures of family life, make better use of family members, and avoid troublesome interactions. Research has found that family therapy—particularly when it is combined with drug therapy—helps reduce tensions within the family and so helps relapse rates go down (Bustillo et al., 2001; Pitschel et al., 2001).

The families of persons with schizophrenia may also turn to *family support groups* and *family psychoeducational programs* for assistance, encouragement, and advice (Herz et al., 2000; Zhang et al., 1998). In such programs, family members meet with others in the same situation to share their thoughts and emotions, provide mutual support, and learn about schizophrenia. Although research has yet to determine the usefulness of these groups, the approach is becoming common.

SOCIAL THERAPY Many clinicians believe that the treatment of people with schizophrenia should include techniques that address social and personal difficulties in the clients' lives. These clinicians offer practical advice; work with clients on problem solving, decision making, and social skills; make sure that the clients are taking their medications properly; and may even help them find work, financial assistance, and proper housing (McGuire, 2000; Penn & Mueser, more than ten times with a chef's knife. Soon after, Laudor was found on the campus of Cornell University, disheveled and spattered with blood. He confessed to attacking Caroline (Chua-Eoan, 1998). No one knew precisely what had caused Laudor to kill his fiancée, but few doubted that a return of psychotic functioning was generally responsible. The police reported that he seemed disoriented at the time of his arrest. His mother had detected delusional ideas in phone conversations that she had had with him during the days preceding the killing. Caroline herself had increasingly been expressing concerns to friends about his mental condition.

What triggered Laudor's relapse and out-of-character behavior (friends had never known him to be violent)? Some friends believe that he had stopped taking his antipsychotic medications; others suggest that the medications had stopped being effective. Then again, Laudor had been experiencing considerable stress in his life. He had not been able to

find work as a law professor despite (or perhaps because of) his fame, and writing the book seemed to place enormous pressure on him, given his perfectionistic ways. Some friends also pointed out that the death of Laudor's father in 1995 had left him without one of his most important sources of support: he had previously credited his father with saving his life.

Whatever the specific trigger, Laudor's fall was a tragedy not only for him and his fiancée but for everyone who saw him as evidence that schizophrenia can be conquered. Although numerous people with this disorder do recover (many without relapse), this highly publicized

case reminds us of how much the clinical field has yet to learn about the causes, course, and treatment of schizophrenia.

Battle lost *(Facing page) Yale Law School student Michael Laudor, who described his inspirational battle against schizophrenia in a 1995 interview with the* New York Times. *(This page) Laudor was taken into custody in 1998 and charged with killing his fiancée in their garden apartment.*

1996). Research finds that this practical, active, and broad approach, called *social therapy* or *personal therapy,* does indeed help keep people out of the hospital (Hogarty et al., 1997, 1986, 1974).

The Community Approach

The broadest approach for the treatment of schizophrenia is the *community approach.* In 1963, partly in response to the terrible conditions in public mental institutions, the U.S. government ordered that patients be released and treated in the community. Congress passed the Community Mental Health Act, which provided that patients with psychological disorders were to receive a range of mental health services—outpatient therapy, inpatient treatment, emergency care, preventive care, and aftercare—in their communities rather than being transported to institutions far from home. The act was aimed at a variety of psychological disorders, but patients with schizophrenia, especially those who had been institutionalized for years, were affected most. Other countries around the world put similar sociocultural treatment programs into action shortly thereafter (Hafner & van der Heiden, 1988).

Thus began three decades of **deinstitutionalization,** an exodus of hundreds of thousands of patients with schizophrenia and other long-term mental disorders from state institutions into the community. On a given day in 1955 close to 600,000 patients were living in state institutions; today only around 70,000 patients reside in those settings (Lang, 1999; Torrey, 1997). Clinicians have learned that patients recovering from schizophrenia can profit greatly from community programs. As we shall see, however, the quality of community care for these people

"If it is possible to rehabilitate two-thirds of patients, why aren't we?"

Ronald Levant, 2000, schizophrenia treatment researcher

DEINSTITUTIONALIZATION The discharge of large numbers of patients from long-term institutional care so that they might be treated in community programs.

has been inadequate throughout the United States. The result is a "revolving door" syndrome: many patients have been released to the community, readmitted to an institution within months, released a second time, admitted yet again, and so on, over and over (Geller, 1992).

WHAT ARE THE FEATURES OF EFFECTIVE COMMUNITY CARE? People recovering from schizophrenia need medication, psychotherapy, help in handling daily pressures and responsibilities, guidance in making decisions, training in social skills, residential supervision, and vocational counseling. Those whose communities help them meet these needs make greater progress than people living in other communities (McGuire, 2000). Some of the key features of effective community care programs are (1) coordination of patient services, (2) short-term hospitalization, (3) partial hospitalization, (4) halfway houses, and (5) occupational training.

COORDINATED SERVICES When the Community Mental Health Act was first passed, it was expected that community care would center on a **community mental health center,** a treatment facility that would provide medication, psychotherapy, and inpatient emergency care to people with severe disturbances, as well as coordinate the services offered by other community agencies. When community mental health centers do in fact provide these services, patients with schizophrenia often make significant progress (Scott & Dixon, 1995). Coordination of services is particularly important for the so-called *mentally ill chemical abusers (MICAs)*, patients with schizophrenia as well as a substance-related disorder (Drake et al., 2001). It is estimated that at least half of all patients with schizophrenia also abuse alcohol or other drugs at some time during their disorder (Cantor-Graae et al., 2001; Buckley, 1998).

"Wild Man of West 96th Street" *The famous case of Larry Hogue, the so-called* Wild Man of West 96th Street, *helped bring the plight of MICAs to public attention. During the 1990s Hogue was repeatedly released from mental hospitals and prisons, each time returning to a life of alcohol abuse and mental illness and a pattern of chasing and frightening his Upper West Side neighbors in Manhattan.*

SHORT-TERM HOSPITALIZATION When people develop schizophrenic symptoms, today's clinicians first try to treat them on an outpatient basis, usually with a combination of antipsychotic medication and psychotherapy (Marder, 1996). If this approach fails, *short-term hospitalization* that lasts a few weeks (rather than months or years) may be tried. Soon after the patients improve, they are released for **aftercare,** a general term for follow-up care and treatment in the community (Sederer, 1992).

PARTIAL HOSPITALIZATION People's needs may fall between full hospitalization and outpatient therapy, and so some communities offer **day centers** or **day hospitals,** all-day programs in which the patients return to their homes for the night (Clay, 1996; Goldberg, 1995). The centers provide patients with daily supervised activities, therapy, and programs to improve social skills. People recovering from schizophrenia in day centers often do better than those who spend extended periods in the hospital or in traditional outpatient therapy (Takano et al., 1995).

HALFWAY HOUSES Halfway houses, also called **group homes,** are homes for people who do not require hospitalization but cannot live alone or with their families. These residences, often large houses in areas where housing is inexpensive, may shelter between one and two dozen people. The live-in staff usually are *paraprofessionals*—lay people who receive training and ongoing supervision from outside mental health professionals. The houses are usually run with a *milieu therapy* philosophy that emphasizes mutual support, resident responsibility, and self-government.

Research indicates that halfway houses help many people recovering from schizophrenia adjust to community life and avoid rehospitalization (McGuire, 2000). Here is how one woman described living in a halfway house after 10 hospitalizations in 12 years:

COMMUNITY MENTAL HEALTH CENTER A treatment facility that provides medication, psychotherapy, and emergency inpatient care for psychological problems and coordinates treatment in the community.

AFTERCARE A program of post-hospitalization care and treatment out in the community.

DAY CENTER A program that offers hospital-like treatment during the day only. Also known as *day hospital.*

> The halfway house changed my life. First of all, I discovered that some of the staff members had once been clients in the program! That one single fact offered me hope. For the first time, I saw proof that a program could help someone, that it was possible to regain control over one's life and become independent. The house was democratically run; all residents had one vote and the staff members, outnumbered 5 to 22, could not make rules or even discharge a client from the program without majority sentiment. There was a house bill of rights that was strictly observed by all. We helped one another and gave support. When residents were in a crisis, no staff member hustled them off or increased their medication to calm them down. Residents could cry, be comforted and hugged until a solution could be found, or until they accepted that it was okay to feel bad. . . . Choices were real, and failure and success were accepted equally.
>
> *(Lovejoy, 1982, pp. 605–609)*

Art that heals *Art and other creative activities can be therapeutic for people with schizophrenia and other severe mental disorders. More than 250,000 pieces of patient-produced art are on display at the Museum of the Unconscious in Rio de Janeiro, Brazil, where supervisors work closely with patients every day. One of the museum's most famous and talented patients, Fernando Diniz, poses with some of his extraordinary artwork.*

OCCUPATIONAL TRAINING Paid employment provides income, independence, self-respect, and the stimulation of working with others. It also brings companionship and order to one's daily life. For these reasons, occupational training and placement are important services for people with schizophrenia (McGuire, 2000; Bell, Lysaker, & Milstein, 1996).

Many people recovering from this disorder receive occupational training in a **sheltered workshop**—a supervised workplace for employees who are not ready for competitive or complicated jobs. For some, the sheltered workshop becomes a permanent workplace. For others, it is an important step toward better-paying and more demanding employment or a return to a previous job (Bustillo et al., 2001; Bell et al., 1996). In the United States occupational training is not consistently available to people with severe psychological disorders (Drake et al., 1996). Some studies find that only 25 percent of such people are employed, fewer than 10 percent outside of sheltered workplaces (MRI, 1998; Mulkern & Manderscheid, 1989).

HOW HAS COMMUNITY TREATMENT FAILED? There is no doubt that effective community programs can help people with schizophrenia recover. However, fewer than half of all people who need them receive appropriate community mental health services (McGuire, 2000; PORT, 1998). In fact, in any given year, almost 40 percent of all people with schizophrenia receive no treatment at all (Torrey, 1997; Regier et al., 1993). Two factors are primarily responsible: *poor coordination* of services and *shortage* of services.

POOR COORDINATION OF SERVICES The various mental health agencies in a community often fail to communicate with one another (Leshner et al., 1992). There may, for example, be an opening at a nearby halfway house and the therapist at the community mental health center may not know about it. In addition, even within a community agency a patient may not have continuing contacts with the same staff members. Still another problem is poor communication between state hospitals and community mental health centers (Torrey, 1997; Leshner et al., 1992). Sometimes community agencies are not even informed when patients are discharged from the hospital.

It is not surprising, then, that a growing number of community therapists are becoming **case managers** for people with schizophrenia (Chan et al., 2000). Like the social therapists described earlier, they offer therapy and advice, teach problem-solving and social skills, and ensure that medications are being taken

HALFWAY HOUSE A residence for people with schizophrenia or other severe problems who cannot live alone or with their families, often staffed by paraprofessionals. Also known as *group home.*

SHELTERED WORKSHOP A supervised workplace for people who are not yet ready for competitive jobs.

CASE MANAGER A community therapist who offers a full range of services for people with schizophrenia or other severe disorders, including therapy, advice, medication, guidance, and protection of patients' rights.

Community care in action *Clinicians have learned that people with schizophrenia and other severe disorders often make great progress in well-coordinated community treatment programs. Here patients begin their day with breakfast at New York City's Fountain House, a day center that provides daily activities and therapy, as well as extensive occupational training.*

THE NEW MENTAL INSTITUTIONS

The Los Angeles County Jail, where 3,300 of the 21,000 inmates require daily mental health services, is now de facto the largest mental institution in the United States (Torrey, 1997; Grinfield, 1993).

properly. In addition, they try to coordinate available community services, guide clients through the community system, and, perhaps most important, help protect clients' rights. Many professionals now believe that effective case management is the key to success for a community program (Dozier, 1996).

SHORTAGE OF SERVICES The number of community programs available to people with schizophrenia falls woefully short. The roughly 800 community mental health centers now operating in the United States are only one-third of the number projected in the early 1960s. Halfway houses and sheltered workshops are in similarly short supply.

Also disturbing, the community mental health centers that do exist generally fail to provide adequate services for people with severe disorders. They tend to devote their efforts and money to people with less disabling problems, such as anxiety disorders or problems in social adjustment. Only a fraction of the patients treated by community mental health centers suffer from schizophrenia (Torrey, 1997, 1988).

Why is there such a shortage of services for people with schizophrenia? First, it appears that most mental health professionals simply prefer to work with people whose problems are less severe and shorter-term (Lee et al., 1993; Harding et al., 1992). Second, neighborhood residents often object to the presence of community programs for patients recovering from schizophrenia (Leshner et al., 1992). But perhaps the primary reason for the shortage of community care is economic. On the one hand, more public funds are available for people with psychological disorders now than in the past (Torrey, 1997, 1988; Redick et al., 1992). On the other hand, rather little of this new money is going to community treatment programs for people with severe disorders. Much of it goes to monthly income payments such as social security disability income, to services for persons with mental disorders in nursing homes and general hospitals, and to community services for people who are less disturbed (Torrey, 1997, 1988; Stein, 1993). Today the financial burden of providing community treatment for persons with long-term severe disorders often falls on local governments and nonprofit organizations rather than the federal or state government, and local resources cannot always meet this challenge.

WHAT ARE THE CONSEQUENCES OF INADEQUATE COMMUNITY TREATMENT? What happens to persons with schizophrenia whose communities do not provide the services they need and whose families cannot afford private treatment? As we have observed, a large number receive no treatment at all; many others spend a short time in a state hospital and are then discharged prematurely, often without adequate follow-up treatment (Torrey, 1997; Torrey et al., 1988).

Many of the people with schizophrenia return to their families and receive medication and perhaps emotional and financial support, but little else in the way of treatment. Between 5 and 15 percent enter an alternative institution such as a nursing home or rest home, where they receive only custodial care and medication (Torrey, 1997; Smyer, 1989). As many as 35 percent are placed in single-room-occupancy hotels, boardinghouses, or rooming houses, typically in run-down inner-city neighborhoods. They survive on government disability payments (Barker et al., 1992), and many spend their days wandering through neighborhood streets. Thus it is sometimes said that persons with schizophrenia are now "dumped" in the community, just as they were once "warehoused" in institutions.

Finally, a great number of people with schizophrenia have become homeless (Herman et al., 2000; Susnick & Belcher, 1995). There are between 350,000 and 1 million homeless people in the United States, and approximately one-third apparently have a severe mental disorder, commonly schizophrenia (Torrey, 1997; Manderscheid & Rosenstein, 1992). Many such persons have been released from hospitals. Others are young adults who were never hospitalized in the first place. Another 150,000 people with severe mental disorders end up in prisons because their disorders have led them to break the law (Torrey, 1997; DeAngelis, 1994). Certainly deinstitutionalization and the community mental health movement have failed these people, and many report actually feeling relieved if they are able to return to hospital life (Drake & Wallach, 1992).

THE PROMISE OF COMMUNITY TREATMENT Despite these very serious problems, proper community care has shown great potential for assisting in the recovery from schizophrenia and other severe disorders, and clinicians and many government officials continue to press to make it more available. In recent years government and professional agencies have created task forces whose purpose is to find more effective ways for the federal government, states, and local organizations to meet the needs of people with such disorders (Knowlton, 1997; Leshner et al., 1992).

Another important development has been the formation of *national interest groups* that push for better community treatment (McGuire, 2000; Torrey, 1997). One, the National Alliance for the Mentally Ill, began in 1979 with 300 members and has expanded to more than 208,000 members in 1,200 chapters (NAMI, 1999). Made up largely of relatives of people with severe mental disorders (particularly schizophrenia, bipolar disorders, and major depressive disorder), this group has become a powerful lobbying force in state legislatures and

Lobbying for better care *In a creative form of protest, members of the Florida Alliance for the Mentally Ill chained together figures without faces in 1997 and placed them outside the state capitol building. The members were reminding state legislators about the needs of the tens of thousands of faceless patients who are held captive by their disorders.*

THE CURRENT SCENE

Coming Full Circle

During the past three decades patients with schizophrenia have journeyed from mental hospitals, where they received poor care, into the community, where many receive no care at all. E. Fuller Torrey describes the ultimate irony in this tragic state of affairs:

> For three quarters of a century . . . part of Manhattan State Hospital [served] patients with severe mental illnesses. Then, as more and more beds became vacant in the 1970s, the building was no longer needed and it was turned over to the City of New York, which reopened it in 1981 as a public shelter [the Keener Shelter] for homeless men. . . .
>
> In 1990, the Keener Shelter housed 800 homeless men. At least 40 percent of them were mentally ill and many had previously been patients at

Manhattan State Hospital. One man with schizophrenia has been living in the Keener Shelter for seven years, the same period of time he had previously been there when it had been a hospital. . . . [The difference is] the

Keener Shelter is merely a shelter and cannot deliver the psychiatric care needed by many of its inhabitants. Nor is the Keener Shelter unique. . . . For many of these homeless, it is like returning home. █

(TORREY, 1997, pp. 23–24)

Consider This

● How might patients react when they find themselves back in the same place where they were confined years earlier, under totally different circumstances? ● Might the Keener Shelter, which is run humanely and efficiently by the Volunteers of America, be more therapeutic than the old state hospitals?

Hospital neglect *Even as countries around the world move away from long-term institutional care and toward community mental health, the horrors of asylums and overcrowded public mental hospitals continue to live in some locations. This heart-wrenching scene inside a mental hospital in the southern Philippines clarifies the point.*

has pressured community mental health centers to treat more persons with schizophrenia and other severe disorders (see Table 12-3).

Today community care is a major feature of treatment for people recovering from schizophrenia in countries throughout the world (Dencker & Dencker, 1995; Fog, 1995). Some countries, learning from the mistakes of deinstitutionalization in the United States, have organized their own community programs better and as a result have had more success with them (Perris, 1988). Both in the United States and abroad, varied and well-coordinated community treatment is seen as an important part of the solution to the problem of schizophrenia (Melle et al., 2000).

Table 12-3 DSM-IV Checklist

An Array of Psychotic Disorders

DISORDER	KEY FEATURES	DURATION	LIFETIME PREVALENCE
Schizophrenia	Various psychotic symptoms such as delusions, hallucinations, disorganized speech, flat or inappropriate affect, and catatonia.	6 months or more	1.0%
Brief psychotic disorder	Various psychotic symptoms such as delusions, hallucinations, disorganized speech, flat or inappropriate affect, and catatonia.	Less than 1 month	Unknown
Schizophreniform disorder	Various psychotic symptoms such as delusions, hallucinations, disorganized speech, flat or inappropriate affect, and catatonia.	1 to 5 months	0.2%
Schizoaffective disorder	Marked symptoms of both schizophrenia and a mood disorder.	6 months or more	Unknown
Delusional disorder	Persistent delusions that are not bizarre and not due to schizophrenia. Persecutory, jealous, grandiose, and somatic delusions are common.	1 month or more	0.1%
Shared psychotic disorder	Person adopts delusions that are held by another individual, such as a parent or sibling. Also known as *folie à deux*.	No minimum length	Unknown
Psychotic disorder due to a general medical condition	Hallucinations or delusions caused by a medical illness or brain damage.	No minimum length	Unknown
Substance-induced psychotic disorder	Hallucinations or delusions caused directly by a substance, such as an abused drug.	No minimum length	Unknown

SUMMING UP

How Is Schizophrenia Treated?

For years all efforts to treat schizophrenia brought only frustration. The disorder is still difficult to treat, but today's therapies are more successful than those of the past.

Institutional Care For more than half of the twentieth century the main treatment for schizophrenia was institutionalization and custodial care. In the 1950s two in-hospital approaches were developed, milieu therapy and the token economy program. They often brought improvement and particularly helped patients to care for themselves and feel better about themselves.

Antipsychotic Drugs The discovery of antipsychotic drugs in the 1950s revolutionized the treatment of schizophrenia. Today they are almost always a part of treatment. Theorists believe that the drugs, at least the conventional ones, operate by reducing excessive dopamine activity in the brain. However, the conventional antipsychotic drugs can also produce dramatic unwanted effects, particularly movement abnormalities. One such effect, tardive dyskinesia, may develop after people have taken the drugs for an extended time. Recently atypical antipsychotic drugs have been developed, which seem to be more effective than the conventional drugs and to cause fewer unwanted effects.

Psychotherapy Today psychotherapy is often employed successfully in combination with antipsychotic drugs. The most helpful forms include insight therapy, family therapy, and social therapy.

The Community Approach A community approach to the treatment of schizophrenia was developed when a policy of deinstitutionalization brought about a mass exodus of hundreds of thousands of patients from state institutions into the community. Among the key elements of effective community care programs are coordination of patient services by a community mental health center, short-term hospitalization, day centers, halfway houses, and occupational training. However, the quality and funding of community care for persons with schizophrenia have been inadequate throughout the United States, often resulting in a "revolving door" syndrome. One result is that many people with schizophrenia are homeless or jailed.

ConsiderThis

○ Why have people with schizophrenia been the victims of mistreatment (lobotomy or deinstitutionalization, for example) more often than people with other disorders?

ALTERNATIVE PLACEMENT

Persons with severe mental disorders account for at least 10 percent of the jail populations in the United States (Torrey, 1999).

CROSSROADS:

An Important Lesson

Schizophrenia—a bizarre and frightening disorder—was studied intensively throughout the twentieth century. Only since the discovery of antipsychotic drugs, however, have clinicians gained much insight into its causes. As with most other psychological disorders, clinical theorists now believe that schizophrenia, in whatever form, is probably caused by a combination of factors (Brennan & Harvey, 2001). At the same time, researchers have been far more successful in identifying the biological influences than the psychological and sociocultural ones. While biological investigations have closed in on specific genes, abnormalities in brain biochemistry and structure, and even viral infections, most of the psychological and sociocultural research has been able to cite only general factors, such as family conflict and diagnostic labeling. Clearly, researchers must identify psychological and sociocultural factors with greater precision if we are to gain a full understanding of this disorder.

The treatment picture for schizophrenia has also improved in recent decades. After years of frustration and failure, clinicians now have an arsenal of weapons to use against the disorder—medication, institutional programs, psychotherapy, and community programs. It has become very clear that antipsychotic medications open the door for recovery from this disorder, but in most cases other kinds

"I doubt if ever the history of the world . . . could show a larger amount of insanity than that of the present day."

John Hawkes, "On the Increase of Insanity," 1857

of treatment are also needed to help the recovery process along. The various approaches must be combined to meet each individual's specific needs.

Working with schizophrenia has taught clinicians an important lesson: no matter how compelling the evidence for biological causes may be, a strictly biological approach to the treatment of psychological disorders is a mistake more often than not (McCabe et al., 1999). Largely on the basis of pharmacological discoveries, hundreds of thousands of patients with schizophrenia and other severe mental disorders were released to the community beginning in the 1960s. Little attention was paid to the psychological and sociocultural needs of these individuals, and many of them have been trapped in their pathology ever since. Clinicians must remember this lesson, especially in today's climate, when managed care and government priorities often promote medication as the sole treatment for psychological problems.

When Emil Kraepelin first described schizophrenia at the turn of the twentieth century, he estimated that only 13 percent of its sufferers ever improved. Today, even with shortages in community care, many more of these individuals show improvement (McGuire, 2000). Certainly the clinical field has advanced considerably since Kraepelin's day, yet it still has far to go. It is unacceptable that the majority of people with this disorder receive few or none of the effective community interventions that have been developed, worse still that tens of thousands have become homeless. It is now up to clinical professionals and public officials to address the needs of all people with schizophrenia.

"To recover rationality after being irrational, to recover normal life, is a great thing."

John Nash, 1994 recipient of Nobel Prize in Economics, after suffering from schizophrenia for 25 years

KEY TERMS

schizophrenia p. 345

psychosis p. 345

positive symptoms p. 348

delusion p. 348

formal thought disorder p. 348

loose associations p. 349

hallucination p. 349

inappropriate affect p. 351

negative symptoms p. 351

alogia p. 351

flat affect p. 351

avolition p. 351

psychomotor symptom p. 351

catatonia p. 352

disorganized type of schizophrenia p. 353

catatonic type of schizophrenia p. 353

paranoid type of schizophrenia p. 353

undifferentiated type of schizophrenia p. 354

residual type of schizophrenia p. 354

Type I schizophrenia p. 354

Type II schizophrenia p. 354

diathesis-stress relationship p. 354

dopamine hypothesis p. 356

antipsychotic drugs p. 356

phenothiazines p. 356

Parkinson's disease p. 356

atypical antipsychotic drugs p. 357

schizophrenogenic mother p. 358

expressed emotion p. 361

institutionalization p. 361

state hospitals p. 361

milieu therapy p. 363

token economy program p. 363

conventional antipsychotic drugs p. 365

atypical antipsychotic drugs p. 365

neuroleptic drugs p. 365

extrapyramidal effects p. 366

tardive dyskinesia p. 366

agranulocytosis p. 367

social therapy p. 369

deinstitutionalization p. 369

community mental health center p. 370

mentally ill chemical abuser (MICA) p. 370

aftercare p. 370

day center p. 370

halfway house p. 371

sheltered workshop p. 371

case manager p. 371

QUICK QUIZ

1. What is schizophrenia, and how prevalent is it? What is its relationship to socioeconomic class, gender, and race? pp. 345–346

2. What are the positive, negative, and psychomotor symptoms of schizophrenia? pp. 348–352

3. What are the most common kinds of delusions, hallucinations, and formal thought disorders in schizophrenia? pp. 348–351

4. What are the five types of schizophrenia identified by DSM-IV? What are the differences between Type I and Type II schizophrenia? pp. 352–354

5. Describe the genetic, biochemical, brain structure, and viral explanations of schizophrenia, and discuss how they have been supported in research. pp. 354–358

6. What are the key features of the psychodynamic, cognitive, social labeling, and family explanations of schizophrenia? pp. 358–360

7. Describe institutional care for people with schizophrenia over the course of the twentieth century. How effective are the milieu and token economy treatment programs? pp. 361–364

8. How do antipsychotic drugs operate on the brain, and how effective are they in the treatment of schizophrenia? What are the unwanted effects of some of these drugs? pp. 364–367

9. What kinds of psychotherapy seem to help people with schizophrenia? pp. 367–369

10. What is deinstitutionalization? What features of community care seem critical for helping people with schizophrenia? pp. 369–371

11. How and why has the community mental health approach been inadequate for people with schizophrenia? pp. 371–374

CYBER STUDY

▲ *Observe hallucinations as they occur.* ▲ *Can you tell whether persons have schizophrenia by looking at them?* ▲ *How do people react to the label "schizophrenia"?* ▲ *Witness past hospital treatments for schizophrenia.*

SEARCH THE *FUNDAMENTALS OF ABNORMAL PSYCHOLOGY* CD ROM FOR

▲ Chapter 12 video cases and discussion
  "Steve"—Schizophrenia
  "Augustine"—Schizophrenia: Pharmacological Treatment

▲ Chapter 12 practice test and feedback

▲ Additional video case and discussion

▲ Early Procedures in Mental Hospitals

LOG ON TO THE COMER WEB PAGE FOR

▲ Suggested Web links, research, exercises, FAQ page, additional Chapter 12 practice test questions
  <www.worthpublishers.com/comer>

UCLA Neuropsychiatric Institute & Hospital

Disorders of Memory and Other Cognitive Functions

Brian was spending Saturday sailing with his wife, Helen. The water was rough but well within what they considered safe limits. They were having a wonderful time and really didn't notice that the sky was getting darker, the wind blowing harder, and the sailboat becoming more difficult to control. After a few hours of sailing, they found themselves far from shore in the middle of a powerful and dangerous storm.

The storm intensified very quickly. Brian had trouble controlling the sailboat amidst the high winds and wild waves. He and Helen tried to put on the safety jackets they had neglected to wear earlier, but the boat turned over before they were finished. Brian, the better swimmer of the two, was able to swim back to the overturned sailboat, grab the side, and hold on for dear life, but Helen simply could not overcome the rough waves and reach the boat. As Brian watched in horror and disbelief, his wife disappeared from view.

After a time, the storm began to lose its strength. Brian managed to restore the sailboat to its proper position and sail back to shore. Finally he reached safety, but the personal consequences of this storm were just beginning. The next days were filled with pain and further horror: the Coast Guard finding Helen's body . . . discussions with authorities . . . breaking the news to Helen's parents . . . conversations with friends . . . self-blame . . . grief . . . and more. On Wednesday, five days after that fateful afternoon, Brian collected himself and attended Helen's funeral and burial. It was the longest and most difficult day of his life. Most of the time, he felt as though he were in a trance.

Soon after awakening on Thursday morning, Brian realized that something was terribly wrong with him. Try though he might, he couldn't remember the events of the past few days. He remembered the accident, Helen's death, and the call from the Coast Guard after they had found her body. But just about everything else was gone—right up through the funeral. At first he had even thought that it was now Sunday, and that his discussions with family and friends and the funeral were all ahead of him. But the newspaper, the funeral guest book, and a phone conversation with his brother soon convinced him that he had lost the past four days of his life.

Most of us experience a sense of wholeness and continuity as we interact with the world. We perceive ourselves as being more than a collection of isolated sensory experiences, feelings, and behaviors. In other words, we have an *identity,* a sense of who we are—unique in our preferences, abilities, characteristics, and needs. Others recognize us and expect certain things of us. But more important, we recognize ourselves and have our own expectations, values, and goals. We have an awareness of where we fit in our environment.

Memory is a key to this sense of wholeness and identity, the link between our past, present, and future. Our recall of past experiences, although not always precisely accurate, helps us react to present events and guides us in making decisions about the future. We recognize our friends and relatives, teachers and employers, and respond to them in appropriate

COMMON OCCURRENCE

In a 1997 survey, doctors reported that 80 percent of their patients over 30 years of age complained of memory loss (Muhammad, 1999).

ways. Without a memory we would always be starting over; with it, life moves forward.

People sometimes experience a major disruption of their memory. They may not be able to remember new information they just learned or old information they once knew well. When, as in Brian's case, such changes in memory lack a clear physical cause, they are called *dissociative disorders.* When the physical causes are clear, the memory disorder is called *organic.* Some memory difficulties have both dissociative and organic elements (Cantagallo et al., 1999).

Dissociative Disorders

People with **dissociative disorders** experience major changes in memory without a clear physical cause. One part of the person's memory seems to be *dissociated,* or separated, from the rest. There are several different kinds of dissociative disorders. The primary symptom of *dissociative amnesia* is an inability to recall important personal events and information. A person with *dissociative fugue* not only forgets the past but travels to a new location and may assume a new identity. Individuals with *multiple personality disorder* (*dissociative identity disorder*) have two or more separate identities that may not always have a knowledge of each other's thoughts, feelings, and behavior.

Several memorable books and movies have portrayed dissociative disorders. Two of the best known are *The Three Faces of Eve* and *Sybil,* each about a woman with multiple personalities. The topic is so fascinating that most television drama series seem to include at least one case of dissociation every season, creating the impression that the disorders are very common. Many clinicians, however, believe that they are rare.

DSM-IV also lists *depersonalization disorder,* persistent feelings of being separated from one's own mental processes or body, as a dissociative disorder. People with this disorder feel as though they are observing themselves from the outside. Because memory problems are not the central feature of this disorder, it will not be discussed here.

Dissociative Amnesia

People with **dissociative amnesia** are unable to recall important information, usually of an upsetting nature, about their lives (APA, 2000, 1994). The loss of memory is much more extensive than normal forgetting and is not caused by organic factors (see Table 13-1). Very often an episode of amnesia is directly triggered by a specific upsetting event (Gershuny & Thayer, 1999).

Dissociative amnesia may be *localized, selective, generalized,* or *continuous.* Any of these kinds of amnesia can be triggered by a traumatic experience such as Brian's, but each represents a particular pattern of forgetting. Brian was suffering from *localized amnesia,* the most common type of dissociative amnesia, in which a person loses all memory of events that took place within a limited period of time, almost always beginning with some very disturbing happening. Recall that Brian awakened on the day after the funeral and could not recall any of the events of the past difficult days, beginning after the boating tragedy. He remembered everything that happened up to and including the accident. He could also recall everything from the morning after the funeral onward, but the days in between remained a total blank. The forgotten period is called the *amnestic episode.* During an amnestic episode, people may appear confused; in some cases they wander about aimlessly. They are already experiencing memory difficulties, but seem unaware of them. Brian, for example, felt as though he were in a trance on the day of Helen's funeral.

People with *selective amnesia,* the second most common form of dissociative amnesia, remember some, but not all, events that

Table 13-1 DSM-IV Checklist

DISSOCIATIVE AMNESIA

1. One or more episodes of inability to recall important personal information, usually of a traumatic or stressful nature, that is too extensive to be explained by ordinary forgetfulness.
2. Significant distress or impairment.

Based on APA, 2000, 1994.

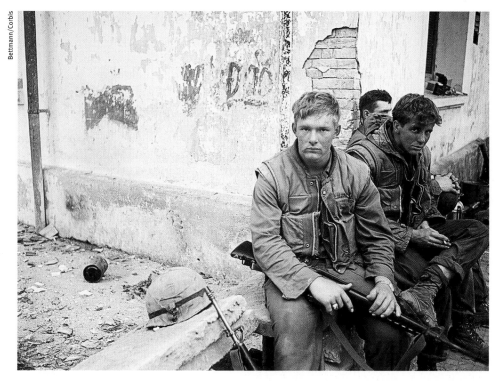

At risk *The stunned looks on the faces of these soldiers suggest confusion, shock, and exhaustion. Combat soldiers are particularly vulnerable to amnesia and other dissociative reactions. They may forget specific horrors, personal information, or even their identities.*

occurred during a period of time. If Brian had selective amnesia, he might remember breaking the news to his in-laws and his conversations with friends, but perhaps not the funeral itself.

In some cases the loss of memory extends back to times long before the upsetting period. Brian might awaken after the funeral and find that, in addition to forgetting events of the past few days, he could not remember events that occurred earlier in his life. In this case, he would be experiencing *generalized amnesia.* In extreme cases, Brian might not even remember who he is and might fail to recognize relatives and friends.

In the forms of dissociative amnesia discussed so far, the period affected by the amnesia has an end. In *continuous amnesia,* however, forgetting continues into the present. Brian might forget new and ongoing experiences as well as what happened before and during the tragedy. Continuous forgetting of this kind is actually quite rare in cases of dissociative amnesia, but, as we shall see, not in cases of organic amnesia.

All these forms of dissociative amnesia are similar in that the amnesia interferes mostly with a person's memory of personal material. Memory for abstract or encyclopedic information usually remains. People with dissociative amnesia are as likely as anyone else to know the name of the president of the United States and how to write, read, drive a car, and so on.

Clinicians do not know how common dissociative amnesia is, but they do know that many cases seem to begin during serious threats to health and safety, as in wartime and natural disasters (Karon & Widener, 1997). Combat veterans often report memory gaps of hours or days, and some forget personal information, such as their names and addresses (van der Hart, Brown, & Graafland, 1999). The 1990s also saw an explosion in the number of case reports of dissociative amnesia linked to child sexual abuse. Dissociative amnesia may also occur under more ordinary circumstances, such as the sudden loss of a loved one through rejection or death (Loewenstein, 1991) or guilt over behavior considered to be immoral (e.g., an extramarital affair).

The personal impact of dissociative amnesia depends on how much is forgotten. Obviously, an amnestic episode of two years is more of a problem than one of two hours. Similarly, an amnestic episode during which a person's life changes in major ways causes more difficulties than one that is quiet and uneventful.

Consider This

⦿ Most people have had odd memory lapses such as forgetting why they are doing something, arriving at a destination without remembering any details of the drive there, forgetting an important appointment or occasion, having trouble remembering the name of a person or where they know someone from, or forgetting an event everyone else seems to remember. What kinds of explanations can you think of for each of these cases?

MEMORY The faculty for recalling past events and past learning.

DISSOCIATIVE DISORDERS Disorders marked by major changes in memory that do not have clear physical causes.

DISSOCIATIVE AMNESIA A dissociative disorder marked by an inability to recall important personal events and information.

Dissociative Fugue

People with **dissociative fugue** not only forget their personal identities and details of their past lives, but also flee to an entirely different location (see Table 13-2). Some individuals travel but a short distance and make few social contacts in the new setting (APA, 2000, 1994). Although confused about their identity, they do not actually take on a new one. Their fugue is brief—a matter of hours or days—and ends suddenly. In other cases, however, the person travels far from home, takes a new name and establishes a new identity, develops new relationships, and even seeks a new line of work. Such people may even display new personality characteristics; often they are more outgoing (APA, 2000, 1994). Some have even been known to travel to foreign countries thousands of miles away. This kind of fugue is seen in the case of the Reverend Ansel Bourne:

> On January 17, 1887, [the Reverend Ansel Bourne, of Greene, R.I.] drew 551 dollars from a bank in Providence with which to pay for a certain lot of land in Greene, paid certain bills, and got into a Pawtucket horsecar. This is the last incident which he remembers. He did not return home that day, and nothing was heard of him for two months. He was published in the papers as missing, and foul play being suspected, the police sought in vain his whereabouts. On the morning of March 14th, however, at Norristown, Pennsylvania, a man calling himself A. I. Brown who had rented a small shop six weeks previously, stocked it with stationery, confectionery, fruit and small articles, and carried on his quiet trade without seeming to anyone unnatural or eccentric, woke up in a fright and called in the people of the house to tell him where he was. He said that his name was Ansel Bourne, that he was entirely ignorant of Norristown, that he knew nothing of shop-keeping, and that the last thing he remembered—it seemed only yesterday—was drawing the money from the bank, etc. in Providence. . . . He was very weak, having lost apparently over twenty pounds of flesh during his escapade, and had such a horror of the idea of the candy-store that he refused to set foot in it again.
>
> *(James, 1890, pp. 391–393)*

Approximately 0.2 percent of the population experience dissociative fugue. Like dissociative amnesia, a fugue usually follows a severely stressful event, such as a wartime experience or a natural disaster, though personal stress, such as financial or legal difficulties or episodes of depression, may also trigger it (APA, 2000, 1994). Some adolescent runaways may be in a state of fugue (Loewenstein, 1991). Like cases of dissociative amnesia, fugues usually affect personal memories from the past rather than encyclopedic or abstract knowledge (Kihlström et al., 1993).

Fugues tend to end suddenly. In some cases, as with Reverend Bourne, the person "awakens" in a strange place, surrounded by unfamiliar faces, and wonders how he or she got there. In other cases, the lack of personal history may arouse suspicion. Perhaps a traffic accident or legal problem leads police to discover the false identity; at other times friends search for and find the missing person. When people are found before their state of fugue has ended, therapists may find it necessary to ask them many questions about the details of their lives, repeatedly remind them who they are, and even begin psychotherapy before they recover their memories. As these people recover their past, some forget the events of the fugue period (APA, 2000, 1994).

DISSOCIATIVE FUGUE

1. Sudden, unexpected travel away from home or one's customary place of work, with inability to recall one's past.
2. Confusion about personal identity, or the assumption of a new identity.
3. Significant distress or impairment.

Based on APA, 2000, 1994.

Lost and found *Cheryl Ann Barnes is helped off a plane by her grandmother and stepmother upon arrival in Florida in 1996. The 17-year-old high school honor student had disappeared from her Florida home and was found one month later in a New York City hospital listed as Jane Doe, apparently suffering from fugue.*

Peter Cosgrove/AP Photo

A CLOSER LOOK

Repressed Childhood Memories or False Memory Syndrome?

In recent years, reports of *repressed childhood memory of abuse* have attracted much public attention. Adults with this type of *dissociative amnesia* seem to recover buried memories of sexual and physical abuse from their childhood. A woman may claim, for example, that her father sexually molested her repeatedly between the ages of 5 and 7. Or a young man may remember that a family friend made sexual advances on several occasions when he was very young. Often the repressed memories surface during therapy for another problem, perhaps for an eating disorder or depression (Gudjonsson, 1997).

Experts are deeply split on this issue (DelMonte, 2000). Some believe that recovered memories are just what they appear to be—horrible memories of abuse that have been buried for years in the person's mind. They point out that at least 200,000 to 300,000 children in the United States are victims of sexual abuse each year, terrible experiences that may leave the children vulnerable to dissociative amnesia. Some studies in fact suggest that 18 to 59 percent of sexual abuse victims have difficulty recalling at least some details of their traumas (Chu et al., 1999; Horn, 1993).

Other experts believe that the memories are actually illusions—false images created by a mind that is confused. In fact, an organization called the False Memory Syndrome Foundation now assists people who claim to be falsely charged with abuse. These theorists note that the details of childhood sexual abuse are usually remembered all too well, not completely wiped from memory (McNally et al., 1998; Loftus, 1993; APA, 1996). They also point out that memory in general is hardly foolproof (Schacter, 1999). Even when recalling events as dramatic as the explosion of the space shuttle *Challenger,* people give inaccurate accounts of where they were at the time of the event or who told them about it. If memory in general is so flawed, questions certainly can be raised about the validity of recovered memories.

If the alleged recovery of childhood memories is not what it appears to be, what is it? According to opponents of the concept, it may be a powerful case of suggestibility (Loftus, 2000, 1997). These theorists hold that both the clinical and public attention has led some therapists to make the diagnosis without sufficient evidence (Frankel, 1993). The therapists may actively search for signs of early sexual abuse in clients and even encourage clients to produce repressed memories (Ganaway, 1989). Certain therapists in fact use special memory recovery techniques, including hypnosis, regression therapy, journal writing, dream interpretation, and interpretation of bodily symptoms (Lindsay, 1996, 1994; Lindsay & Read, 1994). Perhaps some clients respond to the techniques by unknowingly forming false memories of abuse. The apparent memories may then become increasingly familiar to them as a result of repeated therapy discussions of the alleged incidents (Loftus, 1997; Belli et al., 1992). In short, recovered memories may actually be *iatrogenic*—unintentionally caused by the therapist.

Of course, repressed memories of childhood sexual abuse do not emerge only in clinical settings (Leavitt, 2001, 2000; Chu et al., 1999). Many individuals come forward on their own. Opponents of the repressed memory concept explain these cases by pointing to the many books, articles, and television shows that seem to validate repressed memories of childhood sexual abuse (Loftus, 1993). Several books even tell readers how to diagnose repression in themselves, often listing symptoms that are actually rather common—not clinical symptoms at all (Tavris, 1993). Readers who have a number of these symptoms may begin a search for repressed memories of childhood abuse.

It is important to recognize that the experts who question the recovery of repressed childhood memories do not in any way deny the problem of child sexual abuse (Chu, 2000; Knapp & VandeCreek, 2000; APA, 1996). In fact, proponents and opponents alike are greatly concerned that the public may take this debate to mean that clinicians have doubts about the scope of the problem of child sexual abuse. Whatever may be the outcome of the repressed memory debate, the problem of childhood sexual abuse appears to be all too real and all too common.

Early recall *Research suggests that our memories of early childhood may be influenced by the reminiscences of family members, our dreams, television and movie plots, and our present self-image.*

M. Lerner, W. H. Freeman

The majority of people who experience dissociative fugue regain most or all of their memories and never have a recurrence. Since fugues are usually brief and totally reversible, individuals tend to experience few aftereffects (Keller & Shaywitz, 1986). People who have been away for months or years, however, often do

DISSOCIATIVE FUGUE A dissociative disorder in which a person forgets his or her past and travels to a new location.

HIDDEN MOTIVES

In his book *The Psychopathology of Everyday Life,* Freud proposed that all people have a tendency to forget what is disagreeable and that some people develop a greater capacity to forget than others. The forgetting of past events simply cannot be accidental or arbitrary, he argued. The experiences of childhood are too rich and powerful to merely slip away.

have trouble adjusting to the family, social, or job changes that have occurred during their flights. In addition, some people commit illegal or violent acts in their fugue state and later must face the consequences.

Dissociative Identity Disorder (Multiple Personality Disorder)

Multiple personality disorder is both dramatic and disabling, as we see in the case of Eric:

> Dazed and bruised from a beating, Eric, 29, was discovered wandering around a Daytona Beach shopping mall on Feb. 9. . . . Transferred six weeks later to Daytona Beach's Human Resources Center, Eric began talking to doctors in two voices: the infantile rhythms of "young Eric," a dim and frightened child, and the measured tones of "older Eric," who told a tale of terror and child abuse. According to "older Eric," after his immigrant German parents died, a harsh stepfather and his mistress took Eric from his native South Carolina to a drug dealers' hideout in a Florida swamp. Eric said he was raped by several gang members and watched his stepfather murder two men.
>
> One day in late March an alarmed counselor watched Eric's face twist into a violent snarl. Eric let loose an unearthly growl and spat out a stream of obscenities. "It sounded like something out of *The Exorcist,*" says Malcolm Graham, the psychologist who directs the case at the center. "It was the most intense thing I've ever seen in a patient." That disclosure of a new personality, who insolently demanded to be called Mark, was the first indication that Graham had been dealing with a rare and serious emotional disorder: true multiple personality. . . .
>
> Eric's other manifestations emerged over the next weeks: quiet, middle-aged Dwight; the hysterically blind and mute Jeffrey; Michael, an arrogant jock; the coquettish Tian, whom Eric considered a whore; and argumentative Phillip, the lawyer. "Phillip was always asking about Eric's rights," says Graham. "He was kind of obnoxious. Actually, Phillip was a pain."
>
> To Graham's astonishment, Eric gradually unfurled 27 different personalities, including three females. . . . They ranged in age from a fetus to a sordid old man who kept trying to persuade Eric to fight as a mercenary in Haiti. In one therapy session, reports Graham, Eric shifted personality nine times in an hour. "I felt I was losing control of the sessions," says the psychologist, who has eleven years of clinical experience. "Some personalities would not talk to me, and some of them were very insightful into my behavior as well as Eric's."
>
> *(Time, October 25, 1982, p. 70)*

A person with **multiple personality disorder,** or **dissociative identity disorder,** develops two or more distinct personalities, often called **subpersonalities** (or **alternate personalities**), each with a unique set of memories, behaviors, thoughts, and emotions (see Table 13-3). At any given time, one of the subpersonalities takes center stage and dominates the person's functioning. Usually one subpersonality, called the *primary,* or *host, personality,* appears more often than the others.

The transition from one subpersonality to another, called *switching,* is usually sudden and may be dramatic (APA, 2000, 1994; Dell & Eisenhower, 1990). Eric, for example, twisted his face, growled, and yelled obscenities while changing personalities. Switching is usually triggered by a stressful event, although clinicians can also bring about the change with hypnotic suggestion (APA, 2000, 1994).

Cases of multiple personality disorder were first reported almost four centuries ago (Bliss, 1985, 1980). Many clinicians consider the disorder to be rare, but recent reports suggest that it may be more common than was once thought (APA, 2000; Coons, 1998). Most cases are first diagnosed in late adolescence or early adulthood, but the symptoms usually begin in early childhood after episodes of

Table 13-3 DSM-IV Checklist

MULTIPLE PERSONALITY DISORDER (DISSOCIATIVE IDENTITY DISORDER)

1. The presence of two or more distinct identities or personality states.
2. Control of the person's behavior recurrently taken by at least two of these identities or personality states.
3. An inability to recall important personal information that is too extensive to be explained by ordinary forgetfulness.

Based on APA, 2000, 1994.

abuse, typically before the age of 5 (Ross et al., 1991; Sachs, 1986). In fact, studies suggest that as many as 97 percent of patients have been physically, often sexually, abused during their early years (Ross et al., 1991, 1990, 1989). Women receive this diagnosis at least three times as often as men (APA, 2000).

How Do Subpersonalities Interact? How subpersonalities relate to or recall one another varies from case to case. Generally, however, there are three kinds of relationships. In *mutually amnesic relationships,* the subpersonalities have no awareness of one another (Ellenberger, 1970). Conversely, in *mutually cognizant patterns,* each subpersonality is well aware of the rest. They may hear one another's voices and even talk among themselves. Some are on good terms, while others do not get along at all. In *one-way amnesic relationships,* the most common relationship pattern, some subpersonalities are aware of others, but the awareness is not mutual. Those that are aware, called *co-conscious subpersonalities,* are "quiet observers" who watch the actions and thoughts of the other subpersonalities but do not interact with them. Sometimes while another subpersonality is present, the co-conscious personality makes itself known through indirect means, such as auditory hallucinations (perhaps a voice giving commands) or "automatic writing" (the current personality may find itself writing down words over which it has no control).

Investigators used to believe that most cases of multiple personality disorder involved two or three subpersonalities. Studies now suggest, however, that the average number of subpersonalities per patient is much higher—fifteen for women and eight for men (APA, 2000; Ross et al., 1989). In fact, there have been cases in which 100 or more subpersonalities were observed (APA, 2000). Often the subpersonalities emerge in groups of two or three at a time.

In the case of "Eve White," made famous in the book and movie *The Three Faces of Eve,* a woman had three subpersonalities—Eve White, Eve Black, and Jane (Thigpen & Cleckley, 1957). Eve White, the primary personality, was quiet and serious; Eve Black was carefree and mischievous; and Jane was mature and intelligent. According to the book, these three subpersonalities eventually merged into Evelyn, a stable personality who was really an integration of the other three.

The book was wrong, however; this was not to be the end of Eve's dissociation. In an autobiography twenty years later, she revealed that altogether twenty-two subpersonalities had come forth during her life, including nine subpersonalities after Evelyn. Usually they appeared in groups of three, and so the authors of *The Three Faces of Eve* apparently never knew about her previous or subsequent subpersonalities. She has now overcome her disorder, achieving a single, stable identity, and has been known as Chris Sizemore for over twenty-five years (Sizemore & Huber, 1988).

How Do Subpersonalities Differ? As in Chris Sizemore's case, subpersonalities often display dramatically different characteristics. They may also have their own names and different *vital statistics, abilities and preferences,* and even *physiological responses.*

Vital Statistics The subpersonalities may differ in features as basic as age, sex, race, and family history, as in the famous case of Sybil Dorsett. Sybil's multiple personality disorder has been described in fictional form (in the novel *Sybil*), but is based on a real case from the practice of the psychiatrist Cornelia Wilbur (Borch-Jacobsen, 1997; Schreiber, 1973). Sybil displayed seventeen subpersonalities, all with different identifying features. They included adults, a teenager, and a baby named Ruthie; two were male, named Mike and Sid. Sybil's subpersonalities each had particular images of themselves and of each other. The subpersonality named Vicky, for example, saw herself as an attractive blonde, while another, Peggy Lou, was described as a pixie with a pug nose. Mary was plump with dark

Movie madness *One of the cinema's best-known fictional sufferers of multiple personality disorder, Norman Bates, is horrified to discover that his mother (actually his subpersonality) has stabbed a woman to death in the shower in the movie* Psycho.

ConsiderThis

⊙ Women are much more likely to receive a diagnosis of multiple personality disorder than men. What might be some reasons for this difference?

MULTIPLE PERSONALITY DISORDER A dissociative disorder in which a person develops two or more distinct personalities. Also known as *dissociative identity disorder.*

SUBPERSONALITIES The two or more distinct personalities found in individuals suffering from multiple personality disorder, each with a unique set of memories, behaviors, thoughts, and emotions. Also known as *alternate personalities.*

"I'm Eve" *In 1975 Chris Sizemore revealed that she had been the subject of the book and the film* The Three Faces of Eve. *A fully integrated personality for more than 25 years, Ms. Sizemore is now an accomplished author, artist, and mental health spokesperson.*

THE BEGINNINGS OF SYBILIZATION

Several colleagues who worked closely with the author of *Sybil* and with the therapist claim that Sybil was actually a severe "hysteric," highly hypnotizable, extremely suggestible, and anxious to please her therapist, and that her disorder was in fact induced by the treatment techniques of hypnosis and sodium pentothal (Miller & Kantrowitz, 1999; Rieber, 1999).

IATROGENIC DISORDER A disorder that is unintentionally caused by a practitioner.

hair, and Vanessa was a tall redhead with a willowy figure. Mike's olive skin and brown eyes stood in contrast to Sid's fair skin and blue eyes.

ABILITIES AND PREFERENCES Although memories of abstract or encyclopedic information are not usually affected by dissociative amnesia or fugue, they are often disturbed by multiple personality disorder. It is not uncommon for the different subpersonalities to have different areas of expertise or different abilities: one may be able to drive, speak a foreign language, or play a musical instrument, while the others cannot (Coons et al., 1988). Their handwritings can also differ (Coons, 1980). In addition, the subpersonalities usually have different tastes in food, friends, music, and literature. Chris Sizemore ("Eve") displayed such differences. She later pointed out, "If I had learned to sew as one personality and then tried to sew as another, I couldn't do it. Driving a car was the same. Some of my personalities couldn't drive" (1975, p. 4).

PHYSIOLOGICAL RESPONSES Researchers have discovered that subpersonalities may have physiological differences, such as differences in autonomic nervous system activity, blood-pressure levels, and allergies (Putnam, Zahn, & Post, 1990). One study looked at the brain activities of different subpersonalities by measuring their *evoked potentials*—that is, brain response patterns recorded on an electroencephalograph (Putnam, 1984). The brain pattern a person produces in response to a specific stimulus (such as a flashing light) is usually unique and consistent. However, when an evoked potential test was given to four subpersonalities of each of ten people with multiple personality disorder, the results were dramatic. The brain activity pattern of each subpersonality was unique, showing the kinds of variations usually found in totally different people.

HOW COMMON IS MULTIPLE PERSONALITY DISORDER? As we have seen, multiple personality disorder has traditionally been thought of as rare. Some researchers even argue that many or all cases are **iatrogenic**—that is, unintentionally produced by practitioners. They believe that therapists create this disorder by subtly suggesting the existence of other personalities during therapy or by asking a patient to produce different personalities while under hypnosis (Powell & Gee, 1999). In addition, they believe, a therapist who is looking for multiple personalities may reinforce these patterns by displaying greater interest when a patient displays symptoms of dissociation (Merskey, 1995, 1992).

These arguments seem to be supported by the fact that many cases of multiple personality disorder first come to attention while the person is already in treatment for a less serious problem (Allison, 1978). But such is not true of all cases; many other people seek treatment because they have noticed time lapses throughout their lives or because relatives and friends have observed their subpersonalities (Putnam, 2000, 1988, 1985).

The number of people diagnosed with multiple personality disorder has been increasing. Although the disorder is still uncommon, thousands of cases have been diagnosed in the United States and Canada alone (Merskey, 1995). Two factors may account for this increase. First, a growing number of today's clinicians believe that the disorder does exist and are willing to diagnose it (Somer, 2000; Pope et al., 1999). Second, diagnostic procedures tend to be more accurate today than in past years. For much of the twentieth century, schizophrenia was one of the clinical field's most common diagnoses (Rosenbaum, 1980). It was applied, often incorrectly, to a wide range of unusual and mysterious patterns of abnormality, perhaps including multiple personality disorder. Under the stricter criteria of recent editions of the DSM, clinicians are now much more accurate in diagnosing schizophrenia, allowing more cases of multiple personality disorder to

Guilty and Not Guilty

In 1979, Kenneth Bianchi, one of two men known in the media as the "Hillside Strangler," was accused of raping and murdering several women in the Los Angeles area. Bianchi denied the charges, but during an interview in which he underwent hypnosis, another personality, named Steve, emerged. Steve claimed that he, not Kenneth, had committed the crimes.

Bianchi pleaded not guilty by reason of insanity, but the court refused to accept his claim of multiple personality disorder. The second personality, the prosecution pointed out, did not appear until Bianchi was hypnotized, and only after Bianchi was told by the examiner that the procedure would reveal another part of him. Bianchi was found guilty of the crimes.

ConsiderThis

What would have been an appropriate verdict had Bianchi's disorder been ruled genuine? • Might highly publicized trials such as this influence other people to believe that they have a multiple personality disorder? • More than one-quarter of all accused murderers claim to have no memory of their crimes (Noll & Turkington, 1994). Why might a murderer experience amnesia?

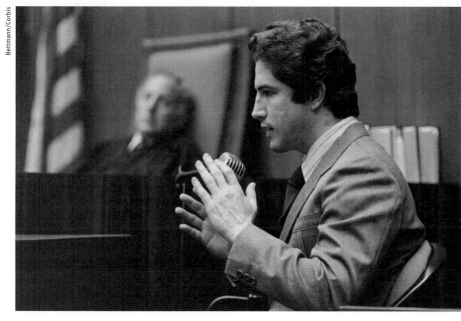

Bettmann/Corbis

Courtroom tactic *Kenneth Bianchi tries to convince a judge that it was his subpersonality who committed the multiple rapes and murders of which he was accused.*

be recognized (APA, 2000; Spiegel, 1994). In addition, several diagnostic tests have been developed to help detect multiple personality disorder (Steinberg & Hall, 1997; Mann, 1995). Despite such changes in professional perceptions, diagnostic practices, and assessment tools, however, many clinicians continue to question the legitimacy of this category and are reluctant to diagnose the disorder (Pope et al., 1999; Muller, 1998).

How Do Theorists Explain Dissociative Disorders?

A variety of theories have been proposed to explain dissociative disorders. Older explanations, such as those offered by psychodynamic and behavioral theorists, have not received much investigation. However, newer viewpoints, which combine cognitive, behavioral, and biological principles and highlight such factors as *state-dependent learning* and *self-hypnosis*, have begun to capture the interest of clinical scientists.

"Memory isn't like reading a book; it's more like writing a book from fragmentary notes."

John F. Kihlström,
psychologist, 1994

THE PSYCHODYNAMIC VIEW Psychodynamic theorists believe that dissociative disorders are caused by *repression*, the most basic ego defense mechanism: people fight off anxiety by unconsciously preventing painful memories, thoughts, or impulses from reaching awareness. Everyone uses repression to a degree, but people with dissociative disorders are thought to repress their memories excessively (Brenner, 1999).

In the psychodynamic view, dissociative amnesia and fugue are *single episodes* of massive repression. In each of these disorders, a person unconsciously blocks

Early beginnings *Chris Sizemore's multiple personality disorder developed long before this photograph of her was taken at age 10. It emerged during her preschool years after she experienced several traumas (witnessing two deaths and a horrifying accident) within a three-month period.*

the memory of an extremely upsetting event to avoid the pain of facing it (Noll & Turkington, 1994). Repression may be the person's only protection from overwhelming anxiety.

In contrast, multiple personality disorder is thought to result from a *lifetime* of excessive repression (Brenner, 1999; Reis, 1993). Psychodynamic theorists believe that such a continuous use of repression is motivated by very traumatic childhood events, particularly abusive parenting. Children who experience such traumas may come to fear the dangerous world they live in and take flight from it, by pretending to be another person who is safely looking on from afar. Abused children may also come to fear the impulses that they believe are the reasons for their excessive punishments. They may try to be "good" and "proper" all of the time by repressing the impulses they consider "bad" and "dangerous." Whenever "bad" thoughts or impulses do break through, the children feel they must disown and deny them, and they unconsciously assign all unacceptable thoughts, impulses, and emotions to other personalities.

Most of the support for the psychodynamic position is drawn from case histories, which report such brutal childhood experiences as beatings, cuttings, burnings with cigarettes, imprisonment in closets, rape, and extreme verbal abuse. Yet some individuals with multiple personality disorder do not seem to have experiences of abuse in their background (Bliss, 1980). Moreover, child abuse appears to be far more common than multiple personality disorder. Why, then, do only a small fraction of abused children develop this disorder?

THE BEHAVIORAL VIEW Behaviorists believe that dissociation is a response learned through operant conditioning. People who experience a horrifying event may later find temporary relief when their minds drift to other subjects. For some, this momentary forgetting, leading to a drop in anxiety, increases the likelihood of future forgetting. In short, they are reinforced for the act of forgetting and learn—without being aware that they are learning—that such acts help them escape anxiety. Thus, like psychodynamic theorists, behaviorists see dissociation as escape behavior. But behaviorists believe that a reinforcement process rather than a hardworking unconscious is keeping the individuals unaware that they are using dissociation as a means of escape.

Like psychodynamic theorists, behaviorists have relied largely on case histories to support their view of dissociative disorders. Such descriptions do often support this view, but they are equally consistent with other kinds of explanations as well: a case that seems to show reinforcement of forgetting can usually also be interpreted as an instance of unconscious repression. In addition, the behavioral explanation fails to explain precisely how temporary and normal escapes from painful memories grow into a complex disorder or why more people do not develop dissociative disorders. Theories that focus on *state-dependent learning* and *self-hypnosis* tackle some of the questions left unanswered by the psychodynamic and behavioral explanations.

STATE-DEPENDENT LEARNING If people learn something when they are in a particular situation or state of mind, they are likely to remember it best when they are again in that same condition. If they are given a learning task while under the influence of alcohol, for example, their later recall of the information may be strongest under the influence of alcohol (Overton, 1966). Similarly, if they smoke cigarettes while learning, they may later have better recall when they are again smoking.

This link between state and recall is called **state-dependent learning.** It was initially observed in studies of animals who learned things while under the influence of certain drugs (Arkhipov, 1999; Overton, 1966, 1964). Research with human subjects later showed that state-dependent learning can be associated with mood states as well: material learned during a happy mood is recalled best

STATE-DEPENDENT LEARNING Learning that becomes associated with the conditions under which it occurred, so that it is best remembered under the same conditions. That is, people may remember an event best when they return to the mental state they were in at the time of the event.

SELF-HYPNOSIS The process of hypnotizing oneself, sometimes for the purpose of forgetting unpleasant events.

when the subject is again happy, and sad-state learning is recalled best during sad states (Eich, 1995; Bower, 1981) (see Figure 13-1).

What causes state-dependent learning? One possibility is that *arousal levels* are an important dimension of learning and memory. That is, a particular level of arousal will have a set of remembered events, thoughts, and skills attached to it. When a situation produces that particular level of arousal, the person is more likely to recall the memories linked to it.

Although people may remember certain events better in some arousal states than in others, most can recall events under a variety of states. However, perhaps people who are prone to develop dissociative disorders have state-to-memory links that are extremely rigid and narrow. Maybe each of their thoughts, memories, and skills is tied *exclusively* to a particular state of arousal, so that they recall a given event from the past only when they experience an arousal state almost identical to the state in which the memory was acquired. When such people are calm, for example, they may forget what occurred during stressful times, thus laying the groundwork for dissociative amnesia or fugue. Similarly, in multiple personality disorder, different arousal levels may produce entirely different groups of memories, thoughts, and abilities—that is, different subpersonalities (Putnam, 1992).

SELF-HYPNOSIS As we first saw in Chapter 1, people who are *hypnotized* enter a sleeplike state in which they become very suggestible. While in this state, they can behave, perceive, and think in ways that would ordinarily seem impossible. They may, for example, become temporarily blind, deaf, or insensitive to pain. Hypnosis can also help people remember events that occurred and were forgotten years ago, a capability used by many psychotherapists. Conversely, it can make people forget facts, events, and even their personal identities—an effect called *hypnotic amnesia* (David et al., 2000).

Most studies of hypnotic amnesia follow similar formats. Subjects are asked to study a word list or other material until they are able to repeat it correctly. Under hypnosis, they are then directed to forget the material until they receive a *cancellation signal* (such as the snap of a finger), at which time they will suddenly recall the learned material. Repeatedly these experiments have found the subjects' memories to be poor during the period of hypnotic amnesia and then restored after the cancellation signal is given (Coe, 1989).

The parallels between hypnotic amnesia and dissociative disorders are striking (Bliss, 1980). Both are conditions in which people forget certain material for a period of time yet later remember it. And in both, the people forget without any insight into why they are forgetting or any awareness that something is being forgotten. Finally, in both situations, personal and specific information is more readily forgotten than abilities or encyclopedic knowledge.

These parallels have led some theorists to conclude that dissociative disorders may be a form of **self-hypnosis** in which people hypnotize themselves to forget unpleasant events (Bliss, 1985, 1980; Hilgard, 1977). Dissociative amnesia, for example, may occur in people who have a heightened capacity to, consciously or unconsciously, hypnotize themselves into forgetting horrifying experiences that have recently occurred in their lives (Bryant et al., 2001). If the self-induced amnesia covers all memories of a person's past and identity, that person may undergo a dissociative fugue.

Self-hypnosis might also be used to explain multiple personality disorder. On the basis of several investigations, some theorists believe that multiple personality disorder often begins between the ages of 4 and 6, a time when children are generally very suggestible and excellent hypnotic subjects (Putnam, 2000; Kluft, 1987; Bliss, 1985, 1980). These theorists argue that some children who experience abuse or other horrifying events manage to escape their threatening world by self-

SUPPRESSED EMOTIONS, SUPPRESSED MEMORY

In one study, subjects who were instructed to suppress their emotions while viewing disturbing photographs later displayed poorer recall of the photographs than did viewers who had been allowed to wince, gasp, and otherwise respond with emotion (Richards & Gross, 1999).

FIGURE 13-1 State-dependent learning
In one study, subjects who learned a list of words while in a hypnotically induced happy state remembered the words better if they were in a happy mood when tested later than if they were in a sad mood. Conversely, subjects who learned the words when in a sad mood recalled them better if they were sad during testing than if they were happy (Bower, 1981).

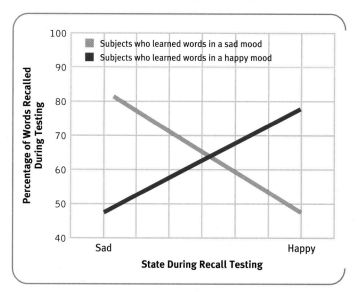

Peculiarities of Memory

*U*sually memory problems must interfere greatly with a person's functioning before they are considered a sign of a disorder. Peculiarities of memory, on the other hand, fill our daily lives. The memory investigators Richard Noll and Carol Turkington (1994) have identified a number of these peculiarities—some familiar, some useful, some problematic, but none abnormal.

- **Absentmindedness** Often we fail to register information because our thoughts are focusing on other things. If we haven't absorbed the information in the first place, it is no surprise that later we can't recall it.

- **Déjà vu** Almost all of us have at some time had the strange sensation of recognizing a scene that we happen upon for the first time. We feel sure we have been there before.

- **Jamais vu** Sometimes we have the opposite experience: a situation or scene that is part of our daily life seems suddenly unfamiliar. "I knew it was my car, but I felt as if I'd never seen it before."

- **The tip-of-the-tongue phenomenon** To have something on the tip of the tongue is an acute "feeling of knowing": we are unable to recall some piece of information, but we know that we know it.

- **Eidetic images** Some people experience visual afterimages so vividly that they can describe a picture in detail after looking at it just once. The images may be memories of pictures, events, fantasies, or dreams.

- **Memory while under anesthesia** Some anesthetized patients may process enough of what is said in their presence during surgery to affect their recovery. In such cases, the ability to understand language has continued under anesthesia, even though the patient cannot explicitly recall it.

- **Memory for music** Even as a small child, Mozart could memorize and reproduce a piece of music after having heard it only once. Although no one yet has matched the genius of Mozart, many musicians can mentally hear whole pieces of music, so that they can rehearse anywhere, far from their instruments.

- **Visual memory** Most people recall visual information better than other kinds of information: they can easily bring to their mind the appearance of places, objects, faces, or the pages of a book. They almost never forget a face, yet they may well forget the name attached to it. Other people have stronger verbal memories: they remember sounds or words particularly well, and the memories that come to their minds are often puns or rhymes.

- **Prenatal memory** Some North American medicine men claim to remember parts of a prenatal existence, an ability they believe is lost to "common" people. Many practicing Buddhists also claim to remember past lives. A few—as did Buddha himself—claim to remember their very first existence.

hypnosis, mentally separating themselves from their bodies and fulfilling their wish to become some other person or persons. One patient with multiple personality disorder observed, "I was in a trance often [during my childhood]. There was a little place where I could sit, close my eyes and imagine, until I felt very relaxed just like hypnosis" (Bliss, 1980, p. 1392).

Treatments for Dissociative Disorders

As we have seen, people with dissociative amnesia and fugue often recover on their own. Only sometimes do their memory problems linger and require treatment (Lyon, 1985). In contrast, people with multiple personality disorder usually require treatment to regain their lost memories and develop an integrated per-

HYPNOTIC THERAPY A treatment in which the patient undergoes hypnosis and is then guided to recall forgotten events or perform other therapeutic activities. Also known as *hypnotherapy*.

sonality. Treatments for dissociative amnesia and fugue tend to be more successful than those for multiple personality disorder.

HOW DO THERAPISTS HELP PEOPLE WITH DISSOCIATIVE AMNESIA AND FUGUE?
The leading treatments for dissociative amnesia and fugue are *psychodynamic therapy, hypnotic therapy,* and *drug therapy.* Psychodynamic therapists ask patients with these disorders to free-associate and search their unconscious in the hope of bringing forgotten experiences back to consciousness (Bartholomew, 2000; Loewenstein, 1991). The focus of psychodynamic therapy seems particularly well suited to the needs of people with these disorders. After all, the patients need to recover lost memories, and the general approach of psychodynamic therapists is to try to uncover memories—as well as other psychological processes—that have been repressed. Thus many theorists, including some who do not ordinarily favor psychodynamic approaches, believe that psychodynamic therapy may be the most appropriate and effective treatment for these disorders.

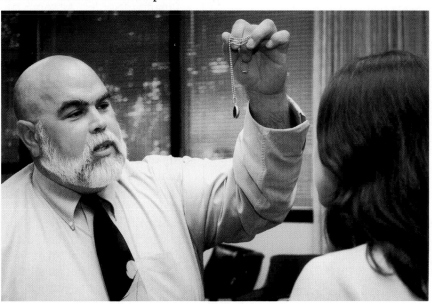

Oscar Sosa/AP Photo

Another common treatment for dissociative amnesia and fugue is **hypnotic therapy,** or **hypnotherapy.** Therapists hypnotize patients and then guide them to recall the forgotten events (Spiegel, 1994; MacHovek, 1981). Given the possibility that dissociative amnesia and fugue may each be a form of self-hypnosis, hypnotherapy may be a particularly appropriate intervention. It has been applied both alone and in combination with other approaches.

Faulty recall *A forensic clinician uses a hypnotic procedure to help a witness recall the details of a crime. Research reveals, however, that such procedures are as capable of creating false memories as they are of uncovering real memories. Thus recollections that initially emerge during hypnosis cannot be used as evidence in criminal cases.*

Sometimes intravenous injections of barbiturates such as *sodium amobarbital* (Amytal) or *sodium pentobarbital* (Pentothal) are used to help patients with dissociative amnesia and fugue regain lost memories (Ruedrich et al., 1985). The drugs are often called "truth serums," but the key to their success is their ability to calm people and free their inhibitions, thus helping them to recall anxiety-producing events (Kluft, 1988; Perry & Jacobs, 1982). These drugs do not always work, however (Spiegel, 1994); and when they do help people recall past events, the individuals may forget upon wakening much of what they said under the drug's influence. For these reasons, the drugs, if used, are likely to be combined with other treatment approaches.

HOW DO THERAPISTS HELP INDIVIDUALS WITH MULTIPLE PERSONALITY DISORDER?
Unlike sufferers of amnesia and fugue, people with multiple personality disorder rarely recover without treatment (Spiegel, 1994). Like the disorder itself, treatment for this pattern is complex and difficult. Therapists usually try to help the clients (1) recognize fully the nature of their disorder, (2) recover the gaps in their memory, and (3) integrate their subpersonalities into one functional personality (Kluft, 2000, 1999, 1992, 1991; Spiegel, 1994).

RECOGNIZING THE DISORDER Once a diagnosis of multiple personality disorder is made, therapists typically try to bond with the primary personality and with each of the subpersonalities (Kluft, 1999, 1992). In general, such bonds are hard to achieve, given the patient's history of abuse and mistrust of others. As bonds are formed, therapists try to educate patients and help them to recognize fully the nature of their disorder (Krakauer, 2001; Allen, 1993). Some therapists actually introduce the subpersonalities to one another under hypnosis, and some have patients look at videotapes of their other personalities (Ross & Gahan, 1988; Sakheim, Hess, & Chivas, 1988). Many therapists have also found that group therapy helps to educate patients (Fine & Madden, 2000). Being with a group of people who all have multiple personality disorder helps relieve a person's feelings of isolation. Family therapy is often included in the treatment program to help

ConsiderThis

● Hypnosis is often used by therapists to help uncover hidden memories, motives, and needs. But hypnotic therapists can also use this suggestive technique to create desires, emotions, and behaviors. How can hypnotists know when they are uncovering a person's state of mind as opposed to creating it?

FUSION The final merging of two or more subpersonalities in multiple personality disorder.

SHORT-TERM MEMORY The memory system that collects new information. Also known as *working memory*.

LONG-TERM MEMORY The memory system that contains all the information that we have stored over the years.

educate spouses and children about the disorder and to gather valuable information about the patient (Kluft, 2000; Porter et al., 1993).

RECOVERING MEMORIES To help patients recover the missing pieces of their past, therapists use many of the approaches applied in other dissociative disorders, including psychodynamic therapy, hypnotherapy, and sodium amobarbital (Kluft, 1999, 1991, 1985). These techniques work slowly for patients with multiple personality disorder, as some subpersonalities may keep denying experiences that the others recall (Lyon, 1992). One of the subpersonalities may even assume a "protector" role, to prevent the primary personality from suffering the pain of recalling traumatic experiences. Some patients become self-destructive and violent during this phase of treatment (Kelly, 1993; Lamberti & Cummings, 1992).

INTEGRATING THE SUBPERSONALITIES The final goal of therapy is to merge the different subpersonalities into a single, integrated identity. Integration is a continuous process that occurs throughout treatment until patients "own" all of their behaviors, emotions, sensations, and knowledge. **Fusion** is the final merging of two or more subpersonalities. Many patients distrust this final treatment goal, and their subpersonalities are likely to see integration as a form of death (Kluft, 1999, 1991; Spiegel, 1994). As one subpersonality said, "There are too many advantages to being multiple. Maybe we're being sold a bill of goods by therapists" (Hale, 1983). Therapists have used a range of approaches to help merge subpersonalities, including psychodynamic, supportive, cognitive, and drug therapies (Goldman, 1995; Fichtner et al., 1990).

Once the subpersonalities are merged, further therapy is needed to maintain the complete personality and to teach social and coping skills that may help prevent later dissociations (Fink, 1992). In case reports, some therapists report high success rates (Kluft, 1999, 1993, 1984), but others find that patients continue to resist full and final integration. A few therapists have in fact questioned the need for full integration.

PROFIT DISTRIBUTIONS

The patient Chris Sizemore received almost no revenues from the 1957 book and movie *The Three Faces of Eve*. In contrast, profits from *Sybil* were shared by the patient, her psychiatrist, and the book's author. Moreover, when the psychiatrist Cornelia Wilbur died in 1992, she left $25,000 and all *Sybil* royalties to the former patient (Miller & Kantrowitz, 1999).

MARITAL OVERSIGHT

Surveys indicate that 16 percent of adults have forgotten their wedding anniversaries (22 percent of men and 11 percent of women). People married only a few years are as likely to forget as those married for many years (Kanner, 1995).

SUMMING UP | **Dissociative Disorders**

Memory plays a key role in our functioning by linking us to the past, present, and future.

Dissociative Disorders People with dissociative disorders experience major changes in memory that are not due to clear physical causes. Typically, one part of the memory is dissociated, or separated, from another. People with dissociative amnesia are suddenly unable to recall important personal information or past events in their lives. Those with dissociative fugue not only lose their memory of their personal identities but flee to a different location and may establish a new identity. In another dissociative disorder, multiple personality disorder, persons display two or more separate subpersonalities. The subpersonalities often have complex relationships with one another and usually differ in vital statistics, abilities and preferences, and even physiological responses. The number of people diagnosed with multiple personality disorder has increased in recent years.

Explanations The dissociative disorders are not yet well understood. Among the factors that have been cited to explain them are extreme depression, operant conditioning, state-dependent learning, and self-hypnosis. The latter two factors have begun to interest clinical scientists. The state-dependent learning explanation argues that the thoughts, memories, and skills of people who develop dissociative disorders are tied exclusively to those states of arousal that were present when the thoughts or memories were first acquired. The self-hypnosis explanation proposes that people with these disorders have hypnotized themselves into forgetting horrifying experiences in their lives.

Treatments Dissociative amnesia and fugue may end on their own or may require treatment. Multiple personality disorder typically requires treatment. Approaches commonly used to help patients with dissociative amnesia and fugue recover their lost memories are psychodynamic therapy, hypnotic therapy, and sodium amobarbital or sodium pentobarbital. Therapists who treat people with multiple personality disorder use the same approaches and, more generally, try to help clients recognize the full scope and nature of their disorder, recover the gaps in their memories, and merge their subpersonalities into one.

Organic Memory Disorders

Some changes in memory have clear organic causes, such as brain injury, medical conditions, and substance misuse. There are two kinds of organic memory disorders: *amnestic disorders,* which primarily affect memory, and *dementias,* which affect both memory and other cognitive functions. Before examining the organic memory disorders, we need to understand some basic information about the biology of memory.

The Biology of Memory

Much of what is known about the biology of memory has come from studies of people who have suffered injuries to specific locations of the brain. Important information has also been gained through experiments in which researchers surgically or chemically damage the brains of animals and then observe the effects on old memories and new learning. Additionally, molecular biology studies have shed light on specific changes that may occur in brain cells as memories form.

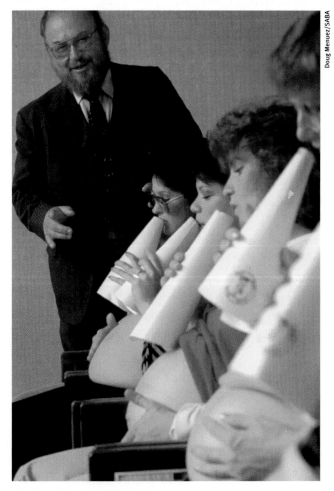

A bit too early *Each mother-to-be in this prenatal program talks to her fetus in order to establish an early relationship with the child. Memory studies suggest that the babies will not remember these early interventions, however; humans cannot intentionally recall events until sometime during their first or second year of life (Bauer, 1996; Mandler & McDonough, 1995).*

Doug Menuez/SABA

WHAT ARE THE DIFFERENT KINDS OF MEMORY? Scientists describe the human brain as having two memory systems that work together to help us learn and recall. **Short-term memory,** or **working memory,** collects new information. **Long-term memory** is the accumulation of information that we have stored over the years—information that first made its way through the short-term memory system. The information held in short-term memory must be transformed, or *consolidated,* into long-term memory if we are to hold on to it. This transformation usually occurs in steps. When short-term information becomes part of our long-term memory, it is said to have been *encoded.* Remembering information that has been stored in long-term memory is called *retrieval* and is described as going into one's long-term memory to bring it out for use again in short-term, or working, memory.

Information in long-term memory can be classified as either procedural or declarative. *Procedural memories* are learned skills we perform without needing to think about them, such as walking, cutting with scissors, or writing. *Declarative memory* consists of names, dates, and other facts that have been learned. Most organic memory disorders interfere far more with declarative memory than with procedural memory (see Table 13-4 on the next page).

WHAT IS THE ANATOMY OF MEMORY? Memories are difficult to locate. Researchers have searched for the place where the content of memory is stored, but they have concluded that no such storehouse exists. They now see memory as a *process* rather than a place, an activity that involves changes in cells throughout the brain. When the process is activated, a memory is triggered and comes forth. Occasionally this process leads to errors of memory (Schacter, 1999), but typically its operation is remarkably effective.

Table 13-4

Comparison of Memory Disorders

	ANTEROGRADE (CONTINUOUS) AMNESIA	RETROGRADE (LOCALIZED, SELECTIVE, AND GENERALIZED) AMNESIA	DECLARATIVE MEMORY LOSS	PROCEDURAL MEMORY LOSS	ORGANIC CAUSES
Dissociative amnesia	Sometimes	Yes	Yes	Sometimes	No
Dissociative fugue	Sometimes	Yes	Yes	Sometimes	No
Multiple personality disorder	Yes	Yes	Yes	Yes	No
Amnestic disorders	Yes	Sometimes	Yes	Sometimes	Yes
Dementias	Yes	Yes	Yes	Yes	Yes

MEMORY BOOSTERS

Popular natural supplements that supposedly boost memory include products named "Brain Fuel," "BrainStorm," "Food for Thought," and "Brain Gum" (Muhammad, 1999). The Chinese herb *Ginkgo biloba* is the most popular memory-enhancing supplement on the market, with sales of over $100 million each year.

MEMORY BUSTERS

Substances that can temporarily impair memory include alcohol, sedative-hypnotic drugs, bromides, antidepressants, analgesics, blood pressure medications, insulin, seasickness patches, antihistamines, and antipsychotic drugs (Noll & Turkington, 1994).

Certain brain structures appear to be especially important in memory (Curran & Schacter, 2000). Among the most important structures in short-term, or working, memory are the **prefrontal lobes,** located just behind the forehead (Anderson, 2000; Thompson, 2000). When animals or humans acquire new information, their prefrontal lobes become more active. Apparently this activity enables them to hold information temporarily and to continue working with the information as long as it is needed.

Among the brain areas most important to long-term memory are the **temporal lobes** (including the *hippocampus* and *amygdala,* key structures under the temporal lobes) and the **diencephalon** (including the *mammillary bodies, thalamus,* and *hypothalamus*), which seem to help transform, or encode, short-term into long-term memory (Anderson, 2000). Cases of organic memory loss involve damage to one or more of these areas (Caine et al., 2001; Cipolotti et al., 2001).

WHAT IS THE BIOCHEMISTRY OF MEMORY? What do the cells in these key areas of the brain do to create and store memories? Although no one has yet discovered the "engram"—the exact physical change in a cell that accounts for a memory—much is known about the electrical and chemical bases of learning and memory. One exciting finding is the role that *long-term potentiation (LTP)* may play (Anderson, 2000; Martinez & Derrick, 1996). Apparently, repeated stimulation of nerve cells in the brain greatly increases the likelihood that the cells will respond—and respond strongly—to future stimulation. This effect can last quite a long time (hence the name "long-term potentiation"), long enough to be a key mechanism in the formation of memories. Think of many sleds ridden one after another down a snowy slope, creating a groove that later sledders can easily find. Perhaps LTP creates a kind of groove that helps memories form, so a person can more easily retrieve a memory later by following the well-worn path.

Memory researchers have also identified biochemical changes that occur in cells as memories form. For example, when new information is acquired, *proteins* are produced in key brain cells. Several chemicals are responsible for the production of proteins, including *acetylcholine, glutamate, RNA (ribonucleic acid),* and *calcium.* If the activity of any of these chemicals is disturbed, the production of proteins may be prevented and the formation of memories interrupted (Martinez & Derrick, 1996; Rosenzweig, 1996). For example, by blocking the activity of glutamate, researchers have prevented both short-term memory and LTP. Similarly, by blocking a cell's production of RNA or of calcium, they have interrupted the formation of long-term memories. Such findings suggest that memory occurs as a result of changes within and between nerve cells.

Amnestic Disorders

Retrograde amnesia is an inability to remember events that occurred before the event that triggered amnesia. **Anterograde amnesia** is an ongoing inability to form new memories after the event. As we have observed, people with dissociative amnesia typically suffer from retrograde amnesia and rarely suffer from anterograde amnesia. However, **amnestic disorders,** organic disorders in which memory loss is the primary symptom, are quite different (see Table 13-5). People with amnestic disorders *sometimes* suffer from retrograde amnesia, depending on the particular disorder, but they almost *always* experience anterograde amnesia.

In anterograde amnesia, it is as though information from short-term memory can no longer cross over into long-term memory. Not surprisingly, the anterograde amnesia observed in amnestic disorders is often the result of damage to the brain's temporal lobes or diencephalon, the areas largely responsible for transforming short-term memory into long-term memory.

In severe forms of anterograde amnesia, new acquaintances are forgotten almost immediately, and problems solved one day must be tackled again the next. The person may not remember anything that has happened since the organic problem first occurred. A middle-aged patient who suffered a physical trauma more than 20 years ago, for example, may still believe that Ronald Reagan is president of the United States. Sufferers of anterograde amnesia may continue to possess all their earlier verbal skills and many problem-solving abilities, however, and their IQ is not changed.

KORSAKOFF'S SYNDROME Fred, a 69-year-old man, was admitted to a mental hospital in a state of confusion, the result of **Korsakoff's syndrome,** an amnestic disorder that causes its victims to keep forgetting newly learned information (anterograde amnesia), although their general knowledge and intelligence remain the same:

> Fred . . . had a history of many years of heavy drinking, although he denied drinking during the past several years. When seen in the admitting ward, the patient was neatly dressed, but there was some deterioration of his personal habits. Although pleasant and sociable with the interviewer and ward personnel, he was definitely confused. He wandered about the ward, investigating objects and trying on other people's clothing. He talked freely, though his speech tended to be rambling and at times incoherent. Most of his spontaneous conversation centered on himself, and there were a number of hypochondriacal complaints. Fred was disoriented for time and place, although he was able to give his name. He could not give his correct address, said his age was 91, and was unable to name the day, the month, or the year. He did not know where he was, although he said he was sent here by his landlord because he had been drinking. He admitted that he had been arrested for fighting and drinking, but he said that he had never had an attack of delirium tremens. [Fred] showed the characteristic symptom picture of Korsakoff's syndrome, with disorientation, confusion, and a strong tendency toward confabulation. When asked where he was, he said he was in a brewery. He gave the name of the brewery, but when asked the same question a few minutes later, he named another brewery. Similarly, he said that he knew the examiner, called him by an incorrect name, and a little later changed the name again. When leaving the examining room, he used still another name when he said politely, "Goodbye, Mr. Wolf!"
>
> *(Kisker, 1977, p. 308)*

As we observed in Chapter 10, approximately 5 percent of people with long-term alcoholism develop Korsakoff's syndrome. A combination of excessive drinking and improper diet produce a deficiency of *vitamin B (thiamine)*, which

---

Table 13-5 DSM-IV Checklist

AMNESTIC DISORDER

1. Memory impairment.
2. Significant impairment in social or occupational functioning, and significant decline from a previous level of functioning.
3. Disturbance is the direct physiological result of a general medical condition or physical trauma.

Based on APA, 2000, 1994.

PREFRONTAL LOBES Regions of the brain that play a key role in short-term memory, among other functions.

TEMPORAL LOBES Regions of the brain that play a key role in transforming short-term to long-term memory, among other functions.

DIENCEPHALON A brain area (consisting of the mammillary bodies, thalamus, and hypothalamus) that plays a key role in transforming short-term to long-term memory, among other functions.

RETROGRADE AMNESIA A lack of memory about events that occurred before the event that triggered amnesia.

ANTEROGRADE AMNESIA The inability to remember new information that is acquired after the event that triggered amnesia.

AMNESTIC DISORDERS Organic disorders in which the primary symptom is memory loss.

KORSAKOFF'S SYNDROME An amnestic disorder caused by long-term alcoholism, an accompanying poor diet, and, in turn, a deficiency of vitamin B (thiamine).

leads to damage in portions of the diencephalon (Harding et al., 2000; Visser et al., 1999). Sufferers of this disorder primarily lose memories of declarative knowledge; they are still able to incorporate new procedural knowledge, such as the way to solve a particular kind of puzzle, and they also maintain their language skills (Verfaellie et al., 1990). This may explain why Korsakoff's patients tend to *confabulate.* Like Fred, they use their general intellectual and language skills to make up elaborate stories and lies in an effort to replace the memories they keep losing.

In addition to severe anterograde amnesia, persons with Korsakoff's syndrome experience some retrograde amnesia. They have trouble remembering events from the years immediately before the onset of the disorder, as opposed to more distant past events (Albert et al., 1979). The syndrome can also affect personality. Aggressive and loud individuals may become quieter and more passive as the disorder continues.

HEAD INJURIES AND BRAIN SURGERY Both *head injuries* and *brain surgery* can cause amnestic disorders (Ahmed et al., 2000; Noll & Turkington, 1994). Television shows and movies often portray bumps on the head as a quick and easy way to lose one's memory. In fact, *mild* head injuries, such as a concussion that does not result in a period of unconsciousness, rarely cause much memory loss, and what loss there is usually disappears within days or at most months. In contrast, almost half of all *severe* head injuries do cause some permanent learning and memory problems, both anterograde and retrograde. When memories do return, older ones typically return first (Searlemen & Herrmann, 1994).

Brain surgery may create more specific memory problems. The most famous case of memory loss as a result of brain surgery is that of H.M., a man whose identity has been protected for decades (Ogden & Corkin, 1991; Corkin, 1984, 1968; Milner, 1971). H.M. suffered from severe *epilepsy,* a disorder that produced seizures in his temporal lobes. To reduce his symptoms, doctors removed parts of both his temporal lobes, along with the amygdala and hippocampus. At that time, the role of these brain areas in the formation of memories was not known. (Today temporal lobe surgery is usually limited to either the right or left side of the brain). H.M. has experienced severe anterograde amnesia ever since his 1953 surgery. He keeps failing to recognize anyone he has met since the operation.

OTHER AMNESTIC DISORDERS Other biological events can also damage the brain areas that play key roles in memory. These include *vascular disease,* which affects the flow of blood to the brain; *heart attacks,* which interrupt the flow of oxygen to the brain; and certain *infectious diseases* (Hokkanen et al., 1995). Each may cause amnestic disorders of various kinds.

Dementias

Dementias, another group of syndromes marked by memory loss, are sometimes difficult to distinguish from the amnestic disorders. In dementia, however, severe memory problems combine with losses in at least one other cognitive function, such as abstract thinking or language (APA, 2000, 1994). People with certain forms of dementia may also undergo personality changes—they may begin to behave inappropriately, for example—and their symptoms may worsen steadily.

Most of us worry from time to time that we are losing our memory and other mental abilities. We rush out the door without our keys; we meet a familiar person and cannot remember her name; or in the middle of an important test our mind goes blank. At such times, we may well believe that we are on our way to dementia. Actually such mishaps are a common and quite normal feature of stress or of aging. As people move through middle age, memory difficulties and lapses of attention increase, and may occur with regularity by the age of 60 or 70. Sometimes, however, people experience memory and other cognitive changes that are far more extensive. They, like Harry, are victims of dementia:

Harry appeared to be in perfect health at age 58. . . . He worked in the municipal water treatment plant of a small city, and it was at work that the first overt signs of Harry's mental illness appeared. While responding to a minor emergency, he became confused about the correct order in which to pull the levers that controlled the flow of fluids. As a result, several thousand gallons of raw sewage were discharged into a river. Harry had been an efficient and diligent worker, so after puzzled questioning, his error was attributed to the flu and overlooked.

Several weeks later, Harry came home with a baking dish his wife had asked him to buy, having forgotten that he had brought home the identical dish two nights before. Later that week, on two successive nights, he went to pick up his daughter at her job in a restaurant, apparently forgetting that she had changed shifts and was now working days. A month after that, he quite uncharacteristically argued with a clerk at the phone company; he was trying to pay a bill that he had already paid three days before. . . .

Months passed and Harry's wife was beside herself. She could see that his problem was worsening. Not only had she been unable to get effective help, but Harry himself was becoming resentful and sometimes suspicious of her attempts. He now insisted there was nothing wrong with him, and she would catch him narrowly watching her every movement. . . . Sometimes he became angry— sudden little storms without apparent cause. . . . More difficult for his wife was Harry's repetitiveness in conversation: He often repeated stories from the past and sometimes repeated isolated phrases and sentences from more recent exchanges. There was no context and little continuity to his choice of subjects. . . .

Two years after Harry had first allowed the sewage to escape, he was clearly a changed man. Most of the time he seemed preoccupied; he usually had a vacant smile on his face, and what little he said was so vague that it lacked meaning. . . . Gradually his wife took over getting him up, toileted, and dressed each morning. . . .

Harry's condition continued to worsen slowly. When his wife's school was in session, his daughter would stay with him some days, and neighbors were able to offer some help. But occasionally he would still manage to wander away. On those occasions he greeted everyone he met—old friends and strangers alike— with "Hi, it's so nice." That was the extent of his conversation, although he might repeat "nice, nice, nice" over and over again. . . . When Harry left a coffee pot on a unit of the electric stove until it melted, his wife, desperate for help, took him to see another doctor. Again Harry was found to be in good health. [However] the doctor ordered a CAT scan [and eventually concluded] that Harry had "Pick-Alzheimer disease" and that there was no known cause and no effective treatment. . . .

Because Harry was a veteran . . . [he qualified for] hospitalization in a regional veterans' hospital about 400 miles away from his home. . . . Desperate, five years after the accident at work, [his wife] accepted with gratitude [this] hospitalization. . . .

At the hospital the nursing staff sat Harry up in a chair each day and, aided by volunteers, made sure he ate enough. Still, he lost weight and became weaker. He would weep when his wife came to see him, but he did not talk, and he gave no other sign that he recognized her. After a year, even the weeping stopped. Harry's wife could no longer bear to visit. Harry lived on until just after his sixty-fifth birthday, when he choked on a piece of bread, developed pneumonia as a consequence, and soon died.

(Heston, 1992, pp. 87–90)

> "Our memory is our coherence, our reason, our feeling, even our action. Without it, we are nothing."
>
> Luis Buñuel, Spanish filmmaker

FIGURE 13-2 Dementia and age *The occurrence of dementia is closely related to age. Fewer than 1 percent of all 60-year-olds have dementia, compared to as many as 50 percent of those who are 85. After 60, the prevalence of dementia doubles every six years up to age 85 or so; then the increase tapers off. (Adapted from Cowley, 2000; Alzheimer's Association, 1997; Ritchie et al., 1992.)*

At any given time, around 3 percent of the world's adult population suffer from dementia (Muir, 1997). Its occurrence is closely related to age (see Figure 13-2). Among people 65 years of age, the prevalence is around 1 to 2 percent,

"You Are the Music, While the Music Lasts"

Clayton S. Collins

Oliver Sacks [a well-known neurologist and writer] danced to the Dead. For three solid hours. At 60. And with "two broken knees." . . .

The power of music— . . . to "bring back" individuals rendered motionless and mute by neurological damage and disorders—is what's driving Sacks these days. The . . . author (*Migraine, A Leg to Stand On, The Man Who Mistook His Wife for a Hat, Seeing Voices,* and *Awakenings*) . . . is working on another case-study book, one that deals in part with the role of music as a stimulus to minds that have thrown up stiff sensory barriers. . . .

"One sees how robust music is neurologically," Sacks says. "You can lose all sorts of particular powers but you don't tend to lose music and identity." . . .

Much of what he has encountered, particularly in working with patients at Beth Abraham Hospital, Bronx, N.Y., . . . relates to music.

Musical awakenings *Over the years, Oliver Sacks has treated neurological disorders with techniques ranging from medication to the music of the Grateful Dead.*

"One saw patients who couldn't take a single step, who couldn't walk, but who could dance," he says. "There were patients who couldn't speak, but who could sing. The power of music in these patients was instantaneous . . . from a frozen Parkinsonian state to a freely flowing, moving, speaking state."

Sacks remembers a woman with Parkinson's who would sit perfectly still until "activated" by the music of Chopin, which she loved and knew by heart. She didn't have to hear a tune played. "It was sometimes sufficient to give her an opus number," Sacks says. "You would just say 'Opus 49,' and the F-minor 'Fantasy' would start playing in her mind. And she could move. . . ."

"Deeply demented people respond to music, babies respond to music, fetuses probably respond to music. Various animals respond to music," Sacks says. "There is something about the animal nervous system . . . which seems to respond to music all the way down . . . ," Sacks says, citing the case of a patient with damage to the frontal lobes of his brain.

"When he sings, one almost has the strange feeling that [music] has given him his frontal lobes back, given him back, temporally, some function that has been lost on an organic basis," Sacks says, adding a quote from T. S. Eliot: "You are the music, while the music lasts."

The effects of music therapy may not always last. Sacks will take what he can get. "To organize a disorganized person for a minute is miraculous. And for half an hour, more so." . . .

The key, says Sacks, is for patients to "learn to be well" again. Music can restore to them, he says, the identity that predates the illness. "There's a health to music, a life to music." . . . Music's been healing for thousands of years, Sacks says. "It's just being looked at now more systematically and with these special populations."

"Greg" was an amnesiac with a brain tumor and no coherent memories of life since about 1969—but an encyclopedic memory of the years that came before, and a real love of Grateful Dead tunes.

Sacks took Greg to that night's [Grateful Dead] performance. "In the first half of the concert they were doing early music, and Greg was enchanted by everything," Sacks recalls. "I mean, he was not an amnesiac. He was completely oriented and organized and with it." Between sets Sacks went backstage and introduced Greg to band member Micky Hart, who was impressed with Greg's knowledge of the group but quite surprised when Greg asked after Pigpen. When told the former band member had died 20 years before, "Greg was very upset," Sacks recalls. "And then 30 seconds later he asked 'How's Pigpen?'"

During the second half, the band played its newer songs. And Greg's world began to fall apart. "He was bewildered and enthralled and frightened. Because the music for him—and this is an extremely musical man, who understands the idiom of the Grateful Dead—was both familiar and unfamiliar. . . . He said, 'This is like the music of the future.'"

Sacks tried to keep the new memories fresh. But the next day, Greg had no memory of the concert. It seemed as if all had been lost. "But—and this is strange—when one played some of the new music, which he had heard for the first time at the concert, he could sing along with it and remember it."

It is an encouraging development. . . . Children have been found to learn quickly lessons that are embedded in song. Sacks, the one-time quiet researcher, is invigorated by the possibilities. He wonders whether music could carry such information, to give his patient back a missing part of his life. To give Greg "some sense of what's been happening in the last 20 years, where he has no autobiography of his own."

That would have Sacks dancing in the aisles.

(EXCERPTED BY PERMISSION FROM *PROFILES,* the magazine of Continental Airlines, February 1994.)

increasing to between 25 and 50 percent for those over the age of 85 (APA, 2000; Cowley, 2000; De Leon et al., 1996). Altogether, 4 million persons in the United States experience some form of dementia (Zal, 1999; Alzheimer's Association, 1997). More than 70 forms have been identified (Noll & Turkington, 1994). Some result from metabolic, nutritional, or other problems that can be corrected. Most forms of dementia, however, are caused by neurological problems, such as Alzheimer's disease and stroke, which are currently difficult or impossible to correct.

ALZHEIMER'S DISEASE The most common form of dementia, usually occurring after the age of 65.

NEUROFIBRILLARY TANGLES Twisted protein fibers that form within certain brain cells as people age.

ALZHEIMER'S DISEASE **Alzheimer's disease,** named after Alois Alzheimer, the German physician who first identified it in 1907, is the most common form of dementia, accounting for at least half of the cases (Muir, 1997). This gradually progressive disease sometimes appears in middle age, but most often it occurs after the age of 65, and its prevalence increases greatly among people in their late 70s and early 80s (see Table 13-6).

Alzheimer's disease may last for as many as 20 years or more. It usually begins with mild memory problems, lapses of attention, and difficulties in language and communication (Small, Kemper, & Lyon, 1997). As symptoms worsen, the person has trouble completing complicated tasks or remembering important appointments (Searleman & Herrmann, 1994). Harry, for example, had problems carrying out his responsibilities at the water treatment plant and repeatedly forgot when to pick up his daughter. Eventually sufferers also have difficulty with simple tasks, distant memories are forgotten, and changes in personality often become very noticeable. For example, a man may become unusually aggressive (Ravetz, 1999).

People with Alzheimer's disease may at first deny that they have a problem, but they soon become anxious or depressed about their state of mind; many also become agitated (Zal, 1999; Devanand et al., 1997). As the dementia progresses, however, they show less and less awareness of their limitations. As we saw in Harry's case, they may withdraw from others during the late stages of the disorder, become more confused about time and place, wander, and show very poor judgment. Eventually they become fully dependent on other people. They may lose almost all knowledge of the past and fail to recognize the faces of even close relatives. They also become more and more uncomfortable at night and take frequent naps during the day. The late phase of the disorder can last from two to five years, with the individuals requiring constant care (Mace & Rabins, 1991).

Like Harry, Alzheimer's victims usually remain in fairly good health until the later stages of the disease. As their mental functioning declines, however, they become less active and spend much of their time just sitting or lying in bed. As a result, they are prone to develop illnesses such as pneumonia, which can result in death. Alzheimer's disease is responsible for 23,000 deaths each year in the United States, which makes it the eighth leading cause of death in elderly people (NCHS, 1999; Alzheimer's Association, 1997).

In most cases, Alzheimer's disease can be diagnosed with certainty only after death (APA, 2000), when structural changes in the person's brain, such as excessive *neurofibrillary tangles* and *senile plaques,* can be fully examined. **Neurofibrillary tangles,** twisted protein fibers found

Table 13-6 **DSM-IV Checklist**

DEMENTIA OF THE ALZHEIMER'S TYPE
 	
 1. The development of multiple cognitive deficits manifested by both memory impairment and at least one of the following cognitive disturbances:
   a. Aphasia.
   b. Apraxia.
   c. Agnosia.
   d. Disturbance in executive functioning.
 2. Significant impairment in social or occupational functioning, along with significant decline from a previous level of functioning.
 3. Gradual onset and continuing cognitive decline.
 	
 Based on APA, 2000, 1994.

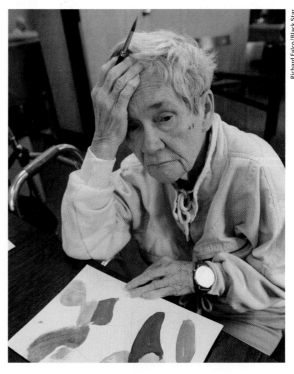

Richard Falco/Black Star

Losing one's mind *Because of their short-term memory problems, people with advanced cases of Alzheimer's disease, one source of dementia, are often unable to complete simple tasks such as painting a picture. In addition, their long-term memory deficits may prevent them from recognizing even close relatives or friends.*

Thalamus
Selected neurons shrink or die

Cerebral cortex
Large neurons shrink
Amyloid deposits develop in spaces between cells

Hypothalamus
Selected neurons die

Mammillary bodies

Basal forebrain
Acetylcholine-secreting
neurons shrink or die

Amygdala
Amyloid deposits develop in spaces between cells
Neurofibrillary tangles develop within neurons

Locus ceruleus
Neurons die

Hippocampus
Large neurons shrink or die
Amyloid deposits develop in spaces between cells
Neurofibrillary tangles develop within neurons

FIGURE 13-3   **The aging brain** *In old age, our brain undergoes changes that affect memory, learning, and reasoning to some degree. These same changes occur to an excessive degree in people with Alzheimer's disease. (Adapted from Selkoe, 1992, p. 136.)*

within the cells of the hippocampus and certain other brain areas, occur in all people as they age (see Figure 13-3), but people with Alzheimer's disease form a very high number of them (Thompson, 2000; Selkoe, 1992). **Senile plaques** are sphere-shaped deposits of a small molecule known as the *beta-amyloid protein* that form in the spaces *between* cells in the hippocampus, cerebral cortex, and certain other brain regions, as well as in some nearby blood vessels. The formation of plaques is also a normal part of aging, but again it is exceptionally high in people with Alzheimer's disease (Selkoe, 2000, 1999, 1992). Plaques may interfere with communications between cells, and so cause cell breakdown or cell death. Scientists do not fully understand why some people develop these problems and the disease. Research has suggested several possible causes, however, including *genetic factors* and *biochemical abnormalities*.

WHAT ARE THE GENETIC CAUSES OF ALZHEIMER'S DISEASE? It appears that Alzheimer's disease often has a genetic basis. Studies have found that particular genes are responsible for the production of proteins called *beta-amyloid precursor protein (beta-APP)* and *presenilin.* Many theorists now believe that some families transmit *mutations,* or abnormal forms, of these genes, increasing the likelihood of plaque formation and, in turn, of Alzheimer's disease (St. George-Hyslop, 2000; Selkoe, 1999, 1998, 1996). Genetic studies have also linked certain kinds of Alzheimer's disease to defects on chromosomes 1, 14, 19, and 21 (Higgins et al., 1997; Roses et al., 1996).

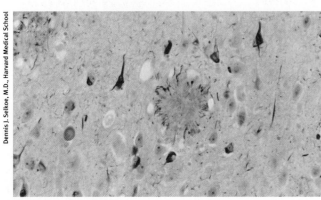

Biological culprits *Tissue from the brain of a 69-year-old man with Alzheimer's disease shows excessive amounts of plaque (large dark-gold sphere), the clusters of beta-amyloid protein that form outside cells, and of neurofibrillary tangles, the twisted fibers within cells that make the cells appear blackened (small dark blobs).*

Dennis J. Selkoe, M.D., Harvard Medical School

WHAT ARE THE BIOCHEMICAL CAUSES OF ALZHEIMER'S DISEASE? Researchers have found that *acetylcholine* and *glutamate,* two of the neurotransmitters that play key roles in memory, are in low supply, or at least function differently, in the brains of Alzheimer victims (Bissette et al., 1996; Lee et al., 1996). Thus some theorists believe that abnormal activity of these neurotransmitters contributes to the disorder. Other scientists believe that a slow-acting infection may help cause Alzheimer's disease (Prusiner, 1991), while still others point to dysfunction of the immune system (Hüll et al., 1996; McGeer & McGeer, 1996). High levels of zinc and aluminum have also been found in the brains of some Alzheimer's victims and have captured the interest of some investigators.

OTHER FORMS OF DEMENTIA A number of other disorders may also lead to dementia. **Vascular dementia,** also known as **multi-infarct dementia,** may follow a cerebrovascular accident, or *stroke,* during which blood flow to specific areas of the brain was cut off, thus damaging the areas. The patient may be aware of the stroke, or it may be "silent"—that is, the person may be unaware that anything has happened. Like Alzheimer's disease, vascular dementia is progressive, but its symptoms begin suddenly rather than gradually. Moreover, cognitive functioning may continue to be normal in areas of the brain that have not been affected by the stroke (Gallagher-Thompson & Thompson, 1995). Inasmuch as men have a higher rate of cardiovascular disease and hypertension as they age, this form of disability occurs more often in men than in women (APA, 2000).

Pick's disease, a rare disorder that affects the frontal and temporal lobes, offers a clinical picture similar to Alzheimer's disease, but the two diseases can be distinguished at autopsy. **Creutzfeldt-Jakob disease,** another source of dementia, is caused by a slow-acting virus that may live in the body for years before the disease develops (APA, 2000). Once launched, however, the disease has a rapid course. **Huntington's disease** is an inherited progressive disease in which memory problems worsen over time, along with personality changes and mood difficulties (Scourfield et al., 1997). Huntington's victims have movement problems, too, such as severe twitching and spasms. Children of people with Huntington's disease have a 50 percent chance of developing it. **Parkinson's disease,** the slowly progressive neurological disorder marked by tremors, rigidity, and unsteadiness, causes dementia in 20 to 60 percent of cases, particularly in older people or people whose cases are advanced (APA, 2000). And lastly, cases of dementia may also be caused by viral and bacterial *infectious disorders* such as HIV and AIDS, meningitis, and advanced syphilis; by *brain seizure disorder;* by *drug abuse;* or by *toxins* such as mercury, lead, or carbon monoxide.

Victim of Parkinson's disease *The world cheered when Muhammad Ali, considered the most skilled and influential athlete of his generation, lit the Olympic flame in 1996. At the same time, Ali's slow gait, halting verbal responses, and shaking hands and limbs demonstrated the impairment that Parkinson's disease can bring.*

What Treatments Are Available for Organic Memory Disorders?

Treating amnestic disorders and dementias is a frustrating and difficult challenge. No single approach or set of approaches is effective in all cases, and treatment tends to offer modest help. However, recent research on causes of these disorders has provided hope that they may be treated more effectively or even prevented in the years to come (Kalb, 2000). Currently the first step in treatment is to identify as clearly as possible the precise type and nature of the disease. Clinicians will typically take a complete history of the patient, do extensive neuropsychological testing, and conduct brain scans to help pinpoint the biological causes of the patient's dysfunctioning (Zal, 1999; Gonzalez, 1996).

A common approach to the treatment of organic memory disorders, particularly dementia, is the use of drugs that affect the neurotransmitters known to play important roles in memory. Two such drugs, *tacrine* (trade name Cognex) and *donepezil* (Aricept), prevent the breakdown of acetylcholine, the neurotransmitter that is in low supply in people with Alzheimer's disease. Some Alzheimer patients who take these drugs improve slightly in short-term memory and reasoning ability, as well as in their use of language and their ability to cope under pressure (Krall, Sramek, & Cutler, 1999; Lyketsos et al., 1996). Although the benefits of the drugs are limited and the risk of undesired effects (particularly for tacrine) is sometimes high, the drugs have been approved by the Food and Drug Administration. Clinicians believe that they may be of most use to those in the early stages of Alzheimer's disease or for those with a mild form of dementia (Krall et al., 1999). Safer and more effective drugs are currently under development (Daly, 1999).

SENILE PLAQUES Sphere-shaped deposits of beta-amyloid protein that form in the spaces between certain brain cells and in certain blood vessels as people age.

VASCULAR DEMENTIA Dementia caused by a cerebrovascular accident, or stroke, which restricts blood flow to certain areas of the brain. Also known as *multi-infarct dementia.*

PICK'S DISEASE A neurological disease that affects the frontal and temporal lobes, causing dementia.

CREUTZFELDT-JAKOB DISEASE A form of dementia caused by a slow-acting virus that may live in the body for years before the disease appears.

HUNTINGTON'S DISEASE An inherited disease in which people develop progressive problems in cognition, emotion, and movement, and which results in dementia.

PARKINSON'S DISEASE A slowly progressive neurological disease, marked by tremors and rigidity, which may also cause dementia.

Mad Human Disease?

In the 1980s British farmers first became aware of *bovine spongiform encephalopathy,* or *mad cow disease.* Cows with this disease became disoriented, uncoordinated, and irritable, and eventually died. Autopsies revealed holes and tangles of protein in their brains. Researchers traced the disease to a particular feeding practice: sick cattle and parts of cattle that could not be sold for meat were ground up and fed to other cattle. British officials promptly banned the practice, but symptoms of the disease do not appear until years after the infection is contracted, so a continuing epidemic of mad cow disease has unfolded (Hileman, 2001). Some 200,000 cattle have now died of the disease (Hileman, 2001).

What does mad cow disease have to do with abnormal psychology in humans? Clinicians have come to appreciate that *Creutzfeldt-Jakob disease (CJD),* a form of human dementia, is somewhat similar, clinically and biologically, to mad cow disease. CJD is a rare progressive dementia—incurable and fatal—apparently caused by an infectious protein that stays in the body for decades before producing symptoms (APA, 2000; Prusiner, 1995).

Although scientists at first believed that it was impossible for mad cow disease to "jump species," many now believe that a new variant of CJD, called *vCJD,* may be contracted by people who eat the meat of cows infected with mad cow disease. To date, about 100 people in Europe have died of vCJD, but nobody knows how many have been infected—like mad cow disease and conventional CJD, vCJD may take years to produce symptoms. Although the absolute number of cases remains small, the rate of residents in the United Kingdom infected with vCJD has grown by 23 percent each year since 1994 (Hileman, 2001).

Once people became aware of the possible connection between mad cow disease and vCJD, panic swept across the United Kingdom and around the world. Most nations banned imports of British beef. Healthy cows could not be distinguished from infected ones, and so the United Kingdom agreed to destroy almost half the nation's herd. By 2000, the number of slaughtered cows had reached 8 million.

The United States appears to have avoided or at least minimized this health problem so far. The government has taken several measures to prevent the spread of mad cow disease and the emergence of vCJD, but some argue that the country is still vulnerable. On the one hand, in 1997 the Food and Drug Administration (FDA) banned the feeding of meat made from cud-chewing animals to other cud-chewing animals (cows and sheep). On the other hand, such banned meals still may be fed to poultry, fish, and pigs, whose remains, in turn, may be fed to cattle (Burros, 2001). Moreover, it appears that some slaughterhouses have difficulty keeping these two types of feed separate. Recently, for example, farmers discovered that 1,000 cattle at a Texas feedlot had inadvertently been given the banned feed; in turn, the cattle had to be destroyed (Burros, 2001).

In still other measures, since 1989 the Department of Agriculture has banned imports of live cattle and sheep from countries where mad cow disease has been identified, and in 1999 the FDA banned blood donations from anyone who lived for more than six months in one of those countries during the 1980s or 1990s. Once again, however, such measures may fall short. The government still does not regulate dietary supplements that may contain tissue from infected cattle, and its testing of farms and slaughterhouses for compliance with feeding regulations and other safeguards has often been unsystematic (Burros, 2001).

Martyn Hayhow/AP/Wide World Photos

Consider This

◉ Initially many scientists argued that mad cow disease could not be transmitted from one species to another, while others countered that such transmissions were indeed possible (Aldhous, 1996). When scientists disagree, how should the public proceed? • Can you suggest other ways of responding to the mad cow disease outbreak that might have been more effective or might have helped prevent the growing panic over its potential dangers?

Tacrine, donepezil, and related drugs are prescribed *after* a person has developed Alzheimer's disease. A number of studies seem to suggest, however, that certain substances may actually help prevent or delay the onset of the disease. For example, one team of researchers concluded that women who take *estrogen,* the female sex hormone, for years after menopause cut their risk of developing Alzheimer's disease in half (Kawas et al., 1997). Similarly, long-term use of *nonsteroid anti-inflammatory drugs* such as *ibuprofen* and *naprosyn* (drugs found in

Advil, Motrin, Nuprin, and other pain relievers) seems to greatly reduce the risk of Alzheimer's disease.

Behavioral and cognitive therapies have also been tried in cases of amnestic disorder and dementia, with modest success. Some people with amnestic disorders, particularly those whose amnesia is caused by a head injury, have successfully been taught special methods for remembering new information; in some cases the teachers have been computers (Schacter et al., 1990). The behavioral techniques applied to dementia typically seek to change everyday patient behaviors that are stressful for the family, such as wandering at night, bed wetting, demands for attention, and inadequate personal care (Fisher & Carstensen, 1990). In these techniques, therapists use a combination of role-playing exercises, modeling, and practice to teach family members how and when to apply reinforcement in order to shape more positive behaviors (Pinkston & Linsk, 1984).

Caregiving can take a heavy toll on the close relatives of people with amnestic disorders or dementia, particularly the latter (Alspaugh et al., 1999; Kiecolt-Glaser et al., 1996). In fact, one of the most frequent reasons for the institutionalization of Alzheimer's victims is that overwhelmed caregivers can no longer cope with the difficulties of keeping them at home (Kaplan, 1998). Many caregivers experience anger and depression, and their own physical and mental health often declines. Clinicians now recognize that one of the most important aspects of treating Alzheimer's disease and other forms of dementia is to focus on the emotional needs of the caregivers: their need for regular time out, for education about the disease, and for psychotherapy when stress begins to build (Clyburn et al., 2000; Kalb, 2000). Some clinicians also provide caregiver classes and support groups (Gallagher-Thompson et al., 2000, 1991).

In recent years, sociocultural approaches have begun to play an important role in the treatment of organic memory disorders, particularly the dementias (Kalb, 2000). A number of *day-care* facilities for patients with Alzheimer's disease have been developed, providing treatment programs and activities for outpatients during the day and returning them to their homes and families at night. In addition, many *assisted-living* facilities have been built, in which individuals suffering from dementia live in cheerful apartments, receive needed supervision, and take part in various activities that bring more joy and stimulation to their lives. These apartments are typically designed to meet the special needs of the residents—providing more light, for example, or enclosing gardens with circular paths so the individuals can go for strolls alone without getting lost (Kalb, 2000). Studies suggest that such facilities often help slow the cognitive decline of residents and increase their enjoyment of life.

Rather than being discouraged by the present limitations in the understanding and treatment of amnestic disorders and dementia, researchers are looking forward to advances in the coming years. The brain changes responsible for cognition are tremendously complex, but given the amount of research under way and reports of progress, most investigators believe that exciting breakthroughs are indeed just over the horizon.

Day treatment *Two women go their separate ways in a New Jersey day-care facility for patients with Alzheimer's disease. Such facilities, which are growing in number, provide special programs and activities for patients. The individuals return to their families each night.*

CAREGIVER STRESS

According to research, caring for a loved one with Alzheimer's disease takes an average of 69 to 100 hours per week. The major worries reported by caregivers are the monetary cost of help (54%), the effects of Alzheimer's-related stress within the family (49%), and lack of time for caregivers to attend to their own needs (49%) (Alzheimer's Association, 1997).

SUMMING UP

Organic Memory Disorders

Amnestic disorders and dementias are organic disorders that cause major problems in short-term memory, long-term memory, or both. Often the disorders are linked to abnormalities in key brain areas, such as the prefrontal lobes, the temporal lobes (including the hippocampus and amygdala, which lie under them), and the diencephalon. Amnestic disorders, disorders that primarily affect memory, may be the result of Korsakoff's syndrome, head injury, brain surgery, or certain other prob-

HOME CARE

Around 70% of people with Alzheimer's disease live at home. Around three-fourths of their caregivers are women (Kalb, 2000).

PEAK CONDITION
Research suggests that memory and other cognitive functions peak at approximately age 25 (McGaugh, 1999).

lems. Dementias, which affect both memory and other cognitive functions, include Alzheimer's disease and vascular dementia.

Explanations Alzheimer's disease has been linked to an unusually high number of neurofibrillary tangles and senile plaques in the brain. Many cases of this disease seem to be caused by genetic factors. Theorists have also proposed such factors as abnormal neurotransmitter activity, slow-acting infections, immune system problems, and high levels of zinc or aluminum in the brain.

Treatments Both drug and behavioral therapies have been applied to organic memory disorders, with limited success. The needs of caregiving are increasingly being addressed in treatment. And new sociocultural approaches such as day-care facilities and assisted-living facilities are now being offered to sufferers of these disorders. The coming years are expected to see major treatment breakthroughs.

DEMENTIA IN DOGS
In 1999 the Food and Drug Administration approved the use of the drug *selegiline* (trade name Anipril) to treat elderly dogs suffering from *canine cognitive dysfunction syndrome*—a disorder characterized by confusion, inability to recognize or respond to familiar household faces, and the loss of house training. Around 70 percent of canine subjects show some improvement with drug treatment.

CROSSROADS:
Enormous Interest but Limited Knowledge

Sometimes scientists ignore a phenomenon that captures the public's interest. Dissociative disorders suffered this fate for many years. The public's interest in dissociative amnesia and fugue was enormous, but scientific studies were limited. Similarly, multiple personality disorder failed to spur much research.

This scientific indifference has since made an about-face. The growing number of reported cases of dissociative disorders, particularly multiple personality disorder, over the past 25 years has convinced many researchers that these patterns do exist and may cause great dysfunctioning. Studies have also begun to suggest that the disorders may have their roots in long-familiar processes, such as state-dependent learning and self-hypnosis.

Still, we do not yet have complete theories about the causes of dissociative disorders—or fully developed treatment programs. Some clinicians further worry that the current degree of interest in dissociative disorders may, in fact, be growing too fast, creating a false impression of their prevalence or importance. They argue that many current diagnoses are based less on a careful assessment of symptoms than on the increasing popularity of these disorders in the field. Of course, such possibilities only highlight the need for continuing investigation.

Less controversial but equally fascinating are the disorders of memory that have organic causes. The complexity of the brain makes amnestic disorders and dementias difficult to understand, diagnose, and treat. However, researchers announce exciting new discoveries almost daily. Because of the organic nature of these disorders, the research is largely biological; but the disorders have such a powerful impact on patients and their families that psychological and sociocultural investigations probably will not lag behind for long.

KEY TERMS

QUICK QUIZ

1. List and describe the different dissociative disorders. pp. 380–387

2. What are four kinds of dissociative amnesia? pp. 380–381

3. What are the different kinds of relationships that the subpersonalities may have in multiple personality disorder? p. 385

4. Describe the psychodynamic, behavioral, state-dependent learning, and self-hypnosis explanations of dissociative disorders. How well is each supported by research? pp. 387–390

5. Discuss the parallels between hypnotic amnesia and dissociative disorders. pp. 389–390

6. What approaches have been used to treat dissociative disorders? What are the key features of treatment for multiple personality disorder? pp. 390–392

7. What brain areas have been tied to memory and to organic disorders of memory? Define short-term and long-term memory, procedural and declarative memory, and long-term potentiation. pp. 393–394

8. What are amnestic disorders? Give two examples of such disorders. pp. 395–396

9. What is dementia? What are the symptoms and possible causes of Alzheimer's disease? pp. 396–400

10. How do today's clinicians treat the various organic disorders of memory? pp. 401–403

CYBER STUDY

▲ *Observe an individual with multiple personality disorder.* ▲ *See "switches" from subpersonality to subpersonality.* ▲ *How do therapists treat multiple personality disorder?* ▲ *What problems are faced by sufferers of Alzheimer's disease and their caregivers?*

SEARCH THE *FUNDAMENTALS OF ABNORMAL PSYCHOLOGY* CD-ROM FOR

▲ Chapter 13 video cases and discussions
  "Tony"—Multiple Personality Disorder
  "Walter"—Alzheimer's Disease

▲ Chapter 13 practice test and feedback

LOG ON TO THE COMER WEB PAGE FOR

▲ Suggested Web links, research exercises, FAQ page, additional Chapter 13 practice test questions
  <www.worthpublishers.com/comer>

The Brain, Second Edition (The Annenberg/CPB Collection, 1997)

CHAPTER

14

Personality
Disorders

While interviewing for the job of editor, Frederick said, "This may sound self-serving, but I am extraordinarily gifted. I am certain that I will do great things in this position, that I and the newspaper will soon set the standard for journalism in this city." The committee was impressed. Certainly, Frederick's credentials were strong, but even more important, his self-confidence and boldness had wowed them.

A year later, many of the same individuals were describing Frederick differently—arrogant, self-serving, cold, ego-maniacal, draining. He had performed well as editor (though not as spectacularly as he seemed to think), but that performance could not outweigh his impossible personality. Colleagues below and above him had grown weary of his manipulations, his emotional outbursts, his refusal ever to take the blame, his nonstop boasting, and his grandiose plans. Once again Frederick had worn out his welcome.

To be sure, Frederick had great charm, and he knew how to make others feel important, when it served his purpose. Thus he always had his share of friends and admirers. But in reality they were just passing through, until Frederick would tire of them or feel betrayed by their lack of enthusiasm for one of his self-serving interpretations or grand plans. Or until they simply could take Frederick no longer.

Bright and successful though he was, Frederick always felt entitled to more than he was receiving—to higher grades at school, greater compensation at work, more attention from girlfriends. If criticized even slightly, he reacted with fury, and was certain that the critic was jealous of his superior intelligence, skill, or looks. At first glance, Frederick seemed to have a lot going for him socially. Typically, he could be found in the midst of a deep, meaningful romantic relationship—one in which he might be tender, attentive, and seemingly devoted to his partner. But Frederick would always tire of his partner within a few weeks or months and would turn cold or even mean. Often he started affairs with other women while still involved with the current partner. The breakups—usually unpleasant and sometimes ugly—rarely brought sadness or remorse to him, and he would almost never think about his former partner again. He always had himself.

definition

Each of us has a **personality**—a unique and long-term pattern of inner experience and outward behavior. We tend to react in our own predictable and consistent ways. These consistencies, often called *personality traits,* may be the result of inherited characteristics, learned responses, or a combination of the two (Millon, 1999). Yet our personalities are also flexible. We learn from experience. As we interact with our surroundings, we try out various responses to see which are more effective. This is a flexibility that people who suffer from a personality disorder usually do not have.

A **personality disorder** is a very rigid pattern of inner experience and outward behavior. The pattern is seen in most of the person's interactions, continues for years, and differs from the experiences and behaviors usually expected of people (see Table 14-1 on the next page). Frederick seems to

PERSONALITY A unique and long-term pattern of inner experience and outward behavior, which leads to consistent reactions across various situations.

PERSONALITY DISORDER A very rigid pattern of inner experience and outward behavior that differs from the expectations of one's culture and leads to dysfunctioning.

Table 14-1 DSM-IV Checklist

PERSONALITY DISORDER

1. An enduring pattern of inner experience and behavior that deviates markedly from the expectations of the individual's culture, with at least two of the following areas affected: • cognition • affectivity • interpersonal functioning • impulse control.
2. Pattern is inflexible and pervasive across a broad range of personal and social situations.
3. Pattern is stable and long-lasting, and its onset can be traced back at least to adolescence or early adulthood.
4. Significant distress or impairment.

Based on APA, 2000, 1994.

Early notions of personality *Scientists have long suspected that biological factors help account for personality and personality disorders. In the theory of* phrenology, *Franz Joseph Gall (1758–1828) held that the brain consists of distinct portions, each responsible for some aspect of personality. Phrenologists tried to assess personality by feeling bumps and indentations on a person's head.*

display such a disorder. For most of his life, his narcissism, grandiosity, outbursts, and insensitivity to others have been excessive and have dominated his functioning. The rigid traits of people with personality disorders often lead to psychological pain for the individual and social or occupational difficulties. The disorders may also bring pain to others. Witness the upset and turmoil experienced by Frederick's co-workers and girlfriends.

Personality disorders typically become recognizable in adolescence or early adulthood, although some start during childhood (APA, 2000, 1994). These are among the most difficult psychological disorders to treat. Many sufferers are not even aware of their personality problems and fail to trace their difficulties to their rigid style of thinking and behaving. It has been estimated that between 4 and 15 percent of all adults may have a personality disorder (Ekselius et al., 2001; Kessler & Zhao, 1999).

As we saw in Chapter 3, DSM-IV separates Axis II disorders, disorders of long standing that usually begin well before adulthood and continue into adult life, from the Axis I disorders, more acute disorders that often begin as a noticeable change in a person's usual behavior and are, in many cases, of limited duration. The personality disorders are Axis II disorders; these patterns are not typically marked by changes in intensity or periods of clear improvement.

It is common for a person with a personality disorder to suffer from an acute (Axis I) disorder at the same time, a relationship called *comorbidity*. Perhaps personality disorders predispose people to develop certain Axis I disorders. For example, people with avoidant personality disorder, who fearfully shy away from all relationships, may be prone to develop a social phobia. Or certain Axis I disorders may set the stage for a personality disorder. Or perhaps some biological factor creates a predisposition to both (Koenigsberg et al., 1999). Whatever the reason for the relationship, research indicates that the presence of a personality disorder reduces a person's chances for a successful recovery from psychological problems (Costello, 1996).

DSM-IV identifies ten personality disorders and separates them into three groups, called *clusters* (APA, 2000, 1994). One group, marked by odd behavior, consists of the *paranoid, schizoid,* and *schizotypal* personality disorders. A second group features dramatic behavior and consists of the *antisocial, borderline, histrionic,* and *narcissistic* personality disorders. The final cluster features a high degree of anxiety, and includes the *avoidant, dependent,* and *obsessive-compulsive* personality disorders.

The various personality disorders overlap so much that it can be difficult to distinguish one from the other (Gunderson & Ronningstam, 2001) (see Figure 14-1). In fact, diagnosticians sometimes determine that particular individuals have more than one personality disorder (Ekselius et al., 2001). In addition, clinicians often disagree as to the correct diagnosis for people with personality disor-

FIGURE 14-1 **Prominent and central features of DSM-IV's ten personality disorders** *The symptoms of the various disorders often overlap greatly, leading to frequent misdiagnosis or to multiple diagnoses for a given client.*

ders. This lack of agreement has raised serious questions about the *validity* (accuracy) and *reliability* (consistency) of the present DSM categories, a concern that we shall return to later in the chapter (O'Connor & Dyce, 1998).

Finally, diagnoses of personality disorder can easily be overdone. We may catch glimpses of ourselves or of people we know in the descriptions of these disorders, and we may be tempted to conclude that we or they have a personality disorder (Maher & Maher, 1994). In the vast majority of instances, such interpretations are incorrect. We all display personality traits. Only rarely are they so rigid, maladaptive, and distressful that they can be considered disorders.

"Odd" Personality Disorders

The cluster of *"odd" personality disorders* consists of the *paranoid*, *schizoid*, and *schizotypal* personality disorders. People with these disorders typically display odd or eccentric behaviors that are similar to but not as extensive as those seen in schizophrenia, including extreme suspiciousness, social withdrawal, and peculiar ways of thinking and perceiving things. Such behaviors often leave the person isolated. Some clinicians believe that these personality disorders are actually

Phrenology update *It appears that old ideas die hard. A 1930 device called the* psychograph *carried on the early nineteenth-century tradition of phrenology, studying and measuring bumps on the head in order to assess an individual's personality.*

related to schizophrenia, and thus they call them *schizophrenia-spectrum disorders.* In support of this idea, people with these personality disorders often qualify for an additional diagnosis of schizophrenia or have close relatives with schizophrenia (APA, 2000, 1994; Solano & DeChavez, 2000).

Clinicians have learned much about the symptoms of the odd personality disorders but have not been so successful in determining their causes or how to treat them. In fact, people with these disorders rarely seek treatment (Fabrega et al., 1991).

Paranoid Personality Disorder

People with **paranoid personality disorder** deeply distrust other people and are suspicious of their motives (APA, 2000, 1994). Because they believe that everyone intends them harm, they avoid close relationships. Their trust in their own ideas and abilities can be excessive, though, as we see in the case of Charles:

> Charles, an only child of poorly educated parents, had been recognized as a "child genius" in early school years. He received a Ph.D. degree at 24, and subsequently held several responsible positions as a research physicist in an industrial firm.
>
> His haughty arrogance and narcissism often resulted in conflicts with his superiors; it was felt that he spent too much time working on his own "harebrained" schemes and not enough on company projects. Charles . . . began to feel that both his superiors and his subordinates were "making fun of him" and not taking him seriously. To remedy this attack upon his status, Charles began to work on a scheme that would "revolutionize the industry," a new thermodynamic principle which, when applied to his company's major product, would prove extremely efficient and economical. After several months . . . he presented his plans to the company president. Brilliant though it was, the plan overlooked certain obvious simple facts of logic and economy.
>
> Upon learning of its rejection, Charles withdrew to his home where he became obsessed with "new ideas," proposing them in intricate schematics and formulas to a number of government officials and industrialists. These resulted in new rebuffs which led to further efforts at self-inflation.
>
> *(Millon, 1969, pp. 329–330)*

DISTRUSTING SOULS

According to surveys, the people who tend to be the most distrustful in the United States are those who were repeatedly warned by their parents against trusting strangers. Other characteristics: they are under 30 years of age, are socially isolated, live in the city, live in poor or crime-ridden neighborhoods, and report having no religious affiliation (Pew Research Center, 1997).

Ever on guard and cautious, and seeing threats everywhere, people like Charles continually expect to be the targets of some trickery (see Figure 14-2). They find "hidden" meanings in everything, which are usually belittling or threatening. In a study that required individuals to role-play, subjects with paranoia were more likely than control subjects to read hostile intentions into the actions of others. In addition, they more often chose anger as the appropriate role-play response (Turkat et al., 1990).

Quick to challenge the loyalty or trustworthiness of those around them, people with paranoid personality disorder remain cold and distant. A woman might avoid confiding in anyone, for example, for fear of being hurt; or a husband might, without any justification, keep questioning his wife's faithfulness. Although inaccurate, their suspicions are not usually *delusional*; the ideas are not so bizarre or so firmly held as to clearly remove the individuals from reality (Fenigstein, 1996).

People with this disorder are critical of weakness and fault in others, particularly at work. They are unable to recognize their own mistakes, however, and are extremely sensitive to criticism. They often blame others for the things that go wrong in their lives, and they repeatedly bear grudges (Fenigstein, 1996). Between 0.5 and 2.5 percent of adults are believed to experience this disorder, apparently more men than women (APA, 2000, 1994).

HOW DO THEORISTS EXPLAIN PARANOID PERSONALITY DISORDER? The proposed explanations of paranoid personality disorder, like those of most other personality disorders, have received little systematic research. Psychodynamic theories, the oldest of the explanations for this disorder, trace the pattern to early interactions with demanding parents, particularly distant, rigid fathers and overcontrolling, rejecting mothers (Manschreck, 1996). (We shall see that psychodynamic explanations for almost all the personality disorders begin the same way—with repeated mistreatment during childhood and lack of love.) According to one psychodynamic view, some individuals come to view their environment as unfriendly as a result of their parents' unreasonable demands. They must always be on the alert because they cannot trust others, and they are likely to develop feelings of extreme anger (Cameron, 1974). They also project these feelings onto others and as a result feel increasingly persecuted (Garfield & Havens, 1991). Similarly, some cognitive theorists suggest that people with paranoid personality disorder generally hold maladaptive assumptions such as "People are evil" and "People will attack you if given the chance" (Beck & Freeman, 1990).

Biological theorists propose that paranoid personality disorder has genetic causes (Fenigstein, 1996). A study that looked at self-reports of suspiciousness in 3,810 Australian twin pairs found that if one twin was excessively suspicious, the other had an increased likelihood of also being suspicious (Kendler et al., 1987). Once again, however, it is important to note that such similarities between twins might also be the result of common environmental experiences.

TREATMENTS FOR PARANOID PERSONALITY DISORDER People with paranoid personality disorder do not typically see themselves as needing help, and few come to treatment willingly (Millon, 1999). Furthermore, many who are in treatment view the role of patient as inferior and distrust and rebel against their therapists (Fenigstein, 1996). Thus it is not surprising that therapy for this disorder, as for most other personality disorders, has limited effect and moves very slowly (Quality Assurance Project, 1990). Object relations therapists, the psychodynamic therapists who give center stage to relationships, try to see past the patient's anger and work on what they view as his or her deep wish for a satisfying relationship (Auchincloss & Weiss, 1992). Behavioral and cognitive therapists, for their part, try to help these individuals control their anxiety and improve their skills at solving interpersonal problems. Cognitive therapists also try to guide the clients to develop more realistic interpretations of other people's words and actions and to become more aware of other people's points of view (Beck & Freeman, 1990). Drug therapy is generally ineffective (Block & Pristach, 1992).

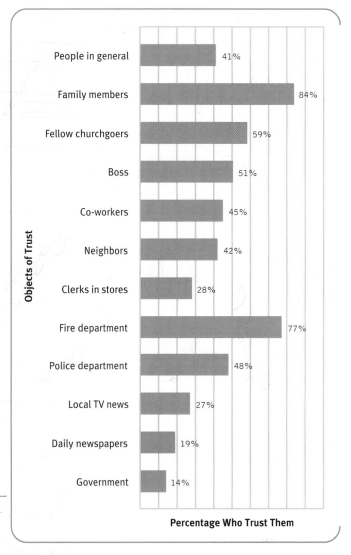

FIGURE 14-2   Whom do you trust? *Although distrust and suspiciousness are the hallmarks of paranoid personality disorder, even persons without this disorder are surprisingly untrusting. In a recent survey of a broad sample of society, only 41 percent of respondents said that they generally trust people. Most do trust their family members and local fire department; however, few trust clerks in stores, daily newspapers, or the government. (Adapted from Pew Research Center for the People and the Press, 1997.)*

PARANOID PERSONALITY DISORDER A personality disorder marked by a pattern of distrust and suspiciousness of others.

Schizoid Personality Disorder

People with **schizoid personality disorder** persistently avoid and are removed from social relationships and show little in the way of emotion (APA, 2000, 1994). Like people with paranoid personality disorder, these individuals do not have close ties with others. The reason they avoid social contact, however, has nothing to do with paranoia—it is that they genuinely prefer to be alone. Take Roy:

> Roy was a successful sanitation engineer involved in the planning and maintenance of water resources for a large city; his job called for considerable foresight and independent judgment but little supervisory responsibility. In general, he was appraised as an undistinguished but competent and reliable employee. There were few demands of an interpersonal nature made of him, and he was viewed by most of his colleagues as reticent and shy and by others as cold and aloof.
>
> Difficulties centered about his relationship with his wife. At her urging they sought marital counseling for, as she put it, "he is unwilling to join in family activities, he fails to take an interest in the children, he lacks affection and is disinterested in sex."
>
> The pattern of social indifference, flatness of affect and personal isolation which characterized much of Roy's behavior was of little consequence to those with whom a deeper or more intimate relationship was not called for; with his immediate family, however, these traits took their toll.
>
> *(Millon, 1969, p. 224)*

People like Roy, often described as "loners," make no effort to start or keep friendships, take little interest in having sexual relationships, and even seem indifferent to their families. They seek out jobs that require little or no contact with others. When necessary, they can form work relations to a degree, but they prefer to keep to themselves. Many live by themselves as well. Not surprisingly, their social skills tend to be weak (Birtchnell, 1996). If they marry, their lack of interest in intimacy may create marital or family problems, as it did for Roy.

People with schizoid personality disorder focus mainly on themselves and are generally unaffected by praise or criticism. They rarely show any feelings, expressing neither joy nor anger. They seem to have no need for attention or acceptance; are typically viewed as cold, humorless, or dull; and generally succeed in being ignored. The prevalence of this disorder is not known, although it is estimated to be present in fewer than 1 percent of the population (Weissman, 1993). It is slightly more likely to occur in men than in women, and men may also be more limited by it (APA, 2000).

Joel Gordon, New York, NY

Alone, either way *Different personality disorders often yield similar behaviors. People with either schizoid or avoidant personality disorder spend much of their time alone. The former, however, truly want to be alone, whereas the latter yearn for but fear social relationships.*

HOW DO THEORISTS EXPLAIN SCHIZOID PERSONALITY DISORDER?

Many psychodynamic theorists, particularly object relations theorists, propose that schizoid personality disorder has its roots in an unsatisfied need for human contact (Carstairs, 1992; Horner, 1991, 1975). The parents of people with this disorder, like those of people with paranoid personality disorder, are believed to have been unaccepting or even abusive of their children. Whereas individuals with paranoid symptoms react to such parenting chiefly with distrust, those with schizoid personality disorder are left unable to give or receive love. They cope by avoiding all relationships.

Cognitive theorists propose, not surprisingly, that people with schizoid personality disorder suffer from deficiencies in their thinking. Their thoughts tend to be vague and empty, and they have trouble scanning the environment to arrive at accurate perceptions (Beck & Freeman, 1990). Unable to pick up emotional cues from others, they simply cannot respond to emotions. As this theory might predict, children with schizoid personality disorder develop language and motor skills very slowly, whatever their level of intelligence (Wolff, 1991).

TREATMENTS FOR SCHIZOID PERSONALITY DISORDER Their social withdrawal prevents most people with schizoid personality disorder from entering therapy unless some other disorder, such as alcoholism, makes treatment necessary. These clients are likely to remain emotionally distant from the therapist, seem not to care about their treatment, and make limited progress at best (Millon, 1999; Quality Assurance Project, 1990).

Cognitive therapists have sometimes been able to help people with this disorder experience more positive emotions and more satisfying social interactions (Beck & Freeman, 1990). Their techniques include presenting clients with lists of emotions to think about or having them write down and remember pleasurable experiences. Behavioral therapists have sometimes had success teaching social skills to such clients, using role playing, exposure techniques, and homework assignments as tools (Millon, 1999). Group therapy is apparently useful when it offers a safe setting for social contact (Vaillant & Perry, 1985), although people with this disorder may resist any pressure to take part (Gabbard, 1990). As with paranoid personality disorder, drug therapy has offered little help (Liebowitz et al., 1986).

Schizotypal Personality Disorder

People with **schizotypal personality disorder** display a range of interpersonal problems marked by extreme discomfort in close relationships, very odd forms of thinking and perceiving, and behavioral eccentricities (APA, 2000, 1994). Anxious around others, they seek isolation and have few close friends. Many feel intensely lonely. The disorder is more severe than the paranoid and schizoid personality disorders, as we see in the case of Harold:

> Harold was the fourth of seven children. . . . "Duckie," as Harold was known, had always been a withdrawn, frightened and "stupid" youngster. The nickname "Duckie" represented a peculiar waddle in his walk; it was used by others as a term of derogation and ridicule. Harold rarely played with his sibs or neighborhood children; he was teased unmercifully because of his "walk" and his fear of pranksters. Harold was a favorite neighborhood scapegoat; he was intimidated even by the most innocuous glance in his direction. . . .
>
> Harold's family was surprised when he performed well in the first few years of schooling. He began to falter, however, upon entrance to junior high school. At about the age of 14, his schoolwork became extremely poor, he refused to go to classes and he complained of a variety of vague, physical pains. By age 15 he had totally withdrawn from school, remaining home in the basement room that he shared with two younger brothers. Everyone in his family began to speak of him as "being touched." He thought about "funny religious things that didn't make sense"; he also began to draw "strange things" and talk to himself. When he was 16, he once ran out of the house screaming "I'm gone, I'm gone, I'm gone . . . ," saying that his "body went to heaven" and that he had to run outside to recover it; rather interestingly, this event occurred shortly after his father had been committed by the courts to a state mental hospital. By age 17, Harold was ruminating all day, often talking aloud in a meaningless jargon; he refused to come to the family table for meals.
>
> *(Millon, 1969, pp. 347–348)*

As with Harold, the thoughts and behaviors of people with schizotypal personality disorder can be noticeably disturbed (Birtchnell, 1996). These symptoms may include *ideas of reference*—beliefs that unrelated events pertain to them in

SCHIZOID PERSONALITY DISORDER A personality disorder in which a person persistently avoids social relationships and shows little emotional expression.

SCHIZOTYPAL PERSONALITY DISORDER A personality disorder in which a person displays a pattern of interpersonal problems marked by extreme discomfort in close relationships, odd forms of thinking and perceiving, and behavioral eccentricities.

"Personality disorders . . . are the only things left in psychiatry where people think you are bad."

Gary M. Flaxenberg, psychiatrist, 1998

some important way—and *bodily illusions*, such as sensing an external "force" or presence. A number of people with this disorder see themselves as having special extrasensory abilities, and some believe that they have magical control over others. Examples of schizotypal eccentricities include repeatedly arranging cans to align their labels, organizing closets extensively, or wearing an odd assortment of clothing. The emotions of these individuals may be inappropriate, flat, or humorless.

People with this personality disorder often have great difficulty keeping their attention focused (Lenzenwerger et al., 1991). Correspondingly, their conversation may be unclear, even sprinkled with loose associations (Caplan et al., 1990). They tend to drift aimlessly and lead an idle, unproductive life (Millon, 1990). They are likely to choose undemanding jobs in which they can work below their capacity and are not required to interact with other people. It has been estimated that around 3 percent of all people—slightly more males than females—may have a schizotypal personality disorder (APA, 2000; Weissman, 1993).

HOW DO THEORISTS EXPLAIN SCHIZOTYPAL PERSONALITY DISORDER? Because the symptoms of this personality disorder so often resemble schizophrenia, researchers have hypothesized that similar factors are at work in both disorders (Raine et al., 1997). They have in fact found that schizotypal symptoms, like schizophrenic patterns, are often linked to poor family communication and to psychological disorders in parents (Asarnow et al., 1991; Nagy & Szatmari, 1986). They have also learned that defects in attention and short-term memory may contribute to schizotypal personality disorder, just as they apparently do to schizophrenia (Roitman et al., 2000, 1997). Finally, researchers have begun to link schizotypal personality disorder to some of the same biological factors found in schizophrenia, such as high activity of the neurotransmitter dopamine, enlarged brain ventricles, smaller temporal lobes, and loss of cortical gray matter (Downhill et al., 2001; Trestman et al., 1996). As we saw in Chapter 12, there are indications that these biological factors may have a genetic base (Kendler et al., 2000, 1994, 1991).

Taxi Driver Some of film's most memorable characters have displayed personality disorders. Travis Bickle, of Taxi Driver fame, seemed to manifest the symptoms of schizotypal personality disorder, including social discomfort and a reduced capacity for interpersonal relationships. He also displayed self-referential interpretations of various events, cognitive distortions, a highly suspicious nature, grandiosity, emotional flatness, and temporary psychotic episodes.

The Kobal Collection

TREATMENTS FOR SCHIZOTYPAL PERSONALITY DISORDER Therapy is as difficult in cases of schizotypal personality disorder as it is in cases of paranoid and schizoid personality disorders (Millon, 1999; McGlashan, 1986). Most therapists agree on the need to help these clients "reconnect" with the world and recognize the limits of their thinking and their powers. The therapists may thus try to set clear limits—for example, by requiring punctuality—and work on helping the clients recognize where their views end and those of the therapist begin (Stone, 1989). Other therapy goals are to increase positive social contacts, ease loneliness, reduce overstimulation, and help the individuals become more aware of their personal feelings (Millon, 1999).

Cognitive therapists further try to teach clients to look at their unusual thoughts or perceptions objectively and to ignore the inappropriate ones (Beck & Freeman, 1990). A therapist may keep track of a person's odd or magical predictions, for example, and later point out their inaccuracy. When a client is speaking and begins to talk loosely or to drift off the subject, the therapist might ask the individual to sum up what he or she is trying to say. On occasion, specific behavioral methods, such as speech lessons, social skills training, and tips on appropriate dress and manners, have helped clients learn to blend in better and be more comfortable around others (Liebowitz et al., 1986).

Antipsychotic drugs have been given to people with schizotypal personality disorder, again because of the disorder's similarity to schizophrenia. In low doses the drugs appear to have helped some people, usually by reducing certain of their thought problems (Coccaro, 1998; Weston & Siever, 1993).

SUMMING UP "Odd" Personality Disorders

A personality disorder is a very rigid pattern of inner experience and outward behavior. The pattern is wide-ranging and long-lasting, differs from that usually expected of people, and leads to dysfunctioning. Explanations for most of the personality disorders have received only limited research support. DSM-IV identifies ten personality disorders and separates them into three groups.

Three of the personality disorders are marked by the kinds of odd or eccentric behavior often seen in the Axis I disorder schizophrenia. People with paranoid personality disorder display a broad pattern of distrust and suspiciousness. Those with schizoid personality disorder generally avoid social relationships and show little emotional expression. Individuals with schizotypal personality disorder display a range of interpersonal problems marked by extreme discomfort in close relationships, very odd forms of thinking and behavior, and behavioral eccentricities. People with these three kinds of disorders usually are resistant to treatment, and treatment gains tend to be modest at best.

"Dramatic" Personality Disorders

The cluster of *"dramatic" personality disorders* includes the *antisocial, borderline, histrionic,* and *narcissistic* personality disorders. The behaviors of people with these problems are so dramatic, emotional, or erratic that it is almost impossible for them to have relationships that are truly giving and satisfying.

These personality disorders are more commonly diagnosed than the others (Fabrega et al., 1991). However, only the antisocial and borderline personality disorders have received much study, partly because they create so many problems for other people. The causes of the disorders, like those of the odd personality disorders, are not well understood. Treatments range from ineffective to moderately effective.

Antisocial Personality Disorder

Sometimes described as *"psychopaths"* or *"sociopaths,"* people with **antisocial personality disorder** persistently disregard and violate others' rights (APA, 2000, 1994). Aside from substance-related disorders, this is the disorder most closely linked to adult criminal behavior. Most people with antisocial personality disorder have displayed some patterns of misbehavior before they were 15, including truancy, running away, physical cruelty to animals or people, destroying property, and setting fires.

Robert Hare (1993), a leading researcher of antisocial personality disorder, recalls an early professional encounter with a prison inmate named Ray:

> In the early 1960s, I found myself employed as the sole psychologist at the British Columbia Penitentiary. . . . I wasn't in my office for more than an hour when my first "client" arrived. He was a tall, slim, dark-haired man in his thirties. The air around him seemed to buzz, and the eye contact he made with me was so direct and intense that I wondered if I had ever really looked anybody in the eye before. That stare was unrelenting—he didn't indulge in the brief glances away that most people use to soften the force of their gaze.
>
> Without waiting for an introduction, the inmate—I'll call him Ray—opened the conversation: "Hey, Doc, how's it going? Look, I've got a problem. I need your help. I'd really like to talk to you about this."

Antisocial and homicidal *Charles Manson, who directed his followers to kill nine people in 1969, fits many of the criteria of antisocial personality disorder, including disregard for and violation of others' rights, impulsivity, disregard for truth, and lack of remorse. In a recent interview Manson bragged, "I was crazy when crazy meant something."*

Bettmann/Corbis

Eager to begin work as a genuine psychotherapist, I asked him to tell me about it. In response, he pulled out a knife and waved it in front of my nose, all the while smiling and maintaining that intense eye contact.

Once he determined that I wasn't going to push the button, he explained that he intended to use the knife not on me but on another inmate who had been making overtures to his "protégé," a prison term for the more passive member of a homosexual pairing. Just why he was telling me this was not immediately clear, but I soon suspected that he was checking me out, trying to determine what sort of a prison employee I was. . . .

From that first meeting on, Ray managed to make my eight-month stint at the prison miserable. His constant demands on my time and his attempts to manipulate me into doing things for him were unending. On one occasion, he convinced me that he would make a good cook . . . and I supported his request for a transfer from the machine shop (where he had apparently made the knife). What I didn't consider was that the kitchen was a source of sugar, potatoes, fruit, and other ingredients that could be turned into alcohol. Several months after I had recommended the transfer, there was a mighty eruption below the floorboards directly under the warden's table. When the commotion died down, we found an elaborate system for distilling alcohol below the floor. Something had gone wrong and one of the pots had exploded. There was nothing unusual about the presence of a still in a maximum-security prison, but the audacity of placing one under the warden's seat shook up a lot of people. When it was discovered that Ray was the brains behind the bootleg operation, he spent some time in solitary confinement.

Once out of "the hole," Ray appeared in my office as if nothing had happened and asked for a transfer from the kitchen to the auto shop—he really felt he had a knack, he saw the need to prepare himself for the outside world, if he only had the time to practice he could have his own body shop on the outside. . . . I was still feeling the sting of having arranged the first transfer, but eventually he wore me down.

Soon afterward I decided to leave the prison to pursue a Ph.D. in psychology, and about a month before I left Ray almost persuaded me to ask my father, a roofing contractor, to offer him a job as part of an application for parole.

Ray had an incredible ability to con not just me but everybody. He could talk, and lie, with a smoothness and a directness that sometimes momentarily disarmed even the most experienced and cynical of the prison staff. When I met him he had a long criminal record behind him (and, as it turned out, ahead of him); about half his adult life had been spent in prison, and many of his crimes had been violent. . . . He lied endlessly, lazily, about everything, and it disturbed him not a whit whenever I pointed out something in his file that contradicted one of his lies. He would simply change the subject and spin off in a different direction. Finally convinced that he might not make the perfect job candidate in my father's firm, I turned down Ray's request—and was shaken by his nastiness at my refusal.

Before I left the prison for the university, I took advantage of the prison policy of letting staff have their cars repaired in the institution's auto shop—where Ray still worked, thanks (he would have said no thanks) to me. The car received a beautiful paint job and the motor and drivetrain were reconditioned.

With all our possessions on top of the car and our baby in a plywood bed in the backseat, my wife and I headed for Ontario. The first problems appeared soon after we left Vancouver, when the motor seemed a bit rough. Later, when we encountered some moderate inclines, the radiator boiled over. A garage mechanic discovered ball bearings in the carburetor's float chamber; he also pointed out where one of the hoses to the radiator had clearly been tampered with. These problems were repaired easily enough, but the next one, which arose while we were going down a long hill, was more serious. The brake pedal became very spongy and then simply dropped to the floor—no brakes, and it was a long hill. Fortunately, we made it to a service station, where we found that the brake line had been cut so that a slow leak would occur. Perhaps it was a co-incidence that Ray was working in the auto shop when the car was being tuned up, but I had no doubt that the prison "telegraph" had informed him of the owner of the car.

(Hare, 1993)

Like Ray, people with antisocial personality disorder lie repeatedly (Seto et al., 1997). Many cannot work consistently at a job; they are absent frequently and are likely to quit their jobs altogether (Bland et al., 1988). Usually they are also careless with money and frequently fail to pay their debts. They are often impulsive, taking action without thinking of the consequences (Lykken, 1995). Correspondingly, they may be irritable, aggressive, and quick to start fights (Vaillant, 1994) (see Figure 14-3). Many travel from place to place.

Recklessness is another common trait: people with antisocial personality disorder have little regard for their own safety or for that of others, even their children. They are self-centered, as well, and likely to have trouble maintaining close relationships (Birtchnell, 1996). Usually they develop a knack for gaining personal profit at the expense of other people. Because the pain or damage they cause seldom concerns them, clinicians commonly say that they lack a moral conscience (Lykken, 1995). They think of their victims as weak and deserving of being conned or robbed.

Surveys indicate that up to 3 percent of people in the United States meet the criteria for antisocial personality disorder (APA, 2000; Kessler et al., 1994). White Americans are somewhat more likely than African Americans to receive the diagnosis (Robins et al., 1991), and the disorder is as much as four times more common among men than women (Kessler & Zhao, 1999).

Because people with this disorder are often arrested, researchers frequently look for people with antisocial patterns in prison populations (Lish et al., 1996). Among men in urban jails, the antisocial personality pattern has been strongly linked to past arrests for crimes of violence (Abram & Teplin, 1990). For many people with this disorder, criminal behavior declines after the age of 40; some, however, continue their criminal activities throughout their lives (Arboleda-Florez & Holley, 1991).

Studies and clinical observations also indicate higher rates of alcoholism and other substance-related disorders among people with antisocial personality disorder than in the rest of the population (Myers, Stewart, & Brown, 1998). Perhaps intoxication and substance abuse help trigger the development of antisocial personality disorder by loosening a person's inhibitions (Kaminer, 1991). Perhaps this personality disorder somehow makes a person more prone to abuse substances (Bukstein et al., 1989). Or perhaps antisocial personality disorder and substance abuse both have the same cause, such as a deep-seated need to take risks (Sher & Trull, 1994). Interestingly, drug users with the personality disorder often cite the recreational aspects of drug use as their reason for starting and continuing it (Mirin & Weiss, 1991).

HOW DO THEORISTS EXPLAIN ANTISOCIAL PERSONALITY DISORDER? Explanations of antisocial personality disorder come from the psychodynamic, behavioral, and biological models. As with many other personality disorders, psychodynamic theorists propose that this one, too, begins with an absence of parental love during infancy, leading to a lack of basic trust (Gabbard, 1990). In this view,

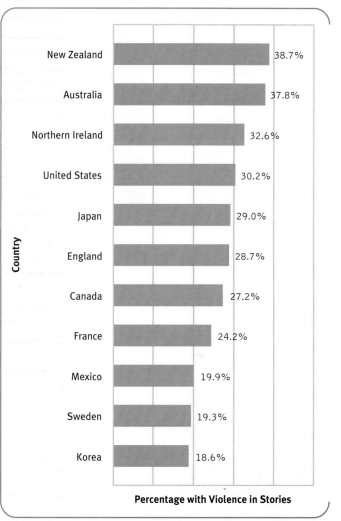

FIGURE 14-3 **Are some cultures more antisocial than others?** *In a cross-cultural study, teenagers were asked to write stories describing how imaginary characters would respond to various conflicts. About one-third of the respondents from New Zealand, Australia, Northern Ireland, and the United States described violent responses, compared to less than one-fifth of the subjects from Korea, Sweden, and Mexico. (Adapted from Archer & McDaniel, 1995.)*

When Life Imitates Art

Oliver Stone's 1994 movie *Natural Born Killers* tells the tale of two sociopathic thrill seekers, Mickey and Mallory, who grow world-famous as they travel the countryside committing brutal murders. Stone meant it to be a satire on our culture's appetite for violence, but the film itself inspired more copycat killings than any other movie ever made (Shnayerson, 1996). Numerous young people went on similar killing sprees, citing *Natural Born Killers* as their inspiration.

The copycat phenomenon is not new (Bushman & Anderson, 2001). When Stanley Kubrick's film *A Clockwork Orange* was released in 1971,

W. B. Productions Ltd./Photofest

critics praised its powerful social statement. But when some British youths copied the actions of the movie's gang leader and raped a woman to the tune of "Singin' in the Rain," Kubrick had the film banned in Britain (Shnayerson, 1996).

ConsiderThis

Must individuals already be antisocial in order to be influenced by films such as these, or do the films confuse people who are not antisocial by glorifying criminal and violent behavior? • Should filmmakers and writers consider the possible psychological influence of their work on suggestible individuals before they undertake such projects?

VIOLENT MODELS

By the age of 18, the average child in the United States has viewed 200,000 acts of violence on television alone (American Academy of Pediatrics, 1999; Prothrow-Stith & Spivak, 1999).

---

some children—the ones who develop antisocial personality disorder—respond to the early inadequacies by becoming emotionally distant, and they bond with others through the use of power and destructiveness. In support of the psychodynamic explanation, researchers have found that people with this disorder are more likely than others to have had significant stress in their childhoods, particularly in such forms as family poverty, family violence, and parental conflict or divorce (Marshall & Cooke, 1999; Farrington, 1991).

Many behavioral theorists have suggested that antisocial symptoms may be learned through *modeling*, or imitation. As evidence, they point to the higher rate of antisocial personality disorder found among the parents of people with this disorder (Lahey et al., 1988). Other behaviorists have suggested that some parents unintentionally teach antisocial behavior by regularly reinforcing a child's aggressive behavior (Capaldi & Patterson, 1994; Patterson, 1986, 1982). When the child misbehaves or becomes violent in reaction to the parents' requests or orders, for example, the parents may give in to restore peace. Without meaning to, they may be teaching the child to be stubborn and perhaps even violent.

Finally, a number of studies suggest that biological factors may play an important role in antisocial personality disorder. Research reveals that people with this disorder often experience less anxiety than do other people, and so may lack a key ingredient for learning (Zuckerman, 1996; Lykken, 1995). This would help explain why they have so much trouble learning from negative life experiences or tuning in to the emotional cues of others. Several studies have found that subjects with antisocial personality disorder are less able than control subjects to learn laboratory tasks, such as finding their way out of a maze, when the key reinforcements are punishments such as shock or loss of money (Newman et al., 1992, 1987; Lykken, 1995, 1957). When experimenters make the punishments very apparent or force subjects to pay attention to them, learning improves; left to their own devices, however, subjects with this disorder are not influenced much by punishments. Perhaps they simply do not react as anxiously as other people to negative events.

Why should people with antisocial personality disorder experience less anxiety than other people? The answer may lie in the biological realm (Raine et al.,

2000). Subjects with the disorder often respond to warnings or expectations of stress with low brain and bodily arousal, such as slow autonomic arousal and slow EEG waves (Dinn & Harris, 2000; Patrick et al., 1993, 1990). Perhaps because of the low arousal, the individuals easily tune out threatening or emotional situations, and so are unaffected by them.

It could also be argued that because of their physical underarousal, people with this disorder will be more likely than other people to take risks and seek thrills. That is, they may be drawn to antisocial activity precisely because it meets an underlying biological need for more excitement and arousal. In support of this idea, as we observed earlier, antisocial personality disorder often goes hand in hand with sensation-seeking behavior (Hasselbrock & Hasselbrock, 1992; Zuckerman, 1989, 1978).

TREATMENTS FOR ANTISOCIAL PERSONALITY DISORDER Approximately one-quarter of all people with antisocial personality disorder receive treatment for it (Regier et al., 1993), yet no treatment appears to be effective. A major problem is the individuals' lack of conscience or desire to change (Millon, 1999). Most of those in therapy have been forced to participate by an employer, their school, or the law, or else they come to the attention of therapists when they also develop another psychological disorder (Fulwiler & Pope, 1987). Not surprisingly, one study found that 70 percent of these patients left treatment prematurely (Gabbard & Coyne, 1987).

Some cognitive therapists try to guide clients with antisocial personality disorder to think about moral issues and about the needs of other people (Beck & Freeman, 1990). In a similar vein, a number of hospitals and prisons have tried to create a therapeutic community for people with this disorder, a structured environment that teaches responsibility toward others (Reid & Burke, 1989; Salama, 1988). Still another popular approach uses physically challenging wilderness programs to build self-confidence, self-esteem, and commitment to others in a group (Reid & Burke, 1989). Some patients seem to profit from such programs. Generally, however, most of today's treatment approaches have little or no impact on people with antisocial personality disorder.

Borderline Personality Disorder

People with **borderline personality disorder** display great instability, including major shifts in mood, an unstable self-image, and impulsivity. These characteristics combine to make their relationships very unstable as well (APA, 2000, 1994). Some of Ellen Farber's difficulties are typical:

> Ellen Farber, a 35-year-old, single insurance company executive, came to a psychiatric emergency room of a university hospital with complaints of depression and the thought of driving her car off a cliff. . . . Ms. Farber appeared to be in considerable distress. She reported a 6-month period of increasingly persistent dysphoria and lack of energy and pleasure. Feeling as if she were "made of lead," Ms. Farber had recently been spending 15–20 hours a day in her bed. She also reported daily episodes of binge eating, when she would consume "anything I can find," including entire chocolate cakes or boxes of cookies. She reported problems with intermittent binge eating since adolescence, but these had recently increased in frequency. . . .
>
> She attributed her increasing symptoms to financial difficulties. Ms. Farber had been fired from her job two weeks before coming to the emergency room. She claimed it was because she "owed a small amount of money." When asked to be more specific, she reported owing $150,000 to her former employers and another $100,000 to various local banks. . . . From age 30 to age 33, she had used her employer's credit cards to finance weekly "buying binges," accumulating the $150,000 debt. [To relieve feelings of distress,] every few days she would impulsively buy expensive jewelry, watches, or multiple pairs of the same shoes. . . .

BORDERLINE PERSONALITY DISORDER A personality disorder in which an individual displays repeated instability in interpersonal relationships, self-image, and mood, as well as impulsive behavior.

CHARACTER INGESTION

As late as the Victorian era, many English parents believed babies absorbed personality and moral uprightness as they took in milk. Thus, if a mother could not nurse, it was important to find a wetnurse of good character (Asimov, 1997).

> In addition to lifelong feelings of emptiness, Ms. Farber described chronic uncertainty about what she wanted to do in life and with whom she wanted to be friends. She had many brief, intense relationships with both men and women, but her quick temper led to frequent arguments and even physical fights. Although she had always thought of her childhood as happy and carefree, when she became depressed, she began to recall [being abused verbally and physically by her mother].
>
> *(Spitzer et al., 1994, pp. 395–397)*

Like Ellen Farber, people with borderline personality disorder swing in and out of very depressive, anxious, and irritable states that last anywhere from a few hours to a few days or more (see Table 14-2). Their emotions seem to be always in conflict with the world around them (Perry & Cooper, 1986). They are prone to bouts of anger, which sometimes result in physical aggression and violence (Lish et al., 1996). Just as often, however, they direct their impulsive anger inward and inflict bodily harm on themselves. Many seem troubled by deep feelings of emptiness (Koenigsberg et al., 1999).

Many of the patients who come to mental health emergency rooms are individuals with borderline personality disorder who have intentionally hurt themselves (Bongar et al., 1990). Their impulsive, self-destructive activities may range from alcohol and substance abuse to delinquency, unsafe sex, reckless driving, and cutting themselves (Trull et al., 2000). Suicidal threats and actions are also common. Studies suggest that 70 percent of people with this disorder attempt suicide at least once in their lives; around 6 to 9 percent actually commit suicide (Davis, Gunderson, & Myers, 1999). Many, like Ellen, try to hurt themselves as a

EXPRESSION OF ANGER
Only 23 percent of adults in the United States report openly expressing their anger (Kanner, 1998). Around 39 percent say that they hide or contain their anger, and 23 percent walk away to try to collect themselves.

Table 14-2

Comparison of Personality Disorders

	DSM-IV CLUSTER	SIMILAR DISORDERS ON AXIS I	RESPONSIVENESS TO TREATMENT
Paranoid	Odd	Schizophrenia; delusional disorder	Modest
Schizoid	Odd	Schizophrenia; delusional disorder	Modest
Schizotypal	Odd	Schizophrenia; delusional disorder	Modest
Antisocial	Dramatic	Conduct disorder	Poor
Borderline	Dramatic	Mood disorders	Moderate
Histrionic	Dramatic	Somatoform disorders; mood disorders	Modest
Narcissistic	Dramatic	Cyclothymic disorder (mild bipolar disorder)	Poor
Avoidant	Anxious	Social phobia	Moderate
Dependent	Anxious	Separation anxiety disorder; dysthymic disorder (mild depressive disorder)	Moderate
Obsessive-compulsive	Anxious	Obsessive-compulsive anxiety disorder	Moderate

way of dealing with their general feelings of emptiness, boredom, and identity confusion.

People with borderline personality disorder frequently form intense, conflict-ridden relationships in which their feelings are not necessarily shared by the other person (Modestin & Villiger, 1989). They often violate the boundaries of relationships (Gunderson, 1996) and may become furious when their expectations are not met; yet they remain very attached to the relationships, paralyzed by a fear of being left alone. Sometimes they cut themselves or carry out other self-destructive acts to prevent partners from leaving.

Around 2 percent of the general population are thought to suffer from borderline personality disorder. Close to 75 percent of the patients who receive this diagnosis are women (APA, 2000; Grilo et al., 1996). The course of the disorder varies from person to person. In the most common pattern, the instability and risk of suicide reach a peak during young adulthood and then gradually lessen with advancing age (APA, 2000).

How Do Theorists Explain Borderline Personality Disorder? Because a fear of abandonment tortures so many people with borderline personality disorder, psychodynamic theorists have looked once again to early parental relationships to explain the disorder (Gunderson, 2001, 1996). Object relations theorists, for example, propose that an early lack of acceptance by parents may lead to a loss of self-esteem, increased dependence, and an inability to cope with separation (Cardasis et al., 1997; Richman & Sokolove, 1992). Research has found that the early childhoods of people with the disorder are often consistent with this view. In many cases, the parents of such individuals neglected or rejected them, verbally abused them, or otherwise behaved inappropriately (Johnson et al., 2001; Ludolph et al., 1990). Similarly, their childhoods were often marked by multiple parent substitutes, divorce, death, or traumas such as physical or sexual abuse (Spoont, 1996; Plakun, 1991). In fact, some theorists believe that the disorder may be an extended form of posttraumatic stress disorder, triggered by early horrors (Shea et al., 2000).

Some features of borderline personality disorder have also been linked to biological abnormalities. Sufferers who are particularly impulsive, as demonstrated by a suicide attempt or aggression against others, apparently have lower brain serotonin activity (Leyton et al., 2001; Gurvits et al., 2000). People with the disorder also experience abnormalities in sleep that are similar to those of depressed persons (Siever & Davis, 1991). In accord with these biological findings, close relatives of those with borderline personality disorder are five times more likely than the general population to have the disorder (Torgersen, 2000, 1984; Kendler et al., 1991).

Finally, some sociocultural theorists suggest that cases of borderline personality disorder are particularly likely to emerge in cultures that change rapidly. As a culture loses its stability, they argue, it inevitably leaves many of its members with problems of identity, a sense of emptiness, heightened anxiety, and fears of abandonment (Paris, 1991). Family units may come apart, leaving people with little sense of belonging. Changes of this kind in society today may explain growing reports of the disorder.

Treatments for Borderline Personality Disorder It appears that psychotherapy can eventually lead to some degree of improvement for people with borderline personality disorder (Gunderson, 2001; APA, 2000). It is not easy, however, for a therapist to strike a balance between empathizing with the patient's dependency and anger and challenging his or her way of thinking (Goin, 2001; Beck, 1997). Furthermore, when such a person does make progress in treatment, ending therapy is sometimes difficult because of the patient's remaining problems with relationships and abandonment (Sansone et al., 1991).

The Myth of Venting

Contrary to the notion that "letting off steam" reduces anger, angry subjects in one study acted much more aggressively after hitting a punching bag than did angry subjects who first sat quietly for a while (Bushman et al., 1999).

An unthinkable act *People around the world felt angry and betrayed in 1994 when they learned that Susan Smith had murdered her two sons by buckling them into the family car and pushing it into a nearby river. For days the woman from South Carolina had tearfully told a story of forced abduction and had begged for the boys' safe return, fooling everyone, including her ex-husband. Some clinicians believe that Smith's impulsive and violent act, her shallow motives, her shifting moods and unstable self-image, and her capacity to convincingly deceive may reflect an antisocial or borderline personality disorder.*

Tim Kimzey, *Union Daily Times*/Sipa Press

Gambling and Other Impulse Problems

Impulsivity is a symptom of many psychological disorders, including the antisocial and borderline personality disorders (Looper & Paris, 2000). DSM-IV also lists several disorders in which impulsivity, rather than personality, is the main feature. People with these *impulse-control disorders* fail to resist an impulse, drive, or temptation to perform acts that are harmful to themselves or others (APA, 2000, 1994). Usually they experience growing tension before the act and relief when they give in to the impulse. Some, but not all, feel regret or guilt afterward. The impulse-control disorders include pyromania, kleptomania, intermittent explosive disorder, trichotillomania, and pathological gambling.

- ❖ *Pyromania* is the deliberate and repeated setting of fires to achieve intense pleasure or relief from tension. It is different from *arson,* the setting of fires for revenge or financial gain.

- ❖ *Kleptomania* is a recurrent failure to resist the impulse to steal. People with this disorder often have more than enough money to pay for the articles they steal.

- ❖ Individuals with *intermittent explosive disorder* have periodic aggressive outbursts in which they may seriously attack people and destroy property. Their explosiveness far exceeds any provocation.

- ❖ People with *trichotillomania* repeatedly pluck hair from various parts of their bodies, particularly the scalp, eyebrows, and eyelashes (Stein, Christenson, & Hollander, 1999; McElroy et al., 1994).

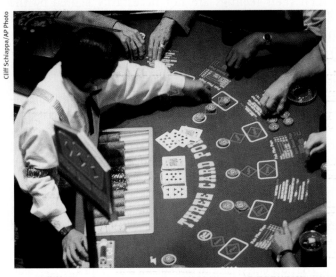

Cliff Schiappa/AP Photo

- ❖ The most common of the impulse-control disorders is *pathological gambling,* persistent and repeated gambling behavior that disrupts one's life at home or at work (APA, 2000, 1994).

It is estimated that as many as 3.4 percent of adults and 3 to 8 percent of teenagers and college students suffer from pathological gambling (APA, 2000; Buckley, 1995). Clinicians are careful, however, to distinguish between pathological and social gambling. Pathological gambling is defined less by the amount of time or money spent in gambling than by the addictive and impulsive nature of the behavior (Petry, 2001). People with this disorder cannot walk away from a bet and are restless and irritable if gambling is denied them. Repeated losses of money lead to more gambling in an ef-

fort to win the money back, and the gambling continues even in the face of financial, social, and health problems. Many people go through four progressive phases during episodes of pathological gambling: winning, losing, desperation, and hopelessness (Rosenthal, 1992).

A great deal of attention has recently been directed toward the treatment of pathological gambling. Treatments that combine cognitive, behavioral, and other approaches and that help build coping skills tend to be the most effective (Echeburúa et al., 2000, 1996; Bujold et al., 1994). People who join self-help support groups, such as *Gamblers Anonymous,* a network patterned after Alcoholics Anonymous, seem to have a higher recovery rate, perhaps in part because they have admitted that they have a problem and are seeking to conquer it.

Journalists and others often ask whether the "medicalization" of gambling has the effect of somehow excusing an irresponsible, often illegal pattern of behavior (Castellani, 2000; Vatz & Weinberg, 1993). However, several studies suggest that pathological gambling and other impulse-control disorders are complex problems that often involve a variety of causes, including even biochemical factors (Blanco et al., 2000).

Psychodynamic therapy has been somewhat effective when it focuses on the patient's central relationship disturbance, poor sense of self, and pervasive loneliness and emptiness (Gunderson, 2001, 1996; Gabbard, 2000). This treatment has sometimes been combined with cognitive-behavioral approaches designed to help people recognize and address the perspectives of others (Koerner & Linehan, 2000; Linehan, 1993, 1992). For example, the therapist may model alternative ways of interpreting and reacting to situations and also arrange for clients to receive social skill training. Group therapy has also been of help to some people with borderline personality disorder. It offers them an opportunity to form close attachments to a number of persons rather than focusing all their emotions and hopes on one or two "chosen" relationships.

Finally, antidepressant, antibipolar, antianxiety, and antipsychotic drugs have helped some individuals to calm their emotional and aggressive storms (Davis et

HISTRIONIC PERSONALITY DISORDER A personality disorder in which an individual displays a pattern of excessive emotionality and attention seeking. Once called *hysterical personality disorder.*

al., 2000, 1999; Soloff, 2000). Given the high risk of suicide attempts by these patients, however, their use of drugs on an outpatient basis is controversial. Some individuals have benefited from a combination of drug therapy and psychotherapy (Livesley, 2000; Stone, 2000).

Histrionic Personality Disorder

People with **histrionic personality disorder,** once called **hysterical personality disorder,** are extremely emotional—they are typically described as "emotionally charged"—and continually seek to be the center of attention (APA, 2000, 1994). Their exaggerated, rapidly changing moods can complicate life considerably, as we see in the case of Suzanne:

> Suzanne, an attractive and vivacious woman, sought therapy in the hope that she might prevent the disintegration of her third marriage. The problem she faced was a recurrent one, her tendency to become "bored" with her husband and increasingly interested in going out with other men. She was on the brink of "another affair" and decided that before "giving way to her impulses again" she had "better stop and take a good look" at herself. . . .
>
> Suzanne was quite popular during her adolescent years. . . . Rather than going on to college, Suzanne attended art school where she met and married a fellow student—a "handsome, wealthy ne'er-do-well." Both she and her husband began "sleeping around" by the end of the first year, and she "wasn't certain" that her husband was the father of her daughter. A divorce took place several months after the birth of this child.
>
> Soon thereafter she met and married a man in his forties who gave both Suzanne and her daughter a "comfortable home, and scads of attention and love." It was a "good life" for the four years that the marriage lasted. . . . In the third year of this marriage she became attracted to a young man, a fellow dancing student. The affair was brief, but was followed by a quick succession of several others. Her husband learned of her exploits, but accepted her regrets and assurances that they would not continue. They did continue, and the marriage was terminated after a stormy court settlement.
>
> Suzanne "knocked about" on her own for the next two years until she met her present husband, a talented writer who "knew the scoop" about her past. . . . She had no inclination to venture afield for the next three years. She enjoyed the titillation of "playing games" with other men, but she remained loyal to her husband, even though he was away on reportorial assignments for periods of one or two months. The last trip, however, brought forth the "old urge" to start an affair. It was at this point that she sought therapy.
>
> *(Millon, 1969, p. 251)*

People with histrionic personality disorder are always "on stage," using theatrical gestures and the most grandiose language to describe ordinary everyday events. They keep changing themselves to attract and impress an audience, and in their pursuit they change not only their surface characteristics—according to the latest fads—but also their opinions and beliefs. In fact, their speech is actually scanty in detail and substance, and they seem to lack a sense of who they really are.

Approval and praise are the life's blood of these individuals; they must have others present to witness their exaggerated emotional states. Vain, self-centered, demanding, and unable to delay gratification for long, they overreact to any minor event that gets in the way of their quest for attention. Some make suicide attempts, often to manipulate others (APA, 2000).

People with this disorder may draw attention to themselves by exaggerating their physical illnesses or feelings of weakness (Morrison, 1989). They may also behave very provocatively and try to achieve their goals through sexual seduction. Most obsess over how they look and how others will perceive them, often wear-

"Oh, What a Tangled Web . . ."

One of the most popular movies of 1997 was *Liar, Liar,* starring Jim Carrey. The movie's plot—a notorious liar loses his capacity to deceive—struck a chord in most viewers.

Melinda Sue Gordon/Photofest

Almost everyone lies from time to time (Ford, 1996). In fact, in one large survey 91 percent of people admitted that they lie regularly (Kanner, 1995). For example, almost 80 percent of adults have given a false name or phone number on occasion. However, many of us know people who, like Carrey's character, lie habitually, almost as if driven to do so (Weston, 1996; Ford et al., 1988). They are not necessarily trying to protect themselves, and their lies often get them in trouble. Interestingly, compulsive lying is not considered a disorder, although it is sometimes characteristic of people with antisocial, histrionic, or narcissistic personality disorder. Nor has lying received much attention from clinical theorists or researchers.

ConsiderThis

- What might be the differences between "normal" lying and "pathological" lying? • How do various institutions in our society—business, government, academia, science, religion—view lying, and how might these views affect the prevalence and nature of individual lies? • Why do people often admire someone who deceives—a flatterer, an art forger, a jewel thief?

ing bright, eye-catching clothes. They exaggerate the depth of their relationships, considering themselves to be the intimate friends of people who see them as no more than casual acquaintances. Often they become involved with romantic partners who may be exciting but who do not treat them well.

This disorder was once believed to be more common in women than in men, and clinicians long described the "hysterical wife" (Reich, 1987; Char, 1985). Research, however, has revealed gender bias in past diagnoses. When reading case studies of people with a mixture of histrionic and antisocial traits, clinicians in several studies gave a diagnosis of histrionic personality disorder to women more than men (Ford & Widiger, 1989; Hamilton et al., 1986). The latest statistics suggest that 2 to 3 percent of adults have this personality disorder, with males and females equally affected (APA, 2000; Nestadt et al., 1990).

HOW DO THEORISTS EXPLAIN HISTRIONIC PERSONALITY DISORDER? The psychodynamic perspective was originally developed to help explain cases of hysteria (see Chapter 8), so it is no surprise that these theorists continue to have a strong interest in histrionic personality disorder today. Most psychodynamic theorists believe that as children, people with this disorder experienced unhealthy relationships in which cold and controlling parents left them feeling unloved and afraid of abandonment (Gunderson, 1988). To defend against deep-seated fears of loss, the individuals learned to behave dramatically, inventing crises that would require other people to act protectively (Kuriansky, 1988).

Cognitive explanations look instead at the lack of substance and extreme suggestibility found in people with histrionic personality disorder. These theories see the individuals as becoming less and less interested in knowing about the world at large because they are so self-focused and emotional. With no detailed memories of what they never learned, they must rely on hunches or on other people to provide them with direction in life (Hollander, 1988). Some cognitive theorists also propose that people with this disorder hold a general assumption that they are helpless to care for themselves; thus, they constantly seek out others who will meet their needs (Beck & Freeman, 1990).

Finally, sociocultural theorists believe that histrionic personality disorder is produced in part by society's norms and expectations. Until recently, our society encouraged girls to hold on to childhood and dependency as they grew up (Hollander, 1988). The vain, dramatic, and selfish behavior of the histrionic person may actually be an exaggeration of femininity as our culture once defined it (Sprock, 2000; Beck & Freeman, 1990).

> **NARCISSISTIC PERSONALITY DISORDER** A personality disorder marked by a broad pattern of grandiosity, need for admiration, and lack of empathy.

TREATMENTS FOR HISTRIONIC PERSONALITY DISORDER Unlike people with most other personality disorders, those with histrionic personality disorder often seek out treatment on their own (Nestadt et al., 1990). Working with them can be very difficult, however, because of the demands, tantrums, and seductiveness they are likely to display (Millon, 1999; Phillips & Gunderson, 1994). Another problem is that these individuals may pretend to have important insights or to experience change during treatment, merely to please the therapist. To head off such problems, therapists must remain objective and maintain strict professional boundaries (Gabbard, 1990).

Cognitive therapists have tried to help people with this disorder to change their belief that they are helpless and also to develop better, more precise ways of thinking and solving problems. Psychodynamic therapy and group therapy have also been applied (Phillips & Gunderson, 1994; Beck & Freeman, 1990). In all these approaches, therapists ultimately aim to help the clients recognize their excessive dependency, find inner satisfaction, and become more independent (Chodoff, 1989). Clinical case reports suggest that each of the approaches can be useful. Drug therapy is less successful, however, except for relieving the depressive symptoms experienced by some patients (Liebowitz et al., 1986).

Narcissistic Personality Disorder

People with **narcissistic personality disorder** are generally grandiose, need much admiration, and feel no empathy with others (APA, 2000, 1994). Convinced of their own great success, power, or beauty, they expect constant attention and admiration from those around them. Frederick, the man whom we met at the beginning of this chapter, was one such person. So is Steven, a 30-year-old artist, married, with one child:

> "To love oneself is the beginning of a life-long romance."
>
> Oscar Wilde, *An Ideal Husband*, 1895

Steven came to the attention of a therapist when his wife insisted that they seek marital counseling. According to her, Steve was "selfish, ungiving and preoccupied with his work." Everything at home had to "revolve about him, his comfort, moods and desires, no one else's." She claimed that he contributed nothing to the marriage, except a rather meager income. He shirked all "normal" responsibilities and kept "throwing chores in her lap," and she was "getting fed up with being the chief cook and bottlewasher, tired of being his mother and sleep-in maid."

On the positive side, Steven's wife felt that he was basically a "gentle and good-natured guy with talent and intelligence." But this wasn't enough. She wanted a husband, someone with whom she could share things. In contrast, he wanted, according to her, "a mother, not a wife"; he didn't want "to grow up, he didn't know how to give affection, only to take it when he felt like it, nothing more, nothing less."

Steve presented a picture of an affable, self-satisfied and somewhat disdainful young man. He was employed as a commercial artist, but looked forward to his evenings and weekends when he could turn his attention to serious painting. He claimed that he had to devote all of his spare time and energies to "fulfill himself," to achieve expression in his creative work. . . .

His relationships with his present co-workers and social acquaintances were pleasant and satisfying, but he did admit that most people viewed him as a "bit self-centered, cold and snobbish." He recognized that he did not know how to share his thoughts and feelings with others, that he was much more interested in himself than in them and that perhaps he always had "preferred the pleasure" of his own company to that of others.

(Millon, 1969, pp. 261–262)

"Call it vanity, call it narcissim, call it egomania. I love you."

People with narcissistic personality disorder exaggerate their achievements and talents, expecting others to recognize them as superior, and often appear arrogant. They are very choosy about their friends and associates, believing that their problems are unique and can be appreciated only by other "special," high-status people. Because of their charm, they often make favorable first impressions. Yet they can rarely maintain long-term relationships.

Like Steven, people with this disorder are seldom interested in the feelings of others. Many take advantage of others to achieve their own ends, perhaps partly out of envy; at the same time they believe others envy them (Wink, 1996). Though grandiose, some of these individuals react to criticism or frustration with bouts of rage or humiliation (Gramzow & Tangney, 1992). Others may react with cold indifference (Messer, 1985). And still others become extremely pessimistic and filled with depression. Periods of zest may alternate with periods of disappointment (Wink, 1996).

Probably less than 1 percent of adults display narcissistic personality disorder, up to 75 percent of them men (APA, 2000; Grilo et al., 1996). Narcissistic-type behaviors and thoughts are common and normal among teenagers and do not usually lead to adult narcissism (APA, 1994).

STEPPING BACK

Personality and the Brain: The Case of Phineas Gage

Most people are aware that damage to particular regions in the brain can cause motor dysfunction, memory or language problems, or even the loss of particular senses such as vision or hearing. However, clinical scientists have come to appreciate that damage to the brain from strokes, injury, or tumors can also bring about major changes in our personality. The tragic story of Phineas Gage provided science with history's most memorable evidence of this fact.

In mid-September of 1848, 25-year-old Gage was laying tracks for a railroad, a hazardous but common occupation in those years. The smart, careful, and friendly Gage was admired and liked by the men he supervised, and the company who wrote his paychecks called him "the most efficient and capable" employee they had. But that was all to change in a few second's time, when a rock-blasting mishap hurled a three-foot long tamping iron under Gage's left cheek and straight through the top of his skull, piercing a one-and-a-half inch hole through his brain's frontal lobes (Damasio, 1994).

Miraculously, Gage's body survived. But you could say that Gage himself, at least as others had known him, did not. From an even-tempered, responsible, and likeable young man, Gage turned "fitful, irreverent, indulging at times in the grossest profanity which was not previously his custom, manifesting but little deference for his fellows, impatient of restraint or advice when it conflicts with his desires, at times pertinaciously obstinate, yet capricious and vacillating, devising many plans of future operation, which are no sooner arranged than they are abandoned" (Harlow, 1868, as cited in Damasio, 1994). Beyond being blind in one eye, Gage suffered no other lasting physical or mental defects. He remained nimble, alert, and able to speak and think. The wound in his head laid waste to his personality alone.

After the accident, Gage could not keep his job, as he no longer had the motivation to perform up to expectations. His newly unpleasant behavior drove friends away and destroyed the possibility of finding a romantic partner to share his life with. Gage moved from

job to job, including a stint in a circus sideshow in New York City. This once-promising and ambitious young man eventually ended up a penniless ward of his mother and sister, dying of a brain seizure at the age of 38 (Damasio, 1994).

What, exactly, was the critical injury suffered by Gage? *Why* did his personality change so profoundly? In his book *Descartes' Error* (1994), neuroscientist Antonio Damasio speculates that the temporal lobe destruction in Gage's brain resulted in an inability to experience appropriate emotion. Imagine being unable to experience shame at saying rude things to your host at a dinner, or anger at being duped by a conman who invests your money in a speculative investment venture, or fear at walking through a dangerous area of town at midnight. Imagine being unable to feel affection toward a spouse or child, or pleasure at engaging in one activity versus another. All of these failures of emotion would leave you socially helpless, indecisive, and unable to behave consistently in ways designed to

How Do Theorists Explain Narcissistic Personality Disorder? Psychodynamic theorists more than others have theorized about narcissistic personality disorder, and, again, they propose that the problem begins with cold, rejecting parents. They argue that some people with this background spend their lives defending against feeling unsatisfied, rejected, unworthy, and frightened of the world (Wink, 1996). They do so by repeatedly telling themselves that they are actually perfect and desirable, and also by seeking admiration from others (Vaillant, 1994). Object relations theorists, the psychodynamic theorists who emphasize relationships, further interpret the grandiose self-image as a way for these people to convince themselves that they are totally self-sufficient and without need of warm relationships with their parents or anyone else (Kernberg, 1989; Siomopoulos, 1988). In support of the psychodynamic theories, research has found that abused children and children of divorce are at particular risk for the development of narcissistic personality disorder. So are children who have been given up for adoption or whose mothers or fathers have died (Kernberg, 1989).

A number of behavioral and cognitive theorists propose that narcissistic personality disorder may develop when people are treated too *positively* rather than too negatively in early life. They hold that certain individuals acquire a superior and grandiose attitude when their "admiring or doting parents" teach them to "overvalue their self-worth" (Millon, 1987). In support of this explanation, first-born and only children, who are often viewed by their parents as having special talents or intelligence, score higher than other children on measures of narcissism (Curtis & Cowell, 1993).

EGOIST VS. EGOTIST
An *egoist* is a person concerned primarily with his or her own interests. An *egotist* has an inflated sense of self-worth. A boastful egotist is not necessarily a self-absorbed egoist.

further your own interests. You would be, in any sense of the word, perfectly unreasonable. In short, you might be much like Phineas Gage.

Gage was far from the last person to lose this critical faculty. Damasio (1994) documents a number of such patients, who display startling results in tests of their emotional capacities. When shown emotion-arousing pictures that raise the galvanic skin responses (GSR) of most people, frontally damaged patients register no GSR reaction at all. When performing "gambling" tasks in certain studies, control subjects adopt low-risk strategies, while frontally damaged patients engage in high-risk and bankrupting tactics. Most telling, when gamblers in such studies are hooked to a polygraph, the GSRs of control subjects increase (signaling increasing dread and nervousness) throughout the task, while those of patients remain constant.

If the ability to *feel* appropriately has such a profound impact on a person's personality and successes, then we shouldn't be surprised to hear that scientists in a relatively new and sometimes controversial field called *evolutionary psychology* have argued persuasively that emotions are adaptive, indeed critical, to an organism's survival. This goes even for those darker emotions we normally view as counterproductive, such as jealousy (Buss, 2000) and vengefulness (Cosmides & Tooby, 2000). Although unpleasant, such emotions may often help us to navigate dangers and respond to social threats where a completely dispassionate, cool-headed person could not.

An 1850s' artist offered these drawings of the injury suffered by Phineas Gage when a three-foot tamping iron penetrated his brain. Although the holes in Gage's head eventually healed, his previous personality did not survive.

AP Photo / Courtesy of Harvard Medical School

Finally, many sociocultural theorists see a link between narcissistic personality disorder and "eras of narcissism" in society (Cooper & Ronningstam, 1992). They suggest that family values and social ideals in certain societies periodically break down, producing generations of youth who are self-centered and materialistic and have short attention spans. Western cultures in particular, which encourage self-expression, individualism, and competitiveness, are considered likely to produce such generations of narcissism.

TREATMENTS FOR NARCISSISTIC PERSONALITY DISORDER Narcissistic personality disorder is one of the most difficult personality patterns to treat (Lawrence, 1987). The clients who consult therapists usually do so because of a related disorder, most commonly depression (Millon, 1999; Beck & Freeman, 1990). Once in treatment, the individuals may try to manipulate the therapist into supporting their sense of superiority. Some also seem to project their grandiose attitudes onto their therapists and develop a love-hate stance toward them (Uchoa, 1985).

Psychodynamic therapists seek to help people with this disorder recognize their basic insecurities and defenses (Adler, 2000). Cognitive therapists, focusing on the self-centered thinking of such clients, try to redirect the clients' focus onto the opinions of others, teach them to interpret criticism more reasonably, increase their ability to empathize, and change their all-or-nothing notions (Beck & Freeman, 1990). None of the approaches has had much success, however.

SUMMING UP | **"Dramatic" Personality Disorders**

Four of the personality disorders are marked by highly dramatic, emotional, or erratic symptoms. Persons with antisocial personality disorder display a pattern of disregard for and violation of the rights of others. No known treatment is particularly effective. People with borderline personality disorder display a pattern of instability in interpersonal relationships, self-image, and mood, along with extreme impulsivity. Treatment apparently can be effective and lead to some improvement for these individuals. Those with histrionic personality disorder (once called hysterical personality disorder) display a pattern of extreme emotionality and attention seeking. Clinical case reports suggest that treatment is helpful on occasion. Finally, people with narcissistic personality disorder display a pattern of grandiosity, need for admiration, and lack of empathy. It is one of the most difficult disorders to treat.

"Anxious" Personality Disorders

The cluster of *"anxious" personality disorders* includes the *avoidant, dependent,* and *obsessive-compulsive* personality disorders. People with these patterns typically display anxious and fearful behavior. Although many of the symptoms of these disorders are similar to those of the anxiety and depressive disorders (Skodol et al., 1999), researchers have not found direct links between the personality disorders and those Axis I disorders (Weston & Siever, 1993). As with most of the other personality disorders, research support for the various explanations is very limited. At the same time, treatments for these disorders appear to be modestly to moderately helpful—considerably better than for other personality disorders.

Avoidant Personality Disorder

People with **avoidant personality disorder** are very uncomfortable and restrained in social situations, overwhelmed by feelings of inadequacy, and extremely sensitive to negative evaluation (APA, 2000, 1994). They are so fearful of

AVOIDANT PERSONALITY DISORDER A personality disorder in which an individual is consistently uncomfortable and restrained in social situations, overwhelmed by feelings of inadequacy, and extremely sensitive to negative evaluation.

being rejected that they give no one an opportunity to reject them—or to accept them either:

> James was a bookkeeper for nine years, having obtained his position upon graduation from high school. He spoke of himself as a shy, fearful and quiet boy ever since early childhood. . . .
>
> James was characterized by his supervisor as a loner, a peculiar young man who did his work quietly and efficiently. They noted that he ate alone in the company cafeteria and never joined in coffee breaks or in the "horsing around" at the office. . . .
>
> As far as his social life was concerned, James had neither dated nor gone to a party in five years. . . . He now spent most of his free time reading, watching TV, daydreaming and fixing things around the house.
>
> James experienced great distress when new employees were assigned to his office section. Some 40 people worked regularly in this office and job turnover resulted in replacement of four or five people a year. . . . In recent months, a clique formed in his office. Although James very much wanted to be a member of this "in-group," he feared attempting to join them because "he had nothing to offer them" and thought he would be rejected. In a short period of time, he, along with two or three others, became the object of jokes and taunting by the leaders of the clique. After a few weeks of "being kidded," he began to miss work, failed to complete his accounts on time, found himself unsure of what he was doing and made a disproportionate number of errors. . . .
>
> *(Millon, 1969, pp. 231-232)*

People like James actively avoid occasions for social contact. At the center of this withdrawal lies not so much poor social skills as a dread of criticism, disapproval, or rejection. They are timid and hesitant in social situations, afraid of saying something foolish or of embarrassing themselves by blushing or acting nervous. Even in intimate relationships they express themselves very carefully, afraid of being shamed or ridiculed.

People with this disorder believe themselves to be unappealing or inferior to others. They exaggerate the potential difficulties of new situations, so they seldom take risks or try out new activities. They usually have few or no close friends, though they actually yearn for intimate relationships, and frequently feel depressed and lonely. As a substitute, some develop an inner world of fantasy and imagination (Millon, 1990).

Avoidant personality disorder is similar to a *social phobia* (see Chapter 4), and many people with one of these disorders also experience the other (Rettew, 2000). The similarities include a fear of humiliation and low confidence. A key difference between the two conditions is that people with a social phobia mainly fear social *circumstances,* while people with the personality disorder tend to fear close social *relationships* (Turner et al., 1986).

Between 0.5 and 1.0 percent of adults have avoidant personality disorder, men as frequently as women (APA, 2000). Many children and teenagers are also painfully shy and avoid other people, but this is usually just a normal part of their development.

How Do Theorists Explain Avoidant Personality Disorder? Theorists often assume that avoidant personality disorder has the same causes as anxiety disorders—such as early traumas, conditioned fears, upsetting beliefs, or biochemical abnormalities. However, research has not yet tied the personality disorder directly to the anxiety disorders (Weston & Siever, 1993). In the meantime, psychodynamic and cognitive explanations are the most popular among clinicians.

Psychodynamic theorists focus mainly on the general sense of shame felt by people with avoidant personality disorder. Some trace the shame to childhood experiences such as early bowel and bladder accidents (Gabbard, 1990). If parents

Mark Richards/PhotoEdit

Just a stage *Many children and teenagers are painfully shy, easily embarrassed, and uncomfortable with people other than their parents, siblings, or close friends. Such reactions are a common and normal part of development, and do not, by themselves, indicate an avoidant or dependent personality disorder.*

repeatedly punish or ridicule a child for having such accidents, the child may develop a negative self-image. This may lead to the individual's feeling unlovable throughout life and distrusting the love of others (Liebowitz et al., 1986). Similarly, cognitive theorists believe that harsh criticism and rejection in early childhood may lead certain people to assume that others in their environment will always judge them negatively. These individuals come to expect rejection, misinterpret the reactions of others to fit that expectation, ignore positive feedback, and generally fear social involvements—setting the stage for avoidant personality disorder (Beck, 1997). In several studies, subjects with this disorder were asked to recall their childhood, and their descriptions supported both the psychodynamic and cognitive theories. They remembered, for example, feeling rejected or isolated, receiving little encouragement from their parents, and experiencing few displays of parental love or pride (Meyer & Carver, 2000; Arbel & Stravynski, 1991).

TREATMENTS FOR AVOIDANT PERSONALITY DISORDER People with avoidant personality disorder come to therapy in the hope of finding acceptance and affection. Keeping them in treatment can be a challenge, however, for many of them soon begin to avoid the sessions (Millon, 1999; Beck & Freeman, 1990). Often they distrust the therapist's sincerity and start to fear his or her rejection. Thus, as with several of the other personality disorders, a key task of the therapist is to gain the individual's trust (Gabbard, 1990).

Beyond building trust, therapists tend to treat people with avoidant personality disorder much as they treat people with social phobias and other anxiety disorders (Reich, 2000). Such approaches have had at least modest success. Psychodynamic therapists try to help clients recognize and overcome the unconscious conflicts that may be operating (Hurt et al., 1991). Cognitive therapists help them change their distressing beliefs and thoughts, carry on in the face of painful emotions, and improve their self-image (Beck & Freeman, 1990; Alden, 1989). Behavioral therapists provide social skills training, as well as exposure treatments that require people to gradually increase their social contacts (Quality Assurance Project, 1991; Stravynski et al., 1987). Group therapy may also be recommended, to provide practice in social interactions (Azima, 1993; Renneberg et al., 1990). Antianxiety and antidepressant drugs are sometimes useful in reducing the social anxiety of people with the disorder, although the symptoms may return when medication is stopped (Liebowitz et al., 1991, 1990).

Dependent Personality Disorder

People with **dependent personality disorder** have a persistent, excessive need to be taken care of (APA, 2000, 1994). As a result, they are clinging and obedient, fearing separation from their parent, spouse, or other close relationship. They rely on others so much that they cannot make the smallest decision for themselves. Mr. G. is a case in point.

> Mr. G.['s] . . . place of employment for the past 15 years had recently closed and he had been without work for several weeks. He appeared less dejected about the loss of his job than about his wife's increasing displeasure with his decision to "stay at home until something came up." She thought he "must be sick" and insisted that he see a doctor. . . .
>
> Mr. G. was born in Europe, the oldest child and only son of a family of six children. . . . His mother kept a careful watch over him, prevented him from engaging in undue exertions and limited his responsibilities; in effect, she precluded his developing many of the ordinary physical skills and competencies that most youngsters learn in the course of growth. . . .
>
> A marriage was arranged by his parents. His wife was a sturdy woman who worked as a seamstress, took care of his home, and bore . . . four children. Mr. G. performed a variety of odds-and-ends jobs in his father's tailoring shop. His

mother saw to it, however, that he did no "hard or dirty work," just helping about and "overlooking" the other employees. As a consequence, Mr. G. learned none of the skills of the tailoring trade.

Shortly before the outbreak of World War II, Mr. G. came to visit two of his sisters who previously had emigrated to the United States; when hostilities erupted in Europe he was unable to return home. All members of his family, with the exception of a young son, perished in the war.

During the ensuing years, he obtained employment at a garment factory owned by his brothers-in-law. Again he served as a helper, not as a skilled workman. Although he bore the brunt of essentially good-humored teasing by his co-workers throughout these years, he maintained a friendly and helpful attitude, pleasing them by getting sandwiches, coffee and cigarettes at their beck and call.

He married again to a hard-working, motherly type woman who provided the greater portion of the family income. Shortly thereafter, the son of his first wife emigrated to this country. Although the son was only 19 at the time, he soon found himself guiding his father's affairs, rather than the other way around.

(Millon, 1969, p. 242)

> "The deepest principle of human nature is the craving to be appreciated."
>
> William James

It is normal and healthy to depend on others, but those with dependent personality disorder constantly need assistance with even the simplest matters and demonstrate extreme feelings of inadequacy and helplessness. Afraid that they cannot care for themselves, they cling desperately to friends or relatives.

We observed earlier that people with avoidant personality disorder have difficulty *starting up* relationships. In contrast, people with dependent personality disorder have difficulty with *separation*. The individuals feel completely helpless and devastated when a close relationship ends, and they quickly seek out another relationship to fill the void. Many cling to relationships with partners who physically or psychologically abuse them.

Lacking confidence in their own ability and judgment, people with this disorder seldom disagree with others and allow even important decisions to be made for them. They may depend on a parent or spouse to decide where to live, what job to have, and which neighbors to like (APA, 2000, 1994; Overholser, 1996). Because they so fear rejection, they are overly sensitive to disapproval and keep trying to meet other people's wishes and expectations, even if it means volunteering for unpleasant or demeaning tasks.

Many people with dependent personality disorder feel distressed, lonely, and sad; often they dislike themselves (Overholser, 1996, 1992). Thus they are at risk for depression and anxiety disorders (Skodol et al., 1999; Reich, 1996). Their fear of separation and their feelings of helplessness may leave them particularly prone to suicidal thoughts, especially when they believe that a relationship is about to end (Kiev, 1989).

The exact prevalence of dependent personality disorder is not known, although some studies suggest that around 2 percent of the population may experience it (Zimmerman & Coryell, 1989). For years clinicians have believed that more women than men display this pattern (Overholser, 1992), but some research suggests that the disorder is just as common in men (APA, 2000; Reich, 1990).

HOW DO THEORISTS EXPLAIN DEPENDENT PERSONALITY DISORDER? Psychodynamic explanations for this personality disorder are very similar to those for depression. Freudian theorists argue, for example, that unresolved conflicts during the oral stage of development can give rise to a lifelong need for nurturance,

Par-Anders Patterson/Black Star

Detachment and separation *One child gazes fearfully out the bus window and another hides his eyes as they cross the border into a refugee camp during Serbia's attempted purge of 850,000 ethnic Albanians from Kosovo in 1999. Clinicians worry that the abrupt and traumatic separations from home and family experienced by thousands of Kosovar children may have produced lingering insecurities and fears of abandonment, leaving them particularly vulnerable to such problems as dependent personality disorder, depression, and anxiety.*

Dysfunctional toons *As the technology of film animation has become more complex over time, so have the personality problems of animated characters. (Left) Troubled characters of the past were usually defined by a single undesirable personality trait, as demonstrated by Snow White's friend Grumpy, second from left. (Right) Today's characters have groups of self-defeating traits. Beavis and Butt-Head, for example, display poor control of impulses, disregard for others' rights, disturbed relationships, emotional and cognitive shallowness, and, in Beavis's case, submissive and clinging behavior.*

increasing the likelihood of a dependent personality disorder (Greenberg & Bornstein, 1988). Similarly, object relations theorists say that early parental loss or rejection may prevent normal experiences of *attachment* and *separation*, leaving some children with fears of abandonment that persist throughout their lives. Still other psychodynamic theorists suggest that, to the contrary, many parents of people with this disorder were overinvolved and overprotective, thus increasing their children's dependency, insecurity, and anxiety over separation (Bornstein, 1996, 1992).

Behaviorists propose that parents of people with dependent personality disorder unintentionally rewarded their children's clinging and "loyal" behavior, while at the same time punishing acts of independence, perhaps through the withdrawal of love. Alternatively, some parents' own dependent behaviors may have served as models for their children.

Finally, cognitive theorists identify two maladaptive attitudes as helping to produce and maintain this disorder: (1) "I am inadequate and helpless to deal with the world," and (2) "I must find a person to provide protection so I can cope" (Beck, 1997; Beck & Freeman, 1990). Dichotomous (black-and-white) thinking may also play a key role: "If I am to be dependent, I must be completely helpless," or "If I am to be independent, I must be alone." Such thinking prevents sufferers of this disorder from making efforts to be independent.

TREATMENTS FOR DEPENDENT PERSONALITY DISORDER In therapy, people with this personality disorder usually place all responsibility for their treatment and well-being on the clinician (Beck, 1997; Perry, 1989). Thus a key task of therapy is to help patients accept responsibility for themselves. Because the domineering behaviors of a spouse or parent may help foster a patient's symptoms, some clinicians propose couple or family therapy as well, or even separate therapy for the partner or parent (Millon, 1999; Liebowitz et al., 1986).

Treatment for dependent personality disorder can be at least modestly helpful. Psychodynamic therapy for this pattern focuses on many of the same issues as therapy for depressed people. In particular, the issue of transference of dependency needs onto the therapist becomes a major treatment concern (Perry, 1989). Behavioral therapists often provide assertiveness training to help clients better express their own wishes in relationships. And cognitive therapists try to help clients challenge and change their assumptions of incompetence and helplessness (Beck & Freeman, 1990).

Finally, as with avoidant personality disorder, a group therapy format can be helpful because it provides opportunities for the client to receive support from a number of peers rather than from a single dominant person (Azima, 1993; Perry, 1989). In addition, group members may serve as models for one another as they practice better ways to express feelings and solve problems (Beck & Freeman, 1990).

OBSESSIVE-COMPULSIVE PERSONALITY DISORDER A personality disorder marked by such an intense focus on orderliness, perfectionism, and control that the individual loses flexibility, openness, and efficiency.

Internet Dependence: A New Kind of Problem

*T*he computer age has apparently brought with it a new psychological problem—an uncontrollable need to be on-line (Davis, 2001; Orzack, 1998). Some clinicians consider it a kind of *substance-related disorder*. Others think it has the qualities of an *impulse-control disorder*. And many note that the pattern resembles *dependent personality disorder,* except that in this new pattern the individual is excessively dependent on a cyberbeing and on numerous fellow users, ever seeking their company, guidance, and reassurance, and fearing separation.

For some people, the Internet, the conglomeration of computer networks that spans the world, has become a black hole. Sufferers spend up to 60 hours a week surfing the Net, participating in chat groups, e-mailing acquaintances, or playing complex computer games (Black, Belsare, & Schlosser, 1999; Young, 1998, 1996). They describe their need to be on-line as an obsession for which they have unintentionally sacrificed their jobs, education, friends, even spouses. University students seem especially prone to the problem:

Randy Jones/*The New York Times*

❙ I was first introduced while I was studying at the university in '91. . . . I discovered by accident one day that you could send little messages to people in other universities and even people in America and other exotic places like Mexico and Finland! Well, that was the point of no return for me and I began spending inordinately large periods of time on-line. That was at the beginning of my final year. . . . [My] attendance record got worse and worse [and] predictably enough I failed in spectacular fashion. But I didn't mind so much because I had the Net to catch me, I'd made many friends on and off-line through it, including my then girlfriend, so life wasn't that bad really, was it? . . .

I've [since] learned to censor out some things, and not to get entwined up to my arse in endless threads of chat. Okay, so this is bad in some ways, but I feel a little more in control of my life. I don't find myself involuntarily glued to my screen at 4 A.M. talking about something that isn't even interesting, begging myself to go to bed. ❙

(ANONYMOUS, 1996)

ConsiderThis

◉ Which clinical disorder does Internet addiction resemble most closely?
• What are the dangers of describing patterns of excessive behavior, such as this, as clinical disorders?

Obsessive-Compulsive Personality Disorder

People with **obsessive-compulsive personality disorder** are so focused on order, perfection, and control that they lose all flexibility, openness, and efficiency. Their concern for doing everything "right" interferes with their productivity, as in the case of Wayne:

Wayne was advised to seek assistance from a therapist following several months of relatively sleepless nights and a growing immobility and indecisiveness at his job. When first seen, he reported feelings of extreme self-doubt and guilt and prolonged periods of tension and diffuse anxiety. It was established early in therapy that he always had experienced these symptoms. They were now merely more pronounced than before.

The precipitant for this sudden increase in discomfort was a forthcoming change in his academic post. New administrative officers had assumed authority at the college, and he was asked to resign his deanship to return to regular departmental instruction. In the early sessions, Wayne spoke largely of his fear of facing classroom students again, wondered if he could organize his material well, and doubted that he could keep classes disciplined and interested in his lectures. It was his preoccupation with these matters that he believed was preventing him from concentrating and completing his present responsibilities.

At no time did Wayne express anger toward the new college officials for the "demotion" he was asked to accept. He repeatedly voiced his "complete confidence" in the "rationality of their decision." Yet, when face-to-face with them, he observed that he stuttered and was extremely tremulous.

Wayne was the second of two sons, younger than his brother by three years. His father was a successful engineer, and his mother a high school teacher. Both were "efficient, orderly and strict" parents. Life at home was "extremely well planned," with "daily and weekly schedules of responsibilities posted" and "vacations arranged a year or two in advance." Nothing apparently was left to chance. . . . Wayne adopted the "good boy" image. Unable to challenge his brother either physically, intellectually or socially, he became a "paragon of virtue." By being punctilious, scrupulous, methodical and orderly, he could avoid antagonizing his perfectionistic parents, and would, at times, obtain preferred treatment from them. He obeyed their advice, took their guidance as gospel and hesitated making any decision before gaining their approval. Although he recalled "fighting" with his brother before he was six or seven, he "restrained his anger from that time on and never upset his parents again."

(Millon, 1969, pp. 278–279)

In Wayne's concern with rules and order and doing things right, he has trouble seeing the larger picture. When faced with a task, he and others with obsessive-compulsive personality disorder may become so focused on organization and details that they fail to grasp the point of the activity. As a result, their work is often behind schedule (some seem unable to finish any job), and they may neglect leisure activities and friendships.

People with this personality disorder set unreasonably high standards for themselves and others. They can never be satisfied with their performance, but they refuse to seek help or to work with a team, convinced that others are too careless or incompetent to do the job right. Because they are so afraid of making mistakes, they may be reluctant to make decisions.

These individuals also tend to be rigid and stubborn, particularly in their morals, ethics, and values. They live by a strict personal code and use it as a yardstick for measuring others. They may have trouble expressing much affection, and their relationships are often stiff and superficial. In addition, they are rarely generous with their time or money. Some cannot even throw away objects that are worn out or useless (APA, 2000, 1994; Warren & Ostrom, 1988).

Around 1 to 2 percent of the population has obsessive-compulsive personality disorder, with white, educated, married, and employed individuals receiving the diagnosis most often (APA, 2000; Weissman, 1993). Men are twice as likely as women to display the disorder.

Many clinicians believe that obsessive-compulsive personality disorder and obsessive-compulsive disorder (the anxiety disorder) are closely related. Certainly, the two disorders share a number of features. Moreover, many people who suffer from the anxiety disorder qualify for the personality disorder diagnosis as well (APA, 2000). However, other personality disorders (avoidant, histrionic, schizotypal, and dependent) may be even more common among those with the anxiety disorder (Steketee, 1990). In fact, researchers have not found a specific link between obsessive-compulsive personality disorder and the obsessive-compulsive anxiety disorder (Mavissakalian et al., 1990).

"An obstinate man does not hold opinions, but they hold him."

Alexander Pope

A CRITICAL DIFFERENCE

People with obsessive-compulsive anxiety disorder typically do not want or like their symptoms; those with obsessive-compulsive personality disorder often embrace their symptoms and rarely wish to resist them (Zohar & Pato, 1991).

Toilet rage *According to Freud, toilet training often produces rage in a child. If parents are too harsh in their approach, the child may become fixated at the anal stage and prone to obsessive-compulsive functioning later in life.*

How Do Theorists Explain Obsessive-Compulsive Personality Disorder?

Most explanations of obsessive-compulsive personality disorder borrow heavily from those of obsessive-compulsive anxiety disorder, despite the doubts concerning a link between the two disorders. As with so many of the personality disorders, psychodynamic explanations dominate and research evidence is limited.

Freudian theorists suggest that people with obsessive-compulsive personality disorder are *anal regressive*. That is, because of overly harsh toilet training during the anal stage, they become filled with anger, and they remain *fixated* at this stage. To keep their anger under control, they persistently resist both their anger and their instincts to have bowel movements. In turn, they become extremely orderly and restrained; many become passionate collectors. Other psychodynamic theorists suggest that any early struggles with parents over control and independence may ignite the aggressive impulses at the root of this personality disorder (Kuriansky, 1988; Mollinger, 1980).

Cognitive theorists have little to say about the origins of obsessive-compulsive personality disorder, but they do propose that illogical thinking processes help keep it going. They point, for example, to dichotomous (black-and-white) thinking, which may produce rigidity and perfectionism. Similarly, they note that people with this disorder tend to misread or exaggerate the potential outcomes of mistakes or errors.

Treatments for Obsessive-Compulsive Personality Disorder

People with obsessive-compulsive personality disorder do not usually believe there is anything wrong with them. They therefore are not likely to seek treatment unless they are also suffering from another disorder, most frequently anxiety or depression, or unless someone close to them insists that they get treatment (Beck & Freeman, 1990). Whereas drug therapy and behavioral therapy have been highly effective for people with obsessive-compulsive anxiety disorder, individuals with the personality disorder often appear to respond better to psychodynamic or cognitive therapy (Primac, 1993; Jenike, 1991, 1990). Psychodynamic therapists typically try to help them recognize, experience, and accept their feelings and underlying insecurities, and perhaps to take risks and accept their personal limitations (Millon, 1999; Salzman, 1989). Cognitive therapists focus on helping clients to change their dichotomous thinking, perfectionism, indecisiveness, procrastination, and chronic worrying.

Personality Disorders and the DSM: A Rocky Relationship

ConsiderThis

○ It is common for people outside the clinical field to mistakenly diagnose mental disorders in themselves, relatives, or acquaintances, and the personality disorders are among the most favored diagnoses. Why do you think these disorders are particularly subject to such efforts at amateur psychology?

Most of today's clinicians believe that personality disorders are important and troubling patterns. Yet these disorders are particularly hard to diagnose and easy to misdiagnose, difficulties that indicate serious problems with the *validity* (accuracy) and *reliability* (consistency) of the DSM categories (O'Connor & Dyce, 1998).

One problem is that some of the criteria used to diagnose personality disorders cannot be observed directly. To separate paranoid from schizoid personality disorder, for example, clinicians must ask not only whether people avoid forming close relationships, but also *why*. In other words, the diagnoses often rely heavily on the impressions of the individual clinician. A related problem is that clinicians differ widely in their judgments about when a normal personality style crosses the line and deserves to be called a disorder (Widiger & Costa, 1994). Some even believe that it is wrong ever to think of personality styles as mental disorders, however troublesome they may be.

The similarity of personality disorders within a cluster, or even between clusters, poses yet another problem. Within the "anxious" cluster, for example, there is considerable overlap between the symptoms of avoidant personality disorder and those of dependent personality disorder (Bornstein, 1998). Faced with similar feelings of inadequacy, fear of disapproval, and the like, is it reasonable for clinicians to consider them separate disorders (Livesley et al., 1994)? Also, the many borderline traits ("dramatic" cluster) found among some people with dependent personality disorder ("anxious" cluster) may indicate that these two disorders are but different versions of one basic pattern (Dolan, Evans, & Norton, 1995; Flick et al., 1993).

Another problem is that people with quite different personalities may be given the same personality disorder diagnosis (Costello, 1996). Individuals must meet a certain number of criteria from DSM-IV to receive a given diagnosis, but no single feature is necessary for any diagnosis (Millon, 1999).

Partly because of these problems, diagnosticians keep changing the criteria used to assess each of the personality disorders. In fact, the general categories themselves have changed more than once, and they will no doubt change again. For example, DSM-IV dropped a past category, **passive-aggressive personality disorder,** a pattern of negative attitudes and resistance to the demands of others, because research failed to show that this was more than a single trait. The pattern is now being studied more carefully and may be included once again in future editions of the DSM.

Given these problems, some theorists believe that the personality disorders actually differ more in *degree* than in *type* of dysfunction and have proposed that the disorders be organized by how severe certain key traits are rather than by the presence or absence of specific traits (Trull, Widiger, & Burr, 2001; Westen & Shedler, 2000). It is not yet clear where these arguments will lead, but at the very least, the growing debate indicates once again that most clinicians believe personality disorders to be important categories in the understanding and treatment of human behavior.

ConsiderThis

○ Try to invent a way of organizing and defining personality disorders that improves upon the present diagnostic system. • How would the current DSM categories fit into your new scheme?

SUMMING UP | **"Anxious" Personality Disorders**

Three of the personality disorders are marked by the kinds of symptoms found in Axis I's anxiety and depressive disorders. People with avoidant personality disorder are consistently uncomfortable and restrained in social situations, overwhelmed by feelings of inadequacy, and extremely sensitive to negative evaluation. People with dependent personality disorder persistently need to be taken care of, are clinging and obedient, and fear separation. Individuals with obsessive-compulsive personality disorder are so focused on orderliness, perfectionism, and control that they lose their flexibility, openness, and efficiency. A variety of treatment strategies have been used for people with these three disorders and apparently have been modestly to moderately helpful.

Diagnostic Problems It appears that personality disorders are commonly misdiagnosed, an indication of some serious problems in the validity and reliability of the diagnostic categories.

PASSIVE-AGGRESSIVE PERSONALITY DISORDER A category of personality disorder listed in past versions of the DSM, marked by a pattern of negative attitudes and resistance to the demands of others.

CROSSROADS:
Disorders of Personality Are Rediscovered

During the first half of the twentieth century, clinicians believed deeply in the unique, enduring patterns we call personality, and they tried to define important personality traits. They then discovered how readily people can be shaped by the situations in which they find themselves, and a backlash developed. The concept of personality seemed to lose legitimacy, and for a while it became almost an obscene word in some circles. The clinical category of personality disorders experienced a similar rejection. When psychodynamic and humanistic theorists dominated the clinical field, personality disorders were considered useful categories (Millon et al., 2000). But their popularity declined as other models grew in influence.

During the past decade, serious interest in personality and personality disorders has rebounded. In case after case, clinicians have concluded that rigid personality traits do seem to pose special problems, and they have developed new objective tests and interview guides to assess these disorders, setting in motion a wave of systematic research (Langbehn et al., 1999; Scarpa et al., 1999). So far, only the antisocial and, to a lesser extent, the borderline personality disorders have received much study. As other personality disorders attract research attention as well, however, clinicians should be better able to answer some pressing questions: How common are the various personality disorders? How useful are the present categories? How are the disorders related? And what treatments are most effective?

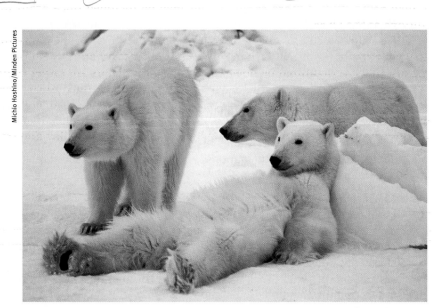

Personality au naturel *As suggested by the varied reactions of these polar bears to events at Canada's Hudson Bay, human beings are not the only creatures who demonstrate differences in personality, mood, and lifestyle. Natural data of this kind have led many theorists to suspect that inborn, biological factors contribute, at least in part, to personality differences and personality disorders.*

Michio Hoshino/Minden Pictures

One of the most important questions is, Why do people develop these patterns? As we have seen, psychological, as opposed to biological and sociocultural, theories have offered the most suggestions so far, but these proposed explanations are not very precise, and they do not have strong research support. Given the current enthusiasm for biological explanations, genetic and biological factors are likely to receive more study in the coming years, helping researchers determine their possible interaction with psychological causes. And we would hope that sociocultural factors will receive investigation as well. As we have seen, sociocultural theorists have only occasionally offered explanations for personality disorders. However, sociocultural factors may well play an important role in these disorders and should be examined more carefully, especially since, by definition, each of the patterns diagnosed as a personality disorder differs markedly from the expectations of a person's culture.

The future will likely bring major changes to the explanations and treatments for personality disorders, and the categories of personality disorders will probably undergo change as well (Widiger, 2000). Such changes, however, are now more likely to be based on research rather than on clinical intuitions and impressions. For the many people caught in the web of rigid and maladaptive personality traits, these changes should make an important, and overdue, difference.

KEY TERMS

personality p. 407
personality traits p. 407
personality disorder p. 407
"odd" personality disorders p. 409
paranoid personality disorder p. 410
schizoid personality disorder p. 412
schizotypal personality disorder p. 413

"dramatic" personality disorders p. 415
antisocial personality disorder p. 415
borderline personality disorder p. 419
histrionic personality disorder p. 423
narcissistic personality disorder p. 425
"anxious" personality disorders p. 428
avoidant personality disorder p. 428

social phobias p. 429
dependent personality disorder p. 430
obsessive-compulsive personality disorder
p. 433
anal regressive p. 435
passive-aggressive personality disorder
p. 436

QUICK QUIZ

1. What is a personality disorder, and why are personality disorders listed on Axis II in DSM-IV? pp. 407–409

2. What are the principal features of the "odd" personality disorders? To what Axis I disorder are these personality disorders similar? pp. 409–410, 420

3. Describe the symptoms of the paranoid, schizoid, and schizotypal personality disorders. What explanations and treatments have been applied to these disorders? pp. 410–415

4. What are the "dramatic" personality disorders, and what are the symptoms of each? pp. 415–428

5. How have theorists explained antisocial personality disorder? How effectively have clinicians treated this disorder? pp. 417–419

6. What are the leading explanations and treatments for the borderline, histrionic, and narcissistic personality disorders? How strongly does research support these explanations and treatments? pp. 421–428

7. To which Axis I disorders are the avoidant, dependent, and obsessive-compulsive personality disorders similar? Has research uncovered strong ties between these personality disorders and the Axis I disorders that they resemble? pp. 428, 420

8. What are the leading explanations for the avoidant, dependent, and obsessive-compulsive personality disorders, and to what extent are they supported by research? How are the disorders treated, and how effective are the treatments? pp. 429–435

9. Describe the social relationship problems caused by each of the personality disorders. pp. 409–435

10. What kinds of problems have clinicians run into when diagnosing personality disorders? What are the causes of these problems, and what solutions have been proposed? p. 436

CYBER STUDY

▲ *How might obsessive-compulsive personality disorder and obsessive-compulsive anxiety disorder overlap?* ▲ *What roles do orderliness, perfection, and the tendency to collect things play in each of these disorders?* ▲ *How do clinicians assess psychopathy, or antisocial personality disorder?* ▲ *Does treatment help people with psychopathy?*

SEARCH THE *FUNDAMENTALS OF ABNORMAL PSYCHOLOGY* CD-ROM FOR

▲ Chapter 14 video case and discussion
  "Bill"—Obsessive-Compulsive Disorder

▲ Chapter 14 practice test and feedback

▲ Additional video cases and discussions
  "Jennifer"—Obsessive-Compulsive Disorder
  The Mind of the Psychopath
  "Pat"—Psychopathy

LOG ON TO THE COMER WEB PAGE FOR

▲ Suggested Web links, research exercises, FAQ page, additional Chapter 14 practice test questions

  <www.worthpublishers.com/comer>

UCLA Neuropsychiatric Institute & Hospital

Disorders of Childhood and Old Age

"Children nowadays are tyrants. They contradict their parents, gobble their food, and tyrannize their teachers."

Socrates, 425 B.C.

Billy, a 7-year-old . . . child, was brought to a mental health clinic by his mother because "he is unhappy and always complaining about feeling sick." . . . His mother describes Billy as a child who has never been very happy and never wanted to play with other children. From the time he started nursery school, he has complained about stomachaches, headaches, and various other physical problems. . . .

Billy did well in first grade, but in second grade he is now having difficulty completing his work. He takes a lot of time to do his assignments and frequently feels he has to do them over again so that they will be "perfect." Because of Billy's frequent somatic complaints, it is hard to get him off to school in the morning. If he is allowed to stay home, he worries that he is falling behind in his schoolwork. When he does go to school, he often is unable to do the work, which makes him feel hopeless about his situation. . . .

His worries have expanded beyond school, and frequently he is clinging and demanding of his parents. He is fearful that if his parents come home late or leave and go somewhere without him something may happen to them. . . .

Although Billy's mother acknowledges that he has never been really happy, in the last 6 months, she feels, he has become much more depressed. He frequently lies around the house, saying that he is too tired to do anything. He has no interest or enjoyment in playing. His appetite has diminished. He has trouble falling asleep at night and often wakes up in the middle of the night or early in the morning. Three weeks ago, he talked, for the first time, about wanting to die. . . .

(Spitzer et al., 1994, pp. 333–334)

[Oscar] was an 83-year-old married man with an episode of major depressive disorder. . . . He said that about one and one-half years prior to beginning treatment, his brother had died. In the following months, two friends whom he had known since childhood died. Following these losses, he became increasingly anxious [and] grew more and more pessimistic. Reluctantly, he acknowledged, "I even thought about ending my life." Review of his symptoms indicated that while [generalized] anxiety was a prominent part of his clinical picture, so was depression. . . .

During . . . treatment, [Oscar] discussed his relationship with his brother. He discussed how distraught he was to watch his brother's physical deterioration from an extended illness. He described the scene at his brother's deathbed and the moment "when he took his final breath." He experienced guilt over the failure to carry out his brother's funeral services in a manner he felt his brother would have wanted. Although initially characterizing his relationship with his brother as loving and amiable, he later acknowledged that he disapproved of many ways in which his brother acted. Later in therapy, he also reviewed different facets of his past relationships with his two deceased friends. He expressed sadness that the long years had ended. . . . [Oscar's] life had been organized around visits to his brother's home and outings with his friends. . . . [While] his wife had encouraged him to visit with other friends and family, it became harder and harder to do so as he became more depressed.

(Hinrichsen, 1999, p. 433)

THE FOUR AGES OF MAN

INFANCY   CHILDHOOD   YOUTH   MATURITY

Billy and Oscar are both suffering from clinical depression. Their conditions are similar in many ways—the feelings of sadness, loss of interest in usual activities, difficulty falling asleep—but they differ in important ways too. Billy has stomachaches and headaches; Oscar has feelings of loneliness, pessimism, and guilt. Billy worries constantly about his parents' safety; Oscar worries about everything. School pressures helped trigger Billy's emotional decline; the losses of his brother and two lifelong friends contributed to Oscar's unhappiness. Various factors may be responsible for these differences. Among the most important are the differences in the individuals' ages and stages of life.

Abnormal functioning can occur at any time in life. Some patterns of abnormality, however, are more likely to emerge during particular periods—during childhood, for example, or at the other end of the spectrum, during old age. Sometimes the special pressures of the particular life stage help trigger the dysfunctioning. In other cases, unique experiences or biological abnormalities may be the key factor. Some age-related forms of abnormality subside rather quickly or can be corrected, whereas others may continue for the rest of a person's life. Still others, particularly certain childhood disorders, change form or give way to different patterns of abnormality as time goes by.

Theorists often view life as a series of stages on the road from birth to death. Most people pass through these stages in the same order, though at their own rates and in their own ways. Freud proposed that each child passes through the same five stages—the *oral, anal, phallic, latency,* and *genital* stages. The influential psychodynamic theorist Erik Erikson (1963) added *old age* as one of life's most meaningful stages. Although theorists may disagree with the details of these schemes, most agree with the idea that we face key pressures during each stage in life and either grow or decline depending on how we meet those pressures. Each stage offers many opportunities for dysfunction.

During much of the twentieth century, clinicians viewed children as small adults and often treated their psychological disorders just as they would adult problems (Peterson & Roberts, 1991). Worse, elderly persons were seen merely as remnants of adulthood, and their psychological disorders were rarely treated at all. Now, however, clinicians recognize that both groups have pressing issues and problems and that all people deserve treatment.

Disorders of Childhood and Adolescence

People often think of childhood as a carefree and happy time—yet it can also be frightening and upsetting. In fact, children of all cultures typically experience at least some emotional and behavioral problems as they encounter new people and situations (Crijnen, Achenbach, & Verhulst, 1999). Surveys reveal that *worry* is a common experience: close to half of all children in the United States have multi-

VARIED LIFE SPANS

Life spans vary from species to species. Marine clams live up to 200 years; giant tortoises 150 years; killer whales 90 years; toads 40 years; male houseflies 17 days (Ash, 1999).

YOUTHFUL CONCERNS

According to surveys, today's teens worry about being victims of violence (59%), getting sexually transmitted diseases (58%), affording college (54%), and finding good jobs in the future (43%) (Begley, 2000).

ple fears, particularly concerning school, health, and personal safety (Silverman, La Greca, & Wasserstein, 1995). Bed-wetting, nightmares, temper tantrums, and restlessness are other problems experienced by many children (King, 1993).

Adolescence can also be a difficult period. Physical and sexual changes, social and academic pressures, personal doubts, and temptations cause many teenagers to feel anxious, confused, and depressed (McNamara, 2000; Arnett, 1999; Takanishi, 1993). Today's teens, although generally happy and optimistic and often spiritual, tend to feel less trusting, more sensitive, and more isolated from their families than adolescents of decades past (Begley, 2000).

Along with these common psychological difficulties, around one-fifth of all children and adolescents in North America also experience a diagnosable psychological disorder (Breton et al., 1999; Kazdin, 1994). Boys with disorders outnumber girls, even though most of the adult psychological disorders are more common among women.

Duck and cover *Childhood anxieties can be caused by society's repeated warnings of possible catastrophes. These schoolchildren in Japan dive for cover during an earthquake drill.*

Childhood Anxiety Disorders

As in adults, the anxiety disorders experienced by children and adolescents include specific phobias, social phobias, generalized anxiety disorder, and obsessive-compulsive disorder (Oest & Treffers, 2001). However, one form of anxiety in children, **separation anxiety disorder,** is different enough from the adult disorders to be listed as a separate category in DSM-IV. Children with this disorder feel extreme anxiety, often panic, whenever they are separated from home or a parent. Carrie, a 9-year-old girl, was referred to a local mental health center by her school counselor when she seemed to become extremely anxious at school for no apparent reason.

> She initially reported feeling sick to her stomach and later became quite concerned over being unable to get her breath. She stated that she was too nervous to stay at school and that she wanted her mother to come get her and take her home. . . . The counselor indicated that a similar incident occurred the next day with Carrie ending up going home again. She had not returned to school since. . . .
>
> At the time of the intake evaluation the mother indicated that she felt Carrie was just too nervous to go to school. She stated that she had encouraged her daughter to go to school on numerous occasions but that she seemed afraid to go and appeared to feel bad, so she had not forced her. . . . When asked if Carrie went places by herself, the mother stated that Carrie didn't like to do that and that the two of them typically did most everything together. The mother went on to note that Carrie really seemed to want to have her (the mother) around all the time and tended to become upset whenever the two of them were separated.
>
> *(Schwartz & Johnson, 1985, p. 188)*

Children like Carrie have great trouble traveling away from their family, and they often refuse to visit friends' houses, go on errands, or attend camp or school. Many cannot even stay alone in a room and cling to their parent around the house. Some also have temper tantrums, cry, or plead to keep their parents from leaving them. The children may fear that they will get lost when separated from their parents or that the parents will meet with an accident or illness (APA, 2000, 1994). It has been estimated that about 4 percent of children and young adolescents suffer from separation anxiety disorder, somewhat more girls than boys (Masi et al., 2001; APA, 2000). In many cases it is triggered by a stressful event such as the death of a parent or pet, moving to a new home, or a change of schools. The symptoms may wax and wane over the course of childhood and adolescence.

"It is an illusion that youth is happy, an illusion of those who have lost it."

W. Somerset Maugham,
Of Human Bondage, 1915

SEPARATION ANXIETY DISORDER A childhood disorder marked by excessive anxiety, even panic, whenever the child is separated from home or a parent.

As in Carrie's case, a separation anxiety disorder sometimes takes the form of a **school phobia,** or **school refusal,** a common problem in which children fear going to school and often stay home for a long period. Many cases of school phobia, however, have causes other than separation fears, such as social or academic fears, depression, and fears of specific objects or persons at school.

A CLOSER LOOK

Child Abuse

❚ What I remember most about my mother was that she was always beating me. She'd beat me with her high-heeled shoes, with my father's belt, with a potato masher. When I was eight, she black and blued my legs so badly, I told her I'd go to the police. She said, "Go, they'll just put you into the darkest prison." So I stayed. When my breasts started growing at 13, she beat me across the chest until I fainted. Then she'd hug me and ask forgiveness. . . . Most kids have nightmares about being taken away from their parents. I would sit on our front porch crooning softly of going far, far away to find another mother. ❚

(*TIME,* SEPTEMBER 5, 1983, p. 20)

A problem that affects all too many children and has an enormous impact on their psychological development is *child abuse,* the nonaccidental use of excessive physical or psychological force by an adult on a child, often with the intention of hurting or destroying the child. About 3 million cases of physical child abuse occur each year (Gallup, 1995; McCurdy & Daro, 1993). Surveys suggest that one of every ten children is the victim of severe violence, such as being kicked, bitten, hit, beaten, or threatened with a knife or a gun. In fact, some observers believe that physical abuse and neglect are the leading causes of death among young children. Girls and boys are abused at approximately the same rate. Although child abuse occurs in all socioeconomic groups, it is apparently more common among the poor (Gallup, 1995; Gelles, 1992).

Abusers are usually the child's parents. Clinical investigators have learned that abusive parents often have poor impulse control and low self-esteem. Many have been abused themselves as children and have had poor role models (Bowen, 2000). In some cases, they are experiencing the stress of marital discord or family unemployment (Whipple, Webster, & Stratton, 1991).

Studies suggest that the victims of child abuse may suffer both immediate and long-term psychological effects. Research has revealed, for example, that abused children have more performance and behavior problems in school. Long-term negative effects include lack of social acceptance, more medical illnesses and psychological disorders, more abuse of alcohol and other substances, more arrests during adolescence and adulthood, a greater risk of becoming criminally violent, a higher unemployment rate, and a higher suicide rate (Widom, 2001, 1991, 1989; Bensley et al., 1999; Johnson et al., 1999). Finally, as many as one-third of abuse victims grow up to be abusive, neglectful, or inadequate parents themselves (Clarke et al., 1999; Oliver, 1993).

Two forms of child abuse have received special attention of late: psychological and sexual abuse. *Psychological abuse* may include severe rejection, excessive discipline, scapegoating and ridicule, isolation, and refusal to provide help for a child with psychological problems. *Child sexual abuse,* the use of a child for gratification of adult sexual desires, may occur outside of or within the home (Davidson et al., 1996). In 25 percent of cases, the child is younger than 7 (Wurtele & Schmitt, 1992). In two surveys, one-fifth of adult female subjects reported having been forced into sexual contact with an adult male as children, many of them with their father or stepfather (Vogeltanz et al., 1999; Eisen, 1993). Boys are also sexually abused, and the incidence of their abuse may be underreported (Romano & DeLuca, 2001).

A variety of therapies have been used in cases of child abuse, including groups offered by the national organization *Parents Anonymous,* which help parents develop insight into their behavior, provide training on alternatives to abuse, and teach parenting skills (Azar & Siegal, 1990; Wolfe et al., 1988). Still other treatments help parents deal more effectively with the stresses that often trigger the abuse, such as unemployment, marital conflict, and feelings of depression.

Research suggests that the psychological needs of the child victims should be addressed as early as possible (Gray et al., 2000; Roesler & McKenzie, 1994). Clinicians and educators have launched *early detection programs* that aim to (1) educate all children about child abuse; (2) teach them skills for avoiding or escaping from abusive situations; (3) encourage children to tell another adult if they are abused; and (4) assure them that abuse is never their own fault (Godenzi & DePuy, 2001; Finkelhor et al., 1995). These programs seem to increase the likelihood that children will report abuse, reduce their tendency to blame themselves for it, and increase their feelings of efficacy (MacIntyre & Carr, 1999; Finkelhor et al., 1995).

Honoré Daumier's *Fatherly Discipline*

Honoré Daumier, Fatherly Discipline, 1851. The Art Institute of Chicago, Arthur Heun Fund, 1952. (1108)

Childhood anxiety disorders are generally explained in much the same way as the adult anxiety disorders (discussed in Chapters 4 and 5). However, the special features of childhood can also play an important role. For example, since children have had fewer experiences than adults, their world is often new and scary. They may be frightened by common events, such as the beginning of school, or by special upsets, such as moving to a new house or becoming seriously ill (Tweed, Schoenbach, & George, 1989). Special features of their world can also frighten children and set the stage for anxiety disorders. Today's children, for example, are repeatedly warned, both at home and at school, about the dangers of kidnapping and of drugs. They are bombarded by violent images in television shows, movies, and news programs. Even fairy tales and nursery rhymes contain frightening images that upset many children.

Psychodynamic, behavioral, cognitive, and family therapies, separately or in combination, have been used to treat anxiety disorders in children, often with success (Barrett, 2001; Kazdin, 1994). Clinicians have also used drug therapy in some cases, but this approach has not yet received much research attention (Riddle et al., 1999). Because children typically have difficulty recognizing and understanding their feelings and motives, many therapists, particularly psychodynamic therapists, use **play therapy** as part of treatment. In this approach, the children play with toys, draw, and make up stories, and in so doing reveal the conflicts in their lives and their related feelings. The therapists then introduce more play and fantasy to help the children work through their conflicts and change their emotions and behavior. In addition, because children are often excellent hypnotic subjects, some therapists use *hypnotherapy* to help them overcome intense fears (Murray, 1996).

Constructive play *Therapists may use play therapy to assess the functioning of children, to help them express their feelings and thoughts, and to help them better understand themselves and others.*

Childhood Depression

Children, like adults, may develop depression (Kendall, 2000; Kovacs, 1997), as did Billy, whom we observed at the beginning of this chapter. Bobby has a similar problem:

> In observing Bobby in the playroom it was obvious that his activity level was well below that expected for a child of 10. He showed a lack of interest in the toys that were available to him, and the interviewer was unable to get him interested in any play activity for more than a few minutes. In questioning him about home and school, Bobby indicated that he didn't like school because he didn't have any friends, and he wasn't good at playing games like baseball and soccer like the other kids were, stating "I'm not really very good at anything." . . . When asked what he would wish for if he could have any three wishes granted he indicated, "I would wish that I was the type of boy my mother and father want, I would wish that I could have friends, and I would wish that I wouldn't feel sad so much."
>
> In speaking with the parents, the mother reported that she and her husband had become increasingly concerned about their son during the past year. She indicated that he always seemed to look sad and cried a lot for no apparent reason and that he appeared to have lost interest in most of the things that he used to enjoy doing. The mother confirmed Bobby's statements that he had no friends, indicating that he had become more and more of a loner during the past 6 to 9 months. She stated that his schoolwork had also suffered in that he is unable to concentrate on school assignments and seems to have "just lost interest." The mother notes, however, that her greatest concern is that he has recently spoken more and more frequently about "killing himself," saying that the parents would be better off if he wasn't around.
>
> *(Schwartz & Johnson, 1985, p. 214)*

SCHOOL PHOBIA A childhood pattern in which children fear going to school and often stay home for a long period of time. Also known as *school refusal*.

PLAY THERAPY An approach to treating childhood disorders that helps children express their conflicts and feelings indirectly by drawing, playing with toys, and making up stories.

April Saul, *The Philadelphia Inquirer*

How could you? *Childhood anxieties and difficulties may be the result of developmental upsets, such as the increasingly common experience of having to share a parent's affection with a new stepparent. The face of this boy after his mother's remarriage says it all.*

Approximately 2 percent of children under 17 years of age experience major depressive disorder (Kazdin, 1994). The rate for teenagers alone is about 7 percent (Petersen et al., 1993, 1991). The symptoms in young sufferers are likely to include physical discomfort (for example, stomachaches or headaches), irritability, and social withdrawal (APA, 2000, 1994). There appears to be no difference in the rates of depression in boys and girls before the age of 11, but by the age of 16, girls are twice as likely as boys to be depressed (Hankin & Abramson, 1999; Angold & Rutter, 1992).

Explanations of childhood depression are similar to those of adult depression. Theorists have pointed to factors such as loss, learned helplessness, negative cognitions, and low serotonin or norepinephrine activity (Garber & Flynn, 2001; Stark et al., 2000). Also, like adult depression, many cases of childhood depression seem to be triggered by a negative life event, major change, rejection, or ongoing abuse.

Like depression among adults, childhood depression often is helped by cognitive therapy or interpersonal approaches such as social skills training (Kazdin & Weisz, 1998). In addition, family therapy can be effective (Beardslee et al., 1996). Antidepressant medications have not proved consistently useful in cases involving children (Wagner & Ambrosini, 2001), but they do seem to help depressed adolescents (Sallee et al., 1997).

Disruptive Behavior Disorders

Children often misbehave. If they consistently display extreme hostility and defiance, however, they may qualify for a diagnosis of oppositional defiant disorder or conduct disorder. Those with **oppositional defiant disorder** argue repeatedly with adults, lose their temper, and feel great anger and resentment. They often ignore adult rules and requests, try to annoy other people, and blame others for their own mistakes and problems. The disorder is more common in boys than in girls before puberty, but equal in both sexes after puberty. Between 2 and 16 percent of children display this pattern (APA, 2000).

Children with **conduct disorder,** a more severe problem, go further and repeatedly violate the basic rights of others. They are often aggressive and may in fact be physically cruel to people or animals, deliberately destroy other people's property, lie and cheat, skip school, or run away from home (see Table 15-1). Many steal from, threaten, or harm their victims, committing such crimes as shoplifting, forgery, breaking into buildings or cars, mugging, and armed robbery. As they get older their acts of physical violence may include rape or, in rare cases, homicide (APA, 2000, 1994).

Conduct disorder usually begins between 7 and 15 years of age (APA, 2000). Between 1 and 10 percent of children display this pattern, boys more than girls. Children with a mild conduct disorder may improve over time, but severe cases frequently continue into adulthood and may develop into antisocial personality disorder or other psychological problems (Myers, Stewart, & Brown, 1998).

Cases of conduct disorder have been linked to genetic and biological factors, drug abuse, poverty, and exposure to community violence (Simonoff, 2001; Steiner & Wilson, 1999). However, they have most often been tied to troubled parent-child relationships, family conflict, and family hostility (Biederman et al., 2001; Hoge et al., 1996). Children whose parents reject them, leave them, or fail to provide consistent discipline and supervision are apparently more likely to develop a conduct disorder (Frick, Christian, & Wooton, 1999; Rosenstein & Horowitz, 1996). Similarly, children seem more prone to this disorder when their parents are antisocial or have substance-related, mood, or schizophrenic disorders (Wozniak et al., 2001; APA, 2000, 1994).

OPPOSITIONAL DEFIANT DISORDER A childhood disorder in which children argue repeatedly with adults, lose their temper, and swear, feeling intense anger and resentment.

CONDUCT DISORDER A childhood disorder in which the child repeatedly violates the basic rights of others, displaying aggression and sometimes destroying others' property, lying, cheating, or running away from home.

Table 15-1 DSM-IV Checklist

CONDUCT DISORDER

1. A repetitive and persistent pattern of behavior in which the basic rights of others or major age-appropriate societal norms or rules are violated, with at least three of the following present in the past twelve months (and at least one in the past six months):

   a. Frequent bullying or threatening of others.
   b. Frequent provoking of physical fights.
   c. Using dangerous weapons.
   d. Physical cruelty to people.
   e. Physical cruelty to animals.
   f. Stealing while confronting a victim.
   g. Forcing someone into sexual activity.
   h. Fire-setting.
   i. Deliberately destroying others' property.
   j. Breaking into a house, building, or car.
   k. Frequent manipulation of others.
   l. Stealing items of nontrivial value without confronting a victim.
   m. Frequent staying out beyond curfews, beginning before the age of 13.
   n. Running away from home overnight at least twice.
   o. Frequent truancy from school, beginning before the age of 13.

2. Significant impairment.

Based on APA, 2000, 1994.

"It's what we had to do."

Dylan Klebold, 1999, explaining in a prerecorded videotape his killings at Columbine High School

Because disruptive behavior patterns become more locked in with age, treatments for conduct disorder are generally most effective with children younger than 13 (Burnette & Murray, 1996). Given the importance of family factors in this disorder, therapists often use family interventions. In the most successful of these approaches, (1) parents are taught more effective ways to deal with their children (for example, they are taught to be consistent about rewarding appropriate behaviors), or (2) parents and children meet together in behavior-oriented family therapy (Kazdin & Wassell, 1999; Kazdin, 1997).

Sociocultural approaches such as residential treatment in the community, programs at school, and group therapy have also helped some children improve (DeAngelis, 1996). Individual approaches are sometimes effective as well, particularly those that teach the child how to cope with anger (Tate et al., 1995). And recently drug therapy has been tried to help control aggressive outbursts in these children (Donovan et al., 1997). Institutionalization in so-called *juvenile training centers* has not met with much success (Tate et al., 1995). In fact, such institutions frequently serve to strengthen delinquent behavior rather than resocialize young offenders (Erickson, 1992) (see Figure 15-1).

It may be that the greatest hope for reducing the problem of conduct disorder lies in *prevention* programs that begin in early childhood (LeMarquand, Tremblay, & Vitaro, 2001; Reid et al., 1999). These programs try to change unfavorable social conditions before a conduct disorder is able to develop. The programs may offer training opportunities for young people, recreational facilities, and health care, and may try to ease the stresses of poverty and improve parents' child-rearing skills. All approaches work best when they educate and involve the family.

FIGURE 15-1 **Teenage crime** *Teenagers in the United States commit crimes at a disproportionately high rate. That is, although people in this age group make up only 14 percent of the total population, they commit around 30 percent of all violent crimes and 34 percent of all murders. Teenagers are also the victims of 33 percent of all violent crimes. (Adapted from FBI Uniform Crime Reports, 1997; Benson, 1996; National Crime Victimization Survey, 1996, 1993.)*

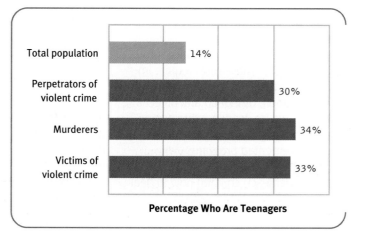

Total population	14%
Perpetrators of violent crime	30%
Murderers	34%
Victims of violent crime	33%

Percentage Who Are Teenagers

Bullying: A Growing Crisis?

Does bullying qualify as a national crisis? Even to pose the question sounds a bit silly, conjuring up images of the schoolyard thug from the *Calvin and Hobbes* comic strip, or Bart's nemesis on *The Simpsons*. But many sober voices say that bullying is no laughing matter and warn that if society continues to overlook this problem, it will place its citizens, particularly its children, at considerable risk.

Last year, the Secret Service released a report examining the 37 school shootings that have taken place across the United States since 1997. It found that bullying was a factor in two-thirds of them (Crisp, 2001). In some cases, the shooters had been bullies; much more often, they had been the *victims* of bullying. A survey released by the Kaiser Family Foundation and Nickelodeon asked a national sample of children aged 8 to 15 what issues in school concerned them most, and all age groups pointed to teasing and bullying as "big problems" that ranked higher than racism, AIDS, and peer pressure to try sex or alcohol (Cukan, 2001). Reports such as these have elevated bullying from a narrow concern that is best dealt with by students themselves (or, perhaps, by the teachers and parents of those directly involved) into a widespread problem that requires the attention of school-level programs and statewide policies.

For instance, in the wake of shooting disasters such as those at Columbine in Colorado (where two students murdered twelve of their peers and a teacher and injured dozens of others, before committing suicide) and Santana in California (where a 15-year-old killed two and injured thirteen at his high school), many schools have put "zero-tolerance" programs in place. These rules require immediate suspension of pupils who bring in any weapon, or indeed any object at all that could be used in a threatening way. A growing number of schools, too, have implemented programs—with names like "Taking the Bully By the Horns"—that teach children how to deal

SW Productions/Photodisc

level-headedly with their tormenters and when to ask a teacher for help.

While acknowledging the important impact and role of bullying in the recent wave of school shootings, some experts worry that the public, school officials, and policymakers are focusing on this issue so intensely that other—more subtle, and perhaps more significant—factors are being ignored by clinicians and researchers. Why has the public centered so much attention on bullying as it tries to sort out school shootings and other unthinkable acts by schoolchildren? Perhaps, some experts argue, because bullying offers a quick explanation and a ready focus for intervention and change. After all, teachers and administrators have been observing and dealing with bullies since the first little red schoolhouse appeared on the prairie. As Charles Ewing, a law professor, psychologist, and expert on homicides by children, puts it, "It's not rocket science to figure out who these unhappy kids are" (Cukan, 2001, n.p.).

At the same time, the commonplace nature of bullying that makes it seem so familiar and treatable might actually render it an elusive problem to address. A recent study published in the *Journal of the American Medical Association* found

that a full 30 percent of American students are involved in moderate or frequent bullying—11 percent have been victims, 13 percent have been bullies, and 6 percent have been both (Tanner, 2001). Other studies report even higher rates (Haynie et al., 2001). How easy can it be for clinicians to identify which children will turn dangerously violent, if indeed one-third of all children have experienced bullying? How can we rid ourselves of a problem as pervasive as this? As one commentator said, "Short of raising kids in isolation chambers . . . bullying behaviors can never be eliminated entirely from the sustained hazing ritual known as growing up" (Angier, 2001).

ConsiderThis

● What kinds of psychological problems may lead a child to bully others? ● What psychological effects might bullying have on its victims? ● Why do many individuals seem able to overcome the trauma of being bullied, while others do not?

Attention-Deficit/Hyperactivity Disorder

Children who display **attention-deficit/hyperactivity disorder (ADHD)** have great difficulty attending to tasks or behave overactively and impulsively, or both (see Table 15-2 on the next page). The disorder often appears before the child starts school, as in the case of Steven:

> Steven's mother cannot remember a time when her son was not into something or in trouble. As a baby he was incredibly active, so active in fact that he nearly rocked his crib apart. All the bolts and screws became loose and had to be tightened periodically. Steven was also always into forbidden places, going through the medicine cabinet or under the kitchen sink. He once swallowed some washing detergent and had to be taken to the emergency room. As a matter of fact, Steven had many more accidents and was more clumsy than his older brother and younger sister. . . . He always seemed to be moving fast. His mother recalls that Steven progressed from the crawling stage to a running stage with very little walking in between.
>
>   Trouble really started to develop for Steven when he entered kindergarten. Since his entry into school, his life has been miserable and so has the teacher's. Steven does not seem capable of attending to assigned tasks and following instructions. He would rather be talking to a neighbor or wandering around the room without the teacher's permission. When he is seated and the teacher is keeping an eye on him to make sure that he works, Steven's body still seems to be in motion. He is either tapping his pencil, fidgeting, or staring out the window and daydreaming. Steven hates kindergarten and has few long-term friends; indeed, school rules and demands appear to be impossible challenges for him. The effects of this mismatch are now showing in Steven's schoolwork and attitude. He has fallen behind academically and has real difficulty mastering new concepts; he no longer follows directions from the teacher and has started to talk back.
>
> *(Gelfand, Jenson, & Drew, 1982, p. 256)*

The symptoms of ADHD often feed into one another. Children who have trouble focusing attention may keep turning from task to task until they end up trying to run in several directions at once. Similarly, constantly moving children may find it hard to attend to tasks or show good judgment. Often one of these symptoms stands out much more than the other (Gaub & Carlson, 1997). About

ATTENTION-DEFICIT/HYPERACTIVITY DISORDER (ADHD) A disorder marked either by inability to focus attention or by overactive and impulsive behavior, or by both.

ADHD ON THE RISE

The numbers of children diagnosed with ADHD more than doubled during the 1990s (Robison et al., 1999).

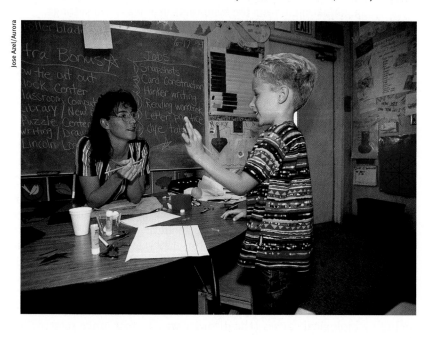

Jose Azel/Aurora

Behavioral intervention *Educational and treatment programs for children with ADHD use behavioral principles that clearly spell out target behaviors and program rewards and systematically reinforce appropriate behaviors by the children.*

Table 15-2 DSM-IV Checklist

ATTENTION-DEFICIT/HYPERACTIVITY DISORDER

1. Either of the following groups:

    A. At least six of the following symptoms of *inattention,* persisting for at least six months to a degree that is maladaptive and inconsistent with development level:
        a. Frequent failure to give close attention to details, or making careless mistakes.
        b. Frequent difficulty in sustaining attention.
        c. Frequent failure to listen when spoken to directly.
        d. Frequent failure to follow through on instructions and failure to finish work.
        e. Difficulty organizing tasks and activities.
        f. Avoidance of, dislike of, and reluctance to engage in tasks that require sustained mental effort.
        g. Frequent loss of items necessary for tasks or activities.
        h. Easy distraction by irrelevant stimuli.
        i. Forgetfulness in daily activities.

    B. At least six of the following symptoms of *hyperactivity-impulsivity,* persisting for at least six months to a degree that is maladaptive and inconsistent with developmental level:
        a. Fidgeting with hands or feet, or squirming in seat.
        b. Frequent wandering from seat in classroom or similar situation.
        c. Frequent running about or climbing excessively in situations in which it is inappropriate.
        d. Frequent difficulty playing or engaging in leisure activities quietly.
        e. Frequent "on the go" activity or acting as if "driven by a motor."
        f. Frequent excessive talking.
        g. Frequent blurting out of answers before questions have been completed.
        h. Frequent difficulty awaiting turn.
        i. Frequent interrupting of or intruding on others.

2. The presence of some symptoms before the age of 7.

3. Impairment from the symptoms in at least two settings.

4. Significant impairment.

Based on APA, 2000, 1994.

DIAGNOSTIC ERRORS?

ADHD can be reliably diagnosed only after a battery of observations, interviews, psychological tests, and physical exams (Buttross, 2000). Yet studies have found that only one-third to one-half of children who receive this diagnosis from pediatricians undergo psychological or educational testing to support the conclusion (Miller, 1999).

METHYLPHENIDATE A stimulant drug, known better by the trade name Ritalin, commonly used to treat ADHD.

ENURESIS A childhood disorder marked by repeated bed-wetting or wetting of one's clothes.

half of the children with ADHD also have learning or communication problems, many perform poorly in school, a number have difficulty interacting with other children, and about 80 percent misbehave, often quite seriously (Mariani & Barkley, 1997; Greene et al., 1996). It is also common for the children to have mood or anxiety problems (Spencer, Biederman, & Wilens, 2000, 1999).

Around 5 percent of schoolchildren display ADHD, as many as 90 percent of them boys. The disorder usually persists throughout childhood (APA, 2000, 1994). Many children show a marked lessening of symptoms as they move into late adolescence, but others continue to have problems. One-third of affected children have ADHD as adults (Trollor, 1999; Lie, 1992). Those whose parents have had ADHD are more likely than others to develop it, and the disorder is more common than usual among relatives of people with the disorder (APA, 2000, 1994; Faraone et al., 1996, 1994).

Today's clinicians generally consider ADHD to have several interacting causes, including biological causes (the disorder was, in fact, once referred to as *minimal brain damage*), high levels of stress, and family dysfunctioning (Baird et al., 2000; Needleman et al., 1996). However, none of these suggested causes, examined alone, has received clear and consistent research support (Anastopoulos & Barkley, 1992). Sociocultural theorists point out that ADHD symptoms and a diagnosis of ADHD may themselves create interpersonal problems and produce additional symptoms in the child. That is, children who are hyperactive tend to be viewed particularly negatively by their peers and by their parents, and they often view themselves negatively as well (APA, 2000; McCormick, 2000).

There is heated disagreement about the most effective treatment for ADHD (Solanto et al., 2001; Hoagwood et al., 2000). The most common approach has been the use of stimulant drugs, such as **methylphenidate (Ritalin)** (see Figure 15-2). These drugs sometimes have a quieting effect on children with ADHD and increase their ability to solve problems, perform academically, and control aggression (Evans et al., 2001). However, some clinicians worry about the possible long-term effects of the drugs (Bennett et al., 1999). Moreover, research suggests that ADHD may be overdiagnosed in the United States, and that many children who receive Ritalin or other such drugs have been inaccurately diagnosed (Miller, 1999; UNINCB, 1996). As many as 12 percent of all American boys may take such drugs, and the number of girls taking them is growing.

Behavioral therapy is also applied widely in cases of ADHD. Here parents and teachers learn how to reward attentiveness or self-control in their children or students. Such operant conditioning treatments have often been helpful, especially when combined with drug therapy (Jensen et al., 2001; Klassen et al., 1999).

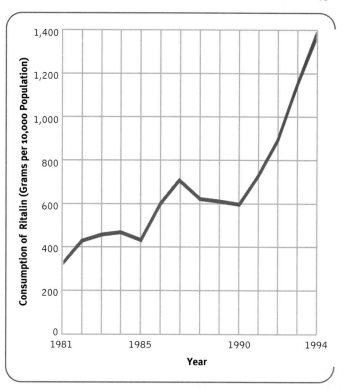

FIGURE 15-2 **The rise of Ritalin** *The use of Ritalin has been increasing since the early 1980s, when researchers discovered that it helped people with ADHD. Sales almost tripled during the 1990s alone. (Adapted from Drug Enforcement Administration, 1996.)*

Elimination Disorders

Children with elimination disorders repeatedly urinate or pass feces in their clothes, in bed, or on the floor. They already have reached an age at which they are expected to control these bodily functions, and their symptoms are not caused by physical illness.

ENURESIS **Enuresis** is repeated involuntary (or in some cases intentional) bedwetting or wetting of one's clothes. It typically occurs at night during sleep but may also occur during the day. Children must be at least 5 years of age to receive this diagnosis (see Table 15-3). The problem may be brought on by a stressful event, such as hospitalization or entrance into school. The prevalence of enuresis decreases with age. As many as 10 percent of children who are 5 years old suffer from this disorder, compared to 3 to 5 percent of 10-year-olds and 1 percent of 15-year-olds (APA, 2000). People with enuresis typically have a close relative (parent, sibling, child) who has had the same disorder (APA, 2000).

Research has not favored one explanation for enuresis beyond the others. Psychodynamic theorists explain it as a symptom of broader anxiety and underlying conflicts (Olmos de Paz, 1990). Family theorists point to disturbed family interactions (Fletcher, 2000). Behaviorists often view it as the result of improper toilet training. And biological theorists suspect that the physical structure of the urinary system develops more slowly in certain children (FDA, 1999; Erickson, 1992).

Most cases of enuresis correct themselves even without treatment. However, therapy, particularly behavioral therapy, can speed up the process (Murphy & Carr, 2000; Moilanen et

Table 15-3 DSM-IV Checklist

ENURESIS

1. Repeated voiding of urine into bed or clothes.
2. Behavior occurring twice a week for at least three consecutive months, or producing significant distress or impairment.
3. A chronological age of at least 5 (or equivalent developmental level).

ENCOPRESIS

1. Repeated passage of feces into inappropriate places (e.g., clothing or floor).
2. Behavior occurring at least once a month for at least three months.
3. A chronological age of at least 4 (or equivalent developmental level).

Based on APA, 2000, 1994.

Early start *A number of theorists worry that in our therapy-oriented society, parents and clinicians are sometimes too quick to subject children to therapy, particularly when the children are merely experiencing the normal anxieties, mood changes, and other struggles that accompany childhood.*

"I wish I'd started therapy at your age."

al., 1998). In a widely used classical conditioning approach, the *bell-and-battery technique,* a bell and a battery are wired to a pad consisting of two metallic foil sheets, and the entire apparatus is placed under the child at bedtime (Mellon & McGrath, 2000; Mowrer & Mowrer, 1938). A single drop of urine sets off the bell, awakening the child as soon as he or she starts to wet. Thus the bell (unconditioned stimulus) paired with the sensation of a full bladder (conditioned stimulus) produces the response of waking. Eventually, a full bladder alone awakens the child.

> "The boy will come to nothing."
>
> Jakob Freud, 1864, referring to his 8-year-old son Sigmund, after he had urinated in his parents' bedroom

ENCOPRESIS **Encopresis,** repeatedly defecating into one's clothing, is less common than enuresis and less well researched. This problem seldom occurs at night during sleep (Levine, 1975). It is usually involuntary, starts after the age of 4, and affects about 1 percent of 5-year-olds. The disorder is more common in boys than in girls (APA, 2000).

Encopresis causes social problems, shame, and embarrassment. Children who suffer from it will usually try to hide their condition and to avoid situations, such as camp or school, in which they might embarrass themselves (APA, 2000, 1994; Ross, 1981). Cases may stem from stress, constipation, or improper toilet training. The most common and successful treatments are behavioral and medical approaches, or combinations of the two (McGrath et al., 2000; Murphy & Carr, 2000). Family therapy has also been helpful (Wells & Hinkle, 1990).

SUMMING UP | Disorders of Childhood and Adolescence

Emotional and behavioral problems are common in childhood and adolescence. A fifth of all children and adolescents in the United States experience a psychological disorder.

Anxiety Disorders and Depression Anxiety disorders among children include adult-like disorders such as specific phobias, social phobia, and generalized anxiety disorder, as well as the unique childhood pattern of separation anxiety disorder, which is marked by excessive anxiety, often panic, whenever a child is separated from a parent. Depression is found among 2 percent of all children under 17 years of age, and among 7 percent of teenagers.

Disruptive Disorders Children with disruptive behavior disorders go beyond the normal breaking of rules and act very aggressively. Those who display an oppositional

ENCOPRESIS A childhood disorder characterized by repeated defecating in inappropriate places, such as one's clothing.

THECURRENT SCENE

Power Play among Kids

Every few years children around the world turn to a new fantasy hero or heroine. Often their fascination with the character arouses adults' concern and interest. The Mighty Morphin Power Rangers—both male and female—have been the center of controversy ever since the television show of the same name became popular several years back (Hellmich, 1995).

Many of today's clinical theorists and parents worry that the Power Rangers are far too violent and teach children that violence solves problems. Others are concerned that aggressive action heroes such as these may create confusion between fantasy and reality.

Terry Gilliam/AP Photo

ConsiderThis

◉ Could violent action heroes help produce psychological disorders among children? • Some experts suggest that superhero play is actually a healthy activity. How might this be so?

See and do *A 4-year-old flexes his muscles in front of the Red Ranger during a Power Rangers Rocket Tour.*

defiant disorder argue repeatedly with adults, lose their temper, and feel great anger and resentment. Those with a conduct disorder, a more severe pattern, repeatedly violate the basic rights of others. They often are violent and cruel and may lie, steal, and run away. Conduct disorder is often related to family dysfunctioning, and so family approaches are often used in treatment. Prevention programs that begin in early childhood have also been tried.

ADHD As many as 5 percent of schoolchildren, mostly boys, display attention-deficit/hyperactivity disorder (ADHD). They attend poorly to tasks or behave overactively and impulsively, or both. It is currently considered a disorder with several interacting causes. Stimulant drugs, such as Ritalin, and behavioral programs are often effective treatments.

Elimination Disorders Children with an elimination disorder—enuresis or encopresis—repeatedly urinate or pass feces in inappropriate places. The prevalence of these disorders falls dramatically as children grow older. A range of factors, from stress to biological, may contribute to the disorders. The behavioral bell-and-battery technique is an effective treatment for enuresis. Encopresis sometimes responds to behavioral, medical, and family approaches.

MASS PRODUCTION

Around 8.5 tons of Ritalin are produced each year, and 90 percent of it is used in the United States (Leutwyler, 1996; UNINCB, 1996).

Long-Term Disorders That Begin in Childhood

Most childhood disorders change or subside as the person ages. Two of the disorders that emerge during childhood, however, are likely to continue unchanged throughout a person's life: *autism* and *mental retardation*. Although it was not always so, clinicians have developed a range of treatment approaches that can make a major difference in the lives of people with these problems.

Autism

A child named Mark presents a typical picture of autism:

In retrospect [Susan, Mark's mother] can recall some things that appeared odd to her. For example, she remembers that . . . Mark never seemed to anticipate being picked up when she approached. In addition, despite Mark's attachment to a pacifier (he would complain if it were mislaid), he showed little interest in toys. In fact, Mark seemed to lack interest in anything. He rarely pointed to things and seemed oblivious to sounds. . . . Mark spent much of his time repetitively tapping on tables, seeming to be lost in his own world.

After his second birthday, Mark's behavior began to trouble his parents. . . . Mark, they said, would "look through" people or past them, but rarely at them. He could say a few words but didn't seem to understand speech. In fact, he did not even respond to his own name. Mark's time was occupied examining familiar objects, which he would hold in front of his eyes while he twisted and turned them. Particularly troublesome were Mark's odd movements—he would jump, flap his arms, twist his hands and fingers, and perform all sorts of facial grimaces, particularly when he was excited—and what Robert [Mark's father] described as Mark's rigidity. Mark would line things up in rows and scream if they were disturbed. He insisted on keeping objects in their place and would become upset whenever Susan attempted to rearrange the living room furniture. . . .

Slowly, beginning at age five, Mark began to improve. . . .

(Wing, 1976)

Mark was displaying **autistic disorder,** also called **autism,** a pattern first identified by the American psychiatrist Leo Kanner in 1943. Children with this disorder are extremely unresponsive to others, uncommunicative, repetitive, and rigid. Their symptoms appear early in life, before 3 years of age. Autism affects only 5 of every 10,000 children (APA, 2000; Fombonne, 1999) (see Table 15-4). Approximately 80 percent of them are boys. Two-thirds of children with autism remain severely disabled into adulthood and are unable to lead independent lives (APA, 2000). Moreover, even the highest-functioning adults with autism typi-

Table 15-4

Comparison of Childhood Disorders

DISORDER	USUAL AGE OF IDENTIFICATION	PREVALENCE AMONG ALL CHILDREN	GENDER WITH GREATER PREVALENCE	ELEVATED FAMILY HISTORY	RECOVERY BY ADULTHOOD
Separation anxiety disorder	Before 12 years	4%	Females	Yes	Often
Conduct disorder	7–15 years	1–10%	Males	Yes	Often
ADHD	Before 12 years	5%	Males	Yes	Often
Enuresis	5–8 years	5%	Males	Yes	Usually
Encopresis	After 4 years	1%	Males	Unclear	Usually
Learning disorders	6–9 years	5%	Males	Yes	Often
Autism	0–3 years	0.05%	Males	Yes	Sometimes
Mental retardation	Before 10 years	1%	Males	Unclear	Sometimes

cally have problems in social interactions and communication and have limited interests and activities (APA, 2000, 1994).

Several other disorders are similar to autism but differ to some degree in symptoms or time of onset. Properly speaking, these different disorders are categorized as *pervasive developmental disorders,* but most clinicians refer to them in general as "autism," and this chapter will do the same.

WHAT ARE THE FEATURES OF AUTISM? The individual's *lack of responsiveness,* including extreme aloofness and lack of interest in other people, has long been considered the central feature of autism. Like Mark, children with this disorder typically do not reach for their parents during infancy. Instead they may arch their backs when they are held and appear not to recognize or care about those around them.

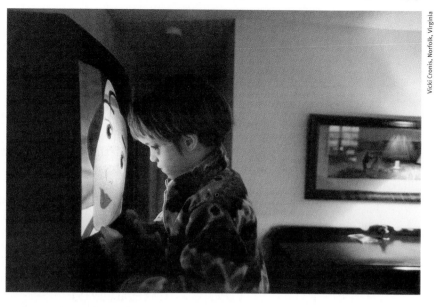

Autistic acts *This autistic child is comforted by standing on her chair and watching television close up, and she often repeats this behavior. People with autism often interact with objects and people in unusual ways that seem to fascinate, stimulate, comfort, or reassure them.*

Language and communication problems take various forms in autism. Approximately half of all sufferers fail to speak or develop language skills (Dawson & Castelloe, 1992). Those who do talk may show peculiarities in their speech. One of the most common speech problems is *echolalia,* the exact echoing of phrases spoken by others. The individuals repeat the words with the same accent, but with no sign of understanding. Some even repeat a sentence days after they have heard it (delayed echolalia). People with autism may also display other speech oddities, such as *pronominal reversal,* or confusion of pronouns—the use of "you" instead of "I." When Mark was hungry, he would say, "Do you want dinner?" In addition, individuals may have problems naming objects, using abstract language, employing a proper tone when speaking, speaking spontaneously, or understanding speech.

Autism is also marked by *limited imaginative play* and *very repetitive and rigid behavior.* Affected children may be unable to play in a varied, spontaneous way or to include others in their play. Typically they become very upset at minor changes of objects, persons, or routine, and resist any efforts to change their repetitive behaviors. Mark, for example, lined things up and screamed if they were disturbed. Similarly, children with autism may react with tantrums if a parent wears an unfamiliar pair of glasses, a chair is moved to a different part of the room, or a word in a song is changed. Kanner (1943) labeled such reactions a *preseveration of sameness.* Furthermore, many sufferers become strongly attached to particular objects—plastic lids, rubber bands, buttons, water. They may collect these objects, carry them, or play with them constantly. Some are fascinated by movement and may watch spinning objects, such as fans, for hours.

The *motor movements* of people with this disorder may also be unusual. Mark would jump, flap his arms, twist his hands and fingers, and make faces. These acts are called *self-stimulatory behaviors.* Some individuals perform *self-injurious behaviors,* such as repeatedly lunging into or banging their head against a wall, pulling their hair, or biting themselves.

These symptoms suggest a very disturbed and contradictory pattern of reactions to stimuli (Wing, 1976; Wing & Wing, 1971). Sometimes the individuals seem *overstimulated* by sights and sounds and to be trying to block them out, whereas at other times they seem *understimulated* and to be performing self-stimulatory actions. They may fail to react to loud noises, for example, yet turn around when they hear soda being poured. Similarly, they may fail to recognize that they have reached the edge of a dangerous high place, yet immediately spot a small object that is out of position in their room.

WHAT CAUSES AUTISM? A variety of explanations have been offered for autism. This is one disorder for which sociocultural explanations have probably been

"97X Bam. The Future of Rock and Roll . . .
97X Bam. The Future of Rock and Roll . . .
97X Bam. The Future of Rock and Roll . . .
97X Bam. The Future of Rock and Roll . . ."

Raymond Babbit, *Rain Man,* 1988
(echolalic response to a radio
advertisement)

AUTISTIC DISORDER A long-term disorder marked by extreme unresponsiveness to others, poor communication skills, and highly repetitive and rigid behavior. Also called *autism.*

overemphasized and initially led investigators in the wrong direction. More recent work in the psychological and biological spheres has persuaded clinical theorists that cognitive limitations and brain abnormalities are the primary causes of autism.

SOCIOCULTURAL CAUSES At first, theorists thought that family dysfunction and social stress were the primary causes of autism. When he first identified autism, for example, Leo Kanner (1954, 1943) argued that *particular personality characteristics of the parents* created an unfavorable climate for development and contributed to the child's disorder. He saw these parents as very intelligent yet cold—"refrigerator parents." These claims had enormous influence on the public and on the self-image of the parents themselves, but research has totally failed to support a picture of rigid, cold, rejecting, or disturbed parents (Roazen, 1992).

Similarly, some other clinicians have proposed that a high degree of *social and environmental stress* is a factor in autism. Once again, however, research has not supported this notion. Investigators who have compared children with autism to children without the disorder have found no differences in the rate of parental death, divorce, separation, financial problems, or environmental stimulation (Cox et al., 1975).

PSYCHOLOGICAL CAUSES According to some theorists, people with autism have a central perceptual or cognitive disturbance that makes normal communication and interactions impossible. One influential explanation holds that individuals with this disorder fail to develop a **theory of mind**—an awareness that other people base their behaviors on their own beliefs, intentions, and other mental states, not on information that they have no way of knowing (Frith, 2000; Happé, 1997, 1995; Leslie, 1997).

By 3 to 5 years of age, most children can take the perspective of another person into account and use it to anticipate what the person will do. In a way, they learn to read others' minds. Let us say, for example, that we watch Jessica place a marble in a container and then we observe Frank move the marble to a nearby room while Jessica is taking a nap. We know that later Jessica will search first in the container for the marble, because she is not aware that Frank moved it. We know that because we take Jessica's perspective into account. A normal child would also anticipate Jessica's search correctly. A person with autism would not. He or she would expect Jessica to look in the nearby room, because that is where the marble actually is. Jessica's own mental processes would be unimportant to the person.

Repeated studies show that people with autism have this kind of "mindblindness." They thus have great difficulty taking part in make-believe play, using language in ways that include the perspectives of others, developing relationships, or participating in interactions. Why do people with autism have this cognitive limitation? Some theorists believe that they suffered early biological problems that prevented them from developing a theory of mind (Frith, 2000; Frith et al., 1991).

BIOLOGICAL CAUSES For years researchers have tried to determine what biological abnormalities might cause theory-of-mind deficits and the other symptoms of autism. They have not yet developed a clear biological explanation, but they have uncovered some very promising leads (Volkmar, 2001; Rodier, 2000; Kemper & Bauman, 1998). First, examinations of the relatives of people with autism keep suggesting a *genetic factor* in this disorder. The prevalence of autism among their siblings, for example, is as high as 6 to 8 per 100 (Piven et al., 1997), a rate up to 200 times higher than the general population's. Moreover, identical twins of people with autism display the highest risk of all. In addition, chromosomal abnormalities have been discovered in 10 to 12 percent of people with the disorder (Sudhalter et al., 1990).

Some studies have also linked autism to *prenatal difficulties* or *birth complications* (Rodier, 2000; Simon, 2000). The chances of developing the disorder are higher when the mother had rubella (German measles) during pregnancy, was

"No two people with autism are the same. Its precise form of expression is different in every case."

Oliver Sacks, 2000

"Autism is . . . genetically lethal [for researchers]. That means people who have it don't usually have children. If it is not passed on, the genetics are difficult to study."

Marvin Schwalb, molecular geneticist, 1999

A CLOSER LOOK

A Special Kind of Talent

Most people are familiar with the savant syndrome, thanks to Dustin Hoffman's portrayal of a man with autism in the movie *Rain Man* (right). The savant skills that Hoffman portrayed—counting 246 toothpicks in the instant after they fall to the floor, memorizing the phone book through the G's, and doing numerical calculations at lightning speed—were based on the astounding talents of certain real-life people who are otherwise limited by autism or mental retardation.

A *savant* (French for "learned" or "clever") is a person with a major mental disorder or intellectual handicap who has some spectacular ability, some area of exceptional brilliance. Often these abilities are remarkable only in light of the handicap, but sometimes they are remarkable by any standard (Yewchuk, 1999).

A common savant skill is calendar calculating, the ability to calculate what day of the week a date will fall on, such as New Year's Day in 2050 (Heavey, Pring, & Hermelin, 1999). A common musical skill such individuals may possess is the ability to play a piece of classical music flawlessly from memory after hearing it only once. Other individuals can paint exact replicas of scenes they saw years ago (Hou et al., 2000).

Some theorists believe that savant skills do indeed represent special forms of cognitive functioning; others propose that the skills are merely a positive side to certain cognitive deficits (Scheuffgen et al., 2000; Miller, 1999). Special memorization skills, for example, may be facilitated by the very narrow and intense focus often found in cases of autism.

Consider This

◉ Why are people so fascinated by the savant syndrome, and might their fascination lead them to glamorize it? • What hidden reminders of human equality or messages of hope may be derived from observations of savant functioning?

---

exposed to toxic chemicals before or during pregnancy, or had complications during labor or delivery. In 1998 one team of investigators proposed that a *postnatal event*—the vaccine for measles, mumps, and rubella—might produce autism in some children, alarming many parents of toddlers. However, subsequent research has found no link between the vaccine and the disorder (Taylor et al., 1999).

Finally, researchers have identified specific *biological abnormalities* that may contribute to autism. Some recent studies have pointed to the **cerebellum,** for example (Carper & Courchesne, 2000; Courchesne & Courchesne, 1997). Brain scans and autopsies reveal abnormal development in this brain area occurring early in the life of people with autism. Scientists have long known that the cerebellum coordinates movement in the body, but they now suspect that it also helps control a person's ability to shift attention rapidly. It may be that people whose cerebellum develops abnormally will have great difficulty adjusting their focus of attention, following verbal and facial cues, and making sense of social information, all key features of autism.

Many researchers believe that autism may in fact have multiple biological causes (Mueller & Courchesne, 2000). Perhaps all relevant biological factors (genetic, prenatal, birth, and postnatal) eventually lead to a common problem in the brain—a "final common pathway," such as neurotransmitter abnormalities, that produces the cognitive problems and other features of the disorder (Tsai, 1999).

HOW IS AUTISM TREATED? Treatment can help people with autism adapt better to their environment, although no treatment yet known totally reverses the autistic pattern. Treatments of particular help are *behavioral therapy, communication training, parent training,* and *community integration.* In addition, psychotropic

THEORY OF MIND Awareness that other people base their behaviors on their own beliefs, intentions, and other mental states, not on information they have no way of knowing.

CEREBELLUM An area of the brain that coordinates movement in the body and perhaps helps control a person's ability to shift attention rapidly.

Learning to speak *Behaviorists have had success teaching many children with autism to speak. The therapist systematically models how to position the mouth and how to make appropriate sounds, and then rewards the child's accurate imitations.*

ConsiderThis

⊙ Clinicians sometimes use punishment to help eliminate the self-injurious behaviors of children with autism. The children may be squirted in the face with water, pinched, or, in extreme cases, shocked whenever they act to hurt themselves. Should self-injurious behaviors reach a certain level of severity before punishments are allowed? • Who should make the decision about whether to use punishments in given cases?

drugs and certain vitamins have sometimes helped when combined with other approaches (Volkmar, 2001; Tsai, 1999).

BEHAVIORAL THERAPY Behavioral approaches have been used in cases of autism for more than 30 years to teach new, appropriate behaviors, including speech, social skills, classroom skills, and self-help skills, while reducing negative, dysfunctional ones. Most often, the therapists use modeling and operant conditioning. In modeling, they demonstrate a desired behavior and guide people with the disorder to imitate it. In operant conditioning, they reinforce such behaviors, first by *shaping* them—breaking them down so they can be learned step by step—and then rewarding each step clearly and consistently (Erba, 2000; Lovaas, 1987). With careful planning and execution, these procedures often produce new, more functional behaviors.

A long-term study compared the progress of two groups of children with autism (McEachin et al., 1993; Lovaas, 1987). Nineteen received intensive behavioral treatments, and 19 served as a control group. The treatment began when the children were 3 years old and continued until they were 7. By the age of 7, those in the behavioral group were doing better in school and scoring higher on intelligence tests than those in the control group. Many were able to go to school in regular classrooms. The gains continued into the subjects' teenage years. In light of such findings, many clinicians now consider early behavioral programs to be the preferred treatment for autism (Harris, 2000, 1995).

Therapies for people with autism, particularly the behavioral therapies, are ideally applied in school while they are young. The children attend special classes, often at special schools, where education and therapy can be combined. Specially trained teachers help the children improve their skills, behaviors, and interactions with the world. Higher-functioning persons with this disorder may spend at least part of their school day in normal classrooms, developing social and academic skills in the company of nonautistic students (Simpson & Sasso, 1992; Tomchek et al., 1992).

COMMUNICATION TRAINING Even when given intensive behavioral treatment, half of the people with autism remain speechless. As a result, many therapists also teach other forms of communication, including *sign language and simultaneous communication,* a method combining sign language and speech. They may also turn to **augmentative communication systems,** such as "communication boards" or computers that use pictures, symbols, or written words to represent objects or needs. A child may point to a picture of a fork to give the message "I am hungry," for example, or point to a radio for "I want music."

PARENT TRAINING Today's treatment programs involve parents in a variety of ways. Behavioral programs, for example, often train parents so that they can apply behavioral techniques at home (Erba, 2000; Love, Matson, & West, 1990). Instruction materials for parents and home visits by teachers and other professionals are often included in such programs. In addition, individual therapy and support groups are becoming more available to help parents deal with their own emotions and needs. A number of parent associations and lobbies also offer emotional support and practical help.

COMMUNITY INTEGRATION Many of today's school-based and home-based programs for autism teach self-help, self-management, and living, social, and work skills as early as possible, to help the children function better in their communities (Koegel et al., 1992). In addition, greater numbers of carefully run *group homes* and *sheltered workshops* are now available for teenagers and young adults with autism (Van Bourgondien & Schopler, 1990). These and related programs help the individuals become a part of their community; they also reduce the concerns of aging parents whose children will always need supervision (Pfeiffer & Nelson, 1992).

Mental Retardation

Ed Murphy, aged 26, can tell us what it's like to be diagnosed as retarded:

> What is retardation? It's hard to say. I guess it's having problems thinking. Some people think that you can tell if a person is retarded by looking at them. If you think that way you don't give people the benefit of the doubt. You judge a person by how they look or how they talk or what the tests show, but you can never really tell what is inside the person.
>
> *(Bogdan & Taylor, 1976, p. 51)*

For much of his life Ed was labeled mentally retarded and was educated and cared for in special institutions. During his adult years, clinicians discovered that Ed's intellect was in fact higher than had been assumed. In the meantime, however, he had lived the childhood and adolescence of a person labeled retarded, and his statement reveals the kinds of difficulties often faced by people with this disorder.

The term "mental retardation" has been applied to a varied population, including children in institutional wards who rock back and forth, young people who work in special job programs, and men and women who raise and support their families by working at undemanding jobs. Approximately one of every 100 persons receives this diagnosis (APA, 2000). Around three-fifths of them are male and the vast majority are considered *mildly* retarded.

According to DSM-IV, people should receive a diagnosis of **mental retardation** when they display general *intellectual functioning* that is well below average, in combination with poor *adaptive behavior* (APA, 2000, 1994). That is, in addition to having a low IQ (a score of 70 or below), a person with mental retardation must have great difficulty in areas such as communication, home living, self-direction, work, or safety (APA, 2000, 1994). The symptoms must also appear before the age of 18 (see Table 15-5). Although these DSM-IV criteria may seem straightforward, they are in fact hard to apply.

ASSESSING INTELLIGENCE Educators and clinicians administer intelligence tests to measure intellectual functioning (see Chapter 3). These tests consist of a variety of questions and tasks that rely on different aspects of intelligence, such as knowledge, reasoning, and judgment. It is an individual's overall test score, or **intelligence quotient (IQ),** that is thought to indicate general intellectual ability.

Many theorists have questioned whether IQ tests are indeed valid. Do they actually measure what they are supposed to measure? The correlation between IQ and school performance is rather high—around .50—indicating that many children with lower IQs do, as one might expect, perform poorly in school, while many of those with higher IQs perform better (Ceci & Williams, 1997). At the same time, the correlation also suggests that the relationship is far from perfect. That is, a particular child's school performance is often higher or lower than his or her IQ might predict. Correlations between IQ and job performance or social effectiveness, other areas that might be expected to rely on intellectual ability, are even lower (Neisser et al., 1996).

AUGMENTATIVE COMMUNICATION SYSTEM A method for enhancing the communication skills of individuals with autism, mental retardation, or cerebral palsy by teaching them to point to pictures, symbols, letters, or words on a communication board or computer.

MENTAL RETARDATION A disorder marked by intellectual functioning and adaptive behavior that are well below average.

INTELLIGENCE QUOTIENT (IQ) A score derived from intelligence tests that theoretically represents a person's overall intellectual capacity.

Table 15-5 DSM-IV Checklist

MENTAL RETARDATION

1. Significantly subaverage intellectual functioning: an IQ of approximately 70 or below on an individually administered IQ test.

2. Concurrent deficits or impairments in present adaptive functioning in at least two of the following areas:
   a. Communication.
   b. Self-care.
   c. Home living.
   d. Social/interpersonal skills.
   e. Use of community resources.
   f. Self-direction.
   g. Functional academic skills.
   h. Work.
   i. Leisure.
   j. Health.
   k. Safety.

3. Onset before the age of 18.

Based on APA, 2000, 1994.

Getting a head start *Studies suggest that IQ scores and school performances of children from poor neighborhoods can be improved by enriching their daily environments at a young age through programs such as Head Start, thus revealing the powerful effect of the environment on IQ scores and intellectual performance.*

"The IQ test was invented to predict academic performance, nothing else. If we wanted something that would predict life success, we'd have to invent another test completely."

Robert Zajonc, psychologist, 1984

Intelligence tests also appear to be socioculturally biased, as we observed in Chapter 3 (Lee, 1999; Neisser et al., 1996). Children reared in households at the middle and upper socioeconomic levels tend to have an advantage on the tests because they are regularly exposed to the kinds of language and thinking that the tests measure. The tests rarely measure the "street sense" needed for survival by people who live in poor, crime-ridden areas—a kind of know-how that certainly requires intellectual skills. Similarly, members of cultural minorities and people for whom English is a second language often appear to be at a disadvantage in taking these tests.

If IQ tests do not always measure intelligence accurately and objectively, then the diagnosis of mental retardation also may be biased (Baroff & Olley, 1999; Wilson, 1992). That is, some people may receive the diagnosis partly because of cultural differences, discomfort with the testing situation, or the bias of a tester.

ASSESSING ADAPTIVE FUNCTIONING Diagnosticians cannot rely solely on a cutoff IQ score of 70 to determine whether a person suffers from mental retardation. Some people with a low IQ are quite capable of managing their lives and functioning independently, while others are not. The cases of Brian and Jeffrey show the range of adaptive abilities.

Brian comes from a lower-income family. He always has functioned adequately at home and in his community. He dresses and feeds himself and even takes care of himself each day until his mother returns home from work. He also plays well with his friends. At school, however, Brian refuses to participate or do his homework. He seems ineffective, at times lost, in the classroom. Referred to a school psychologist by his teacher, he received an IQ score of 60.

Jeffrey comes from an upper-middle-class home. He was always slow to develop, and sat up, stood, and talked late. During his infancy and toddler years, he was put in a special stimulation program and given special help and attention at home. Still Jeffrey has trouble dressing himself today and cannot be left alone in the backyard lest he hurt himself or wander off into the street. Schoolwork is very difficult for him. The teacher must work slowly and provide individual instruction for him. Tested at age 6, Jeffrey received an IQ score of 60.

Brian seems well adapted to his environment outside of school. However, Jeffrey's limitations are widespread. In addition to his low IQ score, Jeffrey has difficulty meeting challenges at home and elsewhere. Thus, a diagnosis of mental retardation may be more appropriate for Jeffrey than for Brian.

Several scales have been developed to assess adaptive behavior (Leland, 1991; Britton & Eaves, 1986). Here again, however, some people function better in their lives than the scales predict, while others fall short. Thus to properly diagnose mental retardation, clinicians should observe the functioning of each individual in his or her everyday environment, taking both the person's background and the community's standards into account. Even then, such judgments can be subjective, and clinicians are not always familiar with the standards of a particular culture or community.

WHAT ARE THE CHARACTERISTICS OF MENTAL RETARDATION? The most consistent sign of mental retardation is that the person learns very slowly (Baroff & Olley, 1999; Kail, 1992). Other areas of difficulty are attention, short-term memory, planning, and language. Those who are institutionalized with mental retardation are particularly likely to have these limitations. It may be that the unstimulating environment and minimal interactions with staff in many institutions contribute to such difficulties.

Reading and 'Riting and 'Rithmetic

*O*ver 20 percent of children, boys more often than girls, develop slowly and function poorly in comparison with their peers in an area such as learning, communication, or coordination (APA, 2000). The children do not suffer from mental retardation, and in fact they are often very bright, yet their problems may interfere with school performance, daily living, and, in some cases, social interactions (Geisthardt & Munsch, 1996). According to DSM-IV, these children may be suffering from a learning disorder, a communication disorder, or a developmental coordination disorder.

The skill in arithmetic, written expression, or reading exhibited by children with *learning disorders* is well below their intellectual capacity and causes academic and personal dysfunctioning (APA, 2000, 1994). For example, children with *reading disorder,* also known as *dyslexia,* have great difficulty recognizing words and comprehending as they read. They typically read slowly and haltingly and may omit, distort, or substitute words as they go.

Children with *communication disorders* have severe difficulty pronouncing words, speaking fluently, or comprehending or expressing language. Those with *expressive language disorder,* for example, may struggle at learning new words, confine their speech to short simple sentences, or show a general lag in language development.

Finally, children with *developmental coordination disorder* perform coordinated motor activities at a level well below that of others their age (APA,

2000, 1994). Younger children with this disorder are clumsy and are slow to master skills such as tying shoelaces, buttoning shirts, and zipping pants. Older children with the disorder may have great difficulty assembling puzzles, building models, playing ball, and printing or writing.

Studies have linked these various developmental disorders to genetic defects, birth injuries, lead poisoning, inappropriate diet, sensory or perceptual dysfunction, and poor teaching (Grigorenko, 2001; Lovett, 2000). Research implicating each of these factors has been limited, however, and the precise causes of the disorders remain unclear.

Some of the disorders respond to special treatment approaches (Pless & Carlsson, 2000; Merzenich et al., 1996). Reading therapy, for example, is very helpful in mild cases of reading disorder. Furthermore, learning, communication, and developmental coordination disorders often disappear before adulthood, even without any treatment (APA, 2000).

The inclusion of learning, communication, and coordination problems in the DSM is controversial. Many clinicians view them as strictly educational or social problems, best addressed at school or at home. The framers of DSM-IV have reasoned, however, that the additional problems created by these disorders and the frequent links to other psychological

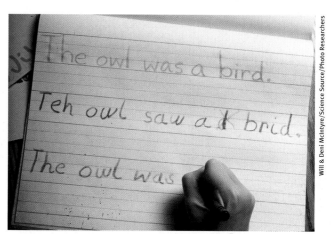

Dyslexic impairment *A student with dyslexia has trouble copying words. His mistakes reflect the difficulties he experiences when reading.*

problems justify their clinical classifications (Mishna, 1996). Of special concern are studies that have found an increased risk of depression and even suicide in adolescents with certain of these problems, particularly the learning disorders (Huntington & Bender, 1993).

ConsiderThis

In past times, a child with one of these problems might simply be called a "weak" reader, "clumsy," or the like. What are the advantages and disadvantages to the child of affixing clinical names to the patterns? • Should these patterns be listed in DSM-IV as psychological disorders?

DSM-IV describes four levels of mental retardation: mild (IQ 50–70), moderate (IQ 35–49), severe (IQ 20–34), and profound (IQ below 20). In contrast, the American Association of Mental Retardation (1992) prefers to distinguish different kinds of mental retardation according to the level of support the person needs—intermittent, limited, extensive, or pervasive.

MILD RETARDATION Approximately 85 percent of all people with mental retardation fall into the category of **mild retardation** (IQ 50–70) (APA, 2000). They are sometimes called "educably retarded" because they can benefit from schooling and can support themselves as adults. Still, they typically need assistance

MILD RETARDATION A level of mental retardation (IQ between 50 and 70) at which people can benefit from education and support themselves as adults.

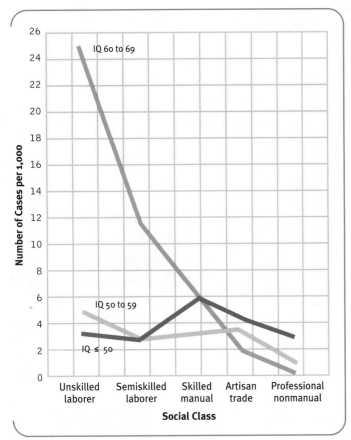

Number of Cases per 1,000

IQ 60 to 69

IQ 50 to 59

IQ ≤ 50

Unskilled laborer • Semiskilled laborer • Skilled manual • Artisan trade • Professional nonmanual

Social Class

FIGURE 15-3 **Mental retardation and socio-economic class** *The prevalence of mild mental retardation is much higher in the lower socio-economic classes than in the upper classes. In contrast, the forms of mental retardation that result in greater impairment are evenly distributed. (Adapted from Popper, 1988; Birch et al., 1970.)*

RESIDENTIAL SHIFT

Around 200,000 people with mental retardation lived in large state institutions in 1967, compared to 60,000 today (Lakin et al., 1999, 1996).

when they are under stress. Their jobs tend to be unskilled or semiskilled. Mild mental retardation is not usually recognized until a child enters school and is assessed there. Interestingly, the intellectual performance of individuals in this category often seems to improve with age; some even seem to leave the label behind when they leave school, and they go on to function well in the community.

Research has linked mild mental retardation mainly to sociocultural and psychological causes, particularly poor and unstimulating environments, inadequate parent-child interactions, and insufficient learning experiences during a child's early years (Stromme & Magnus, 2000). These relationships have been observed in studies comparing deprived and enriched environments (see Figure 15-3). In fact, some community programs have sent workers into the homes of young children with low IQ scores to help enrich the environment there, and their interventions have often improved the children's functioning. When continued, programs of this kind also help improve the children's later performance in school (Ramey & Ramey, 1999, 1998, 1992).

Although these factors seem to be the leading causes of mild mental retardation, at least some biological factors also may be operating. Studies suggest, for example, that a mother's moderate drinking, drug use, or malnutrition during pregnancy may lower her child's intellectual potential (Neisser et al., 1996; Stein et al., 1972). Similarly, malnourishment during a child's early years may hurt his or her intellectual development, although this effect can be reversed at least partly if the child's diet is improved before too much time goes by (Baroff & Olley, 1999; Neisser et al., 1996).

MODERATE, SEVERE, AND PROFOUND RETARDATION Approximately 10 percent of persons with mental retardation function at a level of **moderate retardation** (IQ 35–49). They can learn to care for themselves and can benefit from vocational training, and many can work in unskilled or semiskilled jobs, usually under supervision. Most persons with moderate retardation also function well in the community if they have supervision (APA, 2000, 1994).

Approximately 4 percent of people with mental retardation display **severe retardation** (IQ 20–34). They usually require careful supervision, profit somewhat from vocational training, and can perform only basic work tasks in structured and sheltered settings. Their understanding of communication is usually better than their speech. Most are able to function well in the community if they live in group homes, community nursing homes, or with their families (APA, 2000, 1994).

Around 1 percent of all people with mental retardation fall into the category of **profound retardation** (IQ below 20). With training they may learn or improve basic skills such as walking, some talking, and feeding themselves. They need a very structured environment, with close supervision and considerable help, including a one-to-one relationship with a caregiver, in order to develop to the fullest (APA, 2000, 1994). Severe and profound levels of mental retardation often appear as part of larger syndromes that include severe physical handicaps. In many cases these physical problems are even more limiting than an individual's low intellectual functioning.

The primary causes of moderate, severe, and profound retardation are biological, although people who function at these levels are also greatly affected by their family and social environment (Baroff & Olley, 1999; Bruce et al., 1996). Sometimes genetic factors are at the root of these biological problems, in the form of chromosomal or metabolic disorders. In fact, researchers have identified

1,000 genetic causes of mental retardation, although few of them have undergone much study (Dykens & Hodapp, 2001; Azar, 1995). Other biological causes of these kinds of mental retardation come from unfavorable conditions that occur before, during, or after birth.

CHROMOSOMAL CAUSES The most common of the chromosomal disorders leading to mental retardation is **Down syndrome,** named after Langdon Down, the British physician who first identified it. Fewer than 1 of every 1,000 live births result in Down syndrome, but this rate increases greatly when the mother's age is over 35. Many older expectant mothers are now encouraged to undergo *amniocentesis* (testing of the amniotic fluid that surrounds the fetus) during the fourth month of pregnancy to identify Down syndrome and other chromosomal abnormalities.

Individuals with Down syndrome may have a small head, flat face, slanted eyes, high cheekbones, and, in some cases, a protruding tongue. The latter may affect their ability to pronounce words clearly. They are often very affectionate with family members, but in general display the same range of personality characteristics as people in the general population (Carr, 1994).

Several types of chromosomal abnormalities may cause Down syndrome, but the most common type is *trisomy 21,* in which the individual has three twenty-first chromosomes instead of two (Pueschel & Thuline, 1991). Most people with Down syndrome range in IQ from 35 to 55. The individuals appear to age early, and many even show signs of dementia as they approach 40 (Lawlor et al., 2001; Zigman et al., 1995; Carr, 1994). Studies suggest that Down syndrome and early dementia often occur together because the genes that produce them are located close to each other on chromosome 21 (Selkoe, 1991).

Fragile X syndrome is the second most common chromosomal cause of mental retardation (Zigler & Hodapp, 1991). Children born with a fragile X chromosome (that is, an X chromosome with a genetic abnormality that leaves it prone to breakage and loss) generally have mild to moderate degrees of intellectual dysfunctioning, language impairment, and, in some cases, behavioral problems (Baroff & Olley, 1999).

METABOLIC CAUSES In metabolic disorders, the body's breakdown or production of chemicals is disturbed. The metabolic disorders that affect intelligence and development are typically caused by the pairing of two defective *recessive genes,* one from each parent. Although one such gene would have no influence if it were paired with a normal gene, its pairing with another defective gene leads to major problems for the child.

The most common metabolic disorder to cause mental retardation is *phenylketonuria (PKU),* which strikes 1 of every 17,000 children. Babies with PKU appear normal at birth but cannot break down the amino acid *phenylalanine.* The chemical builds up and is converted into substances that poison the system, causing severe retardation and several other symptoms. Today infants can be screened for PKU, and if started on a special diet before 3 months of age, they may develop normal intelligence.

In *Tay-Sachs disease,* another metabolic disorder resulting from a pairing of recessive genes, children progressively lose their mental functioning, vision, and motor ability over the course of two to four years, and eventually die. One of every 30 persons of Eastern European Jewish ancestry carries the recessive gene responsible for this disorder, so that one of every 900 Jewish couples is at risk for having a child with Tay-Sachs disease.

Brian Davies/The Appeal Democrat

Reaching higher *Until the 1970s, clinicians were pessimistic about the potential of people with Down syndrome. Today they are viewed as individuals who can learn and accomplish many things in their lives. Derek Finstad, a 16-year-old with this disorder, celebrates with his football teammates after the team's 56–0 season-opening victory.*

MODERATE RETARDATION A level of mental retardation (IQ between 35 and 49) at which people can learn to care for themselves and benefit from vocational training.

SEVERE RETARDATION A level of mental retardation (IQ between 20 and 34) at which individuals require careful supervision and can learn to perform basic work in structured and sheltered settings.

PROFOUND RETARDATION A level of mental retardation (IQ below 20) at which individuals need a very structured environment with close supervision.

DOWN SYNDROME A form of mental retardation related to abnormalities of the twenty-first chromosome.

PRENATAL AND BIRTH-RELATED CAUSES As a fetus develops, major physical problems in the pregnant mother can threaten the child's prospects for a normal life (Baroff & Olley, 1999; Neisser et al., 1996). When a pregnant woman has too little iodine in her diet, for example, her child may develop *cretinism,* marked by an abnormal thyroid gland, slow development, mental retardation, and a dwarf-like appearance. The disorder is rare today because the salt in most diets now contains extra iodine. Also, any infant born with this disorder may quickly be given thyroid extract to bring about a normal development.

Other prenatal problems may also cause mental retardation. As we observed in Chapter 10, children whose mothers drink too much alcohol during pregnancy may be born with **fetal alcohol syndrome,** a group of very serious problems that includes lower intellectual functioning. In fact, a generally safe level of alcohol consumption during pregnancy has not been established by research. In addition, certain maternal infections during pregnancy—*rubella* (German measles) and *syphilis,* for example—may cause childhood problems that include mental retardation.

Birth complications can also lead to mental retardation. A prolonged period without oxygen (*anoxia*) during or after delivery can cause brain damage and retardation in a baby (Erickson, 1992). Similarly, although premature birth does not necessarily lead to long-term problems for children, researchers have found that a birth weight of less than 3.5 pounds may sometimes result in retardation (Neisser et al., 1996).

CHILDHOOD PROBLEMS After birth, particularly up to age 6, certain injuries and accidents can affect intellectual functioning and in some cases lead to mental retardation. Poisonings, serious head injuries caused by accident or abuse, excessive exposure to X rays, and excessive use of certain drugs pose special dangers. For example, a serious case of *lead poisoning,* from eating lead-based paints or inhaling high levels of automobile fumes, can cause retardation in children. Mercury, radiation, nitrite, and pesticide poisoning may do the same. In addition, certain infections, such as *meningitis* and *encephalitis,* can lead to mental retardation if they are not diagnosed and treated in time (Baroff & Olley, 1999; Berney, 1993).

INTERVENTIONS FOR PEOPLE WITH MENTAL RETARDATION The quality of life achieved by people with mental retardation depends largely on sociocultural factors: where they live and with whom, how they are educated, and the growth opportunities available at home and in the community. Thus intervention programs for these individuals try to provide comfortable and stimulating residences, social and economic opportunities, and a proper education. Once these needs are met, psychological or biological treatments are also of help in some cases.

WHAT IS THE PROPER RESIDENCE? Until recent decades, parents of children with mental retardation would send them to live in public institutions—**state schools**—as early as possible. These overcrowded institutions provided basic care, but residents were neglected, often abused, and isolated from society.

During the 1960s and 1970s, the public became more aware of these sorry conditions, and, as part of the broader *deinstitutionalization* movement (see Chapter 12), demanded that many people with mental retardation be released from the state schools (Beyer, 1991). In a number of cases, residents were released without adequate preparation or supervision. Like deinstitutionalized people suffering from schizophrenia, the individuals were virtually dumped into the community. Often they failed to adjust and had to be institutionalized once again.

Since that time, reforms have led to the creation of small institutions that teach self-sufficiency, devote more staff time to patient care, and offer educational and medical services. Many of these institutions and other community

Jeff Albertson/Stock Boston

Environmental danger *Children such as this toddler who scrape and eat lead-based paint chips may experience lead poisoning, which can cause mental retardation.*

residences follow the principles of **normalization** first started in Denmark and Sweden—they try to provide living conditions similar to those enjoyed by the rest of society, flexible routines, and normal developmental experiences, including opportunities for self-determination, sexual fulfillment, and economic freedom (Baroff & Olley, 1999). Growing numbers of group homes, small local branches of larger institutions, and independent residences now apply these principles, teaching clients with retardation how to get along in the community.

Today the vast majority of children with mental retardation live at home rather than in an institution (Erickson, 1992). As they approach adulthood and as their parents age, however, the family may become less able to provide the kinds of assistance and experiences these individuals require (Krauss et al., 1992), and a community residence becomes an appropriate alternative for some. Most people with mental retardation, including almost all with mild mental retardation, now spend their adult lives either in the family home or in a community residence (Blacher & Baker, 1994, 1992; Jacobson & Schwartz, 1991).

WHICH EDUCATIONAL PROGRAMS WORK BEST? Because early intervention seems to offer such great promise, educational programs for individuals with mental retardation may begin during the earliest years. The appropriate education depends on the individual's degree of retardation (Patton et al., 2000; Cipani, 1991). Educators hotly debate whether special classes or mainstreaming is most effective once the children enter school (Freeman & Alkin, 2000). In **special education,** children with mental retardation are grouped together in a separate, specially designed educational program. **Mainstreaming,** in contrast, places them in regular classes with nonretarded students. Neither approach seems consistently superior (Gottlieb et al., 1991; Gottlieb, 1981). It may well be that mainstreaming is better for some areas of learning and for some children, special classes for others.

Many teachers use operant conditioning principles to improve the self-help, communication, social, and academic skills of individuals with mental retardation (Erickson, 1992). They break learning tasks down into small steps, giving positive reinforcement as each increment is accomplished. In addition, many institutions, schools, and private homes have set up *token economy programs*—the operant conditioning programs that have also been used to treat institutionalized patients suffering from schizophrenia.

WHEN IS THERAPY NEEDED? Like anyone else, people with mental retardation sometimes experience emotional and behavioral problems. At least 10 percent of them have a diagnosable psychological disorder other than mental retardation (Stromme & Diseth, 2000; Grizenko et al., 1991). Furthermore, some suffer from low self-esteem, interpersonal problems, and difficulties adjusting to community life. These problems are helped to some degree by either individual or group therapy (Rush & Frances, 2000; Baroff & Olley, 1999). In addition, large numbers of people with retardation are given psychotropic medications (Matson et al., 2000). Many clinicians suggest, however, that too often the medications are used simply for the purpose of making the individuals easier to manage.

HOW CAN OPPORTUNITIES FOR PERSONAL, SOCIAL, AND OCCUPATIONAL GROWTH BE INCREASED? People need to feel effective and competent in order to move forward in life. Those with mental retardation are most likely to achieve these feelings if their communities allow them to grow and to make many of their own choices (Wehmeyer, 1992). Denmark and Sweden, where the normalization movement began, are again leaders in this area, developing youth clubs that encourage those with mental retardation to take risks and function independently (Perske, 1972).

Socializing, sex, and marriage are difficult issues for people with mental retardation and their families, but

FETAL ALCOHOL SYNDROME A group of problems in a child, including lower intellectual functioning, head and face irregularities, heart defects, and slow growth, that result from excessive alcohol intake by the mother during pregnancy.

STATE SCHOOL A state-supported institution for individuals with mental retardation.

NORMALIZATION The principle that institutions and community residences should expose people with mental retardation to living conditions and opportunities similar to those found in the rest of society.

SPECIAL EDUCATION An approach to educating children with mental retardation in which they are grouped together and given a separate, specially designed education.

MAINSTREAMING The placement of children with mental retardation in regular school classes with children who are not mentally retarded.

Artistic development *Clinicians have come to recognize that people with mental retardation can benefit from instruction in the arts as well as academic and vocational training. Individuals enrolled in this creative arts course at the center of the Association for Retarded Persons develop greater self-confidence and better communication skills along with improved artistic ability.*

David Creamer/Gamma Liaison

Laura Dwight/Peter Arnold

Normal needs *The interpersonal and sexual needs of people with mental retardation are normal, and many, such as this engaged couple, demonstrate considerable ability to express intimacy.*

with proper training and practice, the individuals can usually learn to use contraceptives and carry out responsible family planning (Lumley & Scotti, 2001; Dowdney & Skuse, 1993). The National Association for Retarded Citizens offers guidance in these matters, and some clinicians have developed *dating skills programs* (Valenti-Hein et al., 1994).

Some states restrict marriage for people with mental retardation (Levesque, 1996). These laws are rarely enforced, however, and in fact between one-quarter and half of all people with mild mental retardation eventually marry (Grinspoon et al., 1986). Contrary to popular myths, the marriages can be very successful. Moreover, although some individuals may be incapable of raising children, many are quite able to do so, either on their own or with special help and community services (Levesque, 1996; Bakken et al., 1993).

Finally, adults with mental retardation—whatever the severity—need the personal and financial rewards that come with holding a job (Kiernan, 2000; AAMR, 1992). Many work in **sheltered workshops,** protected and supervised workplaces that train them at a pace and level tailored to their skills. After training in the workshops, many with mild or moderate retardation move on to hold regular jobs (Moore, Flowers, & Taylor, 2000).

Although training programs for people with mental retardation have improved greatly in quality over the past 30 years, there are too few of them. Consequently, most of these individuals fail to receive a complete range of educational and occupational training services. Additional programs are required so that more people with mental retardation may achieve their full potential, as workers and as human beings.

ConsiderThis

⦿ Those who support special classes for people with mental retardation believe that such programs allow the participants to experience feelings of success and to receive needed special attention, while those who favor mainstreaming argue that this format offers a more normal educational experience and increased interaction between children with and without mental retardation. What are the merits and flaws of each position?

SHELTERED WORKSHOP A protected and supervised workplace that offers job opportunities and training at a pace and level tailored to people with various psychological disabilities.

SUMMING UP

Long-Term Disorders That Begin in Childhood

Autism and mental retardation are problems that emerge early and typically continue throughout a person's life.

Autism People with autism are very unresponsive to others, have poor communication skills, and behave in a very rigid and repetitive manner. They may display, for example, perseveration of sameness, strong attachments to objects, self-stimulatory behaviors, and self-injurious behaviors. The leading explanations of this disorder point to cognitive disturbances, such as failure to develop a theory of mind, and biological abnormalities, such as abnormal development of the cerebellum.

Treatment for autism is designed to help the individuals adapt to their environment. Although no treatment totally reverses the autistic pattern, behavioral treatments, communication training, treatment and training for parents, and community integration have proved very helpful.

Mental Retardation Persons with mental retardation are well below average in intelligence and adaptive ability. Mild retardation, by far the most common level of mental retardation, has been linked mainly to sociocultural and psychological factors such as understimulation, inadequate parent-child interactions, and insufficient early learning experiences. Moderate, severe, and profound mental retardation are caused primarily by biological factors, although individuals who function at these levels are also greatly affected by their family and social environment. The leading biological causes are chromosomal disorders, metabolic disorders, certain prenatal problems, birth complications, and certain childhood diseases and injuries.

Today intervention programs for people with mental retardation try to ensure that individuals live in comfortable and stimulating residences, such as at home with their families or in a small institution or group home that follows the principles of normalization. Other important interventions are proper education, therapy for psychological problems, and programs offering training in such areas as socializing, sex, marriage, parenting, and occupational skills.

Disorders of Later Life

Old age is usually defined in our society as the years past age 65. By this account more than 35 million people in the United States are "old," representing around 15 percent of the total population; this is an elevenfold increase since 1900 (Hobbs, 1997) (see Figure 15-4). Older women outnumber older men by 3 to 2.

Like childhood, old age brings special pressures, unique upsets, and key biological changes. People become more prone to illness and injury as they age, and they are likely to experience the stress of loss—the loss of spouses, friends, and adult children, and the loss of former activities and roles. Many lose their sense of purpose after they retire. Even favored pets and possessions are sometimes lost (Gallagher-Thompson & Thompson, 1995).

The stresses of elderly people need not necessarily result in psychological problems (Schultz & Heckhausen, 1996). In fact, some older persons use the changes that come with aging to help them learn more about themselves and to grow. For others, however, the stresses of old age do lead to psychological difficulties. Studies indicate that as many as 50 percent of elderly people would benefit from mental health services, yet fewer than 20 percent actually receive them. At present fewer than 4 percent of all clinicians work primarily with elderly patients (Birren & Schroots, 2000; Sleek, 1996).

The psychological problems of elderly persons may be divided into two groups. One group consists of disorders that are found in people of all ages but that often are closely connected to the process of aging when they occur in an elderly person. These include depression and anxiety and substance-related disorders. The other group consists of disorders that are most likely to be found in the elderly, such as delirium and dementia.

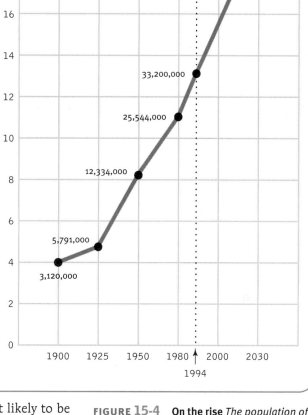

FIGURE 15-4 **On the rise** *The population of people aged 65 and older in the United States increased elevenfold during the twentieth century. The percentage of elderly people in the population increased from 4 percent in 1900 to 12.5 percent in 1994 and is expected to be 20 percent in 2030 (Hobbs, 1997; AARP, 1990).*

Mood, Anxiety, and Substance-Related Disorders

Depression is the most common mental health problem of older adults. As with Oscar, the man whose case description opened this chapter, depression is particularly common among elderly persons who have recently had a trauma, such as the loss of a spouse or close friend or a serious physical illness. Overall, as many as 20 percent of the elderly experience this disorder (Lyness et al., 1999; Koenig & Blazer, 1992). The rate is highest in older women (Fernandez et al., 1995).

Several studies suggest that depression among older people raises their chances of developing significant medical problems. For example, older depressed people with high blood pressure are almost three times as likely to suffer a stroke as older nondepressed people with the same condition (Simonsick et al., 1995). Similarly, elderly people who are depressed recover more slowly and less completely from heart attacks, hip fractures, pneumonia, and other infections and illnesses (Goleman, 1995).

Like younger adults, older individuals who are depressed may be helped by cognitive therapy, interpersonal therapy, antidepressant medications, or a combination of these approaches (Cappeliez, 2000; Katz & Oslin, 2000; Hinrichsen, 1999). Between half and 65 percent of older patients with depression improve with such treatments. At the same time, it is sometimes difficult to use antidepressant drugs safely with older persons because the body breaks the drugs down differently in later life (Bell, 1999). Finally, group therapy can be a useful approach for older people who are depressed.

Anxiety is also common among elderly people (Wetherell & Gatz, 2001; Fuentes & Cox, 2000). Surveys indicate that generalized anxiety disorder and

ConsiderThis

◉ Need aging lead to depression and other psychological problems? What kinds of attitudes, preparations, and activities might help an individual enter old age with peace of mind and even anticipation?

Micheal Heron/Woodfin Camp & Associates

Dreary setting *Most aging persons fear that they will eventually be forced by poor health to reside in a nursing home, separated from their families, friends, and homes. An additional concern is that many of today's nursing homes are unstimulating settings in which residents may be neglected, mistreated, and overmedicated.*

agoraphobia are particularly common, experienced by up to 7 percent and 5 percent, respectively (Flint, 1994). In fact, these numbers may be low, as anxiety in the elderly tends to be underreported (Sleek, 1996). Both the elderly individual and the clinician may interpret physical symptoms of anxiety, such as heart palpitations and sweating, as symptoms of a medical condition.

Older adults with anxiety disorders are often treated with psychotherapy of various kinds, particularly cognitive therapies (Stanley & Averill, 1999; McCarthy et al., 1991). Many also receive benzodiazepines or other antianxiety medications, although more and more of those with obsessive-compulsive disorder are, like younger sufferers, being treated with serotonin-enhancing antidepressant drugs such as *fluoxetine* (Prozac) (Calamari & Cassiday, 1999). Again, however, all such drugs must be used carefully with people over 60 years of age.

Alcohol abuse and other forms of *substance abuse* are another problem for many older persons, although the prevalence of these disorders actually goes down among people over the age of 60 (Stewart & Oslin, 2001; Graham et al., 1996). Nonetheless, 4 to 6 percent of older people, particularly men, experience alcohol-related disorders in any given year (Adams & Cox, 1997). Researchers often distinguish between older problem drinkers who have experienced significant alcohol-related problems for many years, perhaps since their 20s or 30s, and those who do not start the pattern until their 50s or 60s. The latter group typically begin their abusive drinking as a reaction to the negative events and pressures of growing older, such as the death of a spouse or unwanted retirement. Alcohol abuse and dependence in elderly people are treated much as in younger adults (see Chapter 10), with such approaches as detoxification, Antabuse, Alcoholics Anonymous (AA), and cognitive-behavioral therapy (Dupree & Schonfeld, 1999).

A leading kind of substance problem in the elderly is the misuse of prescription drugs (Graham et al., 1996). Most often it is unintentional. Older people receive twice as many prescriptions on average as younger persons, and one-quarter of them take three or more drugs daily (Patterson et al., 1999; Lipton, 1988). Thus their risk of confusing medications or skipping doses is high (Salzman et al., 1995). Physicians and pharmacists are now trying to simplify medications and to educate older patients about their prescriptions, clarifying directions and teaching them to watch for undesired effects.

Delirium and Dementia

Delirium is a clouding of consciousness. As the person's awareness of the environment becomes less clear, he or she has great difficulty concentrating, focusing attention, and thinking clearly, which leads to misinterpretations, illusions, and, on occasion, hallucinations (APA, 2000, 1994). Sufferers may believe that it is morning in the middle of the night or that they are home when actually they are in a hospital room.

This state of massive confusion typically develops over a short period of time, usually hours or days. It may occur in any age group, including children, but is most common in elderly persons. In fact, when elderly people enter a hospital to be treated for a general medical condition, at least one in ten of them shows the symptoms of delirium (Meagher, 2001; APA, 2000, 1994). At least another 10 percent develop delirium during their stay in the hospital (Martin et al., 2000; Inouye et al., 1999; Inouye, 1998).

Fever, infections, poor nutrition, head injuries, certain brain diseases, and stress (including the stress of surgery) may all cause delirium (Litaker et al., 2001). So may intoxication by certain substances, such as prescription drugs. Partly because older people face so many of these problems, they are more likely

DELIRIUM A rapidly developing clouding of consciousness in which a person has great difficulty concentrating, focusing attention, and following an orderly sequence of thought.

DEMENTIA A syndrome marked by severe problems in memory and in at least one other cognitive function.

The Oldest Old

Clinicians suggest that aging need not inevitably lead to psychological problems. Nor apparently does it always lead to physical problems. When researchers recently studied people over 95 years of age—often called the "oldest old"—they were surprised to find that these individuals are on average more healthy, clear-headed, and agile than those in their 80s and early 90s (Perls, 1995). Many, in fact, are still employed, sexually active, and able to enjoy the outdoors and the arts.

Some scientists believe that individuals who live this long carry "longevity" genes that make them resistant to disabling or terminal infections (Perls, 1995). The individuals themselves often credit a good frame of mind or regular behaviors that they have maintained for many years—eating healthful food, pursuing regular exercise, not smoking.

ConsiderThis

- The "oldest old" often seem particularly well adjusted. Does their positive frame of mind lead to longevity, or does outstanding health produce greater happiness? • Why do many in this age group attribute their longevity to psychological factors, while scientists seem to prefer biological explanations?

John Parrish, a 104-year-old medicine man living in Monument Valley, Arizona.

than younger ones to experience delirium. If a health professional accurately identifies delirium, it can often be easy to correct—by treating the underlying infection, for example, or changing the patient's drug prescription. However, delirium is not always recognized for what it is (Monette et al., 2001; Inouye, 1999, 1998). One study on a medical ward found that admission doctors detected only one of fifteen consecutive cases of delirium (Cameron et al., 1987).

As we saw in Chapter 13, **dementia** is a syndrome marked by severe problems in memory and in at least one other cognitive function, such as abstract thinking, judgment, or language. All people experience some cognitive losses as they age, but only a minority develop dementia. People with this syndrome may also undergo extreme personality and behavioral changes, and their symptoms may worsen progressively. Some also react to their disorder with agitation, anxiety, or depression. As we have seen, the occurrence of dementia is closely related to age. Around 1 to 2 percent of people 65 years of age experience it, compared to more than one-quarter of those over the age of 85 (Cowley, 2000; DeLeon et al., 1996). Dementia is sometimes confused with delirium, and in fact the two may occur together.

Like delirium, dementia sometimes has a cause that is reversible. Some sufferers, for example, have nutritional disorders that can be corrected. Similarly, improving vision and hearing can improve the cognitive functioning of some individuals (Evenhuis, 1999). However, most cases of dementia are caused by neurological problems, such as Alzheimer's disease and stroke, which currently are difficult or impossible to change (see pages 396–404).

Issues Affecting the Mental Health of the Elderly

As the study and treatment of elderly people have progressed, three issues have raised concern among clinicians: the problems faced by elderly members of ethnic minority groups, the inadequacies of long-term care, and the need for a health-maintenance approach to medical care in an aging world (Gallagher-Thompson & Thompson, 1995).

Discrimination due to ethnicity has long been a problem in the United States (see Chapter 2), and many people suffer as a result, particularly those who are old (Cavanaugh, 1990). To be both old and a member of a minority group is

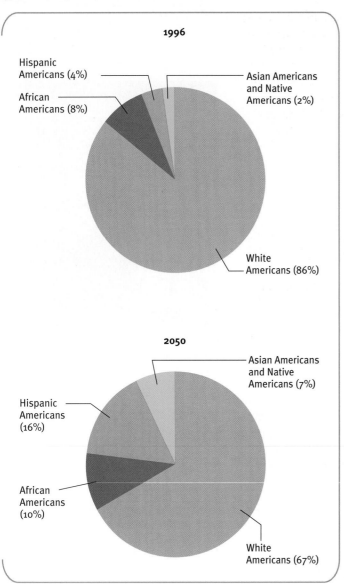

1996

Hispanic Americans (4%)

African Americans (8%)

Asian Americans and Native Americans (2%)

White Americans (86%)

2050

Asian Americans and Native Americans (7%)

Hispanic Americans (16%)

African Americans (10%)

White Americans (67%)

FIGURE 15-5 **Ethnicity and old age** *The elderly population is becoming racially and ethnically more diverse. In the United States today, 86 percent of all people over the age of 65 are white Americans. By 2050, only 67 percent of the elderly will be in this group. (Adapted from Hobbs, 1997; NIA, 1996.)*

considered a kind of "double jeopardy" by many observers. For older women in minority groups, the difficulties are sometimes termed "triple jeopardy," as many more older women than older men live alone, are widowed, and are poor. Clinicians must take into account their older patients' ethnicity as they try to diagnose and treat their mental health problems (Cook et al., 2000; Kelty et al., 2000) (see Figure 15-5).

Some elderly people from ethnic minority groups face language barriers that interfere with their medical and mental health care. Others may hold cultural beliefs that prevent them from seeking services. Moreover, many members of minority groups do not trust the majority establishment or do not know about medical and mental health services that are sensitive to their culture and their particular needs (Ralston, 1991; Jackson, 1988). As a result, it is common for elderly members of ethnic minority groups to rely solely on family members or friends for remedies and health care.

Many older people require *long-term care,* a general term that may refer variously to the services offered in a partially supervised apartment, in a senior housing complex for mildly impaired elderly persons, or in a nursing home where skilled medical and nursing care are available around the clock. The quality of care in such residences varies widely.

At any given time in the United States, only about 5 percent of the elderly population actually live in nursing homes, but most older adults live in fear of being "put away" (NCHS, 1999; Hobbs, 1997). They fear having to move, losing independence, and living in a medical environment. Many elderly people know someone who died shortly after being admitted to a long-term care facility, and this awareness increases their fears about life in such settings (Gallagher-Thompson & Thompson, 1995).

Many also worry about the cost of long-term care facilities. Families today are trying to keep elderly relatives at home longer, and so most older people enter nursing homes only in the last stages of a disease and in need of almost total care. Around-the-clock nursing care is expensive, and nursing home costs continue to rise. The health insurance plans available today do not even begin to cover the costs of long-term or permanent placement (Gallagher-Thompson & Thompson, 1995). Worry over these issues can greatly harm the mental health of older adults, perhaps leading to depression and anxiety as well as family conflict (Banerjee & Macdonald, 1996).

Stimulating effects *When long-term care institutions offer stimulating programs (such as this exercise class for people with Alzheimer's disease), allow patients to control their lives, and involve family members and friends, elderly persons are generally happier and show relatively better cognitive functioning.*

Lynn Johnson/Black Star

Finally, clinicians suggest that the current generation of young adults should take a *health-maintenance,* or *wellness,* approach to their own aging process. In other words, they should do things that promote physical and mental health—avoid smoking, eat well-balanced and healthful meals, exercise regularly, and take advantage of psychoeducational, stress management, and other mental health programs. There is a growing belief that older adults will adapt more readily to changes and negative events if their physical and psychological health is reasonably good (Gallagher-Thompson & Thompson, 1995).

SUMMING UP

Disorders of Later Life

The problems of the elderly are often linked to the losses and other stresses and changes that occur with advancing age. As many as 50 percent of elderly people would benefit from mental health services, yet fewer than 20 percent receive them.

Depression is the most common mental health problem of older adults. Cognitive therapy, antidepressant drugs, or both are often used to treat elderly people with this disorder. Older people may also suffer from generalized anxiety disorder or other anxiety disorders. If identified, these problems are often treated with psychotherapy or drug therapy. In addition, between 3 and 5 percent of older persons have alcohol-related problems in any given year, and many others misuse prescription drugs.

Older people are more likely than people of other age groups to experience delirium, a clouding of consciousness in which individuals have great difficulty concentrating, focusing attention, and keeping a straightforward stream of thought. Dementia, a syndrome characterized by severe memory loss and other cognitive disturbances, also becomes increasingly common in older age groups.

As the study and treatment of the problems of old age have increased, clinicians have become concerned about three issues: discrimination due to ethnicity, inadequacies of long-term care, and the need for health maintenance by young adults.

AGING AND RELIGION

On average, the death rate of elderly people who regularly attend religious services is 46 percent lower than the rate of those who attend infrequently (Koenig et al., 1999).

CROSSROADS:
Clinicians Discover the Young and the Elderly

Early in the twentieth century, mental health professionals virtually ignored children and the elderly. Today the problems of these groups have caught the attention of researchers and clinicians (Jellinek, 1999). Although all of the leading models have been used to help explain and treat these problems, the sociocultural perspective—especially the family perspective—is considered to play a special role.

Because both children and the elderly have limited control over their lives, they are greatly affected by the attitudes and reactions of family members. Clinicians must therefore deal with those attitudes and reactions as they try to address the problems of the young and the old. Treatments for conduct disorder, ADHD, mental retardation, and other problems of childhood typically fall short unless clinicians educate and work with the family as well. Similarly, clinicians who treat elderly patients with dementia are most successful when they also consider the concerns and needs of the family caregivers.

At the same time, clinicians who work with children, adolescents, and the elderly have learned that a narrow focus on any one model can lead to problems. For years autism was explained exclusively by family factors, misleading theorists and therapists alike, and adding to the pain of parents already devastated by their child's disorder. In the past, too, the sociocultural model often led professionals

ConsiderThis

 Although boys with psychological disorders outnumber girls, adult women with such disorders outnumber adult men. Some theorists believe that this age-related shift in prevalence rates reflects the special pressures felt by women in Western society. What kinds of factors might be operating here? • Could there be other explanations for the shift?

wrongly to accept the depression and anxiety of elderly people as inevitable, given the many losses suffered in old age.

The increased clinical focus on the young and the elderly has been accompanied by increased attention to their human and legal rights. More and more clinicians have called on government agencies to protect the rights and safety of these sometimes powerless groups. In doing so, they hope to fuel the fight against child abuse and neglect, sexual abuse, malnourishment, and fetal alcohol syndrome, and to better address the health and financial needs of the elderly.

As the mistreatment of young people receives greater attention and as the elderly population grows larger, the special needs of these groups are becoming more visible. Thus the study and treatment of their psychological problems are likely to continue at a rapid pace. Now that clinicians and public officials have "discovered" these populations, they are not likely to underestimate their needs and importance again.

KEY TERMS

separation anxiety disorder p. 443

school phobia p. 444

play therapy p. 445

oppositional defiant disorder p. 446

conduct disorder p. 446

attention-deficit/hyperactivity disorder (ADHD) p. 449

methylphenidate (Ritalin) p. 451

enuresis p. 451

encopresis p. 452

autistic disorder p. 454

self-stimulatory behavior p. 455

self-injurious behavior p. 455

theory of mind p. 456

cerebellum p. 457

augmentative communication system p. 458

group home p. 458

mental retardation p. 459

intelligence quotient p. 459

mild retardation p. 461

moderate retardation p. 462

severe retardation p. 462

profound retardation p. 462

Down syndrome p. 463

fragile X syndrome p. 463

recessive genes p. 463

phenylketonuria (PKU) p. 463

fetal alcohol syndrome p. 464

lead poisoning p. 464

state school p. 464

deinstitutionalization p. 464

normalization p. 465

special education p. 465

mainstreaming p. 465

token economy program p. 465

sheltered workshop p. 466

delirium p. 468

dementia p. 469

QUICK QUIZ

1. How do anxiety disorders and depression in childhood compare with adult versions of these disorders? What are separation anxiety disorder and school phobia? pp. 443–446

2. What are the prevalence rates and gender ratios for the various childhood disorders? pp. 443, 446, 450, 451, 452, 454

3. Describe oppositional defiant disorder and conduct disorders. What factors help cause conduct disorders, and how are these disorders treated? pp. 446–447

4. What are the symptoms of attention-deficit/hyperactivity disorder? What are the current treatments for it, and how effective are they? pp. 449–451

5. What are enuresis and encopresis? How are these disorders treated? pp. 451–452

6. What are the symptoms and possible causes of autism? pp. 454–457

7. What are the overall goals of treatment for autism, and which interventions have been most helpful for individuals with this disorder? pp. 457–458

8. Describe the different levels of mental retardation, and discuss their causes. pp. 459–464

9. What kinds of residences, educational programs, treatments, and community programs are helpful to persons with mental retardation? pp. 464–466

10. What kinds of psychological problems are common in elderly people, and how are they treated? pp. 467–469

CYBER STUDY

▲ *Observe the symptoms of ADHD in action.* ▲ *When do a child's behaviors call for a clinical diagnosis and treatment?* ▲ *Observe the educational mainstreaming of a young man with autism.* ▲ *Witness savant skills.* ▲ *Observe the symptoms and impact of dementia.*

SEARCH THE *FUNDAMENTALS OF ABNORMAL PSYCHOLOGY* CD-ROM FOR

▲ Chapter 15 video cases and discussions
  "Michael"—ADHD
  "Joseph"—Autism

▲ Chapter 15 practice test and feedback

▲ Additional video case and discussion
  "Walter"—Alzheimer's Disease

LOG ON TO THE COMER WEB PAGE FOR

▲ Suggested Web links, research exercises, FAQ page, additional Chapter 15 practice test questions

  <www.worthpublishers.com/comer>

UCLA Neuropsychiatric Institute & Hospital

Law, Society, and the Mental Health Profession

Dear Jodie:

There is a definite possibility that I will be killed in my attempt to get Reagan. It is for this very reason that I am writing you this letter now. As you well know by now, I love you very much. The past seven months I have left you dozens of poems, letters and messages in the faint hope you would develop an interest in. . . . Jodie, I would abandon this idea of getting Reagan in a second if I could only win your heart and live out the rest of my life with you, whether it be in total obscurity or whatever. I will admit to you that the reason I'm going ahead with this attempt now is because I just cannot wait any longer to impress you. I've got to do something now to make you understand in no uncertain terms that I am doing all of this for your sake. By sacrificing my freedom and possibly my life I hope to change your mind about me. This letter is being written an hour before I leave for the Hilton Hotel. Jodie, I'm asking you please to look into your heart and at least give me the chance with this historical deed to gain your respect and love. I love you forever.

JOHN HINCKLEY

John W. Hinckley, Jr., wrote this letter to the actress Jodie Foster in March 1981. Soon after writing it, he stood waiting, pistol ready, outside the Washington Hilton Hotel. Moments later, President Ronald Reagan came out of the hotel, and the popping of pistol fire was heard. As Secret Service men pushed Reagan into the limousine, a policeman and the president's press secretary fell to the pavement. The president had been shot, and by nightfall most of America had seen the face and heard the name of the disturbed young man from Colorado.

We have observed throughout this book that the psychological dysfunctioning of an individual does not occur in isolation. It is influenced—sometimes caused—by societal and social pressures, and it affects the lives of relatives, friends, and acquaintances. The case of John Hinckley demonstrates in powerful terms that individual dysfunction may, in some cases, also affect the well-being and rights of people the person does not know.

By the same token, clinical scientists and practitioners do not conduct their work in isolation. As they study and treat people with psychological problems, they are affecting and being affected by other institutions of society. We have seen, for example, how the government regulates the use of psychotropic medications, how clinicians have helped carry out the government's policy of deinstitutionalization, and how clinicians have called the psychological ordeal of Vietnam veterans to the attention of society.

In short, like their clients, clinical professionals operate within a complex social system, and in fact, it is the system that assigns responsibilities to these professionals. Just as we must understand the social context in which abnormal behavior occurs in order to understand the behavior, so must we understand the context in which this behavior is studied and treated.

Two social institutions have a particularly strong impact on the mental health profession—the legislative and judicial systems. These institutions—collectively, the legal field—have long been responsible for protecting both the public good and the rights of individuals. Sometimes the relationship between the legal field and the mental health field has been friendly (Bersoff et al., 1997), and they have worked together to protect the rights and meet the needs of troubled individuals and of society at large. At other times, they have clashed, and one field has imposed its will on the other.

This relationship has two aspects. On the one hand, mental health professionals often play a role in the criminal justice system, as when they are called upon to help the courts assess the mental stability of people accused of crimes, for example. They responded to this call in the Hinckley case, as we shall see, and in thousands of other cases. On the other hand, the legislative and judicial systems are responsible for regulating certain aspects of mental health care. The courts may, for example, force some individuals to enter treatment, even against their will. In addition, the law protects the rights of patients.

How Do Clinicians Influence the Criminal Justice System?

To be able to arrive at just and appropriate punishments, the courts need to know whether defendants are *responsible* for the crimes they commit and *capable* of defending themselves in court. If not, it would be inappropriate to find individuals guilty or punish them in the usual manner. The courts have decided that in some instances people who suffer from severe *mental instability* may not be responsible for their actions or may not be able to defend themselves in court, and so should not be punished in the usual way. Although the courts make the final judgment as to mental instability, their decisions are guided to a large degree by the opinions of mental health professionals.

When people accused of crimes are judged to be mentally unstable, they are usually sent to a mental institution for treatment, a process called **criminal commitment.** Actually there are several forms of criminal commitment. In one, individuals are judged mentally unstable *at the time of their crimes* and so innocent of wrongdoing. They may plead **not guilty by reason of insanity (NGRI)** and bring mental health professionals into court to support their claim. When people are found not guilty on this basis, they are committed for treatment until they improve enough to be released.

In a second form of criminal commitment, individuals are judged mentally unstable *at the time of their trial* and so are considered unable to understand the trial procedures and defend themselves in court. They are committed for treatment until they are competent to stand trial. Once again, the testimony of mental health professionals helps determine the defendant's psychological functioning.

These judgments of mental instability have stirred many arguments. Some people consider the judgments to be "loopholes" in the legal system that allow criminals to escape proper punishment for wrongdoing. Others argue that a legal system simply cannot be just unless it allows for extenuating circumstances, such as mental instability. The practice of criminal commitment differs from country to country. In this chapter we shall observe primarily how it operates in the United States. Although the specific principles and procedures of each country may differ, most countries grapple with the same issues, concerns, and decisions that we shall be examining.

Criminal Commitment and Insanity during Commission of a Crime

Consider once again the case of John Hinckley. Was he insane at the time he shot the president? If insane, should he be held responsible for his actions? On June 21, 1982, fifteen months after he shot four men in the nation's capital, a jury pronounced Hinckley not guilty by reason of insanity. Hinckley thus joined Richard Lawrence, a house painter who shot at Andrew Jackson in 1835, and

---

> "Our [legal] confusion is eliminated, we believe, if we resort to that quintessential twentieth-century solution to hard problems: We refer the problem to an expert."
>
> Winslade & Ross, 1983

CRIMINAL COMMITMENT A legal process by which people accused of a crime are instead judged mentally unstable and sent to a mental health facility for treatment.

NOT GUILTY BY REASON OF INSANITY (NGRI) A verdict stating that defendants are not guilty of committing a crime because they were insane at the time of the crime.

M'NAGHTEN TEST A widely used legal test for insanity that holds people to be insane at the time they committed a crime if, because of a mental disorder, they did not know the nature of the act or did not know right from wrong.

IRRESISTIBLE IMPULSE TEST A legal test for insanity that holds people to be insane at the time they committed a crime if they were driven to do so by an uncontrollable "fit of passion."

DURHAM TEST A legal test for insanity that holds people to be insane at the time they committed a crime if their act was the result of a mental disorder or defect.

AMERICAN LAW INSTITUTE TEST A legal test for insanity that holds people to be insane at the time they committed a crime if, because of a mental disorder, they did not know right from wrong or they could not resist an uncontrollable impulse to act.

John Schrank, a saloonkeeper who shot former president Teddy Roosevelt in 1912, as a would-be assassin who was found not guilty by reason of insanity.

It is important to recognize that "insanity" is a *legal* term. That is, the definition of "insanity" used in criminal cases was written by legislators, not by clinicians. Defendants may have mental disorders but not necessarily qualify for a legal definition of insanity. Modern Western definitions of insanity can be traced to the murder case of Daniel M'Naghten in England in 1843. M'Naghten shot and killed Edward Drummond, the secretary to British Prime Minister Robert Peel, while trying to shoot Peel. Because of M'Naghten's apparent delusions of persecution, the jury found him to be not guilty by reason of insanity. The public was outraged by this decision, and their angry outcry forced the British law lords to define the insanity defense more clearly. This legal definition, known as the **M'Naghten test** *or rule,* stated that experiencing a mental disorder at the time of a crime does not by itself mean that the person was insane; the defendant also had to be *unable to know right from wrong.* The state and federal courts in the United States adopted this test as well.

In the late nineteenth century some state and federal courts in the United States, dissatisfied with the M'Naghten rule, adopted a different test—the **irresistible impulse test.** This test, which had first been used in Ohio in 1834, emphasized the inability to control one's actions. A person who committed a crime during an uncontrollable "fit of passion" was considered insane and not guilty under this test.

For years, state and federal courts chose between the M'Naghten test and the irresistible impulse test to determine the sanity of criminal defendants. For a while a third test, called the **Durham test,** also became popular, but it was soon replaced in most courts. This test, based on a decision handed down by the Supreme Court in 1954 in the case of *Durham v. United States,* stated simply that people are not criminally responsible if their "unlawful act was the product of mental disease or mental defect." This test was meant to offer more flexibility in court decisions, but it proved too flexible. Insanity defenses could point to such problems as alcoholism or other forms of substance dependence, and conceivably even headaches or ulcers, which were listed as psychophysiological disorders in DSM-I.

In 1955 the American Law Institute (ALI) developed a test that combined aspects of the M'Naghten, irresistible impulse, and Durham tests. The **American Law Institute test** held that people are not criminally responsible if they had a mental disorder or defect at the time of a crime that prevented them from knowing right from wrong *or* from being able to control themselves and to follow the law. For a time the new test became the most widely accepted legal test of insanity. After the Hinckley verdict, however, there was a public uproar over the "liberal" ALI guidelines, and people called for tougher standards.

Partly in response to this uproar, the American Psychiatric Association recommended in 1983 that people should be found not guilty by reason of insanity *only if* they did not know right from wrong at the time of the crime; an inability to control themselves and to follow the law should no longer be sufficient grounds for a judgment of insanity. In short, the association was calling for a return to the M'Naghten test. This test now is used in all cases tried in federal courts and in about half of the state courts (Steadman et al., 1993). The more liberal ALI standard is still used in the remaining state courts, except in Idaho, Montana, and Utah, which have done away with the insanity plea altogether. Research has not found, however, that the stricter M'Naghten definition actually reduces the likelihood of verdicts of not guilty by reason of insanity (Ogloff et al., 1992; Finkel, 1991, 1990, 1989).

People suffering from severe mental disorders in which confusion is a major feature may not be able to tell right from wrong or to control their behavior

Would-be assassin *Few courtroom decisions have spurred as much debate or legislative action as the jury's verdict that John Hinckley, having been captured in the act of shooting President Ronald Reagan, was not guilty by reason of insanity.*

"[John Hinckley suffers from] schizophrenia."

Expert defense witness, June 7, 1982

"Hinckley does not suffer from schizophrenia."

Expert prosecution witness, June 7, 1982

"[Hinckley had] a very severe depressive disorder."

Expert defense witness, May 20, 1982

"There is little to suggest he was seriously depressed [the day of the shootings]."

Expert prosecution witness, June 4, 1982

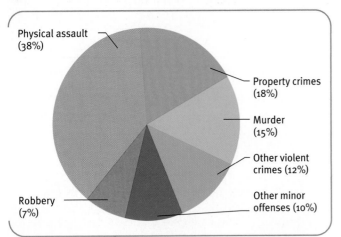

FIGURE 16-1 **Crimes for which persons are found not guilty by reason of insanity (NGRI)** *A review of NGRI verdicts in eight states revealed that most people who were acquitted on this basis had been charged with a crime of violence. (Based on Steadman et al., 1993; Callahan et al., 1991.)*

M'NAGHTEN'S FATE

After being judged not guilty by reason of insanity, Daniel M'Naghten lived in a mental hospital until his death 22 years later (Slovenko, 1995).

ConsiderThis

⦿ After a patient has been criminally committed to an institution, why might a clinician be reluctant to declare that the person is mentally stable and unlikely to commit the same crime again, even if the patient shows significant improvement?

(Nestor & Haycock, 1997; Elliott, 1996). It is therefore not surprising that approximately two-thirds of defendants who are acquitted of a crime by reason of insanity qualify for a diagnosis of schizophrenia (Steadman et al., 1993). The vast majority of these acquitted defendants have a history of past hospitalization, arrest, or both. About half who successfully plead insanity are white, and 86 percent are male. Their mean age is 32 years. The crimes for which defendants are found not guilty by reason of insanity vary greatly. However, approximately 65 percent are violent crimes of some sort (Steadman et al., 1993). Close to 15 percent of those acquitted are accused specifically of murder (see Figure 16-1).

WHAT CONCERNS ARE RAISED BY THE INSANITY DEFENSE? Despite the changes in the insanity tests, criticism of the insanity defense continues (Slovenko, 1995). One concern is the fundamental difference between the law and the science of human behavior. The law assumes that individuals have free will and are generally responsible for their actions. Several models of human behavior, in contrast, assume that physical or psychological forces act to determine the individual's behavior. Inevitably, then, legal definitions of insanity and responsibility will differ from those suggested by clinical research.

A second criticism points to the uncertainty of scientific knowledge about abnormal behavior. During a typical insanity defense trial, the testimony of defense clinicians conflicts with that of clinicians hired by the prosecution, and so the jury must weigh the claims of "experts" who disagree in their assessments. Some people see this lack of professional agreement as evidence that clinical knowledge in some areas may be too incomplete to be allowed to influence important legal decisions (Golding et al., 1999; Slovenko, 1995). Others counter that the field has made great advances—for example, developing several psychological scales to help clinicians discriminate more consistently between the sane and insane according to the M'Naghten standard (Rogers & Shuman, 2000; Rogers & Sewell, 1999).

Even with helpful scales in hand, however, clinicians making judgments of legal insanity face a problem that is hard to overcome: they must evaluate the state of mind a defendant was in during an event that occurred weeks, months, or years earlier. Because mental states can and do change over time and across situations, clinicians can never be entirely certain that their assessments of mental instability at the time of the crime are accurate.

Perhaps the criticism of the insanity defense most often heard is that it allows dangerous criminals to escape punishment. Granted, some people who successfully plead insanity are released from treatment facilities just months after their acquittal. Yet the number of such cases is quite small. According to surveys, the public dramatically overestimates the percentage of defendants who plead insanity, guessing it to be 30 to 40 percent, when in fact it is less than 1 percent (Steadman et al., 1993). Moreover, only a minority of these persons fake or exaggerate their psychological symptoms (Fauteck, 1995), and only one-quarter of defendants who plead insanity are actually found not guilty on this basis (Callahan et al., 1991). In the end, fewer than 1 of every 400 defendants in the United States is found not guilty by reason of insanity.

During most of U.S. history, a successful insanity plea amounted to the equivalent of a long-term prison sentence (Callahan & Silver, 1998). In fact, treatment in a mental hospital often resulted in a longer period of confinement than a verdict of guilty would have brought (Lymburner & Roesch, 1999; Ogloff et al., 1992). Because hospitalization resulted in little, if any, improvement, clinicians were reluctant to predict that the offenders would not repeat their crimes. Today, however, offenders are being released from mental hospitals earlier and earlier. This trend is the result of the increasing effectiveness of drug therapy in institutions, the growing reaction against extended institutionalization, and a greater emphasis on patients' rights (Blackburn, 1993). In 1992, in the case of *Foucha v.*

STEPPING BACK

Famous Insanity Defense Cases

1977 In Michigan, Francine Hughes poured gasoline around the bed where her husband, Mickey, lay in a drunken stupor. Then she lit a match and set him on fire. At her trial she explained that he had beaten her repeatedly for 14 years, and he had threatened to kill her if she tried to leave him. The jury found her not guilty by reason of temporary insanity, making her into a symbol for many abused women across the nation. Some people saw the decision as confirmation of a woman's right to self-defense in her own home.

1978 David "Son of Sam" Berkowitz, a serial killer in New York City, explained that a barking dog had sent him demonic messages to kill. Although two psychiatrists assessed him as psychotic, he was found guilty of his crimes. Long after his trial, he said that he had actually made up the delusions.

1979 Kenneth Bianchi, one of the pair known as the Hillside Stranglers, entered a plea of not guilty by reason of insanity but was found guilty along with his cousin of sexually assaulting and murdering women in the Los Angeles area in late 1977 and early 1978. He claimed that he had multiple personality disorder.

1980 In December, Mark David Chapman murdered John Lennon. Chapman later explained that he had killed the rock music legend because he believed Lennon to be a "sell-out." He also described hearing the voice of God, considered himself his generation's "catcher in the rye" (from the J. D. Salinger novel), and compared himself to Moses. Despite clinical testimony that supported Chapman's plea of not guilty by reason of insanity, he was ultimately convicted of murder.

1981 In an attempt to prove his love for the actress Jodie Foster, John W. Hinckley, Jr., tried to assassinate President Ronald Reagan. Hinckley was found not guilty by reason of insanity and was committed to St. Elizabeth's Hospital for the criminally insane in Washington, where he remains today.

1992 Jeffrey Dahmer, a 31-year-old mass murderer in Milwaukee, was tried for the killings of 15 young men. Dahmer apparently drugged some of his victims and performed crude lobotomies on them in an attempt to create zombielike companions for himself. He also dismembered his victims' bodies and stored their parts to be eaten. Although his defense attorney argued that Dahmer was not guilty by reason of insanity, the jury found him guilty as charged. He was beaten to death by another inmate in 1995.

1994 On June 23, 1993, 24-year-old Lorena Bobbitt cut off her husband's penis with a 12-inch kitchen knife while he slept. During her trial, defense attorneys argued that after years of abuse by John Bobbitt, his wife suffered a brief psychotic episode and was seized by an "irresistible impulse" to cut off his penis after he came home drunk and raped her. In 1994, the jury acquitted her of the charge of malicious wounding by reason of temporary insanity. She was committed to a state mental hospital for further assessment and treatment and released a few months later.

1997 John E. Du Pont, 57-year-old heir to his family's chemical fortune, shot and killed the Olympic wrestling champion Dave Schultz in January 1995. The murder took place on Du Pont's 800-acre estate, where he had built a sports center for amateur athletes. Schultz, his close friend, had coached wrestlers at the center. In 1997, Du Pont was found guilty of third-degree murder, but mentally ill, and he was sentenced to prison for 13 to 30 years. He is currently receiving treatment at the mental health unit of a correctional institution.

Guilty and not insane *Theodore Kaczynski, the so-called Unabomber, who sent mail bombs to unsuspecting victims for 18 years, refused all legal efforts to have himself judged mentally incompetent to stand trial or to plead not guilty by reason of insanity. Preferring a conviction for murder to a label of insanity, he pleaded guilty in a federal court in 1998 and is now serving a life sentence without parole.*

John Youngbear/AP Photo

JOHN HINCKLEY, 1999

In 1999, a U.S. court of appeals ruled that John Hinckley may make supervised day trips away from St. Elizabeth's Hospital, in Washington, D.C., where he is currently confined.

"I feel the insanity defense should be retained. I bear no grudge against John Hinckley, but I sure don't hope he wins the Irish Sweepstakes."

James Brady, presidential news secretary shot by John Hinckley

DAN WHITE: THE AFTERMATH

Dan White was released from prison in 1984 and spent a year on parole. He committed suicide in 1985.

Louisiana, the U.S. Supreme Court clarified that the *only* acceptable basis for determining the release of hospitalized offenders is whether or not they are still "insane"; they cannot be kept indefinitely in mental hospitals solely because they are dangerous. Some states are able to maintain control over offenders even after their release from hospitals (Hiday, 1999). The states may insist on community treatment, monitor the patients closely, and rehospitalize them if necessary.

WHAT OTHER VERDICTS ARE AVAILABLE? In recent years 13 states have added another verdict option—**guilty but mentally ill** (Slovenko, 1995). Defendants who receive this verdict are found to have had a mental illness at the time of their crimes, but the illness was not fully related to or responsible for the crime. The guilty-but-mentally-ill option enables jurors to convict a person they view as dangerous while also suggesting that the individual receive needed treatment. Defendants found to be guilty but mentally ill are given a prison term with the added recommendation that they also undergo treatment if necessary.

In Georgia, juries given the option of finding a person guilty but mentally ill have delivered fewer insanity acquittals (Callahan et al., 1992). Studies with mock juries have found that many jurors prefer having this third option, seeing it as "moral, just and an adequate means of providing for the treatment needs of mentally ill offenders" (Boudouris, 2000; Roberts et al., 1987). However, those who criticize this option point out that appropriate mental health care is supposed to be available to all prisoners anyway, regardless of the verdict. They argue that the new option differs from a guilty verdict in name only (Slovenko, 1995; Tanay, 1992).

Some states allow still another kind of defense, *guilty with diminished capacity.* Here a defendant's mental dysfunctioning is viewed as an extenuating circumstance that the court should take into consideration when determining the precise crime of which he or she is guilty (Clark, 1999). The defense lawyer argues that because of mental dysfunctioning, the defendant could not have *intended* to commit a particular crime. The person can then be found guilty of a lesser crime—of manslaughter (unlawful killing without intent), say, instead of murder in the first degree (planned murder). The case of Dan White, who shot and killed Mayor George Moscone and City Supervisor Harvey Milk of San Francisco in 1978, illustrates the use of this verdict.

. . . Defense attorney Douglas Schmidt argued that a patriotic, civic-minded man like Dan White—high school athlete, decorated war veteran, former fireman, policeman, and city supervisor—could not possibly have committed such an act unless something had snapped inside him. The brutal nature of the two final shots to each man's head only proved that White had lost his wits. White was not fully responsible for his actions because he suffered from "diminished capacity." Although White killed Mayor George Moscone and Supervisor Harvey Milk, he had not planned his actions. On the day of the shootings, White was mentally incapable of planning to kill, or even of wanting to do such a thing.

Well known in forensic psychiatry circles, Martin Blinder, professor of law and psychiatry at the University of California's Hastings Law School in San Francisco, brought a good measure of academic prestige to White's defense. White had been, Blinder explained to the jury, "gorging himself on junk food: Twinkies, Coca-Cola. . . . The more he consumed, the worse he'd feel and he'd respond to his ever-growing depression by consuming ever more junk food." Schmidt later asked Blinder if he could elaborate on this. "Perhaps if it were not for the ingestion of this junk food," Blinder responded, "I would suspect that these homicides would not have taken place." From that moment on, Blinder became known as the author of the Twinkie defense. . . .

Dan White was convicted only of voluntary manslaughter, and was sentenced to seven years, eight months. (He was released on parole January 6, 1984.) Psychiatric testimony convinced the jury that White did not wish to kill George Moscone or Harvey Milk.

(Coleman, 1984, pp. 65-70)

Justice served? *Mass protests took place in San Francisco after Dan White was convicted of voluntary manslaughter rather than premeditated murder in the killings of Mayor George Moscone and Supervisor Harvey Milk, one of the nation's leading gay activists. For many, the 1979 verdict highlighted the serious pitfalls of the "diminished capacity" defense.*

Because of possible miscarriages of justice, many legal experts have argued against the "diminished-capacity" defense (Slovenko, 1992; Coleman, 1984), and a number of states have eliminated it. Some studies find, however, that jurors are often capable of using the option in careful and appropriate ways (Finkel & Duff, 1989; Finkel et al., 1985).

WHAT ARE SEX OFFENDER STATUTES? Since 1937, when Michigan passed the first "sex psychopath" law, some states have placed sex offenders in a special legal category (Bumby & Maddox, 1999; Monahan & Davis, 1983). These states believe that people who are repeatedly found guilty of certain sex crimes have a mental disorder, and so the states categorize them as *mentally disordered sex offenders*.

People classified in this way have been convicted of a criminal offense and are thus judged to be responsible for their actions. Nevertheless, like people found not guilty by reason of insanity, mentally disordered sex offenders are committed to a mental health facility (Small, 1992). In part, such laws reflect a belief held by some legislators that sex offenders are psychologically disturbed. On a practical level, the laws help protect sex offenders from the physical abuse that they often receive in prison society.

Over the last two decades, a growing number of states have been changing or abolishing these sex-offender laws. There are several reasons for this trend. First, some states have found the laws difficult to apply. Some state laws, for example, require that the offender be found "sexually dangerous beyond a reasonable doubt"—a judgment that is often beyond the reach of the clinical field's expertise (Szasz, 1991). Furthermore, there is evidence that racial bias can affect the use of the sex-offender classification (Sturgeon & Taylor, 1980). White Americans are twice as likely to be granted sex-offender status as African Americans or Hispanic Americans who have been convicted of similar crimes.

Criminal Commitment and Incompetence to Stand Trial

Regardless of their state of mind at the time of a crime, defendants may be judged to be **mentally incompetent** to stand trial. The competence requirement is meant to ensure that defendants understand the charges they are facing and can work with their lawyers to prepare and run an adequate defense (Zapf & Roesch, 2001; Gutheil, 1999). This minimum standard of competence was specified by the Supreme Court in the case of *Dusky v. United States* (1960).

GUILTY BUT MENTALLY ILL A verdict stating that defendants are guilty of committing a crime, but are also suffering from a mental illness that should be treated during their imprisonment.

MENTAL INCOMPETENCE A state of mental instability that leaves defendants unable to understand the legal charges and proceedings they are facing and unable to prepare an adequate defense with their attorneys.

CIVIL COMMITMENT A legal process by which an individual can be forced to undergo mental health treatment.

ASSESSING COMPETENCE

Each year in the United States an estimated 25,000 defendants are assessed for their mental competence to stand trial (Winick, 1995).

ConsiderThis

● In some states, the defense must prove that a defendant was not guilty by reason of insanity, whereas in other states the prosecution must prove that a defendant making this plea was not insane. Which burden of proof is more appropriate?

The issue of competence is most often raised by the defendant's attorney, although prosecutors, arresting police officers, and even the judge may raise it as well (Meyer, 1992). They prefer to err on the side of caution, because some convictions have been reversed on appeal when a defendant's competence was not established at the beginning. When the issue of competence is raised, the judge orders a psychological evaluation, usually on an inpatient basis. Approximately 20 percent of defendants who receive such an evaluation are in fact found to be incompetent to stand trial (Hiday, 1999). If the court decides that the defendant is incompetent, the person is assigned to a mental health facility until competent to stand trial (Bennett & Kish, 1990).

Many more cases of criminal commitment result from decisions of mental incompetence than from verdicts of not guilty by reason of insanity (Roesch et al., 1999). However, the majority of criminals currently institutionalized for psychological treatment in the United States are not from either of these two groups. Rather, they are convicted inmates whose psychological problems have led prison officials to decide they need treatment—either in mental health units within the prison or in mental hospitals.

It is possible that an innocent defendant, ruled incompetent to stand trial, could spend years in a mental health facility with no chance to disprove the criminal accusations. Some defendants have, in fact, served longer "sentences" in mental health facilities awaiting a ruling of competence than they would have served in prison had they been convicted (Meyer, 1992). Such a possibility was reduced when the Supreme Court ruled, in the case of *Jackson v. Indiana* (1972), that an incompetent defendant cannot be indefinitely committed. After a reasonable amount of time, he or she should either be found competent and tried, set free, or transferred to a mental health facility under *civil* commitment procedures.

Until the early 1970s, most states required the commitment of mentally incompetent defendants to maximum-security institutions for the "criminally insane" (Winick, 1983). Under current law, the courts have greater flexibility. In some cases, particularly when the charge is a minor one, the defendant may even be treated on an outpatient basis.

SUMMING UP | **How Do Clinicians Influence the Criminal Justice System?**

The mental health profession interacts with the legislative and judicial institutions in two primary ways. First, clinicians may be called on to help assess the mental stability of people accused of crimes. Second, the legislative and judicial branches of government help regulate mental health care.

Criminal Commitment To impose punishment assumes that individuals are responsible for their crimes and are capable of defending themselves in court. Evaluations by clinicians often result in criminal commitment instead of punishment.

Not Guilty by Reason of Insanity If defendants are judged to have been mentally unstable at the time they committed a crime, they may be found not guilty by reason of insanity and placed in a treatment facility rather than a prison. "Insanity" is a legal term, defined by legislators, not by clinicians. In federal courts and about half the state courts, insanity is judged by the M'Naghten test. This test holds that defendants were insane at the time of a criminal act if they did not know the nature or quality of the act or did not know right from wrong at the time they committed it. Other states use the broader American Law Institute test.

The insanity defense has been criticized on several grounds, and some states now also permit a verdict of guilty but mentally ill. Defendants who receive this verdict are sentenced to prison with the expectation that they will also receive psychological treatment. Another verdict option is guilty with diminished capacity. And in some states convicted sex offenders are considered to have a mental disorder and are assigned to treatment in a mental health facility.

Mental Incompetence Regardless of their state of mind at the time of their crimes, defendants may be ruled mentally incompetent to stand trial, that is, incapable of fully understanding the charges or legal proceedings facing them. If so, they are typically sent to a treatment facility until they are competent to stand trial. They may not, however, be institutionalized indefinitely on the basis of incompetence alone.

How Do the Legislative and Judicial Systems Influence Mental Health Care?

Just as the clinical field has influenced the legal system, so has the legal system had a major impact on clinical practice. First, courts and legislatures have developed the process of **civil commitment,** which allows certain people to be forced into mental health treatment. Although many people who show signs of mental disturbance seek treatment voluntarily, a large number are not aware of their problems or are simply not interested in undergoing therapy. What are clinicians to do for these people? Should they force treatment upon them? Or do people have the right to feel miserable and function poorly? The law has answered this question by developing civil commitment guidelines under which certain people can be forced into treatment (Douglas & Koch, 2001).

Second, the legal system, on behalf of the state, has taken on the responsibility for protecting patients' rights during treatment. This protection extends not only to patients who have been involuntarily committed but also to those who seek treatment voluntarily, even on an outpatient basis.

Civil Commitment

Every year in the United States large numbers of people with mental disorders are involuntarily committed to mental institutions. These civil commitments have long caused controversy and debate. In some ways the law provides greater protection for suspected criminals than for people suspected of psychosis (Burton, 1990).

WHY COMMIT? Generally our legal system permits involuntary commitment of individuals when they are considered to be *in need of treatment* and *dangerous to themselves or others.* People may be dangerous to themselves if they are suicidal or if they act recklessly (for example, drinking a drain cleaner to prove that they are immune to its chemicals). They may be dangerous to others if they seek to harm them or if they unintentionally place others at risk. The state's authority to commit disturbed individuals rests on its duties to protect the interests of the individual and of society: the principles of *parens patriae* and police power (Wettstein, 1988). Under *parens patriae* ("parent of the country"), the state can make decisions that further the patient's best interests and provide protection from self-harm, including a decision of involuntary hospitalization. Conversely, *police power* allows the state to take steps to protect society from a person who is violent or otherwise dangerous.

WHAT ARE THE PROCEDURES FOR CIVIL COMMITMENT? Civil commitment laws vary from state to state. Some basic procedures, however, are common to most of these laws. Often family members begin commitment proceedings. In response to a son's psychotic behavior and repeated assaults on other people, for example, his parents may try to persuade him to seek admission to a mental institution. If the son refuses, the parents may go to court and seek an

"When a man says that he is Jesus or Napoleon . . . he is labeled psychotic and locked up in the madhouse. Freedom of speech is only for normal people."

Thomas S. Szasz, *The Second Sin,* 1973

Legal experts *Each segment of the clinical field has its own "forensic" specialists who represent it in the courts and houses of legislature. Forensic psychologists, psychiatrists, and social workers typically receive special training in such duties as evaluating the functioning of criminal defendants, making recommendations concerning patients' rights, and assessing the psychological trauma experienced by crime victims (Ladds, 1997).*

Serial Murderers: Madness or Badness?

▌ A shy, brilliant boy, he skipped two grades in school and entered Harvard at age 16. He went on to receive a Ph.D. in mathematics from the University of Michigan in 1967. Securing a highly prestigious position at the University of California, Berkeley, he seemed destined for fame and success. But . . . two years into his stint at Berkeley, he decided to drop out of society—opting instead for a grubby . . . existence in rural Montana.

It was here, alone in a 10-foot-by-12-foot shack, that this reclusive eccentric produced his most renowned works: sixteen bombs, three deaths, twenty-three maimings, several taunting letters to the *New York Times,* and a 35,000-word antitechnology manifesto. By the end of his eighteen-year rampage, "Unabomber"—his FBI code name— had become a household word. On April 3, 1996, federal agents raided Theodore Kaczynski's Montana cabin, and his reign of mail bomb terror, which had captured the attention of a nation, was finally put to an end. ▌

(DUFFY, 1996; THOMAS, 1996)

*T*heodore Kaczynski has joined a growing list of serial killers who have fascinated and horrified Americans over the years: Ted Bundy, David Berkowitz ("Son of Sam"), Albert DeSalvo, John Wayne Gacy, Jeffrey Dahmer. Serial murderers seem to kill for the sheer thrill of the experience. Clinical theorists do not yet understand these individuals, but they are beginning to use the information that has been gathered about them to speculate on the psychology behind their violence.

Although each follows a different pattern, serial killers appear to have some characteristics in common. Most are white males between 25 and 34 years old, of average to high intelligence, generally clean-cut, smooth-talking, attractive, and skillful manipulators. For the most part,

these men have no permanent ties to any community and move from place to place in pursuit of the kill. They typically select their victims carefully. Many are fascinated by police work and the popular media and follow their crimes closely in the news (Ressler & Schactman, 1992; Holmes & DeBurger, 1985).

Many serial killers have mental disorders, but they do not typically meet the legal criteria of insanity (Fox & Levin, 1999). Park Dietz, a psychiatrist and highly regarded expert on the subject, offers this explanation:

▌ None of the serial killers I've had the occasion to study or examine has been legally insane, but none has been normal, either. They've all been people who've got mental disorders. But despite their mental disorders, which have to do with their sexual interests and their character, they've been people who knew what they were doing, knew what they were doing was wrong, but chose to do it anyway. ▌

(DOUGLAS, 1996, pp. 344–345)

As a result, the plea of not guilty by reason of insanity is generally unsuccessful for serial killers. This outcome may also be influenced by the concern of communities that a defendant found not guilty by reason of insanity may be released too quickly (Gresham, 1993).

A number of serial killers display severe personality disorders (Ferreira, 2000; Scarf, 1996). Lack of conscience and an utter disregard for people and the rules of society—key features of antisocial personality disorder—are typical. Narcissistic thinking is quite common as well. The feeling of being special may even give the killer an unrealistic belief that he will not get caught (Scarf, 1996). Sexual dysfunction and fantasy also seem to play a part in many cases (Ressler &

Schactman, 1992). Studies have found that vivid fantasies, often sexual and sadistic, may help drive the killer's behavior (Lachmann & Lachmann, 1995; Ressler & Schactman, 1992). Some clinicians also believe that the killers may be trying to overcome general feelings of powerlessness by controlling, hurting, or eliminating those who are momentarily weaker (Fox & Levin, 1999; Levin & Fox, 1985). Studies show that the majority of serial killers were abused as children— physically, sexually, and emotionally (Ressler & Schactman, 1992). Despite such profiles and suspicions, clinical theorists are quick to point out that they do not yet really understand why serial killers behave as they do.

This 1994 artist's sketch of the Unabomber has become a powerful symbol of serial murder and terror.

FBI/Jeanne Boylan/AP/Wide World Photo

involuntary commitment order. If the son is a minor, the process is simple. The Supreme Court has ruled that a hearing is not necessary in such cases, as long as a mental health professional considers commitment necessary. If the son is an adult, however, the process is more involved. The court will usually order a mental examination and allow the person to challenge the commitment in court, often represented by a lawyer (Holstein, 1993).

Although the Supreme Court has offered few guidelines concerning specific procedures of civil commitment, one important decision, in the case of *Addington v. Texas* (1979), outlined the *minimum standard of proof* needed for commitment. Here the Court ruled that before an individual can be committed, there must be "clear and convincing" proof that he or she is mentally ill and has met the state's criteria for involuntary commitment. The ruling does not suggest what criteria should be used. That matter is still left to each state. But, whatever the state's criteria, clinicians must offer clear and convincing proof that the individual meets those criteria. When is proof clear and convincing, according to the Court? When it provides 75 percent certainty that the criteria of commitment have been met. This is far less than the near-total certainty ("beyond a reasonable doubt") required to convict people of committing a crime.

EMERGENCY COMMITMENT Many situations require immediate action; no one can wait for commitment proceedings when a life is at stake. Consider, for example, an emergency room patient who is suicidal or hearing voices demanding hostile actions against others. He or she may need immediate treatment and round-the-clock supervision. If treatment could not be given in such situations without the patient's full consent, the consequences could be tragic (Currier, 1999).

Therefore, many states give clinicians the right to certify that certain patients need temporary commitment and medication. In past years, these states required certification by two *physicians* (not necessarily psychiatrists in some of the states). Today states may allow certification by other mental health professionals as well. The clinicians must declare that the state of mind of the patients makes them dangerous to themselves or others. By tradition, the certifications are often referred to as *two-physician certificates,* or *"2 PCs."* The length of such emergency commitments varies from state to state, but three days is often the limit (Holstein, 1993). Should clinicians come to believe that a longer stay is necessary, formal commitment proceedings may be started during the period of emergency commitment.

WHO IS DANGEROUS? In the past, people with mental disorders were actually less likely than others to commit violent or dangerous acts. This low rate of violence was apparently tied to the fact that so many such individuals lived in institutions. As a result of deinstitutionalization, however, hundreds of thousands of people with severe disturbances now live in the community and receive little, if any, treatment. Some of these individuals are indeed dangerous to themselves or others (Hiday, 1999).

Although approximately 90 percent of people with mental disorders are in no way violent or dangerous (Swanson et al., 1990), studies now suggest at least a small relationship between severe mental disorders and violent behavior (Monahan, 2001; Hodgins et al., 1996). After reviewing a number of studies, John Monahan (1993, 1992), a law and psychology professor, concluded that the rate of violent behavior among persons with severe mental disorders, particularly psychotic disorders, is at least somewhat higher than that of people without such disorders:

- Approximately 15 percent of patients in mental hospitals have assaulted another person prior to admission.

- Around 25 percent of patients in mental hospitals assault another person during hospitalization.

- Approximately 12 percent of all people with schizophrenia, major depression, or bipolar disorder have assaulted other people, compared with 2 percent of persons without a mental disorder.

- Approximately 4 percent of people who report having been violent during the past year suffer from schizophrenia, whereas 1 percent of nonviolent persons suffer from schizophrenia.

INVOLUNTARY COMMUNITY TREATMENT

Thirty-seven states and Washington, D.C., now have *involuntary outpatient commitment* laws, under which outpatients who are considered dangerous can be institutionalized if they fail to keep regular outpatient appointments and take their medications (Applebaum, 2001; Warner, 1999). Few of the states, however, impose the laws very often.

SUBSTANCE USE MAY BE THE KEY

A large study of patients discharged from mental hospitals within the previous year found that only 5 percent of those who remained on medication and stayed away from drugs and alcohol committed violent acts, the same percentage as nonpatients who lived in the same neighborhood. In contrast, 10 percent of patients who used drugs or alcohol committed violent acts after discharge from the hospital (Steadman et al., 1998).

Failure to predict *The 1990s witnessed the growth of a new form of dangerousness—children and adolescents who shoot family members, schoolmates, and teachers. A school-cafeteria surveillance camera captures Dylan Klebold and Eric Harris in the midst of their killing rampage at Columbine High School in Littleton, Colorado, on April 20, 1999. Earlier videos made by the two boys suggest that they had planned their attack for more than a year. Despite building a violent Web site, threatening other students, having problems with the law, and, in the case of one boy, receiving treatment for mental health problems, professionals were not able to predict or prevent their violent behavior.*

"This is how we live [in Russia]: without any arrest warrant or any medical justification four policemen and two doctors come to a healthy man's house. The doctors declare that he is crazy, the police Major shouts: 'We are an Organ of Coercion! Get up!' They twist his arms and drive him off to the mad house."

Aleksandr Solzhenitsyn, Russian novelist and political dissident, 1971

Monahan cautions that the findings do not suggest that people with mental disorders are generally dangerous. But they do indicate that a severe mental disorder may in certain cases be more of a risk factor for violence than mental health experts used to believe.

A judgment of *dangerousness* is often required for involuntary civil commitment. But can mental health professionals accurately predict who will commit violent acts? Research suggests that psychiatrists and psychologists are wrong more often than right when they make *long-term* predictions of violence (Buchanan, 1999, 1997). Most often they overestimate the likelihood that a patient will eventually be violent. On the other hand, studies suggest that *short-term* predictions—that is, predictions of imminent violence—can be more accurate (Binder, 1999). Researchers are now working, with some success, to develop new assessment techniques that use statistical approaches and are more objective in their predictions of dangerousness than the subjective judgments of clinicians (Monahan, 2001; Pinard & Pagan, 2001).

WHAT ARE THE PROBLEMS WITH CIVIL COMMITMENT? Civil commitment has been criticized on several grounds. First is the difficulty of assessing a person's dangerousness. If judgments of dangerousness are often inaccurate, how can one justify their being used to deprive people of liberty (Ennis & Emery, 1978)? Second, the legal definitions of "mental illness" and "dangerousness" are vague. The terms may be defined so broadly that they could be applied to almost anyone an evaluator views as undesirable. Indeed, many civil libertarians worry about the use of involuntary commitment to control people, as occurred in the former Soviet Union and certain other countries where mental hospitals routinely housed people with unpopular political views (Morse, 1982; Ennis & Emery, 1978). A third problem is the sometimes questionable therapeutic value of civil commitment. Research suggests that many people committed involuntarily do not respond well to therapy (Wanck, 1984). It may be that people often need a sense of choice or control in order to succeed in treatment (Langer, 1983). On the basis of these and other arguments, some clinicians suggest that involuntary commitment should be abolished (Szasz, 1977, 1963).

The Separation of Mind and State

During the presidential campaigns of 1992 and 1996, the independent candidate Ross Perot was branded "emotionally unbalanced" by some of his detractors. Perot reacted with good humor and even adopted Willie Nelson's "Crazy" as his theme song. The strategy of questioning the psychological stability of political opponents was taken to the extreme in the former Soviet Union, particularly under the rule of Josef Stalin, when many political opponents were placed in mental hospitals to get them out of the way.

Politically motivated labeling was at work during the mid-nineteenth-century debate over slavery in the United States, when those who favored slavery attacked Abraham Lincoln in the press as "insane" for his antislavery stance (Gamwell & Tomes, 1995). Many people, even among those who were against slavery, feared radical abolitionists and called them mentally unbalanced, blaming them for the nation's turmoil.

The trial of the abolitionist John Brown brought the issue out front for all to see. Brown, a white opponent of slavery, organized a small force of African Americans and white Americans to attack the federal armory at Harpers Ferry

in Virginia. He was captured after two days and tried for murder and treason. Many of Brown's supporters, including his own defense attorneys, urged him to plead not guilty by reason of insanity to avoid the death penalty (Gamwell & Tomes, 1995). Some fellow abolitionists, however, were offended by the suggestion that Brown's actions represented insanity, and Brown himself proudly maintained that he was mentally stable. In the end, Brown was convicted and executed.

As the historians Lynn Gamwell and Nancy Tomes (1995) point out, it was in the interests of both sides of the case to have Brown declared legally insane. Many people who opposed slavery believed that an insanity verdict would identify Brown's radical behavior as a special case and thus calm public fears of violence by abolitionists. On the other hand, many of those who defended slavery believed that a judgment of insanity would hurt Brown's reputation and prevent him from becoming a martyr for the abolitionist cause. Obviously, the verdict pleased neither group.

Clinical labels have been used for political gain throughout the ages. We may not always be able to stop the practice,

Last Moments of John Brown *The abolitionist John Brown's journey to execution is portrayed in Thomas Hovenden's painting* The Last Moments of John Brown, *1884.*

Thomas Hovenden, *The Last Moments of John Brown, 1884.* The Metropolitan Museum of Art, New York.

but we should at least be aware of it. As we read about historical events, we must separate mental health labels that are used correctly from those that seek merely to further a political cause.

TRENDS IN CIVIL COMMITMENT The flexibility of the involuntary commitment laws probably reached a peak in 1962. That year, in the case of *Robinson v. California,* the Supreme Court ruled that imprisoning people who suffered from drug addictions might violate the Constitution's ban on cruel and unusual punishment, and it recommended involuntary civil commitment to a mental hospital as a more reasonable action. This ruling encouraged the civil commitment of many kinds of "social deviants." In the years immediately following, civil commitment procedures granted far fewer rights to "defendants" than the criminal courts did (Holstein, 1993). In addition, involuntarily committed patients found it particularly difficult to obtain release.

During the late 1960s and early 1970s, reporters, novelists, civil libertarians, and others spoke out against the ease with which so many people were being unjustifiably committed to mental hospitals. As the public became more aware of these issues, state legislatures started to pass stricter standards for involuntary commitment (Arben, 1999; Holstein, 1993). Some states, for example, spelled out specific types of behavior that had to be observed before an assessment of dangerousness could be made. Rates of involuntary commitment then declined and release rates rose (Wanck, 1984).

ConsiderThis

◉ Today how are people who have been institutionalized viewed and treated by others? • Is the stigma of hospitalization a legitimate argument against civil commitment?

RIGHT TO TREATMENT The legal right of patients, particularly those who are involuntarily committed, to receive adequate treatment.

RIGHT TO REFUSE TREATMENT The legal right of patients to refuse certain forms of treatment.

Today fewer people are institutionalized through civil commitment procedures than in the past. The lower commitment rate has not led to more criminal behavior or more arrests of people who would have been committed under more flexible criteria (Teplin, Abram, & McClelland, 1994; Hiday, 1992). Nevertheless, some states are concerned that commitment criteria are now too strict, and they are moving toward broadening the criteria once again (Beck & Parry, 1992; Belcher & Blank, 1990). It is not yet clear whether this broadening will lead to a return to the vague commitment procedures of the past.

Protecting Patients' Rights

Over the past two decades, court decisions and state and federal laws have greatly expanded the rights of patients with mental disorders, in particular the *right to treatment* and the *right to refuse treatment.*

HOW IS THE RIGHT TO TREATMENT PROTECTED? When people are committed to mental institutions and do not receive treatment, the institutions become, in effect, prisons for the unconvicted. To many patients in the late 1960s and the 1970s, large state mental institutions were just that. Thus some patients and their attorneys began to demand that the state honor their **right to treatment.** In the case of *Wyatt v. Stickney,* a suit on behalf of institutionalized patients in Alabama in 1972, a federal court ruled that the state was constitutionally obligated to provide "adequate treatment" to all people who had been committed involuntarily. Because conditions in the state's hospitals were so terrible, the judge laid out goals that state officials had to meet, including more therapists, better living conditions, more privacy, more social interactions and physical exercise, and a more proper use of physical restraint and medication. Other states have since adopted many of these standards.

Another important decision was handed down in 1975 by the Supreme Court in the case of *O'Connor v. Donaldson.* After being held in a Florida mental institution for more than 14 years, Kenneth Donaldson sued for release. Donaldson had repeatedly sought release and had been overruled by the institution's psychiatrists. He argued that he and his fellow patients were receiving poor treatment, were being largely ignored by the staff, and were allowed little personal freedom. The Supreme Court ruled in his favor, fined the hospital's superintendent, and said that such institutions must review patients' cases periodically. The justices also ruled that the state cannot continue to institutionalize against their will people who are not dangerous and who are capable of surviving on their own or with the willing help of responsible family members or friends. In a later case of importance, *Youngberg v. Romeo* (1982), the Supreme Court further ruled that

Environmental change *During the past two decades, court decisions have set minimum standards for mental health care and for treatment environments. Some older facilities have been closed or redesigned to meet these standards. Shortly after this photograph was taken, this wing of a mental hospital closed.*

Joe McNally/Matrix

people committed involuntarily have a right to "reasonably nonrestrictive confinement conditions" as well as "reasonable care and safety."

To help protect the rights of patients, Congress passed the Protection and Advocacy for Mentally Ill Individuals Act in 1986 (Woodside & Legg, 1990). This law set up *protection and advocacy systems* in all states and U.S. territories and gave public advocates who worked for patients the power to investigate possible abuse and neglect, and to correct those problems legally.

In recent years public advocates have argued that the right to treatment should also be extended to the tens of thousands of people with severe mental disorders who are repeatedly released from hospitals. Many such people have no place to go and are unable to care for themselves, often winding up homeless or in prisons (Torrey, 1997; SAMHSA, 1993). A number of advocates are now suing federal and state agencies throughout the country, demanding that they fulfill the promises of the community mental health movement (see Chapter 12).

HOW IS THE RIGHT TO REFUSE TREATMENT PROTECTED? During the past two decades the courts have also decided that patients, particularly those in institutions, have the **right to refuse treatment** (Wysoker, 1999). The courts have been reluctant to make a single general ruling on this right because there are so many different kinds of treatment, and a general ruling based on one of them might have unintended effects. Therefore, rulings usually target one specific treatment at a time.

Most of the right-to-refuse-treatment rulings center on *biological treatments* (Wettstein, 1999). These treatments are easier to force on patients without their cooperation than psychotherapy, and they often seem more hazardous. For example, state rulings have consistently granted patients the right to refuse *psychosurgery,* the most irreversible form of physical treatment—and therefore the most dangerous.

Some states have also acknowledged a patient's right to refuse *electroconvulsive therapy (ECT),* the treatment used in many cases of severe depression (see Chapter 6). However, the right-to-refuse issue is more complex with regard to ECT than to psychosurgery. ECT is very effective for many people with severe depression, yet it can cause great upset and can also be misused. Today many states grant patients—particularly voluntary patients—the right to refuse ECT. Usually a patient must be informed fully about the nature of the treatment and must give written consent to it. A number of states continue to permit ECT to be forced on committed patients, whereas others require the consent of a close relative or other third party in such cases.

In the past, patients did not have the right to refuse *psychotropic medications.* As we have seen, however, many psychotropic drugs are very powerful, and some produce effects that are unwanted and dangerous. As these harmful effects have become more apparent, a number of states have granted patients the right to refuse medication. Typically, these states require physicians to explain the purpose of the medication to patients and obtain their written consent. If a patient's refusal is considered incompetent, dangerous, or irrational, the state may allow it to be overturned by an independent psychiatrist, medical committee, or local court (Wettstein, 1999, 1988). However, the refusing patient is supported in this process by a lawyer or other patient advocate.

WHAT OTHER RIGHTS DO PATIENTS HAVE? Court decisions have protected still other patient rights over the past several decades. Patients who perform work in mental institutions, particularly private institutions, are now guaranteed at least a minimum wage. In addition, a district court ruled in 1974 that patients released from state mental hospitals have a right to

ARRESTING THE HOMELESS

Many homeless people with severe mental disorders currently wind up in jail rather than in treatment. Most of them are charged with such infractions as disorderly conduct, trespassing, not paying for a meal, menacing, panhandling, loitering, or "lewd and lascivious behavior" (for example, urinating on a street corner) (Mulhern, 1990; Valdiserri, Carroll, & Harti, 1986).

The right to an appropriate community residence *Although "guaranteed" the right to live in community adult homes, many people with chronic and severe mental disorders receive no treatment or guidance and wind up on the streets or in public shelters, such as this shelter for the homeless in Washington, D.C.*

John Ficara/Woodfin Camp Associates

aftercare and to an appropriate community residence, such as a group home. And in the 1975 case of *Dixon v. Weinberger,* another district court ruled that people with psychological disorders should receive treatment in the least restrictive facility available. If an inpatient program at a community mental health center is available, for example, then that is the facility to which they should be assigned, not a mental hospital. In the 1999 case of *Olmstead v. L.C. et al.* the Supreme Court confirmed that patients have a right to community treatment.

THE "RIGHTS" DEBATE   Certainly, people with psychological disorders have civil rights that must be protected at all times. However, many clinicians express concern that the patients' rights rulings and laws may unintentionally deprive these patients of opportunities for recovery. Consider the right to refuse medication (Appelbaum & Grisso, 1995; Grisso & Appelbaum, 1995). If medications can help a patient with schizophrenia to recover, doesn't the patient have the right to that recovery? If confusion causes the patient to refuse medication, can clinicians in good conscience delay medication while legal channels are cleared? The psychologist Marilyn Whiteside raises similar concerns in her description of a 25-year-old patient with mental retardation:

> He was 25 and severely retarded. And after his favorite attendant left, he became self-abusive. He beat his fists against the side of his head until a football helmet had to be ordered for his protection. Then he clawed at his face and gouged out one of his eyes.
>
> The institution psychologists began a behavior program that had mildly aversive consequences: they squirted warm water in his face each time he engaged in self-abuse. When that didn't work, they requested permission to use an electric prod. The Human Rights Committee vetoed this "excessive and inhumane form of correction" because, after all, the young man was retarded, not criminal.
>
> Since nothing effective could be done that abridged the rights and negated the dignity of the developmentally disabled patient, he was verbally reprimanded for his behavior—and allowed to push his thumb through his remaining eye. He is now blind, of course, but he has his rights and presumably his dignity.
>
> *(Whiteside, 1983, p. 13)*

Despite such legitimate concerns, we should keep in mind the fact that the clinical field has not always done an effective job of protecting patients' rights. Over the years, many patients have been overmedicated and received improper treatments (Crane, 1973). Similarly, some institutions have misused patients' labor. Furthermore, one must ask whether the field's present state of knowledge justifies clinicians' overriding of patients' rights. Can clinicians confidently say that a given treatment will help a patient? Can they predict when a treatment will have harmful effects? Since clinicians themselves often disagree, it seems appropriate for patients, their advocates, and outside evaluators to play key roles in decision making.

In What Other Ways Do the Clinical and Legal Fields Interact?

Mental health and legal professionals may influence each other's work in other ways as well. During the past two decades, their paths have crossed in three new areas: *malpractice suits, jury selection,* and *professional boundaries.*

The number of *malpractice lawsuits* against therapists has risen so sharply in recent years that clinicians have coined terms for the fear of being sued—"litigaphobia" and "litigastress." Claims have been made against clinicians in response to a patient's attempted suicide, sexual activity with a patient, failure to obtain informed consent for a treatment, negligent drug therapy, omission of drug therapy that would speed improvement, improper termination of treatment, and wrongful commitment (Malley & Reilly, 1999; Smith, 1991). For better or for worse, a malpractice suit, or the fear of one, can have major effects on clinical decisions and practice.

Another area in which the clinical and legal fields intersect is *jury selection*. During the past 20 years, more and more lawyers have turned to clinicians for advice in conducting trials (Strier, 1999; Gottschalk, 1981). A new breed of clinical specialists, known as "jury specialists," has evolved. They advise lawyers about which jury candidates are likely to favor their side and which strategies are likely to win jurors' support during trials. The jury specialists make their suggestions on the basis of surveys, interviews, analyses of jurors' backgrounds and attitudes, and laboratory enactments of upcoming trials. However, it is not clear that a clinician's advice is more useful than a lawyer's instincts or that either's judgments are particularly accurate.

Finally, during the past several years the legislative and judicial systems have helped to change the *boundaries* that separate one clinical profession from another. In particular, they have given more authority to psychologists and blurred the lines that once separated psychiatry from psychology. In 1991, with the blessings of Congress, the Department of Defense (DOD) started to reconsider the biggest difference of all between the practices of psychiatrists and psychologists— the authority to prescribe drugs, a role heretofore denied to psychologists. The DOD set up a trial training program for Army psychologists in which the psychologists prescribed drugs for psychological problems under the supervision of physicians (DeLeon, 1992). Given the apparent success of this trial program, the American Psychological Association recommended in 1996 that all psychologists be allowed to attend a special educational program in prescription services and receive certification to prescribe medications if they pass. And in recent years, several states have introduced laws regarding the expansion of prescription privileges (Hanson et al., 1999).

As the action by the American Psychological Association suggests, the legislative and judicial systems do not simply take it upon themselves to interfere in the affairs of clinical professionals. In fact, professional associations of psychologists, psychiatrists, and social workers lobby in state legislatures across the country for laws and decisions that may increase the authority of their members. In each instance, clinicians seek the involvement of other institutions as well, demonstrating again how the mental health system interacts with other parts of our society.

A JUDGMENT OF MALPRACTICE

After firing a rifle on a busy street and killing two men in 1995, the delusional law student Wendell Williamson was found not guilty by reason of insanity. From his room in a mental hospital, Williamson later sued the psychiatrist who had seen him a handful of times eight months before the killings, contending that the therapist had not made a correct diagnosis or followed up after the sessions. In 1998 a jury awarded Williamson a judgment of $500,000.

ConsiderThis

⦿ Most psychiatrists do not want psychologists to be granted the authority to prescribe psychotropic medications. Surprisingly, many psychologists oppose the idea as well. Why might they take this position?

SUMMING UP | **How Do the Legislative and Judicial Systems Influence Mental Health Care?**

The legal system often influences and helps regulate the clinical field in various ways.

Civil Commitment The legal system may be called on to commit noncriminals to mental hospitals for treatment, a process called civil commitment. Society allows involuntary commitment of people considered to be in need of treatment and dangerous to themselves or others. Civil commitment procedures vary from state to state, but a minimum standard of proof—clear and convincing evidence of the need to commit—has been defined by the Supreme Court.

Protecting Patients' Rights The courts and legislatures also affect the mental health profession by identifying and ensuring legal rights to which patients are entitled. The rights that have received the most attention are the right to treatment and the right to refuse treatment.

Other Clinical-Legal Interactions The mental health and legal professions also intersect in three other areas. First, malpractice lawsuits against therapists have increased in recent years. Second, lawyers may seek the advice of mental health professionals regarding the selection of jurors and trial strategies. Third, the legislative and judicial systems help set the professional boundaries of clinical practice.

What Ethical Principles Guide Mental Health Professionals?

Discussions of the legal and mental health systems may sometimes give the impression that clinicians are uncaring and are considerate of patients' rights and needs only when forced. This, of course, is not true. Most clinicians care greatly about their clients and try to help them and, at the same time, respect their rights and dignity. In fact, clinicians do not rely exclusively on the legislative and court systems to ensure proper and effective clinical practice. They also regulate themselves by continually developing and revising ethical guidelines for members of the clinical field. Many legal decisions do nothing more than place the power of law behind these already existing professional guidelines.

Each profession within the mental health field has its own **code of ethics** (Ford, 2001; Malley & Reilly, 1999). The code of the American Psychological Association is typical (Nagy, 2000). This code, highly respected by other mental health professionals and public officials, includes a number of specific guidelines, including the following:

1. *Psychologists are permitted to offer advice* in self-help books, on television and radio programs, in newspaper and magazine articles, through mailed material, and in other places, provided they do so responsibly and professionally and base their advice on appropriate psychological literature and practices.

2. *Psychologists may not conduct fraudulent research, plagiarize the work of others, or publish false data.* During the past two decades cases of scientific fraud or misconduct have been discovered in all of the sciences, including psychology. These acts have led to misunderstandings of important issues, taken scientific research in the wrong direction, and damaged public trust. Unfortunately, the impressions created by false findings may continue to influence for years the thinking of both the public and other scientists (Pfeifer & Snodgrass, 1990).

3. *Psychologists must acknowledge their limitations* with regard to patients who are disabled or whose gender, ethnicity, language, socioeconomic status, or sexual orientation differs from that of the therapist. This guideline often requires psychotherapists to obtain additional training or supervision, consult with more knowledgeable colleagues, or refer clients to more appropriate professionals.

4. *Psychologists who make evaluations and testify in legal cases must base their assessments on sufficient information and substantiate their findings appropriately.* If an adequate examination of the individual in question is not possible, psychologists must make clear the limited nature of their testimony.

5. *Psychologists may not take advantage of clients and students, sexually or otherwise.* This guideline relates to the widespread social problem of sexual harassment, as well as the problem of therapists who take sexual advantage of clients in therapy. The code specifically forbids a sexual relationship with a present or former therapy client for at least two years after the end of treatment; and even then such a relationship is permitted only in "the most unusual circumstances." Furthermore, psychologists may not accept as clients people with whom they have previously had a sexual relationship.

Clients may suffer great emotional damage from sexual involvement with their therapists (Malley & Reilly, 1999; Lazarus, 1995). A number of therapists are now treating clients whose primary problem is that they previously experienced some form of sexual misconduct by a therapist (Bloom et al., 1999; Wincze et al., 1996). Many such clients experience the symp-

THE LIMITS OF EXPERTISE

When mental health experts testify at trials, they must base their opinions only on firsthand observations that they have collected outside of court and on information presented at the trial (Federal Rules of Evidence 702).

toms of posttraumatic stress disorder or major depressive disorder (Luepker, 1999; Hankins et al., 1994).

How many therapists actually have a sexual relationship with a client? On the basis of various surveys, reviewers have estimated that some form of sexual misconduct with patients may be engaged in today by around 8 percent of today's male therapists and 2 percent of female therapists (Malley & Reilly, 1999; Illingworth, 1995; Hankins et al., 1994). Although the vast majority of therapists keep their sexual behavior within appropriate professional bounds, their ability to control private feelings is apparently another matter. In surveys, close to 90 percent of therapists reported having been sexually attracted to a client, at least on occasion (Pope, 2000; Pope & Tabachnick, 1993). Although few of these therapists acted on their feelings, most of them felt guilty, anxious, or concerned about the attraction (Pope et al., 1986). Given such sexual feelings and reactions, it is not surprising that in recent years sexual ethics training has been given high priority in many clinical training programs (Housman & Stake, 1999).

6. ***Psychologists must follow the principle of confidentiality.*** All of the state courts uphold laws protecting therapist **confidentiality,** and in the 1996 case of *Jaffee v. Redmond,* the Supreme Court applied this principle to federal courts as well. For peace of mind and to ensure effective therapy, clients must be able to trust that their private exchanges with a therapist will not be repeated to others (Wysoker, 2001). There are times, however, when the principle of confidentiality must be compromised. A therapist in training, for example, must discuss cases on a regular basis with a supervisor. Clients, in turn, must be informed that such discussions are occurring.

A second exception arises in cases of outpatients who are clearly dangerous. The 1976 case of *Tarasoff v. Regents of the University of California,* one of the most important cases to affect client-therapist relationships, concerned an outpatient at a University of California hospital. He had confided to his therapist that he wanted to harm his former girlfriend, Tanya Tarasoff. Several days after ending therapy, the former patient fulfilled his promise. He stabbed Tanya Tarasoff to death.

Should confidentiality have been broken in this case? The therapist, in fact, felt that it should. Campus police were notified, but the patient was released after some questioning. In their suit against the hospital and therapist, the victim's parents argued that the therapist should have also warned them and their daughter that the patient intended to harm Ms. Tarasoff. The California Supreme Court agreed: "The protective privilege ends where the public peril begins."

The current code of ethics for psychologists thus declares that therapists have a **duty to protect**—a responsibility to break confidentiality, even without the client's consent, when it is necessary "to protect the client or others from harm." Since the *Tarasoff* ruling, California's courts have further held that therapists must also protect people who are close to a client's intended victim and thus in danger. A child, for example, is likely to be at risk when a client plans to assault the child's mother. The California courts have also clarified that the duty to protect applies only when the intended victim is readily identifiable, as opposed to the public at large, and only when the intended object of violence is a person, as opposed to property. Many, but not all, states have adopted the California court rulings or similar ones (Bloom, 1990; Pietrofesa et al., 1990), and a number have passed "duty to protect bills" that clarify the rules of confidentiality for therapists and protect them from certain civil suits (Simon, 2001; Bersoff, 1999).

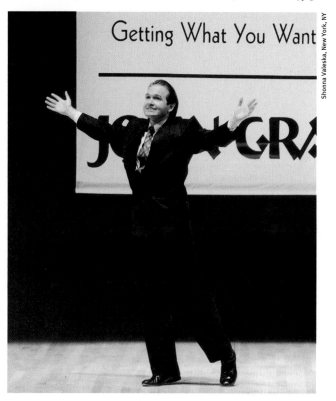

Shonna Valeska, New York, NY

The ethics of giving professional advice *Like John Gray, author of* Men Are from Mars, Women Are from Venus, *many of today's clinicians offer advice to millions of people in books, at workshops, on television and radio programs, and in tape packages. Their presentations often affect people greatly, and so they, too, are bound by the field's ethics codes to act responsibly and professionally and to base their presentations on appropriate psychological literature.*

"Anyhow we are getting tired of making bombs. It's no fun having to spend all your evenings and weekends preparing dangerous mixtures."

Letter from the Unabomber (later identified as Ted Kaczynski) to the *New York Times,* April 1995

EMPLOYEE ASSISTANCE PROGRAM A mental health program offered by a business to its employees.

STRESS-REDUCTION SEMINAR A workshop or series of group sessions offered by a business in which mental health professionals teach employees how to cope with and solve problems and reduce stress. Also known as *problem-solving seminar*.

MANAGED CARE PROGRAM An insurance program in which the insurance company decides the cost, method, provider, and length of treatment.

PEER REVIEW SYSTEM A system by which clinicians paid by an insurance company may periodically review a patient's progress and recommend the continuation or termination of insurance benefits.

Mental Health, Business, and Economics

The legislative and judicial systems are not the only social institutions with which mental health professionals interact. The *business* and *economic* fields are two other sectors that influence and are influenced by clinical practice and study.

Bringing Mental Health Services to the Workplace

Collectively, psychological disorders are among the ten leading categories of work-related disorders and injuries in the United States. In fact, almost 12 percent of all employees are believed to experience psychological problems that are serious enough to affect their work. Psychological problems contribute to 60 percent of all absenteeism from work, up to 90 percent of industrial accidents, and 65 percent of work terminations (Kemp, 1994). Alcohol abuse and other substance-related disorders are particularly damaging, increasing absences by as much as six times, accidents by four times, and workers' compensation claims by five times (Martin, Kraft, & Roman, 1994; Wright, 1984). The business world has often turned to clinical professionals to help prevent and correct such problems (Schott, 1999; Millar, 1990, 1984). Two common means of providing mental health care in the workplace are *employee assistance programs* and *problem-solving seminars*.

Employee assistance programs, mental health services made available by a place of business, are run either by mental health professionals who work directly for a company or by outside mental health agencies (Oher, 1999; Canty, 1996). Companies publicize such programs at the work site, educate workers about psychological dysfunctioning, and teach supervisors how to identify workers who are having psychological problems. Businesses believe that employee assistance programs save them money in the long run by preventing psychological problems from interfering with work performance and by reducing employee insurance claims (Dickens, 1999; Miller, 1998), although these beliefs have yet to undergo extensive testing (Kemp, 1994).

Stress-reduction and **problem-solving seminars** are workshops or group sessions in which mental health professionals teach employees techniques for coping, solving problems, and handling and reducing stress (Daw, 2001; Kagan et al., 1995). Programs of this kind are just as likely to be aimed at high-level executives as at assembly-line workers. Often employees are required to attend such workshops, which may run for several days, and are given time off from their jobs to do so. Again, the businesses expect these programs to save money by helping workers to achieve a healthier state of mind, suffer less dysfunction on the job, and improve their performance.

The Economics of Mental Health

We have already seen how economic decisions by the government may influence the clinical field's treatment of people with severe mental disorders. For example, the desire of the state and federal governments to reduce costs was an important consideration in the country's deinstitutionalization movement, which contributed to the premature release of hospital patients into the community. Economic decisions by government agencies may affect other kinds of clients and treatment programs as well.

On the one hand, government funding for people with psychological disorders has risen sharply over the past three decades, from $3 billion in 1969 to $61 billion today (Torrey, 1997; Redick et al., 1992). On the other hand, much of that money is spent on income support, housing subsidies, and other such expenses, rather than directly on mental health services. Government funding for services actually appears to be decreasing. It currently covers less than half the cost of all mental health services, leaving most of the expense to individual patients and their private insurance companies (Taube, 1990).

"I wish I could help you. The problem is that you're too sick for managed care."

The growing economic role of private insurance companies has had a significant effect on the way clinicians go about their work. In an effort to reduce their expenses and to keep track of the payments they are making, many of these companies have developed **managed care programs,** in which the insurance company decides such questions as which therapists clients may choose, the cost of sessions, and the number of sessions for which a client may be reimbursed (Manderscheid et al., 1999). These and other insurance plans may also control expenses through the use of **peer review systems,** in which clinicians who work for the insurance company periodically review a client's treatment program and recommend that insurance benefits be either continued or stopped. Typically, insurers require detailed reports or session notes from the therapist, often including intimate personal information about the patient (Stoline & Sharfstein, 1996; Appelbaum, 1993).

As we observed in Chapter 1, many therapists and clients dislike managed care programs and peer reviews. They believe that the reports required of therapists breach confidentiality, even when efforts are made to protect anonymity, and that the value of therapy in a given case is sometimes difficult to present in a brief report. They also argue that the priorities of managed care programs inevitably shorten therapy, even if longer-term treatment would be advisable in particular cases. The priorities may also favor treatments that offer short-term results (for example, drug therapy) over more costly approaches that might achieve a more promising long-term improvement. As in the medical field, disturbing stories are often heard about patients who are prematurely cut off from mental health services by their managed care programs. In short, many clinicians fear that the current system amounts to regulation of therapy by insurance companies rather than by therapists.

The Person within the Profession

The actions of clinical researchers and practitioners not only influence and are influenced by other institutions but are closely tied to their personal needs and goals. We have seen that the human strengths, imperfections, wisdom, and clumsiness of clinical professionals may affect their theoretical orientations, their interactions with clients, and the kinds of clients with whom they choose to work.

A PUBLIC VIEW

In a 1999 survey of 1,000 people across the United States, 67 percent of respondents said the government should spend more money to treat people with mental disorders who cannot afford to pay (*Time*/CNN, 1999).

DECLINING COSTS

Mental health expenditures by insurance companies fell 54 percent during the 1990s. Total health-care spending fell just 7 percent during the same decade (*Wall Street Journal*, 1998).

Therapists under Attack

A number of therapists have found out that their rights—including the right to a safe practice—may be violated (Flannery et al., 2000; Brasic & Fogelman, 1999). More than 10 percent of therapists have been attacked by their patients at least once in private therapy, and an even larger percentage have been assaulted in mental hospitals (Tryon, 1987; Bernstein, 1981). In fact, one study found that 40 percent of psychiatrists had been assaulted at least once during their careers (Menninger, 1993). Patients have used a variety of weapons in their attacks, including such common objects as shoes, lamps, fire extinguishers, and canes. Some have used guns or knives and have severely wounded or even killed a therapist.

Many therapists who have been attacked continue to feel anxious and insecure in their work for a long time after. Some try to be more selective in accepting patients and look for cues that signal impending violence. One therapist even studied karate for a year and a half (Tryon, 1987).

Consider This

🔘 How might lingering anxiety affect the behavior and effectiveness of clinicians who have been attacked? • Such attacks seem to be on the rise. Why?

COUNTERTRANSFERENCE

In a national survey of 285 therapists, 87 percent reported having been angry at a client on at least one occasion, and 57 percent have raised their voice at a client (Pope & Tabachnick, 1993).

We have also looked at how personal factors may sometimes override professional standards and scruples and, in extreme cases, lead clinical scientists to commit research fraud and clinical practitioners to engage in sexual misconduct with clients.

A national survey of the mental health of therapists found that 84 percent reported being in therapy at least once (Pope & Brown, 1996; Pope & Tabachnick, 1994). Their reasons were largely the same as those of other clients, with emotional problems, depression, and anxiety topping the list. In fact, 61 percent of the therapists reported having experienced depression, 29 percent reported having had suicidal feelings, and 4 percent said they had attempted suicide (Pope & Tabachnick, 1994). It is not clear why so many therapists report having psychological problems. Perhaps their jobs are highly stressful; perhaps therapists are simply more aware of their own negative feelings or are more likely to pursue treatment for their problems; or perhaps individuals with personal concerns are more inclined to choose clinical work as a profession. Whatever the reason, clinicians bring a set of psychological concerns and emotions to their work that may, along with other important factors, affect how they listen and respond to clients.

The science and profession of abnormal psychology seeks to understand, predict, and change abnormal functioning. But we must not lose sight of the broader environment in which its activities are conducted. Mental health researchers and clinicians are human beings, living within a society of human beings, working to serve human beings. The mixture of discovery, misdirection, promise, and frustration that we have seen throughout this book is thus to be expected. When one thinks about it, could the study and treatment of human behavior really proceed in any other way?

SUMMING UP | **Ethical, Economic, and Personal Factors**

Ethical Guidelines Each clinical profession has a code of ethics. The psychologists' code forbids engaging in fraudulent research and taking advantage of clients or students, sexually or otherwise. It also sets up guidelines for respecting patient confi-

"STOP TRYING TO PSYCHOANALYZE ME WHEN I'M TRYING TO PSYCHOANALYZE YOU."

dentiality. The case of *Tarasoff v. Regents of the University of California* has determined some of the circumstances in which therapists must break confidentiality in order to protect the public.

Mental Health, Business, and Economics The clinical field also intersects with business and economic institutions. For example, clinicians are often employed to help prevent or treat psychological problems in the workplace. In addition, private insurance companies are setting up managed care programs whose procedures influence the nature and length of therapy.

The Person within the Profession Mental health activities are affected by the personal needs and goals of the people who conduct clinical research and provide clinical services. These factors inevitably affect their choices and even the quality of their work.

CROSSROADS:
Operating within a Larger System

At one time clinical researchers and professionals conducted their work largely in isolation. Today, however, their activities have ties to the legislative, judicial, economic, and other established systems. One reason for this growing interconnectedness is that the clinical field has achieved a high level of respect and acceptance in our society. Clinicians now serve millions of people in many ways. They have much to say about almost every aspect of society, from education to ecology, and are widely looked to as sources of expertise. When a field achieves such prominence, it inevitably affects how other institutions are run. It also attracts public attention, and various institutions begin to keep an eye on its activities.

Today, when people with psychological problems seek help from a therapist, they are entering a complex system consisting of many interconnected parts. Just as their personal problems have grown within a social structure, so will their treatment be affected by the various parts of a larger system—the therapist's values and needs, legal and economic forces, societal attitudes, and yet other forces. These many forces influence clinical research as well.

The effects of this larger system on an individual's psychological needs can be positive or negative, like a family's impact on each of its members. When the system protects a client's rights and confidentiality, for example, it is serving the

"I spent . . . two hours chatting with Einstein. . . . He is cheerful, assured and likable, and understands as much about psychology as I do about physics, so we got on together very well."

Sigmund Freud, 1927

client well. When economic, legal, or other societal forces limit treatment options, cut off treatment prematurely, or stigmatize a person, the system is adding to the person's problems.

Because of the enormous growth and impact of the mental health profession in our society, it is important that we understand its strengths and weaknesses. As we have seen throughout this book, the field has gathered much knowledge, especially during the past several decades. What mental health professionals do not know and cannot do, however, still outweighs what they do know and can do. Everyone who turns to the clinical field—directly or indirectly—must recognize that it is young and imperfect. Society is vastly curious about behavior and often in need of information and help. What we as a society must remember, however, is that the field is truly at a *crossroads*.

KEY TERMS

criminal commitment p. 476

not guilty by reason of insanity (NGRI) p. 476

M' Naghten test p. 477

irresistible impulse test p. 477

Durham test p. 477

American Law Institute (ALI) test p. 477

guilty but mentally ill p. 480

guilty with diminished capacity p. 480

mentally disordered sex offenders p. 481

mental incompetence p. 481

civil commitment p. 483

two-physician certificate (2 PC) p. 485

right to treatment p. 488

right to refuse treatment p. 489

malpractice lawsuit p. 490

jury selection p. 491

professional boundaries p. 491

code of ethics p. 492

confidentiality p. 493

duty to protect p. 493

employee assistance programs p. 494

stress-reduction seminars p. 494

managed care program p. 495

peer review system p. 495

QUICK QUIZ

1. Briefly explain the M'Naghten, irresistible impulse, Durham, and ALI tests of insanity. pp. 476–477

2. Which tests are used today to determine whether defendants are not guilty by reason of insanity? pp. 477–478

3. Explain the guilty-but-mentally-ill, diminished-capacity, and mentally-disordered-sex-offender verdicts. pp. 480–481

4. What are the reasons behind and the procedures for determining whether defendants are mentally incompetent to stand trial? pp. 481–482

5. What are the reasons for civil commitment, and how is it carried out? What criticisms have been made of civil commitment? pp. 483–486

6. What rights have court rulings and legislation guaranteed to patients with psychological disorders? pp. 488–490

7. How do the legislative and judicial systems affect the professional boundaries of clinical practice? pp. 490–491

8. What key issues are covered by the psychologist's code of ethics? Under what conditions must therapists break the principle of confidentiality? pp. 492–493

9. What kinds of programs for the prevention and treatment of psychological problems have been established in business settings? p. 494

10. What trends have emerged in recent years in the funding and insurance of mental health care? pp. 494–495

When might people not be responsible for aggressive or violent acts? ▲ *Can clinicians predict antisocial acts, dangerousness, and violence?* ▲ *Did the hospital treatments of past times violate patients' rights?* ▲ *Is it appropriate to commit people who are experiencing suicidal thoughts, depression, or hallucinations?*

SEARCH THE *FUNDAMENTALS OF ABNORMAL PSYCHOLOGY* CD-ROM FOR

▲ Chapter 16 video cases and discussions
    "Mark"—Aggression, Violence, and the Brain
    The Mind of the Psychopath
    "Pat"—Psychopathy

▲ Chapter 16 practice test and feedback

▲ Additional video cases and discussions
    Early Procedures in Mental Hospitals
    Early Electroconvulsive Therapies
    "Andy"—Suicide
    "Steve"—Schizophrenia

LOG ON TO THE COMER WEB PAGE FOR

▲ Suggested Web links, research exercises, FAQ page, additional Chapter 16 practice test questions
    <www.worthpublishers.com/comer>

The Mind, Second Edition (WNET/Worth Publishers, 1999)

glossary

Abnormal psychology The scientific study of abnormal behavior in order to describe, predict, explain, and change abnormal patterns of functioning.

Acute stress disorder An anxiety disorder in which fear and related symptoms are experienced soon after a traumatic event and last less than a month.

Aftercare A program of post-hospitalization care and treatment out in the community.

Agoraphobia An anxiety disorder in which a person is afraid to be in places or situations from which escape might be difficult (or embarrassing) or help unavailable if panic-like symptoms were to occur.

Agranulocytosis A life-threatening reduction in white blood cells. This condition is sometimes produced by clozapine, one of the atypical antipsychotic drugs.

Alcohol Any beverage containing ethyl alcohol, including beer, wine, and liquor.

Alcoholics Anonymous (AA) A self-help organization that provides support and guidance for persons with alcohol abuse or dependence.

Alogia A symptom of schizophrenia in which the person shows a decrease in speech or speech content. Also known as *poverty of speech*.

Altruistic suicide Suicide committed by people who intentionally sacrifice their lives for the well-being of society.

Alzheimer's disease The most common form of dementia, usually occurring after the age of 65.

Amenorrhea Absence of menstrual cycles.

American Law Institute test A legal test for insanity that holds people to be insane at the time they committed a crime if, because of a mental disorder, they did not know right from wrong or they could not resist an uncontrollable impulse to act.

Amnestic disorders Organic disorders in which the primary symptom is memory loss.

Amphetamine A stimulant drug that is manufactured in the laboratory.

Analogue experiment A research method in which the experimenter produces abnormal-like behavior in laboratory subjects and then conducts experiments on the subjects.

Anomic suicide Suicide committed by individuals whose social environment fails to provide stability, thus leaving them without a sense of belonging.

Anorexia nervosa A disorder marked by the pursuit of extreme thinness and by an extreme loss of weight.

Antagonist drugs Drugs that block or change the effects of an addictive drug.

Anterograde amnesia The inability to remember new information that is acquired after the event that triggered amnesia.

Antianxiety drugs Psychotropic drugs that help reduce tension and anxiety.

Antibipolar drugs Psychotropic drugs that help stabilize the moods of people suffering from a bipolar mood disorder.

Antidepressant drugs Psychotropic drugs that improve the moods of people with depression.

Antigen A foreign invader of the body, such as a bacterium or virus.

Antipsychotic drugs Psychotropic drugs that help correct the confusion, hallucinations, and delusions found in psychotic disorders.

Antisocial personality disorder A personality disorder marked by a general pattern of disregard for and violation of other people's rights.

Anxiety The central nervous system's physiological and emotional response to a vague sense of threat or danger.

Anxiety sensitivity A tendency to focus on one's bodily sensations, assess them illogically, and interpret them as harmful.

Assessment The process of collecting and interpreting relevant information about a client or subject.

Asthma A medical problem marked by narrowing of the trachea and bronchi, which results in shortness of breath, wheezing, coughing, and a choking sensation.

Asylum A type of institution that first became popular in the sixteenth century to provide care for persons with mental disorders. Most became virtual prisons.

Attention-deficit/hyperactivity disorder (ADHD) A disorder marked either by inability to focus attention or by overactive and impulsive behavior, or by both.

Attribution An explanation of events as resulting from particular causes.

Atypical antipsychotic drugs A new group of antipsychotic drugs whose biological action is different from that of the traditional antipsychotic drugs.

Augmentative communication system A method for enhancing the communication skills of individuals with autism, mental retardation, or cerebral palsy by teaching them to point to pictures, symbols, letters, or words on a communication board or computer.

Autistic disorder A long-term disorder marked by extreme unresponsiveness to others, poor communication skills, and highly repetitive and rigid behavior.

Automatic thoughts Numerous unpleasant thoughts that help to cause or maintain depression, anxiety, or other forms of psychological dysfunction.

Autonomic nervous system (ANS) The network of nerve fibers that connects the central nervous system to all the other organs of the body.

Aversion therapy A treatment in which clients are repeatedly presented with unpleasant stimuli while performing undesirable behaviors such as taking a drug.

Avoidant personality disorder A personality disorder in which an individual is consistently uncomfortable and restrained in social situations, overwhelmed by feelings of inadequacy, and extremely sensitive to negative evaluation.

Avolition A symptom of schizophrenia marked by apathy and an inability to start or complete a course of action.

Barbiturates Addictive sedative-hypnotic drugs used to reduce anxiety or to help people fall asleep.

Basic irrational assumptions The inaccurate and inappropriate beliefs held by people with various psychological problems, according to Albert Ellis.

Battery A series of tests, each of which produces a different kind of data.

Behavioral medicine A field of treatment that combines psychological and physical interventions to treat or prevent medical problems.

Behavioral self-control training (BSCT) A cognitive-behavioral approach to treating alcohol abuse and dependence in which clients are taught to keep track of their drinking behavior and to apply coping strategies in situations that typically trigger excessive drinking.

Benzodiazepines The most common group of antianxiety drugs, which includes Valium and Xanax.

Binge An episode of uncontrollable eating during which a person ingests a very large quantity of food.

Binge-eating disorder A type of eating disorder in which a person displays a pattern of binge eating without any accompanying compensatory behaviors.

Biofeedback A treatment technique in which a client is given information about physiological reactions as they occur and learns to control the reactions voluntarily.

Biofeedback training A treatment technique in which a client receives information about physiological reactions as they occur and learns to control the reactions voluntarily.

Biological challenge test A procedure used to produce panic in subjects or clients by having them exercise vigorously or perform some other potentially panic-inducing task in the presence of a researcher or therapist.

Biopsychosocial theories Explanations of abnormality as resulting from an interaction of genetic, biological, developmental, emotional, behavioral, cognitive, social, and societal influences.

Bipolar disorder A disorder marked by alternating or intermixed periods of mania and depression.

Bipolar I disorder A type of bipolar disorder marked by full manic and major depressive episodes.

Bipolar II disorder A type of bipolar disorder marked by mildly manic (hypomanic) episodes and major depressive episodes.

Blind design An experiment in which subjects do not know whether they are in the experimental or the control condition.

Body dysmorphic disorder A somatoform disorder marked by excessive worry that some aspect of one's physical appearance is defective. Also known as *dysmorphophobia*.

Borderline personality disorder A personality disorder in which an individual displays repeated instability in interpersonal relationships, self-image, and mood, as well as impulsive behavior.

Bulimia nervosa A disorder marked by frequent eating binges that are followed by forced vomiting or other extreme compensatory behaviors to avoid gaining weight. Also known as *binge-purge syndrome*.

Cannabis drugs Drugs produced from the different varieties of the hemp plant, *Cannabis sativa*. They cause a mixture of hallucinogenic, depressant, and stimulant effects.

Case manager A community therapist who offers a full range of services for people with schizophrenia or other severe disorders, including therapy, advice, medication, guidance, and protection of patients' rights.

Case study A detailed account of a person's life and psychological problems.

Catatonia A pattern of extreme psychomotor symptoms found in some forms of schizophrenia, which may include catatonic stupor, rigidity, or posturing.

Catatonic type of schizophrenia A type of schizophrenia dominated by severe psychomotor disturbances.

Catharsis The reliving of past repressed feelings in order to settle internal conflicts and overcome problems.

Caudate nuclei Structures in the brain, within the region known as the basal ganglia, that help convert sensory information into thoughts and actions.

Cerebellum An area of the brain that coordinates movement in the body and perhaps helps control a person's ability to shift attention rapidly.

Civil commitment A legal process by which an individual can be forced to undergo mental health treatment.

Classical conditioning A process of learning by temporal association in which two events that repeatedly occur close together in time become fused in a person's mind and produce the same response.

Classification system A list of disorders, along with descriptions of symptoms and guidelines for making appropriate diagnoses.

Client-centered therapy The humanistic therapy developed by Carl Rogers in which clinicians try to help clients by being accepting, empathizing accurately, and conveying genuineness.

Clinical interview A face-to-face encounter in which clinicians ask questions of clients, weigh their responses and reactions, and learn about them and their psychological problems.

Cocaine An addictive stimulant obtained from the coca plant. It is the most powerful natural stimulant known.

Code of ethics A body of principles and rules for ethical behavior, designed to guide decisions and actions by members of a profession.

Cognitive therapy A therapy developed by Aaron Beck that helps people identify and change the maladaptive assumptions and ways of thinking that help cause their psychological disorders.

Cognitive triad The three forms of negative thinking that Aaron Beck theorizes lead people to feel depressed. The triad consists of a negative view of one's experiences, oneself, and the future.

Community mental health center A treatment facility that provides medication, psychotherapy, and emergency inpatient care for psychological problems and coordinates treatment in the community.

Community mental health treatment A treatment approach that emphasizes community care.

Compulsion A repetitive and rigid behavior or mental act that a person feels driven to perform in order to prevent or reduce anxiety.

Conditioning A simple form of learning.

Conduct disorder A childhood disorder in which the child repeatedly violates the basic rights of others, displaying aggression and sometimes destroying others' property, lying, cheating, or running away from home.

Confidentiality The principle that certain professionals will not divulge the information they obtain from a client.

Confounds In an experiment, variables other than the independent variable that may also be affecting the dependent variable.

Control group In an experiment, a group of subjects who are not exposed to the independent variable.

Conversion disorder A somatoform disorder in which a psychosocial need or conflict is converted into dramatic physical symptoms that affect voluntary motor or sensory function.

Coronary heart disease Illness of the heart caused by a blocking of the coronary arteries.

Correlation The degree to which events or characteristics vary along with each other.

Correlational method A research procedure used to determine how much events or characteristics vary along with each other.

Corticosteroids A group of hormones, including cortisol, released by the adrenal glands at times of stress.

Couple therapy A therapy format in which the therapist works with two people who share a long-term relationship. Also called *marital therapy*.

Crack A powerful, ready-to-smoke free-base cocaine.

Creutzfeldt-Jakob disease A form of dementia caused by a slow-acting virus that may live in the body for years before the disease appears.

Criminal commitment A legal process by which people accused of a crime are instead judged mentally unstable and sent to a mental health facility for treatment.

Crisis intervention A treatment approach that tries to help people in a psychological crisis to view their situation more accurately, make better decisions, act more constructively, and overcome the crisis.

Critical incident stress debriefing Training in how to help victims talk about their feelings and reactions to traumatic incidents.

Culture A people's common history, values, institutions, habits, skills, technology, and arts.

Cyclothymic disorder A disorder marked by numerous periods of hypomanic symptoms and mild depressive symptoms.

Day center A program that offers hospital-like treatment during the day only. Also known as *day hospital*.

Death darer A person who is ambivalent about the wish to die even as he or she attempts suicide.

Death ignorer A person who attempts suicide without recognizing the finality of death.

Death initiator A person who attempts suicide believing that the process of death is already under way and that he or she is simply hastening the process.

Death seeker A person who clearly intends to end his or her life at the time of a suicide attempt.

Deinstitutionalization The practice, begun in the 1960s, of releasing hundreds of thousands of patients from public mental hospitals so that they might be treated in community programs.

Delirium A rapidly developing clouding of consciousness in which a person has great difficulty concentrating, focusing attention, and following an orderly sequence of thought.

Delirium tremens (DTs) A dramatic withdrawal reaction experienced by some people who are alcohol-dependent. It consists of confusion, clouded consciousness, and terrifying visual hallucinations. Also called *alcohol withdrawal delirium*.

Delusion A strange false belief firmly held despite evidence to the contrary.

Dementia A syndrome marked by severe problems in memory and in at least one other cognitive function.

Dementias Organic syndromes marked by major problems in memory and at least one other cognitive function.

Dependent personality disorder A personality disorder characterized by a pattern of clinging and obedience, fear of separation, and an ongoing need to be taken care of.

Dependent variable The variable in an experiment that is expected to change as the independent variable is manipulated.

Depression A low, sad state marked by significant levels of sadness, lack of energy, low self-worth, guilt, or related symptoms.

Desire phase The phase of the sexual response cycle consisting of an urge to have sex, sexual fantasies, and sexual attraction to others.

Detoxification Systematic and medically supervised withdrawal from a drug.

Diagnosis A determination that a person's problems reflect a particular disorder.

Diathesis-stress explanation The view that a person must first have a predisposition to a disorder and then be subjected to episodes of severe stress in order to develop the disorder.

Dichotomous thinking Viewing problems and solutions in rigid "either/or" terms.

Diencephalon A brain area (consisting of the mammillary bodies, thalamus, and hypothalamus) that plays a key role in transforming short-term to long-term memory, among other functions.

Directed masturbation training A sex therapy approach that teaches women with female arousal or orgasmic disorders how to masturbate effectively and eventually to reach orgasm during sexual interactions.

Disorganized type of schizophrenia A type of schizophrenia marked primarily by confusion, incoherence, and flat or inappropriate affect.

Disregulation model A theory that explains psychophysiological disorders as breakdowns in the body's negative feedback loops, which lead to interruption of the body's smooth, self-regulating operation.

Dissociative amnesia A dissociative disorder marked by an inability to recall important personal events and information.

Dissociative disorders Disorders marked by major changes in memory that do not have clear physical causes.

Dissociative fugue A dissociative disorder in which a person travels to a new location and may assume a new identity, simultaneously forgetting his or her past.

Dopamine hypothesis The theory that schizophrenia results from excessive activity of the neurotransmitter dopamine.

Down syndrome A form of mental retardation related to abnormalities of the twenty-first chromosome.

Dream A series of ideas and images that form during sleep.

DSM-IV The fourth, and current, edition of the *Diagnostic and Statistical Manual of Mental Disorders*.

Durham test A legal test for insanity that holds people to be insane at the time they committed a crime if their act was the result of a mental disorder or defect.

Duty to protect The principle that therapists must break confidentiality in order to protect a person who may be the intended victim of a client.

Dyspareunia A disorder in which a person experiences severe pain in the genitals during sexual activity.

Dysthymic disorder A mood disorder that is similar to but longer lasting and less disabling than a major depressive disorder.

Ego According to Freud, the psychological force that employs reason and operates in accordance with the reality principle.

Ego defense mechanisms According to psychoanalytic theory, strategies developed by the ego to control unacceptable id impulses and to avoid or reduce the anxiety they arouse.

Ego theory The psychodynamic theory that emphasizes the role of the ego and considers it an independent force.

Egoistic suicide Suicide committed by people over whom society has little or no control, people who are not inhibited by the norms or rules of society.

Electroconvulsive therapy (ECT) A form of biological treatment, used primarily on depressed patients, in which a brain seizure is triggered as an electric current passes through electrodes attached to the patient's forehead.

Electromyograph (EMG) A device that provides feedback about the level of muscular tension in the body.

Employee assistance program A mental health program offered by a business to its employees.

Encopresis A childhood disorder characterized by repeated defecating in inappropriate places, such as one's clothing.

Endorphins Neurotransmitters that help relieve pain and reduce emotional tension. They are sometimes referred to as the body's own opioids.

Enmeshed family pattern A family system in which members are overinvolved with each other's affairs and overconcerned about each other's welfare.

Enuresis A childhood disorder marked by repeated bed-wetting or wetting of one's clothes.

Epidemiological study A study that measures the incidence and prevalence of a disorder in a given population.

Excitement phase The phase of the sexual response cycle marked by changes in the pelvic region, general physical arousal, and increases in heart rate, muscle tension, blood pressure, and rate of breathing.

Exhibitionism A paraphilia in which persons have repeated sexually arousing urges or fantasies about exposing their genitals to another person, and may act upon those urges.

Existential anxiety A universal fear of the limits and responsibilities of one's existence.

Existential therapy A therapy that encourages clients to accept responsibility for their lives and to live with greater meaning and values.

Exorcism The practice in early societies of treating abnormality by coaxing evil spirits to leave the person's body.

Experiment A research procedure in which a variable is manipulated and the effect of the manipulation is observed.

Experimental group In an experiment, the subjects who are exposed to the independent variable under investigation.

Exposure and response prevention A behavioral treatment for obsessive-compulsive disorder that exposes clients to anxiety-arousing thoughts or situations and then prevents them from performing their compulsive acts.

Exposure treatments Behavioral treatments in which persons are exposed to the objects or situations they dread.

Expressed emotion The general level of criticism, disapproval, and hostility expressed in a family. People recovering from schizophrenia are considered more likely to relapse if their families rate high in expressed emotion.

Extrapyramidal effects Unwanted movements, such as severe shaking, bizarre-looking grimaces, twisting of the body, and extreme restlessness, sometimes produced by conventional antipsychotic drugs.

Factitious disorder An illness with no identifiable physical cause, in which the patient is believed to be intentionally producing or faking symptoms in order to assume a sick role.

Family pedigree study A research design in which investigators determine how many and which relatives of a person with a disorder have the same disorder.

Family systems theory A theory that views the family as a system of interacting parts whose interactions exhibit consistent patterns and unstated rules.

Family therapy A therapy format in which the therapist meets with all members of a family and helps them to change in therapeutic ways.

Fear The central nervous system's physiological and emotional response to a serious threat to one's well-being.

Fear hierarchy A list of objects or situations that frighten a person, starting with those that are slightly feared and ending with those that are feared greatly.

Female orgasmic disorder A dysfunction in which a woman rarely has an orgasm or repeatedly experiences a very delayed one.

Female sexual arousal disorder A female dysfunction marked by a persistent inability to attain sexual excitement, including adequate lubrication or genital swelling, during sexual activity.

Fetal alcohol syndrome A group of problems in a child, including lower intellectual functioning, hyperactivity, head and face deformities, heart defects, and slow growth, that result from excessive alcohol intake by the mother during pregnancy.

Fetishism A paraphilia consisting of recurrent and intense sexual urges, fantasies, or behaviors that involve the use of a nonliving object, often to the exclusion of all other stimuli.

Fixation According to Freud, a condition in which the id, ego, and superego do not mature properly and are frozen at an early stage of development.

Flashback LSD-induced sensory and emotional changes that recur long after the drug has left the body.

Flat affect A symptom of schizophrenia in which the person shows almost no emotions at all.

Flooding A treatment for phobias in which clients are exposed repeatedly and intensively to a feared object and made to see that it is actually harmless.

Formal thought disorder A disturbance in the production and organization of thought.

Free association A psychodynamic technique in which the patient describes any thought, feeling, or image that comes to mind, even if it seems unimportant.

Free-basing A technique for ingesting cocaine in which the pure cocaine basic alkaloid is chemically separated from processed cocaine, vaporized by heat from a flame, and inhaled with a pipe.

Frotteurism A paraphilia consisting of repeated and intense sexual urges, fantasies, or behaviors that involve touching and rubbing against a nonconsenting person.

Fusion The final merging of two or more subpersonalities in multiple personality disorder.

GABA The neurotransmitter gamma-aminobutyric acid, whose low activity has been linked to generalized anxiety disorder.

Gender identity disorder A disorder in which a person persistently feels extremely uncomfortable about his or her assigned sex and strongly wishes to be a member of the opposite sex. Also known as *transsexualism*.

Gene Chromosome segments that control the characteristics and traits we inherit.

Generalized anxiety disorder A disorder marked by persistent and excessive feelings of anxiety and worry about numerous events and activities.

Gestalt therapy The humanistic therapy developed by Fritz Perls in which clinicians actively move clients toward self-recognition and self-acceptance by using techniques such as role-playing and self-discovery exercises.

Group therapy A therapy format in which a group of people with similar problems meet together with a therapist to work on those problems.

Guilty but mentally ill A verdict stating that defendants are guilty of committing a crime, but are also suffering from a mental illness that should be treated during their imprisonment.

Habituation training A therapeutic technique in which a therapist tries to call forth a client's obsessive thoughts again and again, with the expectation that the thoughts will eventually lose their power to frighten and thus to cause anxiety.

Halfway house A residence for people with schizophrenia or other severe problems who cannot live alone or with their families, often staffed by paraprofessionals. Also known as *group home*.

Hallucination The experiencing of sights, sounds, or other perceptions in the absence of external stimuli.

Hallucinogen A substance that causes powerful changes primarily in sensory perception, including strengthening perceptions and producing illusions and hallucinations. Also called *psychedelic drug*.

Heroin One of the most addictive substances derived from opium, illegal in the United States under all circumstances.

Histrionic personality disorder A personality disorder in which an individual displays a pattern of excessive emotionality and attention seeking. Once called *hysterical personality disorder*.

Hopelessness A pessimistic belief that one's present circumstances, problems, or mood will not change.

Hormones The chemicals released by glands into the bloodstream.

Humors According to Greek and Roman physicians, bodily chemicals that influence mental and physical functioning.

Huntington's disease An inherited disease in which people develop progressive problems in cognition, emotion, and movement, and which results in dementia.

Hypertension Chronic high blood pressure.

Hypnosis A sleeplike suggestible state during which a person can be directed to act in unusual ways, to experience unusual sensations, to remember seemingly forgotten events, or to forget remembered events.

Hypnotic therapy A treatment in which the patient undergoes hypnosis and is then guided to recall forgotten events or perform other therapeutic activities. Also known as *hypnotherapy*.

Hypoactive sexual desire disorder A disorder marked by a lack of interest in sex and hence a low level of sexual activity.

Hypochondriasis A somatoform disorder in which people mistakenly fear that minor changes in their physical functioning indicate a serious disease.

Hypothalamus A part of the brain that helps regulate various bodily functions, including eating and hunger.

Hysterical somatoform disorders Somatoform disorders in which people suffer actual changes in their physical functioning.

Iatrogenic disorder A disorder that is unintentionally caused by a practitioner.

Id According to Freud, the psychological force that produces instinctual needs, drives, and impulses.

Idiopathic understanding An understanding of the behavior of a particular individual.

Immune system The body's network of activities and cells that identify and destroy antigens and cancer cells.

Inappropriate affect A symptom of schizophrenia in which a person displays emotions that are unsuited to the situation.

Incidence The number of new cases of a disorder occurring in a population over a specific period of time.

Independent variable The variable in an experiment that is manipulated to determine whether it has an effect on another variable.

Insomnia Difficulty falling or staying asleep.

Intelligence quotient (IQ) A score derived from intelligence tests that theoretically represents a person's overall intellectual capacity.

Intelligence test A test designed to measure a person's intellectual ability.

Interpersonal psychotherapy (IPT) A treatment for unipolar depression that is based on the belief that clarifying and changing one's interpersonal problems will help lead to recovery.

Irresistible impulse test A legal test for insanity that holds people to be insane at the time they committed a crime if they were driven to do so by an uncontrollable "fit of passion."

Isolation An ego defense mechanism in which people unconsciously isolate and disown undesirable and unwanted thoughts, experiencing them as foreign intrusions.

Korsakoff's syndrome An alcohol-related disorder marked by extreme confusion, memory impairment, and other neurological symptoms.

Lateral hypothalamus (LH) The region of the hypothalamus that, when activated, produces hunger.

Learned helplessness The perception, based on past experiences, that one has no control over one's reinforcements.

Lithium A metallic element that occurs in nature as a mineral salt and is an effective treatment for bipolar disorders.

Locus ceruleus A small area of the brain that seems to be active in the regulation of emotions. Many of its neurons use norepinephrine.

Longitudinal study A study that observes the same subjects on many occasions over a long period of time.

Long-term memory The memory system that contains all the information that we have stored over the years.

Loose associations A common thinking disturbance in schizophrenia, characterized by rapid shifts from one topic of conversation to another. Also known as *derailment*.

Lymphocytes White blood cells that circulate through the lymph system and bloodstream, helping the body identify and destroy antigens and cancer cells.

Lysergic acid diethylamide (LSD) A hallucinogenic drug derived from ergot alkaloids.

Mainstreaming The placement of children with mental retardation in regular school classes with children who are not mentally retarded.

Major depressive disorder A severe pattern of depression that is disabling and is

not caused by such factors as drugs or a general medical condition.

Male erectile disorder A dysfunction in which a man repeatedly fails to attain or maintain an erection during sexual activity.

Male orgasmic disorder A male dysfunction characterized by a repeated inability to reach orgasm or long delays in reaching orgasm after normal sexual excitement.

Managed care program An insurance program in which the insurance company decides the cost, method, provider, and length of treatment.

Mania A state or episode of euphoria or frenzied activity in which people may have an exaggerated belief that the world is theirs for the taking.

MAO inhibitor An antidepressant drug that prevents the action of the enzyme monoamine oxidase.

Marijuana One of the cannabis drugs, derived from the leaves and flowering tops of the hemp plant, *Cannabis sativa*.

Masturbatory satiation A behavioral treatment in which a client masturbates for a very long period of time while fantasizing in detail about a paraphilic object. The procedure is expected to produce a feeling of boredom that in turn becomes linked to the object.

Meditation A technique of turning one's concentration inward and achieving a slightly changed state of consciousness.

Memory The faculty for recalling past events and past learning.

Mental incompetence A state of mental instability that leaves defendants unable to understand the legal charges and proceedings they are facing and unable to prepare an adequate defense with their attorneys.

Mental retardation A disorder marked by intellectual functioning and adaptive behavior that are well below average.

Mental status exam A set of interview questions and observations designed to reveal the degree and nature of a client's abnormal functioning.

Methadone maintenance program An approach to treating heroin dependence in which clients are given legally and medically supervised doses of a substitute drug, methadone.

Methylphenidate A stimulant drug, known better by the trade name Ritalin, commonly used to treat ADHD.

Migraine headache An extremely severe headache that occurs on one side of the head, often preceded by a warning sensation and sometimes accompanied by dizziness, nausea, or vomiting.

Mild retardation A level of mental retardation (IQ between 50 and 70) at which people can benefit from education and support themselves as adults.

Milieu therapy A humanistic approach to institutional treatment based on the belief that institutions can help patients recover by creating a climate that promotes self-respect, responsible behavior, and meaningful activity.

Mind-body dualism René Descartes's position that the mind is separate from the body.

M'naghten test A widely used legal test for insanity that holds people to be insane at the time they committed a crime if, because of a mental disorder, they did not know the nature of the act or did not know right from wrong.

Model A set of assumptions and concepts that help scientists explain and interpret observations. Also called a *paradigm*.

Modeling A process of learning in which a person observes and then imitates others. Also, a therapy approach based on the same principle.

Moderate retardation A level of mental retardation (IQ between 35 and 49) at which people can learn to care for themselves and benefit from vocational training.

Moral treatment A nineteenth-century approach to treating people with mental dysfunction which emphasized moral guidance and humane and respectful treatment.

Morphine A highly addictive substance derived from opium that is particularly effective in relieving pain.

Multidimensional risk perspective A theory that identifies several kinds of risk factors that are thought to combine to help cause a disorder. The more factors present, the greater the risk of developing the disorder.

Multiple personality disorder A dissociative disorder in which a person develops two or more distinct personalities. Also known as *dissociative identity disorder*.

Munchausen syndrome The extreme and chronic form of factitious disorder.

Munchausen syndrome by proxy A disorder in which parents make up or induce physical illnesses in their children.

Muscle contraction headache A headache caused by the narrowing of muscles surrounding the skull. Also known as *tension headache*.

Narcissistic personality disorder A personality disorder marked by a broad pattern of grandiosity, need for admiration, and lack of empathy.

Natural experiment An experiment in which nature, rather than an experimenter, manipulates an independent variable.

Naturalistic observation A method for observing behavior in which clinicians or researchers observe people in their everyday environments.

Negative symptoms Symptoms of schizophrenia that seem to be deficits in normal thought, emotions, or behaviors.

Neurofibrillary tangles Twisted protein fibers that form within certain brain cells as people age.

Neuroleptic drugs Conventional antipsychotic drugs, so called because they often produce undesired effects similar to the symptoms of neurological disorders.

Neurological test A test that directly measures brain structure or activity.

Neuron A nerve cell.

Neuropsychological test A test that detects brain impairment by measuring a person's cognitive, perceptual, and motor performances.

Neurotransmitter A chemical that, released by one neuron, crosses the synaptic space to be received at receptors on the dendrites of neighboring neurons.

Neutralizing An attempt to eliminate unwanted thoughts by thinking or behaving in ways that put matters right internally, that make up for the unacceptable thoughts.

Nocturnal penile tumescence (NPT) Erection during sleep.

Nomothetic understanding A general understanding of the nature, causes, and treatments of abnormal psychological functioning in the form of laws or principles.

Norepinephrine A neurotransmitter whose abnormal activity is linked to panic disorder and depression.

Normalization The principle that institutions and community residences should expose people with mental retardation to living conditions and opportunities similar to those found in the rest of society.

Norms A society's stated and unstated rules for proper conduct.

Not guilty by reason of insanity (NGRI) A verdict stating that defendants are not guilty of committing a crime because they were insane at the time of the crime.

Object relations theory The psychodynamic theory that views the desire for relationships as the key motivating force in human behavior.

Obsession A persistent thought, idea, impulse, or image that is experienced repeatedly, feels intrusive, and causes anxiety.

Obsessive-compulsive disorder A disorder in which a person has recurrent unwanted thoughts, a need to perform repetitive and rigid actions, or both.

Obsessive-compulsive personality disorder A personality disorder marked by such an intense focus on orderliness, perfectionism, and control that the individual loses flexibility, openness, and efficiency.

Operant conditioning A process of learning in which behavior that leads to satisfying consequences is likely to be repeated.

Opioid Opium or any of the drugs derived from opium, including morphine, heroin, and codeine.

Opium A highly addictive substance made from the sap of the opium poppy.

Oppositional defiant disorder A childhood disorder in which children argue repeatedly with adults, lose their temper, and swear, feeling intense anger and resentment.

Orbital frontal cortex A region of the brain in which impulses involving excretion, sexuality, violence, and other primitive activities normally arise.

Orgasm phase The phase of the sexual response cycle during which an individual's sexual pleasure peaks and sexual tension is released as muscles in the pelvic region contract rhythmically.

Orgasmic reorientation A procedure for treating certain paraphilias by teaching clients to respond to new, more appropriate sources of sexual stimulation.

Pain disorder associated with psychological factors A somatoform disorder marked by pain, with psychosocial factors playing a central role in the onset, severity, or continuation of the pain.

Panic attack Periodic short bouts of panic that occur suddenly, reach a peak within minutes, and gradually pass.

Panic disorder An anxiety disorder marked by recurrent and unpredictable panic attacks.

Paranoid personality disorder A personality disorder marked by a pattern of distrust and suspiciousness of others.

Paranoid type of schizophrenia A type of schizophrenia in which the person has an organized system of delusions and hallucinations.

Paraphilias Disorders characterized by recurrent and intense sexual urges, fantasies, or behaviors involving nonhuman objects, children, nonconsenting adults, or experiences of suffering or humiliation.

Parasuicide A suicide attempt that does not result in death.

Parkinson's disease A slowly progressive neurological disease, marked by tremors and rigidity, which may also cause dementia.

Passive-aggressive personality disorder A category of personality disorder listed in past versions of the DSM, marked by a pattern of negative attitudes and resistance to the demands of others.

Pedophilia A paraphilia in which a person has repeated and intense sexual urges or fantasies about watching, touching, or engaging in sexual acts with prepubescent children, and may carry out those urges or fantasies.

Peer review system A system by which clinicians paid by an insurance company may periodically review a patient's progress and recommend the continuation or termination of insurance benefits.

Performance anxiety The fear of performing inadequately and a related tension experienced during sex.

Personality A unique and long-term pattern of inner experience and outward behavior, which leads to consistent reactions across various situations.

Personality disorder A very rigid pattern of inner experience and outward behavior that differs from the expectations of one's culture and leads to dysfunctioning.

Personality inventory A test designed to measure broad personality characteristics, consisting of statements about behaviors, beliefs, and feelings that people evaluate as either characteristic or uncharacteristic of them.

Phenothiazines A group of antihistamine drugs that became the first group of effective antipsychotic medications.

Phobia A persistent and unreasonable fear of a particular object, activity, or situation.

Pick's disease A neurological disease that affects the frontal and temporal lobes, causing dementia.

Placebo A sham treatment that a subject believes to be genuine.

Play therapy An approach to treating childhood disorders that helps children express their conflicts and feelings indirectly by drawing, playing with toys, and making up stories.

Polysubstance-related disorder A long-term pattern of maladaptive behavior centered on abuse of or dependence on a combination of drugs.

Positive symptoms Symptoms of schizophrenia that seem to be excesses of or bizarre additions to normal thoughts, emotions, or behaviors.

Posttraumatic stress disorder An anxiety disorder in which fear and related symptoms continue to be experienced long after a traumatic event.

Prefrontal lobes Regions of the brain that play a key role in short-term memory, among other functions.

Premature ejaculation A dysfunction in which a man reaches orgasm and ejaculates before, on, or shortly after penetration and before he wishes to.

Preoccupation somatoform disorders Somatoform disorders in which people misinterpret and overreact to minor, even normal, bodily symptoms or features.

Preparedness A predisposition to develop certain fears.

Prevalence The total number of cases of a disorder occurring in a population over a specific period of time.

Primary gain In psychodynamic theory, the gain achieved when hysterical symptoms keep internal conflicts out of awareness.

Private psychotherapy An arrangement in which a person directly pays a therapist for counseling services.

Profound retardation A level of mental retardation (IQ below 20) at which individuals need a very structured environment with close supervision.

Projective test A test consisting of ambiguous material that people interpret or respond to.

Psychoanalysis Either the theory or the treatment of abnormal mental functioning that emphasizes unconscious psychological forces as the cause of psychopathology.

Psychogenic perspective The view that the chief causes of abnormal functioning are psychological.

Psychoneuroimmunology The study of the connections between stress, the body's immune system, and illness.

Psychopharmacologist A psychiatrist who primarily prescribes medications. Also known as a *pharmacotherapist*.

Psychophysiological disorders Illnesses that result from an interaction of psychosocial and organic factors. Also known as *psychosomatic disorders*.

Psychophysiological test A test that measures physical responses (such as heart rate and muscle tension) as possible indicators of psychological problems.

Psychosis A state in which a person loses contact with reality in key ways.

Psychosurgery Brain surgery for mental disorders.

Psychotropic medications Drugs that mainly affect the brain and reduce many symptoms of mental dysfunctioning.

Quasi-experiment An experiment in which investigators make use of control and experimental groups that already exist in the world at large. Also called a *mixed design*.

Random assignment A selection procedure that ensures that subjects are randomly placed either in the control group or in the experimental group.

Rap group A group that meets to talk about and explore members' problems in an atmosphere of mutual support.

Rape Forced sexual intercourse or another sexual act upon a nonconsenting person or intercourse with an underage person.

Rapprochement movement An effort to identify a set of common strategies that run through the work of all effective therapists.

Rational-emotive therapy A cognitive therapy developed by Albert Ellis which helps clients to identify and change the irrational assumptions and thinking that help cause their psychological disorder.

Reaction formation An ego defense mechanism whereby a person suppresses an unacceptable desire by taking on a lifestyle that expresses the opposite desire.

Relapse-prevention training An approach to treating alcohol abuse that is similar to BSCT and also has clients plan ahead for risky situations and reactions.

Relaxation training A treatment procedure that teaches clients to relax at will so they can calm themselves in stressful situations.

Reliability A measure of the consistency of test or research results.

Residential treatment center A place where people formerly dependent on drugs live, work, and socialize in a drug-free environment. Also called a *therapeutic community*.

Residual type of schizophrenia A type of schizophrenia in which the acute symptoms of the disorder have lessened in strength and number, yet remain in residual form.

Resistance An unconscious refusal to participate fully in therapy.

Response inventories Tests designed to measure a person's responses in one specific area of functioning, such as affect, social skills, or cognitive processes.

Retrograde amnesia A lack of memory about events that occurred before the event that triggered amnesia.

Retrospective analysis A psychological autopsy in which clinicians and researchers piece together information about a person's suicide from the person's past.

Reward center A dopamine-rich pathway in the brain that produces feelings of pleasure when activated.

Reward-deficiency syndrome A condition, suspected to be present in some individuals, in which the brain's reward center is not readily activated by the usual events in their lives.

Right to refuse treatment The legal right of patients to refuse certain forms of treatment.

Right to treatment The legal right of patients, particularly those who are involuntarily committed, to receive adequate treatment.

Schizoid personality disorder A personality disorder in which a person persistently avoids social relationships and shows little emotional expression.

Schizophrenia A psychotic disorder in which personal, social, and occupational functioning deteriorate as a result of strange perceptions, disturbed thought processes, unusual emotions, and motor abnormalities.

Schizophrenogenic mother A type of mother—supposedly cold, domineering, and uninterested in the needs of others—who was once thought to cause schizophrenia in her child.

Schizotypal personality disorder A personality disorder in which a person displays a pattern of interpersonal problems marked by extreme discomfort in close relationships, odd forms of thinking and perceiving, and behavioral eccentricities.

School phobia A childhood pattern in which children fear going to school and often stay home for a long period of time. Also known as *school refusal*.

Scientific method The process of systematically gathering and evaluating information through careful observations to gain an understanding of a phenomenon.

Second messengers Chemical changes within a neuron just after the neuron receives a neurotransmitter message and just before it responds.

Secondary gain In psychodynamic theory, the gain achieved when hysterical symptoms elicit kindness from others or provide an excuse to avoid unpleasant activities.

Sedative-hypnotic drug A drug used in low doses to reduce anxiety and in higher doses to help people sleep. Also called *anxiolytic drug*.

Selective serotonin reuptake inhibitors (SSRIs) A group of second-generation antidepressant drugs that increase serotonin activity specifically, without affecting other neurotransmitters.

Self-actualization The humanistic process by which people fulfill their potential for goodness and growth.

Self-efficacy The belief that one can master and perform needed behaviors whenever necessary.

Self-help group A group made up of people with similar problems who help and support one another without the direct leadership of a clinician. Also called a *mutual help group*.

Self-hypnosis The process of hypnotizing oneself, sometimes for the purpose of forgetting unpleasant events.

Self-instruction training A cognitive treatment developed by Donald Meichenbaum which teaches clients to use coping self-statements at times of stress. Also known as *stress inoculation training*.

Self-monitoring A technique for observing behavior in which clients observe themselves.

Self theory The psychodynamic theory that emphasizes the role of the self—our unified personality.

Senile plaques Sphere-shaped deposits of beta-amyloid protein that form in the spaces between certain brain cells and in certain blood vessels as people age.

Separation anxiety disorder A childhood disorder marked by excessive anxiety, even panic, whenever the child is separated from home or a parent.

Serotonin A neurotransmitter whose abnormal activity is linked to depression, obsessive-compulsive disorder, and eating disorders.

Severe retardation A level of mental retardation (IQ between 20 and 34) at which individuals require careful supervision and can learn to perform basic work in structured and sheltered settings.

Sex-change surgery A surgical procedure that changes a person's sex organs and features, and, in turn, sexual identity.

Sexual aversion disorder A disorder characterized by an aversion to and avoidance of genital sexual interplay.

Sexual dysfunction A disorder marked by a persistent inability to function normally in some area of the human sexual response cycle.

Sexual masochism A paraphilia characterized by repeated and intense sexual urges, fantasies, or behaviors that involve being humiliated, beaten, bound, or otherwise made to suffer.

Sexual sadism A paraphilia characterized by repeated and intense sexual urges, fantasies, or behaviors that involve inflicting suffering on others.

Sheltered workshop A protected and supervised workplace that offers job opportunities and training at a pace and level tailored to people with various psychological disabilities who are not yet ready for competitive jobs.

Short-term memory The memory system that collects new information. Also known as *working memory*.

Single-subject experiment A research method in which a single subject is observed and measured both before and after the manipulation of an independent variable.

Situation anxiety The various levels of anxiety produced in a person by different situations.

Social phobia A severe and persistent fear of social or performance situations in which embarrassment may occur.

Social skills training A therapy approach that helps people learn or improve social skills and assertiveness through role playing and rehearsing of desirable behaviors.

Somatization disorder A somatoform disorder marked by numerous recurring physical ailments without an organic basis. Also known as *Briquet's syndrome.*

Somatoform disorder A physical illness or ailment that is explained largely by psychosocial causes, in which the patient experiences no sense of wanting or guiding the symptoms.

Somatogenic perspective The view that abnormal psychological functioning has physical causes.

Special education An approach to educating children with mental retardation in which they are grouped together and given a separate, specially designed education.

Specific phobia A severe and persistent fear of a specific object or situation (excluding agoraphobia and social phobia).

Spectator role A state of mind that some people experience during sex, focusing on their sexual performance to such an extent that their performance and their enjoyment are reduced.

Standardization The process in which a test is administered to a large group of persons whose performance then serves as a common standard or norm against which any individual's score can be measured.

State-dependent learning Learning that becomes associated with the conditions under which it occurred, so that it is best remembered under the same conditions. That is, people may remember an event best when they return to the mental state they were in at the time of the event.

State hospitals State-run public mental institutions in the United States.

State school A state-supported institution for individuals with mental retardation.

Stimulus generalization A phenomenon in which responses to one stimulus are also produced by similar stimuli.

Stress management program An approach to treating generalized and other anxiety disorders that teaches clients techniques for reducing and controlling stress.

Stress-reduction seminar A workshop or series of group sessions offered by a business in which mental health professionals teach employees how to cope with and solve problems and reduce stress. Also known as *problem-solving seminar*.

Stress response A person's particular reactions to stress.

Stressor An event that creates a sense of threat by confronting a person with a demand or opportunity for change.

Structured observation A method for observing behavior in which people are observed in artificial settings such as clinicians' offices or laboratories.

Subintentional death A death in which the victim plays an indirect, hidden, partial, or unconscious role.

Subpersonalities The two or more distinct personalities found in individuals suffering from multiple personality disorder, each with a unique set of memories, behaviors, thoughts, and emotions. Also known as *alternate personalities*.

Substance abuse A pattern of behavior in which people rely on a drug excessively and regularly, bringing damage to their relationships, functioning poorly at work, or putting themselves or others in danger.

Substance dependence A pattern of behavior in which people organize their lives around a drug, possibly building a tolerance to it or experiencing withdrawal symptoms when they stop taking it, or both. Also called *addiction*.

Suicide A self-inflicted death in which the person acts intentionally, directly, and consciously.

Suicide prevention program A program that tries to identify people who are at risk of killing themselves and to offer them crisis intervention.

Superego According to Freud, the psychological force that represents a person's values and ideals.

Symbolic loss According to Freudian theory, the loss of a valued object (for example, a loss of employment) which is unconsciously interpreted as the loss of a loved one. Also called *imagined loss*.

Synapse The tiny space between the nerve ending of one neuron and the dendrite of another.

Syndrome A cluster of symptoms that usually occur together.

Synergistic effect In pharmacology, an increase of effects that occurs when more than one substance is acting on the body at the same time.

Systematic desensitization A behavioral treatment that uses relaxation training and a fear hierarchy to help clients with phobias react calmly to the objects or situations they dread.

Tardive dyskinesia Extrapyramidal effects that appear in some patients after they have taken conventional antipsychotic drugs for an extended time.

Temporal lobes Regions of the brain that play a key role in transforming short-term to long-term memory, among other functions.

Test A device for gathering information about a few aspects of a person's psychological functioning from which broader information about the person can be inferred.

Tetrahydrocannabinol (THC) The main active ingredient of cannabis substances.

Theory of mind Awareness that other people base their behaviors on their own beliefs, intentions, and other mental states, not on information they have no way of knowing.

Token economy program A behavioral program in which a person's desirable behaviors are reinforced systematically throughout the day by the awarding of tokens that can be exchanged for goods or privileges.

Tolerance The adjustment that the brain and the body make to the regular use of certain drugs so that even larger doses are needed to achieve the earlier effects.

Trait anxiety The general level of anxiety that a person brings to the various events in his or her life.

Transference According to psychodynamic theorists, a process that occurs during psychotherapy, in which patients act toward the therapist as they did or do toward important figures in their lives.

Transvestic fetishism A paraphilia consisting of repeated and intense sexual urges, fantasies, or behaviors that involve dressing in clothes of the opposite sex. Also known as *transvestism*.

Treatment A procedure designed to help change abnormal behavior into more normal behavior. Also called *therapy*.

Trephination An ancient operation in which a stone instrument was used to cut away a circular section of the skull, perhaps to treat abnormal behavior.

Tricyclic An antidepressant drug such as imipramine that has three rings in its molecular structure.

Type I schizophrenia A type of schizophrenia characterized mainly by positive symptoms, such as delusions, hallucinations, and certain formal thought disorders.

Type II schizophrenia A type of schizophrenia in which the person experiences mostly negative symptoms, such as flat affect, poverty of speech, and loss of volition.

Type A personality style A personality pattern characterized by hostility, cynicism, drivenness, impatience, competitiveness, and ambition.

Type B personality style A personality pattern in which persons are more relaxed, less aggressive, and less concerned about time.

Ulcer A lesion that forms in the wall of the stomach or of the duodenum.

Undifferentiated type of schizophrenia A type of schizophrenia in which no single set of psychotic symptoms (incoherence, psychomotor disturbances, delusions, or hallucinations) dominates.

Undoing An ego defense mechanism whereby a person unconsciously cancels out an unacceptable desire or act by performing another act.

Unipolar depression Depression without a history of mania.

Vaginismus A condition marked by involuntary contractions of the muscles around the outer third of the vagina, preventing entry of the penis.

Validity The accuracy of a test's or study's results; that is, the extent to which the test or study actually measures or shows what it claims.

Vascular dementia Dementia caused by a cerebrovascular accident, or stroke, which restricts blood flow to certain areas of the brain. Also known as *multi-infarct dementia*.

Ventromedial hypothalamus (VMH) The region of the hypothalamus that, when activated, depresses hunger.

Voyeurism A paraphilia in which a person has repeated and intense sexual desires to observe unsuspecting people in secret as they undress or to spy on couples having intercourse, and may act upon those desires.

Weight set point The weight level that a person is predisposed to maintain, controlled in part by the hypothalamus.

Withdrawal Unpleasant, sometimes dangerous reactions that may occur when people who use a drug regularly stop taking or reduce their dosage of the drug.

Working through The psychoanalytic process of facing conflicts, reinterpreting feelings, and overcoming one's problems.

references

Journal Abbreviations

Acta Psychiatr. Scand.—Acta Psychiatrica Scandinavica
Addict. Behav.—Addictive Behaviors
Adolesc. Psychiatry—Adolescent Psychiatry
Adv. Behav. Res. Ther.—Advances in Behavior Research and Therapy
Adv. Drug React. Toxicol. Rev.—Advanced Drug Reaction and Toxicology Review
Adv. Mind-Body Med.—Advances in Mind-Body Medicine
Alcohol Alcohol.—Alcohol and Alcoholism
Am. Health—American Health
Am. J. Addict.—American Journal on Addictions
Am. J. Cardiol.—American Journal of Cardiology
Am. J. Clin. Hypnosis—American Journal of Clinical Hypnosis
Am. J. Clin. Hypnother.—American Journal of Clinical Hypnotherapy
Am. J. Clin. Nutr.—American Journal of Clinical Nutrition
Am. J. Commun. Psychol.—American Journal of Community Psychology
Am. J. Criminal Justice—American Journal of Criminal Justice
Am. J. Forens. Psychol.—American Journal of Forensic Psychology
Am. J. Geriatr. Psychiatry—American Journal of Geriatric Psychiatry
Am. J. Health Syst. Pharmacol.—American Journal of Health Systems and Pharmacology
Am. J. Med. Genet.—American Journal of Medical Genetics
Am. J. Ment. Defic.—American Journal of Mental Deficiency
Am. J. Ment. Retard.—American Journal on Mental Retardation
Am. J. Obstet. Gynecol.—American Journal of Obstetrics and Gynecology
Am. J. Orthopsychiatry—American Journal of Orthopsychiatry
Am. J. Psychiatry—American Journal of Psychiatry
Am. J. Psychother.—American Journal of Psychotherapy
Am. J. Public Health—American Journal of Public Health
Am. Psychol.—American Psychologist
Am. Sci.—American Scientist
Am. Sociol. Rev.—American Sociological Review
Ann. Behav. Med.—Annals of Behavioral Medicine
Ann. Clin. Psychiatry—Annals of Clinical Psychiatry
Ann. Intern. Med.—Annals of Internal Medicine
Ann. Med.—Annals of Medicine
Ann. Neurol.—Annals of Neurology
Ann. Pharmacother.—Annals of Pharmacotherapy
Annu. Rev. Neurosci.—Annual Review of Neuroscience
Annu. Rev. Psychol.—Annual Review of Psychology
Appl. Cognit. Psychol.—Applied Cognitive Psychology
Appl. Neuropsychol.—Applied Neuropsychology
Appl. Prev. Psychol.—Applied and Preventive Psychology
Appl. Psychophysiol. Biofeedback—Applied Psychophysiology and Biofeedback
Arch. Fam. Med.—Archives of Family Medicine
Arch. Gen. Psychiatry—Archives of General Psychiatry
Arch. Intern. Med.—Archives of Internal Medicine
Arch. Neurol.—Archives of Neurology
Arch. Pediatr. Adolesc. Med.—Archives of Pediatric Adolescent Medicine
Arch. Psychiatr. Nurs.—Archives of Psychiatric Nursing
Arch. Sex. Behav.—Archives of Sexual Behavior
Arch. Suicide Res.—Archives of Suicide Research
Aust. J. Clin. Exp. Hypnosis—Australian Journal of Clinical and Experimental Hypnosis
Aust. N. Z. J. Psychiatry—Australian and New Zealand Journal of Psychiatry
Aust. Psychol.—Australian Psychologist

Basic Appl. Soc. Psychol.—Basic and Applied Social Psychology
Behav. Brain Res.—Behavioral Brain Research
Behav.-Change—Behaviour-Change

Behav. Cognit. Psychother.—Behavioral and Cognitive Psychotherapy
Behav. Genet.—Behavioral Genetics
Behav. Med.—Behavioral Medicine
Behav. Modif.—Behavior Modification
Behav. Neurosci.—Behavioral Neuroscience
Behav. Psychother.—Behavioural Psychotherapy
Behav. Res. Methods Instrum. Comput.—Behavioral Research Methods, Instruments and Computers
Behav. Res. Ther.—Behavior Research and Therapy
Behav. Sci.—Behavioral Science
Behav. Sci. Law—Behavioral Science and the Law
Behav. Ther.—Behavior Therapy
Biofeedback Self-Regul.—Biofeedback and Self-Regulation
Biol. Psychiatry—Biological Psychiatry
Biol. Psychol.—Biological Psychology
Brain, Behav. Immun.—Brain, Behavior and Immunity
Brain Injury—Brain Injury
Brain Res.—Brain Research
Br. J. Cognit. Psychother.—British Journal of Cognitive Psychotherapy
Br. J. Dev. Psychol.—British Journal of Developmental Psychology
Br. J. Med. Psychol.—British Journal of Medicinal Psychology
Br. J. Psychiatry—British Journal of Psychiatry
Br. J. Urol.—British Journal of Urology
Br. Med. J.—British Medical Journal
Bull. Am. Acad. Psychiatry Law—Bulletin of the American Academy of Psychiatry Law
Bull. Menninger Clin.—Bulletin of the Menninger Clinic
Bull. Psychol.—Bulletin de Psychologie
Bull. Psychosom. Soc.—Bulletin of the Psychosomatic Society

Can. J. Neurol. Sci.—Canadian Journal of Neurological Science
Can. J. Psychiatry—Canadian Journal of Psychiatry
Can. Psychol.—Canadian Psychology
Child Abuse Neglect—Child Abuse and Neglect
Child Adolesc. Psychiatr. Clin. North Am.—Child and Adolescent Psychiatric Clinics of North America
Child Dev.—Child Development
Child Maltreat.: J. Am. Prof. Soc. Abuse Child.—Child Maltreatment: Journal of the American Professional Society on the Abuse of Children
Child Psychiatry Hum. Dev.—Child Psychiatry and Human Development
Chron. Higher Educ.—Chronicle of Higher Education
Clin. Child Psychol. Psychiatry—Clinical Child Psychology and Psychiatry
Clin. Electroencephalogr.—Clinical Electroencephalography
Clin. Pediatr.—Clinical Pediatrics
Clin. Pharmacol. Ther.—Clinical and Pharmacological Therapy
Clin. Psychol. Rev.—Clinical Psychology Review
Clin. Psychol.: Sci. Pract.—Clinical Psychology: Science and Practice
Clin. Rehabil.—Clinical Rehabilitation
Clin. Soc. Work J.—Clinical Social Work Journal
Clin. Ther.: Int. J. Drug Ther.—Clinical Therapeutics: The International Journal of Drug Therapy
Cognition Emotion—Cognition & Emotion
Cognit. Ther. Res.—Cognitive Therapy and Research
Commun. Res.—Communication Research
Compr. Psychiatry—Comprehensive Psychiatry
Compr. Ther.—Comprehensive Therapy
Contemp. Hypnosis—Contemporary Hypnosis
Contemp. Psychol.—Contemporary Psychology
Criminal Justice Behav.—Criminal Justice and Behavior
Cult. Diversity Ethnic Minority Psychol.—Cultural Diversity and Ethnic Minority Psychology
Cult. Med. Psychiatry—Culture, Medicine and Psychiatry
Curr. Dir. Psychol. Sci.—Current Directions in Psychological Science
Curr. Probl. Pediatr.—Current Problems in Pediatrics

Death Stud.—Death Studies
Dementia Geriatr. Cognit. Disord.—Dementia and Geriatric Cognitive Disorders
Depression Anxiety—Depression and Anxiety
Dev. Neuropsychol.—Developmental Neuropsychology
Dev. Psychol.—Developmental Psychology
Dev. Psychopathol.—Developmental Psychopathology
Dis. Nerv. Syst.—Diseases of the Nervous System
Diss. Abstr. Int. A—Dissertation Abstracts International: Section A: Humanities and Social Sciences
Diss. Abstr. Int. B—Dissertation Abstracts International: Section B: The Sciences and Engineering
Dissoc. Prog. Dissoc. Disord.—Dissociation Progress in the Dissociative Disorders
Drug Alcohol Depend.—Drug and Alcohol Dependence

Eat. Disord.: J. Treat. Prev.—Eating Disorders: The Journal of Treatment and Prevention
Empirical Stud. Arts—Empirical Studies of the Arts
Endocr. Res.—Endocrine Research
Ethics Behav.—Ethics & Behavior
Eur. Arch. Psychiatry Clin. Neurosci.—European Archives of Psychiatry and Clinical Neuroscience
Eur. Arch. Psychiatry Neurol. Sci.—European Archives of Psychiatry and Neurological Science
Eur. J. Med. Res.—European Journal of Medical Research
Eur. J. Pers.—European Journal of Personality
Eur. J. Psychiatry—European Journal of Psychiatry
Eur. J. Psychol. Assess.—European Journal of Psychological Assessment
Eur. Neurol.—European Neurology
Eur. Neuropsychopharmacol.—European Neuropsychopharmacology
Eur. Psychiatry—European Psychiatry
Eur. Urol.—European Urology
Exp. Clin. Psychopharmacol.—Experimental and Clinical Pharmacology

Fam. Process—Family Process
Fed. Probation—Federal Probation

G. Ital. Suicidol.—Giornale Italiano di Suicidologia
Gen. Hosp. Psychiatry—General Hospital Psychiatry
Gender Soc.—Gender and Society

Health Care Women Int.—Health Care for Women International
Health Psychol.—Health Psychology
Homeostasis Health Dis.—Homeostasis Health and Disease
Hosp. Commun. Psychiatry—Hospital and Community Psychiatry
Hum. Mutat.—Human Mutation
Hum. Psychopharmacol. Clin. Exp.—Human Psychopharmacology Clinical and Experimental

Imagination Cognit. Pers.—Imagination, Cognition and Personality
Indian J. Clin. Psychol.—Indian Journal of Clinical Psychology
Individual Psychol.: J. Adlerian Theory Res. Pract.—Individual Psychology: A Journal of Adlerian Theory, Research and Practice
Injury Prev.—Injury Prevention
Integr. Physiol. Behav. Sci.—Integrative Physiological and Behavioral Science
Integr. Psychiatry—Integrated Psychiatry
Int. Clin. Psychopharmacol.—International Clinical Psychopharmacology
Int. Forum Psychoanal.—International Forum of Psychoanalysis
Int. J. Addict.—International Journal of Addiction
Int. J. Aging Hum. Dev.—International Journal of Aging and Human Development
Int. J. Behav. Dev.—International Journal of Behavioral Development

Int. J. Behav. Med.—International Journal of Behavioral Medicine

Int. J. Clin. Exp. Hypnosis—International Journal of Clinical and Experimental Hypnosis

Int. J. Eat. Disord. International—Journal of Eating Disorders

Int. J. Geriatr. Psychiatry—International Journal of Geriatric Psychiatry

Int. J. Group Psychother.—International Journal of Group Psychotherapy

Int. J. Ment. Health—International Journal of Mental Health

Int. J. Methods Psychiatr. Res.—International Journal of Methods in Psychiatric Research

Int. J. Obes.—International Journal of Obesity

Int. J. Offender Ther. Comp. Criminol.—International Journal of Offender Therapy and Comparative Criminology

Int. J. Psychiatry Clin. Pract.—International Journal of Psychiatry in Clinical Practice

Int. J. Psychoanal.—International Journal of Psychoanalysis

Int. J. Psychoanal.-Psychother.—International Journal of Psychoanalytic-Psychotherapy

Int. J. Psychol. Religion—International Journal for the Psychology of Religion

Int. J. Psychophysiol.—International Journal of Psychophysiology

Int. J. Psychosom.—International Journal of Psychosomatics

Int. J. Soc. Psychiatry—International Journal of Social Psychiatry

Int. J. Stress Manag.—International Journal of Stress Management

Int. Med. J.—International Medical Journal

Int. Psychogeriatr.—International Psychogeriatrics

Ir. J. Psychol. Med.—Irish Journal of Psychological Medicine

Issues. Ment. Health Nurs.—Issues in Mental Health Nursing

Ital. J. Neurol. Sci.—Italian Journal of Neurological Sciences

J. Abnorm. Child Psychol.—Journal of Abnormal Child Psychology

J. Abnorm. Psychol.—Journal of Abnormal Psychology

J. Abnorm. Soc. Psychol.—Journal of Abnormal and Social Psychology

J. Adolesc.—Journal of Adolescence

J. Adolesc. Health—Journal of Adolescent Health

J. Adv. Nurs.—Journal of Advanced Nursing

J. Affect. Disord.—Journal of Affective Disorders

J. Alcohol Drug Educ.—Journal of Alcohol and Drug Education

J. Am. Acad. Child Adolesc. Psychiatry—Journal of the American Academy of Child and Adolescent Psychiatry

J. Am. Acad. Psychiatry Law—Journal of the American Academy of Psychiatry and the Law

J. Am. Acad. Psychoanal.—Journal of the American Academy of Psychoanalysis

J. Am. Board Fam. Pract.—Journal of American Board of Family Practitioners

J. Am. Coll. Health—Journal of American College Health

J. Am. Geriatr. Soc.—Journal of the American Geriatric Society

J. Am. Med. Assoc. JAMA—Journal of the American Medical Association

J. Am. Osteopath. Assoc.—Journal of American Osteopathic Association

J. Am. Psychiatr. Nurs. Assoc.—Journal of the American Psychiatric Nurses Association

J. Am. Psychoanal. Assoc.—Journal of the American Psychoanalytical Association

J. Anxiety Disord.—Journal of Anxiety Disorders

J. Appl. Behav. Anal.—Journal of Applied Behavior Analysis

J. Appl. Behav. Sci.—Journal of Applied Behavioral Sciences

J. Appl. Physiol.—Journal of Applied Physiology

J. Appl. Soc. Psychol.—Journal of Applied Social Psychology

J. Appl. Soc. Sci.—Journal of Applied Social Sciences

J. Asthma—Journal of Asthma

J. Autism Child. Schizophr.—Journal of Autism and Childhood Schizophrenia

J. Autism Dev. Disord.—Journal of Autism and Developmental Disorders

J. Behav. Decision Making—Journal of Behavioral Decision Making

J. Behav. Ther. Exp. Psychiatry—Journal of Behavior Therapy and Experimental Psychiatry

J. Cardiovasc. Pharmacol. Ther.—Journal of Cardiovascular Pharmacology and Therapy

J. Child Adolesc. Psychopharmacol.—Journal of Child and Adolescent Psychopharmacology

J. Child Psychol. Psychiatry—Journal of Child Psychology and Psychiatry

J. Child Psychol. Psychiatry Allied Discip.—Journal of Child Psychology, Psychiatry and Allied Disciplines

J. Child Sex. Abuse—Journal of Child Sexual Abuse

J. Clin. Child Psychol.—Journal of Clinical Child Psychology

J. Clin. Geropsychol.—Journal of Clinical Geropsychology

J. Clin. Psychiatry—Journal of Clinical Psychiatry

J. Clin. Psychol.—Journal of Clinical Psychology

J. Clin. Psychol. Med. Settings—Journal of Clinical Psychology in Medical Settings

J. Clin. Psychopharmacol.—Journal of Clinical Psychopharmacology

J. Cognit. Psychother.—Journal of Cognitive Psychotherapy

J. Coll. Stud. Dev.—Journal of College Student Development

J. Commun. Psychol.—Journal of Community Psychology

J. Consult. Clin. Psychol.—Journal of Consulting and Clinical Psychology

J. Counsel. Dev.—Journal of Counseling & Development

J. Counsel. Psychol.—Journal of Counseling Psychology

J. Cross-Cult. Psychol.—Journal of Cross-Cultural Psychology

J. Early Adolesc.—Journal of Early Adolescence

J. Epidemiol. Commun. Health—Journal of Epidemiology and Community Health

J. Exp. Anal. Behav.—Journal of Experimental Analysis of Behavior

J. Exp. Child Psychol.—Journal of Experimental Child Psychology

J. Exp. Psychol.—Journal of Experimental Psychology

J. Exp. Psychol. Gen.—Journal of Experimental Psychology General

J. Exp. Soc. Psychol.—Journal of Experimental Social Psychology

J. Fam. Issues—Journal of Family Issues

J. Fam. Pract.—Journal of Family Practice

J. Fam. Psychother.—Journal of Family Psychotherapy

J. Gambling Stud.—Journal of Gambling Studies

J. Gen. Intern. Med.—Journal of General Internal Medicine

J. Genet. Psychol.—Journal of Genetic Psychology

J. Geriatr. Psychiatry Neurol.—Journal of Geriatric Psychiatry and Neurology

J. Gerontol. A—Journal of Gerontology, A: Biological Science and Medical Science

J. Gerontol. B—Journal of Gerontology, B. Psychological Science and Social Science

J. Health Care Poor Underserved—Journal of Health Care for the Poor and Underserved

J. Health Soc. Behav.—Journal of Health and Social Behavior

J. Hum. Psychol.—Journal of Humanistic Psychology

J. Interpers. Violence—Journal of Interpersonal Violence

J. Learn. Disord.—Journal of Learning Disorders

J. Marital Fam. Ther.—Journal of Marital and Family Therapy

J. Med. Genet.—Journal of Medical Genetics

J. Ment. Health Admin.—Journal of Mental Health Administration

J. Ment. Health Counsel.—Journal of Mental Health Counseling

J. Ment. Health UK—Journal of Mental Health UK

J. Nerv. Ment. Dis.—Journal of Nervous and Mental Diseases

J. Neurochem.—Journal of Neurochemistry

J. Neurol. Neurosurg. Psychiatry—Journal of Neurology and Neurosurgical Psychiatry

J. Neuropsychiatry Clin. Neurosci.—Journal of Neuropsychiatry and Clinical Neurosciences

J. Neurotrauma—Journal of Neurotrauma

J. Occup. Health Psychol.—Journal of Occupational Health Psychology

J. Perinat. Med.—Journal of Perinatal Medicine

J. Pers. Assess.—Journal of Personality Assessment

J. Pers. Disord.—Journal of Personality Disorders

J. Pers. Soc. Psychol.—Journal of Personality and Social Psychology

J. Pharmacol. Exp. Ther.—Journal of Pharmacology and Experimental Therapeutics

J. Pineal Res.—Journal of Pineal Research

Jpn. J. Hypnosis—Japanese Journal of Hypnosis

J. Primary Prev.—Journal of Primary Prevention

J. Psychiatry Neurosci.—Journal of Psychiatry & Neuroscience

J. Psychiatr. Res.—Journal of Psychiatric Research

J. Psychol.—Journal of Psychology

J. Psychopharmacol.—Journal of Psychopharmacology

J. Psychosom. Med.—Journal of Psychosomatic Medicine

J. Psychosom. Res.—Journal of Psychosomatic Research

J. Psychother. Pract. Res.—Journal of Psychotherapy Practice and Research

J. Ration.-Emotive Cognit.-Behav. Ther.—Journal of Rational-Emotive & Cognitive-Behavior Therapy

J. Rehabil.—Journal of Rehabilitation

J. Sci. Study Religion—Journal for the Scientific Study of Religion

J. Sex Educ. Ther.—Journal of Sex Education and Therapy

J. Sex Marital Ther.—Journal of Sex and Marital Therapy

J. Sex Res.—Journal of Sex Research

J. Soc. Behav. Pers.—Journal of Social Behavior and Personality

J. Soc. Clin. Psychol.—Journal of Social and Clinical Psychology

J. Soc. Pers. Relat.—Journal of Social and Personal Relationships

J. Soc. Psychol.—Journal of Social Psychology

J. Sociol. Soc. Welfare—Journal of Sociology and Social Welfare

J. Sport Exercise Psychol.—Journal of Sport and Exercise Psychology

J. Stud. Alcohol—Journal of Studies on Alcohol

J. Subst. Abuse—Journal of Substance Abuse

J. Traumatic Stress—Journal of Traumatic Stress

J. Urol.—Journal of Urology

J. Youth Adolesc.—Journal of Youth and Adolescence

Law Hum. Behav.—Law and Human Behavior

Law Psychol. Rev.—Law and Psychology Review

Marriage Fam. Rev.—Marriage and Family Review

Med. Aspects Hum. Sex.—Mental Aspects of Human Sexuality

Med. J. Aust.—Medical Journal of Australia

Mil. Med.—Military Medicine

MMW Fortschr. Med.—MMW Fortschritte der Medizin

Mol. Psychiatry—Molecular Psychiatry

Ned. Tidjschr. Geneeskd.—Nederlands Tidjschrift voor Geneeskunde

N. Engl. J. Med.—New England Journal of Medicine

Neurol. Clin.—Neurologic Clinics

Neuropsychiatry, Neuropsychol., Behav. Neurol.—Neuropsychiatry, Neuropsychology, and Behavioral Neurology

N. Z. Med. J.—New Zealand Medical Journal
N. Y. State J. Med.—New York State Journal of Medicine

Obes. Health—Obesity and Health
Omega: J. Death Dying—Omega: Journal of Death and
    Dying

Pediatr. Clin North Am.—Pediatric Clinics of North
    America
Percept. Mot. Skills—Perceptual and Motor Skills
Pers. Individual Differ.—Personality and Individual
    Differences
Pers. Soc. Psychol. Bull.—Personality and Social
    Psychology Bulletin
Pharmacol. Biochem. Behav.—Pharmacological
    Biochemical Behavior
Pharmacol. Rev.—Pharmacological Reviews
Philos. Psychiatry Psychol.—Philosophy, Psychiatry, and
    Psychology
Physiol. Behav.—Physiology and Behavior
Postgrad. Med. J.—Postgraduate Medical Journal
Proc. Natl. Acad. Sci. U.S.A.—Proceedings of the National
    Academy of Sciences of the United States of America
Prof. Psychol.—Professional Psychologist
Prof. Psychol.: Res. Pract.—Professional Psychology:
    Research and Practice
Prof. School Counsel.—Professional School Counseling
Prog. Neuropsychopharmacol.—Progressive
    Neuropsychopharmacology
Prog. Neuropsychopharmacol. Biol. Psychiatry—
    Progressive Neuropsychopharmacological Biological
    Psychiatry
Psychiatr. Ann.—Psychiatric Annals
Psychiatr. Clin. North Am.—Psychiatric Clinics of North
    America
Psychiatr. Hosp.—Psychiatric Hospital
Psychiatr. J. Univ. Ottawa—Psychiatric Journal of the
    University of Ottawa
Psychiatr. Q.—Psychiatric Quarterly
Psychiatr. Serv.—Psychiatric Services
Psychiatr. Times—Psychiatric Times
Psychiatry Genet.—Psychiatry and Genetics
Psychiatry Res.—Psychiatry Research
Psychoanal. Psychol.—Psychoanalytic Psychology
Psychol. Addict. Behav.—Psychology of Addictive Behavior
Psychol. Aging—Psychology and Aging
Psychol. Assess.—Psychological Assessment
Psychol. Bull.—Psychological Bulletin
Psychol. Med.—Psychological Medicine
Psychol. Rec.—Psychological Record
Psychol. Rep.—Psychological Reports
Psychol. Rev.—Psychological Review
Psychol. Sch.—Psychology in the Schools
Psychol. Sci.—Psychological Science
Psychol. Women Q.—Psychology of Women Quarterly
Psychopharmacol. Bull.—Psychopharmacology Bulletin
Psychopharmacology (Berlin)—Psychopharmacology
    (Berlin)
Psychosom. Med.—Psychosomatic Medicine
Psychosomatics—Psychosomatics
Psychother. Private Pract.—Psychotherapy in Private
    Practice
Psychother. Res.—Psychotherapy Research
Psychother. Theory Res. Pract.—Psychotherapy: Theory,
    Research and Practice
Public Pers. Manag.—Public Personnel Management

Q. J. Stud. Alcohol.—Quarterly Journal on the Studies of
    Alcoholism

Rehabil. Counsel. Bull.—Rehabilitation Counseling
    Bulletin
Rehabil. Nurs.—Rehabilitation Nursing
Rehabil. Psychol.—Rehabilitation Psychology

Remed. Spec. Educ.—Remedial and Special Education
Reprod. Nutr. Dev.—Reproductive and Nutritional
    Development
Res. Nurs. Health—Research in Nursing and Health
Res. Soc. Work Pract.—Research on Social Work Practice

S. Afr. J. Psychol.—South African Journal of Psychology
Scand. J. Work Environ. Health—Scandinavian Journal
    of Work and Environment Health
Schizophr. Bull.—Schizophrenic Bulletin
Schizophr. Res.—Schizophrenic Research
Sci. Am.—Scientific American
Semin. Neurol.—Seminars in Neurology
Sex. Abuse J. Res. Treat.—Sexual Abuse Journal of
    Research and Treatment
Sex. Disabil.—Sexual Disability
Sex. Marital Ther.—Sexual and Marital Therapy
Soc. Behav. Pers.—Social Behavior and Personality
Soc. Forces—Social Forces
Soc. Psychiatry—Social Psychiatry
Soc. Psychiatry Psychiatr. Epidemiol.—Social Psychiatry
    and Psychiatric Epidemiology
Soc. Sci. Med.—Social Science and Medicine
Soc. Work Health Care—Social Work Health Care
Subst. Use Misuse—Substance Use and Misuse
Suicide Life-Threaten. Behav.—Suicide and Life-
    Threatening Behavior

Top. Early Child. Spec. Educ.—Topics in Early Childhood
    Special Education
Trends Cell Biol.—Trends in Cell Biology
Trends Neurosci.—Trends in Neuroscience

Women Health—Women & Health

References

AA (Alcoholics Anonymous) World Services.
    (1998). Statistics branch, New York (personal
    communication).
AA (Alcoholics Anonymous) World Services.
    (2000).
AAMR (American Association on Mental Retar-
    dation). (1992). Mental retardation: Definition,
    classification, and systems of supports (9th ed.).
    Washington, DC: Author.
AAPC (American Association for Protecting
    Children). (1992). Highlights of official child ne-
    glect and abuse reporting. Denver, CO: American
    Humane Society.
AARP (American Association of Retired Per-
    sons). (1990). A profile of older Americans. Wash-
    ington, DC: Author.
ADVTP (Alaska Domestic Violence Training Pro-
    ject). (1996). Training the Trainers Workshop.
APA (American Psychiatric Association). (1983).
    APA statement on the insanity defense: Insanity
    defense work group. Am. J. Psychiatry, 140(6),
    681–688.
APA (American Psychiatric Association). (1993).
    Practice guideline for major depressive disorder in
    adults. Washington, DC: Author.
APA (American Psychiatric Association). (1994).
    Diagnostic and statistical manual of mental disorders
    (4th ed.). Washington, DC: Author.
APA (American Psychiatric Association). (1995).
    Ethical principles of psychologists and code of conduct.
    Washington, DC: Author.
APA (American Psychiatric Association). (1995,
    May 23). Survey: Healthy mind over matter. USA
    Today, p. 1D.
APA (American Psychiatric Association). (1996).
    Interim report of the working group on investiga-
tion of memories of childhood abuse. In K. Pezdek
    & W. P. Banks (Eds.), The recovered memory/false
    memory debate. San Diego, CA: Academic Press.
APA (American Psychiatric Association). (2000).
    DSM-IV text revision. Washington, DC: Author.
Aasland, O. G., Ekeberg, O., & Schweder, T.
    (2001). Suicide rates from 1960 to 1989 in Norwe-
    gian physicians compared with other educational
    groups. Soc. Sci. Med., 52(2), 259–265.
Abadi, S. (1984). Adiccion: La eterna repeticion de
    un desencuentro (Acerca de la dependencia
    humana) [Addiction: The endless repetition of
    a disencounter]. Rev. Psicoanal. 41(6), 1029–
    1044.
Abel, E. L., & Zeidenberg, P. (1985). Age, alcohol
    and violent death: A postmortem study. J. Stud. Al-
    cohol, 46, 228–231.
Abel, G. G. (1989). Paraphilias. In H. I. Kaplan &
    B. J. Sadock (Eds.), Comprehensive textbook of psy-
    chiatry (5th ed., Vol. 1). Baltimore: Williams &
    Wilkins.
Abel, G. G., Becker, J. V., & Cunningham-
    Rathner, J. (1984). Complications, consent, and
    cognitions in sex between children and adults. Int.
    J. Law Psychiatry, 7, 89–103.
Abel, G. G., & Osborn, C. (1992). The paraphilias:
    The extent and nature of sexually deviant and
    criminal behavior. Psychiatr. Clin. North Am.,
    15(3), 675–687.
Abou-Saleh, M. T. (1992). Lithium. In E. S. Paykel
    (Ed.), Handbook of affective disorders. New York:
    Guilford Press.
Abou-Saleh, M. T., Ghubash, R., Karim, L.,
    Krymski, M., & Anderson, D. N. (1999). The
    role of pterins and related factors in the biology of
    early postpartum depression. Eur. Neuropsychophar-
    macol., 9(4), 295–300.
Abraham, K. (1911). Notes on the psychoanalytic
    investigation and treatment of manic-depressive
    insanity and allied conditions. In Selected papers on
    psychoanalysis (pp. 137–156). New York: Basic
    Books, 1960.
Abraham, K. (1916). The first pregenital stage of the
    libido. In Selected papers on psychoanalysis (pp.
    248–279). New York: Basic Books, 1960.
Abraham, S., & Llewellyn-Jones, D. (1984). Eating
    disorders: The facts. New York: Oxford University
    Press.
Abrams, K. M., & Robinson, G. E. (1998). Stalk-
    ing: Part I. An overview of the problem. Can. J. Psy-
    chiatry, 43(5), 473–476.
Abrams, K. M., & Teplin, L. A. (1990). Drug disor-
    der, mental illness, and violence. Natl. Inst. Drug
    Abuse Res. Monogr. Ser., 103, 222–238.
Abramson, E. E., & Valene, P. (1991). Media use,
    dietary restraint, bulimia and attitudes towards
    obesity: A preliminary study. Br. Rev. Bulimia
    Anorexia Nervosa, 5(2), 73–76.
Abramson, L. Y., Alloy, L. B., Hogan, M. E.,
    Whitehouse, W. G., Donovan, P., Rose, D. T.,
    Panzarella, C., & Raniere, D. (1999). Cognitive
    vulnerability to depression: Theory and evidence.
    J. Cognit. Psychother., 13(1), 5–20.
Abramson, L. Y., Metalsky, G. I., & Alloy, L. B.
    (1989). Hopelessness depression: A theory-based
    subtype of depression. Psychol. Rev., 96(2),
    358–372.
Abramson, L. Y., Seligman, M. E., & Teasdale,
    J. D. (1978). Learned helplessness in humans: Cri-
    tique and reformulation. J. Abnorm. Psychol.,
    87(1), 49–74.
Ackerman, M. D. (1995). Introduction to the spe-
    cial section on contemporary issues in human sex-
    uality: Research and practice. J. Consult. Clin. Psy-
    chol., 63(6), 859–861.
Ackerman, M. D., & Carey, M. P. (1995). Psychol-
    ogy's role in the assessment of erectile dysfunction:
    Historical precedents, current knowledge, and

methods. *J. Consult. Clin. Psychol., 63*(6), 862–876.

Acocella, J. (1999). *Creating hysteria: Women and multiple personality disorder.* San Francisco: Jossey-Bass.

Adam, K. S., Bouckoms, A., & Streiner, D. (1982). Parental loss and family stability in attempted suicide. *Arch. Gen. Psychiatry, 39*(9), 1081–1085.

Adams, C. E., Pantelis, C., Duke, P. J., & Barnes, T. R. E. (1996). Psychopathology, social, and cognitive functioning in a hostel for homeless women. *Br. J. Psychiatry, 168,* 82–86.

Adams, P. R., & Adams, G. R. (1984). Mount Saint Helen's ashfall: Evidence for a disaster stress reaction. *Am. Psychol., 39,* 252–260.

Adams, W. L., & Cox, N. S. (1997). Epidemiology of problem drinking among elderly people. In A. Gurnack (Ed.), *Older adults' misuse of alcohol, medicines, and other drugs.* New York: Springer.

Addington, D. (1995). The use of placebos in clinical trials for acute schizophrenia. *Can. J. Psychiatry, 40*(4), 171–176.

Addis, M. E. (2000). Graduate training in Boulder model clinical psychology programs: The evolving tension between science and art. In S. Soldz & L. McCullough (Eds.), *Reconciling empirical knowledge and clinical experience: The art and science of psychotherapy* (pp. 51–66). Washington, DC: American Psychological Association.

Ader, R., Felten, D. L., & Cohen, N. (Eds.). (2001). *Psychoneuroimmunology* (3rd ed., Vols. 1 & 2). San Diego, CA: Academic Press.

Adler, G. (2000). The alliance and the more disturbed patient. In S. T. Levy et al. (Eds.), *The therapeutic alliance. Workshop series of the American Psychoanalytic Association* [Monogr. 9]. Madison, CT: International Universities Press.

Adler, N. E., Boyce, T., Chesney, M. A., Cohen, S., Folkman, S., Kahn, R. L., & Syme, S. L. (1994). Socioeconomic status and health: The challenge of the gradient. *Am. Psychol., 49*(1), 15–24.

Adler, T. (1992). Prenatal cocaine exposure has subtle, serious effects. *APA Monitor, 23*(11), 17.

Administrative Office of the U.S. Courts. (1998, May 25). Statistics. Cited in *Time,* p. 33.

Advokat, C. P., & Kutlesic, V. (1995). Pharmacotherapy of the eating disorders: A commentary. *Neurosci. Biobehav. Rev., 19*(1), 59–66.

Agid, O., Shapira, B., Zislin, J., Ritsner, M., Hanin, B., Murad, H., Troudart, T., Bloch, M., Heresco-Levy, U., & Lerer, B. (1999). Environment and vulnerability to major psychiatric illnesses: A case control study of early parental loss in major depression, bipolar disorder and schizophrenia. *Mol. Psychiatry, 4*(2), 163–172.

Agras, W. S. (1984). Behavioral medicine: An overview. In A. J. Frances & R. E. Hales (Eds.), *American Psychiatric Association annual review* (Vol. 5). Washington, DC: American Psychiatric Press.

Agras, W. S. (1984). The behavioral treatment of somatic disorders. In W. D. Gentry (Ed.), *Handbook of behavioral medicine.* New York: Guilford Press.

Agras, W. S. (1995). Treatment of eating disorders. In A. F. Schatzberg & C. B. Nemeroff (Eds.), *The American Psychiatric Press textbook of psychopharmacology.* Washington, DC: American Psychiatric Press.

Agras, W. S., Rossiter, E. M., Arnow, B., Telch, C. F. et al. (1994). One-year follow-up of psychosocial and pharmacologic treatments for bulimia nervosa. *J. Clin. Psychiatry, 55*(5), 179–183.

Agras, W. S., Sylvester, D., & Oliveau, D. (1969). The epidemiology of common fears and phobias. *Comp. Psychiatry, 10*(2), 151–156.

Ahmed, S., Bierley, R., Sheikh, J. I., & Date, D. S. (2000). Post-traumatic amnesia after closed head injury: A review of the literature and some sugges-

tions for further research. *Brain Injury, 14*(9), 765–780.

Aiken, L. R. (1985). *Psychological testing and assessment* (5th ed.). Boston: Allyn & Bacon.

Aikins, D. E., & Craske, M. GF. (2001). Cognitive theories of generalized anxiety disorder. *Psychiatr. Clin. North Am., 24*(1), 57–74.

Akechi, T., Okamura, H., Yamawaki, S., & Uchitomi, Y. (2001). Why do some cancer patients with depression desire an early death and others do not? *Psychosomatics, 42*(2), 141–145.

Akhtar, S., Wig, N. H., Verma, V. K., Pershod, D., & Verma, S. K. (1975). A phenomenological analysis of symptoms in obsessive-compulsive neuroses. *Br. J. Psychiatry, 127,* 342–348.

Albert, M. S., Butters, N., & Levin, J. (1979). Temporal gradients in the retrograde amnesia of patients with alcoholic Korsakoff's disease. *Arch. Neurol., 36,* 211–216.

Albertini, R. S., & Phillips, K. A. (1999). Thirty-three cases of body dysmorphic disorder in children and adolescents. *J. Am. Acad. Child Adolesc. Psychiatry, 38*(4), 453–459.

Albucher, R. C., Abelson, J. L., & Nesse, R. (1998). Defense mechanism changes in successfully treating patients with obsessive-compulsive disorder. *Am. J. Psychiatry, 155*(4), 558–559.

Alden, L. (1989). Short-term structured treatment for avoidant personality disorder. *J. Consult. Clin. Psychol., 57*(6), 756–764.

Aldhous, P. (1996, April 27). Matching proteins raise CJD fears. *New Sci.,* p. 21.

Aldridge, D. (1998). *Suicide: The tragedy of hopelessness.* London: Jessica Kingsley.

Aldwin, C. M., Sutton, K. J., Chiara, G., & Spiro, A. (1996). Age differences in stress, coping, and appraisal: Findings from the normative aging study. *J. Gerontol., 51B*(4), 179–188.

Alegria, M., Kessler, R. C., Bijl, R., Lin, E., Heeringa, S. G., Takeuchi, D. T., & Kolody, B. (2000). Comparing data on mental health service use between countries. In G. Andrews & S. Henderson (Eds.), *Unmet need in psychiatry: Problems, resources, responses* (pp. 97–118). New York: Cambridge University Press.

Alexander, B. (1981). Behavioral approaches to the treatment of bronchial asthma. In C. K. Prokop & L. A. Bradley (Eds.), *Medical psychology: Contributions to behavioral medicine.* New York: Academic Press.

Alexander, R. C. (2000). Medical treatment of Munchausen syndrome by proxy. In R. M. Reece (Ed.), *Treatment of child abuse: Common ground for mental health, medical, and legal practitioners* (pp. 236–241). Baltimore: Johns Hopkins University Press.

Allan, C., Smith, I., & Mellin, M. (2000). Detoxification from alcohol: A comparison of home detoxification and hospital-based day patient care. *Alcohol Alcohol., 35*(1), 66–69.

Allard, R., Marshall, M., & Plante, M. C. (1992). Intensive follow-up does not decrease the risk of repeat suicide attempts. *Suicide Life-Threaten. Behav., 22,* 303–314.

Allaz, A. F., Vannotti, M., Desmeules, J., Piguet, V., Celik, Y., Pyroth, O., Guex, P., & Dayer, P. (1998). Use of the label "litigation neurosis" in patients with somatoform pain disorder. *Gen. Hosp. Psychiatry, 20*(2), 91–97.

Allderidge, P. (1979). Hospitals, madhouses and asylums: Cycles in the care of the insane. *Br. J. Psychiatry, 134,* 321–334.

Allen, J. G. (1993). Dissociative processes: Theoretical underpinnings of a working model for clinician and patient. *Bull. Menninger Clin., 57*(3), 287–308.

Allison, R. B. (1978). A rational psychotherapy plan for multiplicity. *Svensk Tidskrift Hypnose, 3,* 9–16.

Alloy, L. B., Kelly, K. A., Mineka, S., & Clements, C. M. (1990). Comorbidity of anxiety and depressive disorders: A helplessness-hopelessness perspective. In J. D. Maser & R. Cloninger (Eds.), *Comorbidity of mood and anxiety disorders.* Washington, DC: American Psychiatric Press.

Allsop, S., Saunders, B., & Phillips, M. (2000). The process of relapse in severely dependent male problem drinkers. *Addiction, 95*(1), 95–106.

Allumbaugh, D. L., & Hoyt, W. T. (1999). Effectiveness of grief therapy: A meta-analysis. *J. Counsel. Psychol., 46*(3), 370–380.

Alspaugh, M. E. L., Stephens, M. A. P., Townsend, A. L., Zarit, S. H., & Greene, R. (1999). Longitudinal patterns of risk for depression in dementia caregivers: Objective and subjective primary stress as predictors. *Psychol. Aging, 14*(1), 34–43.

Althof, S. E. (1995). Pharmacologic treatment of rapid ejaculation [Special issue: Clinical sexuality]. *Psychiatr. Clin. North Am., 18*(1), 85–94.

Althof, S. E., Levine, S. B., Corty, E., Risen, C., & Stern, E. (1994, March). *The role of clomipramine in the treatment of premature ejaculation.* Paper presented at the 16th annual meeting of the Society for Sex Therapy and Research.

Althof, S. E., & Seftel, A. D. (1995). The evaluation and management of erectile dysfunction. *Psychiatr. Clin. North Am., 18*(1), 171–191.

Altman, C. A. (2001). Effects of selective-serotonin reuptake inhibitors on sexual function. *J. Clin. Psychopharmacol., 21*(2), 241–242.

Alvir, J. J., Lieberman, J. A., & Safferman, A. Z. (1995). Do white-cell count spikes predict agranulocytosis in clozapine recipients? *Psychopharmacol. Bull., 31*(2), 311–314.

Alzheimer's Association. (1997, February 17). Survey: Stress on Alzheimer caregivers. Cited in *USA Today,* p. 1D.

Aman, M. G., & Singh, N. N. (1991). Pharmacological intervention. In J. L. Matson & J. A. Mulick (Eds.), *Handbook of mental retardation.* New York: Pergamon Press.

Amass, L., Kamien, J. B., & Mikulich, S. K. (2000). Efficacy of daily and alternate-day dosing regimens with the combination buprenorphine-naloxone tablet. *Drug Alcohol Depend., 58*(1–2), 143–152.

Ambrosini, P. J., Bianchi, M. D., Rabinovich, H., & Elia, J. (1993). Antidepressant treatments in child and adolescents: I. Affective disorders. *J. Am. Acad. Child Adolesc. Psychiatry, 32*(1), 1–6.

Amenson, C., & Lewinsohn, P. (1981). An investigation into the observed sex differences in prevalence of unipolar depression. *J. Abnorm. Psychol., 90,* 1–13.

American Academy of Pediatrics. (1999). *Media alert: AAP addresses Colorado shooting.*

American Medical Association. (1992). *Diagnostic treatment guidelines on domestic violence.* Washington, DC: Author.

Americans Use of Time Project. (1995). Survey. As Cited in J. P. Robinson & G. Godbey, The great American slowdown. *Am. Demogr., 13*(6), 34–41.

Amir, M., Kaplan, Z., Efroni, R., & Kotler, M. (1999). Suicide risk and coping styles in posttraumatic stress disorder patients. *Psychother. Psychosom., 68*(2), 76–81.

Amminger, G. P., Pape, S., Rock, D., Roberts, S. A., Ott, S. L., Squires-Wheeler, E., Kestenbaum, C., & Erlenmeyer, K. L. (1999). Relationship between childhood behavioral disturbance and later schizophrenia in the New York High-Risk Project. *Am. J. Psychiatry, 156*(4), 525–530.

Anastasi, A. (1982). *Psychological testing* (5th ed.). New York: Macmillan.

Anastopoulos, A. D., & Barkley, R. A. (1992). Attention deficit-hyperactivity disorder. In C. E.

Walker & M. C. Roberts (Eds.), *Handbook of clinical child psychology* (2nd ed.). New York: Wiley.

Andersen, A. E. (1985). *Practical comprehensive treatment of anorexia nervosa and bulimia.* Baltimore: Johns Hopkins University Press.

Andersen, A. E. (1992). Eating disorders in males: A special case? In K. D. Brownell, J. Rodin, & J. H. Wilmore (Eds.), *Eating, body weight, and performance in athletes: Disorders of modern society.* Philadelphia: Lea & Febiger.

Andersen, A. E. (1992). Eating disorders in males: Critical questions. In R. Lemberg (Ed.), *Controlling eating disorders with facts, advice, and resources.* Phoenix, AZ: Oryx Press.

Andersen, B. L., Kiecolt-Glaser, J. K., & Glaser, R. (1994). A biobehavioral model of cancer stress and disease course. *Am. Psychol., 49*(5), 389–404.

Andersen, R. E., Bartlett, S. J., Morgan, G. D., & Brownell, K. D. (1995). Weight loss, psychological, and nutritional patterns in competitive male body builders. *Int. J. Eat. Disord., 18,* 49–57.

Anderson, D. (1994). *Breaking the tradition on college campuses: Reducing drug and alcohol misuse.* Fairfax, VA: George Mason University Press.

Anderson, J. R. (2000). *Cognitive psychology and its implications* (5th ed.). New York: Worth.

Anderson, N. B., & Scott, P. A. (1999). Making the case for psychophysiology during the era of molecular biology. *Psychophysiology, 36*(1), 1–13.

Anderson, S. C. (1993). Anti-stalking laws: Will they curb the erotomanic's obsessive pursuit? *Law Psychol. Rev., 17,* 171–191.

Anderson, S. R., Avery, D. L., DiPietro, E. K., Edwards, G. L. et al. (1989). Intensive home-based early intervention with autistic children. *Educ. Treat. Child., 10*(4), 352–366.

Anderson, W. P., Reid, C. M., & Jennings, G. L. Pet ownership and risk factors for cardiovascular disease. *Med. J. Aust., 157*(5), 298–301.

Andrade, V. M. (1996). Superego, narcissism and culture. *Rev. Bras. Psicanal., 30*(2), 385–405.

Andrasik, F. (2000). Biofeedback. In D. I. Mostofsky & D. H. Barlow (Eds.), *The management of stress and anxiety in medical disorders* (pp. 66–83). Needham Heights, MA: Allyn & Bacon.

Andrasik, F., Blanchard, E. B., Neff, D. F., & Rodichok, L. D. (1984). Biofeedback and relaxation training for chronic headache: A controlled comparison of booster treatments and regular contacts for long-term maintenance. *J. Consult. Clin. Psychol., 52*(4), 609–615.

Andreasen, N. C. (1999). Understanding the causes of schizophrenia. *N. Engl. J. Med., 340*(8), 645–647.

Andreasen, N. C. (2000, February). Interviewed in P. A. McGuire, New hope for people with schizophrenia. *Monitor Psychol., 31*(2), 24–28.

Andreasen, N. C., Hoffman, R. E., & Grove, W. M. (1985). Mapping abnormalities in language and cognition. In M. Alpert (Ed.), *Controversies in schizophrenia: Changes and constancies.* New York: Guilford Press.

Andresen, J. (2000). Meditation meets behavioral medicine: The story of experimental research on meditation. *J. Consciousness. Stud., 7*(11–12), 17–73.

Andrews, V. (1998, December 14). Abducted by aliens? Or just a little schizoid? *HealthScout.*

Andrulonis, P. A. (1991). Disruptive behavior disorders in boys and the borderline personality disorder in men. *Ann. Clin. Psychiatry, 3*(1), 23–26.

Angermeyer, K. C., Kuhn, L., & Goldstein, M. M. (1990). Gender and the course of schizophrenia: Differences in treated outcomes. *Schizophr. Bull., 16*(2), 293–307.

Angier, N. (2001, May 20). Bully for you: Why push comes to shove. *New York Times,* Sect. 4, p. 1.

Angold, A., & Rutter, M. (1992). Effects of age and pubertal status on depression in a large clinical sample. *Dev. Psychopathol., 41*(1), 5–28.

Angst, J. (1995). The epidemiology of depressive disorders. *Eur. Neuropsychopharmacol., Suppl.,* pp. 95–98.

Angst, J. (1999). Major depression in 1998: Are we providing optimal therapy? *J. Clin. Psychiatry, 60*(Suppl. 6), 5–9.

Angst, J., & Merikangas, K. R. (2001). Multidimensional criteria for the diagnosis of depression. *J. Affect. Disord., 62*(1–2), 7–15.

Annas, G. J. (1993). Physician-assisted suicide—Michigan's temporary solution. *N. Engl. J. Med., 328*(21), 1573–1574.

Anonymous. (1996). First person account: Social, economic, and medical effects of schizophrenia. *Schizophr. Bull., 22*(1), 183.

Anooshian, J., Streltzer, J., & Goebert, D. (1999). Effectiveness of a psychiatric pain clinic. *Psycosomatics, 40*(3), 226–232.

Anthony, J. C., Arria, A. M., & Johnson, E. O. (1995). Epidemiological and public health issues for tobacco, alcohol, and other drugs. In J. M. Oldham & M. B. Riba (Eds.), *American Psychiatric Press review of psychiatry* (Vol. 14). Washington, DC: American Psychiatric Press.

Anthony, J. C., Warner, L. A., & Kessler, R. C. (1994). Comparative epidemiology of dependence on tobacco, alcohol, controlled substances and inhalants: Basic findings from the National Comorbidity Survey. *Clin. Exp. Psychopharmacol., 2,* 244–268.

Anton, R. F., Moak, D. H., Latham, P. K., Waid, R., Malcolm, R. J., Dias, J. K., & Roberts, J. S. (2001). Posttreatment results of combining naltrexone with cognitive-behavior therapy for the treatment of alcoholism. *J. Clin. Psychopharmacol., 21*(1), 72–77.

Antoni, M. H., Baggett, L., Ironson, G., LaPerriere, A., August, S., Klimas, N., Schneiderman, N., & Fletcher, M. A. (1991). Cognitive-behavioral stress management intervention buffers distress responses and immunologic changes following notification of HIV-1 seropositivity. *J. Consult. Clin. Psychol., 59*(6), 906–915.

Antony, M. M., Brown, T. A., & Barlow, D. H. (1997). Heterogeneity among specific phobia types in DSM-IV. *Behav. Res. Ther., 35,* 1089–1100.

Antony, M. M., & Swinson, R. P. (2000). *Phobic disorders and panic in adults: A guide to assessment and treatment.* Washington, DC: American Psychological Association.

Apelle, S., Lynn, S. J., & Newman, L. (1998, December 14). Cited in V. Andrews, Abducted by aliens? Or just a little schizoid? *HealthScout.*

Appelbaum, P. S. (1993). Legal liability and managed care. *Am. Psychol., 48,* 251–257.

Appelbaum, P. S. (2001). Thinking carefully about outpatient commitment. *Psychiatr. Serv., 52*(3), 347–350.

Appelbaum, P. S., & Grisso, T. (1995). The MacArthur treatment competence study: I. Mental illness and competence to consent to treatment. *Law Hum. Behav., 19*(2), 105–126.

Arata, C. M. (1999). Repeated sexual victimization and mental disorders in women. *J. Child Sex. Abuse, 7*(3), 1–17.

Arbel, N., & Stravynski, A. (1991). A retrospective study of separation in the development of adult avoidant personality disorder. *Acta Psychiatr. Scand., 83*(3), 174–178.

Arben, P. D. (1999). A commentary: Why civil commitment laws don't work the way they're supposed to. *J. Sociol. Soc. Welfare, 26*(3), 61–70.

Arboleda-Florez, J., & Holley, H. L. (1991). Antisocial burnout: An exploratory study. *Bull. Am. Acad. Psychiatry Law, 19*(2), 173–183.

Archer, D., & McDaniel, P. (1995). Violence and gender: Differences and similarities across societies. In R. B. Ruback & N. A. Weiner (Eds.), *Interpersonal violent behaviors: Social and cultural aspects.* New York: Springer.

Archer, R. P. (1997). Future directions for the MMPI-A: Research and clinical issues. *J. Pers. Assess., 68*(1), 95–109.

Arieti, S. (1974). *Interpretation of schizophrenia.* New York: Basic Books.

Arieti, S., & Bemporad, J. (1978). *Severe and mild depression: The psychotherapeutic approach.* New York: Basic Books.

Aring, C. D. (1974). The Gheel experience: Eternal spirit of the chainless mind! *JAMA, J. Am. Med. Assoc., 230*(7), 998–1001.

Aring, C. D. (1975). Gheel: The town that cares. *Fam. Health, 7*(4), 54–55, 58, 60.

Arkhipov, V. I. (1999). Memory dissociation: The approach to the study of retrieval processes. *Behav. Brain Res., 106*(1–2), 39–46.

Arkin, R., Hermann, A., & Leonardelli, G. (1999). *Study on thinking pattern of chronic self-doubters.* Paper presented at the annual meeting of the American Psychological Society, Denver, CO.

Arnett, J. J. (1999). Adolescent storm and stress, reconsidered. *Am. Psychol., 54*(5), 317–326.

Arnette, J. (1996). Physiological effects of chronic grief: A biofeedback treatment approach. *Death Stud., 20,* 59–72.

Arnold, L. E. (1973, October). Is this label necessary? *J. Sch. Health, 43,* 510–514.

Asaad, G. (2000). Somatization disorder. In M. Hersen & M. Biaggio (Eds.), *Effective brief therapies: A clinician's guide* (pp. 179–190). San Diego, CA: Academic Press.

Asarnow, J. R., Asarnow, R. F., Hornstein, N., & Russell, A. (1991). Childhood-onset schizophrenia: Developmental perspectives on schizophrenic disorders. In E. F. Walker (Ed.), *Schizophrenia: A life-course developmental perspective.* San Diego, CA: Academic Press.

Asberg, M., Traskman, L., & Thoren, P. (1976). 5 HIAA in the cerebrospinal fluid: A biochemical suicide predictor? *Arch. Gen. Psychiatry, 33*(10), 1193–1197.

Aserinsky, E., & Kleitman, N. (1953). Eye movements during sleep. *Fed. Process, 13,* 6–7.

Ash, R. (1998). *The top 10 of everything 1999.* New York: DK Publishing.

Ash, R. (1999). *Fantastic book of 1001 facts.* New York: DK Publishing.

Ashton, C. H. (2001). Pharmacology and effects of cannabis: A brief review. *Br. J. Psychiatry, 178,* 101–106.

Ashton, H. (1995). Toxicity and adverse consequences of benzodiazepine use. *Psychiatr. Ann., 25*(3), 158–165.

Ashton, J. R., & Donnan, S. (1981). Suicide by burning as an epidemic phenomenon: An analysis of 82 deaths and inquests in England and Wales in 1978–9. *Psychol. Med., 11*(4), 735–739.

Asimov, I. (1997). *Isaac Asimov's book of facts.* New York: Random House (Wings Books).

Atkinson, D. R., Brown, M. T., Parham, T. A., Matthews, L. G. et al. (1996). African American client skin tone and clinical judgments of African American and European American psychologists. *Prof. Psychol.: Res. Pract., 27*(5), 500–505.

Atlas, J. A. (1995). Association between history of abuse and borderline personality disorder for hospitalized adolescent girls. *Psychol. Rep., 77,* 1346.

Attie, I., & Brooks-Gunn, J. (1992). Developmental issues in the study of eating problems and eating disorders. In J. H. Crowther, D. L. Tennenbaum, S. E. Hobfoll, & M. A. P. Stephens (Eds.), *The etiology of bulimia nervosa: The individual and familial context.* Washington, DC: Hemisphere.

Auchincloss, E. L., & Weiss, R. W. (1992). Paranoid character and the intolerance of indifference. *J. Am. Psychoanal. Assoc., 40*(4), 1013–1037.

Auge, W. K., III, & Auge, S. M. (1999). Naturalistic observation of athletic drug-use patterns and behavior in professional-caliber bodybuilders. *Subst. Use Misuse, 34*(2), 217–249.

Avery, D., & Lubrano, A. (1979). Depression treated with imipramine and ECT: The DeCarolis study reconsidered. *Am. J. Psychiatry, 136,* 559–569.

Avia, M. D., Ruiz, M. A., Olivares, E., Crespo, M. et al. (1996). Shorter communications. The meaning of psychological symptoms: Effectiveness of a group intervention with hypochondriacal patients. *Behav. Res. Ther., 34*(1), 23–31.

Ayd, F. J., & Palma, J. M. (1999, May). Suicide: Risk recognition and prevention. *Psychiatr. Times, 16*(5).

Ayd, F. J., Jr. (1956). A clinical evaluation of Frenquel. *J. Nerv. Ment. Dis., 124,* 507–509.

Ayllon, T. (1963). Intensive treatment of psychotic behavior by stimulus satiation and food reinforcement. *Behav. Res. Ther., 1,* 53–62.

Ayllon, T., & Michael, J. (1959). The psychiatric nurse as a behavioural engineer. *J. Exp. Anal. Behav., 2,* 323–334.

Ayoub, C. C., Deutsch, R. M., & Kinscherff, R. (2000). Munchausen by proxy: Definitions, identification, and evaluation. In R. M. Reece (Ed.), *Treatment of child abuse: Common ground for mental health, medical, and legal practitioners* (pp. 213–226). Baltimore: Johns Hopkins University Press.

Ayoub, C. C., Deutsch, R. M., & Kinscherff, R. (2000). Psychosocial management issues in Munchausen by proxy. In R. M. Reese (Ed.), *Treatment of child abuse: Common ground for mental health, medical, and legal practitioners* (pp. 226–235). Baltimore: Johns Hopkins University Press.

Ayres, J. J. B. (1998). Fear conditioning and avoidance. In W. T. O'Donohue et al. (Eds.), *Learning and behavior therapy.* Boston: Allyn & Bacon.

Azar, B. (1995). Mental disabilities and the brain-gene link. *APA Monitor, 26*(12), 18.

Azar, B. (1996). Intrusive thoughts proven to undermine our health. *APA Monitor, 27*(10), 34.

Azar, S. T., Robinson, D. R., Hekimian, E. E., & Twentyman, C. T. (1984). Unrealistic expectations and problem solving ability in maltreating and comparison mothers. *J. Consult. Clin. Psychol., 52,* 687–691.

Azar, S. T., & Siegal, B. R. (1990). Behavioral treatment of child abuse: A developmental perspective. *Behav. Mod., 14*(3), 279–300.

Azar, S. T., & Wolfe, D. A. (1989). Child abuse and neglect. In E. J. Mash & R. Barkley (Eds.), *Treatment of childhood disorders.* New York: Guilford Press.

Azima, F. J. C. (1993). Group psychotherapy with personality disorders. In H. I. Kaplan & B. J. Sadock (Eds.), *Comprehensive group psychotherapy* (3rd ed.). Baltimore: Williams & Wilkins.

Baberg, H. T., Nelesen, R. A., & Dimsdale, J. E. (1996). Amphetamine use: Return of an old scourge in a consultation psychiatry setting. *Am. J. Psychiatry, 153*(6), 789–793.

Babor, T. F., Steinberg, K., Anton, R., & Del Bocca, F. (2000). Talk is cheap: Measuring drinking outcomes in clinical trials. *J. Stud. Alcohol, 61*(1), 55–63.

Bacon, S. D. (1973). The process of addiction to alcohol: Social aspects. *Q. J. Stud. Alcohol., 34*(1, Pt. A), 1–27.

Baer, L. (2001). *The imp of the mind: Exploring the silent epidemic of obsessive bad thoughts.* New York: Dutton/Penguin Books.

Baer, L., Platman, S. R., Kassir, S., & Fieve, R. R. (1971). Mechanisms of renal lithium handling and their relationship to mineralcorticoids: A dissociation between sodium and lithium ions. *J. Psychiatr. Res., 8*(2), 91–105.

Bagby, E. (1922). The etiology of phobias. *J. Abnorm. Psychol., 17,* 16–18.

Bagley, C. (1991). Poverty and suicide among Native Canadians: A replication. *Psychol. Rep., 69*(1) 149–150.

Bahrick, H. (1996, January). Cited in G. Neimeyer, Anecdotes for education. *Newsl. Abnorm. Psychol.*

Bailey, J. M., & Pillard, R. C. (1991). A genetic study of male sexual orientation. *Arch. Gen. Psychiatry, 48*(12), 1089–1096.

Bailey, J. M., Pillard, R. C., Kitringer, C., & Wilkinson, S. (1997). Sexual orientation: Is it determined by biology? In M. R. Walsh (Ed.), *Women, men, & gender: Ongoing debates* (pp. 181–203). New Haven, CT: Yale University Press.

Bailey, J. M., Pillard, R. C., Neale, M. C. et al. (1993). Heritable factors influence sexual orientation in women. *Arch. Gen. Psychiatry, 50*(3), 217–223.

Bailine, S. H., Rifkin, A., Kayne, E., Selzer, J. A., Vital-Herne, J., Blieka, M., & Pollack, S. (2000). Comparison of bifrontal and bitemporal ECT for major depression. *Am. J. Psychiatry, 157*(1), 121–123.

Baird, J., Stevenson, J. C., & Williams, D. C. (2000). The evolution of ADHD: A disorder of communication? *Q. Rev. Biol., 75*(1), 17–35.

Baker, F. M., & Bell, C. C. (1999). Issues in the psychiatric treatment of African Americans. *Psychiatr. Serv., 50*(3), 362–368.

Baker, T., & Brandon, T. H. (1988). Behavioral treatment strategies. In *A report of the Surgeon General: The health consequences of smoking: Nicotine addiction.* Rockville, MD: U. S. Department of Health and Human Services.

Bakish, D. (1999). The patient with comorbid depression and anxiety: The unmet need. *J. Clin. Psychiatry, 60*(Suppl. 6), 20–24.

Bakken, J., Miltenberger, R. G., & Schauss, S. (1993). Teaching parents with mental retardation: Knowledge versus skills. *Am. J. Ment. Retard., 97*(4), 405–417.

Baldessarini, R. J., Tondo, L., & Hennen, J. (1999). Effects of lithium treatment and its discontinuation on suicidal behavior in bipolar manic-depressive disorders. *J. Clin. Psychiatry, 60*(Suppl. 2), 77–84.

Baldwin, D. S. (1998). Depression and panic: Comorbidity. *Eur. Psychiatry, 13*(Suppl. 2), 65s–70s.

Balk, D. F. (1995). Bereavement research using control groups: Ethical obligations and questions. [Special issue: Ethics and bereavement research]. *Death Stud., 19*(2), 123–138.

Ball, S. G., Baer, L., & Otto, M. W. (1996). Symptom subtypes of obsessive-compulsive disorder in behavioral treatment studies: A quantitative review. *Behav. Res. Ther., 34*(1), 45–51.

Ballenger, J. C. (1988). The clinical use of carbamazepine in affective disorders. *J. Clin. Psychiatry, 49*(Suppl), 13–19.

Ballenger, J. C. (1995). Benzodiazepines. In A. F. Schatzberg & C. B. Nemeroff (Eds.), *The American Psychiatric Press textbook of psychopharmacology.* Washington, DC: American Psychiatric Press.

Ballenger, J. C. (1997). Panic disorder in the medical setting. *J. Clin. Psychiatry, 38*(Suppl. 2), 13–17.

Ballenger, J. C. (1998). Treatment of panic disorder in the general medical setting. *J. Psychosom. Res., 44*(1), 5–15.

Ballenger, J. C. (1999). Current treatments of the anxiety disorders in adults. *Biol. Psychiatry, 46*(11), 1579–1594.

Balon, R. (1998). Pharmacological treatment of paraphilias with a focus on antidepressants. *J. Sex Marital Ther., 24*(4), 241–254.

Balshem, M., Oxman, G., Van Rooyen, D., & Girod, K. (1992). Syphilis, sex, and crack cocaine: Images of risk and morality. *Soc. Sci. Med., 35*(2), 147–160.

Baltaxe, C. A. M., & Simmons, J. Q., III. (1995). Speech and language disorders in children and adolescents with schizophrenia. *Schizophr. Bull., 21*(4), 677–692.

Bancroft, J. (1989). *Human sexuality and its problems.* New York: Churchill-Livingstone.

Bandura, A. (1971). Psychotherapy based upon modeling principles. In A. E. Bergin & S. L. Garfield (Eds.), *Handbook of psychotherapy and behavior change.* New York: Wiley.

Bandura, A. (1971). Vicarious and self-reinforcement processes. In R. Glaser (Ed.), *The nature of reinforcement.* New York: Academic Press.

Bandura, A. (1977). Self-efficacy: Toward a unifying theory of behavioral change. *Psychol. Rev., 84*(2), 191–215.

Bandura, A., Adams, N. E., & Beyer, J. (1977). Cognitive processes mediating behavioral change. *J. Pers. Soc. Psychol., 35*(3), 125–139.

Bandura, A., & Rosenthal, T. (1966). Vicarious classical conditioning as a function of arousal level. *J. Pers. Soc. Psychol., 3,* 54–62.

Bandura, A., Roth, D., & Ross, S. (1963). Imitation of film-mediated aggressive models. *J. Abnorm. Soc. Psychol., 66,* 3–11.

Banerjee, S., & Macdonald, A. (1996). Mental disorder in an elderly home care population: Associations with health and social service use. *Br. J. Psychiatry, 168,* 750–756.

Banister, P., Burman, E., Parker, I., Taylor, M., & Tindall, C. (1994). *Qualitative methods in psychology: A research guide.* Buckingham, UK: Open University Press.

Banner, B. (1998, April). Are you normal? It's a laugh. *Am. Demogr.*

Barak, A. (1999). Psychological applications on the Internet: A discipline on the threshold of a new millennium. *Appl. Prev. Psychol., 8*(4), 231–245.

Barber, A. (1999, March). HerZines. Some yet-to-be exploited niches in the women's magazine market. *Am. Demogr.*

Barber, T. X. (1984). Hypnosis, deep relaxation, and active relaxation: Data, theory and clinical applications. In F. L. Woolfolk & P. M. Lehrer (Eds), *Principles and practice of stress management.* New York: Guilford Press.

Barber, T. X. (1993). Hypnosuggestive approaches to stress reduction: Data, theory, and clinical applications. In P. M. Lehrer & R. L. Woolfolk (Eds.), *Principles and practice of stress management* (2nd ed.). New York: Guilford Press.

Bardenstein, K. K., McGlasham, T. H., & McGlasham, T. H. (1988). The natural history of a residentially treated borderline sample: Gender differences. *J. Pers. Disord., 2*(1), 69–83.

Barker, C., Pistrang, N., & Elliott, R. (1994). *Research methods in clinical and counseling psychology.* Chichester, England: Wiley.

Barker, J. G., & Howell, R. J. (1992). The plethysmograph: A review of recent literature. *Bull. Am. Acad. Psychiatry Law, 20*(1), 13–25.

Barker, P. R., Manderscheid, R. W., Hendershot, G. E., Jack, S. S., Schoenborn, C. A., & Goldstrom, I. (1992). Serious mental illness and disability in the adult household population: United States, 1989. In R. W. Manderscheid & M. A. Sonnenschein (Eds.), *Mental health, United States,*

1992. Washington, DC: U. S. Department of Health and Human Services.

Barker, S. B. (1999, February). Therapeutic aspects of the human-companion animal interaction. *Psychiatr. Times, 16*(2).

Barlow, D. H., Gorman, J. M., Shear, M. K., & Woods, S. W. (2000). Cognitive-behavioral therapy, imipramine, or their combination for panic disorder: A randomized controlled trial. *JAMA, J. Am. Med. Assoc., 283*(19), 2529–2536.

Barnes, G. E., & Prosen, H. (1985). Parental death and depression. *J. Abnorm. Psychol., 94*(1), 64–69.

Baroff, G. S., & Olley, J. G. (1999). *Mental retardation: Nature, cause, and management* (3rd ed.). Philadelphia: Brunner/Mazel.

Baron, M., Barkai, A., Gruen, R., Peselow, E. et al. (1987). Platelet sup 3H imipramine binding and familial transmission of affective disorders. *Neuropsychobiology, 17*(4), 182–186.

Barondes, S. H. (1993). *Molecules and mental illness.* New York: Scientific American Library.

Barraclough, B. M., Bunch, J., Nelson, B. et al. (1974). A hundred cases of suicide: Clinical aspects. *Br. J. Psychiatry, 125,* 355–373.

Barratt, E. S., & Stanford, M. S. (1996). Impulsiveness. In C. G. Costello (Ed.), *Personality characteristics of the personality disordered.* New York: Wiley.

Barrett, G., Pendry, E., Peacock, J., Victor, C., Thakar, R., & Manyonda, I. (1999). Women's sexuality after childbirth: A pilot study. *Arch. Sex. Behav., 28*(2), 179–191.

Barrett, P. (2001). Current issues in the treatment of childhood anxiety. In M. W. Vasey & M. R. Dadds (Eds.), *The developmental psychopathology of anxiety* (pp. 304–324). New York: Oxford University Press.

Barrett, P. M., Duffy, A., Dadds, M. R., & Rapee, R. M. (2001). Cognitive-behavioral treatment of anxiety disorders in children: Long-term (6-year) follow-up. *J. Consult. Clin. Psychol., 69*(1), 135–141.

Barrington, M. R. (1980). Apologia for suicide. In M. P. Battin & D. J. Mayo (Eds.), *Suicide: The philosophical issues.* New York: St. Martin's Press.

Barroso, J. (1999). Long-term nonprogressors with HIV disease. *Nursing.*

Barsky, A. J., & Klerman, G. I. (1983). Overview: Hypochondriasis, bodily complaints and somatic styles. *Am. J. Psychiatry, 140,* 273–283.

Barta, P. E., Pearlson, G. D., Brill, L. B., II, Royall, R. et al. (1997). Planum temporale asymmetry reversal in schizophrenia: Replication and relationship to gray matter abnormalities. *Am. J. Psychiatry, 154*(5), 661–667.

Bartels, S., Teague, G., Drake, R., Clark, R., Bush, P., & Noordsy, D. (1993). Substance abuse in schizophrenia: Replication and relationship to gray matter abnormalities. *Am. J. Psychiatry, 154*(5), 661–667.

Bartels, S., Teague, G., Drake, R., Clark, R., Bush, P., & Noordsy, D. (1993). Substance abuse in schizophrenia: Service utilization and costs. *J. Nerv. Ment. Dis., 181*(4), 227–232.

Bartholomew, K. (2000). Clinical protocol. *Psychoanal. Inquiry, 20*(2), 227–248.

Bartrop, R. W., Lockhurst, E., Lazarus, L., Kiloh, L. G., & Penny, R. (1977). Depressed lymphocyte function after bereavement. *Lancet, 1,* 834–836.

Basson, R., Berman, J., Burnett, A., Derogatis, L., Ferguson, D., Fourcroy, J., Goldstein, I., Graziottin, A., Heiman, J., Laan, E., Leiblum, S., Padma-Nathan, H., Rosen, R., Segraves K., Segraves, R. T., Shabsigh, R., Sipski, M., Wagner, G., & Whipple, B. (2001). Report of the International Consensus Development Conference on Female Dysfunction: Definitions and classifications. *J. Sex Marital Ther., 27*(2), 83–94.

Bastiani, A. M., Altermus, M., Pigott, T. A., Rubenstein, C. et al. (1996). Comparison of obsessions and compulsions in patients with anorexia nervosa and obsessive compulsive disorder. *Biol. Psychiatry, 39,* 966–969.

Bastiani, A. M., Rao, R., Weltzin, T., & Kaye, W. H. (1995). Perfectionism in anorexia nervosa. *Int. J. Eat. Disord., 17*(2), 147–152.

Batchelor, W. F. (1988). AIDS 1988. *Am. Psychol., 43*(11), 853–858.

Bates, G. W., Thompson, J. C., & Flanagan, C. (1999). The effectiveness of individual versus group induction of depressed mood. *J. Psychol., 133*(3), 245–252.

Bateson, G. (1978, April 21). The double-blind theory—Misunderstood? *Psychiatr. News,* p. 40.

Bateson, G., Jackson, D., Haley, J., & Weakland, J. (1956). Toward a theory of schizophrenia. *Behav. Sci., 1,* 251–264.

Battaglia, M., Cavallini, M. C., Macciardi, F., & Bellodi, L. (1997). The structure of DSM-III-R schizotypal personality disorder diagnosed by direct interviews. *Schizophr. Bull., 23*(1), 83–92.

Battaglia, M., Gasperini, M., Sciuto, G., Scherillo, P. et al. (1991). Psychiatric disorders in the families of schizotypal subjects. *Schizophr. Bull., 17*(4), 659–668.

Battin, M. P. (1980). Manipulated suicide. In M. P. Battin & D. J. Mayo (Eds.), *Suicide: The philosophical issues.* New York: St. Martin's Press.

Battin, M. P. (1980). Suicide: A fundamental human right? In M. P. Battin & D. J. Mayo (Eds.), *Suicide: The philosophical issues.* New York: St. Martin's Press.

Battin, M. P. (1982). *Ethical issues in suicide.* Englewood Cliffs, NJ: Prentice-Hall.

Battin, M. P. (1998, December 11). Interviewed in V. Andrews, Beyond Kevorkian: What others say about "last rights." *HealthScout.*

Battin, M. P. (1999). Can suicide be rational? Yes, sometimes. In J. L. Werth, Jr. (Ed.), *Contemporary perspectives on rational suicide.* Philadelphia: Brunner/Mazel.

Battle, E. K., & Brownell, K. D. (1996). Confronting a rising tide of eating disorders and obesity: Treatment vs. prevention and policy. *Addict. Behav., 32*(6), 755–765.

Battle, Y. L., Martin, B. C., Dorfman, J. H., & Miller, L. S. (1999). Seasonality and infectious disease in schizophrenia: The birth hypothesis revisited. *J. Psychiatr. Res., 33*(6), 501–509.

Baucom, D. H., Epstein, N., & Gordon, K. C. (2000). Marital therapy: Theory, practice, and empirical status. In C. R. Snyder & R. E. Ingram (Eds.), *Handbook of psychological change: Psychotherapy processes & practices for the 21st century* (pp. 280–308). New York: Wiley.

Baucom, D. H., Shoham, V., Mueser, K. T., Daiuto, A. D., & Stickle, T. R. (1998). Empirically supported couple and family interventions for marital distress and adult mental health problems. *J. Consult. Clin. Psychol., 66*(1), 53–88.

Bauer, P. J. (1996). What do infants recall of their lives? Memory for specific events by one- to two-year-olds. *Am. Psychol., 51*(1), 29–41.

Bauer, R. M. (2000). The flexible battery approach to neuropsychological assessment. In R. D. Vanderploeg et al. (Eds.), *Clinician's guide to neuropsychological assessment.* Mahwah, NJ: Erlbaum.

Baum, A. (1990). Stress, intrusive imagery, and chronic stress. *Health Psychol., 9,* 653–675.

Baum, A., Gatchel, R. J., & Schaeffer, M. (1983). Emotional, behavioural and physiological effects of chronic stress at Three Mile Island. *J. Consult. Clin. Psychol., 51,* 565–572.

Baxter, L. R., Schwart, J. M., Bergman, K. S., Szuba, M. P., Guze, B. H., Mazziotta, J. C., Alazraki, A., Selin, C. E., Ferng, H. K., Munford, P., & Phelps, M. E. (1992). Caudate glucose metabolic rate changes with both drug and behavior therapy for obsessive-compulsive disorder. *Arch. Gen. Psychiatry, 49,* 681–689.

Baxter, L. R., Schwartz, J. M., Guze, B. H., Bergman, K. S. et al. (1990). PET imaging in obsessive compulsive disorder with and without depression. Symposium: Serotonin and its effects on human behavior (1989, Atlanta, GA). *J. Clin. Psychiatry, 51*(Suppl.), 61–69.

Baxter, L. R., Jr., Clark, E. C., Iqbal, M., & Ackermann, R. F. (2001). Cortical-subcortical systems in the mediation of obsessive-compulsive disorder: Modeling the brain's mediation of a classic "neurosis." In D. G. Lichter & J. L. Cummings (Eds.), *Frontal-subcortical circuits in psychiatric and neurological disorders* (pp. 207–230). New York: Guilford Press.

Beach, S. R. H. (2001). Marital therapy for co-occurring marital discord and depression. In S. R. H. Beach (Ed.), *Marital and family processes in depression: A scientific foundation for clinical practice* (pp. 205–224). Washington, DC: American Psychological Association.

Beach, S. R. H., Sandeen, E. E., & O'Leary, K. D. (1990). Depression in marriage: A model for etiology and treatment. In D. H. Barlow (Ed.), *Treatment manuals for practitioners.* New York: Guilford Press.

Beamish, P. M., Granello, P. F., Granello, D. H., McSteen, P. B. et al. (1996). Outcome studies in the treatment of panic disorder: A review. *J. Counsel. Dev., 74,* 460–467.

Beardslee, W. R., Wright, E., Rothberg, P. C., Salt, P., & Versage, E. (1996). Response of families to two preventive intervention strategies: Long-term differences in behavior and attitude change. *J. Am. Acad. Child Adolesc. Psychiatry, 35*(6), 774–782.

Beaty, L. A. (1999). *Identity development of homosexual youth and parental and familial influences on the coming out process.* Chicago: Northeastern Illinois University Press.

Beautrais, A., Joyce, P., & Mulder, R. (2000). Unmet need following serious suicide attempt: Follow-up of 302 individuals for 30 months. In G. Andrews, S. Henderson et al. (Eds.), *Unmet need in psychiatry: Problems, resources, responses.* New York: Cambridge University Press.

Beauvais, F. (1992). The consequences of drug and alcohol use for Indian youth. *Am. Indian Alaska Native Ment. Health Res., 5*(1), 32–37.

Bebbington, P., & Ramana, R. (1995). The epidemiology of bipolar affective disorder. *Soc. Psychiatry Psychiatr. Epidemiol., 30,* 279–292.

Bebbington, P. E. (1998). Epidemiology of obsessive-compulsive disorder. *Br. J. Psychiatry, 173*(Suppl. 35), 2–6.

Beck, A. T. (1967). *Depression: Clinical, experimental and theoretical aspects.* New York: Harper & Row.

Beck, A. T. (1976). *Cognitive therapy and the emotional disorders.* New York: International University Press.

Beck, A. T. (1985). Theoretical perspectives on clinical anxiety. In A. H. Tuma & J. D. Maser (Eds.), *Anxiety and the anxiety disorders.* Hillsdale, NJ: Erlbaum.

Beck, A. T. (1988). Cognitive approaches to panic disorder: Theory and therapy. In S. Rachman & J. Maser (Eds.), *Panic: Psychological perspectives.* Hillsdale, NJ: Erlbaum.

Beck, A. T. (1991). Cognitive therapy: A 30-year retrospective. *Am. Psychol., 46*(4), 368–375.

Beck, A. T. (1993). Cognitive approaches to stress. In P. M. Lehrer & R. L. Woolfolk (Eds.), *Principles and practice of stress management* (2nd ed.). New York: Guilford Press.

Beck, A. T. (1997). Cognitive therapy: Reflections. In J. K. Zeig (Ed.), *The evolution of psychotherapy: The third conference.* New York: Brunner/Mazel.

Beck, A. T., Emery, G., & Greenberg, R. (1985). *Anxiety disorders and phobias: A cognitive perspective.* New York: Basic Books.

Beck, A. T., & Emery, G., with Greenberg, R. L. (1985). Differentiating anxiety and depression: A test of the cognitive content-specificity hypothesis. *J. Abnorm. Psychol., 96,* 179–183.

Beck, A. T., & Freeman, A. (1990). *Cognitive therapy of personality disorders.* New York: Guilford Press.

Beck, A. T., Laude, R., & Bohnert, M. (1974). Ideational components of anxiety neurosis. *Arch. Gen. Psychiatry, 31,* 319–325.

Beck, A. T., Resnik, H., & Lettieri, D. (Eds.). (1974). *The prediction of suicide.* Philadelphia: Charles Press.

Beck, A. T., Rush, A. J., Shaw, B. F., & Emery, G. (1979). *Cognitive therapy of depression.* New York: Guilford Press.

Beck, A. T., Ward, C. H., Mendelson, M., Mock, J. E., & Erbaugh, J. (1962). Reliability of psychiatric diagnosis: 2. A study of consistency of clinical judgments and ratings. *Am. J. Psychiatry, 119,* 351–357.

Beck, A. T., & Weishaar, M. E. (1995). Cognitive therapy. In R. J. Corsini & D. Wedding (Eds.), *Current psychotherapies* (5th ed.). Itasca, IL: Peacock.

Beck, A. T., Weissman, A., Lester, D. et al. (1974). The measurement of pessimism: The hopelessness scale. *J. Consult. Clin. Psychol., 42,* 861–865.

Beck, A. T. et al. (1985). Treatment of depression with cognitive therapy and amitriptyline. *Arch. Gen. Psychiatry, 42*(2), 142–148.

Beck, J. C., & Parry, J. W. (1992). Incompetence, treatment refusal, and hospitalization. *Bull. Am. Acad. Psychiatry Law, 20*(3), 261–267.

Beck, J. G. (1995). Hypoactive sexual desire disorder: An overview. *J. Consult. Clin. Psychol., 63*(6), 919–927.

Beck, J. G., & Bozman, A. (1996). Gender differences in sexual desire: The effects of anger and anxiety. *Arch. Sex. Behav., 24*(6), 595–612.

Becker, A. (1999, May 31). Fat-phobia in the Fijis: TV-thin is in. *Newsweek,* p. 70.

Becker, E. S., Rinck, M., Roth, W. T., & Margraf, J. (1998). Don't worry and beware of white bears: Thought suppression in anxiety patients. *J. Anxiety Disord. 12*(1), 39–55.

Becker, J. V. (1989). Impact of sexual abuse on sexual functioning. In S. R. Leiblum & R. C. Rosen (Eds.), *Principles and practice of sex therapy* (2nd ed.). New York: Guilford Press.

Becker, P., & Comstock, C. (1992, October). *A retrospective look at one MPD/DD group: Recommendations for future MPD/DD groups.* Paper presented at the 9th International Conference of the International Society for the Study of Multiple Personality and Dissociative Disorders, Chicago.

Becvar, D. S., & Becvar, R. J. (1993). *Family therapy: A systemic integration* (2nd ed.). Boston: Allyn & Bacon.

Bednar, R. L., & Kaul, T. J. (1994). Experiential group research: Can the canon fire? In A. E. Bergin & S. L. Garfiel (Eds.), *Handbook of psychotherapy and behavior change* (4th ed.). New York: Wiley.

Beebe, D. K. (1991). Emergency management of the adult female rape victim. *Am. Fam. Physician 43,* 2041–2046.

Begley, S. (1989, August 14). The stuff that dreams are made of. *Newsweek,* p. 40.

Begley, S. (1995, October 9). Promises, promises. *Newsweek,* pp. 60–62.

Begley, S. (2000, May 8). A world of their own. *Newsweek,* pp. 52–63.

Beidel, D. C., Turner, S. M., & Morris, T. L. (1995). A new inventory to assess childhood social anxiety and phobia: The social phobia and anxiety inventory for children. *Psychol. Assess., 7*(1), 73–79.

Beidel, D. C., Turner, S. M., & Morris, T. L. (2000). Behavioral treatment of childhood social phobia. *J. Consult. Clin. Psychol., 68*(6), 1072–1080.

Bein, E. (1998). How well does long-term psychoanalytically oriented inpatient treatment work? A review of a study by Blatt and Ford. *Psychother. Res., 8*(1), 30–34.

Beiser, M., Shore, J. H., Peters, R., & Tatum, E. (1985). Does community care for the mentally ill make a difference? A tale of two cities. *Am. J. Psychiatry, 142,* 1047–1052.

Beitman, B. D. (1993). Afterword to Section IV. In J. M. Oldham, M. B. Riba, & A. Tasman (Eds.), *Review of psychiatry* (Vol. 12). Washington, DC: American Psychiatric Press.

Beitman, B. D. (1993). Pharmacotherapy and the stages of psychotherapeutic change. In J. M. Oldham, M. B. Riba, & A. Tasman (Eds.), *Review of psychiatry* (Vol. 12). Washington, DC: American Psychiatric Press.

Beitman, B. D. (1996). Integrating pharmacotherapy and psychotherapy: An emerging field of study. *Bull. Menninger Clin., 60*(2), 160–173.

Belcher, J. R. (1988). Defining the service needs of homeless mentally ill persons. *Hosp. Commun. Psychiatry, 39*(11), 1203–1205.

Belcher, J. R. (1988). The future role of state hospitals. *Psychiatr. Hosp., 19*(2), 79–83.

Belcher, J. R., & Blank, H. (1990). Protecting the right to involuntary commitment. *J. Appl. Soc. Sci., 14*(1), 95–115.

Belkin, L. (1990, June 6). Doctor tells of first death using his suicide device. *New York Times,* A1, p. 3.

Bell, I. R. (1999). A guide to current psychopharmacological treatments for affective disorders in older adults: Anxiety, agitation, and depression. In M. Duffy (Ed.), *Handbook of counseling and psychotherapy with older adults.* New York: Wiley.

Bell, M. D., Lysaker, P. H., & Milstein, R. M. (1996). Clinical benefits of paid work activity in schizophrenia. *Schizophr. Bull., 22*(1), 51–67.

Belle, D. (1990). Poverty and women's mental health. *Am. Psychol., 45*(3), 385–389.

Belli, R. F., Windschitl, P. D., McCarthy, T. T., & Winfrey, S. E. (1992). Detecting memory impairment with a modified test procedure: Manipulating retention interval with centrally presented event items. *J. Exp. Psychol.: Learn., Memory, Cognit., 18,* 356–367.

Bellinger, D. L., Madden, K. S., Felten, S. Y., & Felten, D. L. (1994). Neural and endocrine links between the brain and the immune system. In C. S. Lewis, C. O'Sullivan, & J. Barraclough (Eds.), *The psychoimmunology of cancer: Mind and body in the fight for survival.* Oxford, England: Oxford University Press.

Bellivier, F., Leboyer, M., Courtet, P., Feingold, J., Buresi, C., & Malafosse, A. (1999). "Association between the tryptophane hydroxylase gene and manic-depressive illness": Reply. *Arch. Gen. Psychiatry, 56*(1), 101.

Belluck, P. (1996, December 1). The symptoms of Internet addiction. *New York Times,* p. 5.

Belmaker, R. H., Bersudsky, Y., Genjamin, J., Agam, G., Levine, J., & Kofman, O. (1995). Manipulation of Inositol-linked second messenger systems as a therapeutic strategy in psychiatry. In G. Gessa, W. Fratta, L. Pani, & G. Serra (Eds.), *Depression and mania: From neurobiology to treatment.* New York: Raven Press.

Bemporad, J. R. (1992). Psychoanalytically orientated psychotherapy. In E. S. Paykel (Ed.), *Handbook of affective disorders.* New York: Guilford Press.

Bemporad, J. R. (1996). Self-starvation through the ages: Reflections on the pre-history of anorexia nervosa. *Int. J. Eat. Disord., 19*(3), 217–237.

Bemporad, J. R., & Vasile, R. G. (1999). Dynamic psychotherapy. In M. Hersen & A. S. Bellack (Eds.), *Handbook of comparative interventions for adult disorders* (2nd ed.). New York: Wiley.

Bender, K. J. (1998). New prescription for paraphilia? *Psychiatr. Times, 15*(4).

Bender, K. J. (1998). FDA approves reduced clozapine monitoring; increased patient access versus increased risk. *Psychiatr. Times, 15*(5).

Bender, L. (1938). *A visual motor gestalt test and its clinical use.* New York: American Orthopsychiatric Assoc.

Bender, R., Jockel, K. H., Trautner, C., Spraul, M., & Berger, M. (1999). Effect of age on excess mortality in obesity. *JAMA, J. Am. Med. Assoc., 281*(16), 1498–1504.

Benezech, M., DeWitte, J. J. E., & Bourgeois, M. (1989). A lycanthropic murderer. *Am. J. Psychiatry, 146*(7), 942.

Bennett, F. C., Brown, R. T., Craver, J., & Anderson, D. (1999). Stimulant medication for the child with attention-deficit/hyperactivity disorder. *Pediatr. Clin. North Am., 46*(5), 929–944, vii.

Bennett, G. T., & Kish, G. R. (1990). Incompetency to stand trial: Treatment unaffected by demographic variables. *J. Forensic Sci., 35*(2), 403–412.

Bennett, M. B. (1987). Afro-American women, poverty and mental health: A social essay. *Women Health, 12*(3–4), 213–228.

Bennett, M. E., Miller, J. H., & Woodall, W. G. (1999). Drinking, binge drinking and other drug use among southwestern undergraduates: Three-year trends. *Am. J. Drug Alcohol Abuse, 25*(2), 331–350.

Bennett, M. P. (1998). The effect of mirthful laughter on stress and natural killer cell cytotoxicity. *Diss. Abstr. Int. B; 58*(7-B), 3553.

Benowitz, N. (1990). Clinical pharmacology of caffeine. *Annu. Rev. Med., 41,* 277–288.

Ben Shakhar, G., Bar Hillel, M., Bilu, Y., & Shefler, G. (1998). Seek and ye shall find: test results are what you hypothesize they are. *J. Behav. Decision Making, 11*(4), 235–249.

Bensley, L. S., Spieker, S. J., Van Eenwyk, J., & Schoder, J. (1999). Self-reported abuse history and adolescent problem behaviors: II. Alcohol and drug use. *J. Adolesc. Health, 24*(3), 173–180.

Bensley, L. S., Van Eenwyk, J., Spieker, S. J., & Schoder, J. (1999). Self-reported abuse history and adolescent problem behaviors: I. Antisocial and suicidal behaviors. *J. Adolesc. Health, 24*(3), 163–172.

Benson, J. (1996, January 15). Crime: Law and order. *Newsweek,* pp. 48–54.

Bergem, A. L., Engedal, K., & Kringlen, E. (1997). The role of heredity in late-onset alzheimer disease and vascular dementia: A twin study. *Arch. Gen. Psychiatry, 54,* 264–270.

Berger, F. M. (1970). The discovery of meprobamate. In F. Ayd & B. Blackwell (Eds.), *Discoveries in biological psychiatry.* Philadelphia: Lippincott.

Bergler, E. (1951). *Neurotic counterfeit sex.* New York: Grune & Stratton.

Berk, S. N., & Efran, J. S. (1983). Some recent developments in the treatment of neurosis. In C. E. Walker et al. (Eds.), *The handbook of clinical psychology: Theory, research, and practice* (Vol. 2). Homewood, IL: Dow Jones-Irwin.

Berlin, F. S. (2000). The etiology and treatment of sexual offending. In D. H. Fishbein (Ed.), *The science, treatment, and prevention of antisocial behaviors: Application to the criminal justice system* (pp. 21-1-21-15). Kingston, NJ: Civic Research Institute.

Berlin, I. N. (1987). Suicide among American Indian adolescents: An overview. *Suicide Life-Threaten. Behav., 17,* 218–232.

Berliner, R., Solomon, S., Newman, L. C., & Lipton, R. B. (1999). Migraine: Clinical features and diagnosis. *Compr. Ther., 25*(8–10), 397–402.

Berman, A. L. (1986). Helping suicidal adolescents: Needs and responses. In C. A. Corr & J. N. McNeil (Eds.), *Adolescence and death.* New York: Springer.

Berman, A. L., & Jobes, D. A. (1991). *Adolescent suicide: Assessment and intervention.* Washington, DC: American Psychological Association.

Berman, A. L., & Jobes, D. A. (1995). Suicide prevention in adolescents (age 12–18) [Special issue: Suicide prevention: Toward the year 2000]. *Suicide Life-Threaten. Behav., 25*(1), 143–154.

Berman, S., Delaney, N., Gallagher, D., Atkins, P., & Graeber, M. (1987). Respite care: A partnership between a Veterans Administration nursing home and families to care for frail elders at home. *Gerontologist, 27,* 581–584.

Berney, B. (1993). Round and round it goes: The epidemiology of childhood lead poisoning, 1950–1990. *Milbank Q., 71*(1), 3–39.

Bernstein, H. A. (1981). Survey of threats and assaults directed toward psychotherapists. *Am. J. Psychother., 35,* 542–549.

Berrettini, W. H. (2000). Susceptibility loci for bipolar disorder: Overlap with inherited vulnerability to schizophrenia. *Biol. Psychiatry, 47*(3), 245–251.

Bersoff, D. M., & Bersoff, D. N. (1999). Ethical perspectives in clinical research. In P. C. Kendall, J. N. Butcher et al. (Eds.), *Handbook of research methods in clinical psychology* (2nd ed.). New York: Wiley.

Bersoff, D. N. (Ed.). (1995). *Ethical conflicts in psychology.* Washington, DC: American Psychological Association.

Bersoff, D. N. (Ed.). (1999). *Ethical conflicts in psychology* (2nd ed.). Washington, DC: American Psychological Association.

Bersoff, D. N., Goodman-Delahunty, J. G., Grisso, J. T., Hans, V. P., Poythress, N. G., Jr., & Roesch, R. G. (1997). Training in law and psychology. *Am. Psychol., 52*(12), 1301–1310.

Bertani, A., Perna, G., Arancio, C., Caldirola, D., & Bellodi, L. (1997). Pharmacologic effect of imipramine, paroxetine, and sertraline on 35% carbon dioxide hypersensitivity in panic patients: A double-blind, random, placebo-controlled study. *J. Clin. Psychopharmacol., 17*(2), 97–101.

Berthier, M. L., Kulisevsky, J., Gironell, A., & Lopez, O. L. (2001). Obsessive-compulsive disorder and traumatic brain injury: Behavioral, cognitive, and neuroimaging findings. *Neuropsychiatry, Neuropsychol., Behav., Neurol., 14*(1), 23–31.

Beutel, M., Deckardt, R., Von Rad, M., & Weiner, H. (1995). Grief and depression after miscarriage: Their separation, antecedents, and course. *Psychosom. Med., 57,* 517–526.

Beutler, L. E. (1979). Toward specific psychological therapies for specific conditions. *J. Consult. Clin. Psychol., 47,* 882–892.

Beutler, L. E. (1991). Have all won and must all have prizes? Revisiting Luborsky et al.'s verdict. *J. Consult. Clin. Psychol., 59,* 226–232.

Beutler, L. E., Machado, P. P. P., & Neufeldt, S. A. (1994). Therapist variables. In A. E. Bergin & S. L. Garfield (Eds.), *Handbook of psychotherapy and behavior change.* New York: Wiley.

Beutler, L. E., Williams, R. E., Wakefield, P. J., & Entwistle, S. R. (1995). Bridging scientist and practitioner perspectives in clinical psychology. *Am. Psychol., 50*(12), 984–994.

Beyer, H. A. (1991). Litigation involving people with mental retardation. In J. L. Matson & J. A. Mulick (Eds.), *Handbook of mental retardation* (2nd ed.). New York: Pergamon Press.

Bickel, W. K., & Amass, L. (1995). Buprenorphine treatment of opioid dependence: A review. *Exp. Clin. Psychopharmacol., 3*(4), 477–489.

Bickman, L. & Dokecki, P. (1989). Public and private responsibility for mental health services. *Am. Psychol., 44*(8), 1133–1137.

Biddle, S., Akande, D., Armstrong, N., Ashcroft, M., Brooke, R., & Goudes, M. (1996). The self-motivation inventory modified for children: Evidenced on psychometric properties and its use in physical exercise. *Int. J. Sport Psychol., 27*(3), 237–250.

Biederman, J., Mick, E., Faraone, S. V., & Burback, M. (2001). Patterns of remission and symptom decline in conduct disorder: A four-year prospective study of an ADHD sample. *J. Am. Acad. Child Adolesc. Psychiatry, 40*(3), 290–298.

Biederman, J., Rosenbaum, J. F., Hirshfeld, D. R., Farone, S. V., Bolduc, E. A., Gersten, M., Meminger, S. R., Kagan, J., Snidman, N., & Reznick, J. S. (1990). Psychiatric correlates of behavioral inhibition in young children of parents with and without psychiatric disorders. *Arch. Gen. Psychiatry, 47,* 21–26.

Biegon, A., Dillon, K., Volkow, N. D., & Fowler, J. S. (1995). Quantitative autoradiographic localization and characterization of cocaine binding sites in the human brain post-mortem. In A. Biegon & N. D. Volkow (Eds.), *Sites of drug action in the human brain.* Boco Raton, FL: CRC Press.

Biegon, A., & Kerman, I. (1995). Quantitative autoradiography of cannabinoid receptors in the human brain post-mortem. In A. Biegon & N. D. Volkow (Eds.), *Sites of drug action in the human being.* Boca Raton, FL: CRC Press.

Bienvenu, O. J., & Eaton, W. W. (1998). The epidemiology of blood-injection-injury phobia. *Psychol. Med., 28*(5), 1129–1136.

Bijl, R. V., Ravelli, A., & van Zessen, G. (1998). Prevalence of psychiatric disorder in the general population: Results of the Netherlands Mental Health Survey and Incidence Study (NEMESIS). *Soc. Psychiatry Psychiatr. Epidemiol., 33*(12), 587–595.

Bill, W. (1975). *Alcoholics Anonymous comes of age: A brief history of AA.* New York: Alcoholics Anonymous World Services. (Original work published 1957.)

Bilder, R. M., Lipschutz-Broch, L., Reiter, G., Geisler, S. H. et al. (1992). Intellectual deficits in first-episode schizophrenia: Evidence for progressive deterioration. *Schizophr. Bull., 18*(3), 437–448.

Binder, R. L. (1999). Are the mentally ill dangerous? *J. Am. Acad. Psychiatry Law, 27*(2), 189–201.

Binet, A., & Simon, T. (1916). *The development of intelligence in children (The Binet-Simon Scale).* Baltimore: Williams & Wilkins.

Binik, Y. M., Bergeron, S., & Khalife, S. (2000). Dyspareunia. In S. R. Leiblum & R. C. Rosen (Eds.), *Principles and practice of sex therapy* (3rd ed., pp. 154–180). New York: Guilford Press.

Binik, Y. M., Servan-Schreiber, D., Freiwald, S., & Hall, K. S. (1988). Intelligent computer-based assessment and psychotherapy: An expert system for sexual dysfunction. *J. Nerv. Ment. Dis., 176*(7), 387–400.

Birch, H. G., Richardson, S. A., Baird D. et al. (1970). *Mental subnormality in the community—A clinical and epidemiological study.* Baltimore: Williams & Wilkins.

Bird, J. (1979). The behavioral treatment of hysteria. *Br. J. Psychiatry, 134,* 129–137.

Birren, J. E., & Schroots, J. F. (Eds.). (2000). *A history of geropsychology in autobiography.* Washington, DC: American Psychological Association.

Birtchnell, J. (1996). Detachment. In C. G. Costello (Ed.), *Personality characteristics of the personality disordered.* New York: Wiley.

Bissette, G., Seidler, F. J., Nemeroff, C. B., & Slotkin, T. A. (1996). High affinity choline transporter status in Alzheimer's disease tissue from rapid autopsy. In R. J. Wurtman, S. Corkin, J. H. Growdon, & R. M. Nitsch (Eds.), *The neurobiology of Alzheimer's disease.* New York: New York: Academy of Sciences.

Bisson, J. I., & Deahl, M. P. (1994). Psychological debriefing and prevention of post-traumatic stress: More research is needed. *Br. J. Psychiatry, 165*(6), 717–720.

Blacher, J., & Baker, B. L. (1992). Toward meaningful involvement in out-of-home placement settings. *Ment. Retard., 30*(1), 35–43.

Blacher, J., & Baker, B. L. (1994). Family involvement in residential treatment of children with retardation: Is there evidence of detachment? *J. Child Psychol. Psychiatry Allied Discip., 35*(3), 505–520.

Black, D. W., & Andreasen, N. C. (1994). Schizophrenia, schizophreniform disorder, and delusional (paranoid) disorder. In R. E. Hales, S. C. Yudofsky, & J. A. Talbott (Eds.), *The American Psychiatric Press textbook of psychiatry* (2nd ed.). Washington, DC: American Psychiatric Press.

Black, D. W., Belsare, G., & Schlosser, S. (1999). Clinical features, psychiatric comorbidity, and health-related quality of life in persons reporting compulsive computer use behavior. *J. Clin. Psychiatry, 60*(12), 839–844.

Black, D. W., Kehrberg, L. L. D., Flumerfelt, D. L., & Schlosser, S. S. (1997). Characteristics of 36 subjects reporting compulsive sexual behavior. *Am. J. Psychiatry, 154,* 243–249.

Black, D. W., Monahan, P., & Gabel, J. (1997). Fluvoxamine in the treatment of compulsive buying. *J. Clin. Psychiatry, 58*(4), 159–163.

Black, S. T. (1993). Comparing genuine and simulated suicide notes: A new perspective. *J. Consult. Clin. Psychol., 61*(4), 699–702.

Blackburn, R. (1993). *The psychology of criminal conduct: Theory, research, and practice.* New York: Wiley.

Blackman, S. (1998). Is it depression or is it dementia? *Psychiatr. Times, 15*(2).

Blackman, S. (1998). From Mars to Venus—Couples sex therapy. *Psychiatr. Times, 15*(9).

Blair, C. D., & Lanyon, R. I. (1981). Exhibitionism: Etiology and treatment. *Psychol. Bull., 89*(3), 439–463.

Blanchard, E. B. (1994). Behavioral medicine and health psychology. In A. E. Bergin & S. L. Garfield (Eds.), *Handbook of psychotherapy and behavior change.* New York: Wiley.

Blanchard, E. B., & Andrasik, F. (1982). Psychological assessment and treatment of headache: Recent developments and emerging issues. *J. Consult. Clin. Psychol., 50*(6), 859–879.

Blanchard, E. B., Buckley, T. C., Hickling, E. J., & Taylor, A. E. (1998). Posttraumatic stress disorder and comorbid major depression: Is the correlation an illusion? *J. Anxiety Disord., 12*(1), 21–37.

Blanchard, E. B., Schwarz, S. P., Suls, J. M., Gerardi, M. et al. (1992). Two controlled evaluations of multicomponent psychological treatment of irritable bowel syndrome. *Behav. Res. Ther., 30*(2), 175–189.

Blanchard, J. J., Brown, S. A., Horan, W. P., & Sherwood, A. R. (2000). Substance use disorders in schizophrenia: Review, integration, and a proposed model. *Clin. Psychol. Rev., 20*(2), 207–234.

Blanchard, R., & Hucker, S. J. (1991). Age, transvestism, bondage, and concurrent paraphilic activities in 117 fatal cases of autoerotic asphyxia. *Br. J. Psychiatry, 159,* 371–377.

Blanco, C., Ibañez, A., Saiz-Ruiz, J., Blanco-Jerez, C., & Nuñes, E. V. (2000). Epidemiology, pathophysiology and treatment of pathological gambling. *CNS Drugs*, 13(6), 397–407.

Bland, R., & Harrison, C. (2000). Developing and evaluating a psychoeducation program for caregivers of bipolar affective disorder patients: Report of a pilot project. *Res. Soc. Work Pract.*, 10(2), 209–228.

Bland, R. C., Orn, H., & Newman, S. C. (1988). Lifetime prevalence of psychiatric disorders in Edmonton. *Acta Psychiatr. Scand.*, 77(Suppl. 338), 24–32.

Blasko, D. G., Kazmerski, V. A., Corty, E. W., & Kallgren, C. A. (1998). Courseware for observational research (COR): A new approach to teaching naturalistic observation. *Behav. Res. Methods Instrum. Comput.*, 30(2), 217–222.

Blatt, S. J. (1995). The destructiveness of perfectionism. Implications for the treatment of depression. *Am. Psychol.*, 50(12), 1003–1020.

Blatt, S. J. (1999). Personality factors in brief treatment of depression: Further analyses of the NIMH-sponsored Treatment for Depression Collaborative Research Program. In D. S. Janowsky et al. (Eds.), *Psychotherapy indications and outcomes*. Washington, DC: American Psychiatric Press.

Blazer, D. G., George, L. K., & Hughes, D. (1991). The epidemiology of anxiety disorders: An age comparison. In C. Salzman & B. D. Lebowitz (Eds.), *Anxiety in the elderly*. New York: Springer.

Blazer, D. G., Hughes, D., George, L. K., Swartz, M., & Boyer, R. (1991). Generalized anxiety disorder. In L. N. Robins & D. A. Regier (Eds.), *Psychiatric disorders in America: The epidemiologic catchment area study*. New York: Maxwell Macmillan International.

Blehar, M. C., & Oren, D. A. (1995). Women's increased vulnerability to mood disorders: Integrating psychobiology and epidemiology. *Depression, 3,* 3–12.

Blier, P., & de Montigny, C. (1994, July). Current advances and trends in the treatment of depression. *Trends Pharmacol. Sci.*, 15, 220–226.

Blinder, B. J., Blinder, M. C., & Sanathara, V. A. (1998, December). Eating disorders and addiction. *Psychiatr. Times*, 15(12).

Bliss, E. L. (1980). Multiple personalities: A report of 14 cases with implications for schizophrenia and hysteria. *Arch. Gen. Psychiatry*, 37(12), 1388–1397.

Bliss, E. L. (1980). *Multiple personality, allied disorders and hypnosis*. New York: Oxford University Press.

Bliss, E. L. (1985). "How prevalent is multiple personality?": Dr. Bliss replies. *Am. J. Psychiatry, 142*(12), 1527.

Bloch, S., Crouch, E., & Reibstein, J. (1982). Therapeutic factors in group psychotherapy: A review. *Arch. Gen. Psychiatry, 27,* 216–324.

Bloch, S., Szmukler, G. I., Herman, H., Benson, A., & Colussa, S. (1995). Counseling caregivers of relatives with schizophrenia: Themes, interventions, and caveats. *Fam. Process, 34,* 413–425.

Block, B., & Pristach, C. A. (1992). Diagnosis and management of the paranoid patient. *Am. Fam. Physician, 45*(6), 2634–2640.

Bloom, B. L. (1984). *Community mental health: A general introduction* (2nd ed.). Monterey, CA: Brooks/Cole.

Bloom, C., Gitter, A., Gutwill, S., Kogel, L., & Zaphiropoulos, L. (1994). *Eating problems: A feminist psychoanalytic treatment model*. New York: Basic Books.

Bloom, F., Lazerson, A., & Hofstadter, L. (1985). *Brain, mind, and behavior*. New York: Freeman.

Bloom, J. D. (1990). The Tarasoff decision & gun control legislation. *Int. J. Offender Ther. Comp. Criminol., 34*(1), v–viii.

Bloom, J. D., Nadelson, C. C., & Notman, M. T. (Eds.). (1999). *Physician sexual misconduct*. Washington, DC: American Psychiatric Press.

Bloomfield, H. H., Nordfors, M., & McWilliams. P. (1996). *Hypericum & depression*. Los Angeles: Prelude Press.

Bloomingdale, L., & Bloomingdale, E. (1989). Childhood identification and prophylaxis of antisocial personality disorder. In R. Rosner & H. I. Schwartz (Eds.), *Juvenile psychiatry and the law*. New York: Plenum Press.

Blum, K., Braverman, E. R., Holder, J. M., Lubar, J. F., Monastra, V. J., Miller, D., Lubar, J. O., Chen, T. J. H., & Comings, D. E. (2000). Reward deficiency syndrome: A biogenetic model for the diagnosis and treatment of impulsive, addictive, and compulsive behaviors. *J. Psychoact. Drugs, 32*(Suppl.), 1–68.

Blum, K., & Noble, E. (1993). Drug dependence and the A1 allele gene. *Drug Alcohol Depend., 33*(5).

Blum, K., Noble, E., Sheridan, P., Finley, O. et al. (1991). Association of the A1 allele of the D2 dopamine receptor gene with severe alcoholism. *Alcohol, 8*(5), 409–416.

Bocker, F. M. (1984). Soziale Integration und Kontakte zu Bezugspersonen des gewohnten sozialen Umfeldes wahrend stationarer Behandlung im psychiatrischen Krankenhaus. Eine prospektive katamnestische Untersuchung an erstmals aufgenommenen Patienten mit schizophrenen und cyclothymen Psychosen [Social integration and contact with people in the normal social environment during treatment in a psychiatric hospital: A follow-up of first-admission inpatients with schizophrenia and affective disorders]. *Eur. Arch. Psychiatr. Neurol. Sci., 234*(4), 250–257.

Bockoven, J. S. (1963). *Moral treatment in American psychiatry*. New York: Springer.

Boegels, S. M., & Zigterman, D. (2000). Dysfunctional cognitions in children with social phobia, separation anxiety disorder, and generalized anxiety disorder. *J. Abnorm. Child Psychol., 28*(2), 205–211.

Boergers, J., Spirito, A., & Donaldson, D. (1998). Reasons for adolescent suicide attempts: Associations with psychological functioning. *J. Am. Acad. Child Adolesc. Psychiatry, 37*(12), 1287–1293.

Bogdan, R., & Taylor, S. (1976, January). The judged, not the judges: An insider's view of mental retardation. *Am. Psychol., 31*(1), 47–52.

Bolgar, H. (1965). The case study method. In B. B. Wolman (Ed.), *Handbook of clinical psychology*. New York: McGraw-Hill.

Bolla, K. I., McCann, U. D., & Ricaurte, G. A. (1998). Memory impairment in abstinent MDMA ("Ecstasy") users. *Neurology, 51*(6), 1532–1537.

Bolton, D., Luckie, M., & Steinberg, D. (1995). Long-term course of obsessive-compulsive disorder treated in adolescence. *J. Am. Acad. Child Adolesc. Psychiatry, 34*(11), 1441–1450.

Bolund, C. (1985). Suicide and cancer: II. Medical and care factors in suicides by cancer patients in Sweden, 1973–1976. *J. Psychol. Oncol., 3*(1), 31–52.

Bondolfi, G., Dufour, H., Patris, M., May, J. P., Billeter, U., Eap, C. B., & Baumann, P. (1998). Risperidone versus clozapine in treatment-resistant chronic schizophrenia: A randomized double-blind study. *Am. J. Psychiatry, 155*(4), 499–504.

Bongar, B., Peterson, L. G., Golann, S., & Hardiman, J. J. (1990). Self-mutilation and the chronically suicidal patient: An examination of the frequent visitor to the psychiatric emergency room. *Ann. Clin. Psychiatry, 2*(3), 217–222.

Bonn, D. (1996). Melatonin's multifarious marvels: Miracle or myth. *Lancet, 347,* 184.

Bonner, R. L. (1992). Isolation, seclusion, and psychosocial vulnerability as risk factors for suicide behind bars. In R. W. Maris, A. L. Berman, J. T. Maltsberger, & R. I. Yufit (Eds.), *Assessment and prediction of suicide*. New York: Guilford Press.

Booth, R. E., Kwiatkowski, C. F., & Chitwood, D. D. (2000). Sex related HIV risk behaviors: Differential risks among injection drug users, crack smokers and injection drug users who smoke crack. *Drug Alcohol Depend., 58*(3), 219–226.

Borch-Jacobsen, M. (1997). Sybil—The making of a disease: An interview with Dr. Herbert Spiegel. *New York Review of Books, 44*(7), 60–64.

Borison, R. L. (1995). Clinical efficacy of serotonin-dopamine antagonists relative to classic neuroleptics. *J. Clin. Psychopharmacol., 15*(1, Suppl. 1), 24S–29S.

Bornstein, R. A., Schwarzkopf, S. B., Olson, S. C., & Nasrallah, H. A. (1992). Third-ventricle enlargement and neuropsychological deficit in schizophrenia. *Biol. Psychiatry, 31*(9), 954–961.

Bornstein, R. F. (1992). The dependent personality: Developmental, social, and clinical perspectives. *Psychol. Bull., 112*(1), 3–23.

Bornstein, R. F. (1995). Comorbidity of dependent personality disorder and other psychological disorders: An integrative review. *J. Pers. Disord., 9*(4), 286–303.

Bornstein, R. F. (1996). Dependency. In C. G. Costello (Ed.), *Personality characteristics of the personality disordered*. New York: Wiley.

Bornstein, R. F. (1998). Dependency in the personality disorders: Intensity, sight, expression, and defense. *J. Clin. Psychol., 54*(2), 175–189.

Bornstein, R. F. (1999). Criterion validity of objective and projective dependency tests: A meta-analytic assessment of behavioral prediction. *Psychol. Assess., 11*(1), 48–57.

Boros, S., Ophoven, J., Anderson, R., & Brubaker, L. (1995). Munchausen syndrome by proxy: A profile for medical child abuse. *Aust. Fam. Physician, 24*(5), 768–773.

Bortz, W. M., II, Wallace, D. H., & Wiley, D. (1999). Sexual function in 1,202 aging males: Differentiating aspects. *J. Gerontol. A 54*(5), M237–241.

Borum, R. (1996). Improving the clinical practice of violence risk assessment. Technology, guidelines, and training. *Am. Psychol., 51*(9), 945–956.

Borys, D. S., & Pope, K. S. (1989). Dual relationships between therapist and client: A national study of psychologists, psychiatrists and social workers. *Prof. Psychol., 20,* 283–293.

Bosc, M. (2000). Assessment of social functioning in depression. *Comp. Psychiatry, 41*(1), 63–69.

Boscarino, J. A. (1997). Diseases among men 20 years after exposure to severe stress: Implications for clinical research and medical care. *Psychosom. Med., 59,* 605–614.

Bose, J. (1995). Depression. In M. Lionells, J. Fiscalini, C. H. Mann, & D. B. Stern (Eds.), *Handbook of interpersonal psychoanalysis*. Hillsdale, NJ: Analytic Press.

Bott, E. (1928). Teaching of psychology in the medical course. *Bull. Assoc. Am. Med. Coll., 3,* 289–304.

Bouchard, C., Rhéaume, J., & Ladouceur, R. (1999). Responsibility and perfectionism in OCD: An experimental study. *Behav. Res. Ther., 37*(3), 239–248.

Boudewyns, P. A. (1996). Posttraumatic stress disorder: Conceptualization and treatment. In M. Hersen, R. M. Eisler, & P. M. Miller (Eds.), *Progress in behavior modification* (Vol. 30). Pacific Grove, CA: Brooks/Cole.

Boudewyns, P. A., Stwertka, S. A., Hyer, L. A., Albrecht, J. W., & Sperr, E. V. (1991). Eye movement desensitization for PTSD of combat: A treatment outcome pilot study. Paper presented at the convention of the American Psychological Association, San Francisco.

Boudouris, J. (2000). The insanity defense in Polk County, Iowa. *Am. J. Forensic Psychol., 18*(1), 41–79.

Bourgeois, M. (1991). Serotonin, impulsivity and suicide. *Hum. Psychopharmacol. Clin. Exp., 6*(Suppl.), 31–36.

Bourgeois, M. (1995, December). [Importance of DSM IV (APA) and ICD-10 (WHO) in diagnosis and treatment of mood disorders]. *Encephale,* Spec. No. 5, pp. 47–52 (in French).

Bourin, M., Malinge, M., & Guitton, B. (1995). [Provocative agents in panic disorder.] *Therapie, 50*(4), 301–306 (in French).

Bourne, P. G. (1970). *Men, stress & Vietnam.* Boston: Little, Brown.

Boutros, N., Bonnet, K., & Mak, T. (1996). Drug abuse: A significant variable in schizophrenia research. *Biol. Psychiatry, 39,* 1053–1054.

Bowden, C. L. (2001). Strategies to reduce misdiagnosis of bipolar depression. *Psychiatr. Serv., 52*(1), 51–55.

Bowen, K. (2000). Child abuse and domestic violence in families of children seen for suspected sexual abuse. *Clin. Pediatr., 39*(1), 33–40.

Bowen, M. A. (1960). A family concept of schizophrenia. In D. D. Jackson (Ed.), *The etiology of schizophrenia.* New York: Basic Books.

Bower, B. (1995). Moods and the muse. *Sci. News, 147,* 378–380.

Bower, B. (1995). Deceptive appearances: Imagined physical defects take an ugly personal toll. *Sci. News, 148,* 40–41.

Bower, G. H. (1981). Mood and memory. *Am. Psychol., 36*(2), 129–148.

Bowers, K. S., & Woody, E. Z. (1996). Hypnotic amnesia and the paradox of intentional forgetting. *J. Abnorm. Psychol., 105*(3), 381–390.

Bowman, E. S., & Markand, O. N. (1996). Psychodynamic and psychiatric diagnoses of pseudoseizure subjects. *Am. J. Psychiatry, 153*(1), 57–63.

Boyce, W. T., Chesney, M., Alkon, A., Tschann, J. M. et al. (1995). Psychobiologic reactivity to stress and childhood respiratory illnesses: Results of two prospective studies. *Psychosom. Med., 57,* 411–422.

Boyd, J. H., Rae, D. S., Thompson, J. W., Burns, B. J. et al. (1990). Phobia: Prevalence and risk factors. *Soc. Psychiatry Psychiatr. Epidemiol., 25*(6), 314–323.

Bozman, A., & Beck, J. G. (1991). Covariation of sexual desire and sexual arousal: The effects of anger and anxiety. *Arch. Sex. Behav., 20,* 47–60.

Braatvedt, G. D. (1999). Outcome of managing impotence in clinical practice. *N. Z. Med. J., 112*(1092), 272–274.

Bradbury, T. N., & Karney, B. R. (1993). Longitudinal study of marital interaction and dysfunction: Review and analysis. *Clin. Psychol. Rev., 13*(1), 15–27.

Bradford, J. M. (1999). The paraphilias, obsessive compulsive spectrum disorder, and the treatment of sexually deviant behaviour. *Psychiatr. Q., 70*(3), 209–219.

Bradford, J. M. W. (1995). Pharmacological treatment of the paraphilias. In J. M. Oldham & M. B. Riba (Eds.), *American Psychiatric Press review of psychiatry* (Vol. 14). Washington, DC: American Psychiatric Press.

Bradley, B. P., Mogg, K., Falla, S. J., & Hamilton, L. R. (1998). Attentional bias for threatening facial expressions in anxiety: Manipulation of stimulus duration. *Cognition Emotion, 12*(6), 737–753.

Bradley, S. J. (1995). Psychosexual disorders in adolescence. In J. M. Oldham & M. B. Riba (Eds.), *American Psychiatric Press review of psychiatry* (Vol. 14), Washington, DC: American Psychiatric Press.

Brady, J. P., & Lind, D. L. (1961). Experimental analysis of hysterical blindness: Operant condi-

tioning techniques. *Arch. Gen. Psychiatry, 4,* 331–339.

Braff, D. L., & Saccuzzo, D. P. (1985). The time course of information-processing deficits in schizophrenia. *Am. J. Psychiatry, 142*(2), 170–174.

Braginsky, B. M., Braginsky, D. D., & Ring, K. (1969). *Methods of madness: The mental hospital as a last resort.* New York: Holt.

Brandon, S. (1981). The history of shock treatment. In *Electroconvulsive therapy: An appraisal.* Oxford, UK: Oxford University Press.

Brandon, S., Boakes, J., Glaser, D., & Green, R. (1998). Recovered memories of childhood sexual abuse: Implications for clinical practice. *Br. J. Psychiatry, 172,* 296–307.

Brannen, S. J., Bradshaw, R. D., Hamlin, E. R., II, Fogarty, J. P., & Colligan, T. W. (1999). Spouse abuse: Physician guidelines to identification, diagnosis and management in the uniformed services. *Mil. Med., 164*(1), 30–36.

Brasic, J. R., & Fogelman, D. (1999). Clinician safety. *Psychiatr. Clin. North Am., 22*(4), 923–940.

Brauer, A. (1999). Biofeedback and anxiety. *Psychiatr. Times, 16*(2).

Braun, D. L. (1996, July 28). Interview. In S. Gilbert. More men may seek eating-disorder help. *New York Times.*

Braun, D. L., Sunday, S. R., & Halmi, K. A. (1995). Psychiatric comorbidity in patients with eating disorders. *Psychol. Med.*

Brawman-Mintzer, O. (2001). Pharmacologic treatment of generalized anxiety disorder. *Psychiatr. Clin. North Am., 24*(1), 119–137.

Brawman-Mintzer, O., & Lydiar, R. B. (1997). Biological basis of generalized anxiety disorder. *J. Clin. Psychiatry, 58*(Suppl. 3), 16–25.

Bray, G. A., Dahms, W. T., Atkinson, R. L. et al. (1980). Factors controlling food intake: A comparison of dieting and intestinal bypass. *Am. J. Clin. Nutr., 33,* 376–382.

Breggin, P. R. (1998). *Talking back to Ritalin: What doctors aren't telling you about stimulants for children.* Monroe, ME: Common Courage Press.

Breier, A. (1995). Serotonin, schizophrenia and antipsychotic drug action. *Schizophr. Res., 14*(3), 187–202.

Breier, A. (2001). A new era in the pharmacotherapy of psychotic disorders. *J. Clin. Psychiatry 62*(Suppl. 2), 3–5.

Breitbart, W., Rosenfeld, B., & Passik, S. (1996). Interest in physician-assisted suicide among ambulatory HIV-infected patients. *Am. J. Psychiatry, 153*(2), 238–242.

Bremner, J. D. (1999). Does stress damage the brain? *Biol. Psychiatry, 45*(7), 797–805.

Bremner, J. D., Southwick, S. M., & Charney, D. S. (1999). The neurobiology of posttraumatic stress disorder: An integration of animal and human research. In P. A. Saigh, J. D. Bremner et al. (Eds.), *Posttraumatic stress disorder: A comprehensive text.* Boston: Allyn & Bacon.

Bremner, J. D., Southwick, S. M., Johnson, D. R., Yehuda, R., & Charney, D. S. (1993). Childhood physical abuse and combat-related posttraumatic stress disorder in Vietnam veterans. *Am. J. Psychiatry, 150*(2), 235–239.

Bremner, J. D., Steinberg, M., Southwick, S. M., Johnson, D. R., & Charney, D. S. (1993). Use of the structured clinical interview for DSM-IV dissociative disorders for systematic assessment of dissociative symptoms in posttraumatic stress disorder. *Am. J. Psychiatry, 150*(7), 1101–1114.

Brems, C. (1995). Women and depression: A comprehensive analysis. In W. Beckham & W. Leber (Eds.), *Handbook of depression* (2nd ed.). New York: Guilford Press.

Brende, J. O., & Parson, E. R. (1985). *Vietnam veterans.* New York: Plenum Press.

Brende, J. O., & Rinsley, D. B. (1981). A case of multiple personality with psychological automatisms. *J. Am. Acad. Psychoanal., 9*(1), 129–151.

Brennan, P. A., & Harvey, P. D. (2001). Vulnerability to schizophrenia across the lifespan. In R. E. Ingram & J. M. Price (Eds.), *Vulnerability to psychopathology: Risk across the lifespan* (pp. 382–386). New York: Guilford Press.

Brenner, I. (1999). Deconstructing DID. *Am. J. Psychother., 53*(3), 344–360.

Brent, D. A., Bridge, J., Johnson, B. A., & Connolly, J. (1996). Suicidal behavior runs in families. A controlled family study of adolescent suicide victims. *Arch. Gen. Psychiatry, 53,* 1145–1152.

Brent, D. A., Bridge, J., Johnson, B. A., & Connolly, J. (1998). Suicidal behavior runs in families: A controlled family study of adolescent suicide victims. In R. J. Kosky, H. S. Eshkevari, & R. Hassan (Eds.), *Suicide prevention: The global context.* New York: Plenum Press.

Brent, D. A., & Kolko, D. J. (1998). Psychotherapy: Definitions, mechanisms of action, and relationship to etiological models. *J. Abnorm. Child Psychol., 26*(1), 17–25.

Brent, D. A., Kupfer, D. J., Bromet, E. J., & Dew, M. A. (1988). The assessment and treatment of patients at risk for suicide. In A. J. Frances & R. E. Hales (Eds.), *American Psychiatric Press review of psychiatry* (Vol. 7). Washington, DC: American Psychiatric Press.

Brent, D. A., Moritz, G., Liotus, L., Schweers, J., Balach, L., Roth, C., & Perper, J. A. (1998). Familial risk factors for adolescent suicide: A case-control study. In R. J. Kosky, H. S. Eshkevari, & R. Hassan (Eds.), *Suicide prevention: The global context.* New York: Plenum Press.

Breslau, N., Chilcoat, H. D., Kessler, R. C., & Davis, G. C. (1999). Previous exposure to trauma and PTSD effects of subsequent trauma: Results from the Detroit Area Survey of Trauma. *Am. J. Psychiatry, 156*(6), 902–907.

Breton, J. J., Bergeron, L., Valla, J. P., Berthiaume, C., Gaudet, N., Lambert, J., St. Georges, M., Houde, L., & Lepine, S. (1999). Quebec child mental health survey: Prevalence of DSM-III-R mental health disorders. *J. Child Psychol. Psychiatry Allied Discip., 40*(3), 375–384.

Brew, B. J. (1999). AIDS dementia complex. *Neurol. Clin., 17*(4), 861–881.

Brewerton, T. D., Lydiard, R. B., Herzog, D. B., Brotman, A. W. et al. (1995). Comorbidity of Axis I psychiatric disorders in bulimia nervosa. *J. Clin. Psychiatry, 56*(2), 77–80.

Brewin, C. R., Andrews, B., Rose, S., & Kirk, M. (1999). Acute stress disorder and posttraumatic stress disorder in victims of violent crime. *Am. J. Psychiatry, 156*(3), 360–366.

Brisman, J. (1992). Bulimia in the older adolescent: An analytic perspective to a behavioral problem. In J. D. O'Brien, D. J. Pilowsky, & O. W. Lewis (Eds.), *Psychotherapies with children and adolescents: Adapting the psychodynamic process.* Washington, DC: American Psychiatric Press.

Bristow, M., & Bright, J. (1995). Group cognitive therapy in chronic depression: Results from two intervention studies. *Behav. Cognit. Psychother., 23,* 373–380.

Britton, W. H., & Eaves, R. C. (1986). Relationship between the Vineland Adaptive Behavior Scales-Classroom Edition of the Vineland Social Maturity Scales. *Am. J. Ment. Defic., 91*(1), 105–107.

Brodsky, S., & Pothyress, N. (1990). Presentation of the American Psychological Association Convention, Boston.

Bromet, E. J., Hough, L., & Connell, M. (1984). Mental health of children near the Three Mile Island reactor. *J. Prev. Psychiatry, 2,* 275–301.

Bromet, E. J., Schulberg, H. C., & Dunn, L. (1982). Reactions of psychiatric patients to the Three Mile Island nuclear accident. *Arch. Gen. Psychiatry, 39*(6), 725-730.

Brooks, G. R., & Richardson, F. C. (1980). Emotional skills training: A treatment program for duodenal ulcer. *Behav. Ther., 11*(2), 198-207.

Brooner, R. K., King, V. L., Kidorf, M., Schmidt, C. W., & Bigelow, G. E. (1997). Psychiatric and substance use comorbidity among treatment-seeking opioid abusers. *Arch. Gen. Psychiatry, 54,* 71-80.

Brown, A. S. (2001). Prenatal infection and adult schizophrenia: A review and synthesis. *Int. J. Ment. Health, 29*(4), 22-37.

Brown, A. S., Susser, E. S., Butler, P. D., Andrews, R. R. Kaufmann, C. A., & Gorman, J. M. (1996). Neurobiological plausibility of prenatal nutritional deprivation as a risk factor for schizophrenia. *J. Nerv. Ment. Dis., 184*(2), 71-85.

Brown, E. (1972). Assessment from a humanistic perspective. *Psychother. Theory Res. Pract., 9,* 103-106.

Brown, G. L., Ebert, M., Goyer, P., Jimerson, D. C., Klein, W. J., Bunney, W. E., & Goodwin, F. K. (1982). Aggression, suicide, and serotonin: Relationships to CSF amine metabolites. *Am. J. Psychiatry, 139* 741-746.

Brown, G. L., Goodwin, F. K., Ballenger, J. C., Goyer, P. F., & Major, L. F. (1979). Aggression in humans correlates with cerebrospinal fluid metabolites. *Psychiatry Res., 1,* 131-139.

Brown, G. L., Linnoila, M. I., & Goodwin, F. K. (1992). Impulsivity, aggression, and associated affects: Relationship to self-destructive behavior and suicide. In R. W. Maris, A. L. Berman, J. T. Maltsberger, & R. I. Yufit (Eds.), *Assessment and prediction of suicide.* New York: Guilford Press.

Brown, G. W. (1988). Early loss of parent and depression in adult life. In S. Fisher & J. Reason (Eds.), *Handbook of life stress, cognition and health.* Chichester, England: Wiley.

Brown, G. W., & Harris, T. O. (1978). *Social origins of depression: A study of psychiatric disorder in women.* London: Tavistock.

Brown, G. W., Monck, E. M., Carstairs, G. M., & Wing, J. K. (1962). Influence on family life on the course of schizophrenic illness. *Br. J. Prev. Soc. Med., 16,* 55-68.

Brown, J. H., Henteleff, P., Barakat, S., & Rowe, C. J. (1986). Is it normal for terminally ill patients to desire death? *Am. J. Psychiatry, 143*(2), 208-211.

Brown, J. L., & Pollitt, E. (1996, February). Malnutrition, poverty and intellectual development. *Sci. Am.,* pp. 38-43.

Brown, L. (1993). Enrollment of drug abusers in HIV clinical trials: A public health imperative for communities of color. *J. Psychoact. Drugs, 25*(1), 45-48.

Brown, M. W., & Massaro, S. (1998, February 3). *Study identifies mechanism for cocaine-induced stroke and other brain damage.* Washington, DC: National Institutes of Health/National Institute on Drug Abuse (NIH News release).

Brown, P. J., Stout, R. L., & Mueller, T. (1996). Posttraumatic stress disorder and substance abuse relapse among women: A pilot study. *Psychol. Addict. Behav., 10*(2), 124-128.

Brown, S. (1997). Excess mortality of schizophrenia: A meta-analysis. *Br. J. Psychiatry, 171,* 502-508.

Brown, T. A., Hertz, R. M., & Barlow, D. H. (1992). New developments in cognitive-behavioral treatment of anxiety disorders. In A. Tasman & M. B. Riba (Eds.), *Review of psychiatry* (Vol. 11). Washington, DC: American Psychiatric Press.

Brown, W. A. (1998, January). The placebo effect. *Sci. Am.,* pp. 90-95.

Browne, A., & Finklehor, D. (1986). Impact of child sexual abuse: A review of the research. *Psychol. Bull., 99*(1), 66-77.

Brownell, K. D. (1991). Dieting and the search for the perfect body. Where physiology and culture collide. *Behav. Ther., 22,* 1-12.

Brownell, K. D., & Napolitano, M. A. (1995). Distorting reality for children: Body size proportions of Barbie and Ken dolls. *Int. J. Eat. Disord., 18*(3), 295-298.

Brownell, K. D., & O'Neil, P. M. (1993). Obesity. In D. H. Barlow (Ed.), *Clinical handbook of psychological disorders: A step-by-step treatment manual* (2nd ed.). New York: Guilford Press.

Brownell, K. D., & Wadden, T. A. (1992). Etiology and treatment of obesity: Understanding a serious, prevalent, and refractory disorder. *J. Consult. Clin. Psychol., 60*(4), 505-517.

Bruce, E. J., Schultz, C. L., & Smyrnios, K. X. (1996). A longitudinal study of the grief of mothers and fathers of children with intellectual disability. *Br. J. Med. Psychol., 69,* 33-45.

Bruce, M. L., & Kim, K. M. (1992). Differences in the effects of divorce on major depression in men and women. *Am. J. Psychiatry, 149*(7), 914-917.

Bruce, T. J., & Saeed, S. A. (1999). Social anxiety disorder: A common, underrecognized mental disorder. *Am. Fam. Physician, 60*(8), 2311-2320, 2322.

Bruch, H. (1962). Perceptual and conceptual disturbances in anorexia nervosa. *Psychosom. Med., 24,* 187-194.

Bruch, H. (1973). *Eating disorders: Obesity, anorexia nervosa and the person within.* New York: Basic Books.

Bruch, H. (1973). Psychiatric aspects of obesity. *Psychiatr. Ann., 3*(7), 6-10.

Bruch, H. (1978). *The golden cage: The enigma of anorexia nervosa.* Cambridge, MA: Harvard University Press.

Bruch, H. (1981). Developmental considerations of anorexia nervosa and obesity. *Can. J. Psychiatry, 26,* 212-217.

Bruch, H. (1982). Anorexia nervosa: Therapy and theory. *Am. J. Psychiatry, 139,* 1531-1538.

Bruch, H. (1991). The sleeping beauty: Escape from change. In S. I. Greenspan & G. H. Pollock (Eds.), *The course of life: Vol. 4. Adolescence.* Madison, CT: International Universities Press.

Brumberg, J. J. (1988). *Fasting girls: The history of anorexia nervosa.* New York: Penguin Books.

Bruni, F. (1998, November 22). Behind the jokes, a life of pain and delusion; For Letterman stalker, mental illness was family curse and scarring legacy. *New York Times,* Sect. 1, p. 45.

Bryant, R. A., Guthrie, R. M., & Moulds, M. L. (2001). Hypnotizability in acute stress disorder. *Am. J. Psychiatry, 158*(4), 600-604.

Bryant, R. A., & Harvey, A. G. (1995). Posttraumatic stress in volunteer firefighters: Predictors of stress. *J. Nerv. Ment. Dis., 183*(4), 267-271.

Buchan, H., Johnstone, E. C., McPherson, K., Palmer, R. L. et al. (1992). Who benefits from electroconvulsive therapy? Combined results of the Leicester and Northwick Park trials. *Br. J. Psychiatry, 160,* 355-359.

Buchanan, A. (1997). The investigation of acting on delusions as a tool for risk assessment in the mentally disordered. *Br. J. Psychiatry, 170*(Suppl. 32), 12-14.

Buchanan, A. (1999). Risk and dangerousness. *Psychol. Med., 29*(2), 465-473.

Buchanan, R. W., & Carpenter, W. T. (1997). The neuroanatomies of schizophrenia. *Schizophr. Bull., 23*(3), 367-372.

Buchanan, R. W., & Carpenter, W. T., Jr. (2001). Evaluating negative symptom efficacy. In R. S. E. Keefe & J. P. McEvoy (Eds.), *Negative symptom and cognitive deficit treatment response in schizophrenia* (pp. 1-18). Washington, DC: American Psychiatric Press.

Buchele, B. J. (1993). Group psychotherapy for persons with multiple personality and dissociative disorders. *Bull. Menninger Clin., 57*(3), 362-370.

Buchkremer, G., Monking, H. S., Holle, R., & Hornung, W. P. (1995). The impact of therapeutic relatives' groups on the course of illness of schizophrenic patients. *Eur. Psychiatry, 10*(1), 17-27.

Buchsbaum, M. S., & Haier, R. J. (1987). Functional and anatomical brain imaging: Impact on schizophrenia research. *Schizophr. Bull., 13*(1), 115-132.

Buchwald, A. M., & Rudick-Davis, D. (1993). The symptoms of major depression. *J. Abnorm. Psychol., 102*(2), 197-205.

Buckley, J. T. (1995). Nation raising "a generation of gamblers." *USA Today,* pp. 1A-2A.

Buckley, P. F. (1998). Substance abuse in schizophrenia: A review. *J. Clin. Psychiatry, 59*(Suppl. 3), 26-30.

Buffum, J. (1992). Prescription drugs and sexual function. *Psychiatr. Med., 10*(2), 181-198.

Bugental, J. F. T. (1965). The existential crisis in intensive psychotherapy. *Psychother. Theory Res. Pract., 2*(1), 16-20.

Bugental, J. F. T. (1992). The betrayal of the human: Psychotherapy's mission to reclaim our lost identity. In J. K. Zeig (Ed.), *The evolution of psychotherapy: The second conference.* New York: Brunner/Mazel.

Bugental, J. F. T. (1997). There is a fundamental division in how psychotherapy is conceived. In J. K. Zeig (Ed.), *The evolution of psychotherapy: The third conference.* New York: Brunner/Mazel.

Bujold, A., Ladouceur, R., Sylvain, C., & Boisvert, J. M. (1994). Treatment of pathological gamblers: An experimental study. *J. Behav. Ther. Exp. Psychiatry, 25*(4), 275-282.

Bukstein, O. G., Brent, D. A., & Kaminer, Y. (1989). Comorbidity of substance abuse and other psychiatric disorders in adolescents. *Am. J. Psychiatry, 146*(9), 1131-1141.

Bulik, C. M., Sullivan, P. F., Carter, F. A., McIntosh, V. V., & Joyce, P. R. (1998). The role of exposure with response prevention in the cognitive-behavioural therapy for bulimia nervosa. *Psychol. Med., 28*(3), 611-623.

Bumby, K. M., & Maddox, M. C. (1999). Judges' knowledge about sexual offenders, difficulties presiding over sexual offense cases, and opinions on sentencing, treatment, and legislation. *Sex. Abuse J. Res. Treat., 11*(4), 305-315.

Bunney, W. E., & Bunney, B. G. (2000). Molecular clock genes in man and lower animals: Possible implications for circadian abnormalities in depression. *Neuropsychopharmacology, 22*(4), 335-345.

Bunney, W. E., & Davis, J. M. (1965). Norepinephrine in depressive reactions: A review. *Arch. Gen. Psychiatry, 13*(6), 483-493.

Bunney, W. E., & Garland, B. L. (1984). Lithium and its possible modes of actions. In R. M. Post & J. C. Ballenger (Eds.), *Neurobiology of mood disorders: Vol. I. Frontiers of clinical neuroscience.* Baltimore: Williams & Wilkins.

Burd, L., Severud, R., Kerbeshian, J., & Klug, M. G. (1999). Prenatal and perinatal risk factors for autism. *J. Perinat. Med., 27*(6), 441-450.

Bureau of Justice Statistics. (1999). *Report on U.S. prison population.* Washington, DC: U.S. Department of Justice.

Bureau of Justice Statistics. (1999). *Substance abuse and treatment, state and federal prisoners, 1997.* Washington, DC: U.S. Department of Justice.

Burgess, E., & Haaga, D. A. (1994). The Positive Automatic Thoughts Questionnaire (ATQ-P) and the Automatic Thoughts Questionnaire-Revised

(ATQ-RP): Equivalent measures of positive thinking? *Cognit. Ther. Res., 18*(1), 15–23.

Burnett, R., Mallett, R., Bhugra, D., Hutchinson, G., Der, G., & Leff, J. (1999). The first contact of patients with schizophrenia with psychiatric services: Social factors and pathways to care in a multi-ethnic population. *Psychol. Med., 29*(2), 475–483.

Burnette, E. (1996). Urban activists call for hands-on community work. *APA Monitor, 27*(10), 30.

Burnette, E., & Murray, B. (1996). Conduct disorders need early treatment. *APA Monitor, 27*(10), 40.

Burney, J., & Irwin, H. J. (2000). Shame and guilt in women with eating-disorder symptomatology. *J. Clin. Psychol., 56*(1), 51–61.

Burns, L. H. (1995). An overview of sexual dysfunction in the infertile couple. *J. Fam. Psychother., 6*(1), 25–46.

Burns, T. P., & Crisp, A. H. (1985). Factors affecting prognosis in male anorexics. *J. Psychiatr. Res., 19*(2–3), 323–328.

Burr, J. A., Hartman, J. T., & Matteson, D. W. (1999). Black suicide in U.S. metropolitan areas: An examination of the racial inequality and social integration-regulation hypotheses. *Soc. Forces, 77*(3), 1049–1080.

Burros, M. (1996, May 8). Experts see flaws in U.S. mad cow safeguards. *New York Times.*

Burt, D. R., Creese, I., & Snyder, S. H. (1977). Antischizophrenic drugs: Chronic treatment elevates dopamine receptor binding in brain. *Science, 196,* 326–328.

Burton, V. S. (1990). The consequences of official labels: A research note on rights lost by the mentally ill, mentally incompetent, and convicted felons. *Commun. Ment. Health J., 26*(3), 267–276.

Burvill, P. W. (1998). Migrant suicide rates in Australia and in country of birth. *Psychol. Med., 28*(1), 201–208.

Bushman, B. J., & Anderson, C. A. (2001). Media violence and the American public: Scientific facts versus media misinformation. *Am. Psychol., 56*(6/7), 477–489.

Bushman, B. J., Baumeister, R. F., & Stack. A. D. (1999). Catharsis, aggression, and persuasive influence: Self-fulfilling or self-defeating prophecies? *J. Pers. Soc. Psychol., 76*(3), 367–376.

Buss, D. M. (2000). *The dangerous passion: Why jealousy is as necessary as love and sex.* New York: Free Press.

Bustillo, J. R., Lauriello, J., Horan, W. P., & Keith, S. J. (2001). The psychosocial treatment of schizophrenia: An update. *Am. J. Psychiatry, 158*(2), 163–175.

Bustillo, J. R., Thaker, G., Buchanan, R. W., Moran, M. et al. (1997). Visual information-processing impairments in deficit and nondeficit schizophrenia. *Am. J. Psychiatry, 154*(5), 647–654.

Butcher, J. N. (1999). *A beginner's guide to the MMPI-2.* Washington, DC: American Psychological Assoc.

Butcher, J. N., Lim, J., & Nezami, E. (1998). Objective study of abnormal personality in cross-cultural settings: The Minnesota Multiphasic Personality Inventory (MMPI-2). *J. Cross-Cult. Psychol., 29*(1), 189–211.

Butler, G., Fennel, M., Robson, P., & Gelder, M. (1991). A comparison of behavior therapy and cognitive behavior therapy in the treatment of generalized anxiety disorder. *J. Consult. Clin. Psychol., 59*(1), 167–175.

Butler, R. N. (1975). Psychiatry and the elderly: An overview. *Am. J. Psychiatry, 132,* 893–900.

Button, E. (1993). *Eating disorders: Personal construct therapy and change.* Chichester, England: Wiley.

Button, E. J., & Warren, R. L. (2001). Living with anorexia nervosa: The experience of a cohort of sufferers from anorexia nervosa 7.5 years after initial presentation to a specialized eating disorders service. *Eur. Eating Disord. Rev., 9*(2), 74–96.

Buttross, S. (2000). Attention deficit/hyperactivity disorder and its deceivers. *Curr. Probl. Pediatr., 30*(2), 37–50.

Buysse, D. J., Frank, E., Lowe, K. K., Cherry, C. R., & Kupfer, D. J. (1997). Electroencephalographic sleep correlates to episode and vulnerability to recurrence in depression. *Depression, 41,* 406–418.

Buysse, D. J., Reynolds, C. F., & Kupfer, D. J. (1993). Depression. In M. A. Carsakadon (Ed.), *The encyclopedia of sleep and dreaming.* New York: Macmillan.

Buysse, D. J., Tu, X. M., Cherry, C. R., Begley, A. E., Kowalski, J., Kupfer, D. J., & Frank, E. (1999). Pretreatment REM sleep and subjective sleep quality distinguish depressed psychotherapy remitters and nonremitters. *Biol. Psychiatry, 45*(2), 205–213.

Byrnes, G., & Kelly, I. W. (1992). Crisis calls and lunar cycles: A twenty-year review. *Psychol. Rep., 71*(3, Pt. 1), 779–785.

CDC (Centers for Disease Control and Prevention). (1996, December 20). *What CDC is doing to prevent fetal alcohol syndrome and other alcohol-related developmental disabilities.* Atlanta, GA: National Center for Environmental Health (NCEH), Division of Birth Defects and Developmental Disabilities (DBDDD).

CDC (Centers for Disease Control and Prevention). (1997). Cited in NCIPC (National Center for Injury Prevention and Control), *Impaired driving fact sheet.* Atlanta, GA: Author.

CDC (Centers for Disease Control and Prevention). (1998, March 20), *Suicide among black youths.* Atlanta, GA: Office of Communications, Division of Medicine.

CDC (Centers for Disease Control and Prevention). (1998, May 21). *Facts about violence among youth and violence in schools.* Atlanta, GA: Office of Communications, Division of Medicine.

CDC (Centers for Disease Control and Prevention). (1998, December 11). *Impaired driving.* Atlanta, GA: Office of Communications, Division of Medicine.

CDC (Centers for Disease Control and Prevention). (1999, June 29). Cited in S. Uretsky, The world will end tomorrow. *HealthScout.*

Cacciola, J. S., Rutherford, M. J., Alterman, A. I., McKay, J. R., & Snider, E. C. (1996). Personality disorders and treatment outcomes in methadone maintenance patients. *J. Nerv. Ment. Dis., 184*(4), 234–239.

Caces, F., & Harford, T. (1998). Time series analysis of alcohol consumption and suicide mortality in the United States, 1934–1987. *J. Stud. Alcohol, 59*(4), 455–461.

Caddy, G. R. (1985). Cognitive behavior therapy in the treatment of multiple personality. *Behav. Mod., 9*(3), 267–292.

Cadoret, R. J., Yates, W. R., Troughton, E., Woodworth, G., & Stewart, M. A. (1995). Adoption study demonstrating two genetic pathways to drug abuse. *Arch. Gen. Psychiatry, 52,* 42–52.

Cage, M. C. (1992). 42% of college students engage in "binge drinking," survey shows. *Chron. Higher Educ., 39*(6), S30.

Cahill, S. P., Carrigan, M. H., & Frueh, B. C. (1999). Does EMDR work? and if so, why?: A critical review of controlled outcome and dismantling research. *J. Anxiety Disord., 13*(1–2), 5–33.

Caine, D., Patterson, K., Hodges, J. R., Heard, R., & Haliday, G. (2001). Severe anterograde amnesia with extensive hippocampal degeneration in a case of rapidly progressive frontotemporal dementia. *Neurocase, 7*(1), 57–64.

Calamari, J. E., & Cassiday, K. L. (1999). Treating obsessive-compulsive disorder in older adults: A review of strategies. In M. Duffy (Ed.), *Handbook of counseling and psychotherapy with older adults.* New York: Wiley.

Calev, A., Gaudino, E. A., Squires, N. K., Zervas, I. M., & Fink, M. (1995). ECT and non-memory cognition: A review. *Br. J. Clin. Psychol., 34,* 505–515.

Calev, A., Kochav-Lev, E., Tubi, N., Nigal, D. et al. (1991). Change in attitude toward electroconvulsive therapy: Effects of treatment, time since treatment, and severity of depression. *Convulsive Ther., 7*(3), 184–189.

Calev, A., Nigal, D., Shapira, B., Tubi, N. et al. (1991). Early and long-term effects of electroconvulsive therapy and depression on memory and other cognitive functions. *J. Nerv. Ment. Dis., 179*(9), 526–533.

Callahan, C. M., Wolinsky, F. D., Stump, T. E., Nienaber, N. A., Hui, S. L., & Tierney, W. M. (1998). Mortality, symptoms, and functional impairment in late-life depression. *J. Gen. Intern. Med., 13*(11), 746–752.

Callahan, L. A., McGreevy, M. A., Cirincione, C. & Steadman, H. J. (1992). Measuring the effects of the GBMI verdict: Georgia's 1982 GBMI reform. *Law Hum. Behav., 16*(4), 447–461.

Callahan, L. A., & Silver, E. (1998). Factors associated with the conditional release of persons acquitted by reason of insanity: A decision tree approach. *Law. Hum. Behav., 22*(2), 147–163.

Callahan, L. A., Steadman, H. J., McGreevy, M. A., & Robbins, P. C. (1991). The volume and characteristics of insanity defense pleas: An eight-state study. *Bull. Am. Acad. Psychiatry Law, 19*(4), 331–338.

Calsyn, D. A., Fleming, C., Wells, E. A., & Saxon, A. J. (1996). Personality disorder subtypes among opiate addicts in methadone maintenance. *Psychol. Addict. Behav., 10*(1), 3–8.

Camara, W. J., & Schneider, D. L. (1994). Integrity tests: Facts and unresolved issues. *Am. Psychol., 49*(2), 112–119.

Cameron, D. J., Thomas, R. I., Mulvhill, M., & Bronheim, H. (1987). Delirium: A test of the Diagnostic and Statistical Manual III criteria on medical inpatients. *J. Am. Geriatr. Soc., 35,* 1007–1010.

Cameron, N. (1974). Paranoid conditions and paranoia. In S. Arieti & E. Brody (Eds.), *American handbook of psychiatry.* New York: Basic Books.

Cameron, P. M., Leszcz, M., Bebchuk, W., Swinson, R. P., Antony, M. M., Azim, H. F., Doidge, N., Korenblum, M. S., Nigam, T., Perry, J. C., & Seeman, M. V. (1999). The practice and roles of the psychotherapies: A discussion paper. *Can. J. Psychiatry, 44*(Suppl. 1), 18S–31S.

Campbell, J. C. (1995). Prediction of homicide of and by battered women. In J. C. Campbell (Ed.), *Assessing dangerousness: Violence by sexual offenders, batterers, and child abusers.* Thousand Oaks, CA: Sage.

Campbell, R. V., O'Brien, S., Bickett, A. D., & Lutzker, J. R. (1983). In-home parent training of migraine headaches and marital counseling as an ecobehavioral approach to prevent child abuse. *J. Behav. Ther. Exp. Psychiatry, 14,* 147–154.

Campbell, T. L., & Patterson, J. M. (1995). The effectiveness of family interventions in the treatment of physical illness. Special Issue: The effectiveness of marital and family therapy. *J. Marital Fam. Ther., 21*(4), 545–583.

Campbell, T. W. (1999). Challenging the evidentiary reliability of DSM-IV. *Am. J. Forensic Psychol., 17*(1), 47–68.

Campo, J. V., & Negrini, B. J. (2000). Case study: Negative reinforcement and behavioral management of conversion disorder. *J. Am. Acad. Child Adolesc. Psychiatry, 39*(6), 787–790.

Canals, J., Blade, J., Carbvajo, G., & Domenech-Llaberia, E. (2001). The Beck Depression Inventory: Psychometric characteristics and usefulness in nonclinical adolescents. *Eur. J. Psychol. Assess., 17*(1), 63–68.

Canetto, S. S. (1995). Elderly women and suicidal behavior. In S. S. Canetto & D. Lester (Eds.), *Women and suicidal behavior.* New York: Springer.

Canetto, S. S. (1995). Suicidal women: Prevention and intervention strategies. In S. S. Canetto & D. Lester (Eds.), *Women and suicidal behavior.* New York: Springer.

Canetto, S. S., & Lester, D. (1995). The epidemiology of women's suicidal behavior. In S. S. Canetto & D. Lester (Eds.), *Women and suicidal behavior.* New York: Springer.

Canetto, S. S., & Lester, D. (1995). Gender and the primary prevention of suicide mortality [Special issue]. *Suicide Life-Threaten. Behav., 25*(1), 58–69.

Canino, E., Cardona, R., Monsalve, P., Perez, A. F., Lopez, B., & Fragachan, F. (1994). A behavioral treatment program as a therapy in the control of primary hypertension. *Acta Cient. Venez., 45*(1), 23–30.

Cannon, D. S., Baker, T. B., Gino, A., & Nathan, P. E. (1986). Alcohol-aversion therapy: Assessment of conditioning. *J. Consult. Clin. Psychol., 54,* 825–830.

Cannon, D. S., Baker, T. B., & Wehl, W. K. (1981). Emetic and electric shock alcohol aversion therapy: Six- and twelve-month follow-up. *J. Consult. Clin. Psychol., 49,* 360–368.

Cannon, T. D., & Marco, E. (1991). Structural brain abnormalities as indicators of vulnerability to schizophrenia. *Schizophr. Bull., 20*(1), 89–102.

Cannon, W. (1927). The James-Lange theory of emotions: A critical examination and an alternative. *Am. J. Psychol., 39,* 106–124.

Cantagallo, A., Grassi, L., & Della Sala, S. (1999). Dissociative disorder after traumatic brain injury. *Brain Injury, 13*(4), 219–228.

Cantor, C. H., & Baume, P. J. M. (1998). Access to methods of suicide: What impact? *Aust. N. Z. J. Psychiatry, 32*(1), 8–14.

Cantor-Graae, E., Nordström, L. G., & McNeil, T. F. (2001). Substance abuse in schizophrenia: A review of the literature and a study of correlates in Sweden. *Schizophr. Res., 48*(1), 69–82.

Canty, G. F. (1996). Therapists at work. *The Institute Notebook, 5*(2), 1, 4.

Canty, G. F. (1996). A heart to heart on depression. *The Institute Notebook, 5*(3), 1, 4.

Capaldi, D. M., & Patterson, G. R. (1994). Interrelated influences of contextual factors on antisocial behavior in childhood and adolescence for males. In D. C. Fowles, P. Sutker, & S. H. Goodman (Eds.), *Progress in experimental personality and psychopathology research.* New York: Springer.

Caplan, R., Perdue, S., Tanguay, P. E., & Fish, B. (1990). Formal thought disorder in childhood onset schizophrenia and schizotypal personality disorder. *J. Child Psychol. Psychiatry Allied Discip., 31*(7), 1103–1114.

Capleton, R. A. (1996). Cognitive function in schizophrenia: Association with negative and positive symptoms. *Psychol. Rep., 78,* 123–128.

Cappeliez, P. (2000). Presentation of depression and response to group cognitive therapy with older adults. *J. Clin. Geropsychol., 6*(3), 165–174.

Capps, L., Sigman, M., Sena, R., Henker B., & Whalen, C. (1996). Fear, anxiety and perceived control in children of agoraphobic parents. *J. Child Psychol. Psychiatry, 37*(4), 445–452.

Cardasis, W., Hochman, J. A., & Silk, K. R. (1997). Transitional objects and borderline personality disorder. *Am. J. Psychiatry, 154*(2), 250–255.

Carducci, B. (2000, March 13). Taking the pain out of painfully shy. *Los Angeles Times,* Part E, p. 2.

Carek, P. J., & Dickerson, L. M. (1999). Current concepts in the pharmacological management of obesity. *Drugs, 57*(6), 883–904.

Carels, R. A., Baucom, D. H., Leone, P., & Rigney, A. (1998). Psychosocial factors and psychological symptoms: HIV in a public health setting. *J. Commun. Psychol., 26*(2), 145–162.

Carey, A. R., & Mullins, M. E. (1995, July 31). Survey: Caffeine and baby boomers. Cited in *USA Today,* p. 1D.

Carey, G., & Gottesman, I. I. (1981). Twin and family studies of anxiety, phobic, and obsessive disorders. In D. K. Klein & J. Rabkin (Eds.), *Anxiety: New research and changing concepts.* New York: Raven Press.

Carey, K. (1989). Emerging treatment guidelines for mentally ill chemical abusers. *Hosp. Commun. Psychiatry, 40*(4), 341–342.

Carey, K. B., & Carey, M. P. (1995). Reasons for drinking among psychiatric outpatients: Relationship to drinking patterns. *Psychol. Addict. Behav., 9*(4), 251–257.

Carey, M., Carey, K., & Meisler, A. (1991). Psychiatric symptoms in mentally ill chemical abusers. *J. Nerv. Ment. Dis., 179*(3), 136–138.

Carey, M. P., Wincze, J. P., & Meisler, A. W. (1993). Sexual dysfunction: Male erectile disorder. In D. H. Barlow (Ed.), *Clinical handbook of psychological disorders: A step-by-step treatment manual* (2nd ed.). New York: Guilford Press.

Carey, R. J., Pinheiro-Carrera, M., Dai, H., Tomaz, C., & Huston, J. P. (1995). L-Dopa and psychosis: Evidence for L-dopa-induced increases in prefrontal cortex dopamine and in serum corticosterone. *Biol. Psychiatry, 38,* 669–676.

Carlson, G. A., Rich, C. L., Grayson, P., & Fowler, R. C. (1991). Secular trends in psychiatric diagnoses of suicide victims. *J. Affect. Disord., 21,* 127–132.

Carlson, M. (1998, June 22). The best things in life aren't free. *Time, 151,* 21.

Carnahan, H., Elliott, D., & Velamoor, V. R. (1996). Influence of object size on prehension in leukotomized and unleukotomized individuals with schizophrenia. *J. Clin. Exp. Neuropsychol., 18*(1), 136–147.

Carpenter, K. M., & Hasin, D. (1998). A prospective evaluation of the relationship between reasons for drinking and DSM-IV alcohol-use disorders. *Addict. Behav., 23*(1), 41–46.

Carpenter, S. (2001). Research on Teen Smoking Cessation gains momentum. *APA Monitor, 32*(6), 54–55.

Carper, R. A., & Courchesne, E. (2000). Inverse correlation between frontal lobe and cerebellum sizes in children with autism. *Brain, 123*(Pt. 4), 836–844.

Carr, J. (1994). Annotation: Long term outcome for people with Down syndrome. *J. Child Psychol. Psychiatry Allied Discip., 35*(3), 425–439.

Carr, R. E. (1998). Panic disorder and asthma: Causes, effects and research implications. *J. Psychosom. Res., 44*(1), 43–52.

Carrasco, J. L., Diaz-Marsa, M., Hollander, E., Cesar, J., & Saiz-Ruiz, J. (2000). Decreased platelet monoamine oxidase activity in female bulimia nervosa. *Eur. Neuropsychopharmacology, 10*(2), 113–117.

Carrey, N. J., Butter, H. J., Persinger, M. A., & Bialik, R. J. (1995). Physiological and cognitive correlates of child abuse. *J. Am. Acad. Child Adolesc. Psychiatry, 34*(8), 1067–1075.

Carrier, S. (1996, December). The test. *Harper's Magazine,* pp. 31–33.

Carrington, P. (1978). *Clinically standardized meditation (CSM) instructors kit.* Kendall Park, NJ: Pace Educational Systems.

Carrington, P. (1993). Modern forms of meditation. In P. M. Lehrer & R. L. Woolfolk (Eds.), *Principles and practice of stress management* (2nd ed.). New York: Guilford Press.

Carris, M. J., Sheeber, L., & Howe, S. (1998). Family rigidity, adolescent problem-solving deficits, and suicidal ideation: A mediational model. *J. Adolesc., 21*(4), 459–472.

Carroll, K. M., & Rounsaville, B. J. (1995). Psychosocial treatments. In J. M. Oldham & M. B. Riba (Eds.), *American Psychiatric Press review of psychiatry* (Vol. 14). Washington, DC: American Psychiatric Press.

Carstairs K. (1992). Paranoid-schizoid or symbiotic? *Int. J. Psychoanal., 73*(1), 71–85.

Carter, C. S., Servan-Schreiber, D., & Perlstein, W. M. (1997). Anxiety disorders and the syndrome of chest pain with normal coronary arteries: Prevalence and pathophysiology. *J. Clin. Psychiatry, 58*(Suppl. 3), 70–73.

Cartwright, R. D., & Lamberg, L. (1992). *Crisis dreaming: Using your dreams to solve your problems.* New York: HarperCollins.

Cash, T. F., & Henry, P. E. (1995). Women's body images: The results of a national survey in the U.S.A. *Sex Roles, 33*(1/2), 19–28.

Casper, R. C. (1995). Biology of eating disorders. In A. F. Schatzberg & C. B. Nemeroff (Eds.), *The American Psychiatric Press textbook of psychopharmacology.* Washington, DC: American Psychiatric Press.

Cassem, N. H., & Hyman, S. E. (1995). Psychological management of grief and serious illness. In *Scientific American Series: Vol. 13. Psychiatry.* New York: Scientific American.

Castellani, B. (2000). *Pathological gambling: The making of a medical problem.* Albany: State University of New York Press.

Castle, D. J., Abel, K., Takei, N., & Murray, R. M. (1995). Gender differences in schizophrenia: Hormonal effect or subtypes? *Schizophr. Bull., 21*(1), 1–12.

Castrogiovanni, P., Pieraccini, F., & Di Muro, A. (1998). Suicidality and aggressive behavior. *Acta Psychiatr. Scand., 97*(2), 144–148.

Catherall, D. R. (1999). Family as a group treatment for PTSD. In B. H. Young & D. D. Blake (Eds.), *Group treatments for post-traumatic stress disorder.* Philadelphia: Brunner/Mazel.

Caton, C. L. (1982). Effect of length of inpatient treatment for chronic schizophrenia. *Am. J. Psychiatry, 139*(7), 856–861.

Cattell, H., & Jolley, D. J. (1995). One hundred cases of suicide in elderly people. *Br. J. Psychiatry, 166*(4), 451–457.

Cauchon, D. (1995, December 6). Patients often aren't informed of full danger. *USA Today,* pp. 1A–2A.

Cauchon, D. (1999, February). Patients often aren't informed of danger. *USA Today.*

Cautela, J. R. (1966). Treatment of compulsive behavior by covert sensitization. *Psychol. Rec., 16*(1), 33–41.

Cauwels, J. M. (1983). *Bulimia: The binge-purge compulsion.* New York: Doubleday.

Cavenaugh, J. C. (1990). *Adult development and aging.* Belmont, CA: Wadsworth.

Ceci, S. J., & Williams, W. M. (1997). Schooling, intelligence, and income. *Am. Psychol., 52*(10), 1051–1058.

Centorrino, F., Baldessarini, R. J., Frankenburg, F. R., Kando, J., Volpicelli, S. A., & Flood, J. G. (1996). Serum levels of clozapine and norclozapine in patients treated with selective serotonin reuptake inhibitors. *Am. J. Psychiatry, 153*(6), 820–822.

Cerf, C., & Navasky, V. (1998). *The experts speak.* New York: Villard.

Cerletti, U., & Bini, L. (1938). L'elettroshock. *Arch. Gen. Neurol. Psychiatry, Psychoanal., 19,* 266–268.

Chabra, A., Chavez, G. F., Harris, E. S., & Shah, R. (1999). Hospitalization for mental illness in adolescents: Risk groups and impact on the health care system. *J. Adolesc. Health, 24*(5), 349–356.

Chaika, E. O. (1990). *Understanding psychotic speech: Beyond Freud and Chomsky.* Springfield, IL: Thomas.

Chait, L. D., Fishman, M. W., & Schuster, C. R. (1985). "Hangover" effects the morning after marijuana smoking. *Drug Alcohol Depend., 15*(3), 229–238.

Chakos, M. H., Alvir, J. M. J., Woerner, M. G., Koreen, A., Geisler, S., Mayerhoff, D., Sobel, S., Kane, J. M., Borenstein, M., & Lieberman, J. A. (1996). Incidence and correlates of tardive dyskinesia in first episode of schizophrenia. *Arch. Gen. Psychiatry, 53,* 313–319.

Chakos, M. H., Lieberman, J. A., Hoffman, E., Bradford, D., & Sheitman, B. (2001). Effectiveness of second-generation antipsychotics in patients with treatment-resistant schizophrenia: A review and meta-analysis of randomized trials. *Am. J. Psychiatry, 158*(4), 518–526.

Chamberlain, P. (1985). Increasing the attention span of five mentally handicapped children using their parents as agents of change. *Behav. Psychother., 13*(20), 142–153.

Chambless, D. L., & Ollendick, T. H. (2001). Empirically supported psychological interventions. *Annu. Rev. Psychol., 52,* 685–716.

Champion, L. A., & Power, M. J. (1995). Social and cognitive approaches to depression: Towards a new synthesis. *Br. J. Clin. Psychol., 34,* 485–503.

Chan, S., MacKenzie, A., Ng, D. T., & Leung, J. K. (2000). An evaluation of the implementation of case management in the community psychiatric nursing service. *J. Adv. Nurs., 31*(1), 144–156.

Chang, Y., & Gates, D. (1997, March 10). The piano man. *Newsweek,* pp. 62–66.

Char, W. F. (1985). The hysterical spouse. *Med. Aspects Hum. Sex., 19*(9), 123–133.

Charney, D. S., Heninger, G. R., & Redmond, D. E. (1983). Yohimbine induced anxiety and increased noradrenergic function in humans: Effects of diazepam and clonidine. *Life Sci., 33,* 19–29.

Charney, D. S., Heninger, G. R., & Sternberg, D. E. (1984). The effect of mianserin on alpha 2 adrenergic receptor function in depressed patients. *Br. J. Psychiatry, 144,* 407–418.

Charney, D. S., Heninger, G. R., & Redmond, D. E. (1984, May). *Neurobiological mechanism.* Abstracts of the APA annual meeting (Abstract 30C), Los Angeles.

Charney, D. S., Woods, S. W., Goodman, W. K., & Heninger, G. R. (1987). Neurobiological mechanisms of panic anxiety: Biochemical and behavioral correlates of yohimbine-induced anxiety. *Am. J. Psychiatry, 144*(8), 1030–1036.

Charney, D. S., Woods, S. W., Krystal, J. H., Nagy, L. M., & Heninger, G. R. (1992). Noradrenergic neuronal dysregulation in panic disorder: The effects of intravenous yohimbine and clonidine in panic disorder patients. *Acta Psychiatr. Scand., 86,* 273–282.

Charney, D. S., Woods, S. W., Price, L. H., Goodman, W. K., Glazer, W. M., & Heninger, G. R. (1990). Noradrenergic dysregulation in panic disorder. In J. C. Ballenger (Ed.), *Neurobiology of panic disorder.* New York: Wiley-Liss.

Chase, M. (1993, May 28). Psychiatrists declare severe PMS a depressive disorder. *Wall Street Journal,* pp. B1, B6.

Chase, M. (1996, April 15). If you're considering melatonin, weigh facts against all the hype. *Wall Street Journal,* pp. B1–B2.

Chastang, F., Rioux, P., Dupont, I., Baranger, E., Kovess, V., & Zarifian, E. (1998). Suicide attempts and job insecurity: A complex association. *Eur. Psychiatry, 13*(7), 359–364.

Chatlos, C. (1987). *Crack: What you should know about the cocaine epidemic.* New York: Perigee Books.

Chen, X., & Cui, Q. (1995). Effect of biofeedback and relaxation training on patients with 1st or 2nd period primary hypertension. *Chin. Ment. Health J., 9*(3), 126, 125.

Chen, X., Rubin, R. H., & Li, B. (1995). Depressed mood in Chinese children: Relations with school performance and family environment. *J. Consult. Clin. Psychol., 63*(6), 938–947.

Chen, Y. R., Swann, A. C., & Burt, D. B. (1996). Stability of diagnosis in schizophrenia. *Am. J. Psychiatry, 153*(5), 682–686.

Cherland, E., & Fitzpatrick, R. (1999). Psychotic side effects of psychostimulants: A 5-year review. *Can. J. Psychiatry, 44*(8), 811–813.

Childress, A. R., Hole, A. V., Ehrman, R. N. et al. (1993). Cue reactivity and cue reactivity interventions in drug dependence. In L. S. Onken, J. D. Blaine, & J. J. Boren (Eds.), *Behavioral treatments for drug abuse and dependence* (NIDA Res. Monogr. Ser. No. 137). Rockville, MD: National Institute on Drug Abuse.

Childress, A. R., McLellan, A. T., & O'Brien, C. P. (1984). Assessment and extinction of conditioned withdrawal-like responses in an integrated treatment for opiate dependence. In L. S. Harris (Ed.), *Problems of drug dependence* (NIDA Res. Monogr. Ser. No. 55). Rockville, MD: National Institute on Drug Abuse.

Childress, A. R., McLellan, A. T., & O'Brien, C. P. (1988). Classically conditioned responses in cocaine and opioid dependence: A role in relapse? In B. A. Ray (Ed.), *Learning factors in substance abuse* (NIDA Res. Monogr. Ser. No. 84). Rockville, MD: National Institute on Drug Abuse.

Chiu, L. H. (1971). Manifested anxiety in Chinese and American children. *J. Psychol., 79,* 273–284.

Chochinov, H., Wilson, K., Enns, M., Mowchum, N., Lander, S., Levitt, M., & Clinch, J. (1995). Desire for death in the terminally ill. *Am. J. Psychiatry, 152,* 1185–1191.

Chodoff, P. (1989). Histrionic personality disorder. In American Psychiatric Association (Ed), *Treatments of psychiatric disorders: A task force report of the American Psychiatric Association.* Washington, DC: American Psychiatric Press.

Chorpita, B. F., & Lilienfeld, S. O. (1999). Clinical assessment of anxiety sensitivity in children and adolescents: Where do we go from here? *Psychol. Assess., 11*(2), 212–224.

Christensen, A., & Heavey, C. L. (1999). Interventions for couples. *Annu. Rev. Psychol., 50,* 165–190.

Christensen, A. J., Dornick, R., Ehlers, S. L., & Schultz, S. K. (1999). Social environment and longevity in schizophrenia. *Psychosom. Med., 61*(2), 141–145.

Christenson, G. A., & Mackenzie, T. B. (1995). Trichotillomania, body dysmorphic disorder, and obsessive-compulsive disorder. *J. Clin. Psychiatry, 56*(5), 211–212.

Christie, D. (2000). Cognitive-behavioral therapeutic techniques for children with eating disorders. In B. Lask & R. Bryant-Waugh (Eds.), *Anorexia nervosa and related eating disorders in childhood and adolescence* (2nd ed., pp. 205–226). Hove, England: Psychology Press/Taylor & Francis.

Chu, J. A. (2000). "Memories of childhood abuse: Dissociation, amnesia, and corroboration": Reply. *Am. J. Psychiatry, 157*(8), 1348–1349.

Chu, J. A., Frey, L. M., Ganzel, B. L., & Matthews, J. A. (1999). Memories of childhood abuse: Dissociation, amnesia, and corroboration. *Am. J. Psychiatry, 156*(5), 749–755.

Chua-Eoan, H. (1998, June 29). A precarious genius. *Time,* p. 42.

Ciccocioppo, R. (1999). The role of serotonin in craving: From basic research to human studies. *Alcohol Alcohol., 34*(2), 244–253.

Cimons, M. (1999, June 10). Some drugs affect men, women differently, but why? *Miami Herald.*

Ciompi, L., Dauwalder, H., Maier, C., Aebi, E., Trutsch, K., Kupper, Z., & Rutishauser, C. (1992). The pilot project `soteria berne': Clinical experiences and results. *Br. J. Psychiatry, 161*(Suppl. 18), 145–153.

Cipani, E. (1991). Educational classification and placement. In J. L. Matson & J. A. Mulick (Eds.), *Handbook of mental retardation.* New York: Pergamon Press.

Cipolotti, L., Shallice, T., Chan, D., Fox, N., Scahill, R., Harrison, G., Stevens, J., & Rudge, P. (2001). Long-term retrograde amnesia . . . the crucial role of the hippocampus. *Neuropsychologia, 39*(2), 151–172.

Cisin, I. H., & Calahan, D. (1970, July 6). The big drinkers. *Newsweek,* p. 57.

Clark, A. J. (1995). Projective techniques in the counseling process. *J. Councel. Dev., 73*(3), 311–316.

Clark, C. R. (1999). Specific intent and diminished capacity. In A. K. Hess, I. B. Weiner et al. (Eds.), *The handbook of forensic psychology* (2nd ed.). New York: Wiley.

Clark, D. A. (1992). Depressive, anxious and intrusive thoughts in psychiatric inpatients and outpatients. *Behav. Res. Ther., 30,* 93–102.

Clark, D. A., Beck, A. T., & Alford, B. A. (1999). *Scientific foundations of cognitive theory and therapy of depression.* New York: Wiley.

Clark, D. A., & Purdon, C. (1993). New perspectives for a cognitive theory of obsessions. *Aust. Psychol.*

Clark, D. C. (1999). The puzzle of suicide in later life. In M. T. Stimming, M. Stimming et al. (Eds.), *Before their time: Adult children's experiences of parental suicide.* Philadelphia: Temple University Press.

Clark, D. M. (1993). Cognitive mediation of panic attacks induced by biological challenge tests. *Adv. Behav. Res. Ther., 15,* 75–84.

Clark, D. M. (1999). Anxiety disorders: Why they persist and how to treat them. *Behav. Res. Ther., 37*(Suppl. 1), S5–S27.

Clark, D. M., Salkovskis, P. M., Hackmann, A., Middleton, H., Anastasiades, P., & Gelder, M. (1994). A comparison of cognitive therapy, applied relaxation and imipramine in the treatment of panic disorder. *Br. J. Psychiatry, 164*(6), 759–769.

Clark, D. M., & Wells, A. (1997). Cognitive therapy for anxiety disorders. In L. J. Dickstein, M. B. Riba, & J. M. Oldham (Eds.), *Review of psychiatry* (Vol. 16). Washington, DC: American Psychiatric Press.

Clark, H. W. (2001). Residential substance abuse treatment for pregnant and postpartum women and their children: Treatment and policy implications. *Child Welfare, 80*(2), 179–198.

Clark, R., Anderson, N. B., Clark, V. R., & Williams, D. R. (1999). Racism as a stressor for African Americans: A biopsychosocial model. *Am. Psychol., 54*(10), 805–816.

Clarke, G. N., Rohde, P., Lewinsohn, P. M., Hops, H., & Seeley, J. R. (1999). Cognitive-behavioral treatment of adolescent depression: Efficacy of acute group treatment and booster sessions. *J. Am. Acad. Child Adolesc. Psychiatry, 38*(3), 272–279.

Clarke, J., Stein, M. D., Sobota, M., Marisi, M., & Hanna, L. (1999). Victims as victimizers: Physical aggression by persons with a history of childhood abuse. *Arch. Intern. Med., 159*(16), 1920-1924.

Clarke, J. C., & Saunders, J. B. (1988). *Alcoholism and problem drinking: Theories and treatment.* Sydney: Pergamon Press.

Clay, R. A. (1996). Day treatment helps empower patients. *APA Monitor, 26*(5), 31.

Clay, R. A. (1996). Modern hypnosis wins clinical respect, praise. *APA Monitor, 26*(5), 31.

Clay, R. A. (1996). Psychologists' faith in religion begins to grow. *APA Monitor, 27*(8), 1, 48.

Clay, R. A. (1997). Is assisted suicide ever a rational choice? *APA Monitor, 28*(4), 1, 43.

Clay, R. A. (1999, July/August). Psychologists rush to help kosovar refugees. *APA Monitor, 30*(7), 12.

Clayton, A. H. (2001). Recognition and assessment of sexual dysfunction associated with depression. *J. Clin. Psychiatry, 62*(Suppl. 3), 5-9.

Clements, R. (1999). Prevalence of alcohol-use disorders and alcohol-related problems in a college student sample. *J. Am. Coll. Health, 48*(3), 111-118.

Clifford, D. B. (2000). Human immunodeficiency virus-associated dementia. *Arch. Neurol., 57*(3), 321-324.

Clifford, J. S., Norcross, J. C., & Sommer, R. (1999). Autobiographies of mental health clients: Psychologists' uses and recommendations. *Prof. Psychol.: Res. Pract., 30*(1), 56-59.

Clum, G., & Yang, B. (1995). Additional support for the reliability and validity of the Modified Scale for Suicide Ideation. *Psychol. Assess., 7*(1), 122-125.

Clyburn, L. D., Stones, M. J., Hadjistavropoulos, T., & Tuokko, H. (2000). Predicting caregiver burden and depression in Alzheimer's disease. *J. Gerontol. B, 55*(1), S2-S13.

Coambs, R. B., & McAndrews, M. P. (1994). The effects of psychoactive substances on workplace performance. In S. Macdonald &. P. Roman (Eds.), *Research advances in alcohol and drug problems: Vol. 11. Drug testing in the workplace.* New York: Plenum Press.

Cobb, J. M. T., & Steptoe, A. (1998). Psychosocial influences on upper respiratory infectious illness in children. *J. Psychosom. Res., 45*(4), 319-330.

Coccaro, E. F. (1998). Clinical outcome of psychopharmacologic treatment of borderline and schizotypal personality disordered subjects. *J. Clin. Psychiatry, 59*(Suppl. 1), 30-35.

Coe, C. L. (1999). Psychosocial factors and psychoneuroimmunology within a lifespan perspective. In D. P. Keating, C. Hertzman et al. (Eds.), *Developmental health and the wealth of nations: Social, biological, and educational dynamics.* New York: Guilford Press.

Coe, W. C. (1989). Posthypnotic amnesia: Theory and research. In N. P. Spanos & J. F. Chaves (Eds.), *Hypnosis: The cognitive-behavioral perspective.* Buffalo, NY: Prometheus Books.

Cohen, D., Llorente, M., & Eisendorfer, C. (1998). Homicide-suicide in older persons. *Am. J. Psychiatry, 155,* 390-396.

Cohen, L., Ardjoen, R. C., & Sewpersad, K. S. M. (1997). Type A behaviour pattern as a risk factor after myocardial infarction: A review. *Psychol. Health, 12,* 619-632.

Cohen, M. B., Baker, G., Cohen, R. A., Fromm-Reichmann, F., & Weigert, E. V. (1954). An intensive study of twelve cases of manic-depressive psychosis. *Psychiatry, 17,* 103-137.

Cohen, R. M., Semple, W. E., Gross, M., & Nordahl, T. E. (1988). From syndrome to illness: Delineating the pathophysiology of schizophrenia with PET. *Schizphr. Bull., 14*(2), 169-176.

Cohen, S., & Herbert, T. B. (1996). Health psychology: Psychological factors and physical disease

from the perspective of human psychoneuroimmunology. *Annu. Rev. Psychol., 47.*

Cohen-Kettenis, P. T. (2001). Gender identity disorder in DSM? *J. Am. Acad. Child Adolesc. Psychiatry, 40*(4), 391.

Cohen-Kettenis, P. T., & Gooren, L. J. (1999). Transsexualism: A review of etiology, diagnosis and treatment. *J. Psychosom. Res., 46*(4), 315-333.

Cohen-Kettenis, P. T., & van Goozen, S. H. M. (1997). Sex reassignment of adolescent transsexuals: A follow-up study. *J. Am. Acad. Child Adolesc. Psychiatry, 36*(2), 263-271.

Cohl, H. A. (1997). *The book of mosts.* New York: St. Martin's Press.

Colahan, M. (1995). Being a therapist in eating disorder treatment trials: Constraints and creativity. Special Issue: Eating disorders. *J. Fam. Ther., 17*(1), 79-96.

Colahan, M., & Senior, R. (1995). Family patterns in eating disorders: Going round in circles, getting nowhere fasting. In G. Szmukler, C. Dare, & J. Treasure (Eds.), *Handbook of eating disorders: Theory, treatment and research.* Chichester, England: Wiley.

Colburn, D. (1996, November 19). Singer's suicide doesn't lead to "copycat" deaths. *Washington Post Health,* p. 5.

Colby, K. M., Faught, W. S., & Parkison, R. C. (1979). Cognitive therapy of paranoid conditions: Heuristic suggestions based on a computer simulation model. *Cognit. Ther. Res., 3*(1), 55-60.

Cole, D. A., & Turner, J. E., Jr. (1993). Models of cognitive mediation and moderation in child depression. *J. Abnorm. Psychol., 102*(2), 271-281.

Cole, J. O., Klerman, G. L., Goldberg, S. C. et al. (1964). Phenothiazine treatment in acute schizophrenia. *Arch. Gen. Psychiatry, 10,* 246-261.

Cole, J. O., & Yonkers, K. A. (1995). Nonbenzodiazepine anxiolytics. In A. F. Schatzberg & C. B. Nemeroff (Eds.), *The American Psychiatric Press textbook of psychopharmacology.* Washington, DC: American Psychiatric Press.

Coleman, L. (1984). *The reign of error: Psychiatry, authority, and law.* Boston: Beacon.

Colerick, E. J., & George, L. K. (1986). Predictors of institutionalization among caregivers of patients with Alzheimer's disease. *J. Am. Geriatr. Soc., 34,* 493-498.

Collier, D. A., Arranz, M. J., Li, T. et al. (1997). Association between the 5-HT2A gene promoter polymorphism and anorexia nervosa [Letter]. *Lancet, 351,* 499.

Comer, R. (1973). *Therapy interviews with a schizophrenic patient.* Unpublished manuscript.

Compas, B. E., Haaga, D. A. F., Keefe, F. J., Leitenberg, H., & Williams, D. A. (1998). Sampling of empirically supported psychological treatments from health psychology: Smoking, chronic pain, cancer, and bulimia nervosa. *J. Consult. Clin. Psychol., 66*(1), 89-112.

Compton, W. M., Helzer, J. E., Hwu, H., Yeh, E., McEvoy, L., Tipp, J. E., & Spitznagel, E. L. (1991). New methods in cross-cultural psychiatry: Psychiatric illness in Taiwan and the United States. *Am. J. Psychiatry, 148*(12), 1697-1704.

Coney, N. S., & Mackey, W. C. (1998). On whose watch? The silent separation of American children from their fathers. *J. Sociol. Soc. Welfare, 25*(3), 143-178.

Conklin, A., & Westen, D. (2001). Thematic apperception test. In W. I. Dorfman & M. Hersen (Eds.), *Understanding psychological assessment. Perspectives on individual differences* (pp. 107-133). New York: Kluwer Academic/Plenum Press.

Connelly, S. (1999, February 4). The end of Sybilization. *Daily News (New York),* p. 55.

Connors, M. E. (2001). Relationship of sexual abuse to body image and eating problems. In J. K.

Thompson & L. Smolak (Eds.), *Body image, eating disorders, and obesity in youth: Assessment, prevention, and treatment* (pp. 149-167). Washington, DC: American Psychological Association.

Conrad, N. (1992). Stress and knowledge of suicidal others as factors in suicidal behavior of high school adolescents. *Issues Ment. Health Nurs., 13*(2), 95-104.

Conwell, Y., Caine, E. D., & Olsen, K. (1990). Suicide and cancer in late life. *Hosp. Commun. Psychiatry, 43,* 1334-1338.

Conwell, Y., Duberstein, P. R., Cox, C., Herrmann, J., Forbes, N., & Caine, E. D. (1998). Age differences in behaviors leading to completed suicide. *Am. J. Geriatr. Psychiatry, 6*(2), 122-126.

Cook, C. E., Jeffcoat, A. R., & Perez-Reyes, M. (1985). Pharmacokinetic studies of cocaine and phencyclidine in man. In G. Barnett & C. N. Chiang (Eds.), *Pharmacokinetics and pharmacodynamics of psychoactive drugs.* Foster City, CA: Biomedical Publications.

Cook, E. H., Rowlett, R., Jaselskis, C., Leventhal, B. L. (1992). Fluoxetine treatment of children and adults with autistic disorder and mental retardation. *J. Am. Acad. Child Adolesc. Psychiatry, 31*(4), 739-745.

Cook, J. M., Black, B. S., Rabins, P. V., & German, P. (2000). Life satisfaction and symptoms of mental disorder among older African American public housing residents. *J. Clin. Geropsychol., 6*(1), 1-14.

Coon, D. W., Rider, K., Gallagher-Thompson, D., & Thompson, L. (1999). Cognitive-behavioral therapy for the treatment of late-life distress. In M. Duffy (Ed.), *Handbook of counseling and psychotherapy with older adults.* New York: Wiley.

Cooney, N. L., Litt, M. D., Morse, P. A., Bauer, L. O., & Gaupp, L. (1997). Alcohol cue reactivity, negative-mood reactivity, and relapse in treated alcoholic men. *J. Abnorm. Psychol., 106*(2), 243-250.

Coons, P. M. (1980). Multiple personality: Diagnostic considerations. *J. Clin. Psychiatry, 41*(10), 330-336.

Coons, P. M. (1998). The dissociative disorders. Rarely considered and underdiagnosed. *Psychiatr. Clin. North Am., 21*(3), 637-648.

Coons, P. M., Bowman, E. S., & Milstein, V. (1988). Multiple personality disorder: A clinical investigation of 50 cases. *J. Nerv. Ment. Dis., 176*(9), 519-527.

Cooper, A., Scherer, C. R., Boies, S. C., & Gordon, B. L. (1999). Sexuality on the Internet: From sexual exploration to pathological expression. *Prof. Psychol.: Res. Pract., 30*(2), 154-164.

Cooper, A. M., & Ronningstam, E. (1992). Narcissistic personality disorder. In A. Tasman & M. B. Riba (Eds.), *American Psychiatric Press review of psychiatry* (Vol. 11). Washington, DC: American Psychiatric Press.

Cooper, M. L. (1994). Motivations for alcohol use among adolescents: Development and validation of a four-factor model. *Psychol. Asses., 6*(2), 117-128.

Cooper, P. J., & Eke, M. (1999). Childhood shyness and maternal social phobia: A community study. *Br. J. Psychiatry, 174,* 439-443.

Coppen, A. (1994). Depression as a lethal disease: Prevention strategies. *J. Clin. Psychiatry, 55*(Suppl. 4), 37-45.

Cordova, J. V., & Jacobson, N. S. (1993). Couple distress. In D. H. Barlow (Ed.), *Clinical handbook of psychological disorders: A step-by-step treatment manual* (2nd ed.). New York: Guilford Press.

Corey-Bloom, J., Jernigan, T., Archibald, S., Harris, M. J. et al. (1995). Quantitative magnetic resonance imaging of the brain in late-life schizophrenia. *Am. J. Psychiatry, 152*(3), 447-449.

Corkin, S. (1968). Acquisition of motor skill after bilateral medial temporal-lobe excision. *Neuropsychologia, 6,* 255–264.

Corkin, S. (1984). Lasting consequences of bilateral medial temporal lobectomy: Clinical course and experimental findings in H. M. *Semin. Neurol., 4,* 249–259.

Cornblatt, B. A., & Erlenmeyer-Kimling, L. (1985). Global attentional deviance as a marker of risk for schizophrenia: Specificity and predictive validity. *J. Abnorm. Psychol., 94*(4), 31–46.

Cornblatt, B. A., & Keilp, J. G. (1994). Impaired attention, genetics, and the pathophysiology of schizophrenia. *Schizophr. Bull., 20*(1), 31–46.

Cornelius, J. R., Salloum, I. M., Mezzich, J., Cornelius, M. D., Fabrega, H., Ehler, J. G., Ulrich, R. F., Thase, M. E., & Mann, J. J. (1995). Disproportionate suicidality in patients with comorbid major depression and alcoholism. *Am. J. Psychiatry, 152*(3), 358–364.

Cornell, C. P., & Gelles, R. J. (1983). *Intimate violence in families.* Beverly Hills, CA: Sage.

Cornish, J. W., McNicholas, L. F., & O'Brien, C. P. (1995). Treatment of substance-related disorders. In A. F. Schatzberg & C. B. Nemeroff (Eds.), *The American Psychiatric Press textbook of psychopharmacology.* Washington, DC: American Psychiatric Press.

Corwin, M. (1993, May 8). When the law can't protect. *Los Angeles Times,* p. A1.

Coryell, W., Leon, A., Winokur, G., Endicott, J. et al. (1996). Importance of psychotic features to long-term course in major depressive disorder. *Am. J. Psychiatry, 153,* 483–489.

Coryell, W., Miller, D. D., & Perry, P. J. (1998). Haloperidol plasma levels and dose optimization. *Am. J. Psychiatry, 155,* 48–53.

Cosimides, L., & Tooby, J. (2000). Psychology and the emotions. In M. Lewis & J. M. Haviland (Eds.), *Handbook of emotions* (2nd ed.). New York: Guilford Press.

Costa, E. (1983). Are benzodiazepine recognition sites functional entities for the action of endogenous effectors or merely drug receptors? *Adv. Biochem. Psychopharmacol., 38,* 249–259.

Costa, E. (1985). Benzodiazepine-GABA interactions: A model to investigate the neurobiology of anxiety. In A. H. Tuma & J. Maser (eds.), *Anxiety and the anxiety disorders.* Hillsdale, NJ: Erlbaum.

Costa, E., Guidotti, A., Mao, C. C., & Suria, A. (1975). New concepts on the mechanism of action of benzodiazepines. *Life Sci., 17*(2), 167–185.

Costa, E., Guidotti, A., & Toffano, G. (1978). Molecular mechanisms mediating the action of benzodiazepines on GABA receptors. *Br. J. Psychiatry, 133,* 239–248.

Costantino, G., & Malgady, R. G. (2000). Multicultural and cross-cultural utility of the TEMAS (Tell-Me-A-Story) Test. In R. H. Dana (Ed.), *Handbook of cross-cultural and multicultural personality assessment: Personality and clinical psychology series* (pp. 481–513). Mahwah, NJ: Erlbaum.

Constantino, G., Malgady, R. G., & Rogler, L. H. (1986). Cuento therapy: A culturally sensitive modality for Puerto Rican children. *J. Consult. Clin. Psychol., 54*(5), 639–645.

Costantino, G., Malgady, R. G., & Vazquez, C. (1981). A comparison of Murray's TAT and a new thematic apperception test for urban Hispanic children. *Hisp. J. Behav. Sci., 3,* 291–300.

Costanzo, P. R., Musante, G. J., Friedman, K. E., Kern, L. S., & Tomlinson, K. (1999). The gender specificity of emotional, situational, and behavioral indicators of binge eating in a diet-seeking obese population. *Int. J. Eat. Disord., 26*(2), 205–210.

Costello, C. G. (1996). The advantages of focusing on the personality characteristics of the personality disordered. In C. G. Costello (Ed.), *Personality characteristics of the personality disordered.* New York: Wiley.

Council on Psychiatry and the Law. (1992). Peer review of psychiatric testimony. *Bull. Am. Acad. Psychiatry Law, 20*(3), 343–352.

Courchesne, R., & Courchesne, E. (1997). From impasse to insight in autism research: From behavioral symptoms to biological explanations [Special issue]. *Dev. Psychopathol.*

Cowan, D., & Brunero, S. (1997). Group therapy for anxiety disorders using rationale emotive behaviour therapy. *Aust. N. Z. J. Ment. Health Nurs., 6*(4), 164–168.

Cowen, E. L. (1991). In pursuit of wellness. 98th annual convention of the American Psychological Association Distinguished Contributions to Psychology in the Public Interest Award Address (1990, Boston, MA). *Am. Psychol., 46,* 404–408.

Cowley, G. (2000, January 31). Alzheimer's: Unlocking the mystery. *Newsweek,* pp. 46–51.

Cox, A., Rutter, M., Newman, S., & Bartak, L. (1975). A comparative study of infantile autism and specific developmental receptive language disorder: II. Parental characteristics. *Br. J. Psychiatry, 126,* 146–159.

Cox, B. J. (1996). The nature and assessment of catastrophic thoughts in panic disorder. *Behav. Res. Ther., 34*(4), 363–374.

Cox, B. J., Borger, S. C., & Enns, M. W. (1999). Anxiety sensitivity and emotional disorders: Psychometric studies and their theoretical implications. In S. Taylor et al. (Eds.), *Anxiety sensitivity: Theory, research, and treatment of the fear of anxiety. The LEA series in personality and clinical psychology.* Mahwah, NJ: Erlbaum.

Cox, B. J., Enns, M. W., Borger, S. C., & Parker, J. D. A. (1999). The nature of the depressive experience in analogue and clinically depressed samples. *Behav. Res. Ther., 37*(1), 15–24.

Cox, B. J., Rector, N. A., Bagby, R. M., Swinson, R. P., Levitt, A. J., & Joffe, R. T. (2000). Is self-criticism unique for depression? A comparison with social phobia. *J. Affect. Disord., 57*(1–3), 223–228.

Cox, R. H., Robb, M., & Russell, W. D. (1999). Order of scale administration and concurrent validity of the Anxiety Rating Scale. *Percept. Mot. Skills, 88*(1), 271–272.

Coy, T. V. (1998). The effect of repressive coping style on cardiovascular reactivity and speech disturbances during stress. *Diss. Abstr. Int. B; 58*(8-B), 4512.

Coyne, J. C. (1976). Depression and the response of others. *J. Abnorm. Psychol., 85*(2), 186–193.

Coyne, J. C. (2001). Depression and the response of others. In W. G. Parrott (Ed.), *Emotions in social psychology: Essential readings* (pp. 231–238). Philadelphia: Psychology Press/Taylor & Francis.

Coyne, J. C., Schwenk, T. L., & Fechner-Bates, S. (1995). Nondetection of depression by primary care physicians reconsidered. *Gen. Hosp. Psychiatry, 17*(1), 3–12.

Crabbé, J. C. (2001). Use of genetic analyses to refine phenotypes related to alcohol tolerance and dependence. *Alcohol.: Clin. Exp. Res., 252,* 288–292.

Craddock, N., & Jones, I. (1999). Genetics of bipolar disorder. *J. Med. Genet., 36*(8), 585–594.

Craig, R. J., Cannon, B., & Olson, R. E. (1995). Psychological screening of impotence with Finney's MMPI-derived impotence scale. *Psychol. Rep., 77,* 1019–1026.

Cramer, P. (1996). *Storytelling, narrative, and the Thematic Apperception Test.* New York: Guilford Press.

Crandall, C. S., Preisler, J. J., & Aussprung, J. (1992). Measuring life events stress in the lives of college students: The Undergraduate Stress Questionnaire (USQ). *J. Behav. Med., 15*(6), 627–662.

Crane, G. E. (1973). Persistent dyskinesia. *Br. J. Psychiatry, 22,* 395–405.

Craske, M. G., & Rowe, M. K. (1997). Nocturnal panic. *Clin. Psychol.: Sci. Pract., 4,* 153–174.

Cravatta, M. J. (1998, January). Looking for luck. *Am. Demogr.*

Creer, C., & Wing, J. K. (1974). *Schizophrenia at home.* London: National Schizophrenia Fellowship.

Creese, I., Burt, D. R., & Snyder, S. H. (1977). Dopamine receptor binding enhancement accompanies lesion-induced behavioral supersensitivity. *Science, 197,* 596–598.

Crijnen, A. A., Achenbach, T. M., & Verhulst, F. C. (1999). Problems reported by parents of children in multiple cultures: The Child Behavior Checklist syndrome constructs. *Am. J. Psychiatry, 156*(4), 569–574.

Crino, R. D., & Andrews, G. (1996). Obsessive-compulsive disorder and Axis I comorbidity. *J. Anxiety Disord., 10*(1), 37–46.

Crisp, A. H. (1981). Anorexia nervosa at a normal weight?: The abnormal-normal weight control syndrome. *Int. J. Psychiatry Med., 11,* 203–233.

Crisp, A. H., Gelder, M. G., Rix, S., Meltzer, H. I., & Rowlands, O. J. (2000). Stigmatisation of people with mental illnesses. *Br. J. Psychiatry, 177,* 4–71.

Crisp, M. (2001, April 8). Sticks & stones: 'New Kid' puts comic spin on a serious situation. *Sunday News (Lancaster, PA),* p. H-1.

Crits, C. P., Connolly, M. B., Azarian, K., Crits-Cristoph, K., & Shappell, S. (1996). An open trial of brief supportive-expressive psychotherapy in the treatment of generalized anxiety disorder. *Psychotherapy, 33*(3), 418–430.

Crits-Christoph, P., Baranackie, K., Kurcias, J. S., Beck, A. T., Carroll, K., Perry, K., Luborsky, L., McLellan, A. T., Woody, G. E., Thompson, L., Gallagher, D., & Zitrin, C. (1991). Meta-analysis of therapist effects in psychotherapy outcome studies. *Psychother. Res., 1*(2), 81–91.

Crits-Cristoph, P., Crits-Cristoph, K., Wolf-Palacio, D., Fichter, M., & Rudick, D. (1995). Brief supportive-expressive psychodynamic therapy for generalized anxiety disorder. In J. P. Barber, P. Crits-Cristoph et al. (Eds.), *Dynamic therapies for psychiatric disorders.* New York: Basic Books.

Crocker, P. R. (1989). A follow-up of cognitive-affective stress management training. *J. Sport Exercise Psychol., 11,* 236–242.

Crompton, M. R. (1985). Alcohol and violent accidental and suicidal death. *Med. Sci. Law, 25,* 59–62.

Crow, T. J. (1980). Positive and negative schizophrenic symptoms and the role of dopamine: II. *Br. J. Psychiatry, 137,* 383–386.

Crow, T. J. (1982). Positive and negative symptoms and the role of dopamine in schizophrenia. In G. Hemmings (Ed.), *Biological aspects of schizophrenia and addiction.* New York: Wiley.

Crow, T. J. (1985). The two-syndrome concept: Origins and current status. *Schizophr. Bull., 11*(3), 471–486.

Crow, T. J. (1995). Brain changes and negative symptoms in schizophrenia. *Psychopathology, 28*(1), 18–21.

Crowley, T. J., Macdonald, M. J., Whitmore, E. A., & Mikulich, S. K. (1998). Cannabis dependence, withdrawal, and reinforcing effects among adolescents with conduct symptoms and substance use disorder. *Drug Alcohol Depend., 50*(1), 27–37.

Crowther, J. H., Bond, L. A., & Rolf, J. R. (1981). The incidence, prevalence, and severity of behavior disorder among preschool-age children in day care. *J. Abnorm. Child Psychol., 9,* 23–42.

Crowther, J. H., Snaftner, J., Bonifazi, D. Z., & Shepherd, K. L. (2001). The role of daily hassles in binge eating. *Int. J. Eating Disord., 29*(4), 449–454.

Cruise, K. R., & Rogers, R. (1998). An analysis of competency to stand trial: An integration of case law and clinical knowledge. *Behav. Sci. Law, 16,* 35–50.

Crystal, S., & Schlosser, L. R. (1999). The HIV-mental health challenge. In A. V. Horwitz, T. L. Scheid et al. (Eds.), *A handbook for the study of mental health: Social contexts, theories, and systems.* New York: Cambridge University Press.

Cukan, A. (2001, March 8). Confronting a culture of cruelty. General feature release. *United Press International.*

Culbertson, F. M. (1997). Depression and gender: An international review. *Am. Psychol., 52*(1), 25–31.

Cullen, E. A. (1993, August). Iowa becomes the tenth state with a hospital privileges statute for psychologists. *Practitioner Focus, 6*(2), 6.

Culp, A. M., Clyman, M. M., & Culp, R. E. (1995). Adolescent depressed mood, reports of suicide attempts, and asking for help. *Adolescence, 30*(120), 827–837.

Cumming, J., & Cumming, E. (1962). *Ego and milieu: Theory and practice of environmental therapy.* New York: Atherton.

Cunningham, J. (1999, February 16). Health: Hex marks the spot; Many people with mental problems would rather see this man than their GP. John Cunningham on why the NHS is studying voodoo. *The Guardian (London),* p. 16.

Cunningham-Owens, D. G. (2000). The challenges of diagnosis and continuing patient assessment. *Int. J. Psychiatry Clin. Pract., 4*(Suppl. 1), S13–S18.

Curran, T., & Schacter, D. L. (2000). Amnesia II: Cognitive Neuropsychological issues. In M. J. Farah & T. E. Feinberg (Eds.), *Patient-based approaches to cognitive neuroscience. Issues in clinical and cognitive neuropsychology* (pp. 291–299). Cambridge, MA: MIT Press.

Currier, G. W. (Ed.). (1999). *New developments in emergency psychiatry: Medical, legal, and economic.* San Francisco: Jossey-Bass.

Curtis, G. C., Magee, W. J., Eaton, W. W., Wittchen, H.-U., & Kessler, R. C. (1998). Specific fears and phobias: Epidemiology and classification. *Br. J. Psychiatry, 173,* 212–217.

Curtis, J. M., & Cowell, D. R. (1993). Relation of birth order and scores on measures of pathological narcissism. *Psychol. Rep., 72*(1), 311–315.

Cuticchia, A. J. (2000). Future vision of the GDB human genome database. *Hum. Mutat., 15*(1), 62–67.

Cutler, D. M., Glaeser, E. L., & Norberg, K. E. (2001). Explaining the rise in youth suicide. In J. Gruber (Ed.), *Risky behavior among youths: An economic analysis* (pp. 219–269). Chicago: University of Chicago Press.

Cutmore, T. R. H., & James, D. A. (1999). Identifying and reducing noise in psychophysiological recordings. *Int. J. Psychophysiol., 32*(2), 129–150.

Cutright, P., & Fernquist, R. M. (2001). The relative gender gap in suicide: Societal integration, the culture of suicide and period effects in 20 developed countries, 1955–1994. *Soc. Sci. Res., 30*(1), 76–99.

Cutting, J. (1985). *The psychology of schizophrenia.* Edinburgh, UK: Churchill-Livingstone.

Cutting, J., & Murphy, D. (1988). Schizophrenic thought disorder: A psychological and organic interpretation. *Br. J. Psychiatry, 152,* 310–319.

Cutting, J., & Murphy, D. (1990). Impaired ability of schizophrenics, relative to manics or depressives, to appreciate social knowledge about their culture. *Br. J. Psychiatry, 157,* 355–358.

Cyr, J. J., & Kalpin, R. A. (1988). Investigating the lunar-lunacy relationship: A reply to Rotton and Kelly. *Psychol. Rep., 62*(1), 319–322.

Cyranowski, J. M., Frank, E., Young, E., & Shear, K. (2000). Adolescent onset of the gender differences in lifetime rates of major depression. *Arch. Gen. Psychiatry, 57*(1), 21–27.

Cytryn, L., & McKnew, D. H., Jr. (1996). *Growing up sad: Childhood depression and its treatment.* New York: Norton.

DAWN (Drug Abuse Warning Network). (1997). *Highlights from 1996 Report.* Drug Abuse Warning Network.

DAWN (Drug Abuse Warning Network). (1998). *Highlights from 1998 Report.* Drug Abuse Warning Network.

DHM (Discovery Health Media). (1999, August 2). How America measures up. *Newsweek,* pp. 50–53.

Dalby, J. T. (1997). Elizabethan madness: On London's stage. *Psychol. Rep., 81,* 1331–1343.

Daly, M. P. (1999). Diagnosis and management of Alzheimer disease. *J. Am. Board Fam. Pract., 12*(5), 375–385.

Dalzell, H. J. (2000). Whispers: The role of family secrets in eating disorders. *Eat. Disord.: J. Treat. Prev., 8*(1), 43–61.

Damasio, A. R. (1994). *Descartes' error: Emotion, reason, and the human brain.* New York: Avon Books.

Dana, R. H. (1999). Projective assessment of Latinos in the United States: Current realities, problems, and prospects. *Cult. Div. Ethnic Minority Psychol., 4*(3), 165–184.

Dana, R. H. (Ed.). (2000). *Handbook of cross-cultural and multicultural personality assessment.* Mahwah, NJ: Erlbaum.

Dare, C., & Crowther, C. (1995). Living dangerously: Psychoanalytic psychotherapy of anorexia nervosa. In G. Szmukler, C. Dare, & J. Treasure (Eds.), *Handbook of eating disorders: Theory, treatment and research.* Chichester, England: Wiley.

Dare, C., & Crowther, C. (1995). Psychodynamic models of eating disorders. In G. Szmukler, C. Dare, & J. Treasure (Eds.), *Handbook of eating disorders: Theory, treatment and research.* Chichester, England: Wiley.

Dare, C., & Eisler, I. (1992). Family therapy for anorexia nervosa. In P. J. Cooper & A. Stein (Eds.), *Feeding problems and eating disorders in children and adolescents.* Philadelphia: Harwood Academic Publishers.

Dare, C., & Eisler, I. (1995). Family therapy. In G. Szmukler, C. Dare, & J. Treasure (Eds.), *Handbook of eating disorders: Theory, treatment and research.* Chichester, England: Wiley.

Dare, C., & Eisler, I. (1997). Family therapy. In G. I. Szmukler & C. Dare (Eds.), *Handbook of treatment for eating disorders* (2nd ed.). New York: Guilford Press.

Darvres-Bornoz, J., Lemperiere, T., Degiovanni, A., & Gaillard, P. (1995). Sexual victimization in women with schizophrenia and bipolar disorder. *Soc. Psychiatry Psychiatr. Epidemiol., 30*(2), 78–84.

Davanloo, H. (Ed.). (1980). *Short-term dynamic psychotherapy.* New York: Jason Aronson.

Davey, G. C. L., & Levy, S. (1999). Internal statements associated with catastrophic worrying. *Pers. Individual Differ., 26*(1), 21–32.

David. D., Brown, R., Pojoga, C., & David, A. (2000). The impact of posthypnotic amnesia and directed forgetting on implicit and explicit memory: New insights from a modified process dissociation procedure. *Int. J. Clin. Exp. Hypnosis, 48*(3), 267–289.

Davidson, J. R., Hughes, D., Blazer, D. G., & George, L. K. (1991). Posttraumatic stress disor-der in the community: An epidemiological study. *Psychol. Med., 21*(3), 713–721.

Davidson, J. R., Hughes, D., George, L. K., & Blazer, D. G. (1996). The association of sexual assault and attempted suicide within the community. *Arch. Gen. Psychiatry, 53,* 550–555.

Davidson, J. R. T. (1998). Pharmacotherapy of social anxiety disorder. *J. Clin. Psychiatry, 59*(Suppl. 17), 47–53.

Davis, J. D., Kane, J. M., Marder, S. R., Brauzer, B., Gierl, B., Schooler, N., Casey, D. E., & Hassan, M. (1993). Dose response of prophylatic antipsychotics. *J. Clin. Psychiatry, 54*(Suppl. 3), 24–30.

Davis, J. M., Comaty, J. E., & Janicak, P. G. (1988). The psychological effects of antipsychotic drugs. In C. N. Stefanis & A. D. Rabavilis (Eds.), *Schizophrenia: Recent biosocial developments.* New York: Human Sciences Press.

Davis, J. O., & Phelps, J. A. (1995). Twins with schizophrenia: Genes or germs? *Schizophr. Bull., 21*(1), 13–18.

Davis, L. L., Ryan, W., Adinoff, B., & Petty, F. (2000). Comprehensive review of the psychiatric uses of valproate. *J. Clin. Psychopharmacol., 20*(Suppl 1), 1S–17S.

Davis, M. (1992). Analysis of aversive memories using the fear potentiated startle paradigm. In N. Butters & L. R. Squire (Eds.), *The neuropsychology of memory* (2nd ed.). New York: Guilford Press.

Davis, P. J. (1999). Gender differences in autobiographical memory for childhood emotional experiences. *J. Pers. Soc. Psychol., 76*(3), 498–510.

Davis, R., Olmsted, M., Rockert, W., Marques, T., & Dolhanty, J. (1997). Group psychoeducation for bulimia nervosa with and without additional psychotherapy process sessions. *Int. J. Eat. Disord., 22,* 25–34.

Davis, R. A. (2001). A cognitive-behavioral model of pathological Internet use. *Computers Hum. Behav., 17*(2), 187–195.

Davis, R. C., Brickman, E., & Baker, T. (1991). Supportive and unsupportive responses of others to rape victims: Effects on concurrent victim adjustment. *Am. J. Commun. Psychol., 19,* 443–451.

Davis, S. (2000). Testosterone and sexual desire in women. *J. Sex Educ. Ther., 25*(1), 25–32.

Davis, S. F. (1992). Report to the American Psychological Association. *Psychol. Today, 25*(6), 9.

Davis, S. R. (1998). The clinical use of androgens in female sexual disorders. *J. Sex Marital Ther., 24*(3), 153–163.

Davis, T., Gunderson, J. G., & Myers, M. (1999). Borderline personality disorder. In D. G. Jacobs (Ed.), *The Harvard Medical School guide to suicide assessment and intervention.* San Francisco: Jossey-Bass.

Davison, A. N., & Dobbing, J. (1966). Myelination as a vulnerable period in brain development. *Br. Med. Bull., 22,* 40–44.

Daw, J. (2001). Road rage, air rage & now "desk rage." *APA Monitor Psychol., 32*(7), 52–54.

Dawood, K., Pillard, R. C., Horvath, C., Revelle, W., & Bailey, J. M. (2000). Familial aspects of male homosexuality. *Arch. Sex. Behav., 29*(2), 155–163.

Dawson, G., & Castelloe, P. (1992). Autism. In C. E. Walker (Ed.), *Clinical psychology: Historical and research foundations.* New York: Plenum Press.

DeAngelis, T. (1993, September). Controversial diagnosis is voted into latest DSM. *APA Monitor, 24*(9), 32–33.

DeAngelis, T. (1994, March). Poor kids are focus of asthma studies. *APA Monitor, 25*(3), 26–27.

DeAngelis, T. (1994, May). Vets, minorities, single moms make up homeless population. *APA Monitor, 25*(5), 39.

DeAngelis, T. (1996, October). New interventions address teen-age behavior problems. *APA Monitor*, p. 42.

Dearwater, S. R., Coben, J. H., Campbell, J. C., Nah, G., Glass, N., McLoughlin, E., & Bekemeier, B. (1998). Prevalence of intimate partner abuse in women treated at community hospital emergency departments. *JAMA, J. Am. Med. Assoc., 280*, 433–438.

Deaton, A. V. (1998). Treating conversion disorders: Is a pediatric rehabilitation hospital the place? *Rehabil. Psychol., 43*(1), 56–62.

de Castro, J. M., & Pearcey, S. M. (1995). Lunar rhythms of the meal and alcohol intake of humans. *Physiol. Behav., 57*(3), 439–444.

DeCubas, M., & Field, T. (1993). Children of methadone-dependent women: Developmental outcomes. *Am. J. Orthopsychiatry, 63*(2), 266–269.

de Groot, J. M., & Kennedy, S. H. (1995). Integrating clinical and research psychiatry. *J. Psychiatry Neurosci., 20*(2), 150–154.

Deitz, S. M. (1977). An analysis of programming DRL schedules in educational settings. *Behav. Res. Ther., 15*(1), 103–111.

Dekker, J. (1993). Inhibited male orgasm. In W. O'Donohue & J. Geer (Eds.), *Handbook of sexual dysfunctions*. Boston: Allyn & Bacon.

Delahanty, J., Ram, R., Postrado, L., Balis, T., Green-Paden, L., & Dixon, L. (2001). Differences in rates of depression in schizophrenia by race. *Schizophr. Bull., 27*(1), 29–38.

Delay, J., & Deniker, P. (1952). Le traitement des psychoses par une méthode neurolytique dérivée d'hibernothérapie: Le 4560 RP utilisé seul en cure prolongée et continuée. *Cong. Med. Alienistes Neurol. Fr. Pays Lang. Fr., 50*, 503–513.

De Leo, D., Padoani, W., Scocco, P., Lie, D., Bille-Brahe, U., Arensman, E., Hjelmeland, H., Crepet, P., Haring, C., Hawton, K., Lonnqvist, J., Michel, K., Pommereau, X., Querejeta, I., Phillipe, J., Salander-Renberg, E., Schmidtke, A., Fricke, S., Weinacker, B., Tamesvary, B., Wasserman, D., & Faria, S. (2001). Attempted and completed suicide in older subjects: Results from the WHO/EURO Multicentre Study of Suicidal Behavior. *Int. J. Geriatr. Psychiatry, 16*(3), 300–310.

DeLeon, M. J. (1992). Cited in Youngstrom, N. Training brings psychologists closer to prescribing drugs. *APA Monitor, 23*(10).

DeLeon, M. J., Convit, A., George. A. E., Golomb, J., De Santi, S., Tarshish, C., Rusinek, H., Bobinski, M., Ince, C., Miller, D., & Wisniewski, H. (1996). In vivo structural studies of the hippocampus in normal aging and in incipient Alzheimer's disease. In R. J. Wurtman, S. Corkin, J. H. Growdon, & R. M. Nitsch (Eds.), *The neurobiology of Alzheimer's disease*. New York: New York Academy of Sciences.

DeLeon, P. H., & Wiggins, J. G., Jr. (1996). Prescription privileges for psychologists. *Am. Psychol., 51*(3), 225–229.

Delgado, P. L., & Moreno, F. A. (2000). Role of norepinephrine in depression. *J. Clin. Psychiatry, 61*(Suppl.), 5–12.

Delisle, J. R. (1986). Death with honors: Suicide among gifted adolescents [Special issue]. *J. Counsel. Dev., 64*(9), 558–560.

Dell, P. F., & Eisenhower, J. W. (1990). Adolescent multiple personality disorder: A preliminary study of eleven cases. *J. Am. Acad. Child Adolesc. Psychiatry, 29*(3), 359–366.

Del Monte, M. (1995). Silence and emptiness in the service of healing: Lessons from meditation. *Br. J. Psychother., 11*(3), 368–378.

DelMonte, M. M. (2000). Retrieved memories of childhood sexual abuse. *Br. J. Med. Psychol., 73*(1), 1–13.

de Man, A. F., Ludec, C. P., & Labreche-Gauthier, L. (1992). Parental control in child rearing and multidimensional locus of control. *Psychol. Rep., 70*(1), 320–322.

de Messias, E. L. M., Cordeiro, N.-F., Sampaio, J. J. C., Bartko, J. J., & Kirkpatrick, B. (2001). Schizophrenia and season of birth in a tropical region: Relationship to rainfall. *Schizophr. Res., 48*(2–3), 227–234.

Dencker, S. J., & Dencker, K. (1995). The need for quality assurance for a better compliance and increased quality of life in chronic schizophrenic patients. XIIth AEP Congress: Improvement of compliance: Quality assurance: Increased quality of life in community care in schizophrenia. *Int. Clin. Psychopharmacol., 9*(Suppl. 5), 35–40.

DeNelsky, G. Y. (1996). The case against prescription privileges for psychologists. *Am. Psychol., 51*(3), 207–212.

DeRubeis, R. J., & Crits-Christoph, P. (1998). Empirically supported individual and group psychological treatments for adult mental disorders. *J. Consult. Clin. Psychol., 66*(1), 37–52.

DeRubeis, R. J., Tang, T. Z., & Beck, A. T. (2001). Cognitive therapy. In K. S. Dobson (Ed.), *Handbook of cognitive-behavioral therapies* (2nd ed., pp. 349–392). New York: Guilford Press.

DeRubeis, R. J., Tang, T. Z., Gelfand, L. A., & Feeley, M. (2000). Recent findings concerning the processes and outcomes of cognitive therapy for depression. In S. L. Johnson, A. M. Hayes et al. (Eds.), *Stress, coping, and depression*. Mahwah, NJ: Erlbaum.

De Silva, P. (1995). Cognitive-behavioural models of eating disorders. In G. Szmukler, C. Dare, & J. Treasure (Eds.), *Handbook of eating disorders: Theory, treatment and research*. Chichester, England: Wiley.

Desmond, D. W., Morony, J. T., Paik, M. C., Sano, M., Mohr, J. P., Aboumatar, S., Tseng, C. L., Chan, S., Williams, J. B., Remien, R. H., Hauser, W. A., & Stern, Y. (2000). Frequency and clinical determinants of dementia after ischemic stroke. *Neurology, 54*(5), 1124–1131.

Devanand, D. P., Jacobs, D. M., Tang, M. X., Del Castillo-Castaneda, C. et al. (1997). The course of psychopathologic features in mild to moderate Alzheimer disease. *Arch. Gen. Psychiatry, 54*, 257–263.

DeVeaugh-Geiss, J., Moroz, G., Biederman, J., Cantwell, D. P. et al. (1992). Clomipramine hydrochloride in childhood and adolescent obsessive compulsive disorder. A multicenter trial. *J. Am. Acad. Child Adolesc. Psychiatry, 31*(1), 45–49.

DeVita, E. (1996, January–February). Melatonin: The hottest hormone of all. *Am. Health*, pp. 72–73.

Dew, M. A., Bromet, E. J., Brent, D., & Greenhouse, J. B. (1987). A quantitative literature review of the effectiveness of suicide prevention centers. *J. Consult. Clin. Psychol., 55*, 239–244.

de Wilde, E. J., & Kienhorst, I. C. W. M. (1998). Life events and adolescent suicidal behavior. In T. W. Miller et al. (Eds.), *Children of trauma: Stressful life events and their effects on children and adolescents. International Universities Press stress and health series* [Monogr. 8]. Madison, CT: International Universities Press.

de Wilde, E. J., Kienhorst, I. C. W. M., Diekstra, R. F. W., & Wolters, W. H. G. (1992). The relationship between adolescent suicidal behavior and life events in childhood and adolescence. *Am. J. Psychiatry, 149*, 45–51.

Diamond, D. (1987). Psychotherapeutic approaches to the treatment of panic attacks, hypochondriasis and agoraphobia. *Br. J. Med. Psychol., 60*, 85–90.

Dickens, R. S. (1999). The alignment of EAP and business unit goals. In J. M. Oher et al. (Eds.), *The employee assistance handbook*. New York: Wiley.

Diekstra, R. F. W. (1989). Suicidal behavior in adolescents and young adults: The international picture. *Crisis, 10*, 16–35.

Diekstra, R. F. W. (1989). Suicide and attempted suicide: An international perspective. *Acta Psychiatr. Scand., 80*(Suppl. 354), 1–24.

Diekstra, R. F., Kienhorst, C. W. M., & de Wilde, E. J. (1995). Suicide and suicidal behaviour among adolescents. In M. Rutter & D. J. Smith (Eds.), *Psychosocial disorders in young people*. Chichester, England: Wiley.

Diener, E. (2000, January). Subjective well-being: The science of happiness and a proposal for a national index. *Am. Psychol., 55*(1), 34–43.

Diener, E., & Diener, C. (1996). Most people are happy. *Psychol. Sci., 7*(3), 181–185.

Diener, E., Sandvik, E., Pavot, W., & Fujita, F. (1992). Extraversion and subjective well-being in a U.S. national probability sample. *J. Res. Pers., 26*(3), 205–215.

Diener, E., Sandvik, E., Seidlitz, L., & Diener, M. (1993). The relationship between income and subjective well-being: Relative or absolute? *Soc. Indicators Res., 28*(3), 195–223.

Dilsaver, S. C. (1990). Onset of winter depression earlier than generally thought? *J. Clin. Psychiatry, 51*(6), 258.

Dilsaver, S. C., & Swann, A. C. (1995). Mixed mania: Apparent induction by a tricyclic antidepressant in five consecutively treated patients with bipolar depression. *Biol. Psychiatry, 37*(1), 60–62.

Dinn, W. M., & Harris, C. L. (2000). Neurocognitive function in antisocial personality disorder. *Psychiatry Res., 97*(2–3), 173–190.

Dinwiddie, S. H., Heath, A. C., Dunne, M. P., Bucholz, K. K., Madden, P. A. F., Slutske, W. F., Bierut, L. J., Statham, D. B., & Martin, N. G. (2000). Early sexual abuse and lifetime psychopathology: A co-twin-control study. *Psychol. Med., 30*(1), 41–52.

di Tomaso, E., Beltramo, M., & Piomelli, D. (1996, August 22). Brain cannabinoids in chocolate. *Nature (London), 382*, 677–678.

Dixon, L. B., & Lehman, A. F. (1995). Family interventions for schizophrenia. *Schizophr. Bull., 21*(4), 631–643.

Dixon, W. A., Heppner, P. P., Burnett, J. W., & Lips, B. J. (1993). Hopelessness and stress: Evidence for an interactive model of depression. *Cognit. Ther. Res., 17*(1), 39–52.

Doan, B. D., & Bryson, S. E. (1994). Etiological and maintaining factors in multiple personality disorder: A critical review. In R. M. Klein & B. K. Doane (Eds.), *Psychological concepts and dissociative disorders*. Hillsdale, NJ: Erlbaum.

Dobkin, P. L., & Da Costa, D. (2000). Group psychotherapy for medical patients. *Psychol., Health Med., 5*(1), 87–96.

Dobson, D. J. G., McDougall, G., Busheikin, J., & Aldous, J. (1995). Effects of social skills training and social milieu treatment on symptoms of schizophrenia. *Psychiatr. Serv., 46*(4), 376–380.

Docherty, N. M., DeRosa, M., & Andreasen, N. C. (1996). Communication disturbances in schizophrenia and mania. *Arch. Gen. Psychiatry, 53*, 358–364.

Docter, R. F., & Prince, V. (1997). Transvestism: A survey of 1032 cross-dressers. *Arch. Sex. Behav., 26*(6), 589–605.

Doherty, W. (1999, July 1). Interviewed in P. Tucker, Marital therapy field splitting up. *HealthScout*.

Dohrenwend, B. P. (2000). The role of adversity and stress in psychopathology: Some evidence and its implications for theory and research. *J. Health Soc. Behav., 41*(1), 1–19.

Dohrmann, R. J., & Laskin, D. M. (1978). An evaluation of electromyographic feedback in the treatment of myofascial pain-dysfunction syndrome. *JAMA, J. Am. Med. Assoc., 96*, 656–662.

Doka, K. J. (1999). A primer on loss and grief. In J. D. Davidson & K. J. Doka (Eds.), *Living with grief at work, at school, at worship.* Philadelphia: Brunner/Mazel.

Dolan, B., Evans, C., & Norton, K. (1995). Multiple Axis-II diagnoses of personality disorder. *Br. J. Psychiatry, 166*, 107–112.

Dole, V. P., & Nyswander, M. (1965). A medical treatment for heroin addiction. *JAMA, J. Am. Med. Assoc., 193*, 646–650.

Dole, V. P., & Nyswander, M. (1967). Heroin addiction, a metabolic disease. *Arch. Intern. Med., 120*, 19–24.

Dolinski, D., & Nawrat, R. (1998). "Fear-then-relief" procedure for producing compliance: Beware when the danger is over. *J. Exp. Soc. Psychol., 34*(1), 27–50.

Domino, G., & Swain, B. J. (1986). Recognition of suicide lethality and attitudes toward suicide in mental health professions. *Omega: J. Death Dying, 16*(4), 301–308.

Domino, G., & Takahashi, Y. (1991). Attitudes toward suicide in Japanese and American medical students. *Suicide Life-Threaten. Behav., 21*(4), 345–359.

Donaldson, S. K., Klein, D. N., Riso, L. P., & Schwartz, J. E. (1997). Comorbidity between dysthymic and major depressive disorders: A family study analysis. *J. Affect. Disord., 42*, 103–111.

D'Onofrio, G., Rathlev, N. K., Ulrich, A. S., Fish, S. S., & Freedland, E. S. (1999). Lorazepam for the prevention of recurrent seizures related to alcohol. *N. Engl. J. Med., 340*(12), 915–919.

Donohue, J., & Gebhard, P. (1995). The Kinsey Institute/Indiana University report on sexuality and spinal cord injury. *Sex. Disabil., 13*(1), 7–85.

Donovan, S. J., Susser, E. S., Nunes, E. V., Stewart, J. W. et al. (1997). Divalproex treatment of disruptive adolescents: A report of 10 cases. *J. Clin. Psychiatry, 58*(1), 12–15.

Dorfman, W. I., & Leonard, S. (2001). The Minnesota Multiphasic Personality Inventory-2 (MMPI-2). In W. I. Dorfman & M. Hersen (Eds.), *Understanding psychological assessment. Perspectives on individual differences* (pp. 145–171). New York: Kluwer Academic/Plenum Press.

Dorr, N. C. (1999). Blood pressure in African Americans: Examining the role of coping with discrimination. *Diss. Abstr. Int. B; 59*(7-B), 3769.

Dorwart, R. A., & Ostacher, M. J. (1999). A community psychiatry approach to preventing suicide. In D. G. Jacobs (Ed.), *The Harvard Medical School guide to suicide assessment and intervention.* San Francisco: Jossey-Bass.

Dougher, M. J. (1997). Cognitive concepts, behavior analysis, and behavior therapy. *J. Behav. Ther. Exp., Psychiatry, 28*(1), 65–70.

Douglas, J. (1996). *Mind hunter: Inside the FBI's elite serial crime unit.* New York: Pocket Star.

Douglas, K. S., & Koch, W. J. (2001). Civil commitment and civil competence: Psychological issues. In R. A. Schuller & J. R. P. Ogloff (Eds.), *Introduction to psychology and law: Canadian perspectives* (pp. 353–374). Toronto, Ont., Can.: University of Toronto Press.

Douglas, V. I., Barr, R. G., Amin, K., O'Neill, M. E., & Britton, B. G. (1988). Dosage effects and individual responsivity to methylphenidate in attention deficit disorder. *J. Child Psychol. Psychiatry Allied Discip., 29*, 453–475.

Dowdney, L., & Skuse, D. (1993). Parenting provided by adults with mental retardation. *J. Child Psychol. Psychiatry Allied Discip., 34*(1), 25–47.

Doweiko, H. E. (1999). *Concepts of chemical dependency* (4th ed.). Pacific Grove, CA: Brooks/Cole.

Downey, A. M. (1991). The impact of drug abuse upon adolescent suicide. *Omega: J. Death Dying, 22*(4), 261–275.

Downey, R. G., Sinnett, E. R., & Seeberger, W. (1998). The changing face of MMPI practice. *Psychol. Rep., 83*(3, Pt. 2), 1267–1272.

Downhill, J. E., Jr., Buchsbaum, M. S., Hazlett, E. A., Barth, S., Roitman, S. L., Nunn, M., Lekarev, O., Wei, T., Shihabuddin, L., Mitropoulou, V., Silverman, J., & Siever, L. J. (2001). Temporal lobe volume determined by magnetic resonance imaging in schizotypal personality disorder and schizophrenia. *Schizophr. Res., 48*(2–3), 187–199.

Doyle, A. C. (1938). The sign of the four. In *The complete Sherlock Holmes.* Garden City, NY: Doubleday.

Doyle, K. O., & Youn, S. (2000). Exploring the traits of happy people. *Soc. Indicators Res., 52*(2), 195–209.

Dozier, M. (1996). University of Delaware, Newark (personal correspondence).

Drake, R. E., Essock, S. M., Shaner, A., Carey, K. B., Minkoff, K., Kola, L., Lynde, D., Osher, F. C., Clark, R. E., & Richards, L. (2001). Implementing dual diagnosis services for clients with severe mental illness. *Psychiatr. Serv., 52*(4), 469–476.

Drake, R. E., McHugo, G. J., Becker, D. R., Anthony, W. A., & Clark, R. E. (1996). The New Hampshire study of supported employment for people with severe mental illness. *J. Consult. Clin. Psychol., 64*(2), 391–399.

Drake, R. E., Osher, F., & Wallach, M. (1991). Homelessness and dual diagnosis. *Am. Psychol., 46*(11), 1149–1158.

Drake, R. E., & Wallach, M. A. (1992). Mental patients' attraction to the hospital: Correlates of living preference. *Commun. Ment. Health J., 28*(1), 5–12.

Drane, J. (1995). Physician-assisted suicide and voluntary active euthanasia: Social ethics and the role of hospice. *Am. J. Hospice & Palliative Care, 12*(6), 3–10.

Dratcu, L. (2000). Panic, hyperventilation and perpetuation of anxiety. *Prog. Neuro-Psychopharmacol. Biol. Psychiatry, 24*(7), 1069–1089.

Drug Enforcement Administration. (1996). *Consumption of ritalin.* Washington, DC: Author.

Druss, B. G., & Rosenheck, R. A. (1998). Mental disorders and access to medical care in the United States. *Am. J. Psychiatry, 155*(12), 1775–1777.

Dryden, W., & Ellis, A. (2001). Rational emotive behavior therapy. In K. S. Dobson (Ed.), *Handbook of cognitive-behavioral therapies* (2nd ed., pp 295–348). New York: Guilford Press.

Dubbert, P. M. (1995). Behavioral (life-style) modification in the prevention and treatment of hypertension. *Clin. Psychol. Rev., 15*(3), 187–216.

Duberstein, P. R., Conwell, Y., & Cox, C. (1998). Suicide in widowed persons: A psychological autopsy comparison of recently and remotely bereaved older subjects. *Am. J. Geriatr. Psychiatry, 6*(4), 328–334.

Duberstein, P. R., Conwell, Y, Cox, C., Podgorski, C., Glazer, R., & Caine, E. (1995). Attitudes toward self-determined death: A survey of primary care physicians. *J. Am. Geriatr. Soc., 43*, 395–400.

Dubner, A. E., & Motta, R. W. (1999). Sexually and physically abused foster care children and posttraumatic stress disorder. *J. Consult. Clin. Psychol., 67*(3), 367–373.

Duffy, B. (1996, April 15). The mad bomber? *U. S. News & World Report,* pp. 29–36.

Dugas, M. J., Freeston, M. H., Ladouceur, R., Rhéaume, J., Provencher, M., & Boisvert, J. M. (1998). Worry themes in primary GAD, secondary GAD, and other anxiety disorders. *J. Anxiety Disord., 12*(3), 253–261.

Duggan, J. P., & Booth, D. A. (1986). Obesity, overeating, and rapid gastric emptying in rats with ventromedial hypothalamic lesions. *Science, 231,* 609–611.

Dugger, C. W. (1996, October 5). Genital ritual is unyielding in Africa. *New York Times,* pp. 1, 6–7.

Dunbar, F. (1948). *Synopsis of psychosomatic diagnosis and treatment.* St. Louis, MO: Mosby.

Duncan, R. M., & Cheyne, J. A. (1999). Incidence and functions of self-reported private speech in young adults: A self-verbalization. *Can. J. Behav. Sci., 31*(2), 133–136.

Dunn, K. M., Croft, P. R., & Hackett, G. I. (1999). Association of sexual problems with social, psychological, and physical problems in men and women: A cross sectional population survey. *J. Epidemiol. Commun. Health, 53*(3), 144–148.

Dunner, D. L., & Hall, K. S. (1980). Social adjustment and psychological precipitants in mania. In R. H. Belmaker & H. M. van Praag (Eds.), *Mania: An evolving concept.* New York: Spectrum.

Dupont, S. (1995). Multiple sclerosis and sexual functioning: A review. *Clin. Rehabil., 9*(2), 135–141.

Dupree, L. W., & Schonfeld, L. (1999). Management of alcohol abuse in older adults. In M. Duffy (Ed.), *Handbook of counseling and psychotherapy with older adults.* New York: Wiley.

Durkheim, E. (1951). Suicide. New York: Free Press. (Original work published 1897.)

Dweck, C. S. (1976). Children's interpretation of evaluative feedback: The effect of social cues on learned helplessness. *Merrill Palmer Q., 22*(2), 105–109.

Dwyer, J. T., Feldman, J. J., Seltzer, C. C., & Mayer, J. (1969). Body image in adolescents: Attitudes toward weight and perception of appearance. *Am. J. Clin. Nutr., 20,* 1045–1056.

Dykens, E. M., & Hodapp, R. M. (2001). Research in mental retardation: Toward an etiologic approach. *J. Child Psychol. Psychiatry Allied Discipl., 42*(1), 49–71.

Eakes, G. G. (1995). Chronic sorrow: The lived experience of parents of chronically mentally ill individuals. *Arch. Psychiatr. Nurs., 9*(2), 77–84.

Eaton, W. W. (2001). *The sociology of mental disorders* (3rd ed.). Westport, CT: Praeger/Greenwood.

Eaton, W. W., Bilker, W., Haro, J. M., & Herman, H. (1992). Long-term course of hospitalization for schizophrenia: II. Change with passage of time. *Schizophr. Bull., 18*(2), 229–241.

Eaton, W. W., Dryman, A., & Weissman, M. M. (1991). Panic and phobia. In L. N. Robins & D. A. Regier (Eds.), *Psychiatric disorders in America: The Epidemiologic Catchment Area Study.* New York: Maxwell Macmillan International.

Eaton, W. W., & Muntaner, C. (1999). Socioeconomic stratification and mental disorder. In A. V. Horwitz, T. L. Scheid et al. (Eds.), *A handbook for the study of mental health: Social contexts, theories, and systems.* New York: Cambridge University Press.

Ebihara, S., Marks, T., Hudson, D. J., & Menaker, M. (1986). *Science, 231,* 491–493.

Echeburúa, E., Báez, C., & Fernández-Montalvo, J. (1996). Comparative effectiveness of three therapeutic modalities in the psychological treatment of pathological gambling: Long-term outcome. *Behav. Cognit. Psychother., 24,* 51–72.

Echeburúa, E., Fernández-Montalvo, J., & Báez, C. (2000). Relapse prevention in the treatment of slot-machine pathological gambling: Long-term outcome. *Behav. Ther., 31*(2), 351–364.

Eckenrode, J., Laird, M., & Doris, J. (1993). School performance and disciplinary problems among abused and neglected children. *Dev. Psychol., 29*(1), 54–62.

Edelman, R. E., & Chambless, D. L. (1995). Adherence during sessions and homework in cognitive-behavioral group treatment of social phobia. *Behav. Res. Ther.*, 33(5), 573-577.

Edelstein, B. A., & Semenchuk, E. M. (1996). Interviewing older adults. In L. L. Carstensen, B. A. Edelstein et al. (Eds.), *The practical handbook of clinical gerontology.* Thousand Oaks, CA: Sage.

Editors of Roper Reports. (1998, January). Partying like it's 1999. Source: Roper Starch Worldwide, NY. *Am. Demogr.*

Edwards, T. M. (1998, November 9). What the cutters feel. *Behaviour, 152*(19).

Egan, B. M. (1992). Vascular reactivity, sympathetic tone, and stress. In E. H. Johnson, E. D. Gentry, & S. Julius (Eds.), *Personality, elevated blood pressure, and essential hypertension.* Washington, DC: Hemisphere.

Egeland, B. (1991, February). *Presentation.* New York: American Association for the Advancement of Science.

Ehrman, M. (1995, June 25). Reaching out for virtual therapy. *Los Angeles Times,* pp. E1, E4.

Eich, E. (1995). Mood as a mediator of place dependent memory. *J. Exp. Psychol. Gen., 124*(3), 293-308.

Eigan, L. (1991, February). *Alcohol practices, policies, and potentials of American colleges and universities.* An OSAP White Paper, Office for Substance Abuse Prevention, Rockville, MD.

Einarson, T. R., Arikian, S. R., Casciano, J., & Doyle, J. J. (1999). Comparison of extended-release venlafaxine, selective serotonin reuptake inhibitors, and tricyclic antidepressants in the treatment of depression: A meta-analysis of randomized controlled trials. *Clin. Ther.: Int. J. Drug Ther., 21*(2), 296-308.

Eisen, M. R. (1993). The victim's burden: Guilt, shame, and abuse. *Imagination Cognit. Pers., 12*(1), 69-88.

Eisenberg, L. (1958). School phobia: A study in the communication of anxiety. *Am. J. Psychiatry, 114,* 712-718.

Eisendrath, S. J. (1995). Psychiatric aspects of chronic pain. *Neurology, 45*(Suppl. 9), S26-S34.

Eisenthal, S., Koopman, C., & Lazare, A. (1983). Process analysis of two dimensions of the negotiated approach in relation to satisfaction in the initial interview. *J. Nerv. Ment. Dis., 171,* 49-54.

Eisler, I. (1995). Family models of eating disorders. In G. Szmukler, C. Dare, & J. Treasure (Eds.), *Handbook of eating disorders: Theory, treatment and research.* Chichester, UK: Wiley.

Eitinger, L. (1964). *Concentration camp survivors in Norway and Israel.* New York: Humanities Press.

Eitinger, L. (1969). Psychosomatic problems in concentration camp survivors. *J. Psychosom. Res., 13,* 183-190.

Eitinger, L. (1973). A follow-up study of the Norwegian concentration camp survivors: Mortality and morbidity. *Isr. Ann. Psychiatry Relat. Discip., 11,* 199-210.

Ekman, P., O'Sullivan, M., & Frank, M. G. (1999). A few can catch a liar. *Psychol. Sci., 10*(3), 263-266.

Ekselius, L., Tillfors, M., Furmark, T., & Fredrikson, M. (2001). Personality disorders in the general population: DSM-IV and ICD-10 defined prevalence as related to sociodemographic profile. *Pers. Individual Differ., 30*(2), 311-320.

Elias, M. (1993, July 15). Poor odds for heroin recovery. *USA Today,* p. 1D.

Elias, M. (1995, April 18). Therapist's program to go on-line. *USA Today,* p. 1D.

Elias, M. (2000, March 7). Online mental-health therapy in its formative years. *USA Today,* p. 3D.

Elkin, I. (1994). The NIMH Treatment of Depression Collaborative Research Program: Where we began and where we are. In A. E. Bergin & S. L. Garfiel

(Eds.), *Handbook of psychotherapy and behavior change* (4th ed.). New York: Wiley.

Elkin, I., Shea, M. T., Watkins, J. T., Imber, S. D. et al. (1989). National Institute of Mental Health Treatment of Depression Collaborative Research Program: General effectiveness of treatments. *Arch. Gen. Psychiatry, 46*(11), 971-982.

Elkins, D. N. (1999, October). Spirituality: It's what's missing in mental health. *Psychol. Today,* pp. 45-48.

Elkins, I. J., & Cromwell, R. L. (1994). Priming effects in schizophrenia: Associative interference and facilitation as a function of visual context. *J. Abnorm. Psychol., 103*(4), 791-800.

Elkins, R. L. (1991). An appraisal of chemical aversion (emetic therapy) approaches to alcoholism treatment. *Behav. Res. Ther., 29,* 387-414.

Ellenberger, H. F. (1970). *The discovery of the unconscious.* New York: Basic Books.

Ellenberger, H. F. (1972). The story of "Anna O.": A critical review with new data. *J. Hist. Behav. Sci., 8,* 267-279.

Elliot, D. M., & Guy, J. D. (1993). Mental health professionals vs. non-mental health professionals: Childhood trauma and adult functioning. *Prof. Psychol.: Res. Pract., 24*(1), 83-90.

Elliott, C. (1996). *The rules of insanity: Moral responsibility and the mentally ill offender.* Albany: State University of New York Press.

Ellis, A. (1962). *Reason and emotion in psychotherapy.* Secaucus, NJ: Lyle Stuart.

Ellis, A. (1977). The basic clinical theory of rational-emotive therapy. In A. Ellis & R. Grieger (Eds.), *Handbook of rational-emotive therapy.* New York: Springer.

Ellis, A. (1979). A note on the treatment of agoraphobics with cognitive modification versus prolonged exposure in vivo. *Behav. Res. Ther., 17,* 162-164.

Ellis, A. (1979). The theory of rational-emotive therapy. In A. Ellis & J. M. Whitely (Eds.), *Theoretical and empirical foundations of rational-emotive therapy.* Monterey, CA: Brooks/Cole.

Ellis, A. (1995). Rational emotive behavior therapy. In R. J. Corsini & D. Wedding (Eds.), *Current psychotherapies* (5th ed.). Itasca, IL: Peacock.

Ellis, A. (1999). *How to make yourself happy and remarkably less disturbable.* Atascadero, CA: Impact Publishers.

Ellison, C. G., & Levin, J. S. (1998). The religion-health connection: Evidence, theory, and future directions. *Health Educ. Behav., 25*(6), 700-720.

Ellison, J. M. (1998). SSRIs and sexual dysfunction. *Psychiatr. Times, 15*(8).

El-Mallakh, R. S., & Huff, M. O. (2001). Mood stabilizers and ion regulation. *Harv. Rev. Psychiatry, 9*(1), 23-32.

Elsesser, K., Sartory, G., & Maurer, J. (1996). The efficacy of complaints management training in facilitating benzodiazepine withdrawal. *Behav. Res. Ther., 34*(2), 149-156.

Emmanuel, N. P., Ware, M. R., Brawman-Mintzer, O., Ballenger, J. C., & Lydiard, R. B. (1999). Once-weekly dosing of fluoxetine in the maintenance of remission in panic disorder. *J. Clin. Psychiatry, 60*(5), 299-301.

Emmelkamp, P. M. (1982). Exposure in vivo treatments. In A. Goldstein & D. Chambless (Eds.), *Agoraphobia: Multiple perspectives on theory and treatment.* New York: Wiley.

Emmelkamp, P. M. (1982). *Phobic and obsessive-compulsive disorders.* New York: Plenum Press.

Emmelkamp, P. M. (1994). Behavior therapy with adults. In A. E. Bergin & S. L. Garfiel (Eds.), *Handbook of psychotherapy and behavior change* (4th ed.). New York: Wiley.

Emrick, C. D., & Hansen, J. (1983). Assertions regarding effectiveness of treatment for alcoholism: Fact or fantasy? *Am. Psychol., 38,* 1078-1088.

Engel, G. L. (1968). A life setting conducive to illness: The giving-up-given-up complex. *Ann. Intern. Med., 69,* 293.

Ennis, B. J., & Emery, R. D. (1978). *The rights of patients (ACLU Handbook Series).* New York: Avon.

Enoch, M. A., Kaye, W. H., Rotondo, A. et al. (1998). 5-HT2A promoter polymorphism-1438G/A, anorexia nervosa, and obsessive-compulsive disorder [Letter]. *Lancet, 351,* 1785-1786.

Enright, S. J. (1989). Paedophilia: A cognitive/behavioural treatment approach in a single case. *Br. J. Psychiatry, 155,* 399-401.

Ensminger, M. E. (1995, December). Welfare and psychological distress: A longitudinal study of African American urban mothers. *J. Health Soc. Behav., 36,* 346-359.

Epstein, S. (1983). Hypnotherapeutic control of exhibitionism: A brief communication. *Int. J. Clin. Exp. Hypnosis, 31*(2), 63-66.

Erba, H. W. (2000). Early intervention programs for children with autism: Conceptual frameworks for implementation. *Am. J. Orthopsychiatry, 70*(1), 82-94.

Erdelyi, M. H. (1985). *Psychoanalysis: Freud's cognitive psychology.* New York: Freeman.

Erdelyi, M. H. (1992). Psychodynamics and the unconscious. *Am. Psychol., 47*(6), 784-787.

Ereshefsky, L. (1995). Treatment strategies for schizophrenia. New Antipsychotic Treatments for Schizophrenia Symposium. *Psychiatr. Ann., 25*(5), 285-296.

Erickson, D. J., Wolfde, J., King, D. W., King, L. A., & Sharkansky, E. J. (2001). *J. Consult. Clin. Psychol., 69*(1), 41-49.

Erickson, M. T. (1992). *Behavior disorders of children and adolescents.* Englewood Cliffs, NJ: Prentice-Hall.

Erikson, E. (1963). *Childhood and society.* New York: Norton.

Ernst, N. D., & Harlan, W. R. (1991). Obesity and cardiovascular disease in minority populations: Executive summary. Conference highlights, conclusions, and recommendations. *Am. J. Clin. Nutr., 53*(Suppl.), 1507-1511.

Escobar, J. I., Gara, M., Waitzkin, H., Silver, R. C., Holman, A., & Compton, W. (1998). DSM-IV hypochondriasis in primary care. *Gen. Hosp. Psychiatry, 20*(3), 155-159.

Eser, A. (1981). "Sanctity" and "quality" of life in a historical comparative view. In S. E. Wallace & A. Eser (Eds.), *Suicide and euthanasia: The rights of personhood.* Knoxville: University of Tennessee Press.

Essau, C. A., Conradt, J., & Petermann, F. (1999). Frequency of panic attacks and panic disorder in adolescents. *Depression Anxiety, 9*(1), 19-26.

Etzersdorfer, E., & Sonneck, G. (1998). Preventing suicide by influencing mass-media reporting. The Viennese experience 1980-1996. *Arch. Suicide Res., 4*(1), 67-74.

Evans, S. W., Pelham, W. E., Smith, B. H., Bukstein, O., Gnagy, E. M., Greiner, A. R., Altenderfer, L., & Baron-Myak, C. (2001). Dose-response effects of methylphenidate on ecologically valid measures of academic performance and classroom behavior in adolescents with ADHD. *Exp. Clin. Psychopharmacol., 9*(2), 163-175.

Evenhuis, H. M. (1999). Associated medical aspects. In M. P. Janicki & A. P. Dalton (Eds.), *Dementia, aging, and intellectual disabilities: A handbook.* Philadelphia: Brunner/Mazel.

Everson, S. A., Goldberg, D. E., Kaplan, G. A., Cohen, R. D. et al. (1996). Hopelessness and risk of mortality and incidence of myocardial infarction and cancer. *Psychosom. Med., 58,* 113-121.

Exner, J. E. (1993). *The Rorschach: A comprehensive system: Vol. 1. Basic foundations* (3rd ed.). New York: Wiley.

Exner, J. E. (1997). The future of Rorschach in personality assessment. *J. Pers. Assess., 68*(1), 37-46.

Express Scripts. (1999, June 29). *1998 Express Scripts Trend Report.* St. Louis, MO: Author.

FDA (Food and Drug Administration). (1996, March 26). Press release. Cited in A. Manning, Quitter's new tool: Nicotine nasal spray. *USA Today,* p. 1A.

FDA (Food and Drug Administration). (1999, January 13). Bedwetting may be more widespread than thought. *HealthScout.*

Fabrega, H., Ulrich, R., Pilkonis, P., & Mezzich, J. (1991). On the homogeneity of personality disorder clusters. *Compr. Psychiatry, 32*(5), 373–386.

Faedda, G. L., Tondo, L., Teichner, M. H., Baldessarini, R. J., Gelbard, H. A., & Floris, G. F. (1993). Seasonal mood disorders: Patterns of seasonal recurrence in mania and depression. *Arch. Gen. Psychiatry, 50*(1), 17–23.

Fahrenberg, J., Foerster, F., & Wilmers, F. (1995). Is elevated blood pressure level associated with higher cardiovascular responsiveness in laboratory tasks and with response specificity? *Psychophysiology, 32*(1), 81–91.

Fahrenberg, J., Franck, M., Baas, U., & Jost, E. (1995). Awareness of blood pressure: interoception or contextual judgement? *J. Psychosom. Res., 39*(1), 11–18.

Fairbairn, G. J. (1998). Suicide, language, and clinical practice. *Philos. Psychiatry Psychol., 5*(2), 157–169.

Fairbank, J. A., & Keane, T. M. (1982). Flooding for combat-related stress disorders: Assessment of anxiety reduction across traumatic memories. *Behav. Ther., 13,* 499–510.

Fairburn, C. G. (1985). Cognitive-behavioural treatment for bulimia. In D. M. Garner & P. E. Garfinkel (Eds.), *Handbook of psychotherapy for anorexia nervosa and bulimia.* New York: Guilford Press.

Fairburn, C. G. (1985). The management of bulimia nervosa. *J. Psychiatr. Res., 19,* 465–472.

Fairburn, C. G., Jones, R., Peveler, R. C., Hope, R. A., & O'Connor, M. (1993). Psychotherapy and bulimia nervosa: Longer-term effects of interpersonal psychotherapy behavior therapy, and cognitive behavior therapy. *Arch. Gen. Psychiatry, 50,* 419–428.

Fairburn, C. G., Norman, P. A., Welch, S. L., O'Connor, M. E. et al. (1995). A prospective study of outcome in bulimia nervosa and the long-term effects of three psychological treatments. *Arch. Gen. Psychiatry, 52*(4), 304–312.

Fairweather, G. W., Danders, D. H., Maynard, H., & Cressler, D. L. (1969). *Community life for the mentally ill: An alternative to institutional care.* Chicago: Aldine.

Falloon, I. R. H., Coverdale, J. H., & Brooker. C. (1996). Psychosocial interventions in schizophrenia: A review. *Int. J. Ment. Health, 25*(1), 3–21.

Fals, S. W., & Schafer, J. (1992). The treatment of substance abusers diagnosed with obsessive-compulsive disorder: An outcome study. *J. Subst. Abuse Treat., 9*(4), 365–370.

Famy, C., Streissguth, A. P., & Unis, A. S. (1998). Mental illness in adults with fetal alcohol syndrome or fetal alcohol effects. *Am. J. Psychiatry, 155*(4), 552–554.

Faraone, S. V., Biederman, J., Mick, E., Wozniak, J. et al. (1996). Attention deficit hyperactivity disorder in a multigenerational pedigree. *Biol. Psychiatry, 39,* 906–908.

Faraone, S. V., Biederman, J., & Milberger, S. (1994). An exploratory study of ADHD among second-degree relatives of ADHD children. *Biol. Psychiatry, 35*(6), 398–402.

Faraone, S. V., Tsuang, M. T., & Tsuang, D. W. (1999). *Genetics of mental disorders: A guide for students, clinicians, and researchers.* New York: Guilford Press.

Farberow, N. L., & Litman, R. E. (1970). *A comprehensive suicide prevention program.* Unpublished final report, Suicide Prevention Center of Los Angeles, Los Angeles.

Farley, C. J. (1994, April 18). The butt stops here. *Time,* pp. 58–64.

Farrington, D. P. (1991). Psychological contributions to the explanations of offending. *Issues Criminol. & Legal Psychol., 1*(17), 7–19.

Fasko, S. N., & Fasko, D. (1991). Suicidal behavior in children. *Psychol.: J. Hum. Behav., 27*(4)–28(1), 10–16.

Fauber, R. L., & Long, N. (1992). Parenting in a broader context: A reply to Emery, Finchman, and Cummings. *J. Consult. Clin. Psychol., 60*(6), 913–915.

Fauteck, P. K. (1995). Detecting the malingering of psychosis in offenders: No easy solutions. *Criminal Justice Behav., 22*(1), 3–18.

Fava, M. (2000). New approaches to the treatment of refractory depression. *J. Clin. Psychiatry, 61*(Suppl.), 26–32.

Fava, M., Bless, E., Otto, M. W., Pava, J. A., & Rosenbaum, J. F. (1994). Dysfunctional attitudes in major depression. *J. Nerv. Ment. Dis., 182*(1), 45–49.

Fava, M., Rankin, M. A., Wright, E. C., Alpert, J. E., Nierenberg, A. A., Pava, J., & Rosenbaum, J. F. (2000). Anxiety disorders in major depression. *Comp. Psychiatry, 41*(2), 97–102.

Favaro, A., Maiorani, M., Colombo, G., & Santonastaso, P. (1999). Traumatic experiences, posttraumatic stress disorder, and dissociative symptoms in a group of refugees from former Yugoslavia. *J. Nerv. Ment. Dis., 187*(5), 306–308.

Fawcett, J. (1999). Profiles of completed suicides. In D. G. Jacobs (Ed.), *The Harvard Medical School guide to suicide assessment and intervention.* San Francisco: Jossey-Bass.

Fawcett, J., & Busch, K. A. (1995). Stimulants in psychiatry. In A. F. Schatzberg & C. B. Nemeroff (Eds.), *The American Psychiatric Press textbook of psychopharmacology.* Washington, DC: American Psychiatric Press.

Fawcett, J., Scheftner, W., Clark, D., Hedeker, D. et al. (1987). Clinical predictors of suicide in patients with major affective disorders: A controlled prospective study. *Am. J. Psychiatry, 144*(1), 35–40.

Fawzy, F. I., Fawzy, N. W., Hyun, C. S., Elashoff, R., Guthrie, D. et al. (1993). Malignant melanoma: Effects of an early structured psychiatric intervention, coping, and affective state on recurrence and survival six years later. *Arch. Gen. Psychiatry, 50,* 681–689.

Fehre, K., & White, B. J. (Eds.). (1996). *The self-help group directory* (14th ed.). Denville, NJ: Northwest Convenant Medical Center.

Feighner, J. P. (1999). Overview of antidepressants currently used to treat anxiety disorders. *J. Clin. Psychiatry, 60*(Suppl. 22), 18–22.

Feinberg, M. (1999). Pharmacotherapy. In M. Hersen & A. S. Bellack (Eds.), *Handbook of comparative interventions for adult disorders* (2nd ed.). New York: Wiley.

Feldman, H. A., Goldstein, I., Hatzichristou, D. G., Krane, R. J., & McKinlay, J. B. (1994). Impotence and its medical and psychosocial correlates: Results of the Massachusetts Male Aging Study. *J. Urol., 151,* 54–61.

Feldman, M. D., & Feldman, J. M. (1995). Tangled in the web: Countertransference in the therapy of factitious disorders. *Int. J. Psychiatr. Med., 25*(4), 389–399.

Feldman, M. D., Ford, C. V., & Reinhold, T. (1994). *Patient or pretender: Inside the strange world of factitious disorders.* New York: Wiley.

Felix-Ortiz, M., Salazar, M. R., Gonzalex, J. R., Sorensen, J. L., & Plock, D. (2000). A qualitative evaluation of an assisted self-help group for drug-addicted clients in a structured outpatient treatment setting. *Commun. Ment. Health J., 36*(4), 339–350.

Fenichel, O. (1945). *The psychoanalytic theory of neurosis.* New York: Norton.

Fenigstein, A. (1996). Paranoia. In C. G. Costello (Ed.), *Personality characteristics of the personality disordered.* New York: Wiley.

Fenn, D. S., Moussaoui, D., Hoffman, W. F., Kadri, N., Bentounssi, B., Tilane, A., Khomeis, M., & Casey, D. E. (1996). Movements in never-medicated schizophrenics: A preliminary study. *Psychopharmacology, 123,* 206–210.

Fennig, S., Schwartz, J. E., & Bromet, E. J. (1994). Are diagnostic criteria, time of episode and occupational impairment important determinants of the female:male ratio for major depression? *J. Affect. Disord., 30,* 147–154.

Fenton, W. S., & McGlashan, T. H. (1994). Antecedents, symptom progression, and long-term outcome of the deficit syndrome in schizophrenia. *Am. J. Psychiatry, 151*(3), 351–356.

Fenton, W. S., Mosher, L. R., Herrell, J. M., & Blyler, C. R. (1998). Randomized trial of general hospital and residential alternative care for patients with severe and persistent mental illness. *Am. J. Psychiatry, 155*(4), 516–522.

Fergusson, D. M., Woodward, L. J., & Horwood, L. J. (2000). Risk factors and life processes associated with the onset of suicidal behavior during adolescence and early adulthood. *Psychol. Med., 30*(1), 23–39.

Fernandez, F., Levy, J. K., Lachar, B. L., Small, G. W. et al. (1995). The management of depression and anxiety in the elderly. *J. Clin. Psychiatry, 56*(Suppl. 2), 20–29.

Fernandez-Guasti, A., & Lopez-Rubalcava, C. (1998). Modification of the anxiolytic action of 5-HT-sub(1A) compounds by GABA-benzodiazepine agents in rats. *Pharmacol. Biochem. Behav., 60*(1), 27–32.

Ferrada, N. M., Asberg, M., Ormstad, K., & Nordström, P. (1995). Definite and undetermined forensic diagnoses of suicide among immigrants in Sweden. *Acta Psychiatr. Scand., 91*(2), 130–135.

Ferrando, S. J. (2001). Substance abuse and HIV infection. *Psychiatr. Ann., 31*(1), 57–62.

Ferreira, C. (2000). Serial killers—Victims of compulsion or masters of control? In D. H. Fishbein (Ed.), *The science, treatment, and prevention of antisocial behaviors: Application to the criminal justice system* (pp. 15-1-15-18). Kingston, NJ: Civic Research Institute.

Fichter, M. (1990). Psychological therapies in bulimia nervosa. In M. M. Fichter (Ed.), *Bulimia nervosa: Basic research, diagnosis and therapy.* Chichester, England: Wiley.

Fichter, M. M., & Pirke, K. M. (1995). Starvation models and eating disorders. In G. Szmukler, C. Dare, & J. Treasure (Eds.), *Handbook of eating disorders: Theory, treatment and research.* Chichester, England: Wiley.

Fichtner, C. G., Kuhlman, D. T., Gruenfeld, M. J., & Hughes, J. R. (1990). Decreased episodic violence and increased control of dissociation in a carbamazepine-treated case of multiple personality. *Biol. Psychiatry, 27*(9), 1045–1052.

Field, A. P., & Davey, G. C. L. (2001). Conditioning models of childhood anxiety. In W. K. Silverman & P. S. A. Treffers (Eds.), *Anxiety disorders in children and adolescents: Research, assessment and intervention* (pp. 187–211). New York: Cambridge University Press.

Fieve, R. R. (1975). *Moodswing.* New York: Morrow.

Figley, C. R. (1978). Symptoms of delayed combat stress among a college sample of Vietnam veterans. *Mil. Med., 143*(2), 107–110.

Figley, C. R., & Leventman, S. (1990). Introduction: Estrangement and victimization. In C. R. Figley & S. Leventman (Eds.), *Strangers at home: Vietnam veterans since the war.* New York: Praeger.

Fine, C. G., & Madden, N. E. (2000). Group psychotherapy in the treatment of dissociative identity disorder and allied dissociative disorders. In R. H. Klein & V. L. Schermer (Eds.), *Group psychotherapy for psychological trauma* (pp. 298–325). New York: Guilford Press.

Fink, D. (1992). The psychotherapy of multiple personality disorder. A case study. *Psychoanal. Inquiry, 12*(1), 49–70.

Fink, M. (1988). Convulsive therapy: A manual of practice. In A. J. Frances & R. Hales (Eds.), *Review of psychiatry* (Vol. 7). Washington, DC: American Psychiatric Press.

Fink, M. (1992). Electroconvulsive therapy. In E. S. Paykel (Ed.), *Handbook of affective disorders.* New York: Guilford Press.

Fink, M. (1995). Recognizing NMS as a type of catatonia. *Neuropsychiatry, Neuropsyhol., Behav. Neurol., 8*(1), 75–76.

Fink, M. (2001). Convulsive therapy: A review of the first 55 years. *J. Affect. Disord., 63*(1–3), 1–15.

Fink, P. (1995). Psychiatric illness in patients with persistent somatisation. *Br. J. Psychiatry, 166,* 93–99.

Fink, P., Ewald, H., Jensen, J., Sorensen, L., Engberg, M., Holm, M., & Munk-Jorgensen, P. (1999). Screening for somatization and hypochondriasis in primary care and neurological in-patients: A seven-item scale for hypochondriasis and somatization. *J. Psychosom. Res., 46*(3), 261–273.

Fink, P., Sorensen, L., Engberg, M., Holm, M., & Munk-Jorgensen, P. (1999). Somatization in primary care: Prevalence, health care utilization, and general practitioner recognition. *Psychosomatics, 40*(4), 330–338.

Finkel, N. J. (1988). *Insanity on trial.* New York: Plenum Press.

Finkel, N. J. (1989). The Insanity Defense Reform Act of 1984: Much ado about nothing. *J. Behav. Sci. Law, 7*(3), 403–419.

Finkel, N. J. (1990). De facto departures from insanity instructions. *Law Hum. Behav., 14*(2), 105–122.

Finkel, N. J. (1991). The insanity defense. *Law Hum. Behav., 15*(5), 533–555.

Finkel, N. J., & Duff, K. (1989). The insanity defense: Giving jurors a third option. *Forensic Rep., 1,* 65–70.

Finkel, N. J., Shaw, R., Bercaw, S., & Koch, J. (1985). Insanity defenses: From the juror's perspective. *Law Psychol. Rev., 9,* 77–92.

Finkel, S. (1991). Group psychotherapy in later life. In W. A. Myers (Ed.), *New techniques in the psychotherapy of older patients.* Washington, DC: American Psychiatric Press.

Finkelhor, D., Asdigian, N., & Dziuba-Leatherman, J. (1995). Victimization prevention programs for children: A follow-up. *Am. J. Public Health, 85*(12), 1684–1689.

Finkelstein, J. R. J., Cannon, T. D., Gur, R. E., Gur, R. C., & Moberg, P. (1997). Attentional dysfunctions in neuroleptic-naive and neuroleptic-withdrawn schizophrenic patients and their siblings. *J. Abnorm. Psychol., 106*(2), 203–212.

Finn, P. R., Sharkansky, E. J., Brandt, K. M., & Turcotte, N. (2000). The effects of familial risk, personality, and expectancies on alcohol use and abuse. *J. Abnorm. Psychol., 109*(1), 122–133.

Fiscalini, J. (1993). Interpersonal relations and the problem of narcissism. In J. Fiscalini & A. L. Grey (Eds.), *Narcissism and the interpersonal self.* New York: Columbia University Press.

Fischer, C. T., McElwain, B., & DuBoise, J. T. (2000). Existential approaches to psychotherapy. In C. R. Snyder & R. E. Ingram (Eds.), *Handbook of psychological change: Psychotherapy processes & practices for the 21st century* (pp. 243–257). New York: Wiley.

Fishbain, D. A. (2000). Re: The meeting of pain and depression. Comorbidity in women. *Can. J. Psychiatry, 45*(1), 88.

Fishbain, D. A., Cutler, R. B., Rosomoff, H. L., & Rosomoff, R. S. (1998). Do antidepressants have an analgesic effect in psychogenic pain and somatoform pain disorder? A meta-analysis. *Psychosom. Med., 60*(4), 503–509.

Fisher, D., Beech, A., & Browne, K. (2000). The effectiveness of relapse prevention training in a group of incarcerated child molesters. *Psychol. Crime Law, 6*(3), 181–195.

Fisher, J. E., & Carstensen, L. L. (1990). Behavior management of the dementias. *Clin. Psychol. Rev., 10,* 611–629.

Fisher, J. O., & Birch, L. L. (1999). Restricting access to palatable foods affects children's behavioral response, food selection, and intake. *Am. J. Clin. Nutr., 69*(6), 1264–1272.

Fisher, P. L., & Durham, R. C. (1999). Recovery rates in generalized anxiety disorder following psychological therapy: An analysis of clinically significant change in the STAI-T across outcome studies since 1990. *Psychol. Med., 29*(6), 1425–1434.

Fitz, A. (1990). Religious and familial factors in the etiology of obsessive-compulsive disorder: A review. *J. Psychol. Theol., 18*(2), 141–147.

Flaherty, J. A., & Adams, S. (1998). Therapist-patient race and sex matching: Predictors of treatment duration. *Psychiatr. Times, 15*(1).

Flament, M. F., Koby, E., Rapoport, J. L., Berg, C. J. et al. (1991). Childhood obsessive-compulsive disorder: A prospective follow-up study. *Annu. Prog. Child Psychiatry Child Dev.,* pp. 373–394.

Flanagan, O. (2000). *Dreaming souls: Sleep, dreams, and the evolution of the conscious mind.* New York: Oxford University Press.

Flannery, R. B., Jr., Fisher, W., Walker, A., Kolodziej, K., & Spillane, M. J. (2000). Assaults on staff by psychiatric patients in community residences. *Psychiatr. Serv., 51*(1), 111–113.

Flaskerud, J. H. (2000). Ethnicity, culture, and neuropsychiatry. *Issues Ment. Health Nurs., 21*(1), 5–29.

Flaskerud, J. H., & Hu, L. (1992). Racial/ethnic identity and amount and type of psychiatric treatment. *Am. J. Psychiatry, 149*(3), 379–384.

Flaskerud, J. H., & Hu, L. (1992). Relationship of ethnicity to psychiatric diagnosis. *J. Nerv. Ment. Dis., 180*(5), 296–303.

Flavin, D. K., Franklin, J. E., & Frances, R. J. (1990). Substance abuse and suicidal behavior. In S. J. Blumenthal & D. J. Kupfer (Eds.), *Suicide over the life cycle: Risk factors, assessment, and treatment of suicidal patients.* Washington, DC: American Psychiatry Press.

Flaxenberg, G. M. (1998).

Fleer, J., & Pasewark, R. A. (1982). Prior public health agency contacts of individuals committing suicide. *Psychol. Rep., 50*(3, Pt. 2), 1319–1324.

Fletcher, T. B. (2000). Primary nocturnal enuresis: A structural and strategic family systems approach. *J. Ment. Health Counsel. 22*(1), 32–44.

Flett, G. L., Vredenburg, K., & Krames, L. (1997). The continuity of depression in clinical and nonclinical samples. *Psychol. Bull., 121*(3), 395–416.

Flick, S. N., Roy-Byrne, P. P., Cowley, D. S., Shores, M. M., & Dunner, D. L. (1993). DSM-III-R personality disorders in a mood and anxiety disorders clinic: Prevalence, comorbidity, and clinical correlates. *J. Affect. Disord., 27,* 71–79.

Flint, A. J. (1994). Epidemiology and comorbidity of anxiety disorders in the elderly. *Am. J. Psychiatry, 151*(5), 640–649.

Flint, J., Corley, R., DeFries, J. C., Fulker, D. W., Gray, J. A., Miller, S., & Collins, A. C. (1995). Chromosomal mapping of three loci determining quantitative variation of susceptibility to anxiety in the mouse. *Science, 268,* 1432–1435.

Foa, E. B., & Franklin, M. E. (1999). Cognitive behavior therapy. In M. Hersen, A. S. Bellack et al. (Eds.), *Handbook of comparative interventions for adult disorders* (2nd ed.). New York: Wiley.

Foa, E. B., & Kozak, M. J. (1995). DSM-IV field trial: Obsessive compulsive disorder. *Am. J. Psychiatry, 152*(1), 90–96.

Foderaero, L. W. (1993, August 12). Electroshock therapy makes a comeback. *Anchorage Daily News,* p. D3.

Foderaro, L. (1994, March 6). Got problems? Dial a shrink. *New York Times,* p. B4.

Foderaro, L. (1995, June 16). The mentally ill debate what to call themselves. *New York Times,* p. B1.

Fog, R. (1995). New diagnostic vistas. XIIth AEP Congress: Improvement of compliance: Quality assurance: Increased quality of life in community care in schizophrenia. *Int. Clin. Psychopharmacol. 9*(Suppl. 5), 71–73.

Fogel, B. S. (1986). ECT versus tricyclic antidepressants. *Am. J. Psychiatry, 143*(1), 121.

Fombonne, E. (1995). Eating disorders: Time trends and possible explanatory mechanisms. In M. Rutter & D. J. Smith (Eds.), *Psychosocial disorders in young people.* Chichester, England: Wiley.

Fombonne, E. (1999). The epidemiology of autism: A review. *Psychol. Med., 29*(4), 769–786.

Fonagy, P. (1999). Psychoanalytic theory from the viewpoint of attachment theory and research. In J. Cassidy, P. R. Shaver et al. (Eds.), *Handbook of attachment: Theory, research, and clinical applications.* New York: Guilford Press.

Fondacaro, K. M., & Butler, W. M. (1995). Suicidality in female survivors of child sexual abuse. In S. S. Canetto & D. Lester (Eds.), *Women and suicidal behavior.* New York: Springer.

Fong, M. L., & Silien, K. A. (1999). Assessment and diagnosis of DSM-IV anxiety disorders. *J. Counsel. Dev., 77*(2), 209–217.

Ford, C. E., & Hamerton, J. L. (1956). The chromosomes of man. *Nature (London), 178,* 1020–1023.

Ford, C. V. (1996). *Lies! Lies! Lies!!!: The psychology of deceit.* Washington, DC: American Psychiatric Press.

Ford, C. V., King, B. H., & Hollender, M. H. (1988). Lies and liars: Psychiatric aspects of prevarication. *Am. J. Psychiatry, 145*(5), 554–562.

Ford, G. G. (2001). *Ethical reasoning in the mental health professions.* Boca Raton, FL: CRC Press.

Ford, J. D., & Stewart, J. (1999). Group psychotherapy for war-related PTSD with military veterans. In B. H. Young & D. D. Blake (Eds.), *Group treatments for post-traumatic stress disorder.* Philadelphia: Brunner/Mazel.

Ford, M. R., & Widiger, T. A. (1989). Sex bias in the diagnosis of histrionic and antisocial personality disorders. *J. Consult. Clin. Psychol., 57*(2), 301–305.

Foreyt, J. P., Poston, W. S. C., & Goodrick, G. K. (1996). Future directions in obesity and eating disorders. *Addict. Behav., 21*(6), 767–778.

Fortmann, S., & Killen, J. (1995). Nicotine gum and self-help behavioral treatment for smoking relapse prevention: Results from a trial using population-based recruitment. *J. Consult. Clin. Psychol., 63*(3), 460–468.

Foster, P. S., & Eisler, R. M. (2001). An integrative approach to the treatment of obsessive-compulsive disorder. *Compr. Psychiatry, 42*(1), 24–31.

Foster, P. S., Smith, E. W. L., & Webster, D. G. (1999). The psychophysiological differentiation of actual, imagined, and recollected anger. *Imagination Cognit. Pers., 18*(3), 189–203.

Foster-Higgins. (1991, June 8). Cited in L. Block, Mental health expenses make employers anxious. *Business Insurance*, p. 3.

Fowler, J. S., Volkow, N. D., & Wolf, A. P. (1995). PET studies of cocaine in human brain. In A. Biegon & N. D. Volkow (Eds.), *Sites of drug action in the human brain.* Boca Raton, FL: CRC Press.

Fowler, R. (1999, June 10). Cited in Associated Press release (Philadelphia). Outrage over sex abuse study.

Fox, J. A., & Levin, J. (1999). Serial murder: Popular myths and empirical realities. In M. D. Smith, M. A. Zahn et al. (Eds.), *Homicide: A sourcebook of social research.* Thousand Oaks, CA: Sage.

Fox, P. (1992). Implications for expressed emotion therapy within a family therapeutic context. *Health Soc. Work, 17*(3), 207–213.

Fox, V. (2000). Empathy: The wonder quality of mental health treatment. *Psychiatr. Rehabil. J., 23*(3), 292–293.

Foxhall, K. (2001). Preventing relapse: Looking at data differently led to today's influential Relapse Prevention Therapy. *APA Monitor, 32*(6), 46–47.

Frances, A. J., & Egger, H. L. (1999). Whither psychiatric diagnosis. *Aust. N. Z. J. Psychiatry, 33*(2), 161–165.

Frances, R. J., & Franklin, J. E. (1988). Alcohol and other psychoactive substance use disorders. In J. A. Talbott, R. E., Hales, & S. C. Yudofsky (Eds.), *Textbook of psychiatry.* Washington, DC: American Psychiatric Press.

Francis, L. J. (1999). Happiness is a thing called stable extraversion: A further examination of the relationship between the Oxford Happiness Inventory and Eysenck's dimensional model of personality and gender. *Pers. Individual Differ., 26*(1), 5–11.

Francis, M. E., & Pennebaker, J. W. (1992). Putting stress into words: The impact of writing on physiological, absentee, and self-reported emotional well-being measures. *Am. J. Health Promotion, 6*(4), 280–287.

Frank, E. (1997). Enhancing patient outcomes: Treatment adherence. *J. Clin. Psychiatry, 58*(Suppl. 1), 11–14.

Frank, E. (1999). *Bipolar disorder therapy.* 3rd International Conference on Bipolar Disorder, Pittsburgh, PA.

Frank, E., Grochocinski, V. J., Spanier, C. A., Buysse, D. J., Cherry, C. R., Houck, P. R., Stapf, D. M., & Kupfer, D. J. (2000). Interpersonal psychotherapy and antidepressant medication: Evaluation of a sequential treatment strategy in women with recurrent major depression. *J. Clin. Psychiatry, 61*(1), 51–57.

Frank, E., Kupfer, D. J., Perel, J. M., Cornes, C., Jarrett, D. B., Mallinger, A. G. et al. (1990). Three-year outcomes for maintenance therapies in recurrent depression. *Arch. Gen. Psychiatry, 47*(12), 1093–1099.

Frank, E., Kupfer, D. J., Wagner, E. F., McEachran, A. B., & Cornes, C. (1991). Efficacy of interpersonal therapy as a maintenance treatment of recurrent depression: Contributing factors. *Arch. Gen. Psychiatry, 48,* 1053–1059.

Frank, J. D. (1973). *Persuasion and healing* (Rev. ed.). Baltimore: Johns Hopkins University Press.

Frankel, F. H. (1993). Adult reconstruction of childhood events in the multiple personality literature. *Am. J. Psychiatry, 150*(6), 954–958.

Frankish, C. J. (1994). Crisis centers and their role in treatment: Suicide prevention versus health promotion. In A. A. Leenaars, J. T. Maltsberger, & R. A. Neimeyer (Eds.), *Treatment of suicidal people.* Washington, DC: Taylor & Francis.

Frankl, V. E. (1963). *Man's search for meaning.* New York: Washington Square.

Frankl, V. E. (1975). Paradoxical intention and dereflection. *Psychother. Theory: Res. Pract., 12*(3), 226–237.

Franklin, M. E., Jaycox, L. H., & Foa, E. B. (1999). Social skills training. In M. Hersen & A. S. Bellack (Eds.), *Handbook of comparative interventions for adult disorders* (2nd ed.). New York: Wiley.

Frasciello, L. M., & Willard, S. G. (1995). Anorexia nervosa in males: A case report and review of the literature. *Clin. Soc. Work J., 23*(1), 47–58.

Frawley, P., & Smith, J. (1992). One-year follow-up after multimodal inpatient treatment for cocaine and methamphetamine dependencies. *J. Subst. Abuse Treat., 9,* 271–286.

Frayn, D. H. (1991). The incidence and significance of perceptual qualities in the reported dreams of patients with anorexia nervosa. *Can. J. Psychiatry, 36*(7), 517–520.

Fredericks, L. E. (2001). *The use of hypnosis in surgery and anesthesiology: Psychological preparation of the surgical patient.* Springfield, IL: Thomas.

Fredrikson, M., Annas, P., Fischer, H., & Wik, G. (1996). Gender and age differences in the prevalence of specific fears and phobias. *Behav. Res. Ther., 34*(1), 33–39.

Freeman, A., & Oster, C. (1999). Cognitive behavior therapy. In M. Hersen & A. S. Bellack (Eds.), *Handbook of comparative interventions for adult disorders* (2nd ed.). New York: Wiley.

Freeman, C. (1995). Cognitive therapy. In G. Szmukler, C. Dare, & J. Treasure (Eds.), *Handbook of eating disorders: Theory, treatment and research.* Chichester, England: Wiley.

Freeman, L. J., Templer, D. I., & Hill, C. (1999). The relationship between adult happiness and self-appraised childhood happiness and events. *J. Gen. Psychol., 160*(1), 46–54.

Freeman, M. P., & Stoll, A. L. (1998). Mood stabilizer combinations: A review of safety and efficacy. *Am. J. Psychiatry, 155*(1), 12–21.

Freeman, S. F. N., & Alkin, M. C. (2000). Academic and social attainments of children with mental retardation in general education and special education settings. *Remed. Spec. Educ., 21*(1), 3–18.

Freeston, M. H., & Ladouceur, R. (1997). What do patients do with their obsessive thoughts? *Behav. Res. Ther., 35*(4), 335–348.

Freeston, M. H., Ladouceur, R., Gagnon, F., & Thibodeau, N. (1992). *Beliefs about obsessional thoughts.* Unpublished manuscript, Laval University, Quebec City, Quebec.

Freeston, M. H., Rhéaume, J., & Ladouceur, R. (1996). Correcting faulty appraisals of obsessional thoughts. *Behav. Res. Ther., 34*(5/6), 433–446.

Freiberg, P. (1994, April). Gay-rights position takes on significance. *APA Monitor, 25*(4), 40.

French, O. (1987). More on multiple personality disorder. *Am. J. Psychiatry, 144*(1), 123–124.

Freud, S. (1885). On the general effects of cocaine. *Med. Chir. Centralb., 20,* 373–375.

Freud, S. (1894). The neuropsychoses of defense. In J. Strachey (Ed.), *The standard edition of the complete psychological works of Sigmund Freud* (Vol. 3). London: Hogarth Press, 1962.

Freud, S. (1900). *The interpretation of dreams* (J. Strachey, Ed. & Trans.). New York: Wiley.

Freud, S. (1909). Analysis of a phobia in a five-year-old boy. In *Sigmund Freud: Collected Papers* (Vol. 3). New York: Basic Books.

Freud, S. (1915). A case of paranoia counter to psychoanalytic theory. In *Complete psychological works* (Vol. 14). London: Hogarth, 1957.

Freud, S. (1917). *A general introduction to psychoanalysis* (J. Riviere, Trans.). New York: Liveright, 1963.

Freud, S. (1917). Mourning and melancholia. In *Collected Papers* (Vol. 4, pp. 152–172). London: Hogarth Press and the Institute of Psychoanalysis, 1950.

Freud, S. (1924). The loss of reality in neurosis and psychosis. In *Sigmund Freud's collected papers* (Vol. 2, pp. 272–282). London: Hogarth Press.

Freud, S. (1933). *New introductory lectures on psychoanalysis.* New York: Norton.

Freud, S. (1935). *Autobiography.* New York: Norton.

Freud, S. (1957). Mourning and melancholia. In J. Strachey (Ed. & Trans.), *The standard edition of complete psychological works* (Vol. 14). London: Hogarth Press. (Original work published 1917.)

Frey, K. A., Koeppe, R. A., & Holthoff, V. A. (1995). In vivo imaging of benzodiazepine receptors with positron emission tomography. In A. Biegon & N. D. Volkow (Eds.), *Sites of drug action in the human brain.* Boca Raton, FL: CRC Press.

Frick, P. J., Christian, R. E., & Wooton, J. M. (1999). Age trends in association between parenting practices and conduct problems. *Behav. Mod., 23*(1), 106–128.

Frick, W. B. (1995). The subpersonalities controversy: A reply to my critics. *J. Hum. Psychol., 35*(1), 97–101.

Fride, F. (1995). Anandamides: Tolerance and cross-tolerance to delta 9–tetrahydrocannabinol. *Brain Res., 697*(1–2), 83–90.

Friedman, M., & Rosenman, R. (1959). Association of specific overt behavior pattern with blood and cardiovascular findings. *JAMA, J. Am. Med. Assoc., 169,* 1286.

Friedman, M., & Rosenman, R. (1974). *Type A behavior and your heart.* New York: Knopf.

Friedman, M., Thoresen, C., Gill, J. et al. (1984). Alteration of type A behavior and reduction in cardiac recurrences in postmyocardial infarction patients. *Am. Heart J., 108*(2), 653–665.

Friedman, M. J. (1999). Pharmacotherapy for posttraumatic stress disorder. In M. J. Horowitz et al. (Eds.), *Essential papers on posttraumatic stress disorder. Essential papers in psychoanalysis.* New York: New York University Press.

Friend, T. (1996, March 4). Alzheimer's deaths "underestimated." *USA Today,* Sec. D, p. 1.

Friman, P. C., Allen, K. D., Kerwin, M. L. E., & Larzelere, R. (1993). Changes in modern psychology: A citation analysis of the Kuhnian displacement thesis. *Am. Psychol., 48*(6), 658–664.

Friman, P. C., & Warzak, W. J. (1990). Nocturnal enuresis: A prevalent, persistent, yet curable parasomnia. *Pediatrician, 17*(1), 38–45.

Frischholz, E. J., Lipman, L. S., Braun, B. G., & Sachs, R. G. (1992). Psychopathology, hypnotizability, and dissociation. *Am. J. Psychiatry, 149*(11), 1521–1525.

Frith, U. (2000). Cognitive explanations of autism. In K. Lee et al. (Eds.), *Childhood cognitive development: The essential readings. Essential readings in developmental psychology.* Malden, MA: Blackwell.

Frith, U., Morton, J., & Leslie, A. M. (1991). The cognitive basis of a biological disorder. *Autism Trends Neurosci., 14,* 433–438.

Fritz, C., Farver, T. B., & Kass, P. H. (1997). Correlation among three psychological scales used in research of caregivers for patients with Alzheimer's disease. *Psychol. Rep., 80,* 67–80.

Froelich, J., von Gontard, A., Lehmkuhl, G., Pfeiffer, E., & Lehmkuhl, U. (2001). Pericardial effusions in anorexia nervosa. *Eur. Child Adolesc. Psychiatry, 10*(1), 54–57.

Fromm, E., & Nash, M. R. (Eds.). (1992). *Contemporary hypnosis research.* New York: Guilford Press.

Fromm-Reichmann, F. (1943). Psychotherapy of schizophrenia. *Am. J. Psychiatry, 111,* 410–419.

Fromm-Reichmann, F. (1948). Notes on the development of treatment of schizophrenia by psychoanalytic psychotherapy. *Psychiatry, 11,* 263–273.

Fromm-Reichmann, F. (1950). *Principles of intensive psychotherapy.* Chicago: University of Chicago.

Frosch, W. A., Robbins, E. S., & Stern, M. (1965). Untoward reactions to lysergic acid diethylamide (LSD) resulting in hospitalization. *N. Engl. J. Med., 273,* 1235–1239.

Fry, R. (1993). Adult physical illness and childhood sexual abuse. *J. Psychosom. Res., 37*(2), 89–103.

Fuentes, K., & Cox, B. (2000). Assessment of anxiety in older adults: A community-based survey and comparison with younger adults. *Behav. Res. Ther., 38*(3), 297–309.

Fukunishi, I. (1998). Eating attitudes in female college students with self-reported alexithymic characteristics. *Psychol. Rep., 82,* 35–41.

Fukunishi, I., Hosaka, T., Negishi, M., Moriya, H., Hayashi, M., & Matsumoto, T. (1996). Subclinical depressive symptoms in HIV infection are related to avoidance coping responses: A comparison with end-stage renal failure and breast cancer. *Psychol. Rep., 78,* 483–488.

Fuller, R. C. (1982, Fall). Carl Rogers, religion, and the role of psychology in American culture. *J. Hum. Psychol., 22,* 21–32.

Fulwiler, C., & Pope, H. G., Jr. (1987). Depression in personality disorder. In O. G. Cameron (Ed.), *Presentations of depression: Depressive symptoms in medical and other psychiatric disorders.* New York: Wiley.

Funari, D. J., Piekarski, A. M., & Sherwood, R. J. (1991). Treatment outcomes of Vietnam veterans with posttraumatic stress disorder. *Psychol. Rep., 68*(2), 571–578.

Furukawa, T. A., Ogura, A., Hirai, T., Fujihara, S., Kitamura, T., & Takahashi, K. (1999). Early parental separation experiences among patients with bipolar disorder and major depression: A case-control study. *J. Affect. Disord., 52*(1–3), 85–91.

Fyer, A. J., Mannuzza, S., Gallops, M. S., Martin, L. Y., Aaronson, C., Gorman, J. M., Liebowitz, M. R., & Klein, D. F. (1990). Familial transmission of simple phobias and fears: A preliminary report. *Arch. Gen. Psychiatry, 47,* 252–256.

Gabbard, G. O. (1990). *Psychodynamic psychiatry in clinical practice.* Washington, DC: American Psychiatric Press.

Gabbard, G. O. (1998, September). The impact of psychotherapy on the brain. *Psychiatr. Times, 15*(9).

Gabbard, G. O. (2000). Psychodynamic psychotherapy of borderline personality disorder: A contemporary approach. *Bull. Menninger Clin., 65*(1), 41–57.

Gabbard, G. O., & Coyne, L. (1987). Predictors of response of antisocial patients to hospital treatment. *Hosp. Commun. Psychiatry, 38*(11), 1181–1185.

Gabbard, G. O., & Goodwin, F. K. (1996). Integrating biological and psychosocial perspectives. In L. J. Dickstein, M. B. Riba, & J. M. Oldham (Eds.), *Review of psychiatry* (Vol. 15). Washington, DC: American Psychiatric Press.

Gable, S. L., & Shean, G. D. (2000). Perceived social competence and depression. *J. Soc. Pers. Relat., 17*(1), 139–150.

Gaboriau, H., & Graham, H. D. (1999, April). *The desire for cosmetic facial plastic surgery may result from a personality disorder, not vanity.* Paper presented at meeting of American Academy of Facial Plastic and Reconstructive Surgery. Palm Desert, CA.

Galanter, M., & Brook, D. (2001). Network therapy for addiction: Bringing family and peer support into office practice. *Int. J. Group Psychother., 51*(1), 101–122.

Galanter, M., & Castañeda, R. (1999). Psychotherapy and family network therapy. In M. Hersen & A. S. Bellack (Eds.), *Handbook of comparative interventions for adult disorders* (2nd ed.). New York: Wiley.

Galanter, M., Talbott, D., Gallegos, K., & Rubenstone, E. (1990). Combined Alcoholics Anonymous and professional care for addicted physicians. *Am. J. Psychiatry, 147*(1), 64–68.

Gallacher, J. E., Yarnell, J. W. G., Sweetnam, P. M., Elwood, P. C., & Stansfeld, S. A. (1999). Anger and incident heart disease in the Caerphilly study. *Psychosom. Med., 61*(4), 446–453.

Gallagher, R. (1998, December 17). Interviewed in R. Vigoda, More college students showing signs of stress. *The Seattle Times.*

Gallagher-Thompson, D., Lovett, S., & Rose, J. (1991). Psychotherapeutic interventions for stressed family caregivers. In W. A. Myers (Ed.), *New techniques in the psychotherapy of older patients.* Washington, DC: American Psychiatric Press.

Gallagher-Thompson, D., Lovett, S., Rose, J., McKibbin, C., Coon, D., Futterman, A., & Thompson, L. W. (2000). Impact of psychoeducational interventions on distressed family caregivers. *J. Clin. Geropsychol., 6*(2), 91–110.

Gallagher-Thompson, D., & Thompson, L. W. (1995). Problems of aging. In R. J. Comer (Ed.), *Abnormal psychology.* New York: Freeman.

Gallup Organization. (1995). *Child abuse survey.* Princeton, NJ: Author.

Galper, J. (1998, June). Population update for June. *Am. Demogr.*

Gamwell, L., & Tomes, N. (1995). *Madness in America: Cultural and medical perceptions of mental illness before 1914.* Ithaca, NY: Cornell University Press.

Ganaway, G. K. (1989). Historical versus narrative truth: Clarifying the role of exogenous trauma in the etiology of MPD and its variants. *Dissociation, 2,* 205–222.

Ganley, A. (1981). *A participant and trainer's manual for working with men who batter.* Washington, DC: Center for Women Policy Studies.

Gannon, L., Luchetta, T., Rhodes, K., Pardie, L., & Segrist, D. (1992). Sex bias in psychological research: Progress or complacency? *Am. Psychol., 47*(3), 389–396.

Ganzach, Y. (1995). Nonlinear models of clinical judgment: Meehl's data revisited. *Psychol. Bull., 118*(3), 422–429.

Ganzini, L., Leong, G. B., Fenn, D. S., Silva, J. A., & Weinstock, R. (2000). Evaluation of competence to consent to assisted suicide: Views of forensic psychiatrists. *Am. J. Psychiatry, 157*(4), 595–600.

Garb, H. N., Florio, C. M., & Grove, W. M. (1998). The validity of the Rorschach and the Minnesota Multiphasic Personality Inventory: Results from meta-analyses. *Psychol. Sci., 9*(5), 402–404.

Garber, J., & Flynn, C. (2001). Vulnerability to depression in childhood and adolescence. In R. E. Ingram & J. M. Price (Eds.), *Vulnerability to psychopathology: Risk across the lifespan* (pp. 175–225). New York: Guilford Press.

Garber, J., Weiss, B., & Shanley, N. (1993). Cognitions, depressive symptoms, and development in adolescents. *J. Abnorm. Psychol., 102*(1), 47–57.

Gardner, D. L., Leibenluft, E., O'Leary, K. M., & Cowdry, R. W. (1991). Self-ratings of anger and hostility in borderline personality disorder. *J. Nerv. Ment. Dis., 179*(3), 157–161.

Gardner, F. L., McGowan, L. P., DiGiuseppe, R., & Sutton-Simon, K. (1980, November). *A comparison of cognitive and behavioral therapies in the reduction of social anxiety.* Paper presented to the American Association of Behavior Therapy, New York.

Gardner, J. P. (1996). *The effects of sleep deprivation on serotonergic neuronal activity in the dorsal raphe nucleus of the cat.* Unpublished doctoral dissertation, Princeton University, Princeton, NJ.

Gardner, R. (1984, July 12). Full moon lunacy: Fact or fiction. *Trenton Times,* p. B1.

Garety, P. (1991). Reasoning and delusions. *Br. J. Psychiatry, 159*(Suppl. 14), 14–18.

Garfield, D. A., & Havens, L. (1991). Paranoid phenomena and pathological narcissism. *Am. J. Psychother., 45*(2), 160–172.

Garfield, S. L. (1998). Some comments on empirically supported treatments. *J. Consult. Clin. Psychol., 66*(1), 121–125.

Garfinkel, P. E., & Gallop, R. (1992). Eating disorders and borderline personality disorder. In D. Silver & M. Rosenbluth (Eds.), *Handbook of borderline disorders.* Madison, CT: International Universities Press.

Garfinkel, P. E., & Garner, D. M. (1982). *Anorexia nervosa: A multidimensional perspective.* New York: Brunner/Mazel.

Garfinkel, P. E., Lin, E., Goering, P., Spegg, C., Goldbloom, D. S., Kennedy, S., Caplan, A. S., & Woodside, D. B. (1995). Bulimia nervosa in a Canadian community sample: Prevalence in comparison of subgroups. *Am. J. Psychiatry, 152,* 1052–1058.

Garland, A. F., Shaffer, D., & Whittle, B. (1989). A national survey of adolescent suicide prevention programs. *J. Am. Acad. Child Adolesc. Psychiatry, 28,* 931–934.

Garnefski, N., & Diekstra, R. F. W. (1997). Adolescents from one parent, stepparent and intact families: Emotional problems and suicide attempts. *J. Adolesc., 20,* 201–208.

Garner, D. M., & Bemis, K. M. (1982). A cognitive-behavioral approach to anorexia nervosa. *Cognit. Ther. Res., 6*(2), 123–150.

Garner, D. M., & Bemis, K. M. (1985). Cognitive therapy for anorexia nervosa. In D. M. Garner & P. E. Garfinkel (Eds.), *Handbook of psychotherapy for anorexia nervosa and bulimia.* New York: Guilford Press.

Garner, D. M., Cooke, A. K., & Marano, H. E. (1997). The 1997 body image survey results. *Psychol. Today,* pp. 30–44.

Garner, D. M., & Fairburn, C. G. (1988). Relationship between anorexia nervosa and bulimia nervosa: Diagnostic implications. In D. M. Garner & P. E. Garfinkel (Eds.), *Diagnostic issues in anorexia nervosa and bulimia nervosa. Eating disorders monograph series, No. 2.* New York: Brunner/Mazel.

Garner, D. M., Garfinkel, P. E., & O'Shaughnessy, M. (1985). The validity of the distinction between bulimia with and without anorexia nervosa. *Am. J. Psychiatry, 142,* 581–587.

Garner, D. M., Garfinkel, P. E., Schwartz, D., & Thompson, M. (1980). Cultural expectations of thinness in women. *Psychol. Rep., 47,* 483–491.

Garner, D. M., Olmsted, M. P., & Polivy, J. (1984). *The EDI.* Odessa, FL: Psychological Assessment Resources.

Garralda, M. E. (1996). Somatisation in children. *J. Child Psychol. Psychiatry, 37*(1), 13–33.

Garris, P. A., Kilpatrick, M., Bunin, M. A., Michael, D., Walker, Q. D., & Wightman, R. M. (1999). Dissociation of dopamine release in the nucleus accumbens from intracranial self-stimulation. *Nature (London), 398,* 67–69.

Garssen, B., & Goodkin, K. (1999). On the role of immunological factors as mediators between psychosocial factors and cancer progression. *Psychiatr. Res., 85*(1), 51–61.

Garvin, V., Striegel-Moore, R. H., Kaplan, A., Wonderlich, S. A. (2001). The potential of professionally developed self-help interventions for the treatment of eating disorders. In R. H. Striegel-Moore & Smolak (Eds.), *Eating disorders: Innovative directions in research and practice* (pp. 153–172). Washington, DC: American Psychological Association.

Gatchel, R. J., & Baum, A. (1983). *An introduction to health psychology.* New York: Random House.

Gattaz, W. F. (1995). Does vitamin E prevent tardive dyskinesia? *Biol. Psychiatry, 37*(12), 896–897.

Gaub, M., & Carlson, C. L. (1997). Behavioral characteristics of DSM-IV ADHD subtypes in a school-based population. *J. Abnorm. Child Psychol., 25*(2), 103–111.

Gawin, F. H., & Ellinwood, E. H. (1988). Cocaine and other stimulants: Actions, abuse, and treatment. *N. Engl. J. Med., 318,* 1173–1182.

Gay, P. (1999, March 29). Psychoanalyst Sigmund Freud. *Time,* pp. 66–69.

Gaynes, B. N., Magruder, K. M., Burns, B. J., Wagner, H. R., Yarnall, K. S. H., & Broadhead, W. E. (1999). Does a coexisting anxiety disorder predict persistence of depressive illness in primary care patients with major depression? *Gen. Hosp. Psychiatry, 21*(3), 158–167.

Gearty, R. (1999, February 27). Exorcist mom who killed daughter judged insane. *New York Daily News,* p. 40.

Gebhard, P. H. (1965). Situational factors affecting human sexual behavior. In F. Beach (Ed.), *Sex and behavior.* New York: Wiley.

Gebhard, P. H., Gagnon, J. H., Pomeroy, W. B., & Christenson, C. V. (1965). *Sex offenders: An analysis of types.* New York: Harper & Row.

Geisthardt, C., & Munsch, J. (1996). Coping with school stress: A comparison of adolescents with and without learning disabilities. *J. Learn. Disabil., 29*(3), 287–296.

Gelfand, D. M., Jenson, W. R., & Drew, C. J. (1982). *Understanding child behavior disorders.* New York: Holt, Rinehart & Winston.

Geller, J. L. (1992). A historical perspective on the role of state hospitals viewed from the era of the "revolving door." *Am. J. Psychiatry, 149,* 1526–1533.

Gelles, R. J. (1992). Poverty and violence toward children. *Am. Behav. Sci., 35*(3), 258–274.

Gelles, R. J., & Straus, M. A. (1987). Is violence toward children increasing? A comparison of 1975 and 1985 national survey rates. *J. Interpers. Violence, 2,* 212–222.

Gelman, D. (1983, November 7). A great emptiness. *Newsweek,* pp. 120–126.

Gelman, D., & Katel, P. (1993, April 5). The trauma after the storm. *Newsweek.*

General Social Survey, University of Chicago (GSS). (1998, February). Cited in J. Student, *Am. Demogr.*

George, E. L., Friedman, J. C., & Miklowitz, D. J. (2000). Integrated family and individual therapy for bipolar disorder. In S. L. Johnson, A. M. Hayes et al. (Eds.), *Stress, coping, and depression.* Mahwah, NJ: Erlbaum.

George, L. K., Larson, D. B., Koenig, H. G., & McCullough, M. E. (2000). Spirituality and health: What we know, what we need to know. *J. Soc. Clin. Psychol., 19*(1), 102–116.

Gerlach, J., & Hansen, L. (1992). Clozapine and D1/D2 antagonism in extrapyramidal functions. *Br. J. Psychiatry, 160*(Suppl.), 34–37.

Gerlach, J., Lublin, H., & Peacock, L. (1996). Extrapyramidal symptoms during long-term treatment with antipsychotics: Special focus on clozapine and D1 and D2 dopamine antagonists. *Neuropsychopharmacology, 14,* 35S–39S.

Gernsbacher, L. M. (1985). *The suicide syndrome.* New York: Human Sciences Press.

Gershon, E. S. (2000). Bipolar illness and schizophrenia as oligogenic diseases: Implications for the future. *Biol. Psychiatry, 47*(3), 240–244.

Gershon, E. S., & Nurnberger, J. I. (1995). Bipolar illness. In J. M. Oldham & M. B. Riba (Eds.), *American Psychiatric Press review of psychiatry* (Vol. 14). Washington, DC: American Psychiatric Press.

Gershon, E. S., & Rieder, R. O. (1992). Major disorders of mind and brain. *Sci. Am.,* pp. 127–133.

Gershuny, B. S., & Thayer, J. F. (1999). Relations among psychological trauma, dissociative phenomena, and trauma-related distress: A review and integration. *Clin. Psychol. Rev., 19*(5), 631–657.

Ghaemi, S. N., Boiman, E. E., & Goodwin, F. K. (1999). Kindling and second messengers: An approach to the neurobiology of recurrence in bipolar disorder. *Biol. Psychiatry, 45*(2), 137–144.

Gheorghiu, V. A., & Orleanu, P. (1982). Dental implant under hypnosis. *Am. J. Clin. Hypnosis, 25*(1), 68–70.

Gibbs, M. S. (1989). Factors in the victim that mediate between disaster and psychopathology: A review. *J. Traumatic Stress, 2,* 489–514.

Gidron, Y., Davidson, K., & Bata, I. (1999). The short-term effects of a hostility-reduction intervention on male coronary heart disease patients. *Health Psychol., 18*(4), 416–420.

Gilbert, K. (1996). "We've had the same loss, why don't we have the same grief?" Loss and differential grief in families. *Death Stud., 20,* 269–283.

Gilbert, P. L., Harris, M. J., McAdams, L. A., & Jeste, D. V. (1995). Neuroleptic withdrawal in schizophrenic patients: Review of the literature. *Arch. Gen. Psychiatry, 52*(3), 173–188.

Gilbert, S. (1996, May 1). Estrogen patch appears to lift severe depression in new mothers. *New York Times,* p. C12.

Gilbert, S. (1996, July 28). More men may seek eating-disorder help. *New York Times.*

Gill, A. D. (1982). Vulnerability to suicide. In E. L. Bassuk, S. C. Schoonover, & A. D. Gill (Eds.), *Lifelines: Clinical perspectives on suicide.* New York: Plenum Press.

Gillberg, C. (1992). Subgroups in autism: Are there behavioral phenotypes typical of underlying medical conditions? *J. Intell. Disabil. Res., 36*(3), 201–214.

Gillham, J. E., Reivich, K. J., Jaycox, L. H., & Seligman, M. E. (1995). Prevention of depressive symptoms in schoolchildren: Two-year follow-up. *Psychol. Sci., 6*(6), 343–351.

Gillham, J. E., Reivich, K. J., & Shatte, A. J. (2001). Building optimism and preventing depressive symptoms in children. In E. C. Chang (Ed.), *Optimism & pessimism: Implications for theory, research, and practice* (pp. 301–320). Washington, DC: American Psychological Association.

Gilmore, J. H., Jarskog, L. F., & Stroup, T. S. (2001). Medical and surgical illness in patients with schizophrenia. In M. Y. Hwang & P. C. Bermanzohn (Eds.), *Schizophrenia and comorbid conditions: Diagnosis and treatment. Clinical practice.* Washington, DC: American Psychiatric Press.

Ginsberg, B. G. (1984). Beyond behavior modification: Client-centered play therapy with the retarded. *Acad. Psychol. Bull., 6*(3), 321–334.

Girón, M., Manjón-Arce, P., Puerto-Barber, J., Sánchez-García, E., & Gómez-Beneyto, M. (1998). Clinical interview skills and identification of emotional disorders in primary care. *Am. J. Psychiatry, 155*(4), 530–535.

Gist, R., & Woodall, S. J. (1999). There are no simple solutions to complex problems: The rise and fall of critical incident stress debriefing as a response to occupational stress in the fire service. In R. Gist & B. Lubin (Eds.), *Response to disaster.* Philadelphia: Brunner/Mazel.

Given, C. W., Given, B. A., Stommel, M., & Azzouz, F. (1999). The impact of new demands for assistance on caregiver depression: Tests using an inception cohort. *Gerontologist, 39*(1), 76–85.

Gladis, M. M., Wadden, T. A., Vogt, R., Foster, G., Kuehnel, R. H., & Barlett, S. J. (1998). Behavioral treatment of obese binge eaters: Do they need different care? *J. Psychosom. Res., 44*(3/4), 375–384.

Glaser, R., Kiecolt-Glaser, J. K., Bonneau, R. H., Malarkey, W., Kennedy, S., & Hughes, J. (1992). Stress-induced modulation of the immune response to recombinant hepatitis B vaccine. *Psychosom. Med., 54,* 22–29.

Glass, C. R., Arnkoff, D. B., & Rodriquez, B. F. (1998). An overview of directions in psychotherapy integration research. *J. Psychother. Integr., 8*(4), 187–209.

Glass, C. R., & Merluzzi, T. V. (2000). Cognitive and behavioral assessment. In C. E. Watkins, Jr., V. L. Campbell et al. (Eds.), *Testing and assessment in counseling practice* (2nd ed). Mahwah, NJ: Erlbaum.

Glass, R. M. (2001). Electroconvulsive therapy: Time to bring it out of the shadows. *JAMA, J. Am. Med. Assoc., 285*(10).

Glassman, A. H., & Shapiro, P. A. (1998). Depression and the course of coronary artery disease. *Am. J. Psychiatry, 155*(1), 4–11.

Glausiusz, J. (1996, January). The genes of 1995. *Discover,* p. 36.

Glausiusz, J. (1997, January). The genes of 1996. *Discover,* p. 36.

Glazer, S. (1993, February 26). Violence against women: Is the problem more serious than statistics indicate? *CQ Researcher, 3*(8), 169–192.

Gleaves, D. H., Williamson, D. A., & Barker, S. E. (1993). Confirmatory factor analysis of a multidimensional model of bulimia nervosa. *J. Abnorm. Psychol., 102*(1), 173–176.

Gleick, E. (1995, July 10). Sobering times for A. A. *Time,* pp. 49–50.

Glick, I. D. (1999). Family therapies: Efficacy, indications, and treatment outcomes. In D.S. Janowsky et al. (Eds.), *Psychotherapy indications and outcomes.* Washington, DC: American Psychiatric Press.

Globisch, J., Hamm, A. O., Esteves, F., & Oehman, A. (1999). Fear appears fast: Temporal course of startle reflex potentiation in animal fearful subjects. *Psychophysiology, 36*(1), 66–75.

Glogower, F. D., Fremouw, W. J., & McCroskey, J. C. (1978). A component analysis of cognitive restructuring. *Cognit. Ther. Res., 2*(3), 209–223.

Glynn, S. M. (1990). Token economy approaches for psychiatric patients: Progress and pitfalls of chronic psychiatric illness. *Behav. Mod., 14*(4), 383–407.

Glynn, S. M., Eth, S., Randolph, E. T., Foy, D. W. et al. (1995). Behavioral family therapy for Vietnam combat veterans with posttraumatic stress disorder. *J. Psychother. Pract. Res., 4*(3), 214–223.

Goate, A., Chartier, H. M., Mullan, M. et al. (1991). Segregation of a missense mutation in the amyloid precursor protein gene with familial Alzheimer's disease. *Nature (London), 349,* 704–706.

Godding, V., Kruth, M., & Jamart, J. (1997). Joint consultation for high-risk asthmatic children and their families with pediatrician and child psychiatrist as co-therapists: Model and evaluation. *Fam. Process, 36,* 265–280.

Godenzi, A., & De Puy, J. (2001). Overcoming boundaries: A cross-cultural inventory of primary prevention programs against wife abuse and child abuse. *J. Primary Prev., 21*(4), 455–475.

Goetzel, R. Z., Anderson, D. R., Whitmer, R. W., Ozminkowski, R. J., Dunn, R. L., & Wasserman, J. (1998). The relationship between modifiable health risks and health care expenditures. An analysis of the multi-employer HERO health risk and cost database. The Health Enhancement Research Organization (HERO) Research Committee. *J. Occup. Environ. Med., 40*(10), 843–854.

Goin, M. K. (2001). Borderline personality disorder: The importance of establishing a treatment framework. *Psychiatr. Serv., 52*(2), 167–168.

Goisman, R. M., Goldenberg, I., Vasile, R. G., & Keller, M. B. (1995). Comorbidity of anxiety disorders in a multicenter anxiety study. *Compr. Psychiatry, 36*(4), 303–311.

Goisman, R. M., Warshaw, M. G., & Keller, M. B. (1999). Psychosocial treatment prescriptions for generalized anxiety disorder, panic disorder, and social phobia, 1991–1996. *Am. J. Psychiatry, 156*(11), 1819–1821.

Goisman, R. M., Warshaw, M. G., Steketee, G. S., Fierman, E. J. et al. (1995). DSM-IV and the disappearance of agoraphobia without a history of panic disorder: New data on a controversial diagnosis. *Am. J. Psychiatry, 152*(10), 1438–1443.

Gold, E. R. (1986). Long-term effects of sexual victimization in childhood: An attributional approach. *J. Consult. Clin. Psychol., 54*, 471–475.

Gold, J. H. (1998). Gender differences in psychiatric illness and treatments: A critical review. *J. Nerv. Ment. Dis., 186*(12), 769–775.

Goldberg, C. (1999, March 7). Interviewed in M. Jurkowitz, I'm OK; you're OK; Y2K? Does all the worry about deadly computer bugs express our primal fear of entering 2000? *Boston Globe*, p. C1.

Goldberg, D. (1995). Cost effectiveness studies in the evaluation of mental health services in the community: Current knowledge and unsolved problems. XIIth AEP Congress: Improvement of the quality of life in community care in schizophrenia. *Int. Clin. Psychopharmacol., 9*(Suppl. 5), 29–34.

Goldberg, J. F., Harrow, M., & Grossman, L. S. (1995). Recurrent affective syndromes in bipolar and unipolar mood disorders at follow-up. *Br. J. Psychiatry, 166*, 382–385.

Goldbloom, D. S., Hicks, L. K., & Garkinkel, P. E. (1990). Platelet serotonin uptake in bulimia nervosa. *Biol. Psychiatry, 28*(7), 644–647.

Golden, M. (1964). Some effects of combining psychological tests on clinical inferences. *J. Consult. Clin. Psychol., 28*, 440–446.

Golden, R. N., & Gilmore, J. H. (1990). Serotonin and mood disorders. *Psychiatr. Ann., 20*(10), 580–588.

Goldfried, M. R., & Wolfe, B. E. (1996). Psychotherapy practice and research. Repairing a strained alliance. *Am. Psychol., 51*(10), 1007–1016.

Goldfried, M. R., & Wolfe, B. E. (1998). Toward a more clinically valid approach to therapy research. *J. Consult. Clin. Psychol., 66*(1), 143–150.

Goldiamond, I. (1965). Self-control procedures in personal behavior problems. *Psychol. Rep., 17*, 851–868.

Golding, S. L., Skeem, J. L., Roesch, R., & Zapf, P. A. (1999). The assessment of criminal responsibility: Current controversies. In A. K. Hess, I. B. Weiner et al. (Eds.), *The handbook of forensic psychology* (2nd ed.). New York: Wiley.

Goldman, B. D. (1999). The circadian timing system and reproduction in mammals. *Steroids, 64*(9), 679–685.

Goldman, J. G. (1995). A mutual story-telling technique as an aid to integration after abreaction in the treatment of MPD. *Dissoc. Prog. Dissoc. Disord., 8*(1), 53–60.

Goldman, S., & Beardslee, W. R. (1999). Suicide in children and adolescents. In D. G. Jacobs (Ed.), *The Harvard Medical School guide to suicide assessment and intervention*. San Francisco: Jossey-Bass.

Goldney, R. D. (1998). Suicide prevention is possible: A review of recent studies. *Arch. Suicide Res., 4*(4): 329–339.

Goldstein, A. (1994). *Addiction: From biology to drug policy*. New York: Freeman.

Goldstein, G. (1990). Comprehensive neuropsychological assessment batteries. In G. Goldstein & M. Hersen (Eds.), *Handbook of psychological assessment* (2nd ed.). New York: Pergamon Press.

Goldstein, G., & Hersen, M. (1990). Historical perspectives. In G. Goldstein & M. Hersen (Eds.), *Handbook of psychological assessment* (2nd ed.). New York: Pergamon Press.

Goleman, D. (1995, May 2). Biologists find site of working memory. *New York Times*, pp. C1, C9.

Goleman, D. (1995, June 13). Provoking a patient's worst fears to determine the brain's role. *New York Times*, pp. C1, C10.

Goleman, D. (1995, September 6). Depression in the old can be deadly, but the symptoms are often missed. *New York Times*, p. C10.

Goleman, D. (1995, October 4). Eating disorder rates surprise the experts. *New York Times*, p. C11.

Goleman, D. (1996, May 1). Higher suicide risk for perfectionists. *New York Times*, p. C12.

Goleman, D., & Gurin, J. (1993). Mind/body medicine-At last. *Psychol. Today, 26*(2), 16, 80.

Gonzalez, R. G. (1996). Molecular and functional magnetic resonance neuroimaging for the study of dementia. In R. J. Wurtman, S. Corkin, J. H. Growdon, & R. M. Nitsch (Eds.), *The neurobiology of Alzheimer's disease*. New York: New York Academy of Sciences.

Good, M. (1995). A comparison of the effects of jaw relaxation and music on postoperative pain. *Nurs. Res., 44*(1), 52–57.

Good, M., Stanton-Hicks, M., Grass, J. A., Anderson, G. C., Choi, C., Schoolmeesters, L. J., & Salman, A. (1999). Relief of postoperative pain with jaw relaxation, music and their combination. *Pain, 81*(1–2), 163–172.

Goodman, A. (1998). Sexual addiction: Diagnosis and treatment. *Psychiatr. Times, 15*(10).

Goodman, D. (1992). NIMH grantee finds drug responses differ among ethnic groups. *ADAMHA News, 18*(1), p. 5.

Goodman, R. (1990). Technical note: Are perinatal complications causes or consequences of autism? *J. Child Psychol. Psychiatry Allied Discip., 31*(5), 809–812.

Goodman, W. K., McDougle, C., & Price, L. H. (1992). Pharmacotherapy of obsessive compulsive disorder. *J. Clin. Psychiatry, 53*(Suppl. 4), 29–37.

Goodwin, C. J. (1995). *Research in psychology: Methods and design*. New York: Wiley.

Goodwin, D. W. (1976). Adoption studies of alcoholism. *J. Oper. Psychiatry, 7*(1), 54–63.

Goodwin, D. W. (1984). Studies of familial alcoholism: A review. *J. Clin. Psychiatry, 45*(12, Sect. 2), 14–17.

Goodwin, F. K., & Jamison, K. R. (1984). The natural course of manic-depressive illness. In R. M. Post & J. C. Ballenger (Eds.), *Neurobiology of mood disorders*. Baltimore: Williams & Wilkins.

Goodwin, F. K., & Jamison, K. R. (1990). *Manic-depressive illness*. New York: Oxford University Press.

Goodyer, I. M., Herbert, J., Tamplin, A., Secher, S. M., & Pearson, J. (1997). Short-term outcome of major depression: II. Life events, family dysfunction, and friendship difficulties as predictors of persistent disorder. *J. Am. Acad. Child Adolesc. Psychiatry, 36*(4), 474–480.

Gordon, R. A. (1990). *Anorexia and bulimia*. Cambridge, England: Basil Blackwell.

Gordon, R. A. (2000). *Eating disorders: Anatomy of a social epidemic* (2nd ed.). Malden, MA: Blackwell.

Gore, S. M. (1999). Suicide in prisons: Reflection of communities served, or exacerbated risk? *Br. J. Psychiatry, 175*, 50–55.

Gorman, C. (1995, November 13). Trapped in the body of a man? *Time*, pp. 94–95.

Gorman, C. (1998, August 17). E-mail your doctor. *Time*.

Gorman, J. M., & Kent, J. M. (1999). SSRIs and SNRIs: Broad spectrum of efficacy beyond major depression. *J. Clin. Psychiatry, 60*(Suppl. 4), 33–39.

Gorman, J. M., Kent, J. M., Sullivan, G. M., & Coplan, J. D. (2000). Neuroanatomical hypothesis of panic disorder, revised. *Am. J. Psychiatry, 157*(4), 493–505.

Gorman, J. M., Papp, L. A., & Coplan, J. D. (1995). Neuroanatomy and neurotransmitter function in panic disorder. In S. P. Roose & R. A. Glick (Eds.), *Anxiety as symptom and signal*. Hillsdale, NJ: Analytic Press.

Gorwood, P., Bouvard, M., Mouren-Simeoni et al. (1998). Genetics and anorexia nervosa: A review of candidate genes. *Psychiatr. Genet., 8*, 1–12.

Goshen, C. E. (1967). *Documentary history of psychiatry: A source book on historical principles*. New York: Philosophy Library.

Gossop, M., Marsden, J., Stewart, D., & Treacy, S. (2001). Outcomes after methadone maintenance and methadone reduction treatments: Two-year follow-up results from the National Treatment Outcome Research Study. *Drug Alcohol Depend., 62*(3), 255–264.

Gotlib, I. H., & Neubauer, D. L. (2000). Information-processing approaches to the study of cognitive biases in depression. In S. L. Johnson, A. M. Hayes et al. (Eds.), *Stress, coping, and depression*. Mahwah, NJ: Erlbaum.

Gotlib, I. H., & Robinson, L. A. (1982). Responses to depressed individuals: Discrepancies between self-report and observer-related behavior. *J. Abnorm. Behav., 91*(4), 231–240.

Gottesman, I. I. (1991). *Schizophrenia genesis*. New York: Freeman.

Gottlieb, J. (1981). Mainstreaming: Fulfilling the promise? *Am. J. Ment. Defic., 86*(2), 115–126.

Gottlieb, J., Alter, M., & Gottlieb, B. W. (1991). Litigation involving people with mental retardation. In J. L. Matson & J. A. Mulick (Eds.), *Handbook of mental retardation*. New York: Pergamon Press.

Gottschalk, E. C. (1981, April 3). While more firms try jury consultants, debate grows over how much they help. *Wall Street J.*

Gould, M. S., Shaffer, D., & Davies, M. (1990). Truncated pathways from childhood to adulthood: Attrition in follow-up studies due to death. In L. Robins & M. Rutter (Eds.), *Straight and devious pathways from childhood to adulthood*. Cambridge, England: Cambridge University Press.

Gould, R. A., Mueser, K. T., Bolton, E., Mays, V., & Goff, D. (2001). Cognitive therapy for psychosis in schizophrenia: An effect size analysis. *Schizophr. Res., 48*(2–3), 335–342.

Gowers, S. G., North, C. D., & Byram, V. (1996). Life event precipitants of adolescent anorexia nervosa. *J. Child Psychol. Psychiatry, 37*(4), 469–477.

Graham, J., & Gaffan, E. A. (1997). Fear of water in children and adults: Etiology and familial effects. *Behav. Res. Ther., 35*(2), 91–108.

Graham, J. R. (1977). *The MMPI: A practical guide*. New York: Oxford University Press.

Graham, J. R. (1987). *The MMPI: A practical guide* (2nd ed.). New York: Oxford University Press.

Graham, K., Clarke, D., Bois, C., Carver, V. et al. (1996). Addictive behavior of older adults. *Addict. Behav., 21*(3), 331–346.

Gramzow, R., & Tangney, J. P. (1992). Proneness to shame and the narcissistic personality. *Pers. Soc. Psychol. Bull., 18*(3), 369–376.

Grant, B. F., & Dawson, D. A. (1997). Age at onset of alcohol use and its association with DSM-IV alcohol abuse and dependence: Results from the National Longitudinal Alcohol Epidemiologic Survey. *J. Subst. Abuse, 9*, 103–110.

Grant, I., Marcotte, T. D., & Heaton, R. K. (1999). Neurocognitive complications of HIV disease. *Psychol. Sci., 10*(3), 191–195.

Graves, J. S. (1993). Living with mania: a study of outpatient group psychotherapy for bipolar patients. *Am. J. Psychother., 47*(1), 113–126.

Gray, H. (1959). *Anatomy of the human body* (27th ed.). Philadelphia: Lea & Febiger.

Gray, J., Nielsen, D. R., Wood, L. E., Andresen, M., & Dolce, K. (2000). Academic progress of children who attended a preschool for abused children: A follow-up of the Keepsafe Project. *Child Abuse Neglect, 24*(1), 25–32.

Gray, J. A. (1982). *The neuropsychology of anxiety.* New York: Oxford University Press.

Gray, J. A. (1985). Issues in the neuropsychology of anxiety. In A. H. Tuma & J. D. Maser (Eds.), *Anxiety and the anxiety disorders.* Hillside, NJ: Erlbaum.

Gray, J. A. (1995). Neural systems, emotion and personality. In J. Madden, S. Matthysse, & J. Barchas (Eds.), *Adaptation, learning and affect.* New York: Raven Press.

Gray, J. A., & McNaughton, N. (1996). The neuropsychology of anxiety: Reprise. In D. A. Hope (Ed.), *The Nebraska Symposium on Motivation* (Vol. 43). Lincoln: University of Nebraska Press.

Gray-Little, B., & Kaplan, D. (2000). Race and ethnicity in psychotherapy research. In C. R. Snyder & R. E. Ingram (Eds.), *Handbook of psychological change: Psychotherapy processes & practices for the 21st century* (pp. 591–613). New York: Wiley.

Greeley, A. M. (1991). *Faithful attraction.* New York: Tor Books.

Green, R. (2000). Family cooccurrence of "gender dysphoria": Ten siblings or parent-child pairs. *Arch. Sex. Behav., 29*(5), 499–507.

Green, S. A. (1985). *Mind and body: The psychology of physical illness.* Washington, DC: American Psychiatric Press.

Greenberg, D. M. (1998). Sexual recidivism in sex offenders. *Can. J. Psychiatry, 43*(5), 459–465.

Greenberg, I., Chan, S., & Blackburn, G. L. (1999). Nonpharmacologic and pharmacologic management of weight gain. *J. Clin Psychiatry, 60*(Suppl. 21), 31–36.

Greenberg, L., Elliott, R., & Lietaer, G. (1994). Research on experiential psychotherapies. In A. E. Bergin & S. L. Garfield (Eds.), *Handbook of psychotherapy and behavior change.* New York: Wiley.

Greenberg, L. S., Watson, J. C., & Lietaer, G. (Eds.). (1998). *Handbook of experiential psychotherapy.* New York: Guilford Press.

Greenberg, P. E., Sisitsky, T., Kessler, R. C., Finkelstein, S. N., Berndt., E. R., Davidson, J. R., Ballenger, J. C., & Fyer, A. J. (1999). The economic burden of anxiety disorders in the 1990s. *J. Clin. Psychiatry, 60*(7), 427–435.

Greenberg, R. P., & Bornstein, R. F. (1988). The dependent personality: II. Risk for psychological disorders. *J. Pers. Disord., 2*(2), 136–143.

Greene, R. W., Biederman, J., Faraone, S. V., Ouellette, C. et al. (1996). Toward a new psychometric definition of social disability in children with attention-deficit/hyperactivity disorder. *J. Am. Acad. Child Adolesc. Psychiatry, 35*(5), 571–578.

Greenfield, D. (1999, April 1). Virtual addiction survey. Cited in P. Tucker, Are you addicted to the Net? *HealthScout.*

Greenhill, L. L. (1992). Pharmacologic treatment of attention deficit/hyperactivity disorder. *Psychiatr. Clin. North Am., 15*(1), 1–27.

Greer, S. (1999). Mind-body research in psychooncology. *Adv. Mind-Body Med., 15*(4), 236–244.

Grégoire, A. J. P., Kumar, R., Everitt, B., Henderson, A. F., & Studd, J. W. W. (1996, April 6). Transdermal oestrogoen for treatment of severe post-natal depression. *Lancet, 347*, pp. 930–933.

Greist, J. H. (1990). Treatment of obsessive-compulsive disorder: Psychotherapies, drugs, and other somatic treatment. *J. Clin. Psychol., 51*(Suppl. 8), 44–50.

Greist, J. H. (1992). An integrated approach to treatment of obsessive-compulsive disorder. *J. Clin. Psychiatry, 53*(Suppl. 4), 38–41.

Greist, J. H., & Klein, M. H. (1980). Computer programs for patients, clinicians, and researchers in psychiatry. In J. B. Sidowski, J. H. Johnson, & T. A. Williams (Eds.), *Technology in mental health care delivery systems.* Norwood, NJ: Ablex.

Gresham, A. C. (1993). The insanity plea: A futile defense for serial killers. *Law Psychol. Rev., 17,* 193–208.

Griffiths, R., Gross, G., Russell, J., Thornton, C., Beumont, P. J. V., Schotte, D., & Touyz, S. W. (1998). Perceptions of bed rest of anorexic patients. *Int. J. Eat. Disord., 23,* 443–447.

Grigg, J. R. (1988). Imitative suicides in an active duty military population. *Mil. Med., 153*(2), 79–81.

Grigorenko, E. L. (2001). Developmental dyslexia: An update on genes, brains, and environments. *J. Child Psychol. Psychiatry Allied Discip., 42*(1), 91–125.

Grilo, C. M., Becker, D. F., Fehon, D. C., Walker, M. L. et al. (1996). Gender differences in personality disorders in psychiatrically hospitalized adolescents. *Am. J. Psychiatry, 153*(8), 1089–1091.

Grinfield, M. J. (1993, July). Report focuses on jailed mentally ill. *Psychiatr. Times,* pp. 1–3.

Grinfield, M. J. (1997). Mysterious brain disease defies easy solution. *Psychiatr. Times, 14*(11).

Grinfield, M. J. (1998, February). "Patient dumping"—Mentally ill get shortchanged. *Psychiatr. Times, 15*(2).

Grinspoon, L., & Bakalar, J. B. (1986). Can drugs be used to enhance the psychotherapeutic process? *Am. J. Psychother., 40*(3), 393–404.

Grinspoon, L. et al. (Eds.). (1986). Paraphilias. *Harv. Med. Sch. Ment. Health Newsl., 3*(6), 1–5.

Grisso, T., & Appelbaum, P. S. (1995). The MacArthur treatment competence study: III. Abilities of patients to consent to psychiatric and medical treatments. *Law Hum. Behav., 19*(2), 149–174

Grizenko, N., Cvejíc, H., Vida, S., & Sayegh, L. (1991). Behaviour problems of the mentally retarded. *Can. J. Psychiatry, 36*(10), 712–717.

Grob, G. N. (1966). *State and the mentally ill: A history of Worcester State Hospital in Massachusetts, 1830–1920.* Chapel Hill: University of North Carolina Press.

Grossman, J. A., & Kruesi, M. J. P. (2000). Innovative approaches to youth suicide prevention: An update of issues and research findings. In R. W. Maris, S. S. Canetto et al. (Eds.), *Review of suicidology, 2000* (pp. 170–201). New York: Guilford Press.

Grossman, S. P. (1990). Brain mechanisms concerned with food intake and body-weight regulation. In M. M. Fichter (Ed.), *Bulimia nervosa: Basic research, diagnosis and therapy.* Chichester, England: Wiley.

Grotstein, J. C. (1996). Object relations theory. In E. Nersessian, & R. G. Kopff (Eds.), *Textbook of psychoanalysis.* Washington, DC: American Psychiatric Press.

Gruenberg, E. M. (1980). Mental disorders. In J. M. Last (Ed.), *Maxcy-Rosenau public health and preventive medicine* (11th ed.). New York: Appleton-Century-Crofts.

Gruneberg, M. M., & Sykes, R. N. (1993). The generalisability of confidence—accuracy studies in eyewitnessing. *Memory, 1*(3), 185–189.

Guastello, S. J., & Reike, M. L. (1991). A review and critique of honesty test research. *Behav. Sci. Law, 9*(4), 501–523.

Gudjonsson, G. H. (1997). Accusations by adults of childhood sexual abuse: A survey of the members of the British False Memory Society (BFMS). *Appl. Cognit. Psychol., 11,* 3–18.

Guidotti, A., & Costa, E. (1998). Can the antidysphoric and anxiolytic profiles of selective serotonin reuptake inhibitors be related to their ability to increase brain 3alpha, 5alpha-tetrahydroprogesterone (allopregnanolone) availability? *Biol. Psychiatry, 44*(9), 865–873.

Guild, T., & Lowe, G. (1998). Media messages and alcohol education: A school-based study. *Psychol. Rep., 82,* 124–126.

Guillard, P., & Guillard, C. (1987). Suicide and attempted suicide in Martinique. *Psychol. Med., 19*(5), 629–630.

Gunderson, J. G. (1988). Personality disorders. In A. M. Nicholi, Jr. (Ed.), *The new Harvard guide to psychiatry.* Cambridge, MA: Belknap Press.

Gunderson, J. G. (1996). The borderline patient's intolerance of aloneness: Insecure attachments and therapist availability. *Am. J. Psychiatry, 153*(6), 752–758.

Gunderson, J. G. (2001). *Borderline personality disorder: A clinical guide.* Washington, DC: American Psychiatric Publishing.

Gunderson, J. G., & Ronningstam, E. (2001). Differentiating narcissistic and antisocial personality disorders. *J. Pers. Disord., 15*(2), 103–109.

Gupta, M. A., & Johnson, A. M. (2000). Non-weight-related body image concerns among female eating-disordered patients and nonclinical controls: Some preliminary observations. *Int. J. Eat. Disord., 27*(3), 304–309.

Gur, R. E., & Pearlson, G. D. (1993). Neuroimaging in schizophrenia research. *Schizophr. Bull., 19,* 337–353.

Guralnick, M. J. (1998). Effectiveness of early intervention for vulnerable children: A developmental perspective. *Am. J. Ment. Retard., 102*(4), 319–345.

Gurvits, I. G., Koenigsberg, H. W., & Siever, L. J. (2000). Neurotransmitter dysfunction in patients with borderline personality disorder. *Psychiatr. Clin. North Am., 23*(1), 27–40.

Gutheil, T. G. (1999). A confusion of tongues: Competence, insanity, psychiatry, and the law. *Psychiatr. Serv., 50*(6), 767–773.

HEW (Health Education and Welfare). (1976). *Even my kids didn't know I was an alcoholic: An interview with Dick Van Dyke* (ADM 76-348). Washington, DC: U.S. Government Printing Office.

Haaga, D. A. F., & Beck, A. T. (1992). Cognitive therapy. In E. S. Paykel (Ed.), *Handbook of affective disorders.* New York: Guilford Press.

Hackenberg, T. D. (1998). Laboratory methods in human behavioral ecology. In K. A. Lattal, M. Perone et al. (Eds.), *Handbook of research methods in human operant behavior. Applied clinical psychology.* New York: Plenum Press.

Hackman, R. M., Stern, J. S., & Gerschwin, M. E. (2000). Hypnosis and asthma: A critical review. *J. Asthma, 37*(1), 1–15.

Hadley, S. W., & Strupp, H. H. (1976). Contemporary views of negative effects in psychotherapy: An integrated account. *Arch. Gen. Psychiatry, 33*(1), 1291–1302.

Hafner, H., & van der Heiden, W. (1988). The mental health care system in transition: A study in organization, effectiveness, and costs of complementary care for schizophrenic patients. In C. N. Stefanis & A. D. Rabavilis (Eds.), *Schizophrenia: Recent biosocial developments.* New York: Human Sciences Press.

Hage, J. J., & Bouman, F. G. (1992). Silicone genital prosthesis for female-to-male transsexuals. *Plast. Reconstr. Surg., 90*(3), 516–519.

Haight, B. K., Michel, Y., & Hendrix, S. (1998). Life review: Preventing despair in newly relocated nursing home residents: Short- and long-term effects. *Int. J. Aging Hum. Dev., 47*(2), 119–142.

Halaas, J. L., Gajiwala, K. F., Maffei, M., Cohen, S. L. et al. (1995). Weight-reducing effects of the plasma protein encoded by the obese gene. *Science, 269,* 543–546.

Hale, C. A., & Borkowski, J. G. (1991). Attention, memory and cognition. In J. L. Matson & J. A. Mulick (Eds.), *Handbook of mental retardation.* New York: Pergamon Press.

Hale, E. (1983, April 17). Inside the divided mind. *New York Times Magazine,* pp. 100–106.

Hall, C. (1997, March 17). It's not only the string section that's highly strung. *Electronic Telegraph.*

Hall, L., with Cohn, L. (1980). *Eat without fear.* Santa Barbara, CA: Gurze.

Hall, N. W., & Zigler, E. (1997). Drug-abuse prevention efforts for young children: A review and critique of existing programs. *Am. J. Orthopsychiatry, 67*(1), 134–143.

Hall, S. M., Tunstall, C., Rugg, D. et al. (1985). Nicotine gum and behavioral treatment in smoking cessation. *J. Consult. Clin. Psychol., 53,* 256–258.

Hall, W., & Solowij, N. (1997). Long-term cannabis use and mental health. *Br. J. Psychiatry, 171,* 107–108.

Hallam, R. S., & Rachman, S. (1976). Current status of aversion therapy. In M. Hersen, R. Eisler, & P. Miller (Eds.), *Progress in behavior modification* (Vol. 2). New York: Academic Press.

Halmi, K. A. (1985). Behavioral management for anorexia nervosa. In D. M. Garner & P. E. Garfinkel (Eds.), *Handbook of psychotherapy for anorexia nervosa and bulimia.* New York: Guilford Press.

Halmi, K. A. (1985). Classification of the eating disorders. *J. Psychiatr. Res., 19,* 113–119.

Halmi, K. A. (1995). Current concepts and definitions. In G. Szmukler, C. Dare, & J. Treasure (Eds.), *Handbook of eating disorders: Theory, treatment and research.* Chichester, England: Wiley.

Halmi, K. A., Agras, W. S., Kaye, W. H., & Walsh, B. T. (1994). Evaluation of pharmacologic treatments in eating disorders. In R. F. Prien & D. S. Robinson (Eds.), *Clinical evaluation of psychotropic drugs: Principles and guidelines.* New York: Raven Press.

Halmi, K. A., Eckert, E., Marchik, P. A. et al. (1991). Comorbidity of psychiatric diagnoses in anorexia nervosa. *Arch. Gen. Psychiatry, 48,* 712–718.

Halmi, K. A., Sunday, S. R., Puglisi, A. et al. (1989). Hunger and satiety in anorexia and bulimia nervosa. *Ann. N. Y. Acad. Sci., 575,* 431–445.

Halperin, J. M., & McKay, K. E. (1998). Psychological testing for child and adolescent psychiatrists: A review of the past 10 years. *J. Am. Acad. Child Adolesc. Psychiatry, 37*(6), 575–584.

Halstead, W. C. (1947). *Brain and intelligence: A quantitative study of the frontal lobes.* Chicago: University of Chicago.

Hamer, D. H., Hu, S., Magnuson, V. L., Hu, N. et al. (1993). A linkage between DNA markers on the X chromosome and male sexual orienation. *Science, 261,* 321–327.

Hamilton, N. (1991). Intake and diagnosis of drug-dependent women. In *National Conference on Drug Abuse Research and Practice Conference highlights.* Rockville, MD: National Institute on Drug Abuse.

Hamilton, S., Rothbart, M., & Dawes, R. N. (1986). *Sex Roles, 15*(5–6), 269–274.

Hammen, C. (1999). The emergence of an interpersonal approach to depression. In T. Joiner, J. C. Coyne et al. (Eds.), *The interactional nature of depression: Advances in interpersonal approaches.* Washington, DC: American Psychological Association.

Hammen, C., Gitlin, M., & Altshuler, L. (2000). Predictors of work adjustment in bipolar I patients: A naturalistic longitudinal follow-up. *J. Consult. Clin. Psychol., 68*(2), 220–225.

Hammen, C. L., & Glass, D. R. (1975). Expression, activity, and evaluation of reinforcement. *J. Abnorm. Psychol., 84*(6), 718–721.

Hammen, C. L., & Krantz, S. (1976). Effect of success and failure on depressive cognitions. *J. Abnorm. Psychol., 85*(8), 577–588.

Hammond, K. R., & Summers, D. A. (1965). A cognitive dependence on linear and non-linear cues. *Psychol. Rev., 72,* 215–224.

Hancock, L. (2001, May/June). The school shootings: Why context counts. *Columbia J. Rev.,* p. 76.

Hancock, L. N. (1996, March 18). Mother's little helper. *Newsweek,* pp. 51–56.

Handler, L. (1998). Teaching and learning the interpretation of the Wechsler Intelligence Tests as personality instruments. In L. Handler, M. J. Hilsenroth et al. (Eds.), *Teaching and learning personality assessment. The LEA series in personality and clinical psychology.* Mahwah, NJ: Erlbaum.

Handy, B. (1998, May 4). The Viagra craze. *Newsweek,* pp. 56–61.

Hankin, B. L., & Abramson, L. Y. (1999). Development of gender differences in depression: Description and possible explanations. *Ann. Med., 31*(6), 372–379.

Hankin, B. L., Abramson, L. Y., Moffitt, T. E., Silva, P. A., McGee, R., & Angell, K. E. (1998). Development of depression from preadolescence to young adulthood: Emerging gender differences in a 10-year longitudinal study. *J. Abnorm. Psychol., 197*(1), 128–140.

Hankins, G. C., Vera, M. I., Barnard, G. W., & Herkov, M. J. (1994). Patient-therapist sexual involvement: A review of clinical and research data. *Bull. Am. Acad. Psychiatry Law, 22*(1), 109–126.

Hanson, K. M., Louie, C. E., Van Male, L. M., Pugh, A. O., Karl, C., Muhlenbrook, L., Lilly, R. L., & Hagglund, K. J. (1999). Involving the future: The need to consider the views of psychologists-in-training regarding prescription privileges for psychologists. *Prof. Psychol.: Res. Pract., 30*(2), 203–208.

Hantula, D. A., & Reilly, N. A. (1996). Reasonable accommodation for employees with mental disabilities: A mandate for effective supervision? *Behav. Sci. Law, 14,* 107–120.

Happé, F. G. E. (1995). The role of age and verbal ability in the theory of mind task performance of subjects with autism. *Child Dev., 66,* 843–855.

Happé, F. G. E. (1997). Central coherence and theory of mind in autism: Reading homographs in context. *Br. J. Dev. Psychol., 15,* 1–12.

Harding, A., Halliday, G., Caine, D., & Kril, J. (2000). Degeneration of anterior thalamic nuclei differentiates alcoholics with amnesia. *Brain, 123*(1), 141–154.

Harding, C. M., Zubin, J., & Strauss, J. S. (1992). Chronicity in schizophrenia: Revisited. *Br. J. Psychiatry, 161*(Suppl. 18), 27–37.

Hare, R. D. (1980). A research scale for the assessment of psychopathy in criminal populations. *Pers. Individual Differ., 1*(2), 111–119.

Hare, R. D. (1993). *Without conscience: The disturbing world of the psychopaths among us.* New York: Pocket Books.

Hargreaves, R. J., & Shepheard, S. L. (1999). Pathophysiology of migraine—New insights. *Can. J. Neurol. Sci., 26*(Suppl. 3), S12–S19.

Harkavy, J. M., & Asnis, G. (1985). Suicide attempts in adolescence: Prevalence and implications. *N. Engl. J. Med., 313,* 1290–1291.

Harlow, H. F., & Harlow, M. K. (1965). The affectional systems. In A. Schrier, H. Harlow, & F. Stollnitz (Eds.), *Behavior of nonhuman primates* (Vol. 2). New York: Academic Press.

Harrington, R. C., Fudge, H., Rutter, M. L., Bredenkamp, D., Groothues, C., & Pridham, J. (1993). Child and adult depression: A test of continuities with data from a family study. *Br. J. Psychiatry, 162,* 627–633.

Harris, A., Ayers, T., & Leek, M. R. (1985). Auditory span of apprehension deficits in schizophrenia. *J. Nerv. Ment. Dis., 173*(11), 650–657.

Harris, E. C., & Barraclough, B. (1997). Suicide as an outcome for mental disorders. *Br. J. Psychiatry, 170,* 205–228.

Harris, E. C., & Barraclough, B. (1998). Excess mortality of mental disorder. *Br. J. Psychiatry, 173,* 11–53.

Harris, F. C., & Lahey, B. B. (1982). Subject reactivity in direct observation assessment: A review and critical analysis. *Clin. Psychol. Rev., 2,* 523–538.

Harris, G., Rice, M., & Cormier, C. (1991). Length of detention in matched groups of insanity acquittees and convicted offenders. *Int. J. Law Psychiatry, 14,* 223–236.

Harris, L. M., & Menzies, R. G. (1996). Origins of specific fears: A comparison of associative and non-associative accounts. *Anxiety, 2,* 248–250.

Harris, S. (1999, June 22). Schizophrenia drugs often out of reach. *USA Today.*

Harris, S. L. (1995). Autism. In M. Hersen & R. T. Ammerman (Eds.), *Advanced abnormal psychology.* Hillsdale, NJ: Erlbaum.

Harris, S. L. (2000). Pervasive developmental disorders: The spectrum of autism. In M. Hersen, R. T. Ammerman et al. (Eds.), *Advanced abnormal child psychology* (2nd ed.). Mahwah, NJ: Erlbaum.

Harris, S. L., & Milch, R. E. (1981). Training parents as behavior modifiers for their autistic children. *Clin. Psychol. Rev., 1,* 49–63.

Hart, B. (1993). Battered women and the criminal justice system. Special Issue: The impact of arrest on domestic assault. *Am. Behav. Sci., 36*(5), 624–638.

Hart, B. (1993). The legal road to freedom. In M. Hansen & M. Harway (Eds.), *Battering and family therapy: A feminist perspective.* Newbury Park, CA: Sage.

Hart, K., & Kenny, M. E. (1995, August). *Adherence to the superwoman ideal and eating disorder symptoms among college women.* Paper presented at the American Psychological Association, New York.

Hart, S. N., & Brassard, M. R. (1987). A major threat to children's mental health: Psychological maltreatment. *Am. Psychol., 42*(2), 160–165.

Hart, S. N., & Brassard, M. R. (1991). Psychological maltreatment: Progress achieved. *Dev. Psychopathol., 3*(1), 61–70.

Harter, S., & Marold, D. B. (1994). Psychosocial risk factors contributing to adolescent suicidal ideation. In G. G. Naom & S. Borst (Eds.), *Children, youth, and suicide: Developmental perspectives. New directions for child development,* No. 64. San Francisco: Jossey-Bass.

Hartmann, U., & Langer, D. (1993). Combination of psychosexual therapy and intrapenile injections in the treatment of erectile dysfunctions: Rationale and predictors of outcome. *J. Sex Educ. Ther., 19,* 1–12.

Hartung, C. M., & Widiger, T. A. (1998). Gender differences in the diagnosis of mental disorders: Conclusions and controversies of the DSM-IV. *Psychol. Bull., 123*(3), 260–278.

Harvard School of Public Health. (1995). *Binge drinking on American college campuses: A new look at an old problem.* Boston: Author.

Harvey, E. (1999). Short-term and long-term effects of early parental employment on children of the National Longitudinal Survey of Youth. *Dev. Psychol., 35*(2), 445–459.

Harwood, D., Hawton, K., Hope, T., & Jacoby, R. (2001). Psychiatric disorder and personality factors associated with suicide in older people: A descriptive and case-control study. *Int. J. Geriatr. Psychiatry, 16*(2), 155–165.

Hasin, D., Endicott, J., & Lewis, C. (1985). Alcohol and drug abuse in patients with affective syndromes. *Compr. Psychiatry, 26,* 283–295.

Hassan, R. (1998). One hundred years of Emile Durkheim's Suicide: A Study in Sociology. *Aust. N. Z. J. Psychiatry, 32*(2), 168–171.

Hatonen, T., Alila, A., & Laakso, M. L. (1996). Exogenous melatonin fails to counteract the light-induced phase delay of human melatonin rhythm. *Brain Res., 710*(1–2), 125–130.

Hauri, P. J. (2000). The many faces of insomnia. In D. Mostofsky & D. H. Barlow (Eds.), *The management of stress and anxiety in medical disorders* (pp. 143–159). Needham Heights, MA: Allyn & Bacon.

Haworth-Hoeppner, S. (2000). The critical shapes of body image: The role of culture and family in the production of eating disorders. *J. Marriage Fam., 62*(1), 212–227.

Hawton, K. (1986). *Suicide and attempted suicide among children and adolescents.* Beverly Hills, CA: Sage.

Hawton, K. (1998). Why has suicide increased in young males? *Crisis, 19*(3), 119–124.

Hawton, K., Fagg, J., Simkin, S., Bale, E., & Bond, A. (2000). Deliberate self-harm in adolescents in Oxford, 1985–1995. *J. Adolesc., 23*(1), 47–55.

Hay, L. R., Hay, W. R., & Angle, H. V. (1977). The reactivity of self-recording: A case report of a drug abuser. *Behav. Ther., 8*(5), 1004–1007.

Hayden, L. A. (1998). Gender discrimination within the reproductive health care system: Viagra v. birth control. *J. Law Health, 13,* 171–198.

Hayes, L. M., & Rowan, J. R. (1988). *National study of jail suicides: Seven years later.* Alexandria, VA: National Center for Institutions and Alternatives.

Haynes, S. G., Feinleib, M., & Kannel, W. B. (1980). The relationship of psychosocial factors to coronary heart disease in the Framingham study: III. Eight-year incidence of coronary heart disease. *Am. J. Epidemiol., 111,* 37–58.

Haynes, S. N. (2001). Introduction to the special section on clinical applications of analogue behavioral observation. *Psychol. Assess., 13*(1), 3–4.

Haynes, S. N. (2001). Clinical applications of analog behavioral observations: Dimensions of psychometric evaluations. *Psychol. Assess., 13*(1), 73–85.

Haynes, S. N., Nelson, K., & Blaine, D. D. (1999). Psychometric issues in assessment research. In P. C. Kendall, J. N. Butcher et al. (Eds.), *Handbook of research methods in clinical psychology* (2nd ed.). New York: Wiley.

Haynes, S. N., & O'Brien, W. H. (2000). *Principles and practice of behavioral assessment.* New York: Kluwer Academic/Plenum Press.

Haynie, D. L., Nansel, T., Eitel, P., Crump, A. D., Saylor, K., Yu, K., & Simons, M. B. (2001). Bullies, victims, and bully/victims: Distinct groups of at-risk youth. *J. Early Adolesc., 21*(1), 29–49.

Hayward, C., Killen, J. D., Hammer, L. D., Litt, I. F., Wilson, D. M., Simmonds, B., & Taylor, C. B. (1992). Pubertal stage and panic attack history in sixth- and seventh-grade girls. *Am. J. Psychiatry, 149,* 1239–1243.

Hayward, M. D., & Taylor, J. E. (1965). A schizophrenic patient describes the action of intensive psychotherapy. *Psychiatr. Q.,* p. 30.

Haywood, T. W., Kravitz, H. M., Grossman, L. S., Cavanaugh, J. L. et al. (1995). Predicting the "revolving door" phenomenon among patients with schizophrenia, schizoaffective, and affective disorders. *Am. J. Psychiatry, 152*(6), 856–861.

Hazell, P., & Lewin, T. (1993). Friends of adolescent suicide attempters and completers. *J. Am. Acad. Child Adolesc. Psychiatry, 32*(1), 76–81.

He, H., & Richardson, J. S. (1995). A pharmacological, pharmacokinetic and clinical overview of risperidone, a new antipsychotic that blocks serotonin 5-HT2 and dopamine D2 receptors. *Int. Clin. Psychopharmacol., 10*(1), 19–30.

Healy, D., & Williams, J. M. (1988). Dysrhythmia, dysphoria, and depression: The interaction of learned helplessness and circadian dysrhythmia in the pathogenesis of depression. *Psychol. Bull., 103*(2), 163–178.

Heaton, R. K., Baade, L. E., & Johnson, K. L. (1978). Neuropsychological test results associated with psychiatric disorders in adults. *Psychol. Bull., 85,* 141–162.

Heavey, L., Pring, L., & Hermelin, B. (1999). A date to remember: The nature of memory in savant calendrical calculators. *Psychol. Med., 29*(1), 145–160.

Heflinger, C. A., Cook, V. J., & Thackrey, M. (1987). Identification of mental retardation by the System of Multicultural Pluralistic Assessment: Nondiscriminatory or nonexistent? *J. Sch. Psychol., 25*(2), 177–183.

Heilbrun, A. B., & Witt, N. (1990). Distorted body image as a risk factor in anorexia nervosa: Replication and clarification. *Psychol. Rep., 66*(2), 407–416.

Heiman, J. R. (1977). A psychophysiological exploration of sexual-arousal patterns in females and males. *Psychophysiology, 14,* 266–274.

Heiman, J. R. (2000). Organic disorders in women. In S. R. Leiblum & R. C. Rosen (Eds.), *Principles and practice of sex therapy* (3rd ed., pp. 118–153). New York: Guilford Press.

Heiman, J. R., Gladue, B. A., Roberts, C. W., & LoPiccolo, J. (1986). Historical and current factors discriminating sexually functional from sexually dysfunctional married couples. *J. Marital Fam. Ther., 12*(2), 163–174.

Heiman, J. R., & Grafton-Becker, V. (1989). Orgasmic disorders in women. In S. R. Leiblum & R. C. Rosen (Eds.), *Principles and practice of sex therapy: Update for the 1990's.* New York: Guilford Press.

Heiman, J. R., & LoPiccolo, J. (1988). *Becoming orgasmic: A personal and sexual growth program for women.* New York: Prentice Hall.

Heiman, J. R., LoPiccolo, L., & LoPiccolo, J. (1981). Treatment of sexual dysfunction. In A. S. Gurman & D. P. Kniskern (Eds.), *Handbook of family therapy.* New York: Brunner/Mazel.

Heimberg, R. G. (2001). Current status of psychotherapeutic interventions for social phobia. *J. Clin. Psychiatry, 62*(Suppl. 1), 36–42.

Heimberg, R. G., Dodge, C. S., Hope, D. A., Kennedy, C. R. et al. (1990). Cognitive behavioral group treatment for social phobia: Comparison with a credible placebo control. *Cognit. Ther. Res., 14*(1), 1–23.

Heimberg, R. G., Liebowitz, M. R., Hope, D. A., Schneier, F. R., Holt, C. S., Welkowitz, L. A., Juster, H. R., Campeas, R., Bruch, M. A., Cloitre, M., Fallon, B., & Klein, D. F. (1998). Cognitive behavioral group therapy vs. phenelzine therapy for social phobia: 12-week outcome. *Arch. Gen. Psychiatry, 55*(12), 1133–1141.

Heimberg, R. G., Salzman, D. G., Holt, C. S., & Blendall, K. (1991). Cognitive behavioral treatment for social phobia: Effectiveness at five-year follow-up. Manuscript submitted for publication.

Heimberg, R. G., Salzman, D. G., Holt, C. S., & Blendall, K. A. (1993). Cognitive-behavioral group treatment for social phobia: Effectiveness at five-year follow-up. *Cognit. Ther. Res., 17,* 325–339.

Heinrichs, D. W., & Carpenter, W. T., Jr. (1983). The coordination of family therapy with other treatment modalities for schizophrenia. In W. McFarlane (Ed.), *Family therapy in schizophrenia.* New York: Guilford Press.

Heinz, A., Mann, K., Weinberger, D. E., & Goldman, D. (2001). Serotonergic dysfunction, negative mood states, and response to alcohol. *Alcohol.: Clin. Exp. Res., 25*(4), 487–495.

Heise, L., & Chapman, J. R. (1990). Reflections on a movement: The U.S. battle against women abuse. In M. Schuler (Ed.), *Freedom from violence: Women's strategies round the world.* OEF International.

Heller, K. (1996). Coming of age of prevention science: Comments on the 1994 National Institute of Mental Health–Institute of Medicine Prevention Reports. *Am. Psychol., 51*(11), 1123–1127.

Hellerstein, D. J., Rosenthal, R. N., & Miner, C. R. (1995). A prospective study of integrated outpatient treatment for substance-abusing schizophrenic patients. *Am. J. Addict., 4*(1), 33–42.

Hellmich, N. (1995, July 21). Power rangers: Negative or empowering? *USA Today,* p. 4D

Hellström, K., & Öst, L. G. (1996). Prediction of outcome in the treatment of specific phobia. A cross validation study. *Behav. Res. Ther., 34*(5/6), 403–411.

Helms, J. E. (1992). Why is there no study of cultural equivalence in standardized cognitive ability testing? *Am. Psychol., 47*(9), 1083–1101.

Helzer, J. E., Burnam, A., & McEvoy, L. T. (1991). Alcohol abuse and dependence. In L. N. Robins & D. S. Regier (Eds.), *Psychiatric disorders in America: The Epidemiological Catchment Area Study.* New York: Free Press.

Hendin, H. (1995). Assisted suicide, euthanasia, and suicide prevention: The implications of the Dutch experience. *Suicide Life-Threaten. Behav., 25*(1), 193–205.

Hendin, H. (1999). Suicide, assisted suicide, and euthanasia. In D. G. Jacobs (Ed.), *The Harvard Medical School guide to suicide assessment and intervention.* San Francisco: Jossey-Bass.

Hendin, H. (1999). Suicide, assisted suicide, and medical illness. *J. Clin. Psychiatry, 60*(Suppl. 2), 46–50.

Hendren, J. (1999, April 15). Prescription errors blamed on pharmaceutical name game. *Nando Times.*

Henning, C. W., Crabtree, C. R., & Baum, D. (1998). Mental health CPR: Peer contracting as a response to potential suicide in adolescents. *Arch. Suicide Res., 4*(2), 169–187.

Henriksson, M. M., Isometsa, E. T., Hietanen, P. S., Aro, H. M., & Lonnqvist, J. K. (1995). Research report. Mental disorders in cancer suicides. *J. Affect. Disord., 36,* 11–20.

Hepple, J., & Quinton, C. (1997). One hundred cases of attempted suicide in the elderly. *Br. J. Psychiatry, 171,* 42–46.

Herek, G. M., & Capitanio, J. P. (1993). Public reaction to AIDS in the U.S.: A 2nd generation of stigma. *Am. J. Public Health, 83*(4), 574–577.

Herek, G. M., & Capitanio, J. P. (1994). Conspiracies, contagion, and compassion: Trust and public reactions to AIDS. *AIDS Educ. Prev., 6*(4), 365–375.

Herek, G. M., & Capitanio, J. P. (1997). AIDS stigma and contact with persons with AIDS: Effects of direct and vicarious contact. *J. Appl. Soc. Psychol., 27*(1), 1–36.

Herek, G. M., & Capitanio, J. P. (1999). AIDS stigma and sexual prejudice. *Am. Behav. Sci., 42*(7), 1130–1147.

Herman, D., Opler, L., Felix, A., Valencia, E., Wyatt, R. J., & Susser, E. (2000). A critical time intervention with mentally ill homeless men: Impact on psychiatric symptoms. *J. Nerv. Ment. Dis., 188*(3), 135–140.

Hermann, C., Kim, M., & Blanchard, E. B. (1995). Behavioral and prophylactic pharmacological intervention studies of pediatric migraine: An exploratory meta-analysis. *Pain, 60*(3), 239–255.

Hermesh, H., Aizenberg, D., Weizman, A., Lapidot, M., Mayor, C., & Munitz, H. (1992). Risk for definite neuroleptic malignant syndrome: A prospective study in 223 consecutive inpatients. *Br. J. Psychiatry, 161,* 254–257.

Hersen, M., Bellack, A. S., Himmelhoch, J. M., & Thase, M. E. (1984). Effects of social skill training, amitriptyline, and psychotherapy in unipolar depressed women. *Behav. Ther., 15,* 21-40.

Hershman, D. J., & Lieb, J. (1998). *Manic depression and creativity.* Amherst, NY: Prometheus Books.

Hertel, P. (1998). Relation between rumination and impaired memory in dysphoric moods. *J. Abnorm. Psychol., 107*(1), 166-172.

Herz, L. R., Volicer, L., Ross, V., & Rhéaume, Y. (1992). A single-case-study method for treating resistiveness in patients with Alzheimer's disease. *Hosp. Commun. Psychiatry, 43*(7), 720-724.

Herz, M. I., Lamberti, J. S., Mintz, J., Scott, R., O'Dell, S. P., McCartan, L., & Nix, G. (2000). A program for relapse prevention in schizophrenia: A controlled study. *Arch. Gen. Psychiatry, 57*(3), 277-283.

Herz, R. S. (1999). Caffeine effects on mood and memory. *Behav. Res. Ther., 37*(9), 869-879.

Herzog, D. B., Dorer, D. J., Keel, P. K., Selwin, S. E., Ekeblad, E. R., Flores, A. T., Greenwood, D. N., Burwell, R. A., & Keller, M. B. (1999). Recovery and relapse in anorexia and bulimia nervosa: A 7.5-year follow-up study. *J. Am. Acad. Child Adolesc. Psychiatry, 38*(7), 829-837.

Hess, N. (1995). Cancer as a defence against depressive pain. University College Hospital/Middlesex Hospital Psychotherapy Department. *Psychoanal. Psychother., 9*(2), 175-184.

Hester, R. K. (1995). Behavioral self-control training. In R. K. Hester & W. R. Miller (Eds.), *Handbook of alcoholism treatment approaches: Effective alternatives* (2nd ed.). Boston: Allyn & Bacon.

Heston, L. L. (1992). *Mending minds: A guide to the new psychiatry of depression, anxiety, and other serious mental disorders.* New York: Freeman.

Hewitt, P. L., Newton, J., Flett, G. L., & Callander, L. (1997). Perfectionism and suicide ideation in adolescent psychiatric patients. *J. Abnorm. Child Psychol., 25*(2), 95-101.

Hibma, M., & Griffin, J. F. T. (1994). Brief communication: The influence of maternal separation on humoral and cellular immunity in farmed deer. *Brain, Behav. Immun., 8,* 80-85.

Hickie, I., Pols, R. G., Koschera, A., & Davenport, T. (2000). Why are somatoform disorders so poorly recognized and treated? In G. Andrews, S. Henderson et al. (Eds.), *Unmet need in psychiatry: Problems, resources, responses.* New York: Cambridge University Press.

Hiday, V. A. (1992). Coercion in civil commitment: Process, preferences, and outcome. *Int. J. Law Psychiatry, 15*(4), 359-377.

Hiday, V. A. (1999). Mental illness and the criminal justice system. In A. V. Horwitz & T. L. Scheid (Eds.), *A handbook for the study of mental health: Social contexts, theories, and systems.* Cambridge, England: Cambridge University Press.

Higgins, G. A., Large, C. H., Rupniak, H. T., & Barnes, J. C. (1997). Apolipoprotein E and Alzheimer's disease: A review of recent studies. *Pharmacol. Biochem. Behav., 56*(4), 675-685.

Higgins, S. T., Budney, A. J., Bickel, W. K., Hughes, J., Foerg, F., & Badger, G. (1993). Achieving cocaine abstinence with a behavioral approach. *Am. J. Psychiatry, 150*(5), 763-769.

Higuchi, S., Suzuki, K., Yamada, K., Parrish, K., & Kono, H. (1993). Alcoholics with eating disorders: Prevalence and clinical course, A study from Japan. *Br. J. Psychiatry, 162,* 403-406.

Hileman, B. (2001, April 9). The "mad" disease has many forms: Has the U.S. government taken sufficient measures to keep it from infecting humans? *Chem. Eng. News.*

Hilgard, E. R. (1977). Controversies over consciousness and the rise of cognitive psychology. *Aust. Psychol., 12*(1), 7-26.

Hilgard, E. R. (1987). Research advances in hypnosis: Issues and methods. *Int. J. Clin. Exp. Hypnosis, 35,* 248-264.

Hilgard, E. R. (1992). Dissociation and theories of hypnosis. In E. Fromm & M. R. Nash (Eds.), *Contemporary hypnosis research.* New York: Guilford Press.

Hill, A. J., & Franklin, J. A. (1998). Mothers, daughters and dieting: Investigating the transmission of weight control. *Br. J. Clin. Psychol., 37,* 3-13.

Hill, A. J., & Robinson, A. (1991). Dieting concerns have a functional effect on the behaviour of nine-year-old girls. *Br. J. Clin. Psychol., 30*(3), 265-267.

Hill, S. Y., & Muka, D. (1996). Childhood psychopathology in children from families of alcoholic female probands. *J. Am. Acad. Child. Adolesc. Psychiatry, 35*(6), 725-733.

Hiller, W., Rief, W., & Fichter, M. M. (1995). Further evidence for a broader concept of somatization disorder using the Somatic Symptom Index. *Psychosomatics, 36*(3), 285-294.

Hinrichsen, G. A. (1999). Interpersonal psychotherapy for late-life depression In M. Duffy (Ed.), *Handbook of counseling and psychotherapy with older adults.* New York: Wiley.

Hinshaw, S. P. (1991). Stimulant medication and the treatment of aggression in children with attentional deficits. *J. Clin. Child Psychol., 20,* 301-312.

Hiroto, D. S. (1974). Locus of control and learned helplessness. *J. Exp. Psychol., 102*(2), 187-193.

Hirsch, S., Adams, J. K., Frank, L. R., Hudson, W., Keene, K., Krawitz-Keene, G., Richman, D., & Roth, R. (Eds.). (1974). *Madness: Network news reader.* San Francisco: Glide Publications.

Hirsch, S., Bowen, J., Emami, J., Cramer, P., Jolley, A., Haw, C., & Dickinson, M. (1996). A one year prospective study of the effect of life events and medication in the aetiology of schizophrenic relapse. *Br. J. Psychiatry, 168,* 49-56.

Hirsch, S., & Leff, J. (1975). *Abnormalities in parents of schizophrenics.* Oxford, UK: Oxford University Press.

Hirshfeld, D. R., Rosenbaum, J. F., Biederman, J., Bolduc, E. A., Farone, S. V., Snidman, N., Reznick, J. S., & Kagan, J. (1992). Stable behavioral inhibition and its association with anxiety disorder. *J. Am. Acad. Child Adolesc. Psychiatry, 31,* 103-111.

Hirschfeld, R. M. (1992). The clinical course of panic disorder and agoraphobia. In G. D. Burrows, S. M. Roth, & R. Noyes, Jr. (Eds.), *Handbook of anxiety* (Vol. 5). Oxford, UK: Elsevier.

Hirschfeld, R. M. (1999). Efficacy of SSRIs and newer antidepressants in severe depression: Comparison with TCAs. *J. Clin. Psychiatry, 60*(5), 326-335.

Hirschfeld, R. M. (1999). Management of sexual side effects of antidepressant therapy. *J. Clin. Psychiatry, 60*(Suppl. 14), 27-30.

Hirschfeld, R. M. (1999). Personality disorders and depression: Comorbidity. *Depression Anxiety, 10*(4), 142-146.

Hirschfeld, R. M., & Davidson, L. (1988). Clinical risk factors for suicide [Special issue]. *Psychiatr. Ann., 18*(11), 628-635.

Hirschfeld, R. M., & Davidson, L. (1988). Risk factors for suicide. In A. J. Frances & R. E. Hales (Eds.), *American Psychiatric Press review of psychiatry* (Vol. 7). Washington, DC: American Psychiatric Press.

Hirschfeld, R. M., & Russell, J. M. (1997). Assessment and treatment of suicidal patients. *N. Engl. J. Med., 337,* 910-915.

Hlastala, S. A., Frank, E., Mallinger, A. G., Thase, M. E., Ritenour, A. M., & Kupfer, D. J. (1997). Bipolar depression: An underestimated treatment challenge. *Depression Anxiety, 5,* 73-83.

Ho, T. P., Hung, S. F., Lee, C. C., Chung, K. F. et al. (1995). Characteristics of youth suicide in Hong Kong. *Soc. Psychiatry Psychiatr. Epidemiol., 30*(3), 107-112.

Hoagwood, K., Kelleher, K. J., Feil, M., & Comer, D. M. (2000). Treatment services for children with ADHD: A national perspective. *J. Am. Acad. Child Adolesc. Psychiatry, 39*(2), 198-206.

Hobbs, F. B. (1997). *The elderly population. U.S. Census Bureau: The official statistics.* Washington, DC: U.S. Census Bureau.

Hobson, C. J., Kamen, J., Szostek, J., Nethercut, C. M., Tiedmann, J. W., & Wojnarowicz, S. (1998). Stressful life events: A revision and update of the Social Readjustment Rating Scale. *Int. J. Stress Manag., 5*(1), 1-23.

Hobson, J. A., & McCarley, R. W. (1977). The brain as a dream state generator: An activation-synthesis hypothesis of the dream process. *Am. J. Psychiatry, 134*(12), 1335-1348.

Hochhauser, M. (1999). Informed consent and patient's rights documents: A right, a rite, or a rewrite? *Ethics Behav., 9*(1), 1-20.

Hodgins, S., Mednick, S. A., Brennan, P. A., Schulsinger, F., & Engberg, M. (1996). Mental disorder and crime. *Arch. Gen. Psychiatry, 53,* 489-496.

Hodgson, R. J., & Rachman, S. (1972). The effects of contamination and washing in obsessional patients. *Behav. Res. Ther., 10,* 111-117.

Hoebel, B. G., & Teitelbaum, P. (1966). Weight regulation in normal and hypothalamic hyperphagic rats. *J. Comp. Physiol. Psychol., 61*(2), 189-193.

Hogan, R. A. (1968). The implosive technique. *Behav. Res. Ther., 6,* 423-431.

Hogarty, G. E., Greenwald, D., Ulrich, R. F., Kornblith, S. J., DiBarry, A. L., Cooley, S., Carter, M., & Flesher, S. (1997). Three-year trials of personal therapy among schizophrenic patients living with or independent of family: II. Effects on adjustment of patient. *Am. J. Psychiatry, 154*(11), 1514-1524.

Hogarty, G. E. et al. (1974). Drug and sociotherapy in the aftercare of schizophrenic patients: III. Two-year relapse rates. *Arch. Gen. Psychiatry, 31*(5), 609-618.

Hogarty, G. E. et al. (1986). Family psychoeducation, social skills training, and maintenance chemotherapy in the aftercare treatment of schizophrenia: I. One-year effects of a controlled study on relapse and expressed emotion. *Arch. Gen. Psychiatry, 43*(7), 633-642.

Hoge, R. D., Andrews, D. A., & Leschied, A. W. (1996). An investigation of risk and protective factors in a sample of youthful offenders. *J. Child Psychiatry, 37*(4), 419-424.

Hohagen, F., Winkelmann, G., Rasche-Raeuchle, H., Hand, I., Koenig, A., Muenchau, N., Hiss, H., Geiger-Kabisch, C., Kaeppler, C., Schramm, P., Rey, E., Aldenhoff, J., & Berger, M. (1998). Combination of behaviour therapy with fluvoxamine in comparison with behaviour therapy and placebo: Results of a multicentre study. *Br. J. Psychiatry, 173*(Suppl. 35), 71-78.

Hokkanen, L., Launes, J., Vataja, R., Valanne, L. et al. (1995). Isolated retrograde amnesia for autobiographical material associated with acute left temporal lobe encephalitis. *Psychol. Med., 25*(1), 203-213.

Holcomb, H. H., Cascella, N. G., Thaker, G. K., Medoff, D. R., Dannals, R. F., & Tamminga, C. A. (1996). Functional sites of neuroleptic drug action in the human brain: PET/FDG studies with and without Haloperidol. *Am. J. Psychiatry, 153,* 41-49.

Holder, H., Longabaugh, R., Miller, W. et al. (1991). The cost effectiveness of treatment for alcoholism: A first approximation. *J. Stud. Alcohol, 52*, 517–540.

Holinger, P. C., & Offer, D. (1982). Prediction of adolescent suicide: A population model. *Am. J. Psychiatry, 139*, 302–307.

Holinger, P. C., & Offer, D. (1991). Sociodemographic, epidemiologic, and individual attributes. In L. Davidson & M. Linnoila (Eds.), *Risk factors for youth suicide.* New York: Hemisphere.

Holinger, P. C., & Offer, D. (1993). *Adolescent suicide.* New York: Guilford Press.

Holland, J. C. (1996, September). Cancer's psychological challenges. *Sci. Am.*, pp. 158–160.

Holland, R. L., Musch, B. C., & Hindmarch, I. (1999). Specific effects of benzodiazepines and tricyclic antidepressants in panic disorder: Comparisons of clomipramine with alprazolam SR and adinazolam SR. *Hum. Psychopharmacol. Clin. Exp., 14*(2), 119–124.

Hollander, E., & Aronowitz, B. R. (1999). Comorbid social anxiety and body dysmorphic disorder: Managing the complicated patient. *J. Clin. Psychiatry, 60*(Suppl. 9), 27–31.

Hollander, E., Simeon, D., & Gorman, J. M. (1994). Anxiety disorders. In R. E. Hales, S. C. Yudofsky, & J. A. Talbott (Eds.), *The American Psychiatric Press textbook of psychiatry* (2nd ed.). Washington, DC: American Psychiatric Press.

Hollander, M. H. (1988). Hysteria and memory. In H. M. Pettinati (Ed.), *Hypnosis and memory.* New York: Guilford Press.

Hollifield, M., Paine, S., Tuttle, L., & Kellner, R. (1999). Hypochondriasis, somatization, and perceived health and utilization of health care services. *Psychosomatics, 40*(5), 380–386.

Hollifield, M., Tuttle, L., Paine, S., & Kellner, R. (1999). Hypochondriasis and somatization related to personality and attitudes toward self. *Psychosomatics, 40*(5), 387–395.

Hollon, S. D., & Beck, A. T. (1986). Research on cognitive therapies. In S. L. Garfield & A. E. Bergin (Eds.), *Handbook of psychotherapy and behavior change.* New York: Wiley.

Hollon, S. D., & Beck, A. T. (1994). Cognitive and cognitive-behavioral therapies. In A. E. Bergin & S. L. Garfiel (Eds.), *Handbook of psychotherapy and behavior change* (4th ed.). New York: Wiley.

Hollon, S. D., Shelton, R. C., & Davis, D. D. (1993). Cognitive therapy for depression: Conceptual issues and clinical efficacy. *J. Consult. Clin. Psychol., 61*(2), 270–275.

Holmes, R. M., & DeBurger, J. E. (1985). Profiles in terror: The serial murderer. *Fed. Probation, 49*, 29–34.

Holmes, T. H., & Rahe, R. H. (1967). The Social Readjustment Rating Scale. *J. Psychosom. Res., 11*, 213–218.

Holmes, T. H., & Rahe, R. H. (1989). The Social Readjustment Rating Scale. In T. H. Holmes & E. M. David (Eds.), *Life change, life events, and illness: Selected papers.* New York: Praeger.

Holmes, V. F., & Rich, C. L. (1990). Suicide among physicians. In S. J. Blumenthal & D. J. Kupfer (Eds.), *Suicide over the life cycle: Risk factors, assessment, and treatment of suicidal patients.* Washington, DC: American Psychiatric Press.

Holroyd, J. (1996). Hypnosis treatment of clinical pain: Understanding why hypnosis is useful. *Int. J. Clin. Exp. Hypnosis, 54*(1), 33–51.

Holroyd, J. C., & Brodsky, A. M. (1977). Psychologists' attitudes and practices regarding erotic and noneroting physical contact with patients. *Am. Psychol., 32*, 843–849.

Holsboer, F. (2001). Stress, hypercortisolism and corticosteroid receptors in depression: Implications for therapy. *J. Affect. Disord., 62*(1–2), 77–91.

Holstein, J. A. (1993). *Court-ordered insanity: Interpretive practice and involuntary commitment.* New York: de Gruyter.

Holzman, P. S. (1986). Quality of thought disorder in differential diagnosis. *Schizophr. Bull., 12*, 360–372.

Honig, A., Hofman, A., Hilwig, M., Noorthoorn, E., & Ponds, R. (1995). Psychoeducation and expressed emotion in bipolar disorder: Preliminary findings. *Psychiatry Res., 56*(3), 299–301.

Honig, P. (2000). Family work. In B. Lask, R. Bryant-Waugh et al. (Eds.), *Anorexia nervosa and related eating disorders in childhood and adolescence* (2nd ed.). Hove, England: Psychology Press/Taylor & Francis.

Honigfeld, G., Arellano, F., Sethi, J., Bianchini, A., & Schein, J. (1998). Reducing clozapine-related morbidity and mortality: 5 years of experience with the clozaril national registry. *J. Clin. Psychiatry, 59*(Suppl. 3), 3–7.

Honikman, J. I. (1999). Role of self-help techniques for postpartum mood disorders. In L. J. Miller et al. (Eds.), *Postpartum mood disorders.* Washington, DC: American Psychiatric Press.

Hooley, J. M., & Hiller, J. B. (2000). Personality and expressed emotion. *J. Abnorm. Psychol., 109*(1), 40–44.

Hooley, J. M., Orley, J., & Teasdale, J. D. (1986). Levels of expressed emotion and relapse in depressed patients. *Br. J. Psychiatry, 148*, 642–647.

Hooley, J. M., & Teasdale, J. D. (1989). Predictors of relapse in unipolar depressives: Expressed emotions, marital distress, and perceived critcism. *J. Abnorm. Psychol., 98*(3), 229–235.

Hope, D. A., & Heimberg, R. G. (1993). Social phobia and social anxiety. In D. H. Barlow (Ed.), *Clinical handbook of psychological disorders: A step-by-step treatment manual* (2nd ed.). New York: Guilford Press.

Hopkins, J., Marcus, M., & Campbell, S. (1984). Postpartum depression: A critical review. *Psychol. Bull., 95*(3), 498–515.

Hopper, E. (1995). A psychoanalytical theory of 'drug addiction': Unconscious fantasies of homosexuality, compulsions and masturbation within the context of traumatogenic processes. *Int. J. Psychoanal., 76*(6), 1121–1142.

Horesh, N., Apter, A., Lepkifker, E., Ratzoni, G. et al. (1995). Life events and severe anorexia nervosa in adolescence. *Acta Psychiatr. Scand., 91*(1), 5–9.

Horgan, J. (1995, November). Gay genes, revisited. *Sci. Am.*, p. 26.

Horn, M. (1993, November). Memories lost and found. *U.S. News & World Report*, pp. 52–63.

Horner, A. J. (1975). Stages and processes in the development of early object relations and their associated pathologies. *Int. Rev. Psychoanal., 2*, 95–105.

Horner, A. J. (1991). *Psychoanalytic object relations therapy.* Northvale, NJ: Jason Aronson.

Horney, K. (1937). *The neurotic personality of our time.* New York: Norton.

Hornyak, L. M., Green, J. P. et al. (Eds.). (2000). *Healing from within: The use of hypnosis in women's health care. Dissociation, trauma, memory, and hypnosis book series.* Washington, DC: American Psychological Association.

Horowitz, B. (1996, February 20). Portion sizes and fat content "out of control." *USA Today*, pp. 1A–2A.

Horowitz, J., Damato, E., Solon, L., Metzsch, G., & Gill, V. (1995). Postpartum depression: Issues in clinical assessment. *J. Perinatol., 15*(4), 268–278.

Horton, D. (1943). The functions of alcohol in primitive societies: A cross-cultural study. *Q. J. Stud. Alcohol, 4*, 199–320.

Horton, P. C. (1992). A borderline treatment dilemma: To solace or not to solace. In D. Silver & M. Rosenbluth (Eds.), *Handbook of borderline disorders.* Madison, CT: International Universities Press.

Hou, C., Miller, B. L., Cummings, J. L., Goldberg, M., Mychack, P., Bottino, V., & Benson, D. F. (2000). Artistic savants. *Neuropsychiatry, Neuropsychol., Behav. Neurol., 13*(1), 29–38.

Housman, L. M., & Stake, J. E. (1999). The current state of sexual ethics training in clinical psychology: Issues of quantity, quality and effectiveness. *Prof. Psychol.: Res. Pract., 30*(3), 302–311.

Houston, K., Hawton, K., & Sheppard, R. (2001). Suicide in young people aged 15–24: A psychological autopsy study. *J. Affect. Disord., 63*(1–3), 159–170.

Howe, R., & Nugent, T. (1996, April 22). The gory details. *People*, pp. 91–92.

Howells, J. G., & Guirguis, W. R. (1985). *The family and schizophrenia.* New York: International Universities Press.

Howitt, D. (1995). *Paedophiles and sexual offences against children.* Chichester, England: Wiley.

Hsu, L. K. G. (1980). Outcome of anorexia nervosa: A review of literature (1954–1978). *Arch. Gen. Psychiatry, 37*, 1041–1046.

Hsu, L. K. G., Crisp, A. H., & Callender, J. S. (1992). Psychiatric diagnoses in recovered and unrecovered anorectics 22 years after onset of illness: A pilot study. *Compr. Psychiatry, 33*(2), 123–127.

Hsu, L. K. G., Crisp, A. H., & Harding, B. (1979). Outcome of anorexia nervosa. *Lancet, 1*, 61–65.

Hsu, L. K. G., & Holder, D. (1986). Bulimia nervosa: Treatment and short-term outcome. *Psychol. Med., 16*, 65.

Hu, S., Pattatucci, A. M. L., Patterson, C., Li, L. et al. (1995, November). Linkage between sexual orientation and chromosome Xq28 in males but not in females. *Nat. Genet., 11*, 248–256.

Huff, C. O. (1999). Source, recency, and degree of stress in adolescence and suicide ideation. *Adolescence, 34*(133), 81–89.

Hugdahl, K. (1995). *Psychophysiology: The mind-body perspective.* Cambridge, MA: Harvard University Press.

Hughes, J. R., Oliveto, A. H., Bickel, W. K., Higgins, S. T., & Badger, G. J. (1995). The ability of low doses of caffeine to serve as reinforcers in humans: A replication. *Exp. Clin. Psychopharmacol., 3*(4), 358–363.

Hull, J. D. et al. (1995, January 30). Special Report: The State of the Union. *Time*, pp. 53–74.

Hüll, M., Berger, M., Volk, B., & Bauer, J. (1996). Occurrence of interleukin-6 in cortical plaques of Alzheimer's disease patients may precede transformation of diffuse into neuritic plaques. In R. J. Wurtman, S. Corkin, J. H. Growdon, & R. M. Nitsch (Eds.), *The neurobiology of Alzheimer's disease.* New York: New York Academy of Sciences.

Hultman, C. M., Wieselgren, I.-M., & Öhman, A. (1997). Relationships between social support, social coping and life events in the relapse of schizophrenic patients. *Scand. J. Psychol., 38*, 3–13.

Humphrey, D. H., & Dahlstrom, W. G. (1995). The impact of changing from the MMPI to the MMPI-2 on profile configurations. *J. Pers. Assess., 64*(3), 428–439.

Humphreys, K. (1996). Clinical psychologists as psychotherapists. History, future, and alternatives. *Am. Psychol., 51*(3), 190–197.

Humphreys, K., & Rappaport, J. (1993). From the community mental health movement to the war on drugs: A study in the definition of social problems. *Am. Psychol., 48*(8), 892–901.

Humphry, D., & Wickett, A. (1986). *The right to die: Understanding euthanasia.* New York: Harper & Row.

Hunicutt, C. P., & Newman, I.A. (1993). Adolescent dieting practices and nutrition knowledge. Health values. *J. Health Behav., Educ. Promotion, 17*(4), 35-40.

Hunt, C., & Andrews, G. (1995). Comorbidity in the anxiety disorders: The use of a life-chart approach. *J. Psychiatr. Res., 29*(6), 467-480.

Huntington, D. D., & Bender, W. N. (1993). Adolescents with learning disabilities at risk: Emotional well-being, depression, suicide. *J. Learn. Disabil., 26*(3), 159-166.

Hurlbert, D. F. (1991). The role of assertiveness in female sexuality: A comparative study between sexually assertive and sexually nonassertive women. *J. Sex Marital Ther., 17*, 183-190.

Hurlbert, D. F. (1993). A comparative study using orgasm consistency training in the treatment of women reporting hypoactive sexual desire. *J. Sex Marital Ther., 19*, 41-55.

Hurlbert, D. F., & Apt, C. (1995). The coital alignment technique and directed masturbation: A comparative study on female orgasm. *J. Sex Marital Ther., 21*(1), 21-29.

Hurlbert, D. F., White, L. C., Powell, R. D., & Apt, C. (1993). Orgasm consistency training in the treatment of women reporting hypoactive sexual desire: An outcome comparison of women-only groups and couples-only groups. *J. Behav. Ther. Exp. Psychiatry, 24*(1), 3-13.

Hurley, A. D., & Hurley, F. L. (1986). Counseling and psychotherapy with mentally retarded clients: I. The initial interview. *Psychol. Aspects Ment. Retard. Rev., 5*(5), 22-26.

Hurley, J. D., & Meminger, S. R. (1992). A relapse-prevention program: Effects of electromyographic training on high and low levels of state and trait anxiety. *Percept. Mot. Skills, 74*(3, Pt. 1), 699-705.

Hurt, R., Offord, K., Lauger, G., Marusic, Z. et al. (1995). Cessation of long-term nicotine gum use: A prospective, randomized trial. *Addiction, 90*(3), 407-413.

Hurt, S. W., Reznikoff, M., & Clarkin, J. F. (1991). *Psychological assessment, psychiatric diagnosis, and treatment planning.* New York: Brunner/Mazel.

Husaini, B. A. (1997, January). Predictors of depression among the elderly: Racial differences over time. *Am. J. Orthopsychiatry, 67*(1), 48-58.

Hutchinson, R. L., & Little, T. J. (1985). A study of alcohol and drug usage by nine- through thirteen-year-old children in central Indiana. *J. Alcohol Drug Educ., 30*(3), 83-87.

Hwu, H. G., Yeh, E. K., & Chang, L. Y. (1989). Prevalence of psychiatric disorders in Taiwan defined by the Chinese Diagnostic Interview Schedule. *Acta Psychiatr. Scand., 79*, 136-147.

Hyde, A. P., & Goldman, C. R. (1992). Use of a multi-modal family group in the comprehensive treatment and rehabilitation of people with schizophrenia. *Psychosociol. Rehabil. J., 15*(4), 77-86.

Hyde, J. S. (1990). *Understanding human sexuality* (4th ed.). New York: McGraw-Hill.

Hyler, S. E., & Spitzer, R. T. (1978). Hysteria split asunder. *Am. J. Psychiatry, 135*, 1500-1504.

Hyman, S. E. (1999). Looking to the future: The role of genetics and molecular biology in research on mental illness. In S. Weissman, M. Sabshin et al. (Eds.), *Psychiatry in the new millennium.* Washington, DC: American Psychiatric Press.

Iacono, W. G., & Patrick, C. J. (1997). Polygraphy and integrity testing. In R. Rogers et al. (Eds.), *Clinical assessment of malingering and deception* (2nd ed.). New York: Guilford Press.

Iga, M. (1993). Japanese suicide. In A. A. Leenaars (Ed.), *Suicidology.* Northvale, NJ: Jason Aronson.

Iketani, T., Kiriike, N., Nakanishi, S., & Nakasuji, T. (1995). Effects of weight gain and resumption of menses on reduced bone density in patients with anorexia nervosa. *Biol. Psychiatry, 37*(80), 521-527.

Illingworth, P. M. L. (1995). Patient-therapist sex: Criminalization and its discontents. *J. Contemp. Health Law Policy, 11*, 389-416.

Inouye, S. K. (1998). Delirium in hospitalized older patients: Recognition and risk factors. *J. Geriatr. Psychiatry, 11*(3), 118-125.

Inouye, S. K. (1999). Predisposing and precipitating factors for delirium in hospitalized older patients. *Dementia Geriatr. Cognit. Disord., 10*(5), 393-400.

Inouye, S. K., Bogardus, S. T., Jr., Charpentier, P. A., Leo-Summers, L., Acampora, D., Holford, T. R., & Cooney, L. M., Jr. (1999). A multicomponent intervention to prevent delirium in hospitalized older patients. *N. Engl. J. Med., 340*(9), 669-676.

Inouye, J., Flannelly, L., & Flannelly, K. J. (2001). The effectiveness of self-management training for individuals with HIV/AIDS. *JANAC, J. Assoc. Nurses Aids Care, 12*(2), 73-84.

Inouye, S. K., Schlesinger, M. J., & Lydon, T. J. (1999). Delirium: A symptom of how hospital care is failing older persons and a window to improve quality of hospital care. *Am. J. Med., 106*(5), 565-573.

Inskip, H. M., Harris, E. C., & Barraclough, B. (1998). Lifetime risk of suicide for affective disorder, alcoholism and schizophrenia. *Br. J. Psychiatry, 172*, 35-37.

International Narcotics Control Board. (1999, February 23). Annual report. Cited in *Washington Post.*

Ironson G., Friedman, A., Klimas, N., Antoni, M., Fletcher, M. A., LaPerriere, A., Simoneau, J., & Schneiderman, N. (1994). Distress, denial, and low adherence to behavioral interventions predict faster disease progression in gay men infected with human immunodeficiency virus. *Int. J. Behav. Med., 1*, 90-105.

Ironson, G., Taylor, C. B., Boltwood, M. et al. (1992). Effects of anger on left ventricular ejection fraction in coronary artery disease. *Am. J. Cardiol., 70*(3), 281-285.

Isometsae, E. T., & Loennqvist, J. K. (1998). Suicide attempts preceding completed suicide. *Br. J. Psychiatry, 173*, 531-535.

Ito, A., Ichihara, M., Hisanaga, N., Ono, Y. et al. (1992). Prevalence of seasonal mood changes in low latitude area: Seasonal Pattern Assessment Questionnaire score of Quezon City workers. *Jpn. J. Psychiatry, 46*, 249.

Iversen, L. L. (1975). Dopamine receptors in the brain. *Science, 188*, 1084-1089.

Iverson, G. L., & Barton, E. (1999). Interscorer reliability of the MMPI-2: Should TRIN and VRIN be computer scored? *J. Clin. Psychol., 55*(1), 65-69.

Jablensky, A. (1995). Kraepelin's legacy: Paradigm or pitfall for modern psychiatry? [Special issue: Emil Kraepelin and 20th century psychiatry]. *Eur. Arch. Psychiatry Clin. Neurosci., 245*(4-5), 186-188.

Jack, C. R., Jr., Petersen, R. C., Xu, Y. C., O'Brien, P. C., Smith, G. E., Ivnik, R. J., Boeve, B. F., Waring, S. C., Tangalos, E. G., & Kokmen, E. (1999). Prediction of AD with MRI-based hippocampal volume in mild cognitive impairment. *Neurology, 52*(7), 1397-1403.

Jackson, J. L., Calhoun, K. S., Amick, A. A., Madever, H. M., & Habif, V. L. (1990). Young adult women who report childhood intrafamilial sexual abuse: Subsequent adjustment. *Arch. Sex. Behav., 19*(3), 211-221.

Jackson, J. S. (Ed.). (1988). *The black American elderly: Research on physical and psychosocial health.* New York: Springer.

Jacobs, B. L. (Ed.). (1984). *Hallucinogens: Neurochemical, behavioral, and clinical perspectives.* New York: Raven Press.

Jacobs, B. L. (1994). Serotonin, motor activity and depression-related disorders. *Am. Sci., 82*, 456-463.

Jacobs, D. G. (Ed.). (1999). *The Harvard Medical School guide to suicide assessment and intervention.* San Francisco: Jossey-Bass.

Jacobs, D. G., Brewer, M., & Klein-Benheim, M. (1999). Suicide assessment: An overview and recommended protocol. In D. G. Jacobs (Ed.), *The Harvard Medical School guide to suicide assessment and intervention.* San Francisco: Jossey-Bass.

Jacobs, R. (1993). AIDS communication: College students' AIDS knowledge and information sources. *Health Values, J. Health, Behav., Educ., Promotion, 17*(3), 32-41.

Jacobs, S. C. (1999). *Traumatic grief: Diagnosis, treatment, and prevention.* Philadelphia: Brunner/Mazel.

Jacobsen, L. K., Rabinowitz, I., Popper, M. S., Solomon, R. J., Sokol, M. S., & Pfeffer, C. R. (1994). Interviewing prepubertal children about suicidal ideation and behavior. *J. Am. Acad. Child Adolesc. Psychiatry, 33*(4), 439-452.

Jacobson, B., & Thurman-Lacey, S. (1992). Effect of caffeine on motor performance by caffeine-naive and -familiar subjects. *Percept. Mot. Skills, 74*, 151-157.

Jacobson, G. (1999). The inpatient management of suicidality. In D. G. Jacobs (Ed.), *The Harvard Medical School guide to suicide assessment and intervention.* San Francisco: Jossey-Bass.

Jacobson, J. W., & Schwartz, A. A. (1991). Evaluating living situations of people with development disabilities. In J. L. Matson & J. A. Mulick (Eds.), *Handbook of mental retardation.* New York: Pergamon Press.

Jacobson, N. S. (1989). The maintenance of treatment gains following social learning-based marital therapy. *Behav. Ther., 20*(3), 325-336.

Jacobson, N. S., Dobson, K. S., Truax, P. A., Addis, M. E. et al. (1996). A component analysis of cognitive-behavioral treatment for depression. *J. Consult. Clin. Psychol., 64*(2), 295-304.

Jacobson, N. S., & Gortner, E. T. (2000). Can depression be de-medicalized in the 21st century: Scientific revolutions, counter-revolutions and the magnetic field of normal science. *Behav. Res. Ther., 38*(2), 103-117.

Jadad, A. R., Booker, L., Gauld, M., Kakuma, R., Boyle, M., Cunningham, C. E., Kim, M., & Schachar, R. (1999). The treatment of attention-deficit/hyperactivity disorder: An annotated bibliography and critical appraisal of published systematic reviews and metaanalyses. *Can. J. Psychiatry, 44*(10), 1025-1035.

Jaffe, J. H. (1985). Drug addiction and drug abuse. In L. S. Goodman & A. Gilman (Eds.), *The pharmacological basis of therapeutic behavior.* New York: Macmillan.

Jahangir, F., ur-Rehman, H., & Jan., T. (1998). Degree of religiosity and vulnerability to suicidal attempt/plans in depressive patients among Afghan refugees. *Int. J. Psychol. Religion, 8*(4), 265-269.

Jambor, E. (2001). Media involvement and the idea of beauty. In R. McComb & J. Jacalyn (Eds.), *Eating disorders in women and children: Prevention, stress management, and treatment* (pp. 179-183). Boca Raton, FL: CRC Press.

James, W. (1890). *Principles of psychology* (Vol. 1). New York: Holt, Rinehart & Winston.

Jamison, K. R. (1987). Psychotherapeutic issues and suicide prevention in the treatment of bipolar disorders. In R. E. Hales & A. J. Frances (Eds.), *Psychiatric update: American Psychiatric Association annual review* (Vol. 6). Washington, DC: American Psychiatric Press.

Jamison, K. R. (1995, February). Manic-depressive illness and creativity. *Sci. Am.*, pp. 63–67.

Jamison, K. R. (1995). *An unquiet mind.* New York: Vintage Books.

Janowsky, D. S., & Davis, J. M. (1976). Methylphanidate, dextroamphetamine, and levamfetamine: Effects on schizophrenic symptoms. *Arch. Gen. Psychiatry, 33*(3), 304–308.

Janowsky, D. S., El-Yousef, M. K., Davis, J. M., & Sekerke, H. J. (1973). Provocation of schizophrenic symptoms by intravenous administration of methylphenidate. *Arch. Gen. Psychiatry, 28,* 185–191.

Janus, S. S., & Janus, C. L. (1993). *The Janus report on sexual behavior.* New York: Wiley.

Jarrett, R. B., Schaffer, M., McIntire, D., Witt-Browder, A., Kraft, D., & Risser, R. C. (1999). Treatment of atypical depression with cognitive therapy or phenelzine: A double-blind, placebo-controlled trial. *Arch. Gen. Psychiatry, 56*(5), 431–437.

Jefferson, J. W., & Greist, J. H. (1994). Mood disorders. In R. E. Hales, S. C. Yudofsky, & J. A. Talbott (Eds.), *The American Psychiatric Press textbook of psychiatry* (2nd ed.). Washington, DC: American Psychiatric Press.

Jefferson, L. (1948). *These are my sisters.* Tulsa, OK: Vickers.

Jeffries, J. J. (1995). Working with schizophrenia: A clinician's personal experience. *Can. J. Psychiatry, 40*(3, Suppl. 1), S22–S25.

Jellinek, M. S. (1999). Changes in the practice of child and adolescent psychiatry: Are our patients better served? *J. Dev. Behav. Pediatr., 20*(5), 378–380.

Jemmott, J. B. (1987). Social motives and susceptibility to disease: Stalking individual differences in health risks. *J. Pers., 55*(2), 267–298.

Jemmott, J. B., Borysenko, J. Z., Borysenko, M., McClelland, D. C. et al. (1983). Academic stress, power motivation and decrease in secretion rate of salivary immunoglobulin. *Lancet, 12,* 1400–1402.

Jencks, C. (1998). Racial bias in testing. In C. Jencks, M. Phillips et al. (Eds.), *The black-white test score gap.* Washington, DC: Brookings Institution.

Jenike, M. A. (1990). Approaches to the patient with treatment-refractory obsessive-compulsive disorder. *J. Clin. Psychiatry, 51*(Suppl. 2), 15–21.

Jenike, M. A. (1991). Geriatric obsessive-compulsive disorder. *J. Geriatr. Psychiatry Neurol., 4,* 34–39.

Jenike, M. A. (1991). Management of patients with treatment-resistant obsessive-compulsive disorder. In M. T. Pato & J. Zohar (Eds.), *Current treatments of obsessive-compulsive disorder.* Washington, DC: American Psychiatric Press.

Jenike, M. A. (1991). Obsessive-compulsive disorders: A clinical approach. In W. Coryell & G. Winokur (Eds.), *The clinical management of anxiety disorders.* New York: Oxford University Press.

Jenike, M. A. (1992). New developments in treatment of obsessive-compulsive disorder. In A. Tasman & M. B. Riba (Eds.), *Review of psychiatry* (Vol. 11). Washington, DC: American Psychiatric Press.

Jenike, M. A. (Ed.). (1994, October). *J. Geriatr. Psychiatry Neurol.*

Jenike, M. A. (1995). Alzheimer's disease. In *Scientific American Series: Vol. 13. Psychiatry.* New York: Scientific American.

Jenike, M. A., Baer, L., Ballantine, H. T., Martuza, R. L., Tynes, S., Giriunas, I., Buttolph, M. L., & Cassem, N. H. (1991). Cingulotomy for refractory obsessive-compulsive disorder: A long-term follow-up of 33 patients. *Arch. Gen. Psychiatry, 48,* 548–555.

Jenkins, R., Lewis, G., Bibbington, P., Brugha, T. et al. (1997). The National Psychiatric Morbidity Surveys of Great Britain: Initial findings from the household survey. *Psychol. Med., 27*(4), 775–789.

Jenkins, R. L. (1968). The varieties of children's behavioral problems and family dynamics. *Am. J. Psychiatry, 124*(10), 1440–1445.

Jenkins-Hall, K., & Sacco, W. P. (1991). Effect of client race and depression on evaluations by white therapists. *J. Soc. Clin. Psychol., 10*(3), 322–333.

Jensen, G. M. (1998). The experience of injustice: Health consequences of the Japanese American internment. *Diss. Abstr. Int. A; 58*(7-A), 2718.

Jensen, P. S., Hinshaw, S. P., Swanson, J. M., Greenhill, L. L., Conners, C. K., Arnold, L. E., Abikoff, H. B., Elliott, G., Hechtman, L., Hoza, B., March, J. S., Newcorn, J. H., Severe, J. B., Vitiello, B., Wells, K., & Wigal, T. (2001). Findings from the NIMH Multimodal Treatment Study of ADHD (MTA): Implications and applications for primary care providers. *J. Dev. Behav. Pediatr., 22*(1), 60–73.

Jessen, G., Jensen, B. F., Arensman, E., Bille-Brahe, U., Crepet, P., De Leo, D., Hawton, K., Haring, C., Hjelmeland, H., Michel, K., Ostamo, A., Salander-Renberg, E., Schmidtke, A., Temesvary, B., & Wasserman, D. (1999). Attempted suicide and major public holidays in Europe: Findings from the WHO/EURO multicentre study on parasuicide. *Acta Psychiatr. Scand., 99*(6), 412–418.

Jeste, D. V., Eastham, J. H., Lacro, J. P., Gierz, M., Field, M. G., & Harris, M. J. (1996). Management of late-life psychosis. *J. Clin. Psychiatry, 57*(Suppl 3), 39–45.

Ji, J., Klelinman, A., & Becker, A. E. (2001). Suicide in contemporary China: A review of China's distinctive suicide demographics in their sociocultural context. *Harv. Rev. Psychiatry, 9*(1), 1–12.

Joffe, R. T., Singer, W., Levitt, A. J., & MacDonald, C. (1993). A placebo-controlled comparison of lithium and triiodothyronine augmentation of tricyclic antidepressants in unipolar refractory depression. *Arch. Gen. Psychiatry, 50,* 387–393.

Johns, A. (2001). Psychiatric effects of cannabis. *Br. J. Psychiatry, 178,* 116–122.

Johnsen, F. (1994). *The encyclopedia of popular misconceptions.* New York: Citadel Press.

Johnson, B. R., & Becker, J. V. (1997). Natural born killers?: The development of the sexually sadistic serial killer. *J. Am. Acad. Psychiatry Law, 25*(3), 335–348.

Johnson, C. (1995, February 8). National Collegiate Athletic Association study. In *The Hartford Courant.*

Johnson, C., & Wonderlich, S. A. (1992). Personality characteristics as a risk factor in the development of eating disorders. In J. H. Crowther, D. L. Tennenbaum, S. E. Hobfoll, & M. A. P. Stephens (Eds.), *The etiology of bulimia nervosa: The individual and familial context.* Washington, DC: Hemisphere.

Johnson, D. R., Feldman, S., & Lubin, H. (1995). Critical interaction therapy: Couples therapy in combat-related posttraumatic stress disorder. *Fam. Process, 34,* 401–412.

Johnson, D. R., Rosenheck, R., Fontana, A., Lubin, H. et al. (1996). Outcome of intensive inpatient treatment for combat-related posttraumatic stress disorder. *Am. J. Psychiatry, 153,* 771–777.

Johnson, E. H., Gentry, W. D., & Julius, S. (Eds.). (1992). *Personality, elevated blood pressure, and essential hypertension.* Washington, DC: Hemisphere.

Johnson, F. A. (1991). Psychotherapy of the elderly anxious patient. In C. Salzman & B. D. Lebowitz (Eds.), *Anxiety in the elderly.* New York: Springer.

Johnson, J. G., Cohen, P., Brown, J., Smailes, E. M., & Bernstein, D. P. (1999). Childhood maltreatment increases risk for personality disorders

during early adulthood. *Arch. Gen. Psychiatry, 56*(7), 600–606.

Johnson, J. G., Cohen, P., Smailes, E. M., Skodol, A. E., Brown, J., & Oldham, J. M. (2001). Childhood verbal abuse and risk for personality disorders during adolescence and early adulthood. *Compr. Psychiatry, 42*(1), 16–23.

Johnson, K. (1996, December 31). Medical marijuana rejected as "hoax." *USA Today*, p. 4A.

Johnson, M. E., Jones, G., & Brems, C. (1996). Concurrent validity of the MMPI-2 feminine gender role (GF) and masculine gender role (GM) scales. *J. Pers. Assess., 66*(1), 153–168.

Johnson, M. R., & Lydiard, R. B. (1998). Comorbidity of major depression and panic disorder. *J. Clin. Psychol., 54*(2), 201–210.

Johnson, N. R. (1987). Panic at "The Who concert stampede." An empirical assessment. *Soc. Prob., 34,* 362–373.

Johnson, S. K., DeLuca, J., & Natelson, B. H. (1996). Assessing somatization disorder in the chronic fatigue syndrome. *Psychosom. Med., 58,* 50–57.

Johnson, W. D. (1991). Predisposition to emotional distress and psychiatric illness amongst doctors: The role of unconscious and experiential factors. *Br. J. Med. Psychol., 64*(4), 317–329.

Johnson, W. G., Schlundt, D. G., Barclay, D. R., Carr-Nangle, R. E. et al. (1995). A naturalistic functional analysis of binge eating. Special Series: Body dissatisfaction, binge eating, and dieting as interlocking issues in eating disorders research. *Behav. Ther., 26*(1), 101–118.

Johnson-Greene, D., Fatis, M., Sonnek, K., & Shawchuck, C. (1988). A survey of caffeine use and associated side effects in a college population. *J. Drug Educ., 18*(3), 211–219.

Johnston, D. W. (1992). The management of stress in the prevention of coronary heart disease. In S. Maes, H. Leventhal, & M. Johnston (Eds.), *International review of health psychology* (Vol. 1). New York: Wiley.

Johnston, J. (1999, April 9). "Cyber-shrinks" a click away: Traditional therapy too costly for insurers. *HealthScout.*

Johnston, L. D., Bachman, J., & O'Malley, P. (1996). *Monitoring the Future study.* Rockville, MD.: National Institute on Drug Abuse (NIDA).

Johnston, L. D., Bachman, J. G., & O'Malley, P. M. (1998). *Monitoring the Future Study.* Rockville, MD: National Institute on Drug Abuse (NIDA).

Johnston, L. D., O'Malley, P. M., & Bachman, J. G. (1993). *National survey results on drug use from the Monitoring the Future Study, 1975–1992.* Rockville, MD: National Institute on Drug Abuse.

Johnston, L. D., O'Malley, P. M., & Bachman, J. G. (1998). Cited in press release: *Drug use by American young people begins to turn downward.* Ann Arbor: University of Michigan News and Information Services.

Johnston, L. D., O'Malley, P. M., & Bachman, J. G. (1998). Cited in press release: *Smoking among American teens declines some.* Ann Arbor: University of Michigan News and Information Services.

Johnston, L. D., O'Malley, P. M., & Bachman, J. G. (1999). Cited in press release: *Drug trends in 1999 among American teens are mixed.* Ann Arbor: University of Michigan News and Information Services.

Johnston, L. D., O'Malley, P. M., & Bachman, J. G. (1999). Cited in press release: *Cigarette smoking among American teens continues gradual decline.* Ann Arbor: University of Michigan News and Information Services.

Joiner, T. E. (1995). The price of soliciting and receiving negative feedback: Self-verification theory as a vulnerability to depression theory. *J. Abnorm. Psychol., 104*(2), 364–372.

Joiner, T. E., Heatherton, T. F., Rudd, M. D., & Schmidt, N. B. (1997). Perfectionism, perceived weight status, and bulimic symptoms: Two studies testing a diathesis-stress model. *J. Abnorm. Psychol., 106*(1), 145–153.

Joiner, T. E., Metalsky, G. I., & Wonderlich, S. A. (1995). Bulimic symptoms and the development of depressive symptoms: The moderating role of attributional style. *Cognit. Ther. Res., 19*(6), 651–666.

Joiner, T. E., Wonderlich, S. A., Metalsky, G. I., & Schmidt, N. B. (1995). Body dissatisfaction: A feature of bulimia, depression, or both? *J. Soc. Clin. Psychol., 14*(4), 339–355.

Joiner, T. E., Jr. (1999). The clustering and contagion of suicide. *Curr. Dir. Psychol. Sci., 8*(3), 89–92.

Joiner, T. E., Jr. (1999). A test of interpersonal theory of depression in youth psychiatric inpatients. *J. Abnorm. Child Psychol., 27*(1), 77–85.

Joiner, T. E., Jr., Katz, J., & Heatherton, T. F. (2000). Personality features differentiate late adolescent females and males with chronic bulimic symptoms. *Int. J. Eat. Disord., 27*(2), 191–197.

Joiner, T. E., Jr., Vohs, K. D., & Heatherton, T. F. (2000). Three studies on the factorial distinctiveness of binge eating and bulimic symptoms among nonclinical men and women. *Int. J. Eat. Disord., 27*(2), 198–205.

Jones, A., & Schechter, S. (1992). *When love goes wrong.* New York: HarperCollins.

Jones, G. D. (1997). The role of drugs and alcohol in urban minority adolescent suicide attempts. *Death Stud., 21,* 189–202.

Jones, L., Hughes, M., & Unterstaller, U. (2001). Posttraumatic stress disorder (PTSD) in victims of domestic violence: A review of the research. *Trauma Violence Abuse, 2*(2), 99–119.

Jones, M. C. (1968). Personality correlates and antecedants of drinking patterns in males. *J. Consult. Clin. Psychol., 32,* 2–12.

Jones, M. C. (1971). Personality antecedents and correlates of drinking patterns in women. *J. Consult. Clin. Psychol., 36,* 61–69.

Jordan, D. (1993). *1001 facts somebody screwed up.* Atlanta, GA: Longstreet Press.

Jordan, D. (1997). *1001 more facts somebody screwed up.* Atlanta, GA: Longstreet Press.

Jorenby, D. E., Leischow, S. J., Nides, M. A., Rennard, S. I., Johnston, J. A., Hughes, A. R., Smith, S. S., Muramoto, M. L., Daughton, D. M., Doan, K., Fiore, M. C., & Baker, T. B. (1999). A controlled trial of sustained-release bupropion, a nicotine patch, or both for smoking cessation. *N. Engl. J. Med., 340*(9), 685–691.

Jorm, A. F., Korten, A. E., Jacomb, P. A., Rodgers, B., Pollitt, P., Christensen, H., & Henderson, S. (1997). Helpfulness of interventions for mental disorders: Beliefs of health professionals compared with the general public. *Br. J. Psychiatry, 171,* 233–237.

Joyner, C. D., & Swenson, C. C. (1993). Community-level intervention after a disaster. In C. F. Saylor (Ed.), *Children and disasters.* New York: Plenum Press.

Judd, L. L. (1995). Depression as a brain disease. *Depression, 3,* 121–124.

Juel-Nielsen, N., & Videbech, T. (1970). A twin study of suicide. *Acta Genet. Med. Gemellol., 19,* 307–310.

Julien, R. M. (1988). *A primer of drug action* (5th ed.). New York: Freeman.

Julius, S. (1992). Relationship between the sympathetic tone and cardiovascular responsiveness in the course of hypertension. In E. H. Johnson, E. D. Gentry, & S. Julius (Eds.), *Personality, elevated blood pressure, and essential hypertension.* Washington, DC: Hemisphere.

Jung, W., & Irwin, M. (1999). Reduction of natural killer cytotoxic activity in major depression: Interaction between depression and cigarette smoking. *Psychosom. Med., 61*(3), 263–270.

Jurkowitz, M. (1999, March 7). I'm OK; you're OK; Y2K? Does all the worry about deadly computer bugs express our primal fear of entering 2000? *Boston Globe,* p. C1.

Just, N., & Alloy, L. B. (1997). The response styles theory of depression: Tests and an extension of the theory. *J. Abnorm. Psychol., 106*(2), 221–229.

Juster, H. R., Heimberg, R. G., & Holt, C. S. (1996). Social phobia: Diagnostic issues and review of cognitive behavioral treatment strategies. In M. Hersen, R. M. Eisler, & P. M. Miller (Eds.), *Progress in behavior modification* (Vol. 30). Pacific Grove, CA: Brooks/Cole.

Kabat-Zinn, J., Massion, A. O., Kristeller, J., Peterson, L. G. et al. (1992). Effectiveness of a meditation-based stress reduction program in the treatment of anxiety disorders. *Am. J. Psychiatry, 149*(7), 936–943.

Kafka, M. P. (2000). The paraphilia-related disorders: Nonparaphilic hypersexuality and sexual compulsivity/addiction. In S. R. Leiblum & R. C. Raymond (Eds.), *Principles and practice of sex therapy* (3rd ed., pp. 471–503). New York: Guilford Press.

Kagan, J., & Snidman, N. (1991). Infant predictors of inhibited and uninhibited profiles. *Psychol. Sci., 2,* 40–44.

Kagan, J., & Snidman, N. (1999). Early childhood predictors of adult anxiety disorders. *Biol. Psychiatry, 46*(11), 1536–1541.

Kagan, N. I., Kagan, H., & Watson, M. G. (1995). Stress reduction in the workplace: The effectiveness of psychoeducational programs. *J. Counsel. Psychol., 42*(1), 71–78.

Kahn, A. P., & Fawcett, J. (1993). *The encyclopedia of mental health.* New York: Facts on File.

Kaij, L. (1960). *Alcoholism in twins: Studies on the etiology and sequels of abuse of alcohol.* Stockholm: Almquist & Wiksell.

Kail, R. (1992). General slowing of information-processing by persons with mental retardation. *Am. J. Ment. Retard., 97*(3), 333–341.

Kalafat, J., & Elias, M. J. (1995). Suicide prevention in an educational context: Broad and narrow foci [Special issue: Suicide prevention: Toward the year 2000]. *Suicide Life-Threaten. Behav., 25*(1), 123–133.

Kalafat, J., & Ryerson, D. M. (1999). The implementation and institutionalization of a school-based youth suicide prevention program. *J. Primary Prev., 19*(3), 157–175.

Kalayjian, L. A., & Morrell, M. J. (2000). Female sexuality and neurological disease. *J. Sex Educ. Ther., 25*(1), 89–95.

Kalb, C. (2000, January 31). Coping with the darkness: Revolutionary new approaches in providing care for helping people with Alzheimer's stay active and feel productive. *Newsweek,* pp. 52–54.

Kalin, N. H. (1993, May). The neurobiology of fear. *Sci. Am.,* pp. 94–101.

Kalska, H., Punamaeki, R. L., Maekinen-Pelli, T., & Saarinen, M. (1999). Memory and metamemory functioning among depressed patients. *Appl. Neuropsychol., 6*(2), 96–107.

Kaminer, Y. (1991). Adolescent substance abuse. In R. J. Frances & S. I. Miller (Eds.), *Clinical textbook of addictive disorders.* New York: Guilford Press.

Kamphuis, J. H., & Emmelkamp, P. M. G. (2001). Traumatic distress among support-seeking female victims of stalking. *Am. J. Psychiatry, 158*(5), 795–798.

Kanakis, D. M., & Thelen, M. H. (1995, July/August). Parental variables associated with bulimia nervosa. *Addict. Behav., 20,* 491–500.

Kandel, E. R. (1998). A new intellectual framework for psychiatry. *Am. J. Psychiatry, 155*(4), 457–469.

Kane, J. (2001). Progress defined—short-term efficacy, long-term effectiveness. *Int. Clin. Psychopharmacol., 16*(Suppl. 1), S1–S8.

Kane, J. M. (1992). Clinical efficacy of clozapine in treatment-refractory schizophrenia: An overview. *Br. J. Psychiatry, 160*(Suppl. 17), 41–45.

Kanner, B. (1995). *Are you normal?: Do you behave like everyone else?* New York: St. Martin's Press.

Kanner, B. (1998, February). Are you normal? Turning the other cheek. *Am. Demogr.*

Kanner, B. (1998, May). Are you normal? Creatures of habit. *Am. Demogr.*

Kanner, B. (1998, August). Are you normal? Summertime. *Am. Demogr.*

Kanner, B. (1999, January). Hungry, or just bored? *Am. Demogr.*

Kanner, L. (1943). Autistic disturbances of affective contact. *Nerv. Child., 2,* 217.

Kanner, L. (1954). To what extent is early infantile autism determined by constitutional inadequacies? *Proc. Assoc. Res. Nerv. Ment. Dis., 33,* 378–385.

Kaplan, A. (1998, September). Caring for the caregivers: Family interventions and Alzheimer's disease. *Psychiatr. Times, 15*(9).

Kaplan, A. (1999). China's suicide patterns challenge depression theory. *Psychiatr. Times, 16*(1).

Kaplan, A. S., & Garfinkel, P. E. (1999). Difficulties in treating patients with eating disorders: A review of patient and clinician variables. *Can. J. Psychiatry, 44*(7), 665–670.

Kaplan, H. S. (1974). *The new sex therapy: Active treatment of sexual dysfunction.* New York: Brunner/Mazel.

Kaplan, M. D. (1999). Developmental and psychiatric evaluation in the preschool context. *Child Adolesc. Psychiatry Clin. North Am., 8*(2), 379–393.

Kaplan, M. S., Marks, G., & Mertens, S. B. (1997). Distress and coping among women with HIV infection: Preliminary findings from a multiethnic sample. *Am. J. Orthopsychiatry, 67*(1), 80–91.

Kaplan, W. (1984). *The relationship between depression and anti-social behavior among a court-referred adolescent population.* Paper presented to the American Academy of Child Psychiatry, Toronto.

Kapur, S., & Remington, G. (1996). Serotonin-dopamine interaction and its relevance to schizophrenia. *Am. J. Psychiatry, 153*(4), 466–476.

Kardiner, A. (1977). *My analysis with Freud: Reminiscences.* New York: Norton.

Karel, R. (1992, May 1). Hopes of many long-term sufferers dashed as FDA ends medical marijuana program. *Psychiatr. News.*

Karel, R. (1998, December 18). Journals issue mixed verdict on popular alternative therapies. *Psychiatr. News.*

Karlberg, L., Unden, A. L., Elofsson, S., & Krakau, I. (1998). Is there a connection between car accidents, near accidents, and Type A drivers? *Behav. Med., 24*(3), 99–106.

Karon, B. P. (1985). Omission in review of treatment interactions. *Schizophr. Bull., 11*(1), 16–17.

Karon, B. P., & VandenBos, G. R. (1996). *Psychotherapy of schizophrenia: The treatment of choice.* Northvale, NJ: Jason Aronson.

Karon, B. P., & Widener, A. J. (1997). Repressed memories and World War II: Lest we forget. *Prof. Psychol.: Res. Pract., 28*(4), 338–340.

Karp, D.A. (1996). *Speaking of sadness: Depression, disconnection, and the meanings of illness.* New York: Oxford University Press.

Karp, J. F., & Frank, E. (1995). Combination therapy and the depressed woman. *Depression, 3,* 91–98.

Kashani, J. H., Suarez, L., Luchene, L., & Reid, J. C. (1998). Family characteristics and behavior problems of suicidal and non-suicidal children and adolescents. *Child Psychiatry Hum. Dev., 29*(2), 157–168.

Kaslow, N. J., Reviere, S. L., Chance, S. E., Rogers, J. H., Hatcher, C. A., Wasserman, F., Smith, L.,

Jessee, S., James, M. E., & Seelig, B. (1998). An empirical study of the psychodynamics of suicide. *J. Am. Psychoanal. Assoc., 46*(3), 777–796.

Kasper, S., Kauscher, J., Kufferle, B., Barnas, C., Pezawas, L., & Quiner, S. (1999). Dopamine- and serotonin-receptors in schizophrenia: Results of imaging-studies and implications for pharmacotherapy in schizophrenia. *Eur. Arch. Psychiatry Clin. Neurosci., 249*(Suppl. 4), 83–89.

Kassel, J. D., Wagner, E. F., & Unrod, M. (1999). Alcoholism-behavior therapy. In M. Hersen & A. S. Bellack (Eds.), *Handbook of comparative interventions for adult disorders* (2nd ed.). New York: Wiley.

Kate, N. T. (1998, March). How many children? *Am. Demogr.*

Kate, N. T. (1998, April). Two careers, one marriage. *Am. Demogr.*

Kate, N. T. (1998, May). Freshmen get wholesome. *Am. Demogr.*

Katel, P., & Beck, M. (1996, March 29). Sick kid or sick Mom? *Newsweek*, p. 73.

Kato, T., Takahashi, S., Shioiri, T., & Inubushi, T. (1993). Alterations in brain phosphorous metabolism in bipolar disorder detected by in vivo 31 P and 7 Li magnetic resonance spectroscopy. *J. Affect. Disord., 27,* 53–60.

Katon, W. J., & Walker, E. A. (1998). Medically unexplained symptoms in primary care. *J. Clin. Psychiatry, 59*(Suppl. 20), 15–21.

Katona, C. L. E. (1995). Refractory depression: A review with particular reference to the use of lithium augmentation. *Eur. Neuropsychopharmacol., Suppl.,* pp. 109–113.

Katz, E. C., Gruber, K., Chutuape, M. A., & Stitzer, M. L. (2001). Reinforcement-based outpatient treatment for opiate and cocaine abusers. *J. Subst. Abuse Treatm., 20*(1), 93–98.

Katz, I., & Oslin, D. (Eds.). (2000). *Annual review of gerontology and geriatrics: Focus on psychopharmacologic interventions in late life* (Vol. 19). New York: Springer.

Katz, R. J., Lott, M., Landau P., & Waldmeier, P. (1993). A clinical test of noradrenergic involvement in the therapeutic mode of action of an experimental antidepressant. *Biol. Psychiatry, 33,* 261–266.

Katzman, R. (1981, June). Early detection of senile dementia. *Hosp. Practitioner,* pp. 61–76.

Kaufman, M. (1999, June 8). White House decries stigma: "A health issue—no more and no less." *Washington Post,* p. Z07.

Kaufman, M. J., Levin, J. M., Maas, L. C., Rose, S. L., Lukas, S. E., Mendelson, J. H., Cohen, B. M., & Renshaw, P. F. (1998). Cocaine decreases relative cerebral blood volume in humans: A dynamic susceptibility contrast magnetic resonance imaging study. *Psychopharmacology (Berlin), 138*(1), 76–81.

Kaufman, M. J., Siegel, A. J., Mendelson, J. H., Rose, S. L., Kukes, T. J., Sholar, M. B., Lukas, S. E., & Renshaw, P. F. (1998). Cocaine administration induces human splenic constriction and altered hematologic parameters. *J. Appl. Physiol., 85*(5), 1877–1883.

Kawas, C., Resnick, S., Morrison, A., Brookmeyer, R., Corrada, M., Zonderman, A., Bacal, C., Lingle, D. D., & Metter, E. J. (1997). A prospective study of estrogen replacement therapy and the risk of developing Alzheimer's disease: The Baltimore Longtitudinal Study of Aging. *Neurology, 48*(6), 1517–1521.

Kaye, W. H., Gendall, K. A., Fernstrom, M. H., Fernstrom, J. D., McConaha, C. W., & Weltzin, T. E. (2000). Effects of acute tryptophan depletion on mood in bulimia nervosa. *Biol. Psychiatry, 47*(2), 151–157.

Kaye, W. H., Gendall, H., & Strober, M. (1998). Serotonin neuronal function and selective sero-

tonin reuptake inhibitor treatment in anorexia and bulimia nervosa. *Biol. Psychiatry, 44*(9), 825–838.

Kaye, W. H., Greeno, C. G., Moss, H., Fernstrom, J., Fernstrom, M., Lilenfeld, L. R., Weltzin, T. E., & Mann, J. J. (1998). Alterations in serotonin activity and psychiatric symptoms after recovery from bulimia nervosa. *Arch. Gen. Psychiatry, 55*(10), 927–935.

Kazdin, A. E. (1983). Failure of persons to respond to the token economy. In E. B. Foa & P. M. G. Emmelkamp (Eds.), *Failures in behavior therapy.* New York: Wiley.

Kazdin, A. E. (1990). Childhood depression. *J. Child Psychol. Psychiatry Allied Discip., 31,* 121–160.

Kazdin, A. E. (1993). Psychotherapy for children and adolescents: Current progress and future research directions. *Am. Psychol., 48*(6), 644–657.

Kazdin, A. E. (1994). Methodology, design, and evaluation in psychotherapy research. In A. E. Bergin & S. L. Garfiel (Eds.), *Handbook of psychotherapy and behavior change* (4th ed.). New York: Wiley.

Kazdin, A. E. (1994). Psychotherapy for children and adolescents. In A. E. Bergin & S. L. Garfiel (Eds.), *Handbook of psychotherapy and behavior change* (4th ed.). New York: Wiley.

Kazdin, A. E. (1997). Practitioner review: Psychosocial treatments for conduct disorder in children. *J. Child Psychol. Psychiatry, 38*(2), 161–178.

Kazdin, A. E. (2000). Adolescent development, mental disorders, and decision making of delinquent youths. In T. Grisso & R. G. Schwartz (Eds.), *Youth on trial: A developmental perspective on juvenile justice* (pp. 33–65). Chicago: University of Chicago Press.

Kazdin, A. E. (2000). *Psychotherapy for children and adolescents: Directions for research and practice.* New York: Oxford University Press.

Kazdin, A. E., & Wassell, G. (1999). Barriers to treatment participation and therapeutic change among children referred for conduct disorder. *J. Clin. Child Psychol., 28*(2), 160–172.

Kazdin, A. E., & Weisz, J. R. (1998). Identifying and developing empirically supported child and adolescent treatments. *J. Consult. Clin. Psychol., 66*(1), 19–36.

Kazes, M., Danion, J. M., Grange, D., Pradignac, A. et al. (1994). Eating behaviour and depression before and after antidepressant treatment: A prospective, naturalistic study. *J. Affect. Disord., 30,* 193–207.

Kearney, C. A., & Silverman, W. K. (1998). A critical review of pharmacotherapy for youth with anxiety disorders: Things are not as they seem. *J. Anxiety Disord., 12*(2), 83–102.

Kearney-Cooke, A., & Steichen-Asch, P. (1990). Men, body image, and eating disorders. In A. E. Andersen (Ed.), *Males with eating disorders.* New York: Brunner/Mazel.

Kebabian, J. W., Petzold, G. L., & Greengard, P. (1972). Dopamine-sensitive adenylate cyclase in caudate nucleus of rat brain and its similarity to the "dopamine receptor." *Proc. Natl. Acad. Sci. U.S.A., 69,* 2145–2149.

Keel, P. K., Mayer, S. A., & Harnden-Fischer, J. H. (2001). Importance of size in defining binge eating episodes in bulimia nervosa. *Int. J. Eat. Disord., 29*(3), 294–301.

Keel, P. K., & Mitchell, J. E. (1997). Outcome in bulimia nervosa. *Am. J. Psychiatry, 154,* 313–321.

Keel, P. K., Mitchell, J. E., Miller, K. B., Davis, T. L., & Crow, S. J. (1999). Long-term outcome of bulimia nervosa. *Arch. Gen. Psychiatry, 56*(1), 63–69.

Keel, P. K., Mitchell, J. E., Miller, K. B., Davis, T. L., & Crow, S. J. (2000). Predictive validity of bulimia nervosa as a diagnostic category. *Am. J. Psychiatry, 157*(1), 136–138.

Keel, P. K., Mitchell, J. E., Miller, K. B., Davis, T. L., & Crow, S. J. (2000). Social adjustment

over 10 years following diagnosis with bulimia nervosa. *Int. J. Eat. Disord., 27*(1), 21–28.

Keen, E. (1970). *Three faces of being: Toward an existential clinical psychology.* New York: Meredith Corp. (Reprinted by permission of Irvington Publishers.)

Keene, L. C., & Davies, P. H. (1999). Drug-related erectile dysfunction. *Adv. Drug React. Toxicol. Rev., 18*(1), 5–24.

Keesey, R. E., & Corbett, S. W. (1983). Metabolic defense of the body weight set-point. In A. J. Stunkard & E. Stellar (Eds.), *Eating and its disorders.* New York: Raven Press.

Keilman, J. (1999, June 24). E-therapy; affordable counseling is now a click away. *The Times-Picayune,* p. E1.

Keith, S. J., Regier, D. A., & Rae, D. S. (1991). Schizophrenic disorders. In L. N. Robins & D. S. Regier (Eds.), *Psychiatric disorders in America: The Epidemiological Catchment Area Study.* New York: Free Press.

Kelleher, M. J., Chambers, D., Corcoran, P., Williamson, E., & Keeley, H. S. (1998). Religious sanctions and rates of suicide worldwide. *Crisis, 19*(2), 78–86.

Kelleher, M. J., Hynes, F., Kelleher, M. J. A., & Keeley, H. (1998). Suicide as a complication of schizophrenia. *Ir. J. Psychol. Med., 15*(1), 24–25.

Keller, M. B. (1988). Diagnostic issues and clinical course of unipolar illness. In A. J. Frances & R. E. Hales (Eds.), *Review of psychiatry* (Vol. 7). Washington, DC: American Psychiatric Press.

Keller, M. B. (1999, May). *Chronic depression: Psychotherapy and pharmacotherapy: Additive or synergistic?* Paper presented at the annual meeting of the American Psychiatric Association, Washington, DC.

Keller, R., & Shaywitz, B. A. (1986). Amnesia or fugue state: A diagnostic dilemma. *J. Dev. Behav. Pediatr., 7*(8), 131–132.

Kellner, C. (1999, February 2). Interviewed in D. Cauchon, How shock therapy works. *USA Today.*

Kellner, M., & Yehuda, R. (1999). Do panic disorder and posttraumatic stress disorder share a common psychoneuroendocrinology? *Psychoneuroendocrinology, 24*(5), 485–504.

Kelly, K. A. (1993). Multiple personality disorders: Treatment coordination in a partial hospital setting. *Bull. Menninger Clin., 57*(3), 390–398.

Kelly, M. J., Mufson, M. J., & Rogers, M. P. (1999). Medical settings and suicide. In D.G. Jacobs (Ed.), *The Harvard Medical School guide to suicide assessment and intervention.* San Francisco: Jossey-Bass.

Kelly, M. P., Strassberg, D. S., & Kircher, J. R. (1990). Attitudinal and experiental correlates of anorgasmia. *Arch. Sex. Behav., 19,* 165–172.

Kelly, V. A., & Myers, J. E. (1996). Parental alcoholism and coping: A comparison of female children of alcoholics with female children of nonalcoholics. *J. Counsel. Dev., 74*(5), 501–504.

Kelty, M. F., Hoffman, R. R., III, Ory, M. G., & Harden, J. T. (2000). Behavioral and sociocultural aspects of aging, ethnicity, and health. In R. M. Eisler, M. Hersen et al. (Eds.), *Handbook of gender, culture, and health.* Mahwah, NJ: Erlbaum.

Kemeny, M. E., & Laudenslager, M. L. (1999). Beyond stress: The role of individual difference factors in psychoneuroimmunology. *Brain Behav. Immun., 13*(2), 73–75.

Kemp, A., Green, B. L., Hovanitz, C., & Rawlings, E. I. (1995). Incidence and correlates of posttraumatic stress disorder in battered women: Shelter and community samples. *J. Interpers. Violence, 10*(1), 43–55.

Kemp, D. R. (1994). *Mental health in the workplace: An employer's and manager's guide.* Westport, CT: Quorum Books.

Kemper, T. L., & Bauman, M. (1998). Neuropathology of infantile autism. *J. Neuropathol. Exp. Neurol., 57*(7), 645–652.

Kendall, P. C. (1990). Behavioral assessment and methodology. In C. M. Franks, G. T. Wilson, P. C. Kendall, & J. P. Foreyt (Eds.), *Review of behavior therapy: Theory and practice* (Vol. 12). New York: Guilford Press.

Kendall, P. C. (Ed.). (1990). *Child and adolescent therapy: Cognitive-behavioral procedures.* New York: Guilford Press.

Kendall, P. C. (1990). Cognitive processes and procedures in behavior therapy. In C. M. Franks, G. T. Wilson, P. C. Kendall, & J. P. Foreyt (Eds.), *Review of behavior therapy: Theory and practice* (Vol. 12). New York: Guilford Press.

Kendall, P. C. (1998). Empirically supported psychological therapies. *J. Consult. Clin. Psychol., 66*(1), 3–6.

Kendall, P. C. (2000). *Childhood disorders.* Hove, England: Psychology Press/Taylor & Francis.

Kendler, K. S. (1997). The diagnostic validity of melancholic major depression in a population-based sample of female twins. *Arch. Gen. Psychiatry, 54,* 299–304.

Kendler, K. S., & Gardner, C. O., Jr. (1998). Twin studies of adult psychiatric and substance dependence disorders: Are they biased by differences in the environmental experiences of monozygotic and dizygotic twins in childhood and adolescence? *Psychol. Med., 28*(3), 625–633.

Kendler, K. S., Heath, A., & Martin, N. G. (1987). A genetic epidemiologic study of self-report suspiciousness. *Compr. Psychiatry, 28*(3), 187–196.

Kendler, K. S., Heath, A., Neale, M., Kessler, R., & Eaves, L. (1992). A population-based twin study of alcoholism in women. *JAMA, J. Am. Med., Assoc., 268*(14), 1877–1882.

Kendler, K. S., Karkowski, L. M., & Prescott, C. A. (1998). Stressful life events and major depression: Risk period, long-term contextual threat and diagnostic specificity. *J. Nerv. Ment. Dis., 186*(11), 661–669.

Kendler, K. S., Karkowski, L. M., & Prescott, C. A. (1999). Causal relationship between stressful life events and the onset of major depression. *Am. J. Psychiatry, 156*(6), 837–848.

Kendler, K. S., Kessler, R. C., Walters, E. E., MacLean, C., Neale, M. C., Heath, A. C., & Eaves, L. J. (1995). Stressful life events, genetic liability, and onset of an episode of major depression in women. *Am. J. Psychiatry, 152,* 833–842.

Kendler, K. S., McGuire, M., Gruenberg, A. M., O'Hare, A., Spellman, M., & Walsh, D. (1993). The Roscommon Family Study. *Arch. Gen. Psychiatry, 50,* 527–540.

Kendler, K. S., McGuire, M., Gruenberg, A. M., & Walsh, D. (1994). An epidemiological, clinical, and family study of simple schizophrenia in County Roscommon, Ireland. *Am. J. Psychiatry, 151*(1), 27–34.

Kendler, K. S., Myers, J. M., O'Neill, F. A., Martin, R., Murphy, B., MacLean, C. J., Walsh, D., & Straub, R. E. (2000). Clinical features of schizophrenia and linkage to chromosomes 5q, 6p, 8p, and 10p in the Irish study of high-density schizophrenia families. *Am. J. Psychiatry, 157*(3), 402–408.

Kendler, K. S., Neale, M. C., Heath, A. C., Kessler, R. C., & Eaves, L. J. (1994). A twin-family study of alcoholism in women. *Am. J. Psychiatry, 151*(5), 707–715.

Kendler, K. S., Neale, M. C., Kessler, R. C., Heath, A. C., & Eaves, L. J. (1993). Panic disorder in women: A population-based twin study. *Psychol. Med., 23,* 397–406.

Kendler, K. S., Neale, M. C., Kessler, R. C., Heath, A. C. et al. (1992). Generalized anxiety disorder in women: A population-based twin study. *Arch. Gen. Psychiatry, 49*(4), 267–272.

Kendler, K. S., Ochs, A. L., Gorman, A. M., Hewitt, J. K., Ross, D. E., & Mirsky, A. F. (1991). The structure of schizotypy: A pilot multitrait twin study. *Psychiatry Res., 36*(1), 19–36.

Kendler, K. S., Walters., E. E., Neale, M. C., Kessler, R. C. et al. (1995). The structure of the genetic and environmental risk factors for six major psychiatric disorders in women: Phobia, generalized anxiety disorder, panic disorder, bulimia, major depression, and alcoholism. *Arch. Gen. Psychiatry, 52*(5), 374–383.

Kendler, K. S., Walters, E. E., Truett, K. R., Heath, A. C. et al. (1995). A twin-family study of self-report symptoms of panic-phobia and somatization. *Behav. Genet., 25*(6), 499–515.

Kennedy, S. H., Katz, R., Neitzert, C. S., Ralevski, E. et al. (1995). Exposure with response prevention treatment of anorexia nervosa-bulimic subtype and bulimia nervosa. *Behav. Res. Ther., 33*(6), 685–689.

Kent, D. A., Tomasson, K., & Coryell, W. (1995). Course and outcome of conversion and somatization disorders: A four-year follow-up. *Psychosomatics, 36*(2), 138–144.

Kent, G., & Turpin, G. (2000). Attention and information processing: Applications to schizophrenia. In D. Gupta & R.M. Gupta (Eds.), *Psychology for psychiatrists.* London: Whurr Publishers.

Kernberg, O. F. (1976). *Object-relations theory and clinical psychoanalysis.* New York: Jason Aronson.

Kernberg, O. F. (1997). Convergences and divergences in contemporary psychoanalytic technique and psychoanalytic psychotherapy. In J. K. Zeig (Ed.), *The evolution of psychotherapy: The third conference.* New York: Brunner/Mazel.

Kernberg, O. F. (2001). The concept of libido in the light of contemporary psychoanalytic theorizing. In P. Hartocollis (Ed.), *Mankind's oedipal destiny: Libidinal and aggressive aspects of sexuality* (pp. 95–111). Madison, CT: International Universities Press.

Kernberg, P. F. (1989). Narcissistic personality disorder in childhood. *Psychiatr. Clin. North Am., 12*(3), 671–694.

Kessing, L. V., Andersen, P. K., Mortensen, P. B., & Bolwig, T. G. (1998). Recurrence in affective disorder: I. Case register study. *Br. J. Psychiary, 172,* 23–28.

Kessler, R. C., Berglund, P. A., Zhao, S., Leaf, P. J. et al. (1996).The 12-month prevalence and correlates of serious mental illness (SMI). In R. W. Manderscheid & M. A. Sonnenschein (Eds.), *Mental health, United States, 1996* (DHHS Publ. No. SMA 96-3098). Washington, DC: U.S. Department of Health and Human Services.

Kessler, R. C., Crum, R. M., Warner, L. A., Nelson, C. B. et al. (1997). Lifetime co-occurrence of DSM-III-R alcohol abuse and dependence with other psychiatric disorders in the National Comorbidity Survey. *Arch. Gen. Psychiatry, 54,* 313–321.

Kessler, R. C., DuPont, R. L., Berglund, P., & Wittchen, H. U. (1999). Impairment in pure and comorbid generalized anxiety disorder and major depression at 12 months in two national surveys. *Am. J. Psychiatry, 156*(12), 1915–1923.

Kessler, R. C., Keller, M. B., & Wittchen, H. U. (2001). The epidemiology of generalized anxiety disorder. *Psychiatr. Clin. North Am., 24*(1), 19–39.

Kessler, R. C., McGonagle, K. A., Zhao, S., Nelson, C. B., Hughes, M., Eshleman, S., Wittchen, H. U., & Kendler, K. S. (1994). Lifetime and 12-month prevalence of DSM-III-R psychiatric disorders among persons aged 15–54 in the United States: Results from the National Comorbidity Survey. *Arch. Gen. Psychiatry, 51*(1), 8–19.

Kessler, R. C., Olfson, M., & Berglund, P. A. (1998). Patterns and predictors of treatment contact after first onset of psychiatric disorders. *Am. J. Psychiatry, 155*(1), 62–69.

Kessler, R. C., Sonnega, A., Bromet, E., Hughes, M., & Nelson, C. B. (1995). Posttraumatic stress disorder in the National Comorbidity Survey. *Arch. Gen. Psychiatry, 52,* 1048–1060.

Kessler, R. C., Stang, P. E., Wittchen, H.-U., Ustun, T. B., Roy-Burne, P. P., & Walters, E. E. (1998). Lifetime panic-depression comorbidity in the National Comorbidity Survey. *Arch. Gen. Psychiatry, 55,* 801–808.

Kessler, R. C., & Zhao, S. (1999). The prevalence of mental illness. In A. V. Horwitz & T. L. Scheid (Eds.), *A handbook for the study of mental health: Social contexts, theories, and systems.* Cambridge, England: Cambridge University Press.

Kessler, R. C., Greenberg, P. E. et. al. (1999). The economic burden of anxiety disorders in the 1990s. *J. Clin. Psychiatry, 60*(7), 427–435.

Ketter, T. A., George, M. S., Kimbrell, T. A., Benson, B. E., & Post, R. (1996). Functional brain imaging, limbic function, and affective disorders. *Neuroscientist, 2*(1), 55–65.

Kettl, P. (1998). Alaska native suicide: Lessons for elder suicide. *Int. Psychogeriatr., 110*(2), 205–211.

Kety, S. S. (1974). From rationalization to reason. *Am. J. Psychiatry, 131*(9), 957–963.

Kety, S. S. (1988). Schizophrenic illness in the families of schizophrenic adoptees: Findings from the Danish national sample. *Schizophr. Bull., 14*(2), 217–222.

Kety, S. S., Rosenthal, D., Wender, P. H., Schulsinger, F., & Jacobsen, B. (1978). The biologic and adoptive families of adopted individuals who become schizophrenic: Prevalence of mental illness and other characteristics. In L. C. Wynne, R. L. Cromwell, & S. Matthysse (Eds.), *The nature of schizophrenia: New approaches to research and treatment.* New York: Wiley.

Kety, S. S., Rosenthal, D., Wender, P. H. et al. (1968). The types and prevalence of mental illness in the biological and adoptive families of schizophrenics. *J. Psychiatr. Res., 6,* 345–362.

Kety, S. S., Rosenthal, D., Wender, P. H. et al. (1975). Mental illness in the biological and adoptive families of adopted individuals who became schizophrenic: A preliminary report based on psychiatric interviews. In R. R. Fieve, D. Rosenthal, & H. Brill (Eds.), *Genetic research in psychiatry.* Baltimore, MD: Johns Hopkins University Press.

Kewman, D. G., & Tate, D. G. (1998). Suicide in SCI: A psychological autopsy. *Rehabil. Psychol., 43*(2), 143–151.

Keys, A., Brozek, J., Henschel, A., Mickelson, O., & Taylor, H. L. (1950). *The biology of human starvation.* Minneapolis: University of Minnesota Press.

Khanna, R., Das, A., & Damodaran, S. S. (1992). Prospective study of neuroleptic-induced dystonia in mania and schizophrenia. *Am. J. Psychiatry, 149*(4), 511–513.

Khantzian, E. J. (1985). The self-medication hypothesis of addictive disorders: Focus on heroin and cocaine dependence. *Am. J. Psychiatry, 142*(11), 1259–1264.

Kheriaty, E., Kleinknecht, R. A., & Hyman, I. E., Jr. (1999). Recall and validation of phobic origins as a function of a structured interview versus the Phobia Origins Questionnaire. *Behav. Mod., 23*(1), 61–78.

Kiecolt-Glaser, J. K., Dura, J. R., Speicher, C. E., Trask, O. J., & Glaser, R. (1991). Spousal caregivers of dementia victims: Longitudinal changes in immunity and health. *Psychosom. Med., 53,* 345–362.

Kiecolt-Glaser, J. K., Fisher, L., Ogrocki, P., Stout, J. C., Speicher, C. E., & Glaser, R.

(1987). Marital quality, marital disruption, and immune function. *Psychosom. Med., 49,* 13–34.

Kiecolt-Glaser, J. K., Garner, W., Speicher, C., Penn, G. M., Holliday, J., & Glaser, R. (1984). Psychosocial modifiers of immunocompetence in medical students. *Psychosom. Med., 46,* 7–14.

Kiecolt-Glaser, J. K., & Glaser, R. (1988). Methodological issues in behavioral immunology research with humans. *Brain Behav. Immun., 2,* 67–68.

Kiecolt-Glaser, J. K., & Glaser, R. (1988). Psychological influences on immunity: Implications for AIDS. *Am. Psychol., 43*(11), 892–898.

Kiecolt-Glaser, J. K., & Glaser, R. (1999). Psychoneuroimmunology and immunotoxicology: Implications for carcinogenesis. *Psychosom. Med., 61*(3), 271–272.

Kiecolt-Glaser, J. K., Glaser, R., Gravenstein, S., Malarkey, W. B., & Sheridan, J. (1996). Chronic stress alters the immune response to influenza virus vaccine in older adults. *Proc. Natl. Acad. Sci. U.S.A., 93,* 3043–3047.

Kiecolt-Glaser, J. K., Glaser, R., Shuttleworth, E. C., Dyer, C. S., Ogrocki, P., & Speicher, C. E. (1987). Chronic stress and immunity in family caregivers of Alzheimer's disease victims. *Psychosom. Med., 49,* 523–535.

Kiecolt-Glaser, J. K., Kennedy, S., Malkoff, S., Fisher, L., Speicher, C. E., & Glaser, R. (1988). Marital discord and immunity in males. *Psychosom. Med., 50,* 213–229.

Kiecolt-Glaser, J. K., Page, G. G., Marucha, P. T., MacCallum, R. C., & Glaser, R. (1998). Psychological influences on surgical recovery. Perspectives from psychoneuroimmunology. *Am. Psychol., 53*(11), 1209–1218.

Kienhorst, C. W. M., Wolters, W. H. G., Diekstra, R. F. W., & Otte, E. (1987). A study of the frequency of suicidal behaviour in children aged 5 to 14. *J. Child Psychol. Psychiatry Allied Discip., 28*(1), 151–165.

Kienhorst, I. C., de Wilde, E. J., Diekstra, R. F. W., & Wolters, W. H. G. (1995). Adolescents' image of their suicide attempt. *J. Am. Acad. Child Adolesc. Psychiatry, 34*(5), 623–628.

Kiernan, W. (2000). Where we are now: Perspectives on employment of persons with mental retardation. *Focus Autism Other Dev. Disabil., 15*(2), 90–96.

Kiesler, C. A. (1992). U.S. mental health policy: Doomed to fail. *Am. Psychol., 47*(9), 1077–1082.

Kiesler, D. J. (1966). Some myths of psychotherapy research and the search for a paradigm. *Psychol. Bull., 65,* 110–136.

Kiesler, D. J. (1995). Research classic: "Some myths of psychotherapy research and the search for a paradigm": Revisited. *Psychother. Res., 5*(2), 91–101.

Kiev, A. (1989). Suicide in adults. In J. G. Howells (Ed.), *Modern perspectives in the psychiatry of the affective disorders.* New York: Brunner/Mazel.

Kihlstrom, J. F. (1994). *The social construction of memory.* Paper presented at the American Psychological Society convention.

Kihlström, J. F., Tataryn, D. J., & Hoyt, I. P. (1993). Dissociative disorders. In P. B. Sucker & H. E. Adams (Eds.), *Comprehensive handbook of psychopathology* (2nd ed.), New York: Plenum Press.

Killen, J. D. (1996). Development and evaluation of a school-based eating disorder symptoms prevention program. In L. Smolak, M. P. Levine, & R. Striegel-Moore (Eds.), *The developmental psychopathology of eating disorders: Implications for research, prevention, and treatment.* Mahwah, NJ: Erlbaum.

Killen, J. D., Taylor, C. B., Hayward, C., Wilson, D. M., Hammer, L. D., Robinson, T. N., Litt, I., Simmonds, B. A., Varady, A., & Kraemer, M. (1994). The pursuit of thinness and onset of eating disorder symptoms in a community sample of ado-

lescent girls: A three-year prospective analysis. *Int. J. Eat. Disord., 16,* 227–238.

Kilmann, P. R., Sabalis, R. F., Gearing, M. L., Bukstel, L. H., & Scovern, A. W. (1982). The treatment of sexual paraphilias: A review of outcome research. *J. Sex Res., 18,* 193–252.

Kilmann, P. R., Wagner, M. K., & Sotile, W. M. (1977). The differential impact of self-monitoring on smoking behavior: An exploratory study. *J. Clin. Psychol., 33*(3), 912–914.

Kim, J. J., Mohamed, S., Andreasen, N. C., O'Leary, D. S., Watkins, G. L., Ponto, L. L. B., & Hichwa, R. D. (2000). Regional neural dysfunctions in chronic schizophrenia studied with positron emission tomography. *Am. J. Psychiatry, 157*(4), 542–548.

Kimball, A. (1993). Nipping and tucking. In Skin deep: Our national obsession with looks. *Psychol. Today, 26*(3), 96.

King, N. (2001). Young adult women: Reflections on recurring themes and a discussion of the treatment process and setting. In B. Kinoy (Ed.), *Eating disorders: New directions in treatment and recovery* (2nd ed., pp. 148–158). New York: Columbia University Press.

Kimzey, S. L. (1975). The effects of extended spaceflight on hematologic and immunologic systems. *J. Am. Med. Women's Assoc., 30*(5), 218–232.

Kimzey, S. L., Johnson, P. C., Ritzman, S. E., & Mengel, C. E. (1976, April). Hematology and immunology studies: The second manned Skylab mission. *Aviat., Space, Environ. Med.,* pp. 383–390.

Kinard, E. M. (1982). Child abuse and depression: Cause or consequence? *Child Welfare, 61,* 403–413.

Kinderman, P., & Bentall, R. P. (1997). Causal attributions in paranoia and depression: Internal, personal, and situational attributions for negative events. *J. Abnorm. Psychol., 106*(2), 341–345.

King, C. A., & Young, R. D. (1981). Peer popularity and peer communication patterns: Hyperactive vs. active but normal boys. *J. Abnorm. Child Psychol., 9*(4), 465–482.

King, D. W., King, L. A., Foy, D. W., & Gudanowski, D. M. (1996). Prewar factors in combat related posttraumatic stress disorder: Structural equation modeling with a national sample of female and male Vietnam veterans. *J. Consult. Clin. Psychol., 64,* 520–531.

King, D. W., King, L. A., Foy, D. W., Keane, T. M., & Fairbank, J. A. (1999). Posttraumatic stress disorder in a national sample of female and male Vietnam veterans: Risk factors, war-zone stressors, and resilience-recovery variables. *J. Abnorm. Psychol., 108*(1), 164–170.

King, G. A., Polivy, J., & Herman, C. P. (1991). Cognitive aspects of dietary restraint: Effects on person memory. *Int. J. Eat. Disord., 10*(3), 313–321.

King, L. W., Liberman, R. P., & Roberts, J. (1974). *An evaluation of personal effectiveness training (assertive training): A behavior group therapy.* Paper presented at the 31st annual conference of American Group Psychotherapy Association, New York.

King, M., & Bartlett, A. (1999). British psychiatry and homosexuality. *Br. J. Psychiatry, 175,* 106–113.

King, M. B., & Mezey, G. (1987). Eating behaviour of male racing jockeys. *Psychol. Med., 17,* 249–253.

King, M. K., Schmaling, K. B., Cowley, D. S., & Dunner, D. L. (1995). Suicide attempt history in depressed patients with and without a history of panic attacks. *Compr. Psychiatry, 36*(1), 25–30.

King, M. P., & Tucker, J. A. (2000). Behavior change patterns and strategies distinguishing moderation drinking and abstinence during the natural resolution of alcohol problems without treatment. *Psychol. Addict. Behav., 14*(1), 48–55.

King, N. J. (1993). Simple and social phobias. In T. H. Ollendick & R. J. Prinz (Eds.), *Advances in*

clinical child psychology (Vol. 15). New York: Plenum Press.

King, N. J., Eleonora, G., & Ollendick, T. H. (1998). Etiology of childhood phobias: Current status of Rachman's three pathways theory. *Behav. Res. Ther., 36*(3), 297–309.

Kinzie, J., Leung, P., Boehnlein, J., & Matsunaga, D. (1992). Psychiatric epidemiology of an Indian village: A 19-year replication study. *J. Nerv. Ment. Dis., 180*(1), 33–39.

Kirby, M. (2000). Psychiatry, psychology, law and homosexuality—Uncomfortable bedfellows. *Psychiatry, Psychol. Law, 7*(2), 139–149.

Kirk, S. A., & Kutchins, H. (1992). *The selling of DSM: The rhetoric of science in psychiatry.* New York: de Gruyter.

Kirkpatrick, B., Kopelowicz, A., Buchanan, R. W., & Carpenter, W. T., Jr. (2000). Assessing the efficacy of treatments for the deficit syndrome of schizophrenia. *Neuropsychopharmacology, 22*(3), 303–310.

Kirmayer, L. J., Robbins, J. M., & Paris, J. (1994). Somatoform disorders: Personality and the social matrix of somatic distress. *J. Abnorm. Psychol., 103*(1), 125–136.

Kirn, W. (1997, August 18). The ties that bind. *Time,* pp. 48–50.

Kisker, G. W. (1977). *The disorganized personality.* New York: McGraw-Hill.

Klassen, A., Miller, A., Raina, P., Lee, S. K., & Olsen, L. (1999). Attention-deficit hyperactivity disorder in children and youth: A quantitative systematic review of the efficacy of different management strategies. *Can. J. Psychiatry, 44*(10), 1007–1016.

Klausner, J. D., Sweeney, J. A., Deck, M. D., Haas, G. L. et al. (1992). Clinical correlates of cerebral ventricular enlargement in schizophrenia: Further evidence for frontal lobe disease. *J. Nerv. Ment. Dis., 180*(7), 407–412.

Kleber, H. D. (1981). Detoxification from narcotics. In J. H. Lowinson & P. Ruiz (Eds.), *Substance abuse: Clinical problems and perspectives.* Baltimore, MD: William & Wilkins.

Kleber, H. D. (1995). Afterword to section I. In J. M. Oldham & M. B. Riba (Eds.), *American Psychiatric Press review of psychiatry* (Vol. 14). Washington, DC: American Psychiatric Press.

Klein, D. F. (1964). Delineation of two drug-responsive anxiety syndromes. *Psychopharmacologia, 5,* 397–408.

Klein, D. F., & Fink, M. (1962). Psychiatric reaction patterns to imipramine. *Am. J. Psychiatry, 119,* 432–438.

Klein, E., Kreinin, I., Chistyakov, A., Koren, D., Mecz, L., Marmur, S., Ben-Shachar, D., & Feinsod, M. (1999). Therapeutic efficacy of right prefrontal slow repetitive transcranial magnetic stimulation in major depression. *Arch. Gen. Psychiatry, 56*(4), 315–320.

Klein, M. (1998, January). Suicidal states. *Am. Demogr.*

Klein, M. (1998, March). Looking out for Fido. *Am. Demogr.*

Klein, M. (1998, March). Moving experiences. *Am. Demogr.*

Klein, M. (1998, March). Stalking situations. *Am. Demogr.*

Klerman, G. L. (1984). Characterologic manifestations of affective disorders: Toward a new conceptualization: Commentary. *Integr. Psychiatry, 2*(3), 94–96.

Klerman, G. L., & Weissman, M. M. (1992). Interpersonal psychotherapy. In E. S. Paykel (Ed.), *Handbook of affective disorders.* New York: Guilford Press.

Klerman, G. L., Weissman, M. M., Markowitz, J., Glick, I., Wilner, P. J., Mason, B., & Shear,

M. K. (1994). Medication and psychotherapy. In A. E. Bergin & S. L. Garfiel (Eds.), *Handbook of psychotherapy and behavior change* (4th ed.). New York: Wiley.

Klerman, G. L., Weissman, M. M., Rounsaville, B., & Chevron, E. (1984). *Interpersonal psychotherapy of depression.* New York: Basic Books.

Kliewer, W., Lepore, S. J., Oskin, D., & Johnson, P. D. (1998). The role of social and cognitive processes in children's adjustment to community violence. *J. Consult. Clin. Psychol., 66*(1), 199–209.

Klimes-Dougan, B., Free, K., Ronsaville, D., Stilwell, J., Welsh, C. J., & Radke-Yarrow, M. (1999). Suicidal ideation and attempts: A longitudinal investigation of children of depressed and well mothers. *J. Am. Acad. Child Adolesc. Psychiatry, 38*(6), 651–659.

Kline, N. S. (1958). Clinical experience with iproniazid (Marsilid). *J. Clin. Exp. Psychopathol., 19*(1, Suppl.), 72–78.

Kline, P. (1993). *The handbook of psychological testing.* New York: Routledge.

Kling, K. C., Hyde, J. S., Showers, C. J., & Buswell, B. N. (1999). Gender differences in self-esteem: A meta-analysis. *Psychol. Bull., 125*(4), 470–500.

Klocek, J. W., Oliver, J. M., & Ross, M. J. (1997). The role of dysfunctional attitudes, negative life events, and social support in the prediction of depressive dysphoria: A prospective longitudinal study. *Soc. Behav. Pers., 25*(2), 123–136.

Klopfer, B., & Davidson, H. (1962). *The Rorschach technique.* New York: Harcourt, Brace.

Kluft, R. P. (1983). Hypnotherapeutic crisis intervention in multiple personality. *Am. J. Clin. Hypnosis, 26*(2), 73–83.

Kluft, R. P. (1984). Treatment of multiple personality disorder: A study of 33 cases. *Psychiatr. Clin. North Am., 7*(1), 9–29.

Kluft, R. P. (1985). Hypnotherapy of childhood multiple personality disorder. *Am. J. Clin. Hypnosis, 27*(4), 201–210.

Kluft, R. P. (1987). The simulation and dissimulation of multiple personality disorder. *Am. J. Clin. Hypnosis, 30*(2), 104–118.

Kluft, R. P. (1988). The dissociative disorders. In J. Talbott, R. Hales, & S. Yudofsky (Eds.), *Textbook of psychiatry.* Washington, DC: American Psychiatric Press.

Kluft, R. P. (1991). Multiple personality disorder. In A. Tasman & S. M. Goldfinger (Eds.), *American Psychiatric Press review of psychiatry* (Vol. 10). Washington, DC: American Psychiatric Press.

Kluft, R. P. (1992). Discussion: A specialist's perspective on multiple personality disorder. *Psychoanal. Inquiry, 12*(1), 139–171.

Kluft, R. P. (1993). Basic principles in conducting the psychotherapy of multiple personality disorder. In R. P. Kluft & C. G. Fine (Eds.), *Clinical perspectives on multiple personality disorder.* Washington, DC: American Psychiatric Press.

Kluft, R. P. (1999). An overview of the psychotherapy of dissociative identity disorder. *Am. J. Psychother., 53*(3), 289–319.

Kluft, R. P. (2000). The psychoanalytic psychotherapy of dissociative identity disorder in the context of trauma therapy. *Psychoanal. Inquiry, 20*(2), 259–286.

Knapp, S., & VandeCreek, L. (2000). Recovered memories of childhood abuse: Is there an underlying professional consensus? *Prof. Psychol.: Res. Pract., 31*(4), 365–371.

Knesper, D. J., Pagnucco, D. J., & Wheeler, J. R. (1985). Similarities and differences across mental health services providers and practice settings in the United States. *Am. Psychol., 40*(12), 1352–1369.

Knowlton, L. (1995, August 29). Licensed to heal. *Los Angeles Times,* p. E3.

Knowlton, L. (1997, May). Outreach Program aids homeless mentally ill. *Psychiatr. Times, 16*(5).

Knowlton, L. (1998). "Women Healing" conference examines women in recovery. *Psychiatr. Times, 15*(7).

Knutson, B., Wolkowitz, O. M., Cole, S. W., Chan, T., Moore, E. A., Johnson, R. C., Terpstra, J., Turner, R. A., & Reus, V. I. (1998). Selective alteration of personality and social behavior by serotonergic intervention. *Am. J. Psychiatry, 155,* 373–379.

Knutson, J. F. (1995). Psychological characteristics of maltreated children. *Annu. Rev. Psychol., 46,* 401–431.

Kobasa, S. C. (1979). Stressful life events, personality, and health: An inquiry into hardiness. *J. Pers. Soc. Psychol., 37*(1), 1–11.

Kobasa, S. C. (1982). Commitment and coping in stress resistance among lawyers. *J. Pers. Soc. Psychol., 42,* 707–717.

Kobasa, S. C. (1982). The hardy personality: Towards a social psychology of stress and health. In J. Suls & G. Sanders (Eds.), *Social psychology of health and illness.* Hillsdale, NJ: Erlbaum.

Kobasa, S. C. (1984). Barriers to work stress: II. The "hardy" personality. In W. D. Gentry, H. Benson, & C. J. de Wolff (Eds.), *Behavioral medicine: Work, stress and health.* The Hague: Martinus Nijhoff.

Kobasa, S. C. (1987). Stress responses and personality. In R. C. Barnett, L. Biener, & G. K. Baruch (Eds.), *Gender and stress.* New York: Free Press.

Kobasa, S. C. (1990). Stress resistant personality. In R. E. Ornstein & C. Swencionis (Eds.), *The healing brain: A scientific reader.* Oxford, England: Pergamon Press.

Kocsis, J. H., Friedman, R. A., Markowitz, J. C., Miller, N., Gniwesch, L., & Bram, J. (1995). Stability of remission during tricyclic antidepressant continuation therapy for dysthymia. *Psychopharmacol. Bull., 31*(2), 213–216.

Koegel, L. K., Koegel, R. L., Hurley, C., & Frea, W. D. (1992). Improving social skills and disruptive behavior in children with autism through self-management. *J. Appl. Behav. Anal., 25*(2), 341–353.

Koenig, H. G., & Blazer, D. (1992). Epidemiology of geriatric affective disorders. *Clin. Geriatr. Med., 8,* 235–251.

Koenig, H. G., Hays, J. C., Larson, D. B., George, L. K., Cohen, H. J., McCullough, M. E., Meador, K. G., & Blazer, D. G. (1999). Does religious attendance prolong survival? A six-year-follow-up study of 3,968 older adults. *J. Gerontol. A, 54*(7), M370–M376.

Koenigsberg, H. W., Anwunah, I., New, A. S., Mitropoulou, V., Schopick, F., & Siever, L. J. (1999). Relationship between depression and borderline personality disorder. *Depression Anxiety, 10*(4), 158–167.

Koerner, K., & Linehan, M. M. (2000). Research on dialectical behavior therapy for patients with borderline personality disorder. *Psychiatr. Clin. North Am., 23*(1), 151–167.

Kohn, R., & Levav, I. (1995, May 23). Jewish depression study. Cited in *USA Today,* p. 1D.

Kohn, Y., Zislin, J., Agid, O., Hanin, B., Troudart, T., Shapira, B., Bloch, M., Gur, E., Ritsner, M., & Lerer, B. (2001). Increased prevalence of negative life events in subtypes of major depressive disorder. *Compr. Psychiatry, 42*(1), 57–63.

Kohut, H. (1971). *The analysis of the self.* New York: International Universities Press.

Kohut, H. (1977). *The restoration of the self.* New York: International Universities Press.

Kohut, H. (1984). *How does analysis cure?* Chicago: University of Chicago Press.

Kohut, H., & Wolf, E. S. (1978). The disorders of the self and their treatment: An outline. *Int. J. Psychoanal., 59*(4), 413–425.

Kolata, G. (1998, January 11). The fat's in the fire, again. *New York Times,* Sect. 4, p. 4.

Kolbert, E. (1998, January 19). Housing hope of mentally ill is fading away. *New York Times,* p. B1.

Kolff, C. A., & Doan, R. N. (1985). Victims of torture: Two testimonies. In E. Stover & E. O. Nightingale (Eds.), *The breaking of bodies and minds: Torture, psychiatric abuse, and the health professions.* New York: Freeman.

Kolodny, R., Masters, W. H., & Johnson, J. (1979). *Textbook of sexual medicine.* Boston: Little, Brown.

Komara, F. A. (1999). Management of behavioral problems in elderly patients with dementia. *J. Am. Osteopathol. Assoc., 99*(Suppl. 9), S9–12.

Komaroff, A. L., Masuda, M., & Holmes, T. H. (1986). The Social Readjustment Rating Scale: A comparative study of Negro, white, and Mexican Americans. *J. Psychosom. Res., 12,* 121–128.

Komaroff, A. L., Masuda, M., & Holmes, T. H. (1989). The Social Readjustment Rating Scale: A comparative study of Black, white, and Mexican Americans. In T. H. Holmes & E. M. David (Eds.), *Life change, life events, and illness.* New York: Praeger.

Kong, D. (1998, November 18). Still no solution in the struggle on safeguards—Doing harm: Research on the mentally ill. *Boston Globe,* p. A1.

Koopman, C., Hermanson, K., Diamond, S., Angell, K., & Spiegel, D. (1998). Social support, life stress, pain and emotional adjustment to advanced breast cancer. *Psycho-Oncology, 7*(2), 101–111.

Kopelman, M. D. (1995). The Korsakoff syndrome. *Br. J. Psychiatry, 166*(2), 154–173.

Korchin, S. J., & Sands, S. H. (1983). Principles common to all psychotherapies. In C. E. Walker et al. (Eds.), *The handbook of clinical psychology.* Homewood, IL: Dow Jones-Irwin.

Koren, D., Arnon, I., & Klein, E. (1999). Acute stress response and posttraumatic stress disorder in traffic accident victims: A one-year prospective, follow-up study. *Am. J. Psychiatry, 156*(3), 367–373.

Kosik, K. S. (1992). Alzheimer's disease: A cell biological perspective. *Science, 256,* 780–783.

Kosky, R. J., Eshkevari, H. S., Goldney, R. D., & Hassan, R. (1998). *Suicide prevention: The global context.* New York: Plenum Press.

Koss, M. P. (1992). The underdetection of rape: Methodological choices influence incidence estimates. *J. Soc. Issues, 48*(1), 61–75.

Koss, M. P. (1993). Rape: Scope, impact, interventions, and public policy responses. *Am. Psychol., 48*(10), 1062–1069.

Koss, M. P., & Heslet, L. (1992). Somatic consequences of violence against women. *Arch. Fam. Med., 1*(1), 53–59.

Koss, M. P., & Kilpatrick, D. G. (2001). Rape and sexual assault. In E. Gerrity, T. M. Keane et al (Eds.), *The mental health consequences of torture* (pp. 177–193). New York: Kluwer Academic/Plenum.

Koss, M. P., Koss, P., & Woodruff, W. J. (1991). Deleterious effects of criminal victimization on women's health and medical utilization. *Arch. Intern. Med., 151,* 342–357.

Koss, M. P., Woodruff, W. J., & Koss, P. (1991). Criminal victimization among primary care medical patients: Prevalence, incidence, and physician usage. *Behav. Sci. Law, 9,* 85–96.

Kosten, T. R., & McCance-Katz, E. (1995). New pharmacotherapies. In J. M. Oldham & M. B. Riba (Eds.), *American Psychiatric Press review of psychiatry* (Vol. 14). Washington, DC: American Psychiatric Press.

Kotler, M., Iancu, J., Efroni, R., & Amir, M. (2001). Anger, impulsivity, social support, and suicide risk in patients with posttraumatic stress disorder. *J. Nerv. Ment. Dis., 189*(3), 162–167.

Kouri, E. M., & Pope, H. G., Jr. (2000). Abstinence symptoms during withdrawal from chronic marijuana use. *Exp. Clin. Psychopharmacol., 8*(4), 483–492.

Kovacs, M. (1996). Presentation and source of major depression disorder during childhood and later years of the life span. *J. Am. Child Adolesc. Psychiatry, 35*(6), 705–715.

Kovacs, M. (1997). Depressive disorders in childhood: An impressionistic landscape. *J. Child Psychol. Psychiatry, 38*(3), 287–298.

Kovacs, M., Goldston, D., & Gatsonis, C. (1993). Suicidal behaviors and childhood-onset depressive disorders: A longitudinal investigation. *J. Am. Acad. Child Adolesc. Psychiatry, 32*, 8–20.

Krabbendam, L., Visser, P. J., Derix, M. M. A., Verhey, F., Hofman, P., Verhoeven, W., Tuinier, S., & Jolles, J. (2000). Normal cognitive performance in patients with chronic alcoholism in contrast to patients with Korsakoff's syndrome. *J. Neuropsychiatry Clin. Neurosci., 12*(1), 44–50.

Kraines, S. H., & Thetford, E. S. (1972). *Help for the depressed.* Springfield, IL: Thomas.

Krakauer, S. Y. (2001). *Treating dissociative identity disorder: The power of the collective heart.* Philadelphia: Brunner-Routledge.

Krall, W. J., Sramek, J. J., & Cutler, N. R. (1999). Cholinesterase inhibitors: A therapeutic strategy for Alzheimer disease. *Ann. Pharmacother., 33*(4), 441–450.

Kramer, M. (1992). Cited in R. D. Cartwright & L. Lamberg, *Crisis dreaming: Using your dreams to solve your problems.* New York: HarperCollins.

Krantz, L. (1992). *What the odds are.* New York: Harper Perennial.

Kratochwill, T. R. (1992). Single-case research design and analysis: An overview. In T. R. Kratochwill & J. R. Levin (Eds.), *Single-case research design and analysis: New directions for psychology and education.* Hillsdale, NJ: Erlbaum.

Kratzer, L., & Hodgins, S. (1997). Adult outcomes of child conduct problems: A cohort study. *J. Abnorm. Child Psychol., 25*(1), 65–81.

Krauss, M. W., Seltzer, M. M., & Goodman, S. J. (1992). Social support networks of adults with mental retardation who live at home. *Am. J. Ment. Retard., 96*(4), 432–441.

Krausz, M., Muller-Thomsen, T., & Haasen, C. (1995). Suicide among schizophrenic adolescents in the long-term course of illness. *Psychopathology, 28*(2), 95–103.

Kresin, D. (1993). Medical aspects of inhibited sexual desire disorder. In W. O'Donohue & J. Geer (Eds.), *Handbook of sexual dysfunctions.* Boston: Allyn & Bacon.

Kring, A. M., & Neale, J. M. (1996). Do schizophrenic patients show a disjunctive relationship among expressive, experiential, and psychophysiological components of emotion? *J. Abnorm. Psychol., 105*(2), 249–257.

Kring, B. (2000). Psychotherapy of sexual dysfunction. *Am. J. Psychother., 54*(1), 97–101.

Krishnan, K. R. R., Swartz, M. S., Larson, M. J., & Santo-Liquido, G. (1984). Funeral mania in recurrent bipolar affective disorders: Reports of three cases. *J. Clin. Psychiatry, 45*, 310–311.

Krueger, R. G., & Kaplan, M. S. (2000). Evaluation and treatment of sexual disorders: Frottage. In L. Vandecreed & T. L. Jackson (Eds.), *Innovations in clinical practice: A source book* (Vol. 18, pp. 185–197). Sarasota, FL: Professional Resource Press.

Krug, E. G., Kresnow, M. J., Peddicord, J. P., Dahlberg, L. L., Powell, K. E., Crosby, A. E., & Annest, J. L. (1998). Suicide after natural disasters. *N. Engl. J. Med., 338*(6), 373–378.

Kuch, K., & Cox, B. J. (1992). Symptoms of PTSD in 124 survivors of the Holocaust. *Am. J. Psychiatry, 149*(3), 337–340.

Kuczmarski, R., Fiegal, K., Campbell, S., & Johnson, C. (1994). Increasing prevalence of overweight among U.S. adults: The National Health and Nutrition Examination Surveys, 1960–1991. *JAMA, J. Am. Med. Assoc., 272*, 205–211.

Kuhn, R. (1958). The treatment of depressive states with G-22355 (imipramine hydrochloride). *Am. J. Psychiatry, 115*, 459–464.

Kuhn, T. S. (1962). *The structure of scientific revolutions.* Chicago: University of Chicago Press.

Kulhara, P., Basu, D., Mattoo, S. K., Sharan, P., & Chopra, R. (1999). Lithium prophylaxis of recurrent bipolar affective disorder: Long-term outcome and its psychosocial correlates. *J. Affect. Disord., 54*(1–2), 87–96.

Kupeli, S., Aydos, K., & Budak, M. (1999). Penile implants in erectile impotence. The importance of clinical experience on outcome. *Eur. Urol., 36*(2), 129–135.

Kuperman, S., Schlosser, S. S., Lidral, J., & Reich, W. (1999). Relationship of child psychopathology to parental alcoholism and antosicla personality disorder. *J. Am. Acad. Child Adolesc. Psychiatry, 38*(6), 686–692.

Kupfer, D. J. (1995). Acute continuation and maintenance treatment of mood disorders. *Depression, 3*, 137–138.

Kupfer, D. J., & Frank, E. (2001). The interaction of drug- and psychotherapy in the long-term treatment of depression. *J. Affect. Disord., 62*(1–2), 131–137.

Kupfer, D. L. (1999). Cited in L. Rabasca, I'm okay and you're okay, but not so sure about Y2K. *APA Monitor, 30*(1), 1,18.

Kuriansky, J. B. (1988). Personality style and sexuality. In R. A. Brown & J. R. Field (Eds.), *Treatment of sexual problems in individual and couples therapy.* Costa Mesa, CA: PMA Publishing.

Kurtz, D. L., Stewart, R. B., Zweifel, M., Li, T.-K., & Froehlich, J. C. (1996). Genetic differences in tolerance and sensitization to the sedative/hypnotic effects of alcohol. *Pharmacol., Biochem. Behav., 53*(3), 585–591.

Kushner, H. I. (1995). Women and suicidal behavior: Epidemiology, gender and lethality in historical perspective. In S. S. Canetto & D. Lester (Eds.), *Women and suicidal behavior.* New York: Springer.

Kushner, M. G., Riggs, D. S., Foa, E. B., & Miller, S. M. (1992). Perceived controllability and the development of posttraumatic stress disorder (PTSD) in crime victims. *Behav. Res. Ther., 31*(1), 105–110.

Kusumi, I., Ishikane, T., Matsubara, S., & Koyama, T. (1995). Long-term treatment with haloperidol or clozapine does not affect dopamine D[4] receptors in rat frontal cortex. *J. Neural Transm., 101*, 231–235.

LEMAS (Law Enforcement Management and Administrative Statistics Survey). (1990). Cited in U.S. Department of Justice (1994).

Labbate, L. A., & Snow, M. P. (1992). Posttraumatic stress symptoms among soldiers exposed to combat in the Persian Gulf. *Hosp. Commun. Psychiatry, 43*(8), 831–833.

Labbé, E. E. (1995). Treatment of childhood migraine with autogenic training and skin temperature biofeedback: A component analysis. *Headache, 35*(1), 10–13.

Labellarte, M. J., Ginsburg, G. S., Walkup, J. T., & Riddle, M. A. (1999). The treatment of anxiety disorders in children and adolescents. *Biol. Psychiatry, 46*(11), 1567–1578.

Labott, S. M., Preisman, R. C., Popovich, J., & Iannuzzi, M. C. (1995). Health care utilization of somatizing patients in a pulmonary subspecialty clinic. *Psychosomatics, 36*(2), 122–128.

Lachmann, A., & Lachmann, F. M. (1995). The personification of evil: Motivations and fantasies of the serial killer. *Int. Forum Psychoanal., 4*(1), 17–23.

Lachner, G., & Engel, R. R. (1994). Differentiation of dementia and depression by memory tests: A meta-analysis. *J. Nerv. Ment. Dis., 182*(1), 34–39.

Lacks, P. (1984). *Bender Gestalt screening for brain dysfunction.* New York: Wiley.

Lacks, P. (1999). *Bender Gestalt screening for brain dysfunction* (2nd ed.). New York: Wiley.

Ladds, B. (1997). Forensic treatment and rehabilitation: The growing need for more services and more research. *Int. J. Ment. Health, 25*(4), 3–10.

Ladouceur, R., Blais, F., Freeston, M. H., & Dugas, M. J. (1998). Problem solving and problem orientation in generalized anxiety distorder. *J. Anxiety Disord., 12*(2), 139–152.

Ladouceur, R., Freeston, M. H., Gagnon, F., Thibodeau, N. et al. (1995). Cognitive-behavioral treatment of obsessions. *Behav. Mod., 19*(2), 247–257.

Lahey, B. B., Hartdagen, S. E., Frick, P. J., McBurnett, K. et al. (1988). Conduct disorder: Parsing the confounded relation to parental divorce and antisocial personality. *J. Abnorm. Psychol., 97*(3), 334–337.

Lahiri, A. et al. (1998, November). Study on blood pressure. *Circulation.*

Laing, R. D. (1959). *The divided self: An existential study in sanity and madness.* London: Tavistock.

Laing, R. D. (1964). *The divided self* (2nd ed.). London: Pelican.

Laing, R. D. (1967). *The politics of experience.* New York: Pantheon.

Lakin, K. C., Anderson, L., Prouty, R., & Polister, B. (1999). State institution populations less than one third of 197, residents older with more impairments. *Ment. Retard., 37*, 85–86.

Lakin, K. C., Prouty, B., Smith, G., & Braddock, D. (1996). Nixon goal surpassed: Two-fold. *Ment. Retard., 34*, 67.

Lakin, M. (1998). Carl Rogers and the culture of psychotherapy. In G. A. Kimble, M. Wertheimer et al. (Eds.), *Portraits of pioneers in psychology* (Vol. 3). Washington, DC: American Psychological Association.

Lam, R. W., Tam, E. M., Shiah, I.-S., Yatham, L. N., & Zis, A. P. (2000). Effects of light therapy on suicidal ideation in patients with winter depression. *J. Clin. Psychiatry, 61*(1), 30–32.

Lamb, H. R. (1994). Public psychiatry and prevention. In R. E. Hales, S. C. Yudofsky, & J. A. Talbott (Eds.), *The American Psychiatric Press textbook of psychiatry* (2nd ed.). Washington, DC: American Psychiatric Press.

Lamb, M. (1998). Cybersex: Research notes on the characteristics of the visitors to online chat rooms. *Deviant Behav.: Interdiscipl. J., 19*, 121–135.

Lambert, M. J., & Bergin, A. E. (1994). The effectiveness of psychotherapy. In A. E. Bergin & S. L. Garfield (Eds.), *Handbook of psychotherapy and behavioral change* (4th ed.). New York: Wiley.

Lambert, M. J., Shapiro, D. A., & Bergin, A. E. (1986). The effectiveness of psychotherapy. In S. L. Garfield & A. E. Bergin (Eds.), *Handbook of psychotherapy and behavioral change* (3rd ed.). New York: Wiley.

Lambert, M. J., Weber, F. D., & Sykes, J. D. (1993, April). *Psychotherapy versus placebo.* Poster presented at the annual meeting of the Western Psychological Association, Phoenix, AZ.

Lambert, M. T., & Silva, P. S. (1998). An update on the impact of gun control legislation on suicide. *Psychiatr. Q., 69*(2), 127–134.

Lamberti, J. S., & Cummings, S. (1992). Hands-on restraints in the treatment of multiple personality disorder. *Hosp. Commun. Psychiatry, 43*(3), 283–284.

Landes, R. (1999, March 7). Interviewed in M. Jurkowitz, I'm OK; you're OK; Y2K? Does all the worry about deadly computer bugs express our primal fear of entering 2000? *Boston Globe*, p. C1.

Landry, M. J. (1994). *Understanding drugs of abuse: The processes of addiction, treatment, and recovery.* Washington, DC: American Psychiatric Press.

Landsbergis, P. A., Schnall, P. L., Warren, K., Pickering, T. G., & Schwartz, J. E. (1994). Association between ambulatory blood pressure and alternative formulations of job strain. *Scand. J. Work Environ. Health, 20,* 349–363.

Lane, J. (1999). Habitual moderate caffeine consumption elevates blood pressure and levels of stress hormones. Paper presented at the 1999 meeting of the Society of Behavioral Medicine, San Diego, CA.

Lang, J. (1999, April 16). Local jails dumping grounds for mentally ill. *Detroit News.*

Langbehn, D. R., Pfohl, B. M., Reynolds, S., Clark, L. A., Battaglia, M., Bellodi, L., Cadoret, R., Grove, W., Pilkonis, P., & Links, P. (1999). The Iowa Personality Disorder Screen: Development and preliminary validation of a brief screening interview. *J. Pers. Disord., 13*(1), 75–89.

Langer, E. J. (1983). *The psychology of control.* Beverly Hills, CA: Sage.

Langer, S. Z., & Raisman, R. (1983). Binding of (3H) imipramine and (3H) desipramine as biochemical tools for studies in depression. *Neuropharmacology, 22,* 407–413.

Langevin, R., Bain, J., Wortzman, G., Hucker, S. et al. (1988). Sexual sadism: Brain, blood, and behavior. *Ann. N.Y. Acad. Sci., 528,* 163–171.

Langlois, F., Freeston, M. H., & Ladouceur, R. (2000). Differences and similarities between obsessive intrusive thoughts and worry in a nonclinical population: Study 1. *Behav. Res. Ther., 38*(2), 157–173.

Langlois, F., Freeston, M. H., & Ladouceur, R. (2000). Differences and similarities between obsessive intrusive thoughts and worry in a nonclinical population: Study 2. *Behav. Res. Ther., 38*(2), 175–189.

Langs, G., Quehenberger, F., Fabisch, K., Klug, G., Fabisch, H., & Zapotoczky, H. G. (2000). The development of agoraphobis in panic disorder: A predictable process? *J. Affect. Disord., 58*(1), 43–50.

Langwieler, G., & Linden, M. (1993). Therapist individuality in the diagnosis and treatment of depression. *J. Affect. Disord., 27,* 1–12.

Lara, M. E., & Klein, D. N. (1999). Psychosocial processes underlying the maintenance and persistence of depression: Implications for understanding chronic depression. *Clin. Psychol. Rev., 19*(5), 553–570.

Larkin, K. T., & Zvolensky, M. J. (2001). Behavior therapy. In M. Hersen & V. B. Van Hasselt (Eds.), *Advanced abnormal psychology* (2nd ed., pp. 563–578). New York: Kluwer Academic/Plenum Press.

Larsson, B., & Ivarsson, T. (1998). Clinical characteristics of adolescent psychiatric inpatients who have attempted suicide. *Eur. Child Adolesc. Psychiatry, 7*(4), 201–208.

Laruelle, M., & Abi-Dargham, A. (1999). Dopamine as the wind of the psychotic fire: New evidence from brain imaging studies. *J. Psychopharmacol., 13*(4), 358–371.

Lask, B. (2000). Aetiology. In B. Lask, R. Bryant-Waugh et al. (Eds.), *Anorexia nervosa and related eating disorders in childhood and adolescence* (2nd ed.). Hove, England: Psychology Press/Taylor & Francis.

Lask, B., & Bryant-Waugh, R. (Eds.). (2000). *Anorexia nervosa and related eating disorders in childhood and adolescence* (2nd ed.). Hove, England: Psychology Press/Taylor & Francis.

Laumann, E. O., Gagnon, J. H., Michael, R. T., & Michaels, S. (1994). *The social organization of sexuality.* Chicago: University of Chicago Press.

Laumann, E. O., Paik, A., & Rosen, R. C. (1999). Sexual dysfunction in the United States: Prevalence and predictors. *JAMA, J. Am. Med. Assoc., 281*(6), 537–544.

Laumann, E. O., Paik, A., & Rosen, R. C. (1999). Sexual dysfunction in the United States: Prevalence and predictors. *JAMA, J. Am. Med. Assoc., 281*(13), 1174.

Lautenbacher, S., & Rollman, G. B. (1999). Somatization, hypochondriasis, and related conditions. In A. R. Block, E. F. Kremer et al. (Eds.), *Handbook of pain syndromes: Biopsychosocial perspectives.* Mahwah, NJ: Erlbaum.

Lawford, B. R., Young, R. McD., Rowell, J. A., Gibson, J. N. et al. (1997). Association of the D^2 dopamine receptor A1 allele with alcoholism: Medical severity of alcoholism and type of controls. *Biol. Psychiatry, 41,* 386–393.

Lawlor, B. A., McCarron, M., Wilson, G., & McLoughlin, M. (2001). Temporal lobe-oriented CT scanning and dementia in Down's syndrome. *Int. J. Geriatr. Psychiatry, 16*(4), 427–429.

Lawlor, D.A., & Hopker, S. W. (2001). The effectiveness of exercise as an intervention in the management of depression: Systematic review and meta-regression analysis of randomised controlled trials. *Br. Med. J., 322,* 763–766.

Lawrence, C. (1987). An integrated spiritual and psychological growth model in the treatment of narcissism. *J. Psychol. Theol., 15*(3), 205–213.

Lawrence, E., Eldridge, K., Christensen, A., & Jacobson, N. S. (1999). Integrative couple therapy: The dyadic relationship of acceptance and change. In J. Donovan et al. (Eds.), *Short-term couple therapy.* New York: Guilford Press.

Lawrence, G. H. (1986). Using computers for the treatment of psychological problems. *Comput. Hum. Behav., 2*(1), 43–62.

Lazarus, A. A. (1965). The treatment of a sexually inadequate man. In L. P. Ullman & L. Krasner (Eds.), *Case studies in behavior modification.* New York: Holt, Rinehart & Winston.

Lazarus, J. A. (1995). Ethical issues in doctor-patient sexual relationships [Special issue: Clinical sexuality]. *Psychiatr. Clin. North Am., 18*(1), 55–70.

Lazarus, R. S., & Folkman, S. (1984). *Stress, appraisal, and coping.* New York: Springer.

Lean, M. E., Han, T. S., & Seidell, J. C. (1999). Impairment of health and quality of life using new US federal guidelines for the identification of obesity. *Arch. Intern. Med., 159*(8), 837–843.

Leane, W., & Shute, R. (1998). Youth suicide: The knowledge and attitudes of Australian teachers and clergy. *Suicide Life-Threaten. Behav., 28*(2), 165–173.

Leavitt, F. (2000). Surviving roots of trauma: Prevalence of silent signs of sex abuse in patients who recover memories of childhood sex abuse as adults. *J. Pers. Assess., 74*(2), 311–323.

Leavitt, F. (2001). Iatrogenic recovered memories: Examining the empirical evidence. *Am. J. Forens. Psychol., 19*(2), 21–32.

Lebegue, B. (1991). Paraphilias in U.S. pornography titles: "Pornography made me do it" (Ted Bundy). *Bull. Am. Acad. Psychiatry Law, 19*(1), 43–48.

Lebell, M. B., Marder, S. R., Mintz, J., Mintz, L. I., Tompson, M., Wirshing, W., Johnston-Cronk, K., & McKenzie, J. (1993). Patients' perceptions of family emotional climate and outcome in schizophrenia. *Br. J. Psychiatry, 162,* 751–754.

Lecrubier, Y. (1995). Pharmacotherapy and the role of new and classic antidepressants. *Depression, 3,* 134–136.

Lecrubier, Y., Bakker, A., Dunbar, G., and the Collaborative Paroxetine Panic Study Investigators. (1997). A comparison of paroxetine, clomipramine and placebo in the treatment of panic disorder. *Acta Psychiatr. Scand., 95,* 145–152.

Ledoux, S., Choquet, M., & Manfredi, R. (1993). Associated factors for self-reported binge eating among male and female adolescents. *J. Adolesc., 16,* 75–91.

Lee, D. E. (1985). Alternative self-destruction. *Percept. Mot. Skills, 61*(3, Pt. 2), 1065–1066.

Lee, D. Y., Uhlemann, M. R., & Barak, A. (1999). Effects of diagnostic suggestion on the clinical judgments and recall memories of autobiography. *J. Soc. Clin. Psychol., 18*(1), 35–46.

Lee, J. K., Lee, C. H., Park, D. B., Kee, B. S., Na, C., Lee, Y. S., Cho, J. Y., Nam, B. W., Lee, K. H., & Chang, D. S. (1998). Circulating natural killer cell in neurotic patients. *Int. Med. J., 5*(2), 121–126.

Lee, P. W. H., Lieh-Mak, Tu, K. K., & Spinks, J. A. (1993). Coping strategies of schizophrenic patients and their relationship to outcome. *Br. J. Psychiatry, 163,* 177–182.

Lee, R. K. K., Jimenez, J., Cox, A. J., & Wurtman, R. J. (1996). Metabotropic glutamate receptors regulate APP processing in hippocampal neurons and cortical astrocytes derived from fetal rats. In R. J. Wurtman, S. Corkin, J. H. Growdon, & R. M. Nitsch (Eds.), *The neurobiology of Alzheimer's disease.* New York: New York Academy of Sciences.

Lee, T., & Seeman, P. (1980). Elevation of brain neuroleptic/dopamine receptors in schizophrenia. *Am. J. Psychiatry, 137,* 191–197.

Lee, W. M. L. (1999). *An introduction to multicultural counseling.* Philadelphia: Taylor & Francis.

Leenaars, A., Connolly, J., Cantor, C., EchoHawk, M., He, Z.-X., Kokorina, N., Lester, D., Lopatin, A. A., Rodriguez, M., Sclhlebusch, L., Takahashi, Y., & Vijayakuman, L. (2001). Suicide, assisted suicide and euthanasia: International perspectives. *Ir. J. Psychol. Med., 18,* 33–37.

Leenaars, A. A., De Wilde, E. J., Wenckstern, S., & Kral, M. (2001). Suicide notes of adolescents: A life-span comparison. *Can. J. Behav. Sci., 33*(1), 47–57.

Leenaars, A. A., & Lester, D. (1992). Facts and myths of suicide in Canada and the United States. *J. Soc. Psychol., 132*(6), 787–789.

Leenaars, A. A., & Lester, D. (1998). The impact of gun control on suicide: Studies from Canada. *Arch. Suicide Res., 4*(1), 25–40.

Leenaars, A. A., & Lester, D. (1999). Domestic integration and suicide in the provinces of Canada. *Crisis, 20*(2), 59–63.

Leenaars, A. A., & Wenckstern, S. (1998). Principles of postvention: Applications to suicide and trauma in schools. *Death Stud., 22*(4), 357–391.

Leenstra, A. S., Ormel, J., & Giel, R. (1995). Positive life change and recovery from depression and anxiety: A three-stage longitudinal study of primary care attenders. *Br. J. Psychiatry, 166*(3), 333–343.

Lehman, A. F., Myers, C. P., Dixon, L. B., & Johnson, J. L. (1996). Detection of substance use disorders among psychiatric inpatients. *J. Nerv. Ment. Dis., 184*(4), 228–233.

Lehman, R. S. (1991). *Statistics and research design in the behavioral sciences.* Belmont, CA: Wadsworth.

Lehmann, H. E. (1985). Current perspectives on the biology of schizophrenia. In M. N. Menuck & M. V. Seeman. *New perspectives in schizophrenia.* New York: Macmillan.

Lehoux, P. M., Steiger, H., & Jabalpurlawa, S. (2000). State/trait distinctions in bulimic syndromes. *Int. J. Eat. Disord., 27*(1), 36–42.

Lehrer, P. M. (1998). Emotionally triggered asthma: A review of research literature and some hypotheses for self-regulation. *Appl. Psychophysiol. Biofeedback*, 23(1), 13–41.

Leibbrand, R., Hiller, W., & Fichter, M. M. (2000). Hypochondriasis and somatization: Two distinct aspects of somatoform disorders? *J. Clin. Psychol.*, 56(1), 63–72.

Leibenluft, E. (1996). Women with bipolar illness: Clinical and research issues. *Am. J. Psychiatry*, 153(2), 163–173.

Leibenluft, E. (2000). Women and bipolar disorder: An update. *Bull. Menninger Clin.*, 64(1), 5–17.

Leiblum, S. R. (1996). Sexual pain disorders. In *Treatment of psychiatric disorders: The DSM-IV edition*. Washington, DC: American Psychiatric Press.

Leiblum, S. R. (2000). Vagubusnys: A most perplexing problem. In S. R. Leiblum & R. C. Rosen (Eds.), *Principles and practice of sex therapy* (3rd ed., pp. 181–202). New York: Guilford Press.

Leiblum, S. R. (2001). Critical overview of the new consensus-bases definitions and classification of female sexual dysfunction. *J. Sex. Marital Ther.*, 27(2), 159–168.

Leiblum, S. R., & Rosen, R. C. (Eds.). (2000). *Principles and practice of sex therapy* (3rd ed.). New York: Guilford Press.

Leiblum, S. R., & Segraves, R. T. (1995). Sex and aging. In J. M. Oldham & M. B. Riba (Eds.), *American Psychiatric Press review of psychiatry* (Vol. 14). Washington, DC: American Psychiatric Press.

Leichsenring, F. (2001). Comparative effects of short-term psychodynamic psychotherapy and cognitive-behavioral therapy in depression. A meta-analytic approach. *Clin. Psychol. Rev.*, 21(3), 401–419.

Leipsic, J. S., Abraham, H. D., & Halperin, P. (1995). Neuroleptic malignant syndrome in the elderly. *J. Geriatr. Psychiatry Neurol.*, 8(1), 28–31.

Leitenberg, H., Yost, L. W., & Carroll-Wilson, M. (1986). Negative cognitive errors in children: Questionnaire development, normative data, and comparisons between children with and without self-reported symptoms of depression, low self-esteem, and evaluation anxiety. *J. Consult. Clin. Psychol.*, 54, 528–536.

Leland, H. (1991). Adaptive behavior scales. In J. L. Matson & J. A. Mulick (Eds.), *Handbook of mental retardation*. New York: Pergamon Press.

LeMarquand, D., Tremblay, R. E., & Vitaro, F. (2001). The prevention of conduct disorder: A review of successful and unsuccessful experiments. In J. Hill & B. Maughan (Eds.), *Conduct disorders in childhood and adolescence* (pp. 449–477). New York: Cambridge University Press.

Lenderking, W. R., Tennen, H., Nackley, J. F., Hale, M. S., Turner, R. R., & Testa, M. A. (1999). The effects of venlafaxine on social activity level in depressed outpatients. *J. Clin. Psychiatry*, 60(3), 157–163.

Lennkh, C., & Simhandl, C. (2000). Current aspects of valproate in bipolar disorder. *Int. Clin. Psychopharmacol.*, 15(1), 1–11.

Lenox, R. H., McNamara, R. F., Papke, R. L., & Manji, H. K. (1998). Neurobiology of lithium: An update. *J. Clin. Psychiatry*, 59(Suppl. 6), 37–47.

Lenzenweger, M. F., Cornblatt, B. A., & Putnick, M. (1991). Schizotypy and sustained attention. *J. Abnorm. Psychol.*, 100(1), 84–89.

Lenzenweger, M. F., Loranger, A. W., Korfine, L., & Neff, C. (1997). Detecting personality disorders in a non-clinical population: Application of a two-stage procedure for case identification. *Arch. Gen. Psychiatry*, 54, 345–351.

Leo, R. J., & Kim, K. Y. (1995). Clomipramine treatment of paraphilias in elderly demented patients. *J. Geriatr. Psychiatry Neurol.*, 8(2), 123–124.

Leon, G. R. (1977). *Case histories of deviant behavior* (2nd ed.). Boston: Allyn & Bacon.

Leon, G. R. (1984). *Case histories of deviant behavior* (3rd ed.). Boston: Allyn & Bacon.

Leonard, B. E. (1997). Neurotransmitters in depression: Noradrenaline and serotonin and their interactions. *J. Clin. Psychopharmacol.*, 17(2, Suppl. 1), 1S.

Leonard, B. E. (1999). Therapeutic applications of benzodiazepine receptor ligands in anxiety. *Hum. Psychopharmacol. Clin. Exp.*, 14(2), 125–135.

Lerer, B., Shapira, B., Calev, A., Tubi, N., Drexler, H., Kindler, S., Lidsky, D., & Schwartz, J. E. (1995). Antidepressant and cognitive effects of twice- versus three-times-weekly ECT. *Am. J. Psychiatry*, 152(4), 564–570.

Lerner, H. D. (1986). Current developments in the psychoanalytic psychotherapy of anorexia nervosa and bulimia nervosa. *Clin. Psychol.*, 39(2), 39–43.

Lerner, H. D., & Ehrlich, J. (2001). Psychoanalytic model. In M. Hersen & V. B. Van Hasselt (Eds.), *Advanced abnormal psychology* (2nd ed., pp. 65–92). New York: Kluwer Academic/Plenum Press.

Lerner, P. M. (1998). *Psychoanalytic perspectives on the Rorschach*. Hillsdale, NJ: Analytic Press.

Lerner, V., Fotyanov, M., Liberman, M., Shlafman, M., & Bar-El, Y. (1995). Maintenance medication for schizophrenia and schizoaffective patients. *Schizophr. Bull.*, 21(4), 693–701.

Leroux, J. A. (1986). Suicidal behavior and gifted adolescents. *Roeper Rev.*, 9(2), 77–79.

Lesch, K.-P., Bengel, D., Heils, A., Sabol, S. Z., Greenberg, B. D., Petri, S., Benjamin, J., Müller, C. R., Hamer, D. H., & Murphy, D. L. (1996, November 29). Association of anxiety-related traits with a polymorphism in the serotonin transporter gene regulatory region. *Science*, 274, 1527–1531.

Leserman, J., Drossman, D. A., Li, Z., Toomey, T. C. et al. (1996). Sexual and physical abuse history in gastroenterology practice: How types of abuse impact health status. *Psychosom. Med.*, 58(1), 4–15.

Leshner, A. I. et al. (1992). *Outcasts on the main street: Report of the Federal Task Force on Homelessness and Severe Mental Illness*. Washington, DC: Interagency Council on the Homeless.

Leslie, A. (1997, May 23). *Theory of mind impairment in autism: Its nature and significance*. Keynote address at The Eden Institute Foundation Princeton Lecture Series on Autism.

Lester, D. (1972). Myth of suicide prevention. *Compr. Psychiatry*, 13(6), 555–560.

Lester, D. (1974). The effects of suicide prevention centers on suicide rates in the United States. *Public Health Rep.*, 89, 37–39.

Lester, D. (1985). Accidental deaths as disguised suicides. *Psychol. Rep.*, 56(2), 626.

Lester, D. (1985). The quality of life in modern America and suicide and homicide rates. *J. Soc. Psychol.*, 125(6), 779–780.

Lester, D. (1989). *Can we prevent suicide?* New York: AMS Press.

Lester, D. (1991). Do suicide prevention centers prevent suicide? *Homeostasis Health Dis.*, 33(4), 190–194.

Lester, D. (1991). The etiology of suicide and homicide in urban and rural America. *J. Rural Commun. Psychol.*, 12(1), 15–27.

Lester, D. (1992). Alcoholism and drug abuse. In R. W. Maris, A. L. Berman, J. T. Maltsberger, & R. I. Yufit (Eds.), *Assessment and prediction of suicide*. New York: Guilford Press.

Lester, D. (1992). Is there a need for suicide prevention? *Crisis*, 2, 94.

Lester, D. (1992). Suicide and disease. *Loss, Grief & Care*, 6(2–3), 173–181.

Lester, D. (1997). Effect of suicide prevention centers in Ireland and Great Britain. *Psychol. Rep.*, 81, 1186.

Lester, D. (1998). The association of alcohol use, abuse and treatment with suicide and homicide rates. *G. Ital. Suicide*, 8(1), 23–24.

Lester, D. (1998). Judging the sex and age of suicide note writers. *Percept. Mot. Skills*, 86(3, Pt. 2), 1218.

Lester, D. (1998). Differences in content of suicide notes by age and method. *Percept. Mot. Skills*, 87(2), 530.

Lester, D. (1998). Experience of loss in famous suicides. *Psychol. Rep.*, 82(3, Pt. 1), 1090.

Lester, D. (1998). Preventing suicide by restricting access to methods for suicide. *Arch. Suicide Res.*, 4(1), 7–24.

Lester, D. (1998). Suicidal behavior in African-American slaves. *Omega: J. Death Dying*, 37(1), 1–13.

Lester, D. (1998). Suicide and homicide after the fall of communist regimes. *Eur. Psychiatry*, 13(2), 98–100.

Lester, D., & Saito, Y. (1999). The reasons for suicide in Japan. *Omega: J. Death Dying*, 38(1), 65–68.

Leszcz, M. (1992). Group psychotherapy of the borderline patient. In D. Silver & M. Rosenbluth (Eds.), *Handbook of borderline disorders*. Madison, CT: International Universities Press.

Letourneau, E., & O'Donohue, W. (1993). Sexual desire disorders. In W. O'Donohue & J. Geer (Eds.), Handbook of sexual dysfunctions. Boston: Allyn & Bacon.

Le Unes, A. D., Nation, J. R., & Turley, N. M. (1980). Male-female performance in learned helplessness. *J. Psychol.*, 104, 255–258.

Leung, N., Waller, G., & Thomas, G. (2000). Outcome of group cognitive-behavior therapy for bulimia nervosa: The role of core beliefs. *Behav. Res. Ther.*, 38(2), 145–156.

Leutwyler, K. (1996). Paying attention: The controversy over ADHD and the drug Ritalin is obscuring a real look at the disorder and its underpinnings. *Sci. Am.*, 272(2), 12–13.

Leutwyler, K. (1996, February). Schizophrenia revisited: New studies focus on malfunctions in the brain. *Sci. Am.*, 22–23.

Levant, R. F. (2000, February). Interviewed in P. A. McGuire. New hope for people with schizophrenia. *Monit. Psychol.*, 31(2), 24–28.

LeVay, S., & Hamer, D. H. (1994). Evidence for a biological influence in male homosexuality [Review]. *Sci. Am.*, 270(5), 44–49.

Levenson, J. L. (1985). Neuroleptic malignant syndrome. *Am. J. Psychiatry*, 142, 1137–1145.

Levenson, M. R. (1992). Rethinking psychopathy. *Theory Psychol.*, 2(1), 51–71.

Levenstein, S. (2000). The very model of a modern etiology: A biopsychosocial view of peptic ulcer. *Psychosom. Med.*, 62(2), 176–185.

Levesque, R. J. R. (1996). Regulating the private relations of adults with mental disabilities: Old laws, new policies, hollow hopes. *Behav. Sci. Law*, 14, 83–106.

Levin, B. L. (1992). Managed health care: A national perspective. In R. W. Manderscheid & M. A. Sonnenschein (Eds.), *Mental health, United States, 1992*. Washington, DC: U.S. Department of Health and Human Services.

Levin, E. (1983, February 21). A sweet surface hit a troubled soul in the late Karen Carpenter, a victim of anorexia nervosa. *People Weekly* (quoting Cherry Boone O'Neill).

Levin, J., & Fox, J. A. (1985). *Mass murder*. New York: Plenum Press.

Levine, M. D. (1975). Children with encopresis: A descriptive analysis. *Pediatrics*, 56, 412–416.

Levine, M. D. (1987). *How schools can help combat student eating disorders: Anorexia nervosa and bulimia.* Washington, DC: National Education Assoc.

Levinson, V. R. (1985). The compatibility of the disease concept with a psychodynamic approach in the treatment of alcoholism [Special issue: Psychosocial issues in the treatment of alcoholism]. *Alcohol. Treat. Q., 2*, 7–24.

Levitan, H. L. (1981). Implications of certain dreams reported by patients in a bulimic phase of anorexia nervosa. *Can. J. Psychiatry, 26*(4), 228–231.

Levitt, D. H. (2001). Anorexia nervosa: Treatment in the family context. *Fam. J. Counsel. Ther. Couples Fam., 9*(2), 159–163.

Levitt, E. E. (1989). *The clinical application of MMPI Special Scales.* Hillsdale, NJ: Erlbaum.

Levitt, R. (1975). *Psychopharmacology: A biological approach.* New York: Wiley.

Levy, D., Kimhi, R., Barak, Y., Demmer, M. et al. (1996). Brainstem auditory evoked potentials of panic disorder patients. *Neuropsychobiology 33*, 164–167.

Levy, N. B. (1985). The psychophysiological disorders: An overview. In R. C. Simons (Ed.), *Understanding human behavior in health and illness* (3rd ed.). Baltimore, MD: Williams & Wilkins.

Levy, R. L., Cain, K. C., Jarrett, M., & Heitkemper, M. M. (1997). The relationship between daily life stress and gastrointestinal symptoms in women with irritable bowel syndrome. *J. Behav. Med., 20*(2), 177–197.

Lewin, B. D. (1950). *The psychoanalysis of elation.* New York: Norton.

Lewinsohn, P. M. (1988). A prospective study of risk factors for unipolar depression. *J. Abnorm. Psychol., 97*(3), 251–284.

Lewinsohn, P. M., Antonuccio, D. O., Steinmetz, J. L., & Teri, L. (1984). *The coping with depression course.* Eugene, OR: Castalia.

Lewinsohn, P. M., & Clarke, G. N. (1999). Psychosocial treatment for adolescent depression. *Clin. Psychol. Rev., 19*(3), 329–342.

Lewinsohn, P. M., Clarke, G. N., Hops, H., & Andrews, J. (1990). Cognitive-behavioral treatment for depressed adolescents. *Behav. Ther., 21*, 385–401.

Lewinsohn, P. M., Rohde, P., Teri, L., & Tilson, M. (1990, April). Presentation. Western Psychological Association.

Lewinsohn, P. M., Sullivan, J. M., & Grosscup, S. J. (1982). Behavioral therapy: Clinical applications. In A. T. Rush (Ed.), *Short-term psychotherapies for the depressed patient.* New York: Guilford Press.

Lewinsohn, P. M., Youngren, M. A., & Grosscup, S. J. (1979). Reinforcement and depression. In R. A. Depue (Ed.), *The psychobiology of the depressive disorders.* New York: Academic Press.

Lewis, O., & Chatoor, I. (1994). Eating disorders. In J. M. Oldham & M. B. Riba (Eds.), *Review of psychiatry* (Vol. 13). Washington, DC: American Psychiatric Press.

Lewis-Harter, S. (2000). Psychosocial adjustment of adult children of alcoholics: A review of the recent empirical literature. *Clin. Psychol. Rev., 20*(3), 311–337.

Leyton, M., Okazawa, H., Diksic, M., Paris, J., Rosa, P., Mzengeza, S., Young, S. N., Blier, P., & Benkelfat, C. (2001). Brain regional α-[11C]Methyl-L-tryptophan trapping in impulsive subjects with borderline personality disorder. *Am. J. Psychiatry, 158*(5), 775–782.

Li, G., Chanmugam, A., Rothman, R., DiScala, C., Paidas, C. N., & Kelen, G. D. (1999). Alcohol and other psychoactive drugs in trauma patients aged 10–14 years. *Injury Prev., 5*(2), 94–97.

Li, T. K. (2000). Pharmacogenetics of responses to alcohol and genes that influence alcohol drinking. *J. Stud. Alcohol, 61*(1), 5–12.

Liberman, R., Marder, S., Marshall, B. D., Jr., Mintz, J., & Kuehnel, T. (1998). Biobehavioral therapy: Interactions between pharmacotherapy and behavior therapy in schizophrenia. In T. Wykes, N. Tarrier et al. (Eds.), *Outcome and innovation in psychological treatment of schizophrenia.* Chichester, England: Wiley.

Liberman, R. P. (1982). Assessment of social skills. *Schizophr. Bull., 8*(1), 82–84.

Liberman, R. P., & Raskin, D. E. (1971). Depression: A behavioral formulation. *Arch. Gen. Psychiatry, 24*, 515–523.

Lieberman, J. A., Chakos, M., Wu, H., Alvir, J., Hoffman, E., Robinson, D., & Bilder, R. (2001). Longitudinal study of brain morphology in first episode schizophrenia. *Biol. Psychiatry, 49*(6), 487–499.

Libow, J. A. (1995). Munchausen by proxy victims in adulthood: A first look. *Child Abuse Neglect, 19*(9), 1131–1142.

Libow, J. A., & Schreirer, H. A. (1998) Factitious disorder by proxy. In R. T. Ammerman & J. V. Campo (Eds.), *Handbook of pediatric psychology and psychiatry: Vol. 1. Psychological and psychiatric issues in the pediatric setting.* Boston: Allyn & Bacon.

Lichtenberg, J. W., & Kalodner, C. (1997, February 28). *The science-based practice of counseling psychology: A case for empirically-validated interventions.* Paper presented at the midwinter meeting of the Council of Counseling Psychology Training Programs, La Jolla, CA.

Lickey, M. E., & Gordon, B. (1991). *Medicine and mental illness: The use of drugs in psychiatry.* New York: Freeman.

Lidz, T. (1963). *The family and human adaptation.* New York: International Universities Press.

Lidz, T. (1973). *The origin and treatment of schizophrenic disorders.* New York: Basic Books.

Lidz, T., Cornelison, A., & Fleck, S. (1965). *Schizophrenia and the family.* New York: International Universities Press.

Lidz, T., Cornelison, A., Fleck, S., & Terry, D. (1957). The intra-familial environment of the schizophrenic patient: II. Marital schism and marital skew. *Am. J. Psychiatry, 114*, 241–248.

Lie, N. (1992). Follow-ups of children with attention deficit/hyperactivity disorder. *Acta Psychiatr. Scand., 85*, 40.

Lieberman, J. A. (1995). Signs and symptoms: What can they tell us about the clinical course and pathophysiologic processes of schizophrenia. *Arch. Gen. Psychiatry, 52*(5), 361–363.

Lieberman, J. A. (1998). Maximizing Clozapine therapy: Managing side effects. *J. Clin. Psychiatry, 59*(Suppl. 3), 38–43.

Lieberman, J. A., Alvir, J. Ma., Koreen, A., Geisler, S., Chakos, M., Scheitman, B., & Woerner, M. (1996). Psychobiologic correlates of treatment response in schizophrenia. *Neuropsychopharmacology, 14*, 13S–21S.

Liebowitz, M. R. (1992). Diagnostic issues in anxiety disorders. In A. Tasman & M. B. Riba (Eds.), *Review of psychiatry* (Vol. 11). Washington, DC: American Psychiatric Press.

Liebowitz, M. R., Heimberg, R. G., Schneier, F. R., Hope, D. A., Davies, S., Holt, C. S., Goetz, D., Juster, H. R., Lin, S. H., Bruch, M. A., Marshall, R. D., & Klein, D. F. (1999). Cognitive-behavioral group therapy versus phenelzine in social phobia: Long-term outcome. *Depression Anxiety, 10*(3), 89–98.

Liebowitz, M. R., Hollander, E., Schneier, F., Campeas, R. et al. (1990). Reversible and irreversible monoamine oxidase inhibitors in other psychiatric disorders. *Acta Psychiatr. Scand., 82*(Suppl. 360), 29–34.

Liebowitz, M. R., Schneier, F. R., Hollander, E., & Welkowitz, L. A. et al. (1991). Treatment of social phobia with drugs other than benzodiazepines. *J. Clin. Psychiatry, 52*(Suppl.), 10–15.

Liebowitz, M. R., Stone, M., & Turkat, I. D. (1986). Treatment of personality disorders. In A. Frances & R. Hales (Eds.), *American Psychiatric Association annual review* (Vol. 5). Washington, DC: American Psychiatric Press.

Liebowitz, S. F., & Hoebel, B. G. (1998). Behavioral neuroscience of obesity. In G. A. Bray, C. Bouchard, & P. T. James (Eds.), *The handbook of obesity.* New York: Dekker.

Liedl, B. (1999). Sex-adjusting surgery in transsexualism (in German). *MMW Fortschr Med., 141*(23), 41–45.

Lifton, R. J. (1973). *Home from the war: Vietnam veterans, neither victims nor executioners.* New York: Simon & Schuster.

Lilienfeld, S. O., Lynn, S. J., Kirsch, I., Chaves, J. F., Sarbin, T. R., Ganaway, G. K., & Powell, R. A. (1999). Dissociative identity disorder and the sociocognitive model: Recalling the lessons of the past. *Psychol. Bull., 125*(5), 507–523.

Limandri, B. J., & Sheridan, D. J. (1995). Prediction of intentional interpersonal violence: An introduction. In J. C. Campbell (Ed.), *Assessing dangerousness: Violence by sexual offenders, batterers, and child abusers.* Thousand Oaks, CA: Sage.

Linaker, O. M. (2000). Dangerous female psychiatric patients: Prevalences and characteristics. *Acta Psychiatr. Scand., 101*(1), 67–72.

Lindner, M. (1968). *Hereditary and environmental influences upon resistance to stress.* Unpublished doctoral dissertation, University of Pennsylvania, Philadelphia.

Lindsay, D. S. (1994). Contextualizing and clarifying criticisms of memory work in psychotherapy. *Consciousness Cognit., 3*, 426–437.

Lindsay, D. S. (1996). Contextualizing and clarifying criticisms of memory work in psychotherapy. In K. Pezdek & W. P. Banks (Eds.), *The recovered memory/false memory debate.* San Diego: Academic Press.

Lindsay, D. S., & Read, J. D. (1994). Psychotherapy and memories of childhood sexual abuse: A cognitive perspective. *J. Appl. Cognit. Psychol., 8*, 281–338.

Lindstrom, E. M., Ohlund, L. S., Lindstrom, L. H., & Ohman, A. (1992). Symptomatology and electrodermal activity as predictors of neuroleptic response in young male schizophrenic inpatients. *Psychiatry Res., 42*(2), 145–158.

Lindström, L. H. (1996). Clinical and biological markers for outcome in schizophrenia: A review of a longitudinal follow-up study in Uppsala schizophrenia research project. *Neuropsychopharmacology, 14*, 23S–26S.

Linehan, M. M. (1992). Behavior therapy, dialectics, and the treatment of borderline personality disorder. In D. Silver & M. Rosenbluth (Eds.), *Handbook of borderline disorders.* Madison, CT: International Universities Press.

Linehan, M. M. (1993). *Cognitive-behavioral therapy of borderline personality disorder.* New York: Guilford Press.

Linehan, M. M. (1998, June 7). Cited in G. Hochman, On the edge. *Inquirer Magazine*, p. 36.

Linehan, M. M., & Nielsen, S. L. (1981). Assessment of suicide ideation and parasuicide: Hopelessness and social desirability. *J. Consult. Clin. Psychol., 49*(5), 773–775.

Links, P. S. (1996). *Clinical assessment and management of severe personality disorders.* Washington, DC: American Psychiatric Press.

Links, P. S., & Heslegrave, R. J. (2000). Prospective studies of outcome. Understanding mechanisms of change in patients with borderline personality disorder. *Psychiatr. Clin. North Am., 23*(1), 137–150.

Linsky, A. S., Strauss, M. A., & Colby, J. P. (1985). Stressful events, stressful conditions and alcohol problems in the United States: A partial test of Bales's theory. *J. Stud. Alcohol, 46*(1), 72–80.

Linszen, D. H., Dingemans, P. M., Nugter, M. A., Willem, A. J. et al. (1997). Patient attributes and expressed emotion as risk factors for psychotic relapse. *Schizophr. Bull., 23*(1), 119–130.

Linz, D., & Imrich, D. (2001). Child pornography. In S. O. White (Ed.), *Handbook of youth and justice* (pp. 79–111). New York: Kluwer Academic/Plenum Press.

Linz, T. D., Hooper, S. R., Hynd, G. W., Isaac, W. et al. (1990). Frontal lobe functioning in conduct disordered juveniles: Preliminary findings. *Arch. Clin. Neuropsychol., 5*(4), 411–416.

Lipke, H. J., & Botkin, A. L. (1992). Brief case studies of eye movement desensitization and reprocessing (EMD/R) with chronic post-traumatic stress disorder. *Psychotherapy, 29,* 591–595.

Lipowski, Z. J. (1987). Somatization: Medicine's unsolved problem. *Psychosomatics, 28*(6), 294–297.

Lipschitz, A. (1995). Suicide prevention in young adults (age 18–30) [Special issue: Suicide prevention: Toward the year 2000]. *Suicide Life-Threaten. Behav., 25*(1), 155–170.

Lipsky, M. J., Kassinove, H., & Miller, N. J. (1980). Effects of rational-emotive therapy, rational role reversal, and rational-emotive imagery on the emotional adjustment of community mental health center patients. *J. Consult. Clin. Psychol., 48*(3), 366–374.

Lipton, A. A., & Simon, F. S. (1985). Psychiatric diagnosis in a state hospital: Manhattan State revisited. *Hosp. Commun. Psychiatry, 36*(4), 368–373.

Lipton, H. L. (1988). A prescription for change. *Generations, 12*(4), 74–79.

Lisansky-Gomberg, E. (1993). Women and alcohol: Use and abuse. *J. Nerv. Ment. Dis., 181*(4), 211–216.

Lish, J. D., Kavoussi, R. J., & Coccaro, E. F. (1996). Aggressiveness. In C. G. Costello (Ed.), *Personality characteristics of the personality disordered.* New York: Wiley.

Liss, M., & Stahly, G. (1993). Domestic violence and child custody. In M. Hansen & M. Harway (Eds.), *Battering and family therapy. A feminist perspective.* Newbury Park, CA: Sage.

Lissner, L., Odell, P. M., D'Agostino, R. B., Stokes, J., Kreger, B. E., Bélanger, A. J., & Brownell, K. D. (1991). Variability of body weight and health outcomes in the Farmingham population. *N. Engl. J. Med., 324,* 1839–1844.

Litaker, D., Locala, J., Franco, K., Bronson, D. L., & Tannous, Z. (2001). Preoperative risk factors for postoperative delirium. *Gen. Hosp. Psychiatry, 23*(2), 84–89.

Litinsky, A. M., & Haslam, N. (1998). Dichotomous thinking as a sign of suicide risk on the TAT. *J. Pers. Assess., 71*(3), 368–378.

Litman, R. E. (1995). Suicide prevention in a treatment setting [Special issue: Suicide prevention: Toward the year 2000]. *Suicide Life-Threaten. Behav., 25*(1), 134–142.

Litt, M. D. (1996). A model of pain and anxiety associated with acute stressors: Distress in dental procedures. *Behav. Res. Ther., 34*(5/6), 459–476.

Little, K. B., & Shneidman, E. S. (1959). Congruences among interpretations of psychological test and amamnestic data. *Psychol. Monogr., 73*(476).

Liu, L. (1999, March 19). Before you pop that pill . . . Something to know if you're over 65.

Livesley, W. J. (Ed.). (1995). *The DSM-IV personality disorders.* New York: Guilford Press.

Livesley, W. J. (2000). A practical approach to the treatment of patients with borderline personality disorder. *Psychiatr. Clin. North Am., 23*(1), 211–232.

Livesley, W. J., Schroeder, M. L., Jackson, D. N., & Jang, K. L. (1994). Categorical distinctions in the study of personality disorder: Implications for classification. *J. Abnorm. Psychol., 103*(1), 6–17.

Livingston, R., Witt, A., & Smith, G. R. (1995). Families who somatize. *J. Dev. Behav. Pediatry, 16*(1), 42–46.

Lloyd, G. G., & Lishman, W. A. (1975). Effect of depression on the speed of recall of pleasant and unpleasant experiences. *Psychol. Med., 5,* 173–180.

Lloyd, G. K., Fletcher, A., & Minchin, M. C. W. (1992). GABA agonists as potential anxiolytics. In G. D. Burrows, S. M. Roth, & R. Noyes, Jr., *Handbook of anxiety* (Vol. 5). Oxford, England: Elsevier.

Lock, J., & Giammona, A. (1999). Severe somatoform disorder in adolescence: A case series using a rehabilitation model for intervention. *Clin. Child Psychol. Psychiatry, 4*(3), 341–351.

Loebel, J. P., Loebel, J. S., Dager, S. R., Centerwall, B. S. et al. (1991). Anticipation of nursing home placement may be a precipitant of suicide among the elderly. *J. Am. Geriatr. Soc., 39*(4), 407–408.

Loerch, B., Graf-Morgenstern, M., Hautzinger, M., & Schlegel, S. (1999). Randomised placebo-controlled trial of moclobemide, cognitive-behavioural therapy and their combination in panic disorder with agoraphobia. *Br. J. Psychiatry, 174,* 205–212.

Loewenstein, R. J. (1991). Psychogenic amnesia and psychogenic fugue: A comprehensive review. In A. Tasman & S. M. Goldfinger (Eds.), *American Psychiatric Press review of psychiatry* (Vol. 10). Washington, DC: American Psychiatric Press.

Loftus, E. F. (1993). The reality of repressed memories. *Am. Psychol., 48,* 518–537.

Loftus, E. F. (1997). Repressed memory accusations: Devastated families and devastated patients. *Appl. Cognit. Psychol., 11,* 25–30.

Loftus, E.F. (2000). Remembering what never happened. In E. Tulving et al. (Eds.), *Memory, consciousness, and the brain: The Tallinn Conference.* Philadelphia: Psychology Press/Taylor & Francis.

Loge, J. H., Ekeberg, O., & Kaasa, S. (1998). Fatigue in the general Norwegian population: Normative data and associations. *J. Psychosom. Res., 56*(1), 53–65.

Logue, A. W. (1991). *The psychology of eating and drinking.* New York: Freeman.

Loh, E.-W., & Ball, D. (2000). Role of the $GABA_A\beta_2$, $GABA_A\alpha_6$, $GABA_A\alpha_1$ and $GABA_A\gamma_2$ receptor subunit genes cluster in drug responses and the development of alcohol dependence. *Neurochem. Int., 37*(5–6), 413–423.

LoLordo, A., & Sun Foreign Staff. (1998, September 13). Holocaust continues to take toll; Trauma: A portion of Israel's survivors have had to be institutionalized as the horrors they lived through have overwhelmed them. *Baltimore Sun,* p. 2A.

Longo, L. P. (1998). Non-benzodiazepine pharmacotherapy of anxiety and panic in substance abusing patients. *Psychiatr. Ann., 28*(3), 14–153.

Lonigan, C. J., Shannon, M. P., Taylor, C. M. et al. (1994). Children exposed to disaster: II. Risk factors for the development of post-traumatic symptomatology. *J. Am. Acad. Child Adolesc. Psychiatry, 33,* 94–105.

Loomer, H. P., Saunders, J. C., & Kline, N. S. (1957). A clinical and phamacodynamic evaluation of iproniazid as a psychic energizer. *Am. Psy. Assoc. Res. Rep., 8,* 129.

Looper, K. J., & Paris, J. (2000). What dimensions underlie Cluster B personality disorders? *Compr. Psychiatry, 41*(6), 432–437.

López, S. R., & Guarnaccia, P. J. (2000). *Annu. Rev. Psychol., 51,* 571–598.

LoPiccolo, C. J., Goodkin, K., & Baldewicz, T. T. (1999). Current issues in the diagnosis and management of malingering. *Ann. Med., 31*(3), 166–173.

LoPiccolo, J. (1985). Advances in diagnosis and treatment of male sexual dysfunction. *J. Sex Marital Ther., 11*(4), 215–232.

LoPiccolo, J. (1990). Treatment of sexual dysfunction. In A. S. Bellak, M. Hersen, & A. E. Kazdin (Eds.), *International handbook of behavior modification and therapy* (2nd ed.). New York: Plenum Press.

LoPiccolo, J. (1991). Post-modern sex therapy for erectile failure. In R. C. Rosen & S. R. Leiblum (Eds.), *Erectile failure: Diagnosis and treatment.* New York: Guilford Press.

LoPiccolo, J. (1992). Paraphilias. *Nord. Sex., 10*(1), 1–14.

LoPiccolo, J. (1995). Sexual disorders and gender identity disorders. In R. J. Comer (Ed.), *Abnormal psychology* (2nd ed.). New York: Freeman.

LoPiccolo, J. (1997). Sex therapy: A post-modern model. In S. J. Lynn & J. P. Garske (Eds.), *Contemporary psychotherapies: Models and methods* (2nd ed.).

LoPiccolo, J., & Friedman, J. R. (1988). Broad spectrum treatment of low sexual desire: Integration of cognitive, behavioral, and systemic treatment. In S. Leiblum & R. Rosen (Eds.), *Sexual desire disorders.* New York: Guilford Press.

LoPiccolo, J., & Stock, W. E. (1987). Sexual function, dysfunction, and counseling in gynecological practice. In Z. Rosenwaks, F. Benjamin, & M. L. Stone (Eds.), *Gynecology.* New York: Macmillan.

Lorand, S. (1950). *Clinical studies in psychoanalysis.* New York: International Universities Press.

Lorand, S. (1968). Dynamics and therapy of depressive states. In W. Gaylin (Ed.), *The meaning of despair.* New York: Jason Aronson.

Loranger, A. W., Sartoruis, N., Andreoli, A., Berger, P. et al. (1994). The International Personality Disorder Examination. *Arch. Gen. Psychiatry, 51,* 215–224.

Lorenzo, A., & Yankner, B. A. (1996). Amyloid fibril toxicity in Alzheimer's disease and diabetes. In R. J. Wurtman, S. Corkin, J. H. Growdon, & R. M. Nitsch (Eds.), *The neurobiology of Alzheimer's disease.* New York: New York Academy of Sciences.

Losonczy, M. F. et al. (1986). Correlates of lateral ventricular size in chronic schizophrenia: I. Behavioral and treatment response measures. *Am. J. Psychiatry, 143*(8), 976–981.

Lotufo-Neto, F., Trivedi, M., & Thase, M. E. (1999). Meta-analysis of the reversible inhibitors of monoamine oxidase type A moclobemide and brofaromine for the treatment of depression. *Neuropsychopharmacology, 20*(3), 226–247.

Lovaas, O. I. (1987). Behavioral treatment and normal educational/intellectual functioning in young autistic children. *J. Consult. Clin. Psychol., 55,* 3–9.

Love, S. R., Matson, J. L., & West, D. (1990). Mothers as effective therapists for autistic children's phobias. *J. Appl. Behav. Anal., 23*(3), 379–385.

Lovejoy, M. (1982). Expectations and the recovery process. *Schizophr. Bull., 8*(4), 605–609.

Lovejoy, M. (2001). Disturbances in the social body: Differences in body image and eating problems among African-American and white women. *Gender Soc., 15*(2), 239–261.

Lovett, M. W. (2000). Developmental reading disorders. In M. J. Farah & T. E. Feinberg (Eds.), *Patient-*

based approaches to cognitive neuroscience: Issues in clinical and congitive neuropsychology (pp. 247–261). Cambridge, MA: MIT Press.

Low, P., Jeffries, J., Jr., & Bonnie, R. (1986). *The trial of John W. Hinkley, Jr.: A case study in the insanity defense.* Mineola, NY: Foundation Press.

Lowe, M. R., Gleaves, D. H., DiSimone-Weiss, R. T., Forgueson, C. et al. (1996). Restraint, dieting, and the continuum model of bulimia nervosa. *J. Abnorm. Psychol., 105*(4), 508–517.

Lowenstein, L. F. (2001). Post-traumatic stress reactions in victims of motor accidents. *Police J., 74*(1), 9–25.

Lu, L. (1999). Personal or environmental causes of happiness: A longitudinal analysis. *J. Soc. Psychol., 139*(1), 79–90.

Lubetsky, M. J. (1986). The psychiatrist's role in the assessment and treatment of the mentally retarded child. *Child Psychiatry Hum. Dev., 16*(4), 261–273.

Luborsky, L. (1973). Forgetting and remembering (momentary forgetting) during psychotherapy. In M. Mayman (Ed.), *Psychoanalytic research and psychological issues* (Monogr. 30). New York: International Universities Press.

Luborsky, L., Diguer, L., Luborsky, E., & Schmidt, K. A. (1999). The efficacy of dynamic versus other psychotherapies: Is it true that "everyone has won and all must have prizes"?—An Update. In D. S. Janowsky et al. (Eds.), *Psychotherapy indications and outcomes.* Washington, DC: American Psychiatric Press.

Luborsky, L., Singer, B., & Luborsky, L. (1975). Comparative studies of psychotherapies. *Arch. Gen. Psychiatry, 32*, 995–1008.

Ludolph, P. S., Westen, D., Misle, B., Jackson, A. et al. (1990). The borderline diagnosis in adolescents: Symptoms and developmental history. *Am. J. Psychiatry, 147*(4), 470–476.

Ludwig, A. (1994). Creative activity and mental illness in female writers. *Am. J. Psychiatry, 151,* 1650–1656.

Ludwig, A. M. (1995). *The price of greatness: Resolving the creativity and madness controversy.* New York: Guilford Press.

Luechken, L. J. (1998). Childhood attachment and loss experiences affect adult cardiovascular and cortisol function. *Psychosom. Med., 60*(6), 765–772.

Luepker, E. T. (1999). Effects of practitioners' sexual misconduct: A follow-up study. *J. Am. Acad. Psychiatry Law, 27*(1), 51–63.

Lumley, V. A., & Scotti, J. R. (2001). Supporting the sexuality of adults with mental retardation: Current status and future directions. *J. Positive Behav. Interventions, 3*(2), 109–119.

Lundberg, U., Dohns, I. E., Medlin, B., Sandsjoe, L., Palmerud, G., Kadefors, R., Ekstroem, M., & Parr, D. (1999). Psychophysiological stress responses, muscle tension, and neck and shoulder pain among supermarket cashiers. *J. Occup. Health Psychol., 4*(3), 245–255.

Lundholm, J. K., & Waters, J. E. (1991). Dysfunctional family systems: Relationship to disordered eating behaviors among university women. *J. Subst. Abuse, 3*(1), 97–106.

Luntz, B. K., & Widom, C. S. (1994). Antisocial personality disorder in abused and neglected children grown up. *Am. J. Psychiatry, 151*(5), 670–674.

Lutgendorf, S. K., Antoni, M. H., Ironson, G., Klimas, N., Kumar, M., Starr, K., McCabe, P., Cleven, K., Fletcher, M. A., & Schneiderman, N. (1997). Cognitive-behavioral stress management decreases dysphoric mood and herpes simplex virus-type 2 antibody titers in symptomatic HIV-seropositive gay men. *J. Consult. Clin. Psychol., 65,* 31–43.

Lydiard, R. B., & Brawman-Mintzer, O. (1998). Anxious depression. *J. Clin. Psychiatry, 59*(Suppl. 18), 10–17.

Lyketsos, C. G., Hoover, D. R., Guccione, M., Dew, M. A. et al. (1996). Changes in depressive symptoms as AIDS develops. *Am. J. Psychiatry, 153*(11), 1430–1437.

Lykken, D. T. (1957). A study of anxiety in the sociopathic personality. *J. Abnorm. Soc. Psychol., 55,* 6–10.

Lykken, D. T. (1995). *The antisocial personalities.* Hillsdale, NJ: Erlbaum.

Lykken, D. T. (1998). *A tremor in the blood: Uses and abuses of the lie detector.* New York: Plenum Press.

Lykken, D. T., & Tellegen, A. (1996). Happiness is a stochastic phenomenon. *Psychol. Sci., 7*(3), 186–189.

Lyman, B. (1982). The nutritional values and food group characteristics of foods preferred during various emotions. *J. Psychol., 112,* 121–127.

Lymburner, J. A., & Roesch, R. (1999). The insanity defense: Five years of research (1993-1997). *Int. J. Law Psychiatry, 22*(3–4), 213–240.

Lynch, G. (1998). The application of self-psychology to short-term counselling. *Psychodyn. Counsel., 4*(4), 473–485.

Lyness, J. M., Caine, E. D., King, D. A., Cox, C., & Yoediono, Z. (1999). Psychiatric disorders in older primary care patients. *J. Gen. Intern. Med., 14*(4), 249–254.

Lyness, J. M., King, D. A., Cox, C., Yoediono, Z., & Caine, E. D. (1999). The importance of subsyndromal depression in older primary care patients: Prevalenced and associated functional disability. *J. Am. Geriatr. Soc., 47*(6), 647–652.

Lyon, K. A. (1992). Shattered mirror: A fragment of the treatment of a patient with multiple personality disorder. *Psychoanal. Q., 12*(1), 71–94.

Lyon, L. S. (1985). Facilitating telephone number recall in a case of psychogenic amnesia. *J. Behav. Ther. Exp. Psychiatry, 16*(2), 147–149.

Lyon, M., Chatoor, I., Atkins, D., Silber, T. et al. (1997, Spring). Testing the hypothesis of the multidimensional model of anorexia nervosa in adolescents. *Adolescence, 32*(125), 101–111.

Lysaker, P., & Bell, M. (1995). Work and meaning: Disturbance of volition and vocational dysfunction in schizophrenia. *Psychiatry, 58*(4), 392–400.

MORI (Market Opinion Research International). (1999, May 22) Poll on animal experimentation. *New Sci.*

MRI (Matrix Research Institute). (1998). *The facts about mental illness and work.* Philadelphia: Author.

MacDonald, M. L., & Schnur, R. E. (1987). Anxieties and American elders: Proposals for assessment and treatment. In L. Michelson & L. M. Ascher (Eds.), *Anxiety and stress disorders: Cognitive behavioral assessment and treatment.* New York: Guilford Press.

MacDonald, W. L. (1998). The difference between blacks' and whites' attitudes toward voluntary euthanasia. *J. Sci. Study Religion, 37*(3), 411–426.

Mace, N., & Rabins, P. (1991). *The 36-hour day* (2nd ed.). Baltimore: Johns Hopkins University Press.

MacHovek, F. J. (1981). Hypnosis to facilitate recall in psychogenic amnesia and fugue states: Treatment variables. *Am. J. Clin. Hypnosis, 24*(1), 7–13.

Machover, K. (1949). *Personality projection in the drawing of the human figure.* Springfield, IL: Thomas.

MacIntyre, D., & Carr. A. (1999). Evaluation of the effectiveness of the stay safe primary prevention program for child sexual abuse. *Child Abuse Neglect, 23*(12), 1307–1325.

MacIntyre, D., & Carr, A. (1999). Helping children to the other side of silence: A study of the impact of the stay safe program on Irish children's disclosures of sexual victimization. *Child Abuse Neglect, 23*(12), 1327–1340.

MacQueen, G. M., & Young, L. T. (2001). Bipolar II disorder: Symptoms, course, and response to treatment. *Psychiatr. Serv., 52*(3), 358–361.

Madge, N., & Harvey, J. G. (1999). Suicide among the young: The size of the problem. *J. Adolesc., 22*(1), 145–155.

Madianos, M. G., & Madianou, D. (1992). The effects of long-term community care on relapse and adjustment of persons with chronic schizophrenia. *Int. J. Ment. Health, 21*(1), 37–49.

Magee, W. J., Eaton, W. W., Wittchen, H.-U., McGonagle, K. A., & Kessler, R. C. (1996). Agoraphobia, simple phobia, and social phobia in the National Comorbidity Survey. *Arch. Gen. Psychiatry, 53,* 159–168.

Magherini, G., & Biotti, V. (1998). Madness in Florence in the 14th-18th centuries: Judicial inquiry and medical diagnosis, care, and custody. *Int. J. Law Psychiatry, 21*(4), 355–368.

Maguire, T. (1998, December). Web nets the masses. *Am. Demogr.*

Maguire, T. (1999, January). The skinny on Zzzzzzs. *Am. Demogr.*

Maher, B. A. (1974). Delusional thinking and perceptual disorder. *J. Individual Psychol., 30*(1), 98–113.

Maher, B. A., & Maher, W. B. (1994). Personality and psychopathology: A historical perspective. *J. Abnorm. Psychol., 103*(1), 72–77.

Maher, W. B., & Maher, B. A. (1985). Psychopathology: I. From ancient times to the eighteenth century. In G. A. Kimble & K. Schlesinger (Eds.), *Topics in the history of psychology* (Vol. 2). Hillsdale, NJ: Erlbaum.

Maier, S. F. (1997, September). *Stressor controllability, anxiety, and serotonin.* Paper presented at the National Institute of Mental Health Workshop on Cognition and Anxiety, Rockville, MD.

Maier, S. F., Watkins, L. R., & Fleshner, M. (1994). Psychoneuroimmunology. The interface between behavior, brain and immunity. *Am. Psychol., 49*(12), 1004–1017.

Maier, W., Gaensicke, M., Freyberger, H. J., Linz, M., Heun, R., & Lecrubier, Y. (2000). Generalized anxiety disorder (ICD-10) in primary care from a cross-cultural perspective: A valid diagnostic entity? *Acta Psychiatr. Scand., 101*(1), 29–36.

Maier, W., Gaensicke, M., Gater, R., Rezaki, M. Tiemens, B., & Urzua, R. F. (1999). Gender differences in the prevalence of depression: A survey in primary care. *J. Affect. Disord., 53*(3), 241–252.

Maina, G., Albert, U., & Bogetto, F. (2001). Relapses after discontinuation of drugs associated with increased resistance to treatment in obsessivecompulsive disorder. *Int. Clin. Psychopharmacol., 16*(1), 33–38.

Maj, M., Pirozzi, R., Magliano, L., & Bartoli, L. (1998). Long-term outcome of lithium prophylaxis in bipolar disorder: A 5-year prospective study of 402 patients at a lithium clinic. *Am. J. Psychiatry, 155*(1), 30–35.

Maj, M., Satz, P., Janssen, R., Zaudig, M. et al. (1994). WHO neuropsychiatric AIDS study, Cross-sectional phase II. *Arch. Gen. Psychiatry, 51,* 51–61.

Malcolm, A. H. (1990, Jun. 9). Giving death a hand. *New York Times,* p. A6.

Maller, R. G., & Reiss, S. (1992). Anxiety sensitivity in 1984 and panic attacks in 1987. *J. Anxiety Disord., 6*(3), 241–247.

Malley, P. B., & Reilly, E. P. (1999). *Legal and ethical dimensions for mental health professionals.* Philadelphia: Taylor & Francis.

Malone, K. M, Corbitt, E. M., Li, S., & Mann, J. J. (1996). Prolactin response to fenfluramine and suicide attempt lethality in major depression. *Br. J. Psychiatry, 168*, 324–329.

Maltsberger, J. T. (1999). The psychodynamic understanding of suicide. In D. G. Jacobs et al. (Eds.), *The Harvard Medical School guide to suicide assessment and intervention.* San Francisco: Jossey-Bass.

Mandell, A. J., & Knapp, S. (1979). Asymmetry and mood, emergent properties of seratonin regulation: A proposed mechanism of action of lithium. *Arch. Gen. Psychiatry, 36*(8), 909–916.

Manderscheid, R. W., Henderson, M. J., Witkin, M. J., & Atay, J. E. (1999). Contemporary mental health systems and managed care. In A. V. Horwitz & T. L. Scheid (Eds.), *A handbook for the study of mental health: Social contexts, theories, and systems.* Cambridge, England: Cambridge University Press.

Manderscheid, R. W., & Rosenstein, M. (1992). Homeless persons with mental illness and alcohol or other drug abuse: Current research, policy, and prospects. *Curr. Opin. Psychiatry, 5*, 273–278.

Mandler, J. M., & McDonough, L. (1995). Long-term recall of event sequences in infancy. *J. Exp. Child Psychol., 59*, 457–474.

Manji, H. K., Bebchuk, J. M., Moore, G. J., Glitz, D., Hasanat, K. A., & Chen, G. (1999). Modulation of CNS signal transduction pathways and gene expression by mood-stabilizing agents: Therapeutic implications. *J. Clin. Psychiatry, 60*(Suppl. 2), 27–39.

Manley, R. S., & Needham, L. (1995). An anti-bulimia group for adolescent girls. *J. Child Adolesc. Group Ther., 5*(1), 19–33.

Mann, B. J. (1995). The North Carolina Dissociation Index: A measure of dissociation using items from the MMPI-2. *J. Pers. Assess., 64*(2), 349–359.

Mann, J. J., & Arango, V. (1999). The neurobiology of suicidal behavior. In J. D.G. Jacobs (Ed.), *The Harvard Medical School guide to suicide assessment and intervention.* San Francisco: Jossey-Bass.

Mann, J. J., Brent, D. A., & Arango, V. (2001). The neurobiology and genetics of suicide and attempted suicide: A focus on the serotonergic system. *Neurosychopharmacology, 24*(5), 467–477.

Mann, J. J., Oquendo, M., Underwood, M. D., & Arango, V. (1999). The neurobiology of suicide risk: A review for the clinician. *J. Clin. Psychiatry, 60*(Suppl. 2), 7–11.

Manning, A. (1996, January 16). New alcohol programs turn focus to moderation. *USA Today*, p. 6D.

Mannuzza, S., Klein, R. G., Bessler, A., Malloy, P., & LaPadula, M. (1993). Adult outcome of hyperactive boys. *Arch. Gen. Psychiatry, 50*, 565–576.

Mannuzza, S., Klein, R. G., Bressler, A., Malloy, P., & LaPadula, M. (1998). Adult psychiatric status of hyperactive boys grown up. *Am. J. Psychiatry, 155*(4), 493–498.

Manschreck, T. C. (1996). Delusional disorder: The recognition and management of paranoia. *J. Clin. Psychiatry, 57*(Suppl. 3), 32–38.

Manson, J. E., Willett, W. C., Stampfer, M. J., Colditz, G. A. et al. (1995). Body weight and mortality among women. *N. Engl. J. Med., 333*(11), 677–685.

Manson, S. M., & Good, B. J. (1993). *Cultural considerations in the diagnosis of DSM-IV mood disorders. Cultural proposals and supporting papers for DSM-IV.* Submitted to the DSM-IV Task Force by the Steering Committee, NIMH-Sponsored Group on Culture and Diagnosis.

Manuck, S. B., Cohen, S., Rabin, B. S., Muldoon, M. F., & Bachen, E. A. (1991). Individual differences in cellular immune responses to stress. *Psychol. Sci., 2*, 1–5.

Marazziti, D., Akiskal, H. S., Rossi, A., & Cassano, G. B. (1999). Alteration of the platelet sero-tonin transporter in romantic love. *Psychol. Med., 29*(3), 741–745.

March, J. S., & Curry, J. F. (1998). Predicting the outcome of treatment. *J. Abnorm. Child Psychol., 26*(1), 39–51.

Marcus, D. K. (1999). The cognitive-behavioral model of hypochondriasis: Misinformation and triggers. *J. Psychosom. Res., 47*(1), 79–91.

Marder, S. R. (1996). Management of schizophrenia. *J. Clin. Psychiatry, 57*(Suppl. 3), 9–13.

Margo, G. M., & Newman, J. S. (1989). Venesection as a rare form of self-mutilation. *Am. J. Psychother., 43*(3), 427–432.

Margo, J. L. (1985). Anorexia nervosa in adolescents. *Br. J. Med. Psychol., 58*(2), 193–195.

Margraf, J., Ehlers, A., Roth, W. T., Clark, D. B. et al. (1991). How "blind" are double-blind studies? *J. Consult. Clin. Psychol., 59*(1), 184–187.

Mariani, M. A., & Barkley, R. A. (1997). Neuropsychological and academic functioning in preschool boys with attention deficit/hyperactivity disorder. *Dev. Neuropsychol., 13*(1), 111–129.

Maris, R. W. (1992). How are suicides different? In R. W. Maris, A. L. Berman, J. T. Maltsberger, & R. I. Yufit (Eds.), *Assessment and prediction of suicide.* New York: Guilford Press.

Maris, R. W. (1992). Methods of suicide. In R. W. Maris, A. L. Berman, J. T. Maltsberger, & R. I. Yufit (Eds.), *Assessment and prediction of suicide.* New York: Guilford Press.

Maris, R. W. (1992). Overview of the study of suicide assessment and prediction. In R. W. Maris, A. L. Berman, J. T. Maltsberger, & R. I. Yufit (Eds.), *Assessment and prediction of suicide.* New York: Guilford Press.

Maris, R. W., & Silverman, M. M. (1995). Postscript: Summary and synthesis [Special issue: Suicide prevention: Toward the year 2000]. *Suicide Life-Threaten. Behav., 25*(1), 205–209.

Mark, T. L., Woody, G. E., Juday, T., & Kleber, H. D. (2001). The economic costs of heroin addiction in the United States. *Drug Alcohol Depend., 61*(2), 195–206.

Markman, H. J., & Hahlweg, K. (1993). The prediction and prevention of marital distress: An international perspective. *Clin. Psychol. Rev., 13*(1), 29–43.

Marks, I., Green, R., & Mataix-Cols, D. (2000). Adult gender identity disorder can remit. *Compr. Psychiatry, 41*(4), 273–275.

Marks, I. M. (1977). Phobias and obsessions: Clinical phenomena in search of a laboratory model. In J. Maser and M. Seligman (Eds.), *Psychopathology: Experimental models.* San Francisco: Freeman.

Marks, I. M. (1987). Comment on S. Lloyd Williams' "On anxiety and phobia." *J. Anxiety Disord., 1*(2), 181–196.

Marks, I. M. (1987). *Fears, phobias and rituals: Panic, anxiety and their disorders.* New York: Oxford University Press.

Marks, I. M., & Gelder, M. G. (1967). Transvestism and fetishism: Clinical and psychological changes during faradic aversion. *Br. J. Psychiatry, 113*, 711–730.

Marks, I. M., & Swinson, R. (1992). Behavioral and/or drug therapy. In G. D. Burrows, S. M. Roth, & R. Noyes, Jr., *Handbook of anxiety* (Vol. 5). Oxford, England: Elsevier.

Marks, J. (1998, October 12). Mayor vs. drug czar. *U.S. News.*

Marlatt, G. A. (1985). Controlled drinking: The controversy rages on. *Am. Psychologist, 40*(3), 374–375.

Marlatt, G. A., Blume, A. W., & Parks, G. A. (2001). Integrating harm reduction therapy and traditional substance abuse treatment. *J. Psychoact. Drugs, 33*(1), 13–21.

Marlatt, G. A., Kosturn, C. F., & Lang, A. R. (1975). Provocation to anger and opportunity for retaliation as determinants of alcohol consumption in social drinkers. *J. Abnorm. Psychol., 84*(6), 652–659.

Marmar, C. R., Foy, D., Kagan, B., & Pynoos, R. S. (1993). An integrated approach for treating posttraumatic stress. In J. M. Oldham, M. B. Riba, & A. Tasman (Eds.), *Review of psychiatry* (Vol. 12). Washington, DC: American Psychiatric Press.

Marquis, J. N., & Morgan, W. G. (1969). *A guidebook for systematic desensitization.* Palo Alto, CA: Veterans Administration Hospital.

Marsella, A. J. (1980). Depressive experience and disorder across cultures. In H. C. Triandis & J. Draguns (Eds.), *Handbook of cross-cultural psychology* (Vol. 6). Boston: Allyn & Bacon.

Marshall, J. J. (1997). Personal communication.

Marshall, J. R. (1997). Alcohol and substance abuse in panic disorder. *J. Clin. Psychiatry, 58*(Suppl. 2), 46–49.

Marshall, L. A., & Cooke, D. J. (1999). The childhood experiences of psychopaths: A retrospective study of familial and societal factors. *J. Pers. Disord., 13*(3), 211–225.

Marshall, W. L., & Lippens, K. (1977). The clinical value of boredom: A procedure for reducing inappropriate sexual interests. *J. Nerv. Ment. Dis., 165*, 283–287.

Marston, W. M. (1917). Systolic blood pressure changes in deception. *J. Exp. Physiol., 2*, 117–163.

Martin, G. (1998). Media influence to suicide: The search for solutions. *Arch. Suicide Res., 4*(1), 51–66.

Martin, G., & Pear, J. (1999). *Behavior modification: What it is and how to do it* (6th ed.). Upper Saddle River, NJ: Prentice Hall.

Martin, J. K., Kraft, J. M., & Roman, P. M. (1994). Extent and impact of alcohol and drug use problems in the workplace: A review of the empirical evidence. In S. Macdonald & P. Roman (Eds.), *Research advances in alcohol and drug problems: Vol. 11. Drug testing in the workplace.* New York: Plenum Press.

Martin, N. J., Stones, M. J., Young, J. E., & Bedard, M. (2000). Development of delirium: A prospective cohort study in a community hospital. *Int. Psychogeriatr., 12*(1), 117–127.

Martin, P. L. (2000). Potency and pregnancy in Japan: Did Viagra push the Pill? *Tulsa Law. J., 35*, 651–677.

Martin, S. (1996). Improving lives, not just infrastructures. *APA Monitor, 27*(10), 24.

Martin, W. T. (1984). Religiosity and U.S. suicide rates, 1972–1978. *J. Clin. Psychol., 40*(5), 1166–1169.

Martineau, J., Barthelemy, C., Jouve, J., & Muh, J. P. (1992). Monoamines (serotonin and catecholamines) and their derivatives in infantile autism: Age-related changes and drug effects. *Dev. Med. Child Neurol., 34*(7), 593–603.

Martinez, J. L., Jr., & Derrick, B. E. (1996). Long-term potentiation and learning. *Annu. Rev. Psychol., 47.*

Martinez, P., & Richters, J. E. (1993). The NIMH community violence project: II. Children's distress symptoms associated with violence exposure. *Psychiatry, 56*, 22–35.

Marzuk, P. M., Tardiff, K., Leon, A. C., Stajic, M., Morgan, E. B., & Mann, J. J. (1992). Prevalence of cocaine use among residents of New York City who committed suicide during a one-year period. *Am. J. Psychiatry, 149*(3), 371–375.

Masi, G., Mucci, M., & Millepiedi, S. (2001). Separation anxiety disorder in children and adolescents: Epidemiology, diagnosis and management. *CNS Drugs, 15*(2), 93–104.

Maslow, A. H. (1970). *Motivation and personality* (2nd ed.). New York: Harper & Row.

Mâsse, L. C., & Tremblay, R. E. (1997). Behavior of boys in kindergarten and the onset of substance use during adolescence. *Arch. Gen. Psychiatry, 54,* 62–68.

Masters, W. H., & Johnson, V. E. (1966). *Human sexual response.* Boston: Little, Brown.

Masters, W. H., & Johnson, V. E. (1970). *Human sexual inadequacy.* Boston: Little, Brown.

Matarazzo, J. D. (1984). Behavioral health: A 1990 challenge for the health sciences professions. In J. D. Matarazzo, S. M. Weiss, J. A. Herd, N. E. Miller, & S. M. Weiss (Eds.), *Behavioral health: A handbook of health enhancement and disease prevention.* New York: Wiley.

Mathew, R., Wilson, W., Blazer, D., & George, L. (1993). Psychiatric disorders in adult children of alcoholics: Data from the epidemiologic catchment area project. *Am. J. Psychiatry, 150*(5), 793–796.

Mathew, S. J., Yudofsky, S. C., McCullough, L. B., Teasdale, T. A., & Jankovic, J. (1999). Attitudes toward neurosurgical procedures for Parkinson's disease and obsessive-compulsive disorder. *J. Neuropsychiatry Clin. Neurosci., 11*(2), 259–267.

Mathews, A., Whitehead, A., & Hellett, J. (1983). Psychological and hormonal factors in the treatment of female sexual dysfunction. *Psychol. Med., 13,* 83–92.

Matson, J. L., Bamburg, J. W., Mayville, E. A., Pinkston, J., Bielecki, J., Kuhn, D., Smalls, Y., & Logan, J. R. (2000). Psychopharmacology and mental retardation: A 10-year review (1990–1999). *Res. Dev. Disabil., 21*(4), 263–296.

Matsunaga, H., Kaye, W. H., McConaha, C., Plotnicov, K., Pollice, C., & Rao, R. (2000). Personality disorders among subjects recovering from eating disorders. *Int. J. Eat. Disord., 27*(3), 353–357.

Matthys, W., Walterbos, W., Njio, L., & Van Engeland, H. (1988). Person perception of children with conduct disorders. *Tijdschr. Psychiatr., 30*(5), 302–314.

Mattis, S., & Wilson, B. C. (1997). Psychological assessment in a managed care climate: The neuropsychological evaluation. In L. J. Dickstein, M. B. Riba, & J. M. Oldham (Eds.), *Review of psychiatry* (Vol. 16). Washington, DC: American Psychiatric Press.

Maugh, T. H., II. (1995, May 31). Researchers hone in on gene that may cause "werewolf" disorder. *Los Angeles Times,* p. A3.

Mauk, G. W., & Sharpnack, J. D. (1998). A light unto the darkness: The psychoeducational imperative of school-based suicide postvention. In A. H. Esman, L. T. Flaherty, et al. (Eds.), *Adolescent psychiatry: Developmental and clinical studies: Vol. 23. Annals of the American Society for Adolescent Psychiatry.* Hillsdale, NJ: Analytic Press.

Maurer, D. W., & Vogel, V. H. (1978). *Narcotics and narcotic addiction.* Springfield, IL: Thomas.

Mavissakalian, M. R., Hamann, M. S., & Jones, B. (1990). Correlates of DSM III personality disorder in obsessive-compulsive disorder. *Compr. Psychiatry, 31*(6), 481–489.

May, P. R. A., & Tuma, A. H. (1964). Choice of criteria for the assessment of treatment outcome. *J. Psychiatry Res., 2*(3), 16–527.

May, P. R. A., Tuma, A. H., & Dixon, W. J. (1981). Schizophrenia: A follow-up study of the results of five forms of treatment. *Arch. Gen. Psychiatry, 38,* 776–784.

May, R. (1961). *Existential psychology.* New York: Random House.

May, R. (1967). *Psychology and the human dilemma.* New York: Van Nostrand-Reinhold.

May, R. (1987). Therapy in our day. In J. K. Zeig (Ed.), *The evolution of psychotherapy.* New York: Brunner/Mazel.

May, R., Angel, E., & Ellenberger, H. F. (1958). *Existence: A new dimension in psychiatry and psychology.* New York: Basic Books.

May, R., & Yalom, I. (1989). Existential psychotherapy. In R. J. Corsini & D. Wedding (Eds.), *Current psychotherapies.* Itasca, IL: Peacock.

May, R., & Yalom, I. (1995). Existential psychotherapy. In R. J. Corsini & D. Wedding (Eds.), *Current psychotherapies* (5th ed.). Itasca, IL: Peacock.

Mays, D. T., & Franks, C. M. (1985). *Negative outcome in psychotherapy and what to do about it.* New York: Springer.

Mazo, E. (1999, March 23). Studying St. John's wort; Pitt participating in examination of popular herbal anti-depressant. *Pittsburgh Post-Gazette,* p. G5.

McCabe, M. P., & Delaney, S. M. (1992). An evaluation of therapeutic programs for the treatment of secondary inorgasmia in women. *Arch. Sex. Behav., 21*(1), 69–89.

McCabe, R., Roder-Wanner, U. U., Hoffmann, K., & Priebe, S. (1999). Therapeutic relationships and quality of life: Association of two subjective constructs in schizophrenia patients. *Int. J. Soc. Psychiatry, 45*(4), 276–283.

McCarroll, J. E., Fullerton, C. S., Ursano, R. J., & Hermsen, J. M. (1996). Posttraumatic stress symptoms following forensic dental identification: Mt. Carmel, Waco, Texas. *Am. J. Psychiatry, 153,* 778–782.

McCarthy, M. (1990). The thin ideal, depression and eating disorders in women. *Behav. Res. Ther., 28*(3), 205–215.

McCarthy, P. R., Katz, I. R., & Foa, E. B. (1991). Cognitive-behavioral treatment of anxiety in the elderly: A proposed model. In C. Salzman & B. D. Leibowitz (Eds.), *Anxiety in the elderly.* New York: Springer.

McClelland, D. C. (1993). Motives and health. In G. G. Brannigan & M. R. Merrens (Eds.), *The undaunted psychologist.* New York: McGraw-Hill.

McClelland, L., & Crisp, A. (2001). Anorexia nervosa and social class. *Int. J. Eat. Disord., 29*(2), 150–156.

McClelland, S. (1998, September 21). Grief crisis counsellors under fire: Trauma teams were quick to descend on Peggy's Cove. Susan McClelland asks whether they do more harm than good. *Ottawa Citizen,* p. A4.

McCormick, L. H. (2000). Improving social adjustment in children with attention-deficit/hyperactivity disorder. *Arch. Fam. Med., 9*(2), 191–194.

McCoy, S. A. (1976). Clinical judgments of normal childhood behavior. *J. Consult. Clin. Psychol., 44*(5), 710–714.

McCreadie, R. G., Thara, R., Kamath, S., Padmavathy, R., Latha, S., Mathrubootham, N., & Menon, M. S. (1996). Abnormal movements in never-medicated Indian patients with schizophrenia. *Br. J. Psychiatry, 168,* 221–226.

McCurdy, K., & Daro, D. (1993). *Current trends: A fifty state survey.* Washington, DC: National Committee for the Prevention of Child Abuse.

McDaniel, J. S., Moran, M. G., Levenson, J. L., & Stoudemire, A. (1994). Psychological factors affecting medical conditions. In R. E. Hales, S. C. Yudofsky, & J. A. Talbott (Eds.), *The American Psychiatric Press textbook of psychiatry* (2nd ed.). Washington, DC: American Psychiatric Press.

McDaniel, S. H., Lusterman, D. D., & Philpot, C. L. (Eds.). (2001). *Casebook for integrating family therapy: An ecosystemic approach.* Washington, DC: American Psychological Association.

McDermut, W., Miller, I. W., & Brown, R. A. (2001). The efficacy of group psychotherapy for depression: A meta-analysis and review of the empirical research. *Clin. Psychol.: Sci. Pract., 8*(1), 98–116.

McEachin, J. J., Smith, T., & Lovaas, O. I. (1993). Long-term outcome for children with autism who received early intensive behavioral treatment. *Am. J. Ment. Retard., 97*(4), 359–372.

McElroy, S. L., Hudson, J. L., Pope, H. G., & Keck, P. E. (1991). Kleptomania: Clinical characteristics and associated psychopathology. *Psychol. Med., 21*(1), 93–108.

McEvoy, J. (1992). Fragile X syndrome: A brief overview. *Educ. Psychol. Pract., 8*(3), 146–149.

McEwen, B. S. (2000). The neurobiology of stress: From serendipity to clinical relevance. *Brain Res., 886*(1–2), 172–189.

McFarlane, A.C. (1999). Risk factors for the acute biological and psychological response to trauma. In R. Yehuda (Ed.), *Risk factors for posttraumatic stress disorder.* Washington, DC: American Psychiatric Press.

McGaugh, J. (1999, March 30). Interviewed in L. Muhammad. Experts brainstorming over memory loss. *USA Today,* p. 6D.

McGeer, P. L., & McGeer, E. G. (1996). Anti-inflammatory drugs in the fight against Alzheimer's disease. In R. J. Wurtman, S. Corkin, J. H. Growdon, & R. M. Nitsch (Eds.), *The neurobiology of Alzheimer's disease.* New York: New York Academy of Sciences.

McGehee, D. S., Heath, M. J. S., Gelber, S., Devay, P., & Role, L. W. (1995). Nicotine enhancement of fast excitatory synaptic transmission in CNS by presynaptic receptors. *Science, 269,* 1692–1696.

McGhie, A., & Chapman, J. S. (1961). Disorders of attention and perception in early schizophrenia. *Br. J. Med. Psychol., 34,* 103–116.

McGlashan, T. H. (1986). Schizotypal personality disorder: Chestnut Lodge follow-up study: VI. Long-term follow-up perspectives. *Arch. Gen. Psychiatry, 43*(4), 329–334.

McGlynn, F. D., & Bates, L. W. (1999). Cognitive behavior therapy. In M. Hersen & A. S. Bellack (Eds.), *Handbook of comparative interventions for adult disorder* (2nd ed.). New York: Wiley.

McGlynn, F. D., Moore, P. M., Lawyer, S., & Karg, R. (1999). Relaxation training inhibits fear and arousal during in vivo exposure to phobia-cue stimuli. *J. Behav. Ther. Exp. Psychiatry, 30*(3), 155–168.

McGoldrick, M., Gerson, R., & Shellenberger, S. (1999). *Genograms: Assessment and intervention* (2nd ed.). New York: Norton.

McGrady, A., Lynch, D., Nagel, R., & Zsembik, C. (1999). Application of the High Risk Model of Threat Perception to a primary care patient population. *J. Nerv. Ment. Dis., 187*(6), 369–375.

McGrath, M. L., Mellon, M. W., & Murphy, L. (2000). Empirically supported treatments in pediatric psychology: Constipation and encopresis. *J. Pediatr. Psychol., 25*(4), 225–254.

McGrath, P. A., & Hillier, L. M. (2001). Recurrent headache: Triggers, causes, and contributing factors. In P. A. McGrath & L. M. Hiller (Eds.), *The child with headache: Diagnosis and treatment* (pp. 77–107). Seattle, WA: IASP Press.

McGrath, P. H. (1999). Clinical psychology issues in migraine headaches. *Can. J. Neurol. Sci., 26*(Suppl. 3), S33–S36.

McGuffin, P., Katz, R., Watkins, S., & Rutherford, J. (1996). A hospital-based twin register of the heritability of DSM-IV unipolar depression. *Arch. Gen. Psychiatry, 53,* 129–136.

McGuire, D. (1982). The problem of children's suicide: Ages 5–14. *Int. J. Offender Ther. Comp. Criminol., 26*(1), 10–17.

McGuire, P. A. (2000, February). New hope for people with schizophrenia. *Monitor Psychol., 31*(2), 24–28.

McGuire, P. K., Shah, G. M. S., & Murray, R. M. (1993). Increased blood flow in Broca's area during auditory hallucinations in schizophrenia. *Lancet, 342,* 703–706.

McGuire, P. K., Silbersweig, D. A., Wright, I., Murray, R. M., Frackowiak, R. S., & Frith,

C. D. (1996). The neural correlates of inner speech and auditory verbal imagery in schizophrenia: Relationship to auditory verbal hallucinations. *Br. J. Psychiatry, 169*(2), 148–159.

McGuire, P. K., Silbersweig, D. A., Wright, I., Murray, R. M. et al. (1995). Abnormal monitoring of inner speech: A physiological basis for auditory hallucinations. *Lancet, 346,* 596–600.

McIntosh, J. L. (1987). Suicide: Training and education needs with an emphasis on the elderly. *Gerontol. Geriatr. Educ., 7,* 125–139.

McIntosh, J. L. (1991). Epidemiology of suicide in the U.S. In A. A. Leenaars (Ed.), *Life span perspectives of suicide.* New York: Plenum Press.

McIntosh, J. L. (1992). Epidemiology of suicide in the elderly. *Suicide Life-Threaten. Behav., 22*(1), 15–35.

McIntosh, J. L. (1992). Methods of suicide. In R. W. Maris, A. L. Berman, J. T. Maltsberger, & R. I. Yufit (Eds.), *Assessment and prediction of suicide.* New York: Guilford Press.

McIntosh, J. L. (1995). Suicide prevention in the elderly (age 65–99) [Special issue: Suicide prevention: Toward the year 2000]. *Suicide Life-Threaten. Behav., 25*(1), 180–192.

McIntosh, J. L. (1996). *U. S. suicide rates 1932–1992.* Washington, DC: National Center for Health Statistics.

McIntosh, J. L. (1999). Arguments against rational suicide: A gerontologist's perspective. In J. L. Werth, Jr. et al. (Eds.), *Contemporary perspectives on rational suicide. Series in death, dying, and bereavement.* Philadelphia: Brunner/Mazel.

McIntosh, J. L. (1999). Research on survivors of suicide. In M. T. Stimming, M. Stemming et al. (Eds.), *Before their time: Adult children's experiences of parental suicide.* Philadelphia: Temple University Press.

McIntosh, J. L., Hubbard, R. W., & Santos, J. F. (1985). Suicide facts and myths: A study of prevalence. *Death Stud., 9,* 267–281.

McIntosh, J. L., & Santos, J. F. (1982). Changing patterns in methods of suicide by race and sex. *Suicide Life-Threaten. Behav., 12,* 221–233.

McKay, J. R., Alterman, A. I., McLellan, A. T., Snider, E. C., & O'Brien, C. P. (1995). Effect of random versus nonrandom assignment in a comparison of inpatient and day hospital rehabilitation for male alcoholics. *J. Consult. Clin. Psychol., 63*(1), 70–78.

McKee, G. R. (1998). Lethal vs. nonlethal suicide attempts in jail. *Psychol. Rep., 82*(2), 611–614.

McKenzie, S. J., Williamson, D. A., & Cubic, B. A. (1993). Stable and reactive body image disturbances in bulimia nervosa. *Behav. Ther., 24,* 195–207.

McKisack, C., & Waller, G. (1997). Factors influencing the outcome of group psychotherapy for bulimia nervosa. *Int. J. Eat. Disord., 22,* 1–13.

McLean, P. D., & Hakstian, A. R. (1979). Clinical depression: Comparative efficacy of outpatient treatments. *J. Consult. Clin. Psychol., 47*(5), 818–836.

McLean, P. D., & Woody, S. R. (2001). *Anxiety disorders in adults: An evidence-based approach to psychological treatment.* New York: Oxford University Press.

McLeer, S. V., Dixon, J. F., Henry, D., Ruggiero, K., Escovitz, K., Niedda, T., & Scholle, R. (1998). Psychopathology in non-clinically referred sexually abused children. *J. Am. Acad. Child Adolesc. Psychiatry, 37*(12), 1326–1333.

McLellan, A. T., Arndt, I. O., Metzger, D. S. et al. (1993). The effects of psychosocial services in substance abuse treatment. *JAMA, J. Am. Med. Assoc., 269,* 1953–1959.

McLoyd, V. C. (1998). Socioeconomic disadvantage and child development. *Am. Psychol., 53*(2), 185–204.

McNally, R. J. (1999). Anxiety sensitivity and information-processing biases for threat. In S. Taylor et al. (Eds.), *Anxiety sensitivity: Theory, research, and treatment of the fear of anxiety. The LEA series in personality and clinical psychology.* Mahwah, NJ: Erlbaum.

McNally, R. J. (1999). Theoretical approaches to the fear of anxiety. In S. Taylor et al. (Eds.), *Anxiety sensitivity: Theory, research, and treatment of the fear of anxiety. The LEA series in personality and clinical psychology.* Mahwah, NJ: Erlbaum.

McNally, R. J. (2001). Vulnerability to anxiety disorders in adulthood. In R. E. Ingram & J. M. Price (Eds.), *Vulnerability to psychopathology: Risk across the lifespan* (pp. 304–321). New York: Guilford Press.

McNally, R. J., Hornig, C. D., & Donnell, C. D. (1995). Clinical versus nonclinical panic: A test of suffocation false alarm theory. *Behav. Res. Ther., 33*(2), 127–131.

McNally, R. J., & Lukach, B. M. (1991). Behavioral treatment of zoophilic exhibitionism. *J. Behav. Ther. Exp. Psychiatry, 22*(4), 281–284.

McNally, R. J., Metzger, L. J., Lasko, N. B., Clancy, S. A., & Pitman, R. K. (1998). Directed forgetting of trauma cues in adult survivors of childhood sexual abuse with and without posttraumatic stress disorder. *J. Abnorm. Psychol., 107*(4), 596–601.

McNamara, S. (2000). *Stress in young people: What's new and what can we do?* London: ContinuumInternational Publishing Group.

McNeal, E. T., & Cimbolic, P. (1986). Antidepressants and biochemical theories of depression. *Psychol. Bull., 99*(3), 361–374.

McNeil, E. B. (1967). *The quiet furies.* Englewood Cliffs, NJ: Prentice-Hall.

McNeil, T. F., & Cantor-Graae, E. (2001). Obstetric complications as risk factors for schizophrenia. *Int. J. Ment. Health, 29*(4), 73–83.

McNiel, D. E., & Binder, R. L. (1991). Clinical assessment of the risk of violence among psychiatric inpatients. *Am. J. Psychiatry, 148*(10), 1317–1321.

Meagher, D. J. (2001). Delirium: Optimizing management. *Br. Med. J., 322,* 144–149.

Mechanic, D. (1999). Mental health and mental illness: Definitions and perspectives. In A. V. Horwitz & T. L. Scheid (Eds.), *A handbook for the study of mental health: Social contexts, theories, and systems.* Cambridge, England: Cambridge University Press.

Mednick, S. A. (1971). Birth defects and schizophrenia. *Psychol. Today, 4,* 48–50.

Mednick, S. A., Gabrielli, W. F., Jr., & Hutchings, B. (1987). Genetic factors in the etiology of criminal behavior. In S. A. Mednick, T. E. Moffitt, & S. A. Stack (Eds.), *The causes of crime: New biological approaches.* Cambridge, England: Cambridge University Press.

Meehl, P. E. (1960). The cognitive activity of the clinician. *Am. Psychol., 15,* 19–27.

Meehl, P. E. (1996). *Clinical versus statistical prediction: A theoretical analysis and a review of the evidence.* Northvale, NJ: Jason Aronson.

Mehlum, L., Hytten, K., & Gjertsen, F. (1999). Epidemiological trends of youth suicide in Norway. *Arch. Suicide Res., 5*(3), 193–205.

Mehta, U., & Bedient, L. (1999). Update on ECT. *Carrier Clin. Med. Educ. Lett., 200,* 1–4.

Meibach, R. C., Mullane, J. F., & Binstok, G. (1987). A placebo-controlled multicenter trial of propranolol and chlordiazepoxide in the treatment of anxiety. *Curr. Ther. Res., 41,* 65–76.

Meichenbaum, D. H. (1972). Cognitive modification of test-anxious college students. *J. Consult. Clin. Psychol., 39,* 370–380.

Meichenbaum, D. H. (1972). Examination of model characteristics in reducing avoidance behavior. *J. Behav. Ther. Exp. Psychiatry, 3,* 225–227.

Meichenbaum, D. H. (1975). Enhancing creativity by modifying what subjects say to themselves. *Am. Educ. Res. J., 12*(2), 129–145.

Meichenbaum, D. H. (1975). A self-instructional approach to stress management: A proposal for stress inoculation training. In I. Sarason & C. D. Spielberger (Eds.), *Stress and anxiety* (Vol. 2). New York: Wiley.

Meichenbaum, D. H. (1975). Theoretical and treatment implications of development research on verbal control of behavior. *Can. Psychol. Rev., 16*(1), 22–27.

Meichenbaum, D. H. (1975). Toward a cognitive of self-control. In G. Schwartz & D. Shapiro (Eds.), *Consciousness and self-regulation: Advances in research.* New York: Plenum Press.

Meichenbaum, D. H. (1977). *Cognitive-behavior modification: An integrative approach.* New York: Plenum Press.

Meichenbaum, D. H. (1977). Dr. Ellis, please stand up. *Counsel. Psychol., 7*(1), 43–44.

Meichenbaum, D. H. (1992). Evolution of cognitive behavior therapy: Origins, tenets, and clinical examples. In J. K. Zeig (Ed.), *The evolution of psychotherapy: The second conference.* New York: Brunner/Mazel.

Meichenbaum, D. H. (1993). The personal journey of a psychotherapist and his mother. In G. G. Brannigan & M. R. Merrens (Eds.), *The undaunted psychologist: Adventures in research.* New York: McGraw-Hill.

Meichenbaum, D. H. (1993). Stress inoculation training: A 20-year update. In P. M. Lehrer & R. L. Woolfolk (Eds.), *Principles and practice of stress management* (2nd ed.). New York: Guilford Press.

Meichenbaum, D. H. (1997). The evolution of a cognitive-behavior therapist. In J. K. Zeig (Ed.), *The evolution of psychotherapy: The third conference.* New York: Brunner/Mazel.

Meilman, P., Leichliter, J. S., & Presley, C. A. (1999). Greeks and athletes: Who drinks more? *J. Am. Coll. Health, 47*(4), 187–190.

Melfi, C. A., Croghan, T. W., & Hanna, M. P. (1999). Access to treatment for depression in a Medicaid population. *J. Health Care Poor Underserved, 10*(2), 201–215.

Melges, F. T., & Swartz, M. S. (1989). Oscillations of attachment in borderline personality disorder. *Am. J. Psychiatry, 146*(9), 1115–1120.

Melle, I., Friis, S., Hauff, E., & Vaglum, P. (2000). Social functioning of patients with schizophrenia in high-income welfare societies. *Psychiatr. Serv., 51*(2), 223–228.

Mellon, M. W., & McGrath, M. L. (2000). Empirically supported treatments in pediatric psychology: Nocturnal enuresis. *J. Pediatr. Psychol., 25*(4), 193–214.

Melo, J. A., Shendure, J., Pociask, K., & Silver, L. M. (1996, June). Identification of sex-specific quantitative trait loci controlling alcohol preference in C57BL/6 mice. *Nat. Genet., 13,* 147–153.

Meltzer, H. Y. (1991). The mechanism of action of novel antipsychotic drugs. *Schizophr. Bull., 17*(2), 263–287.

Meltzer, H. Y. (1992). Dimensions of outcome with clozapine. *Br. J. Psychiatry, 160*(Suppl. 17), 46–53.

Meltzer, H. Y. (1995). Neuroleptic withdrawal in schizophrenic patients: An idea whose time has come. *Arch. Gen. Psychiatry, 52*(3), 200–202.

Meltzer, H. Y. (1998). Suicide in schizophrenia: Risk factors and clozapine treatment. *J. Clin. Psychiatry, 59*(Suppl. 3), 15–20.

Meltzer, H. Y. (2000). Genetics and etiology of schizophrenia and bipolar disorder. *Biol. Psychiatry, 47*(3), 171–173.

Melville, J. (1978). *Phobias and obsessions.* New York: Penguin.

Mendels, J. (1970). *Concepts of depression.* New York: Wiley.

Mendelson, W., Hatoum, H. T., Kong, S. X., Wong, J. M., & Kania, C. M. (1999). Insomnia and its impact. *Psychiatr. Times, 16*(3).

Mendlewicz, J., Fleiss, J. L., & Fieve, R. R. (1972). Evidence for X-linkage in the transmission of manic-depressive illness. *JAMA, J. Am. Med. Assoc., 222,* 1624-1627.

Mendlewicz, J., Linkowski, P., & Wilmotte, J. (1980). Linkage between glucose-6-phosphate dehydrogenase deficiency in manic depressive psychosis. *Br. J. Psychiatry, 137,* 337-342.

Mendlewicz, J., Simon, P., Sevy, S., Charon, F., Brocas, H., Legros, S., & Vassart, G. (1987). Polymorphic DNA marker on X chromosome and manic depression. *Lancet, 1,* 1230-1232.

Menke, J. A., McClead, R. E., & Hansen, N. B. (1991). Perspectives on perinatal complications associated with mental retardation. In J. L. Matson & J. A. Mulick (Eds.), *Handbook of mental retardation.* New York: Pergamon Press.

Menninger, K. (1938). *Man against himself.* New York: Harcourt.

Menninger, W. W. (1993). Management of the aggressive and dangerous patient. *Bull. Menninger Clin., 57,* 209.

Menzies, R. G., & Clarke, J. C. (1993). A comparison of in vivo and vicarious exposure in the treatment of childhood water phobia. *Behav. Res. Ther., 31*(1), 9-15.

Menzies, R. G., & Clarke, J. C. (1995). The etiology of phobias: A non-associative account. *Clin. Psychol. Rev., 15,* 23-48.

Menzies, R. P. D., Federoff, J. P., Green, C. M., & Isaacson, K. (1995). Prediction of dangerous behaviour in male erotomania. *Br. J. Psychiatry, 116*(4), 529-536.

Merikangas, K. R., Stevens, D. E., & Angst, J. (1994). Psychopathology and headache syndromes in the community. *Headache, 34*(8), S17-S22.

Mersch, P. P., Emmelkamp, P. M., & Lips, C. (1991). Social phobia: Individual response patterns and the long-term effects of behavioural and cognitive interventions. A follow-up study. *Behav. Res. Ther., 29*(4), 357-362.

Merskey, H. (1986). Classification of chronic pain: Descriptions of chronic pain syndromes and definitions of pain terms. *Pain, 3,* 226.

Merskey, H. (1992). The manufacture of personalities: The production of multiple personality disorder. *Br. J. Psychiatry, 160,* 327-340.

Merskey, H. (1995). Multiple personality disorder and false memory syndrome. *Br. J. Psychiatry, 166*(3), 281-283.

Merzenich, M. M., Jenkins, W. M., Johnston, P., Schreiner, C. et al. (1996). Temporal processing deficits of language-learning impaired children ameliorated by training. *Science, 271,* 77-84.

Messer, A. A. (1985). Narcissistic people. *Med. Aspects Hum. Sex., 19*(9), 169-184.

Messer, S. B. (2001). What makes brief psychodynamic therapy time efficient. *Clin. Psychol.: Sci. Pract., 8*(1), 5-22.

Messer, S. B., Tishby, O., & Spillman, A. (1992). Taking context seriously in psychotherapy research: Relating therapist interventions to patient progress in brief psychodynamic therapy. *J. Consult. Clin. Psychol., 60*(5), 678-688.

Metalsky, G. I., Joiner, T. E., Jr., Hardin, T. S., & Abramson, L. Y. (1993). Depressive reactions to failure in a naturalistic setting: A test of the hopelessness and self-esteem theories of depression. *J. Abnorm. Psychol., 102*(1), 101-109.

Metha, A., Weber, B., & Webb, L. D. (1998). Youth suicide prevention: A survey and analysis of policies and efforts in the 50 states. *Suicide Life-Threaten. Behav., 28*(2), 150-164.

Metz, M. E., & Pryor, J. L. (2000). Premature ejaculation: A psychophysiological approach for assessment and management. *J. Sex Marital Ther., 26*(4), 293-320.

Meyer, B., & Carver, C. S. (2000). Negative childhood accounts, sensitivity and pessimism: A study of avoidant personality disorder features in college students. *J. Person. Disord., 14*(3), 233-248.

Meyer, R. E. (1995). Biology of psychoactive substance dependence disorders: Opiates, cocaine, and ethanol. In A. F. Schatzberg & C. B. Nemeroff (Eds.), *The American Psychiatric Press textbook of psychopharmacology.* Washington, DC: American Psychiatric Press.

Meyer, R. E., Murray, R. F., Jr., Thomas, F. B. et al. (1989). *Prevention and treatment of alcohol problems: Research opportunities.* Washington, DC: National Academy Press.

Meyer, R. G. (1992). *Abnormal behavior and the criminal justice system.* New York: Lexington Books.

Meyer, V. (1966). Modification of expectations in cases with obsessional rituals. *Behav. Res. Ther., 4,* 273-280.

Michael, R. T., Gagnon, J. H., Laumann, E. O., & Kolata, G. (1994). *Sex in America: A definitive survey.* Boston: Little, Brown.

Michaelson, R. (1993). Flood volunteers build emotional levees. *APA Monitor, 24*(10), 30.

Mickalide, A. D. (1990). Sociocultural factors influencing weight among males. In A. E. Andersen (Ed.), *Males with eating disorders.* New York: Brunner/Mazel.

Mickley, D. W. (2001). Medical aspects of anorexia and bulimia. In B. Kinoy (Ed.), *Eating disorders: New directions in treatment and recovery* (2nd ed., pp. 7-16). New York: Columbia University Press.

Miklowitz, D. J., Goldstein, M. J., & Nuechterlein, K. H. (1995). Verbal interactions in the families of schizophrenic and bipolar affective patients. *J. Abnorm. Psychol., 104*(2), 268-276.

Miles, C. P. (1977). Conditions predisposing to suicide: A review. *J. Nerv. Ment. Dis., 164*(4), 231-246.

Millar, J. D. (1984). The NIOSH-suggested list of the ten leading work-related diseases and injuries. *J. Occup. Med., 26,* 340-341.

Millar, J. D. (1990). Mental health and the workplace: An interchangeable partnership. *Am. Psychol., 45*(10), 1165-1166.

Millar, M. G., & Millar, K. U. (1996). Effects of message anxiety on disease detection and health promotion behaviors. *Basic Appl. Soc. Psychol., 18*(1), 61-74.

Miller, A. (1998, August 30). Special report: Managed care and mental health; Employee assistance programs. *Atlanta J. Constitution,* p. 07R.

Miller, A. (1999). Appropriateness of psychostimulant prescription to children: Theoretical and empirical perspectives. *Can. J. Psychiatry, 44*(10), 1017-1024.

Miller, G. A. (1999, January 6). Cited in Gap widening between genetic and behavioral research. *Science Daily News Release.*

Miller, I. W., Norman, W. H., & Keitner, G. I. (1999). Combined treatment for patients with double depression. *Psychother. Psychosom., 68*(4), 180-185.

Miller, K. J., Gleaves, D. H., Hirsch, T. G., Green, B. A., Snow, A. C., & Corbett, C. C. (2000). Comparisons of body image dimensions by race-ethnicity and gender in a university population. *Int. J. Eat. Disord., 27*(3), 310-316.

Miller, L. K. (1999). The Savant Syndrome: Intellectual impairment and exceptional skill. *Psychol. Bull., 125*(1), 31-46.

Miller, L. S., Wasserman, G. A., Neugebauer, R., Gorman-Smith, D., & Kamboukos, D. (1999). Witnessed community violence and antisocial behavior in high-risk, urban boys. *J. Clin. Child Psychol., 28*(1), 2-11.

Miller, M., & Kantrowitz, B. (1999, January 25). Unmasking Sybil: A re-examination of the most famous psychiatric patient in history. *Newsweek,* pp. 66-68.

Miller, M. A., & Rahe, R. H. (1997). Life changes scaling for the 1990s. *J. Psychosom. Res., 43*(3), 297-292.

Miller, M. N., & Pumariega, A. (1999). Culture and eating disorders. *Psychiatr. Times, 16*(2).

Miller, N. E. (1948). Studies of fear as an acquirable drive: I. Fear as motivation and fear-reduction as reinforcement in the learning of new responses. *J. Exp. Psychol., 38,* 89-101.

Miller, N. S. (1999). Benzodiazepines: Behavioral and pharmacologic basis of addiction, tolerance, and dependence. In *The Hatherleigh guide to psychopharmacology. The Hatherleigh guides series* (Vol. 11). New York: Hatherleigh Press.

Miller, N. S., & Gold, M. S. (1990). Benzodiazepines: Tolerance, dependence, abuse, and addiction. *J. Psychoact. Drugs, 22*(1), 23-33.

Miller, N. S., Klamen, D. L., & Costa, E. (1998). Medications of abuse and addiction: Benzodiazepines and other sedatives/hypnotics. In R. E. Tarter, R. T. Ammerman et al. (Eds.), *Handbook of substance abuse: Neurobehavioral pharmacology.* New York: Plenum Press.

Miller, P. M. (1996). Redefining success in eating disorders. *Addict. Behav., 21*(6), 745-754.

Miller, P. M., Ingham, J. G., & Davidson, S. (1976). Life events, symptoms, and social support. *J. Psychiatr. Res., 20*(6), 514-522.

Miller, W. R. (1983). Controlled drinking. *Q. J. Stud. Alcohol, 44,* 68-83.

Miller, W. R. (1998). Researching the spiritual dimensions of alcohol and other drug problems. *Addiction, 93*(7), 979-990.

Miller, W. R. (2000). Rediscovering fire: Small interventions, large effects. *Psychol. Addict. Behav., 14*(1), 6-18.

Miller, W. R., Leckman, A. L., Delaney, H. D., & Tinchom, M. (1992). Long-term follow-up of behavioral self-control training. *J. Stud. Alcohol, 51,* 108-115.

Miller, W. R., & Seligman, M. E. (1975). Depression and learned helplessness in man. *J. Abnorm. Psychol., 84*(3), 228-238.

Miller, W. R., Walters, S. T., & Bennett, M. E. (2001). How effective is alcoholism treatment in the United States? *J. Stud. Alcohol, 62*(2), 211-220.

Millin, T., & Davis, R. D. (1998). Ten subtypes of psychopathy. In T. Millon, E, Simonsen et al. (Eds.), *Psychopathy: Antisocial, criminal, and violent behavior* (pp. 161-170). New York: Guilford Press.

Millon, T. (1969). *Modern psychopathology: A biosocial approach to maladaptive learning and functioning.* Philadelphia: Saunders.

Millon, T. (1987). *Millon Clinical Multiaxial Inventory-II: Manual for the MCMI-II* (2nd ed.). Minneapolis, MN: National Computer Systems.

Millon, T. (1990). The disorders of personality. In L. A. Pervin (Ed.), *Handbook of personality theory and practice.* New York: Guilford Press.

Millon, T. (1990). *Toward a new personology.* New York: Wiley.

Millon, T. (1999). *Personality-guided therapy.* New York: Wiley.

Millon, T., Davis, R., Millon, C., Escovar, L., & Meagher, S. (2000). *Personality disorders in modern life.* New York: Wiley.

Millward, D. (1996, June 3). Beware of the dog that is being prescribed Prozac. *Electronic Telegraph,* Issue 397.

Milner, B. (1971). Interhemispheric difference in the localization of psychological processes in man. *Br. Med. Bull., 27,* 272-277.

Mineka, S. (1985). Animal models of anxiety-based disorders: Their usefulness and limitations. In A. H. Tuma & J. Maser (Eds.), *Anxiety and the anxiety disorders*. Hillsdale, NJ: Erlbaum.

Mineka, S., Davidson, M., Cook, M., & Keir, R. (1984). Observational conditioning of snake fear in rhesus monkeys. *J. Abnorm. Psychol., 93*(4), 355–372.

Miner, I. D., & Feldman, M. D. (1998). Factitious deafblindness: An imperceptible variant of factitious disorder. *Gen. Hosp. Psychiatry, 20*(1), 48–51.

Mintzer, J. E., & Brawman-Mintzer, O. (1996). Agitation as a possible expression of generalized anxiety disorder in demented elderly patients toward a treatment approach. *J. Clin. Psychiatry, 57*(Suppl. 7), 55–63.

Minuchin, S. (1974). *Families and family therapy.* Cambridge, MA: Harvard University Press.

Minuchin, S. (1987). My many voices. In J. K. Zeig (Ed.), *The evolution of psychotherapy*. New York: Brunner/Mazel.

Minuchin, S. (1997). The leap to complexity: Supervision in family therapy. In J. K. Zeig (Ed.), *The evolution of psychotherapy: The third conference*. New York: Brunner/Mazel.

Minuchin, S., Rosman, B. L., & Baker, L. (1978). *Psychosomatic families: Anorexia nervosa in context.* Cambridge, MA: Harvard University Press.

Mirin, S. M., & Weiss, R. D. (1991). Substance abuse and mental illness. In R. J. Frances & S. I. Miller (Eds.), *Clinical textbook of addictive disorders*. New York: Guilford Press.

Mirowsky, J., & Ross, C. (1995). Sex differences in distress: Real or artifact? *Am. Sociol. Rev., 60,* 449–468.

Mirsky, I. A. (1958). Physiologic, psychologic, and social determinants of the etiology of duodenal ulcer. *Am. J. Dig. Dis., 3,* 285–314.

Mishara, B. L. (1998). Suicide, euthanasia and AIDS. *Crisis, 19*(2), 87–96.

Mishna, F. (1996). Clinical report. In their own words: Therapeutic factors for adolescents who have learning disabilities. *Int. J. Group Psychother., 46*(2), 265–273.

Mitchell, J. E. (2001). Psychopharmacology of eating disorders: Current knowledge and future directions. In R. H. Striegel-Moore & L. Smolak (Eds.), *Eating disorders: Innovative directions in research and practice* (pp. 197–212). Washington, DC: American Psychological Association.

Mitchell, J. E., & de Zwaan, M. (1993). Pharmacological treatments of binge eating. In C. G. Fairburn & G. T. Wilson (Eds.), *Binge eating: Nature, assessment, and treatment*. New York: Guilford Press.

Mitchell, J. E., & Peterson, C. B. (1997). Cognitive-behavioral treatment of eating disorder. In L. J. Dickstein, M. B. Riba, & J. M. Oldham (Eds.), *Review of psychiatry* (Vol. 16). Washington, D.C.: American Psychiatric Press.

Mitchell, J. E., Pyle, R. L., & Miner, R. A. (1982). Gastric dilation as a complication of bulimia. *Psychosomatics, 23,* 96–97.

Mittleman, M. A., Mintzer, D., Maclure, M., Tofler, G. H., Sherwood, J. B., & Muller, J. E. (1999). Triggering of myocardial infarction by cocaine. *Circulation, 99*(21), 2737–2741.

Mizes, J. S. (1993). Bulimia nervosa. In A. S. Bellack & M. Hersen (Eds.), *Handbook of behavior therapy in the psychiatric setting. Critical issues in psychiatry* (pp. 311–327). New York: Plenum Press.

Mizes, J. S. (1995). Eating disorders. In M. Hersen & R. T. Ammerman (Eds.), *Advanced abnormal child psychology*. Hillsdale, NJ: Erlbaum.

Moberg, P. J., Lazarus, L. W., Mesholam, R. I., Bilker, W., Chuy, I. L., Neyman, I., & Markvart, V. (2001). Comparison of the standard and structured interview guide for the Hamilton Depression Rating Scale in depressed geriatric inpatients. *Am. J. Geriatr. Psychiatry, 9*(1), 35–40.

Modestin, J., & Villiger, C. (1989). Follow-up study on borderline versus nonborderline personality disorders. *Compr. Psychiatry, 30*(3), 236–244.

Modrow, J. (1992). *How to become a schizophrenic: The case against bio. psychiatry.* Everett, WA: Apollyon Press.

Moeller, H. J., Mueller, N., & Hippius, H. (2001). Molecular and clinical aspects of affective disorders—a hundred years after the Kraepelinian concept of manic-depressive psychosis. *J. Affect. Disord., 62*(1–2), 3–5.

Moen, P. (1999, January). *The time squeeze: Work/family strategies in the next century.* Panel presentation at the annual meeting of the American Association for the Advancement of Science, Anaheim, CA.

Moene, F. C., & Hoogduin, K. A. L. (1999). The creative use of unexpected responses in the hypnotherapy of patients with conversion disorders. *Int. J. Clin. Exp. Hypnosis, 47*(3), 209–226.

Moene, F. C., Landberg, E. H., Hoogduin, K. A. L., Spinhoven, P., Hertzberger, L. I., Kleyweg, R. P., & Weeda, J. (2000). Organic syndromes diagnosed as conversion disorder: Identification and frequency in a study of 85 patients. *J. Psychosom. Res., 49*(1), 7–12).

Moffitt, T. E., Brammer, G. L., Caspi, A. et al. (1998). Whole blood serotonin relates to violence in an epidemiological study. *Biol. Psychiatry, 43*(6), 446–457.

Mogale, C. C. (1999). "Moriti wa letswele" (the shadow of the breast)—a stress-related somatoform pain disorder. *S. Afr. J. Psychol., 29*(2), 72–75.

Mogg, K., & Bradley, B. P. (1998). A cognitive motivational analysis of anxiety. *Behav. Res. Ther., 36*(9), 809–848.

Mogg, K., Bradley, B. P., Millar, N., & White, J. (1995). A follow-up study of cognitive bias in generalized anxiety disorder. *Behav. Res. Ther., 33*(8), 927–935.

Mohler, H., & Okada, T. (1977). Benzodiazepine receptor: Demonstration in the central nervous system. *Science, 198,* 849–851.

Mohler, H., Richards, J. G., & Wu, J.-Y. (1981). Autoradiographic localization of benzodiazepine receptors in immunocytochemically identified Y-aminobutyric synapses. *Proc. Natl. Acad. Sci. U.S.A., 78,* 1935–1938.

Mohr, D. C., & Beutler, L. E. (1990). Erectile dysfunction: A review of diagnostic and treatment procedures. *Clin. Psychol. Rev., 10*(1), 123–150.

Mohr, J. W., Turner, R. E., & Jerry, M. B. (1964). *Pedophilia and exhibitionism.* Toronto: University of Toronto Press.

Moilanen, I., Tirkkonen, T., Jarvelin, M. R., Linna, S. L., Almqvist, F., Piha, J., Rasanen, E., & Tamminen, T. (1998). A follow-up of enuresis from childhood to adolescence. *Br. J. Urol., 81*(Suppl. 3), 94–97.

Moldin, S. O., & Gottesman, I. I. (1997). At issue: Genes, experience, and chance in schizophrenia—positioning for the 21st century. *Schizophr. Bull., 23*(4), 547–561.

Moller, H. J. (1999). Effectiveness and safety of benzodiazepines. *J. Clin. Psychopharmacol., 19*(6 Suppl. 2), 2S–11S.

Mollerstrom, W. W., Patchner, M. A., & Milner, J. S. (1992). Family violence in the Air Force: A look at offenders and the role of the Family Advocacy Program. *Mil. Med., 157*(7), 371–374.

Mollinger, R. N. (1980). Antithesis and the obsessive-compulsive. *Psychoanal. Rev., 67*(4), 465–477.

Monahan, J. (1992). Mental disorder and violent behavior: Perceptions and evidence. *Am. Psychol., 47*(4), 511–521.

Monahan, J. (1993). Limiting therapist exposure to Tarasoff liability: Guidelines for risk containment. *Am. Psychol., 48*(3), 242–250.

Monahan, J. (1993). Mental disorder and violence: Another look. In S. Hodgins (Ed.), *Mental disorder and crime*. Newbury Park, CA: Sage.

Monahan, J. (2001). Major mental disorder and violence: Epidemiology and risk assessment. In G. F. Pinard & L. Pagani (Eds.), *Clinical assessment of dangerousness: Empirical contributions* (pp. 89–102). New York: Cambridge University Press.

Monahan, J., & Davis, S. K. (1983). Mentally disordered sex offenders. In J. Monahan & H. J. Steadman (Eds.), *Mentally disordered offenders*. New York: Plenum Press.

Monahan, J., & Steadman, H. J. (Eds.). (1983). *Mentally disordered offenders.* New York: Plenum Press.

Monahan, J., & Steadman, H. J. (1996). Violent storms and violent people. How meteorology can inform risk communication in mental health law. *Am. Psychol., 51*(9), 931–938.

Moncrieff, J. (1997). Lithium: Evidence reconsidered. *Br. J. Psychiatry, 171,* 113–119.

Moncrieff, J., Drummond, C., Candy, B., Checinski, K., & Farmer, R. (1996). Sexual abuse in people with alcohol problems: A study of the prevalence of sexual abuse and its relationship to drinking behavior. *Br. J. Psychiatry, 169,* 355–360.

Monette, J., du Fort, G. G., Fung, S. H., Massoud, F., Moride, Y., Arsenault, L., & Afilalo, M. (2001). Evaluation of the Confusion Assessment Method (CAM) as a screening tool for delirium in the emergency room. *Gen. Hosp. Psychiatry, 23*(1), 20–25.

Monnier, J., Briggs, E. C., Davis, J. L., & Ezzell, C. E. (2001). Group treatment for domestic violence victims with posttraumatic stress disorder and depression. In L. VandeCreek & T. L. Jackson (Eds.), *Innovations in clinical practice: A source book* (Vol. 19, pp. 113–128). Sarasota, FL: Professional Resource Press.

Montgomery, S. A. (1999). Managing the severely ill and long-term depressed. *Int. J. Psychiatry Clin. Pract., 3*(Suppl. 1), S13–S17.

Montgomery, S. A. (1999). Social phobia: Diagnosis, severity and implications for treatment. *Eur. Arch. Psychiatry Clin. Neurosci., 249*(Suppl. 1), S1–S6.

Montgomery, S. A., Bebbington, P., Cowen, P., Deakin, W. et al. (1993). Guidelines for treating depressive illness with antidepressants. *J. Psychopharmacol., 7*(1), 19–23.

Montgomery, S. A., Dufour, H., Brion S., Gailledreau, J. et al. (1988). The prophylactic efficacy of fluoxetine in unipolar depression. *Br. J. Psychiatry, 153*(Suppl. 3), 69–76.

Montgomery, S. A., & Kasper, S. (1995). Comparison of compliance between serotonin reuptake inhibitors and tricyclic antidepressants: A meta-analysis. *Int. Clin. Psychopharmacol., 9*(Suppl. 4), 33–40.

Moore, C. L., Flowers, C. R., & Taylor, D. (2000). Vocational rehabilitation services: Indicators of successful rehabilitation for persons with mental retardation. *J. Appl. Rehabil. Counsel., 31*(2), 36–40.

Moore, M. T. (1997, October 30). Maine initiative would give the vote to all mentally ill. *USA Today,* p. 12A.

Moore, N. C. (2000). A review of EEG biofeedback treatment of anxiety disorders. *Clin. Electroencephalogr., 31*(1), 1–6.

Moos, R. H., & Cronkite, R. C. (1999). Symptom-based predictors of a 10-year chronic course of treated depression. *J. Nerv. Ment. Dis., 187*(6), 360–368.

Morgan, A. H., & Hilgard, E. R. (1973). Age differences in susceptibility to hypnosis. *Int. J. Clin. Exp. Hypnosis, 21,* 78–85.

Morgan, C. D., & Murray, H. A. (1935). A method of investigating fantasies: The Thematic Apperception Test. *Arch. Neurol. Psychiatry, 34,* 289–306.

Morgan, M. J., & London, E. D. (1995). The use of positron emission tomography to study the acute effects of addictive drugs on cerebral metabolism. In A. Biegon & N. D. Volkow (Eds.), *Sites of drug action in the human brain.* Boca Raton, FL: CRC Press.

Morganthaler, A. (1999). Male impotence. *Lancet, 354,* 1713–1718.

Morganthau, T. (1998, June 29). Descent into darkness. *Newsweek,* pp. 54–55.

Moriarty, P. J., Lieber, D., Bennett, A., White, L., Parrella, M., Harvey, P. D., & Davis, K. L. (2001). Gender differences in poor outcome patients with lifelong schizophrenia. *Schizophr. Bull., 27*(1), 103–113.

Morin, C. M., Colecchi, C., Brink, D., Astruc, M. et al. (1995). How "blind" are double-blind placebo-controlled trials of benzodiazepine hypnotics? *Sleep, 18*(4), 240–245.

Morokoff, P. J. (1988). Sexuality in premenopausal and postmenopausal women. *Psychol. Women Q., 12,* 489–511.

Morokoff, P. J. (1993). Female sexual arousal disorder. In W. O'Donohue & J. Geer (Eds.), *Handbook of sexual dysfunctions.* Boston: Allyn & Bacon.

Morokoff, P. J., & Gilliland, R. (1993). Stress, sexual functioning, and marital satisfaction. *J. Sex Res., 30*(1), 43–53.

Morral, A. R., McCaffrey, D., & Iguchi, M. Y. (2000). Hardcore drug users claim to be occasional users: Drug use frequency underreporting. *Drug Alcohol Depend., 57*(3), 193–202.

Morren, M. (1998). Hostility as a risk factor for coronary heart disease. *Psychology, 33*(3), 101–108.

Morris, G. (1983). Acquittal by reason of insanity: Developments in the law. In J. Monahan & H. J. Steadman (Eds.), *Mentally disordered offenders.* New York: Plenum Press.

Morrison, J. (1989). Histrionic personality disorder in women with somatization disorder. *Psychosomatics, 30*(4), 433–437.

Morse, S. J. (1982). A preference for liberty: The case against involuntary commitment of the mentally disordered. *Calif. Law Rev., 70,* 55–106.

Mortensen, P. B., Pedersen, C. B., Westergaard, T., Wohlfahrt, J., Ewald, H., Mors, O., Andersen, P. K., & Melbye, M. (1999). Effects of family history and place and season of birth on the risk of schizophrenia. *N. Engl. J. Med., 340*(8), 603–608.

Moscicki, E. K. (1999). Epidemiology of suicide. In D. G. Jacobs (Ed.), *The Harvard Medical School guide to suicide assessment and intervention.* San Francisco: Jossey-Bass.

Moshinsky, D. (1995). *Things you know that are not so.* Voorhees, NJ: Russet Press.

Moss, D. (1999). Biofeedback, mind-body medicine, and the higher limits of human nature. In D. Moss et al. (Eds.), *Humanistic and transpersonal psychology: A historical and biographical sourcebook.* Westport, CT: Greenwood.

Moss, H. B. (1999). Pharmacotherapy. In M. Hersen & A. S. Bellack (Eds.), *Handbook of comparative interventions for adult disorders* (2nd ed.). New York: Wiley.

Mostofsky, S. (1999, April). *Brain abnormalities in children with ADHD.* Paper presented at the 51st annual meeting of American Academy of Neurology, Toronto.

Motto, J. (1967). Suicide and suggestibility: The role of the press. *Am. J. Psychiatry, 124,* 252–256.

Mowrer, O. H. (1939). *An experimentally produced "social problem" in rats* [Film]. Bethlehem, PA: Lehigh University, Psychological Cinema Register.

Mowrer, O. H. (1939). A stimulus-response analysis of anxiety and its role as a reinforcing agent. *Psychol. Rev., 46,* 553–566.

Mowrer, O. H. (1947). On the dual nature of learning: A reinterpretation of "conditioning" and "problem-solving." *Harv. Educ. Rev., 17,* 102–148.

Mowrer, O. H., & Mowrer, W. M. (1938). Enuresis: A method for its study and treatment. *Am. J. Orthopsychiatry, 8,* 436–459.

Mueller, R. A., & Courchesne, E. (2000). Autism's home in the brain: Reply. *Neurology, 54*(1), 270.

Mueser, K. T., Bellack, A. S., & Brady, E. U. (1990). Hallucinations in schizophrenia. *Acta Psychiatr. Scand., 82*(1), 29–36.

Muhammad, L. (1999, March 30). Experts brainstorming over memory loss. *USA Today,* p. 6D.

Muir, J. L. (1997). Acetylcholine, aging, and Alzheimer's disease. *Pharmacol. Biochem. Behav., 56*(4), 687–696.

Mulder, A. (1996). *Prevention of suicidal behaviour in adolescents: The development and evaluation of a teacher's education programme.* Leiden, The Netherlands: University of Leiden Press.

Mulhern, B. (1990, December 15–18). Everyone's problem, no one's priority. *Capital Times.*

Mulholland, A. M., & Mintz, L. B. (2001). Prevalence of eating disorders among African American women. *J. Counsel. Psychol., 48*(1), 111–116.

Mulkern, V. M., & Manderscheid, R. W. (1989). Characteristics of community support program clients in 1980 and 1984. *Hosp. Commun. Psychiatry, 40*(2), 165–172.

Muller, R. J. (1998). A patient with dissociative identity disorder "switches" in the emergency room. *Psychiatr. Times, 15*(11).

Mullins, L. L., Olson, R. A., & Chaney, J. M. (1992). A social learning/family systems approach to the treatment of somatoform disorders in children and adolescents. *Fam. Syst. Med., 10*(2), 201–212.

Munk, J. P., & Mortensen, P. B. (1992). Social outcome in schizophrenia: A 13-year follow-up. *Soc. Psychiatry Psychiatr. Epidemiol., 27*(3), 129–134.

Muris, P., Merckelbach, H., & Clavan, M. (1997). Abnormal and normal compulsions. *Behav. Res. Ther. 35*(3), 249–252.

Muris, P., Schmidt, H., Merckelbach, H., & Schouten, E. (2001). Anxiety sensitivity in adolescents: Factors structure and relationships to trait and symptoms of anxiety disorders and depression. *Behav. Res. Ther., 39*(1), 89–100.

Murphy, C. M., Meyer, S. L., & O'Leary, K. D. (1994). Dependency characteristics of partner assaultive men. *J. Abnorm. Psychol., 103*(4), 729–735.

Murphy, E., & Carr, A. (2000). Enuresis and encopresis. In A. Carr (Ed.), *What works with children and adolescents?: A critical review of psychological interventions with children, adolescents and their families* (pp. 49–64). Florence, KY: Taylor & Francis/Routledge.

Murphy, G. E. (1998). Why women are less likely than men to commit suicide. *Compr. Psychiatry, 39*(4), 165–175.

Murphy, J. B., & Lipshultz, L. I. (1988). Infertility in the paraplegic male. In E. A. Tanagho, T. F. Lue, & R. D. McClure (Eds.), *Contemporary management of impotence and infertility.* Baltimore: Williams & Wilkins.

Murphy, S. M. (1990). Rape, sexually transmitted diseases and human immunodeficiency virus infection. *Inter. J. Stud. AIDS, 1,* 79–82.

Murray, B. (1996). Computer addictions entangle students. *APA Monitor, 27*(6), 38–39.

Murray, B. (1996). Hypnosis helps children address their many fears. *APA Monitor, 27*(10), 46.

Murray, K. (1993, May 9). When the therapist is a computer. *New York Times,* Sect. 3, p. 25.

Murray, R. M., & Fearon, P. (1999). The developmental "risk factor" model of schizophrenia. *J. Psychiatr. Res., 33*(6), 497–499.

Mussell, M. P., Mitchell, J. E., de Zwaan, M., Crosby, R. D. et al. (1996). Clinical characteristics associated with binge eating in obese females: A descriptive study. *Int. J. Obes., 20,* 324–331.

Mustaine, E. E., & Tewksbury, R. (1998). Specifying the role of alcohol in predatory victimization. *Deviant Behav.: An Interdiscip. J., 19,* 173–199.

Muuss, R. E. (1986). Adolescent eating disorder: Bulimia. *Adolescence, 21*(82), 257–267.

Myatt, R. J., & Greenblatt, M. (1993). Adolescent suicidal behavior. In A. A. Leenaars (Ed.), *Suicidology.* Northvale, NJ: Jason Aronson.

Mydans, S. (1996, October 19). New Thai tourist sight: Burmese "giraffe women." *New York Times,* p. C1.

Myers, D., & Diener, E. (1995). Who is happy? *Psychol. Sci., 6*(1), 10–19.

Myers, D., & Diener, E. (1996, May). The pursuit of happiness. *Sci. Am.,* pp. 70–72.

Myers, D. G. (2000). The funds, friends, and faith of happy people. *Am. Psychol., 55*(1), 56–67.

Myers, M. G., Stewart, D. G., & Bown, S. A. (1998). Progression from conduct disorder to antisocial personality disorder following treatment for adolescent substance abuse. *Am. J. Psychiatry, 155*(4), 479–485.

NAMHC (National Advisory Mental Health Council) Basic Behavioral Science Task Force. (1996). Basic behavioral science research for mental health: Vulnerability and resilience. *Am. Psychol., 51*(1), 22–28.

NAMHC (National Advisory Mental Health Council). (1996). Basic behavioral science research for mental health. Perception, attention, learning, and memory. *Am. Psychol., 51*(2), 133–142.

NAMHC (National Advisory Mental Health Council). (1996). Basic behavioral science research for mental health. *Am. Psychol., 51*(3), 181–189.

NAMHC (National Advisory Mental Health Council). (1996). Basic behavioral science research for mental health. Sociocultural and environmental processes. *Am. Psychol., 51*(7), 722–731.

NAMI (National Alliance for the Mentally Ill). (1994). Personal communication.

NAMI (National Alliance for the Mentally Ill). (1996, February 7). Survey on mental health insurance. Cited in *USA Today,* p. 4D.

NAMI (National Alliance for the Mentally Ill). (1999, March 11). Testimony before House committee on Ways and Means Subcommittee on Social Security, Washington, DC.

NAPHS (National Association of Psychiatric Health Systems). (1999). *The NAPHS 1998 annual survey report—trends in psychiatric health systems: A benchmarking report.* Washington, DC: Author.

NARAL (2001. Insurance coverage for contraception (a state-by-state chart). Directory: *www.naral.org/mediaresources/fact/privateins.html* (last visited May 29, 2001).

NCHS (National Center for Health Statistics). (1990). *Vital statistics of the United States, 1987: Vol. 2. Mortality.* Washington, DC: U.S. Government Printing Office.

NCHS (National Center for Health Statistics). (1994). *Advance report of final mortality statistics, 1992* (Monthly vital statistics report, 43). Hyattsville, MD: Public Health Service.

NCHS (National Center for Health Statistics). (1995). *Advance report of final divorce statistics* (Monthly vital statistics report, 43, (No. 9, Suppl.). Hyattsville, MD: Public Health Service.

NCHS (National Center for Health Statistics). (1999). *Fastats A to Z. Alzheimer's disease.* Washington, DC: Center for Disease Control.

NCHS (National Center for Health Statistics). (1999). *Fastats A to Z. Chronic liver disease/cirrhosis.* Washington, DC: Center for Disease Control.

NCHS (National Center for Health Statistics). (1999). *Fastats A to Z. Divorce.* Washington, DC: Center for Disease Control.

NCHS (National Center for Health Statistics). (1999). *Fastats A to Z. Health of the elderly.* Washington, DC: Center for Disease Control.

NCHS (National Center for Health Statistics). (1999). *Fastats A to Z. Overweight prevalence.* Washington, DC: Center for Disease Control.

NCHS (National Center for Health Statistics). (1999). *National Center for Health Statistics, Health, United States, 1996-1997* (DHHS Publ. No. PHS 97-1232). Hyattsville, MD: Center for Disease Control.

NCHS (National Center for Health Statistics). (1999, September 24). *Fastats. Asthma.* Washington, DC: Center for Disease Control.

NCHS (National Center for Health Statistics). (1999, September 9). *Fastats. Hypertension.* Washington, DC: Center for Disease Control.

NCHS (National Center for Health Statistics). (2000). *Births, marriages, divorces, and deaths: Provisional data for January 1999* (National Vital Statistics Reports, Vol. 48, No. 1). Washington, DC: Centers for Disease Control and Prevention.

NCIPC (National Center for Injury Prevention and Control). (1999, February 20). *Suicide in the United States.* Washington, DC: Centers for Disease Control and Prevention.

NCIPC (National Center for Injury Prevention and Control). (1999, October 25). *Epidemiology of traumatic brain injury in the United States.* Washington, DC: Centers for Disease Control and Prevention.

NCVS (National Crime Victimization Survey). (1993). *Highlights from 20 years of surveying crime victims: The National Crime Victimization Survey, 1973-1992.* Washington, DC: Bureau of Justice Statistics.

NCVS (National Crime Victimization Survey). (1996). Washington, DC: Bureau of Justice Statistics.

NHSDA (National Household Survey on Drug Abuse). (1998). *1998 national estimates of rates of use and other measures related to drugs, alcohol, cigarettes, and other forms of tobacco.* Washington, DC: U.S. Department of Health and Human Services.

NIA (National Institute on Aging). (1996). *Aging America poses unprecendented challenge. 65+.* Washington, DC: Office of the Demography of Aging.

NIAAA (National Institute on Alcohol Abuse and Alcoholism). (1992). *Alcohol alert #15. Alcohol and AIDA.* Rockville, MD: Author.

NIAAA (National Institute on Alcohol Abuse and Alcoholism). (1992). *Alcohol alert #16. Moderate drinking.* Rockville, MD: Author.

NIDA (National Institute on Drug Abuse). (1990). *Substance abuse among blacks in the U. S.* Rockville, MD: Author.

NIDA (National Institute on Drug Abuse). (1990). *Substance abuse among Hispanic Americans.* Rockville, MD: Author.

NIDA (National Institute on Drug Abuse). (1991). *Annual emergency room data, 1991.* Rockville, MD: Author.

NIDA (National Institute on Drug Abuse). (1991). *Annual medical examiner data, 1991.* Rockville, MD: Author.

NIDA (National Institute on Drug Abuse). (1991). *Third triennial report to Congress on drug abuse and drug abuse research.* Rockville, MD: Author.

NIDA (National Institute on Drug Abuse). (1995). *Facts about teenagers and drug abuse. NIDA Capsule.* Rockville, MD: Author.

NIDA (National Institute on Drug Abuse). (1996). *Monitoring the future study, 1975-1996.* Rockville, MD: Author.

NIDA (National Institute on Drug Abuse). (1998). *Economic costs of alcohol and drug abuse.* Washington, DC: Author.

NIH (National Institutes of Health). (1998, October 7). *New "gene map" doubles number of genes* (NIH News Advisory). Washington, DC: Author.

NIH (National Institutes of Health). (1999, February 19). *American Indian: Facts-at-a-glance for women's health.* Washington, DC: Author.

NIMH (National Institute of Mental Health). (1999, June 7). *National Institute of Mental Health launches landmark study* (Press release). Washington, DC: Author.

NMHA (National Mental Health Association). (1999, June 5). Poll. *U.S. Newswire.*

Nagle, D. L., McGrail, S. H., Vitale, J., Woolf, E. A., Dussault, B. J., Jr., DiRocco, L., Holmgren, L., Montagno, J., Bork, P., Huszar, D., Fairchild-Huntress, V., Ge, P., Keilty, J., Ebeling, C., Baldini, L., Gilchrist, J., Voen, P., Carlson, G. A., & Moore, K. J. (1999). The mahogany protein is a receptor involved in suppression of obesity. *Nature, 398,* 148-152.

Nagy, J., & Szatmari, P. (1986). A chart review of schizotypal personality disorders in children. *J. Autism Dev. Disord., 16*(3), 351-367.

Nagy, T. F. (2000). *Ethics in plain English: An illustrative casebook for psychologists.* Washington, DC: American Psychological Association.

Nahas, G. G. (1984). Toxicology and pharmacology. In G. G. Nahas (Ed.), *Marijuana in science and medicine.* New York: Raven Press.

Nahas, G. G., Sutin, K. M., Harvey, D., Agurell, S., Pace, N., & Cancro, R. (Eds.). (1999). *Marihuana and medicine.* Clifton, NJ: Humana Press.

Najavitis, L. M., Gastfriend, D. R., Barber, J. P., Reif, S., Muenz, L. R., Blaine, J., Frank, A., Crits-Christoph, P., Thase, M., & Weiss, R. D. (1998). Cocaine dependence with and without PTSD among subjects in the National Institute on Drug Abuse collaborative cocaine treatment study. *Am. J. Psychiatry, 155*(2), 214-219.

Najman, J. M., Andersen, M. J., Bor, W., O'Callaghan, M. J., & Williams, G. M. (2000). Postnatal depression—Myth and reality: Maternal depression before and after the birth of a child. *Soc. Psychiatry Psychiatr. Epidemiol., 35*(1), 19-27.

Nakao, M., Nomura, S., Shimosawa, T., Fujita, T., & Kuboki, T. (2000). Blood pressure biofeedback treatment of white-coat hypertension. *J. Psychosom. Res., 48*(2), 161-169.

Narrow, W. E., Regier, D. A., Rae, D. S., Manderscheid, R. W., & Locke, B. Z. (1993). Use of services by persons with mental and addictive disorders: Findings from the National Institute of Mental Health Epidemiologic Catchment Area Program. *Arch. Gen. Psychiatry, 50,* 95-107.

Nash, J. M. (1997, May 5). Addicted. *Time,* pp. 68-76.

Nash, J. M. (1997). Special report: Fertile minds. *Newsweek, 149*(5), 48-56.

Nathan, P. E., & Lagenbucher, J. W. (1999). Psychopathology: Description and classification. *Annu. Rev. Psychol., 50,* 79-107.

National Commission on Children. (1991). *Speaking of kids: A national survey of children and parents.* Washington, DC: Author.

National Mental Health Association. (1983). *Myths and realities: A report of the National Commission on the insanity defense.* Arlington VA: Author.

National Opinion Research Center. (1994). *Survey on extramarital relationships.* Washington, DC: Author.

Needleman, H. O., Riess, J. A., Tobin, M. J., Biesecker, G. E. et al. (1996). Bone lead levels and delinquent behavior. *JAMA, J. Am. Med. Assoc., 275*(5), 363-369.

Needleman, L. D. (1999). *Cognitive case conceptualization: A guidebook for practitioners.* Mahwah, NJ: Erlbaum.

Neel, J. V. (1994). *Physician to the gene pool.* New York: Wiley.

Neeleman, J., & Farrell, M. (1997). Suicide and substance misuse. *Br. J. Psychiatry, 171,* 303-304.

Neeleman, J., & Persaud, R. (1995). Why do psychiatrists neglect religion? *Br. J. Med. Psychol., 68*(2), 169-178.

Neeleman, J., Wessely, S., & Lewis, G. (1998). Suicide acceptability in African- and white Americans: The role of religion. *J. Nerv. Ment. Dis., 186*(1), 12-16.

Neimeyer, R. A., & Bonnelle, K. (1997). The suicide intervention response inventory: A revision and validation. *Death Stud., 21,* 59-81.

Neisser, U., Boodoo, G., Bouchard, T. J., Jr., Boykin, A. W. et al. (1996). Intelligence: Knowns and unknowns. *Am. Psychol., 51*(2), 77-101.

Nelson, R., Demas, G., Huang, P., Fishman, M., Dawson, V., Dawson, T., & Snyder, S. (1995). Behavioral abnormalities in male mice lacking neuronal nitric oxide synthase. *Nature, 378,* 383-386.

Nelson, R. O. (1977). Assessment and therapeutic functions of self-monitoring. In M. Hersen, R. M. Eisler, & P. M. Miller (Eds.), *Progress in behavior modification.* New York: Academic Press.

Ness, R. B., Grisso, J. A., Herschinger, N., Markovic, N., Shaw, L. M., Day, N. L., & Kline, J. (1999). Cocaine and tobacco use and the risk of spontaneous abortion. *N. Engl. J. Med., 340*(5), 333-339.

Nesse, R. M. (2000). Is depression an adaptation? *Arch. Gen. Psychiatry, 57*(1), 14-20.

Nestadt, G., Romanoski, A. J., Brown, C. H., Chahal, R. et al. (1991). DSM-III compulsive personality disorder: An epidemiological survey. *Psychol. Med., 21*(2), 461-471.

Nestadt, G., Romanoski, A. J., Chahal, R., Merchant, A., Folstein, M. F., Gruenberg, E. M., & McHugh, P. R. (1990). An epidemiological study of histrionic personality disorder. *Psychol. Med., 29,* 413-422.

Nestor, P. G., & Haycock, J. (1997). Not guilty by reason of insanity of murder: Clinical and neuropsychological characteristics. *J. Am. Acad. Psychiatry Law, 23*(2), 161-171.

Neugebauer, R. (1978). Treatment of the mentally ill in medieval and early modern England: A reappraisal. *J. Hist. Behav. Sci., 14,* 158-169.

Neugebauer, R. (1979). Medieval and early modern theories of mental illness. *Arch. Gen. Psychiatry, 36,* 477-483.

Neumaier, J. F., Petty, F., Kramer, G. L., Szot, P., & Hamblin, M. W. (1997). Learned helplessness increases 5-hydroxytryptamine$_{1B}$ receptor mRNA levels in the rat dorsal raphe nucleus. *Biol. Psychiatry, 41,* 668-674.

Neuman, P. A., & Halvorson, P. A. (1983). *Anorexia nervosa and bulimia: A handbook for counselors and therapists.* New York: Van Nostrand-Reinhold.

Neumarker, K. J. (1997). Mortality and sudden death in anorexia nervosa. *Int. J. Eat. Disord., 21*(3), 205-212.

Newcomb, M. D. (1994). Predictors of drug use and implications for the workplace. In S. Macdonald & P. Roman (Eds.), *Research advances in alcohol and drug problems: Vol. 11. Drug testing in the workplace.* New York: Plenum Press.

Newcomb, M. D., Galaif, E. R., & Locke, T. F. (2001). Substance use diagnosis within a community sample of adults: Distinction, comorbidity, and progression over time. *Prof. Psychol.: Res. Pract., 32*(3), 239–247.

Newman, D. L., Moffitt, T. E., Caspi, A., & Silva, P. A. (1998). Comorbid mental disorders: Implications for treatment and sample selection. *J. Abnorm. Psychol., 107*(2), 305–311.

Newman, J. D., & Farley, M. J. (1995). An ethologically based, stimulus and gender-sensitive nonhuman primate model for anxiety. *Prog. Neuropsychopharmacol. Biol. Psychiatry, 19*(4), 677–685.

Newman, J. P., Kosson, D. S., & Patterson, C. M. (1987). Response perseveration in psychopaths. *J. Abnorm. Psychol., 96,* 145–149.

Newman, J. P., Kosson, D. S., & Patterson, C. M. (1992). Delay of gratification in psychopathic and nonpsychopathic offenders. *J. Abnorm. Psychol., 101*(4), 630–636.

Newman, R. et al. (1996). State leadership conference mobilizes practitioners for community outreach. *Practitioner Update, 4*(1), 1.

Newsweek Poll. (1995). *The state of shame and the union.* Princeton, NJ: Princeton Survey Research Associates.

Newton, J. T. O., Spence, S. H., & Schotte, D. (1995). Cognitive-behavioral therapy versus EMG biofeedback in the treatment of chronic low back pain. *Behav. Res. Ther., 33*(6), 691–697.

Newton, S. E. (1999). Sexual dysfunction in men on chronic hemodialysis: A rehabilitation nursing concern. *Rehab. Nurs., 24*(1), 24–29.

Neziroglu, F. (1998, January). Body dysmorphic disorder: A common but underdiagnosed clinical entity. *Psychiatr. Times, 15*(1).

Neziroglu, F., McKay, D., Todaro, J., & Yaryura-Tobias, J. A. (1996). Effect of cognitive behavior therapy on persons with body dysmorphic disorder and comorbid Axis II diagnoses. *Behav. Ther., 27,* 67–77.

Nezlek, J. B., Hampton, C. P., & Shean, G. D. (2000). Clinical depression and day-to-day social interaction in a community sample. *J. Abnorm. Psychol., 109*(1), 11–19.

Nichols, D. S. (2001). *Essentials of MMPI-2 assessment.* New York: Wiley.

Nichols, M. P. (1984). *Family therapy: Concepts and methods.* New York: Gardner Press.

Nichols, M. P. (1992). *The power of family therapy.* New York: Gardner Press.

Nichols, M. P., & Minuchin, S. (1999). Short-term structural family therapy with couples. In J. Donovan et al. (Eds.), *Short-term couple therapy.* New York: Guilford Press.

Nicholson, P. (1999). Loss, happiness and postpartum depression: The ultimate paradox. *Can. Psychol., 40*(2), 162–178.

Nichter, M., & Nichter, M. (1991). Hype and weight. *Med. Anthropol., 13*(3), 249–284.

Nichter, M., & Vuckovic, N. (1994). Fat talk: Body image among adolescent females. In N. Sault (Ed.), *Mirror, mirror: Body image and social relations.* New Brunswick, NJ: Rutgers University Press.

Nie, N. (1999, July). Tracking our techno future. What are the social consequences of innovation? *Am. Demogr.*

Nielson, S., Møller-Madsen, S., Isager, T., Jørgensen, J., Pagsberg, K., & Theander, S. (1998). Standardized mortality in eating disorders—A quantitative summary of previously published and new evidence. *J. Psychosom. Res., 14*(3/4), 413–434.

Nieman, D. H., Bour, L. J., Linszen, D. H., Goede, J., Koelman, J. H. T. M., Gersons, B. P. R., & Ongerboer de Visser, B. W. (2000). Neuropsychological and clinical correlates of antisaccade task performance in schizophrenia. *Neurology, 54*(4), 866–871.

Nietzel, M. T., Bernstein, D. A., & Milich, R. (1994). *Introduction to clinical psychology* (4th ed.). Englewood Cliffs, NJ: Prentice-Hall.

Nijinsky, V. (1936). *The diary of Vaslav Nijinsky.* New York: Simon & Schuster.

Nishino, S., Mignot, E., & Dement, W. C. (1995). Sedative hypnotics. In A. F. Schatzberg & C. B. Nemeroff (Eds.), *The American Psychiatric Press Textbook of Psychopharmacology.* Washington, DC: American Psychiatric Press.

Nock, M. K., & Marzuk, P. M. (1999) Murder-suicide: Phenomenology and clinical implications. In D.G. Jacobs (Ed.), *The Harvard Medical School guide to suicide assessment and intervention.* San Francisco: Jossey-Bass.

Nolen, W. A. (1999). Pharmacotherapy in bipolar disorder. *Ned. Tijdschr. Geneeskd., 143*(25), 1299–1305.

Nolen-Hoeksema, S. (1987). Sex differences in unipolar depression: Evidence and theory. *Psychol. Bull., 101*(2), 259–282.

Nolen-Hoeksema, S. (1990). *Sex differences in depression.* Stanford, CA: Stanford University Press.

Nolen-Hoeksema, S. (1995). Gender differences in coping with depression across the lifespan. *Depression, 3,* 81–90.

Nolen-Hoeksema, S. (1998). The other end of the continuum: The costs of rumination. *Psychol. Inquiry, 9*(3), 216–219.

Nolen-Hoeksema, S., & Girgus, J. (1995). Explanatory style and achievement, depression, and gender differences in childhood and early adolescence. In G. Buchanan & M. Seligman (Eds.), *Explanatory style.* Hillsdale, NJ: Erlbaum.

Noll, R., & Turkington, C. (1994). *The encyclopedia of memory and memory disorders.* New York: Facts-on-File.

Nonacs, R., & Cohen, L. S. (1998). Postpartum mood disorders: Diagnosis and treatment guidelines. *J. Clin. Psychiatry, 59*(Suppl. 2), 34–40.

Noonan, J. R. (1971). An obsessive-compulsive reaction treated by induced anxiety. *Am. J. Psychother., 25*(2), 293–299.

Norcross, J. C., Beutler, L. E., & Clarkin, J. F. (Eds.). (1998). Prescriptive eclectic psychotherapy. In R. A. Dorfman et al. (Eds.), *Paradigms of clinical social work* (Vol. 2). Philadelphia: Brunner/Mazel.

Norcross, J. C. Karg, R. S., & Prochaska, J. O. (1997). Clinical psychologists in the 1990s. *Clin. Psychol., 50*(2), 4–9.

Norcross, J. C., & Prochaska, J. O. (1984). Where do behavior (and other) therapists take their troubles? II. *Behav. Ther., 7*(2), 26–27.

Norcross, J. C., & Prochaska, J. O. (1986). Psychotherapist heal thyself: I. The psychological distress and self-change of psychologists, counselors, and laypersons. *Psychotherapy, 23,* 102–114.

Norcross, J. C., Prochaska, J. O., & Farber, J. A. (1993). Psychologists conducting psychotherapy: New findings and historical comparisons on the psychotherapy division membership. *Psychotherapy, 30*(4), 692–697.

Norcross, J. C., Strausser, D. J., & Missar, C. D. (1988). The process and outcomes of psychotherapists' personal treatment experiences. *Psychotherapy, 25,* 36–43.

Nordenberg, L. (1998). *Dealing with the depths of depression.* Washington, DC: U.S. Food and Drug Administration.

Nordstrom, P., Samuelsson, M., & Asberg, M. (1995). Survival analysis of suicide risk after attempted suicide. *Acta Psychiatr. Scand., 91*(5), 336–340.

Norman, R. M. G., & Malla, A. K. (1995). Prodromal symptoms of relapse in schizophrenia: A review. *Schizophr. Bull., 21*(4), 527–539.

Norman, R. M. G., & Malla, A. K. (2001). Family history of schizophrenia and the relationship of stress to symptoms: Preliminary findings. *Aust. N. Z. J. Psychiatry, 35*(2), 217–223.

North, C. S., Nixon, S. J., Shariat, S., Mallonee, S., McMillen, J. C., Spitznagel, E. L., & Smith, E. M. (1999). Psychiatric disorders among survivors of the Oklahoma City bombing. *JAMA, J. Am. Med. Assoc., 282*(8), 755–762.

Norton, G. R., Cox, B. J., Asmundson, G. J. G., & Maser, J. D. (1995). The growth of research on anxiety disorders during the 1980s. *J. Anxiety Disord., 9*(1), 75–85.

Norton, G. R., Cox, B. J., Hewitt, P. L., & McLeod, L. (1997). Personality factors associated with generalized and non-generalized social anxiety. *Pers. Individual Differ., 22*(5), 655–660.

Nott, K. H., & Vedhara, K. (1999). Nature and consequences of stressful life events in homosexual HIV-positive men: A review. *AIDS Care, 11*(2), 235–243.

Novaco, R. W. (1977). A stress inoculation approach to anger management in the training of law enforcement officers. *Am. J. Commun. Psychol., 5*(3), 327–346.

Novaco, R. W. (1977). Stress innoculation: A cognitive therapy for anger and its application to a case of depression. *J. Consult. Clin. Psychol., 45*(4), 600–608.

Noyes, R., Jr. (1999). The relationship of hypochondriasis to anxiety disorders. *Gen. Hosp. Psychiatry, 21*(1), 8–17.

Noyes, R., Jr. (2001). Comorbidity in generalized anxiety disorder. *Psychiatr. Clin. North Am., 24*(1), 41–55.

Noyes, R., Jr. (2001). Epidemiology of hypochondriasis. In V. Starcevic & D. R. Lipsitt (Eds.), *Hypochondriasis: Modern perspectives on an ancient malady* (pp. 127–154). New York: Oxford University Press.

Nurnberger, J. I., Jr., & Gershon, E. S. (1984). Genetics of affective disorders. In R. M. Post & J. C. Ballenger (Eds.), *Neurobiology of mood disorders: Vol. 1. Frontiers of clinical neuroscience.* Baltimore: Williams & Wilkins.

Nurnberger, J. I., Jr., & Gershon, E. S. (1992). Genetics. In E. S. Paykel (Ed.), *Handbook of affective disorders.* New York: Guilford Press.

OSAP (Office for Substance Abuse Prevention). (1991). *Children of alcoholics: Alcoholism tends to run in families.* Rockville, MD: Author.

OSAP (Office for Substance Abuse Prevention). (1991). *College youth.* Rockville, MD: Author.

OSAP (Office for Substance Abuse Prevention). (1991). *Crack cocaine: A challenge for prevention.* Rockville, MD: Author.

OSAP (Office for Substance Abuse Prevention). (1991). *Impaired driving.* Rockville, MD: Author.

O'Brien, C. P., O'Brien, T. J., Mintz, J., & Brady, J. P. (1975). Conditioning of narcotic abstinence symptoms in human subjects. *Drug Alcohol Depend., 1,* 115–123.

O'Connor, B. P., & Dyce, J. A. (1998). A test of models of personality disorder configuration. *J. Abnorm. Psychol., 107*(1), 3–16.

O'Connor, S., Deeks, J. J., Hawton, K., Simkin, S., Keen, A., Altman, D. G., Philo, G., & Bulstrode, C. (1999). Effects of a drug overdose in a television drama on knowledge of specific dangers of self poisoning: Population based surveys. *Br. Med. J., 318,* 955–956.

Oei, T. P., Lim, B., & Hennessy, B. (1990). Psychological dysfunction in battle: Combat stress reactions and posttraumatic stress disorder. *Clin. Psychol. Rev.*, 10(3), 355–388.

Oei, T. P. S., Llamas, M., & Devilly, G. J. (1999). The efficacy and cognitive processes of cognitive behaviour therapy in the treatment of panic disorder with agoraphobia. *Behav. Cognit. Psychother.*, 27(1), 63–88.

Oest, L. G., & Treffers, P. D. A. (2001). Onset, course, and outcome for anxiety disorders in children. In W. K. Silverman & P. D. A. Treffers (Eds.), *Anxiety disorders in children and adolescents: Research, assessment and intervention* (pp. 293–312). New York: Cambridge University Press.

Offer, D., Ostrov, E., & Howard, K. I. (1981). The mental health professional's concept of the normal adolescent. *Arch. Gen. Psychiatry*, 38(2), 140–152.

Ogborne, A. C., Smart, R. G., Weber, T., & Birchmore-Timney, C. (2000). Who is using cannabis as a medicine and why: An exploratory study. *J. Psychoact. Drugs*, 32(4), 435–443.

Ogden, J., & Ward, E. (1995). Help-seeking behavior in sufferers of vaginismus. *Sex Marital Ther.*, 10(1), 23–30.

Ogden, J. A., & Corkin, S. (1991). Memories of H. M. In W. C. Abraham, M. C. Corballis, & K. G. White (Eds.), *Memory mechanisms: A tribute to G. V. Goddard*. Hillsdale, NJ: Erlbaum.

Ogloff, J. R. P., Schweighofer, A., Turnbull, S. D., & Whittemore, K. (1992). Empirical research regarding the insanity defense: How much do we really know? In J. R. P. Ogloff (Ed.), *Law and psychology: The broadening of the discipline*.

O'Hare, T. (1992). The substance-abusing chronically mentally ill client: Prevalence, assessment, treatment and policy concerns. *Soc. Work*, 37(2), 185–187.

Ohayon, M. M. (1997). Prevalence of DSM-IV diagnostic criteria of insomnia: Distinguishing insomnia related to mental disorders from sleep disorders. *J. Psychiatr. Res.*, 31(3), 333–346.

Ohberg, A., Penttila, A., & Lonnqvist, J. (1997). Driver suicides. *Br. J. Psychiatry*, 171, 468–472.

Oher, J. M. (1999). *The employee assistance handbook*. New York: Wiley.

Ohman, A., Erixon, G., & Lofberg, I. (1975). Phobias and preparedness: Phobic versus neutral pictures as continued stimuli for human autonomic responses. *J. Abnorm. Psychol.*, 84, 41–45.

Ohman, A., & Soares, J. J. F. (1993). On the automatic nature of phobic fear: Conditioned electrodermal responses to masked fear-relevant stimuli. *J. Abnorm. Psychol.*, 102(1), 121–132.

Oldenburg, D. (1995, August 18). Miserable? Check out self-analysis. *Washington Post*, p. G5.

O'Leary, K. D., & Kent, R. (1973). Behavior modification for social action: Research tactics and problems. In L. A. Hamerlynck, L. C. Handy, & E. J. Mash (Eds.), *Behavior change: Methodology, concepts, and practice*. Champaign, IL: Research Press.

O'Leary, K. M., Brouwers, P., Gardner, D. L., & Cowdry, R. W. (1991). Neuropsychological testing of patients with borderline personality disorder. *Am. J. Psychiatry*, 148(1), 106–111.

O'Leary, K. M., Turner, E. R., Gardner, D., & Cowdry, R. W. (1991). Homogeneous group therapy of borderline personality disorder. *Group*, 15(1), 56–64.

Olfson, M., & Klerman, G. L. (1993). Trends in the prescription of antidepressants by office based psychiatrists. *Am. J. Psychiatry*, 150(4), 571–577.

Olfson, M., Mechanic, D., Hansell, S., Boyer, C.A., Walkup, J., & Weiden, P.J. (2000). Predicting medication noncompliance after hospital discharge among patients with schizophrenia. *Psychiatr. Serv.*, 51(2), 216–222.

Olfson, M., Pincus, H. A., & Dial, T. H. (1994). Professional practice patterns of U. S. psychiatrists. *Am. J. Psychiatry*, 151(1), 89–95.

Oliver, J. E. (1993). Intergenerational transmission of child abuse: Rates, research and clinical implications. *Am. J. Psychiatry*, 150(9).

Ollendick, T. H., & King, N. J. (1998). Empirically supported treatments for children with phobic and anxiety disorders: Current status. *J. Clin. Child Psychol.*, 27(2), 156–167.

Olmos de Paz, T. (1990). Working-through and insight in child psychoanalysis. *Melanie Klein & Object Relations*, 8(1), 99–112.

Olmsted, M. P., Kaplan, A. S., & Rockert, W. (1994). Rate and prediction of relapse in bulimia nervosa. *Am. J. Psychiatry*, 151(5), 738–743.

Olsson, G. I., & von Knorring, A. L. (1999). Adolescent depression: Prevalence in Swedish high-school students. *Acta Psychiatr. Scand.*, 99(5), 324–331.

O'Malley, S. S., Jaffe, A., Chang, G., Schottenfeld, R., Meyer, R., & Rounsaville, B. (1992). Naltrexone and coping skills therapy for alcohol dependence. *Arch. Gen. Psychiatry*, 49, 881–888.

O'Malley, S. S., Jaffe, A. J., Rode, S., & Rounsaville, B. J. (1996). Experience of a "slip" among alcoholics treated with naltrexone or placebo. *Am. J. Psychiatry*, 153, 281–283.

O'Malley, S. S., Krishnan-Sarin, S., Farren, C., & O'Connor, P. G. (2000). Naltrexone-induced nausea in patients treated for alcohol dependence: Clinical predictors and evidence for opioid-mediated effects. *J. Clin. Psychopharmacol.*, 20(1), 69–76.

O'Neill, S. (1997). Therapy for "bereaved" toy owners. *Electronic Telegraph*, p. 728.

Open Minds. (1997). Cited in *The NAMI Advocate*, 19(3), 19.

Oppenheim, S., & Rosenberger, J. (1991). Treatment of a case of obsessional disorder: Family systems and object relations approaches. *Am. J. Fam. Ther.*, 19(4), 327–333.

Orsillo, S. M., Weathers, F. W., Litz, B. T., Steinberg, H. R. et al. (1996). Current and lifetime psychiatric disorders among veterans with war zone-related posttraumatic stress disorder. *J. Nerv. Ment. Dis.*, 184, 307–313.

Orzack, M. H. (1996, December 1). Interview in P. Belluck, The symptoms of Internet addiction. *New York Times*, p. 5.

Orzack, M.H. (1998). Computer addiction: What is it? *Psychiatr. Times*, 15(8).

Öst, L.G. (1989). *Blood phobia: A specific phobia subtype in DSM-IV*. Paper requested by the Simple Phobia Subcommittee of the DSM-IV Anxiety Disorders Work Group.

Osterweis, M., & Townsend, J. (1988). *Understanding bereavement reactions in adults and children: A booklet for lay people*. Rockville, MD: U. S. Department of Health and Human Services.

Ostrow, D. G., Kalichman, S. C. et al. (Eds.). (1999). *Psychosocial and public health impacts of new HIV therapies*. New York: Kluwer Academic/Plenum Press.

Oswalt, R., & Finkelberg, S. (1995). College depression: Causes, duration, and coping. *Psychol. Rep.*, 77, 858.

Otto, M. W. (1999). Cognitive-behavioral therapy for social anxiety disorder: Model, methods, and outcome. *J. Clin. Psychiatry*, 60(Suppl. 9), 14–19.

Overbeek, T., Rikken, J., Schruers, K., & Griez, E. (1998). Suicidal ideation in panic disorder patients. *J. Nerv. Ment. Dis.*, 186(9), 577–580.

Overholser, J. C. (1992). Interpersonal dependency and social loss. *Pers. Individual Differ.*, 13(1), 17–23.

Overholser, J. C. (1996). The dependent personality and interpersonal problems. *J. Nerv. Ment. Dis.*, 184(1), 8–16.

Overholser, J. C., & Hasser, E. H. (2000). Cognitive-behavioral treatment for generalized anxiety disorder. *J. Contemp. Psychother.*, 30(2), 149–161.

Overmeyer, S., Taylor, E., Blanz, B., & Schmidt, M. H. (1999). Psychosocial adversities underestimated in hyperkinetic children. *J. Child Psychol. Psychiatry*, 40(2), 259–263.

Overmier, J. B. (1992). On the nature of animal models of human behavioral dysfunction. In J. B. Overmier & P. D. Burke (Eds.), *Animal models of human pathology: A bibliography of a quarter century of behavioral research 1967-1992*. Washington, DC: American Psychological Association.

Overmier, J. B., & Murison, R. (2000). Anxiety and helplessness in the face of stress precipitates, and sustains gastric ulceration. *Behav. Brain Res.*, 110(1-2), 161–174.

Overstreet, D. H. (1993). The Flinders sensitive line rats: A genetic animal model of depression. *Neurosci. Biobehav. Rev.*, 17, 51–68.

Overton, D. (1964). State-dependent or "dissociated" learning produced with pentobarbital. *J. Comp. Physiol. Psychol.*, 57, 3–12.

Overton, D. (1966). State-dependent learning produced by depressant and atropine-like drugs. *Psychopharmacologia*, 10, 6–31.

Owen, F., Crow, T. J., & Poulter, M. (1987). Central dopaminergic mechanisms in schizophrenia. *Acta Psychiatr. Belg.*, 87(5), 552–565.

Owen, F., Crow, T. J., Poulter, M. et al. (1978). Increased dopamine receptor sensitivity in schizophrenia. *Lancet*, 2, 223–226.

Owen, M. K., Lancee, W. J., & Freeman, S. J. (1986). Psychological factors and depressive symptoms. *J. Nerv. Ment. Dis.*, 174(1), 15–23.

Ozden, A., & Canat, S. (1999). Factitious hemoptysis. *J. Am. Acad. Child Adolesc. Psychiatry*, 38(4), 356–357.

PORT (Patient Outcomes Research Team). (1998). Cited in S. Barlas, Patient outcome research team study on schizophrenia offers grim indictment. *Psychiatr. Times*, 15(6).

Pace, T. M., & Dixon, D. N. (1993). Changes in depressive self-schemata and depressive symptoms following cognitive therapy. *J. Counsel. Psychol.*, 40(3), 288–294.

Padma, N. H. (1999). A new era in the treatment of erectile dysfunction. *Am. J. Cardiol.*, 84(5B), 18N–23N.

Page, S. (1996, February 21). Nationwide hot line to aid abuse victims. *USA Today*, p. 1D.

Pain, S. (1996, March). Ten deaths that may tell a shocking tale. *New Sci.*, p. 6.

Painot, D., Jotterand, S., Kammer, A., Fossati, M., & Golay, A. (2001). Simultaneous nutritional cognitive-behavioral therapy in obese patients. *Patient Educ. Counsel.*, 42(1), 47–52.

Painter, K. (1992, March 25). Drunken-driving casualties aren't the only victims of alcohol abuse. *USA Today*, p. 5D.

Pajer, K. (1995). New strategies in the treatment of depression in women. *J. Clin. Psychiatry*, 56(Suppl. 2), 30–37.

Palmer, C. J., Jr. (2001). African Americans, depression, and suicide risk. *J. Black Psychol.*, 27(1), 100–111.

Palmore, E. B. (1999). Suicide can be rational for senescent or terminal patients. In J. L. Werth, Jr. et al. (Eds.), *Contemporary perspectives on rational suicide. Series in death, dying, and bereavement*. Philadelphia: Brunner/Mazel.

Panikkar, G.P. (1999). Cocaine addiction: Neurobiology and related current research in pharmacotherapy. *Subst. Abuse*, 20(3), 149–166.

Pankratz, L. (1999). Factitious disorders and factitious disorders by proxy. In S. D. Netherton, D.

Holmes et al. (Eds.), *Child and adolescent psychological disorders: A comprehensive textbook.* New York: Oxford University Press.

Pantano, P., Caramia, F., & Pierallini, A. (1999). The role of MRI in dementia. *Ital. J. Neurol. Sci., 20*(8), S250–S253.

Paris, J. (1991). Personality disorders, parasuicide, and culture. *Transcult. Psychiatry Res. Rev., 28*(1), 25–39.

Paris, J., Nowlis, D., & Brown, R. (1988). Developmental factors in the outcome of borderline personality disorder. *Compr. Psychiatry, 29*(2), 147–150.

Park, A. (1996). Health roundup: The human condition. *Time,* p. 82.

Parker, A., & Bhugra, D. (2000). Attitudes of British medical students towards male homosexuality. *Sex. Relat. Ther., 15*(2), 141–149.

Parker, G. (1983). Parental "affectionless control" as an antecedent to adult depression. *Arch. Gen. Psychiatry, 48,* 956–960.

Parker, G. (1992). Early environment. In E. S. Paykel (Ed.), *Handbook of affective disorders.* New York: Guilford Press.

Parker, G., Hadzi-Pavlovic, D., Brodaty, H., Boyce, P., Mitchell, P., Wilhelm, K., Hickie, I., & Eyers, K. (1993). Psychomotor disturbance in depression: Defining the constructs. *J. Affect. Disord., 27,* 255–265.

Parker, G., Hadzi-Pavlovic, D., Greenwald, S., & Weissman, M. (1995). Low parental care as a risk factor to lifetime depression in a community sample. *J. Affect. Disord., 33*(3), 173–180.

Parker, G., Roussos, J., Mitchell, P., Wilhelm, K. et al. (1997). Distinguishing psychotic depression from melancholia. *J. Affect. Disord., 42,* 155–167.

Parker, G., Roy, K., Wilhelm, K., & Mitchell, P. (2001). Assessing the comparative effectiveness of antidepressant therapies: A prospective clinical practice study. *J. Clin. Psychiatry, 62*(2), 117–125.

Parker, G., Wilhelm, K., Mitchell, P., Austin, M. P., Roussos, J., & Gladstone, G. (1999). The influence of anxiety as a risk to early onset depression. *J. Affect. Disord., 52*(1–3), 11–17.

Parker, N. (1991). The Gary David case. *Aust. N. Z. J. Psychiatry, 25*(3), 371–374.

Parker, P. E. (1993). A case report of Munchausen syndrome with mixed psychological features. *Psychosomatics, 34*(4), 360–364.

Parker, S., Nichter, M., Vuckovic, N., Sims, C., & Ritenbaugh, C. (1995). Body image and weight concerns among African American and white adolescent females: Differences that make a difference. *Hum. Organ., 54*(2), 103–114.

Parks, G. A., & Marlatt, G. A. (1999). Relapse prevention therapy for substance-abusing offenders: A cognitive-behavioral approach. In E. L. Lanham (Ed.), *What works: Strategic solutions* (pp. 161–233). New York: American Correctional Association.

Parks, G. A., & Marlatt, G. A. (2000). Relapse prevention therapy: A cognitive-behavioral approach. *Natl. Psychol., 9*(5).

Parnas, J. (1988). Assortative mating in schizophrenia: Results from the Copenhagen high-risk study. *Psychiatry, 51*(1), 58–64.

Parrott, A. C. (1999). Does cigarette smoking cause stress? *Am. Psychol., 54*(10), 817–820.

Parrott, A. C. (2000). Cigarette smoking does cause distress. *Am. Psychol., 55*(10), 1159–1160.

Parry, B. L. (1999). Postpartum depression in relation to other reproductive cycle mood changes. In L. J. Miller et al. (Eds.), *Postpartum mood disorders.* Washington, DC: American Psychiatric Press.

Partonen, T., Vakkuri, O., Lamberg-Allardt, C., & Lönnqvist, J. (1996). Effects of bright light on sleepiness, melatonin, and 25-hydroxyvitamin D_3

in winter seasonal affective disorder. *Biol. Psychiatry, 39,* 865–872.

Pato, M. T., & Pato, C. N. (1997). Obsessive-compulsive disorder in adults. In L. J. Dickstein, M. B. Riba, & J. M. Oldham (Eds.), *Review of psychiatry* (Vol. 16). Washington, DC: American Psychiatric Press.

Patrick, C. J. (1994). Emotion and psychopathy: Startling new insights. *Psychophysiology, 31*(4), 319–330.

Patrick, C. J., Bradley, M. M., & Lang, P. J. (1993). Emotion in the criminal psychopath: Startle reflex modulation. *J. Abnorm. Psychol., 102*(1), 82–92.

Patrick, C. J., Cuthbert, B. N., & Lang, P. J. (1990). Emotion in the criminal psychopath: Fear imagery. *Psychophysiology, 27*(Suppl.), 55.

Patronek, G. (1999, January 13). Interviewed in A. Marcus, Portrait of a pet-o-pile: Animal hoarding often signals mental illness, experts say. *Health-Scout.*

Patterson, C. H. (2000). *Person-centered approach and client-centered therapy: Essential readers.* Ross-on-Wye, England: PCCS Books.

Patterson, G. R. (1982). *Coercive family process.* Eugene, OR: Castalia.

Patterson, G. R. (1986). Performance models for antisocial boys. *Am. Psychol., 41,* 432–444.

Patterson, T. L., Lacro, J. P., & Jeste, D. V. (1999). Abuse and misuse of medications in the elderly. *Psychiatr. Times, 16*(4).

Patton, G.C., Johnson-Sabine, E., Wood, K., Mann, A.H., & Wakeling, A. (1990). Abnormal eating attitudes in London school girls—A prospective epidemiological study: Outcome at twelve month followup. *Psychol. Med., 20,* 383–394.

Patton, G. C., Selzer, R., Coffee, C., Carlin, J. B., & Wolfe, R. (1999). Onset of adolescent eating disorders: Population based cohort study over 3 years. *Br. Med. J., 318,* 765–768.

Patton, J. R., Polloway, E. A., & Smith, T. E. C. (2000). Educating students with mild mental retardation. *Focus Autism Other Dev. Disabil., 15*(2), 80–89.

Paul, G. L. (1967). The strategy of outcome research in psychotherapy. *J. Consult. Psychol., 31,* 109–118.

Paul, G. L., & Lentz, R. (1977). *Psychosocial treatment of the chronic mental patient.* Cambridge, MA: Harvard University Press.

Paurohit, N., Dowd, E. T., & Cottingham, H. F. (1982). The role of verbal and nonverbal cues in the formation of first impressions of black and white counselors. *J. Counsel. Psychol., 4,* 371–378.

Paxton, S. J., & Diggens, J. (1997). Avoidance coping, binge eating, and depression: An examination of the escape theory of binge eating. *Int. J. Eat. Disord., 22,* 83–87.

Paykel, E. S. (Ed.). (1982). *Handbook of affective disorders.* New York: Guilford Press.

Paykel, E. S. (1991). Stress and life events. In L. Davidson & M. Linnoila (Eds.), *Risk factors for youth suicide.* New York: Hemisphere.

Paykel, E. S. (1995). Clinical efficacy of reversible and selective inhibitors of monoamine oxidase A in major depression. *Acta Psychiatr. Scand. Suppl., 91*(386), 22–27.

Paykel, E. S. (1995). Psychotherapy, medication combinations, and compliance. Compliance strategies to optimize antidepressant treatment outcomes. *J. Clin. Psychiatry, 56*(1), 24–30.

Paykel, E. S., & Cooper, Z. (1992). Life events and social stress. In E. S. Paykel (Ed.), *Handbook of affective disorders.* New York: Guilford Press.

Paykel, E. S., Rao, B. M., & Taylor, C. N. (1984). Life stress and symptom pattern in outpatient depression. *Psychol. Med., 14*(3), 559–568.

Payne, A. F. (1928). *Sentence completion.* New York: New York Guidance Clinics.

Payte, T. J. (1989). Combined treatment modalities: The need for innovative approaches. Third National Forum on AIDS and Chemical Dependency of the American Society of Addiction Medicine. *J. Psychoact. Drugs, 21*(4), 431–434.

Pearlin, L. I. (1999). Stress and mental health: A conceptual overview. In A. V. Horwitz & T. L. Scheid (Eds.), *A handbook for the study of mental health: Social contexts, theories, and systems.* Cambridge, England: Cambridge University Press.

Pearson, J. L. (2000). Suicidal behavior in later life: Research update. In R. W. Maris, S. S. Canetto et al. (Eds.), *Review of suicidology, 2000.* New York: Guilford Press.

Peele, S. (1989). *Diseasing of America: Addiction treatment out of control.* Lexington, MA: Lexington Books/D.C. Heath.

Peele, S. (1992). Alcoholism, politics, and bureaucracy: The consensus against controlled-drinking therapy in America. *Addict. Behav., 17,* 49–62.

Peikin, D. (1998, December). Advocacy group promotes unique treatment model for severe illness. *APA Monitor,* p. 8

Pekrun, R. (1992). Expectancy-value theory of anxiety: Overview and implications. In D. G. Forgays, T. Sosnowski, & K. Wrzesniewski (Eds.), *Anxiety: Recent developments in cognitive, psychophysiological, and health research.* Washington, DC: Hemisphere.

Pekrun, R. (1992). The impact of emotions on learning and achievement: Towards a theory of cognitive/motivational mediators. *Appl. Psychol.: Int. Rev., 41*(4), 359–376.

Pendery, M. L., Maltzman, I. M., & West, L. J. (1982). Controlled drinking by alcoholics? New findings and a reevaluation of a major affirmative study. *Science, 217,* 169–175.

Penn, D. L., Corrigan, P. W., Bentall, R. P., Racenstein, J. M., & Newman, L. (1997). Social cognition in schizophrenia. *Psychol. Bull., 121*(1), 114–132.

Penn, D. L., & Mueser, K. T. (1996). Research update on the psychosocial treatment of schizophrenia. *Am. J. Psychiatry, 153,* 607–617.

Pennebaker, J. W. (1997). *Opening up: The healing power of expressing emotions* (Rev. ed.) New York: Guilford Press.

Pennebaker, J. W. (1997). Writing about emotional experiences as a therapeutic process. *Psychol. Sci., 8*(3), 162–166.

Penninx, B. W., Guralnik, J. M., Ferrucci, L., Simonsick, E. M., Deeg, D. J., & Wallace, R. B. (1998). Depressive symptoms and physical decline in community-dwelling older persons. *JAMA, J. Am. Med. Assoc., 279*(21), 1720–1726.

Pentz, M. A. (1999). Prevention in the community. In R. T. Ammerman, P. J. Ott et al. (Eds.), *Prevention and societal impact of drug and alcohol abuse.* Mahwah, NJ: Erlbaum.

Perkins, K., Grobe, J., DiAmico, D., Fonte, C., Wilson, A., & Stiller, R. (1996). Low-dose nicotine nasal spray use and effects during initial smoking cessation. *Exp. Clin. Psychopharmacol., 4*(2), 191–197.

Perls, F. S. (1969). *Gestalt therapy verbatim.* Moab, UT: Real People.

Perls, F. S. (1973). *The Gestalt approach.* Palo Alto, CA: Science Behavior.

Perls, T. T. (1995, January). The oldest old. *Sci. Am.,* pp. 70–75.

Perez, M., Horner, M., & Morval, M. (1998). How do we measure stress: A new approach: Systematic self-observation using a pocket computer. *Bull. Psychol., 51*(436), 427–439.

Perris, C. (1988). Decentralization, sectorization, and the development of alternatives to institutional care in a northern county in Sweden. In

C. N. Stefanis & A. D. Rabavilis (Eds.), *Schizophrenia: Recent biosocial developments*. New York: Human Sciences Press.

Perry, J. C. (1989). Dependent personality disorder. In American Psychiatric Association (Eds.), *Treatments of psychiatric disorders: A task force report of the American Psychiatric Association*. Washington, DC: American Psychiatric Press.

Perry, J. C. (1992). Problems and considerations in the valid assessment of personality disorders. *Am. J. Psychiatry, 149*, 1645-1653.

Perry, J. C. (1993). Longitudinal studies of personality disorders. *J. Pers. Disord., 7*, 63-85.

Perry, J. C., & Cooper, S. H. (1986). A preliminary report on defenses and conflicts associated with borderline personality disorder. *J. Am. Psychoanal. Assoc., 34*(4), 863-893.

Perry, J. C., & Jacobs, D. (1982). Overview: Clinical applications of the amytal interview in psychiatric emergency settings. *Am. J. Psychiatry, 139*(5), 552-559.

Perry, P. J. (2000). Therapeutic drug monitoring of atypical antipsychotics: Is it of potential clinical value? *CNS Drugs, 13*(3), 167-221.

Perry, S., Difede, J., Musngi, G., Frances, A. J. et al. (1992). Predictors of posttraumatic stress disorder after burn injury. *Am. J. Psychiatry, 149*(7), 931-935.

Perske, R. (1972). The dignity of risk and the mentally retarded. *Ment. Retard., 10*, 24-27.

Persons, J. B., & Silberschatz (1998). Are results of randomized controlled trials useful to psychotherapists? *J. Consult. Clin. Psychol., 66*(1), 126-135.

Petersen, A. C., Compas, B., & Brooks-Gunn, J. (1991). *Depression in adolescence: Implications of current research for programs and policy*. Report prepared for the Carnegie Council on Adolescent Development, Washington, DC.

Petersen, A. C., Compas, B. E., Brooks-Gunn, J., Ey, S., & Grant, K. E. (1993). Depression in adolescence. *Am. Psychol., 48*(2), 155-168.

Peterson, A. L., Talcott, G. W., Kelleher, W. J., & Haddock, C. K. (1995). Site specificity of pain and tension in tension-type headaches. *Headache, 35*(2), 89-92.

Peterson, B. D., West, J., Pincus, H. A., Kohout, J. et al. (1996). An update on human resources in mental health. In R. W. Manderscheid & M. A. Sonnenschein (Eds.), *Mental health, United States, 1996* (DHHS Publ. No. SMA 96-3098). Washington, DC: U. S. Department of Health and Human Services.

Peterson, B. S., Leckman, J. F., Arnsten, A., Anderson, G. M., Staib, L. H., Gore, J. C., Bronen, R. A., Malison, R., Scahill, L., & Cohen, D. J. (1998). Neuroanatomical circuitry. In J. F. Leckman, D. J. Cohen et al. (Eds.), *Tourette's syndrome—Tics, obsessions, compulsions: Developmental psychopathology and clinical care*. New York: Wiley.

Peterson, C. (1993). Helpless behavior. *Behav. Res. Ther., 31*(3), 289-295.

Peterson, J. (1996). Healing continues a year after bombing. *APA Monitor, 27*(6), 22.

Peterson, K. S. (1996, February 21). Harm of domestic strife lingers. *USA Today*, p. 3D.

Peterson, L., & Roberts, M. C. (1991). Treatment of children's problems. In C. E. Walker (Ed.), *Clinical psychology: Historical and research foundations*. New York: Plenum Press.

Petry, N. M. (2000). A comprehensive guide to the application of contingency management procedures in clinical settings. *Drug Alcohol Depend., 58*(1-2), 9-25.

Petry, N. M. (2001). Substance abuse, pathological gambling, and impulsiveness. *Drug Alcohol Depend., 63*(1), 29-38.

Peuskens, J., De Hert, M., Cosyns, P., Pieters, G. et al. (1997). Suicide in young schizophrenic patients during and after inpatient treatment. *Int. J. Ment. Health, 25*(4), 39-44.

Pew Research Center for the People and the Press. (1997). *Trust and citizen engagement in metropolitan Philadelphia: A case study*. Washington, DC: Author.

Pfeffer, C. R. (1986). *The suicidal child*. New York: Guilford Press.

Pfeffer, C. R. (1993). Suicidal children. In A. A. Leenaars (Ed.), *Suicidology*. Northvale, NJ: Jason Aronson.

Pfeffer, C. R. (2000). Suicidal behavior in prepubertal children: From the 1980s to the new millennium. In R. W. Maris, S. S. Canetto et al. (Eds.), *Review of suicidology, 2000*. New York: Guilford Press.

Pfeffer, C. R., Klerman, G. L., Hurt, S. W., Kakuma, T. et al. (1993). Suicidal children grow up: Rates and psychosocial risk factors for suicide attempts during follow-up. *J. Am. Acad. Child Adolesc. Psychiatry, 30*, 106-113.

Pfeffer, C. R., Zuckerman, S., Plutchik, R., & Mizruchi, M. S. (1984). Suicidal behavior in normal school children: A comparison with child psychiatric inpatients. *J. Am. Acad. Child Adolesc. Psychiatry, 23*, 416-423.

Pfeifer, M. P., & Snodgrass, G. L. (1990). The continued use of retractable invalid scientific literature. *JAMA, J. Am. Med. Assoc., 263*(10), 1420-1427.

Pfeiffer, S. I., & Nelson, D. D. (1992). The cutting edge in services for people with autism. *J. Autism Dev. Disord., 22*(1), 95-105.

Phares, E. J. (1979). *Clinical psychology: Concepts, methods, and profession*. Homewood, IL: Dorsey.

Phelps, L., & Grabowski, J. (1993). Fetal alcohol syndrome: Diagnostic features and psychoeducational risk factors. *Sch. Psychol. Q., 7*(2), 112-128.

Phillips, D. P. (1974). The influence of suggestion on suicide: Substantive and theoretical implications of the Werther effect. *Am. Sociol. Rev., 39*, 340-354.

Phillips, D. P., Christenfeld, N., Glynn, L. M., & Steinberg, A. (1999). The influence of medical and legal authorities on deaths facilitated by physicians. *Suicide Life-Threaten. Behav., 29*(1), 48-57.

Phillips, D. P., Lesyna, K., & Paight, D. J. (1992). Suicide and the media. In R. W. Maris, A. L. Berman, J. T. Maltsberger, & R. I. Yufit (Eds.), *Assessment and prediction of suicide*. New York: Guilford Press.

Phillips, D. P., & Ruth, T. E. (1993). Adequacy of official suicide statistics for scientific research and public policy. *Suicide Life-Threaten. Behav., 23*(4), 307-319.

Phillips, K. A. (2000). Body dysmorphic disorder: Diagnostic controversies and treatment challenges. *Bull. Menninger Clin., 64*(1), 18-35.

Phillips, K. A. (2000). Connection between obsessive-compulsive disorder and body dysmorphic disorder. In W. K. Goodman & M. V. Rudorfer (Eds.), *Obsessive-compulsive disorder: Contemporary issues in treatment. Personality and clinical psychology series*. Mahwah, NJ: Erlbaum.

Phillips, K. A., & Gunderson, J. G. (1994). Personality disorders. In R. E. Hales, S. C. Yudofsky, & J. A. Talbott (Eds.), *The American Psychiatric Press textbook of psychiatry* (2nd ed.). Washington, DC: American Psychiatric Press.

Phillips, K. A., Kim, J. M., & Hudson, J. I. (1995). Body image disturbance in body dysmorphic disorder and eating disorders: Obsessions or delusions? *Psychiatr. Clin. North Am., 18*(2), 317-334.

Phillips, K. A., McElroy, S. L., Keck, P. E., Pope, H. G. et al. (1993). Body dysmorphic disorder: 30 cases of imagined ugliness. *Am. J. Psychiatry, 150*(2), 302-308.

Phillips, M. R., Liu, H., & Zhang, Y. (1999). Suicide and social change in China. *Cult. Med. Psychiatry, 23*(1), 25-50.

Piacentini, J., Rotheram-Bors, M. J., Gillis, J. R., Graae, F. et al. (1995). Demographic predictors of treatment attendance among adolescent suicide attempters. *J. Consult. Clin. Psychiatry, 63*(3), 469-473.

Pickar, D., Owen, R. R., & Litman, R. E. (1991). New developments in pharmacotherapy of schizophrenia. In A. Tasman & S. M. Goldfinger (Eds.), *American Psychiatric Press review of psychiatry* (Vol. 10). Washington, DC: American Psychiatric Press.

Pickens, R., & Fletcher, B. (1991). Overview of treatment issues. In R. Pickens, C. Leukefeld, & C. Schuster (Eds.), *Improving drug abuse treatment*. Rockville, MD: National Institute on Drug Abuse.

Pietrofesa, J. J. et al. (1990). The mental health counselor and "duty to warn." *J. Ment. Health Counsel., 12*(2), 129-137.

Pike, K. M., & Rodin, J. (1991). Mothers, daughters, and disordered eating. *J. Abnorm. Psychol., 100*(2), 198-204.

Pillard, R. C., & Bailey, J. M. (1995). A biologic perspective on sexual orientation [Special issue: Clinical sexuality]. *Psychiatr. Clin. North Am., 18*(1), 71-84.

Pinard, G. F., & Pagani, L. (Eds.). (2001). *Clinical assessment of dangerousness: Empirical contributions*. New York: Cambridge University Press.

Pincus, H. A., Henderson, B., Blackwood, D., & Dial, T. (1993). Trends in research in two general psychiatric journals in 1969-1990: Research on research. *Am. J. Psychiatry, 150*(1), 135-142.

Pine, D. S. (1999). Pathophysiology of childhood anxiety disorders. *Biol. Psychiatry, 46*(11), 1555-1566.

Pinhas, L., Toner, B. B., Ali, A., Garfinkel, P. E., & Stuckless, N. (1999). The effects of the ideal of female beauty on mood and body satisfaction. *Int. J. Eat. Disord., 25*(2), 223-226.

Pinkston, E. M., & Linsk, N. L. (1984). Behavioral family intervention with the impaired elderly. *Gerontologist, 24*, 576-583.

Piotrowski, C., Belter, R. W., & Keller, J. W. (1998). The impact of "managed care" on the practice of psychological testing: Preliminary findings. *J. Pers. Assess., 70*(3), 441-447.

Pirke, K. M., Kellner, M., Philipp, E., Laessle, R., Krieg, J. C., & Fichter, M. M. (1992). Plasma norepinephrine after a standardized test meal in acute and remitted patients with anorexia nervosa and in healthy controls. *Biol. Psychiatry, 31*, 1074-1077.

Pirkis, J., & Burgess, P. (1998). Suicide and recency of health care contacts: A systematic review. *Br. J. Psychiatry, 173*, 462-474.

Pithers, W. D. (1990). Relapse prevention with sexual aggressors. In W. L. Marshall, D. R. Laws, & H. E. Barbaree (Eds.), *Handbook of sexual assault*. New York: Plenum Press.

Pithers, W. D., & Cumming, G. F. (1989). Can relapses be prevented? Initial outcome data for the Vermont Treatment Program for Sexual Aggressors. In D. R. Laws (Ed.), *Relapse prevention with sex offenders*. New York: Guilford Press.

Pitschel-Waltz, G., Leucht, S., Baeuml, J., Kissling, W., & Engel, R. R. (2001). The effect of family interventions on relapse and rehospitalization in schizophrenia—A meta-analysis. *Schizophr. Bull., 27*(1), 73-92.

Piven, J., Palmer, P., Jacobi, D., Childress, D., & Arndt, S. (1997). Broader autism phenotype: Evidence from a family history study of multiple-incidence autism families. *Am. J. Psychiatry, 154*(2), 185-190.

Plakun, E. M. (1991). Prediction of outcome in borderline personality disorder. *J. Pers. Disord., 5*(2), 93-101.

Plante, T. G. (1999). *Contemporary clinical psychology.* New York: Wiley.

Plasse, T. F. et al. (1991). Recent clinical experience with dronabinol. *Pharmacol. Biochem. Behav., 40,* 695.

Pless, M., & Carlsson, M. (2000). Effects of motor skill intervention on developmental coordination disorder: A meta-analysis. *Adap. Phys. Activ. Q., 17*(4), 381–401.

Plomin, R., DeFries, J. C., McClearn, G. E., & Rutter, M. (1997). *Behavioral genetics: A primer* (3rd ed.). New York: Freeman.

Plous, S. (1996). Attitudes toward the use of animals in psychological research and education: Results from a national survey of psychologists. *Am. Psychol., 51*(11), 1167–1180.

Podoll, K., & Robinson, D. (1999). Lewis Carroll's migraine experiences. *Lancet, 353,* 1366.

Polcin, D. (1992). Issues in the treatment of dual diagnosis clients who have chronic mental illness. *Prof. Psychol.: Res. Pract., 23*(1), 30–37.

Polk, W. M. (1983). Treatment of exhibitionism in a 38-year-old male by hypnotically assisted covert sensitization. *Int. J. Clin. Exp. Hypnosis, 31,* 132–138.

Pollack, J. M. (1987). Relationship of obsessive-compulsive personality to obsessive-compulsive disorder: A review of the literature. *J. Psychol., 121*(2), 137–148.

Pollack, W. (1989). Schizophrenia and the self: Contributions of psychoanalytic self-psychology. *Schizophr. Bull., 15*(2), 311–322.

Pollock, M. H., Kradin, R., Otto, M. W., Worthington, J. et al. (1996). Prevalence of panic in patients referred for pulmonary function testing at a major medical center. *Am. J. Psychiatry, 153,* 110–113.

Polonsky, D. (1998). Interviewed in S. Blackmun, From Mars to Venus—Couples sex therapy. *Psychiatr. Times, 15*(9).

Polonsky, D. C. (2000). Premature ejaculation. In S. R. Leiblum & R. C. Rosen (Eds.), *Principles and practice of sex therapy* (3rd ed., pp. 305–332). New York: Guilford Press.

Polster, E. (1992). The self in action: A Gestalt outlook. In J. K. Zeig (Ed.), *The evolution of psychotherapy: The second conference.* New York: Brunner/Mazel.

Pope, B. (1983). The initial interview. In C. E. Walker (Ed.), *The handbook of clinical psychology: Theory, research, and practice.* Homewood, IL: Dow Jones-Irwin.

Pope, H. G., & Hudson, J. I. (1984). *New hope for binge eaters: Advances in the understanding and treatment of bulimia.* New York: Harper & Row.

Pope, H. G., & Hudson, J. I. (1992). Is childhood sexual abuse a risk factor for bulimia nervosa? *Am. J. Psychiatry, 149,* 455–463.

Pope, H. G., Jr., Oliva, P. S., Hudson, J. I., Bodkin, J. A., & Gruber, A. J. (1999). Attitudes toward DSM-IV dissociative disorders diagnoses among board-certified American psychiatrists. *Am. J. Psychiatry, 156*(2), 321–323.

Pope, K. S. (2000). Therapists' sexual feelings and behaviors: Research, trends, and quandaries. In L. T. Szuchman, F. Muscarella et al. (Eds.), *Psychological perspectives on human sexuality.* New York: Wiley.

Pope, K. S., & Bouhoutsos, J. (1986). *Sexual intimacy between therapists and patients.* New York: Praeger.

Pope, K. S., & Brown, L. S. (1996). *Recovered memories of abuse: Assessment, therapy, forensics.* Washington, DC: American Psychological Association.

Pope, K. S., & Tabachnick, B. G. (1993). Therapists' anger, hate, fear, and sexual feelings: National survey of therapist responses, client characteristics, critical events, formal complaints, and training. *Prof. Psychol.: Res. Pract., 24*(2), 142–152.

Pope, K. S., & Tabachnick, B. G. (1994). Therapists as patients: A national survey of pscyhologists' experiences, problems, and beliefs. *Prof. Psychol.: Res. Pract., 25*(3), 247–258.

Pope, K. S., Tabachnick, B. G., & Keith-Spiegel, P. (1986). Sexual attraction to clients: The human therapist and the (sometimes) inhuman training system. *Am. Psychol., 41*(2), 147–158.

Pope, K. S., Tabachnick, B. G., & Keith-Spiegel, P. (1987). Ethics of practice: The beliefs and behaviors of psychologists as therapists. *Am. Psychol., 42*(11), 993–1166.

Pope, K. S., & Vetter, V. A. (1991). Prior therapist-patient sexual involvement among patients seen by psychologists. *Psychotherapy, 28*(3), 429–438.

Popenhagen, M. P., & Qualley, R. M. (1998). Adolescent suicide: Detection, intervention, and prevention. *Prof. Sch. Counsel., 1*(4), 30–36.

Popper, C. W. (1988). Disorders usually first evident in infancy, childhood, or adolescence. In J. Talbott, R. S. Hales, & S. C. Yudofsky (Eds.), *Textbook of psychiatry.* Washington, DC: American Psychiatric Press.

Poretz, M., & Sinrod, B. (1991). *Do you do it with the lights on?* New York: Ballantine Books.

Porter, S., Kelly, K. A., & Grame, C. J. (1993). Family treatment of spouses and children of patients with multiple personality disorder. *Bull. Menninger Clin., 57*(3), 371–379.

Porzelius, L. K., Berel, S., & Howard, C. (1999). Cognitive behavior therapy. In M. Hersen & A. S. Bellack (Eds.), *Handbook of comparative interventions for adult disorders* (2nd ed.). New York: Wiley.

Post, R. M. et al. (1978). Cerebrospinal fluid norepinephrine in affective illness. *Am. J. Psychiatry, 135*(8), 907–912.

Post, R. M., Ballenger, J. C., & Goodwin, F. K. (1980). Cerebrospinal fluid studies of neurotransmitter function in manic and depressive illness. In J. H. Wood (Ed.), *The neurobiology of cerebrospinal fluid* (Vol. 1). New York: Plenum Press.

Poulos, C. X., Le, A. D., & Parker, J. L. (1995). Impulsivity predicts individual susceptibility to high levels of alcohol self-administration. *Behav. Pharmacol., 6*(8), 810–814.

Poulton, R., Thomson, W. M., Davies, S., Kruger, E. et al. (1997). Good teeth, bad teeth and fear of the dentist. *Behav. Res. Ther., 35*(4), 327–334.

Poulton, R., Waldie, K. E., Menzies, R. G., Craske, M. G., & Silva, P. A. (2001). Failure to overcome 'innate' fear. A developmental test of the non-associative model of fear acquisition. *Behav. Res. Ther., 39*(1), 29–43.

Poulton, R. G., & Andrews, G. (1996). Change in danger cognitions in agoraphobia and social phobia during treatment. *Behav. Res. Ther., 34*(5/6), 413–421.

Powell, J., Bradley, B., & Gray, J. (1992). Classical conditioning and cognitive determinants of subjective craving for opiates: An investigation of their relative contributions. *Br. J. Addict., 87*(8), 1133–1144.

Powell, R. A., & Gee, T. L. (1999). The effects of hypnosis on dissociative identity disorder: A reexamination of the evidence. *Can. J. Psychiatry, 44*(9). 914–916.

Powers, S. W., Mitchell, M. J., Byars, K. C., Bentti, A. L., LeCates, S. L., & Hershey, A.D. (2001). A pilot study of one-session biofeedback training in pediatric headache. *Neurology, 56*(1), 133.

Powis, T. (1990, March 19). *Paying for the past: A brainwashing victim seeks compensation.* Macleans.

Prange, A. J. et al. (1970). Enhancement of imipramine by thyroid stimulating hormone: Clinical and theoretical implications. *Am. J. Psychiatry, 127*(2), 191–199.

Prange, A. J. et al. (1970). Use of a thyroid hormone to accelerate the action of imipramine. *Psychosomatics, 11*(5), 442–444.

Prange, A. J. et al. (1974). L tryptophan in mania: Contribution to a permissive hypothesis of affective disorders. *Arch. Gen. Psychiatry, 30*(1), 56–62.

Prehn, R. A. (1990). Medication refusal: Suggestions for intervention. *Psychiatr. Hosp., 21*(1), 37–40.

Prendergast, P. J. (1995). Integration of psychiatric rehabilitation in the long-term management of schizophrenia. *Can. J. Psychiatry, 40*(3, Suppl. 1), S18–S21.

Preti, A., & Miotto, P. (1998). Seasonality in suicides: The influence of suicide method, gender and age on suicide distribution in Italy. *Psychiatr. Res., 81*(2), 219–231.

Preti, A., & Miotto, P. (2000). Influence of method on seasonal distribution of attempted suicides in Italy. *Neuropsychobiology, 41*(2), 62–72.

Price, L. H. (1990). Serotonin reuptake inhibitors in depression and anxiety: An overview. *Ann. Clin. Psychiatry, 2*(3), 165–172.

Price, R. W., Brew, B., Sidtis, J., Rosenblum, M., Scheck, A. C., & Cleary, P. (1988). The brain in AIDS: Central nervous system HIV-1 infection and AIDS dementia complex. *Science, 239,* 586–592.

Prien, R. F. (1992). Maintenance treatment. In E. S. Paykel (Ed.), *Handbook of affective disorders.* New York: Guilford Press.

Prien, R. F., Caffey, E. M., Jr., & Klett, C. J. (1974). Factors associated with treatment success in lithium carbonate prophylaxis. *Arch. Gen. Psychiatry, 31,* 189–192.

Primac, D. W. (1993). Measuring change in a brief therapy of a compulsive personality. *Psychol. Rep., 72*(1), 309–310.

Prince, M. (1906). *The dissociation of a personality.* New York: Longmans, Green.

Princeton Survey Research Associates. (1996). Adultery in the '90s. In *Newsweek Poll.* New York: Author.

Princeton Survey Research Associates. (1996). *Healthy steps for young children: Survey of parents.* Princeton, NJ: Author.

Prochaska, J. O. (1984). *Systems of psychotherapy.* Chicago: Dorsey.

Prochaska, J. O., & Norcross, J. C. (1994). *Systems of psychotherapy: A transtheoretical analysis* (3rd ed.). Pacific Grove, CA: Brooks/Cole.

Prochaska, J. O., & Norcross, J. C. (1999). *Systems of psychotherapy: A Transtheoretical Analysis* (4th ed.). Pacific Grove, CA: Brooks/Cole.

Prothrow-Stith, D., & Spivak, H. (1999). America's tragedy. *Psychiatr. Times, 16*(6).

Provini, C., Everett, J. R., & Pfeffer, C. R. (2000). Adults mourning suicide: Self-reported concerns about bereavement, needs for assistance, and help-seeking behavior. *Death Stud., 24*(1), 1–19.

Prudic, J., & Sackeim, H. A. (1999). Electroconvulsive therapy and suicide risk. *J. Clin. Psychiatry, 60*(Suppl. 2), 104–110.

Prusiner, S. (1995, January). The prion diseases. *Sci. Am.,* pp. 48–57.

Prusiner, S. B. (1991). Molecular biology of prion diseases. *Science, 252,* 1515–1522.

Prusoff, B. A., Weissman, M. M., Klerman, G. L., & Rounsaville, B. J. (1980). Research diagnostic criteria subtypes of depression: Their role as predictors of differential response to psychotherapy and drug treatment. *Arch. Gen. Psychiatry, 37*(7), 796–801.

Pueschel, S. M., & Thuline, H. C. (1991). Chromosome disorders. In J. L. Matson & J. A. Mulick (Eds.), *Handbook of mental retardation.* New York: Pergamon Press.

Puk, G. (1991). Treating traumatic memories: A case report on the eye movement desensitization procedure. *J. Behav. Ther. Exp. Psychiatry, 22,* 149–151.

Pukall, C. F., Reissing, E. D., Binik, Y. M., Khalife, S., & Abbott, F. V. (2000). New clinical and research perspectives on the sexual pain disorders. *J. Sex Educ. Ther., 25*(1), 36–44.

Pulver, A. E. (2000). Search for schizophrenia susceptibility genes. *Biol. Psychiatry, 47*(3), 221–230.

Purnell, L. A. (1999). Youth violence and posttraumatic stress disorder: Assessment, implications, and promising school-based strategies. In C. W. Branch et al. (Eds.), *Adolescent gangs: Old issues, new approaches.* Philadelphia: Charles Press.

Pusakulich, R. L., & Nielson, H. C. (1976). Cue use in state-dependent learning. *Physiol. Psychol., 4*(4), 421–428.

Putnam, F. W. (1984). The psychophysiologic investigation of multiple personality disorder. *Psychiatr. Clin. North Am., 7,* 31–40.

Putnam, F. W. (1985). Dissociation as a response to extreme trauma. In R. P. Kluft (Ed.), *Childhood antecedents of multiple personality.* Washington, DC: American Psychiatric Press.

Putnam, F. W. (1985). Multiple personality disorder. *Med. Aspects Hum. Sex., 19*(6), 59–74.

Putnam, F. W. (1988). The switch process in multiple personality disorder and other state-change disorders. *Dissociation, 1,* 24–32.

Putnam, F. W. (1992). Are alter personalities fragments of figments? *Psychoanal. Inquiry, 12*(1), 95–111.

Putnam, F. W. (1996). Posttraumatic stress disorder in children and adolescents. In L. J. Dickstein, M. B. Riba, & J. M. Oldham (Eds.), *Review of psychiatry* (Vol. 15). Washington, DC: American Psychiatric Press.

Putnam, F. W. (2000). Dissocative disorders. In A. J. Sameroff, M. Lewis et al. (Eds.), *Handbook of developmental psychopathology* (2nd ed., pp. 739–754). New York: Kluwer Academic/Plenum Press.

Putnam, F. W., Guroff, J. J., Silberman, E. K., Barban, L. et al. (1986). The clinical phenomenology of multiple personality disorder: Review of 100 recent cases. *J. Clin. Psychol., 47*(6), 285–293.

Putnam, F. W., Zahn, T. P., & Post, R. M. (1990). Differential autonomic nervous system activity in multiple personality disorder. *J. Psychiatr. Res., 31*(3), 251–260.

Putnam, K. M., Harvey, P. D., Parrella, M., White, L., Kincaid, M., Powchik, P., & Davidson, M. (1996). Symptom stability in geriatric chronic schizophrenic inpatients: A one-year follow-up study. *Biol. Psychiatry, 39,* 92–99.

Pyle, R. L. (1999). Dynamic psychotherapy. In M. Hersen & A. S. Bellack (Eds.), *Handbook of comparative interventions for adult disorders* (2nd ed.). New York: Wiley.

Quality Assurance Project. (1990). Treatment outlines for paranoid, schizotypal and schizoid personality disorders. *Aust. N. Z. J. Psychiatry, 24,* 339–350.

Quality Assurance Project. (1991). Treatment outlines for avoidant, dependent and passive-aggressive personality disorders. *Aust. N. Z. J. Psychiatry, 25*(3), 311–313.

Quality Assurance Project. (1991). Treatment outlines for borderline, narcissistic and histrionic personality disorders. *Aust. N. Z. J. Psychiatry, 25,* 392–403.

Quality Assurance Project. (1991). Treatment outlines for antisocial personality disorder. *Aust. N. Z. J. Psychiatry, 25,* 541–547.

Quevillon, R. P. (1993). Vaginismus. In W. O'Donohue & J. Geer (Eds.), *Handbook of sexual dysfunctions.* Boston: Allyn & Bacon.

Quinsey, V. L., & Earls, G. M. (1990). The modificator of sexual preferences. In W. L. Marshall, D. R. Laws, & H. E. Barbaree (Eds.), *Handbook of sexual assault.* New York: Plenum Press.

Quiroga, M. (2000). Cannabis: Efectos nocivos sobre la salud fisica [Cannabis: Harmful effects on health]. *Adicciones, 12*(Suppl. 2), 177–183.

Quitkin, F. M. (1999). Placebos, drug effects, and study design: A clinician's guide. *Am. J. Psychiatry, 156*(6), 829–836.

Rabasca, L. (1998). Substance abuse treatment works. *APA Monitor, 29*(11), 7.

Rabasca, L. (1999). I'm okay and you're okay, but not so sure about Y2K. *APA Monitor, 30*(1), 1, 18.

Rabins, P. V., & Folstein, M. F. (1982). Delirium and dementia: Diagnostic criteria and fatality rates. *Br. J. Psychiatry, 140,* 149–153.

Raboch, J., & Raboch, J. (1992). Infrequent orgasm in women. *J. Sex Marital Ther., 18*(2), 114–120.

Rachman, S. (1966). Sexual fetishism: An experimental analog. *Psychol. Rec., 18,* 25–27.

Rachman, S. (1985). A note on the conditioning theory of fear acquisition. *Behav. Ther., 16*(4), 426–428.

Rachman, S. (1985). Obsessional-compulsive disorders. In B. P. Bradley & C. T. Thompson (Eds.), *Psychological applications in psychiatry.* Chichester, England: Wiley.

Rachman, S. (1985). The treatment of anxiety disorders: A critique of the implications for psychopathology. In A. Tuma & J. Maser (Eds.), *Anxiety and the anxiety disorders.* Hillsdale, NJ: Erlbaum.

Rachman, S. (1993). Obsessions, responsibility and guilt. *Behav. Res. Ther., 31*(2), 149–154.

Rachman, S., & Hodgson, R. (1980). *Obsessions and compulsions.* Englewood Cliffs, NJ: Prentice-Hall.

Rachman, S., Hodgson, R., & Marzillier, J. (1970). Treatment of an obsessional-compulsive disorder by modelling. *Behav. Res. Ther., 8,* 385–392.

Ragin, A. B., Pogue-Geile, M. F., & Oltmanns, T. F. (1989). Poverty of speech in schizophrenia and depression during inpatient and post-hospital periods. *Br. J. Psychiatry, 154,* 52–57.

Ragland, J. D., & Berman, A. L. (1991). Farm crisis and suicide: Dying on the vine? *Omega: J. Death Dying, 22*(3), 173–185.

Raguram, R., Weiss, M. G., Channabasavanna, S. M., & Devins, G. M. (1996). Stigma, depression, and somatization in south India. *Am. J. Psychiatry, 153,* 1043–1049.

Rahe, R. H. (1968). Life-change measurement as a predictor of illness. *Proc. R. Soc. Med., 61,* 1124–1126.

Raine, A. (1989). Evoked potentials and psychopathy. *Int. J. Psychophysiol., 8*(1), 1–16.

Raine, A. (1992). Sex differences in schizotypal personality in a nonclinical population. *J. Abnorm. Psychol., 101*(2), 361–364.

Raine, A., Benishay, D., Lencz, T., & Scarpa, A. (1997). Abnormal orienting in schizotypal personality disorder. *Schizophr. Bull., 23*(1), 75–82.

Raine, A., Lencz, T., Bihrle, S., LaCasse, L., & Colletti, P. (2000). Reduced prefrontal gray matter volume and reduced autonomic activity in antisocial personality disorder. *Arch. Gen. Psychiatry, 57*(2), 119–127.

Raison, C. L., Klein, H. M., & Steckler, M. (1999). The moon and madness reconsidered. *J. Affect. Disord., 53*(1), 99–106.

Raja, M., & Miti, G. (1995). Neuroleptic malignant syndrome. *Neuropsychiatry, Neuropsychol., Behav. Neurol., 8*(1), 74.

Raloff, J. (1995). Drug of darkness: Can a pineal hormone head off everything from breast cancer to aging? *Sci. News, 147,* 300–301.

Ralston, P. A. (1991). Senior centers and minority elders: A critical review. *Gerontologist, 31,* 325–331.

Ram, R., Bromet, E. J., Eaton, W. W., & Pato, C. (1992). The natural course of schizophrenia: A re-

view of first-admission studies. *Schizophr. Bull., 18*(2), 185–207.

Ramey, C. T., & Ramey, S. L. (1992). Effective early intervention. *Ment. Retard., 30*(6), 337–345.

Ramey, C. T., & Ramey, S. L. (1998). Early intervention and early experience. *Am. Psychol., 53,* 109–120.

Ramey, C. T., & Ramey, S. L. (1999). *Right from birth: Building your child's foundation for life (birth to 18 months).* New York: Goddard Press.

Ramirez, S. Z., Wassef, A., Paniagua, F. A., & Linskey, A. O. (1996). Mental health providers' perceptions of cultural variables in evaluating ethnically diverse clients. *Prof. Psychol.: Res. Pract., 27,* 284–288.

Ramm, E., Marks, I. M., Yuksel, S., & Stern, R. S. (1981). Anxiety management training for anxiety states: Positive compared with negative self-statements. *Br. J. Psychiatry, 140,* 397–373.

Rampello, L., Nicoletti, F., & Nicoletti, F. (2000). Dopamine and depression: Therapeutic implications. *CNS Drugs, 13*(1), 35–45.

Rand, C. S., & Kuldau, J. M. (1991). Restrained eating (weight concerns) in the general population and among students. *Int. J. Eat. Disord., 10*(6), 699–708.

Randall, L. O. (1982). Discovery of benzodiazepines. In E. Usdin, P. Skolnick, J. F. Tallman, Jr. et al. (Eds.), *Pharmacology of benzodiazepines.* London: Macmillan.

Rao, S. M. (2000). Neuropsychological evaluation. In B. S. Fogel, R. B. Schiffer et al. (Eds.), *Synopsis of neuropsychiatry.* Philadelphia: Lippincott-Raven.

Rapee, R. M. (1993). Psychological factors in panic disorder. *Adv. Behav. Res. Ther., 15*(1), 85–102.

Rapee, R. M., & Hayman, K. (1996). The effects of video feedback on the self-evaluation of performance in socially anxious subjects. *Behav. Res. Ther., 34*(4), 315–322.

Raphling, D. L. (1989). Fetishism in a woman. *J. Am. Psychoanal. Assoc., 37*(2), 465–491.

Rapoport, J. L. (1989, March). The biology of obsessions and compulsions. *Sci. Am.,* pp. 82–89.

Rapoport, J. L. (1991). Recent advances in obsessive-compulsive disorder. *Neuropsychopharmacology, 5*(1), 1–10.

Raskin, D. C. (1982). The scientific basis of polygraph techniques and their uses in the judicial process. In A. Trankell (Ed.), *Reconstructing the past: The role of psychologists in criminal trials.* Stockholm: Norstedt & Soners.

Raskin, M., Peeke, H. V. S., Dickman, W., & Pinkster, H. (1982). Panic and generalized anxiety disorders: Developmental antecedents and precipitants. *Arch. Gen. Psychiatry, 39,* 687–689.

Raskin, N. J., & Rogers, C. R. (1995). Person-centered therapy. In R. J. Corsini & D. Wedding (Eds.), *Current psychotherapies* (5th ed.). Itasca, IL: Peacock.

Rassin, E., Merckelbach, H., Muris, P., & Spaan, V. (1999). Thought-action fusion as a causal factor in the development of intrusions. *Behav. Res. Ther., 37*(3), 231–237.

Ravetz, R. S. (1999). Psychiatric disorders associated with Alzheimer's disease. *J. Am. Osteopathol. Assoc., 99*(Suppl. 9), S13–S16.

Ray, O., & Ksir, C. (1993). *Drugs, society, and human behavior.* St. Louis, MO: Mosby.

Raymond, N. C., Coleman, E., Ohlerking, F., Christenson, G. A., & Miner, M. (1999). Psychiatric comorbidity in pedophilic sex offenders. *Am. J. Psychiatry, 156*(5), 786–788.

Raymont, V. (2001). Suicide in schizophrenia—how can research influence training and clinical practice? *Psychiatr. Bull., 25*(2), 46–50.

Rebert, W. M., Stanton, A. L., & Schwartz, R. M. (1991). Influence of personality attributes and daily moods on bulimic eating patterns. *Addict. Behav., 16*(6), 497–505.

Redick, R. W., Witkin, M. J., Atay, J. E., & Manderscheid, R. W. (1992). Specialty mental health system characteristics. In R. W. Manderscheid & M. A. Sonnenschein (Eds.), *Mental health, United States, 1992.* Washington, DC: U. S. Department of Health and Human Services.

Redick, R. W., Witkin, M. J., Atay, J. E., & Manderscheid, R. W. (1996). Highlights of organized mental health services in 1992 and major national and state trends. In R. W. Manderscheid & M. A. Sonnenschein (Eds.), DHHS Publ. No. SMA 96-3098. Washington, DC: U. S. Department of Health and Human Services.

Redmond, D. E. (1977). Alterations in the function of the nucleus locus coeruleus: A possible model for studies of anxiety. In I. Hanin & E. Usdin (Eds.), *Animal models in psychiatry and neurology.* New York: Pergamon Press.

Redmond, D. E. (1979). New and old evidence for the involvement of a brain norepinephrine system in anxiety. In W. E. Fann, I. Karacan, A. D. Pokorny, & R. L. Williams (Eds.), *Phenomenology and treatment of anxiety.* New York: Spectrum.

Redmond, D. E. (1981). Clonidine and the primate locus coeruleus: Evidence suggesting anxiolytic and anti-withdrawal effects. In H. Lal & S. Fielding (Eds.), *Psychopharmacology of clonidine.* New York: Alan R. Liss.

Redmond, D. E. (1985). Neurochemical basis for anxiety and anxiety disorders: Evidence from drugs which decrease human fear or anxiety. In A. H. Tuma & J. Maser (Eds.), *Anxiety and the anxiety disorders.* Hillsdale, NJ: Erlbaum.

Reeb, R. N. (2000). Classification and diagnosis of psychopathology: Conceptual foundations. *J. Psychol. Pract., 6*(1), 3-18.

Reed, L. J. (Ed.). (1998). *Webster's new world pocket book of facts.* New York: Macmillan.

Rees, K., Allen, D., & Lader, M. (1999). The influences of age and caffeine on psychomotor and cognitive function. *Psychopharmacology, 145*(2), 181-188.

Rees, L. (1964). The importance of psychological, allergic and infective factors in childhood asthma. *J. Psychosom. Res., 7*(4), 253-262.

Rees, W. D., & Lutkin, S. G. (1967). Mortality of bereavement. *Br. Med. J., 4,* 13-16.

Reese, S. (1998, January). Get it together, do-gooders. *Am. Demogr.*

Regehr, C., Cadell, S., & Jansen, K. (1999). Perceptions of control and long-term recovery from rape. *Am. J. Orthopsychiatry, 69*(1), 110-115.

Regier, D. A., Farmer, E., Rae, D. S. et al. (1990). Co-morbidity of mental disorders with alcohol and other drug abuse: Results from the Epidemiologic Catchment Area (ECA) Study. *JAMA, J. Am. Med. Assoc., 264,* 2511-2518.

Regier, D. A., Narrow, W. E., Rae, D. S., Manderscheid, R. W., Locke, B. Z., & Goodwin, F. K. (1993). The de facto US Mental and Addictive Disorders Service System: Epidemiologic Catchment Area prospective 1-year prevalence rates of disorders in services. *Arch. Gen. Psychiatry, 50,* 85-94.

Regier, D. A., Rae, D. S., Narrow, W. E., Kaelber, C. T., & Schatzberg, A. F. (1998). Prevalence of anxiety disorders and their comorbidity with mood and addictive disorders. *Br. J. Psychiatry, 173*(Suppl. 34), 24-28.

Rehman, J., Lazer, S., Benet, A. E., Schaefer, L. C., & Melman, A. (1999). The reported sex and surgery satisfactions of 28 postoperative male-to-female transsexual patients. *Arch. Sex Behav., 28*(1), 71-89.

Reich, J. H. (1987). Sex distribution of DSM-III personality disorders in psychiatric outpatients. *Am. J. Psychiatry, 144*(4), 485-488.

Reich, J. H. (1990). Comparisons of males and females with DSM-III dependent personality disorder. *Psychiatr. Res., 33*(2), 207-214.

Reich, J. H. (1996). The morbidity of DSM-III-R dependent personality disorder. *J. Nerv. Ment. Dis., 184*(1), 22-26.

Reich, J. H. (2000). The relationship of social phobia to avoidant personality disorder: A proposal to reclassify avoidant personality disorder based on clinical empirical findings. *Eur. Psychiatry, 15*(3), 151-159.

Reid, A. H. (1997). Mental handicap or learning disability: A critique of political correctness. *Br. J. Psychiatry, 170,* 1.

Reid, J. B., Eddy, J. M., Fetrow, R. A., & Stoolmiller, M. (1999). Description and immediate impacts of a preventive intervention for conduct problems. *Am. J. Commun. Psychol., 27*(4), 483-517.

Reid, R., & Lininger, T. (1993). Sexual pain disorders in the female. In W. O'Donohue & J. Geer (Eds.), *Handbook of sexual dysfunctions.* Boston: Allyn & Bacon.

Reid, S. (1998). Suicide in schizophrenia: A review of the literature. *J. Ment. Health UK, 7*(4), 345-353.

Reid, W. H., & Burke, W. J. (1989). Antisocial personality disorder. In American Psychiatric Association (Eds.), *Treatments of psychiatric disorders: A task force report of the American Psychiatric Association.* Washington, DC: American Psychiatric Press.

Reis, B. E. (1993). Toward a psychoanalytic understanding of multiple personality disorder. *Bull. Menninger Clin., 57*(3), 309-318.

Reisch, T., Schlatter, P., & Tschacher, W. (1999). Efficacy of crisis intervention. *Crisis, 20*(2), 78-85.

Reiser, M. (2001). The dream in contemporary psychiatry. *Am. J. Psychiatry, 158*(3), 351-359.

Reiss, S. (1985). The mentally retarded, emotionally disturbed adult. In M. Sigman (Ed.), *Children with emotional disorders and developmental disabilities.* New York: Grune & Stratton.

Reiss, S., Peterson, R. A., Gursky, D. M., & McNally, R. J. (1986). Anxiety sensitivity, anxiety frequency, and the prediction of fearfulness. *Behav. Res. Ther., 24,* 1-8.

Reissing, E. D., Binik, Y. M., & Khalife, S. (1999). Does vaginismus exist? A critical review of the literature. *J. Nerv. Ment. Dis., 187*(5), 261-274.

Reitan, R. M., & Wolfson, D. (1985). *The Halstead-Reitan Neuropsychological Test Battery: Theory and clinical interpretation.* Tucson, AZ: Neuropsychology.

Remafedi, G., French, S., Story, M., Resnick, M. D., & Blum. R. (1998). The relationship between suicide risk and sexual orientation: Results of a population-based study. *Am. J. Public Health, 88*(1), 57-60.

Remington, B., Roberts, P., & Glautier, S. (1997). The effect of drink familiarity on tolerance to alcohol. *Addict. Behav., 22*(1), 45-53.

Remington, G., & Kapur, S. (2000). Atypical antipsychotics: Are some more typical than others? *Psychopharmacology, 148*(1), 3-15.

Remington, G., Pollock, B., Voineskos, G., Reed, K., & Coulter, K. (1993). Acutely psychotic patients receiving high-dose Haloperidol therapy. *J. Clin. Psychopharmacol., 13*(1), 41-45.

Reneman, L., Booij, J., Schmand, B., van den Brink, W., & Gunning, B. (2000). Memory disturbances in "ecstasy" users are correlated with an altered brain serotonin neurotransmission. *Psychopharmacology, 148*(3), 322-324.

Renneberg, G., Goldstein, A. J., Phillips, D., & Chambless, D. L. (1990). Intensive behavioral group treatment of avoidant personality disorder. *Behav. Ther., 21*(3), 363-377.

Reppucci, N. D., Woolard, J. L., & Fried. C. S. (1999). Social, community, and preventive interventions. *Annu. Rev. Psychol., 50,* 387-418.

Resick, P. A. (2001). *Stress and trauma.* Philadelphia: Taylor & Francis.

Ressler, R. K., & Schactman, T. (1992). *Whoever fights monsters.* New York: St. Martin's Press.

Rettew. D. C. (2000). Avoidant personality disorder, generalized social phobia, and shyness: Putting the personality back into personality disorders. *Harv. Rev. Psychiatry, 8*(6), 283-297.

Rey, J. M., & Walter, G. (1997). Half a century of ECT use in young people. *Am. J. Psychiatry, 154*(5), 595-602.

Reyna, L. J. (1989). Behavior therapy, applied behavior analysis, and behavior modification. In J. Hobson (Ed.), *Abnormal states of brain and mind.* Boston: Birkhauser.

Reynolds, A. J. (1998, January). Resilience among black urban youth: Prevalence, intervention effects, and mechanisms of influence. *Am. J. Orthopsychiatry, 68*(1), 84-100.

Reynolds, C. F., III, Frank, E., Perel, J. M., Imber, S. D., Cornes, C., Miller, M. D., Mazumdar, S., Houck, P. R., Dew, M. A., Stack, J. A., Pollock, B. G., & Kupfer, D. J. (1999). Nortriptyline and interpersonal psychotherapy as maintenance therapies for recurrent major depression: A randomized controlled trial in patients older than 59 years. *JAMA, J. Am. Med. Assoc., 281*(1), 39-45.

Rhodes, A. E., & Links, P. S. (1998). Suicide and suicidal behaviours: Implications for mental health services. *Can. J. Psychiatry, 43*(8), 785-791.

Rhodes, R. (1999). Cited in L. Rabasca, I'm okay and you're okay, but not so sure about Y2K. *APA Monitor, 30*(1), 18.

Ricca, V., Mannucci, E., Moretti, S., Di Bernardo, M., Zucchi, T., Cabras, P. L., & Rotella, C. M. (2000). Screening for binge eating disorder in obese outpatients. *Compr. Psychiatry, 41*(2), 111-115.

Rice, D. P., & Miller, L. S. (1998). Health economics and cost implications of anxiety and other mental disorders in the United States. *Br. J. Psychiatry, 173*(Suppl. 34), 4-9.

Rice, G., Anderson, C., Risch, N., & Ebers, G. (1999). Male homosexuality: Absence of linkage to microsatellite markers at Xq28. *Science, 284,* 665-667.

Rice, K. M., Blanchard, E. B., & Purcell, M. (1993). Biofeedback treatments of generalized anxiety disorder: Preliminary results. *Biofeedback Self Regul., 18*(2), 93-105.

Rich, C. L., Dhossche, D. M., Ghani, S., & Isacsson, G. (1998). Suicide methods and presence of intoxicating abusable substances: Some clinical and public health implications. *Ann. Clin. Psychiatry, 10*(4), 169-175.

Richards, J. M., & Gross, J. J. (1999). Composure at any cost? The cognitive consequences of emotion suppression. *Pers. Soc. Psychol. Bull., 25*(8), 1033-1044.

Richards, P. S., & Bergin, A. E. (Eds.) (2000). *Handbook of psychotherapy and religious diversity.* Washington, DC: American Psychological Association.

Richardson, S. (1997, January). The second key. *Discover,* pp. 29-30.

Richardson, S. (1997, January). An ancient immunity. *Discover,* p. 30.

Richman, J. (1999). Similarities and differences between younger and older suicidal people. *J. Clin. Geropsychol., 5*(1), 1-17.

Richman, N. E., & Sokolove, R. L. (1992). The experience of aloneness, object representation, and evocative memory in borderline and neurotic patients. *Psychoanal. Psychiatry, 9*(1), 77-91.

Richter, P., Werner, J., Heerlein, A., Kraus, A., & Sauer, H. (1998). On the validity of the Beck Depression Inventory: A review. *Psychopathology, 31*(3), 160-168.

Richters, J. E., & Martinez, P. (1993). The NIMH community violence project: I. Children as victims of and witnesses to violence. *Psychiatry, 56,* 7-21.

Rickels, K., DeMartinis, N., & Aufdembrinke, B. (2000). A double-blind, placebo-controlled trial of abecarnil and diazepam in the treatment of patients with generalized anxiety disorder. *J. Clin. Psychopharmacol., 20*(1), 12-18.

Ricketts, R. W., Singh, N. N., Ellis, C. R., Chambers, S. et al. (1995). Calcium channel blockers and vitamin E for tardive dyskinesia in adults with mental retardation [Special issue: Pharmacotherapy III]. *J. Dev. Phys. Disabil., 7*(2), 161-174.

Riddle, M. (1998). Obsessive-compulsive disorder in children and adolescents. *Br. J. Psychiatry, 173*(Suppl. 35), 91-96.

Riddle, M. A., Bernstein, G. A., Cook, E. H., Leonard, H. L., March, J. S., & Swanson, J. S. (1999). Anxiolytics, adrenergic agents, and naltrexone. *J. Am. Acad. Child Adolesc. Psychiatry, 38*(5), 546-556.

Rieber, R. W. (1999, March). Hypnosis, false memory, and multiple personality: A trinity of affinity. *His. Psychiatry. 10*(37), 3-11.

Riggs, D. S., & Foa, E. B. (1993). Obsessive compulsive disorder. In D. H. Barlow (Ed.), *Clinical handbook of psychological disorders: A step-by-step treatment manual* (2nd ed.). New York: Guilford Press.

Rihmer, Z., Rutz, W., & Pihlgren, H. (1995). Depression and suicide on Gotland. An intensive study of all suicides before and after a depression-training programme for general practitioners. *J. Affect. Disord., 35,* 147-152.

Rimm, D. C., & Litvak, S. B. (1969). Self-verbalization and emotional arousal. *J. Abnorm. Psychol., 74*(2), 181-187.

Rimm, D. C., & Masters, J. C. (1979). *Behavior therapy: Techniques and empirical findings* (2nd ed.). New York: Academic Press.

Ringuette, E., & Kennedy, T. (1966). *J. Abnorm. Psychol., 71,* 136-141.

Risch, S. C., & Janowsky, D. S. (1984). Cholinergic-adrenergic balance in affective illness. In R. M. Post & J. C. Ballenger (Eds.), *Neurobiology of mood disorders: Vol. 1. Frontiers of clinical neuroscience.* Baltimore: Williams & Wilkins.

Ritchie, K., Kildea, D., & Robine, J. M. (1992). The relationship between age and the prevalence of senile dementia: A meta-analysis of recent data. *Int. J. Epidemiol., 21,* 763-769.

Ritter, A. (2001). Buprenorphine for the treatment of heroin dependence. *Drug Alcohol Rev., 20*(1), 5-7.

Rivas-Vazquez, R. A. (2001). Antidepressants as first-line agents in the current pharmacotherapy of anxiety disorders. *Prof. Psychol. Res. Pract., 32*(1), 101-104.

Rivas-Vazquez, R. A. (2001). Reboxetine: Refocusing on the role of norepinephrine in the treatment of depression. *Prof. Psychol. Res. Pract., 32*(2), 211-215.

Roan, S. (1995, September 19) A poor state of mind. *Los Angeles Times,* pp. E1, E7.

Roazen, P. (1992). The rise and fall of Bruno Bettelheim. *Psychohist. Rev., 20*(3), 221-250.

Robbins, S. J., Ehrman, R. N., Childress, A. R., Cornish, J. W., & O'Brien, C. P. (2000). Mood state and recent cocaine use are not associated with levels of cocaine cue reactivity. *Drug Alcohol Depend., 59*(1), 33-42.

Robert, P. H., Rubin-Brunet, V., & Darcourt, G. (1999). Serotonin and the frontal lobes. In B. L. Miller, J. L. Cummings et al. (Eds.), *The human frontal lobes: Functions and disorders. The science and practice of neuropsychology series.* New York: Guilford Press.

Roberts, A. R. (1979). Organization of suicide prevention agencies. In L. D. Hankoff & B. Einsidler

(Eds.), *Suicide: Theory and clinical aspects.* Littleton, MA: PSG Publishing.

Roberts, C. F., Golding, S. L., & Fincham, F. D. (1987). Implicit theories of criminal responsibility. *Law Hum. Behav., 11*(3), 207-232.

Roberts, J. E., Ciesla, J. A., Direnfeld, D. M., & Hewitt, R. G. (2001). Emotional distress among HIV-positive individuals: The roles of acute negative life events and psychological diatheses. *Pers. Individual Differ., 30*(2), 241-257.

Robertson, E. (1992). The challenge of dual diagnosis. *J. Health Care Poor Underserved, 3*(1), 198-207.

Robertson, M. (1992). *Starving in the silences: An exploration of anorexia nervosa.* New York: New York University Press.

Robin, A. L., Siegel, P. T., & Moye, A. (1995). Family versus individual therapy for anorexia: Impact on family conflict. Topical Section: Treatment and therapeutic processes. *Int. J. Eat. Disord., 17*(4), 313-322.

Robins, L. N., Locke, B. Z., & Regier, D. A. (1991). An overview of psychiatric disorders in America. In L. N. Robins & D. A. Regier (Eds.), *Psychiatric disorders in America: The Epidemiological Catchment Area Study.* New York: Free Press.

Robins, L. N., & Regier, D. S. (1991). *Psychiatric disorders in America: The Epidemiological Catchment Area Study.* New York: Free Press.

Robinson, D. J. (2000). *The psychiatric interview—explained.* Port Huron, MI: Rapid Psychler Press.

Robinson, D. J. (2000). *The mental status exam—explained.* Port Huron, MI: Rapid Psychler Press.

Robison, L. M., Sclar, D. A., Skaer, T. L., & Galin, R. S. (1999). National trends in the prevalence of attention-deficit/hyperactivity disorder and the prescribing of methylphenidate among school children: 1990-1995. *Clin. Pediatr., 38*(4), 209-217.

Rodgers, L. N. (1995). Prison suicide: Suggestions from phenomenology. *Deviant Behav., 16*(2), 113-126.

Rodier, P. M. (2000, February). The early origins of autism. *Sci. Am.,* pp. 56-63.

Rodin, J. (1992). Sick of worrying about the way you look? Read this. *Psychol. Today, 25*(1), 56-60.

Roedema, T. M., & Simons, R. F. (1999). Emotion-processing deficit in alexithymia. *Psychophysiology, 36*(3), 379-387.

Roehrich, L., & Kinder, B. N. (1991). Alcohol expectancies and male sexuality: Review and implications for sex therapy. *J. Sex Marital Ther., 17*(1), 45-54.

Roemer, L., Borkovec, M., Posa, S., & Borkovec, T. D. (1995). A self-report diagnostic measure of generalized anxiety disorder. *J. Behav. Ther. Exp. Psychiatry, 26*(4), 345-350.

Roesch, R. (1991). *The encyclopedia of depression.* New York: Facts-on-File.

Roesch, R., Zapf, P. A., Golding, S. L., & Skeem, J. L. (1999). Defining and assessing competence to stand trial. In A. K. Hess, I. B. Weiner et al. (Eds.), *The handbook of forensic psychology* (2nd ed.). New York: Wiley.

Roesler, A., & Witztum, E. (2000). Pharmacotherapy of paraphilias in the next millennium. *Behav. Sci. Law, 18*(1), 43-56.

Roesler, T. A., & McKenzie, N. (1994). Effects of childhood trauma on psychological functioning of adults sexually abused as children. *J. Nerv. Ment. Dis., 182*(3), 145-150.

Rogers, C. R. (1951). *Client-centered therapy.* Boston: Houghton Mifflin.

Rogers, C. R. (1961). *On becoming a person.* Boston: Houghton Mifflin.

Rogers, C. R. (1987). Rogers, Kohut, and Erickson: A personal perspective on some similarities and differences. In J. K. Zeig (Ed.), *The evolution of psychotherapy.* New York: Brunner/Mazel.

Rogers, C. R., & Dymond, R. (1954). *Psychotherapy and personality change.* Chicago: University of Chicago.

Rogers, J. C., & Holloway, R. L. (1990). Assessing threats to the validity of experimental and observational designs. *Fam. Pract. Res. J., 10*(2), 81-95.

Rogers, R. (1987). Assessment of criminal responsibility: Empirical advances and unanswered questions. *J. Psychiatry Law, 51*(1), 73-82.

Rogers, R., & Ewing, C. P. (1992). The measurement of insanity: Debating the merits of the R-CRAS and its alternatives. *Int. J. Law Psychiatry, 15,* 113-123.

Rogers, R., & Sewell, K. W. (1999). The R-CRAS and insanity evaluations: A re-examination of construct validity. *Behav. Sci. Law, 17*(2), 181-194.

Rogers, R., & Shuman, D. W. (2000). *Conducting insanity evaluations* (2nd ed.) New York: Guilford Press.

Roggla, H., & Uhl, A. (1995). Depression and relapses in treated chronic alcoholics. *Int. J. Addict., 30*(3), 337-349.

Rogler, L. H. (1999). Methodological sources of cultural insensitivity in mental health research. *Am. Psychol., 54*(6), 424-433.

Rogler, L. H., Malgady, R. G., & Rodriguea, O. (1989). *Hispanics and mental health: A framework for research.* Malabar, FL: Krieger.

Rohsenow, D. J., Smith, R. E., & Johnson, S. (1985). Stress management training as a prevention program for heavy social drinkers: Cognition, affect, drinking, and individual differences. *Addict. Behav., 10*(1), 45-54.

Roitman, S. E. L., Cornblatt, B. A., Bergman, A., Obuchowski, M. et al. (1997). Attention functioning in schizotypal personality disorder. *Am. J. Psychiatry, 154*(5), 655-660.

Roitman, S. E. L., Mitropoulou, V., Keefe, R. S. E., Silverman, J. M., Serby, M., Harvey, P. D., Reynolds, D. A., Mohs, R. C., & Siever, L. J. (2000). Visuospatial working memory in schizotypal personality disorder patients. *Schizophr. Res., 41*(3), 447-455.

Rokke, P. D., & Rehm, L. P. (2001). Self-management therapies. In K. S. Dobson (Ed.), *Handbook of cognitive-behavioral therapies* (2nd ed., pp. 173-210). New York: Guilford Press.

Rolland, J. S., & Walsh, F. (1994). Family therapy: Systems approaches to assessment and treatment. In R. E. Hales, S. C. Yudofsky, & J. A. Talbott (Eds.), *The American Psychiatric Press textbook of psychiatry* (2nd ed.). Washington, DC: American Psychiatric Press.

Rollin, H. R. (1980). *Coping with schizophrenia.* London: Burnett.

Rolls, B. J., Fedroff, I. C., & Guthrie, J. F. (1991). Gender differences in eating behavior and body weight regulation. *Health Psychol., 10*(2), 133-142.

Roloff, P. (2001). The nurse's role in a pilot program using a modified cognitive-behavioral approach. In B. Kinoy (Ed.), *Eating disorders: New directions in treatment and recovery* (2nd ed., pp. 127-132). New York: Columbia University Press.

Romano, E., & De Luca, R. V. (2001). Male sexual abuse: A review of effects, abuse characteristics, and links with later psychological functioning. *Agress. Violent Behav., 6*(1), 55-78.

Romans, S. E., Gendall, K. A., Martin, J. L., & Mullen, P. E. (2001). Child sexual abuse and later disordered eating: A New Zealand epidemiological study. *Int. J. Eat. Disord., 29*(4), 380-392.

Roper, G., Rachman, S., & Hodgson, R. (1973). An experiment on obsessional checking. *Behav. Res. Ther., 11,* 271-277.

Roper Reports. (1998, February). Marriage: The art of compromise. *Am. Demogr.*

Roper Reports. (1998, August). How old is old? *Am. Demogr.*

Rosen, E. F., Anthony, D. L., Booker, K. M., Brown, T. L. et al. (1991). A comparison of eating disorder scores among African American and white college females. *Bull. Psychon. Soc., 29*(1), 65–66.

Rosen, J. C., & Leitenberg, H. (1982). Bulimia nervosa: Treatment with exposure and response prevention. *Behav. Ther., 13*(1), 117–124.

Rosen, J. C., & Leitenberg, H. (1985). Exposure plus response prevention treatment of bulimia. In D. M. Garner & P. E. Garfinkel (Eds.), *Handbook of psychotherapy for anorexia nervosa and bulimia.* New York: Guilford Press.

Rosen, J. C., Orosan, P., & Reiter, J. (1995). Cognitive behavior therapy for negative body image in obese women. *Behav. Ther., 26,* 25–42.

Rosen, L. W., & Hough, D. O. (1988). Pathogenic weight-control behaviors of female college gymnasts. *Physician Sports Med., 16*(9), 141–144.

Rosen, L. W., McKeag, D. B., Hough, D. O., & Curley, V. (1986). Pathogenic weight-control behavior in female athletes. *Physician Sports Med., 14*(1), 79–86.

Rosen, M. I., McMahon, T. J., Hameedi, F. A., Pearsall, H. R., Woods, S. W., Kreek, M. J., & Kosten, T. R. (1996). Effect of clonidine pretreatment on naloxone-precipitated opiate withdrawal. *J. Pharmacol. Exp. Ther., 276,* 1128–1135.

Rosen, R. C. (2000). Medical and psychological interventions for erectile dysfunction: Toward a combined treatment approach. In S. R. Leiblum & R. C. Rosen (Eds.), *Principles and practice of sex therapy* (3rd ed., pp. 276–304). New York: Guilford Press.

Rosen, R. C., Lane, R. M., & Menza, M. (1999). Effects of SSRIs on sexual function: A critical review. *J. Clin. Psychopharmacol., 19*(1), 67–85.

Rosen, R. C., & Leiblum, S. R. (1993). Treatment of male erectile disorder: Current options and dilemmas. *J. Sex Marital Ther., 8*(1), 5–8.

Rosen, R. C., & Leiblum, S. R. (1995). Hypoactive sexual desire. *Psychiatr. Clin. North Am., 13*(1), 107–121.

Rosen, R. C., & Leiblum, S. R. (1995). Hypoactive sexual desire [Special issue: Clinical sexuality]. *Psychiatr. Clin. North Am., 18*(1), 107–121.

Rosen, R. C., & Leiblum, S. R. (1995). Treatment of sexual disorders in the 1990s: An integrated approach. *J. Consult. Clin. Psychol., 63*(6), 877–890.

Rosen, R. C., Leiblum, S. R., & Spector, I. (1994). Psychologically based treatment for male erectile disorder: A cognitive-interpersonal model. *J. Sex Marital Ther., 20,* 78–85.

Rosen, R. C., & Rosen, L. R. (1981). *Human sexuality.* New York: Knopf.

Rosen, R. C., Taylor, J. F., Leiblum, S. R., & Bachmann, G. A. (1993). Prevalence of sexual dysfunction in women: Results of a survey study of 329 women in an outpatient gynecological clinic. *J. Sex Marital Ther., 19,* 171–188.

Rosenbaum, M. (1980). The role of the term schizophrenia in the decline of diagnoses of multiple personality. *Arch. Gen. Psychiatry, 37*(12), 1383–1385.

Rosenberg, H. (1993). Prediction of controlled drinking by alcoholics and problem drinkers. *Psychol. Bull., 113*(1), 129–139.

Rosenfarb, I. S., Goldstein, M. J., Mintz, J., & Nuechterlein, K. H. (1995). Expressed emotion and subclinical psychopathology observable within the transactions between schizophrenic patients and their family members. *J. Abnorm. Psychol., 104*(2), 259–267.

Rosenfeld, M. (1998, November 22). Van Gogh's madness: Long after the painter's death, the diagnosis debate lives on. *Washington Post,* p. G1.

Rosenhan, D. L. (1973). On being sane in insane places. *Science, 179,* 250–258.

Rosenman, R. H. (1990). Type A behavior pattern: A personal overview. *J. Soc. Behav. Pers., 5,* 1–24.

Rosenstein, D. S., & Horowitz, H. A. (1996). Adolescent attachment and psychopathology. *J. Consult. Clin. Psychol., 64*(2), 244–253.

Rosenthal, D. A., & Berven, N. L. (1999). Effects of client race on clinical judgment. *Rehabil. Counsel. Bull., 42*(3), 243–264.

Rosenthal, N. E., & Blehar, M. C. (Eds.). (1989). *Seasonal affective disorders and phototherapy.* New York: Guilford Press.

Rosenthal, R. (1966). *Experimenter effects in behavioral research.* New York: Appleton-Century-Crofts.

Rosenthal, R. J. (1992). Pathological gambling. *Psychiatr. Ann., 22*(2), 72–78.

Rosenzweig, M. R. (1996). Aspects of the search for neural mechanisms of memory. *Annu. Rev. Psychol., 47.*

Rosenzweig, S. (1933). The recall of finished and unfinished tasks as affected by the purpose with which they were performed. *Psychol. Bull., 30,* 698.

Rosenzweig, S. (1943). An experimental study of repression with special reference to need-persistive and ego-defensive reactions to frustration. *J. Exp. Psychol., 32,* 64–74.

Roses, A. D., Einstein, G., Gilbert, J., Goedert, M., Han, S. H., Huang, D., Hulette, C., Masliah, E., Pericak-Vance, M. A., Saunders, A. M., Schmechel, D. E., Strittmatter, W. J., Weisgraber, K. H., & Xi, P. T. (1996). Morphological, biochemical, and genetic support for an apolipoprotein E effect on microtubular metabolism. In R. J. Wurtman, S. Corkin, J. H. Growdon, & R. M. Nitsch (Eds.), *The neurobiology of Alzheimer's disease.* New York: New York Academy of Sciences.

Ross, A. O. (1981). *Child behavior therapy: Principles, procedures and empirical basis.* New York: Wiley.

Ross, C. A., & Ellason, J. (1999). Comment on the effectiveness of treatment for dissociative identity disorder. *Psychol. Rep., 84*(3, Pt. 2), 1109–1110.

Ross, C. A., & Gahan, P. (1988). Techniques in the treatment of multiple personality disorder. *Am. J. Psychother., 42*(1), 40–52.

Ross, C. A., Miller, S. D., Bjornson, L., Reagor, P., Fraser, G. A., & Anderson, G. (1991). Abuse histories in 102 cases of multiple personality disorder. *Can. J. Psychiatry, 36,* 97–101.

Ross, C. A., Miller, S. D., Reagor, P., & Bjornson, L. et al. (1990). Structured interview data on 102 cases of multiple personality disorder from four centers. *Am. J. Psychiatry, 147*(5), 596–601.

Ross, C. A., Norton, G. R., & Wozney, K. (1989). Multiple personality disorder: An analysis of 236 cases. *Can. J. Psychiatry, 34*(5), 413–418.

Ross, D. M., & Ross, S. A. (1982). *Hyperactivity: Current issues, research and theory* (2nd ed.). New York: Wiley.

Rosselli, M., & Ardila, A. (1996). Cognitive effects of cocaine and polydrug abuse. *J. Clin. Exp. Neuropsychol., 18*(1), 122–135.

Rossi, A., Bustini, M., Prosperini, P., Marinangeli, M. G., Splendiani, A., Daneluzzo, E., & Stratta, P. (2000). Neuromorphological abnormalities in schizophrenic patients with good and poor outcome. *Acta Psychiatr. Scand., 101*(2), 161–166.

Rossor, M. N., Kennedy, A. M., & Frackowiak, R. S. J. (1996). Clinical and neuroimaging features of familial Alzheimer's disease. In R. J. Wurtman, S. Corkin, J. H. Growdon, & R. M. Nitsch (Eds.), *The neurobiology of Alzheimer's disease.* New York: New York Academy of Sciences.

Rossow, I., & Amundsen, A. (1995). Alcohol abuse and suicide: A 40-year prospective study of Norwegian conscripts. *Addiction, 90*(5), 685–691.

Rossow, I., & Lauritzen, G. (2001). Shattered childhood: A key issue in suicidal behavior among drug addicts? *Addiction, 96*(2), 227–240.

Rotenberg, V., Kayumov, L., Indursky, P., Kimhi, R., Venger, A., Melamed, Y., & Elizur, A.

(1999). Slow wave sleep redistribution and REM sleep eye movement density in depression: Towards the adaptive function of REM sleep. *Homeostasis Health Dis., 39*(3–4), 81–89.

Roth, R. S. (2000). Psychogenic models of chronic pain: A selective review and critique. In M. J. Massie (Ed.), *Pain: What psychiatrists need to know* (Vol. 19, No. 2, pp. 89–131). Washington, DC: American Psychiatric Press.

Rothbaum, B. O., Foa, E. B., Riggs, D. S., Murdock, T., & Walsh, W. (1992). A prospective examination of posttraumatic stress disorder in rape victims. *J. Traumatic Stress, 5*(3), 455–475.

Rothblum, E. D. (1992). The stigma of women's weight: Social and economic realities. *Feminism Psychol., 2*(1), 61–73.

Rowa, K., Kerig, P. K., & Geller, J. (2001). The family and anorexia nervosa: Examining parent-child boundary problems. *Eur. Eat. Disord. Rev., 9*(2), 97–114.

Rowlands, P. (1995). Schizophrenia and sexuality. *J. Sex Marital Ther. 10*(1), 47–61.

Roy, A. (1982). Suicide in chronic schizophrenics. *Br. J. Psychiatry, 141,* 171–177.

Rozin, P., & Stoess, C. (1993). Is there a general tendency to become addicted? *Addict. Behav., 18,* 81–87.

Rubinstein, S., & Caballero, B. (2000). Is Miss America an undernourished role model? *JAMA, J. Am. Med. Assoc., 283*(12), 1569.

Rudd, M. D. (2000). Integrating science into the practice of clinical suicidology: A review of the psychotherapy literature and a research agenda for the future. In R. W. Maris, S. S. Canetto et al. (Eds.), *Review of suicidology, 2000.* New York: Guilford Press.

Rudd, M. D., Joiner, T., & Rajah, M. H. (2001). *Treating suicidal behavior: An effective time-limited approach.* New York: Guilford Press.

Rudolph, K. D., Hammen, C., Burge, D., Lindberg, N., Herzberg, D., & Daley, S. E. (2000). Toward an interpersonal life-stress model of depression: The developmental context of stress generation. *Dev. Psychopathol., 12,* 215–234.

Ruedrich, S. L., Chu, C., & Wadle, C. V. (1985). The amytal interview in the treatment of psychogenic amnesia [Special issue]. *Hosp. Commun. Psychiatry, 36*(10), 1045–1046.

Rush, A. J., & Frances, A. (2000). Expert consensus guideline series: Treatment of psychiatric and behavioral problems in mental retardation. *Am. J. Ment. Retard., 105*(3), 159–228.

Rush, A. J., Weissenburger, J., & Eaves, G. (1986). Do thinking patterns predict depressive symptoms? *Cognit. Ther. Res., 10*(2), 225–235.

Rushford, N., & Ostermeyer, A. (1997). Body image disturbances and their change with videofeedback in anorexia nervosa. *Behav. Res. Ther., 35*(5), 389–398.

Rushton, J. L. (1999). *Prescribing of SSRIs in child and adolescent populations.* Paper presented at the Pediatric Academic Societies annual meeting, San Francisco.

Russell, G. (1979). Bulimia nervosa: An ominous variant of anorexia nervosa. *Psychol. Med., 9*(3), 429–448.

Russell, G. F. M. (1995). Anorexia nervosa through time. In G. Szmukler, C. Dare, & J. Treasure (Eds.), *Handbook of eating disorders: Theory, treatment and research.* Chichester, England: Wiley.

Russell, R. J., & Hulson, B. (1992). Physical and psychological abuse of heterosexual partners. *Pers. Individual Differ., 13*(4), 457–473.

Russell, R. M. et al. (1992). In K. Halmi (Ed.), *Psychobiology and treatment of anorexia nervosa and bulimia.* Washington, DC: American Psychiatric Press.

Rychtarik, R. G., Connors, G. J., Whitney, R. B., McGillicuddy, N. B., Fitterling, J. M., & Wirtz,

P. W. (2000). Treatment settings for persons with alcoholism: Evidence for matching clients to inpatient versus outpatient care. *J. Consult. Clin. Psychol., 68*(2), 277–289.

SAMHSA (Substance Abuse and Mental Health Services Administration). (1996). Preliminary estimates from the drug abuse warning network. Advance report number 17. Washington, DC: U. S. Department of Health and Human Services.

SAMHSA. (1996). *National Household Survey on Drug Abuse, 1994 and 1995.* Office of Applied Studies.

SAMHSA News. (1993, Spring). *Agencies improve mental health services in jails* (Vol. 1, No. 2.). U.S. Department of Health and Human Services.

Saarinen, P. I., Viinamaeki, H., Hintikka, J., Lehtonen, J., & Koennqvist, J. (1999). Psychological symptoms of close relatives of suicide victims. *Eur. J. Psychiatry, 13*(1), 33–39.

Sachs, R. G. (1986). The adjunctive role of social support systems. In B. G. Braun (Ed.), *The treatment of multiple personality disorder.* Washington, DC: American Psychiatric Press.

Sackeim, H. A. (1988). Mechanisms of action of electroconvulsive therapy. In A. J. Frances & R. E. Hales (Eds.), *American Psychiatric Press review of psychiatry* (Vol. 7). Washington, DC: American Psychiatric Press.

Sacks, O. (2000, May). *An anthropologist on Mars: Some personal perspectives on autism.* Keynote address. Eden Institute Foundation's sixth annual Princeton Lecture Series on Autism, Princeton, NJ.

Safer, D. (1994). The impact of recent lawsuits on methylphenidates sales. *Clin. Pediatr., 33*(3), 166–168.

Safer, D., & Krager, J. (1992). Effect of a media blitz and a threatened lawsuit on stimulant treatment. *JAMA, J. Am. Med. Assoc., 268*(8), 1004–1007.

Safer, D., & Krager, J. (1993). Reply to "Treatment of ADHD" (Letter). *JAMA, J. Am. Med. Assoc., 269*(18), 2369.

Saftig, P., Hartmann, D., & De Strooper, B. (1999). The function of presenilin-1 in amyloid beta-peptide generation and brain development. *Eur. Arch. Psychiatry Clin. Neurosci., 249*(6), 271–279.

Sagawa, K., Kawakatsu, S., Shibuya, I., Oiji, A. et al. (1990). Correlation of regional cerebral blood flow with performance on neuropsychological tests in schizophrenic patients. *Schizophr. Res., 3*(4), 241–246.

Sakado, K., Sato, T., Uehara, T., Sakado, M., & Someya, T. (1999). Perceived parenting pattern and response to antidepressants in patients with major depression. *J. Affect. Disord., 52*(1–3), 59–66.

Sakheim, D. K., Hess, E. P., & Chivas, A. (1988). General principles for short-term inpatient work with multiple personality-disorder patients. *Psychotherapy, 24,* 117–124.

Sakurai, S. (1998). Hypnotic approaches to a college female student with personality disorder suffering from somatization disorder. *Jpn. J. Hypnosis, 43*(1), 11–19.

Salama, A. A. (1988). The antisocial personality (the sociopathic personality). *Psychiat. J. Univ. Ottawa, 13*(3), 149–151.

Sales, E., Baum, M., & Shore, B. (1984). Victim readjustment following assault. *J. Soc. Issues, 40*(1), 117–136.

Salkovskis, P. M. (1985). Obsessional-compulsive problems: A cognitive-behavioral analysis. *Behav. Res. Ther., 23,* 571–584.

Salkovskis, P. M. (1989). Cognitive-behavioural factors and the persistence of intrusive thoughts in obsessional problems. *Behav. Res. Ther., 27,* 677–682.

Salkovskis, P. M. (1999). Understanding and treating obsessive-compulsive disorder. *Behav. Res. Ther., 37*(Suppl. 1), S29–S52.

Salkovskis, P. M., Atha, C., & Storer, D. (1990). Cognitive behavioural problem solving in the treatment of patients who repeatedly attempt suicide: A controlled trial. *Br. J. Psychiatry, 157,* 871–876.

Salkovskis, P. M., & Warwick, H. M. C. (2001). Meaning, misinterpretations, and medicine: A cognitive-behavioral approach to understanding health anxiety and hypochondriasis. In V. Starcevic & D. R. Lipsitt (Eds.), *Hypochondriasis: Modern perspectives on an ancient malady* (pp. 202–222). New York: Oxford University Press.

Salkovskis, P. M., & Westbrook, D. (1989). Behaviour therapy and obsessional ruminations: Can failure be turned into success? *Behav. Res. Ther., 27,* 149–160.

Sallee, F. R., Vrindavanam, N. S., Deas-Nesmith, D., Carson, S. W., & Sethuraman, G. (1997). Pulse intravenous clomipramine for depressed adolescents: Double-blind, controlled trial. *Am. J. Psychiatry, 154*(5), 668–673.

Salzman, C. (1999). Treatment of the suicidal patient with psychotropic drugs and ECT. In D.G. Jacobs (Ed.), *The Harvard Medical School guide to suicide assessment and intervention.* San Francisco: Jossey-Bass.

Salzman, C., Vaccaro, B., Lieff, J., & Weiner, A. (1995). Clozapine in older patients with psychosis and behavioral disruption. *Am. J. Geriatr. Psychiatry, 3*(1), 26–33.

Salzman, L. (1980). *Psychotherapy of the obsessive personality.* New York: Jason Aronson.

Salzman, L. (1985). Psychotherapeutic management of obsessive-compulsive patients. *Am. J. Psychother., 39*(3), 323–330.

Salzman, L. (1989). *Compulsive personality disorder.* In *Treatments of psychiatric disorders.* Washington, DC: American Psychiatric Press.

Sampath, G., Shah, A., Kraska, J., & Soni, S. D. (1992). Neuroleptic discontinuation in the very stable schizophrenic patient: Relapse rates and serum neuroleptic levels. *Hum. Psychopharmacol. Clin. Exp., 7*(4), 255–264.

Sanchez-Canovas, J., Botella-Arbona, C., Ballestin, G. P., & Soriano-Pastor, J. (1991). Intervencion comportamental y analisis ipsativo normativo en un trastorno de ansiedad [Behavioral intervention and ipsative-normative analysis in an anxiety disorder]. *Anal. Modif. Conducta, 17*(51), 115–151.

Sandelowski, M. (1995). Sample size in qualitative research. *Res. Nurs. Health, 18*(2), 179–183.

Sanders, S. K., & Shekhar, A. (1995). Anxiolytic effects of chlordiazepoxide blocked by injection of GABA-sub(A) and benzodiazepine receptor antagonists in the region of the anterior basolateral amygdala of rats. *Biol. Psychiatry, 37*(7), 473–476.

Sanders, S. K., & Shekhar, A. (1995). Regulation of anxiety by GABAA receptors in the rat amygdala. *Pharmacol. Biochem. Behav., 52*(4), 701–706.

Sanderson, R. E., Campbell, D., & Laverty, S. G. (1963). An investigation of a new aversive conditioning treatment for alcoholism. *Q. J. Stud. Alcohol., 24,* 261–275.

Sandler, M. (1990). Monoamine oxidase inhibitors in depression: History and mythology. *J. Psychopharmacol., 4*(3), 136–139.

Sanftner, J. L., Barlow, D. H., Marschall, D. E., & Tangney, J. P. (1995). The relation of shame and guilt to eating disorder symptomatology. *J. Soc. Clin. Psychol., 14*(4), 315–324.

Sansone, R. A., Fine, M. A., & Dennis, A. B. (1991). Treatment impressions and termination experiences with borderline patients. *Am. J. Psychother., 45*(2), 173–180.

Sansone, R.A., Wiederman, M., & Sansone, L.A. (2000). Medically self-harming behavior and its relationship to borderline personality symptoms and somatic preoccupation among internal medicine patients. *J. Nerv. Ment. Dis., 188*(1), 45–47.

Santa Mina, E. E., & Gallop, R. M. (1998). Childhood sexual and physical abuse and adult self-harm and suicidal behaviour: A literature review. *Can. J. Psychiatry, 43*(8), 793–800.

Santor, D. A., & Kusumakar, V. (2001). Open trial of interpersonal therapy in adolescents with moderate to severe major depression: Effectiveness of novice IPT therapists. *Am. Acad. Child Adolesc. Psychiatry, 40*(2), 236–240.

Satir, V. (1964). *Conjoint family therapy: A guide to therapy and technique.* Palo Alto, CA: Science & Behavior Books.

Satir, V. (1967). *Conjoint family therapy* (Rev. ed.). Palo Alto, CA: Science & Behavior Books.

Satir, V. (1987). Going behind the obvious: The psychotherapeutic journey. In J. K. Zeig (Ed.), *The evolution of psychotherapy.* New York: Brunner/Mazel.

Sato, T., Sakado, K., Uehara, T., Nichioka, K., & Kasahara, Y. (1997). Perceived parental styles in a Japanese sample of depressive disorders. A replication outside Western culture. *Br. J. Psychiatry, 170,* 173–175.

Saudino, J. J., Pedersen, N. L., Lichenstein, P., McClearn, G. E., & Plomin, R. (1997). Can personality explain genetic influence on life events? *J. Pers. Soc. Psychol., 72*(1), 196–206.

Saunders, D. G. (1992). A typology of men who batter: Three types derived from cluster analysis. *Am. J. Orthopsychiatry, 62*(2), 264–275.

Scarf, M. (1996, June 10). The mind of the Unabomber. *New Republic,* pp. 20–23.

Scarpa, A., Luscher, K. A., Smalley, K. J., Pilkonis, P. A., Kim, Y., & Williams, W. C. (1999). Screening for personality disorders in a nonclinical population. *J. Pers. Disord., 13*(4), 345–360.

Scarr, S., Phillips, D., & McCartney, K. (1989). Working mothers and their families. *Am. Psychol., 44*(11), 1402–1409.

Scarr, S., Phillips, D., & McCartney, K. (1990). Working mothers and their families. *Ann. Prog. Child Psychiatry Child Dev.,* pp. 261–278.

Schachar, R. J., & Wachsmuth, R. (1990). Hyperactivity and parental psychopathology. *J. Child Psychol. Psychiatry Allied Discip., 31,* 381–392.

Schacter, D. L. (1999). The seven sins of memory: Insights from psychology and cognitive neuroscience. *Am. Psychol., 54*(3), 182–203.

Schacter, D. L., Glisky, E. L., & McGlynn, S. M. (1990). Impact of memory disorder on everyday life: Awareness of deficits and return to work. In D. Tupper & K. Cicerone (Eds.), *The neuropsychology of everyday life: Vol. 1. Theories and basic competencies.* Boston: Martinus Nijhoff.

Schatzberg, A. T. et al. (1982). Toward a biochemical classification of depressive disorders: V. Heterogeneity of unipolar depressions. *Am. J. Psychiatry, 130*(4), 471–475.

Schechter, D., Singer, T. M., Kuperman, J., & Endicott, J. (1998). Selection of "normal" control subjects for psychiatric research: Update on a model for centralized recruitment. *Psychiatry Res., 79*(2), 175–185.

Scheel, K. R. (2000). The empirical basis of dialectical behavior therapy: Summary, critique, and implications. *Clin. Psychol.: Sci. Pract., 7*(1), 68–86.

Scheff, T. J. (1975). *Labeling madness.* Englewood Cliffs, NJ: Prentice Hall.

Scheff, T. J. (1999). *Being mentally ill: A sociological theory.* Hawthorne, NY: de Gruyter.

Scheier, L. M., & Botvin, G. J. (1997). Expectancies as mediators of the effects of social influences and alcohol knowledge on adolescent alcohol use: A prospective analysis. *Psychol. Addict. Behav., 11*(1), 48–64.

Scheuffgen, K., Happe, F., Anderson, M., & Frith, U. (2000). High "intelligence," low "IQ"? Speed of processing and measured IQ in children with autism. *Dev. Psychopathol., 12*(1), 83–90.

Schiavi, R. C., White, D., Mandeli, J., & Schreiner-Engel, P. (1993). Hormones and nocturnal penile tumescence in healthy aging men. *Arch. Sex. Behav., 22*(2), 207–216.

Schildkraut, J. J. (1965). The catecholamine hypothesis of affective disorders: A review of supporting evidence. *Am. J. Psychiatry, 122*(5), 509–522.

Schleifer, J. S., Keller, S. E., Bartlett, J. A., Eckholdt, H. M., & Delaney, B. R. (1996). Immunity in young adults with major depressive disorder. *Am. J. Psychiatry, 153*, 477–482.

Schleifer, S. J., Keller, S. E., & Bartlett, J. A. (1999). Depression and immunity: Clinical factors and therapeutic course. *Psychiatry Res., 85*(1), 63–69.

Schlenger, W. E., Fairbank, J. A., Jordan, B. K., & Caddell, J. M. (1998). Combat-related posttraumatic stress disorder: Prevalence, risk factors, and comorbidity. In P. A. Saigh, J. D. Bremner et al. (Eds.), *Posttraumatic stress disorder: A comprehensive text*. Boston: Allyn & Bacon.

Schlesinger, M., Dorwart, R., Hoover, C., & Epstein, S. (1997). Competition, ownership, and access to hospital services: Evidence from psychiatric hospitals. *Med. Care, 35*(9), 974–992.

Schlundt, O. G., & Johnson, W. G. (1990). *Eating disorders: Assessment and treatment*. Boston: Allyn & Bacon.

Schmidt, L.G., Dufeu, P., Kuhn, S., Smolka, M., & Rommelspacher, H. (2000). Transition to alcohol dependence: Clinical and neurobiological considerations. *Compr. Psychiatry, 41*(2, Suppl 1), 90–94.

Schmidt, U., Tiller, J., & Treasure, J. (1993). Psychosocial factors in the origins of bulimia nervosa. *Int. Rev. Psychiatry, 5*(1), 51–59.

Schmidt, U., Tiller, J., & Treasure, J. (1993). Self-treatment of bulimia nervosa: A pilot study. *Int. J. Eat. Disord., 13*(3), 273–277.

Schmidtke, A., & Häfner, H. (1988). The Werther effect after television films: New evidence for an old hypothesis. *Psychol. Med., 18*, 665–676.

Schmidtke, A., Weinacker, B., Apter, A., Batt, A., Berman, A., Bille-Brahe, U., Botsis, A., DeLeo, D., Doneux, A., Goldney, R., Grad, O., Haring, C., Hawton, K., Hjelmeland, H., Kelleher, M., Kerkhof, A., Leenaars, A., Lonnqvist, J., Michel, K., Ostamo, A., Salander-Renberg, E., Sayil, I., Takahashi, Y., Van Heeringen, C., Varnik, A., & Wasserman, D. (1999). Suicide rates in the world: Update. *Arch. Suicide Res., 5*, 81–89.

Schmidtke, A., Weinacker, B., Stack, S., & Lester, D. (1999). The impact of the reunification of Germany on the suicide rate. *Arch. Suicide Res., 5*(3), 233–239.

Schneider, K. J. (1998). Existential processes. In L. S. Greenberg, J. C. Watson et al. (Eds.), *Handbook of experiential psychotherapy*. New York: Guilford Press.

Schneider, L. S. (1996). Overview of generalized anxiety disorder in the elderly. *J. Clin. Psychiatry, 57*(Suppl. 7), 34–45.

Schneiderman, N., & Baum, A. (1992). Acute and chronic stress and the immune system. In N. Schneiderman, P. McCabe, & A. Baum (Eds.), *Perspectives in behavioral medicine: Stress and disease processes*. Hillsdale, NJ: Erlbaum.

Schneiderman, N. (1999). Behavioral medicine and the management of HIV/AIDS. *Int. J. Behav. Med., 6*(1), 3–12.

Schneidman, E. S. (1998). Perspectives on suicidology: Further reflections on suicide and psyche. *Suicide Life-Threaten. Behav., 28*(3), 245–250.

Schneier, F. R. (2001). Treatment of social phobia with antidepressants. *J. Clin. Psychiatry, 62*(Suppl. 1), 43–49.

Schnurr, P. P., & Spiro, A., III. (1999). Combat disorder, posttraumatic stress disorder symptoms, and health behaviors as predictors of self-reported physical health in older veterans. *J. Nerv. Ment. Dis., 187*(6), 353–359.

Schnurr, P. P., & Vielhauer, M. J. (1999). Personality as a risk factor for PTSD. In R. Yehuda et al. (Eds.), *Risk factors for posttraumatic stress disorder*. Washington, DC: American Psychiatric Press.

Schnyder, U., Valach, L., Bichsel, K., & Michel, K. (1999). Attempted suicide: Do we understand the patients' reasons? *Gen. Hosp. Psychiatry, 21*(1), 62–69.

Scholing, A., & Emmelkamp, P. M. G. (1996). Treatment of generalized social phobia: Results at long-term follow-up. *Behav. Res. Ther., 34*(5/6), 447–452.

Scholing, A., & Emmelkamp, P. M. G. (1999). Prediction of treatment outcome in social phobia: A cross-validation. *Behav. Res. Ther., 37*(7), 659–670.

Schott, R. L. (1999). Managers and mental health: Mental illness and the workplace. *Public Pers. Manag., 28*(2), 161–183.

Schou, M. (1997). Forty years of lithium treatment. *Arch. Gen. Psychiatry, 54*, 9–13.

Schover, L. R. (2000). Sexual problems in chronic illness. In S. R. Leiblum & R. C. Rosen (Eds.), *Principles and practice of sex therapy* (3rd ed., pp. 398–422). New York: Guilford Press.

Schover, L. R., & LoPiccolo, J. (1982). Treatment effectiveness for dysfunctions of sexual desires. *J. Sex Marital Ther., 8*(3), 179–197.

Schrader, E. (2000). Equivalence of St. John's wort extract (Ze 117) and fluoxetine: A randomized, controlled study in mild-moderate depression. *Int. Clin. Psychopharmacol., 15*(2), 61–68.

Schreiber, F. R. (1973). *Sybil*. Chicago: Regnery.

Schreiber, R. (2001). Wandering in the dark: Women's experiences with depression. *Health Care for Women Int., 22*(1–2), 85–98.

Schuckit, M. (1999). Cited in C. Ginther, Schuckit addresses state-of-the-art addiction treatments. *Psychiatr. Times, 16*(4).

Schuckit, M. (2000). *Drug and alcohol abuse: A clinical guide to diagnosis and treatment* (5th ed.). New York: Kluwer Academic/Plenum Press.

Schuckit, M. A., Danko, G. P., Raimo, E. B., Smith, T. L., Eng, M. Y., Carpenter, K. K. T., & Hesselbrock, V. M. (2001). A preliminary evaluation of the potential usefulness of the diagnoses of polysubstance dependence. *J. Stud. Alcohol, 62*(1), 54–61.

Schuldberg, D., French, C., Stone, B. L., & Heberle, J. (1988). Creativity and schizotypal traits: Creativity test scores and perceptual aberration, magical ideation, and impulsive nonconformity. *J. Nerv. Ment. Dis., 176*(11), 648–657.

Schulenberg, J., Maggs, J. L., Long, S. W., Sher, K. J., Gotham, H. J., Baer, J. S., Kivlahan, D. R., Marlatt, G. A., & Zucker, R. A. (2001). The problem of college drinking: Insights from a developmental perspective. *Alcohol: Clin. Exp. Res., 25*(3), 473–477.

Schultz, R., & Heckhausen, J. (1996). A life span model of successful aging. *Am. Psychol., 51*(7), 702–714.

Schultz, S. C. (2000). New antipsychotic medications: More than old wine and new bottles. *Bull. Menninger Clin., 64*(1), 60–75.

Schultz, S. K., Miller, D. D., Arndt, S., Ziebell, S., Gupta, S., & Andreasen, N. (1995). Withdrawal-emergent dyskinesia in patients with schizophrenia during antipsychotic discontinuation. *Biol. Psychiatry, 38*, 713–719.

Schulz, P. M. et al. (1986). Diagnoses of the relatives of schizotypal outpatients. *J. Nerv. Ment. Dis., 174*(8), 457–463.

Schwalb, M. (1999). Interviewed in M. S. Baum, Autism: Locked in a solitary world. *HealthState, 17*(2), 18–22.

Schwartz, G. (1977). College students as contingency managers for adolescents in a program to develop reading skills. *J. Appl. Behav. Anal., 10*, 645–655.

Schwartz, G. E. (1977). Psychosomatic disorders and biofeedback: A psychobiological model of disregulation. In J. D. Maser & M. E. P. Seligman (Eds.), *Psychopathology: Experimental models*. San Francisco: Freeman.

Schwartz, G. E. (1982). Testing the biopsychosocial model: The ultimate challenge facing behavioral medicine? *J. Consult Clin. Psychol., 50*(6), 1040–1053.

Schwartz, J. M., Stoessel, P. W., Baxter, L. R., Jr., Martin, K. M., & Phelps, M. E. (1996). Systematic changes in cerebral glucose metabolic rate after successful behavior modification treatment of obsessive-compulsive disorder. *Arch. Gen. Psychiatry, 53*, 109–113.

Schwartz, S. (1993). *Classic studies in abnormal psychology*. Mountain View, CA: Mayfield Publishing.

Schwartz, S. (1999). Biological approaches to psychiatric disorders. In A. V. Horwitz & T. L. Scheid (Eds.), *A handbook for the study of mental health: Social contexts, theories, and systems*. Cambridge, England: Cambridge University Press.

Schwartz, S., & Johnson, J. J. (1985). *Psychopathology of childhood*. New York: Pergamon Press.

Schwarz, K., Harding, R., Harrington, D., & Farr, B. (1993). Hospital management of a patient with intractable factitious disorder. *Psychosomatics, 34*(3), 265–267.

Schwarz, N. (1999). Self-reports: How the questions shape the answers. *Am. Psychol., 54*(2), 93–105.

Schweizer, E. S., & Rickels, K. (1997). Strategies for treatment of generalized anxiety in the primary care setting. *J. Clin. Psychiatry, 58*(Suppl. 3), 27–31.

Scola, P. S. (1991). Classification and social status. In J. L. Matson & J. A. Mulick (Eds.), *Handbook of mental retardation*. New York: Pergamon Press.

Scott, A. (1995). "Reclaimed once more by the realities of life": Hysteria and the location of memory. *Br. J. Psychother., 11*(3), 398–405.

Scott, J. (1990, July 25). Vertigo, not madness, may have tormented Van Gogh. *Los Angeles Times*, p. A14.

Scott, J. (1995). Psychotherapy for bipolar disorder. *Br. J. Psychiatry, 167*(5), 581–588.

Scott, J., & Wright, J. H. (1997). Cognitive therapy for chronic and severe mental disorders. In L. J. Dickstein, M. B. Riba, & J. M. Oldham (Eds.), *Review of psychiatry* (Vol. 16). Washington, DC: American Psychiatric Press.

Scott, J. E., & Dixon, L. B. (1995). Psychological interventions for schizophrenia. *Schizophr. Bull., 21*(4), 621–630.

Scott, J. E., & Dixon, L. B. (1995). Assertive community treatment and case management for schizophrenia. *Schizophr. Bull., 21*(4), 657–668.

Scott, R. D., Fagin, L., & Winter, D. (1993). The importance of the role of the patient in the outcome of schizophrenia. *Br. J. Psychiatry, 163*, 62–68.

Scott, W. D., Winters, R. W., & Beevers, C. G. (2000). Affective distress as a central and organizing sympton in depression: Psychological mechanisms. In S. L. Johnson & A. M. Hayes (Eds.), *Stress, coping, and depression* (pp. 145–175). Mahwah, NJ: Erlbaum.

Scotti, J. R., & Morris, T. L. (2000). Diagnosis and classification. In M. Hersen & R. T. Ammerman (Eds.), *Advanced abnormal child psychology* (2nd ed., pp. 15–32). Mahwah, NJ: Erlbaum.

Scourfield, J., Soldan, J., Gray, J., Houlihan, G., & Harper, P. S. (1997). Huntington's disease: Psychiatric practice in molecular genetic prediction and diagnosis. *Br. J. Psychiatry, 170*, 146–149.

Seale, C., & Addington-Hall, J. (1995). Euthanasia: The role of good care. *Soc. Sci. Med., 40*(5), 581–587.

Seale, C., & Addington-Hall, J. (1995). Dying at the best time. *Soc. Sci. Med., 40*(5), 589–595.

Searleman, A., & Herrmann, D. (1994). *Memory from a broader perspective.* New York: McGraw-Hall.

Sebregts, E. H. W. J., Falger, P. R. J., & Baer, F. W. H. M. (2000). Risk factor modification through nonpharmacological interventions in patients with coronary heart disease. *J. Psychosom. Res., 48*(4–5), 425–441.

Sederer, L. I. (1992). Brief hospitalization. In A. Tasman & M. B. Riba (Eds.), *Review of psychiatry* (Vol. 11). Washington, DC: American Psychiatric Press.

Sedvall, G. (1990). Monoamines and schizophrenia. International Symposium: Development of a new antipsychotic: Remoxipride. *Acta Psychiatr. Scand., 82*(Suppl. 358), 7–13.

Sedvall, G. (1990). PET imaging of dopamine receptors in human basal ganglia: Relevance to mental illness. *Trends Neurosci., 13*(7), 302–308.

Seeman, M. (1982). Gender differences in schizophrenia. *Can. J. Psychiatry, 27*, 108–111.

Seeman, P., Lee, T., Chau Wong, M., & Wong, K. (1976). Antipsychotic drug doses and neuroleptic/dopamine receptors. *Nature, 281*, 717–718.

Segal, Z. V., Gemar, M., & Williams, S. (1999). Differential cognitive response to a mood challenge following successful cognitive therapy or pharmacotherapy for unipolar depression. *J. Abnorm. Psychol., 108*(1), 3–10.

Segraves, K. B., & Segraves, R. T. (1991). Hypoactive sexual desire disorder: Prevalence and comorbidity in 906 subjects. *J. Sex Marital Ther., 17*, 55–58.

Segraves, R. T. (1993). Treatment-emergent sexual dysfunction in affective disorder: A review and management strategies. *J. Clin. Psychiatry, Monogr. Ser., 11*, 7–63.

Segraves, R. T. (1995). Psychopharmacological influences on human sexual behavior. In J. M. Oldham & M. B. Riba (Eds.), *American Psychiatric Press review of psychiatry* (Vol. 14). Washington, DC: American Psychiatric Press.

Segraves, R. T. (1998). Antidepressant-induced sexual dysfunction. *J. Clin. Psychiatry, 59*(Suppl. 4), 48–54.

Segrin, C. (2000). Social skills deficits associated with depression. *Clin. Psychol. Rev., 20*(3), 379–403.

Seiden, R. H. (1981). Mellowing with age: Factors influencing the nonwhite suicide rate. *Int. J. Aging Hum. Dev., 13*, 265–284.

Seidman, L. J. (1990). The neuropsychology of schizophrenia: A neurodevelopmental and case study approach. *J. Neuropsychiatry Clin. Neurosci., 2*(3), 301–312.

Seidman, S. N., & Rieder, R. O. (1995). Sexual behavior through the life cycle: An empirical approach. In J. M. Oldham & M. B. Riba (Eds.), *American Psychiatric Press review of psychiatry* (Vol. 14). Washington, DC: American Psychiatric Press.

Seligman, M. E. P. (1971). Phobias and preparedness. *Behav. Ther., 2*, 307–320.

Seligman, M. E. P. (1975). *Helplessness.* San Francisco: Freeman.

Seligman, M. E. P. (1992). Wednesday's children. *Psychol. Today, 25*(1), 61.

Seligman, M. E. P. (1995). The effectiveness of psychotherapy. The Consumer Reports study. *Am. Psychol., 50*(12), 965–974.

Seligman, M. E. P., Castellon, C., Cacciola, J., Schulman, P. et al. (1988). Explanatory style change during cognitive therapy for unipolar depression. *J. Abnorm. Psychol., 97*(1), 13–18.

Selkoe, D. J. (1991). Amyloid protein and Alzheimer's disease. *Sci. Am., 265*, 68–78.

Selkoe, D. J. (1992). Alzheimer's disease: New insights into an emerging epidemic. *J. Geriatr. Psychiatry, 25*(2), 211–227.

Selkoe, D. J. (1998). The cell biology of beta-amyloid precursor protein and presenilin in Alzheimer's disease. *Trends Cell Biol., 8*(11), 447–453.

Selkoe, D. J. (1999). Translating cell biology into therapeutic advances in Alzheimer's disease. *Nature, 399*, A23–A31.

Selkoe, D. J. (2000). The origins of Alzheimer disease: A is for amyloid. *JAMA, J. Am. Med. Assoc., 283*(12), 1615–1617.

Selkoe, D. J., Yamazaki, T., Citron, M., Podlisny, M. B., Koo, E. H., Teplow, D. B., & Haass, C. (1996). The role of APP processing and trafficking pathways in the formation of amyloid B-protein. In R. J. Wurtman, S. Corkin, J. H. Growdon, & R. M. Nitsch (Eds.), *The neurobiology of Alzheimer's disease.* New York: New York Academy of Sciences.

Selling, L. S. (1940). *Men against madness.* New York: Greenberg.

Selye, H. (1974). *Stress without distress.* Philadelphia: Lippincott.

Selye, H. (1976). *Stress in health and disease.* Woburn, MA: Butterworth.

Seppa, N. (1996). Helping people identify and cope with anxieties. *APA Monitor, 27*(6), 24.

Seppa, N. (1996). Bullies spend less time with adults. *APA Monitor, 27*(10), 41.

Seppa, N. (1996). Psychologist testifies on handling disasters. *APA Monitor, 27*(11), 38.

Sereno, A. B., & Holzman, P. S. (1995). Antisaccades and smooth pursuit eye movements in schizophrenia. *Biol. Psychiatry, 37*(6), 394–401.

Seto, M. C., Khattar, N. A., Lalumière, M. L., & Quinsey, V. L. (1997). Deception and sexual strategy in psychopathy. *Pers. Individual Differ., 22*(3), 301–307.

Shadlen, M. F., & Larson, E. B. (1999). What's new in Alzheimer's disease treatment? Reasons for optimism about future pharmacologic options. *Postgrad. Med. J., 105*(1), 109–118.

Shaffer, D., & Craft, L. (1999). Methods of adolescent suicide prevention. *J. Clin. Psychiatry, 60*(Suppl. 2), 70–74.

Shafii, M., Carrigan, S., Whittinghill, J. R., & Derrick, A. (1985). Psychological autopsy of completed suicide in children and adolescents. *Am. J. Psychiatry, 142*(9), 1061–1064.

Shah, R., & Waller, G. (2000). Parental style and vulnerability to depression: The role of core beliefs. *J. Nerv. Ment. Dis., 188*(1), 19–25.

Shain, M. (1994). Alternatives to drug testing: Employee assistance and health promotion programs. In S. Macdonald & P. Roman (Eds.), *Research advances in alcohol and drug problems: Vol. 11. Drug testing in the workplace.* New York: Plenum Press.

Shalev, A. Y. (1999). Psychophysiological and expression of risk factors for PTSD. In R. Yehuda (Ed.), *Risk factors for posttraumatic stress disorder.* Washington, DC: American Psychiatric Press.

Shalev, A. Y., Bonne, O., & Eth, S. (1996). Treatment of posttraumatic stress disorder: A review. *Psychosom. Med., 58*, 165–182.

Shalev, A. Y., Peri, T., Canetti, L., & Schreiber, S. (1996). Predictors of PTSD in injured trauma survivors: A prospective study. *Am. J. Psychiatry, 153*, 219–225.

Shaner, A., Khalsa, M., Roberts, L., Wilkins, J., Anglin, D., & Hsieh, S. (1993). Unrecognized cocaine use among schizophrenic patients. *Am. J. Psychiatry, 150*(5), 758–762.

Shapiro, L. (1996, January 22). To your health? *Newsweek,* pp. 52–53.

Sharp, C. W., & Freeman, C. P. L. (1993). The medical complications of anorexia nervosa. *Br. J. Psychiatry, 162*, 452–462.

Shaw, B. F. (1976). A systematic investigation of two psychological treatments of depression. *Diss. Abstr. Int. B 36*(8-B), 4179–4180.

Shaw, B. F. (1977). Comparison of cognitive therapy and behavior therapy in the treatment of depression. *J. Clin. Psychol., 45*, 543–551.

Shaw, B. F., & Segal, Z. V. (1999). Efficacy, indications, and mechanisms of action of cognitive therapy of depression. In D. S. Janowsky et al. (Eds.), *Psychotherapy indications and outcomes.* Washington, DC: American Psychiatric Press.

Shay, J., & Munroe, J. (1999). Group and milieu therapy for veterans with complex posttraumatic stress disorder. In P. A. Saigh, J. D. Bremner et al. (Eds.), *Posttraumatic stress disorder: A comprehensive text.* Boston: Allyn & Bacon.

Shea, M. T., Zlotnick, C., Dolan, R., Warshaw, M. G., Phillips, K. A., Brown, P., & Keller, M. B. (2000). Personality disorders, history of trauma, and posttraumatic stress disorder in subjects with anxiety disorders. *Compr. Psychiatry, 41*(5), 315–325.

Shea, S. (1990). Contemporary psychiatric interviewing: Integration of DSM-III-R, psychodynamic concerns and mental health. In G. Goldstein & M. Hersen (Eds.), *Handbook of psychological assessment* (2nd ed.). New York: Pergamon Press.

Shea, T., Elkin, I., Imber, S., Sotsky, S., Watkins, J., Collins, J. et al. (1992). Course of depressive symptoms over follow-up: Findings from the National Institute of Mental Health treatment of depression collaborative research program. *Arch. Gen. Psychiatry, 49*, 782–787.

Shear, M. K., & Beidel, D. C. (1998). Psychotherapy in the overall management strategy for social anxiety disorder. *J. Clin Psychiatry, 59*(Suppl. 17), 39–46.

Shear, M. K., Brown, T. A., Barlow, D. H., Money, R., Sholomskas, D. E., Woods, S. W., Gorman, J. M., & Papp, L. A. (1997). Multicenter collaborative panic disorder severity scale. *Am. J. Psychiatry, 154*, 1571–1575.

Shedler, J., & Block, J. (1990). Adolescent drug use and psychological health: A longitudinal inquiry. *Am. Psychol., 45*(5), 612–630.

Shedler, J., Mayman, M., & Manis, M. (1993). The illusion of mental health. *Am. Psychol., 48*(11), 1117–1131.

Shellenbarger, S. (1998, September 28). Workers are taking more "mental health" days off. *Star Tribune,* p. 10D.

Shelton, R. C. (1999). Mood-stabilizing drugs in depression. *J. Clin. Psychiatry, 60*(Suppl. 5), 37–40.

Shelton, R. C., Davidson, J., Yonkers, K. A., Koran, L. et al. (1997). The undertreatment of dysthymia. *J. Clin. Psychiatry, 58*(2), 59–65.

Shemberg, K. M., & Doherty, M. E. (1999). Is diagnostic judgment influenced by a bias to see pathology? *J. Clin Psychol., 55*(4), 513–518.

Sher, K. J., & Trull, T. J. (1994). Personality and disinhibitry psychopathology: Alcoholism and antisocial personality disorder. *J. Abnorm. Psychol., 103*(1), 92–102.

Sher, L. (2000). Psychological factors, immunity, and heart disease. *Psychosomatics, 41*(4), 372–373.

Sheras, P., & Worchel, S. (1979). *Clinical psychology: A social psychological approach.* New York: Van Nostrand.

Sheras, P. L. (2001). Problems of adolescence. In C. E. Walker & M. C. Roberts (Eds.), *Handbook of clinical child psychology* (3rd ed., pp. 619–803). New York: Wiley.

Sherbourne, C. D., Hays, R. D., & Wells, K. B. (1995). Personal and psychosocial risk factors for physical and mental health outcomes and course of depression among depressed patients. *J. Consult. Clin. Psychol., 63*(3), 345–355.

Sherbourne, C. D., Jackson, C. A., Meredith, L. S., Camp, P., & Wells, K. B. (1996). Prevalence of comorbid anxiety disorders in primary care outpatients. *Arch. Fam. Med., 5*(1), 27–34.

Sherlock, R. (1983). Suicide and public policy: A critique of the "new consensus." *J. Bioethics, 4,* 58–70.

Sherman, C. (1993). Behind closed doors: Therapist-client sex. *Psychol. Today, 26*(3), 64–72.

Sherman, D. K., McGue, M. K., & Iacono, W. G. (1997). Twin concordance for attention deficit hyperactivity disorder: A comparison of teachers' and mothers' reports. *Am. J. Psychiatry, 154*(4), 532–535.

Sherman, R., & Thompson, R. (1990). *Bulimia: A guide for family and friends.* Lexington, MA: Lexington Books.

Shi, J. M., Benowitz, N., Denaro, C., & Sheiner, L. (1993). Pharmacokinetic-pharmacodynamic modeling of caffeine: Tolerance to pressor effects. *Clin. Pharmacol. Ther., 53*(1), 6–15.

Shi, J. M., O'Connor, P. G., Constantino, J. A. et al. (1993). Three methods of ambulatory opiate detoxification. In L. S. Harris (Ed.), *Preliminary results of a randomized clinical trial* (NIDA Res. Monogr. Ser. No. 132, NIH Publ. No. 93-3505). Washington, DC: U. S. Government Printing Office.

Shipherd, J. C., & Beck, J. G. (1999). The effects of suppressing trauma-related thoughts on women with rape-related posttraumatic stress disorder. *Behav. Res. Ther., 37*(2), 99–112.

Shisslak, C. M., Crago, M., McKnight, K. M., Estes, L. S., Gray, G., & Parnaby, O. G. (1998). Potential risk factors associated with weight control behaviors in elementary and middle school girls. *J. Psychosom. Res., 44*(3/4), 301–313.

Shnayerson, M. (1996, July). Natural opponents. *Vanity Fair,* pp. 98–105.

Shneidman, E. S. (1963). Orientations toward death: Subintentioned death and indirect suicide. In R. W. White (Ed.), *The study of lives.* New York: Atherton.

Shneidman, E. S. (1979). An overview: Personality, motivation, and behavior theories. In L. D. Hankoff & B. Einsidler (Eds.), *Suicide: Theory and clinical aspects.* Littleton, MA: PSG Publishing.

Shneidman, E. S. (1981). Suicide. *Suicide Life-Threaten. Behav., 11*(4), 198–220.

Shneidman, E. S. (1985). *Definition of suicide.* New York: Wiley.

Shneidman, E. S. (1987, March). At the point of no return. *Psychol. Today.*

Shneidman, E. S. (1991). The key to suicide. In personal correspondence.

Shneidman, E. S. (1993). *Suicide as psychache: A clinical approach to self-destructive behavior.* Northvale, NJ: Jason Aronson.

Shneidman, E. S. (1999). Perturbation and lethality: A psychological approach to assessment and intervention. In D. G. Jacobs et al. (Eds.). *The Harvard Medical School guide to suicide assessment and intervention.* San Francisco: Jossey-Bass.

Schneidman, E. S. (2001). *Comprehending suicide: Landmarks in 20th-century suicidology.* Washington, DC: American Psychological Association.

Shneidman, E. S., & Farberow, N. (1968). The Suicide Prevention Center of Los Angeles. In H. L. P. Resnick (Ed.), *Suicidal behaviors: Diagnosis and management.* Boston: Little, Brown.

Shotton, M.A. (1998). *Caught in the net: How to recognize the signs of Internet addiction and a winning strategy for recovery.* New York: Wiley.

Shrivastava, R. K., Shrivastava, S., Overweg, N., & Schmitt, M. (1995). Amantadine in the treatment of sexual dysfunction associated with selective serotonin reuptake inhibitors. *J. Clin. Psychopharmacol., 15*(1), 83–84.

Shtasel, D. L., Gur, R. E., Gallacher, F., Heimburg, C. et al. (1992). Gender differences in the clinical expression of schizophrenia. *Schizophr. Res., 7*(3), 225–231.

Shucksmith, J., Glendinning, A., & Hendry, L. (1997). Adolescent drinking behaviour and the role of family life: A Scottish perspective. *J. Adolesc., 20,* 85–101.

Shuller, D. Y., & McNamara, J. R. (1980). The use of information derived from norms and from a credible source to counter expectancy effects in behavioral assessment. *Behav. Assess., 2,* 183–196.

Shultis, C. L. (1999). Music therapy for inpatient psychiatric care in the 1990s. *Psychiatr. Times, 16*(2).

Siegel, J. M. (1990). Stressful life events and use of physician services among the elderly: The moderating role of pet ownership. *J. Pers. Soc. Psychol., 58*(6), 1081–1086.

Siegel, R. K. (1990). In J. Sherlock, Getting high—Animals do it, too. *USA Today,* p. 1A.

Siegert, R. J. (1999). Some thoughts about reasoning in clinical neuropsychology. *Behav. Change, 16*(1), 37–48.

Siegman, A. W., Townsend, S. T., Civelek, A. C., & Blumenthal, R. S. (2000). Antagonistic behavior, dominance, hostility, and coronary heart disease. *Psychosom. Med., 62*(2), 248–257.

Siever, L. J. (1992). Schizophrenia spectrum personality disorders. In A. Tasman & M. B. Riba (Eds.), *American Psychiatric Press review of psychiatry* (Vol. 11). Washington, DC: American Psychiatric Press.

Siever, L. J., & Davis, K. L. (1991). A psychobiological perspective on the personality disorders. *Am. J. Psychiatry, 148*(12), 1647–1658.

Siever, L. J., Davis, K. L., & Gorman, L. K. (1991). Pathogenesis of mood disorders. In K. Davis, H. Klar, & J. T. Coyle (Eds.), *Foundations of psychiatry.* Philadelphia: Saunders.

Sifneos, P. E. (1987). *Short term dynamic psychotherapy evaluation and technique* (2nd ed.). New York: Plenum Press.

Sifneos, P. E. (1992). *Short-term anxiety-provoking psychotherapy: A treatment manual.* New York: Basic Books.

Sigerist, H. E. (1943). *Civilization and disease.* Ithaca, NY: Cornell University Press.

Sigmon, S. T. (1995). Ethical practices and beliefs of psychopathology researchers. *Ethics Behav., 5*(4), 295–309.

Sigmundsson, R., Suckling, J., Maier, M., Williams, S. C. R., Bullmore, E. T., Greenwood, K. E., Fukuka, R., Ron, M. A., & Toone, B. K. (2001). Structural abnormalities in frontal, temporal, and limbic regions and interconnecting white matter tracts in schizophrenic patients with prominent negative symptoms. *Am. J. Psychiatry, 158*(2), 234–243.

Silberman, E. K. (1999). Pharmacotherapy. In M. Hersen & A. S. Bellack (Eds.), *Handbook of comparative interventions for adult disorders* (2nd ed.). New York: Wiley.

Silberswieg, D. A., Stern, E., Frith, C., Cahill, C. et al. (1995). A functional neuroanatomy of hallucinations in schizophrenia. *Nature, 378,* 176–179.

Silva, J. A., Derecho, D. V., Leong, G. B., & Ferrari, M.M. (2000). Stalking behavior in delusional jealousy. *J. Forensic Sci., 45*(1), 77–82.

Silver, E. (1995). Punishment or treatment? Comparing the lengths of confinement of successful and unsuccessful insanity defendants. *Law Hum. Behav., 19*(4), 375–388.

Silver, H., Geraisy, N., & Schwartz, M. (1995). No difference in the effect of biperiden and amantadine on parkinsonian- and tardive dyskinesia-type involuntary movements: A double-blind crossover, placebo-controlled study in medicated chronic schizophrenic patients. *J. Clin. Psychiatry, 56*(4), 167–170.

Silverman, K., Evans, S. M., Strain, E. C., & Griffiths, R. R. (1992). Withdrawal syndrome after the double-blind cessation of caffeine consumption. *N. Engl. J. Med., 327*(16), 1109–1114.

Silverman, M. M., Meyer, P. M., Sloane, F., Raffel, M., & Pratt, D. (1997). The Big Ten Student Suicide Study: A 10-year study of suicides on midwestern university campuses. *Suicide Life-Threaten. Behav., 27*(3), 285–303.

Silverman, P. (1992). An introduction to self-help groups. In B. J. White & E. J. Madara (Eds.), *The self-help sourcebook: Finding & forming mutual aid self-help groups.* Denville, NJ: St. Clares-Riverside Medical Center.

Silverman, W. K., La Greca, A. M., & Wasserstein, S. (1995). What do children worry about? Worries and their relation to anxiety. *Child Dev., 66,* 671–686.

Silverstein, B. (1999). Gender differences in the prevalence of clinical depression: The role played by depression associated with somatic symptoms. *Am. J. Psychiatry, 156*(3), 480–482.

Silverstone, P. H. (1990). Low self-esteem in eating disordered patients in the absence of depression. *Psychol. Rep., 67*(1), 276–278.

Silverstone, T., & Hunt, N. (1992). Symptoms and assessment of mania. In E. S. Paykel (Ed.), *Handbook of affective disorders.* New York: Guilford Press.

Simeon, J. G., Ferguson, H. B., Knott, V., Roberts, N. et al. (1992). Clinical, cognitive, and neurophysiological effects of alprazolam in children and adolescents with overanxious and avoidant disorders. Special section: New developments in pediatric psychopharmacology. *J. Am. Acad. Child Adolesc. Psychiatry, 31*(1), 29–33.

Simeonsson, N., Lorimer, M., Shelley, B., & Sturtz, J. L. (1995). Asthma: New information for the early interventionist. *Top. Early Child. Spec. Educ., 15*(1), 32–43.

Simmon (1990). Media and market study. In skin deep: Our national obsession with looks. *Psychol. Today, 26*(3), 96.

Simon, G. E. (1998). Management of somatoform and factitious disorders. In P. E. Nathan, J. M. Gorman et al. (Eds.), *A guide to treatments that work.* New York: Oxford University Press.

Simon, G. E., & Gureje, O. (1999). Stability of somatization disorder and somatization symptoms among primary care patients. *Arch. Gen. Psychiatry, 56*(1), 90–95.

Simon, G. E., & Katzelnick, D. J. (1997). Depression, use of medical services and cost-offset effects. *J. Psychosom. Res., 42*(4), 333–344.

Simon, N. (2000). Autism's home in the brain. *Neurology, 54*(1), 269.

Simon, R. I. (2001). Duty to foresee, forewarn, and protecct against violent behavior: A psychiatric perspective. In M. Shafi & S. L. Shafi (Eds.), *School violence: Assessment, management, prevention* (pp. 201–215). Washington, DC: American Psychiatric Press.

Simonoff, E. (2001). Genetic influences on conduct disorder. In J. Hill & B. Maughan (Eds.), *Conduct disorders in childhood and adolescence* (pp. 202–234). New York: Cambridge University Press.

Simonsick, E. M., Wallace, R. B., Blazer, D. G., & Berkman, L. F. (1995). Depressive symptomatology and hypertension-associated morbidity and mortality in older adults. *Psychosom. Med., 57*(5), 427–435.

Simpson, C. J., Hyde, C. E., & Faragher, E. B. (1989). The chronically mentally ill in community facilities: A study of quality of life. *Br. J. Psychiatry, 154,* 77–82.

Simpson, R. L., & Sasso, G. M. (1992). Full inclusion of students with autism in general education settings: Values versus science. *Focus Autistic Behav., 7*(3), 1–13.

Simpson, R. O., & Halpin, G. (1986). Agreement between parents and teachers in using the Revised Behavior Problem Checklist to identify deviant behavior in children. *Behav. Disord., 12*(1), 54–58.

Simpson, S. G. (1996, January 17). Cited in W. Leary, As fellow traveler of other illness, depression often goes in disguise. *New York Times,* p. C9.

Simpson, S. G., & Jamison, K. R. (1999). The risk of suicide in patients with bipolar disorders. *J. Clin. Psychiatry, 60*(Suppl. 2), 53–56.

Sines, L. K. (1959). The relative contribution of four kinds of data to accuracy in personality assessment. *J. Consult. Psychol., 23,* 483–495.

Siomopoulos, V. (1988). Narcissistic personality disorder: Clinical features. *Am. J. Psychother., 42*(2), 240–253.

Sirey, J. A., Meyers, B. S., Bruce, M. L., Alexopoulos, G. S., Perlick, D. A., & Raue, P. (1999). Predictors of antidepressant prescription and early use among depressed outpatients. *Am. J. Psychiatry, 156*(5), 690–696.

Sizemore, C., & Pittillo, E. S. (1977). *I'm Eve.* Garden City, NY: Doubleday.

Sizemore, C. C., & Huber, R. J. (1988). The twenty-two faces of Eve. *Individual Psychol. J. Adlerian Theory Res. Pract., 44*(1), 53–62.

Skau, K., & Mouridsen, S. (1995). Munchausen syndrome by proxy: A review. *Acta Paediatr., 84,* 977–982.

Skodol, A. E., Stout, R. L., McGlashan, T. H., Grilo, C. M., Gunderson, J. G., Shea, M. T., Morey, L. C., Zanarini, M. C., Dyck, I. R., & Oldham, J. M. (1999). Co-occurrence of mood and personality disorders: A report from the Collaborative Longitudinal Personality Disorders Study (CLPS). *Depression Anxiety, 10*(4), 175–182.

Slade, P. (1995). Prospects for prevention. In G. Szmukler, C. Dare, & J. Treasure (Eds.), *Handbook of eating disorders: Theory, treatment and research.* Chichester, England: Wiley.

Slater, E., & Shields, J. (1969). Genetical aspects of anxiety. Special Publication No. 3. M. H. Lader (Ed.). *Br. J. Psychiatry,* pp. 62–71.

Sleek, S. (1995). Online therapy services raise ethical questions. *APA Monitor, 26*(11), 9.

Sleek, S. (1995). Rallying the troops inside our bodies. *APA Monitor, 26*(12), 1, 24.

Sleek, S. (1996). AIDS therapy: Patchwork of pain, hope. *APA Monitor, 27*(6), 1, 31.

Sleek, S. (1996). Practitioners will eventually have to meet steeper criteria to practice geropsychology, experts predict. *APA Monitor, 27*(10), 17.

Sleek, S. (1997). Treating people who live life on the borderline. *APA Monitory, 28*(7), 20–21.

Sleek, S. (1997). Disaster victims need most long-term care, report says. *APA Monitor, 28*(10), 18.

Sleek, S. (1997). Novel approach offers hope for treating severe disorders. *APA Monitor, 28*(12), 23.

Slife, B. D., & Weaver, C. A., III. (1992). Depression, cognitive skill, and metacognitive skill in problem solving. *Cognit. Emot., 6*(1), 1–22.

Sloan, E. P., Natarajan, M., Baker, B., Dorian, P., Mironov, D., Barr, A., Newman, D. M., & Shapiro, C. M. (1999). Nocturnal and daytime panic attacks—Comparison of sleep architecture, heart rate variability, and response to sodium lactate challenge. *Biol. Psychiatry, 45*(10), 1313–1320.

Slome, L. R., Mitchell, T. F., Charlebois, E., Benevedes, J. M., & Abrams, D. I. (1997). Physician-assisted suicide and patients with human immunodeficiency virus disease. *N. Engl. J. Med., 336*(6), 417–421.

Slovenko, R. (1992). Is diminished capacity really dead? *Psychiat. Ann., 22*(11), 566–570.

Slovenko, R. (1995). *Psychiatry and criminal culpability.* New York: Wiley-Interscience.

Slutske, W. S., Heath, A. C., Dinwiddie, S. H., Madden, P. A. F. et al. (1997). Modeling genetic and environmental influences in the etiology of conduct disorder: A study of 2,682 adult twin pairs. *J. Abnorm. Psychol., 106*(2), 266–279.

Small, G. W., Mazziotta, J. C., Collins, M. T., Baxter, W. R. et al. (1995). Apolipoprotein E type 4 allele and cerebral glucose metabolism in relatives at risk for familial Alzheimer disease. *JAMA, J. Am. Med. Assoc., 273*(12), 942–947.

Small, J. A., Kemper, S., & Lyon, K. (1997). Sentence comprehension in Alzheimer's disease: Effects of grammatical complexity, speech rate, and repetition. *Psychol. Aging, 12*(1), 3–11.

Small, M. A. (1992). The legal context of mentally disordered sex offender (MDSO) treatment programs. *Criminal Justice Behav., 19*(2), 127–142.

Small, S. A., Perera, G. M., DeLaPaz, R., Mayeus, R., & Stern, Y. (1999). Differential regional dysfunction of the hippocampal formation among elderly with memory decline and Alzheimer's disease. *Ann. Neurol., 45*(4), 466–472.

Small, S. A. et al. (1999, January 17). *Diagnosing early stage Alzheimer's disease.* Paper presented at American Academy of Neurology 51st annual meeting, Toronto.

Smith, A. L., & Weissman, M. M. (1992). Epidemiology. In E. S. Paykel (Ed.), *Handbook of affective disorders.* New York: Guilford Press.

Smith, B. L. (1998). The impossible takes a little longer: The role of theory in teaching psychological assessment. In L. Handler, M. J. Hilsenroth et al. (Eds.), *Teaching and learning personality assessment. The LEA series in personality and clinical psychology.* Mahwah, NJ: Erlbaum.

Smith, D. (2001). Prevention: Still a young field. *APA Monitor, 32*(6), 70–72.

Smith, D. F. (2001). Negative emotions and coronary heart disease: Causally related or merely coexistent? *Scand. J. Psychol., 42*(1), 57–69.

Smith, E., North, C., & Spitznagel, E. (1993). Alcohol, drugs, and psychiatric comorbidity among homeless women: An epidemiologic study. *J. Clin. Psychiatry, 54*(3), 82–87.

Smith, G. R., Rost, K., & Kashner, T. M. (1995). A trial of the effect of a standardized psychiatric consultation on health outcomes and costs in somatizing patients. *Arch. Gen. Psychiatry, 52*(3), 238–243.

Smith, K. (1991). Comments on "Teen suicide and changing cause-of-death certification, 1953-1987." *Suicide Life-Threaten. Behav., 21*(3), 260–262.

Smith, K., & Killam, P. (1994). Munchausen syndrome by proxy. *MCN, 19,* 214–221.

Smith, K. A., Fairburn, C. G., & Cowen, P. J. (1999). Symptomatic repalse in bulimia nervosa following acute tryptophan depletion. *Arch. Gen. Psychiatry, 56*(2), 171–176.

Smith, M. J., Brebion, G., Banquet, J. P., & Cohen, L. (1995). Retardation of mentation in depressives: Posner's covert orientation of visual attention test. *J. Affect. Disord., 35,* 107–115.

Smith, M. L., & Glass, G. V. (1977). Meta-analysis of psychotherapy outcome studies. *Am. Psychol., 32*(9), 752–760.

Smith, M. L., Glass, G. V., & Miller, T. I. (1980). *The benefits of psychotherapy.* Baltimore: Johns Hopkins University Press.

Smith, R. E. (1988). The logic and design of case study research. *Sport Psychol., 2*(1), 1–12.

Smith, S. (1991). Mental health malpractice in the 1990s. *Houston Law Rev., 28,* 209–283.

Smith, W. H. (1993). Incorporating hypnosis into the psychotherapy of patients with multiple personality disorder. *Bull. Menninger Clin., 57*(3), 344–354.

Smolak, L., & Murnen, S. K. (2001). Gender and eating problems. In R. H. Striegel-Moore & L. Smolak (Eds.), *Eating disorders: Innovative directions in research and practice* (pp. 91–110). Washington, DC: American Psychological Association.

Smolan, R., Moffitt, P., & Naythons, M. (1990). *The power to heal: Ancient arts & modern medicine.* New York: Prentice Hall.

Smyer, M. A. (1989). Nursing homes as a setting for psychological practice: Public policy perspectives. *Am. Psychol., 44*(10), 1307–1314.

Smyth, J. M. (1998). Written emotional expression: Effect sizes, outcome types, and moderating variables. *J. Consult. Clin. Psychol., 66*(1), 174–184.

Smyth, J. M., Stone, A. A., Hurewitz, A., & Kaell, A. (1999). Effects of writing about stressful experiences on symptom reduction in patients with asthma or rheumatoid arthritis: A randomized trial. *JAMA, J. Am. Med. Assoc., 281*(14), 1304–1309.

Snow, E. (1976, December). In the snow. *Tex. Mon. Mag.*

Snowden, P. (1997). Practical aspects of clinical risk assessment and management. *Br. J. Psychiatry, 170*(Suppl. 32), 32–34.

Snyder, D. K., Wills, R. M., & Grady-Fletcher, A. (1991). Risks and challenges of long-term psychotherapy outcome research: Reply to Jacobson. *J. Consult. Clin. Psychol., 59*(1), 146–149.

Snyder, S. (1976). Dopamine and schizophrenia. *Psychiatr. Ann., 8*(1), 53–84.

Snyder, S. (1976). The dopamine hypotheses of schizophrenia: Focus on the dopamine receptor. *Am. J. Psychiatry, 133*(2), 197–202.

Snyder, S. (1980). *Biological aspects of mental disorder.* New York: Oxford University Press.

Snyder, S. (1986). *Drugs and the brain.* New York: Scientific American Library.

Snyder, S. (1991). Drugs, neurotransmitters, and the brain. In P. Corsi (Ed.), *The enchanted loom: Chapters in the history of neuroscience.* New York: Oxford University Press.

Snyder, W. V. (1947). *Casebook of non-directive counseling.* Boston: Houghton Mifflin.

Soares, J. C., Mallinger, A. G., Dippold, C. S., Frank, E., & Kupfer, D. J. (1999). Platelet membrane phospholipids in euthymic bipolar disorder patients: Are they affected by lithium treatment? *Biol. Psychiatry, 45*(4), 453–457.

Sobell, M. B., & Sobell, L. C. (1973). Individualized behavior therapy for alcoholics. *Behav. Ther., 4*(1), 49–72.

Sobell, M. B., & Sobell, L. C. (1976). Second year treatment outcome of alcoholics treated by individualized behavior therapy: Results. *Behav. Res. Ther., 14*(3), 195–215.

Sobell, M. B., & Sobell, L. C. (1984). The aftermath of heresy: A response to Pendery et al.'s (1982) critique of "Individualized Behavior Therapy for Alcoholics." *Behav. Res. Ther., 22*(4), 413–440.

Sobell, M. B., & Sobell, L. C. (1984). Under the microscope yet again: A commentary on Walker and Roach's critique of the Dickens Committee's enquiry into our research. *Br. J. Addict., 79*(2), 157–168.

Sobin, C., & Sackeim, H. A. (1997). Psychomotor symptoms of depression. *Am. J. Psychiatry, 154,* 4–17.

Sobin, C., Blundell, M. L., Conry, A., Weiller, F., Gavigan, C., Haiman, C., & Karayiorgou, M. (2001). Early, non-psychotic deviant behavior in schizophrenia: A possible endophenotypic marker for genetic studies. *Psychiatr. Res., 101*(2), 101–113.

Sobin, C., Blundell, M., Weiller, F., Gavigan, C., Haiman, C., & Karayiorgou, M. (1999). Phenotypic characteristics of obsessive-compulsive disorder ascertained in adulthood. *J. Psychiatr. Res., 33*(3), 265–273.

Sobo, S. (1999). The inadequacy of 15-minute med checks as standard psychiatric practice. *Psychiatr. Times, 16*(4).

Sohlberg, S., & Norring, C. (1992). A three-year prospective study of life events and course for adults with anorexia nervosa/bulimia nervosa. *Psychosom. Med., 54*(1), 59–70.

Solano, J. J. R., & De Chavez, M. G. (2000). Premorbid personality disorders in schizophrenia. *Schizophr. Res., 44*(2), 137–144.

Solanto, M. V., Arnsten, A. F. T., & Castellanos, F. X. (Eds.). (2001). *Stimulant drugs and ADHD: Basic and clinical neuroscience.* New York: Oxford University Press.

Soloff, P. H. (2000). Psychopharmacology of borderline personality disorder. *Psychiatr. Clin. North Am., 23*(1), 169–192.

Solomon, D. A., Keitner, G. I., Miller, I. W., Shea, M. T., & Keller, M. B. (1995). Course of illness and maintenance treatments for patients with bipolar disorder. *J. Clin. Psychiatry, 56*(1), 5–13.

Solomon, R. L. (1980). The opponent-process theory of acquired motivation: The costs of pleasure and the benefits of pain. *Am. Psychol., 35*, 691–712.

Somasundaram, D. J., & Rajadurai, S. (1995). War and suicide in northern Sri Lanka. *Acta Psychiatr. Scand., 91*(1), 1–4.

Somer, E. (2000). Israeli mental health professionals' attitudes towards dissociative disorders, reported incidence and alternative diagnoses considered. *J. Trauma Dissociation, 1*(1), 21–44.

Sorbi, S., Nacmias, B., Tedde, A. et al. (1998). 5-HT2A promotor polymorphism in anorexia nervosa [letter]. *Lancet, 351*, 1785.

Sorensen, J. L., & Copeland, A. L. (2000). Drug abuse treatment as an HIV prevention strategy: A review. *Drug Alcohol Depend., 59*(1) 17–31.

Soric, I. (1999). Anxiety and coping in the context of a school examination. *Soc. Behav. Pers., 27*(3), 319–330.

Sorokin, J. E., Giordani, B., Mohs, R. C., Losonczy, M. F. et al. (1988). Memory impairment in schizophrenic patients with tardive dyskinesia. *Biol. Psychiatry, 23*(2), 129–135.

Sourander, A., Helstelae, L., Haavisto, A., & Bergroth, L. (2001). Suicidal thoughts and attempts among adolescents: A longitudinal 8-year follow-up study. *J. Affect. Disord., 63*(1–3), 59–66.

Spalter, A. R., Gwirtsman, H. E., Demitrack, M. A., & Gold, P. W. (1993). Thyroid function in bulimia nervosa. *Biol. Psychiatry, 33*, 408–414.

Spangenberg, J. J., & Theron, J. C. (1999). Stress and coping strategies in spouses of depressed patients. *J. Psychol., 133*(3), 253–262.

Spanier, C., Shiffman, S., Maurer, A., Reynolds, W., & Quick, D. (1996). Rebound following failure to quit smoking: The effects of attributions and self-efficacy. *Exp. Clin. Psychopharmacol., 4*(2), 191–197.

Spanier, C. A., Frank, E., McEachran, A. B., Grochocinski, V. J., & Kupfer, D. J. (1999). Maintenance interpersonal psychotherapy for recurrent depression: Biological and clinical correlates and future directions. In D. S. Janowsky et al. (Eds.), *Psychotherapy indications and outcomes.* Washington, DC: American Psychiatric Press.

Spanos, N. P., Burgess, C. A., DuBreuil, S. C., Liddy, S. et al. (1995). The effects of simulation and expectancy instructions on responses to cognitive skill training for enhancing hypnotizability [Special Issue: To the memory of Nicholas Spanos]. *Contemp. Hypnosis, 12*(1), 1–11.

Spanos, N. P., & Coe, W. C. (1992). A social-psychological approach to hypnosis. In E. Fromm & M. R. Nash (Eds.), *Contemporary hypnosis research.* New York: Guilford Press.

Sparks, G., & Cantor, J. (1998, October 30). Cited in V. Andrews, Heart-stopping fear: Why the body keeps coming back for more. *HealthScout.*

Sparks, G. G., Pellechia, M., & Irvine, C. (1999). The repressive coping style and fright reactions to mass media. *Commun. Res., 26*(2), 176–192.

Speakman, M. T., & Kloner, R. A. (1999). Viagra and cardiovascular disease. *J. Cardiovasc. Pharmacol. Ther., 4*(4), 259–267.

Spector, I. P., & Carey, M. P. (1990). Incidence and prevalence of sexual dysfunctions: A critical review of the empirical literature. *Arch. Sex. Behav., 19*(4), 389–408.

Spence, S. H., Donovan, C., & Brechman-Toussaint, M. (2000). The treatment of childhood social phobia: The effectiveness of a social skills training-based, cognitive-behavioral intervention, with and without parental involvement. *J. Child Psychol. Psychiatry Allied Discip., 41*(6), 713–726.

Spencer, T., Biederman, J., & Wilens, T. (1999). Attention-deficit/hyperactivity disorder and comorbidity. *Pediatr. Clin. North Am., 46*(5), 915–927.

Spencer, T., Biederman, J., & Wilens, T. (2000). Pharmacotherapy of attention deficit hyperactivity disorder. *Child Adol. Psychiatry Clin. North Am., 9*(1), 77–97.

Spiegel, D. (1994). Dissociative disorders. In R. E. Hales, S. C. Yudofsky, & J. A. Talbott (Eds.), *The American Psychiatric Press textbook of psychiatry* (2nd ed.). Washington, DC: American Psychiatric Press.

Spiegel, D., Bloom, J. R., Kraemer, H. C., & Gottheil, E. (1989). The beneficial effect of psychosocial treatment on survival of metastatic breast cancer patients: A randomized prospective outcome study. *Lancet, 2*, 888.

Spiegel, D., Bloom, J., Kraemer, H. C., & Gottheil, E. (1989). Effect of psychosocial treatment on survival of patients with metastic breast cancer. *Lancet, 2*, 888–891.

Spiegel, D., & Classen, C. (2000). *Group therapy for cancer patients: A research-based handbook of psychosocial care.* New York: Basic Books.

Spiegel, D., & Diamond, S. (2001). Psychosocial interventions in cancer: Group therapy techniques. In A. Baum & B. L. Andersen (Eds.), *Psychosocial interventions for cancer* (pp. 215–233). Washington, DC: American Psychological Association.

Spielberger, C. D. (1966). Theory and research on anxiety. In C. D. Spielberger (Ed.), *Anxiety and behavior.* New York: Academic Press.

Spielberger, C. D. (1972). Anxiety as an emotional state. In C. D. Spielberger (Ed.), *Anxiety: Current trends in theory and research* (Vol. 1). New York: Academic Press.

Spielberger, C. D. (1972). Conceptual and methodological issues in anxiety research. In C. D. Spielberger (Ed.), *Anxiety: Current trends in theory and research* (Vol. 2). New York: Academic Press.

Spielberger, C. D. (1985). Anxiety, cognition, and affect: A state-trait perspective. In A. H. Tuma & J. Maser (Eds.), *Anxiety and the anxiety disorders.* Hillsdale, NJ: Erlbaum.

Spielrein, S. (1995). [On the psychological content of a case of schizophrenia (dementia praecox).] *Evol. Psychiatr., 60*(1), 69–95. (French)

Spignesi, S. J. (1994). *The odd index.* New York: Penguin.

Spitz, H. H. (1994). Lewis Carroll's formula for calendar calculating. *Am. J. Ment. Retard., 98*(5), 601–606.

Spitz, R. A. (1945). Hospitalization: An inquiry into the genesis of psychiatric conditions of early child-hood. In R. S. Eissler, A. Freud, H. Hartman, & E. Kris (Eds.), *The psychoanalytic study of the child* (Vol. 1). New York: International Universities Press.

Spitz, R. A. (1946). *Anaclitic depression. The psychoanalytic study of the child* (Vol. 2). New York: International Universities Press.

Spitzer, J. (1990). On treating patients diagnosed with narcissistic personality disorder: The induction phase. *Issues Ego Psychol., 13*(1), 54–65.

Spitzer, R. L., Devlin, M. J., Walsh, B. T., & Hasin, D. (1992). Binge eating disorder: A multisite field trial of the diagnostic criteria. *Int. J. Eat. Disord., 11*, 191–203.

Spitzer, R. L., Gibbon, M., Skodol, A. E., Williams, J. B. W., & First, M. B. (Eds.). (1994). *DSM-IV casebook: A learning companion to the diagnostic and statistical manual of mental disorders* (4th ed.). Washington, DC: American Psychiatric Press.

Spitzer, R. L., Skodol, A., Gibbon, M., & Williams, J. B. W. (1981). *DSM-III case book* (1st ed.). Washington, DC: American Psychiatric Press.

Spitzer, R. L., Skodol, A., Gibbon, M., & Williams, J. B. W. (1983). *Psychopathology: A case book.* New York: McGraw-Hill.

Sponheim, S. R., Iacono, W. G., Clementz, B. A., & Beiser, M. (1997). Season of birth and electroencephalogram power abnormalities in schizophrenia. *Biol. Psychiatry, 41*, 1020–1027.

Spoont, M. R. (1996). Emotional instability. In C. G. Costello (Ed.), *Personality characteristics of the personality disordered.* New York: Wiley.

Sporer, K. A. (1999). Acute heroin overdose. *Ann. Intern. Med., 130*(7), 584–590.

Sprock, J. (2000). Gender-typed behavioral examples of histrionic personality disorder. *J. Psychopathol. Behav. Assess., 22*(2), 107–122.

Squire, L. R. (1977). ECT and memory loss. *Am. J. Psychiatry, 134*, 997–1001.

Squire, L. R., & Slater, P. C. (1983). Electroconvulsive therapy and complaints of memory dysfunction: A prospective three-year follow-up study. *Br. J. Psychiatry, 142*, 1–8.

Squires, R. F., & Braestrup, C. (1977). Benzodiazepine receptors in rat brain. *Nature, 266*, 732–734.

Stacey, J. (1996, February 12). Family life: A changing national portrait. *USA Today*, p. 6D.

Stack, S. (1981). Comparative analysis of immigration and suicide. *Psychol. Rep., 49*(2), 509–510.

Stack, S. (1987). Celebrities and suicide: A taxonomy and analysis, 1948–1983. *Am. Sociol. Rev., 52*, 401–412.

Stack, S. (1998). Heavy metal, religiosity, and suicide acceptability. *Suicide Life-Threaten. Behav., 28*(4), 388–394.

Stack, S. (1998). Research on controlling suicide: Methodological issues. *Arch. Suicide Res., 4*(1), 95–99.

Stack, S. (1998). The relationship of female labor force participation to suicide: A comparative analysis. *Arch. Suicide Res., 4*(3), 249–261.

Stader, S. R., & Hokanson, J. E. (1998). Psychosocial antecedents of depressive symptoms: An evaluation using daily experiences methodology. *J. Abnorm. Psychol., 107*(1), 17–26.

Stahl, S. M. (1998). Basic psychopharmacology of antidepressants, Part 1: Antidepressants have seven distinct mechanisms of action. *J. Clin. Psychiatry, 59*(Suppl. 4), 5–14.

Stahl, S. M. (1998). How psychiatrists can build new therapies for impotence. *J. Clin. Psychiatry, 59*(2), 47–48.

Stahl, S. M. (2001). The psychopharmacology of sex. Part 2: Effects of drugs and disease on the 3 phases of human sexual response. *J. Clin. Psychiatry, 62*(3), 147–148.

Stahl, S. M., & Soefje, S. (1995). Panic attacks and panic disorder: The great neurologic imposters. *Semin. Neurol., 15*(2), 126–132.

Stanley, B., Molcho, A., Stanley, M., Winchel, R., Gameroff, M. J., Parsons, B., & Mann, J. J. (2000). Association of aggressive behavior with altered serotonergic function in patients who are not suicidal. *Am. J. Psychiatry, 157*(4), 609–614.

Stanley, M., Stanley, B., Traskman-Bendz, L., Mann, J. J., & Meyendorff, E. (1986). Neurochemical findings in suicide completers and suicide attempters. In R. W. Maris (Ed.), *Biology of suicide.* New York: Guilford Press.

Stanley, M., Virgilio, J., & Gershon, S. (1982). Tritiated imipramine binding sites are decreased in the frontal cortex of suicides. *Science, 216,* 1337–1339.

Stanley, M. A., & Averill, P. M. (1999). Strategies for treating generalized anxiety in the elderly. In M. Duffy (Ed.), *Handbook of counseling and psychotherapy with older adults.* New York: Wiley.

Staples, S. L. (1996). Human response to environmental noise. *Am. Psychol., 51*(2), 143–150.

Stark, K. D., Bronik, M. D., Wong, S., Wells, G., & Ostrander, R. (2000). Depressive disorders. In M. Hersen, R. T. Ammerman et al. (Eds.), *Advanced abnormal child psychology* (2nd ed.) Mahwah, NJ: Erlbaum.

Stark-Adamek, C. (1992). Sexism in research: The limits of academic freedom. *Women Ther., 12*(4), 103–111.

Staub, E. (1996). Cultural-societal roots of violence. The examples of genocidal violence and of contemporary youth violence in the United States. *Am. Psychol., 51*(2), 117–132.

Steadman, H., Monahan, J., Hartstone, E., Davis, S., & Robbins, P. (1982). Mentally disordered offenders: A national survey of patients and facilities. *Law Hum. Behav., 6,* 31–38.

Steadman, H. J., Monahan, J., Robbins, P. C., Appelbaum, P., Grisso, T., Klassen, D., Mulvey, E. P., & Roth, L. (1993). From dangerousness to risk assessment: Implications for appropriate research strategies. In S. Hodgins (Ed.), *Mental disorder and crime.* New York: Sage.

Steadman, H. J., Mulvey, E. P., Monahan, J., Robbins, P. C., Appelbaum, P. S., Grisso, T., Roth, L. H., & Silver, E. (1998). Violence by people discarded from acute psychiatric inpatient facilities and by others in the same neighborhoods. *Arch. Gen. Psychiatry, 55*(5), 393–401.

Steckler, M.A. (1998). The effects of music on healing. *J. Long Term Home Health Care: Pride Inst. J., 17*(1), 42–48.

Steege, J. F., & Ling, F. W. (1993). Dyspareunia: A special type of chronic pelvic pain. *Obstet. Gynecol. Clin. North Am., 20,* 779–793.

Steen, S. N., Oppliger, R. A., & Brownell, K. D. (1988). Metabolic effects of repeated weight loss and regain in adolescent wrestlers. *JAMA, J. Am. Med. Assoc., 260,* 47–50.

Steffens, D. C., & Blazer, D. G. (1999). Suicide in the elderly. In D. G. Jacobs et al. (Eds.), *The Harvard Medical School guide to suicide assessment and intervention.* San Francisco: Jossey-Bass.

Stein, D. J., Apter, A., Ratzoni, G., Har-Even, D., & Avidan, G. (1998). Association between multiple suicide attempts and negative affects in adolescents. *J. Am. Acad. Child Adolesc. Psychiatry, 37*(5), 488–494.

Stein, D. J., Christenson, G. A., & Hollander, E. (Eds.). (1999). *Trichotillomania.* Washington, DC: American Psychiatric Press.

Stein, L. I. (1993). A system approach to reducing relapse in schizophrenia. *J. Clin. Psychiatry, 54*(3 Suppl.), 7–12.

Stein, M. B., Fyer, A. J., Davidson, J. R. T., Pollack, M. H., & Wiita, B. (1999). Fluvoxamine treatment of social phobia (social anxiety disorder): A double-blind, placebo-controlled study. *Am. J. Psychiatry, 156*(5), 756–760.

Stein, M. B., Jang, K. L., & Livesley, W. J. (1999). Heritability of anxiety sensitivity: A twin study. *Am. J. Psychiatry, 156*(2), 246–251.

Stein, M. B., Liebowitz, M. R., Lydiard, R. B., Pitts, C. D., Bushnell, W., & Gergel, I. (1998). Paroxetine treatment of generalized social phobia (social anxiety disorder): A randomized controlled trial. *JAMA, J. Am. Med. Assoc., 280*(8), 708–713.

Stein, M. B., McQuaid, J. R., Laffaye, C., & McCahill, M. E. (1999). Social phobia in the primary care medical setting. *J. Fam. Pract., 48*(7), 514–519.

Stein, M. B., & Rapee, R. M. (1999). Biological aspects of anxiety sensitivity: Is it all in the head? In S. Taylor et al. (Eds.), *Anxiety sensitivity: Theory, research, and treatment of the fear of anxiety. The LEA series in personality and clinical psychology.* Mahwah, NJ: Erlbaum.

Stein, M. B., & Uhde, T. W. (1995). In A. F. Schatzberg & C. B. Nemeroff (Eds.), *The American Psychiatric Press textbook of psychopharmacology.* Washington, DC: American Psychiatric Press.

Stein, M. B., Walker, J. R., Anderson, G., Hazen, A. L. et al. (1996). Childhood physical and sexual abuse in patients with anxiety disorders and in a community sample. *Am. J. Psychiatry, 153*(2), 275–277.

Stein, M. B., Walker, J. R., & Forde, D. R. (1994). Setting diagnostic thresholds for social phobia: Considerations from a community survey of social anxiety. *Am. J. Psychiatry, 151*(3), 408–412.

Stein, Z., Susser, M., Saenger, G., & Marolla, F. (1972). Nutrition and mental performance. *Science, 178,* 708–713.

Steinberg, J. (1996, March 17). Implant to help dog get over post-neutering trauma. *Fresno Bee,* p. B1.

Steinberg, M., & Hall, P. (1997). The SCID-D diagnostic interview and treatment planning in dissociative disorders. *Bull. Menninger Clin., 61*(1), 108–120.

Steinbrook, R. (1992). The polygraph test: A flawed diagnostic method. *N. Engl. J. Med., 327*(2), 122–123.

Steiner, H., Smith, C., Rosenkranz, R. T., & Litt, I. (1991). The early care and feeding of anorexics. *Child Psychiatry Hum. Dev., 21*(3), 163–167.

Steiner, M., & Tam, W. Y. K. (1999). Postpartum depression in relation to other psychiatric disorders. In L. J. Miller et al. (Eds.), *Postpartum mood disorders.* Washington, DC: American Psychiatric Press.

Steiner, H., & Wilson, J. (1999). Conduct disorder. In R. L. Hendren (Ed.), *Disruptive behavior disorders in children and adolescents. Review of psychiatry series.* Washington, DC: American Psychiatric Press.

Steiner-Adair, C. (1986). The body politic: Normal female adolescent development and the development of eating disorders. *J. Am. Acad. Psychoanal., 14*(1), 95–114.

Steinhausen, H. C. (1997). Annotation: Outcome of anorexia nervosa in the younger patient. *J. Child Psychol. Psychiatry, 38*(3), 271–276.

Steinhausen, H. C., Boyadjieva, S., Grigoroiu-Serbanescu, M., Seidel, R., & Winkler-Metzke, C. (2000). A transcultural outcome study of adolescent eating disorders. *Acta Psychiatr. Scand., 101*(1), 60–66.

Steketee, G. (1990). Personality traits and disorders in obsessive-compulsives. *J. Anxiety Disord., 4*(4), 351–364.

Steketee, G., Chambless, D. L., Tran, G. Q., Worden, H., & Gillis, M. M. (1996). Behavioral avoidance test for obsessive compulsive disorder. *Behav. Res. Ther., 34*(1), 73–83.

Stephens, R. S., & Curtin, L. (1995). Alcohol and depression: Effects on mood and biased processing of self-relevant information. *Psychol. Addict. Behav., 9*(4), 211–222.

Stern, T. A., & Cremens, M. C. (1998). Factitious pheochromocytoma: One patient history and literature review. *Psychosomatics, 39*(3), 283–287.

Sternbach, L. H. (1982). The discovery of CNS active 1,4–benzodiazepines (chemistry). In E. Usdin, P. Skolnick, J. F. Tallman, Jr. et al. (Eds.), *Pharmacology of benzodiazepines.* London: Macmillan.

Sternberg, R. J., Grigorenko, E. L., & Bundy, D. A. (2001). The predictive value of IQ. *Merrill-Palmer Q., 47*(1), 1–41.

Sternberg, S. (1996). Human version of mad cow disease? *Sci. News, 149,* 228.

Sternberg, S. (1996). Of mad cows and Englishmen. *Sci. News, 150,* 238–239.

Stewart, D., & Oslin, D. W. (2001). Recognition and treatment of late-life addictions in medical settings. *J. Clin. Geropsychol., 7*(2), 145–158.

Stewart, J. W., Mercier, M. A., Agosti, V., Guardino, M., & Quitkin, F. M. (1993). Imipramine is effective after unsuccessful cognitive therapy: Sequential use of cognitive therapy and imipramine in depressed outpatients. *J. Clin. Psychopharmacol., 13,* 114–119.

Stewart, S. H., Taylor, S., Jang, K. L., Cox, B. J., Watt, M. C., Fedoroff, I. C., & Borger, S. C. (2001). Causal modeling of relations among learning history, anxiety sensitivity, and panic attacks. *Behav. Res. Ther., 39*(4), 443–456.

St. George-Hyslop, P. H. (2000). Molecular genetics of Alzheimer's disease. *Biol. Psychiatry, 47*(3), 183–199.

Stillion, J. M. (1985). *Death and the sexes: An examination of differential longevity, attitudes, behaviors, and coping skills.* Washington, DC: Hemisphere.

Stillion, J. M. (1995). Through a glass darkly: Women and attitudes toward suicidal behavior. In S. S. Canetto & D. Lester (Eds.), *Women and suicidal behavior.* New York: Springer.

Stillion, J. M., & McDowell, E. E. (1996). *Suicide across the life span: Premature exits* (2nd ed.) Washington, DC: Taylor & Francis.

Stimming, M. T., & Stimming, M. (Eds.). (1999). *Before their time: Adult children's experiences of parental suicide.* Philadelphia: Temple University Press.

St. Lawrence, J. S., & Madakasira, S. (1992). Evaluation and treatment of premature ejaculation: A critical review. *Int. J. Psychiatry Med., 22,* 77–97.

Stock, W. (1993). Inhibited female orgasm. In W. O'Donohue & J. Geer (Eds.), *Handbook of sexual dysfunctions.* Boston: Allyn & Bacon.

Stodghill, R., II. (1999, March 12). Where'd you learn that? *Time.*

Stokes, T. E., & Osnes, P. G. (1989). An operant pursuit of generalization. *Behav. Ther., 20*(3), 337–355.

Stolerman, I., & Jarvis, M. (1995). The scientific case that nicotine is addictive. *Psychopharmacology, 117*(1), 2–10.

Stoline, A. M., & Sharfstein, S. S. (1996). Practice in the eye of a hurricane, or how does the psychiatrist survive in an era of change? In L. J. Dickstein, M. B. Riba, & J. M. Oldham (Eds.), *Review of psychiatry* (Vol. 15). Washington, DC: American Psychiatric Press.

Stone, M. H. (1989). Schizoid personality disorder. In American Psychiatric Association (Eds.), *Treatments of psychiatric disorders: A task force report of the American Psychiatric Association.* Washington, DC: American Psychiatric Press.

Stone, M. H. (2000). Clinical guidelines for psychotherapy for patients with borderline personality disorder. *Psychiatr. Clin. North Am., 23*(1), 193–210.

Stone, T. H., Winslade, W. J., & Klugman, C. M. (2000). Sex offenders, sentencing laws and pharmaceutical treatment: A prescription for failure. *Behav. Sci. Law,* 18(1), 83–110.

Stoppard, J. M. (2000). *Understanding depression: Feminist social constructionist approaches.* New York: Routledge.

Stores, G. (1996). Practitioner review: Assessment and treatment of sleep disorders in children and adolescents. *J. Child Psychol. Psychiatry,* 37(8), 907–925.

Stowe, Z., Casarella, J., Landry, J., & Nemeroff, C. (1995). Sertraline in the treatment of women with postpartum major depression. *Depression,* 3, 49–55.

Stoyva, J. M., & Budzynski, T. H. (1993). Biofeedback methods in the treatment of anxiety and stress disorders. In P. M. Lehrer & R. L. Woolfolk (Eds.), *Principles and practice of stress management* (2nd ed.). New York: Guilford Press.

St. Pierre, T. L. (2001). Strategies for community/school collaborations to prevent youth substance abuse. *J. Primary Prev.,* 21(3), 381–398.

Strain, E. C., Bigelow, G. E., Liebson, I. A., & Stitzer, M. L. (1999). Moderate vs. high-dose methadone in the treatment of opioid dependence: A randomized trial. *JAMA, J. Am. Med. Assoc.,* 281(11), 1000–1005.

Strange, P. G. (1992). *Brain biochemistry and brain disorders.* New York: Oxford University Press.

Stratton, V. N., & Zalanowski, A. H. (1994). Affective impact of music vs. lyrics. *Emp. Stud. Arts,* 12(2), 173–184.

Stratton, V. N., & Zalanowski, A. (1999). *Study on music and emotion.* Papaer presented at the annual meeting of the Eastern Psychological Association.

Strauss, J., & Ryan, R. (1987). Autonomy disturbances in subtypes of anorexia nervosa. *J. Abnorm. Psychol.,* 96(3), 254–258.

Straussner, S. L. A. (Ed.). (2001). *Ethnocultural factors in substance abuse treatment.* New York: Guilford Press.

Stravynski, A., Gaudette, G., Lesage, A., Arbel, N. et al. (1997). The treatment of sexually dysfunctional men without partners: A controlled study of three behavioural group approaches. *Br. J. Psychiatry,* 170, 338–344.

Stravynski, A., & Greenberg, D. (1992). The psychological management of depression. *Acta Psychiatr. Scand.,* 85(6), 407–414.

Stravynski, A., Grey, S., & Elie, R. (1987). Outline of the therapeutic process in social skills training with socially dysfunctional patients. *J. Consult. Clin. Psychol.,* 55(2), 224–228.

Street, A. E., & Arias, I. (2001). Psychological abuse and posttraumatic stress disorder in battered women: Examining the roles of shame and guilt. *Violence Victims,* 16(1), 65–78.

Streiner, D. L. (1999). Placebo-controlled trials: When are they needed? *Schizophr. Res.,* 35(3), 201–210.

Stricker, G., & Trierweiler, S. J. (1995). The local clinical scientist. A bridge between science and practice. *Am. Psychol.,* 50(12), 995–1002.

Strickland, B. R., Hale, W. D., & Anderson, L. K. (1975). Effect of induced mood states on activity and self-reported affect. *J. Consult. Clin. Psychol.,* 43(4), 587.

Strickland, C. J. (1997). Suicide among American Indian, Alaskan Native, and Canadian Aboriginal youth: Advancing the research agenda. *Int. J. Ment. Health,* 25(4), 11–32.

Striegel-Moore, R. H., Cachelin, F. M., Dohm, F. A., Pike, K. M., Wilfley, D. E., & Fairburn, C. G. (2001). Comparison of binge eating disorder and bulimia nervosa in a community sample. *Int. J. Eat. Disord.,* 29(2), 157–165.

Striegel-Moore, R. H., Silberstein, L. R., & Rodin, J. (1986). Toward an understanding of risk factors for bulimia. *Am. Psychol.,* 41(3), 246–263.

Striegel-Moore, R. H., Silberstein, L. R., & Rodin, J. (1993). The social self in bulimia nervosa: Public self-consciousness, social anxiety, and perceived fraudulence. *J. Abnorm. Psychol.,* 102(2), 297–303.

Striegel-Moore, R. H., & Smolak, L. (2000). The influence of ethnicity on eating disorders in women. In R. M. Eisler, M. Hersen et al. (Eds.), *Handbook of gender, culture, and health.* Mahwah, NJ: Erlbaum.

Strier, F. (1999). Whither trial consulting: Issues and projections. *Law Hum. Behav.,* 23(1), 93–115.

Strober, M., Freeman, R., Lampert, C., Diamond, J., & Kaye, W. (2000). Controlled family study of anorexia nervosa and bulimia nervosa: Evidence of shared liability and transmission of partial syndromes. *Am. J. Psychiatry,* 157(3), 393–401.

Strober, M., Freeman, R., Lampert, C., Diamond, J., & Kaye, W. (2001). Males with anorexia nervosa: A controlled study of eating disorders in first-degree relatives. *Int. J. Eat. Disord.,* 29(3), 264–269.

Strober, M., Freeman, R., & Morrell, W. (1997). The long-term course of severe anorexia nervosa in adolescents: Survival analysis of recovery, relapse, and outcome predictors over 10–15 years in a prospective study. *Int. J. Eat. Disord.,* 22(4), 339–360.

Strober, M., & Humphrey, L. L. (1987). Familial contributions to the etiology and course of anorexia nervosa and bulimia [Special Issue: Eating disorders]. *J. Consult. Clin. Psychol.,* 55(5), 654–659.

Strober, M., & Yager, J. (1985). A developmental perspective on the treatment of anorexia nervosa in adolescents. In D. M. Garner & P. E. Garfinkel (Eds.), *Handbook of psychotherapy for anorexia nervosa and bulimia.* New York: Guilford Press.

Stroebe, M., Gergen, M. M., Gergen, K. J., & Stroebe, W. (1992). Broken hearts or broken bonds: Love and death in historical perspectives. *Am. Psychol.,* 47(10), 1205–1212.

Stroebe, M., van Son, M., Stroebe, W., Kleber, R., Schut, H., & van den Bout, J. (2000). On the classification and diagnosis of pathological grief. *Clin. Psychol. Rev.,* 20(1), 57–75.

Stromme, P., & Diseth, T. H. (2000). Prevalence of psychiatric diagnoses in children with mental retardation: Data from a population-based study. *Dev. Med. Child Neurol.,* 42(4), 266–270.

Stromme, P., & Magnus, P. (2000). Correlations between socioeconomic status, IQ and aetiology in mental retardation: A population-based study of Norwegian children. *Soc. Psychiatry Psychiatr. Epidemiol.,* 35(1), 12–18.

Strous, R. D., Shtain, M., Oselka-Goren, H., Lustig, M., Stryjer, R., Zerzion, M., Baruch, Y., & Chelben, J. (2000). Anticipatory reactions of psychiatric inpatients to the year 2000. *J. Nerv. Ment. Dis.,* 188(11), 786–788.

Strupp, H. H. (1989). Psychotherapy: Can the practitioner learn from the researcher? *Am. Psychol.,* 44, 717–724.

Strupp, H. H. (1996). The tripartite model and the Consumer Reports study. *Am. Psychol.,* 51(10), 1017–1024.

Stuart, G. L., Treat, T. A., & Wade, W. A. (2000). Effectiveness of an empirically based treatment for panic disorder delivered in a service clinic setting: 1-year follow-up. *J. Consult. Clin. Psychol.,* 68(3), 506–512.

Stuart, S., & Noyes, R., Jr. (1999). Attachment and interpersonal communication in somatization. *Psychosomatics,* 40(1), 34–43.

Stuart, S., & O'Hara, M. W. (1995). Interpersonal psychotherapy for postpartum depression: A treatment program. *J. Psychother. Pract.. Res.,* 4(1), 18–29.

Stuart, S. P. (1999). Interpersonal psychotherapy for postpartum depression. In L. J. Miller et al. (Eds.), *Postpartum mood disorders.* Washington, DC: American Psychiatric Press.

Stunkard, A. J. (1975). From explanation to action in psychosomatic medicine: The case of obesity. *Psychosom. Med.,* 37, 195–236.

Stunkard, A. J., Sorenson, T. I. A., Hanis, C., Teasdale, T. W. et al. (1986). An adoption study of human obesity. *N. Engl. J. Med.,* 314, 193–198.

Sturgeon, V., & Taylor, J. (1980). Report of a five-year follow-up study of mentally disordered sex offenders released from Atascadero State Hospital in 1973. *Criminal Justice J. West. State Univ., San Diego,* 4, 31–64.

Styron, W. (1990). *Darkness visible: A memoir of madness.* New York: Random House.

Sudhalter, V., Cohen, I. L., Silverman, W., & Wolf-Schein, E. G. (1990). Conversational analyses of males with fragile X, Down syndrome, and autism: Comparison of the emergence of deviant language. *Am. J. Ment. Retard.,* 94, 431–441.

Sue, S., Zane, N., & Young, K. (1994). Research on psychotherapy with culturally diverse populations. In A. E. Bergin & S. L. Garfield (Eds.), *Handbook of psychotherapy and behavior change.* New York: Wiley.

Sugar, M. (1995). A clinical approach to childhood gender identity disorder. *Am. J. Psychother.,* 49(2), 260–281.

Sugarman, A., & Kanner, K. (2000). The contribution of psychoanalytic theory to psychological testing. *Psychoanal. Psychol.,* 17(1), 1–21.

Suh, E., Diener, E., & Fujita, F. (1996). Events and subjective well-being: Only recent events matter. *J. Pers. Soc. Psychol.,* 70(5), 1091–1102.

Sullivan, C. M., Tan, C., Basta, J., Rumptz, M. et al. (1992). An advocacy intervention program for women with abusive partners: Initial evaluation. *Am. J. Commun. Psychol.,* 20(3), 309–332.

Sullivan, H. S. (1953). *The interpersonal theory of psychiatry.* New York: Norton.

Sullivan, H. S. (1962). *Schizophrenia as a human process.* New York: Norton.

Summers, M. (1996, December 9). Mister clean. *People,* pp. 139–140.

Sundbom, E., Binzer, M., & Kullgren, G. (1999). Psychological defense strategies according to the Defense Mechanism Test among patients with severe conversion disorder. *Psychother. Res.,* 9(2), 184–198.

Suokas, J., & Lonnqvist, J. (1995). Suicide attempts in which alcohol is involved: A special group in general hospital emergency rooms. *Acta Psychiatr. Scand.,* 91(1), 36–40.

Suppes, T., Baldessarini, R. J., Faedda, G. L., & Tohen, M. (1991). Risk of recurrence following discontinuation of lithium treatment in bipolar disorder. *Arch. Gen. Psychiatry,* 48(12), 1082–1088.

Susnick, L. C., & Belcher, J. R. (1995). Why are they homeless?: The chronically mentally ill in Washington, DC. *Int. J. Ment. Health,* 24(4), 70–84.

Susser, E., Miller, M., Valencia, E., Colson, P. et al. (1996). Injection drug use and risk of HIV transmission among homeless men with mental illness. *Am. J. Psychiatry,* 153(6), 794–798.

Susser, E., Neugebauer, R., Hoek, H. W., Brown, A. S., Lin, S., Labovitz, D., & Gorman, J. M. (1996). Schizophrenia after prenatal famine. *Arch. Gen. Psychiatry,* 53(1), 25–31.

Sutherland, G. (1999, February 4). Regarding definitions of love and of psycho-analyst. *The Times (London).*

Suzuki, L. A., & Valencia, R. R. (1997). Race-ethnicity and measured intelligence. *Am. Psychol.*, 52(10), 1103-1114.

Svartberg, M., & Stiles, T. C. (1991). Comparative effects of short-term psychodynamic psychotherapy: A meta-analysis. *J. Consult. Clin. Psychol.*, 59, 704-714.

Svensson, B., Hansson, L., & Nyman, K. (2000). Stability of outcome in a comprehensive, cognitive therapy based treatment programme for long-term mentally ill patients. A 2-year follow-up study. *J. Ment. Health UK*, 9(1), 51-61.

Swanson, J., Holzer, C., Ganju, V., & Jono, R. (1990). Violence and psychiatric disorder in the community: Evidence from the Epidemiological Catchment Area Surveys. *Hosp. Commun. Psychiatry*, 41, 761-770.

Swartz, H. A. (1999). Interpersonal psychotherapy. In M. Hersen & A. S. Bellack (Eds.), *Handbook of comparative interventions for adult disorders* (2nd ed.). New York: Wiley.

Swayze, V. W. (1995). Frontal leukotomy and related psychosurgical procedures in the era before antipsychotics (1935-1954): A historical overview. *Am. J. Psychiatry*, 152(4), 505-515.

Swedo, S. E., Pietrini, P., Leonard, H. L., Schapiro, M. B. et al. (1992). Cerebral glucose metabolism in childhood-onset obsessive-compulsive disorder: Revisualization during pharmacotherapy. *Arch. Gen. Psychiatry*, 49(9), 690-694.

Swendsen, J. D., & Mazure, C. M. (2000). Life stress as a risk factor for postpartum depression: Current research and methodology. *Clin. Psychol.: Sci. Pract.*, 7(1), 17-31.

Swendsen, J. D., & Merikangas, K. R. (2000). The comorbidity of depression and substance use disorders. *Clin. Psychol. Rev.*, 20(2), 173-189.

Swerdlow, J. L. (1995). Quiet miracles of the brain. *Natl. Geogr.*, 187(6), 12-13.

Swonger, A. K., & Constantine, L. L. (1983). *Drugs and therapy: A handbook of psychotropic drugs* (2nd ed.). Boston: Little, Brown.

Szanto, K., Reynolds, C. F., III, Conwell, Y., Begley, A. E., & Houck, P. (1998). High levels of hopelessness persist in geriatric patients with remitted depression and a history of attempted suicide. *J. Am. Geriatr. Soc.*, 46(11), 1401-1406.

Szasz, T. S. (1961). *The myth of mental illness: Foundations of a theory of personal conduct.* New York: Harper (Hoeber).

Szasz, T. S. (1963). *Law, liberty, and psychiatry.* Englewood Cliffs, NJ: Prentice-Hall.

Szasz, T. S. (1963). *The manufacture of madness.* New York: Harper & Row.

Szasz, T. S. (1977). *Psychiatric slavery.* New York: Free Press.

Szasz, T. S. (1987). Justifying coercion through theology and therapy. In J. K. Zeig (Ed.), *The evolution of psychotherapy.* New York: Brunner/Mazel.

Szasz, T. S. (1991). The medicalization of sex. *J. Hum. Psychol.*, 31(3), 34-42.

Szasz, T. (1997). The healing word: Its past, present, and future. In J. K. Zeig (Ed.), *The evolution of psychotherapy: The third conference.* New York: Brunner/Mazel.

Szmukler, G. I., & Patton, G. (1995). Sociocultural models of eating disorders. In G. Szmukler, C. Dare, & J. Treasure (Eds.), *Handbook of eating disorders: Theory, treatment and research.* Chichester, England: Wiley.

Szymanski, S., Cannon, T. D., Gallacher, F., Erwin, R. J., & Gur, R. E. (1996). Course of treatment response in first-episode and chronic schizophrenia. *Am. J. Psychiatry*, 153(4), 519-525.

Szymanski, S., Lieberman, J., Alvir, J. M., Mayerhoff, D. et al. (1995). Gender differences in onset of illness, treatment response, course, and biologic

indexes in first-episode schizophrenic patients. *Am. J. Psychiatry*, 152(5), 698-703.

Swora, M. G. (2001). Personhood and disease in Alcoholics Anonymous: A perspective from the anthropology of religious healing. *Ment. Health, Religion Cult.*, 4(1), 1-21.

Szasz, T. (2000). Second commentary on "Aristotle's function argument." *Philos. Psychiatry, Psychol.*, 7(1), 3-16.

Szasz, T. S. (1973). *The second sin.* Garden City, NY: Anchor Press.

Szymanski, S., Lieberman, J., Pollack, S., Kane, J. M., Safferman, A., Munne, R., Umbricht, D., Woerner, M., Masiar, S., & Kronig, M. (1996). Gender differences in neuroleptic nonresponsive clozapine-treated schizophrenics. *Biol. Psychiatry*, 39, 249-254.

Taber, K. H., Lewis, D. A., & Hurley, R. A. (2001). Schizophrenia: What's under the microscope? *J. Neuropsychiatry Clin. Neurosci.*, 13(1), 1-4.

Tacon, A., & Caldera, Y. (2001). Behavior modification. In R. McComb & J. Jacalyn (Eds.), *Eating disorders in women and children: Prevention, stress management, and treatment* (pp. 263-272). Boca Raton, FL: CRC Press.

Taft, C. T., Stern, A. S., King, L. A., & King, D. W. (1999). Modeling physical health and functional health status: The role of combat exposure, posttraumatic stress disorder and personal resource attributes. *J. Traumatic Stress*, 12(1), 3-23.

Takahashi, Y. (1998). Suicide in Japan: What are the problems? In R. J. Kosky, H. S. Eshkevari, & R. Hassan (Eds.), *Suicide prevention: The global context.* New York: Plenum Press.

Takano, Y., Tsukahara, T., Suzuki, T., Hara, T. et al. (1995). The improvement of psychiatric symptoms of schizophrenic patients during day care treatment. *Seishin Igaku*, 37(4), 369-376.

Takeuchi, D. T., Uehara, E., & Maramba, G. (1999). Cultural diversity and mental health treatment. In A. V. Horwitz & T. L. Scheid (Eds.), *A handbook for the study of mental health: Social contexts, theories, and systems.* Cambridge, England: Cambridge University Press.

Tallis, F. (1996). Compulsive washing in the absence of phobia and illness anxiety. *Behav. Res. Ther.*, 34(4), 361-362.

Tam, W. C. C., & Sewell, K. W. (1995). Seasonality of birth in schizophrenia in Taiwan. *Schizophr. Bull.*, 21(1), 117-127.

Tambs, K., Harris, J. R., & Magnus, P. (1995). Sex-specific causal factors and effects of common environment for symptoms of anxiety and depression in twins. *Behav. Genet.*, 25(1), 33-44.

Tamplin, A., Goodyer, I. M., & Herbert, J. (1998). Family functioning and parent general health in families of adolescents with major depressive disorder. *J. Affect. Disord.*, 48, 1-13.

Tan, S. Y., & Dong, N. J. (2000). Psychotherapy with members of Asian American churches and spiritual traditions. In P. S. Richards, A. E. Bergin et al. (Eds.), *Handbook of psychotherapy and religious diversity.* Washington, DC: American Psychological Association.

Tanay, E. (1992). The verdict with two names. *Psychiatr. Ann.*, 22(11), 571-573.

Tanner, L. (2001, April 25). Study: 30% of kids deal with bullying: 'Serious problem' shouldn't be accepted as normal, author says. *The Dallas Morning News*, p. 1A.

Tanzi, R. C., St. George Hyslop, P. H., & Gusella, J. T. (1989). Molecular genetic approaches to Alzheimer's disease. *Trends Neurosci.*, 12(4), 152-158.

Tariot, P. N., Erb, R., Podgorski, C. A., Cox, C., Patel, S., Jakimovich, L., & Irvine, C. (1998). Efficacy and tolerability of carbamazepine for agi-

tation and aggression in dementia. *Am. J. Psychiatry*, 155(1), 54-61.

Tartaglia, L. A., Dembski, M., Weng, X., Deng, N. et al. (1995). Identification and expression cloning of a leptin receptor, OB-R. *Cell*, 83, 1263-1271.

Tataranni, P. A., Gautier, J. F., Chen, K., Uecker, A., Bandy, D., Salbe, A. D., Pratley, R. E., Lawson, M., Reiman, E. M., & Ravussin, E. (1999). Neuroanatomical correlates of hunger and satiation in humans using positron emission tomography. *Proc. Natl. Acad. Sci. U.S.A.*, 96(8), 4569-4574.

Tate, D. C., Reppucci, N. D., & Mulvey, E. P. (1995). Violent juvenile delinquents. *Am. Psychol.*, 50(9), 777-781.

Taube, C. A. (1990). Funding and expenditures for mental illness. In R. W. Manderscheid & M. A. Sonnenschein (Eds.), *Mental health, United States, 1990* (DHHS Publ. No. ADM 90-1708). Washington, DC: U. S. Department of Health and Human Services.

Tavris, C. (1993). Beware the incest-survivor machine. *New York Times Book Review.*

Taylor, B., Miller, E., Farrington, C. P., Petropoulos, M. C., Favot-Mayaud, I., Li, J., & Waight, P. A. (1999). Autism and measles, mumps, and rubella vaccine: No epidemiological evidence for a causal association. *Lancet*, 353, 2026-2029.

Taylor, C. B., Farquhar, J. W., Nelson, E., & Agras, S. (1977). Relaxation therapy and high blood pressure. *Arch. Gen. Psychiatry*, 34, 339-342.

Taylor, E. A., & Stansfeld, S. A. (1984). Children who poison themselves. *Br. J. Psychiatry*, 145, 127-135.

Taylor, E. R., Amodei, N., & Mangos, R. (1996). The presence of psychiatric disorders in HIV-infected women. *J. Counsel. Dev.*, 74, 345-351.

Taylor, G. M., & Ste. Marie, D. M. (2001). Eating disorders symptoms in Canadian female pair and dance figure skaters. *Int. J. Sport Psychol.*, 32(1), 21-28.

Taylor, J. R., & Carroll, J. L. (1987). Current issues in electroconvulsive therapy. *Psychol. Rep.*, 60(3, Pt. 1).

Taylor, P. J., Leese, M., Williams, D., Butwell, M., Daly, R., & Larkin, E. (1998). Mental disorder and violence: A special (high security) hospital study. *Br. J. Psychiatry*, 172, 218-226.

Taylor, R. (1975). Electroconvulsive treatment (ECT): The control of therapeutic power. *Exchange.*

Taylor, S. (1995). Anxiety sensitivity: Theoretical perspectives and recent findings. *Behav. Res. Ther.*, 33(3), 243-258.

Taylor, S., Kuch, K., Koch, W. J., Crockett, D. J., & Passey, G. (1998). The structure of posttraumatic stress symptoms. *J. Abnorm. Psychol.*, 107(1), 154-160.

Taylor, S., Woody, S., Koch, W. J., McLeon, P. D., & Anderson, K. W. (1996). Suffocation false alarms and efficacy of cognitive behavioral therapy for panic disorder. *Behav. Ther.*, 27, 115-126.

Taylor, S. E., Kemeny, M. E., Reed, G. M., Bower, J. E., & Gruenewald, T. L. (2000). Psychological resources, positive illusions, and health. *Am. Psychol.*, 55(1), 99-109.

Taylor, V. (1999). Gender and social movements: Gender processes in women's self-help movements. *Gender Soc.*, 13(1), 8-33.

Telch, C. F., & Agras, W. S. (1993). The effects of a very low calorie diet on binge eating. *Behav. Ther.*, 24, 177-193.

Teller, V., & Dalh, H. (1995). What psychoanalysis needs is more empirical research. In T. Shapiro & R. N. Emde (Eds.), *Research in psychoanalysis: Process, development, outcome.* Madison, CT: International Universities Press.

Telner, J. I., Lapierre, Y. D., Horn, E., & Browne, M. (1986). Rapid reduction of mania by means of reserpine therapy. *Am. J. Psychiatry, 143*(8), 1058.

Temes, R. (Ed.). (1999). *Medical hypnosis: An introduction and clinical guide.* New York: Churchill-Livingstone.

Teng, C. T., Akerman, D., Cordas, T. A., Kasper, S. et al. (1995). Seasonal affective disorder in a tropical country: A case report. *Psychiatr. Res., 56*(1), 11-15.

Ten Kate, N. (1998, February). The marketplace for medicine. *Am. Demogr.*

Teplin, L. A., Abram, K. M., & McClelland, G. M. (1994). Does psychiatric disorder predict violent crime among released jail detainees? *Am. Psychol., 49*(4), 335-342.

Teri, L., & Lewinsohn, P. M. (1986). Individual and group treatment of unipolar depression: Comparison of treatment outcome and identification of predictors of successful treatment outcome. *Behav. Ther., 17*(3), 215-228.

Terp, I. M., Engholm, G., Moller, H., & Mortensen, P. B. (1999). A follow-up study of postpartum psychoses: Prognosis and risk factors for readmission. *Acta Psychiatr. Scand., 1000*(1), 40-46.

Terr, L. (1988). What happens to early memories of trauma? A study of twenty children under age five at the time of documented traumatic events. Annual Meeting of the American Psychiatry Association. *J. Am. Acad. Child Adolesc. Psychiatry, 27*(1), 96-104.

Terry, D., Mayocchi, L., & Hynes, G. (1996). Depressive symptomatology in new mothers: A stress and coping perspective. *J. Abnorm. Psychol., 105*(2), 220-231.

Thalen, B. E., Kjellman, B. F., Morkrid, L., Wibom, R. et al. (1995). Light treatment in seasonal and nonseasonal depression. *Acta Psychiatr. Scand., 91*(5), 352-360.

Thapar, A., Davies, G., Jones, T., & Rivett, M. (1992). Treatment of childhood encopresis: A review. *Child Care, Health Dev., 18*(6), 343-353.

Thase, M. E. (1998). Depression, sleep, and antidepressants. *J. Clin. Psychiatry, 59*(Suppl. 4), 55-65.

Thase, M. E., Buysse, D. J., Frank, E., Cherry, C. R. et al. (1997). Which depressed patients will respond to interpersonal psychotherapy? The role of abnormal EEG sleep profiles. *Am. J. Psychiatry, 154*(4), 502-509.

Thase, M. E., Kupfer, D. J., Fasiczka, A. J., Buysse, D. J. et al. (1997). Identifying an abnormal electroencephalographic sleep profile to characterize major depressive disorder. *Biol. Psychiatry, 41*, 964-973.

Theander, S. (1970). Anorexia nervosa. *Acta Psychiatr. Scand., Suppl.*, pp. 1-194.

Thielman, S. B. (1998). Reflections on the role of religion in the history of psychiatry. In H.G. Koenig et al. (Eds.), *Handbook of religion and mental health.* San Diego, CA: Academic Press.

Thigpen, C. H., & Cleckley, H. M. (1957). *The three faces of Eve.* New York: McGraw-Hill.

Thoits, P. A. (1999). Sociological approaches to mental illness. In A. V. Horwitz & T. L. Scheid (Eds.), *A handbook for the study of mental health: Social contexts, theories, and systems.* Cambridge, England: Cambridge University Press.

Thomas, E. (1996, April 15). What the unabomber did to me. *Newsweek*, pp. 40-41.

Thompson, M. P., & Kingree, J. B. (1998). Brief report: The frequency and impact of violent trauma among pregnant substance abusers. *Addict. Behav., 23*(2), 257-262.

Thompson, R. A., & Sherman, R. T. (1993). *Helping athletes with eating disorders.* Champaign, IL: Human Kinetics.

Thompson, R. A., & Sherman, R. T. (1999). "Good athlete" traits and characteristics of anorexia nervosa: Are they similar? *Eat. Disord.: J. Treat. Prev., 7*(3), 181-190.

Thompson, R. F. (2000). *The brain: A neuroscience primer.* New York: Worth.

Thorn, B. E., Shealy, R. C., & Briggs, S. D. (1993). Sexual misconduct in psychotherapy: Reactions to a consumer-oriented brochure. *Prof. Psychol.: Res. Pract., 24*(1), 75-82.

Thorne, B., & Lambers, E. (Eds.) (1998). *Person-centered therapy: A European perspective.* London: Sage.

Thulesius, H., & Hakansson, A. (1999). Screening of posttraumatic stress disorder symptoms among Bosnian refugees. *J. Traumatic Stress, 12*(1), 167-174.

Thyer, B. A. (1999). Cognitive behavioral group therapy and phenelzine both effects in social phobia.

Tierney, A. J. (2000). Egas Moniz and the origins of psychosurgery: A review commemorating the 50th anniversary of Moniz's Nobel Prize. *J. Hist. Neurosci., 9*(1), 22-36.

Tiggeman, M., & Wilson-Barrett, E. (1998). Children's figure ratings: Relationship to self-esteem and negative stereotyping. *Int. J. Eat. Disord., 23*, 83-88.

Tiihonen, J., Kuikka, J., Viinamaki, H., Lehtonen, J. et al. (1995). Altered cerebral blood flow during hysterical paresthesia. *Biol. Psychiatry, 37*(2), 134-135.

Tiller, J. W. G., Bouwer, C., Behnke, K. et al. (1999). Moclobemide and fluoxetine for panic disorder. *Eur. Arch. Psychiatr. Clin. Neurosci., 249*(Suppl. 1), S7-S10.

Tillich, P. (1952, December). Anxiety, religion, and medicine. *Pastoral Psychol., 3*, 11-17.

Time. (1983, September 5). *Time.*

Time. (1998, October 12). Numbers. *Time.*

Time/CNN Poll. (1998). From what sources do teenagers today mainly learn about sex? In R. Stodghill, II. (1999, March 12). Where'd you learn that? *Time, 151*(23).

Time/CNN Poll. (1999, June 7). *Time, 153*(22), 56.

Timko, C., Moos, R. H., Finney, J. W., & Lesar, M. D. (2000). Long-term outcomes of alcohol use disorders: Comparing untreated individuals with those in Alcoholics Anonymous and formal treatment. *J. Stud. Alcohol, 61*(4), 529-540.

Tishler, C. L., McKenry, P. C., & Morgan, K. C. (1981). Adolescent suicide attempts: Some significant factors. *Suicide Life-Threaten. Behav., 11*(2), 86-92.

Tkachuk, G. A., & Martin, G. L. (1999). Exercise therapy for patients with psychiatric disorders: Research and clinical implications. *Prof. Psychol.: Res. Pract., 30*(3), 275-282.

Tobin, D. L. (2000). *Coping strategies therapy for bulimia nervosa.* Washington, DC: American Psychological Association.

Tobin, J. P. (2001). Post traumatic stress disorder and the adrenal gland. *Ir. J. Psychol. Med., 18*(1), 27-29.

Todd, T. C., & Stanton, M. D. (1983). Research on marital and family therapy: Answers, issues, and recommendations for the future. In B. B. Wolman & G. Stricker (Eds.), *Handbook of family and marital therapy.* New York: Plenum Press.

Tohen, M., & Grundy, S. (1999). Management of acute mania. *J. Clin. Psychiatry, 60*(Suppl. 5), 31-34.

Tolbert, H. A. (1996). Psychoses in children and adolescents: A review. *J. Clin. Psychiatry, 57*(Suppl. 3), 4-8.

Tomasson, K., Kent, D., & Coryell, W. (1991). Somatization and conversion disorders: Comorbidity and demographics at presentation. *Acta Psychiatr. Scand., 84*(3), 288-293.

Tomchek, L. B., Gordon, R., Arnold, M., & Handleman, J. (1992). Teaching preschool children with autism and their normally developing peers: Meeting the challenges of integrated education. *Focus Autistic Behav., 7*(2), 1-17.

Tonigan, J. S. (2001). Benefits of Alcoholics Anonymous attendance: Replication of findings between clinical research sites in project MATCH. *Alcohol. Treat Q., 19*(1), 67-77.

Torgersen, S. (1983). Genetic factors in anxiety disorders. *Arch. Gen. Psychiatry, 40*, 1085-1089.

Torgersen, S. (1983). Genetics of neurosis: The effects of sampling variation upon the twin concordance ratio. *Br. J. Psychiatry, 142*, 126-132.

Torgersen, S. (1984). Genetic and nosological aspects of schizotypal and borderline personality disorders: A twin study. *Arch. Gen. Psychiatry, 41*, 546-554.

Torgersen, S. (1990). Comorbidity of major depression and anxiety disorders in twin pairs. *Am. J. Psychiatry, 147*, 1199-1202.

Torgersen, S. (2000). Genetics of patients with borderline personality disorder. *Psychiatr. Clin. North Am., 23*(1), 1-9.

Torrey, E. F. (1988). *Nowhere to go: The tragic odyssey of the homeless mentally ill.* New York: Harper & Row.

Torrey, E. F. (1991). A viral-anatomical explanation of schizophrenia. *Schizophr. Bull., 17*(1), 15-18.

Torrey, E. F. (1992). Are we overestimating the genetic contribution to schizophrenia? *Schizophr. Bull., 18*(2), 159-170.

Torrey, E. F. (1997). *Out of the shadows: Confronting America's mental illness crisis.* New York: Wiley.

Torrey, E. F. (1999, April 16). Interviewed in J. Lang, Local jails dumping grounds for mentally ill: 700,000 acutely ill held yearly. *Detroit News.*

Torrey, E. F., Bowler, A. E., Rawlings, R., & Terrazas, A. (1993). Seasonality of schizophrenia and stillbirths. *Schizophr. Bull., 19*(3), 557-562.

Torrey, E. F., Bowler, A. E., Taylor, E. H., & Gottesman, I. I. (1994). *Schizophrenia and manic-depressive disorder.* New York: Basic Books.

Torrey, E. F., Miller, J., Rawlings, R., & Yolken, R. H. (1997). Seasonality of births in schizophrenia and bipolar disorder: A review of the literature. *Schizophr. Res., 28*(1), 1-38.

Torrey, E. F., Wolfe, S. M., & Flynn, L. M. (1988). *Care of the seriously mentally ill: A rating of state programs* (2nd ed.). Washington, DC: Public Citizen Health Research Group and National Alliance for the Mentally Ill.

Travis, J. (1996, March 23). AIDS update '96: New drugs, new tests, new optimism mark recent AIDS research. *Science News, 149*, 184-186.

Treaster, J. B. (1992, September 20). After hurricane, Floridians show symptoms seen in war. *New York Times.*

Treasure, J., & Szmukler, G. I. (1995). Medical complications of chronic anorexia nervosa. In G. I. Szmukler, C. Dare, & J. Treasure (Eds.), *Handbook on eating disorders: Theory, treatment and research.* Chichester, England: Wiley.

Treasure, J., Todd, G., & Szmukler, G. (1995). The inpatient treatment of anorexia nervosa. In G. Szmukler, C. Dare, & J. Treasure (Eds.), *Handbook of eating disorders: Theory, treatment and research.* Chichester, England: Wiley.

Treatment Advocacy Center. (1999, April 16). Cited in J. Lang, Local jails dumping grounds for mentally ill: 700,000 acutely ill held yearly. *Detroit News.*

Trestman, R. L., Horvath, T., Kalus, O., Peterson, A. E. et al. (1996). Event-related potentials in schizotypal personality disorder. *J. Neuropsychiatry Clin. Neurosci., 8*, 33-40.

Troiano, R. P., Frongillo, E. A., Sobal, J., & Levitsky, D. A. (1996). The relationship between body weight and mortality: A quantitative analysis of combined information from existing studies. *Int. J. Obes., 20,* 63–75.

Trollor, J. N. (1999). Attention deficit hyperactivity disorder in adults: Conceptual and clinical issues. *Med. J. Aust., 171*(8), 421–425.

Trotter, R. J. (1985, November). Geschwind's syndrome: Van Gogh's malady. *Psychol. Today,* p. 46.

True, W. R., Heath, A. C., Scherrer, J. F., Xian, H., Lin, N., Eisen, S. A., Lyons, M. J., Goldberg, J., & Tsuang, M. T. (1999). Interrelationship of genetic and environmental influences on conduct disorder and alcohol and marijuana dependence symptoms. *Am. J. Med. Genet., 88*(4), 391–397.

True, W. R., & Lyons, M. J. (1999). Genetic risk factors for PTSD: A twin study. In R. Yehuda et al. (Eds.), *Risk factors for posttraumatic stress disorder.* Washington, DC: American Psychiatric Press.

True, W., Rice, L., Eisen, S. A. et al. (1993). A twin study of genetic and environmental contributions to the liability for posttraumatic stress symptoms. *Arch. Gen. Psychiatry, 50,* 257–264.

Trujillo, A. (2000). Psychotherapy with Native Americans: A view into the role of religion and spirituality. In P. S. Richards, A. E. Bergin et al. (Eds.), *Handbook of psychotherapy and religious diversity.* Washington, DC: American Psychological Association.

Trujillo, K. A., & Akil, H. (1991). The NMDA receptor antagonist MK-801 increases morphine catalepsy and lethality. *Pharmacol. Biochem. Behav., 38*(3), 673–675.

Trull, T. J., Sher, K. J., Minks-Brown, C., Durbin, J., & Burr, R. (2000). Borderline personality disorder and substance use disorders: A review and integration. *Clin. Psychol. Rev., 20*(2), 235–253.

Trull, T. J., Widiger, T. A., & Burr, R. (2001). A structured interview for the assessment of the Five-Factor Model of personality: Facet-level relations to the Axis II personality disorders. *J. Pers., 69*(2), 175–198.

Trumbetta, S. L., & Mueser, K. T. (2001). Social functioning and its relationship to cognitive deficits over the course of schizophrenia. In R. S. E. Keefe & J. P. McEvoy (Eds.), *Negative symptom and cognitive deficit treatment response in schizophrenia* (pp. 33–67). Washington, DC: American Psychiatric Press.

Tryon, G. (1987). *Prof. Psychol., 17,* 357–363.

Tsai, L. Y. (1999). Psychopharmacology in autism. *Psychosom. Med., 61*(5), 651–665.

Tsoi, W. F. (1992). Male and female transsexuals: a comparison. *Singapore Med. J., 33*(2), 182–185.

Tsuang, M. (2000). Schizophrenia: Genes and environment. *Biol. Psychiatry, 47*(3), 210–220.

Tsuang, M.-T., Fleming, J. A., & Simpson, J. C. (1999). Suicide and schizophrenia. In D.G. Jacobs (Ed.), *The Harvard Medical School guide to suicide assessment and intervention.* San Francisco: Jossey-Bass.

Tsuang, M.-T., Stone, W. S., & Faraone, S. V. (2001). Genes, environment and schizophrenia. *Br. J. Psychiatry, 178*(Suppl. 40), s18–s24.

Tucker, G. J. (1998). Putting DSM-IV in perspective. *Am. J. Psychiatry, 155*(2), 159–161.

Tucker, P. (1999, February 18). Health is hot online: Depression is No. 1 topic. *HealthScout.*

Turek, F. (1996). Melatonin hype hard to swallow. *Nature, 379,* 295–296.

Turk, C. L., Fresco, D. M., & Heimberg, R. G. (1999). Cognitive behavior therapy. In M. Hersen & A.S. Bellack (Eds.), *Handbook of comparative interventions for adult disorders* (2nd ed.). New York: Wiley.

Turkat, I. D., Keane, S. P., & Thompson-Pope, S. K. (1990). Social processing errors among paranoid personalities. *J. Psychopathol. Behav. Assess., 12*(3), 263–269.

Turner, E., Ewing, J., Shilling, P., Smith, T., Irwin, M., Schuckit, M., & Kelsoe, J. (1992). Lack of association between an RFLP near the D2 dopamine receptor gene and severe alcoholism. *Biol. Psychiatry, 31*(3), 285–290.

Turner, J., Batik, M., Palmer, L. J., Forbes, D., & McDermott, B. M. (2000). Detection and importance of laxative use in adolescents with anorexia nervosa. *J. Am. Acad. Child Adolesc. Psychiatry, 39*(3), 378–385.

Turner, L. A., Althof, S. E., Levine, S. B., Bodner, D. R., Kursh, E. D., & Resnick, M. I. (1991). External vacuum devices in the treatment of erectile dysfunction: A one-year study of sexual and psychosocial impact. *J. Sex Marital Ther., 17*(2), 81–93.

Turner, R. J., & Lloyd, D. A. (1995, December). Lifetime traumas and mental health: The significance of cumulative adversity. *J. Health Soc. Behav., 36,* 360–376.

Turner, S. M., Beidel, D. C., Borden, J. W., Stanley, M. A. et al. (1991). Social phobia: Axis I and II correlates. *J. Abnorm. Psychol., 100*(1), 102–106.

Turner, S. M., Beidel, D. C., Dancu, C. V., & Keys, D. J. (1986). Psychopathology of social phobia and comparison to avoidant personality disorder. *J. Abnorm. Psychol., 95*(4), 389–394.

Turner, S. M., Beidel, D. C., Long, P. J., & Greenhouse, J. (1992). Reduction of fear in social phobics: An examination of extinction patterns. *Behav. Ther., 23*(3), 389–403.

Turner, S. M., Hersen, M., & Bellack, A. S. (1977). Effects of social disruption, stimulus interference, and aversive conditioning on auditory hallucinations. *Behav. Mod., 1*(2), 249–258.

Turner, W. J. (1995). Homosexuality, Type 1: An Xq28 phenomenon. *Arch. Sex. Behav., 24*(2), 109–134.

Turton, M. D., O'Shea, D., Gunn, I., Beak, S. A. et al. (1996, January 4). A role for glucagon-like peptide-1 in the central regulation of feeding. *Nature, 379,* 69–72.

Twain, M. (1885). *The adventures of Huckleberry Finn.*

Tweed, J. L., Schoenbach, V. J., & George, L. K. (1989). The effects of childhood parental death and divorce on six-month history of anxiety disorders. *Br. J. Psychiatry, 154,* 823–828.

Tyrer, P. (1992). Anxiolytics not acting at the benzodiazepine receptor: Beta blockers. *Prog. Neuropsychopharmacol. Biol. Psychiatry, 16*(1), 17–26.

UNINCB (United Nations International Narcotics Control Board) Report. (1996). Cited in J. Roberts, Behavioral disorders are overdiagnosed in U.S. *Br. Med. J., 312,* 657.

UTMB (University of Texas Medical Branch at Galveston). (1999, May 14). *Mania drugs cut hospitalization costs.* Study presented at the meeting of the American Psychiatric Association, May 17, 1999.

Uchino, B. N., & Garvey, T. S. (1997). The availability of social support reduces cardiovascular reactivity to acute psychological stress. *J. Behav. Med., 20*(1), 15–27.

Uchoa, D. D. (1985). Narcissistic transference? *Rev. Bras. Psicanal., 19*(1), 87–96.

Uhlenhuth, E. H., Balter, M. B., Ban, T. A., & Yang, K. (1995). International study of expert judgment on therapeutic use of benzodiazepines and other psychotherapeutic medications: III. Clinical features affecting experts' therapeutic recommendations in anxiety disorders. *Psychopharmacol. Bull., 31*(2), 289–296.

Uhlenhuth, E. H., Balter, M. B., Ban, T. A., & Yang, K. (1999). Trends in recommendations for the pharmacotherapy of anxiety disorders by an international expert panel, 1992–1997. *Eur. Neuropsychopharmacol., 9*(Suppl. 6), S393–S398.

Uhlig, R. (1996, October 31). Prosthetics improve a dog's life. *Electronic Telegraph, Issue 526.*

Ullmann, L. P., & Krasner, L. (1975). *A psychological approach to abnormal behavior* (2nd ed.). Englewood Cliffs, NJ: Prentice-Hall.

Ulrich, R. S. (1984). View from a window may influence recovery from surgery. *Science, 224,* 420–421.

Uniform Crime Reports. (1997). *Crime in the United States: 1996 Uniform Crime Reports.* Washington, DC: FBI.

Uretsky, S. (1999, June 25). Clear as mud: They call it informed consent. *HealthScout.*

Uretsky, S. (1999, June 28). Mate in two: Ideas of perfection vary. *HealthScout.*

Ursano, R. J., Boydstun, J. A., & Wheatley, R. D. (1981). Psychiatric illness in U. S. Air Force Vietnam prisoners of war: A five-year follow-up. *Am. J. Psychiatry, 138*(3), 310–314.

Ursano, R. J., Fullerton, C. S., Epstein, R. S., Crowley, B., Kao, T. C., Vance, K., Craig, K. J., Dougall, A. L., & Baum, A. (1999). Acute and chronic posttraumatic stress disorder in motor vehicle accident victims. *Am. J. Psychiatry, 156*(4), 589–595.

Ursano, R. J., Fullerton, C. S., Vance, K., & Kao, T. C. (1999). Posttraumatic stress disorder and identification in disaster workers. *Am. J. Psychiatry, 156*(3), 353–359.

U.S. Bureau of the Census. (1990). *Statistical abstract of the United States.* Washington, DC: U. S. Government Printing Office.

U.S. Bureau of the Census. (1994). *Statistical abstract of the United States.* Washington, DC: U.S. Government Printing Office.

U.S. Department of Justice. (1994). *Violence between inmates: Domestic violence.* Annapolis Junction, MD: Bureau of Justice Statistics Clearinghouse.

U.S. Department of Justice. (1995). *Violence against women: Estimates from the redesigned National Crime Victimization Survey.* Annapolis Junction, MD: Bureau of Justice Statistics Clearinghouse.

U.S. Department of Justice. (1997, September 6). Cited in T. Daunt, Jails must alter care of mentally ill. *Los Angeles Times,* Pt. B, p. 1.

U.S. Public Health Service. (1999, April 16). Report. Cited in J. Lang, Local jails dumping grounds for mentally ill: 700,000 acutely ill held yearly. *Detroit News.*

Vacc, N. A., & Juhnke, G. A. (1997). The use of structured clinical interviews for assessment in counseling. *J. Counsel. Dev., 75*(6), 470–480.

Vaillant, G. E. (1993). *The wisdom of the ego.* Cambridge, MA: Harvard University Press.

Vaillant, G. E. (1994). Ego mechanisms of defense and personality psychopathology. *J. Abnorm. Psychol., 103*(1), 44–50.

Vaillant, G. E., & Milofsky, E. S. (1982). Natural history of male alcoholism: IV. Paths to recovery. *Arch. Gen. Psychiatry, 39,* 127–133.

Vaillant, G. E., & Perry, J. C. (1985). Personality disorders. In H. I. Kaplan & B. J. Sadock (Eds.), *Comprehensive textbook of psychiatry* (4th ed.). Baltimore: Williams & Wilkins.

Vaillant, P. M., & Antonowicz, D. H. (1992). Rapists, incest offenders, and child molesters in treatment: Cognitive and social skills training. *Int. J. Offender Ther. Compr. Criminol., 36*(3), 221–230.

Valbak, K. (2001). Good outcome for bulimic patients in long-term group analysis: A single-group study. *Eur. Eat. Disord. Rev., 9*(1), 19–32.

Valdisseri, E.V., Carroll, K. R., & Hartl, A. J. (1986). A study of offenses committed by psychotic inmates in a county jail. *Hosp. Commun. Psychiatry, 37,* 163–165.

Valenstein, E. S. (1986). *Great and desperate cures.* New York: Basic Books.

Valente, S. M., & Saunders, J. M. (1995). Women, physical illness and suicidal behavior. In S. S. Canetto & D. Lester (Eds.), *Women and suicidal behavior.* New York: Springer.

Valenti-Hein, D. C., Yarnold, P. R., & Mueser, K. T. (1994). Evaluation of the dating skills program for improving heterosocial interactions in people with mental retardation. *Behav. Mod., 18*(1), 32–46.

Vanathy, S., Sharma, P. S. V. N., & Kumar, K. B. (1998). The efficacy of alpha and theta neurofeedback training in treatment of generalized anxiety disorder. *Indian J. Clin Psychol., 25*(2), 136–143.

van Bommel, H. (1992). *Dying for care: Hospice care or euthanasia.* Toronto: NC Press.

Van Bourgondien, M. E., & Schopler, E. (1990). Critical issues in the residential care of people with autism. *J. Autism Dev. Disord., 20*(3), 391–399.

van Dam Baggen, R., & Kraaimaat, F. (2000). Group social skills training or cognitive group therapy as the clinical treatment of choice for generalized social phobia? *J. Anxiety Disord., 14*(5), 437–451.

Van de Castle, R. (1993). Content of dreams. In M. A. Carskadon (Ed.), *Encyclopedia of sleep and dreams.* New York: Macmillan.

VandenBos, G. R. (1996). Outcome assessment of psychotherapy. *Am. Psychol., 51*(10), 1005–1006.

Vandereycken, W. (1994). Parental rearing behaviour and eating disorders. In C. Perris, W. A. Arrindell, & M. Eisemann (Eds.), *Parenting and psychopathology.* Chichester, England: Wiley.

Van der Ham, T., Meulman, J. J., Van Strien, D. C., & Van Engeland, H. (1997). Empirically based subgrouping of eating disorders in adolescents: A longitudinal perspective. *Br. J. Psychiatry, 170,* 363–368.

van der Hart, O., Brown, P., & Graafland, M. (1999). Trauma-induced dissociative amnesia in World War I combat soldiers. *Aust. N. Z. J. Psychiatry, 33*(1), 37–46.

van der Kolk, B. A. (2001). The psychobiology and psychopharmacology of PTSD. *Hum. Psychopharmacol. Clin. Exp., 16*(Suppl. 1), S49–S64.

van der Kolk, B. A., McFarlane, A. C., van der Hart, O., & Rice-Smith, E. (1999). Treatment of posttraumatic stress disorder and other trauma-related disorders. In D. Spiegel et al. (Eds.), *Efficacy and cost-effectiveness of psychotherapy. Clinical practice.* Washington, DC: American Psychiatric Association.

Van der Molen, H. T., Nijenhuis, J. T., & Keen, G. (1995). The effects of intelligence test preparation. *Eur. J. Pers., 9*(1), 43–56.

VanGent, E. M., & Zwart, F. M. (1991). Psychoeducation of partners of bipolar-manic patients. *J. Affect. Disord., 21*(1), 15–18.

Van Hasselt, V., Null, J., Kempton, T., & Buckstein, O. (1993). Social skills and depression in adolescent substance abusers. *Addict. Behav., 18,* 9–18.

van Os, J., Fañanas, L., Cannon, M., Macdonald, A., & Murray, R. (1997). Dermatoglyphic abnormalities in psychosis: A twin study. *Biol. Psychiatry, 41,* 624–626.

Van Praag, H. M. (1983). CSF 5-HIAA and suicide in non-depressed schizophrenics. *Lancet, 2,* 977–978.

Van Praag, H. M. (1983). In search of the action mechanism of antidepressants. 5-HTP/tyrosine mixtures in depression. *Neuropharmacology, 22,* 433–440.

Van Praag, H. M. (1986). Affective disorders and aggression disorders: Evidence for a common biologi-

cal mechanism. In R. W. Maris (Ed.), *Biology of suicide.* New York: Guilford Press.

Vatz, R., & Weinberg, L. (1993, January 10). Keno krazy? *Washington Post,* p. C5.

Vaughan, K., Doyle, M., McConaghy, N., & Blaszcznski, A. (1992). The relationship between relative's expressed emotion and schizophrenic relapse: An Australian replication. *Soc. Psychiatry Psychiatr. Epidemiol., 27*(1), 10–15.

Velamoor, V. R., Norman, R. M., & Caroff, S. N. et al. (1994). Progression of symptoms in neuroleptic malignant syndrome. *J. Nerv. Ment. Dis., 182,* 168–173.

Velleman, R., & Orford, J. (1993). The adult adjustment of offspring of parents with drinking problems. *Br. J. Psychiatry, 162,* 503–516.

Velligan, D. I., Funderburg, L. G., Giesecke, S. L., & Miller, A. L. (1995). Longitudinal analysis of communication deviance in the families of schizophrenic patients. *Psychiatr. Interpers. Biol. Process., 58*(1), 6–19.

Velting, D. M., Shaffer, D., Gould, M. S., Garfinkel, R., Fisher, P., & Davies, M. (1998). Parent-victim agreement in adolescent suicide research. *J. Am. Acad. Child Adolesc. Psychiatry, 37*(11), 1161–1166.

Venditti, E., Wing, R., Jakicic, J., Butler, B., & Marcus, M. (1996). Weight cycling, psychological health, and binge eating in obese women. *J. Consult. Clin. Psychol., 64*(2), 400–405.

Verburg, K., Griez, E., Meijer, J., & Pols, H. (1995). Respiratory disorders as a possible predisposing factor for panic disorder. *J. Affect Disord., 33*(2), 129–134.

Verfaellie, M., Cermak, L. S., Blackford, S. P. et al. (1990). Strategic and automatic priming of semantic memory in alcoholic Korsakoff patients. *Brain Cognit., 13*(2), 178–192.

Vernberg, E. M., La Greca, A. M., Silverman, W. K., & Prinstein, M. J. (1996). Prediction of posttraumatic stress symptoms in children after Hurricane Andrew. *J. Abnorm. Psychol., 105*(2), 237–248.

Vertosick, F. T., Jr. (1997, October). Lobotomy's back. *Discover,* pp. 66–71.

Vetter, H. J. (1969). *Language behavior and psychopathology.* Chicago: Rand McNally.

Vetter, P. H., von Pritzbuer, J., Jungmann, K., Kropp, P., & Koller, O. (2001). The validity of the ICD-10 classification of recurrent affective disorders: Do endogenous and psychogenic depressions form a homogeneous diagnostic group? *Psychopathology, 34*(1), 36–42.

Vieira, C. (1993). Nudity in dreams. In M. A. Carskadon (Ed.), *Encyclopedia of sleep and dreams.* New York: Macmillan.

Viguera, A. C., Nonacs, R., Cohen, L. S., Tondo, L., Murray, A., & Baldessarini, R. J. (2000). Risk of recurrence of bipolar disorder in pregnant and nonpregnant women after discontinuing lithium maintenance. *Am. J. Psychiatry, 157*(2), 179–184.

Vinogradov, S., & Yalom, I. D. (1994). Group therapy. In R. E. Hales, S. C. Yudofsky, & J. A. Talbott (Eds.), *The American Psychiatric Press textbook of psychiatry* (2nd ed.). Washington, DC: American Psychiatric Press.

Vinson, D. (1994). Therapy for attention-deficit hyperactivity disorder. *Arch. Fam. Med., 3,* 445–451.

Visser, P. J., Krabbendam, L., Verhey, F. R., Hofman, P. A., Verhoeven, W. M., Tuinier, S., Wester, A., Den Berg, Y. W., Goessens, L. F., Werf, Y. D., & Jolles, J. (1999). Brain correlates of memory dysfunction in alcoholic Korsakoff's syndrome. *J. Neurol., Neurosurg. Psychiatry, 67*(6), 774–778.

Vlaeyen, J. W. S., Haazen, I. W. C. J., Schuerman, J. A., Kole-Snijders, A. M. J. et al. (1995). Be-

haviloural rehabilitation of chronic low back pain: Comparison of an operant treatment, an operant-cognitive treatment and an operant-respondent treatment. *Br. J. Clin. Psychol., 34*(1), 95–118.

Vogele, C., & Steptoe, A. (1993). Anger inhibition and family history as modulators of cardiovascular responses to mental stress in adolescent boys. *J. Psychosom. Res., 37*(5), 503–514.

Vogeltanz, N. D., Wilsnack, S. C., Harris, T. R., Wilsnack, R. W., Wonderlich, S. A., & Kristjanson, A. F. (1999). Prevalence and risk factors for childhood sexual abuse in women: National survey findings. *Child Abuse Neglect, 23*(6), 579–592.

Volavka, J. (1995). *Neurobiology of violence.* Washington, DC: American Psychiatric Press.

Volkmar, F. R. (2001). Pharmacological interventions in autism: Theoretical and practical issues. *J. Clin. Child Psychol., 30*(1), 80–87.

Volkmar, F. R., Carter, A., Sparrow, S. S., & Cicchetti, D. V. (1993). Quantifying social development in autism. *J. Am. Acad. Child Adolesc. Psychiatry, 32*(3), 627–632.

Volkow, N. D., & Fowler, J. S. (2000). Addiction, a disease of compulsion and drive: Involvement of the orbitofrontal cortex. *Cereb. Cortex, 10*(3), 318–325.

Volkow, N. D., Fowler, J. S., & Wang, G. J. (1999). Imaging studies on the role of dopamine in cocaine reinforcement and addiction in humans. *J. Psychopharmacol., 13*(4), 337–345.

Volkow, N. D., Gillespie, H., Tancredi, L., & Hollister, L. (1995). The effects of marijuana in the human brain measured with regional brain glucose metabolism. In A. Biegon & N. D. Volkow (Eds.), *Sites of drug action in the human brain.* Boca Raton, FL: CRC Press.

Volkow, N. D., Wang, G. J., Fowler, J. S., Logan, J., Gatley, S. J., Hitzemann, R., Chen, A. D., Dewey, S. L., & Pappas, N. (1997). Decreased striatal dopaminergic responsiveness in detoxified cocaine-dependent subjects. *Nature, 386,* 830–833.

Volkow, N. D., Wang, G. J., Fowler, J. S., Logan, J., Gatley, S. J., Wong, C., Hiutzemann, R., & Pappas, N. R. (1999). Reinforcing effects of psychostimulants in humans are associated with increases in brain dopamine and occupancy of D_2 receptors. *J. Pharmacol. Exp. Ther., 291*(1), 409–415.

Volpicelli, J., Alterman, A., Hayashida, M., & O'Brien, C. (1992). Naltrexone in the treatment of alcohol dependence. *Arch. Gen. Psychiatry, 49,* 876–880.

Volz, H. P., & Laux, P. (2000). Potential treatment for subthreshold and mild depression: A comparison of St. John's wort extracts and fluoxetine. *Compr. Psychiatry, 41*(2, Suppl. 1), 133–137.

von Burg, M., & Hibbard, R. (1995). Munchausen syndrome by proxy: A different kind of child abuse. *Indiana Med., 88*(5), 378–382.

Vonnegut, M. (1974, April). Why I want to bite R. D. Laing. *Harper's, 248,* 80–92.

Vostanis, P., Feehan, C., Grattan, E., & Bickerton, W.-L. (1996). A randomised controlled outpatient trial of cognitive-behavioural treatment for children and adolescents with depression: 9-month follow-up. *J. Affect. Disord., 40,* 105–116.

Vredenburg, K., Flett, G. L., & Krames, L. (1993). Analogue versus clinical depression: A critical reappraisal. *Psychol. Bull., 113*(2), 327–344.

WHO (World Health Organization). (1992). World health statistics annual. Geneva: Author.

Wade, T. D., Bulik, C. M., Neale, M., & Kendler, K. S. (2000). Anorexia nervosa and major depression: Shared genetic and environmental risk factors. *Am. J. Psychiatry, 157*(3), 469–471.

Wagenaar, A. C., Murray, D. M., & Toomey, T. L. (2000). Communities mobilizing for change on alcohol (CMCA): Effects of a randomized trial on arrests and traffic crashes. *Addiction, 95*(2), 209–217.

Wagner, K. D., & Ambrosini, P. J. (2001). Childhood depression: Pharmacological therapy/treatment (pharmacotherapy of childhood depression). *J. Clin. Child Psychol., 30*(1), 88–97.

Wahl, O. F., & Hunter, J. (1992). Are gender effects being neglected in schizophrenia research? *Schizophr. Bull., 18*(2), 313–318.

Wahlberg, K.-E., Wynne, L. C., Oja, H., Keskitalo, P. et al. (1997). Gene-environment interaction in vulnerability to schizophrenia: Findings from the Finnish Adoptive Family Study of Schizophrenia. *Am. J. Psychiatry, 154*(3), 355–362.

Waikar, S. V., & Craske, M. G. (1997). Cognitive correlates of anxious and depressive symptomatology: An examination of the helplessness/hopelessness model. *J. Anxiety Disord., 11*(1), 1–16.

Wakefield, J. C. (1999). The measurement of mental disorder. In A. V. Horwitz & T. L. Scheid (Eds.), *A handbook for the study of mental health: Social contexts, theories, and systems.* Cambridge, England: Cambridge University Press.

Wakeling, A. (1995). Physical treatments. In G. Szmukler, C. Dare, & J. Treasure (Eds.), *Handbook of eating disorders: Theory, treatment and research.* Chichester, England: Wiley.

Walker, E., & Young, T. D. (1986). *A killing cure.* New York: Henry Holt.

Walker, E. A., Gelfand, A., Katon, W. J., Koss, M. P., von Korff, M., Bernstein, D., & Russo, J. (1999). Adult health status of women with histories of childhood abuse and neglect. *Am. J. Med., 107*(4), 332–339.

Walker, L. E. (1979). *The battered woman.* New York: Harper & Row.

Walker, L. E. (1984). *The battered woman syndrome.* New York: Springer.

Walker, L. E. (1984). Battered women, psychology, and public policy. *Am. Psychol., 39*(10), 1178–1182.

Walker, L. E. (1999). Psychology and domestic violence around the world. *Am. Psychol., 54*(1), 21–29.

Walker, R. D., Howard, M. O., Walker, P. S., Lambert, M. D., Maloy, F., & Suchinsky, R. T. (1996). Essential and reactive alcoholism: A review. *J. Clin. Psychol., 52*(1), 80–95.

Wall, T. L., Shea, S. H., Chan, K. K., & Carr, L. G. (2001). A genetic association with the development of alcohol and other substance use behavior in Asian Americans. *J. Abnorm. Psychol., 110*(1), 173–178.

Walsh, B. T., Wilson, G. R., Loeb, K. L., Devlin, M. J. et al. (1997). Medication and psychotherapy in the treatment of bulimia nervosa. *Am. J. Psychiatry, 154,* 523–531.

Walters, E. E., & Kendler, K. S. (1995). Anorexia nervosa and anorexia-like syndromes in a population based female twin sample. *Am. J. Psychiatry, 152,* 64–71.

Walters, G. D. (2000). Behavioral self-control training for problem drinkers: A metal-analysis of randomized control studies. *Behav. Ther., 31*(1), 135–149.

Walton, J. W., Johnson, S. B., & Algina, J. (1999). Mother and child perceptions of child anxiety: Effects of race, health status, and stress. *J. Pediatr. Psychol., 24*(1), 29–39.

Wanck, B. (1984). Two decades of involuntary hospitalization legislation. *Am. J. Psychiatry, 41,* 33–38.

Wang, C., & Chen, W. (2000). The efficacy of behavior therapy in 9 patients with phobia. *Chin. Ment. Health J., 14*(5), 351–352.

Wang, H. Y., Markowitz, P., Levinson, D., Undie, A. S., & Friedman, E. (1999). Increased membrane-associated protein kinase C activity and translocation in blood platelets from bipolar affective disorder patients. *J. Psychiatr. Res., 33*(2), 171–179.

Wang, S., Sun, C., Walczak, C. A., Ziegle, J. S. et al. (1995, May). Evidence for a susceptibility locus for schizophrenia on chromosome 6pter-p22. *Nat. Genet., 10,* 41–46.

Warga, C. (1988, September). You are what you think. *Psychol. Today,* pp. 54–58.

Waring, M., & Ricks, D. (1965). Family patterns of children who become adult schizophrenics. *J. Nerv. Ment. Dis., 140*(5), 351–364.

Warner, G. (1999, January 29). Spitzer seeks law on medication for the mentally ill. *Buffalo News,* p. 1C.

Warnock, J. K., Bundren, J. C., & Morris, D. W. (1997). Female hypoactive sexual desire disorder due to androgen deficiency: Clinical and psychometric issues. *Psychopharmacol. Bull., 33*(4), 761–766.

Warnock, J. K., Bundren, J. C., & Morris, D. W. (1999). Female hypoactive sexual disorder: Case studies of physiologic androgen replacement. *J. Sex Marital Ther., 25*(3), 175–182.

Warren, G., & Sampson, G. (1995). Medical audit of an assessment clinic for male erectile dysfunction. *J. Sex Marital Ther., 10*(1), 39–46.

Warren, L. W., & Ostrom, J. C. (1988). Pack rats: World-class savers. *Psychol. Today, 22*(2), 58–62.

Warren, R. (1997). REBT and generalized anxiety disorder. In J. Yankura, W. Dryden et al. (Eds.), *Using REBT with common psychological problems: A therapist's casebook.* New York: Springer.

Warwick, H. M. C., & Salkovskis, P. M. (2001). Cognitive-behavioral treatment of hypochondriasis. In V. Starcevic & D. R. Lipsitt (Eds.), *Hypochondriasis: Modern perspectives on an ancient malady* (pp. 314–328). New York: Oxford University Press.

Washton, A. M., & Gold, M. S. (1984). Chronic cocaine abuse: Evidence for adverse effects on health and functioning. *Psychiatr. Ann., 14*(10), 733–743.

Wasik, J.F. (1999). The truth about herbal supplements. *Consum. Dig., 38*(4), 75–82.

Wasserman, I. M. (1992). The impact of epidemic, war, prohibition and media on suicide: United States, 1910–1920. *Suicide Life-Threaten. Behav., 22*(2), 240–254.

Wasserman, I. M., & Stack, S. (2000). The relationship between occupation and suicide among African American males: Ohio, 1989–1991. In R. W. Maris, S. S. Canetto et al. (Eds.), *Review of suicidology, 2000.* New York: Guilford Press.

Waters, L. (1990). Reinforcing the empty fortress: An examination of recent research into the treatment of autism. *Educ. Stud., 16*(1), 3–16.

Watkins, C. E., Jr., & Campbell, V. L. (Eds.). (2000). *Testing and assessment in counseling practice* (2nd ed.). Mahwah, NJ: Erlbaum.

Watson, C. G. (1987). Recidivism in "controlled drinker" alcoholics: A longitudinal study. *J. Clin. Psychol., 43*(3), 404–412.

Watson, C. G., Hancock, M., Gearhart, L. P. Mendez, C. M. et al. (1997). A comparative outcome study of frequent, moderate, occasional, and nonattenders of Alcoholics Anonymous. *J. Clin. Psychol., 53*(3), 209–214.

Watson, D., Clark, L. A., & Harkness, A. R. (1994). Structures of personality and their relevance to psychopathology. *J. Abnorm. Psychol., 103*(1), 18–31.

Watson, J. B. (1930). *Behaviorism* (Rev. ed.). Chicago: University of Chicago Press.

Watson, J. B., & Rayner, R. (1920). Conditioned emotional reaction. *J. Exp. Psychol., 3,* 1–14.

Watson, S. J., Benson, J. A., Jr., & Joy, J. E. (2000). Marijuana and medicine: Assessing the science base: A summary of the 1999 Institute of Medicine Report. *Arch. Gen. Psychiatry, 57*(6), 547–552.

Watson Wyatt Worldwide. (1995, July 26). Job satisfaction survey. Cited in M. Reinemer, Work happy. *Am. Demogr.*

Waxweiler, R. J. et al. (1995). Monitoring the impact of traumatic brain injury: A review and update. *J. Neurotrauma, 12*(4).

Wechsler, H., Davenport, A., Dowdall, G., Moeykens, B., & Castillo, S. (1994). Health and behavioral consequences of binge drinking in college. *JAMA, J. Am. Med. Assoc., 272*(21), 1672–1677.

Wechsler, H., Dowdell, G. W., Davenport, A., & Castllo, S. (1995). Correlates of college student binge drinking. *Am. J. Public Health, 85*(7), 921–926.

Wechsler, H., Dowdell, G. W., Davenport, A., & Rimm, E. (1995). A gender-specific measure of binge drinking among college students. *Am. J. Public Health, 85*(7), 982–985.

Wechsler, H., & Isaac, N. (1992). "Binge" drinkers at Massachusetts colleges: Prevalence, drinking styles, time trends, and associated problems. *JAMA, J. Am. Med. Assoc., 267,* 2929–2931.

Wechsler, H., Lee, J. E., Kuo, M., & Lee, H. (2000). College binge drinking in the 1990s: A continuing problem: Results of the Harvard School of Public Health 1999 College Alcohol Study. *J. Am. Coll. Health, 48*(5), 199–210.

Wechsler, H. et al. (1997). *Survey on college binge drinking.* Reported by Harvard University School of Public Health, Cambridge, MA.

Weeks, D., & James, J. (1995). *Eccentrics: A study of sanity and strangeness.* New York: Villard.

Wegner, J. T., & Wegner, A. Z. (2001). Cognitive-behavioral therapy and other short-term approaches in the treatment of eating disorders. In B. P. Kinoy (Ed.), *Eating disorders: New directions in treatment and recovery* (2nd ed., pp. 112–126). New York: Columbia University Press.

Wehmeyer, M. L. (1992). Self-determination and the education of students with mental retardation. *Educ. Training Ment. Retard., 27*(4), 302–314.

Weinberg, M. K., Tronick, E. Z., Beeghly, M., Olson, K. L., Kernan, H., & Riley, J. M. (2001). Subsyndromal depressive symptoms and major depression in postpartum women. *Am. J. Orthopsychiatry, 71*(1), 87–97.

Weiner, H. (1977). *Psychobiology and human disease.* New York: Elsevier.

Weiner, H., Thaler, M., Reiser, M. F., & Mirsky, I. A. (1957). Etiology of duodenal ulcer: I. Relation of specific psychological characteristics to rate of gastric secretion (serum pepsinogen). *Psychosom. Med., 19,* 1–10.

Weiner, I. B. (1995). Methodological considerations in Rorschach research [Special issue: Methodological issues in psychological assessment research]. *Psychol. Assess., 7*(3), 330–337.

Weiner, I. B. (1998). Teaching the Rorschach comprehensive system. In L. Handler, M. J. Hilsenroth et al. (Eds.), *Teaching and learning personality assessment. The LEA series in personality and clinical psychology.* Mahwah, NJ: Erlbaum.

Weiner, I. B. (1999). Contemporary perspectives on Rorschach assessment. *Eur. J. Psychol. Assess., 15*(1), 78–86.

Weiner, I. B. (2000). Making Rorschach interpretation as good as it can be. *J. Pers. Assess., 74*(2), 164–174.

Weiner, I. B. (2000). Using the Rorschach properly in practice and research. *J. Clin. Psychol., 56*(3), 435–438.

Weiner, I. W. (1969). The effectiveness of suicide prevention programs. *Ment. Hyg., 53,* 357–373.

Weingarten, S. M. (1999). Psychosurgery. In B. L. Miller, J. L. Cummings et al. (Eds.), *The human* frontal lobes: Functions and disorders. The science and practice of neuropsychology series. New York: Guilford Press.

Weingarten, S. M., & Cummings, J. L. (2001). Psychosurgery of frontal-subcortical circuits. In D. G. Lichter & J. L. Cummings (Eds.), *Frontal-subcortical circuits in psychiatric and neurological disorders* (pp. 421–435). New York: Guilford Press.

Weinstock, L. S. (1999). Gender differences in the presentation and management of social anxiety disorder. *J. Clin. Psychiatry, 60*(Suppl. 9), 9–13.

Weintraub, M., Segal, R. M., & Beck, A. T. (1974). An investigation of cognition and affect in the depressive experience of normal men. *J. Consult. Clin. Psychol., 42,* 911.

Weir, R. F. (1992). The morality of physician-assisted suicide. *Law, Med. Health Care, 20*(1–2), 116–126.

Weishaar, M. E. (2000). Cognitive risk factors in suicide. In R. W. Maris, S. S. Canetto et al. (Eds.), *Review of suicidology, 2000.* New York: Guilford Press.

Weisheit, R. A. (1990). Domestic marijuana growers: Mainstreaming deviance. *Deviant Behav., 11*(2), 107–129.

Weiss, D. E. (1991). *The great divide.* New York: Poseidon Press/Simon & Schuster.

Weiss, D. S., Marmar, C. R., Schlenger, W. E., & Fairback, J. A. et al. (1992). The prevalence of lifetime and partial posttraumatic stress disorder in Vietnam theater veterans. *J. Traumatic Stress, 5*(3), 365–376.

Weiss, R. (1997, January 3). Study takes a new tack on asthma. *Philadelphia Inquirer,* pp. A1, A22.

Weiss, R. D., & Hufford, M. R. (1999). Substance abuse and suicide. In D.G. Jacobs (Ed.), *The Harvard Medical School guide to suicide assessment and intervention.* San Francisco: Jossey-Bass.

Weissman, M. M. (1993, Spring). The epidemiology of personality disorders. A 1990 update. *J. Pers. Disord., Suppl.,* pp. 44–62.

Weissman, M. M. (2000). Social functioning and the treatment of depression. *J. Clin. Psychiatry, 61*(Suppl.), 33–38.

Weissman, M. M., Bland, R. C., Canino, G. J., Faravelli, C., Greenwald, S., Hwu, H. G., Joyce, P. R., Karam, E. G., Lee, C., Lellouch, J., Lepine, J. P., Newman, S. C., Oakley-Browne, M. A., Rubio-Stipec, M., Wells, J. E., Wickramaratne, P. J., Wittchen, H. U., & Yeh, E. K. (1997). The cross-national epidemiology of panic disorder. *Arch. Gen. Psychiatry, 54*(4), 305–309.

Weissman, M. M., Bland, R. C., Canino, G. J., Greenwald, S., Hwu, H. G., Joyce, P. R., Karam, E. G., Lee, C. K., Lellouch, J., Lepine, J. P., Newman, S. C., Rubio-Stipec, M., Wells, J. E., Wickramaratne, P. J., Wittchen, H. U., & Yeh, E. K. (1999). Prevalence of suicide ideation and suicide attempts in nine countries. *Psychol. Med., 29*(1), 9–17.

Weissman, M. M., & Boyd, J. H. (1984). The epidemiology of mental disorders. In R. M. Post & J. C. Ballenger (Eds.), *Neurobiology of mood disorders.* Baltimore: Williams & Wilkins.

Weissman, M. M., Livingston Bruce, M., Leaf, P. J., Florio, L. P., & Holzer, C., III. (1991). Affective disorders. In L. N. Robins & D. A. Regier (Eds.), *Psychiatric disorders in America: The Epidemiologic Catchment Area Study.* New York: Free Press.

Weissman, M. M., Myers, J. K., & Harding, P. S. (1978). Psychiatric disorders in a U. S. urban community. *Am. J. Psychiatry, 135,* 459–462.

Weissman, M. M., & Olfson, M. (1995). Depression in women: Implications for health care research. *Science, 269,* 799–801.

Weissman, M. M. et al. (1992). The changing rate of major depression: Cross-national comparisons. *JAMA, J. Am. Med. Assoc., 268*(21), 3098–3105.

Weissman, R. X. (1999, February). Getting bigger all the time. Americans say they're dieting and exercising, but the bathroom scale tells a different story. *Am. Demogr.*

Weissman, R. X. (1999, July). Head's up! *Am. Demogr.*

Welch, S., & Fairburn, C. (1994). Sexual abuse and bulimia nervosa: Three integrated case control comparisons. 11th National Conference on Eating Disorders (1992, Columbus, Ohio). *Am. J. Psychiatry, 151,* 402–407.

Welch, S., & Fairburn, C. (1996). Childhood sexual and physical abuse as risk factors for the development of bulimia nervosa: A community-based case control study. *Child Abuse Neglect, 20,* 633–642.

Welch, S. S. (2001). A review of the literature on the epidemiology of parasuicide in the general population. *Psychiatr. Serv., 52*(3), 368–375.

Wells, A., Clark, M. D., Salkovskis, P., Ludgate, J. et al. (1995). Social phobia: The role of in-situation safety behaviors in maintaining anxiety and negative beliefs. *Behav. Ther., 26*(1), 153–161.

Wells, G. L., Small, M., Penrod, S., Malpass, R. S., Fulero, S. M., & Brimacombe, C. A. E. (1998). Eyewitness identification procedures: Recommendations for lineups and photospreads. *Law Hum. Behav., 22*(6), 603–647.

Wells, M. E., & Hinkle, J. S. (1990). Elimination of childhood encopresis: A family systems approach. *J. Ment. Health Counsel., 12*(4), 520–526.

Wender, P. H., Kety, S. S., Rosenthal, D., Schulsinger, F., Ortmann, J., & Lunde, I. (1986). Psychiatric disorders in the biological and adoptive families of adopted individuals with affective disorders. *Arch. Gen. Psychiatry, 43,* 923–929.

Werder, S. F. (1995). An update on the diagnosis and treatment of mania in bipolar disorder. *Am. Fam. Physician, 51*(5), 1126–1136.

Werth, J. (1995). Rational suicide reconsidered: AIDS as an impetus for change. Annual Conference of the Association for Death Education & Counseling. *Death Stud., 19*(1), 65–80.

Werth, J. (1996). *Rational suicide? Implications for mental health professionals.* Washington, DC: Taylor & Francis.

Werth, J. L., Jr. (Ed.) (1999). *Contemporary perspectives on rational suicide.* Philadelphia: Brunner/Mazel.

Werth, J.L., Jr. (1999). Introduction to the issue of rational suicide. In J. L. Werth, Jr. (Ed.), *Contemporary perspectives on rational suicide.* Philadelphia: Brunner/Mazel.

Werth, J. L., Jr. (2000). Recent developments in the debate over physician-assisted death. In R. W. Maris, S. S. Canetto et al. (Eds.), *Review of suicidology, 2000.* New York: Guilford Press.

Wertheim, E. H., Paxton, S. J., Schutz, H. K., & Muir, S. L. (1997). Why do adolescent girls watch their weight? An interview study examining sociocultural pressures to be thin. *J. Psychosom. Med., 42*(4), 345–355.

Westen, D., Feit, A., & Zittel, C. (1999). Focus chapter: Methodological issues in research using projective methods. In P. C. Kendall, J. N. Butcher et al. (Eds.), *Handbook of research methods in clinical psychology* (2nd ed.). New York: Wiley.

Westen, D., & Shedler, J. (2000). "Theoretical clinical empirical approach to classifying Axis II disorders": Reply. *Am. J. Psychiatry, 157*(2), 309.

Weston, S. C., & Siever, L. J. (1993, Spring). Biological correlates of personality disorders. *J. Pers. Disord., Suppl.,* pp. 129–148.

Weston, W. A. (1996). Pseudologia fantastica and pathological lying: A forensic issue. In L. B. Schlesinger (Ed.), *Explorations in criminal psychopathology: Clinical syndromes with forensic implications* (pp. 98–115). Springfield, IL: Thomas.

Wetherell, J. L., & Gatz, M. (2001). Recruiting anxious older adults for a psychotherapy outcome study. *J. Clin. Geropsychol., 7*(1), 29–38.

Wetterberg, L. (1999). Melatonin and clinical application. *Reprod. Nutr. Dev., 39*(3), 367–382.

Wettstein, R. M. (1988). Psychiatry and the law. In J. A. Talbott, R. E. Hales, & S. C. Yudofsky (Eds.), *American Psychiatric Press textbook of psychiatry.* Washington, DC: American Psychiatric Press.

Wettstein, R. M. (1989). Psychiatric malpractice. In A. Tasman, R. E. Hales, & A. J. Frances (Eds.), *American Psychiatric Press review of psychiatry* (Vol. 8). Washington, DC: American Psychiatric Press.

Wettstein, R. M. (1999). The right to refuse psychiatric treatment. *Psychiatr. Clin. North Am., 22*(1), 173–182.

Wexler, D. B. (1983). The structure of civil commitment. *Law Hum. Behav., 7,* 1–18.

Wexler, D. B. (1999). The broken mirror: A self psychological treatment perspective for relationship violence. *J. Psychother. Pract. Res., 8*(2), 129–141.

Whaley, A. L. (1998, January). Racism in the provision of mental health services: A social-cognitive analysis. *Am. J. Orthopsychiatry, 68*(1), 48–59.

Whipple, E. E., Webster, S. C., & Stratton, C. (1991). The role of parental stress in physically abusive families. *Child Abuse Neglect: Int. J., 15*(3), 279.

Whisman, M. A. (2001). The association between depression and marital dissatisfaction. In S. R. H. Beach (Ed.), *Marital and family processes in depression: A scientific foundation for clinical practice* (pp. 3–24). Washington, DC: American Psychological Association.

Whisman, M. A., & McGarvey, A. L. (1995). Attachment, depressotypic cognitions, and dysphoria. *Cognit. Ther. Res., 19*(6), 633–650.

Whitaker, R. (1998, November 17). Lure of riches fuels testing—Doing harm: Research on the mentally ill. *Boston Globe,* p. A1.

Whitby, P. (1996). Spider phobia control (Spider PC). *Behav. Res. Methods Instrum. Comput., 28*(1), 131–133.

Whitehead, W. E., Crowell, M. D., Heller, B. R., Robinson, J. C. et al. (1994). Modeling and reinforcement of the sick role during childhood predicts adult illness behavior. *Psychosom. Med., 56,* 541–550.

Whitehorn, J. C., & Betz, B. J. (1975). *Effective psychotherapy with the schizophrenic patient.* New York: Jason Aronson.

Whiteside, M. (1983, September 12). A bedeviling new hysteria. *Newsweek.*

Whiting, J. W. et al. (1966). I. *Field guide for a study of socialization. Six cultures series.* New York: Wiley.

Whooley, M. A., & Browner, W. S. (1998). Association between depressive symptoms and mortality in older women. Study of Osteoporotic Fractures Research Group. *Arch. Intern. Med., 158*(19), 2129–2135.

Whorley, L. W. (1996). Cognitive therapy techniques in continuing care planning with substance-dependent patients. *Addict. Behav., 21*(2), 223–231.

Whybrow, P. (1994). Of the muse and moods mundane. *Am. J. Psychiatry, 151*(4), 477–479.

Wichniak, A., Riemann, D., Kiemen, A., Voderholzer, U., & Jernajczyk, W. (2000). Comparison between eye movement latency and REM sleep parameters in major depression. *Eur. Arch. Psychiatry Clin. Neurosci., 250*(1), 48–52.

Wichstrom, L. (1999). The emergence of gender difference in depressed mood during adolescence: The role of intensified gender socialization. *Dev. Psychol., 35*(1), 232–245.

Widiger, T. A. (1992). Categorical versus dimensional classification: Implications from and for research. *J. Pers. Disord., 6,* 287–300.

Widiger, T. A. (1993). The DSM-III-R categorical personality disorder diagnoses: A critique and an alternative. *Psychol. Inquiry, 4*, 75–90.

Widiger, T. A. (2000). Personality disorders in the 21st century. *J. Pers. Disord., 14*(1), 3–16.

Widiger, T. A., & Costa, P. T. (1994). Personality and personality disorders. *J. Abnorm. Psychol., 103*(1), 78–91.

Widiger, T. A., & Sankis, L. M. (2000). Adult psychopathology: Issues and controversies. *Annu. Rev. Psychol., 51*, 377–404.

Widloecher, D. (2001). The treatment of affects: An interdisciplinary issue. *Psychoanal. Q., 70*(1), 243–264.

Widom, C. S. (1989). The cycle of violence. *Science, 244*, 160–166.

Widom, C. S. (1991, February). *Presentation.* Washington, DC: American Association for the Advancement of Science.

Widom, C. S. (2001). Child abuse and neglect. In S. O. White (Ed.), *Handbook of youth and justice* (pp. 31–47). New York: Kluwer Academic/Plenum Press.

Wiederman, M. W. (2001). "Don't look now": The role of self-focus in sexual dysfunction. *Fam. J. Counsel. Ther. Couples Fam., 9*(2), 210–214.

Wiederman, M. W., & Pryor, T. (1996). Substance use and impulsive behaviors among adolescents with eating disorders. *Addict. Behav., 21*(2), 269–272.

Wiederman, M. W., & Pryor, T. L. (2000). Body dissatisfaction, bulimia, and depression among women: The mediating role of drive for thinness. *Int. J. Eat. Disord., 27*(1), 90–95.

Wiegner, K. (1995, April 19). Shrink software. *New York Times*, p. D5.

Wiens, A. N., Mueller, E. A., & Bryan, J. E. (2001). Assessment strategies. In M. Hersen & V. B. Van Hasselt (Eds.), *Advanced abnormal psychology* (2nd ed., pp. 23–41). New York: Kluwer Academic/Plenum Press.

Wierzbicki, M., & Pekarik, G. (1993). A meta-analysis of psychotherapy dropout. *Prof. Psychol.: Res. Pract., 24*(2), 190–195.

Wiggins, J. S., & Trobst, K. K. (1997). Prospects for the assessment of normal and abnormal interpersonal behavior. *J. Pers. Assess., 68*(1), 110–126.

Wikan, U. (1991). *Managing turbulent hearts.* Chicago: University of Chicago Press.

Wilcock, M., Mackenzie, I., & Bolt, J. (1999). Country-wide survey of the repeat prescription of hypnotics. *Br. J. Psychiatry, 174*, 277.

Wilcox, J. A. (1990). Fluoxetine and bulimia. *J. Psychoact. Drugs, 22*(1), 81–82.

Wilde, E. J., Kienhorst, I. C. W. M., Diekstra, R. F. W., & Wolters, W. H. G. (1992). The relationship between adolescent suicidal behavior and life events in childhood and adolescence. *Am. J. Psychiatry, 149*, 45–51.

Wilfley, D. E., Agras, W. S., Telch, C. F., Rossiter, E. M., Schneider, J. A., Cole, A. G., Sifford, L., & Raeburn, S. D. (1993). Group cognitive-behavioral therapy and group interpersonal psychotherapy for the nonpurging bulimic individual: A controlled comparison. *J. Consult. Clin. Psychol., 61*(2), 296–305.

Wilfley, D. E., & Cohen, L. R. (1997). Psychological treatment of bulimia nervosa and binge-eating disorder. *Psychopharmacol. Bull., 33*(3), 437–454.

Wilhelm, S., Otto, M. W., Lohr, B., & Deckersbach, T. (1999). Cognitive behavior group therapy for body dysmorphic disorder: A case series. *Behav. Res. Ther., 37*(1), 71–75.

Will, O. A. (1961). Paranoid development and the concept of self: Psychotherapeutic intervention. *Psychiatry, 24*(2), 16–530.

Will, O. A. (1967). Psychological treatment of schizophrenia. In A. M. Freedman & H. I. Kaplan (Eds.), *Comprehensive textbook of psychiatry.* Baltimore: Williams & Wilkins.

Willard, W. (1979). American Indians. In L. D. Hankoff & B. Einsidler (Eds.), *Suicide: Theory and clinical aspects.* Littleton, MA: PSG Publishing.

Willershausen, B., Azrak, A., & Wilms, S. (1999). Fear of dental treatment and its possible effects on oral health. *Eur. J. Med. Res., 4*(2), 72–77.

Williams, C. C. (1983). The mental foxhole: The Viet Nam veterans' search for meaning. *Am. J. Orthopsychiatry, 53*(1), 4–17.

Williams, R. (1999). Personality and post-traumatic stress disorder. In W. Yule et al. (Eds.), *Post-traumatic stress disorders: Concepts and therapy.* Wiley series in clinical psychology. Chichester, England: Wiley.

Williams, R. B. (1989). Biological mechanisms mediating the relationship between behavior and coronary heart disease. In A. W. Siegman & T. M. Dembroski (Eds.), *In search of coronary behavior.* Hillsdale, NJ: Erlbaum.

Williams, R. B. (1989). *The trusting heart: Great news about Type A behavior.* New York: Times Books.

Williams, S. L., Kinney, P. J., Harap, S. T., & Liebmann, M. (1997). Thoughts of agoraphobic people during scary tasks. *J. Abnorm. Psychol., 106*(4), 511–520.

Williams, S. S., Michela, J. L., Contento, I. R., Gladis, M. M., & Pierce, N. T. (1996). Restrained eating among adolescents: Dieters are not always bingers and bingers are not always dieters. *Health Psychol., 15*(3), 176–184.

Williamson, D. A., Netemeyer, R. G., Jackman, L. P., Anderson, D. A. et al. (1995). Structural equation modeling of risk factors for the development of eating disorder symptoms in female athletes. *Int. J. Eat. Disord., 17*(4), 387–393.

Williamson, L. (1998). Eating disorders and the cultural forces behind the drive for thinness: Are African American women really protected? *Soc. Work Health Care, 28*(1), 61–73.

Willick, M. S. (2001). Psychoanalysis and schizophrenia: A cautionary tale. *J. Am. Psychoanal. Assoc., 49*(1), 27–56.

Willick, M. S., Milrod, D., & Karush, R. K. (1998). Psychoanalysis and the psychoses. In M. Furer, E. Nersessian et al. (Eds.), *Controversies in contemporary psychoanalysis: Lectures from the faculty of the New York Psychoanalytic Institute.* Madison, CT: International Universities Press.

Willing, R. (1998, November 19). Survey doubles rape estimate. Researchers say assaults exceed 876,000 in a year. *USA Today*, p. 3A.

Wills, T. A., McNamara, G., Vaccaro, D., & Hirky, A. E. (1996). Escalated substance use: A longitudinal grouping analysis from early to middle adolescence. *J. Abnorm. Psychol., 105*(2), 166–180.

Wilsnack, R. W., Vogeltanz, N. D., Wilsnack, S. C., & Harris, T. R. (2000). Gender differences in alcohol consumption and adverse drinking consequences: Cross-cultural patterns. *Addiction, 95*(2), 251–265.

Wilson, G. T. (1993). Psychological and pharmacological treatments of bulimia nervosa: A research update. *Appl. Prev. Psychol., 2*, 35–42.

Wilson, G. T. (1994). Behavioral treatment of obesity: Thirty years and counting. *Adv. Behav. Res. Ther., 16*, 31–75.

Wilson, G. T., Rossiter, E., Kleifield, E. I., & Lindholm, L. (1986). Cognitive-behavioral treatment of bulimia nervosa: A controlled evaluation. *Behav. Res. Ther., 24*(3), 277–288.

Wilson, K. A., & Chambless, D. L. (1999). Inflated perceptions of responsibility and obsessive-compulsive symptoms. *Behav. Res. Ther., 37*(4), 325–335.

Wilson, K. G., Hayes, S. C., & Gifford, E. V. (1997). Cognition in behavior therapy: Agreements and differences. *J. Behav. Ther. Exp. Psychiatry, 28*(1), 53–63.

Wilson, W. M. (1992). The Stanford-Binet: Fourth Edition and Form L-M in assessment of young children with mental retardation. *Ment. Retard., 30*(2), 81–84.

Wincze, J. P., & Lange, J. D. (1981). Assessment of sexual behavior. In D. H. Barlow (Ed.), *Behavioral assessment of adult disorders.* New York: Guilford Press.

Wincze, J. P., Richards, J., Parsons, J., & Bailey, S. (1996). A comparative survey of therapist sexual misconduct between an American state and an Australian state. *Prof. Psychol:. Res. Pract., 27*(3), 289–294.

Wing, L. (1976). *Early childhood autism.* Oxford, England: Pergamon Press.

Wing, L., & Wing, J. K. (1971). Multiple impairments in early childhood autism. *J. Autism Child. Schizophr., 1*, 256–266.

Winick, B. J. (1983). Incompetency to stand trial: Developments in the law. In J. Monahan & H. J. Steadman (Eds.), *Mentally disordered offenders.* New York: Plenum Press.

Winick, B. J. (1995). The side effects of incompetency labeling and the implcations for mental health law. *Psychol., Public Policy, Law, 1*, 6–42.

Winick, M., Meyer, K., & Harris, R. C. (1975). Malnutrition and environmental enrichment by early adoption. *Science*, pp. 1173–1175.

Wink, P. (1996). Narcissism. In C. G. Costello (Ed.), *Personality characteristics of the personality disordered.* New York: Wiley.

Winslade, W. J., & Ross, J. (1983). *The insanity plea.* New York: Scribner's.

Winter, L. B., Steer, R. A., Jones-Hicks, L., & Beck, A. T. (1999). Screening for major depression disorders in adolescent medical outpatients with the Beck Depression Inventory for Primary Care. *J. Adolesc. Health, 24*(6), 389–394.

Winton, M. A. (2000). The medicalization of male sexual dysfunction: An analysis of sex therapy journals. *J. Sex Educ. Ther., 25*(4), 231–239.

Wirz-Justice, A., Graw, P., Kräuchi, K., Sarrafzadeh, A. et al. (1996). "Natural" light treatment of seasonal affective disorder. *J. Affect. Disord., 37*, 109–120.

Wirz-Justice, A., & Van den Hoofdakker, R. H. (1999). Sleep deprivation in depression: What do we know, where do we go? *Biol. Psychiatry, 46*(4), 445–453.

Wise, R. A. (1996). Neurobiology of addiction. *Curr. Opin. Neurobiol., 6*, 243–251.

Wise, T. N. (1985). Fetishism—Etiology and treatment: A review from multiple perspectives. *Compr. Psychiatry, 26*, 249–257.

Wiseman, C. V., Gray, J. J., Mosimann, J. E., & Ahrens, A. H. (1992). Cultural expectations of thinness in women: An update. *Int. J. Eat. Disord., 11*(1), 85–89.

Witteman, C., & Koele, P. (1999). Explaining treatment decisions. *Psychother. Res., 9*(1), 100–114.

Wittrock, D. A., & Blanchard, E. B. (1992). Thermal biofeedback treatment of mild hypertension: A comparison of effects on conventional and ambulatory blood pressure measures. *Behav. Mod., 16*(3), 283–304.

Wittrock, D. A., Blanchard, E. B., McCoy, G. C., McCaffrey, R. J. et al. (1995). The relationship of expectancies to outcome in stress management treatment of essential hypertensions: Results from the joint USSR-USA Behavioral Hypertension Project. *Biofeedback Self-Regul., 20*(1), 51–68.

Wlazlo, Z., Schroeder-Hartwig, K., Hand, I., Kaiser, G., & Munchau, N. (1990). Exposure in vivo vs. social skills training for social phobia: Long term outcome and differential effects. *Behav. Res. Ther., 28*, 181–193.

Wolberg, L. R. (1967). *The technique of psychotherapy.* New York: Grune & Stratton.

Wolfe, D. A., Edwards, B., Manion, I., & Koverola, C. (1988). Early intervention for parents at risk for child abuse and neglect: A preliminary investigation. *J. Consult. Clin. Psychol., 56*, 40–47.

Wolfe, J. K. L., & Fodor, I. G. (1977). Modifying assertive behavior in women: Comparison of three approaches. *Behav. Ther., 8*, 567–574.

Wolfe, J. L., & Russianoff, P. (1997). Overcoming self-negation in women. *J. Ration.-Emotive Cognit.-Behav. Ther., 15*(1), 81–92.

Wolfe, S. M., Fugate, L., Hulstrand, E. P., & Kamimoto, L. E. (1988). *Worst pills best pills: The older adult's guide to avoiding drug-induced death or illness.* Washington, DC: Public Citizen Health Research Group.

Wolfensberger, W. (1972). *The principle of normalization in human services.* Toronto: National Institute on Mental Retardation.

Wolff, N., Helminiak, T. W., Morse, G. A., Calsyn, R. J. et al. (1997). Cost-effectiveness evaluation of three approaches to case management for homeless mentally ill clients. *Am. J. Psychiatry, 154*(3), 341–348.

Wolff, S. (1991). Schizoid personality in childhood and adult life I: The vagaries of diagnostic labeling. *Br. J. Psychiatry, 159*, 615–620.

Wolpe, J. (1958). *Psychotherapy by reciprocal inhibition.* Stanford, CA: Stanford University Press.

Wolpe, J. (1969). *The practice of behavior therapy.* Oxford, England: Pergamon Press.

Wolpe, J. (1987). The promotion of scientific psychotherapy: A long voyage. In J. K. Zeig (Ed.), *The evolution of psychotherapy.* New York: Brunner/Mazel.

Wolpe, J. (1990). *The practice of behavior therapy* (4th ed.). Elmsford, NY: Pergamon Press.

Wolpe, J. (1997). From psychoanalytic to behavioral methods in anxiety disorders: A continuing evolution. In J. K. Zeig (Ed.), *The evolution of psychotherapy: The third conference.* New York: Brunner/Mazel.

Wolpe, J. *The case of Mrs. Schmidt* [Transcript and record]. Nashville, TN: Counselor Recording and Tests.

Wolpe, J., & Plaud, J. J. (1997). Pavlov's contributions to behavior therapy. *Am. Psychol., 52*(9), 966–972.

Woo, S. M., Goldstein, M. J., & Nuechterlein, K. H. (1997). Relatives' expressed emotion and non-verbal signs of subclinical psychopathology in schizophrenic patients. *Br. J. Psychiatry, 170*, 58–61.

Wood, J. M., Nezworski, M. T., & Stejskal, W. J. (1996). The comprehensive system for the Rorschach: A critical examination. *Psychol. Sci., 7*(1), 3–10

Woodside, M. R., & Legg, B. H. (1990). Patient advocacy: A mental health perspective. *J. Ment. Health Counsel., 12*(1), 38–50.

Woodward, B., Duckworth, K. S., & Gutheil, T. G. (1993). The pharmacotherapist-psychotherapist collaboration. In J. M. Oldham, M. B. Riba, & A. Tasman (Eds.), *Review of psychiatry* (Vol. 12). Washington, DC: American Psychiatric Press.

Woodward, S. H., Drescher, K. D., Murphy, R. T., Ruzek, J. I. et al. (1997). Heart rate during group flooding therapy for PTSD. *Integr. Physiol. Behav. Sci., 32*(1), 19–30.

Woody, G. E., McLellan, A. T., & Bedrick, J. (1995). Dual diagnosis. In J. M. Oldham & M. B. Riba (Eds.), *American Psychiatric Press review of psychiatry* (Vol. 14). Washington, DC: American Psychiatric Press.

Woody, G. E., McLellan, A. T., Luborsky, L., & O'Brien, C. P. (1998). Psychotherapy with opioid-dependent patients. *Psychiatr. Times, 15*(11).

Woody, S. R., Chambless, D. L., & Glass, C. R. (1997). Self-focused attention in the treatment of social phobia. *Behav. Res. Ther., 35*(2), 117–129.

Wooley, S. C., & Wooley, O. W. (1985). Intensive outpatient and residential treatment for bulimia. In D. M. Garner & P. E. Garfinkel (Eds.), *Handbook of psychotherapy for anorexia nervosa and bulimia.* New York: Guilford Press.

Woolfolk, R. L., Carr-Kaffashan, L., McNulty, T. F., & Lehrer, P. M. (1976). Meditation training as a treatment for insomnia. *Behav. Ther. 7*(3), 359–365.

World Health Organization. (1948). World Health Organization constitution. In *Basic documents.* Geneva: Author.

Worrel, J. A., Marken, P. A., Beckman, S. E., & Ruehter, V. L. (2000). Atypical antipsychotic agents: A critical review. *Am. J. Health Syst. Pharmacol., 57*(3), 238–255.

Wozniak, J., Biederman, J., Faraone, S. V., Blier, H., & Monuteaux, M. C. (2001). Heterogeneity of childhood conduct disorder. Further evidence of a subtype of conduct disorder linked to bipolar disorder. *J. Affect. Disord., 64*(2–3), 121–131.

Wragg, M., Hutton, M., Talbot, C., & Alzheimer's Disease Collaborative Group. (1996). Genetic association between intronic polymorphism in presenilin-1 gene and late-onset Alzheimer's disease. *Lancet, 347*, 509–512.

Wright, I. C., Rabe, H. S., Woodruff, P. W. R., David, A. S., Murray, R. M., & Bullmore, E. T. (2000). Meta-analysis of regional brain volumes in schizophrenia. *Am. J. Psychiatry, 157*(1), 16–25.

Wright, J. (1984). EAP: An important supervisory tool. *Supervisory Manag., 29*(12), 16–17.

Wrobleski, A. (1999). "Rational suicide": A contradiction in terms. In J. L. Werth, Jr. et al. (Eds.), *Contemporary perspectives on rational suicide. Series in death, dying, and bereavement.* Philadelphia: Brunner/Mazel.

Wu, J., Kramer, G. L., Kram, M., Steciuk, M., Crawford, I. L., & Petty, F. (1999). Serotonin and learned helplessness: A regional study of 5–HT-sub(1A), 5–HT-sub(2A) receptors and the serotonin transport site in rat brain. *J. Psychiatr. Res., 33*(1), 17–22.

Wu, X., & DeMaris, A. (1996). Gender and marital status differences in depression: The effects of chronic strains. *Sex Roles, 34*(5–6), 299–319.

Wulsin, L., Bachop, M., & Hoffman, D. (1988). Group therapy in manic-depressive illness. *Am. J. Psychother., 42*, 263–271.

Wulsin, L. R., Vaillant, G. E., & Wells, V. E. (1999). A systematic review of the mortality of depression. *Psychosom. Med., 61*(1), 6–17.

Wunderlich, U., Bronisch, T., & Wittchen, H. U. (1998). Comorbidity patterns in adolescents and young adults with suicide attempts. *Eur. Arch. Psychiatry Clin. Neurosci., 248*(2), 87–95.

Wurtele, S. K., & Schmitt, A. (1992). Child care workers' knowledge about reporting suspected child sexual abuse. *Child Abuse Neglect, 16*(3) 385–390.

Wurtman, J. J. (1987). Disorders of food intake: Excessive carbohydrate snack intake among a class of obese people. *Ann. N. Y. Acad. Sci., 499*, 197–202.

Wurtman, R. (1995, October 17). Interview cited in Roan., S., Super pill. *Los Angeles Times*, pp. E1–E5.

Wyatt, R. J. (1995). Risks of withdawing antipsychotic medications. *Arch. Gen. Psychiatry, 52*(3), 205–208.

Wysoker, A. (1999). Thoughts for the millenium: The rights of the mentally ill. *J. Am. Psychiatry Nurs. Assoc., 5*(6), 197–200.

Wysoker, A. (2001). Confidentiality. *J. Am. Psychiatr. Nurs. Assoc., 7*(2), 57–58.

Yabe, K., Tsukahar, R., Mita, K., & Aoki, H. (1985). Developmental trends of jumping reaction time by means of EMG in mentally retarded children. *J. Ment. Def. Res., 29*(2), 137–145.

Yager, J. (1985). The outpatient treatment of bulimia. *Bull. Menninger Clin., 49*(3), 203–226.

Yager, J., Rorty M., & Rossoto E. (1995). Coping styles differ between recovered and nonrecovered women with bulimia nervosa, but not between recovered women and non-eating-disordered control subjects. *J. Nerv. Ment. Dis., 183*(2), 86–94.

Yalom, I. D. (1985). *The theory and practice of group psychotherapy* (3rd ed.). New York: Basic Books.

Yama, M., Fogas, B., Teegarden, L., & Hastings, B. (1993). Childhood sexual abuse and parental alcoholism: Interactive effects in adult women. *Am. J. Orthopsychiatry, 63*(2), 300–305.

Yang, B., & Lester, D. (1995). Suicidal behavior and employment. In S. S. Canetto & D. Lester (Eds.), *Women and suicidal behavior.* New York: Springer.

Yang, B., Stack, S., & Lester, D. (1992). Suicide and unemployment: Predicting the smoothed trend and yearly fluctuations. *J. Socioecon., 21*(1), 39–41.

Yank, G. R., Bentley, K. J., & Hargrove, D. S. (1993). The vulnerability-stress model of schizophrenia: Advances in psychosocial treatment. *Am. J. Orthopsychiatry, 63*(1), 55–69.

Yankelovich Youth Monitor. (1994, January 10). Survey: What children fear. Cited in *Newsweek*, p. 50.

Yehuda, R., Giller, E. L., Southwick, S. M. et al. (1994). The relationship between catecholamine excretion and PTSD symptoms in Vietnam combat veterans and Holocaust survivors. In M. M. Marburg (Ed.), *Catecholamine function in post-traumatic stress disorder.* Washington, DC: American Psychiatric Press.

Yehuda, R., Kahana, B., Binder-Brynes, K., Southwick, S. M. et al. (1995). Low urinary cortisol excretion in Holocaust survivors with posttraumatic stress disorder. *Am. J. Psychiatry, 152*(7), 982–986.

Yehuda, R., McFarlane, A. C., & Shalev, A. Y. (1998). Predicting the development of posttraumatic stress disorder from the acute response to a traumatic event. *Biol. Psychiatry, 44*(12), 1305–1313.

Yeung, W. J. (1999, June 11). Dads spending more time with kids. Interviewed in *Reuters Health.*

Yewchuk, C. (1999). Savant syndrome: Intuitive excellence amidst general deficit. *Dev. Disabil. Bull., 27*(1), 58–76.

Yoder, K. A., Hoyt, D. R., & Whitbeck, L. B. (1998). Suicidal behavior among homeless and runaway adolescents. *J. Youth Adolesc., 27*(6), 753–771.

Yolken, R. H., Karlsson, H., Yee, F., Johnston-Wilson, N. L., & Torrey, E. F. (2000). Endogenous retroviruses and schizophrenia. *Brain Res. Rev., 31*(2–3), 193–199.

Yontef, G. (1998). Dialogic gestalt therapy. In L. S. Greenberg, J. C. Watson et al. (Eds.), *Handbook of experiential psychotherapy.* New York: Guilford Press.

Yost, E., Beutler, L., Corbishley, A. M., & Allender, J. (1986). *Group cognitive therapy: A treatment approach for depressed older adults.* New York: Pergamon Press.

Young, E., & Korszun, A. (1999). Women, stress, and depression: Sex differences in hypothalamic-pituitary-adrenal axis regulation. In E. Leibenluft et al. (Eds.), *Gender differences in mood and anxiety disorders: From bench to bedside. Review of psychiatry series* (Vol. 18, No. 3). Washington, DC: American Psychiatric Press.

Young, E. A., Abelson, J. L., Curtis, G. C., & Nesse, R. M. (1997). Childhood adversity and vulnerability to mood and anxiety disorders. *Depression Anxiety, 5*, 66–72.

Young, J. E., Beck, A. T., & Weinberger, A. (1993). Depression. In D. H. Barlow (Ed.), *Clinical handbook of psychological disorders: A step-by-step treatment manual* (2nd ed.). New York: Guilford Press.

Young, K. S. (1996). Cited in Middle-aged women are more at risk for Internet addiction. *APA Monitor, 27*(10), 10.

Young, K. S. (1996). Psychology of computer use: XL. Addictive use of the Internet: A case that breaks the stereotype. *Psychol. Rep., 79*(3, Pt. 1), 899–902.

Young, K. S. (1998). Internet addiction: The emergence of a new clinical disorder. *CyberPsychol. Behav., 1*(3), 237–244.

Young, K. S. (1999). Evaluation and treatment of Internet addiction. In L. VandeCreek & T. L. Jackson (Eds.), *Innovations in clinical practice: A source book* (Vol. 17, pp. 19–31). Sarasota, FL: Professional Resource Press/Professional Resource Exchange.

Young, M., Benjamin, B., & Wallis, C. (1963). Mortality of widowers. *Lancet, 2*, 454–456.

Young, T. J. (1991). Suicide and homicide among Native Americans: Anomie or social learning? *Psychol. Rep., 68*(3, Pt. 2), 1137–1138.

Young, W. C., Young, L. J., & Lehl, K. (1991). Restraints in the treatment of dissociative disorders: A follow-up of twenty patients. *Dissoc. Prog. Dissoc. Disord., 4*(2), 74–78.

Youngren, M. A., & Lewinsohn, P. M. (1980). The functional relation between depression and problematic interpersonal behavior. *J. Abnorm. Psychol., 89*(3), 333–341.

Youngstrom, N. (1990). Six offender types are identified. *APA Monitor, 21*(10), 21.

Youngstrom, N. (1992). Grim news from national study of rape. *APA Monitor, 23*(7), 38.

Youngstrom, N. (1992). Psychology helps a shattered L. A. *APA Monitor, 23*(7), 1, 12.

Yudofsky, S., Silver, J., & Hales, R. (1993). Cocaine and aggressive behavior: Neurobiological and clinical perspectives. *Bull. Menninger Clin., 57*(2), 218–226.

Yule, W., Perrin, S., & Smith, P. (2001). Traumatic events and post-traumatic stress disorder. In W. K. Silverman & P. D. A. Treffers (Eds.), *Anxiety disorders in children and adolescents: Research, assessment and intervention* (pp. 212–234). New York: Cambridge University Press.

Yuwiler, A., Shih, J. C., Chen, C., & Ritvo, E. R. (1992). Hyperserotoninemia and antiserotonin antibodies in autism and other disorders. *J. Autism Dev. Disord., 22*(1), 33–45.

Zacharakis, C. A., Madianos, M. G., Papadimitriou, G. N., & Stefanis, C. N. (1998). Suicide in Greece 1980–1995: Patterns and social factors. *Soc. Psychiatry Psychiatr. Epidemiol., 33*(10), 471–476.

Zal, H. M. (1999). Agitation in the elderly. *Psychiatr. Times, 16*(1).

Zamichow, N. (1993, February 15). The dark corner of psychology. *Los Angeles Times*, p. A1.

Zapf, P. A., & Roesch, R. (2001). A comparison of MacCAT-CA and the FIT for making determinations of competency to stand trial. *Int. J. Law Psychiatry, 24*(1), 81–92.

Zarin, D. A., Pincus, H. A., Peterson, B. D., West, J. C., Suarez, A. P., Marcus, S. C., & McIntyre, J. S. (1998). Characterizing psychiatry with findings from the 1996 national survey of psychiatric practice. *Am. J. Psychiatry, 155*(3), 397–404.

Zaubler, T. S., & Katon, W. (1998). Panic disorder in the general medical setting. *J. Psychosom. Res., 44*(1), 25–42.

Zax, M., & Cowen, E. L. (1969). Research on early detection and prevention of emotional dysfunction in young school children. In C. D. Speilberger (Ed.), *Current topics in clinical and community psychology* (Vol. 1). New York: Academic Press.

Zax, M., & Cowen, E. L. (1976). *Abnormal psychology: Changing conceptions*. New York: Holt, Rinehart & Winston.

Zemishlany, Z., Alexander, G. E., Prohovnik, I., Goldman, R. G., Mukherjee, S., & Sackeim, H. (1996). Cortical blood flow and negative symptoms in schizophrenia. *Neuropsychobiology, 33*, 127–131.

Zerbe, K. J. (1990). Through the storm: Psychoanalytic theory in the psychotherapy of the anxiety disorders. *Bull. Menninger Clin., 54*(2), 171–183.

Zerbe, K. J. (1993). Whose body is it anyway? Understanding and treating psychosomatic aspects of eating disorders. *Bull. Menninger Clin., 57*(2), 161–177.

Zerssen, D. et al. (1985). Circadian rhythms in endogenous depression. *Psychiatr. Res., 16*, 51–63.

Zhang, M., He, Y., Gittelman, M., Wong, Z., & Yan, H. (1998). Group psychoeducation of relatives of schizophrenic patients: Two-year experiences. *Psychiatry Clin. Neurosci., 52*(Suppl.), S344–S347.

Zhou, J.-N., Hofman, M. A., Gooren, L. J. G., & Swaab, D. F. (1995). A sex difference in the human brain and its relation to transsexuality. *Nature, 378*, 68–70.

Ziedonis, D., Williams, J., Corrigan, P., & Smelson, D. (2000). Management of substance abuse in schizophrenia. *Psychiatr. Ann., 30*(1), 67–75.

Zigler, E., & Hodapp, R. M. (1991). Behavioral functioning in individuals with mental retardation. *Annu. Rev. Psychol., 42*, 29–50.

Zigler, E., Taussig, C., & Black, K. (1992). Early childhood intervention: A promising preventative for juvenile delinquency. *Am. Psychol., 47*(8), 997–1006.

Zigman, W. B., Schupf, N., Sersen, E., & Silverman, W. (1995). Prevalence of dementia in adults with and without Down syndrome. *Am. J. Ment. Retard., 100*(4), 403–412.

Zilbergeld, B. (1978). *Male sexuality*. Boston: Little, Brown.

Zilboorg, G., & Henry, G. W. (1941). *A history of medical psychology*. New York: Norton.

Zill, N., & Schoenborn, C. A. (1990, November). *Developmental, learning, and emotional problems: Health of our nation's children, United States, 1988* (No. 190). Advance Data: National Center for Health Statistics.

Zima, B. T., Wells, K. B., Benjamin, B., & Duan, N. (1996). Mental health problems among homeless mothers. *Arch. Gen. Psychiatry, 53*, 332–338.

Zimbardo, P. (1976). *Rational paths to madness*. Presentation at Princeton University, Princeton, NJ.

Zimmerman, M., & Coryell, W. (1989). DSM-III personality disorder diagnoses in a nonpatient sample: Demographic correlates and comorbidity. *Arch. Gen. Psychiatry, 46*(8), 682–689.

Zito, J. M., Safer, D. J., dos Reis, S., Gardner, J. F., Boles, M., & Lynch, F. (2000). Trends in prescribing of psychotropic medications to preschoolers. *JAMA, J. Am. Med. Assoc., 283*(8), 1025–1030.

Zohar, J., & Pato, M. T. (1991). Diagnostic considerations. In M. T. Pato & J. Zohar (Eds.), *Current treatments of obsessive-compulsive disorder*. Washington, DC: American Psychiatric Press.

Zucker, K. J. (2000). Gender identity disorder. In A. J. Sameroff, M. Lewis et al. (Eds.), *Handbook of developmental psychopathology* (2nd ed., pp. 671–686). New York: Kluwer Academic/Plenum Press.

Zuckerman, M. (1978). Sensation seeking and psychopathy. In R. D. Hare & D. Schalling (Eds.), *Psychopathic behavior: Approaches to research*. New York: Wiley.

Zuckerman, M. (1989). Personality in the third dimension: A psychobiological approach. *Pers. Individual Differ., 10*, 391–418.

Zuckerman, M. (1996). Sensation seeking. In C. G. Costello (Ed.), *Personality characteristics of the personality disordered*. New York: Wiley.

Zuravin, S. J., & Fontanella, C. (1999). The relationship between child sexual abuse and major depression among low-income women: A function of growing up experiences? *Child Maltreat.: J. Am. Prof. Soc. Abuse Child., 4*(1), 3–12.

Zwaigenbaum, L., Szatmari, P., Boyle, M. H., & Offord, D. R. (1999). Highly somatizing young adolescents and the risk of depression. *Pediatrics, 103*(6) 1203–1209.

name index

subject index*

ABAB design, 27
Abnormal psychology, 2. *See also* Psychological abnormality
definition of, 3
Absentmindedness, 390b
Abuse. *See* Child abuse; Domestic violence; Sexual abuse
Acetylcholine, in Alzheimer's disease, 400
Acquired immunodeficiency syndrome
psychological complications of, 237b
substance abuse and, 283, 302
Acute stress disorder, 143. *See also* Stress disorders
Addiction. *See also* Substance abuse
definition of, 274
Addington v. Texas, 485
s-Adenosylmethionine (SAMe), 167
Adjunctive psychotherapy, 91, 186–187
Adjustment disorders, 96b
Adolescents. *See also* Children
binge drinking by, 279b
criminal behavior of, 446–447, 447f
eating disorders in. *See* Eating disorders
school shootings and, 448b, 486f
sexual behavior of, 312b
substance abuse rates for, 277, 277f
suicide by, 207–208
Adrenal glands, 98
Aerophobia, 114
Affect
blunted/flat, in schizophrenia, 351
inappropriate, in schizophrenia, 351
Affective inventories, 76, 76t
Affectual awareness, 326
African Americans. *See* Race/ethnicity
Aftercare, 370
Age, suicide and, 196, 197f
Aggression
cultural differences in, 417f
mental illness and, 485–486
modeling of, 453b
predictors of, 485–486
against psychologists, 496b
serotonin and, 206
stress disorders and, 145–147, 150b
suicide and, 198
Aggressive id impulses, 137
Agoraphobia, 113, 128–129
Agranulocytosis, antipsychotics and, 367
AIDS
psychological complications of, 237b
substance abuse and, 283, 302
AIDS dementia complex, 237b
Alcohol, 275–280
blood levels of, 276–277, 276t
effects of, 275–277
Alcohol abuse/dependence, 275–280
in adolescents and young adults, 277, 277f, 279b
Alcoholics Anonymous for, 303–304, 303b
binge drinking and, 279b
causes of, 293–298
cultural factors in, 278
delirium tremens in, 278
detoxification in, 300
disulfiram (Antabuse) for, 301

in elderly, 468
fetal alcohol syndrome and, 280, 464
genetic factors in, 296–297
health problems in, 278, 279–280
Korsakoff's syndrome and, 280, 395–396
patterns of, 278
personal and social consequences of, 278–280, 281t
in pregnancy, 280, 464
prevalence of, 277–278, 294t
risks and consequences of, 278–280, 281t
suicide and, 199, 200
treatment of, 298–305
withdrawal in, 278
Alcohol dehydrogenase, 276–277
Alcoholics Anonymous, 303–304, 303b
Alogia, 351
Alprazolam (Xanax), 36
for panic disorder, 131, 132–133
Alternate personalities, 384–386
Altruistic suicide, 203–204
Alzheimer's disease, 399–400, 399t. *See also* Dementia
brain lesions in, 399–400, 400f
causes of, 400
prevention of, 402–403
treatment of, 401–403
Amenorrhea, in anorexia nervosa, 249, 266
American Law Institute test, 477
American Psychological Association (APA), code of ethics of, 492–493
Amnesia
anterograde, 394t, 395
continuous, 381, 394t
dissociative, 380–381, 380t
treatment of, 391
generalized, 381, 394t
hypnotic, 389
localized, 380, 394t
retrograde, 394t, 395
selective, 380–381, 394t
Amnestic disorders, 394t, 395–396, 395t
treatment of, 401–403
Amnestic episode, 380
Amniocentesis, 463
Amphetamine abuse, 281t, 287–288. *See also* Substance abuse
Amphetamine psychosis, 356–357
Amygdala, 33, 33f
age-related changes in, 400f
in memory, 394
Amytal (sodium amobarbital), for dissociative disorders, 391, 392
Anafranil (clomipramine), for obsessive-compulsive disorder, 141, 142
Analogue experiments, 26
Anal regressive, 435
Anal stage, 39, 137, 435, 442
Anandamides, 297
Anesthesia, memory during, 390b
Animal experiments, 24b
Anomic suicide, 203–204
Anorexia nervosa, 245–249
age at onset of, 246
amenorrhea in, 249, 266
in athletes, 247b, 253b, 256f

binge-eating/purging-type, 246
biological factors in, 261–262
body image in, 248, 248b
vs. bulimia nervosa, 253–255, 254t
cognitive disturbances and, 258–260, 265
definition of, 245
depression and, 260–261, 269
diagnostic criteria for, 246t
distorted thinking in, 248
ego deficiencies and, 258–260
family factors in, 258, 265
gender and, 246
medical problems in, 249, 255
outcome in, 266–267
preoccupation with food in, 246–248
prevention of, 269
psychological problems in, 248–249
recurrence of, 267
restricting-type, 246
social pressures and, 255–258
support groups for, 270
symptoms of, 246, 254t
treatment of, 262–266, 264–267
Antabuse (disulfiram), 301
Anterograde amnesia, 394t, 395
Antiandrogens, for paraphilias, 331
Antianxiety drugs, 36, 109, 110–111, 111t
abuse of, 280–281
for elderly, 468
for stress disorders, 149
Antibipolar drugs, 36
Anticonvulsives, for bipolar disorder, 186
Antidepressants, 36, 165–167, 165t, 166f
for body dysmorphic disorder, 227–228
for bulimia nervosa, 269
continuation therapy for, 165
MAO inhibitor, 165, 165t
for obsessive-compulsive disorder, 141, 142
for panic disorder, 130
second-generation, 165, 165t, 166
selective norepinephrine reuptake inhibitor, 166–167
selective serotonin reuptake inhibitor, 165t, 166–167
sexual dysfunction and, 319
for social phobia, 121
tricyclic, 165–166, 165t, 166f
Antigens, 236
Antipsychotic drugs, 36, 364–367
agranulocytosis and, 367
atypical, 357, 365, 365t, 366–367
conventional, 365, 365t
discovery of, 356, 364–365
effectiveness of, 365–366
extrapyramidal effects of, 366
Parkinsonian symptoms and, 356, 366
side effects of, 366, 367
tardive dyskinesia and, 366
types of, 365t
Antiseizure drugs, for bipolar disorder, 186
Antisocial personality disorder, 409f, 415–419, 484b
Anxiety, 95–96
antisocial personality disorder and, 418
definition of, 95
eating disorders and, 260–261

*Note: Page numbers followed by f indicate figures, those followed by b indicate boxed material, and those followed by t indicate tables.

subject index | SI–1

Fetal alcohol syndrome, 280, 464
Fetal memory, 390b
Fetishism, 331–332
    transvestic, 332–333
Fixation, 38
Flashbacks, LSD, 289
Flat affect, 351
Flooding, 120, 121
Fluoxetine (Prozac), 36, 166, 167b
    for dogs, 167b
    for obsessive-compulsive disorder, 141, 142
    for premature ejaculation, 328
Fluvoxamine (Luvox), for obsessive-
        compulsive disorder, 141, 142
Forced feeding, for anorexia nervosa, 264
Forebrain, 33, 33f
Formal thought disorders, in schizophrenia,
    348–349
Foucha v. Louisiana, 478–480
Fragile X syndrome, 463
Free association, 40–41
Free-basing, 286
Free-floating anxiety, 99
Freudian theory, 13–14, 37–39
Frontal cortex, orbital, in obsessive-
    compulsive disorder, 141, 141f
Frotteurism, 334
Fugue, dissociative, 382–384
    treatment of, 391

GABA (gamma-aminobutyric acid)
    alcohol and, 276, 297
    in anxiety disorders, 34
    generalized anxiety disorder and, 109–110,
        111
GABA-A receptors, 111
Galvanic skin responses, 76, 77, 119, 427b
Gambling, 422b
Gamma-aminobutyric acid (GABA). *See*
    GABA (gamma-aminobutyric acid)
Gastric ulcers, 229
Gender
    depression and, 158, 162t, 172b–173b
    generalized anxiety disorder and, 109t
    obsessive-compulsive disorder and, 130t,
        134
    panic disorder and, 129, 130t
    psychological abnormalities and, 57
    schizophrenia and, 345–346
    sexual attitudes and, 320b, 321f, 325f
    stress disorders and, 130t, 144
    suicide and, 196, 197f
Gender identity disorder, 338–341, 338t
Generalized amnesia, 381
Generalized anxiety disorder, 99–113. *See
    also* Anxiety; Anxiety disorders
    age at onset of, 109t
    biofeedback for, 111–112, 112f
    biologic perspective on, 109–112
    client-centered therapy for, 104
    cognitive perspective on, 105–108
    cognitive therapy for, 107–108
    definition of, 99
    diagnostic criteria for, 99t
    diathesis-stress model for, 123–124
    drug therapy for, 109, 110–111, 111t

existential perspective on, 104–105
    gender and, 109t
    humanistic perspective on, 103–104
    prevalence of, 100, 109t
    psychodynamic perspective on, 101–103
    psychodynamic therapy for, 102–103
    rational-emotive therapy for, 107–108
    relaxation training for, 111–112
    sociocultural perspective on, 100, 101f
General paresis, 12
Genes, 34
    recessive, 463
Genetic factors. *See also* Family pedigree
        studies; Twin studies
    in psychological abnormality, 34
Genetic linkage studies, 185
    of schizophrenia, 355–356
Genitals
    female, 310f
    male, 317f
Genital stage, 39, 442
Geschwind's syndrome, 69b
Gestalt therapy, 52–53
Ginkgo biloba, 35b
Global assessment of functioning, 84–85
Glove anesthesia, 223, 223f
Glucagon-like peptide (GLP-1)
    in eating disorders, 261–262
    in obesity, 262b
Glutamate, in Alzheimer's disease, 400
Greece, ancient, psychological theory and
        treatment in, 8–9
Grief, 169b
    depression and, 167–168
Group homes, 370–371
Group suicide, 10b, 194
Group therapy, 58–59
    for social phobia, 121, 122
Guilty but mentally ill verdict, 480
Guilty with diminished capacity verdict,
    480–481
Gustatory hallucinations, 350

Habitual lying, 424b
Habituation training, 140–141
Halfway houses, 370–371
Hallucinations
    auditory, 349–350
    in depression, 161
    in schizophrenia, 349–351
Hallucinogens, 288–289
Hallucinosis, 274
Haloperidol (Haldol), 36
Happiness, correlates of, 179b
Hashish, 289
Headache
    migraine, 230
    muscle contraction, 230
Head injuries, memory impairment in, 396
Health problems. *See* Physical disorders
Heart attack, 230
Heart disease, 230
    personality type and, 232–233
Heaven's Gate cult, 10b, 194, 213f
Helper T-cells, 236, 236f
Helplessness, learned, 171–174

Herbal remedies, 35b, 167
Heroin, 281–283, 281t. *See also* Substance
        abuse
    methadone for, 282, 301–302
Hippocampus, 33, 33f
    age-related changes in, 400f
    in memory, 394
Hispanics. *See* Race/ethnicity
Histrionic personality disorder, 409f, 420t,
    423–425
HIV infection
    psychological complications of, 237b
    substance abuse and, 283, 302
Homelessness, 15, 372–373, 373b
Homosexuality, 340b
Hopelessness
    depression and, 174
    suicide and, 198–199
Hormones, 34, 98
    in depression, 162–163, 172b
    sex, 313. *See also* Estrogen; Testosterone
    stress and, 236–238
    supplemental, 35b
Hormone therapy
    for paraphilias, 331
    for transsexualism, 339
Hospitalization/institutionalization
    for Alzheimer's disease, 403
    civil commitment and, 483–488
    deinstitutionalization and, 15, 15f, 369
    for elderly, 470
    for mentally retarded, 464–465
    partial, 370
    for schizophrenia, 361–365, 369–370
    short-term, 15, 370
    for substance abuse, 304
Human immunodeficiency virus infection
    psychological complications of, 237b
    substance abuse and, 283, 302
Humanism, 50
Humanistic-existential model, 50–55, 63t
    assessment of, 54–55
    client-centered therapy and, 51–52
    existentialism and, 50–51
    existential therapy and, 54
    gestalt therapy and, 52–53
    humanism and, 50
    self-actualization in, 50
    unconditional positive regard in, 51, 52
Humors, 8, 8f
Huntington's disease, 33, 401
Hypersomnia, 232b
Hypertension, 230
Hypertrichosis, congenital generalized, 353b
Hyperventilation, in panic disorder, 132
Hypnosis, 13, 240–241
    self-induced, 389–390
Hypnotherapy, for dissociative disorders,
    391
Hypnotic amnesia, 389
Hypoactive sexual desire, 311–313, 311t
    sex therapy for, 326–327
Hypochondriasis, 223–224, 224t. *See also*
        Somatoform disorders
Hypothalamus, 33, 33f
    age-related changes in, 400f

Masochism, sexual, 335–336
Mass madness, 9, 62f
Mass suicide, 10b, 194, 213f
Masturbatory satiation, 332
Matched control subjects, 25
MDMA (ecstasy), 289
Medical disorders. *See* Physical disorders
Medical model. *See* Biological model
Medical symptoms, vs. hysterical symptoms, 223
Medications. *See* Drug(s)
Meditation, 111–112, 240
Medulla, 33, 33f
Melatonin, 35b
   depression and, 163
Memory
   during anesthesia, 390b
   arousal and, 389
   auditory, 390b
   biochemistry of, 394
   biology of, 393–394
   brain structures in, 394
   consolidation of, 393
   declarative, 393, 394t
   definition of, 379–380
   encoding of, 393
   impaired
      in amnestic disorders, 394t, 395–396, 395t
      in dementias, 394t, 396–401
      in dissociative disorders, 380–393, 394t
      in head trauma, 396
      in organic disorders, 393–404, 394t
   long-term, 393
   long-term potentiation in, 394
   for music, 390b
   peculiarities of, 390b
   prenatal, 390b
   procedural, 393, 394t
   repressed childhood, 383b
   retrieval of, 393
   short-term, 393
   state-dependent learning and, 388–389
   storage of, 393–394
   visual, 390b
Memory disorders
   dissociative, 380–393, 394t
   organic, 393–404, 394t
Memory recovery techniques, 392
Men. *See also* Gender
   eating disorders in, 253b
Ménière's syndrome, 69b
Mental illness. *See* Psychological abnormality
Mental incompetence, 481–482
Mentally ill chemical abusers, 370
Mental retardation, 459–466
   assessment in, 459–460, 459t
   causes of, 463–464
   characteristics of, 460–462
   in chromosomal disorders, 463
   classification of, 461–462
   diagnostic criteria for, 459, 459t
   in Down syndrome, 463
   DSM-IV classification of, 84
   education in, 465

in fetal alcohol syndrome, 280, 464
IQ in, 459–460, 459t
living situations for, 464–465
marriage in, 466
in metabolic disorders, 463
mild, 461–462
moderate, 462
profound, 462
psychological abnormalities in, 465
severe, 462
social needs in, 465–466
socioeconomic status and, 462, 462f
Mental status exam, 71
Meprobamate (Miltown), 110–111
Mesmerism, 13
Meta-analysis, 90
Metabolic disorders, mental retardation in, 463
Methadone, 282, 301–302
Methamphetamine, 281t, 287–288
Methylenedioxmethamphetamine (MDMA), 289
Methylphenidate (Ritalin), 451, 451f
Metrazol, 163
Mexican Americans. *See* Race/ethnicity
Midbrain, 33, 33f
Middle Ages, psychological theory and treatment in, 9
Mighty Morphin Power Rangers, 453b
Migraine headache, 230
Milieu therapy, for schizophrenia, 363
Mind-body dualism, 218
Minimal brain damage, 450–451
Minnesota Multiphasic Personality Inventory (MMPI), 74–76, 75f
Minorities. *See* Race/ethnicity
Minor tranquilizers, 36
Misdiagnosis, 86–87
Mixed experiments, 25
MMPI (Minnesota Multiphasic Personality Inventory), 74–76, 75f
Modeling, 44, 45f
   of aggression, 453b
   antisocial personality disorder and, 418
   participant, 120
   phobias and, 117, 120–121
   of suicide, 200–202, 209
Models. *See also* Psychological abnormality, models of
   definition of, 32
Monoamine oxidase (MAO) inhibitors, 165, 165t
Mood disorders, 156–188. *See also* Bipolar disorder; Depression
   causes of, 187–188
   creativity and, 184b
   DSM-IV classification of, 84
   eating disorders and, 260–261
   substance abuse and, 295
   suicide and, 199–200
   treatment of, 188
Moral anxiety, 101–102
Moral treatment, 11–12
Morphine, 281
Mother. *See also* Family; Parent
   schizophrenogenic, 358–359

Mourning, 169b
   depression and, 167–168
Movement disorders, antipsychotics and, 366
Multi-infarct dementia, 401
Multiple personality disorder, 384–387, 384t. *See also* Dissociative disorders
   fusion in, 391
   treatment of, 391
Munchausen syndrome, 218
Munchausen syndrome by proxy, 218–219, 219b
Muscle atrophy, 223
Muscle contraction headache, 230
Music, memory for, 390b
Music therapy, 52
   for dementia, 398b
Mutual help groups, 58–59
Mutually amnesic relationships, 385
Mutually cognizant patterns, 385
Myocardial infarction, 230

Naltrexone, 301
Narcissistic personality disorder, 409f, 420t, 425–428
Narcolepsy, 232b
Narcotic antagonists, 301
Narcotics
   abuse of, 281–283, 281t. *See also* Substance abuse
   methadone for, 282, 301–302
National Comorbidity Survey, 22
National interest groups, for community treatment, 373–374
Native Americans. *See* Race/ethnicity
Natural disasters, stress disorders and, 144–145, 145t, 152–153, 152b
Natural experiments, 25–26
Naturalistic observation, 80–81
Negative correlation, 20
Negative thinking, depression and, 174–175
Neologisms, 349
Nerve endings, 33, 33f
Neurofibrillary tangles, in Alzheimer's disease, 399–400, 400f
Neuroimaging techniques, 78, 78f
Neuroleptics, 365. *See also* Antipsychotic drugs
Neurological tests, 78, 78f
Neurons, 33, 34f
   firing of, 186
   ion flow and, 185, 185f
Neuropsychological tests, 78, 79f
Neurosyphilis, 12
Neurotic anxiety, 101
Neurotransmitters, 33, 33f. *See also* specific neurotransmitters
   antidepressants and, 131
   bipolar disorder and, 184–185
   cocaine and, 285
   depression and, 162–163
   in obsessive-compulsive disorder, 141
   in panic disorder, 130, 131
   second messengers and, 186
   stress and, 236
   in substance abuse, 287, 297

DSM-IV CLASSIFICATION

From the American Psychiatric Association: *Diagnostic and Statistical Manual of Mental Disorders, Fourth Edition*, Washington, DC, American Psychiatric Association, 1994. Reprinted by permission.

(All categories are on Axis I except those indicated otherwise.)

Disorders Usually First Diagnosed in Infancy, Childhood, or Adolescence

Mental Retardation

Note: These are coded on Axis II.
Mild mental retardation
Moderate mental retardation
Severe mental retardation
Profound mental retardation
Mental retardation, severity unspecified

Learning Disorders

Reading disorder
Mathematics disorder
Disorder of written expression
Learning disorder NOS*

Motor Skills Disorder

Developmental coordination disorder

Communication Disorders

Expressive language disorder
Mixed receptive-expressive language disorder
Phonological disorder
Stuttering
Communication disorder NOS*

Pervasive Developmental Disorders

Autistic disorder
Rett's disorder
Childhood disintegrative disorder
Asperger's disorder
Pervasive development disorder NOS*

Attention-Deficit and Disruptive Behavior Disorders

Attention-deficit/hyperactivity disorder
    Combined type
    Predominantly inattentive type
    Predominantly hyperactive-impulsive type
Attention-deficit/hyperactivity disorder NOS*
Conduct disorder
Oppositional defiant disorder
Disruptive behavior disorder NOS*

Feeding and Eating Disorders of Infancy or Early Childhood

Pica
Rumination disorder
Feeding disorder of infancy or early childhood

Tic Disorders

Tourette's disorder
Chronic motor or vocal tic disorder
Transient tic disorder
Tic disorder NOS*

Elimination Disorders

Encopresis
    With constipation and overflow incontinence
    Without constipation and overflow incontinence
Enuresis (not due to a general medical condition)

Other Disorders of Infancy, Childhood, or Adolescence

Separation anxiety disorder
Selective mutism
Reactive attachment disorder of infancy or early childhood
Stereotypic movement disorder
Disorder of infancy, childhood, or adolescence NOS*

Delirium, Dementia, and Amnestic and Other Cognitive Disorders

Delirium

Delirium due to . . . *(indicate the general medical condition)*
Substance intoxication delirium
Substance withdrawal delirium
Delirium due to multiple etiologies
Delirium NOS*

Dementia

Dementia of the Alzheimer's type, with early onset
Dementia of the Alzheimer's type, with late onset
Vascular dementia

Dementia Due to Other General Medical Conditions

Dementia due to HIV disease
Dementia due to head trauma
Dementia due to Parkinson's disease
Dementia due to Huntington's disease
Dementia due to Pick's disease
Dementia due to Creutzfeldt-Jakob disease
Dementia due to . . . *(indicate the general medical condition not listed above)*
Substance-induced persisting dementia
Dementia due to multiple etiologies
Dementia NOS*

Amnestic Disorders

Amnestic disorders due to . . . *(indicate the general medical condition)*
Substance-induced persisting amnestic disorder
Amnestic disorder NOS*

Other Cognitive Disorders

Cognitive disorder NOS*

Mental Disorders Due to a General Medical Condition Not Elsewhere Classified

Catatonic disorder due to . . . *(indicate the general medical condition)*
Personality change due to . . . *(indicate the general medical condition)*
Mental disorder NOS* due to . . . *(indicate the general medical condition)*

Substance-Related Disorders

[Alcohol; Amphetamine; Caffeine; Cannabis; Cocaine; Hallucinogen; Inhalant; Nicotine; Opioid; Phencyclidine; Sedative, Hypnotic, or Anxiolytic; Polysubstance; Other]

Substance Use Disorders

Substance dependence
Substance abuse

Substance-Induced Disorders

Substance intoxication
Substance withdrawal
Substance intoxication delirium
Substance withdrawal delirium
Substance-induced persisting dementia
Substance-induced persisting amnestic disorder
Substance-induced psychotic disorder
Substance-induced mood disorder
Substance-induced anxiety disorder
Substance-induced sexual dysfunction
Substance-induced sleep disorder
Substance-related disorder NOS*

Schizophrenia and Other Psychotic Disorders

Schizophrenia
    Paranoid type
    Disorganized type
    Catatonic type
    Undifferentiated type
    Residual type
Schizophreniform disorder
Schizoaffective disorder
Delusional disorder
Brief psychotic disorder
Shared psychotic disorder
Psychotic disorder due to . . . *(indicate the general medical condition)*
Substance-induced psychotic disorder
Psychotic disorder NOS*

Mood Disorders

Depressive Disorders

Major depressive disorder
Dysthymic disorder
Depressive disorder NOS*

Bipolar Disorders

Bipolar I disorder
Bipolar II disorder
Cyclothymic disorder
Bipolar disorder NOS*
Mood disorder due to . . . *(indicate the general medical condition)*
Substance-induced mood disorder
Mood disorder NOS*

Anxiety Disorders

Panic disorder without agoraphobia
Panic disorder with agoraphobia
Agoraphobia without history of panic disorder
Specific phobia
Social phobia
Obsessive-compulsive disorder
Posttraumatic stress disorder

*NOS= Not otherwise specified